THE OXFORD COMPANION TO
Italian Literature

THE OXFORD COMPANION TO
Italian Literature

Edited by

PETER HAINSWORTH
AND
DAVID ROBEY

OXFORD
UNIVERSITY PRESS

OXFORD
UNIVERSITY PRESS

Great Clarendon Street, Oxford OX2 6DP
Oxford University Press is a department of the University of Oxford.
It furthers the University's objective of excellence in research, scholarship,
and education by publishing worldwide in

Oxford New York

Auckland Bangkok Buenos Aires Cape Town Chennai
Dar es Salaam Delhi Hong Kong Istanbul Karachi Kolkata
Kuala Lumpur Madrid Melbourne Mexico City Mumbai Nairobi
São Paulo Shanghai Singapore Taipei Tokyo Toronto

Oxford is a registered trade mark of Oxford University Press
in the UK and in certain other countries

Published in the United States
by Oxford University Press Inc., New York

Introduction © Peter Hainsworth and David Robey 2002
Text © Oxford University Press 2002

The moral rights of the authors have been asserted
Database right Oxford University Press (maker)

First published 2002

British Library Cataloguing in Publication Data
Data available

Library of Congress Cataloging in Publication Data
The Oxford companion to Italian literature / edited by
Peter Hainsworth and David Robey.
p. cm.
1. Italian literature—Dictionaries. 2. Italian literature—
Bio-bibliography. 3. Authors, Italian—Biography—Dictionaries.
I. Hainsworth, Peter. II. Robey, David.
PQ4006 .O84 2002 850.9'003—dc21 2001059301

ISBN 0-19-818332-1

1 3 5 7 9 10 8 6 4 2

Typeset in Plantin by
Jayvee, Trivandrum, India
Printed in Great Britain
on acid-free paper by
Biddles Ltd.,
Guildford and King's Lynn

Contents

Introduction

Oxford Companions to the world's literatures have a long history. The first versions of those for English and French were produced long enough ago to have been recently rewritten under new editors; German is now in its third edition. This is the first *Oxford Companion to Italian Literature*; indeed it is the first attempt in English to provide a reference work of similar scope on Italian literature, and aiming to serve the needs of specialist and non-specialist alike. It also differs from literary encyclopedias produced in Italy, mainly through the range of entries containing contextual or technical information or general accounts of social and political history, literary criticism and theory, and other branches of culture. A list divided by category of the more important of these entries follows below (pp. xvii–xxi). There are over 500 of them in all, comprising over a third of the total number of words, an emphasis which not only accords with the general character of Oxford Companions but also reflects the broad shift of attention in modern literary criticism and scholarship, in Italy and elsewhere, away from the traditional concentration on the literary canon—a concentration particularly marked in the Italian academic world as a result of the dominant influence of Benedetto Croce's 'aesthetic criticism' in the first half of the 20th century.

Altogether there are almost 2,400 substantive entries. The majority relate to literature written in one form or another of the Italian language, from the early 13th to the end of the 20th century. These constitute the core of the Companion and its primary justification. But there are also numerous entries relating to writing by natives of Italy in other languages (most importantly Latin and Provençal), and to writing in dialect, which is usually not considered a form of Italian but linguistically and often culturally separate. In all these respects we have followed standard Italian practice as regards 'Italian' literature. We have similarly aimed to reflect the traditional canon of texts; the recognized great authors of Italian literature and their works are all given generous space, particularly of course Dante. But the idea of the canon, and indeed the idea of literature itself, have been increasingly called into question by modern theory, a trend we have attempted to accommodate through the inclusion of a large number of short entries on figures who may often be classified as minor and sometimes not even literary, but who have cultural, historical, or aesthetic interest, and who have often played significant roles for writers from other countries. Here, of course, there may be what some readers feel are omissions or, alternatively, surprising inclusions. Especially as regards writers of the last decade of the 20th century, we have frequently found ourselves making additions and modifications to the volume in the course of compilation, and are very likely to have omitted some readers' favourites.

Following established Italian views, the volume has attempted some readjustment of the image of Italian literatures (such as it is) that has tended to be the norm in English-speaking countries. The space given to dialect writers such as Belli and Carlo Porta reflects the increasing recognition of their real interest and importance. Similarly, substantial attention is paid to the 17th and 18th centuries, in many respects centuries of decline and stagnation, but whose characteristic literary and intellectual production, from Baroque poetry and fiction to neoclassical tragedy, is now appreciated without the interference of Romantic prejudices. Above all we have given space (about a quarter of the total number of substantive entries) to the 20th century, which for much of its course was often felt, inside Italy as well as abroad, to be the tail end of a great tradition. Yet it easily bears comparison with the modern literature of similar European countries, and is also one of the routes to understanding the complex and dramatic evolution of Italian society and culture since Unification.

The idea of a unitary tradition of Italian literature was given its most forceful expression by the great critic Francesco De Sanctis in the immediate wake of Unification, and has proved remarkably durable. It too has been called into question in the last fifty years or so. It is plain that a concern with tradition has always been a distinctive feature of Italian literary culture. Even early writers—Dante is the exemplary case—are eager to situate themselves in relation to their literary fathers, and a sense of predecessors' practices and achievements is dominant, at times overridingly so, in Italian literature of all periods. However, the widely held modern view is that the idea of a central tradition running from the 13th century to the present must allow for interruptions and deviations. The spectre of cultural, political, and literary unity may be stronger or weaker at different times in the country's history. It is probably more profitable and in many ways more accurate to think in terms of multiple traditions, allowing for varying degrees of autonomy both in different regions and within the different strands of literature (lyric poetry or the *novella*, for instance). It is from a complex and shifting blend of unity and diversity that the features emerge which most define Italian literature in relation to other European literatures.

The political and cultural diversity of the country must be the most decisive factor in any such definition. Unification was only completed with the occupation of Papal Rome by Italian troops in 1870. Rome is the political capital today, but Milan is frequently considered the economic and intellectual capital, and until at least the start of World War II Florence could reasonably claim to be the cultural capital. Absence of political unity has meant that, in marked contrast, for instance, to Britain and France, the difference between metropolis and provinces does not apply to Italy, and is simply not a factor in the history of the country's literature. The regions and major cities cited under 'Social and Political Context' in the list of general entries below, ranging from Lombardy to Sicily, from Venice to Naples, all have distinctive though interlocking histories, and the families that dominated them (the Borgia, Este, Medici, and others) were in no sense members of a provincial aristocracy. While some parts of the country are noticeable by their absence from this list (especially in the South— but see also the entry on the Mezzogiorno), small urban centres such as Padua, Ferrara, and Mantua merit relatively long entries in view of the role that they played in the Middle Ages and Renaissance. The cultural importance of so many Italian cities was not simply a consequence of disunity; it also resulted from the fundamental continuity of urban life in the peninsula from late antiquity to the Middle Ages, when the social and economic prominence of the Italian cities contrasted with the much more rural world north of the Alps: at the beginning of the 14th century Florence and Venice were the largest cities in Europe after Paris, and about twice the size of London. The existence of so many major urban centres in medieval Italy is probably the main reason why the classical revival of the Renaissance began here earlier than anywhere else.

A further major consequence of political disunity, from the Renaissance onwards, was the prolonged domination of much of Italy by Spain and then Austria, a domination which helps to account for the relative backwardness of Italy during the 17th, 18th, and even much of the 19th century (see the entries on Austria and on Spain and Spanish Influences). But disunity was also the condition for a remarkable feature of Italian literature from the earliest times, the depth of political involvement of so many of its major writers in all periods; hence the entries on a wide range of political and social topics, ranging from the communes and *condottieri* to nationalism and the Christian Democrats. The *Divine Comedy* is a political as much as a religious and philosophical poem, and Dante himself was an active participant in the struggles between Guelfs and Ghibellines, Blacks and Whites. Petrarch, who was much more inclined to turn his back on the world, expressed strong views on the political state of his country and Church as, in the Renaissance, did not only Machiavelli but also Ariosto, the poet of chivalry and love.

In later centuries, alongside a vigorous tradition of political thought, the Enlightenment and then the Risorgimento produce new social and political themes in literature: Alfieri's work is obsessed with the subject of tyranny, while Foscolo, Leopardi, and Manzoni all respond vigorously to the issues of foreign domination and domestic absolutism. Nor is Italian literature any less political after Unification: post-Risorgimento problems figure largely in the work of the *veristi*, who share a strong right-wing bias with the Futurists. During the Fascist period a few major writers, such as Pirandello and Vittorini, actively supported the regime, though with a variety of reservations and qualifications. Even the hermetic poets did not turn their backs on politics as resolutely as has often been claimed. Before Mussolini's fall in 1943, overtly anti-Fascist writing, such as that of Silone, tended necessarily to be produced in exile. But the Resistance that followed the establishment of the Nazi–Fascist Republic of Salò in 1943 reawakened Italian writers to politics, as Calvino has testified, and gave the culture of the postwar decades its distinctive left-wing commitment (*impegno*), the heritage of which is still evident in writing of the 1990s by Tabucchi and others.

The other major consequence of political disunity was linguistic, and is reflected in the number of substantial entries listed below under 'Language'. Only in the second half of the 20th century did Italian become the spoken language of the majority of the country's population, thanks in part to improvements in education and literacy, but even more to the influence of radio, film, and above all television. Up until then Italian existed almost entirely as a written language for the literate minority, and most Italians spoke dialect for everyday purposes (see the entries on Dialect, History of the Italian Language, and Literacy). From the time of Dante up to Unification there was a continuing debate about the Italian language, the *questione della lingua*: given the diversity of dialects in the peninsula and the absence of a dominant cultural centre, what language should literature be written in? In practice the debate was resolved in the 16th century, when the refined version of Florentine used by Petrarch and Boccaccio became the standard vehicle for serious literature, its status being consecrated by the Accademia della Crusca and its dictionary. As a result, literary Italian changed little from the 14th century to the 20th, unlike languages such as English, French, and German; Boccaccio is still far easier for modern Italians to read than his near-contemporary Chaucer for modern English-speakers.

Nevertheless the privileged status of Florentine and the appropriateness of fixing the literary language in that of the 14th century remained a subject for theoretical dispute; and the increasing chronological distance between the language and contemporary reality acted as a major constraint on literary writing, particularly in prose. In the early 19th century Manzoni was much exercised by the need to bring the language up to date, which he famously did by modelling it on the Florentine of his own day; but despite all the Romantics' talk about a literature for the people, at the end of the same century writers like Verga were still struggling to find an Italian suitable for the representation of everyday life (see Spoken Language in Literature). Arguably it is only in the last few decades that the distance between language and reality has ceased to be a practical problem for writers—at a time when, paradoxically, it has come to be a central conceptual problem in literary and cultural theory. Moreover, the relatively narrow and conservative nature of the Italian literary language has reinforced the marginal status of literature in dialect and more popular forms of writing (see Dialect Writing, Folk and Popular Literature). It has also tended to restrict linguistic freedom and experimentation to certain well-defined categories of writing, such as the hybrid Italo-Latin of Renaissance macaronic literature or the *poesia giocosa* of the 13th and 14th centuries. In this respect some of the most important authors, including Dante and more recently Gadda, are exceptions to the general trend.

Another major reason for the distinctive coherence and continuity of the literary language is what we may loosely call the influence of the academy—that is, of a self-consciously learned, classicizing culture. As we have already observed, Renaissance humanism began earlier in Italy than anywhere else, and it has been a central factor in the development of Italian literature; hence the substantial entries on Humanism and Imitation, and further entries covering Antiquarianism, Classical Scholarship, Classicism, Greek Influences and Greek Writing in Italy, Latin Influences, Latin Poetry in Italy, and Latin Prose in Italy. A substantial part of Renaissance as well as medieval Italian literature was written in Latin, particularly in the 15th century; equally, classical theories and models were by far the most important influence on vernacular writing from the time of Dante onwards, and particularly with the development of vernacular humanism in the 16th century. Indeed, a major reason for the imposition of 14th-century Florentine as the literary standard was to be found in the classical principle that the language of literature should be elevated above that of everyday life; from a classical point of view, the anachronistic nature of the standard was an advantage, not a limitation. (For broad pictures of literature and culture of the two periods, see the substantial entries on Middle Ages and Renaissance.)

Humanism led to the historical academies, independent societies which, at their best, acted as forums for the scientific, intellectual, and literary energies of the country from the Renaissance to the 19th century (see the entries on individual academies, as well as on the subject in general). The most influential academy of all, the Accademia dell'Arcadia, was founded in 1690 as a classicizing reaction against the Baroque, whose so-called excesses are charted in the entries on *concettismo, Marinismo, secentismo*, all of which can themselves only be understood within the framework of a broad classical culture. The prevailing neoclassicism of the century that followed in its turn gave an unusual urgency to the Romantics' arguments, at the beginning of the 19th century, that classical models and standards should be abandoned in favour of more natural, spontaneous, and popular modes of writing. Yet classical influences remain strong throughout most of the century; for all his insistence on the use of contemporary Florentine and his avowedly Romantic principles, the complex structures of Manzoni's prose still link it with that of his Renaissance predecessors.

The influence of the academy (and academies) on Italian literature is intimately connected with the importance of literary theories and programmes. Most literature, of course, presupposes in one way or another a relationship between ideas of what literature should do and creative practice, but in the case of Italian literature the former have played a particularly prominent role. The entry on Literary Theory is by far the longest in this volume, and is supported by related entries on individual theories and programmes, listed below under 'Literary Movements, Themes, and Issues' (such as Petrarchism, neoclassicism, Romanticism, and Neorealism), and 'Cultural Contexts and Institutions' (such as Aristotelianism, Enlightenment, and positivism). A strong theoretical component is already evident in 13th-century lyric poetry. It is then taken up and developed in much greater depth and with much greater dynamism by Dante, whose work shows a constant interplay between theory and literary practice. Theoretical reflection made a major contribution to the intensely self-aware quality of Italian literature from Petrarch and Boccaccio through to the Renaissance, though the debates of the later 16th century eventually drove Torquato Tasso to rewrite the *Gerusalemme liberata* as the more conventionally classical (and, in the view of most, much less interesting) *Gerusalemme conquistata*. During the first half of the last century, Crocean idealism with its privileging of mind over matter, theory over practice, exerted an influence over Italian cultural life that was probably without parallel in any period in any other country. Postwar Italian writers tended strongly to assimilate the role of the writer to that of the intellectual, with a resultant inclination not only to develop sophisticated literary programmes but also to incorporate abstract general views in their work; Calvino is probably the best example of this, but there are many others.

The great majority of Italians have historically been members of the Catholic Church, which has played a crucial role in Italian society and which has in turn, in spite of its universalism, been dominated by Italians at the highest level. In particular the great majority of Popes have been from Italy. As well, of course, as entries on Catholic writers and thinkers, we have entries covering religious movements and institutions, relevant religious genres, and the influences of religion on literature, including, for example, the Bible, the Counter-Reformation, Franciscans, hagiography, the Inquisition, Jesuits, sermons, and the Vatican Library. The largest related entry is that on the Papacy and the Catholic Church, significantly on the Church as institution rather than on the development of Catholic thought. For one of the most striking signs of the detachment of literature from the mass of the population is the strongly secular orientation of much of the most important writing, from Sicilian poetry of the 13th century onwards. Dante, Petrarch, and Boccaccio, the *Tre Corone* of the 14th century who have so dominated succeeding periods, all display notable secular interests which proved historically more influential than their explorations of issues of belief. Classical humanism, when it develops in the 14th and 15th centuries, tends to sidestep rather than confront religious authority, and its writings, and the educational system which it developed, are strikingly worldly in character.

In spite of figures such as Savonarola and the fact that many writers were members of the clergy, the early 16th century saw this tendency reach a peak with Machiavelli and Ariosto, whose works define the High Renaissance in terms of literature.

As in the rest of Catholic Europe, the Counter-Reformation considerably increased the Church's cultural dominance in Italy and brought a thematics of inner torment into literature in the work of figures such as Torquato Tasso. But by the 17th century it is Giordano Bruno and the Libertines who now seem to have most to say, not the endless exaltations of piety and orthodoxy. The tension between faith and rationalism only achieves a new compelling urgency in Manzoni, Italy's most famous Catholic writer after Dante. But his contemporary and Italy's greatest poet of the 19th century, Leopardi, was an atheist. Most subsequent Italian writers were convinced supporters of the post-Unification Italian state, which was institutionally anti-Catholic up to the Lateran Pacts of 1929. They were philosophical positivists or, like Croce, idealists; a Catholic writer such as Fogazzaro, who campaigned to bring Church and state together, was something of a literary exception, though he undoubtedly expressed the aspirations of a large percentage of the Italian bourgeoisie. The Christian Democrats dominated Italian politics from the end of World War II to the early 1990s, but postwar Italian literature was no more religious than that of any other Western state; Marxism, if anything, had more influence on writers than Catholicism. None of this is to deny that religion has played an important role as far as Italian writers are concerned, only to make the point that it has certainly not dominated literature in a way that might have been the case if the popular component had been stronger or writers less resistant to institutional power.

Minoritarian within Italy until recently, Italian literature has flourished abroad only to a very limited degree. What has been produced in nearby European countries has generally been in the shadow of writing in Italy itself, with only modern Italian Switzerland (see the entry on Italian writing in Switzerland) developing a significant independent tradition. Italians have written about their travels outside and inside Italy since Marco Polo, but neither the emigration which brought millions to South and North America in the later 19th and early 20th centuries, nor the Italian colonies of the post-Unification and Fascist decades, brought about an *italofonia* corresponding to *francophonie*. All the same, though most emigrants who did write quickly adopted English as their literary medium, a slender current of poetry and fiction in Italian developed amongst first-generation emigrants in some countries (see the entries on Italian writing in America and Australia). Vice versa, with the influx of African immigrants to Italy in the 1980s and 1990s, for the first time in Italian literature a small number of individuals who are not of Italian birth or nationality have published works in Italian (see the entry on immigrant literature).

Contemporary Italian literature displays many of the features that characterize American and other European literatures. As late as the early 20th century the novel remained suspect, as a non-classical genre, to the academic cast of mind in Italy, and was simultaneously beset by the educational and linguistic difficulties we have mentioned. Since then it has come to occupy the centre of the literary stage. Its various forms range from those aimed at a mass market, such as the detective novel and the romantic novel, to demanding post-modernist play. Since Tomasi Di Lampedusa's *Gattopardo* of 1958, best-sellers have had sales of hundreds of thousands and occasionally millions. Conversely, poetry, acknowledged until about the same time as the supreme literary genre, has become a minority activity. Criticism has been absorbed almost entirely into the universities after having survived, even in its more elaborate forms, as an independent branch of literary journalism until the mid-20th century. And literary practitioners, in whatever field, now write in full awareness of the ostensible power of other media, and frequently themselves move more or less comfortably between print, film, radio, and television. At the same time, the historically distinctive features that we have outlined have continued to be evident, in the form of self-awareness, an aspiration to literariness, a sense of literary tradition as well as of the modern condition and modern culture, together with, in the best writers, a refusal to simplify in the name of the market, and a sense of literature having intellectual and political responsibilities which cannot be shirked.

This is a remarkably international Companion. Our almost 200 contributors are drawn from universities (and occasionally from other walks of life) in a range of countries where Italian literature is read and studied. The majority are from the UK and Ireland, and in this sense the Companion is very much the product of the Italian studies community in these countries; but we have been enormously gratified by the willingness of many of the most distinguished Italianists working in Italy, the USA, and Australia to contribute to the volume. For certain specific topics relating principally to influences on Italian literature, we have been aided by colleagues in Spain and France. We asked contributors to focus on the important and interesting features of their topics, but otherwise did not attempt to impose uniformity of approach or judgement. We have been pleasantly surprised by the degree of consensus that seemed spontaneously to emerge.

Warm thanks are due to our Advisory Board. As well as helping with general guidance, each member has been responsible for providing advice and assistance with particular areas of study: Zygmunt Barański for the period up to 1400, Letizia Panizza for the 15th century, Laura Lepschy for the 16th, Paul Diffley for the 17th, John Lindon for the 18th, Michael Caesar for the period 1800–70, Ann Caesar for 1870–1918, David Forgacs for the period from 1918 onwards, and Giulio Lepschy for entries relating to language. Their help has been indispensable for filling the gaps in our knowledge, and they have been a major source of ideas and inspiration, as well as of lists of potential contributors.

Others too have been generous with their time and efforts. Beth Crutch of Oxford University Computing Services gave training in the use of the Ingres Database; Andrew Slater and Chris Turner of the Faculty of Medieval Languages supplied essential computing backup in Oxford; Giulio Lepschy and the late Giovanni Aquilecchia provided additional reading of draft contributions; the late Giovanna Gronda found contributors in Italy on topics for which we would otherwise have been at a complete loss; Nicoletta Simborowski and John Johnson provided drafts of translations of most of the Italian contributions; David Thomas of the Taylor Institution Library in Oxford repeatedly solved library problems; and Jane Hainsworth helped compile the initial list of entries. We are also grateful to both colleagues and friends in Manchester, Oxford, and Reading, and to our families for their support and tolerance over what proved to be more years than we anticipated. Last but certainly not least, we owe a large debt of gratitude to the staff at the Oxford University Press responsible for this project: Sophie Goldsworthy, Frances Whistler, Sarah Barrett, and particularly the late and much-missed Kim Scott Walwyn, who persuaded us to undertake the volume in the first place.

List of General Entries

The more important general entries are listed below.

LITERARY GENRES AND TYPES

Autobiography
Bestiaries
Biography
Cantari
Canti carnascialeschi
Canzoniere
Children's Literature
Chronicles
Colonial Literature
Comedy
Commedia dell'arte
Commentaries
Dante Commentaries
Detective Fiction
Dialogues, Renaissance
Diaries
Encyclopedism
Epic
Epistolary Novel
Fantastic
Folk and Popular Literature
Hagiography
Historical Novel
Historiography
Improvised Poetry

Laudi
Letter-Writing and *Epistolari*
Lyric Poetry
Macaronic Literature
Mock-Heroic Poetry
Novel
Novella and *Racconto*
Novella in versi
Parody and Pastiche
Pastoral
Petrarch Commentaries
Poesia giocosa
Proverbs
Religious Literature
Romance
Sacra rappresentazione
Satire
Science Fiction
Sermons
Sonnet
Tragedy
Tragicomedy
Translations
Travel Writing
Travellers in Italy

LITERARY MOVEMENTS, THEMES, AND ISSUES

Allegory
Arcadia (2)
Arthurian Literature

Baroque
Classicism
Concettismo

CULTURAL CONTEXTS AND INSTITUTIONS

Journalism
Law
Libraries
Literacy
Literary Criticism
Literary Prizes
Magic
Manuscripts and Manuscript
  Production
Marxism
Medicine
Mysticism
Nationalism
Nuns
Patronage
Periodicals
Phenomenology

Platonic Academy
Political Thought
Positivism
Printing
Psychoanalysis
Publishing
Radio
Reading
Scepticism
Scholasticism
Sensismo
Television
Textual Criticism
Theatre
Universities
Vatican Library

LANGUAGE

Dialect
Dialect Writing
Dictionaries
Grammars
History of the Italian Language
Purism

Questione della lingua
Slang
Spelling
Spoken Language in Literature
Vocabolario della Crusca

SOCIAL AND POLITICAL CONTEXT

Armed Forces and Police
Austria
Bankers
Bologna
BORGIA
Byzantium
Censorship
Christian Democrats
Clergy
COLONNA
Communes
Communism
Condottieri

Counter-Reformation
Emigration
ESTE
Exile
Fascism
Ferrara
Feudalism
Florence
Franciscans
Genoa
Inquisition
Jacobinism
Jesuits

NON-ITALIAN WRITING AND INFLUENCES

OTHER ARTS

* In common with the other numerical entries, 1848 and 900 (*Novecento*), this is placed as it would be if spelt out as words.

SOURCES FOR FURTHER REFERENCE

Contributors

ABr	Alison Brown	Royal Holloway, University of London
ABu	Alan Bullock	University of Leeds
AC	Alberto Cadioli	University of Milan
ACdelaM	†Albinia de la Mare	King's College, London
AD	Anna Dolfi	University of Florence
ADelC	Anna Del Conte	London
ADiB	Arnaldo Di Benedetto	University of Turin
ADP	Tony Pagliaro	La Trobe University
AHC	Ann Caesar	University of Warwick
AJT	Anthony Julian Tamburri	Purdue University, Indiana
ALB	Anna Laura Bellina	University of Padua
ALL	Ann Lawson Lucas	University of Hull
AM	Alan Millen	University of Kent
AR	Albert Rabil Jr.	State University of New York, Old Westbury
AS	Aldo Scaglione	New York University
ASP	Anna Proudfoot	Oxford Brookes University
AWM	Anne Mullen	Royal Holloway, University of London
BB	Bojan Bujic	Magdalen College, Oxford
BC	Barry Collett	University of Melbourne
BG	Barbara Garvin	University College, London
BK	Benjamin Kohl	Vassar College
BLT	Brian Trowell	University of Oxford
BR	Brian Richardson	University of Leeds
CCa	Carlo Caruso	University of St Andrews
CC-B	Claude Cazalé-Bérard	University of Paris
CCi	Claudio Ciociola	Università per Stranieri, Siena
CD	Christopher Duggan	University of Reading
CDellaC	Cristina Della Coletta	University of Virginia
CEH	Claire Honess	University of Reading
CEJG	Clive Griffiths	University of Manchester
CF	Conor Fahy	University College, London
CFB	Charles Burdett	University of Bristol

CG	Caterina Griffante	University of Venice
CGW	Chris Wagstaff	University of Reading
CJ	Carolyn James	Monash University
CJF	Claire Farago	University of Colorado
CK	Christopher Kleinhenz	University of Wisconsin
CO'B	Catherine O'Brien	University College, Galway
CPB	Peter Brand	University of Edinburgh
CR	Clare Robertson	University of Reading
DCH	Deborah Holmes	New College, Oxford
DD	Derek Duncan	University of Bristol
DER	Dennis Rhodes	British Library, London
DF	David Forgacs	University College, London
DG	David Gibbons	University of Edinburgh
DieZ	Diego Zancani	Balliol College, Oxford
DK	Dilwyn Knox	University College, London
DO'G	Deirdre O'Grady	University College, Dublin
DomZ	Domenico Zanrè	University of Glasgow
DR	David Robey	University of Reading
DRBK	David Kimbell	University of Edinburgh
DS	Darrow Schecter	University of Sussex
EAM	Eileen Anne Millar	University of Glasgow
ECMR	Christina Roaf	Somerville College, Oxford
EE	Edoardo Esposito	University of Milan
EGH	Eric Haywood	University College, Dublin
ELM	Erika Milburn	St John's College, Oxford
EMcG	Elizabeth McGrath	Warburg Institute, University of London
EP	Eugenia Paulicelli	City University of New York
ES	Elizabeth Schachter	University of Kent
ET	Emmanuela Tandello	Christ Church, Oxford
FC	Francesca Chiarelli	Royal Holloway, University of London
FD'I	Franco D'Intino	University of Birmingham
FF	Franco Fido	Harvard University
FWK	William Kent	Monash University
GAq	†Giovanni Aquilecchia	Royal Holloway, University of London
GBB	Giovanni Bogliolo	University of Urbino
GC	Giovanni Carsaniga	University of Sydney
GCL	Giulio Lepschy	University of Reading
GDP	Giovanni Da Pozzo	University of Padua
GG	Guglielmo Gorni	University of Geneva
GH	George Holmes	All Souls College, Oxford
GLCB	Gino Bedani	University of Swansea
GM	Guido Mazzoni	University of Siena

GN-S	Geoffrey Nowell-Smith	University of Luton
GP	Giuliana Pieri	Royal Holloway, University of London
GPTW	Giles Walker	Oriel College, Oxford
GS	Giuseppe Stellardi	St Hugh's College, Oxford
GT	George Talbot	University of Hull
GUB	Guido Bonsaver	Royal Holloway, University of London
HMcW	†Harry McWilliam	University of Leicester
HS	Hugh Shankland	University of Durham
IC	Ilaria Crotti	University of Venice
IMC	Ilaria Magnani Campanacci	University of Bologna
IWFM	Ian Maclean	All Souls College, Oxford
JAL	Jennifer Lorch	University of Warwick
JAS	John Scott	University of Western Australia
JCB	John Barnes	University College, Dublin
JD	John Dickie	University College, London
JEB	Jennifer Burns	University of Warwick
JEE	Jane Everson	Royal Holloway, University of London
JEL	John Law	University of Swansea
JF	Joe Farrell	University of Strathclyde
JG-R	John Gatt-Rutter	La Trobe University, Victoria
JHB	Judith Bryce	University of Bristol
JJ	John Johnson	Lady Margaret Hall, Oxford
JK	Jill Kraye	Warburg Institute, University of London
JMAL	John Lindon	University College, London
JMD	Jonathan Dunnage	University of Swansea
JMS	June Salmons	University of Swansea
JP	Jennifer Petrie	University College, Dublin
JP	John Pollard	Anglia Polytechnic University
JR	Judy Rawson	University of Warwick
JRW	John Woodhouse	Magdalen College, Oxford
JT	John Took	University College, London
JU	Jonathan Usher	University of Edinburgh
JV	Juliann Vitullo	Arizona State University
KP	Katia Pizzi	University of Kent
KR	Kenneth Richards	University of Manchester
LAP	Letizia Panizza	Royal Holloway, University of London
LB	Lorenzo Bartoli	University of Glasgow

LChe	Luciano Cheles	University of Lancaster
LChi	Loredana Chines	University of Bologna
LL	Laura Lepschy	University College, London
LM	Luigina Morini	University of Pavia
LPer	Lino Pertile	Harvard University
LPol	Loredana Polezzi	University of Warwick
LR	Lucy Riall	Birkbeck College, London
LS	Luigi Surdich	University of Genoa
MA	Michael Allen	University of California, Los Angeles
MB	Massimo Bacigalupo	University of Genoa
MC	Martino Capucci	University of Bologna
MCD	Manuel Carrera Díaz	University of Seville
MD	Michel David	University of Grenoble
MGD	Marco Dorigatti	St Peter's College, Oxford
MH	†Manfred Hardt	Gerhard Mercator University, Duisburg
MLS	Marialuisa Stazio	University of Naples
MM	Martin Maiden	Trinity College, Oxford
MMcL	Martin McLaughlin	Magdalen College, Oxford
MP	Michelangelo Picone	University of Zurich
MPC	Michael Caesar	University of Birmingham
MPS	Maurice Slawinski	University of Lancaster
NC	Nadia Cannata	University of Reading
NG	Nella Giannetto	Università IULM di Milano e Feltre
NL	Nigella Lawson	London
NMS	Nicoletta Simborowski	Christ Church, Oxford
NSD	Nicholas Davidson	St Edmund Hall, Oxford
PA	Peter Armour	Royal Holloway, University of London
PBarn	Paul Barnaby	University of Edinburgh
PBart	Paolo Bartoloni	La Trobe University, Victoria
PBD	Paul Diffley	University of Exeter
PBert	Paola Bertoldi	Wolfson College, Oxford
PC	Philip Cooke	University of Strathclyde
PGB	Pietro Beltrami	University of Pisa
PH	Peter Hainsworth	Lady Margaret Hall, Oxford
PLR	Paolo Rossi	University of Lancaster
PMcN	Philip McNair	University of Birmingham
PP	Pietro Puliatti	Biblioteca Estense, Modena
PRD	Peter Denley	Queen Mary and Westfield College, London
PRH	Philip Horne	Oxford
PS	Prue Shaw	University College, London
RAA	Richard Andrews	University of Leeds

RABGH	Robert Hastings	University of Manchester
RAbs	Roger Absalom	Sheffield Hallam University
RAC	Richard Cooper	Brasenose College, Oxford
RD	Raffaele Donnarumma	University of Pisa
RDB	Robert Black	University of Leeds
RDC	Remo Catani	University of Wales, Cardiff
REL	Robert Lumley	University College, London
RGF	Ronnie Ferguson	University of Durham
RH	Robert Hollander	Princeton University
RL	Romano Luperini	University of Siena
RMD	Mark Davie	University of Exeter
RPB	Richard Bellamy	University of Reading
RS	Rosa Solinas	St Cross College, Oxford
RSCG	Robert Gordon	Gonville and Caius College, Cambridge
RSD	†Robert Dombroski	City University of New York
SC	Stefano Calabrese	University of Udine
SCS	Sybil Sheringham	Oxford
SD	Simon Ditchfield	University of York
SE	Silvia Evangelisti	University of Birmingham
SG	Stephen Gundle	Royal Holloway, University of London
SJM	Stephen Milner	University of Bristol
SNB	Steven Botterill	University of California, Berkeley
SPC	Spencer Pearce	University of Manchester
SR	Silvia Rotondella	University of Bologna
SV	Shirley Vinall	University of Reading
SVM	Sarah Morgan	University of Bristol
SW	Sharon Wood	University of Leicester
TC	Tim Carter	Royal Holloway, University of London
TGG	Gwyn Griffith	University of Manchester
UJF	Ursula Fanning	University College, Dublin
UPB	Peter Burke	Emmanuel College, Cambridge
VB	Vittore Branca	Fondazione Cini, Venice
VBM	Vincenzo Moleta	University of Western Australia
VRJ	Verina Jones	University of Reading
VS-H	Vivienne Suvini-Hand	Royal Holloway, University of London
ZB	Zygmunt Barański	University of Cambridge

Reader's Guide

Entries are arranged in strict alphabetical order. The three entries which are purely numerical (1848, 1968, and 900) are placed where they would be found if spelt out as words—that is, under E, E, and N respectively. Where the heading consists of more than one word, the full sequence of letters is used to determine the place of entries; no account is taken of spaces, apostrophes, and diacritics: DIACCETO precedes DI BREME, DANIELLO precedes D'ANNUNZIO. The definite article (*La, Il,* etc.) is placed after the main name in titles, institutions, etc. (*Promessi sposi, I; Caffè, Il*). *Di, Del, Della,* etc., are conserved at the beginning of book titles (*Dei delitti e delle pene*), as is *Una* (*Una vita, Una donna*).

We have followed normal Italian practice in ordering authors and other figures by family names from the Renaissance onwards. Many medieval writers are classified under their first name (e.g. GIACOMO DA LENTINI, DANTE, BONVESIN DE LA RIVA), but the family name is used where it is commonly employed as a short form of reference (CAVALCANTI, FRESCOBALDI). *Di, Del, Della,* etc. are placed first where they are perceived as part of the name, as is normal with modern names (DELLA VALLE, D'ANNUNZIO), but in some earlier instances the family name is preferred, again in accordance with common practice (MEDICI, LORENZO DE'). Cross-references are given where there are notable alternative spellings (IACOPO DA LENTINI, see GIACOMO DA LENTINI). In some instances of medieval and even Renaissance names Italian practice is variable, and the reader should be ready to look up the other component, if the first selected proves fruitless.

For names of persons and places the normal modern spelling is given. English forms are only adopted if well known (Petrarch, St Francis, Milan, Piedmont, *Divine Comedy*).

In book titles and quotations we have used the form which is normal in current Italian scholarly usage. That may mean that for some medieval and Renaissance texts there are departures from modern Italian spelling (e.g. the use of 'et' instead of 'e').

A short list of the abbreviations used will be found on p. xxxi.

Dates are given as accurately as possible. The indication 1325/30 means some time between 1325 and 1330. For printed books the dates given in brackets indicate the date of first publication or printing. For books of the pre-printing era (up to the later 15th century) the dates are dates of composition. For plays and operas the dates are those of first performance.

An asterisk (*) before a word indicates that there is a separate entry for that word. Asterisks appear only at the first mention of that word in a given entry. Frequently the asterisked word refers to the cognate term used for the entry: e.g. *historian refers to the entry Historiography, *papal to the entry Papacy and the Catholic Church.

Short entries devoted to individual works are intended to give a bare indication of contents. There are commonly fuller discussions of the significance of the work in the entry devoted to the author.

The suggestions for further reading can be supplemented by reference to articles listing resources for more detailed study: see 'Sources for Further Reference' on p. xxi. Editions cited are the most up-to-date scholarly editions of the author in question.

Maps of Italy at different periods are given on pp. xlii–xlv.

Entries devoted to individual writers should be seen in the context of the more general entries—on genres, movements, etc.—listed on pp. xvii–xxi.

The cut-off date for most entries is 2000.

Abbreviations

Canz.	Petrarch, *Canzoniere* (poem number)
Conv.	Dante, *Convivio* (book and chapter numbers)
DVE	Dante, *De vulgari eloquentia* (book and chapter numbers)
Ger. lib.	Tasso, *Gerusalemme liberata* (canto and stanza numbers)
Inf.	Dante, *Divine Comedy, Inferno* (canto and line numbers)
Mon.	Dante, *Monarchia* (book and chapter numbers)
OF	Ariosto, *Orlando furioso* (canto and stanza number)
Para.	Dante, *Divine Comedy, Paradiso* (canto and line numbers)
Purg.	Dante, *Divine Comedy, Purgatorio* (canto and line numbers)
VN	Dante, *Vita nova* (chapter numbers)

Chronology

Dates given for rulers are those of their reigns. The third column places authors and artists at a point corresponding as nearly as possible to the time when they were most active. Virtually all the terms and names introduced here are the subject of entries in the main part of the volume.

Political and social history	Cultural events	Authors and artists
1100–1200 Rise of the communes		
	12th–c. Renaissance	
	Early vernacular literary texts	
1200–1400 Later Middle Ages and the birth of humanism		
13th c.: Rise of Florence and flourishing of Northern and Central communes; Guelf and Ghibelline struggles	Early 13th c. Provençal poetry by N. Italians	Sordello
	c.1225 St Francis, 'Cantico di frate sole'	
1220–50 Frederick II Emperor	c.1220–67 Sicilian School	Giacomo da Lentini
1229 Gregory IX founds the Inquisition	1222 Padua University founded	St Thomas Aquinas
1258–66 Manfredi, King in Sicily and South	c.1250–c.1290 Siculo-Tuscan poetry	Bonagiunta da Lucca
1260 Defeat of Florence at the Battle of Montaperti		Guittone d'Arezzo
1265 Charles of Anjou enters Italy		Cimabue
1266 Battle of Benevento ends Hohenstaufen power		
Late 13th c.: Rise of Northern *signorie*: Visconti (Milan), Della Scala (Verona), Este (Ferrara), Carrara (Padua), etc.		
1282 Revolt of the Sicilian Vespers (Palermo)		Guinizzelli
1282–1372 Anjou–Aragonese War		Brunetto Latini

Events	Literature	Authors
1289 Florence defeats Arezzo at Campaldino	c.1280–1300 *dolce stil novo*	Cavalcanti
	c.1250–1320 Umbrian *laudi*	Iacopone da Todi
		Bonvesin da la Riva
	1295 Dante, *Vita nova*	Cecco Angiolieri
	c.1298 Marco Polo, *Il milione*	
1294 Celestine V Pope		Cino da Pistoia
1294–1303 Boniface VIII Pope	c.1302–21 Dante in exile	Giotto
Late 1290s Black and White conflicts in Florence	c.1305–7 Dante, *Convivio*	Francesco da Barberino
1301 Whites exiled from Florence	c.1305–7 Dante, *De vulgari eloquentia*	
	c.1307–21 Dante, *Divine Comedy*	Marsilio da Padova
1306–77 Papacy in Avignon	14th c.: Early humanism	
1310–13 Invasion and death of Henry VII of Luxemburg	*Ars nova* in Florence	
1309–43 Robert of Anjou, King of Naples	*Cantari*	
	1320s First Dante commentaries	Giovanni Villani
	c.1333 Boccaccio, *Filostrato*	
1345 Bankruptcy of Bardi and Peruzzi banks; continuing decline of international economic importance of Florence	c.1342 Boccaccio, *Teseida*	Simone Martini
1347 Cola di Rienzo proclaims himself tribune (Rome)	1342–74 Petrarch, *Canzoniere*	Fazio degli Uberti
1348 Black Death	1349 Foundation of the University of Florence	Albertino Mussato
1351–7 Egidio d'Albornoz consolidates papal control over the Papal States	1350 Boccaccio, *Decameron*	
	1351 Petrarch and Boccaccio meet	
	1353 Petrarch's definitive return to Italy	
	1351–74 Petrarch's main Latin works	
	1351–76 Boccaccio's main Latin works	St Caterina of Siena
1378 Revolt of Ciompi (Florence)	c.1392 Sacchetti, *Trecentonovelle*	Coluccio Salutati
1378–1402 Giangaleazzo Visconti ruler of Milan		
1400–1600 The Renaissance		
1401 Bentivoglio rule established in Bologna	Growth of study of Greek	Leonardo Bruni

Political and social history	Cultural events	Authors and artists
Early 15th c.: Venetian expansion in Veneto and Dalmatia	Arrival of Byzantine scholars in Italy	Donatello
1406 Florence acquires Pisa		Poggio Bracciolini
1417 End of the Great Schism; election of Martin V as Pope at Council of Constance		Burchiello
	1433–41 Alberti, *Della famiglia*	Masaccio
1434 Cosimo de' Medici takes power in Florence	1436 Brunelleschi's dome for Florence Cathedral completed	Andrea da Barberino
	1444 Cosimo de' Medici founds Medicean Library	Piero della Francesca
1450 The Sforza replace the Visconti in Milan		il Pistoia
1453 Fall of Constantinople		
1454 Treaty of Lodi, guaranteeing peace in Italy		
1458 Enea Silvio Piccolomini elected Pope Pius II	1459 Michelozzo completes the Medici Palace (Florence)	
	1460 Accademia Romana	Ficino
	1460s Platonic Academy in Florence	Landino
	1460s First books printed in Italy	
1466 The Habsburg domination of Trieste begins	c.1465 Accademia Pontaniana	Pontano
1469–92 Lorenzo de' Medici effective ruler of Florence		Mantegna
1474 Federigo da Montefeltro becomes Duke of Urbino	1475 Poliziano, *Stanze*	Botticelli
1478 Pazzi Conspiracy against the Medici	1476 *Raccolta aragonese*	Masuccio Salernitano
	1480 Poliziano, *Orfeo*	Perugino
	1483 Pulci, *Morgante*	Pico della Mirandola
1492 Columbus reaches America	1495 Leonardo da Vinci, *Last Supper* (Milan)	Luca Signorelli
1492 Ludovico il Moro becomes Duke of Milan	1494 Boiardo breaks off *Orlando innamorato*	Serafino Aquilano
1494 Charles VIII of France invades Italy		il Cariteo
1492–1503 Alexander VI Pope (Alessandro Borgia)	1499 Francesco Colonna, *Hypnerotomachia Poliphili*	Manuzio
1494–1512 Florentine Republic		

1494–1525 French and Spanish struggle for Italy		Tebaldeo
1498 Execution of Savonarola	1501 Michelangelo, *David*	
1499–1503 Cesare Borgia in Romagna	1504 Sannazaro, *Arcadia*	
1509 Venice defeated at Agnadello by League of Cambrai (Pope, France, Spain, and Emperor)	1506 New St Peter's begun in Rome	
	Early 1500s: Growth of vernacular humanism	
1512 French defeat at battle of Ravenna	1513 Machiavelli, *Principe*	Bramante
1512 Return of Medici to Florence	1516 Ariosto, *Orlando furioso*	Giorgione
1513–21 Pope Leo X (Giovanni de' Medici)	1508–19 Raphael, *Stanze vaticane*	Folengo
1517 Luther publishes theses	1518 Machiavelli, *Mandragola*	
1523–34 Pope Clement VII (Giulio de' Medici)	1525 Bembo, *Prose della volgar lingua*	Trissino
1525 France defeated at battle of Pavia and Francis I captured		
1526 League of Cognac against the Spanish		
1527 Sack of Rome	1528 Castiglione, *Cortegiano*	Berni
1527–30 Republic restored in Florence	1531 Accademia degli Intronati, *Gli ingannati*	
1530 Coronation of Emperor Charles V in Bologna seals Spanish dominance	1534 Aretino, *Sei giornate* (first part)	Gaspara Stampa
1532 Alessandro de' Medici Duke of Florence	1536–41 Michelangelo, Sistine Chapel	Cellini
1535 Milan annexed by Spain	1536–40 Guicciardini writes *Storia d'Italia*	Vittoria Colonna
	1548 Robortello's commentary on Aristotle's *Poetics*	Titian
	1545–63 Council of Trent initiates Counter-Reformation	Palestrina
	1550 Vasari, *Vite*	Tintoretto
	1553 Della Casa writes *Il Galateo*	Palladio
		Tansillo
1559 Spanish rule of Lombardy, Sardinia, Naples, and Sicily confirmed by the Treaty of Cateau–Cambrésis		Caro
		Varchi
		Giraldi Cinzio

Political and social history	Cultural events	Authors and artists
1571 Battle of Lepanto halts Turkish expansion	Mid-16th c.: Rise of *commedia dell'arte*	Bandello
	1573 Tasso, *Aminta*	
	1575 Tasso, *Gerusalemme liberata*	
	1582 Accademia della Crusca founded	Grazzini
	1590 Guarini, *Pastor fido*	Giordano Bruno
	1598 Jacopo Peri sets Rinuccini's *Dafne* to music (first opera)	

1600–1796 From Baroque to Enlightenment and Neoclassicism

Political and social history	Cultural events	Authors and artists
1605–6 Interdict of Venice by Pope Paul V	17th c.:: *Marinismo* and the Baroque	Sarpi
	1607 Monteverdi, *Orfeo*	Giulio Cesare Croce
17th c.:: Savoy allied with France against Spain	1612 First Crusca dictionary	Carracci brothers
	1623 Campanella, *Città del sole*	Caravaggio
1620 Massacre of Protestants of Valtellina	1623 Marino, *Adone*	Achillini
	1624 Tassoni, *Secchia rapita*	Basile
17th.–18th c.:: Frequent wars between Venice and Turks	1628 Della Valle, *Reina di Scozia*	Chiabrera
	1632 Galileo, *Dialogo sopra i due massimi sistemi*	Borromini
1647 Revolt of Masaniello (Naples)	Mid-17th c.:: Libertines and libertinism	Bernini
1655 Massacre of Waldensians in Piedmont	1668 Foundation of *Giornale de' letterati*	Ferrante Pallavicino
1686 Venetians take Athens (destruction of Parthenon)		Guercino
		Boccalini
1687 Savoy joins anti-French League of Augusta	Later 17th c.:: numerous academies founded	Alessandro Scarlatti
	1690 Accademia dell' Arcadia founded (Rome)	Redi
		Carlo Maria Maggi
		Salvator Rosa
1701–13 War of Spanish Succession	18th c.:: the Enlightenment (*Illuminismo*)	Gravina
1713 Peace of Utrecht		Scipione Maffei

18th c.: Austria takes control of Lombardy

1729 Revolt of Corsica against Genoa
1730s Bourbons become rulers of Naples
1768 Genoa cedes Corsica to France

1724 Metastasio, *Didone abbandonata*
1725 Vico, *Scienza nuova*
1748 Excavations of Pompei begun
1750 Goldoni publishes first volume of *Commedie*
1760 Piranesi, *Carceri*
1763–5 Baretti, *Frusta letteraria*
1764 Beccaria, *Dei delitti e delle pene*

1782 Alfieri, *Saul*

1791–6 Parini, *Il giorno*

Apostolo Zeno
Pietro Giannone
Canaletto
Vivaldi
Muratori

Pietro Chiari
Bettinelli
Gasparo and Carlo Gozzi
Cesarotti
Pietro Verri
Tiraboschi
Frugoni
Casanova
Pindemonte
Cimarosa

1796–1870 Romanticism and Risorgimento

1796 Napoleon invades Italy
1797 Repubblica Cisalpina; Treaty of Campoformio (end of Venetian independence)
1799 Repubblica Partenopea (Naples)
1800 Siege of Genoa by Austrians
1805 Napoleon crowned King of Italy (Milan)
1814 Austrians occupy Milan
1815 Congress of Vienna; Restoration of Austrians in North and Bourbons in Naples

1807 Foscolo, *Dei sepolcri*

1816 Italian Romanticism begins with Berchet, *Lettera semiseria di Grisostomo*
1818–19 *Il Conciliatore*
1819–21 Leopardi writes first *idilli*
1820 Arrest of Silvio Pellico

Canova

Rossini

Settembrini
Donizetti
Belli

Political and social history	Cultural events	Authors and artists
	1827 Manzoni, *I promessi sposi* (first version)	Verdi
1831 Mazzini founds *Giovine Italia*	1831 Leopardi, *Canti*	Tommaseo
1847 Reforms of Carlo Alberto in Piedmont		Gioberti
1848 Uprisings in Naples, Rome, Venice, and elsewhere; First War of Independence		Aleardi
1855 Alliance of Piedmont with England and France	1857–8 Nievo writes *Confessioni di un italiano*	Mastriani
1859 Second War of Independence		Rovani
1860 Garibaldi's expedition to Sicily	1860–70 *Scapigliatura*	Tarchetti
1861 Unification: Vittorio Emanuele of Piedmont proclaimed King of Italy	1858–79 Tommaseo e Bellini, *Dizionario della lingua italiana*	Emilio Praga
1864–70 Florence capital of Italy		G. C. Abba

1870–1918 Italy unified: from *verismo* to Futurism

Political and social history	Cultural events	Authors and artists
1870 Cadorna enters Rome	1872 De Sanctis, *Storia della letteratura italiana*	D'Azeglio
1871 Rome becomes capital of Italy		Dossi
	1870s Development of *verismo*	Giacosa
	1881 Verga, *I Malavoglia*	Capuana
	1887 Carducci, *Rime nuove*	Arrigo Boito
1885 Italian troops enter Massaua (Eritrea)		Pascarella
1887 First Crispi government	1889 D'Annunzio, *Il piacere*; development of *decadentismo*	Serao
1890 Eritrea recognized as Italian colony		
1892 Socialist Party founded (Reggio Emilia)	1891 Pascoli, *Myricae*	De Amicis
1893 Unrest in Sicily (Fasci siciliani)	1894 De Roberto, *I viceré*	De Marchi
1899 Foundation of FIAT (Turin)	1895 Fogazzaro, *Piccolo mondo antico*	
1900 Assassination of Umberto I of Savoy	1903–44 Croce, *La critica*	
1901–19 Giolitti dominates Italian politics	1904 Pirandello, *Il fu Mattia Pascal*	
	1906 Aleramo, *Una donna*	Papini

History	Literature	Authors
	1908–16 *La Voce* (Florence)	Boccioni
	1909 Marinetti, *Manifesto del futurismo*	Carrà
	1910s The *Crepuscolari*	Modigliani
	1911 Gozzano, *I colloqui*	Corazzini
	1914 Campana, *Canti orfici*	Deledda
	1916 Ungaretti, *Il porto sepolto*	Papini
		Palazzeschi
		Sbarbaro
1915 Italy enters World War I		
1917 Defeat at Caporetto		
1918 Trieste becomes part of Italy		
1918–2000 Fascism and after		Cardarelli
1919 Mussolini founds 'fasci di combattimento'		
1919 D'Annunzio occupies Fiume (Rijeka)		
1920 Occupation of the factories	1921 Pirandello, *Sei personaggi in cerca d'autore*	Gobetti
1921 Foundation of Italian Communist Party (PCI)		
1921 Foundation of Fascist Party		
1922 Fascist march on Rome	1923 Svevo, *La coscienza di Zeno*	Bacchelli
1924 Murder of Giacomo Matteotti	1925 Montale, *Ossi di seppia*	Panzini
1929 Carlo Rosselli founds *Giustizia e Libertà*	1929 Moravia, *Gli indifferenti*	Govoni
1929 Lateran Pacts reconcile Papacy and Italian state	1929–35 *Solaria*	Alvaro
1935 Invasion of Ethiopia: international sanctions against Italy	1930 Silone, *Fontamara*	Bontempelli
1938 Racial laws against Jews	1933 Ungaretti, *Sentimento del tempo*	Malaparte
1939 Alliance with Germany (Pact of Steel)	1936 Pavese, *Lavorare stanca*	Quasimodo
1940 Italy enters World War II; invasion of Greece	1930s Hermetic poetry	Cecchi
1940–3 N. African and Russian campaigns	1941 Vittorini, *Conversazione in Sicilia*	Morandi
1943 Allied invasion of Sicily; Mussolini deposed		Trilussa
1943–5 Repubblica Sociale Italiana (Salò); Resistance struggle against Germans and Fascists; Allied campaign against Germans in Italy	*c.*1940–55 Neorealism	Gatto
		Bilenchi

Political and social history	Cultural events	Authors and artists
1945 Mussolini captured and shot	1945 Carlo Levi, *Cristo si è fermato a Eboli*	Guareschi
	1945 Rossellini, *Roma città aperta*	
	1945 Saba, *Canzoniere*	De Filippo
1946 Italy becomes a republic	1945–7 *Il Politecnico*	
	1947 Primo Levi, *Se questo è un uomo*	Betti
1948 Elections establish Christian Democrat hegemony	1948 De Sica, *Ladri di bicicletta*	
1950 Cassa per il Mezzogiorno founded	1952 Calvino, *Il visconte dimezzato*	
	1955 Pratolini, *Metello*	
1957 Italy enters European Economic Community	1955 Pasolini, *Ragazzi di vita*	Berto
	1955–9 *Officina*	
	1956 Montale, *La bufera e altro*	Luzi
1958–63 Economic miracle transforms Italy into a modern industrial state	1958 Tomasi di Lampedusa, *Il gattopardo*	
	1960s *Neoavanguardia*	
	1960s *Arte povera*	Cassola
	1960 Fellini, *La dolce vita*	Sanguineti
	1961 Sciascia, *Il giorno della civetta*	Antonioni
	1962 Bassani, *Il giardino dei Finzi-Contini*	Arbasino
	1963 Gruppo 63	Balestrini
1963 First centre-left government under Aldo Moro	1963 Gadda, *La cognizione del dolore*	Ginzburg
	1965 Asor Rosa, *Scrittori e popolo*	Volponi
1968–72 Student and worker unrest	1968 Zanzotto, *La beltà*	Manganelli
1969 Right-wing killings in Milan's Piazza Fontana begin the terrorism of the *anni di piombo* (1969–78)	1969 Fenoglio, *Il partigiano Johnny*	Fortini
	1970 Fo, *Morte accidentale di un anarchico*	D'Arrigo
		Attilio Bertolucci
1974 Divorce referendum	1974 Morante, *La storia*	Penna

1975 Murder of Pasolini		Sereni
1978 Aldo Moro kidnapped and killed by Brigate Rosse		Caproni
	1979 Eco, *Il nome della rosa*	Bufalino
	1979 Calvino, *Se una notte d'inverno*	Bernardo Bertolucci
1981 P2 scandals discredit Italy's political and financial elite		Consolo
		Giudici
		Celati
1983–7 Socialist government under Craxi	1983 Vattimo and Rovatti, *Pensiero debole*	Busi
		Sanvitale
		Magrelli
		Tondelli
		Loy
		Tabucchi
1990 Foundation of Lega Nord		Nanni Moretti
1991 Communist Party divides		Camilleri
1992 Mafia murders of judges Falcone and Borsellino (Palermo)		
1993 Dissolution of Christian Democrat Party		Capriolo
1994 Silvio Berlusconi Prime Minister	1995– *Cannibali*	Tamaro
2001 Berlusconi re-elected		

MAP 1. Medieval Italy (*c.*1250)

MAP 2. Counter-Reformation Italy (*c.*1559)

GERMAN CONFEDERATION

SWITZERLAND

TYROL

AUSTRIAN EMPIRE

Geneva

SAVOY

Alto Adige

Aosta

Varese

Como

Sondrio

Bolzano
Trentino

Udine

Gorizia

Turin

PIEDMONT

K. OF

SARDINIA

Pavia

Milan

Brescia

Cremona

Mantua

Vicenza

Verona

Padua

Rovigo

Treviso

Venice

Trieste

ISTRIA

Fiume

CROATIA

Cuneo

LIGURIA

Genoa

D. OF
PARMA

Parma

D. OF MODENA

Ferrara

Bologna

Ravenna

MASSA-
CARRARA

LUCCA

Pistoia

Forli

Florence

REP. OF SAN MARINO

OTTOMAN
EMPIRE

Nice

PR. OF MONACO

Pisa

Livorno

Arezzo

GR.
D. OF
TUSCANY

Siena

Perugia

UMBRIA

Grosseto

ELBA

CORSICA

Ajaccio

Civitavecchia

LAZIO

Rome

Teramo
Aquila

Chieti

ABRUZZO

MOLISE

Ancona

LE MARCHE

PAPAL
STATE

ADRIATIC SEA

Sassari

K. OF
SARDINIA

Monte Reale

Cagliari

TYRRHENIAN SEA

Gaeta

Caserta

Capua

Naples

Salerno

Eboli

Benevento

Potenza

BASILICATA

Sapri

Foggia

Bari

Taranto

Brindisi

Lecce

K. OF THE
TWO SICILIES

Cosenza

Catanzaro

Cotrone

CALABRIA

MEDITERRANEAN SEA

LIPARI IS.

Trapani

EGADI IS.

Marsala

Palermo

Calatafimi

SICILY

Caltanissetta

Girgenti

Messina

Reggio

Catania

Siracusa

TUNISIA

ALGERIA

GOZO

MALTA

Boundary of Northern Italy

0   200 km

MAP 3. Restoration Italy (c.1815)

MAP 4. Contemporary Italy

A

For the entries 1848, 1968, and *900* (*Novecento*), see under the initial letter in question.

ABATI, ANTONIO (*c.*1600–67). *Satirical poet in the *Baroque style from Gubbio. His nine *Satire* were published in 1651; eight of them form part of his *Frascherie*, a mixture of prose and poetry in various genres. While satires in the Tuscan manner tended towards the classical in style, Abati's are extreme in their use of puns, conceits, and witticisms. The most well-known is *Pegasino*, which attacks the vices of poets. He was at one time close to Salvatore *Rosa, and there is some overlap of content between their works. [PBD]

ABATI, MEGLIORE DEGLI, see SICULO-TUSCAN POETS.

ABBA, GIUSEPPE CESARE (1838–1910). Novelist, poet, and patriot. Born in Cairo Montenotte near Savona, he abandoned literary and artistic studies in *Genoa and enrolled at the age of 17 in the *Piedmontese army. He then joined *Garibaldi. The experience of the invasion of *Sicily in 1860 and the mainland battles that followed provided the material and the inspiration for most of his writings. In 1862 he settled in *Pisa, where he resumed literary studies and completed a narrative poem in five cantos, *Arrigo. Da Quarto al Volturno* (1866). After again fighting with Garibaldi against the *Austrians in 1866, he became a teacher in Cairo Montenotte, where he also served as mayor. He subsequently taught in Faenza and Brescia, where he remained until his death. He published a *historical novel, *Le rive della Bormida nel 1794* (1875), and more importantly his memoirs. These first appeared as *Noterelle d'uno dei Mille edite dopo vent'anni* (1880). In their definitive version (1891) they acquired the title under which they are generally known, *Da Quarto al Volturno. Noterelle d'uno dei Mille*. Making the most of a direct and simple style, they offer a first-hand account of some of the most significant and dramatic moments in modern Italian history. [DO'G]

ABBAGNANO, NICOLA, see EXISTENTIALISM.

ABBONDANTI, ANTONIO (*c.*1600–after 1641). Author of one of the liveliest burlesque poems of the 17th c. His *Viaggio in Colonia* (first published in 1625) recounts in *mock-heroic terms the journey from Fermo to Cologne, which he undertook in the service of the governor of Fermo. Combining real events with imaginary ones, the poem proved immensely popular. In 1630 Abbondanti completed a journey to the Low Countries, publishing in Antwerp a similar narrative poem on the figure of Judith together with a collection of sacred and moral poems. As a result of his trip he later (1641) published his *Breviario delle guerre dei Paesi Bassi*, in which, on the basis of literary sources and in grave tones, he recounts the events of the anti-Spanish revolt in Holland. [PBD]

Abbondio, Don, the weak-willed village priest in *Manzoni's *I *promessi sposi*.

ABRAVANEL, YEHUDAH, see LEONE EBREO.

ABRIANI, PAOLO (1607–99). *Venetian poet and *translator. His *Poesie*, first published in 1663, belong to the Venetian branch of *Marinismo, in which sensuality is strictly controlled by moral, even moralistic, considerations. Abriani is most famous for his translations of Lucan's *Pharsalia* (1668) and *Horace's *Ars poetica* (1663) and *Odes* (1680). In these he made considerable efforts to find Italian equivalents for Latin verse forms. He published a defence of Torquato *Tasso's

Academies

Gerusalemme liberata (1662), and in 1657 a collection of eighteen academic discourses entitled *Fonghi* ('Mushrooms'), because, he said, they grew up by chance in his uncultivated brain.   [PBD]

Academies in the post-classical sense began in the 15th c. as another aspect of the *humanists' discovery of the Graeco-Roman past. What the *Renaissance believed to be the academies of ancient Greece (as discerned in the idyllic settings of Platonic and other *dialogues) came to be imitated in what were initially free-thinking gatherings of like-minded individuals, whose informal discussions were essentially concerned with the new learning, largely in the humanities, and particularly philosophy and literature; significantly, they met outside the environment of a standard *university, whose teaching and academic policies might be controlled by a ruling prince or by the Church. Indeed, one of the earliest gatherings, the *Accademia Romana, the circle of humanists presided over by Giulio Pomponio *Leto, was repressed by Pope Paul II in 1468, when freedom of thought risked becoming subversive; in his campaign to control over-enthusiastic humanists, the Pope succeeded in banning certain texts, especially Plautus, Terence, and *Ovid. By contrast, in *Naples Alfonso I of *Aragon encouraged intellectuals to meet in his library, so creating the Academy known initially as the Antoniana, and subsequently the *Accademia Pontaniana after Giovanni *Pontano. Contemporaneously in Florence, the Elder Cosimo de' Medici encouraged research into fashionable Platonic and *Neoplatonic philosophy, and funded Marsilio *Ficino's so-called *Platonic Academy, providing him with a large villa at Careggi, and manuscripts of Neoplatonists collected by his agents [see also MEDICI]. The informality and private nature of early academies, such as meetings in Florence's Orti Oricellari, the gardens of the wealthy Bernardo *Rucellai (where *Machiavelli, Pietro *Bembo, *Michelangelo Buonarroti, and other luminaries met), allowed small groups of learned and intelligent persons to discuss cross-cultural issues without inhibitions or formality.

At the same time members of academies had many occupations in common: government functionaries, *lawyers, *bankers, university teachers, secretaries, diplomats. By the end of the 15th c. such associates communicated eagerly through their normal correspondence, as well as through the increasing exchange of printed volumes and essays. The *dialogue form of Platonic philosophical disputes continued to be seen as a model for such academies, seeming more egalitarian and creative to their members than other genres, encouraging free discussion and conviction through argument, as opposed to crushingly *ex cathedra* statements or the apparently stifling logic-chopping of *scholasticism. The academic and private nature of some academies is typified by the *Venetian Accademia Aldina, founded in 1500 by Aldo *Manuzio to include some of the authors he published; among its members were Pietro Bembo and Marin *Sanudo (the Younger). The academies also afforded a refuge from the sycophancy (and tyranny) of the *courts and, after the French invasion of 1499, the colonialization of the peninsula by foreign powers, notably French and *Spanish and later *Austrian.

Yet, particularly after 1550, hierarchical political establishments in most regions tried to formalize those academies which risked becoming too free-thinking and democratic, a good example being the anarchic Accademia degli Umidi (originally formed in 1540), which contained such engaging individualists as Giovan Battista *Gelli and Anton Francesco *Grazzini, and which, under Duke Cosimo I de' Medici, was soon taken over and restyled as the conformist Accademia Fiorentina (1541), the proceedings of which usually included formalized *ex cathedra* lectures. With this academy and elsewhere, the popularity, or at least political importance (and modishness), of the institution led inevitably to the invention of regulatory codes to restrict numbers and formalize procedures, rules being based on the statutes of the old *guilds or of religious orders. (More extreme than the conformity imposed by the Medici were the repressive tactics of the Spanish *Bourbons, who twice suppressed the academies in Naples (1647) and Messina (1674).)

Closely associated with the Fiorentina, the Accademia della *Crusca was one of Florence's most successful academies, founded in 1583 under the aegis of the Medici in order to lay down rules for the Tuscan language, though the original Cruscanti had to find their own funds to publish the first *Vocabolario della Crusca* (and at Venice!) in 1611. The Academy has created some of the most authoritative *dictionaries of Italian, a process that still continues from the beautiful Medici villa at Castello which it has now acquired. Also authoritative and important was the more independent Accademia dei *Lincei, founded in 1603 and directly linked with the empirical philosophy of the 17th c.; its members were initially proud to set reason, empiricism, and technical advances (such as telescope and microscope) against received belief.

Local organizations, with self-deprecating insouciance, adopted titles such as Insensati ('senseless') at Pistoia, or Insipidi ('insipid') at *Siena, Smarriti ('lost') at Faenza, Sventati ('deflated') at Udine, Balordi ('absurd') at Lucca, and a host of such groups at *Bologna, including the *Oziosi ('idle' or 'lazy'). Certain academies, such as the Lincei themselves, included in their closed membership the intellectual elite of their cities; and the Accademia del *Cimento (1657), under Lorenzo *Magalotti and Francesco *Redi, had close connections with London's Royal Society, as did the contemporary Neapolitan Accademia degli *Investiganti (1663), which, while essentially a grouping of scientists (particularly experts in *medicine and chemistry), acquired the latest work of fashionable thinkers such as Bacon, Descartes, and Boyle. These last two academies consciously continued the tradition of the Lincei and linked it and themselves with the figure and work of *Galileo Galilei. A great modern survivor of the *Enlightenment is the Accademia dell'Arcadia, founded in 1690 in an attempt to reform what was seen as the literary decadence of the 17th c.; it continues as a learned society largely for the promotion of literary-critical work [see ARCADIA (2)].

During the Enlightenment certain wealthy liberals encouraged academies; for instance Giuseppe *Parini's employer the Count Giuseppe Maria Imbonati, who profited by the presence of brilliant individuals in *Milan to recreate the Accademia dei Trasformati (1743), with Pietro *Verri, Cesare *Beccaria, and Parini himself as members (later in Milan Verri was to found his own Accademia dei Pugni); in the less patron-orientated atmosphere of Venice, Carlo *Gozzi was one of the co-founders of the Granelleschi (1747). Nevertheless during the 18th c. more and more literary academies yielded in importance to apparently practical institutions (such as the Florentine Accademia dei Georgofili and the Società Botanica Fiorentina, or the Società Agraria of *Turin), while there was also a concentration on didactic institutions which might promote both science and the humanities (Accademie delle Scienze e delle Belle Lettere). Even Florence's ancient *Accademia delle Arti del Disegno, founded by Giorgio *Vasari as early as 1563, and by 1572 chaired by Vincenzio *Borghini, was generalized as an Accademia delle Belle Arti in 1748. Despite attempts to restore earlier academies (such as Vin-

cenzo *Cuoco's revival of the Neapolitan Pontaniana in 1808), few ancient academies survive and thrive today. During the *Fascist period, academics undesirable to the regime (such as Benedetto *Croce) were excluded from national academies. In 1945 Croce's eulogy of the Arcadia (which had kept his name on its books during the Fascist period) testified to its free-thinking character, and that of some other academies, at a time when the Fascists were attempting to collect academics under the aegis of the Reale *Accademia d'Italia founded in 1926. [See also GELATI, ACCADEMIA DEI; INCOGNITI, ACCADEMIA DEGLI; INTRONATI, ACCADEMIA DEGLI; UMORISTI, ACCADEMIA DEGLI.]   [JRW]

See M. Maylender, *Storia delle accademie d'Italia* (1926–30); F. Yates, *Renaissance and Reform: The Italian Contribution* (1983); D. S. Chambers and F. Quiviger (eds.), *Italian Academies of the Sixteenth Century* (1995).

Accademia, see ACCADEMIES.

Accademia delle Arti del Disegno. As Grand Duke of *Florence, Cosimo I de' *Medici saw the potential use of art for politics, and gave his official approval to the proposal for an academy to provide teaching and training for artists. The Accademia was set up on 31 January 1563, and incorporated as a guild in its own right in 1584. There were forty-eight founding members, with Vincenzio *Borghini acting as the Duke's deputy and first administrative head. [See also ACADEMIES.]   [PLR]

Accademia d'Italia, Reale. Founded in 1926, the Accademia d'Italia (as it was usually termed) was one of the principal initiatives taken by *Fascism in the field of culture. Located in *Rome, its purpose was to promote and coordinate research in the arts and sciences, to preserve the national character of Italian culture, and to assist its expansion beyond national boundaries. It awarded annual prizes to authors, editors, cultural organizations, and journals, sponsored scientific expeditions, administered the Fondazione Volta (which promoted international conferences on scientific and cultural matters), and published books, especially on the work of Italians abroad. Its presidents were Tommaso Tittoni, Guglielmo Marconi, Gabriele *D'Annunzio, and Luigi *Federzoni. Among other notable writers and artists, *Pirandello, *Marinetti, *Bontempelli, and *Ungaretti were members at various times. [See also ACADEMIES.]
                    [RSD]

3

Accademia Fiorentina

Accademia Fiorentina, see ACADEMIES.

Accademia Pontaniana. Originally an informal meeting of intellectuals and civil servants in the *Naples of King Alfonso I of *Aragon, organized by *Panormita in the 1440s. The formal title of Accademia Pontaniana was later created by Giovanni *Pontano. The purpose of the meetings was discussion and debate, and the members were given personal nicknames. Unlike most other *academies, they used the vernacular as well as Latin in their deliberations. [PLR]

Accademia Romana. Under the leadership of Giulio Pomponio *Leto, a group of *humanists living in *Rome and mostly connected to the *papal curia held informal discussions of classical literature, went on archaeological field trips, collected Latin inscriptions, and put on Roman plays. In 1468 Pope Paul II accused members of the Accademia of conspiring against him and imprisoned Leto, *Platina and others for some months. The truth of the allegations remains unclear; but it is possible that Filippo *Buonaccorsi (Callimachus Experiens), who fled Rome to escape imprisonment, was involved in an anti-papal plot with the Turkish sultan. [See also ACADEMIES.] [JK]

ACCETTO, TORQUATO (*c.*1590–after 1641), the author of a famous work on the art of dissimulation, left behind few clues about his life. In *Naples he served the Dukes Carafa d'Adria as secretary, and frequented the Accademia degli *Oziosi, presided over by Giambattista *Manso. He published his lyric verse in three notable collections (1621, 1626, 1638), largely in the tradition of *Petrarchism, as mediated by Pietro *Bembo, *Della Casa, Torquato *Tasso, and the early *Marino. The arrangement of the first two collections owes much to *Petrarch: poems celebrating the beloved while she lived are followed by poems 'in morte', rounded off with a spiritual 'exercise'. In the second part of the 1626 collection the poems follow a specifically religious pattern, graduating from sin to penitence, and salvation. The final collection is arranged according to subject, with the theme of love predominant. Accetto's prose work, *Della dissimulazione onesta*, is a fascinating guide to survival in a world of appearance, hypocrisy, and selfishness. We must at all times hold onto truth, but in our inner selves; in our dealings with the outside world, we should aim to practise dissimulation, the art of concealing the truth. Dissimulation is not a permanent state: rather it is a temporary strategy for social accommodation, and to practise it successfully, man must have complete self-knowledge and control over his emotions and words.

Much of Accetto's treatise is unoriginal and can be traced to the classics, as well as to *Castiglione, Virgilio *Malvezzi, and Tasso. But it is original in that it opens dissimulation out for all men rather than restricting it to the claustrophobic world of the *court and palace. It is also remarkable for the way in which its limpid structure and laconic style enact the honest dissimulation that they describe. The work has been associated by critics with 17th-c. *Quietism. [PBD]

ACCIAIUOLI. Leading *Florentine *mercantile and *banking family during the 14th and 15th c., who assumed a major role in the republic's political life, beginning with the support of the *signoria* of Walter of Brienne in 1342 by Angelo Acciaiuolo (1298–1357), then Bishop of Florence. Opposed to the Albizzi [see ALBIZZI, RINALDO DEGLI], they allied their interests with the *Medici family's, although Angelo Acciaiuoli (d.1470) sided with Luca *Pitti against Piero di Cosimo de' Medici in 1465, and Giovanni Acciaiuoli (1460–1527) supported the restored republican regime after the Medici's exile in 1494. Donato *Acciaiuoli (1429–78) was a leading *humanist, taught by Francesco da Castiglione, Carlo *Marsuppini, and *Argyropoulos. The family maintained strong links with the court of *Naples, Neri (d.1394) being granted the hereditary title of Duke of Athens by King Ladislao in 1394. [SJM]

ACCIAIUOLI, ALAMANNO (14th c.–15th c.). One of the *priori* of *Florence in 1378, he is considered the author of the *Caso o tumulto dei Ciompi dell'anno 1378*, a historical chronicle of the eponymous popular revolt seemingly written by somebody close to the positions of the Florentine government. [LB]

ACCIAIUOLI, DONATO (1429–78). *Humanist and member of the ancient *Florentine noble family, who prospered politically under Piero and Lorenzo de' *Medici. He studied Greek under *Marsuppini and *Argyropoulos. His compositions included a Latin life of Charlemagne, dedicated to Louis XI; he also translated Plutarch into Latin. His rich Latin correspondence is still unedited; among his contemporaries he achieved particular renown for his Italian translation of Leonardo *Bruni's history of Florence. Together with Alamanno

*Rinuccini, he disseminated in Florence Argyropoulos' Byzantine view of a broad philosophical culture, preparing the way for the revival of speculative philosophy in the city under *Ficino and *Pico della Mirandola. [RDB]

ACCIAIUOLI, FILIPPO (1637–1700). *Roman impresario and *theatre producer, highly rated by contemporaries for his powerful backstage control. He devised *L'empio punito*, based on the Don Juan story, for a production in 1667 at the palazzo Colonna with music by Melani. He was impresario at the Tordinona theatre, the first public *opera house in Rome, from 1671 to 1673. [FC]

ACCIAIUOLI, NICCOLÒ (1310–65). Statesman at the court of *Naples, where he arrived with his father's *Florentine *bank in 1331. In 1335 Robert of *Anjou appointed him guardian of his nephew Luigi di Taranto, and in 1347 Niccolò arranged a marriage between Luigi and Robert's successor, Queen Joan. In the subsequent civil war he supported the couple against Louis of Hungary, and on the coronation of Luigi in 1352 became grand seneschal of the kingdom. He was a friend of writers and *humanists, including *Petrarch and *Boccaccio. Some of his letters, one of them auto-biographical, have survived.
[JP & JMS]

ACCOLTI, BENEDETTO (THE ELDER) (1415–64). Aretine who, after a successful legal career became first chancellor of *Florence. Following some vernacular poetry composed in his youth, his principal works were both in Latin: a *dialogue comparing the ancients and moderns, and a history of the First *Crusade, both dating from the 1460s. [RDB]

ACCOLTI, BERNARDO, see IMPROVISED POETRY.

ACCROCCA, ELIO FILIPPO (1923–96). Poet and critic. Born near Latina, he studied at *Rome University under *Ungaretti, who greatly influenced his work. *Neorealist influences too are evident in his first collection, *Portonaccio* (1949). He was later drawn to the *Neoavanguardia and then to more *autobiographical forms of poetry.
[JJ]

ACCURSIUS (Francesco Accursio or Accorso) (c.1181/5–1259/63). Professor of law at *Bologna

whose *Glossa*, an extensive collection of comments and interpretations of Justinian's *Corpus iuris civilis*, was the authoritative guide to Roman law until the 17th c. His son, Francesco d'Accorso, also professor of law at Bologna, appears in a story about avarice in the *Novellino* (story 50) and is mentioned by *Dante (*Inf.* 15.110). [PA]

Acerba, see CECCO D'ASCOLI.

ACERBI, GIUSEPPE (1773–1846). Born in Castelgoffredo near *Mantua, he trained as a lawyer at Pavia and became a diplomat working principally for the *Austrians. He was the first editor (1815–26) of *Biblioteca italiana* and the author of its annual *Proemio* summarizing the previous year's literary events. Earlier he had published, in English, an account of his travels through Sweden, Finland, and Lapland (1802). [MPC]

ACHILLINI, CLAUDIO (1574–1640). A significant figure in the history of *Baroque poetry, he belonged to a dynasty of academics, and was himself a law professor at *Bologna—a career interrupted only by two periods in *Rome, when he unsuccessfully sought preferment under the popes most sympathetic to the new literary style of *concettismo, Clement VII and Gregory XV. His literary fame is due principally to a twenty-year association with Giovanbattista *Marino, whom he met in 1602. He championed Marino's primacy particularly in two letters, included respectively in the preface to the latter's *Sampogna* (1620) and in the postface to his first *biography (1625). In spite of this association, and an academic reputation that led to his becoming the highest-paid Bologna professor of his generation, his own literary output, partly published posthumously, is modest and not as akin to that of Marino as once thought. There are hints of youthful heterodoxy, perhaps deriving from his philosophical studies with Cesare *Cremonini; but he takes *concettismo* in the direction of sententious, conventional grandiloquence, promoting virtue and extolling princes, as in his most famous sonnet, 'Sudate fuochi a preparar metalli', to Louis XIII of France. [MPS]

ACQUAVIVA D'ARAGONA. One of the most powerful baronial families in *Naples. Andrea Matteo (1458–1529), Duke of Atri, and Belisario (1464–1528), Duke of Nardo, were warlords and writers (tutored by *Pontano) who played a leading part in the cultural and political life of the kingdom,

Belisario staying loyal to the *Aragonese and *Spanish, his elder and more learned brother siding with the French. Belisario's treatise on the *education of princes, first published in Naples (1519), was later published in Basle (1578) as an antidote to *Machiavelli's *Principe*.   [EGH]

Adalgisa, L'. Collection of prose sketches of *Milanese bourgeois life by *Gadda, published in 1944 with the sub-title *Disegni milanesi*. As so often with Gadda, some of the material came from other works in progress, in particular *La *cognizione del dolore*. The book was republished as part of *I sogni e la folgore* (1955).   [GS]

Adelchi (1822, first performed 1843) is Alessandro *Manzoni's second *tragedy, and follows the same anti-classicizing criteria as *Il *conte di Carmagnola*. Set in the 8th c. during the struggle between Franks and Longobards for the domination of Italy, it dramatizes the defeat and death of the Longobard prince Adelchi, and his sister Ermengarda's death following her repudiation by the Frankish emperor Charlemagne.   [VRJ]

Adelonda, see DELLA VALLE, FEDERICO.

Adelphi, see BAZLEN, ROBERTO; CALASSO, ROBERTO.

ADIMARI, ALESSANDRO (1579–1649). *Florentine patrician who studied classical literature, was secretary of the Accademia Fiorentina [see ACADEMIES], and held minor government offices. In his verse he practised both *concettismo* and the Pindaric mode, as he theorized in his *Lettera sopra la poesia ditirambica* (1629). He also wrote a religious drama, *L'adorazione de' Magi* (1642).   [MPS]

ADIMARI, LUDOVICO (1644–1708). Lyrical and satirical poet and dramatist. He studied in *Pisa and *Florence, and after a period of exile joined the Accademia della *Crusca, and worked on the academy's edition of *Petrarch and the fourth edition of the *Vocabolario della Crusca*. He succeeded Francesco *Redi in the Florentine chair of Tuscan language. He is best known for his five *satires, composed between 1690 and 1700, which are violently anti-*feminist (earlier, in 1685, he was accused of killing his wife). His three volumes of *sonnets (1671, 1693, and 1696) bear some debt to *Marino's early lyric poetry, but shun excessive displays of metaphor and sensuality. He published

three *comedies, two of which are reworkings of works by J. de Herrera and Thomas Corneille.
                                                    [PBD]

Adone (1623). *Marino's most ambitious work, a vast epic without feats of arms, in twenty cantos of *ottava rima*. Reacting against the classicizing *epic of Torquato *Tasso and the moral preoccupations of the later 16th c., the poem revels in the senses, especially sexuality, and in a corresponding stylistic excess. Each canto has a title and tends to be self-contained. The poem as a whole is rich in set pieces and digressions and becomes progressively slower as it develops. Its central story is the passionate love of Adonis and Venus. Adonis, a beautiful prince born of an incestuous union, is led by Cupid to Cyprus, where he is eventually united with the goddess. After scenes celebrating poetry and the sciences, in their ancient and modern guises (including the achievements of *Galileo), Mars puts Adonis to flight. He is changed into a parrot by a witch whose advances he has rejected, and is an unhappy witness to the lovemaking of Venus and Mars. On returning to human form he goes through further improbable adventures, but is finally allowed to return to Cyprus, where he is reunited with Venus. However, he is wounded by a wild boar, urged on by jealous Mars. He dies in Venus' arms, and the poem ends, at extreme length, with his funeral.   [PBD]

Advertising. The earliest examples of advertising in Italy date back to Roman times: inscriptions on the walls of premises in Pompei illustrated the wares or services on offer. Product advertising on a mass scale, however, came only with the boom years of the 1950s and 1960s and the increased availability of consumer goods. Confined initially to the press, particularly women's journals, advertising later spread its wings on *radio, *television, and more recently the Internet. The relative novelty of television advertisements, or *spot pubblicitari*, during the 1960s and 1970s gave the advertising feature *Carosello* (1957–77) cult status.

The content of Italian advertising over the last four decades—both on television and on the printed page—is a mirror image, somewhat distorted, of Italian society. The housewife of the 1950s, dreaming of a kitchen where the latest gadgets would give her freedom from domestic chores, gave way to the emancipated couple who share the same chores and the same aspirations. In more recent advertisements, the couple has given way to single

30-something women, either unmarried or married-but-separated, where the implication is clearly that 'single is fun', reflecting the move away from the nuclear family as the focus of aspirations. With longer working hours and shortage of domestic help now a feature of Italian life, ready-prepared meals are gaining in acceptance. Older advertisements for pasta sauces had to emphasise that they were 'genuine' or 'natural'; now both men and women manage to produce instant meals for crowds of friends, implying spontaneity, modernity, and most importantly popularity. Yet women in Italian advertising can still occupy a position of inferiority which would not be acceptable to a British or American audience. In many instances there is a strong element of sexuality and often ambiguity in male–female interaction that hints of dangerous liaisons. Even the Catholic Church no longer enjoys immunity from such suggestion: advertisements featuring nuns include those for Diesel jeans and Emozioni chocolates.

For a reader or viewer used to the subtleties and tongue-in-cheek style of British advertising, Italian advertising does not appear to offer a high level of sophistication or a wide range of styles: the message is generally delivered in a direct and unsubtle fashion. But literary devices are used. Some advertisers adopt the format of a serialized novel in visual form. Other devices include the story within a story, and the textual reference: the advertisement may arouse memories of a literary classic, a film, or even another advertisement, through textual or visual recall; one such example was the Volkswagen Golf advertisement, which echoed the 'safe sex' reminders of the AIDS awareness campaign. In an unintentional echo of the *novella*, the advertisements of *Carosello* adopted a short story format, where the 'moral' or message was contained in the coda. An important feature of printed advertisements is the symbolic use of English. It is a cultural symbol when advertising products such as Scotch whisky or American jeans. It is used for high-technology products such as computers, stereo systems, cars, and watches, to suggest quality and reliability. And finally it is used for snob value; magazines such as *Capital* or *Gente money* abound in advertisements for Swatch watches, airlines, frequent-flyer schemes, and outdoor clothing.　　　[ASP]

See L. Minestroni, *Casa dolce casa* (1996); A. Borgarelli Bacoccoli, *Lo spot pubblicitario* (1995).

AFFÒ, IRENEO (1741–97). Ducal librarian at Parma from 1778 and a prolific scholar. His *Memorie degli scrittori e letterati parmigiani* (1789–97) is a monument of local literary erudition, which was later continued by Angelo Pezzana (1825–33). In 1776 he published the *Orphei tragoedia*, an anonymous 16th-c. adaptation, which he presented as the original of *Poliziano's *Orfeo.　　　[JMAL]

***Africa.** *Petrarch's Latin *epic in classical hexameters which he began in 1338–41 but never completed, books 4 and 9 still showing many lacunae. Only the thirty-four lines of the lament of the dying Mago were released during his life, partly in commemoration of the death of Robert of *Anjou, who had championed Petrarch's coronation as poet laureate, and partly as a foretaste of an eagerly awaited masterpiece. The subject matter combines historical narrative of the Second Punic war, following Livy, and celebration of the figure of Scipio Africanus, following Cicero, whilst the epic and elegiac treatment is indebted to *Virgil and *Ovid. But overt imitation of classical models is subordinated to a biblical view of history, and the poetry is conditioned by ideas of Christian truth.　　　[MP]

AGAMBEN, GIORGIO (1942–). Philosopher who has published important studies on aesthetics. He graduated at *Rome University with a thesis on Simone Weil and currently teaches at Verona. Deeply influenced by Walter Benjamin, his thought combines political commitment, theoretical synthesis, and critical attention to specific cultural phenomena, together with a pessimistic interpretation of modernity. He attempts to go beyond *idealism and to redraw the relationship between universality and singularity, assigning a central role to the renovatory potential of language and literature, perhaps most notably in *Stanze* (1977). More recently he has written on the holocaust in *Quel che resta di Auschwitz* (1998).　　　[GS]

AGANOOR POMPILIJ, VITTORIA (1855–1910) wrote semi-autobiographical love poetry, tinged with *Leopardian pessimism and prefiguring *Pirandello in its hints of tensions between outer masks and inner dualities. Of noble Armenian extraction, she grew up in *Padua and lived later in *Naples and *Perugia, publishing her first collection, *Leggenda eterna*, only in 1900.　　　[UJF]

AGLI, ANTONIO DEGLI (*c.*1400–77). Distinguished *Florentine cleric and *humanist. He was tutor to the future Pope Paul II, briefly Bishop of

Fiesole, and in 1470 Bishop of Volterra. A mentor and patron of *Ficino, he supposedly attended the banquet at Careggi on 7 November 1468 celebrating Plato's birthday. [MA]

AGLIARDI, BONIFACIO (1612–67). *Theatine monk, Bishop of Adria from 1656, and a central figure in the cultural life of Bergamo. He wrote a sacred novel, *Mosè* (1638), and various essays and discourses based on his activities as a member of Bergamo's Accademia degli Eccitati. [PBD]

Agnese va a morire, L', see VIGANÒ, RENATA.

AGNESI, MARIA GAETANA, see WOMEN WRITERS, 2.

AGNIOLO DI COSIMO DI MARIANO TORI, see BRONZINO, AGNOLO.

AGOSTI, STEFANO, see SEMIOTICS; STRUCTURALISM AND POST-STRUCTURALISM.

AGOSTINI, NICOLÒ DEGLI, see BOIARDO, MATTEO MARIA.

ALAMANNI, LUIGI (1495–1556). Poet and politician. As a member of the Orti Oricellari [see RUCELLAI, BERNARDO] he wrote verse and studied the classics while opposing the *Medici in *Florence. In 1522, following the exposure of a conspiracy in which he was involved, he fled to Lyons, joining the court of Francis I and undertaking various diplomatic missions. In 1527 he returned to Florence after the expulsion of the Medici, leaving again for France after their return in 1530 and remaining there until his death. An eclectic writer, he produced *epic poems, love poetry, religious verse, and *satires. He is traditionally seen as a competent but conventional *Petrarchist. [ABu]

Alassio, see LITERARY PRIZES.

ALBANZANI, DONATO DEGLI (?1328–1411) taught grammar and rhetoric in his native Arezzo and in Ravenna, *Venice, and *Ferrara. He was a friend and correspondent of *Petrarch and *Boccaccio. The former dedicated his *De sui ipsius et multorum ignorantia* to him and the latter his *Buccolicum carmen*. He in turn translated Petrarch's *De viris illustribus* and Boccaccio's *De claris mulieribus*. [MP]

ALBERGATI CAPACELLI, FRANCESCO (1728–1804). Aristocrat and playwright, who had a 300-seat auditorium in his villa at Zola, outside *Bologna. He was an adversary of Carlo *Gozzi, and a friend of Carlo *Goldoni, whom he met in 1752, and wrote numerous *comedies and farces. He was a member of the Accademia dell'*Arcadia and head of the Accademia dei *Gelati, and translated Addison, Racine, and Voltaire, with whom he corresponded. He also published *Novelle morali ad uso dei fanciulli* (1779) and various collections of letters. His moderately innovative treatise *Della drammatica* (1798) led to his being appointed press censor in 1800, then inspector of the *theatre, and finally head of primary schools in Bologna. [ALB]

ALBERICO DA MONTECASSINO. Major representative of the golden age of the monastery of Montecassino, where he was a monk (1057–86). He wrote two rhetorical works, *Dictaminum radii* and *Flores rhetorici*, which are pioneering expressions of the *ars dictaminis*. Probably his too are a number of other works on *papal–imperial relations and *heresy. [JT]

ALBERINI, MASSIMO, see COOKERY BOOKS.

ALBERTANO DA BRESCIA (early 13th c.–c.1270). Judge who represented Brescia in the Lombard League against *Frederick II. Captured at the siege of Ancona (1237), he began writing in prison. His moral and didactic treatises were widely known in vernacular translations, and influenced Brunetto *Latini and Chaucer. [CEH]

ALBERTAZZI, ADOLFO (1865–1924). *Bolognese writer, critic, and literary historian. He is principally known for collections of short stories such as *Novelle umoristiche* (1900), *Il zucchetto rosso* (1910), and *Amore e amore* (1913). Influenced by both the *Renaissance *novella and the psychological realism of Maupassant, his best work approaches *Pirandello's *umorismo. [PBarn]

ALBERTI, ANTONIO DEGLI (c.1360–1415). *Florentine aristocrat and politician, exiled for conspiracy in 1400 to *Bologna, where he died. Though himself a lyric poet, he is remembered as the sponsor of literary and intellectual gatherings at his villa, 'Il Paradiso', immortalized in lightly fictionalized form by *Giovanni da Prato. [SNB]

ALBERTI, FRANCESCO D'ALTOBIANCO (1401–79) was born in *Florence and a close relative of Leon Battista *Alberti, who addressed the *Proemio* of book 3 of *Della famiglia* to him. Like Leon Battista, Francesco spent much of his youth in exile. Returning to Florence in 1430, he subsequently found favour in *Medici circles. A prolific poet and associate of *Burchiello, whose tastes he shared, he is known for his *satirical and burlesque poetry and was a contributor to the *Certame coronario* (1441). [JEE]

ALBERTI, LEON BATTISTA (1404–72) has become, like *Leonardo da Vinci and *Michelangelo, an embodiment of the myth of the *Renaissance man, thanks largely to Jacob *Burckhardt's famous description of him. But even a strictly factual account of his achievements tends to confirm rather than undermine the myth of a man haunted throughout his life by the pursuit of versatility and originality. Born illegitimate and in exile from the Alberti family's native *Florence, he braved relatives' disapproval in order to study canon *law at *Bologna *University in the 1420s, at the same time writing amatory and *pastoral works in the vernacular, and a youthful *comedy, *Philodoxeos*, in a Latin so authentic that it was initially thought to be by an ancient writer. According to the Latin *Vita*, written by Alberti himself, because of poor health he turned to mathematical and scientific subjects, which made lighter demands on memory. In 1428 the exile ban was lifted on the Alberti family, and he returned soon after to *Tuscany, where he wrote his first Latin treatise, *De commodis litterarum atque incommodis* (1428), a work in the tradition of *Petrarch's and *Boccaccio's defences of poetry and of *humanism, which lamented the plight of the humanities student in a materialistic society. He was in *Rome by 1432 as a *papal secretary (*abbreviator*), but he was already experimenting with a *camera obscura* and measuring the city's ancient monuments, studies that would lead to his *Descriptio urbis Romae* and his later treatise on architecture. In what he claimed were ninety days, between 1433 and 1434, he wrote books 1–3 of his first moral *dialogue in the vernacular, *Della famiglia* (book 4 was added in 1441)—at the time a revolutionary choice of language for the dialogue, which had become the flagship genre of 15th-c. humanism. The work meditates on the Alberti family's misfortunes, and articulates, though not without hesitation, its civic and mercantile values in a more positive tone than the *De commodis*, its proem constituting one of the most emphatic humanist assertions of the power of *virtù* over *fortuna*.

Alberti returned to Florence in 1434, where his appreciation of contemporary artistic achievement led him to write his first technical treatise in Latin, *De pictura* (1435). Because of its usefulness to painters, he soon translated it into the vernacular (1436), with an important dedicatory prologue to *Brunelleschi, which also praises the works of Masaccio, *Ghiberti, and Luca della Robbia, and proudly proclaims the superiority of the moderns over antiquity. His second technical treatise, on sculpture (*De statua*), was also written around this time. Alberti remained mostly in Florence until 1443, when, taking advantage of clerical benefices, he returned to Rome, where he wrote a short vernacular piece on agriculture (*Villa*) and Latin works on legal topics (*De iure, Pontifex*), as well as 100 short Latin fables (*Apologi*). His second, much briefer, vernacular dialogue, *Theogenius* (1439–43), reflects a more Stoic, detached mood than *Della famiglia*, similar to the darker, pessimistic tone found in his contemporary Latin work *Fatum et fortuna*, one of his *Intercenales* (1425–39). The latter constitute one of Alberti's most original and characteristic contributions to 15th-c. literature. In these short pieces he develops a mordant tone, imitating an unusual model for the time, Lucian, and the cult of *serio ludere* ('serious playfulness'), a model which also lay behind his famous Latin eulogies of his dog (*Canis*) and the fly (*Musca*). The importance of the *Intercenales* resides both in their content (revealing a more pessimistic streak in Burckhardt's sunny hero) and their style: his claims in the proems that he deliberately chooses non-*Ciceronian Latin are both a conventional topos and a genuine justification of a different rhetorical ideal—the fully rounded Ciceronian period would not suit these brief, *satirical pieces. Along with the *Intercenales* and the technical treatises, *Momus* (1450) is one of Alberti's most ambitious contributions to Renaissance Latin literature in Italy. Its proem stresses the difficulty of writing anything in the shadow of antiquity's achievements, and concludes that if anything is worth writing at all, it has to be original either in content or at least in language and style.

Alberti's interest in the *questione della lingua* continued with his composition of the first *grammar of the Tuscan language (*c.*1440), and his promotion of the *Certame coronario*, a literary contest to promote compositions in the vernacular. His third vernacular dialogue, *Profugiorum ab aerumna*

libri (1441–2), celebrates the peace of mind of the educated intellect which can withstand the arrows of fortune. The start of book 2 contains a key passage about the invention of mosaics, which stands as a symbol for Alberti's approach to originality: as mosaics were invented by piecing together in a new pattern the fragments left over during the construction of the temple at Ephesus, so the humanist writer incorporates classical motifs, but in a new pattern to maintain his originality. After this, Alberti wrote only one more vernacular dialogue—*De iciarchia* (1469), about the duties of the ideal prince or head of a family—and concentrated more on the practical concerns of the architect, concerns which led to his most ambitious technical work, the ten books on architecture of the *De re aedificatoria* (1452). Around 1450 he drew up the plans for Palazzo Rucellai in Florence and for the classical façade of the Tempio Malatestiano in Rimini, and in 1471 he completed the drawings for S. Andrea in *Mantua; but his most emblematic architectural achievement was his Pantheon-inspired upper façade for S. Maria Novella in Florence, the classical proportions above the gothic arches reflecting his own remarkable hybrid style in Italian, with its combination of a broadly vernacular lexis and a classicizing syntax. Alberti's achievements in Latin and the vernacular consistently exemplify his theoretical programme of originality in content or language: his Latin works revive forgotten genres (comedy, technical treatises, Lucianic dialogues, *autobiography, fables), and are composed in an individual non-Ciceronian style; his vernacular works often stitch together classical maxims and ideas, but in a new form of the vernacular, the development of which he vigorously promoted in an age (the first half of the 15th c.) when most intellectual effort in Italy was being channelled into Latin. [See also CLASSICISM; LATIN INFLUENCES; IMITATION; LATIN PROSE IN ITALY.]   [MMcL]
   See G. Ponte, *Leon Battista Alberti* (1981); C. Grayson, *Studi su Leon Battista Alberti*, ed. P. Claut (1998); A. Grafton, *Leon Battista Alberti: Master Builder of the Italian Renaissance* (2000).

ALBERTINI, FRANCESCO, see ANTIQUAR-IANISM.

ALBIZZI,   FRANCESCHINO   DEGLI (d.1348). *Florentine friend of *Petrarch and *Boccaccio who died of the *plague. He was well thought of as a poet in his own time, but only one *ballata* by him survives.

ALBIZZI, RINALDO DEGLI (1370–1442), from an ancient *Florentine noble family, succeeded to the leadership of the city's oligarchy on the death of Niccolò da Uzzano in 1431. Rinaldo had Cosimo de' *Medici exiled in 1433 but was himself banished the following year, when Cosimo's return signalled the triumph of the Medici faction. He was the dedicatee of Leonardo *Bruni's *De militia* (1421) and one of the interlocutors in Francesco *Filelfo's *dialogue *Commentationes florentinae de exilio* (c.1440).   [RDB]

ALCIATO, ANDREA (1492–1550). Legal historian and *humanist who is best known for his collections of *emblems, the *Emblematum liber* (1531, with an expanded version in 1536). The emblem was originally conceived as a kind of epigram without illustrations. The latter were introduced by the publisher (Heinrich Steyner), who established their future format with motto, picture, and verse.   [PLR]

Alcina. A witch in the *Orlando furioso* of *Ariosto.

'Al cor gentil', see GUINIZZELLI, GUIDO.

Alcyone, see D'ANNUNZIO, GABRIELE.

Aldine Press, see MANUZIO, ALDO.

ALEARDI, ALEARDO (1812–78). One of the most popular poets of the 19th c., along with his friend Giovanni *Prati, whom he met at the University of *Padua, where he graduated in law. From an aristocratic Veronese family, he took an active part in the political events of the *Risorgimento, particularly in the revolution of *1848, when he was sent by the Republic of *Venice to Paris in order to obtain the support of the French troops against the *Austrians. His first poetic attempts follow in the footsteps of *Manzoni, especially the historical narrative poem *Arnalda di Roca* (1844), but his extraordinarily successful career and popularity are due to his combination of idyllic and sentimental tones with historical and patriotic themes, as in *Il monte Circello* (1856), *Le antiche città italiane marinare e commercianti* (1856), and *Raffaello e la fornarina* (1858). He was imprisoned by the Austrians in the 1850s. After his release his poetry became even more nationalistic with *I sette soldati* (1861) and *Il canto politico* (1862). In later life he settled in *Florence, where he produced two editions of his collected poems and taught history of art at the Accademia di Belle Arti.   [FD'I]

ALEOTTI,   GIOVANBATTISTA,   see THEATRE (3).

ALERAMO, SIBILLA (pseud. of Rina Faccio) (1876–1950). The most famous of early *feminist writers in Italy. She was born in Alessandria, which her family left in 1888 for the countryside near Ancona, where her father managed a glass-making factory. At 15 she was raped by one of her father's employees, who soon afterwards married her. She gave birth to a son two years later. Her interest in feminism dates from 1897, when she began to send articles and reviews to journals in the North. In 1899 Aleramo and her husband lived briefly in *Milan, where she became editor of the magazine *L'Italia femminile*. Two years after their return home she took the difficult decision to leave her husband and move to *Rome, where she could work as a writer and journalist, although it meant the definitive separation from her son. She took a lover, Giovanni Cena, who suggested her pseudonym and encouraged her to write her highly autobiographical feminist novel *Una donna* (1906). A *cause célèbre* on publication, it has continued to have a significant impact since it was rediscovered by the women's movement in 1970.

Aleramo's life and writing—the two are inseparable—were informed by a combination of a highly romantic, subjective lyricism and a left-wing, emancipatory political realism. Her humanitarian commitment led to her setting up with Cena a health clinic, schools, and nurseries for migrant workers in the malaria-infested Agro romano south of Rome. Until 1910 she took a leading role in the debate around the woman question. The importance she gives to the relationship between private and public, her conviction that women will only attain personal autonomy when they are economically independent, and her interest in literary culture and its role in sustaining a specific female subjectivity, all continue to give her writings resonance today.

After Cena came a succession of tormented affairs with many of the most famous writers and poets of the period, including *Slataper, *Papini, *Cardarelli, *Campana, *Boine, and *Quasimodo. These provided the inspiration for subsequent prose and poetry, such as the fragmentary, confessional narrative *Il passaggio* (1919) and the *D'Annunzian *Amo dunque sono* (1927). In the

postwar years she was active in the Italian *Communist Party. She showed herself an outstanding *diarist in *Dal mio diario* (1945) and *Diario di una donna* (1960). [See also WOMEN WRITERS, 3.]
                                                            [AHC]
        See R. Guerricchio, *Storia di Sibilla* (1974).

ALESSANDRI, BALDASSARRE OLIMPO DEGLI (*c*.1486–*c*.1540). Friar from Sassoferrato and poetic improviser, whose work mixes the stilted forms of 16th-c. *Petrarchism with themes, metres, and imagery drawn from popular literature. His books were among the best-sellers published in *Venice between 1520 and 1530.   [NC]

Alexander Romances. Alexander the Great (356–323 BC) was the hero of many medieval stories and legends which influenced the *romances, especially accounts of marvellous journeys. The principal versions in Italy were Quilichino da Spoleto's *Historia Alexandri Magni* in Latin hexameters (*c*.1236), *I nobili fatti di Alessandro Magno* in Italian prose (late 13th c.), and Domenico Scolari's *Istoria di Alessandro Magno* in *ottava rima* (1355).   [PA]

Alfabeta (1979–88). Monthly *periodical edited in *Milan by a group of intellectuals which included *Balestrini, Antonio *Porta, *Eco, and *Corti. It adopted the format, title, and distribution methods of a newspaper and aimed to reach a wider readership than that of ordinary literary magazines. Its approach to cultural debates was anti-academic, non-programmatic, and interdisciplinary. As well as literature it reviewed films, plays, and exhibitions, and published original poems and photographs. It became an important forum for the discussion of *semiotics, *psychoanalysis, and the role of literature, as well as of the significance of terrorism and other contentious contemporary issues.
                                                            [GS]

ALFANI, GIANNI DEGLI. *Florentine poet of the late 13th c. Biographical details are uncertain, though he seems to have been exiled shortly before his friend Guido *Cavalcanti in 1300. His six *ballate and one *sonnet competently imitate Cavalcanti, to whom one of his poems ('Guido quel Gianni') is addressed. [See also DOLCE STIL NOVO.]
                                                            [JU]

ALFIERI, VITTORIO (1749–1803). Dramatist, lyric poet, and political theorist. Born in Asti, *Piedmont, into an old aristocratic family, he was tutored

11

at home then sent to study at the Accademia Reale in *Turin. In 1766 he joined the army and set off on the first of his travels, through Italy and then on to France, England, and Holland. At Versailles he was presented to Louis XV. He returned to Turin in 1768 with a library of books acquired in Geneva, and during the winter read Montesquieu, Helvétius, Voltaire, Rousseau, perhaps La Bruyère, and Plutarch's *Lives*, at the time virtually a bible for many European men of letters. In May 1769 he set off on another journey, to Austria, Hungary, Germany, Denmark, Sweden, Finland, Russia, and England. In London he was involved in a duel with Lord Edward Ligonier, provoked by Alfieri's close relationship with his wife. He then went on to France, Spain, and Portugal. In Lisbon he met Tomaso *Valperga di Caluso, who urged him to devote himself to literature. He was entranced by the frozen landscapes of Northern Europe, the majestic Rhine, and the torrid scenery of Aragon. Returning to Turin in 1773, he founded the Société des Sanguignons, an academy of sorts where he gave readings of his satirical compositions in French. Between 1773 and 1774 he drafted a few scenes of a *tragedy, *Cleopatra*, or *Antonio e Cleopatra*. In 1774 he resigned from the army.

The year 1775 marks a key moment in his career, when, encouraged by the successful staging of *Antonio e Cleopatra* in Turin, he decided to dedicate himself to writing. He drafted three new tragedies and immersed himself in study. He read *Shakespeare in a French translation, but his admiration for the poet was such that he stopped reading for fear of imitating him. In 1776 and 1777 he made two literary journeys to *Tuscany. In Siena he wrote the first draft of the treatise *Della tirannide*, and worked on a number of tragedies. In November 1777, in *Florence, he met the love of his life, Louise Maximilienne Caroline Emmanuèle, Princess of Stolberg-Gedern and Countess of Albany, married a few years earlier to Charles Edward Stuart, the Young Pretender Bonnie Prince Charlie (1720–88). In 1778 Alfieri made over all his belongings to his sister in exchange for an annuity, in order to release himself from all ties of subjection, as a Piedmont aristocrat, to the King of Sardinia. Inspired by the American revolution, between 1781 and 1783 he composed the five odes of *America libera*. While there is evidence of his membership of the *Freemasons from 1782, he was to leave the organization in the 1790s. In 1783 and 1785 he published ten tragedies in three volumes in Siena, and in 1783–4 made his third trip to

England. In Paris he brought out a new edition of the nineteen tragedies so far composed with the publisher Didot (1787–9). In 1791 he went with the Countess of Albany on his last major journey, to England, Holland, and Belgium, then returning to Paris. Disillusioned by the excesses of the Revolution, in 1792 he fled France and settled definitively in Florence, where he died on 8 October 1803. He was buried in the church of S. Croce.

Steeped in *Enlightenment culture, particularly that of France, Alfieri nevertheless assumes a position of partial detachment from it. The supposed harmony between reason and nature is radically denied, nor does the conviction of the essential benevolence of nature find any echo in his work. He shared the materialism of the 18th c., but perceived it as a barely tolerable limitation, nor is there any significant evidence in his work of the century's utilitarianism. His poetry seems born from the disappointment of a heroic dream, showing a new conception of the poet as an exceptional and superior being, sometimes opposed, in an era which did not yet know the division between the 'two cultures', to the man of science. In the political field, his polemic against the ideology of enlightened despotism seems to foreshadow, in its passionately negative stance more than in its positive aims, the age of Revolution. Benedetto *Croce found in him a partial affinity with the German *Sturm und Drang*, and defined him as a 'protoromantic'.

His writing career begins with *satire: an example is the *Esquisse du jugement universel* (1773–4), written in French, in which members of the Turin court and friends of his are lampooned, including a noteworthy self-portrait in which the author presents himself as a 'tissu d'inconséquences'. This self-portrait is confirmed in the analytical *Giornale*, kept first in French (1774–5) and then in Italian (1777), which is an intimate, worldly confession of his own weaknesses, prejudices, and contradictions. His first tragedy, *Antonio e Cleopatra*, an immature work which he later disowned, is already constructed on the fundamental situation of Alfieri's poetic world, that of the pure, disinterested hero crushed by the man of power, the tyrant, here split into the two rival characters of Cleopatra and Augustus. The unfinished *Charles premier*, written in French prose, is of particular interest for the Shakespearean influences on its characterization; the doomed English king is contrasted with the pitiless Cromwell, prepared to sacrifice even the sincere republican Fairfax to his own ambitions.

Filippo has as its protagonist the Spanish

sovereign Philip II who, inhuman and merciless in his persecution mania, suppresses any hint of independence and generosity in those around him. More than on any historical sources, the tragedy was based on the legend surrrounding the death of Philip's son Don Carlos, a feature characteristic of Alfieri's *theatre, which, even when it deals with historical subjects, never shows any interest in the faithful reconstruction of settings or characters. *Polinice* presents in the character of Eteocles an almost monstrous hero, who identifies his very existence with absolute power and sacrifices all feeling to it. Filippo is dark and impenetrable; Eteocles is barbarically explicit. *Antigone* belongs to the same cycle of myths; here the protagonist's drama is a determined and heroic desire for death, veined however with doubts and uncertainties. The true protagonist of *Agamennone* is Clytemnestra, who loves the treacherous Aegistus (a character who may owe something to Shakespeare's Iago), aware all the while of the degrading nature of her passion and continually tempted to return to a normal family life. The idea of *Oreste* was conceived on the same day as that of *Agamennone*, and is based on the themes of revenge and blood: blinded by passion, Orestes kills not only Aegisthus but, involuntarily, his own mother too, and falls deep into mad delirium.

Alfieri's political treatise *Della tirannide*, first composed in 1777 in a single draft then revised in 1787 and 1789, is a vehement condemnation of absolute monarchy, which the writer equates with tyranny itself [see also POLITICAL THOUGHT]. At a time when the model of the enlightened despot, characteristic of European Enlightenment thought, was beginning to be called into question, Alfieri was among the first to reject it. Along with the tyrant he condemns the 'pillars' that support him: the prime minister, the nobles, the military, and also religion; all are oppressed by fear, including the tyrant himself. Like Rousseau and others, Alfieri also condemns luxury. In place of absolute rule the writer proposes republican constitutionalism, taken also to include constitutional monarchy of the English type.

Close to the ideology and psychology of *Della tirannide* are the three tragedies on the theme of freedom conceived between 1777 and 1779: *Virginia*, *La congiura de' Pazzi*, and *Timoleone*. At the Countess of Albany's suggestion, Alfieri wrote the over-complex *Maria Stuarda*, rated poorly by the poet himself. *Don Garzia* also has a complicated and sensational plot, based on a harrowing anecdote then current in Florence regarding Cosimo I de' *Medici and his son Piero. Uneven, but powerful in parts owing to the characterization of the protagonist, is *Rosamunda*, a tragedy about implacable hatred. The artistic strength of *Ottavia* resides primarily in the timorous dignity of the protagonist, one of the most successful female characters in Alfieri's theatre.

Merope and *Saul* were both written in 1782. The first never goes beyond the limits of a refined literary exercise, designed to compare with Scipione *Maffei's *Merope* and Voltaire's work on the same subject. *Saul*, however, is Alfieri's masterpiece; the biblical king is a kind of Übermensch—the term was coined in Germany in the late 18th c. and used by Alfieri's contemporary Goethe—who gradually discovers his own limitations; his pride in the end can only be expressed in the act of suicide. Following the less successful *Agide* (dedicated to the memory of the English King Charles I) and *Sofonisba*, there came another powerful work, *Mirra* (1784–6). The protagonist is a young girl devastated by her incestuous love for her father; unlike the character in *Ovid's fable, from which the subject is taken, Alfieri's Mirra does not seek to satisfy her insane passion, but tries desperately to thwart it.

In 1786 Alfieri completed his other political treatise, *Del principe e delle lettere*. Begun in 1778, with a final revision in 1789, it is less unified than *Della tirannide*; its main theme is that of the independence of the man of letters; 'natural' impulse is viewed as the only stimulus capable of producing sublime poetry, whilst poets moved by 'artificial' impulse can only achieve elegance at best. Between 1785 and 1786 he composed the *Panegirico di Plinio a Trajano*, a paradoxical but significant invitation addressed to an absolute ruler to accept the status of a simple citizen, and the *dialogue *La virtù sconosciuta*, a bitter reflection on political and moral themes. In 1786 he also completed the poem *L'Etruria vendicata* on the assassination of Alessandro de' Medici by his cousin Lorenzino, a forced and troubled work of little value. The tragedies *Bruto primo* (dedicated to George Washington) and *Bruto secondo* show considerable artistic skill but little power, yet both had widespread success in the late 18th c., no doubt on account of their rhetorical aspirations and the conventional sublimity of the deeds they represent. With these two works the poet considered his career as a tragedian closed, though his last tragedy might be said to be *Abele* (1790–8), conceived as a 'tramelogedia', a neologism invented by the poet for a new and somewhat bizarre theatrical genre, a mixture of tragedy and *melodramma or *opera. The true protagonist of *Abele* is Cain, an anti-hero possessed by envy who redeems artistically a work that is often cold and overly intellectual. *Alceste seconda* (1796–8) cannot be considered more than a brilliant amusement, a rewriting of Euripides's *Alcestis*, which Alfieri himself translated in 1796–7.

The technical innovations of Alfieri's theatre consist in the reduction in the number of characters, the elimination of the confidant, and the extensive use of monologue. All of this would not amount to much if it were not so firmly motivated; Alfieri's typical character is in thrall to his own burning passions and, unlike for example those of Corneille or Racine, is unable to analyse or define himself. In this context even the observance of the unities of time and space emphasize, in the most successful dramas, the restrictions within which the characters exist. The *Rime*, in two volumes, make Alfieri the foremost Italian lyric poet between *Parini and *Foscolo. Another important work is his *Vita*, one of the most notable *autobiographies of the 18th c. His excellent satire, the *Misogallo* (a pamphlet violently attacking the France of the Revolution), and six satirical comedies complete the list of Alfieri's last works. [ADiB]

See M. Fubini, *Vittorio Alfieri (Il pensiero, la tragedia)* (1953); A. Di Benedetto, *Le passioni e il limite: un'interpretazione di Vittorio Alfieri* (1994); W. Binni, *Studi alfieriani* (1995); J. Lindon, *L'Inghilterra di Vittorio Alfieri e altri studi alfieriani* (1995).

ALGAROTTI, FRANCESCO (1712–64). Cosmopolitan *Enlightenment intellectual, who was amongst the first Italians of his century to visit Eastern Europe and a fervent enthusiast of the idea of European renewal. Born into a rich *Venetian merchant family, he was drawn first to France and Voltaire, and then to England and Newtonian science, writing *Neutonianismo per le dame* (1737), an entertaining essay on Newton's ideas on optics. In 1739 he visited Holland, Denmark, Sweden, and St Petersburg with Lord Baltimore, later describing his journey (with particular attention to commerce) in *Viaggi di Russia*. He then held various posts at the court of Frederick II of Prussia, including at one point responsibility for collecting works of art in Italy for the Dresden gallery. He also spent a brief period with Augustus III, the King of Poland and

Elector of Saxony, returning to Italy in 1757. He wrote essays on a wide variety of subjects, from the classics and the arts to the influence of climate and the nature of the Inca empire. He compiled equally wide-ranging collections of letters, such as *Lettere militari* and *Lettere di Polianzio ad Ermogene*, whilst his *Pensieri diversi* revive the maxim tradition. He also published extensively in verse, joining with Carlo Innocenzo *Frugoni and Saverio *Bettinelli in the *Versi sciolti di tre eccellenti moderni autori* (1757). [GDP]

ALICATA, MARIO (1918–66). Southern intellectual based in *Rome. He contributed to *Primato but became a *Communist in 1941. He worked on *Visconti's *Ossessione* and persuaded *Vittorini, amongst others, to join the party. A close collaborator of *Togliatti, he directed the Communist Party's cultural policy between 1955 and 1962. He helped develop new policies in relation to *education and mass communications. His writings are collected in *Intellettuali e azione politica* (1975). [SG]

ALIGHIERI, IACOPO, see DANTE COMMENTARIES.

ALIGHIERI, PIETRO (c.1295–1364). Second son of *Dante and his wife, Gemma Donati. He followed his father into exile, studied at *Bologna, and spent most of his political and literary career in Verona. He corresponded with *Petrarch, and wrote lyric poems which show the understandably strong influence of his father. His major work is an influential Latin commentary on the *Divine Comedy*, which survives in three significantly different versions, dating from c.1340, 1350–5, and c.1358. In all three Pietro goes against contemporaries who saw Dante as an inspired visionary, and stresses his achievement as the author of a poetic fiction. [See also DANTE COMMENTARIES.] [SNB]

ALIONE, GIAN GIORGIO (c.1460–1521), was born of an aristocratic family in Asti in *Piedmont. He wrote poems, plays, and carnival farces in *macaronic Latin, French, and the *dialects of Asti and *Milan. His principal works were *Chapitre de liberté* in honour of the French who ruled Asti, *Maccaronea contra maccaroneam Bassani* against the anti-French Lombards, and ten farces in the Asti dialect, which also utilize French, Lombard, and a variety of other Piedmontese dialects for comic purposes. [VRJ]

ALLACCI, LEONE (Leon Allatios) (1586–1652) was a Greek from Chios, who made his way to *Rome, where he studied theology, Latin, and Greek. He held a prominent post in the *Vatican Library and published some sixty learned works beginning with *Apes Urbanae* (1633), a list of eminent men of letters in Rome between 1630 and 1632. He is perhaps best known for his bibliography of the Italian theatre, *Drammaturgia* (1666).
[DER]

ALLATIOS, LEON, see ALLACCI, LEONE.

Allegoria, see PERIODICALS, 1.

Allegory was one of the dominant concerns of early Italian literature, as it had been for all European writers since the classical period. Some defined it as an extended metaphor, as in *Petrarch's 'Passa la nave mia' (*Canz.* 189). Others saw it as a series of personifications linked to produce a narrative; the popularity of the Roman de la Rose in Italy ensured that this type of allegory was common, as in Brunetto *Latini's *Tesoretto*, *Bono Giamboni's *Libro de' vizi e delle virtudi*, and the *Fiore* and *Detto d'amore* attributed to *Dante. Indeed, allegory could be any kind of verbal expression which said one thing while at the same time signifying something else. As a result, medieval Italian writers also understood allegory as a way of interpreting and not just as a way of writing, one which explored the other meanings present beneath the 'letter', the literal level, of any text. Allegory was thus both a rhetorical device and an exegetical method. Repeating well-established hermeneutic notions, at the beginning of the second book of the *Convivio* Dante defined poetic allegory as 'truth hidden beneath a beautiful lie' ('une veritate ascosa, sotto bella menzogna'), referring to a text's moral sense. He further distinguished poetic allegory from theological allegory, in which the events narrated at the literal level, as in the *Bible, are not just historically true but also refer to salvation history, as well as concealing three spiritual senses: the allegorical, the moral, and the anagogical.

What is original about Dante's presentation of exegetical allegory in the *Convivio* is not its substance, but the fact that he intended to apply the conventions of poetic allegory to his own vernacular verse, rather than, as was the custom, to the works of the great writers of antiquity. In the *Divine Comedy*, Dante made even more startling claims regarding the interpretation and hence the status of his great poem. He proposed, quite radically and uniquely, that the *Divine Comedy* offered an account of an actual, divinely ordained journey through the afterlife, and thus had to be read according to the norms of theological allegory. Dante also continued to make use of rhetorical allegory in the poem, inviting readers to look for the 'hidden' meanings beyond the letter of the more overtly symbolic parts of his text, such as the opening canto of *Inferno* and the processions in the Earthly Paradise at the end of *Purgatorio*. Commentators, including Dante's sons Iacopo and Pietro *Alighieri, *Boccaccio, even *Pascoli in the 19th c., proved eager to take up the author's invitation. *Virgil was interpreted as representing human reason and *Beatrice as theology, to name just the two most obvious examples, but now critics generally agree that rhetorical allegory in the *Comedy* is a sporadic phenomenon, not applicable to the text as a whole. [See also COMMENTARIES; DANTE COMMENTARIES; MIDDLE AGES.]

The distinction between allegory as a mode of writing and a mode of reading is also evident in the literature of the *Renaissance. As a mode of writing it can be clearly seen in parts of *Ariosto's *Orlando furioso*, such as the episode of Astolfo on the moon (35.18–30); as a mode of reading it is especially associated with the *Neoplatonism of exegetes such as *Pico della Mirandola and Cristoforo *Landino. A striking example of how allegorical exegesis could provide interpretative autonomy at the expense of authorial intention was Torquato *Tasso's allegory of his own *Gerusalemme liberata*, from the end of the 16th c. Whilst admitting that he had intended nothing of the kind when writing the poem, Tasso concocted an allegorical significance to the events narrated in an attempt to convince sceptical critics of its moral worth. After the rise of *Romanticism with its more suggestive, less rigid theories of symbolism, allegory suffered something of a critical demise. The indications are, however, that it is finding favour once again, and the work of Romano Luperini should be noted in this regard. Apart from numerous articles and books revealing the allegorical structure of texts by 19th- and 20th-c. authors including *Verga and *Montale, he has founded the journal *Allegoria* to provide a focus for debate on the subject.
[DG]

See R. Hollander, *Allegory in Dante's 'Commedia'* (1969); R. Luperini, *L'allegoria del moderno* (1990); A. J. Minnis and A. B. Scott, *Medieval Literary Theory and Criticism* (1991).

Allegria, L'

Allegria, L', see UNGARETTI, GIUSEPPE.

All'Insegna del Pesce d'Oro, see SCHEIWILLER, VANNI.

Althénopis, see RAMONDINO, FABRIZIA.

ALTOMARE, LIBERO (pseud. of Remo Mannoni) (1883–1966). Poet best known for his association with *Futurism. His first collection, *Rime dell'Urbe e del suburbio* (1908), was in the manner of the *Crepuscolari. In 1909, he sent his next collection, *Procellarie,* to *Marinetti and adhered to the Futurist movement, adopting the heroic pseudonym 'Libero Altomare'. His poem 'Apocalisse' was published in Marinetti's journal *Poesia.* He subsequently contributed to Futurist *serate,* and signed manifestos such as *Il manifesto dei drammaturghi futuristi* (1911). After 1913 he detached himself from the movement, and, clashing with Marinetti, formally severed links in June 1915. In 1954 he wrote a memoir of his Futurist experiences, *Incontri con Marinetti e il futurismo.*   [RSCG]

Altrieri, L', see DOSSI, CARLO.

ALVARO, CORRADO (1895–1956). Calabrian novelist. He was educated by the *Jesuits and at *Rome and *Naples universities, and fought on the Isonzo in *World War I. After some early poetry, he began to publish fiction in the 1920s. He also worked for Giovanni *Amendola's *Il *Mondo and co-edited *Bontempelli's *900 (*Novecento*). Uncomfortable with the *Fascist régime, he travelled widely, writing books on Turkey and the Soviet Union. After the liberation he was active on the literary left and was a founder and president of the Sindacato degli Scrittori Italiani.

His fiction began with the stories of *La siepe e l'orto* (1920) and *L'amata alla finestra* (1929) and the novel *L'uomo nel labirinto* (1926, but serialized in 1922). In general its themes alternate between archaic *peasant revolt in the South and modern urban alienation. The former led to the stories of *Gente in Aspromonte* (1930), which was suppressed by the regime, and later seen as a precursor of *Neorealism in its rural aspect; the latter issued in *L'uomo è forte* (1938), Alvaro's most popular work, which conveys the atmosphere of life under a totalitarian regime. This theme, supplemented by the disappointing sequel of the liberation, is articulated with autobiographical conviction in *Quasi una vita* (1950), the writer's discursive journal of the years

1927–47. Dystopian social fantasy of an over-regulated consumer society after a third world war is the subject of the unfinished *Belmoro* (1957). But Alvaro's most ambitious project was the trilogy *Memorie del mondo sommerso.* In the first volume, *L'età breve* (1946), the peasant seminarist Rinaldo Diacono gives up the Church to find himself adrift in the city. The unfinished *Mastrangelina* (1960) and *Tutto è accaduto* (1961) carry him through the period of *Mussolini's dictatorship with its atmosphere of arbitrary power and corrupt sexuality, to end in utter negativity with the war.   [JG-R]

See M. I. Tancredi, *Corrado Alvaro* (1969); L. Reina, *Cultura e storia di Alvaro* (1973).

AMARI, MICHELE, see SICILY.

AMARILLI ETRUSCA, see BANDETTINI, TERESA.

AMBROGINI, AGNOLO, see POLIZIANO, ANGELO.

Ambrosiana, Biblioteca, see LIBRARIES; MAI, ANGELO; MURATORI, LUDOVICO ANTONIO.

AMBROSOLI, FRANCESCO (1797–1868) wrote several textbooks, including an influential four-volume *Manuale della letteratura italiana* (1831–2), and translated F. Schlegel's *Storia della letteratura antica e moderna* (1828). An eclectic rather than original thinker, he was a close friend of *Giordani and admired *Manzoni.   [MPC]

AMELIO, GIANNI, see CINEMA.

AMENDOLA, GIOVANNI (1882–1926). Moral philosopher and militant *journalist before *World War I, who then worked for the *Corriere della sera* during the conflict. He then entered parliament as a liberal under *Nitti's banner and became leader of the constitutional opposition to *Fascism. He died of injuries inflicted by the regime's thugs.   [JD]

American Influences. It was only in the second half of the 19th c. that the study and appreciation of American literature acquired some momentum in Italy, although the limited knowledge of English amongst educated Italians meant that texts were often read in French *translation. The scholar and poet Enrico Nencioni was largely responsible for introducing writers such as Poe and Whitman to

Italian readers. He also presented a view of American literature which would become deeply rooted in Italy, namely of a powerful but fundamentally naïve body of writing in sharp contrast with the convoluted sophistications of European culture.

It is possible to find traces of American poets in *Carducci, *Pascoli, and *D'Annunzio. But the poetry of Pound, Eliot, and others of their generation was only slowly assimilated, even though Pound lived in Italy and was personally acquainted with *Montale and others. However in the interwar period contemporary American fiction became popular and influential. Scores of novels were translated in the 1930s, with *Pavese and *Vittorini playing a prominent part both as translators and as editors. The orthodox voices speaking of America and American literature were Carlo *Linati and Emilio *Cecchi, but the younger generation of critics and writers, with Vittorini and Pavese at their head, had more dynamic and controversial views. Following on from Nencioni, they admired the stylistic directness and simplicity of American fiction, whilst what they saw as the clash between primal natural forces and the creation of a modern society proved immensely fertile artistically. Their appreciation of the narrative techniques of Hemingway, Caldwell, Saroyan, and others exerted an enormous influence on their own work and that of other Italian novelists in the years immediately before and after *World War II. Though their approach ran implicitly against the nationalist policies of the *Fascist regime, the authorities do not appear to have worried; even pro-Fascist magazines, such as *900 (*Novecento*) and *L'*Italiano published articles and short stories by American writers. Only with the outbreak of war did censorship become significantly stricter. The most stimulating work on American literature to appear so far in Italy, Vittorini's anthology *Americana* (1941), had to be republished with the introductory sections by Vittorini replaced by more critical assessments from Emilio Cecchi. Important novels that emerged from the war, such as Vittorini's *Uomini e no* (1945), *Calvino's *Il sentiero dei nidi di ragno* (1947), and Pavese's *La casa in collina* (1948), all implicitly paid tribute to the narrative technique of American novelists. In fact the spare, unadorned style, with long stretches of dialogue and an avoidance of psychological introspection, that was characteristic of *Neorealism was largely American in origin.

But the dominant left-wing culture of the postwar years drew Italian writers away from American models, as Pavese acknowledged in his later

writings. The 'American way of life' and its consequences for Italian culture tended to be treated critically by writers such as Ennio *Flaiano. However, the protest movements of the 1960s and 1970s found the beat generation and pop art inspirational as expressions of political dissent and anti-bourgeois anarchy. The effects are evident in the poetry of the *Neoavanguardia*, which was also indebted to Pound's *Cantos*, and in fiction such as Nanni *Balestrini's *La violenza illustrata* (1976) and the less sophisticated *Porci con le ali* (1976) by the fictitious Rocco e Antonia [see RAVERA, LIDIA]. More recent Italian fiction writers often acknowledge their debts to American authors as diverse as Salinger, Heller, Coover, and Mailer. [See also ENGLISH INFLUENCES.]   [GUB]

See D. Heiney, *America in Modern Italian Literature* (1964); P. P. D'Attorre (ed.), *Nemici per la pelle: sogno americano e mito sovietico nell'Italia contemporanea* (1991).

Ameto, or *Comedìa delle ninfe,* or (in the 15th c.) *Ninfale d'Ameto* (1341–2). Prose narrative by *Boccaccio, interspersed with poems in *terza rima*, after the example of Boethius and *Dante's *Vita nova*. It tells how Ameto is transformed from rough shepherd to noble lover, through hearing the nymph Lia and her six companions recount their experiences of love. At least four of the narrators have been identified with specific upper-class women. The *pastoral framework strongly influenced subsequent *Arcadian literature.   [VB]

AMICO DI DANTE. The author of five *canzoni and sixty-one *sonnets which appear at the end of the main *Vatican manuscript collection of 13th-c. lyrics (Vat. Lat. 3793). The name was coined because the first *canzone*, 'Ben aggia l'amoroso e dolce core', is a reply, using the same rhymes, to 'Donne ch'avete', the manifesto of the *dolce stil novo* in *Dante's *Vita nova*. The anonymous *Florentine poet himself writes in the old *Siculo-Tuscan manner. He was once thought to be Guido *Cavalcanti, traces of whose style can be discerned in the sonnets. Now he is more commonly believed to be Lippo Pasci de' *Bardi.
                    [GG]

Aminta (1581). *Pastoral play by Torquato *Tasso, written in 1573 and published in 1580. Aminta is a young shepherd and poet who is scorned by his childhood companion Silvia in favour of the hunt. Silvia is also courted by the

Satyr, who attempts to rape her but is chased off by Aminta. She flees and is reported killed by a wolf, whereupon Aminta flings himself from a cliff. But Silvia is safe and is touched with pity to hear of Aminta's attempted suicide. She determines to die too but is prevented by the arrival of a messenger with news of Aminta's safe landing from his fall, and the two are united. A sub-plot shows us the mature Dafne discreetly wooing Tirsi, who keeps her at a distance.   [CPB]

AMMANITI, NICCOLÒ, see CANNIBALI.

AMMANNATI, BARTOLOMEO (1511–92) was an architect and sculptor who was moved by the spiritual message of the *Counter-Reformation to write a treatise in the form of a letter to the members of the *Accademia delle Arti del Disegno, dated 22 August 1582, in which he denounced the depiction of the nude on moral grounds and called for clothing to be mandatory.   [PLR]

AMMIRATO, SCIPIONE (1531–1601) studied rhetoric and moved in the circles of Sperone *Speroni, Vittoria *Colonna, and Pietro *Aretino. He contributed the *Argomenti dei canti* to the 1556 edition of Ludovico *Ariosto's *Orlando furioso*. In 1558 he returned to his native city, Lecce, where he founded the Accademia dei Trasformati. After an unsuccessful attempt to become the official historian of *Naples, he moved to *Florence in 1569 and became an influential figure in Florentine cultural circles. His scholarly activities and literary output as poet, historian, and philosopher seemed so various and impressive to his contemporaries that he was given the name Proteo (Proteus).   [PLR]

Amore, see ANDREAS CAPELLANUS; DETTO D'AMORE, IL.

Amorosa visione, L' (1342, revised c.1365). Narrative poem by *Boccaccio, full of echoes of the *Divine Comedy* and consisting of 50 canti in *terza rima*. It tells of a dream in which the poet sees, in sequence, the triumphs of Wisdom, Earthly Glory, Wealth, Love, all-destroying Fortune (and her servant Death), and thereby becomes worthy of the now heavenly love of *Fiammetta. The triumphs include mythological, classical and contemporary medieval figures. Their moral, cultural, and historical architecture was without precedent, and led *Petrarch to create his own *Trionfi* on the same model. Among contemporaries *Giotto and *Dante stand out, the latter being celebrated over and above any other artist, ancient or modern.
                                            [VB]

ANCESCHI, LUCIANO, see ANTHOLOGIES; NEOAVANGUARDIA; VERRI, IL.

ANDALÒ DEL NEGRO, see BOCCACCIO, GIOVANNI.

ANDREA DA BARBERINO (Andrea de' Mangiabotti) (c.1370–1431/3). *Florentine author of the most compendious prose versions of the Carolingian *chivalric narratives, which gather material from a wide range of French and *Franco-Veneto texts to form a complex tapestry of interrelated dynasties and adventures. Of the works attributed to Andrea, definitely his are *I reali di Francia, Aspramonte,* and *Ugone d'Avernia,* on the exploits of the Carolingian dynasty from their supposed ancestor Constantine to Hugh Capet, and including Charlemagne's nephew Orlando whose childhood and early triumphs are set in Italy; *Storie nerbonesi* and *Aiolfo del Barbicone,* both based on French *chansons de geste*; and *Guerrin meschino,* whose hero has a series of exotic encounters in the course of his quest for his parents. Andrea's works provided a widely used repertoire of material for later writers, including Luigi *Pulci, *Boiardo, and *Ariosto. Their influence continued into modern times; they have been regularly reprinted, and provide the basis for the plots of *Sicilian puppet theatre.   [RMD]

ANDREAS CAPELLANUS (later 12th c.). Author of a famous Latin love manual, *De amore* (c.1185). Composed at the court of Eléonore d'Aquitaine and of *Ovidian inspiration, it offers rules of behaviour for lovers, with exemplary dialogues and an orthodox moral conclusion. It was known in Italy and translated into Tuscan by the 14th c. Its influence is visible in *Dante's *Francesca da Rimini (*Inf. 5) and *Boccaccio's *Filocolo*.   [JU]

ANDREINI, FRANCESCO (1548–1624) was a *commedia dell'arte* actor of Tuscan birth, and devoted husband of Isabella *Andreini Canali. He played the role of the braggart *Capitano, and published some of his repertoire as *Bravure del Capitan Spavento* (1607). He also edited two volumes of Isabella's repertoire pieces under the titles of *Lettere,* though they are not letters, and *Fragmenti.* [See also ANDREINI, GIOVAN BATTISTA; THEATRE, I.]
                                            [RAA]

ANDREINI, GIOVAN BATTISTA (1576–1654), son of Francesco *Andreini and Isabella *Andreini Canali, was a leading actor-manager and dramatist, spending successful periods in Paris in the 1620s and from 1643 to 1647. On the one hand his twenty plays record the influence of *commedia dell'arte masks and techniques on written drama, and have been shown to adapt themselves to the talents of specific actors. On the other hand, they are documents of the *Baroque fashion for mixed (*tragicomic) emotions and for 'total theatre', involving words, action, gestures, improvisation, and the spectacle provided by sophisticated stage machinery. [See also THEATRE,1.]   [RAA]

ANDREINI CANALI, ISABELLA (1562–1604). *Commedia dell'arte actress, born in *Padua, and wife of Francesco *Andreini. One generation after Vincenza *Armani, she was the first European actress to acquire social and cultural respectability as well as fame. Exceptionally for a woman, she was elected to the Accademia degli Intenti, having published in her lifetime a *pastoral drama, Mirtilla (1588), and a substantial body of Rime (1601). [See also ANDREINI, GIOVAN BATTISTA; THEATRE,1.]
          [RAA]

ANDRÉS, JUAN (1740–1817). A native of Alicante, who settled in Italy when Spain banished the *Jesuits (1767). He was librarian successively at Parma and at *Naples, and made his mark in Italian scholarship by compiling Dell'origine, progressi e stato attuale di ogni letteratura (1782–9), a universal history of literature. [See also HISTORIES OF ITALIAN LITERATURE.]   [JMAL]

ANGELA DA FOLIGNO (1248–1309). *Franciscan mystic, a tertiary (lay sister) until the death of her husband and children, when she sold her property and became an anchoress. Her account of her life and spiritual experiences was taken down somewhat fitfully in Latin by her confessor and kinsman Fra Arnaldo da Foligno. This was later enlarged through the addition of letters, meditations, and visions recorded by other hands.
          [JP & JMS]

Angelica. The daughter of Galafrone, King of Cathay, a character invented by *Boiardo for his *Orlando innamorato (1483). Her irresistible yet unattainable beauty, and especially her virginity (her unplucked 'rose'), make her a magnet for male desire. Her most characteristic role, the repeated flight from unrelenting pursuers, was epitomized in *Ariosto's *Orlando furioso, which introduced a significant transformation when, coveted by the greatest knights in the Christian and pagan worlds, she chooses to give up her virginity to the humble Medoro. Variations and continuations were introduced in Pietro *Aretino's De le lagrime di Angelica (1533), Vincenzo *Brusantino's Angelica innamorata (1550), and Marco Bandarini's L'amorosa vendetta di Angelica (1551). Sir John Harington's translation of Orlando furioso (1591) was the main source of Angelica's popularity in Elizabethan literature. [See also RECEPTION OF ITALIAN LITERATURE IN BRITAIN.]   [MGD]

ANGELO CLARENO (Pietro da Fossombrone) (d.1337). Militant *Franciscan. His ascetic side finds expression in the Expositio regulae fratrum minorum and his rebellious side in the Historia septem tribulationum ordinis minorum, both belonging to the last part of his life. A fervent mystic, much influenced by *Gioachino da Fiore, he inspired generations of Franciscan reformers.
          [JT]

ANGIOLETTI, GIOVANNI BATTISTA (1896–1961). Literary critic, *journalist, and novelist. In 1914 he founded the *nationalistic and interventionist La terza Italia, followed, after *World War I, by another review, Trifalco. From 1929 to 1936 he co-edited Italia letteraria with Curzio *Malaparte, and was again its editor (as La *Fiera letteraria) after the war. As a critic, he was an eclectic *modernist, who encouraged Italian authors to absorb French and British contemporary literature. In his own writing he sought to achieve a refined and lyrical prose style after the canons of La *Ronda, but was already developing a firmer narrative structure in Amici di strada (1933).
          [SVM]

ANGIOLIERI, CECCO, see CECCO ANGIOLIERI.

ANGUILLARA, GIOVANNI ANDREA DELL' (c.1517–?1572) began his literary career in *Rome and then sought success in France, *Florence, *Venice, and again Rome. His verse adaptation of *Ovid's Metamorphoses (the complete version was published in 1561) was often reprinted; a partial translation of *Virgil's Aeneid enjoyed less success. Anguillara wrote a comedy (Anfitrione), a *tragedy (Edipo), and Rime.   [BR]

ANGUISSOLA, LANCILLOTTO (*c.*1280/90–1359). Soldier and writer from a noble Piacenza family, he was active in city affairs until moving to *Padua in 1350. He wrote Latin prose and verse letters and some vernacular lyrics, which include an exchange with *Antonio da Ferrara. He was a friend of the *Visconti, one of whom used his name to attack *Petrarch, until Lancillotto disclaimed any involvement. [JP & JMS]

ANIANTE, ANTONIO, see *900 (Novecento).*

ANJOU. French dynasty implanted in Italy by Charles I (1227–85), youngest son of Louis VIII. Supporting *papal claims against the Hohen-staufen [see FREDERICK II], Charles defeated *Man-fredi at Benevento (1266) and crushed the revolt by Conradin. Though he became King of *Naples and *Sicily, his success was checked by the outbreak of the War of the Sicilian Vespers (1282). His son Charles II the Lame failed to retake Sicily from the *Aragonese. Charles II's son Charles Martel died young, but made a good impression on *Dante (see *Para.* 8). More successful, but disliked by Dante, was Charles Martel's younger brother, Robert the Wise (1275–1343), whose rule from 1309 stabilized finances, maintained *Guelf supremacy, and pro-vided enlightened patronage for *Giotto, *Petrarch, *Boccaccio, and other writers and artists. After Robert the succession became contested as a result of the complicated love life of Joan I, Robert's granddaughter. Further confusion over the succes-sors of Joan II (1371–1435) meant that power passed to the Aragonese in 1442 with Alfonso V. Anjou influence in Italy, apart from its crucial con-tribution to the Guelf–Ghibelline power struggle, was important for reinforcing models of French aristocratic culture in Southern Italy, whether in the form of Gothic architecture, *chivalric pursuits such as jousting and tournaments, or the decidedly Gallic literary tastes of the young Boccaccio.
[JU]

ANNIO DA VITERBO, see ANTIQUARIANISM.

ANONIMO GENOVESE (late 13th c.). Name given to an anonymous *Genoese writer with a legal background, who wrote Latin verse and also com-posed substantial quantities of ingenuous verse in the Genoese vernacular. Some is religious-didactic, whilst the more lively compositions celebrate Genoa and its victories over the *Venetians. His best work has an epigrammatic brevity. [JU]

ANONIMO ROMANO, see CRONICA DI ANONI-MO ROMANO.

ANONIMO TRIESTINO, see VOGHERA, GUIDO.

ANONIMO VERONESE (13th c.). Author of a didactic *sirventese, written in a mixture of deca-syllables and *hendecasyllables, advising a certain Guglielmo to behave morally and prudently, avoid-ing such pitfalls as drink, whoring, bad company, and bad table manners. It is the earliest vernacular poem we have from Verona. Its author was prob-ably a *giullare. [JP & JMS]

Anthologies, or collections of texts, usually by different authors, brought together for deliberate reasons, whether private or public, have played an important role throughout the history of Italian lit-erary culture. They continue to be important today, especially for the use made of them in them in the *education system.

Anthogies of verse [see CANZONIERE] played a decisive role in the transmission and shaping of the early Italian lyric tradition in the 13th and early 14th c. They not only are the sole sources for the texts we have from the *Sicilians to the *dolce stil novo, but also, through their selection and configu-ration of the material, largely conditioned how early poetry and those who wrote it would be approached by subsequent readers. Anthologies of *novelle and *exempla from the same period demonstrate the general tendency to collect and preserve on them-atic or generic principles. Overarching structures, such as *Boccaccio's frame for the *Decameron, will mark the passage from mere record to conscious aesthetic or expository purpose. So too *Petrarch's *Canzoniere is an artfully simulated anthology, in which the process of selection and juxtaposition characteristic of the non-authorial anthologizer is elaborated into a sophisticated autobiographical fiction.

Petrarch and Boccaccio came to provide the models for authorial anthologies of lyric verse and *novelle* throughout the *Renaissance. But multi-author anthologies continued to be produced. One with a more consciously scholarly historical and aesthetic programme is the *Raccolta aragonese* (1476–7), produced by Lorenzo de' *Medici with *Poliziano's assistance, for Frederick of *Aragon. This anthology, and its accompanying letter, is a key document for modern reconstructions of the canonic programme of vernacular *humanism. A more widely read anthology of vernacular verse, which may itself have had a polemical purpose in debates about the status of *Florentine language and culture, is the *Giuntina di rime antiche of 1527. [See also PETRARCHISM.]

The diffusion of printing led to the range of anthologies being expanded to include a wider variety of genres, most importantly letters [see LETTER-WRITING AND EPISTOLARI]. By the 18th c. collections of texts, both verse and prose, were increasingly produced for didactic purposes. *Muratori appended one to Della perfetta poesia italiana (1706) to illustrate by example his aesthetic. *Leopardi's two Crestomazie italiane (1827–8), one of poetry, the other of prose, though written primarily for financial reasons, struck out in a new and fertile direction. Rather than providing examples of 'good' writing (often organized by genres), they brought together what the author considered to be the best writing in Italian over the centuries. Their Greek-derived title (etymologically 'useful for learning') also established in the language a new learned term for anthology.

In the 20th c. anthologies have been the means by which groups or currents have defined themselves. Turning points in modern Italian poetry are signalled above all by *Marinetti's Poeti futuristi (1912), *Pancrazi and Papini's Poeti d'oggi (1920), Anceschi's Lirici nuovi (1943), and Alfredo *Giuliani's I novissimi (1961). *Vittorini's anthology of American writing, Americana (1942), was in effect the portrayal of a mythic America deliberately at odds with the prevailing aesthetic of the *Fascist regime, and was published only after cuts by the *censors [see AMERICAN INFLUENCES]. In the postwar period anthologies representing fresh standpoints, such as women's writing, have proved important devices for redefining canons [see FEMINISM]. But anthologies have also reshaped academic perspectives and practices. *Contini's Poeti del Duecento (1960) set new standards of scholarship, and introduced an explanatory and critical methodology which has been widely influential.

Substantial and wide-ranging literary anthologies are still an important element in school and university education in Italy. Though there is continuing debate about the effectiveness of the approach, commented passages by a selection of authors are seen as a legitimate way of offering a sense of values, periodization, and ideological contextualization. [JU]

See V. Branca, 'Le raccolte di rime e le collezioni di classici', in A. Momigliano (ed.), Problemi ed orientamenti critici di lingua e di letteratura italiana: notizie introduttive e sussidi bibliografici, vol. iii (1960); A. Quondam, Petrarchismo mediato: per una critica della forma 'antologia' (1974).

Anti-clericalism, see FREEMASONRY; PAPACY AND THE CATHOLIC CHURCH; POLITICAL THOUGHT.

Antiquarianism. Although some earlier Italian writers, including *Dante, show an interest in the relics of antiquity, and although some remains were mentioned in pilgrim guides such as the *Mirabilia urbis Romae, and archaeological finds caught the attention of *humanist historians in *Padua and Verona, *Petrarch can be considered as the first Italian antiquarian. He describes in letters the awe and melancholy felt visiting the ruins of *Rome in 1337, he attempts to reconstruct them in book 8 of the *Africa, and he makes use of archaeological sources, especially coins. *Cola di Rienzo responded by seeking unsuccessfully to restore the political glory of Rome; but most humanist energies went into surveys of monuments, statues, and inscriptions by figures like *Boccaccio or Giovanni *Dondi dall'Orologio, who compared them with literary evidence. Antiquarian circles sprang up elsewhere, notably in *Florence around Coluccio *Salutati, Pier Paolo *Vergerio (the Elder) and Giovanni *Rucellai, but the principal impetus in the 15th c. came from curial officials following the return of the *Papacy to Rome, notably Poggio *Bracciolini, Flavio *Biondo, and Leon Battista *Alberti. Poggio's topographical studies, included in his De varietate fortunae of 1447, use the ruins as moral examples of transience; but it is the systematic detailed research in Biondo's Roma instaurata (1446), or Alberti's Descriptio urbis Romae, which created the new science of archaeology, whilst also arguing passionately for the preservation of marble remains, fast disappearing into the lime-kilns. Attention was turned to monuments throughout Italy, especially in the picturesque descriptions of Enea Silvio *Piccolomini's Commentarii, or further afield in the extensive manuscripts of the tireless traveller in the eastern Mediterranean, *Ciriaco d'Ancona.

Activity in Rome focused around the *Accademia Romana set up by Giulio Pomponio *Leto, which produced some major studies, notably Bernardo *Rucellai's De Urbe Roma (c.1495), Raffaele Maffei Volaterrano's Commentaria (1506), and Francesco Albertini's De mirabilibus novae et veteris urbis Romae (1510), editions of which reached a wider public and replaced the older pilgrim guides. Literary repercussions are evident both in Francesco *Colonna's pseudo-antiquarian novel, *Hypnerotomachia Poliphili* (1499) and in Annio da Viterbo's forged *chronicles (1498), as well as in the chorus of poetry which greeted major discoveries such as the Laocöon (1506). Enthusiasm for archaeology and topography culminated in *Raphael's project to map the ancient city, in collaboration with *Castiglione and Andrea Fulvio, a project interrupted by Raphael's death but preserved in part in Fulvio's *Antiquitates urbis* and in Marco Fabio Calvo's reconstruction of the ancient city, *Antiquae urbis Romae cum regionibus simulachrum*, both works published immediately before the disastrous *Sack of Rome of 1527.

Activity resumed with the work of the Milanese Bartolommeo Marliani's *Topographia antiquae Romae* (1534 and 1544), and with new campaigns of excavation. These produced discoveries like the *Fasti*, which went to adorn the private collections of families like the Massimi and the Cesi, and the great villas of the *Farnese and the *Este, soon rivalling the papal collections at the Belvedere or the Villa Giulia. Major collections of inscriptions were formed by scholars like Benedetto Egio; ambitious projects were launched to map the ancient city, notably the copious manuscripts of Pirro Ligorio, which also include forgeries; and authoritative topographical surveys were carried out by Fulvio Orsini and Onofrio Panvinio, both left unfinished. Antiquarian taste was also reflected in art, notably in the engravings published in Rome by Antonio Lafreri (*Speculum romanae magnificentiae* (1579)), anticipating the *Vedute* (1745) and *Antichità romane* (1756) of Giovanni Battista Piranesi, and the ruin paintings of Gianpaolo Panini, which helped inspire a *Romantic vision of antiquity. [See also CLASSICAL SCHOLARSHIP; CLASSICISM; LATIN INFLUENCES.] [RAC]

See R. Weiss, *The Renaissance Discovery of Classical Antiquity* (1969); A. Schnapp, *La Conquête du passé* (1993); J.-L. Ferrary, *Onofrio Panvinio et les antiquités romaines* (1996).

Anti-semitism, see JEWS AND JUDAISM.

Antologia (1821–33). Monthly journal of literature, arts, and sciences founded in *Florence by G. P. *Vieusseux in January 1821. The idea came out of discussions between Vieusseux and the circle of leading *Tuscan intellectuals who frequented his reading-room in Palazzo Buondelmonti. It was initially a miscellany of selected book extracts, articles, and reviews translated from the principal European journals, but already in the third number Vieusseux announced that it would include original Italian work. Its founders were eager to give it a national character and, as its reputation grew, it attracted more and more contributors from all over the peninsula. Amongst leading regular contributors were the literary critics Giuseppe *Montani and Niccolò *Tommaseo, the historians Carlo *Botta and Pietro *Colletta, and the social reformer Raffaello *Lambruschini. Although the layout changed over the years, it maintained a broad balance between reviews and substantive articles. The political and social engagement of the journal—to inform, but also to promote improvement and reform—was never concealed. After the disturbances of 1830–1 the Grand Duchy's police and *censors' office became more suspicious and interfering. The journal was finally suppressed in March 1833. [MPC]

ANTONA-TRAVERSI, CAMILLO (1857–1934), prolific playwright, literary critic, and man of the *theatre, was born in *Milan, studied literature in *Naples, and spent eleven years as a teacher of Italian literature in a military college in *Rome. He moved in 1907 to Paris, where a number of his plays were produced. The plays, popular in their time, concentrated on the petite bourgeoisie, adapting the tenets of *verismo to the stage. His *literary criticism, for which he is now better known, includes works on *Boccaccio, *Foscolo, *Leopardi, and *D'Annunzio, and a useful collection of theatrical memoirs. [JAL]

ANTONELLI, LUIGI (1882–1942), author of over 30 plays, is associated with the *teatro *grottesco*. He is known particularly for *L'uomo che incontrò se stesso* (1918), which by dividing a man into two persons, one young and one middle-aged, shows the inability of human beings to shape their lives even when given a second chance. More intellectually and theatrically innovative than *Chiarelli, Antonelli can be seen to herald the *theatre of the absurd. He was also a *journalist and editor.

[JAL]

ANTONIO DA FERRARA (Antonio Beccari) (1315–before 1374). *Ferrarese poet, whose father was probably a butcher (*beccaio*). He moved between various Northern Italian *courts, having a somewhat ambiguous status between courtier and *giullare*. His poems show a considerable formal and thematic range; they include *poesia giocosa*, love poetry imitating the *dolce stil novo*, political *sonnets and *canzoni*, religious poetry in *terza rima*, as well as court poetry praising his patrons, and other occasional verse. Some poems are of an autobiographical, confessional character, referring with sometimes grotesque self-dramatization to the brawling and gambling to which he claims to have been addicted.

Antonio's language draws on Tuscan poetic usage but has many Northern features which, together with a somewhat heavy-handed use of classical commonplaces, give his verse a certain awkwardness. At the same time the technical skill he shows in constructing symmetries and antitheses, combined with the autobiographical content of his work, suggests an indebtedness to *Petrarch. The two exchanged poems on various occasions, and Antonio wrote a long lament for Petrarch when he was falsely reported to have died in 1343. [JP & JMS]

ANTONIO DA RHO (Antonio Raudense) (*c.*1398–1450/3). *Humanist and *Franciscan, who succeeded to Gasparino *Barzizza's chair of rhetoric in *Milan in 1431. He became a friend of *Valla, who made him the Christian spokesman and model preacher in *De vero falsoque bono*. But Valla then accused him of plagiarizing his *Elegantiae* in his *De imitatione* and of gross linguistic misunderstandings. He also worked on the text of Lactantius and wrote a *dialogue against his doctrinal errors. [LAP]

ANTONIO DA TEMPO (14th c.) was a *Paduan judge, versifier, and author of the first influential treatise on Italian metrical forms, the *Summa artis rithimici vulgaris dictaminis* (1332). As a North Italian, Antonio was distant from the mainstream *lyric tradition, though he mentions *Dante and acknowledges the growing supremacy of Tuscan as a literary language. He writes at length about the *sonnet form, offering a number of metrical variants to it; and his *ballate* also correspond with the structures used by leading authors. However, his attempt at demonstrating the *canzone* shows that he neither understood the form nor gave it the prestige which it had for early Tuscan poets and *Petrarch; the form declined after 1400 perhaps partly as a result. His choice and treatment of minor metres shows *French influences. By 1500 Antonio's *Summa* had acquired a series of anonymous additions, including an exposition of *ottava

rima. It was better known than Dante's unfinished *De vulgari eloquentia*, and was only superseded in 1525 by the work of Pietro *Bembo, who in his *Prose della volgar lingua* effectively reinvented the terminology of Italian metrics. [See also VERSIFICATION.] [RAA]

ANTONIO DE FERRARIIS, see GALATEO, IL, I.

ANTONIONI, MICHELANGELO (1912–) sprang to fame with a series of films made with the actress Monica Vitti in the early 1960s—*L'avventura* (1960), *La notte* (1961), *L'eclisse* (1962), and *Il deserto rosso* (1964, in colour)—which seemed to many to express aspects of modernity with a subtlety and precision rare in the *cinema. This sudden success came after a decade and more of obscurity when his pared-down, elliptical style was equally at odds with the critical penchant for realism and with popular taste for melodrama. He was then invited to make three films in English for international audiences. *Blow-Up* (1966) was acknowledged as a brilliant portrayal of 'swinging London', but *Zabriskie Point* (1969), which tried to do something similar for the America of hippiedom and student revolt, was not appreciated in its host country. He displeased a different set of hosts with his documentary on China, *Chung Kuo Cina* (1972), but *Professione: reporter* (1975: English title, *The Passenger*) retrieved his reputation. His later career has been dogged by the effects of a stroke suffered in the late 1980s. [GN-S]

ANTONIO OF PADUA, ST, see SERMONS.

APROSIO, ANGELICO (1607–81). Born Ludovico in Ventimiglia, he took the name 'Angelico' upon becoming an Augustinian monk. Moving from monastery to monastery, he met most of the literary luminaries of the age, drawing on these encounters in the *Biblioteca aprosiana* (1673), which intersperses comments on books and authors with autobiographical notes, and *Grillaia* (1673), a miscellany of literary and antiquarian researches. In his critical writings he defends *Marino against *Stigliani, but he also opposed Arcangela *Tarabotti in the debate over the oppression of women. His extensive book collection formed the basis of the Ventimiglia civic library. [MPS]

AQUINAS, ST THOMAS (1225–74). The leading theologian and philosopher of *scholasticism. Son of Landolfo, Count of Aquino (near *Naples), he became a *Dominican in 1244, studied under Albertus Magnus in Cologne (1248–52), and taught theology in Paris (1252–9, 1269–72) and Italy, mainly *Rome (1259–69) and Naples (1272–4). His vast output, in Latin, includes commentaries on the Scriptures and Aristotle; many *Quaestiones*; the *Summa contra Gentiles* (argued with non-Christians in mind); the unfinished *Summa theologiae*; a treatise on kingship (completed by Tolomeo da Lucca); and some Eucharistic hymns. His chief aim was to enrol *Aristotelian philosophy in the service of Christian dogmatic and moral theology, whilst maintaining the essential distinction between truths that are knowable by reason alone and those, revealed in the Scriptures, that are believed by faith. His *Summa theologiae*, in three books (the second in two parts, Ia IIae and IIa IIae), divided into *quaestiones* and articles, is noted for its rigorous method of argumentation, each article consisting of several initial propositions (the 'objections'), his own judgement, and the resolution of the objections. He was canonized in 1323 and declared the Church's supreme theologian by Leo XIII (1879). In the *Divine Comedy* he is a major interlocutor among the souls of the wise in the Heaven of the Sun (*Para.* 10–14).

[PA]

ARAGON. *Spanish dynasty implanted in *Sicily by Peter I as a result of the anti-French revolt of the Sicilian Vespers (1282). Under Alfonso I 'the Magnanimous', the Castilian branch took *Naples from the House of *Anjou in 1442, creating the first Kingdom of the Two Sicilies. With brief interludes Spanish domination was to continue, through Aragonese and *Bourbon lines, until 1861. Aragonese involvement with literature can be seen in particular in the *Renaissance, with Alfonso I's backing for Lorenzo *Valla's famous exposure (1440) of the *Donation of Constantine, and later with the *Medicean *Raccolta aragonese* (1476–7).

[JU]

ARBASINO, ALBERTO (1930–). Essayist and novelist, who first became generally known as a member of the *Gruppo 63. He has campaigned constantly for the de-provincialization of Italian literature and culture. His own writing is hypersophisticated in its parodic, knowing style, swift changes of direction, and a dense texture of historical and literary allusiveness. His novels—*Le piccole vacanze* (1957), *Fratelli d'Italia* (1963),

Super-Eliogabalo (1969), *Specchio delle mie brame* (1975)—belong mostly to the earlier phases of his career, though an expanded and revised version of *Fratelli d'Italia* was a best-seller in 1993. His horror at the state of Italy becomes a demand for the active intervention of intellectuals in public affairs, as is probably most evident in the mini-essays of *Un paese senza* (1980), which present a kaleidoscope of the deficiencies and misdemeanours of Italian society. He has also published poetry and travel journalism. He was a member of parliament for the Republican Party from 1983 to 1987.

[PBart]

Arcadia (1). Iacopo *Sannazaro's *pastoral novel, which launched a long, and fruitful vogue for highly refined pastoral literature. An incomplete version of *Il libro pastorale nominato Arcadia* circulated in the mid-1480s, but the final edition was published only in 1504, followed by sixty editions in Italy alone, and imitations in France, Spain, Portugal, and England.

Ignoring Christian pastoral *allegories of the *Middle Ages, Sannazaro blended classicizing pastoral settings, characters, and themes taken from *Virgil and Theocritus with the idiom and motifs of the modern vernacular lyric, *Petrarch especially, and transformed the purely poetic classical eclogue into a mixture of prose narrative and verse, using forms such as *terza rima*, the *sestina*, and the *frottola*. Twelve consecutive episodes take place over an unspecified number of days in spring, and are loosely united by interconnecting themes—love, death, friendship, betrayal—and most of all by an overriding melancholy.

Poetry and song provide relief from life's woes, and mutual singing, listening, and commenting create a literary community, a form of republic of letters. For despite the distant, timeless setting, the minute descriptions of ancient games, funerary rites, festivities in honour of the goddess Pales, and nostalgic evocations of a lost Golden Age, Arcadia, it emerges, stands for the poets and writers belonging to the *Accademia Pontaniana in *Naples. There, bonds of friendship surpass social class, titles, and, above all, wealth, inherited or earnt. The shepherd Sincero is Sannazaro himself. The wise elderly shepherd, Uranio, is *Pontano, the author of the cosmological poem *Urania*, and the Aragonese king's prime minister. Ergasto's affectionate lament for Arcadia's leader, Androgeo, is a tribute to *Panormita, the founder of the Academy; and Meliseo's lament for his beloved Filli is a transposition into the vernacular of a Latin eclogue by Pontano in honour of his dead wife.

Although Sannazaro claims in his *Proemio* that his poetry is humble, compared to the lofty subject matter and style of epic, he is conscious of its worth. He would like us to think that the shepherds' songs, accompanied by the *zampogna*, or pan pipes, may give more pleasure than highly sophisticated performances. But he is also confident that he has revived bucolic poetry in Naples after a thousand years of neglect. Poussin captured the essence of Sannazaro's mournful lyrics in his painting of a speaking tomb surrounded by shepherds gazing at the inscription: 'Et in Arcadia ego'.   [LAP]

    Ed. E. Carrara (1967). See K. Kidwell, *Sannazaro and Arcadia* (1993).

Arcadia (2). The publication of **Arcadia* (1504), Iacopo *Sannazaro's influential compilation of *pastoral eclogues, and the foundation of the *Roman *Accademia dell'Arcadia (1690) signal two key dates in the fashion which idealized the pastoral life as a refuge from contemporary problems. As a general aspiration 'Et in Arcadia ego' ('I too shall be in Arcadia') provides a loose definition of the desires of a whole range of society during the century following the foundation of the homonymous academy, informing cultural patterns and social mores until 1789. Yet the Arcadian ideal was by no means as bland as hindsight would have us believe. Enlightened reform, not pastoral ease, was the motive behind the original proposal for an academy, inspired by the enthusiasm of the self-exiled Queen *Christina of Sweden for the cultural improvement of Italy. Christina died in 1689, surrounded by a group of admiring members of Rome's intelligentsia, desirous of opposing the complexities of *Baroque culture with a return to classical simplicity and directness. They applauded her desire to get back to basic (and classical) literary values of sincerity and simplicity in an Italy which, she believed, was allowing its national heritage to waste and decay, because of that Baroque concentration on over-ingenious conceits to the detriment of meaningful content.

The new academy's two most distinguished founding members, Giovanni Mario *Crescimbeni and Gian Vincenzo *Gravina, had respectable intellectual pedigrees, though their divergent personalities caused an early clash and an unfortunate split in the ranks, resolved only by the death of Gravina. Just as Sannazaro's *Arcadia*, though begun by 1489, may have reflected the poet's desire

to withdraw from a troubled world threatened after 1484 and 1499 by French invasions, so the idyll of a bucolic existence, however illusory, proved pleasing when the peninsula was a cockpit for the major European powers. Unlike other *academies, which were invariably limited to individual *courts or cities, Arcadia struck an immediately national note, answering a need for the ideal of the simple rustic life, troubled as the peninsula was by foreign colonialization and religious wars (one aspect of this view of a rural retreat reached its apogee in France a century later with Marie Antoinette and her shepherdesses at Le Hameau). Arcadia, as an academy or as an idealized concept, soon became the symbol of a literary movement, and 'colonies' of the original Roman institution were soon flourishing in every part of Italy, offering the dream of a golden age, not only of literary and other culture but also of political equality and freedom.

But while the academy's ambitions may have been laudably high-minded, from the beginning it risked being taken over by the very forces that it sought to oppose. Its trappings lent themselves to parody, though its earliest members were well aware of the risible side of their accoutrements. Its insignia was a Pan pipe crowned with pine and laurel, its protector was the Christ-child worshipped by shepherds. Members assumed pseudonyms, a forename of Graeco-Roman bucolic form and a second derived from a region of Arcadia (for instance Uledomo Miceneo, or 'Wood-dweller of Mycenae'). These superficialities came to be associated with the movement, even when Arcadian influences spread beyond the salons which housed its members, and posterity was to deride it as superficial not least because of this less serious social side. Severe critics included Giuseppe *Baretti, who was fiercely opposed to what he considered the emptiness and fundamentally frivolous quality of the compositions of the Arcadians, while Luigi *Settembrini saw the movement as a *Jesuitical attempt to reduce the Italian intelligentsia to childish decadence. In truth the reforming aims of the original founding fathers had no creative men of genius to sustain them; Pietro *Metastasio was lauded as the highest exponent of the movement, while inept occasional writers such as Carlo Innocenzo *Frugoni were regarded as divine exponents of their art by decadent 18th-c. society. Surprisingly, greater minds, such as Giuseppe *Parini and Vittorio *Alfieri, were co-opted as members, despite (or because of) their greater achievements outside the Arcadian ambit.

Arcadia, Accademia dell'

Following Baretti, the 19th-c. critic Francesco *De Sanctis, with his *Romantic emphasis on national liberation and patriotic values, reviled what he saw as the effeminate and uncommitted attitudes of the movement, though he appreciated the technical achievements of some of the Arcadian poets, particularly Metastasio. Giosue *Carducci robustly took up De Sanctis's nationalistic attack, but 20th-c. critics, notably Benedetto *Croce and Mario Fubini, have concentrated rather on the reforming side of the academy, claiming that without its early revolutionary and enlightened aims, writers such as *Goldoni, Alfieri, and Parini would not so easily have been able to achieve their particular originality; and that it helped enlightened critics, such as Gravina and *Muratori, to lay down critical rules for judging and defining literary and particularly poetic creations, and thus to stem the tide of mediocrity which threatened Italian letters before the advent of Alfieri. Nor perhaps would it have been so easy for Italian cultural, or at least literary, *nationalism to make itself heard through the literary histories of Crescimbeni (*Istoria della volgar poesia*) and of *Tiraboschi (*Storia della letteratura italiana*), which led directly to the patriotic history of Italian literature created by De Sanctis. The polemics surrounding the usefulness or otherwise of the academy continue today, as its hierarchy becomes another organization for academic patronage. But Arcadia has demonstrated its resilience and its independent stance, not least during the *Fascist era, when alone of the Italian academies, it refused to remove Croce's name from its register of fellows. In its modern guise as promoter of literary criticism, its conservative programme shows every sign of outliving the theories of postwar criticism, and currently the Academy has long waiting lists for its keenly contested membership.   [JRW]

See A. M. Giorgetti Vichi, *Gli Arcadi dal 1690 al 1800* (1977); B. Croce, *La letteratura italiana del Settecento* (1949); M. Fubini, *Dal Muratori al Baretti* (1954).

Arcadia, Accademia dell', see ARCADIA (2).

Archaeology, see ANTIQUARIANISM.

Architecture, see VISUAL ARTS AND LITERATURE.

Archives, see LIBRARIES; MANUSCRIPTS AND MANUSCRIPT PRODUCTION.

ARDIGÒ, ROBERTO (1828–1920) trained as a priest and religious teacher but became one of the most important *Positivist thinkers in Italy, working principally at *Padua University. His treatise *La psicologia come scienza positiva* (1870) is an important contribution to the birth of modern European psychology, showing the influence of *Darwin and John Stuart Mill and proposing that psychic phenomena depend on physiological ones. His writings on pedagogy and moral philosophy (many put on the *Index by the Church) include *La morale dei positivisti* (1879), in which he argues that morality is independent of religion and criticizes contemporary spiritualism.   [GP]

ARESE, PAOLO (1574–1644). Preacher and religious writer. He joined the order of *Theatines in 1589, changing his Christian name from Cesare. His austere piety earned him the respect of the Church and he was made Bishop of Tortona. He composed numerous works in Latin and Italian. His *Arte di predicare bene* (1611) became a popular manual, reprinted many times, on how to construct and embellish a sermon; the work contained treatises on memory and on imitation. His *Imprese sacre* (1613) was an ambitious effort to improve the art of preaching by applying the *impresa* technique, drawn from early 17th-c. art and literature, to sacred material. [See also EMBLEMS.]   [PBD]

ARETINO, PIETRO (1492–1556). The major representative of a group of writers active mainly in *Venice who, in the period 1530–60, reacted against the stilted *classicism of vernacular writing by adopting a more natural style derived from alternative classical models, notably Lucian, under the influence of Erasmus [see also GREEK INFLUENCES; LATIN INFLUENCES].

Born in Arezzo, he published his first work—*Opera nova* (1512), a collection of conventional poems—while practising painting in *Perugia. By 1517 he was in *Rome at the *court of Leo X, on the death of whom in 1521 he produced a series of *pasquinate* favouring the candidature of Giuliano de' *Medici; the latter, however, was only elected Pope (as Clement VII) in 1523, following the death of the austere Adrian VI. Having also written *pasquinate* against Adrian VI, Aretino had to stay away from Rome during his reign. In 1525 he wrote the brilliant first version of *Cortigiana*, a cynical *comedy reflecting the by then carefree life of the Roman court, a more regular version of which was published in 1534.

Following a two-year stay at the court of

*Mantua, having lost the Pope's protection when an attempt was made on his life, he found shelter from 1527 onwards in Venice. Here he found the ideal place to develop his multifarious literary production, thanks to the liberality of the Venetian state and the extraordinary flourishing of the Venetian presses [see also PRINTING]. With the editions of his works produced in Venice by Francesco Marcolini between 1535 and 1545, he initiated a period of close collaboration between authors and *printer-publishers. In 1533 he had published his second comedy, the *Marescalco*, set at the court of Mantua, while in 1534 the first part of the *Sei giornate* followed, as well as the *Passione di Giesù* and *Sette salmi*, these religious works coinciding with the development of an Italian evangelical movement. In 1537 he published the love poetry of the *Stanze* in praise of Angela Serena, and in the following January inaugurated a successful new genre in vernacular literature with the publication of the first of his six books of *Lettere* (1538–57), the last being posthumous [see also LETTER-WRITING AND EPISTOLARI]. Other religious and *chivalric works appeared in 1538–40, followed by three comedies, *Talanta* and *Hipocrito* (1542), *Filosofo* (1549), and (also in 1549) the *tragedy *Orazia*, which marked the culminating point of his literary prestige. In 1553, under the delusion that Pope Julius III would make him a cardinal, he went to Rome; returning to Venice, he died in 1556.

Aretino's production reflects a period of deep social change in Italian history, due to the disruption caused by the wars between France and Empire in the peninsula, with the consequent loss of political equilibrium and destabilization of the aristocratic *courts. The successful attempt by writers such as Pietro *Bembo and *Castiglione to compensate for these losses through the development of an elitist vernacular literature unwittingly opened the doors to parvenu writers who, following the example of Aretino, used the vernacular in alternative ways to express their own iconoclastic and paradoxical views. [GAq]

Teatro, ed. G. Petrocchi (1970); *Poesie varie*, vol. i, ed. G. Aquilecchia and A. Romano (1992); *Lettere*, vol. i, ed. P. Procaccioli (1997). See C. Cairns, *Pietro Aretino and the Republic of Venice* (1985).

ARGENTERIO, GIOVANNI, see MEDICINE.

ARGYROPOULOS, JOHANNES (1415–87) was a *Byzantine philosopher who studied at

*Padua from 1441 to 1444 and settled in Italy after the fall of Constantinople in 1453. He gained a chair at the *University of *Florence in 1456, where he lectured on *Aristotle. In 1471 he moved to *Rome, but returned to Florence in 1477 and resumed his teaching until 1481, spending his last years again in Rome. His Florentine lectures were attended by Angelo *Poliziano and Lorenzo de' *Medici. He produced widely read Latin translations of many works by Aristotle, whom he regarded as the greatest of ancient philosophers. [See also GREEK INFLUENCES; HUMANISM.] [JK]

ARICI, CESARE (1782–1836). Poet from Brescia, who imitated Vincenzo *Monti in his celebratory political poetry and Callimachus in his neoclassical hymns, which he attributed to Bacchylides. He also wrote a series of didactic poems culminating in *La pastorizia* (1814). A critique of one of them, *Il corallo* (1810), actually by *Borsieri but believed to be by *Foscolo, contributed to the latter's estrangement from Monti. Arici later became the target of attacks by the Lombard *Romantics. [JMAL]

ARIENTI, GIOVANNI SABADINO DEGLI (c.1445–1510). Vernacular prose writer. Born in *Bologna, he first served Andrea Bentivoglio, and then from 1491 Ercole d'*Este in *Ferrara. He also acted as a literary advisor to Isabella d'Este *Gonzaga in *Mantua. He is best known for *Le porretane* (1483), a collection of sixty-one *novelle, told by members of the nobility at Porretta, a spa near Bologna, over five days of 1475. The stories are often historical and social anecdotes and aim to provide lively entertainment for men and women at court. As well as histories and moral treatises, Sabadino wrote in 1492 a collection of thirty-three lives of famous 15th-c. women, *Gynevera de le clare donne*, inspired by *Boccaccio's *De claris mulieribus* and dedicated to Ginevra *Sforza Bentivoglio, wife of Duke Ercole; and a *De triumphis religionis*, completed about 1499, which contains descriptions of major buildings in Bologna and Ferrara that have since been destroyed. [LAP]

ARIOSTO, LUDOVICO (1474–1533) owes his fame to his long narrative poem, *Orlando furioso*, published in its definitive edition in 1532, which crowns a long tradition of *chivalrous narrative popular in Italy since the *Middle Ages [see also FRENCH INFLUENCES, 1]. Ariosto had a comparatively uneventful career in the service of the *Este rulers of *Ferrara, and his life is really all in his writing. Apart from a spell of three years as governor of the Garfagnana, in the west of Ferrarese territory, and occasional diplomatic missions to other Italian courts, he was for all his life, as he tells us, within the sight and sound of the bells of Ferrara cathedral, and he was never really happy away from the city, or from the woman who was for many years his mistress and finally his wife, Alessandra Benucci. As a dependent of the Este he was closely involved in the varied and colourful life of the *court, which at this time was one of the most brilliant in Europe, attracting artists, musicians, and men of letters of great distinction.

The initial impetus for the writing of the *Furioso* came from the interruption of *Boiardo's *Orlando innamorato*, which had remained unfinished in 1494 on the invasion of the French under Charles VIII, leaving a public, in Ferrara and elsewhere, eager for a continuation. Ariosto's poem can be seen as a continuation of Boiardo's in many ways: he echoes Boiardo's title, adopts Boiardo's main characters, and completes some eight or nine tales left unfinished in the *Innamorato*. The *Furioso* was in fact criticized later for lacking its own beginning, and it also seems to lack a clear ending: we are left with the disturbing information that the union of Bradamante and Ruggiero, with which the poem ends, will be broken by Ruggiero's premature death. A sense of timelessness, matching the continuum of real life, is paralleled by a similar vagueness of spatial boundaries in the action, which stretches over the entire globe (and the moon), thanks in part to the flying horse (*ippogrifo*), and fuelled by the new maps and tales arriving in Ferrara in the wake of recent discoveries. The frequent intrusion of contemporary events and local characters into the fictitious world of medieval *romance is a characteristic feature of Ariosto's poem, distinguishing it from the *Innamorato*, as is his regular resort to classical as well as romance sources, in response to the increased awareness of the ancient world which the *humanists had brought, and which takes the traditional romance closer to the classical *epic. New too was Ariosto's mastery of his craft as a writer, his care and skill both as poet and narrator, and his insight into the relevance of the traditional chivalrous material for an understanding of human behaviour of all ages.

Thus the 'fury' of Orlando (set in the precise middle of the poem, canto 23) is provoked by Angelica's jilting him, the first knight in all Christendom, for an unknown young Moorish soldier,

while he had just witnessed the steadfast fidelity to her lover of Isabella, who would ultimately trick a would-be rapist into chopping off her head rather than submit to his advances. The complexity of relations between the sexes has rarely been better explored than in the twenty or so love stories embedded in the poem. And the other traditional chivalrous theme of arms is no less delicately exploited. Ariosto's combatants are real people, fighting for their lives but still conscious of their honour and self-respect. The old chivalrous ideals might seem outdated on the modern battlefield which *Machiavelli analysed, but they were by no means dead in Ariosto's time: a knight fought at Pavia in 1525 with one arm bare for love of his lady. Ariosto's knights, some of them, will dismount to face an opponent on foot and then get stabbed for their pains. The ambivalence of our motivation, the irrationality of our conduct, and the interplay of our illusions and experience are a constant source of wonder for the poet.

In much of this Ariosto's attitude is one of amusement, a smile at human folly and pretentiousness. The tone is set in the first canto where the Christian knight Rinaldo and the pagan Ferraù are fighting for possession of Angelica and the lady quietly slips away from these unwanted lovers. The men agree to defer their combat and first secure the prize, but Ferraù has lost his horse and so Rinaldo kindly gives him a lift: 'Oh gran bontà de' cavalieri antiqui' ('Oh the great goodness of the knights of old'), says the poet slyly of the two knights ganging up to seize a fleeing lady (1.22.1). This lighthearted, ironical tone, which has often been seen as typical of the *Furioso*, should not, however, blind us to another serious and earnest note which counterbalances it. The poet is certainly serious in his celebration of the House of Este, for he could not afford to be otherwise with his patrons; and his commentary relating his action to the contemporary world is serious and often highly critical. He deplores the conduct of his fellow Italians: rapacious soldiers, incompetent generals, tyrannical princes and chauvinist husbands, and his admiration for the old-fashioned chivalrous values of compassion, trust, and loyalty is clear. One of the most moving episodes concerns the bravery and comradeship of the pagan warriors Cloridano and Medoro (cantos 18–19) who make a sortie from their besieged camp to recover their king's body and are mown down by the Christians—an incident based on a serious classical source (*Virgil's Euryalus and Nisus in the *Aeneid*). A pessimistic, even bitter note colours some of the material added in the final edition and some of the discarded drafts, especially the so-called *Cinque canti*, seeming to reflect the increasingly despondent mood of the country as foreign invasions and economic decline brought a crisis in the earlier confidence of the humanists.

Ariosto's skill in handling his lengthy narrative is legendary. He preserves the traditional format, giving us forty-six cantos averaging just over 100 octaves each, in the serial technique, ending each canto at a point of suspense, often with a fictitious *cantastorie*'s oral farewell to his audience (although there would be more readers than listeners by Ariosto's time) and beginning the next one with a stanza of introduction or explanation. His technique of interweaving his main actions with a string of subsidiary tales serves to vary his material and keep the reader's interest, and also allows the poet to manipulate his overall pattern into a tapestry of human experience, as he confides to us at one point (2.30), referring to the different threads that he is weaving for different cloths. These brief, often ironical asides, in which the poet takes his audience into his confidence about his characters and his handling of his tale, are a characteristic feature of the poem and have been much admired and imitated by subsequent writers (Walter Scott, for example.)

Less easily imitated was Ariosto's mastery of the arts of poetry, of the subtle blending of sound and image to hold the reader in the spell of his narrative. Much effort has gone into attempts to analyse and explain this, particularly his masterly handling of *ottava rima*. In this he built on the achievements of his recent predecessors, combining the narrative fluency of Boiardo and lyrical skills of *Poliziano, endlessly varying the quadripartite structure of the octave and carefully regulating enjambement between lines and stanzas for special effects [see also VERSIFICATION]. Scholars have also noted the effects he achieves with patterns or clusters of identical phonemes, with changes of tone and of linguistic register, and with intertextual resonances. The poet's contemporaries were, many of them, closely familiar with Ariosto's literary sources, and the poet's conscious reminder of previous works gave a richness to his narrative that is easily missed today.

The text we now read is the third edition which the poet published in 1532, the earlier versions having appeared in 1516 and 1521. Thus, assuming he began writing about 1505, his poem occupied him intermittently over the whole of his working life,

and it is quite likely that he would have gone on revising and extending it further but for his death in 1533. The changes he made for the 1532 edition include four additional sections, probably intended to improve the overall balance of the poem: they comprise the episodes concerning Olimpia (cantos 9–11), the Rocca di Tristano (32–3), Marganorre (37), and Leone (44–6). The earlier editions also underwent a thorough linguistic revision under the guidance of Ariosto's friend, Pietro *Bembo. This mainly meant correcting his two main departures from Bembo's norm, Latinisms and regionalisms, which Ariosto did so effectively as to earn a place as a linguistic no less than a literary model for future generations [see also QUESTIONE DELLA LINGUA].

There were translations of the *Furioso* into French (1543), Spanish (1549), and English (1591), and soon into all the other European languages. However, despite its enormous popularity with the public, the poem was not immediately accepted by a group of critics. By the mid-century a furious quarrel erupted between Ariosto's supporters and literary theorists who objected to his 'romance' and sought more 'epic' qualities, especially a more unified structure, a more elevated style, and a more moral tone; it was in these directions that Torquato *Tasso would attempt to improve on Ariosto [see also ALLEGORY; LITERARY THEORY, 3]. The later 16th c. editions of the *Furioso* were invariably equipped with 'allegories' attempting to show its moral lessons, and Spenser, like so many later readers, had these in mind when he wrote the *Faerie Queene* in an explicit attempt to 'overgo' Ariosto. With Spenser, Tasso, Ronsard, and Lope de Vega the narrative poem took off in new directions, but always with Ariosto's shining example in the background.

Ariosto's minor works are comparatively little known today, but they play a significant role in the history of two other genres. His seven *satires (*Satire*), in *terza rima*, all written between 1517 and 1524 and inspired by *Horace and Juvenal, deal with events in the poet's life and his reactions to the problems facing him: promotion, debts, moving house, etc. His irony embraces his own attitudes as much as the deficiencies of his fellow men, and contemporary institutions, such as the Church, come in for some sharp criticism. This little group of poems, with its sharply observed pictures of everyday life and its witty, conversational style, effectively established a genre in 16th-c. Italian literature and beyond.

The other genre in which Ariosto played an important part was the five-act *comedy in the ancient Roman mould. His *Cassaria* (1508) and *I *suppositi* (1509), if not the first such comedies to be written, were the first to make their mark in performance and set off the long tradition of dramatic comedy which would give us Molière and *Shakespeare. These two plays, and the later *Negromante* and *Lena* (both 1528), represent a conscious attempt to provide a comic *theatre in imitation of Plautus and Terence, with stock characters, love intrigues, discovery of unknown identities, etc. Characteristically Ariosto adapts the Roman model to a local and contemporary context, setting his scenes in the Ferrara of his day and the everyday life of a 16th-c. Italian city. His primacy in the field gave him enormous influence, but his reputation as a playwright has been overshadowed by Machiavelli; the latter perhaps put his finger on a weak spot when he criticized his Ferrarese contemporary for the lack of that wit which only Tuscans were linguistically equipped to deploy effectively. Ariosto reciprocated by leaving Machiavelli out of the crowds of Italian celebrities welcoming him into port at the end of the *Furioso*.   [CPB]

> *Orlando furioso*, ed. L. Caretti (1954); *Opere minori*, ed. C. Segre (1954). See L. Caretti, *Ariosto e Tasso* (1967); C. P. Brand, *Ludovico Ariosto: A Preface to the Orlando Furioso* (1974); E. Saccone, *Il soggetto del 'Furioso' e altri saggi* (1974).

ARISI, FRANCESCO (1657–1743). Cremonese lawyer, historian, and poet, friend to many literary men of his time and member of many academies. He published volumes of *Petrarchan verse (some of which has been described as 'senile'), orations, dithyrambs, and 325 sacred *sonnets. In his *Cremona literata* he aimed to publish all surviving biographical and bibliographical information pertaining to the literary activity of his native town. He allowed himself an enormous chronological range (from the 1st c. BC to his own time), and was not always the most considerate of scholars, preferring summaries to publishing original documents. His work was admired by *Muratori whom he undoubtedly influenced.   [PBD]

ARISTARCO SCANNABUE, see BARETTI, GIUSEPPE MARC'ANTONIO; FRUSTA LETTERARIA, LA.

Aristodemo, see DOTTORI, CARLO DE'.

Aristotelianism. Throughout the *Renaissance and well into the 17th c. Aristotelianism remained the dominant philosophical system in Italy, particularly in the *universities [for Aristotelianism in the *Middle Ages, see SCHOLASTICISM]. *Petrarch, in *De sui ipsius et multorum ignorantia*, attacked contemporary Aristotelians for their impiety and unthinking subservience to the philosopher. Some later *humanists shared his distaste for Aristotelianism; others such as Leonardo *Bruni sought to recover the genuine Aristotle of antiquity by producing classically correct Latin translations of his works and abandoning the elaborate scholastic method of commenting on them. Angelo *Poliziano, in his lectures on Aristotle in the early 1490s, continued this humanist programme by replacing medieval Latin and Arabic commentators, still widely used in universities, with ancient Greek interpreters. Although this new approach slowly gained ground, the vast majority of 15th-c. Aristotelians adopted the traditional scholastic manner of exposition and relied on the standard medieval authorities.

In 1516 Pietro *Pomponazzi challenged a decree of the Fifth Lateran Council constraining philosophers to interpret Aristotle's views on the immortality of the soul in the light of Christian dogma. The ensuing controversy resulted in philosophers achieving a greater degree of freedom from Church interference, as long as they left theological issues to the theologians. 16th-c. Aristotelianism at its best, in the figure of Iacopo Zabarella, combined scholastic rigour with a humanist emphasis on reading Aristotle in Greek and drawing on his ancient commentators. A few philosophers incorporated into Aristotelianism material based on their own direct observation of nature: Andrea Cesalpino, for instance, adapted Aristotle's classificatory scheme to include plants recently discovered in the New World. By the early 17th c., however, Aristotelianism had largely lost the vitality and openness to new trends which had allowed it to survive and flourish since the late Middle Ages. Its leading representatives were entrenched and bookish defenders of Aristotelian orthodoxy like Cesare *Cremonini, who, though a colleague of *Galileo, is said to have refused to look through his telescope, preferring to study the heavens by reading Aristotle's *De caelo*.   [JK]

> See C. B. Schmitt, *Aristotle and the Renaissance* (1983); C. H. Lohr, *Latin Aristotle Commentaries*, vol. ii (1988); D. A. Iorio, *The Aristotelians of Renaissance Italy* (1991).

ARISTOTLE, see SCHOLASTICISM for the *Middle Ages; ARISTOTELIANISM for the *Renaissance onwards.

Arlecchino, a *zanni,* or servant, of the *commedia dell'arte.* The name is possibly of medieval French derivation, illustrations of it dating from as early as 1577. Performers wore a black half-mask covering cheeks, eyes, and forehead, a tunic and trousers of multi-coloured, lozenge-shaped patches, a loose-fitting cap, and a belt into which was thrust a short baton. An archetypal figure of comic performance, its first major interpreter was Tristano *Martinelli. In the early 18th c. the mask was translated into the Harlequin of the English pantomime.   [KR]

ARLOTTO DE' MAINARDI, see MOTTI E FACEZIE DEL PIOVANO ARLOTTO.

ARMANI, VINCENZA (d.1569) was the first European star actress (conceivably the first in any theatrical culture) whose name has survived for posterity. In tributes during and after her life she was credited with great verbal, musical, and rhetorical skills, and her on-stage air of virtuous scorn could silence ribald audiences, despite her probably promiscuous private life. [See also THEATRE, 1.]
                                                            [RAA]

Armed Forces and Police. The Italian army has been characterized by negative images since soon after *Unification. Major military defeats, such as Adua (Ethiopia) in 1896, involved troops of mostly *peasant origin with little understanding of the campaigns they were fighting, though Caporetto (1917) was the only major defeat suffered during *World War I. Internally the army and police were used to repress brigandage in the South (1860–5) and to suffocate left-wing political movements and social unrest during the 1890s. Lack of funding, numerical weaknesses, and inadequate training were often the cause of conflict and bloodshed. Policing was also plagued by the coexistence of several forces with hierarchies in conflict; the Carabinieri, for instance, were part of the army, whilst the Interior Ministry police were not.

The army and police helped the *Fascist movement destroy the forces of the Left. But once securely in power, *Mussolini chose not to 'fascistize' them, since he needed both professionally trained personnel and the means to counter challenges from within the Fascist Party. Nevertheless, the Interior Ministry police (especially OVRA, the

secret police) provided an efficient and often brutal means of fighting anti-Fascism, while the Carabinieri, being ultimately loyal to the *monarchy, not Mussolini, had their role restricted to the maintenance of law and order. The Ethiopian campaign (1935) and the Spanish Civil War (1936–9) brought prestige to the armed forces. However, contrary to propaganda claims, they entered *World War II in 1940 without the modern equipment essential for a long and large-scale conflict.

The alignment of Italian Fascism with Nazism and the number and scale of the military disasters prompted most military and police commanders to distance themselves from the regime and to support General Badoglio after the fall of Mussolini in July 1943. All the same, a significant number of soldiers and policemen went on to fight for the Republic of Salò alongside the Germans, though many later deserted to the *Resistance. The armed forces and police emerged from the war and the ensuing anti-Fascist purges relatively unscathed, and provided the postwar Republic with an anti-*Communist instrument for often brutal use during strikes and demonstrations. At various times the military high command, now under the umbrella of NATO, was itself subverted by its own secret services.

Recently the Italian armed forces have played an increasing role in international humanitarian missions. They also made a significant contribution to the Gulf War (1991). Since the 1980s the Italian police have become more democratic in outlook, and abandoned their more repressive methods.
                                                            [JMD]
See N. Labanca, 'Militari', in B. Bongiovanni and N. Tranfaglia (eds.), *Dizionario storico dell'Italia unita* (1996); J. Dunnage, 'Continuity in Policing Politics in Italy, 1920–1960', in M. Mazower (ed.), *The Policing of Politics in the Twentieth Century* (1997).

Armida. A witch in the *Gerusalemme liberata* of Torquato *Tasso, who falls in love with the hero, *Rinaldo.

Arms, see ARMED FORCES AND POLICE; CHIVALRY; CONDOTTIERI; FEUDALISM.

Arnaldo da Brescia, see NICCOLINI, GIOVAN BATTISTA.

ARNALDO DA FOLIGNO, see ANGELA DA FOLIGNO.

ARNAUT DANIEL (late 12th c.). Provençal *troubadour, acknowledged as the major practitioner of the difficult style (*trobar clus*). He influences Italian *lyric poets from the *Sicilians to *Petrarch. In the *rime petrose *Dante plunders the *sestina from him and competes with him. He confirms his esteem for the 'miglior fabbro del parlar materno' (as *Guinizzelli is made to call him in *Purg.* 26.117) by making him the only character to speak Provençal in the *Divine Comedy.* [PH]

AROMATARI, GIUSEPPE DEGLI ASSISI (1587–1660). *Venetian physician and literary polemicist. He came to prominence in a debate over *Tassoni's criticism of *Petrarch in the *Considerazioni sopra le rime del Petrarca* (1609). Aromatari replied in 1611, with an ineffectual *Aristotelian analysis of ten of Petrarch's poems. A further exchange took place under pseudonyms, but the polemic had grown personal, and the final word was had by Tassoni in the *Tenda rossa,* in chapters whose titles represent the final stages of a battle. Though all this seems to be jocular, behind it lies a serious point concerning authority. Aromatari was also the author of Latin works on rabies and on spontaneous generation (which he argues against). [PBD]

ARPINO, GIOVANNI (1927–87). Novelist. Originally from Istria, he worked in *journalism and *publishing while pursuing his literary vocation, first as a poet and then as a playwright, but most of all as a prolific fiction-writer. His first novel, *Sei stato felice, Giovanni* (1952), caught the tail-end of *Resistance *Neorealism, but Arpino proved adept at updating narrative content, form, and tone, edging away from political commitment to the history of the emotions in *Gli anni del giudizio* (1958) and in *La suora giovane* (1959), and taking up the more broadly social theme of the jealous husband's right to kill his wife in *Un delitto d'onore* (1961). *Una nuvola d'ira* (1962) presciently explores the interplay of individualistic and class aspirations, and the prize-winning *L'ombra delle colline* (1964) is the protagonist's revisitation of the unrealized hopes of the Resistance from the perspective of an uninspiring present. Arpino's later novels, with two more prizes, testify to his continuing ability to match literary facility with readership appeal. [JG-R]

ARRIGHI, CLETTO (pseud. of Carlo Righetti) (1830–1906). *Milanese writer, who fought in the Wars of Independence, as he describes in *Memorie di un soldato lombardo* (1863). His second and best-known novel, *La *scapigliatura e il sei febbraio* (1862), gave a name and identity to Italy's first avant-garde movement, which he modelled on the French *bohème.* His interest in Milanese life led to a series of *dialect plays and a disappointing novel, *La canaglia felice* (1885). He also compiled a Milanese–Italian dictionary (1896). He became editor of *L'Unione,* worked on *Cronaca grigia,* and was later elected to parliament. [AHC]

ARRIGHI, LUDOVICO, see MANUSCRIPTS AND MANUSCRIPT PRODUCTION.

ARRIGO DA SETTIMELLO (12th c.). Latin poet. Born into a humble family, Arrigo studied at *Bologna before becoming a priest. Having fallen out of favour with the Bishop of *Florence, he was deprived of his wealthy parish and ended his life in poverty. He wrote his *De diversitate fortunae et philosophiae consolatione* or *Elegia* in 1193. The poem is divided into four parts, each of 250 lines; the first two lament the cruelty of Fortune, whilst the third and fourth describe the comfort brought to Arrigo by philosophy. The work draws widely on classical and religious authorities, and was extremely well known thanks to various 14th-c. translations. [CEH]

Ars dictaminis. The medieval Latin rhetorical 'art' of *letter-writing whose codification and development were primarily the work of Italian scholars. Although the Roman rhetorician C. Julius Victor introduced a section 'on letters' in his 4th-c. treatise on rhetoric, the first surviving work specifically to deal with composing letters was written around 1087 by *Alberico da Montecassino, whose *Dictaminum radii* offers a systematic treatment and compendium of epistolary practices which had long been in use. During the 12th and 13th c. the major centre for the *ars dictaminis* was *Bologna, where it became part of the *university curriculum. Adapting the traditional six-part *Ciceronian oration, an anonymous text, the *Rationes dictandi* (*c.*1135), established what were to become the canonical five sections of a letter: greeting, securing goodwill, presentation of facts, request, and conclusion. However, it was in the writings of two 13th-c. Bolognese teachers, *Boncompagno da Signa and Guido *Fava, that the *ars dictaminis* reached its apogee; Fava was in fact the first to provide instruction on letter-writing not just in Latin but also in the vernacular.

The many extant treatises on the subject are highly practical in character and reflect the demands of living in complex social and political environments. They offer epistolary rules and models for ecclesiastical and government officials, notaries, judges, teachers, students, and merchants. Abounding in rhetorical and linguistic formulae which are supposed to cover a wide range of real-life eventualities, they are often little more than catalogues and rarely reveal any sense of the broader and theoretical implications of rhetoric. But despite its practical functions, the ars dictaminis did help to enrich the quality of prose writing, especially by disseminating the *cursus, and inspired at least one work of lasting literary and intellectual merit, *Guittone d'Arezzo's vernacular letters. [See also LITERARY THEORY, I.]   [ZB]

See H. Wieruszowski, *Politics and Culture in Medieval Spain and Italy* (1971); M. Camargo, *Ars dictaminis, ars dictandi* (1991).

Ars Nova. Originally used to describe the reformed notation and the style of French music in the 14th c., the term has been extended to include the predominantly secular repertory of Italian music between c.1325 and c.1415. An often used alternative is 'Trecento music', in order to stress that the Italian music uses a system of notation and melodic and rhythmic styles which differ from the French idiom. The earlier music is written for two parts, the later for three, in an exuberant rhythmic style which captures the vitality of improvised performance, particularly in the early settings of *madrigals. In the later 14th c. the *ballata became the favoured form, and the style grew more measured and refined. *Francesco da Barberino and *Antonio da Tempo testify to the existence of musical settings of madrigals, *cacce, and ballate at the beginning of the century, but the earliest surviving compositions date from c.1340 and reflect the repertory circulating in the Veneto and at the *Visconti court in *Milan. Later in the century *Florence became an important centre thanks to the presence of Francesco Landini (c.1325–97) and others. Much of the poetry set to music is anonymous, though the settings of Franco *Sacchetti's poems (some of them by the author himself) enjoyed some popularity.   [BB]

ARTALE, GIUSEPPE (1628–79). A nobleman who made a hurried departure from his native Catania, where he had killed a rival in a duel, and thereafter combined a hectic military career with equally frenzied literary activity. He began with a vast *Enciclopedia poetica* (1658), a notable example

of the *Baroque attempt to produce collections of poems covering every conceivable theme and topic, which pushes *concettismo to some of its most extreme and hyperbolic forms. Whilst no less affected, his second collection, *L'Alloro fruttuoso* (1672), is more conventionally moralizing. As well as an opera *libretto, he also wrote *Cordimarte* (1660), a late example of Baroque *chivalric *romance, in elaborate, densely metaphoric prose, and *Guerra tra i vivi e i morti* (1679), a 'tragedia a lieto fine', which in a theoretical preface he distinguished from *tragicomedy, appealing directly to *Aristotle and Greek *theatre.   [MPS]

Art Criticism, see VISUAL ARTS AND LITERATURE.

Arte della guerra, L', see MACHIAVELLI, NICCOLÒ.

Arte e poesia, see LETTERATURA (2).

Artemisia, see BANTI, ANNA.

Arthurian Literature. Evidence for the diffusion of Arthurian stories in Italy in the 12th c. comes from the visual arts (a carved archivolt in Modena cathedral, a mosaic pavement at Otranto), folklore (the belief that Arthur was alive and dwelling in the crater of Etna, reported by an English visitor to Sicily around 1190), and the use of Arthurian personal names. In the 13th c. allusions to Tristan, Lancelot and other Arthurian figures are part of the repertoire of the *Sicilian school and the *Siculo-Tuscan poets; and *Dante in his *De vulgari eloquentia acknowledged the supremacy of French as the language of prose narrative, thanks to its 'Arturi regis ambages pulcerrime' ('delightful fables about King Arthur'). The most popular of the Arthurian legends in Italy was that of the tragic love of Tristan and Iseult, and most of the Italian versions draw on the French texts of the Tristan cycle. Rustichello da Pisa's *Meliadus* (after 1273), in French prose, is based on the *Roman de Palamedes* and centres on the exploits of Tristan's father. The *Tristano riccardiano* is a Tuscan *translation of the first part of the prose *Tristan*, with some extraneous episodes, from around 1300. The most varied and original of the Tuscan prose versions is the *Tavola ritonda* (before c.1330), a systematic compilation of all the main Arthurian legends. In verse, from the mid-14th c. the *cantari narrate episodes from the prose cycles, or independent stories on Arthurian themes such as the secret love of a knight for a supernatural lady.

In a distinctively Italian development the Arthurian tradition, with its magic and its all-powerful love element, was extended to embrace other bodies of narrative material, a development which found its fullest expression in the poems of *Boiardo and *Ariosto. Boiardo expressed his preference for the 'matter of Britain' over the 'matter of France' (the Carolingian legends), because the latter ignored the power of love, and he promised to remedy this deficiency by showing his readers Roland in love. Boiardo's *Orlando innamorato and, even more, Ariosto's *Orlando furioso, show the adaptability of the Arthurian world, as they make it the vantage-point from which to cast a critical eye on the problematic reality of their own day. [See also CHIVALRY.]   [RMD]

> See E. G. Gardner, *The Arthurian Legend in Italian Literature* (1930); D. Delcorno Branca, *Tristano e Lancilotto in Italia: studi di letteratura arturiana* (1998).

ARTUSI, PELLEGRINO, see COOKERY BOOKS.

ASCOLI, GRAZIADIO ISAIA (1829–1907), the greatest Italian linguist of his time, was born in Gorizia of a *Jewish family. Growing up in a multilingual society he manifested a precocious interest in different linguistic areas and, committed to socialist ideals, was passionate about *education. Among his many works there are studies on Friulian, on the language of the Gypsies, and on Semitic and Indo-European and their relationship. Particularly important is his contribution to Romance linguistics, and he can be considered the founder of Italian dialectology. The work which is best known is the 'Proemio' (1873) to the first issue of the *Archivio glottologico italiano*. Ascoli took as his starting point the publication of the first volume of a dictionary of *Florentine usage, edited by G. Giorgini and E. Broglio, inspired by *Manzoni's suggestion that colloquial educated Florentine should become the model for the Italian national language. The 'Proemio' vigorously argued that languages cannot be modified by decree, and that in Italy a national literary language already existed. The problem was the prevalence of illiteracy, and the remedy could only lie in the spread of education. The 'Proemio' is a masterful essay, offering insights which are still relevant today. [See also DIALECT; HISTORY OF THE ITALIAN LANGUAGE; QUESTIONE DELLA LINGUA.]   [GCL]

ASINARI, FEDERICO (1527/8–1575), Count of Camerano (*Piedmont). His works include *Tancredi*, a verse *tragedy based on a tale from the *Decameron (published 1588); *L'ira di *Orlando*, an attempt to combine *chivalric narrative with a Homeric structure; and *Le trasformazioni*, based on *Ovid's *Metamorphoses*. His complete works were published only in 1795.   [RMD]

Asolani, Gli (1505, revised 1530). *Dialogue by Pietro *Bembo set in Asolo (Veneto), which focuses in its first two parts on sad and happy love. The third part suggests that the good lover should desire both spiritual and physical beauty. The work reflects the influence of *Neoplatonism and the esteem professed for women in *courtly society.   [BR]

ASOR ROSA, ALBERTO (1933–). Cultural and literary historian. In the 1960s he was a prominent left critic of the cultural policy of the *Communist Party (PCI), theorizing a revolutionary role for the intellectual in the essays collected in *Intellettuali e classe operaia* (1971). In *Scrittori e popolo* (1965) he argued that the Italian literary and critical tradition had been afflicted since the *Risorgimento by *populism—intellectuals writing sympathetically about the people to neutralize class conflict. In this tradition he included *Neorealism and *Gramsci's defence of national-popular literature. He joined the PCI as a left-winger in the 1970s and criticized its failure to represent the growing numbers of unemployed and marginalized people in *Le due società* (1977). Appointed professor of Italian literature at the University of *Rome, he has continued to write on the history of culture in Italy, and edited *Einaudi's multi-volume *Letteratura italiana* (1982–).   [DF]

'Aspasia', see LEOPARDI, GIACOMO.

ASSARINO, LUCA (1602–72). *Genoese writer, probably born in Potosì in Bolivia, who led a turbulent life as a political informer, with several spells in prison. He compiled *Il sincero*, the first Italian newspaper, and historical works, such as *Delle rivoluzioni di Catalogna* (1644) and *Delle guerre e successi d'Italia* (1662). His extremely successful novels included *La Stratonica* (1635), which was translated into French, English, and German, and *L'Almerinda* (1640), later expanded and completely reworked in *I giuochi di fortuna* (1655).   [MC]

Astolfo. English knight in *Ariosto's *Orlando furioso*.

Astrology. The important part played by *magic, astrology, witchcraft, superstition, and popular belief in the mentalities of the early modern period has now been acknowledged and has been the subject of much scholarly investigation. Of these, astrology was the most deeply rooted in belief systems and the most influential in terms of social behaviour. It was a legitimate part of astronomy, supported by *Aristotle's writings, and was an essential part of learned *medicine. In the *University of *Bologna the professor of astrology was obliged to produce a yearly almanac for the faculty of medicine which gave astronomical data with attendant astrological interpretations. This practice came to end in the mid-15th c., probably as a result of intervention by the *Inquisition. For the lower classes, astrology was often restricted to the phases of the moon, and popular calendars imparted brief summaries of aspects relevant to agriculture, the weather, and medicine. That its influence permeated all levels of society can be seen from the widespread panic that spread across Europe in the expectation of another universal deluge in February 1524, due to the conjunction of the planets in Pisces. The printed reactions to this event also show how such beliefs could be manipulated for religious and political ends.

Astrological symbols were a means of conveying complex personal and public information. Paintings with astrological themes, whose main function was the glorification of a *patron's virtues and destiny, became widespread. For men like Benvenuto *Cellini, Gerolamo *Cardano, Ascanio *Condivi, *Michelangelo, and Duke Cosimo I de' *Medici, the stars were a fundamental force in their destiny, and their natal charts were erected and used for propaganda as well as for self-analysis. Astrology was linked to magic and posed problems in terms of predestination and free will, problems which led to heated controversy and frequent attacks, especially at the end of the 15th and the beginning of the 16th c. But despite the reaction of the religious authorities, astrology continued to play an important part in the lives of men and women. In the 17th c. the Barberini Pope, Urban VIII, both banned and indulged in astrological speculation. [See also COSMOLOGY; FICINO, MARSILIO; NEOPLATONISM.]   [PLR]
See E. Garin, *Astrology in the Renaissance* (1976); J. C. Eade, *The Forgotten Sky* (1984); J. Tester, *A History of Western Astrology* (1987).

ATTABALIBBA DEL PERÙ, see BANCHIERI, ADRIANO.

AUGURELLI, GIOVANNI AURELIO (1456–1524). Author of both Latin and *Petrarchist poetry. He was a protégé of Pietro *Bembo, and belonged to the most distinguished *humanist circles in *Venice. He contributed to the revision of the first two books of Bembo's *Prose della volgar lingua* before their publication in 1525.   [NC]

AUGUSTINE, ST (354–430). Christian thinker of major importance thoughout the *Middle Ages and *Renaissance. Important as far as the West is concerned for his exploration of Christianity in *Neoplatonic categories, he was influential also in his insistence on the idea of a single creative principle in the universe (over against the Manichaeans) and on the absolute dependence of the soul on the saving grace of God (over against Pelagius). Influential too were his autobiographical *Confessions*, his lengthy account of worldly and other-worldly happiness in *De civitate Dei*, and his essay in biblical interpretation in the *De doctrina christiana*. Everywhere subliminally present in *Dante (though rarely mentioned by name), he figures prominently in *Petrarch's *Secretum* as the voice of conscience.   [JT]

Aulica, poesia. Poetry in the high style, serious love poetry, from the Latin word for 'courtly'; *Dante uses the term *aulicum* to characterize the 'illustrious' vernacular that is the subject of his *De vulgari eloquentia* (1.18).

AULIVER (early 14th c.). The self-naming author of a unique *canzone* on the pains of love in the vernacular of Treviso, beginning 'En rima greuf a far, dir e stravolger' ('In verse that's hard to make, compose and turn'). He may be identifiable with a 'Dominus Auliverius de Robegano' active in Trevisan civic affairs between 1314 and 1319.   [CK]

AURISPA, GIOVANNI (1376–1459). *Sicilian *humanist who travelled to the East, returning with important Greek *manuscripts. In Germany he also discovered Pliny the Younger's *Panegyricus* and Donatus' commentary on Terence. His main interest was in collecting manuscripts and selling them for profit, but he also translated works of Lucian and Plutarch into Latin.   [JK]

Australia, see ITALIAN WRITERS IN AUSTRALIA.

Austria. The War of the Spanish Succession and the Treaty of Utrecht (1713) ended over

150 years of *Spanish domination in Italy. Eventually the Wars of the Austrian and Polish Succession, culminating in the Treaty of Aix-la-Chapelle (1748), firmly established Austrian rule in *Lombardy, *Tuscany, and the Duchies of Parma, Modena, and *Mantua, whilst *Trieste was already Austria's principal Mediterranean port. Austrian influence was also felt in the Kingdom of *Naples and *Sicily through marriage ties with the *Habsburgs.

As capital of the Holy Roman Empire and a cultural centre for the whole of Europe, Vienna attracted many Italian writers in the course of the 18th c. Apostolo *Zeno, *Metastasio, *Da Ponte, among others, all held the post of imperial poet at the Habsburg court. From 1748 to 1796 there was peace and to a large extent acceptance of Austrian rule in Italy. Progressive legislation was initiated in taxation, *education, and the legal and penal system, with the participation of major figures in the Italian *Enlightenment such as Pietro *Verri, Cesare *Beccaria, and Giuseppe *Parini. After the French occupation of the peninsula during the *Napoleonic period (1796–1815), Austrian rule was restored and extended to include *Venice. Opposition to foreign rule and the desire for independence and unity grew apace during the *Risorgimento, culminating in the successful expulsion of Austria from most of Northern Italy in 1859. But after *Unification, Austria retained Venezia Giulia, the Trentino, and the Alto Adige until the end of *World War I. [See also IRREDENTISM; GERMAN INFLUENCES.]   [ES]

Aut-Aut (1951–). Philosophical and cultural review founded by Enzo Paci in *Milan, currently published every two months and edited by Pier Aldo Rovatti. Noted for the high quality of its writing, it has published contributions from Giorgio *Agamben, Gianni *Vattimo, and others, and is a significant reference point for the most recent developments in contemporary thought.   [MPC]

Autobiography in the modern, generic sense of the word originates in the late 18th c., Rousseau's *Confessions* appearing in 1782–9, but the two most prevalent forms of writing about the self in the Italian tradition can both be traced back at least to the 13th c.: the spiritual autobiography or confession, often centred around conversion, and the memoir, a record of a professional or public life.

The spiritual autobiography looks to St *Augustine's *Confessions* as its model, but also draws on the flourishing parallel traditions of saints' lives. It finds an early embodiment in St *Francis of Assisi's *Testamentum,* and it provides the templates for the extraordinary explorations of self in *Dante and *Petrarch. Both these use the confessional model literally and allegorically, to create a history of the self as lover and poet (the life becoming the work), as well as sinner. Dante's most formally autobiographical work is the *Vita nova,* in which, drawing on 'il libro de la mia memoria' (ch. 1), he schematically narrates the history both of his love for *Beatrice and of his poetry and himself as poet. Both the *Convivio* and the *Divine Comedy* have strong autobiographical strands. The former cites Boethius and Augustine as authorities for speaking about oneself (2.1), and offers elements of both anecdotal and intellectual autobiography (e.g. commenting on his eyesight as well as recounting his conversion to philosophy). In the *Comedy,* running beneath its encyclopedic and universal scope, there is a strong thread of spiritual and literary autobiography, by turns apologetic and self-mythologizing.

Far more than Dante, Petrarch's *Canzoniere* was the fountainhead of several centuries of European representations of the self. Despite its skeletal sense of chronology and narrative sequence, the *Canzoniere*'s obsession with the self as contradictory and changing, by turns self-deluding and excruciatingly self-knowing, chimes remarkably with the concerns of modern autobiography. The powerful influence of Augustine on Petrarch's autobiographical work is evident in the *Canzoniere,* the *Secretum,* and the letter on his ascent of Mont Ventoux (*Familiares* 4.1), which promises a work modelled on the *Confessions,* though the closest he came to fulfilling the promise was the *Letter to Posterity* (*Posteritati*).

The period from the 14th to the 18th c. saw a fading of the spiritual form and a flourishing of the memoir. This probably originated in 13th-c. *merchants' private records (e.g. Donato Velluti, Bonaccorso *Pitti) and the more personal of the medieval *chroniclers (e.g. *Compagni), but was also influenced by models of classical *biography, and their modern revival in Petrarch and *Boccaccio. These models—part historical, part biographical and part autobiographical—fed into a tradition of artists' records of their work and their workshops, paralleling the biographical tradition which reaches its apogee in *Vasari. The great monument to emerge from this tradition is Benvenuto *Cellini's extraordinarily vivid, arrogant, and self-promoting *Vita* (written in 1550s and 1560s, but first published in 1728).

*Humanists at times also turned to autobiographical work, for instance Leon Battista *Alberti, Aeneas Sylvius *Piccolomini's chronicle of his papacy as Pius II, *Cardano. It is no coincidence that Cellini's *Vita* was first published in the 18th c., since this century saw autobiography established as a major modern literary genre. In response to a request from a *Venetian *letterato*, the philosopher Giambattista *Vico wrote his *Autobiografia* (1725, expanded 1731), a heroic account of his stoic struggles with ideas, men, and the injustices of fate, for the sake of intellectual enlightenment. In a comparable vein, *Alfieri's *Vita* (published posthumously in 1804) also tapped into a sense of heroic struggle and destiny, making it the key work of *Romantic autobiography in Italy. More prevalent than these, however, were memoirs with strong, picaresque narrative drives, such as the anecdotal professional memoirs by the playwrights *Goldoni (1787) and Carlo *Gozzi (1797–9) and the notorious libertine Giacomo *Casanova's *Histoire de ma vie* (written 1798–90).

Elements of Petrarchan and Romantic modes are found in *Leopardi's tortured self-scrutiny and use of memory, but autobiography in 19th-c. Italy tends rather to be associated with the *Risorgimento, either through writings by its historical players (e.g. *Pellico, Massimo *D'Azeglio, *Settembrini, *Tommaseo) or through imaginary heroes, as in *Foscolo's semi-autobiographical *Ultime lettere di Jacopo Ortis*. Both types display elements of Romantic self-heroicization and patriotic pedagogy. The same also could be said of *De Sanctis's late fragment *Giovinezza*.

From the late 19th c. onwards there is a striking proliferation of autobiographical writing in a broad sense, bent on self-scrutiny and scrutiny of the very nature of selfhood. This is evident in the introspective, psychological narratives of *Svevo and *Pirandello; in the self-conscious conflation of life and art in *D'Annunzio; in the elaborate autobiographical fictions by writers around *La *Voce*; in much *Hermetic poetry, and the lyric and narrative poetry of *Saba, *Penna, *Pasolini, and Attilio *Bertolucci, especially in his *Camera da letto* (1988). Women writers have found in autobiographical writing a means to a voice and an autonomy previously denied them, from *Aleramo's *Una donna* (1906) to diverse works by Natalia *Ginzburg, *Fallaci, *Maraini, *Sanvitale, and others, as have at times homosexual writers such as *Busi and *Tondelli.

Another strand of autobiographical writing, exemplified by Giorgio *Bassani, fathoms history and the self through memory. Historical events, from *Fascism, the *Resistance, and the Holocaust to 1960 and 1970s social movements, have produced waves of 'testimonial' autobiography, often with an oral, non-literary, and non-introspective quality, as evidenced in many *Neorealists, in Primo *Levi, and in the work of the oral historian Luisa Passerini; although several of the more literary Neorealists, such as Carlo *Levi, *Vittorini, and *Pavese, were also ambivalently steeped in introspective autobiography. More conventional but nevertheless interesting memoirs have continued to appear, by philosophers such as *Croce and *Bobbio, politicians such as *Bottai, scientists such as Rita Levi Montalcini and Primo Levi (in *Il sistema periodico*), and so on.

Despite this proliferation, a general suspicion of autobiographical writing remains prevalent in Italian literary culture, with its source in three influential lines of thought. Crocean *idealism was suspicious of its *positivist view of lives as the data of experience; *Marxism mistrusted its *decadent or hermeticist introspection; and high-literary or formalist culture has been generally suspicious of 'simply' speaking about oneself. As a result autobiography has continued to exist either at the literary, social and commerical margins or buried beneath the surface and interests of much modern Italian literature. [See also BIOGRAPHY; DIARIES.]   [RSCG]

See M. Guglielminetti, *Memoria e scrittura: l'autobiografia da Dante a Cellini* (1977); P. Briganti (ed.), 'Autobiography', *Annali d'Italianistica*, 4 (1986); A. Forti-Lewis, *L'Italia autobiografica* (1986).

AVALLE, D'ARCO SILVIO (1920–2002). Romance philologist and theorist of literature who taught at the Universities of *Turin and *Florence. Starting as a specialist in medieval literature and language, he was one of the founders of the journal *Strumenti critici*. He wrote influential discussions and illustrations of *structuralism and *semiotics in the field of literary studies, notably *Gli orecchini di Montale* (1965), and *L'analisi letteraria in Italia: formalismo, strutturalismo, semiologia* (1970).   [DR]

Avanti! Daily newspaper of the Italian *Socialist Party.

AVERLINO, ANTONIO DI PIETRO, see FILARETE, FRANCESCO.

AVERSA, TOMMASO (1623–63). *Sicilian poet and dramatist, who studied in Palermo and subsequently accompanied his patron, Don Pietro d'Aragona, on missions to Spain, Vienna, and *Rome. After his wife's death he entered the priesthood. He wrote *comedies, religious *tragedies, and narrative poetry. His *Le notti di Palermo* (1638) is the first comedy written in Sicilian *dialect, though he also published an Italian version in 1657.

[DO'G]

Avignon, adjoining the papal territory of Venaissin, became part of the county of Provence in the 13th c. In 1309 Pope Clement V took up residence there, and it was the centre of the administration of the Church until Gregory XI returned to *Rome in 1376. *Dante represented this transfer of the *papacy from Rome in apocalyptic terms (*Purg.* 32.148–60), and *Petrarch attacked it as the Church's exile in 'Babylon' (*Canz.* 114, 137, 138). Ruled by anti-Popes during the Great Schism (1376–1423), it was then governed by papal legates until its annexation by France in 1791.

[PA]

Azzeccagarbugli. Character in *Manzoni's *I *promessi sposi*, a dishonest lawyer.

AZZOLINI, LORENZO (or Azzolino) (1583–1632) followed an ecclesiastical career, serving in *Rome first *Urban VIII and then his cousin Cardinal Francesco Barberini, whom he accompanied on a diplomatic trip to Paris and Madrid. The result of this was his *Diario*, which recounts the return journey made between August and October 1626. He also wrote poetry, much of it still unpublished, including *satires, encomiastic poems, and *religious verse.

[PBD]

B

BACCELLI, ALFREDO (1863–1955). Poet, novelist and critic, who published his first book of verse, *Germina* (1883), as a student in *Rome. He became a parliamentary deputy and, after the March on Rome, a supporter of *Fascism. His various volumes of prose and verse display a *Positivist view of the natural world. [DCH]

BACCHELLI, RICCARDO (1891–1985). One of the few modern Italian novelists with a vast and varied production to his credit. Born into a well-off *liberal family in *Bologna, he studied literature at university there under *Pascoli, though he did not take his degree. He published his first novel, *Il filo meraviglioso di Lodovico Clò*, in 1911, and was already writing for *La *Voce* and *Il Resto del Carlino* before *World War I, in which he served as an artillery officer. He was among the founders of *La *Ronda* in 1919 with Emilio *Cecchi and Vincenzo *Cardarelli. He wrote and published extensively during the *Fascist period, and was recognized as a major literary figure, becoming a member of the *Accademia d'Italia in 1941. The works for which he was most highly regarded were his historical novels, beginning with *Lo sa il tonno* (1923) and *Il diavolo al Pontelungo* (1927). These look back to *Manzoni for their mixture of factuality and invention, though Bacchelli was constantly reshaping his style, bringing together popular, literary, and erudite strands in often distinctive combinations. His most famous work, a best-seller in the 1950s thanks to a TV adaptation, is the three-volume *Il mulino del Po* (1938–40), which presents the story of a family from the *Napoleonic era to *World War I. In addition Bacchelli's creative work includes a large number of *novelle (among them some fables), poetry, and plays. He also published various books of *travel writing and critical essays on 19th-c. Italian literature and *opera.

[PBart]

See M. Saccenti, *Riccardo Bacchelli* (1973);

E. Calura, *Riccardo Bacchelli e 'Il mulino del Po'* (1987).

BACCHINI, BENEDETTO (1651–1721). Ecclesistical historian and scholar, who published erudite historical treatises and essays in the *Giornale dei letterati* (1686–97). Professor of Scripture at *Bologna University, court theologian in Parma, and Prefect of the *Estense Library, he was a friend of Mabillon, De Montfaucon, and Leibniz, and influenced *Muratori and Scipione *Maffei.

[PBert]

BACCINI, IDA (1850–1911), a *Florentine teacher, was one of the first *women writers for children and combined a socio-educational mission with modern *journalism, being editor for thirty years of *Cordelia*, a weekly paper for girls. Her most important story, *Le memorie di un pulcino* (1875), anticipates *Pinocchio in presenting an anthropomorphic protagonist who is more convincingly childlike than the usual exemplary humans. [See also CHILDREN'S LITERATURE.] [ALL]

Bacco in Toscana, see REDI, FRANCESCO.

BAFFO, GIORGIO (1694–1768). *Venetian *dialect poet. Born into a patrician family, he held important posts in government administration. His poetry, however, concentrates on licentious, often pornographic themes, though it is underpinned by a coherent *libertine philosophy [see also EROTICISM AND PORNOGRAPHY]. It consists mainly of *sonnets written in colloquial Venetian and was initially known in manuscript, a first edition appearing only in 1771. Baffo sided with *Chiari in his polemic against *Goldoni's theatrical reforms, writing a verse-letter criticizing the latter's play *Il filosofo inglese* (1754). He became well known abroad with the publication in 1910 of a selection of his poems edited by Guillaume Apollinaire. [SC]

Bagutta, see LITERARY PRIZES.

BAIARDI, ANDREA (before ?1459–1511). Soldier and poet, Baiardi spent much of his life in Parma, but was for a while resident in Paris in the service of Louis XII. Author of a mediocre *Petrarchist *canzoniere* and some political poems on contemporary events, such as the French siege of Parma, Baiardi also composed a *romance in *ottava rima* entitled *Philogine* (1507). The *Tromba di Orlando,* a popular *chivalrous *epic, is attributed to him.   [JEE]

BAITELLI, ANGELICA, see NUNS.

BALBO, CESARE (1789–1853). *Turinese *liberal *historian. He was influenced by *Gioberti's Neoguelf theories, and in his most famous work, *Delle speranze d'Italia* (1844), he proposed that Italy should become a federation of independent states under the Pope. He himself served as a moderate deputy and (in *1848) as a minister in the *Piedmontese parliament.   [EAM]

BALDINUCCI, FILIPPO (1625–75). *Florentine painter, important for his artistic erudition and connoisseurship. He was greatly esteemed by the *Medici court and was entrusted with the organization and expansion of Cardinal Leopoldo de' Medici's collections of drawings and self-portraits (now in the Uffizi). His *Notizie de' professori di disegno,* published in six volumes between 1681 and 1728, anticipate 19th-c. scholarship in the use they make of documentary material to link artists' lives and their works. He also published a dictionary of artistic terms (1681) and became a member of the Accademia della *Crusca.   [FC]

BALDO DEGLI UBALDI, see LAW.

BALDOVINI, FRANCESCO (1634–1716). *Florentine famous as a writer of rustic verse and *comedy. His early studies with the *Jesuits led to a degree in *law, rather than in natural philosophy, in which he was also interested. He worked as a secretary, became a priest in 1674, and moved steadily up the ecclesiastical ladder. His most famous work, written in 1661, was the *Lamento di Cecco di Varlungo,* a rustic idyll in forty stanzas in *ottava rima,* in which the *peasant Cecco sings of his unrequited love for the peasant girl Sandra. In its stylistic freshness and authenticity the work has some connection with *Boccaccio's story of Monna Belcolore

(*Decameron* 8.2), but it lies more in the tradition of peasant *satire of the *Nencia da Barberino* attributed to Lorenzo de' *Medici, of Luigi *Pulci, and of later works by *Berni. Like much Tuscan poetry of the second half of the 17th c., Baldovino's work eschews *Marinismo* and *concettismo.* He wrote a three-act comedy, *Chi la sorte ha nemica, usi l'ingegno* (published in 1763), and five one-act dramatic works of a farcical character, for the *carnival of 1670.   [PBD]

BALDUCCI, FRANCESCO (1579–1642). *Sicilian poet who eventually settled in *Rome, participating in the Accademia degli *Umoristi and befriending Tommaso *Stigliani, for whom he wrote prefaces. Some of his *lyrics are in a classical style imitating Anacreon; others adopt a moderate *concettismo.* He also produced *libretti for two of the earliest oratorios.   [MPS]

Baldus, see FOLENGO, TEOFILO; MACARONIC LITERATURE.

BALESTRIERI, DOMENICO (1714–80), a member of the Accademia dei Trasformati in *Milan, wrote poems in Milanese *dialect and Italian, publishing *Rimm milanes* (1744) and *Rime toscane e milanesi* (1774–9). He also translated the *Gerusalemme liberata* into Milanese (1773). His anthology for his cat, *Lagrime in morte di un gatto* (1741), included contributions from *Baretti and Carlo and Gasparo *Gozzi.   [CCa]

BALESTRINI, NANNI (1935–). Poet, novelist and cultural and political activist. He played an influential role in several leading avant-garde movements and institutions, including the *Gruppo 63, Area Cooperativa Scrittori, and *Alfabeta.* He was a founder member of Potere Operaio (1968) and fled Italy on terrorism charges (later dropped) in 1979. His strongly ideological approach to writing led him to view literature as a form of opposition to the inertia of language in the modern, mediatized world. Poetry is for him an instrument of defamiliarization. In collections such as *Il sasso appeso* (1961), *Come si agisce* (1963), *Ma noi facciamone un'altra* (1968), *Poesie pratiche* (1976), *Le ballate della signora Richmond* (1977), *Blackout* (1980), and *Ipocalisse* (1986), he manages to surprise and entertain the reader with his recycling of pre-existing language, his use of collage techniques, and his debunking wit. He is a master of metre, and was an early experimenter with computer-generated poetry. Some of the same experimental techniques appear in his first novel, *Tristano* (1966), and are put to effective political use in *Vogliamo tutto* (1971) and *La violenza illustrata* (1976). He returns to the consequences and residues of 1960s and 1970s activism in *Gli invisibili* (1987) and *L'editore* (1989), which, however, are more didactic and conventional in form.

[MPC]

BALLA, GIACOMO (1871–1958) was the oldest and most established of the *Futurist painters. He was co-signatory of the *Manifesto dei pittori futuristi* (1910) and *Ricostruzione futurista dell'universo* (1915). His Futurist work, often signed 'FuturBalla', became increasingly abstract, depicting rapid movement, electric light, and geometric dynamics. He also worked in Futurist decorative art.

[RSCG]

Ballata. *Lyric form, originally a dance song, which is characterized by a refrain (*ripresa*). This may be of four lines (*ballata grande*), three (*mezzana*), two (*minore*), or one (*minima*, only from the 14th c. onwards), or more than four (*stravagante*, only in the 13th c.). The stanzas contain two (very occasionally three) 'mutations' (*mutazioni*) analogous to the *piedi* of a *canzone*, plus a *volta* constructed in the same way as the refrain and usually with the same final rhyme. Very often, particularly in poems set to music, there is only a single stanza. The ballad can end with a *replicazione* constructed like the refrain. [See also VERSIFICATION.]

[PGB]

BALLESTRA, SILVIA (1969–). Novelist from the Marche, now living in *Milan. Beginning with *Compleanno dell'iguana* (1991), she made her name with slangy, self-aware fiction about the urban young that drew on Pier Vittorio *Tondelli and also on recent *American writing. *Nina* (2000) marks a move to a more overtly literary manner.

[PH]

BALSAMO-CRIVELLI, GUSTAVO (1869–1929). Editor of many Italian classics, but chiefly associated with *Gioberti studies. He produced editions of major works, discovered material thought lost, catalogued the manuscripts, and began editing the correspondence. He also published poetry and a novel as a young man, and was a *socialist *journalist and councillor in his native *Turin.

[JD]

BALSAMO-CRIVELLI, RICCARDO (1874–1938). Author of a burlesque verse account of *Boccaccio's youth, *Boccaccino* (1920), which was championed by *Croce and betrays a long-standing passion for 14th- and 15th-c. literature. His copious subsequent output includes verse, as well as some inferior novels and other prose.

[JD]

BAMBAGLIOLI, GRAZIOLO DEI (1291–1343). The author of some Latin glosses on *Dante's *Inferno*, which he wrote in his native *Bologna about 1324. A jurist, he was exiled from Bologna for his active support of the *Guelfs, and moved to *Naples, where he may have known the young *Boccaccio. A vernacular *Trattato delle volgari sentenze sopra le virtù morali* has also been attributed to him. [See also DANTE COMMENTARIES.]

[SNB]

Bancarella, see LITERARY PRIZES.

BANCHIERI, ADRIANO (1568–1634). *Bolognese composer, organist, theorist, and author. An Olivetan monk, he spent much of his career in S. Michele in Bosco just outside Bologna, where in 1615 he established the musical Accademia dei Floridi (later dei Filomusi). His theoretical works, notably the *Cartella musicale* (1601) and *L'organo suonarino* (1605), did much to popularize new musical developments. His light *madrigal *comedies such as *La pazzia senile* (1598) and *Festino nella sera del giovedì grasso* (1608) followed precedents set by Orazio *Vecchi. He also published *satirical and other works under the pseudonyms Camillo Scaligero della Fratta and Attabalibba del Perù, such as *La nobiltà dell'asino* (1592). His *novella Cacasenno* was added to G. C. *Croce's *Bertoldo e Bertoldino* (1621). [TC]

BANDARINI, MARCO, see ANGELICA.

BANDELLO, MATTEO (1485–1561) was a *Dominican friar, writer of fluent Latin, translator from the Greek, minor poet, courtier, and occasional diplomat, but above all he was a prolific writer of *novelle. He enjoyed favour at the *Gonzaga court at *Mantua in the time of Isabella d'*Este. Later, while in the service of the Fregoso family, he was tutor to the orphaned Lucrezia Gonzaga; in his *Canti XI* he sang her praises and expressed his Platonic love. After the death of Cesare Fregoso in 1541, Bandello accompanied his widow and two sons to France, and thereafter he lived mainly in their castle at Bassens, near Agen. He became Bishop of Agen in 1550, resigning in favour of Giano Fregoso in 1555.

In the framework and language of his 214 *Novelle* (of which parts 1, 2 and 3 were published in 1554, part 4 posthumously in 1573), Bandello moved away from the *Boccaccian model so frequently imitated in *Renaissance Italy. Each of his tales is preceded by a dedicatory letter which purports to tell us where and when he heard it narrated. These letters contain valuable descriptions of *court life, but their claims concerning the genesis of the stories must be treated with caution: it can be demonstrated that Bandello was often deeply indebted to previous written sources, and that his reading extended from Greek and Latin, through Italian and French, to Spanish. He declared that, not being *Florentine like Boccaccio, he had no style, but was convinced that 'history and this sort of *novella* could please, no matter in what language it was written. History (particularly contemporary history) was certainly of overwhelming interest to him, and he often gave the impression that he wished to be accepted merely as a reliable *chronicler of remarkable happenings. But he was capable of a notable imaginative response to certain themes, as can be seen particularly in his treatment of tragic scenes, and in his analysis of the emotions of occasional characters (sometimes in memorable dramatic speeches). His tales soon attracted the attention of translators and adapters in France and England, and some became important sources for dramatists like *Shakespeare, Webster, and Lope de Vega. [TGG]

> *Tutte le opere*, ed. F. Flora (1934). See R. Pruvost, *Matteo Bandello and Elizabethan Fiction* (1937); T. G. Griffith, *Bandello's Fiction* (1955).

BANDETTINI, TERESA (1763–1837). Poetic *improviser from Lucca. Orphaned at an early age, she started her career as a dancer, and then became a poet, entering the *Arcadia *academy as Amarilli Etrusca. She was renowned for her improvisations both on stage and at the meetings of literary academies. [CCa]

BANDI, GIUSEPPE (1834–94). Author of a much-anthologized account of his part in *Garibaldi's 1860 campaign, *I mille* (1886), which is amongst the best of its kind. He also wrote several *historical novels. Born near Grosseto, he was a *journalist and editor, principally in Livorno. His political affiliations followed Francesco Crispi's drift to the right. [JD]

BANDINELLI, BACCIO (1488–1560), whose real name was Bartolomeo Brandini, was a sculptor and painter. A rival and enemy of *Cellini, he wrote a *Memoriale* to promote his noble lineage, character, and learning. He changed his name in 1530 to receive the Order of the Knights of Santiago, which was restricted to the nobility, from the Emperor. [PLR]

BANDINI, ANTON MARIA (1726–1800). *Librarian who catalogued the *manuscripts of the Biblioteca Laurenziana in *Florence (published 1776–93). He is also noted for bio-bibliographical and documentary contributions on Tuscan writers, such as the *Specimen litteraturae Florentiae saeculi XV* (1747–51), which is important for the history of Florentine *humanism. [JMAL]

BANDINI, FERNANDO (1931–). Poet and critic from Vicenza. He has published verse in Italian, Veneto *dialect, and, in *De itinere reginae Sabae* (1989), Latin. His work is highly conscious of literary tradition (in particular *Montale and *Pascoli), and is frequently concerned—in *Santi di dicembre* (1994), for example—with the transformation of Italian culture through industrialization. [JJ]

BANFI, ANTONIO (1886–1957). *Milanese philosopher with *idealist tendencies who became a *Communist member of the *Resistance and then a parliamentary deputy. His wide-ranging philosophical writings reflect his political and social concerns, and emphasize the importance of the individual as a counterbalance to the impersonal power of the modern state. [DCH]

Bankers. During the 13th c. the importance of the itinerant merchant was increasingly eclipsed by the more settled figure of the banker, who worked largely through correspondence and was able to employ company representatives all over Europe. Banking developed rapidly in many Central and Northern city-states. The *Florentines in particular took advantage of new techniques such as double-entry book-keeping and bills of exchange, which allowed money advanced in one currency to be repaid in another. The Florentine florin also began to be minted on a large scale. Despite the Church's condemnation of usury, interest was charged on loans at up to 20 per cent. Since popes and prelates were among the most prominent customers of the great banking families such as the *Bardi, the Peruzzi, and the Frescobaldi, no real attempt could be made to stamp out this practice. Money was also lent to kings and nobles to finance wars, leading to the downfall of many banks in the 1340s, when Edward III of England proved unable to repay the huge debts incurred during the Hundred Years War. But the Florentine and Italian bankers weathered these and other challenges (in particular the *plague of 1348). New family companies appeared, and in the 15th c. the *Medici established even greater economic and and political powers for themselves. Italian banking lost its pre-eminence with the European discovery of the Americas and the shifts in trading patterns which followed. At the time of their greatest profits, however, the banking families were among the most important artistic patrons of the *Middle Ages and *Renaissance. [See also MERCHANTS.]

[CEH]

BANTI, ANNA (pseud. of Lucia Lopresti) (1895–1985). Novelist born in *Florence who studied history of art in *Rome, where she met and married the art historian Roberto *Longhi. Her last work, *Un grido lacerante* (1981), presents a fictionalized account of their marriage. She co-founded and co-edited the journal *Paragone* with Longhi, taking over the editorship entirely after his death and regularly writing on *cinema and literature (especially women writers). Her publications include studies of painters, literary *translations, and *biographies, as well as novels and short stories. *Itinerario di Paolina* (1937) marked the start of her literary career and was followed by a collection of stories, *Il coraggio delle donne* (1940). Today she is best known for *Artemisia* (1947), a creative reworking of the life of the artist Artemisia Gentileschi; it is one of a group of historical novels which includes *Noi credevamo* (1967) and *La camicia bruciata* (1973). [AHC]

BARATELLA, ANTONIO (1358–1448). Prolific Latin poet, most of whose poems are still unpublished. He studied arts and *law at *Padua, and alternated the profession of notary with that of grammar teacher in many Veneto cities. He experimented with a range of metres in his *Ecatometrologia*. Other poems are encomiastic addresses to cultural and political personages or celebrate his native countryside in elegiac, *Virgilian tones. [See also LATIN POETRY IN ITALY.] [CG]

BARATOTTI, GALERANA, see TARABOTTI, ARCANGELA.

Barbara, Metrica (or *Poesia*), see CARDUCCI, GIOSUE; VERSIFICATION.

BARBARANI, BERTO (1872–1945). Veronese *dialect poet, who worked as a *journalist in Verona for most of his life. His poetry, mostly collected by him in *canzonieri*, expresses simple feelings of joy and sadness in the manner of *Pascoli's earlier poetry, and centres on the people and landscape of Verona and the surrounding region. [JJ]

BARBARO, ERMOLAO (THE ELDER) (1410–71). *Venetian patrician and *humanist educated at *Guarino da Verona's school, who went on to serve Popes Eugene IV and Pius II, becoming Bishop of Treviso (1443) and Verona (1453). His *Orationes contra poetas* (written 1455–9) take up the much-discussed issue of the acceptability of pagan poetry. While rejecting the arguments going back to Albertino *Mussato and *Boccaccio that classical myths were *allegories concealing moral, philosophical, and theological truths, he allowed that *Virgil and *Horace were morally sound, but deprecated other poets as erotic and obscene. [LAP]

BARBARO, ERMOLAO (THE YOUNGER) (1454–93). The most illustrious *Venetian *humanist of the 15th c. In his youth he set out to reform the teaching of *Aristotle at its stronghold, the University of *Padua, arguing that, rather than Latin *scholastic manuals, it was necessary to study the Greek text and Greek commentators like Themistius and Simplicius. He is most celebrated for his emendation of the text of the Elder Pliny's *Natural History*, as well as the Latin geographer Pomponius Mela and the Greek botanist Dioscorides, to which he added information about the plants from other sources. His correspondence includes a comic reply to *Pico della Mirandola on the appropriate style for philosophers. [See also GREEK INFLUENCES.] [LAP]

BARBARO, FRANCESCO (c.1390–1454). *Venetian patrician and *humanist, who built up a large library of Greek *manuscripts. He launched a new kind of treatise on marriage and the family in his *De re uxoria*, written after a visit to *Florence in 1415. This adapted material from recently discovered texts by Xenophon and Plutarch in the light of contemporary concerns with the preservation of family dynasties in republics like Florence and Venice. [See also GREEK INFLUENCES; HOUSE-HOLD TREATISES.] [LAP]

BARBARO, GIOSAPHAT (1413–94). *Venetian nobleman, statesman, *merchant, and traveller. He was ambassador to Persia from 1473 to 1477, and his linguistic knowledge allowed him to collect information for the text of *Viaggi fatti da Vinetia alla Tana, in Persia, in India et in Costantinopoli* (1543), included by G. B. *Ramusio in his *Navigationi et viaggi* (1559). [See also TRAVEL WRITING.] [LL]

BARBARO, UMBERTO (1902–55). *Marxist film theorist, who introduced German and Russian thinking about film to Italy. He attempted to develop a new aesthetic for the *cinema, which he believed had spontaneous and collective features that made it superior to *theatre. Born in Catania, he was appointed lecturer at the experimental cinema centre in *Rome in 1935. He also directed films, published some fiction, and translated writers as diverse as Gogol and Diderot. [DCH]

BARBATO DA SULMONA (c.1300–63). Early *humanist and chancellor to Robert of *Anjou in *Naples. He was a friend of *Petrarch, who dedicated his collection of Latin verse letters to him, and also of *Boccaccio. Some of his Latin *letters survive. [JP & JMS]

BARBAZZA, ANDREA (1581/2–1656). Aristocrat who occupied senior legal and administrative offices in his native *Bologna and was renowned as an expert on questions of honour. His friendship with *Marino led him to attack Tommaso *Stigliani in his *Strigliate* (1629). He also published a *pastoral drama, and a small number of *lyrics in contemporary *anthologies. [MPS]

BARBERINI, MAFFEO, see URBAN VIII.

BARBI, MICHELE (1867–1941). Literary scholar who applied the *Positivist historical method to *Dante studies. He directed the *Bullettino della Società Dantesca Italiana* (1893–1905) and founded *Studi danteschi* (1920). His advocacy of the 'nuova *filologia', which patiently reconstructed a work's socio-linguistic context, profoundly influenced Italian criticism after *World War I. [See also LITERARY CRITICISM.] [PBarn]

BARBIERI, GIOVANNI MARIA (1519–74), of Modena, was one of the leading vernacular scholars of his age. A period in France (1538–45) helped him acquire an exceptional knowledge of French and Provençal literature. He planned an edition of the *troubadours with *Castelvetro. The only completed book of a projected *Arte del rimare*, published by *Tiraboschi as *Dell'origine della poesia rimata* (1790), traces the early history of rhymed poetry from the Arabs through French and Provençal to the *Sicilian School, and thence to mainland Italy. Reproducing some Sicilian School verse in untuscanized form, the book provided unique evidence of its original nature. Barbieri also reworked a *Franco-Veneto poem, *La guerra di Attila*, in prose (1568). [BR]

BARBIERI, ULISSE (1842–99). Prolific popular dramatist from *Mantua, who had his greatest successes between 1866 and 1874. His most important works include *Gesù Cristo o il Messia* (1868), *Giulio Cesare* (1874), *Ali tarpate* (1879), and *Caprera* (1888). A collection of political poetry, *Ribellione* (1887), voices his *socialist, anti-establishment views. [JD]

BARCITOTTI, GALERANA, see TARABOTTI, ARCANGELA.

BARDI. Important *Florentine noble family which, in the 13th and 14th c., became one of the most important *mercantile and *banking families in Europe. It was particularly active in *Naples, where it employed *Boccaccio's father, and in England. It attempted to institute a *signoria* in Florence in 1340 but failed. It was an important patron of the arts, commissioning a chapel in Santa Croce decorated by *Giotto. The company made huge losses when Edward III was unable to repay his debts after the Hundred Years War, and went bankrupt in 1346, precipitating a financial crisis throughout Europe. [CEH]

BARDI, LIPPO PASCI DE' (d. before 1332). Author of four surviving *sonnets and the likely addressee of *Dante's double sonnet 'Se Lippo amico se' tu che mi leggi' and its accompanying *canzone* stanza. He may be identifiable with the otherwise anonymous *Amico di Dante. [GG]

BARETTI, GIUSEPPE MARC'ANTONIO (1719–89). *Piedmontese critic, traveller, and *journalist. His early translations from Corneille, his

Poesie piacevoli in *Berni's manner, and some polemical tracts failed to secure him a situation in *Turin, and he left in 1751 for a nine-year stay in London, during which he taught Italian and made friends with Johnson, Garrick, Goldsmith, Burney, and others. Among works connected with his teaching, a successful *Dictionary of the English and Italian languages* (1760) enabled him to return to Italy, through Portugal, Spain, and France. The first two volumes of his lively, outspoken account of the journey appeared as *Lettere familiari ai suoi tre fratelli* in 1762 and 1763, but publication of the last two volumes was forbidden by *Venetian *censorship. In 1763-4 he published in Venice the journal *La *Frusta letteraria*, through which he aimed to modernize Italian literature with stinging criticism of current frivolous or antiquated books. When *La Frusta* too was suppressed in January 1765, Baretti returned to England, and resumed tutoring, writing in 1775 a delightful *Easy Phraseology for the Use of Young Ladies, who Intend to Learn . . . Italian* for his pupil Queeny, daughter of Hester Thrale Piozzi. He spent the rest of his life there, except for some trips to the Continent.

To answer Samuel Sharp's slanderous *Letters from Italy*, he published *An Account of the Manners and Customs of Italy, with Observations on the Mistakes of Some Travellers, with Regard to That Country* (1768). In 1769 he was appointed Secretary for Foreign Correspondence to the Royal Academy, presided over by Joshua Reynolds. He published a translation of the entire *Lettere familiari* as *A Journey from London to Genoa, through England, Portugal, Spain, and France* (1770), and an edition of *Machiavelli's works, with an important Preface (1772). His most mature works were *Discours sur Shakespeare et sur Monsieur de Voltaire* (1777), in which, following Johnson's ideas, he brilliantly defended the free inventions and powerful genius of *Shakespeare against Voltaire's narrow-minded criticism, and *Scelta di lettere familiari fatta per uso degli studiosi di lingua italiana* (1779)—letters attributed to fictitious authors, which beyond any didactic purpose are a kind of intellectual autobiography, showing the conversion of an Italian conservative to more liberal, modern English ideas. Baretti's *Strictures on Signora Piozzi's Publication of Doctor Johnson's Letters* (1788) make him the most probable author of *The Sentimental Mother*, an anonymous *comedy satirizing Thrale Piozzi, published just after his death. [See also ENGLISH INFLUENCES; RECEPTION OF ITALIAN LITERATURE IN BRITAIN.] [FF]

See M. L. Astaldi, *Baretti* (1977).

Baretti, Il (1924-8). Cultural and literary *journal founded in *Turin by Piero *Gobetti, who remained as editor until 1926. It became the means of continuing his opposition to *Fascism, when his overtly political journal, *La *rivoluzione liberale*, had to cease publication in 1925. As Gobetti stated in the first issue, the main objectives were to resist dogmatism and provincialism, whilst avoiding the rhetoric of the earlier avant-garde, to defend the integrity of the intellectual, and to extend knowledge in Italy of modern European culture. Contributors included various notable figures opposed to Fascism, such as Leone *Ginzburg, Benedetto *Croce, Eugenio *Montale, and Gaetano *Salvemini. [CFB]

BARGAGLI, GIROLAMO, see INTRONATI, ACCADEMIA DEGLI.

BARGAGLI, SCIPIONE (1540-1612) set the discussions and stories of *I trattenimenti* (1587) in his native *Siena. *Il Turamino* (1602) describes the Sienese variety of Tuscan and justifies its literary use, in reaction to the dominance of Florentine [see also QUESTIONE DELLA LINGUA]. Bargagli's interest in *iconography led to a *dialogue on the *emblem, *Dell'imprese* (1594), and other works. [BR]

BARGELLINI, PIERO (1897-1980). *Florentine Catholic writer, who founded *Il *Frontespizio* with Carlo *Betocchi and Nicola *Lisi in 1929 and was its guiding force throughout its existence. His own largely popularizing writing covered studies of the figurative arts, *biographies of saints and poets, histories of places or events especially relating to *Tuscany and Florence. Between 1945 and 1952 he published *Pian dei Giullari*, a twelve-volume *history of Italian literature. He worked for much of his life as a teacher in Florence. [CO'B]

Bargello, Il (1929-43). The weekly review of the *Fascist federation of *Florence. From 1932 to 1937 its editorial staff included Elio *Vittorini and Vasco *Pratolini. In that period it voiced the antibourgeois and anti-conformist attitudes of young intellectuals who had grown up under Fascism, and believed it to be a revolutionary force that would advance the cause of Italian *peasants and workers. Though they left the paper as Fascist policies became more patently reactionary, it was able to draw contributions from a wide range of Florentine critics and writers for some time. [RSD]

BARICCO, ALESSANDRO (1958–). Novelist and *journalist, who was born and works in *Turin. His first book, *Castelli di rabbia* (1991), interwove two separate fantastical narratives. After *Oceano mare* (1993) came the very successful *Seta* (1996), the story of a 19th-c. silk farmer, which blends exoticism and minimalist *modernism. Baricco has also written a theatrical monologue, *Novecento* (1994), and an essay on modernism in music, *L'anima di Hegel e le mucche di Wisconsin* (1992). [PH]

BARILE, ANGELO (1880–1967). Poet. After serving in *World War I he spent most of his life in Liguria in Albissola Marina, where he was born. He published his first collection, *Primasera*, in 1933, but generally preferred to publish in reviews, including *Solaria* and *Il *Frontespizio*. His poetry is highly literary and elegiac in tone, although his later work has a more modern air. [JJ]

BARILLI, BRUNO (1880–1952). A music critic and composer, Barilli composed two moderately successful *operas, *Medusa* (1910) and *Emiral* (1915). He made more of an impact, however, with the insightful articles on 18th-c. Italian opera and on *Verdi, which he published in various *journals between 1915 and 1933. [RS]

BARILLI, RENATO (1935–). Critic and aesthetic theorist, with strong *phenomenological interests. He first came to prominence as a member of the *Neoavanguardia, of which he later published a detailed history (1995). His studies of 19th- and 20th-c. literature begin with the impressive *La barriera del naturalismo* (1964). [PH]

BARLAAM, see BYZANTIUM; GREEK WRITING IN ITALY.

Barlaam e Giosafat. Originally an oriental story of a hermit and his son fleeing the temptations of the world, it was transformed in 10th-c. *Byzantium into an account of St Thomas the Apostle's conversion of India. A century later it was turned into Latin in *Naples, and entered *Iacopo da Varagine's *Legenda aurea*. Thence it passed into most European vernaculars. *Boccaccio parodied it in the story of Filippo Balducci in the Introduction to *Decameron*, Day 4. [LAP]

Barone rampante, Il (1957), the second part of Italo *Calvino's trilogy *I nostri antenati*, is a modern *conte philosophique*, set in the 18th c. In thirty chapters, like Voltaire's *Candide*, it is Calvino's longest continuous novel, tracing the life of Cosimo di Rondò from his flight at the age of 12 into the trees (rejecting his aristocratic family and embracing *Enlightenment ideals), through his intellectual and emotional maturing, down to his final disappearance in a balloon. This private *Bildungsroman* is paralleled by history (in turn symbolic of 1950s events): the French Revolution, *Napoleon's rise and fall, the *Bourbon restoration, and the collapse of revolutionary ideals. The narrative brio is underpinned by intertextual allusions to Diderot, Defoe, and Fielding. [MMcL]

BARONIO, CESARE, see PAPACY AND THE CATHOLIC CHURCH (1).

Baroque (*barocco*) is a term most often used to describe the literature and culture of the period between the death of Torquato *Tasso (1595) and the birth of the Accademia dell'*Arcadia (1690). The term was current towards the end of the 16th and throughout the 17th c. in the phrase 'argomenti in barocco', a type of logically defective syllogism. It carried the derogatory sense of imperfection and irregularity, perhaps aided by the Portuguese and Spanish term for an irregular pearl (*barrueca*). It was not used in relation to art and architecture until the 18th c., and was first used to refer to literature in the dictionary of *Tommaseo and Bernardo *Bellini in the second half of the 19th c. The Italian use of the term, like the French, carried from the start strongly negative associations: the Baroque was not only extremely bizarre, it was also decadent. No doubt the idiosyncratic and perverse titles chosen by writers of the Baroque period helped to contribute to this mistaken view, which, as far as Italian scholarship is concerned, persisted well into the works of 20th-c. critics and historians. It seemed to be confirmed by the apparent moral decline of Italy under foreign occupation during the 17th c. The term has also been used widely as a negative synonym for *Marinismo and *secentismo. [See also CONCETTISMO.]

The fundamental fallacy was to hold that the Baroque in literature was primarily and wholly a question of style. No one asked whether the style of *Marino and the Marinists, or of *Tassoni and the novelists, might be the result of a different world view from that of the *Renaissance. Most scholars would now agree, however, that the Baroque in Italy was not merely stylistic strangeness masking decadence; deeper causes were at work, which created a shift in cultural values. In the first two decades of the 17th c. Italian culture had reached an extreme crisis. The old *humanist authorities were tried and found severely wanting; the enterprise of humanism from the 14th up to the early 17th c. had burnt itself out applying the very methods and values it had itself taught the world. These had remained valid as long as the world remained static. But with the Copernican revolution, the voyages of discovery, and the overwhelming evidence that experience was at variance with classical authority, the old order could no longer hold.

Baroque culture may be seen, from this perspective, to involve a radical questioning of authority. Tassoni and Marino led the field in rejecting the authority of *Petrarchism, and in this they differed fundamentally from Tasso; *Galileo and his followers rejected the dogma derived from *Aristotle and Ptolemy. Altogether the early 17th c. saw a significant growth in modernism in Italy, the belief that modern science and creativity was at least equal, if not superior, to those of the ancient world [see QUERELLE DES ANCIENS ET DES MODERNES]. The extension of the Baroque world view, spatially, geographically, poetically, and artistically, was for some an occasion for joyous confidence: in their different spheres this is apparent in the irrepressible energy and sense of mission of Galileo, Marino, *Campanella, Bernini, and others. The world seemed a bigger place, and a place where personal experience (and experiments) had gained a new value of their own. The concomitant of this in the art and literature of the 17th c. was an intensification of the human senses and passions; and the human condition became the subject for extreme reactions in the portrayal of the favourite Baroque situations of martyrdom, sacrifice, heroic glory, self-control, grandeur, sensuality, strangeness, and otherness. However, different Baroque writers reacted differently to the expansion of the universe: while some celebrated, some deplored it; some tried to contain its growth (Cesare *Cremonini), others withdrew into an inner world of their own (Federico *Della Valle, Torquato *Accetto), and yet others set off to widen their experience through world travel (Pietro *Della Valle, Francesco *Carletti).

In comparison with the Renaissance, much writing of the Italian Baroque now seems excessive, exaggerated, unwieldy, an over-demanding. Such features spring from an effort to reflect a new world

with suitable dynamic tools. Baroque writers such as Daniello *Bartoli and Emanuele *Tesauro believed that the human condition was literally a theatrical experience, in which man is confronted by a dramatic world whose every element is a sign that cries out for interpretation and identification. To theatricalize experience is to intensify it, and heighten its impact, as Tasso had done in his staging of scenes in the *Gerusalemme liberata. [See also CLASSICISM.]   [PBD]

See G. Getto, 'La polemica sul barocco', in *Orientamenti culturali: letteratura italiana: le correnti*, vol. i (1956); F. Croce, 'Critica e trattatista del Barocco', in E. Cecchi and N. Sapegno (eds.), *Storia della letteratura italiana*, vol. v (1965); H. G. Koenigsberger, 'Decadence or Shift? Changes in the Civilization of Italy and Europe in the Sixteenth and Seventeenth Centuries', in *Estates and Revolutions: Essays in Early Modern European History* (1971).

BAROZZI, FRANCESCO, see NUMEROLOGY.

BARRILI, ANTON GIULIO (1836–1908). *Journalist and prolific writer of contemporary and historical narratives and plays. His patriotic memoirs, *Con Garibaldi alle porte* (1895), present a vivid evocation of the Wars of Independence. He became professor of Italian literature in his native *Genoa, and was elected to parliament in 1876.
[AHC]

BARRILI, GIOVANNI, see BOCCACCIO, GIOVANNI.

BARTOLI, ADOLFO (1833–94). Important member of the *Florentine school of *Positivist *literary critics and scholars, and a pioneering researcher into the origins of Italian literature. His major work is an unfinished *Storia della letteratura italiana* (1878–89) which argues that worldly, sensual realism reinvigorated Italian literature after the ascetic *Middle Ages. [See also HISTORIES OF ITALIAN LITERATURE.]   [PBarn]

BARTOLI, DANIELLO (1608–85), is best known for his history of the *Jesuits and his rhetorical and linguistic theory. He studied with the Jesuits in *Ferrara before entering the order in 1623. His highly successful career as a preacher began in 1637 and continued to 1648, when ill health prevented him from preaching. He dedicated the rest of his life to writing.

Always alive to literary and linguistic questions, he made his debut with his *Dell'uomo di lettere difeso e emendato* (1645). Here he equates the pleasure of literature with the act of understanding: the scholar-writer is like a spectator in a theatre full of uplifting novel wonders [see BAROQUE]. Yet he upholds the moral as well as aesthetic value of literature, arguing against the vacuity, as he sees it, of much contemporary *concettismo*. His famous *Il torto e 'l diritto del non si può* (1655), argues against the restrictive and prescriptive principles of the *Vocabolario della Crusca* in favour of an openness based on educated good taste and judgement. His contribution to the question of Italian spelling practice, *Dell'ortografia italiana* (1670), uses the same criteria. But he did not sanction linguistic freedom and licence: self-control and moderation are his aims. His works of moral philosophy include *L'huomo al punto* (1667), a contemplation of man in the face of imminent death, where death is not a fearful prospect but a future of truth, light, and life. In *La geografia trasportata al morale* (1664) and *Dei simboli trasportati al morale* (1676) the physical world is described as a repository of symbols, *emblems, and signs of a higher spiritual world of contemplation.

This fervent interest in higher reality tends to reduce the usefulness of Bartoli's specifically scientific writings (on gravity, sound and hearing, and ice formation). In fact his life's work, *Istoria della Compagnia di Gesù*, published between 1650 and 1673, involved much archival work which was not congenial to him. The work is a celebration of the activities of the Order across the world, and was intended to cover the continents of Africa, America, Asia, and Europe. Bartoli had no chance of finishing this project, but produced volumes on St Ignatius, Asia, Japan, China, England, and Italy, as well as biographies of famous Jesuits. What is remarkable about the work is that its detailed descriptions of far-away lands are based upon second-hand evidence. In the past critics have dismissed this as a work more of imagination than of history; but recent research has shown that Bartoli did indeed draw on much archival material. [See also TRAVEL WRITING.] [PBD]

BARTOLINI, LUIGI (1892–1963). Poet, novelist, and artist. Born in Ancona, he studied art in *Siena and *Rome before service in *World War I, after which he became a schoolteacher. He wrote extensively against contemporary intellectualism, especially that of the *hermetic poets, but he also quarrelled with the *Fascist regime, and was sentenced to a period of *confino* [see EXILE]. His own poetry has a vigorous, popular style. His novel, *Ladri di biciclette* (1946), was used as the basis for the famous film by *De Sica, with script by *Zavattini. As an artist he is best known for his etchings. [SVM]

BARTOLO DA SASSOFERRATO (1313/14–1357). The most influential jurist of his time, he studied civil *law under *Cino da Pistoia in *Perugia and then in *Bologna; he was professor of law in *Pisa (1339–43) and Perugia (1343–57). His writings include *Lecturae* on the various sections of the *Corpus iuris civilis*, many *quaestiones* on points of Roman law, and treatises on tyranny and the *Guelfs and Ghibellines. His *De regimine civitatis* attributes supreme legislative autonomy to the Italian *commune. [See also POLITICAL THOUGHT.] [PA]

BARTOLOMEO DA SAN CONCORDIO (d.1347). *Dominican who was for a time lector at Santa Maria Novella in *Florence before *Dante's exile in 1302. His works include *De documentis antiquorum*, a collection of sayings of the ancients, with commentary, and *Summa casuum conscientiae*, a compendium of canon and civil *law. Vernacular versions of both exist, that of the second being probably by *Giovanni delle Celle. Bartolomeo also made *translations from Sallust. [JT]

BARTOLOMEO DELLA FONTE, see FONZIO, BARTOLOMEO.

BARTOLOMEO DI CASTEL DELLA PIEVE (later 14th c.). Umbrian schoolmaster and minor poet. He lived an impoverished wandering life in *Lombardy, Emilia, and *Tuscany, but was respected as a literary figure. His seventeen surviving poems include love *lyrics, political *canzoni, and *autobiographical verse in *tenzoni*. Two Latin letters also survive. [JP & JMS]

BARUFFALDI, GIROLAMO (1665–1755). *Ferrarese poet and critic, who championed the doctrine of strict imitation and inaugurated the 18th-c. georgic revival with *Il canapajo* (1741). The best of his copious output lies, however, in his dithyrambic *Baccanali*, most notably the *Tabaccheide* (1714), a celebration of snuff modelled on *Redi's *Bacco in Toscana*. [JMAL]

BARZINI, LUIGI (1874–1947) was a foreign correspondent for the *Corriere della sera* and then edited newspapers in New York and Italy. He was made a senator in 1934. He became famous as a colourful *travel writer, especially for *La metà del mondo vista da un'automobile* (1908). [See also JOURNALISM.] [REL]

BARZIZZA, GASPARINO (1360–1430), *educator and *humanist, was born near Bergamo and educated at the University of Pavia, where he taught Latin grammar before becoming professor of rhetoric at *Padua from 1407 to 1421. Here he lectured on *Cicero's *De oratore* and Aristotle's *Rhetoric*, while he taught boarders at home, including *Vittorino da Feltre, Francesco *Filelfo, and George *Trapezuntios. As a professor at Pavia and *Bologna, Barzizza wrote treatises on correct Latin orthography and model openings, or *exordia*, for speeches. A transitional figure, he continued to use traditional medieval grammars, while he inculcated his love of newer humanist works in a number of able pupils. [BK]

BARZIZZA, GUINIFORTE (1406–63), *educator, courtier, and son of Gasparino *Barzizza, was born at Pavia, where he earned his degree in arts. He taught rhetoric and moral philosophy at Pavia and *Padua before entering the service of Alfonso of *Aragon. From 1434 to 1447 he taught at *Milan, where he commented on *Dante's *Divine Comedy*. After service at the *Este court, Barzizza ended his days in Milan as tutor to Galeazzo Maria *Sforza. [See also DANTE COMMENTARIES.] [BK]

BASILE, GIAMBATTISTA (1566/75–1632). The most outstanding writer of *novelle* of the 17th c. Born in *Naples, he served with a *Venetian regiment on Crete around 1606. On his return he had a successful career as a courtier and administrator, during which he published idylls, eclogues, and lyric poems, *drammi per musica* [see LIBRETTO; MELODRAMMA], and editions of Pietro *Bembo, *Della Casa, and other contemporary poets. His masterpiece, however, is *Lo cunto de li cunti, overo Lo trattenemiento de' peccerille* ('The Tale of Tales, or Entertainment for the Little Ones'), also called the *Pentamerone* (because the tales are told over five days), which was published posthumously between 1634 and 1636 by his sister, the singer Adriana Basile. It gathers together the largest collection hitherto of *fiabe*, that is, tales of *folk or at least oral origin, though it includes some of classical and oriental derivation, and has become the treasure trove of the European fairy tale. It was imitated in France by Perrault and in Germany by the Brothers Grimm, and is credited as the source for 'Cinderella', 'Puss-in-Boots', 'Sun, Moon and Talia', 'Beauty and the Beast', and 'The Three Oranges'.

But Basile is neither naïve nor sentimental. His Cinderella, for example, murders her stepmother, and the magic cat helps a totally undeserving young lad who turns on him. The frame story itself, while ending in a wedding, has the Prince kill his cunning slave-wife, who is pregnant, to marry the beautiful, virtuous Princess Zoza. The dedicatory letters of early editions show that the intended readers of the work were sophisticated Neapolitans, proud of their linguistic and cultural heritage and eager to break loose from the domination of Florentine and Northern Italian models of language and literature. Some structural elements of *Boccaccio's *Decameron* are preserved—the frame story, the division into days, the number of storytellers, and some form of entertainment in poetry at the end of each day—but Basile also subverts Boccaccio, both linguistically and in content. The storytellers are grotesque, maimed hags; the values they convey glorify the powers of blind luck bringing blessings and misfortunes in quick succession, with magical interventions of fairies and ogres, spells and curses. There is no providence or rational order in things, and laughter at life's absurdity and madness replaces a belief that human ingenuity can triumph over fortune. In Basile's subversive moral universe the powerful are seen from below as no better and no worse than anyone else. The poor and the ugly, on the other hand, can sometimes strike it lucky. Their language, too, crammed with popular proverbs and rude comical metaphors, exhibits a boisterous vitality far richer than the higher linguistic register associated with the upper classes.

The first four days end with 'eclogues' that have little in common with conventional *pastoral and which were removed from later editions. Recited by household servants dressed as *commedia dell'arte characters, they are *satires of Neapolitan society. All, and especially people at *court, deceive or are deceived; even writers pass off other people's thoughts and expressions as their own, and all amusement ends sooner or later in boredom. One player concludes that true wisdom lies in the possession of virtue and gold, for you can never have enough of either. [LAP]

Lo cunto de li cunti, ed. M. Rak (1999).

Basinio Da Parma

BASINIO DA PARMA (1425–57). *Humanist, who was born in the castle of Tizzano near Parma, from a family of *Mantuan origin, and studied at Mantua with *Vittorino da Feltre and at *Ferrara, where he probably met *Guarino da Verona. In 1449 he established himself in Rimini, where he wrote a large part of his romance, the *Liber Isottaeus*. His most important work, written to celebrate the magnificence of Sigismondo *Malatesta, is *Hesperis*, a Latin *epic poem in thirteen books, in which occasional direct *translations from Homer have been detected. The poem is also a reliable source of historical information, some provided by Malatesta himself.   [DieZ]

BASSANI, GIORGIO (1916–2000). One of the most important and best-known writers of the second half of the 20th c., he grew up in his native *Ferrara and studied at the University of *Bologna, where he was taught by Roberto *Longhi; friends from this early period were Attilio *Bertolucci and *Dessì. The promulgation of the racial laws in Italy in 1938 led to his joining the *Resistance, rapidly giving him a degree of political awareness and a sense of his role as a writer that remained with him for the rest of his career. Unable to use his own name because of its recognizably *Jewish origin, in 1940 he published his first collection of stories, *Una città di pianura*, under the pseudonymn of Giacomo Marchi. After the war he moved to *Rome, editing *Botteghe oscure* (1948–60) and *Paragone*, acting as consultant to the publisher *Feltrinelli (he discovered *Tomasi di Lampedusa's *Gattopardo*), and eventually becoming chairman of the heritage society, Italia Nostra. *Una città di pianura* was followed over the years by a series of novels and short stories all centring on the tragedy of the deportation and extermination of the Italian Jews in 1943. The collected edition *Il romanzo di Ferrara* gathers together in six books, with numerous corrections and revisions, all the fiction to which Bassani gave his authorial seal of approval: *Dentro le mura* (1974) (a rewriting of *Cinque storie ferraresi* of 1956), *Gli occhiali d'oro* (1958), Il *giardino dei Finzi-Contini* (1962), *Dietro la porta* (1964), *L'airone* (1968), and *L'odore del fieno* (1972).

Memory, time, and the membrane effect of distance are the fundamental elements of Bassani's narrative world, with a constant emphasis on collective boundaries that act as barriers or prisons, from the city walls of Ferrara to the social and cultural structures that marginalize those who are different. This is accompanied by an uncompromising

analysis of the Jewish middle class in Ferrara, accused of hypocrisy, conservatism, and connivance with *Fascism. But the events and characters which in *Cinque storie ferraresi* were conveyed by an impersonal, external, and judgemental narrator are filtered, from *Gli occhiali d'oro* onwards, through a partly *autobiographical self who evokes, with the inevitable involvement and emotion of a first-person narrator, the memory of a world that has ended, to which he testifies, almost as a form of compensation, an irrevocable allegiance. Pious affection is accompanied by awareness, and horror at silence in the face of the Holocaust is mixed with remorse and a desperate regret for the lost figures of the past, as well as for those who, disillusioned by the new Italy and trapped in the sickness of melancholy, are unable to find a reason for living— notably illustrated in the suicide of Edgardo Limentani at the end of *L'airone*, significantly the concluding volume of the *Romanzo di Ferrara*.

Alongside his narrative work, from his youth onwards Bassani had a strong vocation for poetry. A collection of *lyric poems was published in 1951 as *Un'altra libertà*. With the completion of the *Romanzo di Ferrara*, this side of Bassani's work became a form of confession made increasingly private and anguished by the weight of time passing. Through a mixture of dialogue and epitaph on the model of Edgar Lee Masters' *Spoon River Anthology*, and with some of the violence and anger of more recent American writers, this has its most splendid and mature results in *Epitaffio* (1974) and *In gran segreto* (1978), where Bassani involves himself and his characters in a last journey that seems to go beyond death itself. The definitive title of his collected essays, *Di là dal cuore* (1984), can be read in the same key.   [AD]

> See A. Dolfi, *Le forme del sentimento: prosa e poesia in Giorgio Bassani* (1981); Various, *Le intermittenze del cuore: Bassani e Ferrara* (1995).

BASSANO DA MANTOVA, see MACARONIC LITERATURE.

BASSI, LAURA (1711–78). A graduate of *Bologna University (1732), she became the first and most famous of several women who taught there in the 18th c., rising in 1776 to the chair of physics. She was the subject of much literary adulation and a favourite reference point for champions of women's *education. [See also FEMINISM; WOMEN WRITERS, 2.]   [JMAL]

BASSI, UGO (1801–49). Priest renowned as a preacher with *liberal ideas. Baptized Giuseppe, he changed his name to Ugo in honour of *Foscolo. Eventually excommunicated, he acted as army chaplain for *Garibaldi's troops in 1849, and was arrested and executed by the *Austrians. He published poems, *tragedies, and various works on sacred themes. [FD'I]

Bassvilliana, La, see MONTI, VINCENZO.

BATACCHI, DOMENICO LUIGI (1748–1802). Poet and impoverished aristocrat, who worked in customs and excise at *Pisa and Livorno. His lively, licentious narrative poetry, which includes *novelle in versi* and longer *mock-heroic burlesques, was much admired during the *Romantic period. He also published a *translation of the first volume of Richardson's *Clarissa.* [JMAL]

Battaglia di Benevento, La, see GUERRAZZI, FRANCESCO DOMENICO.

BATTIFERRI AMMANNATI, LAURA (1523–89), born in *Urbino, resided in *Florence after her second marriage to the architect and sculptor Bartolomeo *Ammannati in 1550. She was a member of the Accademia degli *Intronati of *Siena and friend of many contemporary writers. Her principal work is a poetic miscellany, the *Primo libro delle opere toscane* (1560). [See also WOMEN WRITERS, 1.] [JHB]

BATTISTA, GIUSEPPE (1610–75). A late follower of *concettismo.* He was born into the provincial middle class in Grottaglie near Taranto, educated by the *Jesuits, and, having taken holy orders, graduated as a doctor of theology. He served as a parish priest in Grottaglie until 1645, when, following the death of his first literary *patron, Giambattista *Manso, he moved to *Naples, and the household of Prince Francesco Caracciolo. There he published extensive collections of verse, the Latin *Epigrammatum centuriae tres* (1653), and the Italian *Poesie meliche* (in four parts, 1653–70), and *Epicedi eroici* (1667). Then followed a biblical *tragedy, *Assalone* (1676), a *Poetica* (1676), and a collection of *Lettere* (1678). These latter posthumous publications, all printed in *Venice, testify to his ambitions as a literary all-rounder, and to the importance attributed to his work throughout Italy. He is now generally held to be an imitator of

*Marino, but the extent of his debt may be doubted: Battista's convoluted brand of *concettismo* alternates solemn moral reflections with explicitly *autobiographical elements common in mid-17th-c. poetry, and the celebration of the ceremonies and pastimes of Neapolitan literary and aristocratic society. [MPS]

BAZLEN, ROBERTO (Bobi) (1902–65). Eccentric *Triestine intellectual of *Jewish origins with a wide range of recondite interests. He *translated Freud's *Interpretation of Dreams* (1949), and was the first promoter of Jungian *psychoanalysis in Italy. He worked as editorial adviser for various *publishers, including Adelphi, which he helped to found. Convinced that everything had already been written, he refused to publish anything of his own. His writings were posthumously edited by Roberto *Calasso as *Scritti* (1984), and include fragments of a Joycean novel, *Il capitano di lungo corso* (1973). He was a long-standing friend of *Montale. [KP]

BAZZARINI, ANTONIO, see ENCYCLOPEDIAS.

BAZZONI, GIOVANNI BATTISTA (1803–50). *Historical novelist. Born in Novara, he studied at Pavia and then followed a legal career in *Milan. His novels, strongly influenced by Scott, Hugo, and *Manzoni, begin with *Il castello di Trezzo* (1827). He also published two collections of *Racconti storici* (1832 and 1839) and a *translation of Scott's *Waverley.* [DO'G]

Beatrice (?1266–90), the *Florentine lady whom *Dante loved, is the principal subject of his earlier *rime and the *Vita nova,* and his guide through the heavens in the *Paradiso.* *Boccaccio identified her as Bice, daughter of Folco Portinari (d.1289) and wife of Simone de' Bardi. Dante calls her 'Bice' once in the *Vita nova* (24.8), records her father's death (22), and gives her date of death as 8 June 1290 (29). A later poem by *Cino da Pistoia consoled Dante on her death. Elsewhere Dante uses the full name 'Beatrice' ('she who brings blessedness'), and many commentators have emphasized her function in his poetry as an *allegory of Theology, the Scriptures, or Grace. More generally, she became an archetypal image of idealized, spiritualized, or Platonic love for later poets in Italy and elsewhere, notably, during the *Romantic period, for Dante Gabriel *Rossetti in his poetry and in paintings, such as *Beata Beatrix.*

In the *Vita nova* Dante presents events and

Beatrice Del Sera

poems associated with Beatrice from his first meeting with her in childhood until she refused him her greeting (2–12). In poems influenced principally by Guido *Cavalcanti, he expressed the anguish of his love, especially after her mockery of him (13–16). Then, adopting *Guinizzelli's doctrine of love and moral nobility ('gentilezza'), he developed his 'sweet new style' (*dolce stil novo) of praising her as the origin and bearer of love and virtue (17–27). After her death, and his short-lived attraction to another lady, the Donna gentile (28–38), he experienced two visions of Beatrice which made him decide to write of her what had never been said before about any other woman (39, 42). She is virtually absent from the the *Convivio, though she is mentioned as a soul in Heaven who remains at the summit of his thoughts (2.2). In the *Divine Comedy, she sends *Virgil to rescue Dante from the dark wood (Inf. 2), is the goal of his ascent of Purgatory (Purg. 6.46–51; 27.34–42), and eventually appears to him in the Earthly Paradise. After his confession that he strayed from her following her death, she reveals to him the love in her eyes and in her smile (Purg. 30–1), which in the Paradiso transport him through the heavens until she takes her place in the Rose of the Blessed in the Empyrean (Para. 31.58–93).   [PA]

See V. Moleta (ed.), La gloriosa donna de la mia mente: A Commentary on the Vita nova (1994); M. Picchio Simonelli (ed.), Beatrice nell'opera di Dante e nella memoria europea 1290–1990 (1994).

BEATRICE DEL SERA, see NUNS.

BECCADELLI, ANTONIO, see PANORMITA, IL.

BECCADELLI, LUDOVICO (1501–72). Born in *Bologna, he was a *humanist and poet, and friend of Giovanni *Della Casa. A secretary of cardinals Gasparo Contarini and Reginald Pole, in 1555 he became Archbishop of Ragusa and took part in the Council of Trent [see COUNTER-REFORMATION]. He is the author of verse in Latin and the vernacular, and of *biographies, including one of *Petrarch, whom he studied and imitated.
[LPer]

BECCARI, AGOSTINO DE' (?1510–?1590) was the Ferrarese author of the first 'regular' *pastoral drama in five acts, Il sacrificio, first performed in *Ferrara in 1554. With its chain of nymph and shepherd lovers, and its intrusive satyr, the play established a standard set of topoi followed by many others in the genre.   [RAA]

BECCARI, ANTONIO, see ANTONIO DA FERRARA.

BECCARIA, CESARE (1738–94). *Milanese philosopher and reformer, and along with Pietro *Verri a founder member of the *journal Il *Caffè, Beccaria achieved international fame with his work on penal reform *Dei delitti e delle pene (1764). He also wrote on economics (Elementi di economia pubblica, 1804) and aesthetics (Ricerche intorno alla natura dello stile, 1770). From 1771 he served as a state official in the Milanese administration.

Among Beccaria's contributions to Il Caffè were discussions of the purpose and nature of the journal as a genre, the pleasures of the imagination, and issues of literary style and aesthetic theory. On the question of style, Beccaria rejected the archaisms and rhetoric of the *Vocabolario della Crusca in favour of a language closer to common usage. Influenced by the sensism of Condillac, he replaced the theory of words as simple signs for thoughts by one which gave the meaning of words an associative dimension derived from individually determined sense impressions. His writings on aesthetics, also influenced by sensism, examined the relationship between passions and reflection. [See also ENLIGHTENMENT; SENSISMO.]

Easily his most important work, Dei delitti e delle pene was immediately translated into French by Morellet, annotated by Voltaire and Diderot, and read in the rest of Europe and America, becoming a fundamental point of reference for reform movements. Beccaria's critique of the system of justice highlighted its backwardness in sanctioning capital punishment and torture, and the repressive nature of a system in which laws were unclear and interpreted by magistrates with unlimited discretionary powers. By establishing a contractual theory of society as the basis of legislative power, with equality of standing for all citizens before its tribunal, he was mounting a powerful assault on the whole social system of the ancien régime. In claiming that it was crime as a breach of the social pact which was punishable by law, and not sin, he was establishing the basis of a secular system of justice which drew upon his work the condemnation of the Church. Thomas Jefferson copied sections of Beccaria's work in his notebooks, and it had an important influence on Jeremy Bentham's utilitarianism.
[GLCB]

Edizione nazionale delle opere di Cesare Beccaria, ed. L. Firpo (1984). See F. Venturi, *Italy and the Enlightenment* (1972); M. T. Maestro, *Cesare Beccaria and the Origins of Penal Reform* (1973).

BECCHI, GENTILE (d.1497), from Urbino, became Latin tutor to Giuliano and Lorenzo de' *Medici, who secured for him the bishopric of Arezzo in 1473. His vehement defence of Lorenzo after the *Pazzi conspiracy probably prevented his elevation to the cardinalate. He served *Florence and the Medici as ambassador on many important missions, retiring to his diocese after the fall of the Medici in 1494. He was an interlocutor in *Landino's *De nobilitate* and the dedicatee of one of *Poliziano's finest odes; he wrote *Latin poetry and orations, which, like his striking correspondence, remain unedited. [RDB]

BECELLI, GIULIO CESARE (1686–1750). Veronese writer and critic, and a friend of Scipione *Maffei. His innovatory *Della novella poesia* (1732) points to what is new in the Italian literary tradition and rejects classical *imitation. Elsewhere he argues against the use of Greek mythology. In linguistic matters, however, he anticipates Antonio *Cesari in championing 14th-c. usage. [See also QUESTIONE DELLA LINGUA.] [JMAL]

Beffa is an Italian term for 'mockery'. In literature and drama it refers to any narrative plot in which one character gets the upper hand over another— usually in the form of a practical joke, and almost always involving some kind of deception. There may be a practical advantage to be achieved (financial, or sexual), or the trick may be motivated by sheer love of the game. This sets up a simple opposition of a winning trickster against a losing sucker, and it is assumed that the reader or spectator is going to participate vicariously on the side of the winner. [See also COMEDY; FACEZIE.] [RAA]

Belacqua.. Character in *Dante's *Purgatorio*, an indolent figure in Ante-Purgatory.

BELCARI, FEO (1410–84) was a *Florentine whose strict religious education informed his literary compositions after a period in which he worked for the *Monte*, the *commune's funded debt. He translated Ambrogio *Traversari's Latin lives of the saints in the *Prato spirituale*, compiled a version of the *Vita* of the religious leader Giovanni Colombini, and composed numerous *laudi*. Belcari is best known for his *sacre rappresentazioni* in *ottava rima* on Abraham and Isaac, John the Baptist, the Annunciation, and an expanded version of Antonio di *Meglio's *Dì del giudizio*. A *Medici supporter, he held various public offices from 1454. A performance of his Annunciation in 1471 confirmed his place among Florence's cultural elite. [GPTW]

Belfagor (1945–). Fortnightly magazine of politics and culture, taking its name from the arch-devil in *Machiavelli's satirical *novella*. Founded by the literary historian Luigi Russo, it was published initially by D'Anna in *Florence. After Russo's death in 1961 it was published by *Olschki and edited by a team including Eugenio *Garin and Delio Cantimori. It was, throughout this period and subsequently, an important platform for left-liberal opinion and debate on a variety of subjects, including literature, art, philosophy, history, sociology, *theatre, and *cinema. [DF]

Bel Gherardino, Il, see CANTARI.

BELGIOIOSO, CRISTINA (1808–71). *Milanese *journalist and writer. She worked to improve the condition of the *peasants and was actively involved in the *1848 revolution in Milan, on which she wrote an essay. Many of her writings were in French: subjects include the condition of women, *Vico, and her travels in Asia Minor. [See also FEMINISM; WOMEN WRITERS, 3.] [VRJ]

BELLARMINO, ROBERTO (1542–1621) joined the *Jesuit order and studied philosophy in *Rome at the Collegio Romano and theology at *Padua and Louvain. He was made Cardinal by Pope Clement VIII in 1599, and was an important protagonist in the *Galileo controversy. His *autobiographical work, *Memorie autobiografiche* (published posthumously in 1675), gives an insight, as all his writings do, into a personal religious journey. [PLR]

BELLEZZA, DARIO (1944–96). Poet and novelist. He was born and lived in *Rome, where he was a committed member of the *homosexual community and eventually died of an AIDS-related illness. From early in his career he looked to the examples of *Pasolini and *Penna, as well as to French writers such as Gide, Cocteau, and Sartre. His novel, *L'innocenza* (1970), and his first collection of poems, *Invettive e licenze* (1971), are both *autobiographical and focus on perverse but bitter-sweet pleasures. The *epistolary novel *Lettere da Sodoma* (1972) continues in the confessional vein, emphasizing an instinctive compulsion for self-destruction. *Il carnefice* (1973) is less directly personal in its depiction of a world of drug and sex addicts vindictively rebelling against the norms and mores of bourgeois society. But the virulent vitality of these works sinks into nihilistic acceptance in later poetry collections—*Morte segreta* (1976), *Serpenta* (1987), and *Libro di poesia* (1990). In *Morte di Pasolini* (1981) Bellezza creates a moving reconstruction of the death of Pasolini. [VS-H]

BELLI, GIUSEPPE GIOACHINO (1791–1863) is one of the most original poetic voices in the history of Italian literature. Often relegated to its margins as *dialectal, Belli is now considered a major poet. His most important writings are the 2,279 *sonnets in the vernacular of *Rome, in which he presents a human comedy embracing ancient and modern history and the lives and customs of a variety of characters, high and low. Popes, ghetto *Jews, prostitutes, and plebeian Romans are represented, within the sonnet form, struggling with basic issues of hunger, poverty, sex, greed, power, faith, and death. Emphasizing the harsher aspects of *romanesco* (partly through prominent use of double consonants), Belli makes plebeian speech the normal, though not exclusive, register of the poems, and the means whereby his characters voice their opinions and feelings in a natural and convincing manner that has more in common with contemporary *realist fiction than with most *Romantic poetry. Yet, though resolutely antisubjective, Belli presents a plainly *satirical and deeply pessimistic vision of life in general, and of Roman life in particular, which he sees as torn between rebellion and religious belief. Though some poems did appear in periodicals during his lifetime and others circulated in manuscript, the subject matter and mode of expression of many were too obscene for them to be published or publicly acknowledged by their author. His entire œuvre in *romanesco* was first published in 1896.

Belli lived through a historically turbulent time. The French occupation of Rome in 1798, the unenlightened rule of Pope Gregory XVI, and the short-lived Roman republic of 1849 were events which affected both his life and his literary work. He was born into a well-to-do upper-middle class family, the eldest of three children, his father being employed as a papal accountant. After his father's death from cholera in 1802, and that of his mother

in 1807, the young Belli was faced with the need to earn a living, and in 1809 he was taken on as an accountant in the Demanio, the public tax authority then under *Napoleonic rule. But he continued with his education, studying French, English, mathematics, and chemistry. He was also active in the *neoclassical cultural life of the city, being a founder member in 1813 of the Accademia Tiberina, and later its secretary.

His marriage in 1816 to Maria Conti, a wealthy widow, freed him from financial worries. He embarked on a series of travels, going firstly to the Marche to oversee his wife's properties, and then to *Florence and *Milan. The latter visits are described in a French *Journal de voyage* of 1827. His reading of Carlo *Porta's poetry in Milanese dialect spurred him, in 1831, to write over thirty erotic sonnets. Though some of his sonnets in *romanesco* date from 1820, the majority were written between 1827 and 1847. The years 1837 to 1842, however, were a period of deep insecurity, marked by his wife's death, the worsening of his financial circumstances, and the need to provide for his son, Ciro. During this period he composed only seven sonnets and wrote a will stipulating that his sonnets should be destroyed. Though he later retracted that will, he made the same stipulation in a later will of 1849. In that year he wrote just one sonnet, which was also his last. Throughout his life he wrote verse prolifically in Italian in a variety of metres, some 45,000 verses in all. Little of that vast production is of literary interest. [See also DIALECT WRITING.] [BG]

See C. Muscetta, *Cultura e poesia di G. G. Belli* (1961); P. Gibellini, *I panni in Tevere: Belli romano e altri romaneschi* (1989).

BELLINCIONI, BERNARDO (1452–92). *Florentine poet, from a poor family, but, like Luigi *Pulci, and later *Poliziano, he early attracted the attention of Lorenzo de' *Medici, becoming from 1469/70 part of Lorenzo's inner circle, and also enjoying the support of Lucrezia *Tornabuoni. In 1482 he left Florence for the household of Cardinal Francesco *Gonzaga and then that of the Marquis Federigo Gonzaga, before gaining the *patronage of Lodovico *Sforza. With the help of *Niccolò da Correggio he joined *court circles in *Milan, remaining there until his death. In addition to the *lyric poetry that constitutes his chief literary output, ranging from occasional pieces to political poetry and burlesque, Bellincioni also wrote a play, *Festa del Paradiso* (1490), for which *Leonardo da Vinci produced the sets, and served as producer-director of the *theatrical spectacles and festivities which were a significant aspect of the culture of Milan under Lodovico. [JEE]

BELLINI, BERNARDO (1792–1876). Poet and lexicographer, who studied at Pavia and then taught literature in various cities, also founding a *printing-firm in Cremona in 1820. He wrote narrative poems and *tragedies. He is best known for his work with *Tommaseo on the latter's *Dizionario della lingua italiana.* [See also DICTIONARIES.]
[DO'G]

BELLINI, LORENZO (1643–1704). Doctor and poet. Born in *Florence, he studied philosophy and medicine at *Pisa and subsequently became professor of anatomy (1668), doctor to Cosimo III de' *Medici, and medical adviser to Clement IX. His precocious *Exercitatio anatomica* (1662) revolutionized understanding of the function of the kidney. He was admitted to the Accademia dell'*Arcadia in 1691. His verse, much less original than his scientific work, includes the *Bucchereide* (1729), a long poem showing a taste for erudition, exoticism, and metrical and linguistic variety.
[FC]

BELLINI, VINCENZO (1801–35) was the first of *Rossini's successors to find a distinctive tone of voice. Early success in *Naples took him to *Milan, where he established a close professional relationship with the *theatre-poet Felice *Romani, and produced two *operas, *Il pirata* (1827) and *La straniera* (1829), in which the Rossinian format is transformed by a new *Romantic directness of expression. The sentimental *La sonnambula* and the heroic *Norma* (both 1831) represent *bel canto* opera in its ripest style. After estrangement from Romani, Bellini composed his last opera, *I puritani* (1833), for Paris, aiming for a new harmonic and instrumental sophistication. [See also LIBRETTO.]
[DRBK]

BELLO, FRANCESCO, see FRANCESCO CIECO DA FERRARA.

BELLOCCHIO, PIERGIORGIO, see QUADERNI PIACENTINI.

BELLONCI, GOFFREDO (1882–1964). *Journalist and critic, born in *Bologna, where he studied as a pupil of *Carducci. In 1907 he became a journalist and later the head of the political section

of the *Resto del Carlino.* He published essays on a wide range of cultural and political issues, but remained independent of literary and political groups. His criticism shows the influence of *Crocean aesthetics, and includes an *Introduzione alla letteratura italiana di oggi* (1932), a study of 20th-c. *theatre, and an edition of *Sette secoli di *novelle italiane* (1953). He was married to Maria *Bellonci Villavecchia. [DieZ]

BELLONCI VILLAVECCHIA, MARIA (1902–86). *Roman *journalist and novelist. She and her husband, Goffredo *Bellonci, were instrumental in founding the Strega prize in 1947 [see LITERARY PRIZES]. Her novels are largely historical and set principally in the *Renaissance. Her last novel, for example, *Un rinascimento privato* (1985), which was awarded the Strega prize in 1986, is a fictionalized autobiography of Isabella d'*Este. Other subjects included the *Gonzaga family and Lucrezia *Borgia. [SW]

BELLONDI, PUCCIO (13th c.). Florentine author of a small number of poems in the manner of *Guittone d'Arezzo, including one *sonnet in *tenzone* with *Monte Andrea and probably at least one other addressed to *Dante. He was active in the civic affairs of *Florence in the later 13th c.
[PH]

BELLORI, GIOVAN PIETRO (1613–96). *Roman scholar of antique and modern art, with strongly classical sensibilities, who eventually became supervisor of antiquities in Rome. His major work, *Vite de' pittori, scultori e architetti moderni* (1672), the preface to which is the essay 'L'idea del pittore' (1664), discusses twelve modern painters (ranging from Annibale Carracci to Poussin) on the basis of *Neoplatonic criteria that in some ways anticipate *Milizia and Winckelmann. He also wrote a description of *Raphael's paintings and an account of Roman antiquities. He assisted his teacher, Francesco Angeloni, to assemble a private museum of ancient remains, contemporary art, and natural history. [See also ANTIQUARIANISM.] [FC]

BELO, FRANCESCO (16th c.) was a *Roman comic dramatist, author of *El beco* and *El pedante,* both published in 1538. Little is known of him personally; but the sour and scurrilous tone of his *comedies arguably influenced Giordano *Bruno's more famous *Candelaio* of 1582. [RAA]

BELTRAME, ACHILLE, see DOMENICA DEL CORRIERE, LA.

BELTRAMELLI, ANTONIO (1879–1930). Writer and *journalist. His first novel, *Gli uomini rossi* (1904), is a Romeo and Juliet tale of conflict in his native Romagna between Catholics and republicans (*rossi*); in the sequel, *Il cavalier Mostardo* (1922), republicans fight *socialists. Himself a republican *nationalist, Beltramelli volunteered in *World War I and subsequently joined the *Fascist militia. He wrote an early eulogy of *Mussolini, *L'uomo nuovo* (1923), and in 1925 signed *Gentile's *Manifesto degli intellettuali fascisti.* He was a journalist on *Il popolo d'Italia* and founded and co-edited *Il Raduno,* the weekly of the Sindacati fascisti degli autori e scrittori. [DF]

BEMBO, BERNARDO (1433–1519). *Venetian *humanist and politician, who was in contact with figures such as Lorenzo de' *Medici, *Ficino, *Landino, and *Castiglione. He himself wrote speeches and letters, mostly in Latin. His impressive library was fundamental for his son Pietro *Bembo. As *podestà* of Ravenna in 1483, Bernardo was responsible for the restoration of *Dante's tomb. [NG]

BEMBO, ILLUMINATA, see NUNS.

BEMBO, PIETRO (1470–1547) transformed, through his theories and his own example, the language of Italian literature and the nature of *lyric poetry in the 16th c. and beyond. He was born into the *Venetian patrician class: his father, Bernardo *Bembo, was a cultured diplomat and writer. He received a *humanist *education, which included a period studying Greek in Messina (1492–4). His Latin *dialogue *De Aetna* was printed by Aldo *Manuzio (1496), as was his first major vernacular work, *Gli *Asolani* (1505), also written in his favoured dialogue form, and dedicated to Lucrezia *Borgia, whom Bembo had known and loved at the court of *Ferrara (1502–3). The elegantly wrought *Asolani* marked a turning point in the history of the Italian language: Bembo took the decision to imitate 14th-c. literary Florentine consistently, eliminating the contamination by contemporary language and by Latin which had become normal in the 15th c. In the same period he prepared editions of *Petrarch (1501) and *Dante's *Divine Comedy* (1502), both printed by *Manuzio, which reflect Bembo's concern for *textual criticism but also his

precocious desire for uniformity of language and *spelling. In 1506 he moved to the court of *Urbino, and is portrayed in this setting in *Castiglione's *Libro del cortegiano.* There he wrote some *Stanze* (1507), inviting the ladies of the court to love, which show his ability in the relatively humble medium of *ottava rima,* and were influential in the development of this verse form. In 1508 he committed himself to an ecclesiastical career. He moved to *Rome in 1512 and was appointed as a papal secretary in 1513. He left Rome in 1521, making his home in *Padua in 1522; here he had three children by his companion, Morosina.

In 1513 Bembo set out, in a letter *De imitatione* to Giovanfrancesco *Pico, his doctrine of imitating the best authors (*Cicero and *Virgil) in Latin. By 1512 he had written two books of the dialogue which expounded a parallel doctrine for the vernacular, the *Prose della volgar lingua,* and in 1525 he saw the completed work through the press in Venice. Thereafter Bembo's main focus of interest in the vernacular became the Petrarchan lyric poetry which he had been writing since his youth. In 1530 he had his collected *Rime* printed; an augmented and revised edition followed in 1535. His last major work was an official Latin history of Venice (*Historiae venetae*) since 1487, which he was commissioned to write in 1530 and which he translated into the vernacular from 1544; the original and the translation were printed in 1551 and 1552 respectively. In 1539 Bembo was appointed cardinal and moved from Padua to Rome, being ordained priest in the same year. He became Bishop of Gubbio (1541) and Bergamo (1544). In his last years he collected his Latin and vernacular letters for posthumous publication.

The rigour of Bembo's standards aroused some hostility but also explains their profound and lasting influence. He was criticized for his rejection of the living language, by supporters of a courtly language (e.g. Castiglione) and by some Tuscans, but his linguistic principles revolutionized the practice of authors such as *Ariosto and underpinned the *purism later typified by the Accademia della *Crusca. His texts of Petrarch and Dante helped to set new editorial standards for the vernacular. Although Bembo's own poetic inspiration is uneven, his *Rime* and his Petrarchan scholarship played a major part in determining the success of *Petrarchism and the demise of the linguistic and metrical freedom of courtly poetry. [See also IMITATION; LINGUA CORTIGIANA; QUESTIONE DELLA LINGUA.] [BR]

Prose e rime, ed. C. Dionisotti (1966); *Lettere*, ed. E. Travi (1987–93).

BEMPORAD, ENRICO (1868–1944). *Florentine *publisher. He inherited the family firm Paggi and published under his own name from 1906, specializing in children's literature and textbooks, then publishing *Dante, *Verga, and *Moravia. In the 1920s, with Sansoni, he dominated Florentine publishing and developed a strong bookselling arm. In 1935 he was ousted from the board and in 1939 the firm was merged with Barbèra to become *Marzocco, in turn absorbed in 1972 by *Giunti. [DF]

BENAMATI, GUIDUBALDO (*c*.1595–1653). Exceptionally prolific imitator and supporter of *Marino, who served the dukes of Parma, writing numerous works in their praise, as well as *pastorals and a vast *Canzoniere* (1616). In middle age he retired to his native Gubbio, producing yet more lyrics, plays, a prose *romance, and what he believed his masterpiece, *La battaglia navale* (1646), an *epic poem celebrating the Christian victory at the Battle of Lepanto. [MPS]

BENCI, TOMMASO (1427–70). *Florentine *merchant patrician, bibliophile, and poet. He translated *Virgil's *Georgics*, Seneca's *Medea*, *Ficino's *De divino furore*, and in 1463, most significantly, the latter's pioneer Latin rendering of the fourteen treatises in the *Corpus Hermeticum*, known collectively as the *Pimander* [see HERMETICISM]. Benci was a close friend and patron of Ficino, whose *De amore* assigns him the starring role of speaking for Socrates in the re-enactment of Plato's *Symposium* at the (fictive?) banquet at Careggi on 7 November 1468 celebrating Plato's birthday. [MA]

BENCO, ENEA SILVIO (1874–1949). Prolific and influential *journalist, with interests in every aspect of the culture, history, and geography of his native *Trieste. His *irredentism is particularly evident in his three-volume *Gli ultimi anni della dominazione austriaca a Trieste* (1919), which recounts the city's transition from *Austrian to Italian rule. He was a friend of *Svevo and Joyce, and wrote plays and fiction as well as literary, art, and music criticism. His novel, *La contemplazione del disordine* (1946), is an apocalyptic vision of the end of European civilization. [KP]

BENDEDEI DA FERRARA, TIMOTEO (1447–1522). Born in *Ferrara into a noble family from Reggio, he was the author of verses in Latin (now lost) and Italian, and courtier to Ercole I d'*Este and later Cardinal Ippolito I. He moved to *Mantua in 1494, and then to Gazzuolo, where he was associated with the revival of classical *comedies sponsored by Antonia del Balzo. Bendedei's poetry shows the influence of *Tebaldeo, and was well regarded by Ercole *Strozzi and *Ariosto; but little now remains. [JEE]

BENE, CARMELO (1937–2002). The most exciting and innovative figure in Italian avant-garde *theatre since the 1960s. He was an experimental director and actor, known particularly for his many radical adaptations of canonical and popular works, for example *Amleto* (1962) and *Pinocchio* (1962), and for his multi-sensory, often violent performances. He also acted in and directed films, such as *Nostra signora dei turchi* (1968). [RSCG]

BENE DA FIRENZE (late 12th c.–1239), succeeded, not without controversy, *Boncompagno da Signa in the chair of grammar at *Bologna. He is the author of influential works on metrics, in particular *De accentu*. He also produced an important rhetorical manual, the *Candelabrum*, and commented on Priscian's *Grammar*. [JU]

BENEDETTA (pseud. of Benedetta Cappa) (1899–1977). Novelist, painter, and essayist who became part of the *Futurist movement in *Rome and married F. T. *Marinetti. Though she signed various manifestos and wrote extensively about the role of women, she was essentially a traditionalist who considered motherhood the only true female vocation. [See also WOMEN WRITERS, 3.] [UJF]

BENEDETTI, ARRIGO (1910–76). Journalist and novelist from Lucca. After early *journalism for *Il *Selvaggio*, he wrote for *Oggi* and *Omnibus* in *Rome and gradually distanced himself from *Fascism. He began publishing fiction in the 1930s. His most acclaimed novel, *Il passo dei Longobardi* (1964), combines memories of childhood with stories of the *Resistance. [DCH]

BENEDETTO DA MANTOVA, see TRATTATO DEL BENEFICIO DI CRISTO.

Benedictines. Monastic order originating with St Benedict of Norcia in Umbria (*c*.480–543), who fled from the corruption of *Rome to live as a hermit at Subiaco and around 520 founded the monastery of Montecassino. The Rule which he drew up was decisive for the development of all Western monasticism, and led to monasteries becoming centres of learning and high culture. In spite of periodic reforms, by the 12th c. a certain laxity had crept in, and new reforming orders, such as the *Franciscans and the *Dominicans, were founded during the next century. Montecassino itself survived in splendour, but was almost totally destroyed by the British in 1944. [See also RELIGIOUS LITERATURE.]   [JT]

Beneficio di Cristo, Trattato del. Anonymous religious tract (written by Benedetto da Mantova in *Sicily) which draws on both *Benedictine spirituality and the writings of Protestant Reformers to teach the doctrine of justification by faith. It circulated widely in Italy after 1540, but was effectively suppressed by the Roman *Inquisition. [See also REFORMATION; RELIGIOUS LITERATURE.]   [PMcN]

BENELLI, SEM (1877–1949), poet, playwright, *journalist, and man of letters, is best known for his historical dramas in verse. The first of these was *La maschera di Bruto* (1908), in which Lorenzaccio, the murderer of Duke Alessandro de' *Medici, is likened to the Roman Brutus. The second and better known, *La cena delle beffe* (1909), is a theatrical adaptation of a story by *Grazzini set in *Renaissance *Florence. A revenge drama, it caught the popular taste of the period and its leading role, Giannetto, attracted great actors such as John Barrymore and Sarah Bernhardt. Benelli's *tragedies can be compared to *D'Annunzio's for their use of verse, elaborate sets, and costume, but they had a stronger appeal to middle-class audiences and might usefully be regarded as caricatures of D'Annunzio's more lofty attempts at tragic revival.

Benelli also wrote several prose plays; his bourgeois *comedy, *Tignola* (1908), treated the same themes as *Chiarelli's *La maschera e il volto* (1916) some eight years earlier. After serving in *World War I, Benelli joined the *Fascist movement, but left the party after the Matteotti affair (1924). The book *Io in Affrica* (1936) gives his impressions of the war in Ethiopia, in which he served as a volunteer. At the outbreak of *World War II, however, he rejected Fascism again and emigrated to Switzerland, returning to Italy only after *Mussolini's downfall. [See also THEATRE, 2.]   [JAL]

BENI, PAOLO (1553–c.1625) was the leading

*humanist scholar, *literary critic, theologian, and linguist of his day, important for his role in the early stages of the *Querelle des anciens et des modernes in Italy. Born in Gubbio and educated by the *Jesuits, after graduating in theology he worked in *Rome, entering the order in 1581, and remaining there until he was expelled in 1593. Thereafter he taught theology at Rome and composed occasional works for the Pope. In 1600 he moved to *Padua to take up the chair of humanities, and remained there until his death, teaching and publishing well into old age.

He produced an enormous number of works, many published during his lifetime, and many others which are still unpublished. His humanism spawned Latin *commentaries of vast proportions on a range of classical texts, and on the three related topics of poetics and rhetoric (after Aristotle), and history. As a commentator he shares with *Galileo, *Marino, and *Tassoni a willingness to question authority in the name, not of freedom, but of reason. The result of this modernism was not *Baroque decadence (as has often been thought), but a strong thrust towards independence of judgement, human progress, and historical insight. He also published, in Italian, texts on vernacular writing. His polemical work on Battista *Guarini's *Pastor fido* is poorly focused; his *Comparatione* of Homer, *Virgil, *Ariosto, and Torquato *Tasso (1607 and 1612), and his vast commentary on the latter's *Gerusalemme liberata*, interpret Tasso's poetry within the *Renaissance rhetorical tradition, using the example of *Dante to illustrate his achievement. Beni's concept of poetry is classical rather than Baroque, a *classicism which also informs his linguistic writings. The *Anticrusca* (1612) and the *Cavalcanti* (1614) argue against the geographical and temporal restrictions of the *Vocabolario della Crusca*, in the name of a modern Italian language that combines the best of 14th-c. usage in a non-regional, regulated, up-to-date vernacular.   [PBD]

See P. B. Diffley, *Paolo Beni: A Biographical and Critical Study* (1988).

BENIGNI, ROBERTO, see CINEMA.

BENIVIENI, GIROLAMO (1453–1542). *Florentine *humanist with both Greek and Hebrew, a passionate student of *Dante, and in his youth an elegant and subtle love poet. He became a close friend and admirer of Giovanni *Pico della Mirandola, with whom he shares a tomb in San Marco in Florence, and his *Ficinian 'Canzona dell'amor celeste e divino' was the subject of a commentary by Pico. Among the first of the humanists to succumb to the spell of *Savonarola, and the composer thereafter of sacred lyrics, *laudi and *canzoni morali, he remained till the end of his long life a devoted follower of Savonarola's teaching, much admired for his piety and literary accomplishment.   [MA]

BENNI, STEFANO (1947–). *Satirical novelist and poet, with an exuberantly inventive manner. After the comic but straightforward satire of contemporary Italy in the stories of *Bar sport* (1976), he exploits the possibilities offered by *science fiction in his first novel *Terra!* (1983), and plunges into *surrealism in the stories of *Il bar sotto il mare* (1987). His poetry, from *Prima o poi l'amore arriva* (1981), presents similarly engaging combinations of playfulness and seriousness. Amongst his recent works are the novels *Baol* (1990) and *L'ultima lacrima* (1994), the latter being an interesting satire of technological excess. He has written regular *journalism for *Il Manifesto* and *L'Espresso*.

[PBart]

BENTIVOGLIO, CORNELIO (pseud. Selvaggio Porpora) (1668–1732) was well known for his blank verse *translation of *Statius's *Thebaid* (1729). Born in *Ferrara, he belongs to the Ferrarese *epic tradition, and in effect his translation is an adaptation of Statius to the style of Torquato *Tasso. The work was popular with contemporaries, but fell into disfavour after *Alfieri criticized it.

[PBD]

BENTIVOGLIO, ERCOLE (1507–?1573) was born in *Mantua, following the exile of his family from *Bologna, and educated at the *court of Alfonso I d'*Este in *Ferrara. Friend and associate of *humanists and poets, including *Ariosto and *Tullia d'Aragona, Bentivoglio was a gifted musician, contributing to the literary and musical culture of Ferrara and *Venice. His literary output includes several *comedies, but he is best known for his six *Horatian *Satire* with their amused, ironic comments on contemporary life.   [JEE]

BENTIVOGLIO, GINEVRA SFORZA, see ARIENTI, GIOVANNI SABADINO DEGLI; PATRONAGE.

BENTIVOGLIO, GUIDO (1577–1644). Born in *Ferrara, of a patrician family from *Bologna, he studied at *Padua before entering the Church. His experience as a *papal nuncio in Flanders and France and his access to diplomatic sources informed his most famous book, a history of the revolt of the Netherlands, the *Guerra di Fiandra* (1632–9), praised at the time for its style as well as its content. His *Relazioni* were published in 1629 and his memoirs after his death. [See also HISTORIOGRAPHY.]   [UPB]

BENVENUTO DA IMOLA (c.1338–90). Author of a huge, and hugely learned, Latin commentary on the *Divine Comedy* (c.1385), based on lectures he began giving at *Bologna in 1375. The commentary is notable for its critical intelligence as well as its learning, and rich in (generally reliable) historical and cultural information. It is perhaps the greatest achievement of the voluminous 14th-c. tradition of commentary on *Dante's poem and remains remarkably useful for the modern reader. Benvenuto taught grammar at Bologna and *Ferrara and also wrote *commentaries on classical and contemporary authors (Lucan, Valerius Maximus, *Petrarch). [See also DANTE COMMENTARIES.]

[SNB]

BEOLCO, ANGELO, see RUZANTE.

BERARDINELLI, ALFONSO (1943–). Unusually readable critic and occasional poet. In books such as *Il critico senza mestiere* (1983) and *La poesia verso la prosa* (1994), he takes issue with the specialization of critical discourse, the loss of dialogue between high and popular culture, and the self-regardingness of much contemporary poetry. [See also LITERARY CRITICISM; LYRIC POETRY.]

[JJ]

BERCHET, GIOVANNI (1783–1851). *Milanese poet. Destined by his father for a commercial career, he acquired a knowledge of English, German, and Spanish, which he used to acquaint himself with recent literary developments. As a poet he had a *neoclassical apprenticeship but became one of the leading Milanese *Romantics. His knowledge of languages and his interest in popular literature gave his contributions to the literary debates of 1816–19 a markedly democratic (and occasionally exotic) flavour. The central theme of his main critical essay, *Lettera semiseria di Grisostomo al suo figliuolo* (1816), was the call for a morally and politically educative poetry accessible to 'il popolo', which he located between the hyperrefined *Parigini* on one side and the *Ottentoti*, as he called the unlettered masses, on the other, and which was in effect the increasingly literate and numerically expanding middle class. [See also LITERARY THEORY, 5.]

Berchet was closely involved in the conception and subsequent vicissitudes of Il *Conciliatore, to which he contributed a number of reviews under the name of 'Grisostomo', notably on Bouterwek's Storia della poesia e dell'eloquenza (October–November 1818) and 'Sulla Sacontala, ossia L'anello fatale, dramma indiano di Calidasa' (March 1819). He was caught up in the anti-*Austrian conspiracies of 1821 and went into *exile, working first in a London bank (1822–9) and then, like *Scalvini, as tutor to the expatriate Arconati family at Gaesbeek in Belgium. Here he published a translation of Spanish ballads, Vecchie romanze spagnuole (1837). He returned to Italy in 1845; after the revolutions of *1848 he settled definitively in *Turin, ending his days as a moderate deputy in the *Piedmontese parliament.

His most important poetry was written during the time of his greatest political involvement and the early years of his exile. From I profughi di Parga (published in Paris in 1823) to Le fantasie (1829) with its moving introductory letter, 'Agli amici miei in Italia', the poems of the 1820s are romantically eclectic in form and metre, with a predilection for the ballad-like romanza [see BALLATA], and draw on contemporary political events and remote episodes of national history to articulate both the sufferings of a people under foreign domination and those of exiles like Berchet himself. With its accompanying hope in a redemptive future founded on the values of religion, the family, and the nation, his poetry sets the tone for much subsequent *Risorgimento writing.   [MPC]

See A. Cadioli, Introduzione a Berchet (1991).

BERGALLI, LUISA (1703–79). *Venetian poet and playwright. She was a pupil of Apostolo *Zeno and Rosalba Carriera, and wife of Gasparo *Gozzi. From her first work, Agide (1725), and throughout her life her main interest was the *theatre, both *tragedy and *comedy. She translated plays by Terence, Racine, and Molière, and wrote a perceptive and erudite work on poetry written by women (Componimenti poetici delle più illustri rimatrici di ogni secolo of 1726), which led to a new edition (1738) of the Rime of Gaspara *Stampa. [See also WOMEN WRITERS, 2.]   [IC]

BERLINGHIERI, FRANCESCO (1440–1500). *Florentine patrician, *humanist and geographer, friend of Lorenzo de' *Medici and pupil of *Ficino. He is best known for his vernacular version, inappropriately in *terza rima, of Ptolemy's Geography. It included a laudatory proem and thirty-one maps and stimulated a revival of interest in Ptolemy.   [MA]

Bernard, St, see DIVINE COMEDY; PARADISO.

BERNARDINO OF SIENA, ST (1380–1444) was a famous preacher twice cleared of *heresy before becoming head of the *Franciscan Order in 1438. Many of his Latin and vernacular *sermons survive. His persuasive oratory disguised its learned preparation, and relied on imaginary *dialogues between preacher and public. He was canonized in 1450. [See also RELIGIOUS LITERATURE.]   [GPTW]

BERNARI, CARLO (1909–93). *Neapolitan novelist of French origin, who was forced to change his surname from Bernard under *Fascism. Expelled from school at 13, he was self-taught, but quickly entered literary *journalism in *Naples. He made his name with the working-class novel Tre operai (1934), which anticipated the sharper aspects of *Neorealism. But, though well-respected, he never captured a mass readership. Apart from straightforward reportage, notably Il gigante Cina (1957) and his writings on Naples, his numerous novels and short stories use diverse narrative modes that lift them above the documentary. But they remain committed fiction [see IMPEGNO] and are boldly embedded in history, from Quasi un secolo (1940) to Il grande letto (1988), or in the present, from Speranzella (1949) and Vesuvio e pane (1953) to the complex novel of ideas, Era l'anno del sole inquieto (1964).   [JG-R]

BERNERI, GIUSEPPE (1634–1701). *Roman playwright, stage director, and actor, most of whose plays have a sacred, edifying character. His best known work is Meo Patacca (1695), a *mock-heroic poem in twelve canti of *ottava rima, which makes use of Roman *dialect in an attempt to rouse the city's population against the Turks. [See also THEATRE, 2.]   [FC]

BERNI, FRANCESCO (1497/8–1535). Poet. Born at Lamporecchio in *Tuscany, and educated in *Florence, he moved to *Rome in 1517, joining first the household of Bernardo *Dovizi (Cardinal Bibbiena), then, from 1524, that of Giovan Mattia

Giberti, the papal archivist and bishop of Verona, and, between 1532 and 1534, that of Ippolito de' *Medici. Berni took minor orders in Rome and later became apostolic protonotary and a canon of the cathedral in Florence.

His literary output began early, in 1518, and is both prolific and varied, reflecting the dictates of his various *patrons. Much of it is occasional, deriving from political circumstances or events of his life. In addition to his early Latin lyrics, his output in Italian included *parodies and attacks on individuals in the form of sonetti caudati [see SONNET], burlesque letters in capitoli [see CANTO], usually obscene *canti carnascialeschi, paradoxical encomia, and an early rustic farce. His best-known work nowadays is the rifacimento of the *Orlando innamorato of *Boiardo, produced in the period following the *Sack of Rome in 1527, but not published until 1542, after his death. Although Berni himself was dissatisfied with this attempt to produce an *epic fit in theme and language for the times, his rifacimento was extremely popular in the later 16th c., becoming better known than Boiardo's original. Berni's Rime were edited and commented on after death by Anton Francesco *Grazzini, *Della Casa, and *Varchi, and established him as a master of lyric style in the later 16th and 17th c. Modern opinion tends to praise his humour and sense of the burlesque, but to be critical of his excessive *classicism in style and content.

[JEE]

BEROALDO, FILIPPO (THE ELDER) (1453–1505) was the most important exponent of *humanism in *Bologna in the Bentivoglio period. A friend of Ermolao *Barbaro the Younger and *Poliziano, he is best remembered for his textual work on Latin authors gathered together in his Adnotationes centum (1489), and, most famously of all, for his voluminous commentary on Apuleius (1500). Reacting against the *Ciceronianism of the time, he cultivated a *Baroque style, based on archaic and late Latin authors such as Plautus and Apuleius, full of lexical rarities, diminutives and compounds. His pupil G. B. Pio carried the style to further extremes, but the fashion died out in the early 16th c. under Pietro *Bembo's Ciceronianism. [See also CLASSICAL SCHOLARSHIP; LATIN PROSE IN ITALY.] [MMcL]

BERRINI, NINO (1880–1962). *Piedmontese playwright who enjoyed popular success with historical dramas inspired by *D'Annunzio and Sem

*Benelli, such as Il tramonto d'un re (1912) and Il beffardo (1919). These have sometimes been likened to animated school history books. Attentive to *theatrical fashions, he also wrote domestic *comedies and, later, imitated the *grotteschi.

[PBarn]

BERSEZIO, VITTORIO (1828–1900). *Piedmontese playwright, novelist, and *journalist, who founded the Gazzetta piemontese (1865) and edited other newspapers. His articles are collected in Il regno di *Vittorio Emanuele II (1878–95). His many novels are conventional in flavour, with contemporary French fiction as their models, but Bersezio had fought in the wars of independence and infuses them with patriotic spirit, as in La plebe (1867–9), Mentore a Calipso (1872), and Aristocrazia (1881). His most interesting work is in his plays, some of which are in Piedmontese. The best and most famous is Le miserie d'monssù Travet (1863), which depicts the everyday life of a low-ranking civil servant. [See also DIALECT WRITING; THEATRE, 2.] [AC]

BERTACCHI, GIOVANNI (1869–1942). Poet from the Valtellina, who was professor of literature at *Padua (1916–38) but, as a lifelong *socialist, forced to resign by the *Fascist regime. Much of his verse, beginning with the Canzoniere delle Alpi (1895), is centred on his native valley, but he was also inspired by travel and his students. [DCH]

BERTATI, GIOVANNI (1735–1815) lived for most of his life in *Venice, though he gained his greatest recognition in Vienna, where he was appointed imperial poet in 1791 in succession to *Da Ponte. He wrote some seventy drammi per musica, mostly comic in character: among them Don Giovanni o sia il Convitato di pietra, performed in Venice in 1787, the first edition of which (1782) is believed by some scholars to have influenced Mozart's famous opera. [See also AUSTRIA; LIBRETTO; OPERA.] [SC]

BERTELLI, LUIGI, see VAMBA.

BERTO, GIUSEPPE (1914–78). Novelist and playwright. Born in the Veneto, he served as a volunteer in the Ethiopian war, and then in North Africa in *World War II. He was captured in Tunisia in 1943, and sent to a prisoner-of-war camp in Texas. Here he wrote his first novels and stories. These are set in wartime Italy, and, whilst influenced by contemporary American fiction, are assimilable to Italian *Neorealism. His first published novel, *Il cielo è rosso* (1947), was immediately successful with critics and public alike. His later account of his North African experiences, *Guerra in camicia nera* (1955), is based upon notes taken at the time and in diary form. It lucidly confronts Berto's adherence to *Fascism, as well as recounting a growing disillusionment with Fascist ideology that is mirrored in the disastrous progression of the war. After a long period of illness and personal crisis, Berto departs radically from his earlier style in *Il male oscuro* (1964), exploring his own psychological fragility in a stream-of-consciousness manner that is influenced by his experience of *psychoanalysis. It was widely acclaimed as a masterpiece.   [SVM]

BERTOLA DE' GIORGI, AURELIO (1753–98). Born in Rimini, he entered the Olivetan Order, then fled to Hungary, where he joined the Imperial army. He later re-entered the Order as a college teacher, made a name for himself with his odes and other poems, and became a professor of history and geography at the Accademia di Marina in *Naples (1779). In 1784 he was appointed to the chair of Storia Universale at Pavia. He travelled in Germany and Switzerland, where he met Salomon Gessner, writing an *Elogio di Gessner* (1789) and a *Viaggio sul Reno e ne' suoi contorni* (1795), and becoming a key figure in cultural relationships between the German-speaking countries and Italy. [See also GERMAN INFLUENCES; PRE-ROMANTICISM.]
                                     [CCa]

BERTOLAZZI, CARLO (1870–1916) is best respected for his early plays in *Milanese *dialect. His most famous play, *El nost Milan* (1893) ('Our Milan') depicts the life of Milan in two parts through two different social environments, the poor and the corrupt nobility. He turned later to psychological drama in Italian, the most important of which is *La Gibigianna* (1898). [See also DIALECT WRITING; THEATRE, 2.]   [JAL]

Bertoldo (1). The protagonist of Giulio Cesare *Croce's *Le sottilissime astuzie di Bertoldo* (1605). He is a peasant of legendary ugliness, endowed with an extraordinarily refined wit, who can answer all questions from the King of the Lombards who summons him to his court. He is also the father of the simpleton Bertoldino.
                                     [DieZ]

Bertoldo (2) (1936–43). Fortnightly humorous review, published in *Milan and named after G. C. *Croce's character *Bertoldo, promoting what it saw as traditional popular values. It was edited by Giovanni Mosca and included Giovanni *Guareschi on its staff.   [PH]

BERTOLOTTI, DAVIDE (1784–1860). A native of *Turin, he celebrated successive political regimes in verse, wrote *tragedies, and won considerable popularity with sentimental narratives aimed at women, notably *L'isoletta de' cipressi* (1822). *La calata degli Ungheri* (1823) is one of Italy's earliest *historical novels. Later he turned to religious narrative poetry in *Il Salvatore* (1844).   [JMAL]

BERTOLUCCI, ATTILIO (1911–2000). One of the most important poets of the generation after *Montale. Born near Parma, he took a degree in literature at *Bologna. After university he taught in Parma until moving to *Rome in 1950 and working in *radio, *television, and *publishing, mostly in the area of literature and *cinema. His two director sons, Bernardo *Bertolucci and Giuseppe, entered the cinema partly as a result—their father being a close friend of *Pasolini.

His poetic career began very early with the landscape lyricism of *Sirio* (1929), followed by a shift in a narrative direction in *Fuochi in novembre* (1934). But Bertolucci really finds his voice after the war. *Lettera da casa* (1951) firmly establishes his themes as the family, provincial life in the country and the city, and the passage of the seasons. The simple, precise language is attuned to everyday realities, whilst the flow of the sentences combines movement with moments of stillness. This modern *classicism is evident too in the long idyll of *La capanna indiana*, also published in 1951, which centres on the flow of natural time, the cycles of which cancel out individual existences in its 'miele indistinto'.

Viaggio d'inverno (1971) is one of the most significant collections of poetry published in postwar Italy. The themes of the previous collections return in a less tranquil vein. Bertolucci now casts himself as, on the one hand, a man of property and paterfamilias, with the values of the provincial middle classes, and a 'uomo malato' on the other, away from home and a prey to neurosis. With the self in crisis and the task of giving a conscious order to his experience beyond him, he again resorts to cyclical natural patterns. His classicism now returns to ancient models, *Horace in particular, but without trying to ward off or exorcise his neuroses or the loss of a sense of values, both of which are absorbed into poetry as a way of overcoming them.

La camera da letto—the first book appeared in 1984, the shorter second one in 1988—is Bertolucci's main verse-narrative work. It is a linear account of his personal and family history. He himself plays the part of narrator-protagonist, registering but not controlling the natural flow of events to which he trustingly abandons himself, and seeing his prime duty as the protection of private space against the threatening, blundering power of historical change. Bertolucci subsequently returns to the shorter *lyric with the mannerist sophistication and sometimes loose structures of *Verso le sorgenti del Cinghio* (1993) and *La lucertola di Casarola* (1997).   [RD]

See P. Lagazzi, *Bertolucci* (1981); S. Giovannuzzi, *Invito alla lettura di Attilio Bertolucci* (1997).

BERTOLUCCI, BERNARDO (1941–), son of the poet Attilio *Bertolucci, is the most international of major Italian film-makers. The film with which he made his mark, *Prima della rivoluzione* (1964), was set in his home city of Parma, and he has used Parma and the Po Valley as the setting for some of his later films (*Strategia del ragno*, 1970, *1900*, 1980, *La luna*, 1979), but most of his films since *Last Tango in Paris* (1975) have been made abroad and in English—notably his so-called 'oriental trilogy' of *The Last Emperor* (1987), *The Sheltering Sky* (1990), and *Little Buddha* (1993). Although he has access to Hollywood funding, he strenuously denies being anything other than a European film-maker, and continues to make smaller films with Italian settings—e.g. *Io ballo da sola* / *Stealing Beauty* (1996). [See also CINEMA.]
     [GN-S]

Bertran de Born. Provençal *troubadour and a character in *Dante's *Inferno* 28.

BESSARION, BASIL (c.1403–72), a Greek émigré to Italy, became a leading figure in the Catholic Church and devoted himself to preserving the intellectual heritage of *Byzantium. Born in Trebizond and educated in Constantinople, he entered the Basilian Order in 1423. In the early 1430s he studied philosophy in Mistra under the Platonist *Pletho. He became metropolitan of Nicaea in 1437 and the following year attended the Council of Ferrara–Florence as leader of the party in favour of union between the Eastern and Western churches. Converting to Roman Catholicism in 1439, he was immediately made a cardinal. He held

various bishoprics, served as a papal legate, and was a candidate for the *papacy in 1455 and 1471; in 1463 he became titular patriarch of Constantinople. He promoted the study of Greek and encouraged the translation of classical Greek works into Latin, himself producing versions of Xenophon, *Aristotle, and Theophrastus. In 1469 he published *Adversus calumniatorem Platonis*, in which he defended the philosopher against George *Trapezuntios and also provided a learned exposition of Platonism, stressing its compatibility with Christianity. He donated his *library, containing 482 Greek volumes, to *Venice, where it became the core of the Biblioteca Marciana. [See also GREEK INFLUENCES; GREEK WRITING IN ITALY; NEOPLATONISM.]   [JK]

Bestiaries were a sub-genre of the medieval *encyclopedia, dealing with real or fabulous animals, their symbolism, and their magical powers or virtues. So, for example, the panther was ascribed sweet-smelling breath which was often *allegorized as an image of the sanctity of Christ. Deriving from the 4th-c. *Physiologus*, a Latin version of a Greek original, the bestiary tradition is represented in various 13th- and 14th-c. vernacular versions, notably the *sonnet sequence of the 14th-c. Umbrian *Bestiario moralizzato di Gubbio* (as it is usually called). The early *lyric treats the bestiary as an important source of imagery, as when *Stefano Protonotaro's 'Pir meu cori alligrari' compares his falling in love with the tigress being bewitched by her image in the mirror the hunter has set before her. *Dante may well be presuming familiarity with bestiary symbolism in the three beasts in *Inferno* 1. The most concentrated use of bestiary material in Italian appears in *Boccaccio's early *Caccia di Diana*. But the fashion largely disappeared from more refined literature in the course of the 14th c., a few isolated examples (such as the salamander's imperviousness to fire) surviving into *Renaissance poetry.
     [JU]

Bestiario moralizzato di Gubbio, see BESTIARIES.

BETOCCHI, CARLO (1899–1986). Poet. Born in *Turin, he grew up in *Florence and fought in *World War I, subsequently working as a surveyor in the road-building industry. A friend of *Lisi and *Bargellini, he founded with them the Catholic and initially anti-*hermetic *periodical *Il *Frontespizio* in 1929. His first volume of poetry,

Realtà vince il sogno (1932), initiates a search for a poetic language fusing spiritual *Catholicism with an unsentimental view of everyday reality which he continued throughout his subsequent production.

[JJ]

BETTELONI, VITTORIO (1840–1910). Veronese poet. He and *Stecchetti were acclaimed as the foremost poets of *verismo*. In the poems collected as *In primavera* (1869), he rejects *Romantic grandiloquence and celebrates worldly love affairs in everyday language which anticipates the *Crepuscolari*. His later poems are more in the manner of *Carducci. His novel *Prima lotta* (1896) acutely dissects the marriage market. [PBarn]

BETTI, LAURA (1934–) Singer and charismatic theatre and *cinema actress, who worked with Bernardo *Bertolucci, *Fellini, *Rossellini, and *Visconti, among others. She is most associated with *Pasolini, acting in several of his films, and is now director of the Fondo Pier Paolo Pasolini in Rome. She is the author of a novel, *Teta veleta* (1982). [RSCG]

BETTI, UGO (1892–1953). Dramatist, poet, short-story writer, translator, and essayist. Still at school, he published a blank-verse *translation of Catullus' *Epithalamium of Thetis and Peleus* (1910). After graduating in law at Parma in 1915, he volunteered for service as a dispatch rider, then took a commission in the artillery. Captured at Caporetto in 1917, he spent the next two years in a German prisoner-of-war camp, where he made lasting friendships with his fellow prisoners Bonaventura *Tecchi and Carlo Emilio *Gadda. On returning to Italy he resumed his legal studies, publishing a thesis on the responsibilities of railway carriers. Having served as a magistrate in and around Parma, he moved in 1930 to *Rome to become a judge in the Italian supreme court (Corte di Cassazione). After the collapse of the *Fascist regime in 1943, he was relegated in a purge of the judiciary to the humbler calling of archivist in the Roman law courts, later becoming legal adviser to the Società Italiana Autori e Editori.

Betti wrote twenty-five full-length plays, four volumes of poetry, four of short stories, a novel, two important essays, and countless newspaper articles. The theme of justice occupies a prominent position in his drama. In *Frana allo scalo nord* (1935), a judge concludes his investigation into a fatal accident by prescribing compassion as the only meaningful

form of justice. In *Corruzione al palazzo di giustizia* (1944) members of an unspecified judiciary are engaged in a ruthless power struggle, showing them to be more corrupt than the people they are called upon to judge. *L'aiuola bruciata* (1952), Betti's finest play, explores in fascinating detail the morality and motivations of political leaders, and also probes possible causes of what was later to be termed the generation gap. [See also THEATRE, 2.]

[HMcW]

See G. H. McWilliam, Introduction to Ugo Betti, *Two Plays* (1965); F. Doglio and W. Raspolini (eds.), *Betti drammaturgo* (1984).

BETTINELLI, SAVERIO (1718–1808), a *Mantuan who became a *Jesuit at 20 and taught rhetoric first in Brescia, then *Bologna, then in *Venice from 1748 to 1751. There he wrote the *satirical poem *Le raccolte* (1751), in which he called for a reform of the Italian poetic tradition, aimed at both the literary elite and the public. Between 1757 and 1759 he travelled to France and Switzerland, where he met Rousseau, Voltaire, and Helvétius. In the course of a long and productive literary career he turned his hand to literary polemic and critical innovation (*Lettere virgiliane*, *Lettere inglesi*, *Dell'entusiasmo delle belle arti*). Later he wrote a cultural and political history of Italy (*Del risorgimento d'Italia* of 1775), in which anti-*Enlightenment polemic is combined with restrained historicism. [See also HISTORIOGRAPHY, 2.] [IC]

BEVILACQUA, ALBERTO (1934–). *Novelist who is also a prolific *journalist and *cinema director. He achieved widespread popularity with *La califfa* (1964), which he adapted as his first film in 1966. His numerous other novels resuscitate traditional *realism in a variety of ways. Most coherent are *autobiographical novels of his native Parma, such as *La festa parmigiana* (1980). Formally and stylistically more adventurous explorations of relations between the sexes, such as *L'occhio del gatto* (1968), have had a mixed reception. Bevilacqua has also published various collections of poems.

[GUB]

BEZZI, GIULIANO (1592–1674). The town clerk of his native Forlì, who produced a long, somewhat mechanical series of humorous variations on the stock themes of *Baroque poetry in his *Disgrazie poetiche* (1654). He also composed more conventional *Rime* (1645), a *pastoral *comedy, and short religious and celebratory poems. [MPS]

BIAGI, ENZO (1920–). Popular *journalist and *television commentator and presenter. He has written for Il *Corriere della sera and then for La Repubblica, and edited Il *Resto del Carlino in his home city of *Bologna. He has published collections of travel journalism, a biography of the head of FIAT, Gianni Agnelli, and various *novels, beginning with Disonora il padre (1975).   [REL]

BIAMONTI, FRANCESCO (1933–2001). *Novelist. He was born and lived in Liguria, in a small upland village near Ventimiglia. This is the main setting for his tautly lyrical novels, beginning with L'angelo d'Avrigue (1983). They represent an existential disquiet closely linked with the landscape of the region and with the changing nature of its society and economy.   [PH]

BIANCHI, GIOVANNI ANTONIO (1686–1758). *Franciscan who championed ecclesiastical authority against *Giannone in 1739. He also composed *tragedies on sacred subjects for his pupils in *Rome, which were performed to general acclaim, and in 1753 defended the theatre against the rigorist strictures of Daniele Concina (1687–1756).   [JMAL]

BIANCHINI, FRANCESCO (1662–1729). *Antiquarian and scientific thinker. Born in Verona, he studied theology and astronomy at *Padua and subsequently worked in the *papal administration in *Rome, becoming supervisor of antiquities in 1703 and undertaking systematic excavations on the Aventine and Palatine. As well as archaeological studies, he wrote a universal history (1697), and edited the *Liber pontificalis (1718–35). He also produced astronomical studies and investigated, at the behest of the Pope, the timing of Easter and other calendar problems. He travelled widely, including a visit to England during which he met Newton—there is an account of his visit in Iter in Britanniam (1713)—and was an active member of various scientific *academies in Italy and abroad. [See also TRAVEL WRITING.]   [FC]

BIANCIARDI, LUCIANO (1922–71). *Tuscan writer who worked as a librarian after his degree at *Pisa, then as a teacher in Grosseto before moving into *publishing in *Milan. His first book, I minatori della Maremma (1956), written jointly with Carlo *Cassola, was a sociological inquiry into workers' conditions in Tuscany. In Il lavoro cultur-ale (1957) he satirized the new culture industry, and the disillusioned leftist intellectuals involved in it. His first and most successful *novel, La vita agra (1962), is a grotesque portrayal of a provincial intellectual protesting against the mindlessness of the economic miracle in Milan, but being absorbed into it all the same. Later works also deal with the problems of modern Italy.   [JEB]

BIANCO, DANTE LIVIO, see RESISTANCE.

BIANCONI, GIOVANNI LUDOVICO (1717–81). *Bolognese polygraph [see POLIGRAFI] noted for his elegant essays on scientific and historical subjects. He resided at the courts of Darmstadt and Dresden from 1744 to 1764. Subsequently he became Saxony's diplomatic representative to the Vatican and a leading light in literary *Rome.   [JMAL]

BIANCONI, GIUSEPPE, see DARWINISM.

BIAVA, SAMUELE (1792–1870). Poet. After graduating in law, he taught in *Milan and his native Bergamo. A convinced *Romantic who believed in the ideal of popular poetry, he wrote simple melodious lyrics inspired by medieval and Christian themes. His language is traditional and his metres taken from Giovanni *Berchet.   [FD'I]

BIBBIENA, see DOVIZI, BERNARDO.

Bible. The Judaeo-Christian Scriptures of the Old and New Testaments have proved an incomparable source of inspiration for poets, painters, sculptors, and saints from the time of St *Francis to the present day. As elsewhere in Christendom, over the centuries the art and literature of Catholic Italy has drawn on biblical characterization, imagery, narrative and wisdom for its major themes, as witness the works of *Dante, *Giotto, *Michelangelo, and Torquato *Tasso.

For more than a thousand years St Jerome's Latin Vulgate (AD 382–404) remained unrivalled in the Christian West. This was the form in which the Bible was known to literate laymen such as *Petrarch and *Boccaccio. But the medieval Catholic Church did not altogether prohibit vernacular versions, and from 1250 onwards parts of the Scriptures began to appear in Italian, particularly in *Florence. They probably derived from French and Provençal sources, and owed their initial impetus to the *Waldensians, though the *Dominican

Bibliographies of Italian Literature

Domenico *Cavalca produced a remarkable Tuscan version of the Acts of the Apostles in the early 14th c. But all such versions were made from the Latin and not from the Hebrew and Greek: it was the *humanist Lorenzo *Valla—a forerunner of Erasmus—who first scrutinized the New Testament's original text.

The *Reformation brought the Bible into enhanced focus, and set a landmark in Italy with the popular translation from Greek and Hebrew by the Florentine layman Antonio Brucioli (c.1495–1566), printed in *Venice in 1530–2 but banned by the papal *Index in 1559. Because all 'heretics' claimed Scripture as their authority in faith and practice, the *Counter-Reformation did not encourage Bible-reading among the laity; indeed from the time of the Council of Trent until 1757 it was actively discouraged. However, a splendid translation by Giovanni Diodati, a Swiss Calvinist of Lucchese extraction, was published at Geneva in 1607. This was based on original texts, and in significant ways akin to the contemporary English Authorized Version of 1611. It was unequalled for clarity, accuracy, and literary quality among non-Catholic Italians for 300 years. Finally, in 1897, Leo XIII allowed the faithful to use approved vernacular versions of Scripture, and in 1943 Pius XII's encyclical, Divino afflante spiritu, opened the way for Catholics to apply modern critical methods to biblical studies. [See also PAPACY AND THE CATHOLIC CHURCH; RELIGIOUS LITERATURE.]

[PMcN]

See P. R. Ackroyd and others, The Cambridge History of the Bible (1963–70).

Bibliographies of Italian Literature. For general information on Italian authors, including bibliographical references, it is useful to consult standard reference works such as the *Treccani *Enciclopedia italiana (1929–37), with appendices: i (1938), ii (1948–9), iii (1961), iv (1978–81), v (1991–5), vi (2000); and the subsequent reference works from the Istituto della Enciclopedia Italiana: Dizionario enciclopedico italiano (1955–61), Lessico universale italiano (1968–81), and Dizionario biografico degli italiani (1960–). Also useful are the Grande dizionario enciclopedico italiano, founded by P. Fedele, and published by UTET (1933–40), now in a 4th edn. (1984–93) with appendix (1997). In the World Bibliographical Series, see Italy, by L. Sponza and D. Zancani (Oxford, 1995). For books printed in Italy one can use CLIO: Catalogo dei libri italiani dell'Ottocento (1801–1900) (1991); CUBI:

Centro nazionale per il catalogo unico delle biblioteche italiane. Catalogo cumulativo 1886–1957 (1968); BNI: Bibliografia nazionale italiana (1958–) (1961–). The quarterly L'informazione bibliografica (1974–) offers full bibliographical listings and useful review articles on specific topics.

Still important, even though limited to the letters A and B, are the volumes by G. M. *Mazzuchelli, Gli scrittori d'Italia (1753–63). A useful collection of references for biographical information is L. Ferrari, Onomasticon (1501–1850) (1947). Among the literary encyclopedias are: *Laterza-Unedi's Dizionario enciclopedico della letteratura italiana, ed. G. Petronio (1966–70); UTET's Dizionario critico della letteratura italiana, ed. V. Branca (1974, 2nd enlarged edn. 1986); Rizzoli's Dizionario della letteratura italiana, ed. E. Bonora (1977); The Macmillan Dictionary of Italian Literature, ed. P. Bondanella and J. Conaway Bondanella (1979); the Dizionario Bompiani degli autori di tutti i tempi e di tutte le letterature (1987, 1st edn. 1956); *Einaudi's Letteratura italiana: gli autori, ed. A. *Asor Rosa (1990–1); Zanichelli's Dizionario biografico degli scrittori italiani, ed. N. Cannata (1997).

A precious research tool is C. Dionisotti, Indice sistematico dei primi cento volumi del *Giornale storico della letteratura italiana, 1883–1932 (1948). For Lettere italiane there is the Indice trentennale (1949–1978), ed. N. Giannetto (1991); for Italian Studies, the Index to volumes I–L (1937–95) by M. D. Groves (1995). Other standard works are: G. Prezzolini, Repertorio bibliografico della storia e della critica della letteratura italiana dal 1902 al 1932 (1930–6), and for the years from 1932–6 (1946–8); U. Bosco, Repertorio bibliografico della letteratura italiana, vol. i, 1948–9 (1953), vol. ii, 1950–3 (1960), vol. iii, 1943–7 (1969); Letteratura italiana: Aggiornamento bibliografico (1991–) is published twice a year; important for systematic coverage is BiGLLI, Bibliografia generale della lingua e della letteratura italiana, directed by E. Malato (1991–), which is also available in CD-ROM format.

Background information, including works of bibliographical interest, is found in the main introductions to the study of Italian literature, such as G. Mazzoni, Avviamento allo studio critico delle lettere italiane (1907, 1st edn. 1892); M. Puppo, Manuale critico-bibliografico per lo studio della letteratura italiana (1954); W. Binni and R. Scrivano, Introduzione ai problemi critici della letteratura italiana (1967); E. Pasquini (ed.), Guida allo studio della letteratura italiana (1985); G. Barberi Squarotti (ed.), L'italianistica: introduzione allo studio della *letteratura e della lingua italiana* (1992). Many journals offer regular reviews and bibliographical listings; in particular those in the *Rassegna della letteratura italiana* (1953–), and in *Studi e problemi di critica testuale* (1970–). Useful for bibliographical information are the volumes of the *Modern Language Association of America* (1919–), since 1956 with international coverage; and *YWMLS: The Year's Work in Modern Language Studies* (1930–), which also offer a concise critical appreciation of works mentioned.

For the history of the language there are linguistic bibliographies which include many references of literary interest, such as R. A. Hall, *Bibliografia della linguistica italiana* (1958) with supplements in 1969, 1980, 1988; Ž. Muljačić, *Introduzione allo studio della lingua italiana* (1971); R. A. Hall, *Bibliografia essenziale della linguistica italiana e romanza* (1973); Ž. Muljačić, *Scaffale italiano: Avviamento bibliografico allo studio della lingua italiana* (1991); and the review sections of *Zeitschrift für romanische Philologie* (1877–); *L'Italia dialettale* (1925–); *Lingua nostra* (1939–); *Studi di filologia italiana* (1943–); *Studi linguistici italiani* (1960–); *Studi di grammatica italiana* (1971–). [See also DICTIONARIES OF ITALIAN LITERATURE; HISTORIES OF ITALIAN LITERATURE.]   [LL & GCL]

Biblioteca Apostolica Vaticana, see VATICAN LIBRARY.

Biblioteca italiana (1816–40). Monthly review founded in *Milan at the express wish of the newly restored *Austrian administration, which thereby wanted to influence public opinion in Italy. *Foscolo having refused it, the editorship was entrusted to Giuseppe *Acerbi. The first issue carried *Giordani's version of Mme de Staël's essay on *translation which sparked an intense debate on *Romanticism. The review kept silent on politics and tended to be conservative in literature, but its articles, which covered literature, the arts, science, and technology, were often informative, fair-minded, and up to date. Although many Romantics boycotted it, it drew on such ideologically divergent contributors as *Romagnosi, *Scalvini, and Zaiotti.   [MPC]

Biblioteca Nazionale, see LIBRARIES; MAGLIABECHI, ANTONIO.

BIFFI, GIAMBATTISTA, see ENLIGHTENMENT.

BIGIARETTI, LIBERO (1906–93). Novelist and poet. Born in Matelica, he worked as a *journalist in *Rome. He first published *hermetic poetry, but soon concentrated on fiction, focusing on issues of moral ambiguity. A lyrical vein is evident in *Neorealist works such as *La scuola dei ladri* (1952) and still present in depictions of neo-capitalist routine such as *Il congresso* (1963).   [JJ]

BIGONGIARI, PIERO (1914–97). Poet, *translator, and critic and one of the main protagonists of the *Florentine *hermetic movement in the 1930s. Though he had previously published in journals, his first collection, *La figlia di Babilonia*, did not appear until 1942. His poetry, strongly influenced by Mallarmé and *Ungaretti, attempted to voice what he recognized as inaccessible truths, making much use of metaphors of travel and observation, which represented the search for immediate knowledge of the world. Although his style developed over the years, he rarely deviated from the fundamental hermetic model. He was professor of contemporary literature at Florence University and wrote extensively on *Leopardi and on modern Italian poetry.   [CO'B]

BILENCHI, ROMANO (1909–89). *Tuscan novelist whose career is paradigmatic of that of the Italian left-wing writer and intellectual of his generation. Born and bred in Colle di Val d'Elsa, near *Siena, he was a personal friend of Mino *Maccari and first published in his violently satirical fortnightly, *Il *Selvaggio*. He continued to express revolutionary *Fascism in his *Storia dei socialisti di Colle*, published in *Il *Bargello* in 1931–3. His early fiction had a strong lyrical component, best evidenced in the stories of *Anna e Bruno e altri racconti* (1938), though social *realism is already present in the earlier collection, *Il capofabbrica* (1935). In the later 1930s he wrote for more literary journals such as *Letteratura* and *Campo di Marte*, and steadily distanced himself from Fascism. He joined the *Communist Party in 1942 and took part in the *Resistance. After the war he devoted himself to political *journalism, becoming editor of *Il Nuovo Corriere* (1948–53) and contributing extensively to other communist *periodicals until he left the party in 1956. Apart from revising earlier work (sometimes in depth), he did not write any new fiction until *Il bottone di Stalingrad* (1972). He published an interesting collection of memoirs of his interwar friendships with *Vittorini, *Rosai, and others in *Amici* (1988).   [PBart]

Billanovich, Giuseppe

BILLANOVICH, GIUSEPPE, see LITERARY
CRITICISM.

BINI, CARLO (1806–42). Writer born in
Livorno. Imprisoned in 1833 in Portoferraio for his
activities as a member of *Mazzini's *Giovine Italia*,
he wrote *Manoscritto di un prigioniero* in a reflective
*Foscolian vein. He also published *translations of
Sterne, Byron, and Werner, and further Mazzinian
writings.   [EAM]

Biography. Whilst biographical writing has a long
history in Italy, it has never been as popular as in
English-speaking countries amongst either readers
or writers, and has produced no works that are generally considered literary classics. Even modern
biographies have been cautious about probing the
private lives of their subjects and retained something of the celebratory, exemplary manner of pre-
modern practice.

The medieval *hagiographic tradition challenges
many modern expectations. It treated historical fact
as less important than the demonstration of spiritual exemplarity, and sacrificed individuality and
factual accuracy to familiar topoi. Hence the first
biography of St *Francis of Assisi, for instance,
which was written by *Tommaso da Celano in
1228–9 in Latin, only two years after his death, was
commissioned by Pope Gregory IX with the clear
intent of edifying the faithful.

In the 1330s *Petrarch makes a decisive move
away from the hagiographic tradition in his *De viris
illustribus*, in which he recounts the lives of classical
and subsequently biblical heroes in terms of their
exemplary actions. *Boccaccio's *De mulieribus claris*
(begun about 1361) is a celebration of great women,
though the didactic ambitions of the genre are
revealed through the stress the author places on ideal
standards of female behaviour. Overall, women are
poorly represented in the medieval and *Renaissance
biographical tradition both as writers and subjects.
The only exceptions are religious figures such as
*Angela da Foligno and St *Caterina of Siena.

Boccaccio also wrote biographies of *Dante and
Petrarch, which contain important historical information but which become a means of justifying and
celebrating creative literature, with reverberations
for his own work as a writer. The chronicler Filippo
*Villani also decided to include men of letters in his
book on famous Florentines because they added
lustre to the city. In the 16th c. Giorgio *Vasari's
Vite (1550) validate artists through similar celebrations of their gifts and achievements.

With Vasari the historiographical dimension is
already as important as moral encouragement and
reflects the *humanist tendency, springing from the
rediscovery of Plutarch, to give significance to the
individual life. But biographies were still written for
specific audiences and could easily fall into panegyric, as was often the case with the biographies of
popes. Classical models also could also entice biographers away from historical fact. *Machiavelli's
Vita di Castruccio Castracani (1520), for instance,
owes more to the writer's adherence to the conventions of heroic biography than to historical record.
A similar type of biographical writing flourished in
the 19th c. In the years following *Unification
approving biographies of *Garibaldi, *Cavour,
and *Vittorio Emanuele II appeared, constituting
a significant, if partial, historical record of the
period.

The formal impurity of biography continues to
the present day, although the genre now looks for its
models to other sources. The novel tends to provide
narrative strategies, whilst in more academic biography *historiography provides techniques of documentation and analysis. *D'Annunzio argued that
the role of the biographer was to bring out the
uniqueness of the subject's personality and trace its
development, rather than to dwell on its place in
history. This emphasis on the subject's inner self is
marked even in politically motivated biographies
such as Margherita *Sarfatti's life of *Mussolini
(1926), though the more recent seven-volume
biography by Renzo De Felice is really a barely disguised history of Italian *Fascism.

Popular biography still favours exemplary lives,
although these lives are usually crowned by fame or
notoriety rather than religiosity. As a genre, biography continues to develop through film, oral history, and the magazine profile.   [DD]
See A. Battistini, *Lo specchio di Dedalo: autobiografia e biografia* (1990).

BIONDI, GIAN FRANCESCO (1572–1644).
Novelist and *historian. Born in Istria, he served as
a *Venetian diplomat, but was a friend of *Sarpi
and a supporter of the *Reformation who objected
to *papal interference. From 1612 he served the
English court in London, but in 1640, when
Charles I's position weakened, he moved to
Switzerland, where he died. He wrote an *Istoria
delle guerre civili d'Inghilterra tra le due case di Lan-
castro ed Iorc* (1637) and a successful trilogy of
novels—*L'Eromena* (1624), *La donzella desterrada*
(1627), and *Il Coralbo* (1632). In all these works

(and particularly in *L'Eromena*, which is the first significant Italian *novel) he analysed with great perception the destructive effects of political power on human life. [MC]

BIONDO, FLAVIO (1392–1463), from Forlì, worked as an itinerant chancellor and secretary until he was taken into *papal service in *Rome in 1433, where, with only brief interruption, he spent the rest of his life. Biondo composed several *humanist works, including *De verbis Romanae locutionis* (1435), in which he was one of the first to suggest that the vernacular grew directly out of ancient Latin, against Leonardo *Bruni's defence of the long-standing view that the two languages had always existed alongside one another. He was also, like many other humanists, an ardent advocate of the *Crusade. But his greatest achievements were as a pioneer of *Renaissance archaeology, geography, and history.

His *Decades ab inclinatione Romanorum* (1435–53) began as a contemporary history, but Biondo became one of the earliest genuine medievalists when he extended their scope back to late antiquity. Although in this work he failed to put aside medieval historical methods, in his archaeological treatises, *Romae instauratae* (1444–6) and *Roma triumphans* (1455–63), he began the systematic study of Roman topography, institutions, and private life, relying on such evidence as inscriptions, classical citations, and coins, and putting medieval legendary sources to one side. With his *Italia illustrata* (1453) he virtually founded the discipline of historical geography, recording the notable personages, monuments, and events of Italy's localities from the Alps to *Naples. [See also ANTIQUARIANISM; CLASSICAL SCHOLARSHIP; HISTORIOGRAPHY, 1.] [RDB]

BISACCIONI, MAIOLINO (1582–1663). Historian and novelist. Born in *Ferrara, he led an adventurous life as a soldier and administrator for *Venice and other powers but died in poverty. His mainly historical interests led to accounts of recent German wars (1633–7), recent civil wars (1652), and the Masaniello uprising in *Naples (1660), and are evident in his novel *Il Demetrio moscovita* (1639), in which he recounts the Tsar's rise to power and tragic death. He was the foremost *translator of French *romances of his time. Between 1637 and 1664 he also published sixty-two *novelle, all lively tales of adventure, in four collections—*La nave*, *L'albergo*, *L'isola*, and *Il porto*. [MC]

BISSARI, PIETRO PAOLO (1595–1663). Count of Costafabbrica. He spent much of his life writing *libretti and producing *operas in commercial theatres in his native Vicenza (where he held public office), as well as in *Venice and Munich. An unremarkable practitioner of *concettismo, he also published *novelle, academic discourses, and copious collections of verse. [MPS]

BIZZONI, ACHILLE (1841–1904). Ardent Republican and *Garibaldian from Pavia, whose *journalism attacked the post-*Unification government and its policies. He founded and directed a number of papers, his longest association being with the *Gazzettino rosa*. Novels such as *Un matrimonio* (1886) and *L'onorevole* (1895) also indict contemporary politics and society. [AHC]

Blacks and Whites. Although the names *Neri* and *Bianchi* probably originated in Pistoia, they are most commonly used to refer to the two factions within the *Florentine *Guelf party, which emerged in 1300 as result of a long-standing family feud between the Donati and Cerchi families. Whereas the Blacks favoured bringing the city under the control of Pope *Boniface VIII and his *Anjou allies, the primary aim of the Whites was to safeguard Florentine independence. By the end of 1301 the Blacks had gained control of the city, exiling their White enemies (*Dante among them) and confiscating their property. [CEH]

BLASETTI, ALESSANDRO (1900–87). Italy's foremost film director in the 1930s, very active after *World War II, but known mostly for his historical films, such as *1860* (1933) on *Garibaldi's first expedition. His *Quattro passi tra le nuvole* (1942) prefigured *Neorealism, while *Vecchia guardia* (1934) is considered one of the few significant *Fascist films made. [See also CINEMA.] [CGW]

BO, CARLO (1911–2001). *Literary critic, originally from near *Genoa, who studied French literature in *Florence and contributed significant essays on modern French and Italian literature to various reviews in the 1930s. His article 'Letteratura e vita', published in *Il *Frontespizio* in 1938, proposed the need for an interaction, albeit ambiguous and abstract, between literature and life. It became the manifesto of Florentine *hermetic poetry and led to the hermetics' departure from the *Frontespizio* circle. Bo wrote extensively on French,

Spanish, and Italian literature. He became professor of French literature at *Urbino University, of which he was appointed life president in 1950.

[CO'B]

BOBBIO, NORBERTO (1909–). *Turinese philosopher in the *Enlightenment tradition. Already established academically by the end of *World War II, he achieved fame with books such as *Politica e cultura* (1955), becoming one of the few prominent European political thinkers to disagree with Sartre that *Marxism was central to all contemporary intellectual endeavour. In so doing he joined the ranks of figures like Jürgen Habermas in West Germany who believed that there is nothing essentially capitalistic about ideas of law and rights. Bobbio too argued that workers had just as much interest in the impartial administration of universal norms of justice as any other social class. He defended this position against the strong pro-Soviet faction in the Italian *Communist Party which openly advocated the abolition of parliamentary democracy and the establishment of the dictatorship of the proletariat. In later books such as *Saggi sulla scienza politica in Italia* (1969) and *Il futuro della democrazia* (1984) he continued to defend legal constitutionalism and parliamentary institutions, and played a major role in promoting the ideas of the Italian tradition of liberal *socialism as represented by such figures as Piero *Gobetti and Carlo Rosselli. [See GIUSTIZIA E LIBERTÀ; ROSSELLI, AMELIA.] [DS]

BOCCA, GIORGIO (1920–). *Piedmontese *journalist and writer. After taking part in the *Resistance, he worked first for *Milan's *La Gazzetta del popolo*. A *liberal with *socialist sympathies, he has since written for many other papers, notably *Il Giorno* in the 1960s and *La Repubblica* since its foundation in 1975. Bocca made his name with investigative reports into the boom years in Italy, which appeared in book form as *Il miracolo all'italiana* (1961) and *La scoperta dell'Italia* (1963). As well as many other books on contemporary Italy, he has written a highly critical *biography of Palmiro *Togliatti (1977) and an *autobiography, *Il provinciale* (1991). [SG]

BOCCACCIO, GIOVANNI (1313–75). One of Italy's most important and versatile authors. He developed Italian prose and verse narrative in new directions, achieving an undisputed masterpiece in the *Decameron* but also exerting a European influence with works such as the *Teseida* (whence Chaucer's *Knight's Tale*) and the *Filostrato* (whence the story of Troilus and Cressida). His prose became the model for Italian writers in the 16th c., as theorized in *Bembo's *Prose della volgar lingua*, and exerted a determining influence for at least three centuries. He also played a major role in the development of *humanism, and in many ways looks forwards to the *Renaissance, though he also produced one of the highest articulations of the complex culture of the later *Middle Ages.

His early works are studded with cryptic *autobiographical hints, from which a legendary version of his life emerged which was long accepted as true. According to this, he was born in Paris as a result of an affair between a merchant and a lady or perhaps a princess, and then as a young man in *Naples became the lover of *Fiammetta, the beautiful illegitimate daughter of Robert of *Anjou. In reality his father, Boccaccio di Chellino, worked for the powerful *Bardi company. He was indeed in Paris between 1312 and 1313, but Boccaccio was born illegitimately either in Certaldo near *Florence, or more probably in Florence itself. His childhood was spent in the S. Pier Maggiore quarter in the house of his father, who had married Margherita de' Mardoli, a relative of the Portinari family and hence of *Dante's *Beatrice. It was perhaps Margherita and his first teacher, Giovanni Mazzuoli da Strada, who first awakened his interest in Dante.

Around 1327 Boccaccio was sent as a trainee to the Bardi bank in Naples, where the company effectively ran the finances of the Angevin court. Working for the Bardi was an unhappy experience, followed by another equally unhappy one studying canon law, after which he dedicated himself to literary studies, helped by prominent men of letters active at the court. His first highly scholastic letters indicate that the whole Neapolitan period of his life, which lasted until 1340, was characterized by an anxious, disorganized thirst for literature and a willingness to take risks on a large scale in his own writing. In effect he was an autodidact and as such was particularly drawn to the texts and literary forms that were most admired in the late Middle Ages. The stars in this youthful literary firmament were Paolino Veneto, the chronicler and treatise-writer, who was also Bishop of Pozzuoli, Paolo da Perugia, King Robert's learned librarian, Andalò del Negro, the influential astronomer, and possibly Barlaam, the Calabrian monk who seemed an inexhaustible mine of knowledge about Greek culture. *Dionigi da Borgo San Sepolcro, *Barbato da Sulmona, and

Giovanni Barrili, who were admirers of the young *Petrarch, brought his already considerable achievements to Boccaccio's attention. Classical poetry and culture became a passion, and so too did the new vernacular literature, which already had classics of its own that were comparable with the old. But Boccaccio's development as a writer was also deeply influenced by the pleasures and refinements of a court and city which combined Italo-French culture with that of the Arab and *Byzantine world.

It was against this cultivated, sensual background that he constructed his own love story. He made Fiammetta an enchanting noble lady, embellishing her figure with the most splendid literary motifs of the time as a focal point around which to rework the inspiring experiences of his youth. She is not depicted in the *Caccia di Diana* (1334) or the *Filostrato* (c.1335), but dominates, directly or indirectly, all the subsequent works up to the *Decameron*: *Filocolo* (1336–8), *Teseida* (1339–41), *Ameto* (1341–2), *Amorosa visione* (first drafted in 1342–3), and the *Elegia di Madonna Fiammetta* (1343–4).

The Bardi crisis obliged Boccaccio to return to Florence in the winter of 1340–1. His domestic circumstances are reflected in the complaints which punctuate the works and letters of the following years. But contact with the harsh necessities of life, far from undermining his commitment to literature, opened the way to more realistic writing based on direct knowledge of the city and of the complex and intrepid lives of the *merchants to whose society he himself belonged. There were brief sojourns abroad, at the court of Ostasio da Polenta in Ravenna (1345–6) and then at that of Francesco Ordelaffi in Forlì (1347), but in 1348 he was back in Florence, where he witnessed the terrible *plague described in the introduction to the *Decameron*. A short while before he had completed the *Ninfale fiesolano* (probably 1344–6). He probably wrote the *Decameron* between 1349 and 1351. It is the work which crowns the first phase of his literary career, and concludes his narrative and *romance production with a *summa* of medieval story-telling.

His father died in 1349, and Boccaccio had to give even more attention to supporting his family. But his literary reputation was now assured. He was given various official tasks by the city of Florence. In 1350 he was sent as ambassador to the Lords of Romagna. Then, on a more attractive mission, he delivered ten gold florins to Sister Beatrice, Dante's daughter, in recompense for damages suffered by

her family. In 1351 he was elected Chamberlain of the *commune. As representative of the Republic, he was present at the purchase of Prato, and visited the court of Lodovico of Bavaria. In 1354 and 1365 he was Florence's ambassador in *Avignon at the papal courts of Innocent VI and Urban V. In 1367 he conveyed the homage of the Florentines to Urban V on his return to *Rome. But these honorific missions were not sufficient to extricate him from the straitened circumstances which had followed the ruin of the Bardi. Encouraged by happy memories of his youth and the friendship of Niccolò *Acciaiuoli, now the real power at the Angevin court, he went back to Naples in 1362 and 1370, hoping to find a satisfactory solution to his problems. The result, though, was a series of painful disappointments, and he returned embittered to the house in Certaldo, which had been his retreat since 1362.

His passion for culture took a *humanist turn in these later years and a new religious dimension emerged in his moral thought. The changes are already a dominant feature of the *Lettera consolatoria a Pino de' Rossi* (1362), and are visible in the *Corbaccio* (?1365). But they take hold fully as a result of his friendship with Petrarch, a friendship which had decisive influence on Italian and European culture of the later 14th c. Boccaccio first had personal contact with Petrarch in 1350, when he had hurried out of Florence to welcome him as his guest. He had then spent some weeks in the spring of 1351 in Petrarch's house in *Padua, during which the two had established a profound understanding of each other's thought and work. He was Petrarch's guest again in 1359 in *Milan and in 1363 in *Venice. But actual meetings were rare, though much desired on both sides. But whilst they were 'separated in the body, they were spiritually united' (as Petrarch put it in a letter), regularly corresponding, and exchanging books and literary news, with a host of loyal friends in common. By 1360 Boccaccio's house was one of the main centres of early Italian humanism. Meetings there shaped the thinking of Coluccio *Salutati, Filippo *Villani, Luigi *Marsili, and many other early humanists. And it was the centre from which knowledge of newly discovered texts and authors— Varro, Martial, Tacitus, the *Priapea*, etc.—spread through Italy and Europe, as well as the new knowledge of ancient Greek.

Boccaccio acquired the knowledge of Greek that put him ahead of his literary contemporaries from *Leonzio Pilato in 1360–2. As a result, for the first time the world of post-classical learning gained a sense of the ideal unity of the two great ancient cultures. Boccaccio was so conscious of the decisiveness of his achievement that, for the first and only time in his career, he could not resist a moment of humble pride in his discussion of poetry in his *Genealogiae deorum gentilium* (15.7): 'It was I who first and at my own expense brought the books of Homer and various other Greek authors back to Tuscany, from where they had disappeared many centuries ago with no hope of returning.'

Petrarch was always the first to be informed of his latest discoveries, though Boccaccio plainly had a more open-minded approach to Latin culture. He sent Petrarch not only ancient classics but also the great Christian fathers. In 1351, with some nervousness but with frankness and firmness, he presented him with another 'sacred' volume, the *Divine Comedy*, with an introductory Latin poem, 'Ytalie iam certus honos'. Here again Boccaccio's humanism seems less committed to canonical ideas of style and rhetoric than that of Petrarch. But, if it is generally less refined and more eclectic, his writing is always underpinned by an intense commitment to poetry, which he claims in the *Genealogiae* (15.10) went back to when he was in the womb. As the first apostle of the cult of Dante, he perceived more clearly than Petrarch an unbroken continuity in intellectual life, poetry, and culture from antiquity through to his own time. And by uncovering the treasures of ancient Greece, he opened Latin culture to the immense world beyond its borders. He also boldly extended its limits to include Christian authors, certain medieval writers, and Dante as the great vernacular poet.

These early humanist attitudes characterize his mature writings, which he continued to work on until the very end of his life, often producing more than one version—*Genealogiae* (?1350–75), *Buccolicum carmen* (1351–?1366), *De mulieribus claris* (1361–?1375), *De casibus virorum illustrium* (1355–?1374), and *De montibus* (1351–?1374). Aided by Petrarch's calmer but profound Christian beliefs, in these years Boccaccio relinquished the emotional restlessness of his youth for firm religious conviction. As a confirmation of his spiritual progress, he took minor orders, and in 1360 he was granted full holy orders. He devoted himself with ever more enthusiasm to the cult of Dante, writing various versions of his *biography, the *Trattatello in laude di Dante* (1351–71), and lecturing on his 'poema sacro' in the church of S. Stefano di Badia in 1373–4.

Petrarch died in 1374, leaving Boccaccio in his will a vair-lined robe to keep him warm at night whilst studying. The loss of his friend left an unfillable void, which Boccaccio's writings from then on constantly lament. He was old before his time, alone in his house in Certaldo, tormented first by dropsy and then by a painful form of scabies. He was still bitterly mourning the death in about 1358 of his little daughter Violante, who is tenderly remembered in the eclogue *Olympia*. He found relief only in literary labour. He made a careful, serious revision and transcription of the *Decameron*, the autograph of which is now in Berlin; he embarked on a punctilious reworking of the *Genealogiae*, on which he was still working in the last hours of his life; and in his *Esposizioni* he wrote the first great commentary by an important writer on the *Divine Comedy* [see DANTE COMMENTARIES].

On his death on 21 December 1375, Boccaccio was immediately saluted and mourned by his contemporaries as the champion of the idea that poetry has its source in God, and the last of the three great figures of Italian literature. In his lament Franco *Sacchetti mourns in his death the passing of poetry itself. [VB]

See V. Branca, *Giovanni Boccaccio: profilo biografico* (1997); V. Branca, *Boccaccio: The Man and His Works* (1976).

BOCCALINI, TRAIANO (1556–1613). Political *satirist and historian. He was educated by the *Jesuits in Loreto, studied *law in *Perugia and *Padua, and held various administrative and judicial posts. He is best known for his *Ragguagli di Parnaso* (*Centuria Prima* published in 1612, *Centuria Seconda* in 1613, and twenty-nine *ragguagli* published posthumously as *Pietra di paragone politico* ('Political Touchstone') in 1615). Taking his cue from Cesare *Caporali's poems, *Viaggio in Parnaso* and *Avvisi di Parnaso*, but moving to prose, Boccalini developed the highly influential form of the report (*ragguaglio*), ostensibly penned by an impartial gazetteer, of the latest goings-on in the realm of Parnaso, a mythological afterlife inhabited by ancient and modern writers and presided over by Apollo. The work cleverly deflects censure while containing numerous ironic and humorous denunciations of the tyrannical nature of Spanish domination and of the hypocrisy, immorality, and narrowness inherent in current notions of *ragion di stato*.

In Boccalini's broad view of politics as a truth-seeking and virtuous activity, literary culture (*buone* *lettere*) plays a central role: the cultivation of literature is precisely what makes it possible for men to identify and unmask tyranny. Such an ideal 'republic of letters' is also, for Boccalini, necessarily a political republic (best exemplified for him by *Venice, with its long-matured values of tolerance and freedom). Though not spelled out, Boccalini's view of the potential of *education has democratic implications, for, once able to read, all men may be influenced by the likes of Tacitus and *Machiavelli and will thus have access to moral and political truth. In this Boccalini shows little patience with reactionary pedants of his day and with the uncritical observance of authority [see QUERELLE DES ANCIENS ET DES MODERNES]. He is also known as the author of a vast commentary on the works of Tacitus, which was in part published in 1677.

[PBD]

BOCCHINI, BARTOLOMEO (1604–48/53). *Bolognese painter of theatrical scenes, associated with the *commedia dell'arte*, particularly in Bologna and *Venice. He used the name Zan Muzzina and may himself have been a **zanni*. As well as *dialect verse and plays, he wrote a *mock-heroic poem, *Le pazzie de' savi* (1641). His *La corona maccheronica* (1665) is informative about the *zanni's* art and life.

[FC]

BOCCIONI, UMBERTO (1882–1916). *Futurist painter and sculptor. Born in Reggio Calabria, he studied Divisionist techniques with Gino Severini and Giacomo *Balla in *Rome and then with Previtali in *Milan. After meeting *Marinetti, he signed the *Manifesto dei pittori futuristi* and the *Manifesto tecnico della pittura futurista* in 1910, and developed his own distinctive style of Futurist painting. Influenced by Cubism through the 1912 Futurist exhibition in Paris, he summarized his later theories in *Pittura scultura futuriste* (1914). He strongly supported Italian intervention in *World War I, signing the *Sintesi futurista della guerra* in 1914. He served in the army alongside Marinetti and other Futurists, but died as the result of a riding accident.

[AM]

BODINI, VITTORIO (1914–70). *Surrealist poet, who became professor of Spanish in his home town of Bari. His verse blends Spanish surrealism with *Florentine *hermetic poetry, creating novel deployments of traditional images of the moon, motherhood, and southern Italian scenes.

[JJ]

BODONI, GIAMBATTISTA (1740–1813). Born in Saluzzo and trained in *Rome, he raised the art of *printing to new heights as printer to the Duke of Parma. He was influenced by the fine arts, and designed new typefaces in pursuit of *neoclassical perfection. *Napoleon rewarded him handsomely for prestige editions of the classics and other works of more immediate propaganda value. He left an important *Manuale tipografico* (1788).

[JMAL]

BOETHIUS, ANICIUS MANLIUS SEVERINUS (*c*.480–524). Important philosopher and poet, who was a major influence on the *Middle Ages and *Renaissance. He held high office under Emperor Theodoric, but was eventually imprisoned in Pavia and put to death for alleged treason. His *Consolatio philosophiae*, written during his imprisonment, represents Lady Philosophy gradually pulling him back from the brink of despair through a blend of argument and song. Blind, inconstant Fortuna revolving her wheel is actually powerless against the real harmony of the universe and Divine Providence. *Dante attributes his love for philosophy to his reading of Boethius (*Conv.* 2.12). Torquato *Tasso is indebted to him in *Il mondo creato*, and thought his poetry rivalled that of Lucretius.

[LAP]

BOIARDO, MATTEO MARIA (?1441–94), Count of Scandiano, poet and *humanist, was born in the family's ancestral castle at Scandiano, in the Apennines near Reggio in Emilia, some time between 21 May and 20 June and probably in the year 1441. His mother Lucia was the sister of the humanist poet Tito Vespasiano *Strozzi, his father Giovanni the son of Feltrino Boiardo, whom Nicolò III d'Este, Marquis of *Ferrara, had made Lord of Scandiano in 1423. With this investiture the fortunes of the Boiardo family became tied to those of the *Este, who were to play a major role in the poet's life.

In 1441 the family moved to Ferrara, where Matteo Maria grew up until his father died in 1451, when they returned to Scandiano. Here Matteo Maria continued his humanist education under the guidance of his grandfather Feltrino and the family chaplain Bartolomeo da Prato. When Feltrino also died in 1460, he and his cousin Giovanni inherited the fief of Scandiano with its attached lands, but the joint administration gave rise to family feuds culminating in 1474, when Matteo Maria narrowly averted poisoning at the instigation of his aunt

Boiardo, Matteo Maria

Taddea Pio, Giovanni's mother. This caused the lands to be divided, and Boiardo became Lord of Scandiano. But already in 1461 disputes with relatives had forced him to take up residence in Ferrara. In the *court of Borso d'Este he established friendly relations with the young princes, Sigismondo and especially Ercole, who was to inherit the dukedom in 1471. For Ercole Boiardo produced his first humanist works in Latin, the *Carmina de laudibus Estensium* and the *Pastoralia*, both dating from 1463–4; he also undertook a number of free *translations into the vernacular, from Cornelius Nepos, Xenophon, Apuleius, Herodotus, and the *chronicler Ricobaldo of Ferrara.

While in Reggio in 1469 Boiardo met Antonia Caprara, who inspired his *canzoniere*, his first original work in the vernacular, now regarded as one of the highest poetic achievements of the 15th c. Entitled *Amorum libri tres* and comprising 180 *sonnets, *canzoni*, and *madrigals, it recounts in *Petrarchan mode the three phases of the poet's love, from initial joy to subsequent disillusionment and final mourning. In 1476, when he probably finished his *canzoniere*, Boiardo returned to Ferrara to become Duke Ercole's companion; here he witnessed the unfolding of Nicolò d'Este's conspiracy against Ercole, his cousin, whose victory Boiardo promptly celebrated in his Latin *Epigrammata*. It is around this time that he began his major work, *Orlando innamorato*, originally also called *Inamoramento de Orlando*, a three-book *chivalric *romance absorbing the poetic experience of the *canzoniere* and the encomiastic intent of the earlier Latin works. Book 1, dedicated to Ercole, was completed in 1478, and the following year Boiardo married Taddea dei Gonzaga of Novellara, by whom he had six children. In 1480 Ercole appointed him governor of Reggio, where in 1482 he completed book 2; but the outbreak of war between Ferrara and *Venice, the vicissitudes of which are reflected in his *Ecloghe volgari*, and his concern for his native Scandiano, forced him to relinquish the post. 1483 saw the first edition of books 1 and 2, one of the earliest vernacular works by a living author to be printed; however, no copy of this edition has survived.

In 1487 Ercole appointed Boiardo ducal emissary for Reggio, an office which he was to hold until his death, and which has left us the largest nucleus of his *Lettere*, mostly of an administrative nature. A new edition of *Orlando innamorato*, published in Venice that year, provides the earliest extant copy of the poem. Dating probably from this time there is also *Timone*, a *comedy loosely based on the *dia-

logue of the same name by Lucian. About this time he wrote another work for the entertainment of the Este court, the *Capitoli del giuoco dei Tarocchi*. Meanwhile composition of book 3 of *Orlando innamorato* had proved slow and intermittent. When Charles VIII of France invaded Italy, in September 1494, Boiardo's health had deteriorated. He died in Reggio on 19 December, his death, with that of *Poliziano and Giovanni *Pico della Mirandola in the same year, marking the end of an era. The unfinished book 3 appeared posthumously in Venice in 1495; a single copy of this edition remains, and no copies at all of the poem's first complete edition, published in Scandiano later that year.

Within the chivalric tradition *Orlando innamorato* is the first poem to effect a deliberate fusion of the Carolingian and Arthurian narrative cycles [see also EPIC]; hence the poem's novelty, the fact that Orlando, the hero of the *Chanson de Roland*, is in love. Seen as a cosmic force as well as an essential attribute to chivalry, love is by far the main theme, alongside other major themes of arms, *magic, honour, and adventure. Fabulous and anachronistic as this narrative material may seem, the poet relates it to the present by creating the illusion of a live recitation to a courtly audience, whose reactions he registers at various points. Within this frame the narration itself unfolds at a relentless pace, governed by the so-called *entrelacement* technique of suspending one story and shifting to another at the point of maximum expectation. The uniqueness of Boiardo's art lies in his youthful vitality, his grammatically free yet vivid language, and above all his inexhaustible inventiveness. He writes as one of his time who knows at first hand the sorrows of living, yet in art remains unrepentant in his celebration of life.

Boiardo's poem enjoyed great popularity amongst his contemporaries, its unfinished state prompting a number of sequels by, amongst others, Nicolò degli Agostini, Raffaele Valcieco, and above all Ludovico *Ariosto in his *Orlando furioso*. But Pietro *Bembo's reformation of the language in 1525, the rediscovery of Aristotle's *Poetics* in the 1530s, and the incipient *Counter-Reformation in the 1540s all caused it to fall from favour amongst critics and writers, including Torquato *Tasso, who found it lacking on linguistic, theoretical, and moral grounds [see also LITERARY THEORY, 2]. Gradually, Boiardo's original version was supplanted by Francesco *Berni's *rifacimento* (1542), a recasting of the poem in literary Tuscan, and by

Lodovico *Domenichi's contemporary revision, the publication of which (1544), significantly, coincided with the last edition of Boiardo to appear in the *Renaissance in the original text.

Following centuries of neglect, the rediscovery of Boiardo took place in England during the *Romantic period. Starting in 1830 Antonio *Panizzi, the expatriate Italian professor later to become librarian of the British Museum, produced a historic combined edition of Boiardo's *Orlando innamorato* and Ariosto's *Orlando furioso*. This marked both the restoration of the *Innamorato*'s original text and the beginning of modern Boiardo criticism. Described by the critic Carlo *Dionisotti as the most misunderstood poet in Italian literature, and for a long time overshadowed by Ariosto, Boiardo has since emerged as one of the most forceful poets of the Renaissance, his work recognized as the first vernacular masterpiece by a Northern Italian author. As a result of this critical acclaim he now seems set to rival Ariosto's long-standing supremacy.

The first translation of Boiardo into English was Robert Tofte's *Orlando Inamorato: The Three First Bookes* (1598), in reality the first three cantos of book 1 in Domenichi's version. The Italian text was known to Spenser and Milton, but it was not until the 19th c. that other partial translations were attempted, by Richard Wharton (1804), William Stewart Rose (1823), and Leigh Hunt (1846).

[MGD]

Tutte le opere di Matteo Maria Boiardo, ed. A. Zottoli (1944); *L'Inamoramento de Orlando*, ed. A. Tissoni Benvenuti and C. Montagnani (1999). See N. Harris, *Bibliografia dell' 'Orlando innamorato'* (1988–91); M. Praloran, '*Meraviglioso artificio'. Tecniche narrative e rappresentative nell' 'Orlando innamorato'* (1990).

BOINE, GIOVANNI (1887–1917). Modernizing Catholic writer. Born in Liguria, he was educated in *Milan, where he graduated in philosophy with a thesis on Blondel. From 1907 to 1909 he was a contributor to the Catholic journal *Rinnovamento*. Forced by tuberculosis to return to Liguria, he worked as a librarian in Porto Maurizio and wrote religious articles for *La *Voce* that were informed by his interest in Hegelianism and Italian *idealism. At the start of *World War I he published his most successful work, *Discorsi militari*, and the novel he is now best remembered for, *Il peccato*, the story of a love affair between an intellectual and a nun. A year later he abandoned fiction for the short pieces of poetic prose that were collected and published posthumously as *Frantumi* (1918). The critical articles which he wrote from 1914 under the title *Plausi e botte* for *Riviera ligure* showed him to be one of the finest critics of his time; a collection with the same title was published in 1918. [AHC]

BOITO, ARRIGO (1842–1918). Writer, composer and librettist. Born in *Padua, he studied at the *Milan Conservatoire. On graduating in 1861, he spent a year in Paris with his fellow student, the composer Franco Faccio, for whom he wrote his first *libretto, *Amleto* (1862). Back in Milan, he became a major exponent of the *Scapigliatura. His poetry, almost avant-garde in its experimentalism, includes the polymetric *Re Orso* (1865). From this period also date his short stories and critical essays, mostly published in the *Figaro* (1864), which he founded and co-edited with Emilio *Praga. His *opera *Mefistofele*, disastrously premiered in 1868, eventually made him world-famous in its revised version in 1875. Under the pseudonym Tobia Gorrio, he wrote librettos for other composers, including *La gioconda* (1875) for Ponchielli. Later work includes translations of Wagner's operas and *Shakespeare's plays. His most successful collaboration was with *Verdi, for whom he wrote the librettos of *Otello*, *Falstaff*, and the revised *Simon Boccanegra*. Boito's second opera, *Nerone*, begun in 1862, was premiered posthumously in 1924. His successful career, which culminated in the directorship of the Parma Conservatoire (which now bears his name) and a seat in the Senate (1912), has been too readily considered a repudiation of his iconoclastic youth. [RS]

BOITO, CAMILLO, see SCAPIGLIATURA.

Bolgia. Name for each of the ten divisions of the eighth circle (Malebolge) of *Dante's *Inferno, in which sins of fraud are punished.

Bologna. First a *commune and then a *signoria in the *Middle Ages, Bologna was dominated by the Bentivoglio family for much of the 15th c., and became part of the *Papal States from 1506 onwards. The city is the home of the oldest *university in Europe, founded in the late 11th c. and renowned for the study of Roman *law. This gave rise to the medieval genre of the *commentary, which was then extended to Latin and Greek literature, and enjoyed considerable success at the university in later centuries with such teachers as

Bombicci Porta, Luigi

Filippo *Beroaldo and Antonio Urceo. In 1563 the schools of the university, or *studio*, which had been located in different parts of the town, were brought under one roof in the Archiginnasio, where famous scholars such as Andrea *Alciato, Carlo *Sigonio, Girolamo *Cardano, and Pietro *Pomponazzi all taught. The monasteries and convents of the religious orders and their *libraries (San Domenico, San Francesco and San Salvatore) were also of great cultural importance for the city, and from the beginning of the 17th c. the *studio* suffered from the competition of the *Jesuits, who offered more up-to-date teaching methods than those of the university.

In the second half of the 17th c. the proliferation of the *Academies spread to Bologna as well, the most famous being the Accademia degli Incamminati, where the Carracci school of painting was based, the Accademia Filarmonica, and the Accademia delle Scienze. In 1714 Luigi Ferdinando Marsili, a scientist and naturalist, founded the Istituto delle Scienze, which employed new experimental methods and combined the Accademia delle Scienze and the artists' Accademia Clementina; a member of the Institute was Luigi Galvani, famous for his work on electricity, later continued by Alessandro *Volta.

In the 19th and 20th c. Bologna also established its prestige in literature and poetry. Giosue *Carducci taught Italian literature at the university from 1860 to 1904, followed by Giovanni *Pascoli in 1905. This was the era too of the great scientists, such as the physicist Guglielmo Marconi (Nobel Prize in 1909), Augusto Murri (the greatest Italian clinician of the late 19th c.), and Federico Enriques (mathematician and philosopher of science, and friend of Einstein). [LChi]

See W. Tega (ed.), *Storia illustrata di Bologna* (1987–91).

BOMBICCI PORTA, LUIGI, see DARWINISM.

Bompiani. *Milanese *publishing firm founded in 1929 by Valentino Bompiani, formerly an editor at *Mondadori. It is notable for its many *translations of American and British literature, its *Almanacco letterario* and literary reference works. Bompiani's Italian authors include *Moravia, *Vittorini, *Brancati, and *Eco. In the 1980s it merged into the Fabbri–Etas–Sonzogno conglomerate. [DF]

BOMPIANI, GINEVRA (1939–). Novelist, critic, and professor of English at *Siena University.

Her fiction is informed by linguistics, *feminism, and *literary theory, and verges on the *surreal and the *fantastic, as was evident from her first novel, *Bàrtelemi all'ombra* (1967). *Mondanità* (1980) charts a woman's search for an alternative space and identity in a world constructed on fixed roles and myths of gender, whilst metamorphoses and magical happenings abound in the tales of *L'incanto* (1987). *Vecchio cielo, nuova terra* (1988) explores the paradoxes inherent in what is ostensibly banal. [SW]

BON, FRANCESCO AUGUSTO (1788–1858). Actor from Verona who worked in various *Venetian companies and wrote successful *comedies. His most important work, the trilogy *Ludro e la sua gran giornata* (1832), *Il matrimonio di Ludro* (1836), and *La vecchiaia di Ludro* (1837), combines the humour of *Goldoni with the social *satire of Beaumarchais. [DO'G]

BONAGIUNTA DA LUCCA (Bonagiunta Orbicciani) (d. before 1300). *Lyric poet best known for *Dante's representation of him (*Purg.* 24.19–63). Little is known of his life other than that he was a notary. He is usually credited with playing a leading role amongst the *Siculo-Tuscans who established the high style of lyric poetry in central Italy. The twenty-five or so poems of his which survive betray obvious debts to the *Sicilian School, but make more insistent use of nature and animal imagery derived from the *troubadours. In a *tenzone* with *Guinizzelli he is openly hostile towards the poetic intellectualism that the latter was bringing into vogue. When his shade appears to Dante on the terrace of the gluttons in Purgatory, he alludes, rather obscurely, to a future meeting between Dante and an otherwise unknown girl named Gentucca in his native city. He then asks Dante if he is the author of the *canzone* 'Donne ch'avete intelletto d'amore' (in *Vita nova* 19). Dante's reply that he is merely a scribe following the dictates of love leads Bonagiunta to acknowledge the uninspired character of his own work and that of *Giacomo da Lentini and *Guittone d'Arezzo in comparison to the *dolce stil novo*. [PH]

BONARDI, LUIGI, see MALERBA, LUIGI.

BONARELLI, GUIDUBALDO, see BONARELLI, PROSPERO.

BONARELLI, PROSPERO (1588–1659),

born in Ancona, was the younger brother of Guidubaldo Bonarelli (1563–1608), who wrote the influential *pastoral drama *Filli di Sciro* (1607). Prospero was a dramatist, *librettist, and musician, who composed both words and music for intermezzi and *operas, principally in *Florence and Ancona. He founded an Academy in his home town, where his *tragedy *Solimano* was performed in 1611, reportedly to 4,000 spectators. He eliminated prologues, choruses, and supernatural Senecan spectres from his tragedies, and introduced romantic fictional subjects as opposed to historical or mythological ones. In general he sought a balance between the academic tradition of the genre and the increasing fashion for stage spectacle. His *L'Allegrezza del mondo* was the first opera ever performed in Vienna, in 1631. [See also THEATRE, 1.]   [RAA]

BONAVENTURE, ST (Bonaventura da Bagnoregio) (1221–74). *Franciscan theologian and mystic. He studied and taught at the University of Paris at the same time as his *Dominican contemporary, St Thomas *Aquinas. He was Minister General of the Franciscans (1257–74), and strove to resolve dissension within the order. In 1260 he was commissioned to write the official life of St Francis, the *Legenda maior*. He has much in common with Aquinas, but puts more emphasis on feeling and less on rational understanding. His works, which combine formal elegance with intellectual subtlety, include a manual of theology for Franciscan novitiates, mystical texts, of which the best known is the *Itinerarium mentis in Deum*, *commentaries, and many sermons. His immense popularity can be gauged from the fact that there are more than 50,000 extant manuscripts of his works. In the *Divine Comedy* he appears with Aquinas in the Heaven of the Sun (*Para.* 10–14).
[PH]

BONAVIRI, GIUSEPPE (1924–). *Sicilian writer, and a medical doctor by profession. His first novel, *Il sarto della stradalunga* (1954), gave a poetic colouring to *Neorealism. His novels and poetry as a whole combine *realism, *autobiography, *fantasy, and the picaresque, blending scientific curiosity and linguistic experimentation with Sicilian myths and traditional story-telling techniques. He achieves remarkable results in the fantasy novels of the late 1960s and early 1970s, notably the trilogy *La divina foresta* (1969), *Notti sull'altura* (1971), and *L'isola amorosa* (1973).   [AWM]

BONCIANI, ANTONIO (1417–*c*.1469/80). Poet, born in *Florence, who about 1448 followed Astorre II Manfredi to Faenza. Whilst there he wrote *Il giardino*, a *terza rima* poem in five *capitoli* [see CANTO], depicting an idealized *locus amoenus* with minute listing of herbs, vegetables, trees, flowers, and fruit, but also including advice on government. His commissioned poems include a *capitolo* for Lorenzo Manetti praising his lady, Diamante, as a gift from Venus herself. The *Caccia di Belfiore*, a poem in *ottava rima* influenced by Lorenzo de' *Medici's *Uccellagione di starne*, has also been attributed to him.   [DieZ]

BONCOMPAGNO DA SIGNA (*c*.1165–after 1240). Teacher of rhetoric and the *ars dictaminis* at *Bologna. He is chiefly remembered for the *Boncompagnus* and the *Rhetorica novissima*, containing lively models of Latin *letter-writing, which are invaluable for their picture of *university culture, particularly amongst law students. Though technically sophisticated, employing elaborate rhetorical devices and the *cursus, Boncompagno's examples demonstrate humour and narrative verve, and anticipate the vernacular *novella.   [JU]

BONDI, CLEMENTE (1742–1821). Prolific versifier, who achieved his best results in the playful and *satirical poems first collected in *Poemetti e rime varie* (1778) and in *translations from *Virgil and *Ovid (1790–1811). A *Jesuit turned librarian, he entered *Austrian service and passed from *Milan to Brno, and finally (1810) to Vienna, where he was last in the line of Italian laureates.   [JMAL]

BONDIE DIETAIUTI (mid-13th c.). *Florentine poet, of whom we have four *canzoni* and three *sonnets. He is strongly influenced by Provençal *troubadour models, though without the mediation of *Guittone, and uses imagery enriched by material from *bestiaries. He exchanges poems with Brunetto *Latini, whilst other compositions link him with *Pallamidesse di Bellindote and *Rustico Filippi.   [JU]

BONELLI, LUIGI, see COMICS.

BONGHI, RUGGERO (1826–95). Politician and writer, exiled in *1848. As minister of *education (1874–6) he was responsible for the introduction of compulsory elementary schooling. In *Perché la letteratura italiana non sia popolare in Italia* (1855) he argues for the use of more ordinary language in literature, on the model of *Manzoni. [See also LITERACY.] [MPC]

BONGO, PIETRO, see NUMEROLOGY.

BONI, ADA, see COOKERY BOOKS.

BONI, GIOVANNI DE' (*c*.1350–*c*.1404). Aretine poet, active principally at the *Visconti *court in *Milan. He wrote Latin eclogues and verse letters, and Italian lyrics much influenced by *Petrarch. He also wrote a poem in *terza rima* in fifty-three canti on the defeat and sack of Arezzo in 1381–2. [JP & JMS]

BONICHI, GINO, see SCIPIONE.

BONIFACE VIII (Benedetto *Caetani) (?1235–1303), Pope 1294–1303, was fiercely attacked in the poetry of *Iacopone da Todi (*Laude*, 83) and *Dante, who attributed his exile to Boniface's alliance with the *Black *Guelfs (*Inf.* 6.69; *Para.* 17.49–51) and condemned his simony, his crusade against the *Colonna cardinals, and his effective usurpation of the papal throne (*Inf.* 19.52–7; 27.85–111; *Para.* 27.22–7). Boniface authorized the centenary indulgence (Jubilee) of 1300. His Bull *Unam sanctam* (1302) asserted papal supremacy in the temporal sphere—a doctrine opposed by Dante in *Monarchia*, book 3. For three days in September 1303 he was held hostage by French agents at Anagni (*Purg.* 20.85–90). [PA]

BONIFACIO CALVO (13th c.). *Genoese *troubadour who wrote mostly in Provençal. The little information that we have on him derives exclusively from his poetry. Born into a noble Genoese family, he stayed for a long time in Toledo at the court of Alphonso X of Castille. The twenty-one poems we have belong to the years 1253–66 approximately and include two in Portuguese. Bonifacio is more original in his *sirventesi* than in his few love poems. He shows notable technical ability and an interest in formal experiment, particularly in 'Un nou sirventes ses tardar' (*c*.1266), which focuses on Spanish issues and mixes Provençal, Portuguese, and French. [LM]

BONO GIAMBONI (d. *c*.1292). *Florentine judge and one of the earliest writers of Italian prose, including *translations of Orosius and Vegetius from Latin. His *allegorical *Libro de' vizî e delle virtudi* describes how, accompanied by Lady

Filosofia, he witnessed the victory of *Fede Cristiana* and the four Cardinal Virtues over *Fede Giudea*, six heresies, the Vices, and *Fede Pagana* (Islam). [PA]

BONSANTI, ALESSANDRO (1904–84). *Florentine writer, who edited *Solaria* with Alberto *Carocci from 1930 to 1933, and in 1937 founded *Letteratura*. He succeeded *Montale as director of the *Vieusseux library in 1938, and founded *Il *Mondo* with Montale and Arturo *Loria in 1945. His highly introspective novels and stories, such as *Racconto militare* (1937), are generally considered to hold closely to the ideals of *Solaria*, combining European influences, especially that of Proust, with the Italian tradition. [SVM]

BONTEMPELLI, MASSIMO (1878–1960). One of the protagonists of literary *modernism in Italy. He was born in Como, but his father worked for the railways and his family was frequently on the move. After school in *Milan, he studied literature at the University of *Turin. On graduation he worked in various cities as a schoolteacher until 1910 when he settled in *Florence and began a life-long career in *journalism, with contributions principally to *Il *Marzocco* and *Cronache letterarie*. His career as a creative writer was now also under way. After five collections of traditional verse between 1904 and 1910, he showed an up-to-date interest in psychological analysis in collections of stories such as *Socrate moderno* (1908), *Amori* (1910), and *Sette savi* (1912). In 1915 he moved to Milan, where he developed an interest in *theatre, writing plays such as *Guardia alla luna* (1916) and *Siepe a nordovest* (1919). During *World War I he served as a war correspondent and then as an artillery officer. When he returned to Milan in 1918, the desire to break with the past already evident in his prewar work led to a brief flirtation with *Futurism. He also wrote *Vita intensa* (1919), which consists of ten short avant-garde novels.

In 1920 he moved to *Rome, where he continued to write literary and cultural journalism for a variety of papers, including the *Corriere della sera*, *Il Secolo*, *La Stampa*, and *La Gazzetta del popolo*. His interest in theatre was now given fresh stimulation through friendship with *Pirandello. In 1924 he was one of the founders of the Teatro degli Undici for which he wrote *Nostra Dea* (1925) and *Minnie la candida* (1929), as well as adapting other works for the theatre, often writing musical accompaniments—including one for Pirandello's *La Salamandra*. In

1926 he and Curzio *Malaparte founded the journal *900 (*Novecento*), which, until it closed down in 1929, represented an important opening towards European culture. It was largely in its pages that he formulated his ideas on *realismo magico and on the sort of modernism which he thought would be appropriate to the new *Fascist Italy. His emphasis on the metaphysical and on the irrational led to the surreal stories of *La donna dei miei sogni* (1925) and *Mia vita morte e miracoli* (1931), and to critically acclaimed works such as the children's book *La scacchiera davanti allo specchio* (1922) and *Eva ultima* (1923), a novel based on an earlier play of the same title, which consists almost entirely of a dramatic dialogue.

He had joined the Fascist Party in 1924 and was made a member of the *Accademia d'Italia in 1930. He was a strong advocate of the regime but became more critical in the later 1930s, and was banned for a while from journalistic and literary activity. All the same he published a major collection of his modernist articles, *L'avventura novecentesca*, in 1938 and wrote a highly successful column for the weekly *Tempo* until 1943. During *World War II he moved towards *Communism, but his election to the Senate in 1948 was declared null and void because of his previous Fascism. Isolated and ill, he largely withdrew from cultural and public life in the 1950s, although he was awarded the Premio Strega for *L'amante fedele* (1953).   [AHC]

See F. Tempesti, *Bontempelli* (1974); E. Urgnani, *Sogni e visioni: Massimo Bontempelli fra surrealismo e futurismo* (1991).

BONVESIN DE LA RIVA (*c.*1240–*c.*1314). One of the most important Northern Italian poets of the 13th c. Born into a wealthy *Milanese family, he became a teacher and a member of the Third Order of the Humiliati. He was a prolific writer both in Latin and in the Milanese vernacular, for the most part, of moral and didactic works.

All his Milanese writings, which are conventionally given Latin titles, are in verse, their exclusive metrical form being alexandrines in monorhymed four-line stanzas. The most important is probably the *Libro delle tre scritture*, completed before 1274. Over 2,000 lines long and divided into three parts, it describes the torments of Hell, Christ's Passion, and the rewards of Paradise. There is no mention of Purgatory, a fact which has sometimes led to accusations of heresy. The work is tightly constructed and contains quite powerful depictions of the punishments of the sinners, which show a talent for grotesque, even fearsome realism. A similar talent emerges in the *De elemosynis*, an account of contemporary hospitals in Milan, containing some grim descriptions of patients and their illnesses. In fact, Bonvesin seems to have had a particular interest in the care of the sick, leaving money to hospitals in his wills of 1304 and 1313.

A rather more cheerful and engaging insight into contemporary society is afforded by the *De quinquaginta curialitatibus ad mensam*, which lists the fifty rules of good table manners (don't slurp from a spoon, don't dip your bread in a communal wine-cup, etc.). Another picture of contemporary Milan is painted by the Latin *De magnalibus urbis Mediolani* of 1288, which differs from earlier descriptions in not focusing on saints and churches, but rather praises the city for its size and wealth, backing up its claims with extensive facts and figures.

Bonvesin's many religious works include a number of lives of saints and a series of vernacular *contrasti—dialogues between, for example, the soul and the body, or the Devil and the Virgin Mary. He also composed *allegorical *contrasti*. In the *Disputatio mensium* the months of the year rebel against their king, January, taking turns to boast of their qualities and benefits, whilst in the *Disputatio rosae cum viola* the most humble of flowers, the violet, puts forward a case for its superiority over the most magnificent, the rose.   [CEH]

Volgari scelti: Select Poems, ed. and trans. P. S. Diehl and R. Stefanini (1987).

Book Production or Trade, see PRINTING; PUBLISHING.

BORGESE, GIUSEPPE ANTONIO (1882–1952) was a novelist and one of the most important Italian *literary critics of his time. He was one the few Italian non-*Marxist intellectuals forced to leave Italy for refusing to proclaim allegiance to *Fascism.

A *Sicilian who studied in *Florence, he wrote a thesis on the *Storia della critica romantica in Italia*, published by *Croce in 1903 in his *La *Critica* series, which is still regarded as one of the most important works on the subject. For a while he combined Crocean aesthetic principles with *D'Annunzian *nationalism, an orientation that became manifest in the review *Hermes* (1904–6) which he founded. Distancing himself later from both Croce and D'Annunzio, he subsequently supported a morally constructive, value-laden, and humane literature; in the collection of essays of

Borghini, Vincenzio

La vita e il libro (1910–13), he tests his critical mind against the major European writers of the time, and in Tempo di edificare (1923) he reacts against the impressionism and 'fragmentism' then in vogue in Italy, supporting a fiction based on history and psychology of the kind cultivated by *Verga and Federico *Tozzi. He was one of the few critics to recognize immediately the importance of *Moravia's Gli *indifferenti.

In Rubé (1921), the novel which establishes his reputation as a writer, Borgese reflects critically on the subversive culture of his time and the role he once played in promoting it. It is the story of Filippo Rubé, a Sicilian intellectual from the lower middle class who seeks to compensate for his ineptitude and identity problems through the mystique of vitalism and irrationality. The novel is an important representation of the ideological habits of the petty bourgeoisie in the transition from interventionism to the rise of Fascism as a result of the social conflicts following *World War I.

Borgese taught German literature at the universities of *Turin and *Rome, and then aesthetics at *Milan. He left Fascist Italy for the USA in 1931, and taught at the universities of California and Chicago, and at Smith College. During his stay in America, he wrote (in English) Goliath: The March of Fascism in which he demonstrates the 'petty bourgeois' character of *Mussolini's regime. Later, while at the University of Chicago, he developed the project for a 'World Constitution', based on the tenets of a liberal, universal pacifism. He returned to his chair in Milan in 1945.   [RSD]

See S. D'Alberti, Giuseppe Antonio Borgese (1971); F. Mezzetti, Borgese e il fascismo (1978).

BORGHINI, VINCENZIO (1515–80). Florentine scholar and essayist of many talents. He was ordained a *Benedictine priest in 1540, and became Prior of the Foundlings Hospital in *Florence, and simultaneously one of the most influential and faithful courtiers of Cosimo and later Francesco de' *Medici. Benedetto *Croce described him as the first modern *literary critic, notably for his awareness of individual poetic creativity and the need to judge literary works as individual creations. Michele *Barbi regarded him as the first modern *textual critic, and used his method and ideas for his own 'new philology' and for his national edition of the *Divine Comedy [see also FILOLOGIA].

An éminence grise fiercely protective of Florence's intellectual and artistic heritage, he engineered the 1573 *Giunti edition of the *Decameron and the subsequent Annotazioni (1574), which explained the textual changes and examined *Boccaccio's language diachronically and synchronically. He was the inspiration behind the foundation of the Accademia della *Crusca (1583), suggesting to Grand Duke Cosimo the names of a committee, including its future president Lionardo *Salviati. And the fundamental work he did on the Annotazioni would later form the basis for the work of Salviati and for the first *Vocabolario della Crusca of 1611. A great collaborator with contemporary artists, he proposed designs for many artistic enterprises, including themes for the decoration of the Palazzo Vecchio in Florence, especially the *Vasari designs in the Sala dei Cinquecento. After 1572 he acted as the grand ducal lieutenant in Florence's *Accademia delle Arti del Disegno, commissioning and paying artists such as Benvenuto *Cellini and Vincenzio Danti.

Borghini's vast output remains largely unpublished, not least because of his unsystematic method of jotting down sporadic notes, and the difficulty of some of his handwriting, though two large volumes of historical Discorsi (1584–5) were published after his death, containing essays and studies on the history of *Tuscany, Tuscan bishoprics, numismatics, Florentine archaeology and architecture, Tuscany's Roman inheritance, and many other topics. His important correspondence with some of the most notable literary figures of the time, published as Prose fiorentine (1745), marks him out as one of the most significant of cultural advisers, on subjects ranging from Roman archaeological remains to linguistic theory. Borghini's fame reached a new height in the 19th c., and selections from his manuscripts were published sporadically, notably La Ruscelleide (1898), a satirical polemic against the linguistic ineptitude of Girolamo *Ruscelli, and the brief autobiographical notes Ricordi intorno alla sua vita (1909). Most recently some 2,000 of his letters were discovered in the Florentine foundlings' hospital.   [JRW]

Scritti inediti o rari sulla lingua, ed. J. R. Woodhouse (1971); Storia della nobiltà fiorentina, ed. J. R. Woodhouse (1978). See M. Barbi, Degli studi di Vincenzio Borghini sopra la storia e la lingua di Firenze (1889).

BORGIA. Noble Catalan family who successfully insinuated themselves into the *papal court, and challenged the pre-eminence of the traditional Roman barons, especially the *Orsini and *Colonna. They came to prominence as a consequence of the election of Alonso Borgia (1378–1458) as Pope Callistus III. Eleven Borgias became cardinals and Rodrigo Borgia (1431–1503) was elected Alexander VI in 1492, overseeing the pacification of the Romagna and papal domination of the Roman barons.

Two of his illegitimate offspring, Lucrezia Borgia (1480–1519) and the 'Duke Valentino' Cesare Borgia (1475–1507), figure amongst the most famous names in Italian history, both the result of Rodrigo's liaison with Vanozza Catanei. Lucrezia was married three times, to Giovanni *Sforza, to a son of King Alfonso II of *Naples, and to Alfonso d'*Este, becoming Duchess of *Ferrara in 1505. Rumours of her complicity in politically motivated Borgia poisonings, and of incestuous relationships with her father and brother, were largely the result of anti-Borgia invective. At Ferrara she showed herself to be a discerning *patroness of art and literature, sustaining a famous correspondence with Pietro *Bembo, and involving herself in religious works until her death in 1519. Cesare was made Archbishop of Valencia by his father in 1492, but renounced his religious offices in 1498 to concentrate on military affairs, specifically the subjection of the Papal States to Borgia control. This involved successfully defeating many of the dissident *signori, as a result of which Alexander created him Duke of Romagna in 1501. After the so-called revolt of Magione of 1502 Cesare had a number of his military commanders murdered in an infamous act of revenge, as narrated in *Machiavelli's Principe. On the election of Julius II as Pope after Alexander's death, Cesare's fortunes waned and he was forced to flee Italy.

The family's infamous reputation is partly a consequence of the depth of hatred they engendered in their opponents and victims. Julius II had sought to depose Alexander earlier, in 1494, and did much to stigmatize the family whilst seeking to eradicate papal nepotism in the wake of Borgia excesses. *Humanists and historians like *Pontano, Stefano Infessura, and Paolo *Giovio all chronicled Borgia vices whilst in the patronage of their enemies. *Guicciardini's Storia d'Italia in particular provides vivid detail of Borgia depravity, whilst Machiavelli's Principe, on the other hand, celebrated both Alexander VI's and Cesare Borgia's virtù as political leaders.   [SJM]

See M. Mallett, The Borgias: The Rise and Fall of the Most Infamous Family in History (1969).

BORROMEO, FEDERICO (1564–1631).

Cousin of St Carlo *Borromeo, and a famous ecclesiastical historian and philosopher. Born in *Milan, he studied theology at Pavia, and in 1586 moved to *Rome to begin a high-profile career in the Church. In 1595 he became Archbishop of Milan, and held the post for thirty-six years. One of his greatest achievements was the founding of the Biblioteca Ambrosiana in Milan, for which he donated from his own funds [see also LIBRARIES]. He sent agents all over Europe and the Near East in search of new acquisitions, and was able to launch the library with a collection of 12,000 codices and 30,000 printed books. He opened it to the clergy in 1609, with the aim of improving standards in theology and ecclesiastical history. In 1618 he added a picture gallery, donating his own considerable collection of sacred paintings.

His published works, mainly in Latin, number over 100. They show his interest in ecclesiastical archaeology, sacred painting, and collecting. He was interested in the diabolic possession of women, and wrote much on 'ecstatic women', 'sacred virgins', possessed nuns, and St *Caterina of Siena. However, the majority of his works concern themes of contemplation and mysticism. His vision of the soul in contemplation losing itself in a deep sea may have suggested to the Church authorities that he held views associated with *Quietism, and led to his not being canonized. He appears in *Manzoni's *Promessi sposi, where he emerges more as a man of action than as the scholar and contemplative that he also was.   [PBD]

BORROMEO, ST CARLO (1538–84). Cardinal and, from 1565, Archbishop of *Milan. His reforms and asceticism brought him repeatedly into conflict with both clergy and laity enjoying privileges he wanted to curtail. Similarly, the civil authorities and Spanish governors of Milan vigorously fought his attempts to assert autonomy of ecclesiastical jurisdiction for the Milanese See. In earlier life he organized the *humanist Accademia delle Notti Vaticane, which, after the death of his elder brother Federico in 1562, he directed towards theological issues. He left a large body of *religious writings. Canonized in 1610, he became the model Catholic bishop for later generations.
                                                    [DK]

BORSA, MATTEO (1752–98). *Mantuan doctor and nephew to Saverio *Bettinelli by marriage, who won the Mantua Academy's 1783 essay competition with Del gusto presente in letteratura italiana, denouncing neologisms, 'philosophy', and the mingling of styles and genres. The victory is symptomatic of a mounting reaction against foreign influence during the 1780s.   [JMAL]

BORSIERI, PIETRO (1788–1852). *Milanese polemicist and patriot who trained as a lawyer at Pavia but quickly entered literary circles in Milan. He attacked Cesare *Arici for kowtowing to the *Napoleonic regime (1810), joined the editorial board of the *Austrian-inspired *Biblioteca italiana, denounced the deference of men of letters to political power, and promptly resigned (1815). He made various contributions to the debate over *Romanticism, including the lively *Avventure letterarie di un giorno* (1816), which stands up for middlebrow alongside elevated literature. He was a co-founder of *Il*Conciliatore*. In 1821 he was imprisoned by the Austrians in Spielberg, being eventually deported to America in 1836. He returned to Italy depressed and in poor health, but took part in the struggles against Austria in *1848–9.   [MPC]

BOSCHINI, MARCO (c.1605–81). Painter, engraver, cartographer, and dealer in Venetian art in touch with major collectors. He published a guide to *Venice, *Le minere della pittura* (1644), later expanded as *Ricche minere* (1674), and then a guide to Vicenza, *I gioielli pittoreschi* (1676). His masterpiece is his *Carta del navegar pitoresco* (1660), which recounts, in 5370 rhyming quatrains in Venetian *dialect, a metaphorical voyage over the great sea of Venetian painting, polemically asserting, against *Vasari, its absolute supremacy within Italian art. However, the real originality of the work lies in its new critical language and a direct approach to the individual painting, unconstrained by theoretical preconceptions.   [MC]

BOSI, PINO, see ITALIAN WRITERS IN AUSTRALIA.

BOSONE DA GUBBIO (d. after 1349). Primarily a soldier and politician, he was *podestà* of various cities in the 1320s and elected senator in *Rome in 1337. He also wrote *lyric poetry, participating in a celebrated exchange of *sonnets with *Immanuel Romano lamenting the death of *Dante in 1321.   [SNB]

BOTERO, GIOVANNI (1544–1617) joined the *Jesuits and taught in Italy and France but left the order in 1580, becoming secretary first to Cardinal

Carlo *Borromeo in *Milan under whose influence he wrote *De regia sapientia* (1583), and then to his cousin, Federico *Borromeo, with whom he moved to *Rome. In Rome he wrote his best known works, acquiring a European reputation as an original political writer: *Delle cause della grandezza e magnificenza delle città* (1588) is the first work to analyse urban growth; *Della ragion di stato* (1589) argues against *Machiavelli's dissociation of ethics from politics; the *Relazioni universali* (1591–6) is a geopolitical survey in four parts of the world's states.

From 1599 to 1610 Botero was tutor to the sons of Duke Carlo Emanuele of *Savoy, for whom he composed three collections of *biographies of illustrious men from antiquity to modern times. After a period in Spain with the Savoy princes, which resulted in two treatises on monarchy and nobility, he returned to *Turin and was reconciled with the Jesuit order. The final years of his life brought an increased piety and asceticism, leading to works such as *Rime spirituali* (1609), *Discorso della lega contro il Turco* (1614), the *Carmina selecta* (1615), and *Del Purgatorio* (1615). [See also RAGION DI STATO.]
          [PBert]

BOTTA, CARLO (1766–1837). *Piedmontese doctor and historian, forced into permanent exile in France. His advocacy of Italian *Unification and his reformist ideas cost him both the favour of *Napoleon and his academic post in Rouen after the *Restoration. His major work is *Storia d'Italia dal 1789 al 1814* (1824). His ashes were buried in S. Croce in Florence in 1875.   [EAM]

BOTTAI, GIUSEPPE (1895–1959). *Journalist and politician. As a young man he wrote poetry in the manner of the *Crepuscolari, but he was also a *Futurist. He was one of the first *Fascist deputies, taking part in the March on Rome and then rising rapidly through the party hierarchy. He held various important posts, including the ministries of corporations (1929–32) and education (1936–42), as well as leading a machine-gun battalion in the Ethiopian campaign. He worked hard to make Fascism a modernizing and reforming force in Italy and was responsible for some important cultural initiatives, notably the reviews *Critica fascista* and *Primato. As a member of the Fascist Grand Council, he was a prime mover in the deposition of *Mussolini on 25 July 1943. He then disappeared, eventually joining the French Foreign Legion and fighting against the Germans. After the war he published his *autobiography, *Vent'anni e un giorno* (1951), and his diaries. [PH]

BOTTARI, GIOVANNI GAETANO (1689–1775). *Florentine polymath long resident in *Rome. He indulged a passion for archaeology and the fine arts, and edited Italian texts, while *Vatican librarian and professor of ecclesiastical history. His intellectual openness incurred *Jesuit displeasure. He was chief lexicographer for the 1729–37 edition of the *Crusca dictionary. [JMAL]

Bottega del caffè, La, see GOLDONI, CARLO.

Botteghe oscure. Shorthand term to indicate the headquarters of the *Communist Party (PCI) and later the Democratic Party of the Left (PDS) in *Rome's Via delle botteghe oscure. It has always been seen by activists as the party's power centre and by adversaries as a symbol of the threat it posed. The name was also given to a journal founded by Marguerite *Caetani in 1948. [SG]

BOTTICELLI, SANDRO (1444/5–1510). Major figure in *Florentine *Renaissance painting, whose *patrons included the *Medici. Among his most controversial works are the celebrated *Primavera* (1477–8) and *Birth of Venus* (1482). These have often been interpreted as alluding to the poetry of *Poliziano, in particular the *Stanze*. Others have seen them as expressions of the *Neoplatonic philosophy of Marsilio *Ficino. [CR]

BOURBON. European ruling house, descended from the 14th-c. Dukes of Bourbon, which furnished France with kings in the 17th and 18th c. and, through its Spanish connections, also provided parts of Italy with their rulers. In the 1730s the future Charles III of Spain established a Bourbon dukedom in Parma and then a Bourbon monarchy in *Naples. With interruptions, the most significant of which was in the *Napoleonic period, both lasted until the *Unification of Italy in 1860. There was also briefly a Bourbon kingdom of Etruria (1801–7), and a Bourbon dukedom of Lucca (1815–47). [PH]

Bozzetto, see FUCINI, RENATO; NOVELLA AND RACCONTO, 2.

BRACCESI, ALESSANDRO (1445–1503). *Florentine poet, who was a notary from 1467 until

his death, though he also served on important diplomatic missions and as secretary of the Florentine *signoria*. He put together three books of Latin verse, containing elegiac love poetry and more spontaneous verse to his friends, and an *Epigrammatum libellus* dedicated to Lorenzo de' *Medici. His vernacular *Canzoniere* contains *Petrarchan love poems in the first part, while the second is made up of 200 *sonetti caudati* [see SONNET] in the sarcastic, jocular vein of *Burchiello. Some of his letters have also survived. [DieZ]

BRACCIOLINI, FRANCESCO (1566–1645). *Mock-heroic poet. He was born in Pistoia and studied *law, but was drawn to creative writing from an early age. He served Federico *Borromeo in *Milan from around 1595 to 1600, and Maffeo Barberini, the future Pope *Urban VIII, from 1601 in *Rome. He is best known for his mock-heroic poem *Lo scherno degli dei*, composed in fourteen cantos in 1617 and published in 1618; a second edition in twenty cantos was published in 1626. The work immediately gave rise to a polemic with *Tassoni over whether he or Bracciolini first invented the mock-heroic genre in Italian. Though Tassoni's *Secchia rapita* was not published till 1622, it is now accepted, and indeed was widely accepted then, that it was in existence in an advanced state of composition in 1615, two years before Bracciolini put pen to paper. Bracciolini's work, whose purpose was to mock pagan deities and their use in Italian literature, centres on Venus's revenge against her husband Vulcan, who caught her in adultery with Mars. When all the gods are expelled from heaven, they descend to earth and are slaughtered by humankind, led by Prometheus. Like Tassoni's, this work relies on *parody and the grotesque, and shows some interesting Tuscan linguistic touches. Bracciolini's other works include *epic poems in the style of Torquato *Tasso (*La croce racquistata* (1605 and 1611) and *La Bulgheria convertita* (1637)), as well as dramas and historical works. [PBD]

BRACCIOLINI, IACOPO (1442–78), son of Poggio *Bracciolini, enjoyed the friendship of *Ficino and Alessandro *Braccesi, participating in the informal gatherings known as the *Platonic Academy. Best known for his vernacular *translations (including that of his father's *Florentine history), he became involved in the *Pazzi conspiracy against the *Medici, as a result of which he was apprehended and immediately hanged. [RDB]

Bracciolini, Poggio

BRACCIOLINI, POGGIO (1380–1459), from Terranuova in the Valdarno, was a disciple of *Salutati, leaving *Florence in the early 15th c. for the *Roman curia and remaining in *papal service for half a century. He was largely responsible for the creation of *humanist script, rejecting gothic bookhand in favour of Caroline models [see also MANUSCRIPTS AND MANUSCRIPT PRODUCTION]. The most fortunate of all early humanist bookhunters, he personally recovered many lost Latin classics. With his *De varietate fortunae* (1448) he helped to found the serious study of Roman archaeology. He also composed several lively *Ciceronian *dialogues, but as an author he achieved greatest renown for his salacious anecdotes, the *Facetiae* [see FACEZIE].

Poggio was always an intimate friend of Cosimo de' *Medici, and on the death of *Marsuppini in 1453, he left Nicholas V's Rome, now dominated by a new humanist avant-garde (including his enemy Lorenzo *Valla), to become Florentine chancellor. But he was too old for the bureaucratic demands of the chancery, which nearly collapsed under his direction; his only achievement was the composition of a new history of Florence (*Historiae florentini populi*), even more classical than Leonardo *Bruni's. In 1456 he was dismissed as chancellor, much to the embarrassment of Cosimo de' Medici, whose own position in Florence was near to collapse in the mid-1450s. [See also CLASSICAL SCHOLARSHIP.] [RDB]

BRACCO, ROBERTO (1861–1943), author of over thirty plays, was also a short-story writer, *librettist, and drama critic, who championed the works of Ibsen and Wagner. His early plays, *Una donna* (1893), *Infedele* (1894), *Il trionfo* (1895), and *Don Pietro Caruso* (1895), all well received, showed links with southern *verismo. His plays with a female protagonist, the best of which are *Notte di neve* (1905) and *La piccola fonte* (1905), were followed by the acclaimed *tragedy *Il piccolo santo* (1910), in which the past catches up with the curate of a mountain village, considered saintly by his parishioners. It is in this play that Bracco's talent for dramatizing psychological forces is best seen. In the early 20th c. he was recognized as a major dramatist in Italy and abroad, both for the outspokenness of his themes, in particular in *Sperduti nel buio* (1901), later filmed by *Martoglio, and for his innovations in the dramatic representation of psychological processes. He would be better known today had he not been overshadowed by *Pirandello and had his opposition to *Fascism not reduced him to silence. [JAL]

Bradamante. One of the heroines of *Ariosto's *Orlando furioso*.

BRAGAGLIA, ANTON GIULIO (1890–1960). *Photographer, stage designer, *theatre and film director, gallery proprietor (his Casa d'Arte Bragaglia was pivotal in the interwar avant-garde) and *Futurist theorist. He was one of four brothers who often worked together, the others being the painter and writer Alberto, the photographer and actor Arturo, and the stage and film director Carlo Ludovico. He created a form of multiple-exposure photography, *Fotodinamismo futurista* (1911), and in 1923 founded the Teatro degli Indipendenti, which both embraced current innovation and explored earlier theatrical forms. [CGW]

BRANCA, VITTORE (1913–). One of the most authoritative modern Italian critics. He studied at the Scuola Normale Superiore of *Pisa and taught in *Florence, Catania, *Rome, and from 1953 in *Padua. The foremost expert on *Boccaccio, he has produced the standard annotated edition of the *Decameron*, and has published important works on *Poliziano, *Venetian *humanism, *Alfieri, and *De Marchi. He founded and edits the *periodicals *Studi sul Boccaccio* (1963) and *Lettere italiane* (1949). As a critic he rejected prevailing *Crocean and *Marxist influences in the name both of a severe philological approach and of a robust Catholic inspiration. [See also FILOLOGIA.] [LL]

BRANCATI, VITALIANO (1907–54). *Sicilian novelist and playwright. He published a verse drama, *Fedor* (1928), whilst still a student at Catania University, followed by a one-act play, *Everest* (staged in 1930). His first *novel, *L'amico del vincitore* (1932), was a plainly *Fascist work. By now Brancati was working in *Rome as a *journalist. He met other young intellectuals, including Alberto *Moravia, Leo *Longanesi, Marco Pannunzio, and Arrigo *Benedetti, and in the course of the 1930s distanced himself from both the regime and his own earlier work.

A change of direction was signalled by the novel *Singolare avventura di viaggio* (1934), which was banned by the *censor for its eroticism. In 1938 he returned to Sicily as a teacher, but continued to write for *Omnibus* and *Oggi*. He alternated between Rome and Sicily from 1941 onwards. *Gli anni perduti* (published in 1941, but written in the mid-1930s) is the first of his mature novels. It has the irony, the sense of the grotesque, and the moral lucidity that characterize *Don Giovanni in Sicilia* (1941), *Il bell'Antonio* (1949), and the incomplete *Paolo il caldo* (1955). The characters in these novels live in a stagnating, vacuous Sicilian society, and the protagonists are males obsessed by fantasies of seduction and sexual prowess. Their folly is indicative of a more general human condition, and is used by Brancati to point up the need for a harmonious balance between reason and the senses. However, he soon became convinced that the real world prevented such a harmony from being anything but another illusion, as he charted in articles, essays, and his *Diario romano* (1961). The conflict between external masks and inner realities becomes satire of the pretensions and hollowness of Fascism in much of his fiction, particularly in the short stories of *Il vecchio con gli stivali e altri racconti* (1945).

Brancati's extensive work for the *theatre, which included *Questo matrimonio si deve fare* (1939) and *Don Giovanni involontario* (1943), led him into trouble with the censor again in 1951 over the lesbian content of *La governante*. He responded with the pamphlet *Ritorno alla censura* (1952), which expressed his disillusionment as a radical-liberal intellectual in postwar Italy. Brancati also wrote screenplays for films by Luigi Zampa, Steno and Mario Monicelli, and Roberto *Rossellini.   [AC]
See G. C. Ferretti, *L'infelicità della ragione* (1998).

BRASCA, SANTO (1444/5–after 1522). *Milanese administrator and statesman under the *Sforza. In 1480 he went on a pilgrimage to the Holy Land, and left a detailed account (partly based on the previous one by Gabriele *Capodilista), which includes a lively description of *Venice. [See also TRAVEL WRITING.]   [LL]

Bravure del Capitano Spavento, see ANDREINI, FRANCESCO.

BRESCIANI, ANTONIO, see JEWS AND JUDAISM.

BRESCIANI BORSA, ANTONIO (1798–1862). *Jesuit educator and writer, who became head of the College for the Propagation of the Faith in *Rome. He was an editor of *Civiltà cattolica* from its inception (1850) and published in it both

socio-economic essays and a series of pedagogic *romanzi d'appendice* which *Gramsci was later to attack as the model of anti-*Risorgimento individualism.   [MPC]

BRICCIO, GIOVANNI, see COMMEDIA RIDIC-OLOSA.

Brighella. A mask of the *commedia dell'arte*, a *zanni* or servant, who was invariably clad in a white smock and stockings. The characteristics of this mask changed more than most: originally an intriguing and manipulative figure, he later took on the more solid qualities of the reliable, faithful retainer, often a foil to *Arlecchino, and later transferring easily to the innkeeper or majordomo of *Goldonian comedy.   [KR]

BRIGNOLE SALE, ANTON GIULIO (1605–62). *Novelist and writer, who was born into an eminent *Genoese family, and held various public offices, including serving as ambassador to Madrid (1643–7) at a difficult period in relations between Genoa and *Spain. After his wife's death (1648) he took holy orders and eventually became a *Jesuit.

His literary refinement is evident in *Le instabilità dell'ingegno* (1635), a conversation-novel, including discussions of love, portraits of high society, conventional verse-exercises and a few tragic *novelle*. But *Maria Maddalena peccatrice convertita* (1636) is the masterpiece of the 17th-c. religious novel, depicting the Magdalen's tormented journey to repentance convincingly and with psychological subtlety. *L'istoria spagnuola* (1640–2), set against the backdrop of the wars with the Moors, is more intricately plotted, and full of twists and surprises. Brignole is an elegant portrayer of aristocratic life, whose fineness of touch in his descriptions is without equal in the Italian novel. Nine speeches, delivered in 1636 in the Accademia degli Addormentati and published in 1643 as *Tacito aburattato*, demand that political action should be ruled by a rigorous, modern morality.   [MC]

BRIZZI, ENRICO, see CANNIBALI.

Broadcasting, see RADIO; TELEVISION.

BROCARDO, ANTONIO, see SLANG.

BROCARDO, DOMIZIO (*c.*1390–after 1448). *Paduan poet who enjoyed a good reputation in

Northern Italy. He composed a *canzoniere* which follows, with cold elegance, the *Petrarchan manner. But he also wrote poems inspired by family misfortunes, especially on the death of his beloved daughter Rachele, in which, forsaking literary conventions, he expresses himself in popular forms of touching simplicity. [CG]

BROCCHI, VIRGILIO (1876–1961). *Novelist who enjoyed tremendous success with the public during his lifetime. His mature fiction, largely constructed in cycles of novels, was in the vein of *Fogazzaro, and offered Christian *Socialist representations of petit bourgeois life in the Northern provinces. He combined teaching and writing for many years, and was active in *Milanese politics until his *Secondo il cuor mio* (1919) led to prosecution for defeatism. Though absolved, he withdrew to Liguria where he gave himself over to writing and to editorial work for *Mondadori. [SVM]

BROFFERIO, ANGELO (1802–66). Writer and patriot, born near Asti, who became a politically active *journalist in *Turin and was elected in *1848 to the *Piedmontese parliament, where he consistently opposed *Cavour. He published *Alfierian *tragedies, such as *Eudossia* (1825), poems in Piedmontese *dialect, historical works, and the *autobiographical *I miei tempi*. [DO'G]

BROGLIO, MARIO, see VALORI PLASTICI.

BRONZINO, AGNOLO (Agniolo di Cosimo di Mariano Tori) (1503–72) was court artist to Cosimo I de' *Medici, and a major presence in the *Florentine artistic milieu until the advent of Giorgio *Vasari. He supported Annibale *Caro in his literary dispute with Ludovico *Castelvetro, and himself wrote a considerable corpus of poetry, though very little was published in his own lifetime. [PLR]

BRUCIOLI, ANTONIO (1490/1500–66). *Florentine *humanist who studied under *Diacceto and was well versed in Greek, Latin, and Hebrew. He attended meetings at the Orti Oricellari [see ACADEMIES; RUCELLAI, BERNARDO] and was forced to flee Florence after the failed conspiracy against Giulio de' *Medici in 1522. After coming into contact with Lutheran ideas in *Venice and France, he finally settled in Venice, where he translated the *Bible into the vernacular, and wrote an important commentary on the Old and New Testaments. [See also COUNTER-REFORMATION.] [PLR]

BRUCURELLI, CASSIO (Cassio da Narni) (c.1480–c.1536). Poet. Born at Narni, Cassio was educated at *Ferrara, where he entered the service of Alfonso I d'*Este, and became a close associate of *Niccolò da Correggio, *Tebaldeo, and *Ariosto, whom he regarded as his master in verse. He was author of a *romance *epic, *La morte del Danese* (1521), whose main themes are the rivalry between *Orlando and *Rinaldo, the adventures of the latter, and a journey to the underworld. It is heavily derivative and its language hybrid. [JEE]

BRUNELLESCHI, FILIPPO (1377–1461). *Florentine sculptor and architect, most famous for the dome of Florence cathedral, who struck the imagination of his contemporaries for his extraordinary intelligence in solving apparently irresolvable dilemmas. These are qualities recorded in Brunelleschi's own vernacular *sonnets; in the *Novella del grasso legnaiuolo*, which records a *beffa or practical joke in which he was involved; and in Antonio *Manetti's biography of him. [LB]

BRUNI, ANTONIO (1593–1635). One of the most successful of *Marino's southern followers, who worked principally in *Urbino and *Rome. His *concettismo* was more conventional in content than Marino's, and he expressed reservations concerning his *Adone. He retained the favour of *Urban VIII when *concettismo* fell from grace in Rome, and his lyrics, contained in *Le tre grazie* (1630), continued to be appreciated into the 18th c. His most original works are the *Epistole eroiche* (1626), ostensibly verse letters written by historical and literary characters, which combine imitation of *Ovid and Marino with other sources from Tacitus to Torquato *Tasso. [MPS]

BRUNI, LEONARDO (?1370–1444). *Humanist and native of Arezzo, hence also known as Leonardo Aretino. A disciple of Coluccio *Salutati, Bruni was among the first generation of humanists to know *Greek, which he learnt from Manuel *Chrysoloras in *Florence (1397–1400). Becoming a *papal secretary, he returned briefly in 1410–11 to assume the Florentine chancellorship. He returned to the papal curia and attended the Council of Constance in 1415, then went back to Florence permanently in the same year, becoming a Florentine citizen in 1416. In 1412 Bruni married Tommasa da Filicaia, the daughter of a leading Florentine patrician; his close links with the Florentine oligarchy were confirmed by his only son Donato's marriage into the Castellani family in 1431. Although Bruni superficially cultivated the *Medici, who were challenging the Florentine oligarchy's power in the later 1420s and early 1430s, he remained closer to the opposing *Albizzi faction. In 1427, when the Florentine bureaucracy became embroiled in this factional conflict, Bruni was appointed chancellor, widely regarded as a compromise candidate. Following the division of the chancery into two sections in 1437, he became first chancellor, nominally in charge of administering Florentine diplomacy, but any loss of bureaucratic importance was compensated when at the same time he was all but officially admitted to the ruling group, holding a series of the city's most important political offices until his death.

Bruni became the most celebrated humanist between *Petrarch and Erasmus: there are nearly 3,200 manuscripts and about 200 incunables of his works and translations. He made a significant contribution to Italian vernacular prose with his lives of *Dante, *Boccaccio, and Petrarch. His Latin versions of Greek classics established a new style of humanist *translation, in which the medieval word-for-word method was replaced by an attempt to render the overall meaning of the text in *Ciceronian Latin. He was the first to revive the *Livian model of the history of a city-state with his *Historia florentini populi* [see also HISTORIOGRAPHY, 1]. Bruni also initiated the great revival of the Ciceronian *dialogue in *Renaissance literature with his dialogues addressed to Pier Paolo *Vergerio the Elder, *Dialogi ad Petrum Histrum,* on the status and value of Dante, Petrarch, and Boccaccio. He was once argued to have been a keen 'civic humanist', but his Florentine patriotism and commitment to active civic participation actually vacillated throughout his life; in the field of political thought, his greatest contribution may have been to reconcile the popular republican tradition of Florence with the rise of oligarchy, dominated successively by the Albizzi and Medici regimes.

[RDB]

See H. Baron, *The Crisis of the Early Italian Renaissance* (1966); J. Hankins, *Repertorium Brunianum: A Critical Guide to the Writings of Leonardo Bruni,* vol. i (1997); A. Field, 'Leonardo Bruni, Florentine Traitor', *Renaissance Quarterly,* vol. 51 (1998).

BRUNO, GIORDANO (1548–1600), the most inspiring philosopher of the late Italian *Renaissance, was born at Nola, near *Naples, and in 1565 entered the Neapolitan monastery of S. Domenico Maggiore, where he was ordained in 1573. However, in February 1576, as a consequence of two infractions which revealed his rebellious temperament as well as his unorthodox religious views, he fled to *Rome in order to avoid a trial, then abandoned the *Dominican Order, and proceeded to the North of Italy. There he wandered for two years until, in 1578, he moved to Geneva, where he formally embraced Calvinism; but he soon fell into trouble with the local Church, by which he was excommunicated though subsequently reprieved. However, resentful of the way he had been treated, he moved to Toulouse, where he obtained a lectureship in philosophy, which he kept for two years, moving to Paris in 1581. Henry III, who initially had shown interest in Bruno's art of memory, appointed him one of his *lecteurs royaux,* who lectured outside the Sorbonne in opposition to its *Aristotelian conformism. Still in Paris, he published two works on the art of memory, which anticipate some of the cosmological and ethical ideas developed in his later works, followed by a work on the philosophy of knowledge inspired by Ramon Llull's *Ars magna,* and the comedy *Candelaio.*

In the first months of 1583 Bruno's presence in Paris became an embarrassment to the tolerant Henry III, as a result of increasing pressures from the French Catholic League, and he was dispatched to the service of the French ambassador in London, with either a political or a diplomatic role, or simply as a gentleman in the ambassador's retinue. In 1583 Bruno twice visited Oxford, where he held a public dispute on Aristotelian logic with John Underhill, and gave a course of lectures on the human soul and on Copernican cosmology; but these incurred the displeasure of the audience, and he was forced to terminate them. Back in London, Bruno aligned himself with a group of scientific writers under court patronage (including Thomas Digges), who sympathized with Copernican theory and, unlike the Oxford *humanists, wrote in English. In London in 1583–5 Bruno published a volume containing three works in Latin on the art of memory and six philosophical *dialogues in the vernacular: three on cosmology (*La cena de le ceneri, De la causa, principio et uno, De l'infinito universo et mondi*), in which he intuitively goes beyond Copernican theory to envisage the infinity of the world; and three on moral topics (*Spaccio de la bestia trionfante, Cabala* *del cavallo pegaseo, De gli heroici furori*), the first two satirizing traditional philosophical theories as well as Christian beliefs, and the third exalting, both in poetry and in prose, the universal immanence of God as opposed to the Christian idea of transcendence.

Back in Paris in autumn 1585, he found himself deprived of the support of the moderate party of the King, owing to increased Catholic pressure on the latter. However, he did not refrain from attacking in print a protégé of the Catholic Duke of Guise, or from attacking Aristotle in a debate at the Collège de Cambrai. Once again he had to flee, this time to Germany (June 1586), where he wandered from one university city to another: Marburg, Wittenberg, Prague, and Helmsted (where he was excommunicated by the Lutheran church), publishing some minor Latin works, and lecturing when allowed to do so. By June 1590 he had reached Frankfurt, where his three Latin poems were published in 1591: *De minimo, De monade, De immenso* (written in a style reminiscent of Lucretius's *De rerum natura*), which constitute the second systematic exposition of his thought, and are partly connected with his previous cosmological dialogues in the vernacular. In the late summer of 1591 Bruno imprudently moved to *Venice, at the invitation of the patrician Mocenigo, but really attracted by the *University of *Padua, where he delivered his *Praelectiones geometricae*, his last known work. In May 1592 his host denounced him to the Venetian *Inquisition, and after an inconclusive trial he was transferred in February 1593 to Rome, where, at the end of a second trial which lasted seven years, he was sentenced to death and burnt alive on 17 February 1600. [GAq]

Œuvres complètes, vols. i–vii (*Opere italiane*), ed. G. Aquilecchia (1993–9); *Opera latine conscripta*, ed. F. Fiorentino *et al.* (1879–91). See G. Aquilecchia, *Giordano Bruno* (1971); F. A. Yates, *Giordano Bruno and the Hermetic Tradition* (1964).

BRUSANTINO, VINCENZO (d.1556). *Ferrarese nobleman, and author of *Angelica innamorata* (1550), a sequel to the *Orlando furioso*, in which the elusive heroine of *Ariosto's poem is ensnared by a magic spell which makes her fall in love with every available male. He also wrote a verse version of *Boccaccio's *Decameron* (1554). [RMD]

BRUSONI, GIROLAMO (1614–after 1686)

led a restless life as monk, ex-monk, *poligrafo, and political correspondent, but his literary production, mainly linked to the Accademia degli *Incogniti, was immense—historical works, *biographies, stories, *novels, plays, *translations, scurrilous pamphlets, and other literary and political articles. From 1676, he served the House of *Savoy as a *historiographer, and devoted himself to writing the *Istoria d'Italia*, reworking his earlier *Guerre d'Italia dall'anno 1635 fino al 1655*, the definitive edition being published in 1680. Court intrigues forced him to leave in July 1686, after which nothing is known of him. He is best known for a sequence of three novels, *La gondola a tre remi* (1657), *Il carrozzino alla moda* (1658), and *La peota smarrita* (1662), which recounts the vicissitudes of an adventurer, Glisomiro, and his entourage of friends and hangers-on, and provides a portrait of contemporary life in the *Venetian territories. [MC]

Bucolicum carmen, see PETRARCH, FRANCESCO.

BUFALINO, GESUALDO (1920–96). *Sicilian writer. After teaching in a *liceo* in his home town of Comiso for most of his life, he published his first novel, *Diceria dell'untore*, in 1981 at the age of 61, largely thanks to the encouragement of Leonardo *Sciascia and his publisher, *Sellerio. It was a remarkable success, and from 1981 until his death in a car accident, Bufalino wrote and published with impressive intensity. He and Vincenzo *Consolo were the main figures in the resurgence of Sicilian fiction in the 1980s.

Diceria dell'untore was loosely based on his experiences in a TB sanatorium outside Palermo at the end of *World War II. *Argo il cieco* (1984) was similarly autobiographical, looking back to a year spent away from Comiso as a young teacher in the 1950s. He also published a collection of short stories, *L'uomo invaso* (1986), historical fiction, notably *Le menzogne della notte* (1988), a parody of a *detective novel, *Qui pro quo* (1991), and a collection of poetry, *L'amaro miele* (1988). Amongst his most evocative writings are collections of short prose pieces, some of them originally newspaper articles, on Sicily and Sicilian culture, especially *Museo d'ombre* (1982) and *La luce e il lutto* (1988).

Though situating himself in a wider European tradition, Bufalino looks back particularly to his fellow Sicilians, *Pirandello and *Brancati, taking up their concerns with the multiplicity of character, the search for identity, and the meaninglessness of existence, though his primary theme is the absurd, inimical, and ineluctable power of death. But his pessimism is offset by irony and humour, and even more by the exuberance of his highly literary style. Unlike Sciascia and Consolo, Bufalino is not moralistic in his representations of Sicily and does not polemicize against the *Mafia or political malaise. He is more concerned with the destruction by time and modern society of age-old practices and, more positively, with following back the tradition of Sicilian culture and thought to ancient Sicilians such as Empedocles and Gorgias, whose cast of mind he sees as still evident in Pirandello.   [AWM]

   See N. Zago, *Gesualdo Bufalino* (1981); P. Hainsworth, 'Gesualdo Bufalino', in L. Pertile and Z. Baranski (eds.), *The New Italian Novel* (1993).

Bufera e altro, La, see MONTALE, EUGENIO.

BUONACCORSI, FILIPPO (Callimachus Experiens) (1437–96) was a member of the *Accademia Romana. In 1468 he had to leave *Rome in connection with a conspiracy against the Pope, and ended his life in Poland. He is the author of *Epigrammata*, and an important figure in the 15th-c. revival of *Epicureanism.   [LB]

BUONACCORSO DA MONTEMAGNO (?1390–1429). Poet and lawyer from Pistoia. He was active in the Florentine *studio* from 1421 and undertook political and diplomatic missions for Pistoia and *Florence. He composed a short *Petrarchan *canzoniere* (twenty-six *sonnets, one stanza of a *canzone*, and a *madrigal), in which some poems by his grandfather, the elder Buonaccorso da Montemagno, were confusingly inserted at an early date. He also wrote some Italian *Orazioni*, connected with his political activities, and a Latin treatise, *De nobilitate*, on the typically *humanist topic of whether nobility stems from birth or virtue.   [MP]

BUONAFEDE, APPIANO (1716–93). Celestine monk and polygraph [see POLIGRAFI], noted for his attempts to out-reason contemporary rationalism. He composed Italy's first full-length history of philosophy in his seven-volume *Della istoria e dell'indole d'ogni filosofia* (1766–81), a lively but superficial summary-cum-refutation, belittling non-Christian thought, of J. J. Brucker's *Historia critica philosophiae* (1742–4). His name is indissolubly linked to that of *Baretti, whose slashing review of his comedy *I filosofi fanciulli*, in *La Frusta*

letteraria, provoked a vitriolic pamphlet, *Il bue pedagogo* (1764), subsequently outdone by Baretti in witty vituperation.   [JMAL]

BUONARROTI, FILIPPO, see NAPOLEON AND THE FRENCH REVOLUTION.

BUONARROTI, MICHELANGELO (THE YOUNGER) (1568–1646) was the *Florentine nephew of the older *Michelangelo Buonarroti. He composed and staged a number of entertainments for the *Medici *court, and contributed to the *Vocabolario della Crusca*. His interest in popular language contributed to two dramatic spectacles of notable importance, which adapt an established genre of Tuscan rustic comedy for the courtly stage. *La fiera* is a set of five five-act *comedies portraying genre scenes of country life in the market place; *La Tancia* deals with a contest between a citizen and a rustic for the hand of a village maiden, which the citizen loses. Like contemporary *pastoral drama, these plays fashionably romanticize the supposedly simple rural life, but draw on different *theatre traditions. Opinions may differ as to whether Buonarroti is genuinely sympathetic to his characters or merely patronizing; but his serious interest in vernacular speech gives him at least one link to reality.   [RAA]

BUONINSEGNI, FRANCESCO, see TARABOTTI, ARCANGELA.

BUONTALENTI, BERNARDO (1523–1608) was raised at the court of Cosimo I de' *Medici, and served as an architect, engineer, painter, designer, and inventor. He was an important *theatre designer, developing the perspective for the staging of Giovan Battista *Cini's *Il Baratto* in 1577. He was also responsible for the stage effects and costumes of the *intermezzi* for the Medici wedding of 1589.
          [PLR]

BURCHIELLO, IL (1404–49). The pseudonym of Domenico di Giovanni, a *Florentine barber in the quarter of Calimala, who took his name from the poems he wrote *alla burchia*, that is, in an (ostensibly) casual fashion. He was a friend in Florence of wits and artists, including Leon Battista *Alberti, and, possibly, *Brunelleschi. Perhaps on account of hostility to the *Medici, he left Florence for *Siena, where his misdemeanours earned him a spell in prison. In 1443 he moved to *Rome, where he spent the rest of his life.

His characteristic *sonetti caudati* [see SONNET] are largely comical and *satirical, and cover literary polemics as well as everyday life. With their tendency to riddle and paradox they have often, for the modern reader, a surreal air, which is accentuated by the use of ambiguity, rare slang, and obscure topical references. But the style is generally more referential than metaphorical, and the poems were intended to be recited rather than to be read, though they probably do not represent a popular everyday *Tuscan trend, as was once thought. Burchiello is, if anything, a literary expressionist, whose consummate art presupposes a knowledge of poetry and rhetoric.

His production is large but its limits are difficult to determine. Already in his own lifetime his manner had been taken up by others and many sonnets were passed off under his name. *Sonetti burchielleschi* continued to be written in Florence until well into the 16th c.   [DieZ]

BURCKHARDT, JACOB (1818–97). A professor of history at the University of Basel for most of his career, he was the main originator of the modern conception of the *Renaissance through his essay *Die Kultur der Renaissance in Italien* (1860), translated as *The Civilization of the Renaissance in Italy*. With its themes of the development of the individual and the discovery of the world and of man, the book showed the key role of Italy in the development of a new culture in Europe.   [DR]

Burle, see FACEZIE.

Burlesque, see PARODY AND PASTICHE; POESIA GIOCOSA; SATIRE.

BUSENELLO, GIOVAN FRANCESCO (1598–1659). *Venetian lawyer who wrote *libretti for various *operas, including *Monteverdi's *Incoronazione di Poppea*, defended *Marino, and also wrote occasional verse of his own. A pupil of Paolo *Sarpi and Cesare *Cremonini, he has been associated with Gian Francesco *Loredan and Venetian *libertinism, though his writings and legal career suggest a fairly conventional member of his class.   [MPS]

BUSI, ALDO (1948–) is one of Italy's most prominent and prolific contemporary writers. He has also established himself as a media celebrity, famous for his outrageous charm, and as an acute critic of conventional morality, who makes no secret of his *homosexuality nor of his scepticism towards the conventions of gay society. *Seminario sulla gioventù* (1984), *Vita standard di un venditore provvisorio di collant* (1985), and *La delfina bizantina* (1986) are three extravagantly plotted novels that he published in quick succession. His subsequent work has included idiosyncratic *travel writing, a version of *Boccaccio's *Decameron*, a controversial book on women, and a collection of his replies to problem-page letters. He has also written for the *cinema.

His work consistently confounds conventional expectations of genre and is characterized by great semantic richness, combining standard Italian with *dialect and popular forms particularly from his home town of Brescia. The content of his work is equally challenging, especially his explicit depiction of sex between men. His aims are clearest in the travel narrative *Sodomie in corpo 11* (1988), which uses sex as a prism through which to explore different cultures and understand what he sees as the grotesque and corrupt cruelty of social relations.
                                                        [DD]

BUTI, see FRANCESCO DI BARTOLO DA BUTI.

BUTTI, ENRICO ANNIBALE (1868–1912). *Milanese playwright and novelist who pioneered an Ibsenian *theatre of ideas in Italy. In his *Trilogia degli atei* (1900–1), *La fine di un ideale* (1900), and *Sempre così* (1911), he examines *Positivism, atheism, *feminism, and *socialism from a conservative prospective. His novel *L'automa* (1892) foreshadows *Svevo and *Tozzi in portraying an 'inetto'.   [PBarn]

BUTTITTA, IGNAZIO (1899–1997). *Sicilian poet and *cantautore. With little formal education, he published his first verse and songs (in the *dialect of Bagheria) in the 1920s. His work centres on events in the political and social struggles of the *peasant and working classes in Sicily and Italy as a whole.   [SVM]

BUZZATI, DINO (1906–72) was a *journalist on the *Milanese *Corriere della sera* from 1928 until his death. Unlike most contemporary authors, he never committed himself to any political party. He wrote short stories and novels, children's books, poems, several plays, and opera *libretti, with a tinge of fantasy and sometimes *allegory [see also CHILDREN'S LITERATURE; FANTASTIC; NOVELLA AND RACCONTO, 2]. He was also a painter, dealing with subjects as fantastic as his stories. His concerns were with unspoken longings and fears, the search for and the horror of the unknown, the passing of time, and in particular death.

His first novel, *Bàrnabo delle montagne* (1933), started to explore this private world through a figure who comes to terms with a moment of cowardice by chosing to face the challenge again in the solitude of the mountain peaks. With an air of fairy-tale *Il segreto del Bosco Vecchio* (1935) sees a young boy, Benvenuto, initiated into his inheritance. Giovanni Drogo in *Il*deserto dei tartari* (1940) goes heroically to an ignominious death. The prince in the title story of *I sette messaggeri* (1942) searches for the boundary of his father's kingdom, but through Buzzati's mastery of ambiguity the reader sees the enterprise either dwindling into uncertainty and death or becoming a triumphant and transcendent progress into the unknown. *Il grande ritratto* (1960) is Buzzati's nearest approach to *science fiction, set in a secret scientific establishment which has taken on the persona of a woman, Laura, and become a predatory labyrinth. *Un amore* (1963) features another woman, a Milanese prostitute, Laide, with whom an architect, Antonio Dorigo, falls hopelessly in love.

Buzzati was at his best in his short stories, sixty of which were collected in *Sessanta racconti* (1958). Other collections are *Paura alla Scala* (1949), *Il crollo della Baliverna* (1957), *Il colombre* (1966), and *Le notti difficili* (1971). *In quel preciso momento* (1950) and *Egregio signore, siamo spiacenti di . . .* (1960) capture the finesse of his briefer narrative moments. *Poema a fumetti* (1969) is a strip cartoon on the Orpheus and Eurydice story, set in contemporary Milan, and mixing surrealistic illustrations with poetic narrative. He has been discussed lately in terms of *post-modernism and *realismo magico.

[JR]

See G. Oli, *Dino Buzzati* (1988); N. Giannetto, *Il coraggio della fantasia: studi e ricerche intorno a Dino Buzzati* (1989).

BUZZI, PAOLO (1874-1956) was a *Milanese civil servant and a prolific poet and writer. His most interesting work is associated with the *Futurist movement. After a period under neo-classical, *symbolist, and *Scapigliatura influence, during which he wrote poetry and drama, he collaborated with *Marinetti upon the latter's return from Paris. They co-founded with *Benelli the cosmopolitan review *Poesia* (1905).

After joining the Futurist movement in 1909, Buzzi contributed to the anthology *I poeti futuristi* (1912) with several poems and an important essay on *free verse. His two collections of Futurist poetry, *Aeroplani* (1909) and *Versi liberi* (1913), both maintain a conventional free-verse format, and are less visually experimental than Futurist 'parole in libertà', but draw on Futurist technique in their subject matter and use of striking analogies. Much more experimental are his long prose poem, *L'esilio* (1906), his so-called 'film+parole in libertà', *L'ellisse e la spirale* (1915), and *Conflagrazione* (written in 1915–18 but published posthumously). He also wrote some Futurist *theatre sketches, or 'sintesi'. Several collections, such as *Bel canto* (1916), followed after this avant-garde period; they alternate between Futurist and more traditional poetic forms. He later translated Baudelaire (1922), and wrote further drama, criticism, and narrative.

[RSCG]

Byzantium. From the 6th to the 11th c. parts of Italy, particularly in the South, were under Byzantine political control. The presence in *Sicily, Calabria, and Terra d'Otranto of Basilian monasteries, which used the Greek rite and liturgy, ensured that Byzantine cultural influence would remain strong in Southern Italy long after the fall of Constantinople in 1453, with Greek surviving as a spoken language in rural villages into the 20th c. Barlaam of Calabria, *Petrarch's Greek teacher, and *Leonzio Pilato, who translated Homer into Latin for *Boccaccio, were products of this Italo-Greek culture.

Close commercial and diplomatic ties existed between Italy and Byzantium throughout the *Middle Ages. Increasingly desperate attempts to reunite the Eastern and Western churches to counter the Turkish threat, though fruitless, nevertheless brought Italian and Greek ecclesiastics into contact, culminating in the Council of *Ferrara–*Florence in 1438–9, attended by the Byzantine emperor and leading Orthodox churchmen. Some 15th-c. Italian *humanists travelled to Constantinople to learn Greek; others were taught by Byzantine émigrés to Italy. These scholars further contributed to the revival of Greek studies by bringing manuscripts of works unknown in the West, which they copied as scribes, edited for printers like Aldo *Manuzio, commented upon, and translated into Latin. [See also CLASSICAL SCHOLARSHIP; GREEK WRITING IN ITALY.]

[JK]

C

Caccia. Originally a lyric poem set to music. Designed for two voices, the lyrics were alternated with instrumental interludes. Of 13th-c. French origin, the genre spread to Italy at the beginning of the 14th c. Despite its name, the *caccia* was used to describe not only hunting but also festivals and idyllic scenes as well as tumultuous events such as fires or crushes of crowds, although its nomenclature almost certainly indicates its original subject. Those who used the form include Niccolò *Soldanieri, Franco *Sacchetti, and Lorenzo de' *Medici; elements of it can also be seen in *Poliziano's *Stanze per la giostra*. The genre quickly reached the height of its popularity and then declined, although it endured until the 17th c.

[GPTW]

CACCIA DA SIENA, see SICULO-TUSCAN POETS.

Caccia di Belfiore, see BONCIANI, ANTONIO.

Caccia di Diana (1334). Narrative poem by *Boccaccio and one of his earliest works. It consists of eighteen *canti in *terza rima*, each exactly fifty-eight lines long, and represents a morning's *hunting by a band of *Neapolitan noble ladies under the leadership of Diana, concluding however with her rejection and the triumph of a probably allegorical Venus.

[PH]

Cacciaguida. *Dante's ancestor, whom he meets in *Paradiso*.

CACCIANIGA, ANTONIO (1823–1909). Prolific novelist and writer who lived and worked in principally in his native Treviso. Much of his writing extols rural virtues and evokes the dangers of the city. The rural Veneto is also the setting for his *Risorgimento *historical novels, such as his most ambitious work, the generational saga *La famiglia Bonifazio* (1886).

[JD]

CACCIARI, MASSIMO (1944–). *Venetian philosopher who teaches in the faculty of architecture at Venice University. He founded the radical journal *Contropiano* (1968) with *Asor Rosa, and was a *Communist member of parliament (1976–83). He has written extensively on German philosophy, though a more theological and mystical strain is present in *L'angelo necessario* (1986). He has since continued both with his political activities, becoming a highly public figure as mayor of Venice, and with his philosophical writing, which is notable for its idiosyncratically discordant style.

[JEB]

CACCINI, GIULIO, see CAMERATA DE' BARDI.

CAETANI. A powerful *Roman family whose position was greatly strengthened by the election of Benedetto Caetani as Pope *Boniface VIII. In later centuries its members were also prominent in the culture of the Kingdom of *Naples. Scipione (d. before 1612) wrote sonnets for his aunt Lavinia and maritime poetry. Filippo (*c.*1565–1614), governor of Salerno from 1605, poet and author of the comedies *Ortensia, La schiava,* and *Li due vecchi,* helped to found the Accademia di Belle Arti of Naples in 1611. Onorato (1742–97), a priest, wrote historical works and a guide to *Sicily, founded the Biblioteca Caetani between 1775 and 1785, and established the Specola Caetani with his brother Francesco (1738–1810) to promote scientific studies. Marguerite (née Chapin, 1880–1963) held literary and cultural soirées and founded the reviews *Commerce* (Paris, 1918–39) and *Botteghe oscure* (Rome, 1948–60).

[GPTW]

Cafés. The main venues for literary society in the *Renaissance were the villa and *court. Both retained their importance during the period of the *Arcadian *academies, but the 18th c. saw the emergence in Italy of the coffee-house as a social, commercial and cultural meeting-point. A lightly satirized but fairly innocuous image of *Venetian coffee society is presented by *Goldoni in *La botte-ga del caffè* (1750). But, as in France and England, coffee-houses were often the seedbeds of reformist, *Enlightenment thinking. The periodical *Il *Caffè* (1764–6), which aimed at opening up the terms of intellectual debate after the manner of the *Spectator* and the *Tatler*, pretended to report discussions that took place in Demetrio's coffee-house in *Milan.

Cafés became the customary meeting-places for writers and artists during the 19th c., particularly for groups and movements of a more rebellious nature. The *Scapigliati* frequented the Caffè Martini and the Caffè Gnocchi in Milan, as well as various *osterie*, one of which, the Osteria Marietta, became the principal location for *Rovani's talks on aesthetics to an audience of writers, artists, and musicians. By the earlier 20th c. literary society was generally more staid, but aspiring writers and artists still found cafés congenial—warm in winter, inexpensive (if you bought only one coffee), and independent of patrons and authority. Certain cafés became almost literary clubs in the 1920s and 1930s. In *Rome there was the Caffè Aragno, frequented by *Ungaretti and his circle. In *Florence, which with some justification considered itself the literary and artistic capital of the country, the most famous café was the Giubbe Rosse in what is now Piazza della Repubblica. This was the meeting-point for *Montale and writers of the *Solaria* group, both those who lived in Florence and others like *Gadda or *Saba who visited at intervals. Opposite the Giubbe Rosse was the Paszkowski, the café of writers more committed to the *Fascist regime such as Berto *Ricci, *Bilenchi, and Dino Garrone, who gathered around the painter Ottone *Rosai. For a while the Caffè San Marco near the university was the centre for a more *hermetic group, which included *Bo, *Luzi, and *Landolfi, though after a while there was a migration to the Giubbe Rosse.

Postwar *impegno* was ideologically opposed to the leisurely style of prewar café society, and the changing nature of the intellectuals' situation and role saw the functions of the literary café displaced into the *universities or rendered public by television and other media. A late example was the Caffè Mazzara in Palermo, where in the 1950s *Tomasi di Lampedusa met his younger disciples and wrote part of the *Gattopardo*. [PH]

See S. Guarnieri, *L'ultimo testimone* (1989).

CAFFARO, see CHRONICLES.

Caffè, Il (1764–1766). *Periodical founded in *Milan by Pietro *Verri with the support of his brother Alessandro, *Beccaria, Gianrinaldo *Carli, and other figures of the Lombard *Enlightenment. Printed in Brescia (which was then under the rule of *Venice), it was one of a number of journals making their appearance on the peninsula influenced by English reviews such as the *Spectator* and the *Tatler*. It nevertheless differed greatly from its Italian counterparts in style and orientation. Articles took the form of reported discussions between the cultured clients of Demetrio, the Greek owner of a Milanese *café. The aim was to challenge the reader. On social and economic matters, the journal reflected the arguments and proposals for reform which emerged from the debates of the members of the Accademia dei Pugni, the name given to the group of intellectuals who met under the inspiration of Pietro Verri. In other areas it contained contributions by Beccaria on aesthetics, Pietro Verri's defence of *Goldoni's *theatre against the attacks of *Baretti, Gianrinaldo *Carli's essay on the cultural unity of Italians, and the anti-*purist arguments of the Verri brothers for an Italian language closer to common usage. [GLCB]

CAGNA, GIOVANNI, see SCAPIGLIATURA.

CAJUMI, ARRIGO (1899–1955). *Journalist and critic from *Turin, who wrote for *La Stampa* and for the anti-*Fascist *Il *Baretti* and *La *rivoluzione liberale*. He was one of the main figures behind the *periodical *La Cultura* until its suppression in 1935. *Pensieri di un libertino* (1947) is a collection of reflections stemming from his travails under Fascism. After *World War II he returned to journalism, writing for *Il *Mondo* and again for *La Stampa*. Cajumi's critical work focuses on French literature, but he also joined in debates on Italian *modernism. [DCH]

CALAMANDREI, PIERO (1899–1956). Academic lawyer from *Florence who became an anti-*Fascist politician. As a representative of the *Partito d'Azione, he played an important role in establishing Italy's new constitution after *World War II. He wrote extensively on contemporary politics and founded the review *Il *Ponte* in 1945. He also published children's stories earlier in his career. [DCH]

CALANDRA, EDOARDO (1852–1911). *Turinese novelist, best known for *historical novels set in *Piedmont during the *Napoleonic Wars, in particular *La bufera* (1899), and winning the admiration of *Croce for his even-handedness and humanity. He also wrote fantastic *novelle* resembling those of the *Scapigliati*. He was a professional illustrator who illustrated books by *Giacosa and *Verga. [PBarn]

Calandra, La (1513) by Bernardo *Dovizi (il Bibbiena) is the first *comedy to involve twins of opposite sexes. Lidio and Santilla, circulating separately in cross-dressed disguise, wreak havoc among lovers and acquaintances by being constantly mistaken for one another. Meanwhile Calandro, the archetypal idiot, is humiliated and cuckolded by his servant and his wife. [RAA]

Calandrino. Foolish and gullible character in *Boccaccio's *Decameron*.

CALARELLI, NAZARENO, see CARDARELLI, VINCENZO.

CALASSO, ROBERTO (1941–). Writer and director of the Adelphi *publishing house. He has published numerous essays and some distinctive narrative works, which incorporate *literary criticism, anthropology, and philosophy. His major project, inaugurated by *La rovina di Kasch* (1983), is to retell ancient, culture-specific mythologies on a pan-cultural scale. His greatest international success, the encyclopedic *Le nozze di Cadmo e Armonia* (1988), rewrites classical European mythology from a modern perspective, rigorously and self-critically examining the distorting effect of scholarship and received ideas, but celebrating the value of myths as the source understanding human behaviour and aesthetics. *Ka* (1996) explores the origins of Buddhism. [JEB]

CALCAGNINI, CELIO (1479–1541). *Ferrarese *humanist, philosopher, polymath, diplomat, and, in early life, soldier. His (Latin) writings, which cover a vast range of topics, include some anti-Lutheran polemic, and an astronomical treatise (1518–19) proposing that the earth moves around its axis at the centre of the universe [see COSMOLOGY]. He was a friend of *Ariosto and Erasmus. [DK]

CALCOLONA, ETTORE, see CELANO, CARLO.

CALDERINI, DOMIZIO (1445–*c.*1478) was a gifted *humanist whose lectures in *Rome attracted students away from those of Giulio Pomponio *Leto. After taking minor orders in 1471, he became a papal secretary but continued his humanist labours. The most famous of these was an edition and commentary on Martial, which provoked a polemic with the other great contemporary Martial critic, Niccolò Perotti. He also established editions of Juvenal and Statius, but his textual methods were soon eclipsed by the more rigorous philology of *Poliziano, whose readings were based on the most authoritative manuscripts, and who attacked Calderini in his *Miscellanea* for his purely conjectural emendations. [See also CLASSICAL SCHOLARSHIP.] [MMcL]

CALDERINI, GIOVANNI (*c.*1300–1365). Canon lawyer from *Bologna, where he taught until 1359. His influential works on canon law were widely diffused after the invention of *printing. He had an unusally large personal library containing vernacular as well as Latin texts. [JP & JMS]

CALDERONI, ANSELMO (1393–1446). *Florentine poet, who spent some time in in the service of Guidantonio da *Montefeltro in *Urbino. He was known for his dissipated way of life, though he was appointed herald to the Signoria in 1442. His not extensive production includes two outstanding political *canzoni, and some satirical *sonnets written against *Burchiello, whose friend he had once been. [DieZ]

CALEPIO, PIETRO (1693–1762). Bergamasque noble who played a major role in Italo-German literary relations through his thirty-year correspondence (1728–61) with G. G. Bodmer of Zurich, whom he introduced to *Arcadian aesthetics. In 1732 Bodmer published his *Paragone della poesia tragica d'Italia con quella di Francia*, which foreshadows Lessing's *Hamburgische Dramaturgie* (1767–9) in its critique of French classical drama. [JMAL]

CALEPIO, TRUSSARDO (1784–?1834). One of the more extreme *classicist voices in the verbal battle over *Romanticism of 1816. Deeply hostile to the liberalism of *Il *Conciliatore*, he made his views known in his weekly *L'accattabrighe, ossia classico-romanticomachia*, which enjoyed a brief existence in *Milan in 1818. [MPC]

CALIFRONIA, ROSA, see WOMEN WRITERS, 2.

Calligrafismo, see SOLDATI, MARIO.

Callimaco, see MANDRAGOLA, LA.

CALLONI, SILVIO, see ITALIAN WRITERS IN SWITZERLAND.

CALMETA, IL (c.1460–1508), born Vincenzo Colli, was from Castelnuovo Scrivia not far from Pavia. Little is known of his early life until 1490–1, when he appeared in *Rome in the circle of Paolo *Cortesi. Here he probably took the name by which he is known (from the figure of a shepherd in Boccaccio's *Filocolo), and formed a lasting friendship with *Serafino Aquilano, whose *biography he later wrote (1504), giving an interesting account of intellectual life at the Italian *courts. Moving to *Milan in 1494 as secretary to Beatrice d'*Este, he lamented her death in 1497 in five *Triumphi*. Following a period spent in the service of Cesare *Borgia, whom he accompanied on campaigns throughout Italy, he established himself at the *Urbino court of Ercole Pio, and later of Francesco Maria della Rovere. Here he supposedly formulated the theory of the *lingua cortigiana attacked by Pietro *Bembo in the *Prose della volgar lingua, and defended by *Castiglione. Unfortunately, the work in which these ideas were probably explained, the *Nove libri della volgar poesia*, has been lost. As testimony to Calmeta's much-vaunted critical abilities there remains a prose miscellany, the *Annotationi e iudici*, which contains discussions on a variety of subjects, including a famous criticism of the lyrics of *Tebaldeo. [See also QUESTIONE DELLA LINGUA.]

[ELM]

CALMO, ANDREA (1510–71). Venetian actor, playwright, and poet. From an artisan background, Calmo became the outstanding exponent of *polyglot theatre in *Venice in the mid-16th c., performing before socially mixed audiences. His farcical *comedies feature an entertaining babel of languages, pidgins, and accents, and demand to be seen rather than read: *Las Spagnolas* (1549), *Saltuzza* (1551), *La potione* (1552), *La Rodiana* (1553), *La Fiorina* (1553), and *Travaglia* (1556). Calmo neglects coherent storyline and character in favour of sub-plots, types, gags, and linguistic virtuosity, thus pointing decisively towards the improvised *theatre of the *commedia dell'arte. He employed the dialect of the Venetian lagoon to parody *letter-

writing in his influential *Lettere* (1547–52, 1566), the *Petrarchan *sonnet in *Rime piscatorie* (1553), and the *pastoral genre in the *Egloghe pastorali* (1553).

[RGF]

CALOGERÀ, ANGELO (1699–1768). *Benedictine monk, who played a leading role in *Venetian state *censorship of books and also in scholarly *journalism. He edited *Biblioteca universale* (1725–6), *Raccolta di opuscoli scientifici e filologici* (1728–87), and *Minerva, ossia nuovo Giornale dei letterati d'Italia* (1762–7).

[JMAL]

CALVINO, ITALO (1923–85) was, at the time of his death, the best known and most translated Italian prosewriter of the second half of the 20th c. Though born in Cuba, where his father taught agriculture and floriculture, he returned with his parents in 1925 to his father's home town San Remo, where Mario Calvino continued his researches into agronomy, becoming the first person to introduce into Europe then exotic fruits such as grapefruit and avocado; the luxuriant flora to be found especially in Calvino's early fiction derive partly from this paternal legacy. As his mother's side of the family also pursued scientific careers, the young Calvino felt himself to be something of a black sheep, on account of his literary interests and initial rejection of the sciences; but if the flora dominated the early works, the sciences were to reappear with particular emphasis in his later fiction. At secondary school his exemption from religious instruction forced him to explain and defend this anticonformist stance, a salutary experience for any young person, he later claimed, and its echoes resound through his early works.

His first literary exploits involved comic scenes for the stage, drawing cartoons, writing short stories and fables, and even some poetry, inspired by his fellow Ligurian *Montale. In 1941–3 he passed a number of university exams in the faculty of agriculture first at *Turin then *Florence, but by the end of that year, refusing to be a conscript for the *Fascist Republic of Salò, he was forced into hiding. In spring 1944 he joined *Communist-led partisans in the Alpi Marittime; as a result of his refusal to sign up for military service his parents were taken hostage, thus increasing the burden of the choice he had made—a motif reflected in his earliest stories. But his partisan experiences in the 'mondo della storia', as he put it, proved as formative as those encountered in the world of nature, providing the material for his earliest

Calvino, Italo

racconti and his first novel [see NOVELLA AND RACCONTO, 2].

After the Liberation, Calvino completed a degree in English at the University of Turin, graduating with a thesis on Joseph Conrad in 1946–7. In the meantime his first articles (on Ligurian socio-political issues) came out in local papers, and in 1946 his first short stories were published. Also in 1946 he became a regular contributor of both articles and short fiction to the Communist daily *L'Unità*, sharing with Marcello Venturi at the end of that year the newspaper's prize for best *racconto*, for 'Campo di mine'. Encouraged by this success, he completed his first novel in December 1946, *Il *sentiero dei nidi di ragno*, which won the Premio Riccione. In order to support himself as an aspiring writer, Calvino worked in the contiguous fields of *publishing and *journalism (for *L'Unità*), joining the publishers *Einaudi in 1947. His first collection of thirty short fictions, *Ultimo viene il corvo* (1949), was published to considerable acclaim, though his subsequent attempts at a second novel were more problematic: of *Il bianco veliero* (1947–9) only one chapter was deemed publishable, the short story 'Va' così che vai bene'; while *I giovani del Po* (1950–1) and *La collana della regina* (1952–4), both dealing with urban realities of the time, were also left unpublished. It took Calvino eighteen months to finish *I giovani del Po* and, to compensate for this laboured attempt at socialist *realism, he decided to write the kind of fantasy story he himself would have liked to read, composing in 1951 in little over a month *Il *visconte dimezzato*, the work that was to become the first part of his fantasy trilogy *I nostri antenati*. The death of his father in October 1951 also affected him deeply, eliciting homages to his parent in the final paragraph of the *autobiographical trilogy *L'entrata in guerra* (1954), and in the semi-autobiographical work *La strada di San Giovanni* (1962), written just after the tenth anniversary of his father's death.

From 1954 to 1956 Calvino was engaged in collecting and then rewriting the *Fiabe italiane* (1956), his collection of Italian fairy tales—an experience which was to confirm his own taste for non-realist fiction, as well as alerting him to the structural similarities of all stories. De-Stalinization and the violent suppression by Soviet troops of the Hungarian uprising in 1956 caused him at first to dissent and then to resign from the Italian Communist Party (PCI), in 1957. Shortly after his resignation, he wrote a satirical allegory against the PCI's inactivity, 'La gran bonaccia delle Antille', provoking the ire of the party leaders. In these years he also wrote one of his most autobiographical novels, *La speculazione edilizia* (1957), which took fifteen months to complete, but while composing it and again to compensate for the heaviness of its socio-political content, he wrote in a mere two months between 1956 and 1957 the lengthy *Il *barone rampante*, the second volume of *I nostri antenati*. In 1958 he collected in *I racconti* a corpus of over fifty of his short stories, and the following year, just before his first trip to the USA, he completed the third part of the trilogy, *Il *cavaliere inesistente*. Also in 1959 he became co-director with *Vittorini of *Il *Menabò di letteratura*, a cultural journal which explored the role of literature in the new industrial age.

There now followed four years in which Calvino published no major work, and letters of the time testify to his growing dissatisfaction with the contemporary novel, and his anxiety about having nothing more to say. But the period 1963–4 proved to be a turning point in many ways. In 1963 he published: his last realist 'novel' (though, consisting of fewer than 100 pages, it is more a *novella*), *La giornata di uno scrutatore*, which he had begun ten years previously; his last militant essay as a *Marxist, 'L'antitesi operaia'; and *Marcovaldo ovvero le stagioni in città*, his first work in a new modular manner, composed of a series of microtexts forming an overarching macrotext, a format that was to be used for the rest of his output. In 1964 he bade farewell to his realist phase by reissuing *Il sentiero*, with an important new preface which offers a canonical definition of the *Neorealism which had spawned the novel.

Another important change around this time was his wedding in Cuba in February 1964 to Esther Singer, an Argentinian translator for UNESCO whom he had met in Paris. Initially they settled in Rome, but in 1967 the family, including a daughter Giovanna (b.1965), moved to Paris, where they remained until 1979. At least one critic has suggested a connection between the author's new married state and the fact that all his fiction from this point on also has a kind of barrier or frame surrounding it, whether in the scientific epigraphs of *Le cosmicomiche* (1965), the structural grids of *Le città invisibili* (1972) and *Palomar* (1983), the Tarot cards in the margin of *Il castello dei destini incrociati* (1973), or the elaborate framework surrounding *Se una notte d'inverno un viaggiatore* (1979). Calvino himself wrote that once he had decided to be a full-time writer, and to abandon his work in the adjacent fields of journalism and publishing, he had no more 'screens' to put between himself and the world.

But perhaps the most significant transformation around this time, as Calvino admitted in an interview, was the fact that he also lost interest in direct political action, cultivating instead a deeply rooted desire to be a bookworm.

In 1965 Calvino published *Le cosmicomiche*, a series of twelve tales each preceded by an epigraph announcing some important scientific law, followed by a fictional, often humorous account of the events alluded to in the epigraph (the Big Bang, the emergence of light, the development of the first mammals). This new narrative style was an attempt to expand the confines of literature, by putting it on a par with the advances of contemporary science. It is no coincidence that this was the period of the first satellites, the first space shots, and the first men on the moon: the moon is one of the dominant themes of the cosmicomic tales. The style is also Calvino's response to the rejection of traditional realist narrative expressed by his contemporaries in the *Neo-avanguardia* and the *Gruppo 63*. *Ti con zero* (1967) was in the same mode, but in its last four stories it combines not so much literature and science as literature, mathematical logic, and deductive reasoning; this coincided with the writer's move to Paris in 1967, and his interest in the mathematical-combinatory enthusiasms of Raymond Queneau (whose *Les Fleurs bleues* he translated in this same year). Through Queneau Calvino came to know Roland Barthes and the members of the Ouvroir de Littérature Potentielle (OULIPO), including Georges Perec. It was an association that would strongly influence his subsequent output.

Calvino followed the European student upheavals of 1967–70 with detached interest, his own ideas moving in a utopian direction through his reading of the French utopian Charles Fourier, a selection of whose works he prepared for Einaudi in these years. In 1969 he agreed to write a text, 'Il castello dei destini incrociati', to accompany Franco Maria Ricci's lavish edition of the 15th-c. Bergamo Tarot cards; this text was eventually published along with its sequel, which illustrated the ordinary tarot cards ('La taverna dei destini incrociati'), taking *Il castello dei destini incrociati* (1973) as its overall title. But in the meantime Calvino wrote and published *Le *città invisibili* (1972), which brought together his interests in utopias, the city, and the Orient. In 1973 he became a full foreign member of OULIPO. There then followed an unparalleled period of six years in which he wrote no major work. Not surprisingly, when his next volume did appear, it was a novel about writer's block and creativity, *Se una notte d'inverno un viaggiatore* (1979). However, as early as August 1975 Calvino had written for the newspaper *Il Corriere della sera* the first tales centring on a new character, Mr Palomar, who would be the protagonist of the last book to be published in the author's lifetime. Although the newspaper tales were often different from those eventually included in the book *Palomar* (1983), what emerges from all of them is that in the late 1970s the author was trying to write completely contrasting kinds of work, shifting from the metafictional *summa* of all novels in *Se una notte* to, in *Palomar*, minute localized analyses of reality.

In 1980 Calvino selected his essays from the period 1955–79, some political, most literary, in *Una pietra sopra* (1980), a volume which amounts, as its title suggests, almost to a valedictory on a particular phase of his committed socio-political journalism. In his final years his writing was stimulated particularly by the other arts. He wrote serious and ludic pieces inspired by photography, paintings (notably works by Domenico Gnoli, *De Chirico, and Arakawa) and music, including a *libretto for Mozart's *Zaide*, and libretti for his friend Luciano Berio [see also MUSIC]. He continued to work on more cosmicomic tales, reissuing an expanded corpus of *Cosmicomiche vecchie e nuove* (1984), and published another collection of essays, mostly cultural rather than political or literary, under the title *Collezione di sabbia* (1984). He also wrote three of a projected five tales about the five senses (posthumously published as *Sotto il sole giaguaro* (1986)).

Invited in 1985 to deliver the Charles Eliot Norton lectures at Harvard University, he completed five of them before dying from a sudden brain haemorrhage in September 1985. They were published posthumously as *Lezioni americane: sei proposte per il prossimo millennio* (1988). These lectures, especially the five literary qualities enshrined in them, enjoy a considerable vogue; the qualities are those inherent in Calvino's own work, and those that he bequeathed as his literary testament for the next millennium: *leggerezza, rapidità, esattezza, visibilità, molteplicità*. Other previously unpublished fictions have been published since his death, together with his collected literary-critical essays. These demonstrate that, even in periods of creative crisis, Calvino never ceased to read, and to write about what he read in reviews and essays; even if he had never written a single story, he would have been one of the foremost critics of the second half of the century. [MMcL]

See C. Milanini, *L'utopia discontinua* (1990);

Calvo, Edoardo Ignazio

K. Hume, *Calvino's Fictions: Cogito and Cosmos* (1992); M. McLaughlin, *Italo Calvino* (1998).

CALVO, EDOARDO IGNAZIO (1733–1804). *Piedmontese *dialect poet. A doctor by profession, in 1799 he fled to France to escape Austro-Russian persecution, but on his return became a critic of French domination. His *Favole morali* (1801) denounce perfidy in the oppressor and hypocrisy, intrigue, and imposture among the oppressed. [JMAL]

CALVO, MARCO FABIO, see ANTI-QUARIANISM.

CALZABIGI, RANIERI DE' (1714–95). *Librettist. Born into a middle-class Livorno family—he himself added the noble 'de''—he worked in various European *courts after first making his name in the 1740s. Whilst in Paris he wrote *La Lulliade*, a *mock-heroic poem published posthumously, on the 'querelle des bouffons' about the respective merits of Italian and French *opera. In Vienna in the late 1750s, he joined Gluck and the choreographer Gasparo Angiolini in their reform of the opera, composing programmes in French for the ballets *Le Festin de pierre* (1761) and *Sémiramis* (1765), and the libretti for *Orfeo ed Euridice* (1762), *Alceste* (1767), and *Paride ed Elena* (1770). These employ few characters, and take their subjects from mythological rather than historical sources, in contrast with *Metastasio's practice. He satirized opera in *L'opera seria* (1769) and wrote the comic *dramma per musica Amiti e Ontario* (1772). Moving to *Pisa in 1773, he drew on *Ossian for the libretto for *Comala* (1780), and published his *Poesie* (1774), which include *translations of Milton, Gray, and Thompson. When he finally settled in *Naples in 1779, he continued to take part in literary polemics, writing among other things a violent criticism of *Metastasio and an appreciative *Lettera ad *Alfieri* (1783), on Alfieri's first four *tragedies. He also wrote the tragic libretti *Elfrida* (1792) and *Elvira* (1794), which his friend Giovanni Paisiello set to music. He was a member of the Accademia dell'*Arcadia. [ALB]

CAMASIO, SANDRO, see OXILIA, NINO.

CAMBIASI NEGRETTI, AMALIANA, see LIALA.

CAMBOSU, SALVATORE, see SARDINIA.

CAMERANA, GIOVANNI (1845–1905). *Piedmontese poet and magistrate who eventually committed suicide. His poetry initially borrowed from the *Milanese *Scapigliatura*, and later from Baudelaire and the French Parnassians. He was active in *Turinese cultural life as a painter and art critic and a friend of *Faldella and *Giacosa. [AHC]

CAMERATA, GIOVANNI, see SCAPI-GLIATURA.

Camerata de' Bardi. Group of musicians and intellectuals who met at Giovanni de' *Bardi's palace in *Florence between 1573 and 1587. Members included Vincenzo *Galilei, Giulio Caccini, Iacopo Peri, and Ottavio *Rinuccini. Their central concern, developed particularly by Galilei, was a return to the music of classical times. This led them to develop theories for the reform of contemporary polyphony. They also proposed a return to what they thought was the ancient tragic practice of giving equal weight to words and music. Caccini's and Peri's ensuing experiments in monody were a fundamental step in the creation of *opera. [FC]

CAMERINI, MARIO (1895–1981). Film director known mostly for his comedies of the 1930s. These are subtle, sentimental, and satirical of petit bourgeois society, but warm-hearted, the most representative being the tetralogy starring Vittorio *De Sica: *Gli uomini che mascalzoni!* (1932), *Darò un milione* (1935), *Il signor Max* (1937), and *I grandi magazzini* (1939). [CGW]

CAMILLERI, ANDREA (1925–). *Sicilian novelist who was formerly a theatre director and television producer in *Rome. After a first novel, *Il corso delle cose* (1978), he did not publish again seriously until the 1990s. He has had remarkable successes with *detective novels set in the fictional Sicilian town of Vigàta and featuring Ispettore Salvo Montalbano (the first was *La forma dell'acqua* (1994)), but also with *historical novels about post-*Risorgimento Sicily, such as *La mossa del cavallo* (1999). His writing is often comic and characterized by an original mxiture of Italian and Sicilian. [GP]

CAMILLO, DON, see GUARESCHI, GIOVANNI.

CAMILLO, GIULIO (also known as Delminio) (*c.*1480–1544) studied at *Padua and *Venice, and was a friend of Pietro *Bembo and *Aretino. In 1521 he began a lifetime's project to develop a memory theatre, a structure in which places and images would give the adept access to universal knowledge. In 1530, encouraged by King Francis I, he went to France, where he presented his *Theatro della sapientia*. He returned to Italy at the end of 1543, and obtained the *patronage of Alfonso d'Avalos, Governor of *Milan, to whom he dedicated his *Theatro della memoria* of 1544.　　[PLR]

CAMINER TURRA, ELISABETTA (1751–96). The daughter of the *Venetian journalist Domenico Caminer, who introduced her to *journalism. She replaced him as editor of the *Giornale enciclopedico*, which she eventually transferred to Vicenza. She translated plays, collected as *Composizioni teatrali moderne* (4 vols., 1772) and *Nuova raccolta di composizioni teatrali* (6 vols., 1774–6).　　[CCa]

CAMMELLI, ANTONIO, see PISTOIA, IL.

CAMON, FERDINANDO (1935–). Poet, novelist, and critic. His creative writing focuses on social change in the province of *Padua, depicting the decline of *peasant life, the effects of terrorism, and, in his most recent novel, *Mai visti sole e luna* (1994), the *Resistance movement. His most influential critical work, starting with *Letteratura e classi subalterne* (1974), analyses literature from a sociological perspective. Camon has also published interviews with other poets and novelists, notably *Il mestiere di poeta* (1965) and *Il mestiere di scrittore* (1973).　　[PC]

CAMPAGNA, GIUSEPPE (1799–1868). Born near Cosenza, he lived most of his life in *Naples, where he was a friend of Basilio *Puoti, whose linguistic *purism he shared. He wrote *lyric poems, *novelle in versi*, and *tragedies. His choice of some modern subjects shows an openness to moderate *Romanticism.　　[MPC]

CAMPANA, DINO (1885–1932). The most visionary of modern Italian poets. He was born in the Apennine village of Marradi and had an irregular school *education, first in Faenza, then in *Turin and Carmagnola, before registering as a student of chemistry at *Bologna University, though he quickly transferred to *Florence. He had shown signs of instability since his early youth, and in 1906 he spent some time in a mental hospital in Imola.

When he came out, he embarked on travels which took him to France, South America, and Belgium, where he went into hospital in Tournai. He spent another period in hospital in Florence, but in 1912 he again registered as a chemistry student at Bologna. In 1914 he published *Canti orfici*. There were other travels, an attempt to be accepted as a volunteer for service in *World War I, and an affair with Sibilla *Aleramo. But after a spell in gaol, Campana was finally admitted to the hospital of Castel Pulci near Florence, where he remained until his death. An expanded version of *Canti orfici* was published in 1928.

Campana imported the style of poetry (and of life) of the French *poètes maudits* into Italy. Baudelaire and above all Rimbaud were models, who provided themes—drunkenness, erotic desire, travel—poetic forms, and a series of existential attitudes. But for Campana, as for other poets of the time such as *D'Annunzio or even *Carducci, French influences had to coexist with the Italian tradition, not always with happy consequences. His best poems do not allow *symbolism or *orphism to cancel out sensory and visual aspects of the real world, but give them a strangely hallucinatory quality, as occurs in 'La chimera', 'L'invetriata', 'Viaggio a Montevideo', and 'Genova'. Campana's inclusion of *prose poems in the *Canti orfici* was an innovation so far as Italian poetry was concerned.

　　[GM]
Canti orfici, ed. F. Ceragioli (1985). See F. Bernardini Napoletano, *Dino Campana nel Novecento: il progetto e l'opera* (1992).

CAMPANELLA, TOMMASO (1568–1639) was a poet, political reformer, philosopher, and theologian. Born in Calabria, he became a *Dominican monk in 1582. His *Philosophia sensibus demonstrata* (1591) earned him the instant disfavour of the Church, which sentenced him to exile in Calabria, but he escaped to *Rome, and went on to *Florence, *Bologna, and *Padua, where he was tried for sodomy. In 1597 he was accused of *heresy and banished to Calabria, where, in 1599, he led a popular uprising to free his fellow citizens into a utopian City of the Sun in the mountains. He was betrayed by his fellow conspirators and captured. In 1600 he was moved to *Naples and tortured on the rack. He made a full confession and would have been put to death if he had not feigned madness and set his cell on fire. He was tortured further and then, crippled and ill, sentenced to life imprisonment, from which he was eventually released in 1629.

The last years of his life were spent in Rome and Paris.

During his long period of incarceration he composed his main works. His *Poesie*, published in 1622, consist of eighty-nine poems in various metrical forms. Some are *autobiographical, but all are stamped with a seriousness and directness which bypasses the literary fashions of his day. He wrote in Latin on dialectics, rhetoric, poetics, and historiography, as well as the Italian *Del senso delle cose e della magia*, composed in 1604 and published in 1620. In this fascinating work, influenced by the teachings of Bernardino *Telesio, Campanella imagines the world as a living statue of God, in which all aspects of reality have meaning and sense. With its animism and sensuality this vision foreshadows in many ways the views of Daniello *Bartoli and *Tesauro. Campanella's theological work, closely connected with his philosophical writings, includes the *Atheismus triumphatus* and the thirty-volume *Theologia* (1613–24).

His most famous work, and the one that brings together all his interests, is *La città del sole*, first drafted in 1602 in Italian and then later translated into Latin in 1613 and 1631. In it a *Genoese sailor from Christopher Columbus's crew describes the ideal state of the City of the Sun ruled over in both temporal and spiritual matters by the Prince Priest, called Sun or Metaphysician. Under him there are three ministers: Power (concerned with war and peace), Wisdom (concerned with science and art, all written down in one book), and Love (concerned with procreation and education of the citizens of the Sun). The life of the citizens is based on a system of communism: all property is held publicly, there are no families, no rights of inheritance, no marriage, and sexual relations are regulated by the state. Everyone has his or her function in the society, and certain duties are required of all citizens. *Education is the perfect training of the mind and the body, and it is radically opposed to the bookish and academic culture of *Renaissance Italy: the objects of study should be not 'dead things' but nature and the mathematical and physical laws that govern the physical world. There are links here with the burgeoning modernism of the *Querelle des anciens et des modernes*, and with the methods and scientific aspirations of *Galileo, whom Campanella defended in writing in 1616. [PBD]

> *Tutte le opere*, ed. L. Firpo (1954); *Lettere 1595–1638*, ed. G. Ernst (2000). See A. Corsano, *Tommaso Campanella* (1961); V. Paladino (ed.), *Ultimi studi campanelliani* (1978).

CAMPANI, NICCOLÒ, see CONGREGA DEI ROZZI.

CAMPANILE, ACHILLE (1900–77). *Roman playwright, novelist, and *journalist. His *Futurist theatrical works, such as *Centocinquanta la gallina canta* (1925), won critical acclaim. But he had more popular success with novels such as *Ma che cos'è questo amore?* (1927). Both his novels and plays show a passion for nonsense and linguistic ambiguity, although the humour often disguises a strong critique of bourgeois mores. Always a prolific contributor to newspapers and periodicals, Campanile was most active in the postwar period as a *television and *cinema critic. [JJ]

CAMPANO, GIANNANTONIO (1429–77). Teacher, ecclesiastic, papal official, and man of letters. He collaborated with the first Roman typographers and left a varied literary production in Latin, including *letters, *biographies of the *condottiere Braccio Da Montone and of Enea Silvio *Piccolomini (Pope Pius II), and a collection of *Carmina*. [LB]

CAMPEGGI, RIDOLFO (1565–1624). *Bolognese dramatist, poet, and *librettist. As well as musical dramas, lyric and sacred poetry, he wrote the *pastoral play *Il Filarmindo* (1605) and the *tragedy *Tancredi* (1614). His *Andromeda* was possibly the first *opera to be performed in Bologna (1610). He may also have recast Michelangelo *Buonarroti the Younger's *La Tancia* in Bolognese dialect as *La Togna*. [FC]

CAMPI, PIETRO MARIA, see HAGIOGRAPHY.

Campiello, see LITERARY PRIZES.

CAMPIGLIA, MADDALENA (d.1595). Poet who lived all her life in Vicenza. She became a *Dominican tertiary (lay sister) but maintained her cultural interests. As well as a *Discorso intorno all'Annunciazione della Vergine* (1585), her output includes an eclogue and a *pastoral drama, *Flori* (1588). She was in contact with Torquato *Tasso and other writers. [ABu]

CAMPO, CRISTINA (1923–77) (pseud. of Vittoria Guerrini). Writer born into a musical *Bologna family who spent much of her life in literary circles in *Florence and subsequently *Rome, but published little during her lifetime. An intense attention to absolute spiritual and literary values dominates her work—most notably, the essays of *Gli imperdonabili* (1987), the ostensibly private *Lettere a un amico lontano* (1989), and the verse of *La tigre assenza* (1991). [PH]

Campo di Marte (1938–9). Fortnightly *periodical founded and edited by Alfonso *Gatto and Vasco *Pratolini in *Florence. Whilst proclaiming its political orthodoxy, and recognizing that the possibilities for independent thought and action were narrowing sharply in the difficult period preceding *World War II, it attempted to continue the modern, non-dogmatic approach to literature and culture of *Solaria*, and began to articulate some of the ideas that would lead to a literature of *impegno* after the fall of *Fascism. Its idiom, however, remained generally allusive and abstract. As well as plainly *hermetic poets and critics, such as *Luzi and *Bo, contributors included *Betocchi, *Bilenchi, *Gadda, *Montale, and *Vittorini. [PH]

Campoformio, Treaty of, see NAPOLEON AND THE FRENCH REVOLUTION.

Canace, see SPERONI, SPERONE.

CANALI, LUCA (1925–) is a scholar of classical literature, a militant critic, a novelist, and a poet. He has published several *translations and studies of Lucretius, *Virgil, *Horace, and Petronius. This activity has always been accompanied by his commitment as a militant left-wing critic, writing for periodicals such as *Città aperta*, *il *verri*, and *Il *Contemporaneo*. As a poet he has published several collections, among which are *La follia lucida* (1967) and *Zapping* (1993). His fictional output has intensified in recent years, with a series of *autobiographical novels running from *Il sorriso di Giulia* (1980) to *Pietà per le spie* (1996). [GUB]

CANCOGNI, MANLIO (1916–). *Novelist and *journalist from *Bologna, who published his first short stories in *Letteratura* and *Il *Frontespizio* in the 1930s. He began to write political journalism during *World War II and subsequently became a regular contributor to *L'Europeo*, *L'Espresso*, and other magazines and newspapers. Autobiographical experiences and a new-found simplicity of style came together in a first short novel, *La carriera di Pimlico* (1956). The many novels which followed

reveal an independent, modern morality, affiliated neither to the right nor to the left of the political spectrum. [DCH]

Candelaio (1582), Giordano *Bruno's only *comedy, is set in *Naples and satirizes the unnatural passions of society, as exemplified by Bonifacio's infatuation for a *courtesan, Bartolomeo's obsession with gold, and Mamfurio's grammatical pedantry, all contrasted with Giovan Bernardo's genuine (albeit illicit) love for Carubina, Bonifacio's beautiful wife. *Candelaio* means 'candlestick' or 'candle-maker' when referring to the former pederast Bonifacio, 'chandelier' when referring to the comedy's philosophy of light. [GAq]

Cane di Diogene, see FRUGONI, FRANCESCO FULVIO.

CANGIULLO, FRANCESCO (1888–1977). *Neapolitan writer and painter who made an important contribution to *Futurism's experiments in poetry and drama. The performance of his *parole in libertà*, 'Piedigrotta', on 29 March 1914 at the Futurist Gallery in *Rome became a legendary event in the development of 'dynamic and synoptic declamation'. But many of his other poetry experiments were largely, or purely, visual in character, such as his *Caffèconcerto: alfabeto a sorpresa* (1918), which is a series of pictures composed of letters in various fonts. He composed many witty or absurd dramatic sketches for the *Teatro sintetico* which Futurism had first launched in 1915; the extreme example 'Detonazione' consisted solely of the sound of a gunshot, and was intended to encapsulate the action of much more wordy plays. In 1921, with *Marinetti, he wrote the manifesto *Il teatro della sorpresa*, which emphasized the comic element in Futurist drama. He then began a series of tours of Italian cities, with an acting company led by Rodolfo De Angelis, performing Futurist plays. His *Le serate futuriste* (1930) is a lively account of his Futurist experiences. He later moved away from Futurism and enjoyed popular success with his novel *Nini Champagne* (1938). [SV]

Canne al vento (1913). Novel by Grazia *Deledda. Set in rural *Sardinia and centred on her characteristic theme of unwise passion, it depicts the decline of the aristocratic Pintor family, though the most significant character is the servant, Efix, who goes through life trying to atone for a murder committed long ago in self-defence. [UJF]

Cannibali. Publicity term devised in the mid-1990s for a heterogeneous group of young writers cultivating 'pulp' fiction (after the manner of Quentin Tarantino), with a stress on violent, comic, and nihilistic action and a generally calculated use of modern urban *slang. Some of the most interesting examples are Enrico Brizzi's *Jack Frusciante è uscito dal gruppo* (1994), Niccolò Ammaniti's *Fango* (1995), and Aldo Nove's *Woobinda* (1996).   [PH]

CANONIERI, PIETRO ANDREA (d.1639). Prolific and eclectic occasional writer, who came to concentrate on politics. Of a large number of *political tracts, the best known are *Il perfetto cortegiano et dell'uffizio del prencipe verso il cortegiano* and *commentaries on Tacitus (both 1609), and *Dell'introduzione alla politica, alla ragion di stato e alla pratica del buon governo* (1614). He drew on *Campanella extensively, often without acknowledgement. [See also RAGION DI STATO.]   [PBert]

CANOVA, ANTONIO (1757–1822). Italy's foremost *neoclassical sculptor. Born near Treviso, and educated in *Venice, at 22 he settled permanently in *Rome, where his patrons included popes, distinguished foreign visitors, and the Bonaparte family. His work was celebrated by poets such as Keats and Byron. *Foscolo projected *Le grazie* after admiring Canova statues in *Florence and hearing of *The Three Graces* commissioned by ex-Empress Josephine.   [JMAL]

Cantari. The generic name given to a range of narrative verse texts from the 14th and 15th c., originally composed, as the name implies, for recitation to music; however, no musical settings survive, and it is impossible to know how closely the extant texts correspond to any oral version. The essential qualities of the genre remain linked to its oral origins: *cantari* are straightforwardly narrative and descriptive, with a marked preference for strong emotion and dramatic action, manifested in prodigious feats of bravery or endurance, and often including the supernatural, the exotic, and the fabulous. Their characteristic tone is one of ingenuous wonder, in which hyperbole is so pervasive as to become a narrative principle. The texts are either short enough to be recited in a single session (around fifty stanzas, or 400 lines) or, if longer, subdivided into units—*cantari*—of about this length; at the beginning and end of each *cantare* there are lines addressing the real or imagined audience. Most *cantari* (if not, as some critics would argue, *cantari* by definition) are in *ottava rima*, the verse form whose earliest datable examples are *Boccaccio's *Filostrato* and *Teseida*, of the mid- to late 1330s. Their subject matter encompasses the whole range of late medieval narrative: classical and mythological (*Guerra di Troia, Fatti di Cesare, Piramo e Tisbe*), courtly and amatory (*Fiorio e Biancifiore, La donna del Vergiù, Ponzela Gaia*), pious and hagiographical (*Passione di Cristo, Leggenda di Santo Giosafà*). Those containing Carolingian narratives (about the Emperor Charlemagne) appear always to have been longer, both in their *Franco-Veneto form and in the relatively late (mid-15th c.) versions in *ottava rima*, which run to forty or more *cantari* (the *Spagna*, and the *Orlando*, which is the probable source for Luigi *Pulci's *Morgante*).

The origins of the *cantari* have been much debated. The earliest datable manuscript, of *Fiorio e Biancifiore* (also the subject of Boccaccio's *Filocolo*), dates from the 1340s, and the titles of several other extant *cantari* (*Febus, Donna del Vergiù, Bel Gherardino*) are cited in Boccaccio's other works. However, given the collective, fluid nature of the genre, in which each retelling of a story is a new 'performance' rather than a reproduction of a canonical text, it cannot be assumed that the poems in their present form pre-date the manuscripts (mostly 15th-c.) or printed editions (from the turn of the 16th c.) in which they are preserved. With the exception of the *Florentine Antonio *Pucci, most *cantare* authors are anonymous, which gives much scope for speculation about their social standing, level of education and professional activity. The *cantari* show some knowledge, albeit fairly superficial, of the poets of the *dolce stil novo* and of the *Divine Comedy*, and Boccaccio's verse romances seem clearly to have been instrumental in establishing the genre in its definitive form.

Both in their origins and in their influence on subsequent writers, the *cantari* represent one of the most fruitful meeting-points between popular and literary culture in Italy. Varied though they are in character and quality, they have at their best a fairytale character (*fiabesco* is Vittore *Branca's influential term) which persists, notwithstanding the sophistication and irony with which it is overlaid, in the *chivalric poems of Pulci, *Boiardo, and *Ariosto. [See also ARTHURIAN LITERATURE; EPIC.]   [RMD]

Cantari del Trecento, ed. A. Balduino, (1970). See M. Picone and M. Bendinelli Predelli (eds.), *I cantari: struttura e tradizione* (1984).

Cantastorie. Oral performers of verse narratives at festivals or in city squares for a popular audience. The subject matter and techniques were traditional, with probably some room for individual variation and innovation. The earliest *cantari* (14th c.) which have survived are conditioned by the practice of *cantastorie*, though they are probably not direct transcriptions. *Cantastorie* survived in rural areas until the mid-20th c. [See FOLK AND POPULAR LITERATURE; GIULLARI.]   [PH]

Cantautori, or singer-songwriters, first appeared in the early 1960s when Italian popular song was trying to adapt to consumer culture. Influenced by figures like Georges Brassens, Frank Sinatra, and Nat King Cole, Gino Paoli, Fabrizio D'André, Sergio Endrigo, and Luigi Tenco introduced new themes and a new intellectual aura, in some ways privileging the words over the music. Then came Francesco Guccini, Francesco De Gregori, Eugenio Finardi, and others, who owed more to Bob Dylan and Joan Baez. Most *cantautori* were associated with the left, even if not all were politically engaged. Notable women *cantautori* emerged in the 1980s, including Teresa De Sio, Grazia Di Michele, and Paola Turci.   [SG]

Canti, I, see LEOPARDI, GIACOMO.

Cantica, see DIVINE COMEDY.

Canti carnascialeschi. Genre of songs for *carnival time, particularly associated with *Florence in the time of Lorenzo de' *Medici. Essentially popular, they are characterized by the fundamental element of carnival, the subversion of social norms and accepted manners and morals, and they focus usually on the scatological and obscene as sources of ribald humour. Lorenzo de' Medici is sometimes credited as the inventor, but his contribution is probably another example of the adoption and transformation of popular literary genres typified in his *Nencia da Barberino* and Luigi *Pulci's *Beca di Dicomano.* Lorenzo's 'Canzona dei confortini' (1475) nevertheless marks the beginning of the period of greatest output, and, like all the major examples, is constructed around a series of elaborate metaphors for sexual acts and the sexual organs. In most cases the genre involved describing simultaneously and in detail a sexual encounter and the activity of a given trade, establishing a series of exact metaphorical parallels between the two. The celebration of carnival was suspended for a ten-year period after the *Pazzi conspiracy, and when it revived in the late 1480s the themes of the *canti carnascialeschi* became notably more literary and less obscene, drawing on classical mythology and even *Neoplatonism, though Lorenzo's famous 'Canzona a Bacco' dates from the earlier period. *Canti carnascialeschi* were also composed by *Poliziano, Luigi Pulci, Bernardo *Giambullari, and later *Machiavelli. The genre continued, more sporadically, in the first half of the 16th c., but Lasca's anthology (1559) marks effectively the end of the period in which it flourished [see GRAZZINI, ANTON FRANCESCO].   [JEE]

Cantico di frate sole, see FRANCIS, ST.

Canti di Castelvecchio, see PASCOLI, GIOVANNI.

Canti orfici, see CAMPANA, DINO.

Canto. The name given by *Dante to the main metrical units of the *Divine Comedy,* the divisions between which sometimes match and sometimes conflict with the divisions of the narrative. After Dante, a text or part of a text in *terza rima* is normally called a *capitolo.* More generally, *canto* in the technical sense designates the parts into which a poem is divided, as an alternative to *libro* or 'book'. In its broadest sense it is the name given to a piece of poetry, *lyric or otherwise, following the early tradition linking poetry to music. The most famous example is the *Canti* of *Leopardi. [See also VERSIFICATION].   [PGB]

CANTONI, ALBERTO (1841–1904). Writer best known (largely thanks to *Pirandello) as a *humorist. Born into a *Jewish landowning family near *Mantua, he studied in *Venice, and travelled widely until his father's death in 1885 necessitated his return home to manage the family's estates. *Manzoni's influence is very marked in the sketches and stories of rural life which began to appear in *Nuova antologia in 1875. *Tre madamine* (1876) and *Bastianino* (1877) share their narrative energy while foreshadowing the more moralistic tendencies of his later writing. His best-known work, the novel *L'illustrissimo,* takes as its subject provincial life in lower *Lombardy. It was begun in 1881 but only appeared after his death in 1906, with an introduction by Pirandello, which identifies humorism as its most significant characteristic. A similar humorism is also evident in what Cantoni himself defined as 'novelle critiche'—works such as *Un re umorista*

(1891), *Il demonio dello stile* (1887), and *Humor classico e moderno* (1899). [AHC]

Canto novo, see D'ANNUNZIO, GABRIELE.

CANTÙ, CESARE (1804–95). Immensely prolific writer and historian. At 17 he was a literature teacher at the *liceo* in his native Brivio, near Como. He went on to teach in Como, and in 1832 in *Milan. He was and would remain a committed Catholic moralist, but at this stage he was strongly influenced by *Romanticism. He had published a *novella in versi, Algiso,* in Como in 1828. There now followed a string of poems, stories, and *historical novels, the best and most successful of which was the 14th-c. *Margherita Pusterla* (1838). In 1833 he was imprisoned for anti-*Austrian activities and, losing his job as a teacher, was forced into exile in *Piedmont. Though he took part in the revolution of *1848, he gradually moved to the right, as became particularly clear when he was elected to the national parliament in 1860. He had been publishing historical works since the 1830s, including many on Lombard history and histories of Greek, Roman, and Italian literature. His major historical work is the 35-volume *Storia universale* (1838–47), which makes progress and the flourishing of the arts and sciences dependent on the guidance of the Catholic Church. He also wrote moralizing tracts, of which *Il giovinetto drizzato alla bontà, al sapere, all'industria* (1837) is an early example. [DO'G]

CANTÙ, IGNAZIO (1810–77). Brother of Cesare *Cantù, and, like him, a teacher and prolific writer, principally of historical and educational works of a strongly moralizing nature. His best-known fiction is the *historical novel *Il marchese Annibale Perrone* (1842), which, like its *Manzonian model, is set in the 17th c. [DO'G]

Canzone. The major metrical form in early Italian *lyric poetry. It is divided into strophes (*stanze*) each consisting of two *piedi* ('feet'), each with the same metrical structure (of two to six lines), rhymed in varying ways, but so that no line remains without a rhyme; followed by a *sirma* which cannot be divided into two similarly corresponding parts and which has varying rhyme schemes (often the first line of the *sirma* rhymes with the last line of the *piedi*). Instead of the *sirma* (more infrequently and mainly in the 13th c.) the *canzone* can have two *volte* constructed in the same way as the *piedi*. It

normally ends with an indivisible last verse or *congedo* ('farewell') which is shorter than the stanza. [PGB]

Canzonetta, see VERSIFICATION.

Canzoniere. The term is commonly used to indicate a collection of poems with unitary aspirations. It is used most frequently (but not exclusively) with reference to *Renaissance and medieval poetry. Broadly speaking it can refer to one of three types of collection: (a) an *anthology of poems by several authors; (b) a selection of poems from the production of a single author arranged in a significant order, usually aiming at tracing the story of the poet's self through the story of his poetry, the model here being *Petrarch's *Canzoniere*; (c) the collected lyric poems of an author, whether or not the collector is the author himself—for example, *Dante's *Canzoniere,* which is the product of modern editing.

Type (a) is the main means by which lyric poems were transmitted in and through the medieval period and the early Renaissance. The models here were the *troubadour *chansonniers* (though the original Provençal designation is *libres*), which normally order the poems they contain by metre or by author. There may be subdivisions within which the poems are often arranged chronologically. There are three major manuscripts containing early collections of Italian lyrics, all compiled towards the end of the 13th c.—Palatino 418 and Laurenziano Rediano 9, both now in *Florence, and Vatican Latino 3793 in the *Vatican library. All three arrange their poems according to metre, putting the weightier and more demanding *canzoni* before *sonnets and poems in other metres. However, the second of these, which contains poems by a number of *Sicilian and Tuscan poets, gives pride of place to the poems (and letters) of *Guittone d'Arezzo, the ordering of which takes account of his moral and religious conversion. This manuscript, therefore, represents the first emergence in Italian of a type (b) *canzoniere.* Dante's *Vita nova* is sometimes deemed the first example on the grounds that it contains poems selected and arranged by the author in such a way as to tell a story, but, since the work combines poetry with prose, and the latter builds the links between poems and elucidates the narrative, it is doubtful whether it should be considered a *canzoniere* at all.

Canzonieri of type (b) are given their canonical expression by Petrarch. He undoubtedly drew on the *Vita nova* and was also not alone in his cultivation of the form. A much less significant poet, Nicolò de' *Rossi, was working on his collection of lyrics at much the same time. But it was Petrarch who, in the eyes of the Renaissance and subsequent centuries, explored and realized the formal, narrative, and expressive possibilities of a collection of lyric poems, as well as setting the standard of poetic perfection in individual lyrics. He himself never used the term *canzoniere* and entitled the final version of the collection—completed, if it was completed, after more than thirty years of intermittent work not long before his death in 1374—*Rerum vulgarium fragmenta*. His references in his correspondence to *nugellae vulgares* or *sparsa fragmenta* possibly signify the effort, as well as the impossibility, of retracing a narrative unity in the story of his self and his poetry, though a progression from earthly to divine love and from sinfulness to repentance has always proved easy to read into the collection.

Canzonieri of type (a) continued to be produced in the 15th and 16th c., particularly of poems to be set to music. But *canzonieri* of type (b) became increasingly frequent towards the end of the 15th c., especially in *Naples. In his *Asolani* (1505) and *Prose della volgar lingua* (1525) Pietro *Bembo proposed Petrarch as an exclusive poetic model. As his theses came generally to be accepted, the number of Petrarchizing *canzonieri* increased enormously. Though many poets did not actually make their collected lyrics cohere as much as those of Petrarch himself (or those of Bembo), the paradigm seems to haunt their work, even if it veers towards the type (c) *canzoniere*. This is the case with various poets who step outside the *Petrarchist mould or shape it in new ways—for instance, *Michelangelo, *Della Casa, or even Torquato *Tasso. At the same time, just as parodies of Petrarchism appear at the level of the individual poem, so parodies were written of *canzonieri*, such as Camillo *Scroffa's collection for his ostensibly beloved Fidenzio of about 1550. By the early 17th c. the type (b) *canzoniere* was waning in its strict Petrarchan form, and poets were increasingly releasing partial collections of their work. But the aspiration to a Petrarchan *canzoniere* systemizing the poet's lyric production in a form of autobiographical narrative, absent to all intents and purposes from the 17th to the 19th c., reappears in the 20th c. in *Saba, who entitles his collected poems *Il canzoniere*, and *Ungaretti, who prefers *Vita di un uomo*, and is discernible in *Montale, whose poetic œuvre

constitutes one of the major literary autobiographies of the century.

The *Vocabolario della *Crusca* and later Italian dictionaries derive Italian *canzoniere* from French *chansonnier*, itself first recorded in 1328 and meaning a manuscript containing poetry, probably to be accompanied by music, though it was not used again in a comparable sense until the 18th c. The Crusca dates the first use of the Italian form to *Grazzini's *Cene* (c.1550), where it means a collection of poetry for music, and to *Salviati (1584), who uses it of Petrarch's collection. On this account meanings (a) and (b) have therefore both been present since the term's first appearance, with meaning (c) being added subsequently. *Canzoniero*, however, is used of Petrarch's poems in a commentary on them probably dating from the 14th c., attributed to *Antonio da Tempo. *Canzoniere* is also used as the title for Petrarch's collection in a 1516 Bologna edition and becomes its normal designation in the mid-16th c. It is also used in sense (c) as early as 1492 by *Perleoni in Naples.

[NC]

See M. Santagata, *Dal sonetto al canzoniere* (1982); G. Gorni, 'Le forme primarie del testo poetico', in A. Asor Rosa (ed.), *Letteratura italiana*, vol. iii, *Le forme del testo* 1: *Teoria e poesia* (1984); D'A. S. Avalle, 'I canzonieri: definizione di genere e problemi di edizione', in *La critica del testo. Atti del Convegno di Lecce* (1985).

Canzoniere, Il. The traditional title for *Petrarch's collected lyric poems in Italian, first devised by 16th-c. editors, who were indifferent to the fact that it was misleading and historically inappropriate [see CANZONIERE]. It is now generally used in preference to *Rime sparse* (from the opening line of the first poem), which leads to confusion with the *Rime disperse*, the uncollected poems. Petrarch himself (followed by most modern scholars) uses the Latin title *Rerum vulgarium fragmenta* in the manuscript (Vat. Lat. 3195) transcribed, in the years leading up to his death in 1374, partly by himself and partly by Giovanni *Malpaghini working under his supervision. This contains 366 poems (317 *sonnets, 29 *canzoni, 9 *sestine, 7 *ballate, and 4 *madrigals) divided into two parts. The latter acquired at some point the headings 'in vita di madonna Laura' (263 poems) and 'in morte di madonna Laura' (103 poems), with the *canzone* 'I' vo pensando' (264) marking a critical turning point, as the poet struggles to renounce the erotic love and worldly glory that had been the dominant themes of the first part, and devote himself to the search for eternal salvation in the second.

The final ordering was probably not intended to be definitive, though the process of selection and revision of existing poems or the composition of new ones specifically for inclusion had been going on for years. E. H. Wilkins identified nine stages, each more complex than the last; the first goes back to 1342 and can be reconstructed from Petrarch's autograph drafts (Vat. Lat. 3196). The final version recounts the story of the poet's love for *Laura, beginning with the first sight of her on Good Friday, 6 April 1327 (*Canz.* 3 and 221), and continuing long after her death exactly twenty-one years later (*Canz.* 336). But earthly love is seen as either merging with or impeding spiritual progress. The theme of conversion is proposed in the very first poem and developed in various penitential poems, such as the famous 'Padre del ciel' (*Canz.* 62), reaching its climax and conclusion in the *canzone* to the Virgin (*Canz.* 366). The unresolved and irresolvable tension which results is the defining key to Petrarch's art. [MP]

Canzoniere and *Trionfi; Rime estravaganti; Codice degli abbozzi*, ed. M. Santagata (1996). See E. H. Wilkins, *The Making of the Canzoniere* (1951).

CAPASSO, ALDO (1909–97). Poet and critic from *Venice who lived much of his life in Liguria. He founded the movement *Realismo lirico*, which enjoyed the support of *Borgese and *Cardarelli, and edited a journal of the same name. He also contributed to *Solaria* and *La Nazione* as a young man. Though he wrote poems celebrating *Fascism, for instance, *9 poesie per il Duce* (1933), he continued in more meditative vein after *World War II. He also wrote critical studies of French and Italian writers. [DCH]

CAPASSO, NICOLÒ (1671–1745). Law professor at *Naples and a friend of the elder Pietro *Giannone and *Vico, who excelled in Neapolitan dialect poetry, writing *satirical *sonnets (1713–30) and the *macaronic Neapolitan–Latin *De curiositatibus Romae strangulapreticon* (1726). His masterpiece is a *parody of Homer's *Iliad*, books 1–6 and part of book 7 (1737). [JMAL]

Capitan Fracassa (1880–91, 1901–5). *Roman daily paper, founded by a group of *journalists, which was made popular by its caricatures and its distinctive humorous and satirical columns, largely published under pseudonyms. Contributors included *De Amicis, *Guerrini, *Pascarella, and *Serao. Initially liberal and progressive, it became steadily more conformist as its editorial personnel changed. [PH]

Capitano, Il. An important unmasked role of the *commedia dell'arte*, often distinctive for being a social outsider, capable of complicating the action, introducing a bravura note, and serving as *amoroso* to one of the female characters. Often accompanied by a *zanni*, he was frequently a species of *miles gloriosus*, the exchanges between him and his servant providing opportunities for extravagant rhetoric, nicely instanced in Francesco *Andreini's *Bravure del Capitan Spavento* (1607). Elegant and fashionable of dress, frequently bearing the air of a Spanish hidalgo, the role declined in importance in the early 17th c. [KR]

Capitolo, see CANTO.

CAPNIST, GIOVANNI, see COOKERY BOOKS.

CAPODILISTA, GABRIELE (d. 1477). *Paduan doctor in canon *law (1460), who acted as *podestà* in *Perugia (1473). He described his 1458 journey to the Holy Land in an influential *Itinerario in Terra Santa*, which is one of the sources of Santo *Brasca. [See also TRAVEL WRITING.] [LL]

CAPORALI, CESARE (1531–1601). Poet who served various noble *patrons in *Rome, *Florence, and his native *Perugia. His early poems satirize *court life in the manner of *Berni. His *Viaggio in Parnaso* and *Avvisi di Parnaso* are humorous fantasies which anticipate the better-known *Ragguagli* of Traiano *Boccalini; the *Vita di Mecenate* and *Esequie di Mecenate* are poetic versions of Roman history centred on Maecenas, the model patron of poetry. [RMD]

CAPPA, BENEDETTA, see BENEDETTA.

CAPPELLO, BERNARDO (1498–1565). Minor poet, who was the son of a Venetian diplomat and a friend of Pietro *Bembo, Bernardo *Tasso, and Giovanni *Della Casa. Exiled from *Venice for political reasons in 1540, he spent the rest of his life in *court service between *Rome, *Urbino, and Parma. [LPer]

Cappello del prete, Il, see DE MARCHI, EMILIO.

CAPPIELLO, ROSA, see ITALIAN WRITERS IN AUSTRALIA.

CAPPONI, GINO (1792–1876). *Florentine noble active in politics as a *liberal throughout the *Risorgimento period. He also played a leading part in the cultural life of Florence. He was a friend of *Foscolo, *Tommaseo, *Leopardi, and *Manzoni (with whom he had important exchanges on linguistic topics). He also promoted the *Antologia and the *Archivio storico italiano*. [FD'I]

Cappuccini, see FRANCISCANS.

CAPRANICA, LUIGI (1821–91). *Roman noble who served in the Papal Guards and was encouraged by Pius IX to pursue a literary career. After settling in *Milan, he published a series of patriotic *historical novels, beginning with *Giovanni dalle bande nere* (1857), and some collections of stories. [DO'G]

CAPRIN, GIUSEPPE (1843–1904). Writer and *journalist who promoted Italian *nationalist feeling in Friuli and his native *Trieste. Fighting under *Garibaldi, he was wounded at Bezzecca (1866). His historical works include *I tempi andati* (1891), on Trieste in the 1830s and 1840s, and *Il Trecento a Trieste* (1897). *Sfumature* (1876) and *A suon di campane* (1877) contain short regional *novelle*. [PBarn]

CAPRIOLO, PAOLA (1962–). Novelist, who was born and lives in *Milan. The stories of *La grande Eulalia* (1988) and *novels such as *La spettatrice* (1995), *Un uomo di carattere* (1996), and *Una di loro* (2001) are all composed in lucid, classically literary Italian, and focus largely on the neurotically ordered existence of the protagonists. Her aesthetics are made plain in her study of Gottfried Benn, *L'assoluto artificiale* (1996). [PH]

CAPRONI, GIORGIO (1912–90). One of the most individual of modern Italian poets. He spent his early years in Livorno, but soon moved to *Genoa, where he studied literature and music. From 1939 onwards he lived in *Rome. He fought in *World War II as a soldier and then as a partisan in the *Resistance. After the war he earned his living as a teacher and translator. His poetry, collected in *L'opera in versi* (1998), begins with realistic sketches and anecdotes that look back to *Pascoli and even more to *Saba, though the principal theme is

an almost sensual love of life in all its aspects. From the mid-1960s his work takes on forms that are increasingly ironic, theatrical, and meta-literary. It is now marked by an unaggressive nihilism, and reworks the 18th-c. *canzonetta* [see VERSIFICATION] or *operatic aria to sing of the death of God and the vanity of all things, following a poetics of lightness that in many ways comes close to that of the later *Calvino. [GM]

CAPUANA, LUIGI (1839–1915). Writer and critic who was one of the most active *Sicilian *veristi* and the most instrumental in introducing the principles of French naturalism into Italian literary culture.

Born in Mineo in the province of Catania (Sicily), Capuana studied law at the University of Catania. In 1864, he moved to *Florence, then capital of Italy, where he met Giovanni *Verga, with whom he developed a lifelong friendship. For the greater part of his adult life Capuana was involved in local politics, and was twice elected mayor of Mineo. He also worked as theatre critic for *La Nazione* and the *Corriere della sera*, and was editor of *Il *Fanfulla della domenica*. His employment as a teacher of literature included positions at the Istituto Superiore Femminile in *Rome and at the University of Catania. His cultural interests were just as varied as his professional activities, ranging from prose fiction and drama to parapsychology, folklore, popular poetry [see FOLK AND POPULAR LITERATURE] and *photography. His literary production includes the novels *Giacinta* (1879), *Profumo* (1890), *La sfinge* (1895), *Rassegnazione* (1900), and *Il *marchese di Roccaverdina* (1901), a large number of *novelle*, including stories written for children, plays in Sicilian *dialect, and a collection of poems.

In his conversations with Verga, Capuana became concerned with the creation of a new literature attentive to social and psychological truth ('il vero'). He took as his model the experimental method elaborated in France by Émile Zola, according to which the writer, in imitation of the scientist, observed reality impassively without inquiring into its ultimate causes. Capuana, however, combined his interest in French realism with readings of Hegel and *De Sanctis, from whom he acquired the concept of 'typicality' (*tipicità*), which was to alter his faith in naturalism. In fact, Capuana's positive attitude toward Zola and the experimental novel changed considerably during the course of his literary development, as he distanced himself from *Positivism and the hopes associated with its progressive social philosophy. In his essay 'La crisi del romanzo' (1898), he claims that Zola could never have taken seriously his own formula for 'experimental' fiction. The novel, rather than being a scientific programme that examines cause and effect relations, must give characters and events the liberty to be what they naturally are. Positivism and naturalism, Capuana argues in his study of Verga and *D'Annunzio, must exert their influence on the form rather than on the content of the work, which only in this way would become truly objective and impersonal.

Yet the influence of Zola on Capuana, especially in the novel *Giacinta*, is decisive. The work is dedicated to him, and reflects both Zola's and his own belief that modern studies of heredity had made it possible to understand both the unity and variety of human life. Capuana's naturalism consisted much less in scientific and photographic accuracy than in the depiction of the individual as a product of the laws of nature and heredity. It also lent to Zola's Positivism a strong aesthetic dimension, in the belief that the work of art perfects science by giving a life to characters and events that is more complete that anything that scientific testing could provide. Capuana thus held that the novel was the work of both science and art in that it made possible the representation of case studies of eccentric people and situations within the general, determining conditions of life. Both in *Giacinta* and in the more complex *Il marchese di Roccaverdina*, Capuana takes as his focus the psychology of a protagonist whose actions contest immutable social norms and who is destined to meet defeat in madness and death. [RSD]

See V. P. Traversa, *Luigi Capuana, Critic and Novelist* (1968); C. A. Madrignani, *Capuana e il naturalismo* (1970).

Capuismo, see DI CAPUA, LIONARDO.

Carabinieri, see ARMED FORCES AND POLICE.

CARACCIO, ANTONIO (1630–?1702) was a member of the Accademia degli *Investiganti in *Naples, and a prolific poet who joined the Accademia dell'*Arcadia in 1690. His *Impero vendicato*, published first in 1679 in twenty cantos, and then in 1690 in forty cantos, is an *epic or *romance about the Fourth *Crusade of 1202–4. The work interweaves an epic subject (the conquest of Constantinople) with love episodes, and is closer to the *Orlando furioso* than to the *Gerusalemme*

liberata. He also wrote wedding poems (1650–71), *lyric poetry (1689), and a *tragedy (1694).
[PBD]

CARAFA, DIOMEDE (?1406–87). A member of one of the most powerful baronial families of *Naples, who served the *Aragonese kings as soldier, administrator, diplomat, and adviser, rising to great prominence under Ferrante I. In his thirteen *Memoriali* (only one of which, on the perfect courtier, was published in his lifetime, and not all of which have survived) he gives advice, mostly to members of the royal family, on the financial and military implications of politics and on matters of etiquette. Composed in a strongly dialectal vernacular, the *Memoriali* are striking for their realism and the attention they pay to economic issues.
[EGH]

Carbonari (literally 'charcoal-burners'). The most successful of all the secret societies which developed in opposition to *Napoleonic rule in Italy and which owed allegiance to the *Jacobin Filippo Buonarroti. Apart from loyalty to the ideas of the French Revolution, the movement was characterized by intense secrecy and by a strict hierarchy which often compromised its activities. Disappointed by the *Restoration, carbonarist movements spread northwards from Southern Italy but, despite official alarm, were rarely a genuine threat. In 1820 *carbonari* were briefly successful in winning constitutions in *Naples and Palermo and were also active in revolutions in Spain and *Piedmont. After the failure of the 1831 revolution, the movement was superseded by *Mazzini's *Giovine Italia*.
[LR]

CARBONE, LUDOVICO (1430–85). *Humanist, probably a native of Cremona, who taught rhetoric and classics at the University of *Ferrara. The funeral oration he gave there for *Guarino da Verona in 1460 contains a wealth of information about Ferrarese learning of the time. He remained in Ferrara, though he was invited to England in 1460 by one of his pupils, John Tiptof, and later invited to Hungary by King Matthias. His collection of *Facezie, dedicated to Borso d'*Este, in markedly regional Italian, is inferior to Poggio *Bracciolini's but shows elements of originality.
[DieZ]

CARBONI, RAFFAELLO, see ITALIAN WRITERS IN AUSTRALIA.

CARCANO, GIULIO (1812–82). *Milanese poet, playwright, and novelist. His fiction, notably the contemporary novel *Angiola Maria* (1839), has a moralizing, rather sentimental quality. He was the addressee of Cesare *Correnti's 'Della letteratura rusticale', and attempted to represent the *peasantry with understanding and compassion. He took part in the revolution of *1848 and later became a senator. In his retirement he *translated the whole of *Shakespeare (1875–82).   [DO'G]

CARDANO, GEROLAMO (1501–76) studied *medicine and mathematics in *Padua, though his wide-ranging intellectual interests led to works on many subjects. He held chairs of medicine at Pavia and *Bologna and travelled widely. He was arrested by the *Inquisition in Bologna in 1570 but released. Between 1575 and 1576 he wrote his *De propria vita*, a complex work that seeks to justify the trials and tribulations of his personal, religious, and professional life, and which betrays his belief in astral powers. During his lifetime he acquired an international reputation for producing horoscopes and for his works on *medicine, mathematics, *astrology, natural philosophy, and dreams.
                                    [PLR]

CARDARELLI, VINCENZO (pseud. of Nazareno Calarelli) (1887–1959). Poet and literary *journalist. Born in Corneto Tarquinia in the Tuscan Maremma, he began his career as a journalist for *Avanti!*, but became disillusioned with *Socialism and increasingly attracted to *nationalism. Before *World War I he wrote for La *Voce and a number of other avant-garde journals. His first work, *Prologhi* (1916), was an aggressive *autobiography made up of fragments of prose and poetry. It was close in style to a number of other autobiographical experiments by avant-garde writers in *Florence, where Cardarelli lived for a time.

After the war he abandoned experimental *modernism. He moved to *Rome and, heading a band of close associates, founded his own journal, La *Ronda* (1919–23), which aimed to liquidate the experience of the avant-garde and to promote a classically balanced form of expression. He was now drawn to *prosa d'arte* and began to write a series of short and elegantly crafted prose pieces, first exemplified in *Favole e memorie* (1925). In the immediate postwar years he argued for the separation of art and politics, but his attempt to impose a form of literary order paralleled some *Fascist cultural policies, and he became a convinced supporter of *Mussolini. In the late 1920s he expounded the reasons for his allegiance to Fascism in journals such as Il *Selvaggio* and L'*Italiano,* in which he became an important voice of *strapaese.* Two further collections of poetic prose, *Il sole a picco* (1929) and *Il cielo sulle città* (1939), celebrated regional and national culture while showing a clear antipathy for the modern world. The poetry of these years, which was collected in *Poesie* (1936), displays a more decadent sensibility and an occasional closeness to certain *hermetic verse.

After *World War II he edited the journal La *fiera letteraria* for a time, and produced some autobiographical volumes, but otherwise his career as a creative writer was at an end. His work has been much criticized since his death; his poetry has been dismissed as abstract and discursive, while his notion of *classicism has been interpreted as essentially restrictive. But he remains a figure who cannot be easily dismissed, and not solely for historical reasons.   [CFB]

See G. Grasso, *La poesia di Vincenzo Cardarelli* (1982); C. Burdett, *Vincenzo Cardarelli and his Contemporaries* (1999).

CARDELLA, LARA (1967–) shot to prominence in 1989 with the publication of *Volevo i pantaloni,* a semi-autobiographical account of a *Sicilian childhood. The novel provoked outraged national debate with its denunciation of repressive, humiliating attitudes to girls and of widespread sexual abuse. The novels *Una ragazza normale* (1995) and *Detesto il soft* (1997) continue her exploration of issues of female sexuality.   [SW]

CARDUCCI, GIOSUE (1835–1907). Poet, literary scholar, and the first Italian Nobel prize winner for literature (1906). He was born of educated parents near Versilia, studied philosophy and philology at the Scuola Normale Superiore in *Pisa, rose from teacher in a *liceo* to the Chair of Italian Literature at the University of *Bologna, married, had various mistresses, and ended his life as a widely respected establishment figure. The metaphor of a parable was used by *Sapegno to characterize the life of a man who turned from an unruly student into a professorial patriarch, himself the butt of student protests, and from an ardent republican into a member of Italy's royalist establishment. The student who declared himself xenophobic and parochial to the core later adapted and translated foreign poets. He had written the *Inno a Satana*

Carducci, Giosue

(1865), which naïvely pictured progress as an unstoppable surge of sensual pleasures, heresies, and steam engines, and drew on him the ire of the Church; but he also wrote 'La chiesa di Polenta' (in 1897), which raised the possibility of his tardy conversion to Christianity. The scourge of politicians and governments in *Giambi ed epodi* (1882) became the panegyrist of united Italy in *Rime e ritmi* (1899).

The parable metaphor is, however, misleading. A closer look at Carducci's life shows that it was less a continuous curve linking youthful radicalism, moderate maturity, and respectable old age than a summation of apparent contradictions. The coexistence of professed *classicism with instinctive *Romanticism was typical also of *Foscolo and *Leopardi, after whom nobody could write classicist verse in the style of *Parini or Vincenzo *Monti. Yet no serious aspiring poet could call himself a Romantic, considering the poverty of much that the movement generated in Italy. Romantic forms, furthermore, restricted poets to romantic themes and contents, whereas classical forms were traditionally used for the most varied purposes, from the celebration of one's beloved or the deeds of *Napoleon to the description of botanical gardens and hot-air balloons, and the condemnation of air pollution, allowing maximum latitude. Carducci used them to experiment with a large variety of themes—political diatribe, love, history, landscape, patriotism—which from 1850 onwards he began to express also through imitations of ancient classical stanza forms, such as the Alcaic and the Sapphic. Since they were based on stress and not on syllabic quantity, he believed they would have sounded 'barbaric' to classical poets: hence the title *Odi barbare* (1877), followed by *Nuove odi barbare* (1882), *Terze odi barbare* (1889), all collected as *Odi barbare* (1893) [see also VERSIFICATION].

The coexistence of Carducci's *Mazzinian radicalism with his acceptance of the new *monarchy seems less contradictory when one realizes that his republicanism was directed against the petty tyrants of pre-*Unification Italy, destined to be swept away by the 'bianca croce di Savoia', as he writes in 1859 in 'Alla croce di Savoia'; and his praises of Queen Margherita in 'Alla Regina d'Italia' of 1878 were consonant with the general feeling of relief when Victor Emmanuel II's mistress, the uncouth daughter of an army sergeant whom the late king had married morganatically, was at last eclipsed by a cultured, high-born queen. When in 1883 Carducci published a collection of twelve *sonnets entitled *Ça ira*, he was celebrating not so

much, in a new volte-face, the victory of republicanism over monarchy, as the triumph of the bourgeois revolution and the hegemony of the middle classes to which he himself belonged. Because of the mediocrity and corruption of the contemporary Italian ruling class, however, the kind of lofty bourgeois hegemony he aspired to was destined to remain a distant ideal. His criticism of his contemporaries was so hard-hitting as to appear radical and revolutionary; but, however enlightened, it was nevertheless bound by bourgeois ideology, and rarely able to rise above satirical moralism. When bourgeois interests were threatened from below, Carducci predictably and coherently embraced and defended anti-democratic and repressive principles.

It is therefore not surprising that generations of readers who survived two world wars and *Fascism turned away from Carducci's poetry, even if there remained a widespread consensus regarding his status as the most important writer of his generation. A sense of lassitude at his steady and magniloquent output, punctuating almost every important event in Italy after Unification, had already set in shortly after his death, when he was unkindly defined as a 'poeta professore', whose poetry was the pedantic product of erudition. It would be truer to say that Carducci's lifelong interest in poetry stimulated his remarkable scholarship. He left a considerable body of critical writing, in which the lack of the kind of overall aesthetic and philosophical principles adopted by *De Sanctis (whom Carducci disliked) is compensated for by a technical and rhetorical mastery of the highest order in dealing with questions of detail, coupled with unfailing good taste. Much of it can still be read with pleasure and profit.

Carducci saw himself in the 'Congedo' of the *Rime nuove* (his main collection of non-'barbarous' poetry published in 1887) as a poet-prophet-blacksmith forging beautiful and useful cultural tools for his people. Unfortunately, this productive and open-ended metaphor was soon treated as a definitive critical formula. Carducci himself was made into a monument, in part thanks to *Pascoli, who needed a master to set off his own humility, and to *D'Annunzio, who needed a national bard he could succeed to. The metaphor of Carducci's life as a parable leading to a predictable conclusion obscures the real variety and fecundity of his poetry. Much of it has a lasting appeal. In the *Rime nuove* he proves a skilful reworker of medieval themes in poems such as 'Il comune rustico', 'Sui campi di Marengo', and 'Faida di comune' (as also in *La canzone di Legnano* of 1879); whilst he achieves remarkable blends of neoclassical and romantic motifs in 'Primavere elleniche' and pure moments of autobiographical lyricism in 'Idillio maremmano', 'Pianto antico', and 'Davanti a San Guido'. Of the *Odi barbare* 'Alla stazione in una mattina d'autunno', which culminates in the image of the steam engine carrying his beloved away from him like a fiery Moloch, is one of the most impressive Italian poems of all time.   [GC]

Edizione Nazionale delle opere di G. Carducci (1935–40). See M. Biagini, *G. Carducci: biografia critica* (1976); G. Carducci, *Selected Verse*, ed. and trans. D. H. Higgins (with introductory essay) (1994).

CARIGNANO, GIUSEPPINA DI LORENA, see WOMEN WRITERS, 2.

CARITEO, IL (sobriquet of Benedetto Gareth) (*c.*1450–1514). Poet of Catalan origins, born in Barcelona, who moved to *Naples in 1467/8. He made his name at the *Aragonese court as a speaker, poet, and musician, and rose to hold various offices under Ferdinand II. A friend of both *Pontano and *Sannazaro, he was given the name 'Il Chariteo' or 'the son of the Graces', by fellow-members of the Accademia Pontaniana. He was a *Petrarchist, and composed a *canzoniere entitled *Endimione alla luna*, 'Luna' being the name he used for his beloved. First published in 1506 and then again in 1509, it is remarkable for the originality with which it enriches the formal restraint of 16th-c. Petrarchism with imitations of *Virgil, *Ovid, *Horace, and other Latin poets. In 1501–3 Cariteo was part of Angelo *Colocci's circle in *Rome for a while. He brought to Rome, probably at this time, the Provençal manuscript M, which provided the basis for the study of *troubadour poetry in Italy by Pietro *Bembo and his successors, and which remained in Rome until it was taken to Paris by French troops in 1799.   [NC]

CARLETTI, FRANCESCO (1573–1636). *Florentine *merchant and *travel writer. His *Ragionamenti sopra le cose da lui vedute ne' suoi viaggi dell'Indie occidentali come d'altri paesi*, published posthumously by *Magalotti in 1701, narrate a round-the-world journey that lasted from 1594 to 1606. Highlights of his tales include the slave market at Santiago, where he haggles over seventy-five slaves and reveals contemporary Florentine racial views; his year-long stay in Mexico city; the fire at Manila that destroyed all his accumulated treasures; the amazing and horrifying (for him) sexual practices of the Filipinos; the peculiarities of China and Japan; his imprisonment at the hands of the Portuguese in Macao; his stay in Goa; and the dangerous return journey, via Lisbon and Paris, to Florence. By the time the work, written between 1609 and 1636, was published, most of the places and many of the customs were known in Italy; but, with its elegant classical prose, its vivid attention to detail, and its mercantile focus, it remains a valuable insight into its times, and a corrective to the *Jesuit-inspired accounts of Daniello *Bartoli.   [PBD]

CARLI, GIANRINALDO (1720–95). Istrian intellectual with encyclopedic interests. He wrote an early work on *tragic *theatre showing a predilection for love themes. He subsequently produced influential writings on monetary reform, and was called to *Milan to preside over the Supreme Council of the Economy (1765). He became a collaborator of Pietro *Verri in the Milanese administration, and supported *Il *Caffè*, to which he contributed a famous article, 'Della patria degli italiani', seen as foreshadowing a united Italy. The most moderate of the Lombard reformers, Carli became increasingly conservative, and his later writings display a sceptical detachment from the belief in liberty and equality.   [GLCB]

CARLI, MARIO (1889–1935). *Tuscan writer associated with the *Florentine periodical *L'Italia futurista* (1916–18), who became one of *Futurism's leading political activists. He started the ex-combatant Arditi association (1919) and participated in *D'Annunzio's Fiume expedition. He was a committed *Fascist and founded and edited *L'Impero* (1923–9) with Emilio Settimelli.   [SV]

Carlomagno, see CAROLINGIAN.

Carmen in victoriam Pisanorum. Anonymous *Pisan poem of 146 assonanced Latin couplets. Presumably composed soon after August 1087, it celebrates a victorious naval campaign of that month led by Pisa against Mahdia (Muslim North Africa). It foreshadows the concept of holy warfare underlying the *Crusades.   [JCB]

CARNEVALI, EMANUELE, see ITALIAN WRITERS IN THE UNITED STATES.

CARNINO GHIBERTI, see SICULO-TUSCAN POETS.

Carnival is the festival immediately prior to Lent. The Italian term *carnevale* derives from the Latin *carnem levare*, to put away flesh. All classes took part in exuberant celebrations in which eating and drinking, activities restricted during Lent, played a prominent part. Revellers wore masks representing classical or recent heroes, pagan divinities, and symbolic figures, as well as different social groups and professions. Music and dancing always accompanied the merrymaking, and in 15th-c. *Florence a form of verse composition in eight-syllable lines, the *canti carnascialeschi*, emerged as a celebration of the festivities and the figures depicted on the masks. [See also FARSE CAVAIOLE; FESTIVALS.]
[GPTW]

CARO, ANNIBALE (1507–66). Writer, translator, critic, and *academician. Born and educated in Civitanova Marche, he moved to *Florence in 1525 as tutor to Lorenzo Lenzi, curtailing his own studies but coming into contact with Florentine literary and cultural circles, including that of Benedetto *Varchi. Throughout his life Caro was dependent on the *patronage of others; in 1529 he followed his first patron, Giovanni Gaddi, to *Rome, joined the household of Duke Pier Luigi *Farnese in 1543 in Piacenza, and accompanied him to France and Flanders, before returning to Rome in 1547 under the patronage of Cardinal Alessandro Farnese. He retired from *court life in 1563 and died in Rome three years later.

Caro's many *translations from the classics are typical of the times in being free paraphrases rather than close renderings of the original; they include a version of the *Aeneid* in *ottava rima, and, among many translations of Greek classics, a version of Longus' *Daphnis and Chloe*. His own vernacular works include *lyric poetry of various kinds, influenced by *Petrarch and classical poets; he also came under the influence of *Berni. His best-known work, the *comedy *Gli straccioni* (1543–4), owes much to classical models, but is based on the struggle between two well-known contemporary Romans for an inheritance. Caro's assertion of the supremacy of the lyric and defence of *Petrarchism led him (in *Apologia degli accademici di Banchi*) into a fierce polemic with *Castelvetro, in which he had the support of Florentine literary circles. More than 1,000 of his letters survive, collected by himself.
[JEE]

CAROCCI, ALBERTO (1904–72). Novelist and poet, best known as a founder and editor of literary *journals, particularly in 1930s *Florence. He was principally responsible for *Solaria* (1926–35). On its closure by the *Fascist authorities, he founded *La Riforma letteraria* (1936–9) with Giacomo *Noventa. In 1941 he founded *Argomenti* with Raffaello Ramat, and in 1953 in Rome *Nuovi argomenti* with Alberto *Moravia.
[SVM]

Carolingian, relating to the Emperor Charlemagne (Carlomagno). See CHIVALRY; EPIC; ROMANCE; SPAGNA, LA.

CARRÀ, CARLO (1881–1962). Painter. Of *Piedmontese origin, he began as a member of the Divisionist school in *Milan. He joined the *Futurist movement in 1910, but quite soon distanced himself from Milanese Futurism, writing for *Lacerba* and *La *Voce* in *Florence and then for *Valori plastici* in *Rome. An association with *De Chirico led to 'metaphysical' art, of which he wrote a polemical account in *La scuola metafisica* (1919). From 1921 onwards he settled into a classicizing form of *realismo magico*.
[AM]

Carrara dynasty. See PADUA.

CARRER, LUIGI (1801–50). *Venetian poet and critic who gained early notoriety as an *improviser of verse *tragedies. He then worked both in teaching and *publishing. He wrote three volumes of essays on *Goldoni (1825), and founded the literary-political magazine *La Moda*, later re-named *Il Gondoliere* (1833–43). His *Ballate* (1834) focus on historical themes and were a popular success.
[MPC]

CARTARI, VINCENZO, see ICONOGRAPHY.

Casa in collina, La (1949). Semi-autobiographical novel by *Pavese. A teacher is caught up in the turmoil of war in *Piedmont in 1943, but is unable to commit himself either to the *Resistance or to a woman and her child, possibly his own son. His moral dilemmas are seen against both larger historical changes and the unchanging cycles of nature.
[NMS]

CASALICCHIO, CARLO (1624–1700). Short-story and religious writer who lived in *Naples. His *L'utile col dolce*, published in two parts in 1671–8 and 1733, contains 300 chapters each with a *novella* and its moral. He drew on many literary sources to entertain and educate his readers. He attempted to import into the written *novella* techniques developed in the art of preaching, aiming to stimulate the senses of the reader in order to drive his point home. He also wrote religious works, many of them entitled *Stimoli*.   [PBD]

CASANOVA, GIOVANNI GIACOMO (1725–98). Writer of memoirs and much else, mostly in French, who was also a spy, swindler, and seducer. Born in *Venice, he took a degree in law at *Padua, and soon after embarked on his career as an adventurer. Escaping from prison in Venice, he spent periods in various European countries, each time being forced to leave, until in his last years he became librarian to Count Waldstein in Bohemia. His works include histories, political and satirical pamphlets, utopian novels such as *Icosameron* (1788), mathematical treatises such as *Solution du problème déliaque* (1790), and plays such as *Le Polé-moscope ou La Calomnie démasquée* (1791). He had already published the autobiographical *Il duello* (1780) and *Histoire de ma fuite* (1788), when in 1789 in Bohemia he began his vast *L'Histoire de ma vie*. This minutely detailed reconstruction of his life up to 1774, which was put on the *Index even before it was finished, is less an account of *libertine excess than a masterpiece of 18th-c. *autobiog-raphy—structurally opulent, evocatively written, and displaying the breadth of education and vast range of interests of its author.   [SC]

Casella. *Florentine musician and friend of *Dante's, whom he meets in *Purgatorio* 2.

CASONI, GUIDO (1561–1642). A practising lawyer in Treviso and *Venice, he is generally held to be one of the earliest exponents of *concettismo*. His *Ode* (1602, expanded 1639) celebrate social and political events in the two cities (he was knighted for civic merits). His copious writings also include a treatise on love, *Magia d'amore* (1591), and the discourses in verse *Emblemi politici* (1632) and *Meditazioni divote* (1636).   [MPS]

CASSARINO, ANTONIO, see SICILY.

CASSIANI, GIULIANO (1712–78). Professor of rhetoric at Modena University. His *Saggio di rime* (1730), with 'Il ratto di Proserpina', 'La caduta d'Icaro', and 'Susanna', set an example of descrip-tive *sonnets based on episodes from the Bible or

Greek myth which was followed by Onofrio *Minzoni, Vincenzo *Monti, *Alfieri, and others.   [JMAL]

CASSIO DA NARNI, see BRUCURELLI, CASSIO.

CASSOLA, CARLO (1917–87). Novelist. Ori-ginally from *Rome, where he took a degree in law, Cassola gravitated as a schoolteacher to the Tuscan Maremma, where he took part in the *Resistance during *World War II and which became the set-ting for much of his fiction.

Cassola considered himself to belong to no specific literary current, though he has always been closely linked with *Neorealism. His writing identi-fies intensely with the emotional experience and material life of working people, though it was often criticized in the postwar years for lack of political *impegno, and his Resistance novel, *Fausto e Anna* (1952), was attacked for its unflattering character-ization of the partisans. His strengths are evident in *Il taglio del bosco* (1959, but first published in 1949 in *Paragone*). It is an austerely poetic narrative: the woodcutter Guglielmo directs a felling operation through a seasonal cycle, aching unceasingly from the loss of his wife. That is all, but this was also Cassola's own experience in 1949, and led to a deep pessimism which is also found in subsequent novels. The private dimension controls the political dimension even in the sociological enquiry of *I minatori della Maremma* (1956), written jointly with Luciano *Bianciardi, which stays close to human reality, and culminates in the life histories of seventeen miners. Cassola almost explicitly declares his withdrawal from socio-political con-cerns in *La ragazza di Bube* (1960), which centres on a heroine persisting in self-denying devotion to the dubious Bube, in prison for a crime committed in the name of the Resistance. Here, where emo-tions run deep, matter-of-fact registration of every-day detail becomes poetic intensity. Negativity takes over in the pointedly titled *Un cuore arido* (1961), and triteness becomes a risk in the small-scale life histories of *Ferrovia locale* (1968) and the larger life history of Anna in *Paura e tristezza* (1970). Everyday conversation makes up much of *Troppo tardi* (1975), an autobiographically based novel set in wartime middle-class Rome.

Cassola took up a pacifist, anti-nuclear, and environmentalist stance in the 1970s, which led to the campaigning writing of *Ultima frontiera* (1975), *Contro le armi* (1980), and *La rivoluzione disarmista* (1983). Their fictional counterparts were *La morale del branco* (1980) and *Il mondo di nessuno* (1982). [JG-R]

See R. Bertacchini, *Carlo Cassola* (1979); P. N. Pedroni, *Existence as Theme in Carlo Cassola's Fiction* (1985).

CASSOLI, FRANCESCO (1749–1812), from Reggio Emilia, is now considered the finest poet of the Emilian *Scuola oraziana*, thanks to the subjective vein of his verse—for example in the ode 'Alla lucerna'. A *liberal aristocrat, he held office in Reggio during the revolutionary years 1796–9. [JMAL]

CASTELLANETA, CARLO (1930–). *Milanese novelist, whose productive literary career opened with *Viaggio col padre* (1958), a broadly *Neorealist account of his adolescence in wartime Milan. The city remains the setting and reference point for his subsequent work. But from the mid-1960s the focus alternates between individual psychology, as in *Gli incantesimi* (1968), and political themes, as in *La paloma* (1972). He remains a dedicated chronicler of the issues of contemporary everyday life. [JEB]

CASTELLANI, CASTELLANO (1461– *c.*1519). Poet and playwright, born in *Florence, who graduated in canon law at *Pisa. Apart from some *canti carnascialeschi*, his best poetry is of religious inspiration in the manner of *Savonarola, under whose spell he fell briefly. It includes a powerful *Meditatio mortis* in Italian. Numerous *sacre rappresentazioni* are also attributed to him. [DieZ]

CASTELVETRO, LUDOVICO (*c.*1505–71), of Modena, was one of the outstanding scholars and *literary critics of his century, and a friend of Giovanni Maria *Barbieri. From 1553 he became involved in a polemic with Annibale *Caro. Following interrogation on charges of *heresy, Castelvetro fled *Rome in 1560, moving eventually to Geneva, Lyon, and Chiavenna, where he died.

He translated and commented on *Aristotle's *Poetics* (1570) and studied vernacular verse: a commentary on *Petrarch, begun in 1545, appeared in 1582; another commentary on *Dante's *Divine Comedy* was partly destroyed, but the section on *Inferno* 1–39 was printed in 1886 (see also DANTE COMMENTARIES; PETRARCH COMMENTARIES). Some notes on *Boccaccio's *Decameron* are unpublished. A *Correttione* (correction) of *Varchi's *Ercolano*,

which had been conceived in Caro's defence, was printed in 1572 together with a *Giunta* (supplement) to *Bembo's *Prose della volgar lingua*, book 1; *Giunte* to books 2 and 3 appeared in 1714. The first *Giunta* is important for its anticipation of the concept of popular or vulgar Latin, its analysis of different stages in the influence of Germanic tongues on the evolution of Latin, and its identification of the origin of such features of Italian as the future tense and the definite article. [BR]

CASTI, GIOVANNI BATTISTA (1724– 1803). Writer who, in typically *Enlightenment fashion, experiments with different genres whilst keeping socio-political issues constantly in view. Born in Acquapendente near Viterbo, he moved to *Rome in 1760/1 and made his debut as an *Arcadian poet. Then, following in the steps of *Metastasio and *Da Ponte, he became poet to the imperial court in Vienna, where he stayed effectively until 1796, though with a period at St Petersburg and another in Italy, this last giving rise to *Relazione di un mio viaggio da Venezia a Costantinopoli* (1802). In Russia and Vienna he made his name mostly as a writer of *libretti. In 1798 he moved to Paris and was able to publish works that had been unacceptable in Italy—the *ottava rima Poema tartaro* (1797), which satirizes Russia and Catherine II, and the philosophically materialist and often licentious *Novelle galanti* (definitive edition 1802), satirizing relations between the sexes. In Paris he also wrote his most famous work, *Animali parlanti* (1802), a poem in twenty-six *canti of six-line stanzas, which uses the classical fable to depict the political battle between the aristocracy and democracy then under way. Though it attracted stinging criticism, it was lauded by *Leopardi, who treated it as a model of political *satire. [SC]

CASTIGLIA, RODERIGO DI, see RINASCITA; TOGLIATTI, PALMIRO.

CASTIGLIONE, BALDASSARRE (Baldesar) (1478– 1529) is most famous as the author of the *Libro del cortegiano*. Born at Casatico in the territory of *Mantua into an ancient noble family, Castiglione was related to the ruling *Gonzaga family through his mother, Aloisia. Sent to *Milan to complete his education, he experienced the brilliance of the *Sforza *court in its most vibrant period. His literary and courtly formation began in these years, but was cut short on the death of his father, in 1499, from wounds sustained at the battle of Fornovo

(1495). Castiglione therefore witnessed the entry of the French King Louis XII into Milan, but not the subsequent decline of the court after the fall of Ludovico il Moro.

His career as courtier and diplomat began immediately on his return to Mantua, when he became a soldier and courtier of Francesco Gonzaga, accompanying him on the military campaigns of this troubled period (1500–4). On one such mission he made the acquaintance of Guidobaldo da *Montefeltro and left Mantua for *Urbino, partly through the inducements of his cousin Cesare. Francesco Gonzaga reluctantly granted him leave to transfer his allegiance, and Castiglione was appointed as captain-at-arms to the Duke of Urbino from 1504. The period between 1504 and 1508 constituted the golden age of Castiglione's life and career, and provided the material for the Libro del cortegiano. In these years, in addition to participating in the flourishing cultural life of the Urbino court, Castiglione travelled widely on diplomatic business, including a visit to England in 1506.

Following the succession of Franceso Maria della Rovere as Duke of Urbino in 1508, Castiglione took part in military and political missions during the campaigns of Pope Julius II in central Italy. The election of Pope Leo X in 1513, when he was based mainly in *Rome, seemed to Castiglione to mark the beginning of a new golden age; but this Roman period came to an abrupt end in 1516, with the enforced deposition of Francesco Maria della Rovere and the installation as duke of the younger Lorenzo de' *Medici. Unable or unwilling to accept the political coup, Castiglione returned to Mantua and to a few years of domestic and married life. Between 1516 and 1521 he was once again in the service of the Gonzaga. When his wife died giving birth to their third child, he began to think of entering the Church. He took orders in 1521 and entered the papal diplomatic service in 1524. He was made papal nuncio to Spain, and spent the last five years of his life at the Spanish court. In Spain he was bedevilled by the constant indecision and changes of policy of his master, Pope Clement VII, and hindered by his own admiration for the Emperor Charles V. His earlier experiences of the small courts and internal politics of Italy did not prepare him for the international power-broking of the 1520s, but it did clearly reveal to him that the world celebrated in the Cortegiano was ineluctably passing away. He spent the last years of his life completing the revisions to his major work, which was finally printed in 1528, a year before his death in Toledo.

Apart from the Libro del cortegiano, he wrote lyrics in both Latin (Carmina) and Italian (Rime), and a *pastoral poem, Tirsi (1506), composed as a court entertainment at Urbino. He also provided the prologue for the first performance of Bernardo *Dovizi's *Calandra (1513), which he was also responsible for staging. The Epistola de vita et gestis Guidubaldi Urbini Ducis, a commemoration of the award of the Order of the Garter to Guidobaldo by Henry VII, looks forward in part to some of the chapters of the Cortegiano.

The four books of the Cortegiano purport to record a series of conversations which took place on consecutive evenings at the court of Urbino in 1507. The use of the *dialogue form owes much to the *humanist debates of the 15th c., though there are reflections too of the debates of the brigata in the cornice of *Boccaccio's *Decameron, and a significant dependence on handbooks for the *education of the public servant, stemming originally from *Cicero and Quintilian. In essence each book is centred on a particular theme, debated between a presenter and a chief opponent. Book 1 deals with the intrinsic qualities of the courtier, in particular nobility and the essential attributes of grazia and sprezzatura, a concept best defined as the art of doing difficult things naturally and easily; book 2 deals with how the courtier puts these qualities into effect; book 3 turns attention to the lady at court and her attributes; book 4 returns to the male courtier and considers his relationships to his prince and to society, but ends with a celebration by one of the participants, Pietro *Bembo, of the *Neoplatonic ideal of love.

The Cortegiano has been interpreted in many ways, which is a measure of the richness of the material it contains. The setting and the debates were fictionalized by Castiglione, and often modified in emphasis during the twenty-year period of the book's gestation, but the book is deeply concerned with contemporary realities. Behind the courtly etiquette and urbane exchanges is discernible a set of political and practical preoccupations similar to those which concerned *Machiavelli in the Principe. Discussions range far beyond the immediate behaviour and talents of the courtier and the court lady, to include some of the most topical issues of the day: the *questione della lingua, aesthetics, Neoplatonism, the role of women in society, the best type of government, the influence of Fortune. Many of the elements of the debate spring from Castiglione's own experiences, both positive and negative, of serving a prince and of life at court, with its intense rivalry for the prince's favour. The practical usefulness of the book was immediately apparent to its first readers, and it rapidly became extremely influential, especially in the courts of Europe outside Italy. It was much translated and imitated, and spawned a whole new genre of books of manners that continues to this day.

Castiglione, who espoused a form of *lingua cortigiana*, writes in a prose style that is both elegant and lively. He is also well aware of the need to practise variety in tone and structure. Thus discourses by one speaker alternate with brief exchanges between several participants; serious philosophical or moralizing is punctured by witty interruptions and jokes at the speaker's expense; and midway through the work Castiglione introduces a whole series of chapters ostensibly to exemplify types of humour, but in fact to present a series of short witty tales that constitute his own contribution, if not a very original one, to the burgeoning genre of the *novella*.   [JEE]

    Il libro del Cortegiano, ed. B. Maier (1981). See J. Woodhouse, *Baldesar Castiglione: A Reassessment of 'The Courtier'* (1978); V. Cox, *The Renaissance Dialogue* (1992); P. Burke, *The Fortunes of the Courtier* (1995).

CASTRA (13th c.). *Florentine author of the humorous *canzone*, 'Una fermana scopai', which is grudgingly admired by *Dante (*DVE* 1.11). The poem uses rustic language with great effect to parody contemporary motifs in the love *lyric.   [JU]

CASULA, ANTIOCO, see SARDINIA.

CATANI, VITTORIO, see SCIENCE FICTION.

CATERINA OF BOLOGNA, ST, see VIGRI, CATERINA.

CATERINA OF GENOA, ST, see FIESCHI ADORNO, CATERINA.

CATERINA OF SIENA, ST (1347–80). Saint and writer. The daughter of a *Sienese dyer, she is traditionally believed to have shown as a child signs of mystical rapture. She became a *Dominican tertiary or lay sister in 1365, the first unmarried woman to join an order intended solely for widows, and, assisted by her Dominican guides, acquired a good education, possibly learning Latin. Her asceticism aroused the suspicions of the Church authorities, as did her interventions in public

affairs. In 1374 she was examined by the General Chapter of the Dominicans in *Florence and given a spiritual guide, Frate *Raimondo da Capua, who later wrote an account of her life, the *Legenda maior*. In 1376 she travelled to *Avignon to try to bring about a return of the *papacy to Rome, and after her return continued to press the need for reform within the Church. She wrote a *Libro della Divina Provvidenza*, but her main writings are her letters, of which nearly 400 survive, though not all are genuine. They were dictated by her, and document in a vigorous and effective style both her religious and mystical experiences and her political activity. Caterina is believed to have received the stigmata in 1375. She was canonized in 1461.   [NC]

CATHOLICISM AND THE CATHOLIC CHURCH, see PAPACY AND THE CATHOLIC CHURCH.

CATTAFI, BARTOLO (1922–79). Poet. Born in the province of Messina in *Sicily, he trained as a lawyer and then worked in advertising in *Milan. Travels in Africa and Europe were the inspiration behind earlier poetry, such as *Partenza da Greenwich* (1955). On returning to Sicily in 1967, he made his native landscape the focus of the poems of *L'aria secca del fuoco* (1972), turning, in *Montalian fashion, the sun-scorched terrain into a metaphor for a barren existential condition. The last poems, especially the posthumous *Chiromanzia d'inverno* (1983), are barer (at times Beckettian) confrontations with the absurdity of existence and the approach of death.   [VS-H]

CATTANEO, CARLO (1801–69). *Milanese philosopher, economist, and lawyer. A disciple of *Romagnosi, in 1839 he founded *Il *Politecnico*, the most important cultural *journal of the period. As its editor he placed great importance on scientific and technological issues as an essential part of progress and social renewal. His writings generally emphasize the link between knowledge and responsible citizenship, and combine discussions of scientific, historical, economic, social, and educational issues. Cattaneo bitterly opposed the hegemony of *Piedmont, believing that Italy's best interests lay in a federal republic. He was one of the leaders of the *Cinque giornate* of Milan in *1848. On the return of the *Austrians he fled to Paris and then Lugano, where he taught philosophy in a school. In Paris he wrote and published the controversial *L'insurrection de Milan* (1848), which he translated and expanded as *Dell'insurrezione di Milano nel 1848 e della successiva guerra* (1849) and *Archivio triennale delle cose d'Italia* (3 vols., 1850–5). Though Switzerland remained his base, he joined *Garibaldi in *Naples in 1860 and was elected three times to the Italian parliament. He resigned rather than take the oath of allegiance to the *monarchy.   [EAM]

CATTANI DA DIACCETO, FRANCESCO, see DIACCETO, FRANCESCO CATTANI DA.

CATTERMOLE, EVELINA, see CONTESSA LARA.

CAVACCHIOLI, ENRICO (1885–1954) began his literary career as a poet with *L'incubo velato* (1906) and signed the *Futurist manifesto in 1909, but moved away from the movement in 1914. A distinguished *journalist, editing *La Stampa* and *Il Secolo* and for many years *Illustrazione italiana,* he is better known as a playwright associated with the *grotteschi*. The best of his plays, *L'uccello del paradiso* (1920), enhances a traditional theme, the love of a mother and daughter for the same man, with the addition of an innovative metatextual figure, who comments on the action and acts as puppet master and *deus ex machina*.   [JAL]

CAVALCA, DOMENICO (d.1342). *Pisan *Dominican who compiled a wealth of moral and ascetic vernacular treatises. His main concern was with fallen women, for whom he founded the convent of Santa Maria in Pisa towards the end of his life. He was essentially a popularizer, but his versions of some of the *Church Fathers were later highly valued by linguistic *purists. [See also BIBLE.]   [JT]

CAVALCANTI, BARTOLOMEO (1503–62). *Florentine scholar-diplomat who served the Republic (1527–30), went into exile (1537), and spent his remaining years working for the *Este and *Farnese families. He died in poverty in *Padua. His works reflect his interest in politics and scholarship: an oration to the Florentine militia (1530), political memoranda, diplomatic letters, translations from Polybius, essays on classical *political thought (1571), and an amazingly successful *Retorica* (ten editions from 1559 to 1585). The last, a comprehensive compendium of classical rhetoric written in Italian with Italian examples, maintains that the function of rhetoric is civic and practical rather than literary.   [ECMR]

CAVALCANTI, GUIDO (?1260–1300). The most intellectual and most imaginative voice in Italian *lyric poetry of his time, and for a while a dominant influence on the young *Dante. He was born into the *Florentine aristocracy, and took enough part in politics to gain the enmity of the powerful Donati faction [see BLACKS AND WHITES]. Corso Donati apparently tried to have him assassinated in the course of a pilgrimage to Compostella. He was briefly exiled in 1300, presumably in the wake of these disturbances, and died soon after his return, perhaps as a result of illness contracted in the unhealthy Lunigiana. Contemporary anecdotes represent him as haughty and solitary, absorbed in philosophical speculation. True or not, this image fits with the tone of his poetry. He may have studied at *Bologna or at least have been acquainted with *university circles there. If he did not actually meet his closest predecessor, Guido *Guinizzelli, in Bologna, he certainly knew his poetry and at some stage, presumably in the later 1270s, imported his new intellectual style of poetry to Florence.

Just over fifty of his poems survive. Perhaps the earliest is a delicate *canzone, 'Fresca rosa novella', celebrating an angelically beautiful girl in an unproblematically Guinizzellian manner. But his characteristic poetry, written, it seems, for a number of women and never made into a formal collection by him, is much more complex and contradictory. He dismissed *Guittone d'Arezzo and others of the previous generation of Tuscan poets as rhetorically inept and intellectually slovenly (in 'Da più a uno face un sollegismo'), and brought to Florentine poetry a new musicality and refinement of tone that became the model for what is now usually called the *dolce stil novo*. Unlike his younger contemporaries, however, Cavalcanti himself gave more emphasis to the destructiveness of desire than to its transcendental potential. His most famous canzone, 'Donna me prega', is a virtuoso display of complex rhyming and simultaneously a coherent, if difficult, exposition of his theory of love. It links the start of passion with the baleful influence of Mars and explains its deathly progress and effects in terms derived from contemporary philosophy and psychology; at the same time it asserts the intellectual nobility of those afflicted by it, and disdain for those unable to follow the reasoning of the poem.

Most of his poems are more approachable and more obviously imaginative. They are particularly notable for the creation of stylized poetic dramas, in which personifications of his mind, eyes, heart, or what he calls his 'spiriti' (the contemporary academic term for psycho-physical motor forces) voice their sufferings, reproach each other, or try to find mutual consolation in the face of female images endowed with destructive power and beauty. But any straightforward allegory dissolves: the poems achieve force and strangeness by bringing together dialogue exchanges, highly visual metaphors, and carefully selected and poetically potent abstractions. In a very strong sense Cavalcanti asserts the distinctiveness of poetic language and experience, though he can also parody it (in 'Pegli occhi fere un spirito sottile'). Deviations from his dominant manner are to be found in some *tenzone poems, at least one of which ('Guata, Manetto, quella scrignatuzza') veers off into *poesia giocosa. One or two other poems (often thought to be amongst his earliest) are experiments in a delicate *pastoral mode.

The singularity and obscurity of 'Donna me prega' earned it a Latin *commentary from the doctor *Dino del Garbo early in the 14th c., and Cavalcantian influence is still evident in much 14th- and 15th-c. lyric poetry, including that of *Petrarch. Dante in the *Vita nova speaks with pride of the 'primo de li miei amici', but already represents himself as going beyond a negative vision of love. A *sonnet by Cavalcanti to Dante upbraiding him for his feebleness of character ('viltà'), probably in the wake of the death of *Beatrice, seems to mark a cooling of relations. But Dante seems to have been torn. He mentions his poetry with admiration in the De vulgari eloquentia (1.13 and 2.6), but then chooses to point up his absence from the *Divine Comedy (Inf. 10.58) almost as if it were embarrassing. He later again seems to express admiration whilst at the same time recognizing his own poetic superiority (Purg. 11.97–9).

Some poems were translated into English by Dante Gabriel *Rossetti. Ezra Pound then published imaginative translations of all of them, and wrote an influential essay contrasting Cavalcanti's poetic precision with Petrarchan prettiness and ornament. T. S. Eliot drew on the *ballata 'Perch' i' no spero di tornar giammai' in Ash Wednesday.

[PH]

G. Contini (ed.), Poeti del Duecento (1960), vol. ii. See J. E. Shaw, Guido Cavalcanti's Theory of Love (1949); E. Pound, 'Cavalcanti', in T. S. Eliot (ed.), Literary Essays of Ezra Pound (1954); M. Marti, Storia dello stil nuovo (1973).

CAVALCHINI, RINALDO (d. ?1362). Early *humanist *educator. His school in his native Verona followed ancient models and anticipates that of *Guarino da Verona. *Petrarch sent his son Giovanni there in 1345. A few Latin poems by him have survived. [JP & JMS]

Cavaliere inesistente, Il (1959), the conclusion to *Calvino's trilogy I nostri antenati, is a parody of *Ariosto's *Orlando furioso, and an *allegory of life in the modern world. The nonexistent knight of the title is a negative model for young Rambaldo, who with his lover, Bradamante, is the real protagonist. The narrator Suor Teodora's narratological speculations overlay the story, and she turns out to be Bradamante herself. [MMcL]

CAVALIERI, BONAVENTURA (1591/8–1647). *Milanese *Jesuit who studied with *Galileo's pupil Castelli at *Pisa, and was later helped by Galileo to obtain a chair at *Bologna. His Geometria indivisibilium (1635) completes Archimedes' method for measuring areas and volumes. He is considered by some the last ancient mathematician, while for others he formulated the first mathematical approach to infinitesimals. [FC]

Cavalier servente, see CICISBEISMO.

Cavalleria rusticana, see VERGA, GIOVANNI.

CAVALLI, GIAN GIACOMO (1590–1658). A notary and the most important *Genoese *dialect poet of the 17th c. His most significant work is Rà cittara zeneise (1656), that is, 'La città genovese'. He also wrote celebratory poems for ceremonial events. [DO'G]

CAVALLI, PATRIZIA (1949–). Poet born in Todi, who now lives in *Rome. Her first three collections, beginning with Le mie poesie non cambieranno il mondo (1974), and gathered together in Poesie (1974–92) (1992), show a preference for brief, oblique epigrams, centred on everyday experience, with a troubled, self-aware undercurrent. In Sempre aperto teatro (1999) the expressiveness becomes rather more forceful and direct. Cavalli has also *translated plays by Molière and *Shakespeare. [PH]

CAVALLO, MARCO, see TROMBA, FRANCESCO.

CAVALLOTTI, FELICE (1842–98). Flamboyant poet, playwright, and parliamentarian of the radical left. As a boy he ran away from home in *Milan to take part in *Garibaldi's expedition. The rest of his life was marked by love affairs, quarrels, and imprisonments. He first gained notoriety as a polemical *journalist and versifier associated with the *Scapigliatura. His early plays were historical dramas. The first, I pezzenti (1871), was a commercial success and thereafter he relied on the income from his dramas to maintain his political activities. In 1873, he wrote what is considered his best work, Alcibiade, which was the first of a series on classical Greek subjects, though in the 1880s he turned to contemporary themes. He entered parliament in 1873, and by the mid-1880s he was the popular and undisputed leader of the radicals. His epic parliamentary battles with Francesco *Crispi in 1894-5 put him in the forefront of public life. He seemed set to rise further when he was killed in the last of many duels. Although successful in his lifetime, his work has since met with almost unanimous disfavour: his verse is thought formulaic and his *theatre frequently maudlin and psychologically superficial. [JD]

CAVANI, LILIANA, see CINEMA.

CAVICEO, IACOPO (1443–1511). An unwilling priest from Parma who lived a nomadic life in Italy and the Near East, wrote various Latin works and opened up new directions for vernacular fiction with his Libro del Peregrino. In it the protagonist, Peregrino, tells the shade of *Boccaccio of his adventures searching for his beloved Ginevra, which are eventualy concluded with a brief reunion prior to her death in childbirth. Peregrino's travels to the Near East reflect the author's own, and place the *romance in concrete contemporary settings. But there are evident debts to Boccaccio, especially the *Filocolo, whilst linguistically the *novel adopts a Latinate vernacular like the Hypnerotomachia Poliphili [see COLONNA, FRANCESCO]. It was written for Lucrezia *Borgia, when she was Duchess of Ferrara, and may well be the first novel written explicitly for a real woman. First printed in Parma in 1508, it went through many editions and was translated into French and Spanish. [LAP]

CAVOUR (1810–61). Camillo Benso, Conte di Cavour, the second son of a minor *Piedmontese noble, was a leading moderate *liberal in the *Risorgimento and the main architect of Italian *Unification. Well-travelled, energetic, and up-to-date in his running of his father's estates, he only

entered the Piedmontese parliament after the failure of the *1848 revolutions. But he was prime minister by 1852 and introduced sweeping economic and political reforms. In 1859, with France's help, he provoked the war with *Austria which led to the establishment of the Kingdom of Italy. His premature death left the *liberals, and Italy, without a clear leader. [LR]

CA' ZORZI, GIACOMO, see NOVENTA, GIACOMO.

CEBÀ, ANSALDO (1565–1623). Poet and literary critic who studied in *Padua but lived mostly in his native *Genoa. His conservative intellectual outlook was typical of the poorer Genoese nobility, but conflicted with an inclination to *Baroque novelty. He followed a heavily moralized *Petrarchism in his Rime (1601 and 1611), which are dedicated chiefly to repenting his already anaemic youthful passions. In Il Gonzaga, ovvero del poema eroico (1621) he tried somewhat unsuccessfully to prove that *Ariosto and Torquato *Tasso had adhered to the Aristotelian poetic unities in their *epics. He himself attempted biblical epic, most notably La reina Esther (1615), and his theoretical writings may be seen as an attempt to justify the vast, loosely episodic structure of this work. His several attempts at *tragedy were no more successful. [MPS]

CECCHI, EMILIO (1884–1966). Essayist and writer of *prosa d'arte, who was also a prolific and influential critic, *journalist, and art historian. He began his career as a *literary critic in *Florence, where he was born, writing for the avant-garde journal *Leonardo, and then for La *Voce, to which he contributed regularly on the work of authors from a number of different countries in the years leading up to *World War I. He was particularly interested in Anglo-American culture, and published a history of 19th-c. English literature in 1915. He continued to review books for important national dailies until the end of his life.

In 1919 he was one of the founders of La *Ronda, and in the essays he wrote for the review he developed a form of prosa d'arte which took off from the observation of minor details and circumstances but which was striking for its formal intricacy. He published the first of several collections of essays in this manner in Pesci rossi (1920). The later 1920s and early 1930s saw his first serious work as an art-historian, which centred on medieval and

Cecchi, Giovanni Maria

*Renaissance Tuscan painting and on 19th-c. Italian art. In the 1930s he journeyed to Mexico, Greece, and the United States, teaching Italian culture at Berkeley in 1930–1, and also establishing himself as a *travel writer. His *America amara* (1939) presented a highly negative picture of Roosevelt's America, which was entirely at odds with the enthusiasm of writers such as *Vittorini and *Pavese. Though he had been a member of *Mussolini's *Accademia d'Italia, he retained his position as an influential critic after *World War II, and continued to publish essays on art, literature, and *cinema. He has been strongly criticized for his cultural and political conservatism. But he remains a quirky, intelligent voice, whose *prosa d'arte* now seems less superficial than it once did, and who had much of interest to say on a vast range of topics.   [CFB]

See R. Fedi (ed.), *Emilio Cecchi oggi* (1981); C. Di Biase, *Emilio Cecchi* (1983).

CECCHI, GIOVANNI MARIA (1518–87) was an extremely prolific *Florentine dramatist. Of his fifty plays (some still unpublished), half were *humanist-style social and moral *comedies and the remainder religious dramas. His work seems to have been performed chiefly by local confraternities, but sometimes with the support of the Grand Dukes of *Tuscany. [See also THEATRE, 1.]

[RAA]

CECCHINI, PIER MARIA (1563–1645), *Ferrarese by origin, was a versatile and influential *commedia dell'arte* actor-manager, who played a range of masks including 'Fritellino'. Frustrated in his career by quarrels with colleagues and patrons, he expressed his thoughtful and perfectionist vision of improvised *theatre in a series of treatises and observations published between 1610 and 1630.

[RAA]

CECCO ANGIOLIERI (*c.*1260–1311/13). Strikingly original *Sienese exponent of *poesia giocosa*. He projects an image of himself as a dissipated profligate, and surviving legal documents attest to his being involved in a vicious brawl and having to sell off some of his property. We have possibly 112 poems by him, all *sonnets. The two major themes are a decidedly profane, physical love for a woman he calls Becchina, and violent antipathy towards his parents for their meanness, which leads to a number of poems about money and poverty, very much in the goliardic Latin tradition. The popular, realistic tone of his love poetry is not, however, an expression of some native, ingenuous feeling, and still less of romantic rebellion, but rather a studied reaction to the rarefied treatment of the lady in the *lyric tradition, showing awareness of the literary effects of using low language and far-fetched hyperbole. Some of the best involve verbal duels with Becchina, often dividing each line of the sonnet between the two participants to create a comedy in miniature. His most famous poem is the splendidly misanthropic 'S'i' fosse foco' in which he declares that, if he were death, he would visit his parents, and, if he were life, he would flee them.

Like *Dante, he was present at the battle of Campaldino in 1289, when the *Florentines and the Sienese defeated the Aretines. Three of his poems are addressed to Dante. 'Dante Alighier, Cecco, 'l tu' serv' e amico' is a reply to the last sonnet in the *Vita nova*, 'Oltre la spera'; probably Dante's commentary in the *Vita nova* on that poem responds to Cecco's accusations of inconsistency about the heavenly *Beatrice's audibility. The poem 'Dante Alighier, s'io so' bon begolardo' refers to the misfortunes of *exile and is a response to a poem of Dante's now lost.   [JU]

Poeti giocosi del tempo di Dante, ed. M. Marti (1956). See M. Marti, *Cultura e stile nei poeti giocosi del tempo di Dante* (1953).

CECCO D'ASCOLI (?1269–1327), the name by which Francesco degli Stabili, who was born in or near Ascoli Piceno, is commonly known. He was professor of *astrology at *Bologna until dismissed for *heresy in 1324. He then followed Charles of Calabria (son of Robert of *Anjou) to *Florence in 1327 as doctor and astrologer, but was again investigated by the *Inquisition (charges included drawing up Christ's horoscope) and died at the stake.

He wrote Latin *commentaries, not all of which have survived, on canonical astrological treatises, but is best known for his didactic poem on astrology, the *Acerba*. Though broken off at the start of the fifth book on his death, it is still a compendium of contemporary natural science—the order and influences of the heavens, the characteristics and properties of animals and precious stones, the causes of phenomena such as meteors and earthquakes—and of commonplace moral philosophy. It is addressed to a generic youth of 'acèrba età', hence both the title and the use of the vernacular. Written between 1324 and 1327 with explicitly anti-*Dantesque aims, it is nonetheless the earliest significant example of an author drawing on Dante's style in the *Divine Comedy*, from which it also takes its metre, a variety of *terza rima* in six-line stanzas rhyming ABA CBC. Cecco wrote a partial Latin commentary on book 1 and part of book 2. He is also the author of a number of *sonnets, one in *tenzone* with *Cino da Pistoia, who was his colleague in Bologna.   [CCi]

CECCOLI, MARINO, see POESIA GIOCOSA.

CECCO NUCCOLI (?1290–?1350). *Perugian poet and notary, who produced a small corpus of *lyric poetry, including several *tenzoni* with other Perugians. His poems are distinguished by the technical skill and emotive power with which he adapts the traditional rhetoric of the vernacular love lyric to the expression of homoerotic feeling.
[SNB]

CEDERNA, CAMILLA (1921–97). *Milanese *journalist, who was one of the founders of *L'Europeo* in 1945. Her collections of her articles include *Il lato debole: diario italiano 1956–1962* (1977). She is best known for books of investigative journalism such as *Pinelli: una finestra sulla strage* (1971) and *Giovanni Leone: la carriera di un presidente* (1978).   [RE]

CELANO, CARLO (pseud. Ettore Calcolona) (1617–93). *Neapolitan writer who studied law, and then, after being imprisoned for defending the Masaniello uprising (1647), became a cleric. He wrote successful verse *comedies, and also *Degli avanzi delle poste* (1676 and 1681), prose *satires modelled on *Boccalini with *libertine elements. His *Notizie del bello, dell'antico e del curioso della città di Napoli* (1692) is conceived as a modern guide and divided into itineraries.   [FC]

CELANO, LIVIO, see GRILLO, ANGELO.

CELATI, GIANNI (1937–). Writer. He has taught English and American literature at *Bologna University, though his work shows an affinity rather for the oral culture of marginal and subordinate groups. He was close to the *Neoavanguardia in the 1960s and wrote on James Joyce and *literary theory, developing a critique of institutional forms of language and literature in *Finzioni occidentali* (1975). The anarchic streak of his heroes Buster Keaton and the Marx Brothers burst through the pages of his fiction from *Comiche* (1971) to *Le avventure di Guizzardi* (1973) and *Lunario del paradiso* (1978), all of which show youth endlessly at

loggerheads with authority figures. *Narratori delle pianure* (1984) retains the faux naïf tone, but allows its characters and narrators to be dominated by the flatness of the Po Valley, where they live. *Quattro novelle sulle apparenze* (1987) is in a similar vein but with philosophical questioning of an unpretentious sort now to the fore. In the 1990s Celati translated Melville, Stendhal, and Swift, and rewrote *Boiardo's *Orlando innamorato* in *Orlando innamorato raccontato in prosa* (1994). The theme of the relationship between written and oral language returns in the *sonnet sequence *Recita dell'attore Vecchiatto nel teatro di Rio Saliceto* (1996), while *Avventure in Africa* (1998) subverts the unthinking Eurocentrism of traditional European *travel writing.   [RE]

CELESTINE V (Pietro da Morrone) (1209/10–96). A hermit in the Abruzzi, who was elected Pope in July 1294 and abdicated in December. *Iacopone da Todi addressed a poem to him on his election (*Laude* 74). *Dante's phrase, 'colui che fece per viltade il gran rifiuto', probably refers to him (*Inf.* 3.59–60), as his successor was Dante's enemy *Boniface VIII. He was canonized in 1313.
[PA]

CELLINI, BENVENUTO (1500–71) was a *Florentine goldsmith, silversmith, and sculptor. In 1513 he began his apprenticeship as a goldsmith, and in 1518 paid his first visit to *Rome. He returned to his native city in 1521, but soon fell foul of the law and had to flee to Rome, where he entered the service of the *Medici Pope, Clement VII. On the death of Clement in 1534 and the election of the *Farnese pope, Paul III, Cellini lost the *patronage he had enjoyed under the Medici. In the same year he was arrested on a charge of murder. Though he was guilty, the charges were dropped due to the Pope's intervention. In 1538 he was imprisoned for embezzlement and released only after pressure had been put on the authorities by influential patrons. He then moved to France in 1540, where he entered the service of King Francis I. Despite a number of important commissions, including the exquisite Salt Cellar, it was not a successful sojourn. He returned to Florence in 1545, where he completed the statue of Perseus for Duke Cosimo's Piazza della Signoria. He did not, however, find peace or prosperity. Commissions were few and far between. He did not get on with the dominant figure in artistic circles, Giorgio *Vasari, and his irascible nature led to petty squabbles, brawls, and, inevitably, appearances in court and imprisonment.

He began to write his *autobiography, the *Vita*, in 1558 after his release from prison and during his period of house arrest, when he began to have serious doubts about the fate of his eternal soul (he took the first steps to holy orders on 2 June 1558). In the *Vita* he combats all his adversaries and rises above them at the end to greet his maker in triumph. The work is not primarily concerned with the superficial truth of everyday events. Its purpose is to ensure everlasting glory for its protagonist. It was a literary venture, a reworking of specific themes to recreate, not the real man, but a carefully delineated image. Cellini stopped writing almost in mid-sentence between 1566 and 1567, and the work was not published until 1728. Aside from its literary interest, it is an invaluable source of information about patronage and artists' activities.

Cellini also wrote a significant body of poetry which was not published in his lifetime, and an important technical treatise on goldsmithing and sculpture, the *Trattati*. The manuscript version of the *Trattati* was dedicated to Prince Francesco de' Medici and written in 1565, whereas the emended printed version (dated 1568 but really 1569) was dedicated to Cardinal Ferdinando de' Medici.

[PLR]

See J. Pope-Hennessy, *Cellini* (1985); I. Arnaldi, *La vita violenta di Benvenuto Cellini* (1986).

Ceneri di Gramsci, Le, see PASOLINI, PIER PAOLO.

CENNE DALLA CHITARRA (d. before 1336). Aretine and probably a *giullare*, who wrote thirteen *sonnets on the months of the year, responding parodistically to the famous sequence by *Folgore da Sangimignano. The poems' irony and verve make Cenne an important figure in the history of *poesia giocosa.   [SNB]

Censorship of the printed word and performing arts has been applied in varying measure and by diverse means throughout the modern era. Before *Unification the *theatre, as an almost universal means of communication, was the principal focus of attention for the authorities throughout the peninsula. Expressions of patriotic fervour, or criticism of the political or social establishment or of powerful neighbours or institutions, were likely to lead to the withholding of permission for performance, though not necessarily for publication of the printed text. However, given the political divisions of the peninsula and the essentially local system of control, consistency was entirely lacking. After Unification, local control was retained and censorship powers were vested with prefects, who were encouraged, certainly as far as plays were concerned, to pay more attention to moral rather than political issues.

Under *Fascism, censorship became an important weapon of social control and one of the means by which the regime prevented the propagation of ideas it disliked. Press freedom was limited by decree in 1923, and by 1925 was effectively abolished, though the regime was content initially to operate, largely unchanged, the pre-existing mechanisms of censorship for the theatre and the *cinema. From 1931 onwards a much more rigorous, centralized approach to the preventive censorship both of plays and films was instituted, but not until the second half of the 1930s did the regime embark upon the systematic censorship of literature, one famous victim of which was *Vittorini's *Garofano rosso*. When it introduced the race laws in 1938 [see JEWS AND JUDAISM], the regime also began a wholesale purge of printed texts ('la bonifica libraria'), aimed at removing from circulation the works of authors it perceived as subversive. The advent of *World War II meant that this process was slow. *Moravia's Gli *indifferenti*, for instance, clearly classifiable as the subversive work of a Jewish author, was not actually banned until the beginning of 1943.

The damaging effects of censorship on Italian cultural life and creative achievement told particularly during the Fascist period. However, whilst Article 21 of the 1948 Republican constitution guaranteed freedom of speech (and specifically outlawed censorship of the press), the Fascist laws on censorship of theatre and cinema remained in force. Together with new regulations concerning, for example, the exporting of Italian films, they were frequently invoked by a politically and culturally conservative establishment. Challenging dramas or works considered risqué—even a *Renaissance classic such as La *mandragola*—were refused permission for performance, and many *Neorealist directors either had the distribution of their films obstructed or were forced to make cuts. The Catholic Church also operated a system of censorship. Although in many cases this amounted to little more than advice to the faithful, its control of many local cinemas meant it could limit the audience of films if it judged them unworthy or immoral.

Censorship of *television remained largely internal during the era of the state broadcasting (RAI) monopoly, but was at least as strict as that operated directly by the state.

The new law regarding censorship, which finally replaced the Fascist legislation in 1962, did little to enhance artistic freedom. Reviews, musicals, and films were still subject to bureaucratic control, and could be banned outright. It remained wise to submit play-texts to the Ministero del Turismo e dello Spettacolo prior to performance, in order to avoid unnecessary interference by over-zealous local authorities. Anti-establishment playwrights such as Dario *Fo found a whole range of public-order regulations used to prevent even private performances of their plays. Since the early 1980s, however, political and generational changes have led to increased artistic freedom. By the late 1990s the state retained only minimal powers of control, and the main threats to freedom of expression came from commercial interests dictating the directions to be taken by television and cinema. [See also INDEX LIBRO-RUM PROHIBITORUM; INQUISITION; JOURNALISM; PAPACY AND THE CATHOLIC CHURCH.]   [CEJG]

See M. Cesari, *La censura nel periodo fascista* (1978); M. Quargnolo, *La censura ieri e oggi nel cinema e nel teatro* (1982).

Cento anni, see ROVANI, GIUSEPPE.

Cento novelle antiche, Le, see NOVELLINO, IL.

CERAVOLO, MARY, see ITALIAN WRITERS IN AUSTRALIA.

CERETA, LAURA (1469–99) was eldest of six children in an upper-middle-class Brescian family. Between the ages of 7 and 11 she studied Latin in a nearby convent, then was called home to care for her siblings. She continued to study after they were asleep. In 1485 she married Pietro Serina, a merchant, who died of the *plague eighteen months later. She herself died aged 30, leaving behind eighty-two Latin letters and a *dialogue on the death of an ass, all written when she was between 16 and 19, and published in manuscript in 1488. She deals with characteristic *humanist themes, but her Latin style is singular and her point of view *feminist in defence of herself as a humanist writer. [See also WOMEN WRITERS, 1.]   [AR]

CERRETTI, LUIGI (1738–1808). Professor at Modena until appointed by *Napoleon to Pavia's chair of eloquence between Vincenzo *Monti and *Foscolo. He was the most prolific of the Emilian *Scuola oraziana of poets. His verse reflects a variety of influences and ranges easily from the religious to the licentious.   [JMAL]

Certame coronario. A literary contest, organized mainly by Leon Battista *Alberti, sponsored by Piero de' *Medici, and held in October 1441 in *Florence. Modelled on ancient literary competitions, the aim of the initiative was to promote vernacular literature by inviting a number of writers to submit poetic compositions in Italian, on the classical theme of friendship. Amongst the competitors were Benedetto *Accolti, Leonardo *Dati, and *Ciriaco d'Ancona. A jury of *humanists, including Poggio *Bracciolini, Flavio *Biondo, Antonio *Loschi, and probably Leonardo *Bruni, was to award a silver crown to the author of the winning composition, but in the end the jury, unable to reach a decision, witheld the prize. Alberti wrote a *Protesta* complaining that the humanists, who understood how even Latin had developed from humble beginnings, had demanded of the young vernacular a standard that they would never have expected of the classical language at a similar stage of development. Though the initiative ended in stalemate, it did lead to Alberti writing the first Tuscan *grammar, and ultimately it paved the way for the flourishing of the vernacular in the age of Lorenzo de' *Medici, with five of the contributions being included in the *Raccolta aragonese.*

[MMcL]

CERVONI, ISABELLA (16th–17th c.) wrote ceremonial poetry. She published three *canzoni* for Maria de' *Medici and Henry IV's wedding (1600), and an oration to Pope Clement VIII (1598). She was a native of Colle Val d'Elsa near *Siena.   [FC]

CESALPINO, ANDREA, see ARISTOTELIAN-ISM.

CESARI, ANTONIO (1760–1828). Veronese lexicographer who published a revised edition of the *Crusca dictionary (1806–11). He represents the most extreme form of reaction against French influence on Italian, and against the 'corrupting' modernist positions of *Cesarotti's *Saggio sulla filosofia delle lingue*, in favour of the linguistic 'purity' of 14th-c. Tuscan texts. He also published appropriately *purist poems, *novelle*, and religious works. [See also QUESTIONE DELLA LINGUA.]   [JMAL]

CESARINI, VIRGINIO (1595–1624). *Roman poet of noble origins, who was a member of the Barberini circle and the Accademia dei *Lincei, and a representative of the more moderate strand of 17th-c. *Baroque poetry. He wrote Latin and vernacular poetry (*Carmina* (1658), *Poesie liriche toscane* (1664)), but was also interested in mathematics and astronomy. He encouraged *Galileo to write *Il saggiatore* in 1623 and revised it for publication. [PBert]

CESAROTTI, MELCHIORRE (1730–1808). *Paduan essayist and poet who lived and worked in *Venice and Padua, first as a tutor to noble families and eventually as a lecturer in Greek and Hebrew literature. In old age he served on the *education commission set up in Padua by supporters of *Napoleon. He introduced *Ossianism to Italy with his extremely influential *translations of Macpherson (1763). He also translated Voltaire, Gray, Homer, Pindar, Aeschylus, and Demosthenes. His essays begin with *Sopra l'origine e i progressi dell'arte poetica* and *Intorno al diletto della tragedia*, published with his Voltaire translations in 1762, but the later *Saggio sulla filosofia del buon gusto* (1785) and *Saggio sulla filosofia delle lingue applicato alla lingua italiana* (1788) are more distinctive. Developing his ideas from a moderate *sensismo*, Cesarotti tends to interpret literature in relation to the way in which traditions and different forms of civilization evolve, whilst also allowing for the creative genius. He divides language into a stable part, constituted by grammatical norms, and a variable part, made up of individual styles and rhetorical figures, governed exclusively by reason and taste. He himself experimented constantly in his own poetry. [SC]

CESI, FEDERICO (1585–1630). An important figure in the development of 17th-c. science. At barely 18 years of age (in 1603) he founded the Accademia dei *Lincei in *Rome, and master-minded its organization, drafting and redrafting the statutes over many years. In his Latin scientific writings he laid the foundations of the modern study of botany. He doubted the veracity of Ptolemaic *cosmology, and came to *Galileo's defence in his *Del naturale desiderio di sapere*, published in 1616. [PBD]

CETTI, GIAN MENICO, see ITALIAN WRITERS IN SWITZERLAND.

CEVA, TOMMASO (1649–1737). Mathematics professor at Brera, *Milan's *Jesuit College, who defended *scholastic philosophy against Descartes and Gassendi in *Philosophia novo-antiqua* (1704). In the literary field he shared the *Arcadian reaction against the *Baroque, and summed it up in his oft-quoted definition of poetry as 'un sogno che si fa in presenza della ragione'. His *Jesus puer* (1690), a Latin narrative poem in hexameters, is marked, and marred, by its excessive pictorial detail. [JMAL]

CHALCONDYLAS, DEMETRIOS, see GREEK INFLUENCES; PLATONIC ACADEMY.

CHAULA, TOMMASO (later 14th c.–1433/4), from Chiaramonte, was the author of *epic poems and *tragedies in Latin, many of which have been lost. Active in *Sicily, he is best known for his *Gestorum per Alphonsum Aragonum et Siciliae Regem libri quinque*, a long historical and encomiastic work discussing important events between 1420 and 1424. [ELM]

CHIABRERA, GABRIELLO (1552–1638). Poet. He received a classical *education from the *Jesuits at the Collegio Romano. In 1572 he entered the court of Luigi Cornaro in *Rome, where he met Sperone *Speroni, Torquato *Tasso, and Marc-Antoine Muret, who made him aware of the poetry of the Pléiade. He left Rome in 1581, after killing a man in a duel, and travelled to *Venice, Savona, *Turin, and *Florence. Chiabrera was constantly experimenting with new poetic forms. His study of Greek led to the writing of Pindaric odes; he popularized the *canzonetta* form; and he participated in the contemporary fashion for anacreontic verse. His poetic œuvre included *sonnets, odes, *Horatian *satire, and the *epic. His *Gotiade* (1582) took up the theme of Giangiorgio *Trissino's *Italia liberata dai Goti*, though its form reflected the style of Torquato Tasso. For the marriage of Maria de' *Medici to King Henry IV of France he composed *Il rapimento di Cefalo* (1600). He produced other works for the marriages of Francesco *Gonzaga to Margherita of Savoy, and Cosimo de' Medici to Maria Maddalena of Austria. He wrote a short *autobiography after 1625. [See also VERSIFICATION.] [PLR]

CHIARA, PIERO (1913–86). *Novelist. After years of travel and temporary work in northern Italy and abroad, he began to contribute to *Paragone* and other journals in the 1950s. He became popular in the 1960s with spirited novels of Lombard life, beginning with *Il piatto piange* (1962), several of which have been adapted for the *cinema. The vivid narrative embraces ironic exposés of provincial society in novels such as *Il pretore di Cuviò* (1973) and *erotic vitality is counteracted by a sense of mortal transience. [JEB]

CHIARA OF ASSISI, ST, see FIORETTI DI SAN FRANCESCO; NUNS.

CHIARELLI, LUIGI (1880–1947), the author of forty-eight plays, is best known for *La maschera e il volto* (1916), defined by *Pirandello as a 'transcendental farce'. This play, popular abroad as well as in Italy, uses the structure of the well-made play [see THEATRE, 2] to point up the contradictions in an ill-made society. When Paolo assumes the mask of the jealous husband and pretends to kill his wife on discovering her adultery, he is treated lightly by the law and adulated by the public; when it is discovered that the wife is alive and well, the law pursues him for deception and the public turns against him. Beneath the manic farce, the bitter undertone implies that society can only accommodate the mask, not the newly discovered face. By calling his play 'grottesco in 3 atti' Chiarelli gave a name to the dramatic movement known as *teatro *grottesco*. This and subsequent plays, such as *Chimere* (1920) and *La scala di seta* (1922), show the distrust of traditional values and institutions typical of Italian literature produced immediately after *World War I. Chiarelli's themes of the mask, the face, and social hypocrisy suggest comparisons with Pirandello, though his plays revealed neither the ontological despair nor the incisive thought of Pirandello's theatre. Chiarelli was also a *journalist and in addition briefly ran his own theatrical company. [JAL]

CHIARI, PIETRO (1711–85) a versatile writer and cleric from Brescia, very active in *Venice from 1746. He was sensitive to public taste as well as open to *French influences and to *Enlightenment ideas, which he promptly assimilated into his work. He began his successful career as a *novelist in 1753 with *La filosofessa italiana*, and he continued to mine this productive seam well into his old age in Brescia. Earlier he had contributed to the fashionable genre of fictional letters with his *Lettere scelte* (1750–2). His output for the *theatre presents an interesting counterpoint to that of his rival *Goldoni. In 1749 Chiari was working for the Teatro S. Samuele with Giuseppe Imer's company,

and found himself at the centre of a bitter polemic with Goldoni, who was working for Medebach at the Teatro S. Angelo. The bloodiest theatrical conflict took place in the years 1753–4 and 1754–5. In 1761–2 he worked for Gasparo *Gozzi as editor on the *Gazzetta veneta*, before retiring to Brescia. [IC]

CHIARO DAVANZATI (13th c.). One of the most important *Siculo-Tuscan poets, about whose life we know nothing other than that he was *Florentine. He took part in *tenzoni with *Monte Andrea, *Pallamidesse di Bellindote, and *Dante da Maiano, and seems to have belonged to the same generation. His large poetic production (more than sixty *canzoni and 120 *sonnets) shows a less anguished use of language than that of *Guittone d'Arezzo, and the obvious refinement of his verse has been likened to the early *dolce stil novo*, though Provençal influence is more likely [see TROUBADOURS]. His production has been preserved in a single manuscript, and appears not to have been influential. *Dante notably neglects to mention him when castigating Guittone and his followers. But he was technically innovative in his verse forms, and showed impresssive skill in handling traditional motifs and images. A controversial sonnet, 'Di penne di paone', accusing *Bonagiunta da Lucca of plagiarizing *Giacomo da Lentini, has been ascribed to him. [JU]

CHIAROMONTE, NICOLA (1905–72). *Literary critic and left-wing intellectual. He was a radical anti-*Fascist who wrote for *Solaria in *Florence, fought in Spain, and then went to America, where he wrote for *Giustizia e libertà and for American liberal reviews. After the war he founded *Tempo presente* (1956–68) with Ignazio *Silone. [SVM]

CHIAVES, CARLO, see CREPUSCOLARI.

CHIESA, FRANCESCO (1871–1971). Italian-Swiss writer who taught Italian in Lugano and Zurich and made love of Italy and its language a major theme of his poetry and fiction. His most successful novel, *Tempo di marzo* (1925), tells of his boyhood in Ticino. [See also ITALIAN WRITERS IN SWITZERLAND.] [DCH]

Children's Literature. Though children's literature as a recognized genre emerged in Italy only with the *Risorgimento, it owed much to *folk literature, literary fairy tales, and Aesopian fables.

Two early texts for adults have an incalculable importance for children's literature everywhere. *Straparola's *Le piacevoli notti* (1550–3) included, among Eastern tales and animal fables, the first known Puss-in-Boots, albeit female and unshod, whilst *Basile's Neapolitan *Lo cunto de li cunti* (1634–6) contains early fairy tales, combining magical and Oriental elements with low-life experience. An early book written expressly for children is Padre Soave's *Novelle morali* (1782), which attempts to make moral tales the antidote to fancy. Pietro Thouar launched *Il giornalino dei fanciulli* (1834) and L. A. Parravicini made instruction more appealing in his encyclopedic storybook *Il Giannetto* (1837), whilst the critic and historian Cesare *Cantù published a collection of poems for children in 1846 entitled *Fior di memoria pei bambini*. Production for children increased rapidly after *Unification, with works such as Antonio *Stoppani's nation-building *Il bel paese* (1875), Ida *Baccini's *Le memorie di un pulcino* (1875), *Collodi's Perrault translation (1875) and his amusingly didactic *Giannettino* (1877), and *Capuana's reworking of *Sicilian folk tales in *C'era una volta* (1882). Collodi's *Le avventure di *Pinocchio* (1883) displayed a new (and subversive) sophistication, as well as a social conscience, in its blend of the real and the imaginary, and was one of the first works for children which really appealed to its intended audience as well as to parents and teachers. De Amicis' *Cuore* (1886), with its moralizing Risorgimento patriotism, was adopted in Italian schools, as were G. C. *Abba's deliberately simple war memoirs (1891). A radical new departure was offered by the adventure novels of Emilio *Salgari, which presented adult characters in exotic places and periods, and were imaginatively stimulating without being obviously didactic.

*Journalism for children attained a high level in *Il Giornalino della domenica* (1906–27) and in *Il Corriere dei piccoli* (1908–), as did illustration in the innovative work of Sergio Tofano ('Sto') and others. Whilst illustrated *comics emerged in the 1920s for both adults and children on the American model, *Fascism attempted indoctrination of schoolchildren through syllabus control and children's newspapers such as *Il Balilla*, first launched in 1923. Imaginative writing of a high order re-emerged with *Calvino's retelling of Italian fairy tales in his *Fiabe italiane* (1956) and his Marcovaldo stories (1963), though the most

impressive of specialist children's writers was Gianni *Rodari, with his emphasis on education through imagination. More recently Paola *Capriolo, Susanna *Tamaro, and Roberto Piumini have all published interesting work addressed to children.

[ALL]

See A. Faeti, *Letteratura per l'infanzia* (1977); P. Boero and C. De Luca, *La letteratura per l'infanzia* (1995).

CHIODI, PIETRO, see RESISTANCE.

Chivalry originated in France in the 11th c., when developments in warfare gave a new prominence to the knight (in French *chevalier*) as one who had the economic means and the personal skill and bravery to fulfil the key role of the mounted warrior in battle. But the chivalric code was never narrowly military, and in the course of the 12th c. its scope broadened into a comprehensive ideal of devotion to one's lord, generosity, and heedlessness of danger or discomfort in defence of the weak and of one's own honour. The *troubadour love lyric with its cult of *courtly love added the final ingredient to the ethical ideal embodied in the French *romances of the 12th and 13th c., which found a receptive audience in Italy.

Chivalry in Italy had a distinctive quality because of the predominantly urban character of the Italian ruling elite in the late *Middle Ages. But there was still a need for the military leadership which a knightly class provided, and it is clear that the status and ideals of knighthood were as important to the upper classes of the Italian cities as to their rural counterparts elsewhere. The appeal of chivalric values in *Florence around 1300 is accurately reflected by *Dante, in figures such as the noble Florentines of *Inferno* 16, Guido del Duca in *Purgatorio* 14, and the poet's (knighted) ancestor Cacciaguida in *Paradiso* 15–17, not to mention the seductive appeal of courtly love represented by *Francesca da Rimini in *Inferno* 5. *Boccaccio's *Decameron* too, while it has rightly been called a 'mercantile epic' (Vittore *Branca), reveals an aspiration to the chivalric virtues of boldness and magnanimity. The splendour and idealism of an imagined chivalric world, embodied in the *Arthurian and Carolingian legends, inspired the ingenuous hyperbole of the *cantari*, and it was in these texts that, in the 15th c., chivalric narrative was read in the courts of the ruling families of Northern Italy, notably the *Gonzaga of *Mantua and the *Este of *Ferrara. It was at the latter court that the tales of chivalry received their last ambivalent celebration in the poems of *Boiardo and *Ariosto, epitomized by the only half-ironic exclamation in the opening canto of the latter's *Orlando furioso, 'O gran bontà dei cavalieri antiqui' (1.22.1). [See also EPIC; FEUDALISM.] [RMD]

See J. Larner, *Italy in the Age of Dante and Petrarch* (1980); M. Keen, *Chivalry* (1984).

Christian Democrats (Democrazia Cristiana). The Christian Democratic Party was the central political component of all Italian governments between 1948 and 1992. As a political force it established a hegemony within the institutional fabric of the country such as to justify describing the first forty-four years of the Republic as those of the Christian Democrat regime.

Until the mid-1950s the politics of the party were dominated by Alcide *De Gasperi (1881–1954), who believed that the nation's democratic instincts were fragile and that, if they were to develop, they needed the stability which could only be provided by a large centrist party that was *interclassista* in coalition with other centre parties. He used support from the USA and the Church, industry and agriculture, to strengthen the position of his party. By drawing diverse interest groups into a single 'interclassist' party he unwittingly prepared the ground for a *partitocrazia* which would replace the State as the terrain for mediating conflicting interests. The second generation of Christian Democrat leaders had served their apprenticeship in the ranks of *Azione cattolica* during the *Fascist period, and were initially inspired by the idea of spreading Catholic values into all sectors of Italian society. From the mid-1950s, under the vigorous leadership of Amintore Fanfani (1908–99), party structures were reorganized partly for this purpose. Given Catholicism's weak grasp on *liberal principles of institutional correctness, the ensuing Christian Democrat penetration of the country's institutions bred increasingly corrupt and anomalous practices.

Despite the attempts by Aldo Moro (1916–78) from the mid-1960s to theorize a new type of centrality for the party in a rapidly changing society, the liberalization of Catholic thinking following Vatican II (1962–5) made it increasingly difficult for the party to remain the point of reference for all Italian Catholics. Institutionalized corruption and the weakening of ideological loyalty to the party throughout the 1970s and 1980s eventually led to the dissolution of the Christian Democratic Party in 1994, and the recreation of Catholic parties with a

clearer distinction between religious and political affiliations. The two main ones were the CCD (Centro Cristiano Democratico), on the right of the political spectrum, and the PPI (Partito Popolare Italiano), a centrist party with leanings to the left. [See also PAPACY AND THE CATHOLIC CHURCH.]
[GLCB]

See R. Leonardi and D. A. Wertman, *Italian Christian Democracy: The Politics of Dominance* (1989); A. Giovagnoli, *Il partito italiano: la democrazia cristiana dal 1942 al 1994* (1996).

CHRISTINA, QUEEN OF SWEDEN (1626–89). A patron of intellectuals (notably Descartes), she declined marriage, abdicated, converted to Catholicism, and settled in *Rome. Her house became the haunt of poets and writers, a number of whom continued to meet after her death and in 1690 founded the academy of *Arcadia.
[JMAL]

Chronicles, the dominant form of historical writing throughout the *Middle Ages, differ from both classical and modern *historiography. They tend to be structured according to the haphazard occurrence of events, and to group disparate materials in a year-by-year arrangement. Since knowledge was regarded as finite, many chroniclers—for example *Salimbene da Parma—tried to embrace the whole course of world history from the beginning of time and interpreted it as the working out of God's providential plan, though this habit gradually disappeared from the 14th c. onwards.

Despite their frequent universalism, chronicles are essentially local in character. 13th-c. Southern chronicles focus on the *Hohenstaufen monarchs and their *Anjou successors, while a fresh spate of *Sicilian chronicles was stimulated by the Sicilian Vespers (1282). The deeds of Ezzelino da Romano are the focus of 13th-c. chronicles in the mainland Veneto, the best of which is by Rolandino da Padova (1200–76). Generally in Northern and Central Italy chronicles reflect and embody the local patriotism and nascent *political thought engendered by the growth of city-states, some of which appointed official chroniclers, such as Caffaro (d.1166) and his successors in *Genoa. *Venice, on the other hand, retrospectively conferred official status on two chronicles by Andrea *Dandolo (1306–54), which were written in Venetian and bear comparison with Giovanni *Villani's *Nuova cronica*. An isolated masterpiece is the lively vernacular *Cronica* by an Anonimo Romano, written in 1357–8 and in its later chapters covering the career of *Cola di Rienzo [see CRONICA DI ANONIMO ROMANO].

In the 13th c. the customary language for chronicles continued to be Latin. Only Lucca can incontrovertibly boast a (short) chronicle in its own vernacular. Martino da Canal wrote *Les Estoires de Venise* (1267–75) in French because he wanted Venice's praises to be heard in the land that was at the forefront of contemporary culture. But the next century saw a change. The earliest extant *Florentine vernacular chronicle (once erroneously attributed to Brunetto *Latini) covers the period 1180–1303. Thereafter all Florentine chronicles were written in Florentine, including those of *Compagni, the Villani family, and Gregorio *Dati. Besides those from Florence, *Rome, and Venice, 14th-c. vernacular chronicles survive from *Padua, *Bologna, Rimini, *Pisa, Pistoia, *Siena, Orvieto, and *Naples.

Chronicles tended to be ousted in the 15th c. with the onset of *humanist history-writing, though they were still being written in the 16th. [See also MALISPINI, RICORDANO.]   [JCB]

See E. Cochrane, *Historians and Historiography in the Italian Renaissance* (1981).

CHRYSOLORAS, MANUEL (*c.*1350–1415), a *Byzantine scholar and diplomat, taught Greek in *Florence from 1397 to 1400 at the invitation of *Salutati, training *humanists to translate according to sense rather than literally. He *translated Plato's *Republic* into Latin, and a Latin version of his elementary grammar, *Erotemata* ('Questions'), was widely used to teach Greek in Italy. [See also GREEK INFLUENCES.]   [JK]

Church, see PAPACY AND THE CATHOLIC CHURCH.

Church Fathers. The term is used of the Greek and Latin authors who came to be venerated as the guardians of Christian wisdom and orthodoxy from the 1st c. through to the mid-9th c. At the heart of 'patristics' lies a concern to define and preserve the orthodoxy of the faith against those forces threatening its unity and stability both from within and from beyond it. Three phases are traditionally identified: the original or Apostolic phase, including Clement of Rome, Ignatius, and Polycarp; the golden age of patristic literature in the 4th and 5th c., including Gregory of Nazianzus, John Chrysostom, Gregory of Nyssa, Ambrose, and *Augustine; and the age of Christological controversy from the mid-5th c. to the mid-9th c., including the Councils

of Ephesus and Constantinople. In the late 9th c. the patristic era begins to give way to the *scholastic age, which culminates in the great syntheses of the 13th and 14th c. associated with *Aquinas, Duns Scotus, and others, where it is a question, however, of a fresh encounter with ancient philosophy and a greater attention to methodology.

Augustine is especially important for *Dante and *Petrarch, though every kind of Christian moral or dogmatic discourse from the scholastic age onwards presupposes, implicitly or explicitly, the great achievements of the patristic era.   [JT]

See P. J. Hamell, *Introduction to Patrology* (1966).

CIALENTE, FAUSTA (1898–1994) was born in *Sardinia, but moved with her husband in 1921 to Alexandria in Egypt. An anti-*Fascist, she founded the newspaper *Fronte unito* for Italian prisoners during *World War II, and made daily broadcasts from Radio Cairo. Her first major novel, *Cortile a Cleopatra* (1936), uses a male protagonist to tackle questions of freedom, identity, and bourgeois conformity. She returned to Italy after the war and wrote for various *Communist papers. In subsequent novels, such as *Ballata levantina* (1961), *Un inverno freddissimo* (1966), and the *autobiograph-ical *Le quattro ragazze Wieselberger* (1976), she uses her exclusively female protagonists to debate the role of women in contemporary Italian society.   [VS-H]

CIAMBELLI, BERNARDO, see ITALIAN WRITERS IN THE UNITED STATES.

CIANO, GALEAZZO (1903–44). *Mussolini's son-in-law and foreign minister. Ciano was wary of Nazi Germany and supported the move by the *Fascist Grand Council to depose Mussolini in 1943. Following Mussolini's return he sought refuge in Germany, but was handed over by Hitler and executed in Verona on 11 January 1944. His *diary is one of the most important documentary sources for the later years of the Fascist regime.
                    [PC]

CICERO (106–43 BC). Marcus Tullius Cicero, the greatest classical Roman orator, was still read throughout the *Middle Ages but exercised most influence in the *Renaissance. Mentioned by *Dante for his philosophical tracts, he became *Petrarch's idol not just for his ethical instruction but also for the sheer sound of his Latin. His popularity reached its apogee in the 15th and early 16th c., when, in the *imitation debate, the Ciceronians Paolo *Cortesi and Pietro *Bembo championed his status as the sole model for writing Latin. His influence remained unchallenged until the end of the 16th c., when Seneca and Tacitus were advanced as more appropriate models in an absolutist age. [See also CLASSICAL SCHOLARSHIP; CLASSICISM; HUMANISM; LATIN INFLUENCES; LATIN PROSE IN ITALY.]

[MMcL]

Cicisbeismo indicates the socially sanctioned practice of appointing an unmarried young nobleman to attend a married noblewoman. It originated in *Genoa in the early 18th c, and soon spread to all major Italian cities. The *cicisbeo* was supposed to help his lady through all her daily tasks and ceremonies, from morning *toilette* in the dressing-room to visits to public places. The appointment of a *cicisbeo*, sometimes of more than one, was often part of the contract of marriage and not always one about which the bride herself was consulted. The term is probably is probably onomatopoeic in origin, suggesting whispering, and was often replaced by the grander *cavalier servente*.

Foreigners found the practice deplorable and many Italian writers treat it comically or satirically. The most sustained *satire of its dreary futility and ambiguous morality comes in *Parini's *Il *giorno* (1763–5), which describes the daily routine of a *cicisbeo*. It also provided material for numerous *comedies, including *Goldoni's *Il cavaliere e la dama* (1749) and *La famiglia dell'antiquario* (1750) and *Alfieri's *Il divorzio* (1803). But whilst *cicisbeismo* was commonly pictured as symbolic of the decadence and snobbery of the Italian nobility, it found a rare champion in Giuseppe *Baretti, whose English essay, *An Account of the Manners and Customs of Italy* (1768), was an attempt to counter the exceedingly condemnatory account of Italian life in Samuel Sharp's *Letters from Italy* (1766). Baretti argued that *cicisbeismo* continued the *chivalrous spirit of *Neoplatonic love praised by *Renaissance artists and philosophers. Other writers put forwards the more prosaic justification that *cicisbeismo* provided noblewomen with constant protection in public places. Arguments about it continued into the early 19th c., by which time the fashion was rapidly disappearing from society. Ugo *Foscolo offered some final ironic comments from London in his *Lettere scritte dall'Inghilterra* (1816).

[GUB]

See M. Vaussard, *La vita quotidiana in Italia nel Settecento* (1990).

CICOGNANI, BRUNO (1879–1971). Productive *Florentine novelist, who also practised as a lawyer and contributed to *journals such as *Pegaso* and *Nuova antologia*. Earlier works, beginning with *Sei storielle di nòvo cònio* (1917) and the novel *La Velia* (1923), oscillate between documentary *realism and irrational *expressionism. Like his friend *Papini, he eventually converted to *Catholicism. In *L'età favolosa* (1940), which is an evocation of childhood, he reduces the realist elements in his writing and starts on the search for spiritual values which characterizes his later novels.   [DCH]

CICOGNINI, GIACINTO ANDREA (1606–60) was a dramatist and *librettist like his father, Iacopo *Cicognini. He has left over fifty titles under his name, though in some cases there are doubts as to attribution. He was one of the most important contributors to the growing fashion in Italy for drama in the *Spanish style, offering complex romantic intrigues, social moralities around the concept of honour, and mixtures of comic and serious tones in a single play. His *Convitato di pietra* (1671)—if it is his—may be the first Italian stage version of the Don Juan legend. [See also THEATRE, 1.]   [RAA]

CICOGNINI, IACOPO (1577–1633). Playwright, poet, and actor who lived and worked in *Florence and *Rome, largely in the service of various cardinals. In spite of a successful career, he committed suicide. He was a friend and follower of *Chiabrera, and wrote and often acted the spoken parts in musical productions sponsored by the *Medici court or Florentine *academies. His plays alternate between sacred and secular subjects. Later ones show the influence of Lope de Vega, anticipating the more extensive Spanish influence in the work of his son, Giacinto Andrea *Cicognini.
[FC]

CIECO DI ADRIA, IL, see GROTO, LUIGI.

CIELO D'ALCAMO (13th c.) is known exclusively for his 'Contrasto', a comic dialogue in 160 lines of verse composed probably in *Sicily between 1231 and 1250. In it a disreputable and irrepressible *giullare tries to persuade a reasonably wealthy but not noble Sicilian girl to yield him her favours, which, in the end, she does. Presumably the poem was intended for dramatic performance. It has an irony and local colour unique amongst poems of the *Sicilian school, and also a unique metrical form—six-line stanzas of what are basically alexandrines, alternating between the two speakers. Rather than to the *troubadours, it probably looks to popular poetry with roots ultimately in Arab or Andalusian traditions. [See also VERSIFICATION.]

[PH]

CIGALA, LANFRANCO (early 13th c.–before 1274). *Genoese judge who wrote highly refined love *lyrics in Provençal, dwelling on the subsequently influential motif of the smile. Lanfranco was one of a generation moving from a sensual to a spiritual definition of love, a development culminating in devotional poems to the Virgin. [See also TROUBADOURS.]

[JU]

Cimento, Accademia del. With the Accademia dei *Lincei, one of the two most important scientific *academies in 17th-c. Italy. Never as organized as the Lincei had been, it began informally in *Florence in 1642 as a meeting of disciples of *Galileo, all of whom were interested in the progress of the experimental sciences. Official status came in 1657, when Duke Leopoldo de' *Medici sponsored the academy's foundation. With the motto 'provando e riprovando', the members, including Carlo Roberto *Dati, Lorenzo *Magalotti, and Vincenzo *Viviani, set seriously about their work. Unlike Galileo, who tackled large-scale issues, the Cimento worked on a smaller scale. This change of direction was no doubt the result of a cautious attitude towards the *Inquisition and its machinations.

One of the legacies of the Cimento is the elegant Italian prose, capable of describing things accurately, that characterizes the *Saggi di naturali esperienze* edited by Magalotti and published in 1667. However, the academy closed in the same year, partly because its patron moved to *Rome. The diaries of its members remain unpublished in the Biblioteca Nazionale in Florence.

[PBD]

CIMINELLI, SERAFINO, see SERAFINO AQUILANO.

Cinema plays an important role in Italian cultural life, being both popular and respected as art and as entertainment. Even from the early 1920s, home-produced films had to compete in the marketplace with American products. For a brief period just before *World War I this was not the case, and Italy led the world in the production of lush melodramas and lavish spectaculars. This style of film-making did not survive the war and its aftermath, however,

and it was not until the coming of sound in the 1930s that Italian cinema recovered its position.

Surprisingly, the *Fascist government that came to power in 1922 at first did nothing to support or even influence cinema. It acted quickly to nationalize documentary and newsreel production, but was slow to awaken to the consequences—cultural as well as economic—of Italy's heavy dependence on mainly American imports. Then, from around 1930, it set out to make the industry 'autarkic', or economically self-sufficient. Even so, it remained sceptical of attempts by film-makers such as Alessandro *Blasetti to make films actively in support of Fascist 'revolution'. Celebration of the nation was encouraged (e.g. in Blasetti's own *1860*), but political intervention tended to be negative, in the form of a heavy *censorship both of domestic production and of imports (whose soundtracks could be altered by discreet redubbing). Artistically, the government's main achievement was permissive: enabling film-makers such as Mario *Camerini to make films every bit as entertaining as their American counterparts, while retaining a certain relevance to the life of ordinary people in Italy. Direct criticism of the regime was of course impossible, but the blanket portrayal of the Italian cinema of the 1930s as alternating between bombastic epics and insipid 'white telephone' comedies is an unfair postwar concoction.

The fall of Fascism and the *Resistance of 1943–5 created brand new conditions for Italian film-making. With the studios at Cinecittà (first opened in 1937) out of action, film-makers took to the streets to produce the kind of films soon dubbed *Neorealist. First of these was Roberto *Rossellini's *Roma città aperta* (1945), a harrowing account of the liberation of *Rome the previous year. This was followed by Vittorio *De Sica and Cesare *Zavattini's *Sciuscià* (1946), about boys living rough in the city, and Luchino *Visconti's *La terra trema* (1948), an epic tale (loosely based on *Verga's *I Malavoglia*) about a *Sicilian fishing family. The Neorealist movement reached its peak around 1948, the year not only of *La terra trema* but of De Sica and Zavattini's *Ladri di biciclette*, and then declined. Faced with competition both from Hollywood and from a revived commercial industry, Neorealist films proved on the whole unpopular at the box office, unless (as with Giuseppe De Santis's *Riso amaro* of 1949, with Silvana Mangano) they were dressed up like the genre films audiences were accustomed to. The characteristics attributed to Neorealist cinema—an anti-dramatic style and a setting in the world of the Resistance and postwar reconstruction—actually apply only to a small number of films, but these few were very influential, not only in Europe but also, and especially, in the Third World.

In the 1950s the cinema continued to flourish. *Television (introduced in 1954) was slow to make inroads into the mass audience. Co-production, first with France and then with other European countries, enabled Italian (or part-Italian) films to reach wider audiences. For a while Italy became an offshore base for American production companies. Then, when the Americans left, Italian film-makers filled the gap by making, first, inexpensive costume films set in the ancient world (dubbed 'peplums' by the French), and then the famous 'Westerns all'italiana' (known in English as 'spaghetti Westerns'), of which the most famous are those directed by Sergio Leone (1921–89) in the mid-1960s. The fading away of Neorealism made room for new film-makers who did not share its aesthetic. Foremost among these were Federico *Fellini and Michelangelo *Antonioni. The success of Fellini's La dolce vita in 1960 convinced producers and distributors that there was a large market for 'art' cinema. Flamboyant producers like Dino De Laurentiis (1919–) and Carlo Ponti (1910–), with grand ambitions to conquer the American market, were joined by more modest figures such as Franco Cristaldi (1924–92), who saw the future of Italian cinema mainly in terms of the exploitation of niche markets within Europe.

In this favourable climate, artists from other fields were tempted to try their hand at cinema. Novelist and poet Pier Paolo *Pasolini, who had beeen an occasional scriptwriter in the 1950s, directed his first film, Accattone, in 1961, and went on to make many others, including adaptations of the stories of Oedipus (Edipo re, 1967, after Sophocles) and Medea (1970, after Euripides). The multi-talented Bernardo *Bertolucci also opted for a film career. Among the generation which had come of age in 1945, Visconti and De Sica continued to thrive, while Rossellini took the surprising decision to abandon the cinema in favour of television. The 1960s and early 1970s also saw the emergence of women film-makers for the first time since the silent period, notably Lina Wertmueller and Liliana Cavani.

Until the late 1970s Italian cinema could still be considered a national cinema. It produced films in a variety of genres which both addressed national concerns and offered a comprehensive image of Italy to audiences elsewhere. But about 1980 a decline set in. The mass audience was deserting the cinema. Traditional popular genres, such as the commedia all'italiana, lost their appeal. The new comic genre that emerged in the 1980s around the figures of Paolo Villaggio, Massimo Troisi, and Roberto Benigni was narrower in its appeal. Only Benigni, with La vita è bella (1998), and to some extent Nanni Moretti (Caro diario, 1993), have had any success in appealing to international audiences. Meanwhile the collapse of the art cinema market has meant that important films by serious film-makers such as Gianni Amelio (e.g. Lamerica, 1996) have difficulty in finding distribution outside Italy. Saddest of all, from an Italian perspective, is the decline in audiences at home. These are now less than a quarter of what they were in the 1960s, while the proportion of box office receipts for Italian films now stands at 15 per cent, compared to a peak of over 50 per cent in 1960.   [GN-S]

See P. Bondanella, Italian Cinema: From Neorealism to the Present (1990); G. Nowell-Smith with J. Hay and G. Volpi (eds.), The Companion to Italian Cinema (1996).

CINI, GIOVAN BATTISTA (d.1586) was a *Florentine ducal secretary and man of letters, author of a biography, some poems, and two stage *comedies: Il Baratto (1577) is still unpublished; La vedova (1569) stands out among Florentine comedies for its use of regional *dialects, as in professional *commedia dell'arte.   [RAA]

CINO DA PISTOIA (c.1270–1336/7) (Guittoncino di ser Francesco Sigi[s]buldi or Sinibuldi). *Lyric poet usually associated with the *dolce stil novo, and illustrious canon lawyer. Exiled from Pistoia in 1302, he was able (unlike *Dante) to return to his native city after a few years and hold public office. He supported the Emperor *Henry VII, and composed a *canzone on his death in 1313. He was a judge in Pistoia (1316–19) and in the Marche. From 1321 he was a professor of *law, teaching in *Siena and *Perugia and also in *Naples when the young *Boccaccio was there. His works as Latin jurist include a Lectura in Codicem and an unfinished Lectura in Digestum vetus. In Italian he is the most prolific writer of lyric poetry between *Guittone d'Arezzo and *Petrarch, with a secure surviving corpus of twenty canzoni, eleven *ballate and 134 *sonnets. Most of these are love-poems celebrating Selvaggia dei Vergiolesi (d.1310). In the *De vulgari eloquentia (2.2) Dante assigns him prime place amongst love poets in Italian.

His friendship with Dante appears to have been a long-standing one, although it may be that Terino da Castelfiorentino, not Cino (as has been thought), was the author of one of the replies to Dante's early 'A ciascun alma presa e gentil core' (*VN* 3). Cino composed a *canzone* on the death of *Beatrice in 1290, and there are another six sonnets to Dante from Cino and five by Dante to Cino, with Dante initiating the exchange in two cases. They seem to have been particularly close during the first years of Dante's *exile. In the *De vulgari eloquentia* Dante links the two of them in his poetic rolls of honour as 'Cynus et amicus eius'. He also addresses the third of his letters (1306?) 'to the Pistoian exile'. On the death of Dante in 1321 Cino wrote the celebratory 'Su per la costa, Amor, de l'alto monte'. There are, however, two sonnets (one of which is not definitely by Cino) which are critical of the *Divine Comedy.

Cino is the link between the *dolce stil novo* and the greater lyric poetry of Petrarch, whose musicality his own practice anticipates. His poetic correspondents include Guido *Cavalcanti and *Onesto da Bologna, who jibed at the dreaminess of the *dolce stil novo*. The opening of the *canzone*, 'La dolce vista e'l bel guardo soave', is cited respectfully by Petrarch (*Canz.* 70) and the whole poem is re-written in *ottava rima* in Boccaccio's *Filocolo* (5.62–5). Petrarch also wrote a sonnet on his death (*Canz.* 92).   [GG]

Poeti del dolce stil novo, ed. M. Marti (1969).

Cinque maggio, Il, see MANZONI, ALESSANDRO.

CIONE BAGLIONI (mid-13th c.). *Florentine notary and author of a small but uncertain number of poems. Around 1278 he took part in a famous *tenzone* with five other poets, including *Monte Andrea and *Chiaro Davanzati, supporting imperial claims in Italy.   [JU]

CIPRIANI, LEONETTO (1812–88). Born into a *Florentine family living in Corsica, he fought against *Austria in *1848 and was imprisoned and exiled. In the 1859 War of Independence he was a member of Napoleon III's headquarters and became briefly governor of the Romagna. His memoirs, *Avventure della mia vita*, were published only in 1934.   [EAM]

CIRIACO D'ANCONA (Ciriaco de' Pizzicolli) (1390–*c.*1455) travelled extensively in his career as a *merchant in Greece, Egypt, and Asia Minor,

perfecting his knowledge of ancient Greek and collecting inscriptions and descriptions of monuments, some of which are preserved in his *Commentaria*. In 1433 he moved to *Rome and then to *Florence, where he came into contact with the Florentine *humanists. In 1441 he took part in the *Certame coronario* with a *sonnet.   [LB]

CIRO DI PERS (1599–1663). One of the most interesting of *Baroque poets. He was educated at *Bologna, where his teachers included Claudio *Achillini. His studies were interrupted by the death of his father (1618) and his inheritance of the lordship of Pers, near Udine. Disappointed in his suit for Taddea di Colloredo (the 'Nicea' to whom much of his verse is addressed), he took vows as a Friar Knight of Malta, and fought the Turks in the Mediterranean, writing on the subject a long *autobiographical verse narrative known as 'A Iola' after its addressee. After 1630 he returned to Pers, where he remained for the rest of his life, except for occasional visits to *Venice and *Padua, where he was in contact with Giovan Francesco *Loredan and Carlo de' *Dottori. These authors, a *libertine and a *classicist respectively, mark the opposite yet complementary poles of his interests, which were essentially those of a brilliant, original, and restless aristocratic amateur. His works were largely published posthumously.

While long recognized as a major literary personality, Ciro has been wrongly classified as a follower of *Marino. His *concettismo* is notable not for rhetorical extravagance or ideological radicalism but for its personal, introspective, often dramatic qualities: he has an unusual intensity, rejecting established platitudes, and working to isolate from within the Baroque canon a coherent, restricted body of metaphors, which he develops with considerable imaginative force. Furthermore, *concettismo* is only one aspect of his poetry, which also includes odes and long narratives closer to the classicism of Fulvio *Testi and Gabriello *Chiabrera.

[MPS]

Poesie, ed. M. Rak (1978).

CITATI, PIETRO (1930–). *Literary critic who has turned increasingly to forms of narrative. Since the early 1970s he has developed the idea of criticism as a 'double' of the work of art. His studies of Goethe (1970), Katherine Mansfield (1980), Tolstoy (1983), and Kafka (1987) offer a dramatic reconstruction of the artist through *biography and critical interpretation. He turned to his own family's past with the *epistolary *Storia prima felice, poi dolentissima e funesta* (1989). [JJ]

CITOLINI, ALESSANDRO (*c.*1500–*c.*1583). Linguistic theorist. Born in Serravalle in the Friuli, he was forced to flee Italy for religious reasons and spent his later years in London, apparently teaching Italian. He was in favour of Tuscan as a literary language, and corresponded with Claudio *Tolomei. He also wrote a still unpublished Italian *grammar, in which special letters distinguish open from closed vowels. [See also QUESTIONE DELLA LINGUA.] [DieZ]

Città del sole, La, see CAMPANELLA, TOMMASO.

CITTADINI, CELSO (1553–1627), born in *Rome, worked as a secretary in courts before moving to his family's city of *Siena. Here in 1598 he became professor of the Tuscan language. He recognized Claudio *Tolomei as his master, but in his *Trattato della vera origine . . . della nostra lingua* (1601) he made original use of epigraphic and literary evidence to argue that Latin evolved into the vernacular independently of the 'barbarian' invasions. *Le origini della volgar toscana favella* (1604, 1628) identify ten forces which determined the nature of the vernacular. [See also HISTORY OF THE ITALIAN LANGUAGE.] [BR]

Città invisibili, Le (1973), *Calvino's novel inspired by Marco *Polo and Thomas More's *Utopia,* consists of descriptions by Marco of fifty-five fantastic cities with framing dialogues between him and Kublai Kan. The elaborate structure, dividing the cities into different categories, deliberately gives the impression of a symmetrical pattern which fails to contain reality's irregularity. [MMcL]

CIVININI, GUELFO (1873–1954). Prolific and versatile writer and *journalist. He has been dubbed a *crepuscolare* poet in *L'urna* (1901), though he remains close to *D'Annunzio, *Carducci, and *Pascoli. Later books cover his adventures as war reporter (for the *Corriere della sera*), African explorer, and ardent *Fascist. He also published fiction and drama. He co-wrote (with Carlo Zangarini) the *libretto of *Puccini's *La fanciulla del West* (1910). [PBarn]

CLARE OF ASSISI, ST, see FIORETTI DI SAN FRANCESCO; NUNS.

Classical Influences, see GREEK INFLUENCES; LATIN INFLUENCES.

Classical Scholarship in Italy reached an early apogee during the *Renaissance, when philological and interpretive skills formed a major strand in *humanism. Here as in other respects *Petrarch was the pioneer: apart from discovering *Cicero's *Pro Archia* (Liège, 1333), and his letters to Atticus (Verona, 1345), he assembled the most complete codex of Livy since antiquity, now in the British Library (MS Harleian 2493). *Boccaccio followed his mentor's lead, unearthing Tacitus' *Annals* and Apuleius from Montecassino in 1355, but it was in the 15th c. that *manuscript discovery reached its peak. Poggio *Bracciolini made the most important finds, of the complete Quintilian (St Gall, 1416), Lucretius, and *Statius' *Silvae* (1417), as well as Petronius (1423). There were other significant discoveries: the Lodi manuscript of Cicero's rhetorical works (1421), the twelve new Plautus plays brought to Italy by *Nicholas of Cusa (1429), and Tacitus' minor works recovered by Enoch of Ascoli (1455). By 1508, when the Corvey manuscript containing Tacitus' *Annals* 1–6 reached *Rome, the bulk of the Latin texts we possess today were known to Italian humanists. After this date, the only source of new classical texts was either palimpsests or papyri, the most spectacular example of the former being the discovery by the *Vatican librarian Angelo *Mai of Cicero's lost *De re publica* (1819). The acquisition of Greek manuscripts began only in the 15th c. with the journeys to the East of *Guarino da Verona, Francesco *Filelfo, and *Aurispa. Apart from classical Greek writers, *Poliziano championed Hellenistic authors such as Callimachus and Theocritus, while *Bessarion left his huge library of Greek texts to *Venice (1468), which became a natural centre of Greek studies, particularly with the establishment of the Greek academy and printing press of Aldo *Manuzio.

Apart from discovering texts, Italian humanists also led the way in the philology and interpretation of ancient literature. *Biondo and *Ciriaco d'Ancona testify to the antiquarian strain in Italian scholarship, while *Valla's emendations on Petrarch's manuscript of Livy (1446–7) still enjoy authority today, and Poliziano's recognition of the importance of the oldest manuscripts in a tradition was a textual principle he established centuries before Lachmann [see TEXTUAL CRITICISM]. His *Miscellanea* (1489) was a milestone in classical erudition, solving a wide range of problems from

Classicism

difficult manuscript readings to the meaning of philosophical technical terms. Expertise was further sharpened by the rise of major *libraries, notably those of *Federigo da Montefeltro in *Urbino, Lorenzo de' *Medici in *Florence, Pope Nicholas V in Rome, and Alfonso of *Aragon in *Naples. After 1500 the leadership in classical studies passed to northern Europe, even though Italy still produced excellent scholars such as Pier *Vettori (who did major work on Aeschylus) and *Robortello (whose commentary on Aristotle's *Poetics* (1548) would be influential in 16th-c. *literary theory. [See also ANTIQUARIANISM; BYZANTIUM; CLASSICISM; GREEK INFLUENCES; GREEK WRITING IN ITALY; LATIN INFLUENCES; LATIN POETRY IN ITALY; LATIN PROSE IN ITALY.]   [MMcL]

See L. D. Reynolds, *Texts and Transmission: A Survey of the Latin Classics* (1983); L. D. Reynolds and N. G. Wilson, *Scribes and Scholars: A Guide to the Transmission of Greek and Latin Literature* (1991); J. Kraye (ed.), *The Cambridge Companion to Renaissance Humanism* (1996).

Classicism refers in a strict sense to works influenced by the texts of Graeco-Roman antiquity, but in a broad sense to works informed by the qualities thought to typify ancient literature: balance, restraint, conformity with rules. Much of the Italian literary canon even down to modern and *postmodern times continues a dialogue with ancient texts, so that in that first sense nearly every period of Italian literature displays classical influence (though *Latin influences predominate over *Greek influences).

As for classicism in the broad sense of balance and regularity, in its early centuries the new vernacular, aspiring to the regularity of Latin, was very much concerned with rules for both language and style, as is evident from *Dante's *De vulgari eloquentia, *Petrarch's strictures on *imitation, *Castiglione's views on language, Torquato *Tasso's theoretical *Discorsi* on *epic poetry, and the debate on the *questione della lingua, with decisively classicizing contributions from Pietro *Bembo and the *Crusca. Similarly, the practice of literature evinces harmony and restraint, notably in *Petrarch's *Canzoniere, the serene *cornice* of *Boccaccio's *Decameron which counterbalances any impropriety in the stories, and Torquato *Tasso's *Gerusalemme liberata, which exudes balance in plot, structure, and style.

Later, as in other European countries, Italian literature manifests a series of dialectical shifts (*Renaissance, *Baroque, *neoclassicism, *Romanticism), in which rule-making and rule-breaking alternate. *Marino's work typifies Baroque excess, but it is steeped in classical culture. Reacting against the Baroque, neoclassicism's prime rule-followers are *Alfieri and Vincenzo *Monti, but Romanticism is more ambiguous in its attitude to classicism: *Leopardi could reject the *sonnet form, but his poetry and thought are indebted to ancient ideas, while *Foscolo's Romanticism has explicit neoclassical qualities. *Carducci's use of classical metres and subjects is in turn a reaction against Romanticism, while *D'Annunzio celebrates pagan myth over modern reality in an overwrought style.

The classicizing aesthetic and the appeal to ancient literature retained their force in much 20th-c. Italian literature. Although *Futurism wanted to abolish canonical traditions, *Ungaretti, *Montale, and other major poets remain indebted to classical ideas and traditional metres. Classicism was explicitly pursued by the writers of *La *Ronda* immediately after *World War I; and classical restraint can be discerned in Primo *Levi and classical symmetries in *Calvino. Though *Gadda's Baroque vision and style was immensely influential in the 1960s and 1970s, the style at least of some of the most highly rated recent writing (e.g. by *Capriolo, *Del Giudice, and Rosetta *Loy) seems drawn again to classical values. [See also CLASSICAL SCHOLARSHIP; GREEK WRITING IN ITALY; HUMANISM; LATIN POETRY IN ITALY; LATIN PROSE IN ITALY; VERSIFICATION.]   [MMcL]

See G. Highet, *The Classical Tradition* (1985); D. Secretan, *Classicism* (1973); J. T. Kirby, *Secret of the Muses Retold* (2000).

CLEMENT IX (Giulio Rospigliosi) (1600–69). Pope from 1667, who reconciled the Church with France and brought about some reform of its financial administration. His literary work belongs to his earlier career in *Rome, which included a period as secretary to Cardinal Francesco Barberini. He is best known for his *theatrical works. He provided the text for *Sant'Alessio* (1632, published 1634), a sacred music-drama with settings designed by Bernini and music by Stefano Landi, which inaugurated the theatre at the Barberini palace, with the flying machines and trapdoors typical of *Baroque *opera. Subsequent work included the musical *comedy *Chi soffre speri* (1637), a love story taken from *Decameron* 5.9 about an impoverished nobleman, and the drama *Dal male il bene* (1653), a contemporary love story with a complicated and varied plot inspired by Calderón.   [FC]

Clergy. The Roman Catholic Church includes both secular clergy, who live among the laity, and regular clergy, who live in their own communities. Clergy in major orders—bishops, priests, deacons, and (until 1972) subdeacons—perform the most significant pastoral duties of the Church. Bishops are assigned by the Pope to a diocese; they alone may administer the sacraments of confirmation and ordination. Priests administer the other sacraments, and are usually responsible for pastoral care at parish level. Deacons are entrusted with non-sacramental and liturgical duties. Four minor orders were traditionally permitted to perform only lesser duties, but since the reforms of Pope Paul VI in 1972, only two minor orders, acolytes and lectors, have survived, and they are now accorded only lay status. Cardinals are not ordained to any separate clerical order. Nominated by the Pope, and responsible for papal elections, they perform senior administrative duties in the Church; only in modern times has it been necessary for them to be in orders when nominated.

Roman Catholic tradition admits only baptized and confirmed males to ordination; the prohibition on female ordination was reaffirmed by Pope John Paul II in 1994. Clergy in major orders are obliged to the daily recitation of a cycle of specified prayers and readings known as the Divine Office; they are also bound to celibacy, a requirement restated by Paul VI in 1967. Since 1983, however, it has been possible for older married men to be ordained as deacons; and in recent years, dispensations from celibacy have been granted to men who have converted to Catholicism after ordination in another denomination, or who have left the active ministry of the Church. Ordination to any order is seen as conveying an indelible character, however, and even a degraded cleric does not revert to lay status.

Many writers before the 19th c. took orders, since clerical status offered access to *education and the possibility of economic security. In some cases ordination was essential for career advancement, especially in *Rome and the Papal States; and for men in minor orders, religious duties were few. Prominent clerics have often been generous patrons of letters, but criticism of the clergy is a common theme in literature. Some of the most fiercely anticlerical texts have been written by disaffected clerics, though Italian writers (and censors) became more wary of anticlericalism after

the *Reformation of the 16th c. [See also BENE-DICTINES; COUNTER-REFORMATION; DOMINICANS; FRANCISCANS; INQUISITION; JESUITS; PAPACY AND THE CATHOLIC CHURCH; RELIGIOUS LITERATURE.]   [NSD]
See C. Dionisotti, 'Chierici e laici', in *Geografia e storia della letteratura italiana* (1967).

Clorinda, one of the heroines of Torquato *Tasso's *Gerusalemme liberata.

COCAI, MERLIN, see FOLENGO, TEOFILO; MAC-ARONIC LITERATURE.

COCCHI, ANTONIO (1695–1758). Professor of anatomy in *Florence, who visited England (1723–6) and was known for his advanced ideas. In 1732 he became the first Tuscan *freemason. His *Discorsi toscani* (1761) include a dissertation on vegetarianism. In 1728 he published the first edition of *Cellini's *Vita. He was regarded as a model of linguistic propriety in his own prose and second only to Francesco *Redi as a medical writer.   [JMAL]

COCCOLUTO FERRIGNI, PIETRO FRANCESCO LEOPOLDO, see YORICK.

CODEMO, LUIGIA (1828–98). Prolific popular novelist, who was born in Treviso but began to publish after settling in *Venice with her husband in 1851. Inspired by George Sand, her early fiction contrasted country life with urban corruption and was to influence *verismo. She later draws on Balzac, producing her major work in *La rivoluzione in casa* (1869), a portrayal of the *1848 revolution in the Veneto.   [PBarn]

CODIGNOLA, ERNESTO (1885–1965). Educationalist. Born in *Genoa, he spent much of his career at *Florence University. He was close to *Gentile and worked with him on the school reform of 1923. His writings are mostly on the history and theory of *education, though he also published a study of Italian *Jansenism (1947).   [PH]

Cognizione del dolore, La (1963). *Gadda's masterpiece, first published in instalments in *Letteratura* in 1938–41. The setting is the *Milanese hinterland of the post-*World War I years transposed to an imaginary South American country, where the local dialect is Milanese with a Spanish patina. The protagonist, Gonzalo Pirobutirro, is clearly an *autobiographical fiction. He is an impoverished noble, engineer, and failed writer, who lives with his mother in their isolated villa. Much of the novel is concerned with his inner conflicts, alternating intense lyricism and irrepressible comedy. The unexpected tragic dénouement represents an attack on his mother by unknown assailants.

[GS]

COLA DI RIENZO (c.1313–54). *Roman notary and popular leader, who was inspired both by ancient republican Rome and by contemporary apocalyptic ideas. In 1343 he represented the anti-aristocratic Roman *guilds in *Avignon, where he met *Petrarch. On 19–20 May 1347 in Rome, supported by the *papal vicar, Cola successfully staged a coup, proclaiming a Roman republic with himself as tribune. Petrarch compared him to Brutus. In the next few months he made ever more extreme claims, including the Roman people's right to elect the Holy Roman Emperor. Losing both papal and popular support, he abdicated that December. In 1350, at the imperial court at Prague, he was charged with *heresy, and in 1352 sent as a prisoner to Avignon. Reconciled with the Pope, he returned to Rome as senator in 1354. He was subsequently lynched in a riot.   [JP & JMS]

COLAJANNI, NAPOLEONE, see DARWINISM.

Collegio Romano, *Jesuit college in *Rome [see also RELIGIOUS LITERATURE].

COLLENUCCIO, PANDOLFO (1444–1504). Born in Pesaro and educated in *Padua, Collenuccio first served the *Sforza rulers of Pesaro, but was dismissed when Giovanni Sforza succeeded in 1483. He moved to the service of Lorenzo de' *Medici, then that of Ercole d'*Este in *Ferrara. Ercole valued his diplomatic skills and employed him on sensitive missions to Pope Alexander VI (1494) and Cesare *Borgia (1500). He was arrested and executed as a traitor by Giovanni Sforza after his return to power. In addition to his *humanist learning—he was a skilled orator—Collenuccio is known as the author of a *sacra rappresentazione, Comedia de Jacob e de Joseph (also known as the Vita di Iosep figliolo de Iacob), written and produced in Ferrara at Passiontide in 1504, and a translation of Plautus' Amphitryon, performed in 1487. His six Latin and Italian *dialogues, the Apologi (published in 1526), draw on Aesop and Lucian to promote a pleasant, practical

morality. He also composed a substantial collection of *lyric poetry in Latin and Italian, and a Compendio de le istorie del Regno di Napoli, which is unfinished.

[JEE]

COLLETTA, PIETRO (1775–1831). *Neapolitan soldier and *historian. He fought with the republicans in 1799, and subsequently served Murat in 1814–15 and the *Bourbons in 1817. Exiled from Naples in 1821, he completed his major work, Storia del reame di Napoli dal 1734 al 1825 (1834), in *Florence, where his friends included *Capponi, *Giordani, and *Leopardi.

[EAM]

COLLI, VINCENZO, see CALMETA, IL.

COLLODI, CARLO (1826–90) (pseud. of Carlo Lorenzini), author of the greatest classic of Italian *children's literature, Le avventure di *Pinocchio. Born in *Florence, he worked for the *Tuscan civil service but also as a *journalist. After fighting in the *1848 war of independence, he founded a satirical paper, Il lampione, which was soon suppressed for political reasons. He later enlisted to fight again as the *Risorgimento reached its climax in 1859. As well as founding the satirical paper Lo scaramuccia, he wrote a prodigious number of newspaper articles, many of them polemical. He published plays, novels, collections of his humorous articles and memoirs, but made most impression with his children's books, which, like those of *De Amicis, were both entertaining and inspired by his political and educational ideals. The first was Giannettino (1877), which followed close after his translation of Perrault's fairy tales (1875). Le avventure di Pinocchio, serialized in 1881–3 in the Giornale per i bambini, was published in book form in 1883. It was an immediate success and was translated into many other languages.   [ALL]

Colloqui, I, see GOZZANO, GUIDO.

COLLOREDO, ERMES DI, see ERMES DI COLLOREDO.

COLOCCI, ANGELO (1474–1549). *Humanist and bibliophile. Born in Iesi, he became secretary to Leo X and Clement VII, and later Bishop of Nocera. His remarkable library, now mostly in the *Vatican, included *manuscripts of major importance—one of the earliest Italian *canzonieri (Vat. Lat. 3793), *Petrarch's final version and drafts of his *Canzoniere* (Vat. Lat. 3195 and 3196), and manuscripts of early *troubadour and Portuguese poetry, as well as of classical and humanist texts in Latin and Greek. His pioneering work as a scholar of modern vernacular literatures and his promotion of the study of Greek in *Rome led to intellectual partnership with Pietro *Bembo. The only text he published, the *Apologia delle rime di *Serafino Aquilano* (1503), is the first 16th-c. work to argue in favour of a *lingua cortigiana*. [NC]

Colombina. This *servetta* role of the *commedia dell'arte* was invariably elegantly clad in black shoes, white stockings, and colourful smock broken by a small decorative apron. Pert, flirtatious, and quick of repartee, the role became important in the Parisian Comédie-Italienne after 1660, thanks to the refined and sentimental emphases given it by Caterina Biancolleli, daughter of the great *Arlecchino, Domenico. The role was later paired with a wistful Pierrot. [KR]

COLOMBO, LUIGI, see FILLIA.

COLOMBO, REALDO, see MEDICINE.

Colonial Literature. *Mussolini's *Fascist regime treated colonial literature as a tool for ideological propaganda, which would illustrate the epic march of Fascist expansionism in a style that was both instructive and widely accessible. The regime saw the African works by *D'Annunzio and *Marinetti as model examples of how to infuse aesthetic worth into a political agenda. D'Annunzio, who was already producing colonial texts before *World War I, furnished the prototype of the writer-soldier, who blended thought and action in the service of expansion abroad. While providing easily reproducible examples of propaganda, he supported the colonial adventure by interpreting it as the rightful reappropriation of a long-lost empire in *Canzoni delle gesta d'Oltremare* (1911). In works such as *Poema africano della divisione 28 ottobre* (1936), Marinetti championed the opposition between European dynamism and African immobility, and viewed colonialism as a way to bring technological progress to countries otherwise doomed to stagnation.

While other professional writers such as Riccardo *Bacchelli occasionally wrote colonial narratives, disrupting the genre's stock themes with novels like *Mal d'Africa* (1935), colonial authors were often functionaries or military officials who narrated their colonial experiences to support the imperialist cause. The results were neither best-sellers nor works of art. A typical example is Mario dei Gaslini's *Piccolo amore beduino* (1925), a novel of questionable aesthetic value written by a professional military officer who had turned to fiction in order to commemorate the regime's colonial campaigns. Similarly, Gino Mitrano Sani's novels—*E per i solchi millenari delle carovaniere, romanzo di uno spahis* (1926), *La reclusa di Giarabub* (1931), and *Femina somala* (1932)—promoted a kind of counter-exoticism, which emphasized African fascination with the Fascist way of life. Colonial narratives degenerated into pamphlets espousing eugenic theories with Vittorio Tedesco Zammarano's *Azanagò non pianse* (1934) and *Auhér, mio sogno* (1935). The demise of the genre paralleled that of Fascist imperialist politics. [CDellaC]

See G. Tomasello, *La letteratura coloniale italiana dalle avanguardie al fascismo* (1984).

COLONNA. Powerful *Roman baronial family of Ghibelline allegiance [see GUELFS AND GHIBELLINES], with extensive landholdings in the southern *Papal States and the Kingdom of *Naples. They came to prominence in the 14th c., providing a host of Roman senators and cardinals. The family's fortunes blossomed under the aegis of the nepotistic Oddone di Agapito, who was elected Pope Martin V in 1407. Implacable enemies of the *Orsini family, their power was temporarily crushed by the *Borgia Pope Alexander VI, who exiled them and sequestered their estates in 1501. The family were *patrons of *Petrarch, at least until he compromised himself with *Cola di Rienzo. He was particularly close to Giacomo Colonna (c.1300–41) and Cardinal Giovanni Colonna (d.1348). The most famous member of the family during the *Renaissance was Vittoria *Colonna, whose religious and *Neoplatonic *Rime* were praised by *Michelangelo, and who frequented *humanist circles in *Rome, establishing friendships with Pietro *Bembo, Iacopo *Sadoleto, and *Castiglione. [SJM]

COLONNA, FRANCESCO (1433/4–1527). *Dominican friar from Treviso, based in *Venice, who is now believed beyond reasonable doubt to be the author of one of the most remarkable *novels of the *Renaissance, the *Hypnerotomachia Poliphili* (that is, 'the dream of the strife of love of the one who loves Polia'). It is a *classicizing, *allegorical romance, describing Polifilo's dream-journey through classical ruins adorned with Latin, Greek, and Arabic inscriptions, as well as sacred hieroglyphs. He meets his nymph, and after an initiation into love's secrets, marries her and completes his journey on the island of Venus. It was the first vernacular book printed by Aldo *Manuzio in 1499, and was exquisitely illustrated by an unknown master. But the intended readership is unclear. The hybrid language requires considerable Latin—one early editor felt obliged to give a summary in Italian—just as the allusions assume a grounding in ancient mythology and religious rites. It is also undetermined whether the allegory is profane or sacred or both. The novel has been a gift to Jungian literary analysts. [See also MACARONIC LITERATURE.] [LAP]

COLONNA, VITTORIA (1492–1547). The most famous name amongst women *Renaissance poets, though traditionally her verse has been unjustly seen as an example of arid *Petrarchism. She was married at an early age to Ferrante d'Avalos, Marquis of Pescara. Her early love poems mostly follow on his death in 1525 from wounds sustained at the battle of Pavia, and reveal a depth of sorrow and an intense desire for reunion after death which transcend the *Neoplatonic conventions of the genre. They are succeeded by similarly heartfelt expressions of religious devotion in which the figure of Ferrante is replaced by that of Christ.

Contemporaries thought highly of her both as a model widow and as a poet. She addressed poems to writers such as Veronica *Gambara, Francesco *Molza, and Pietro *Bembo, and was particularly close to *Michelangelo between 1538 and 1542. Occasional poems to powerful figures such as Pope Paul III and the Emperor Charles V testify to her interest in secular matters. Her numerous letters cover a wide range of subjects—the management of her estate, literary topics, and the spiritual issues which she discusses with religious reformers like Bernardino *Ochino and Pietro Carnesecchi. Her links with these eventually led to her being suspected of heretical tendencies, but she died in a *Benedictine convent in Rome before she could be formally investigated by the *Inquisition.
[ABu]

Rime, ed. A. Bullock (1982). See P. Wend, *The Female Voice* (1995).

Colonna infame, La, see STORIA DELLA COLONNA INFAME.

COLPANI, GIUSEPPE (1739–1822). Associate of the *Verri brothers from Brescia, who put *Enlightenment themes into blank verse. In 'Il commercio' (1766) and 'Il gusto' (1767) he opposes the views expressed by *Parini in *Il mezzogiorno* (1765), and turns his ironic prescriptions into serious instruction in 'La toletta' and 'Emilia'. [JMAL]

COLTELLINI, MARCO (1719–77). *Librettist from Livorno who became court poet at St Petersburg. He achieved his best results in *Almeria, Antigone,* and *Amore e Psiche.* In the 1760s he owned Livorno's foremost printing press, which published the first edition of *Beccaria's *Dei delitti e delle pene* in 1764. [JMAL]

COLUMBUS, CHRISTOPHER, see TRAVEL WRITING.

Comédie-Italienne, see COMMEDIA DELL'ARTE.

Comedy. In the medieval period, the Latin terms *comedia* and *tragedia* had been interpreted as stylistic categories applicable to all forms of writing. It was only with the rise of *humanist scholarship that comedy was seen principally as a genre of theatrical composition; and in this context, heavy reliance was placed on classical models in order to define it. The models used were the accessible ones of Plautus and Terence: ancient Greek comedy was known only by hearsay. In the late 15th and early 16th c., Roman comedy acted as a practical guide, and the 'rules' were intuited rather than treated as written dogma [see also LATIN INFLUENCES]. It was only after around 1540 that theoretical proposals and debates, based on authorities such as *Aristotle and *Horace, came seriously to affect and constrain dramaturgical and performing practice. The practical models were nonetheless crucial and revolutionary: it was through the genre of comedy, at least initially, that the Italians 'classicized', and thus modernized, the European conception of *theatre.

From the practice of Plautus and Terence, and from the Terentian commentaries of Donatus and Evanthius, humanists learned that comedy was a performed story which attempted to mimic and mock psychological and social behaviour, without resorting either to abstract symbolism or to poetic complexity. It set up a contest between a limited range of standardized characters—young and old, masters and servants—leading to an outcome of which the audience would approve, often a marriage or reconciliation between young people. Most importantly, it dealt with a strictly limited range of people in society—affluent urban citizens and their servants (or slaves) and hangers-on. It did not depict rural life; and noble characters with public as well as private concerns were to be portrayed separately in *tragedy. This class distinction was strongly felt, and for three centuries comedy was to deal with private crises rather than public ones, concentrating in the great majority of cases on events and conflicts within the middle-class family. Although there were a few *Boccaccian plots which ended in the triumph of roguery or adultery, the main tendency was for social and moral order to be restored in a comic denouement, after a period of entertaining subversion and anarchy. However, the plot models of Roman comedy soon proved too restrictive; and the *Sienese comedies of the Accademia degli *Intronati, from 1532, introduced more sentimental formats based on *romance, which were also able to give more prominence and autonomy to female characters.

Commedia erudita, as humanist comedy is now called, was developed by such authors as *Ariosto (the prime innovator), *Dovizi, *Machiavelli, and *Aretino, as well as the Intronati and numerous *Florentines. From the start the genre tended to favour prose over verse—thus introducing a separate, almost accidental revolution into European theatre. It was a hard-edged comedy based on mockery, with few characters who could be seen as really sympathetic, and a considerable dose of farcical implausibility in its intrigue and trickery (though the term 'farce' itself never had a clear-cut meaning in Italy until the French genre was imitated in the late 19th c.) [see also BEFFA; FACEZIE; FARSE CAVAIOLE]. In the Venetian area, more plebeian tendencies were introduced by *Ruzante, and followed up by other writer-performers. This led to the split in theory and practice between gentlemen and professional players, and the rise of *commedia dell'arte* troupes who performed without scripts from outline scenarios. The professionals pillaged *commedia erudita* plots and formats, but shook them into a dramaturgical form which was more fragmentary and performance-oriented: their use of indestructible 'masks', which entered popular folklore, created great comic energy, but also produced a tendency to dehumanize some central characters. Writers of comic scripts learned in their turn from the improvisers, and both erudite and *commedia dell'arte* models spread into European theatre.

In Italy itself, comedy borrowed elements from tragedy or sentimental *pastoral to extend its range,

as in the plays of *Oddi and *Della Porta. Scripts must also have been influenced, as improvised performances certainly were, by the revolutionary involvement of female performers. After around 1630 there was less invention, apart from the interesting case of so-called *commedia ridicolosa*: the lack of a single cultural centre or capital seems to have impeded any of the quite different developments which took place in Spain, England, and France. In the 17th and 18th c., France was in fact the centre of creativity in strictly classical-style comedy, but figures such as Molière and Marivaux were surrounded and heavily influenced by Italian emigrant practitioners.

By the middle of the 18th c., Italian comic invention was centred on two genres: the *commedia dell'arte*, now becoming rather stale and predictable, and *opera buffa* [see OPERA]. *Venice had been the most important performance centre since the founding of public commercial theatres there even before 1600. It was the Venetian Carlo *Goldoni who embarked on a conscious reform of comic drama, moving his audience's taste and tolerance by carefully graded steps, over time, away from established formats. He reduced, and eventually abolished, the presence of the old puppet-like *commedia dell'arte* masks, and also got rid of the unthinking and repetitive scurrility. He aimed instead at a combination of greater social realism in comedy with a clear (but not always indulgent or benign) moral message. The fact that he was ultimately successful, despite polemics and setbacks, indicates that he was genuinely moving with the times. In fact French *sensibilité* had taken European society away from a comedy based purely on mockery and derision, and created a demand for something more probing and subtle on the one hand, and more sympathetic on the other; it was necessary now to offer some characters who won the audience's full approval, as well as others who were roundly mocked. This mingling of moods foreshadowed the breakup of rigid genre distinctions which came with *Romanticism: after 1800 it becomes harder to distinguish comedy as a separate genre.

The last, and most enduringly successful, achievement of Italian stage comedy as a genre must be Lorenzo *Da Ponte's three *libretti for Mozart.   [RAA]

See M. Pieri, *La nascita del teatro moderno in Italia tra XV e XVI secolo* (1989); R. Andrews, *Scripts and Scenarios: The Performance of Comedy in Renaissance Italy* (1993).

Come le foglie

Come le foglie, see GIACOSA, GIUSEPPE.

Comics (*fumetti*) have traditionally enjoyed a large readership in Italy, a fact often attributed to the country's notoriously low rates of *literacy. The forms taken by comic art have varied, however, although American influences have been strong since at least the 1930s, and the influence of the French *bande dessinée* was marked in the 1980s.

From the early years of the century to the 1970s, there was a robust tradition of Italian children's comics, reflected most strongly in the *Corriere dei piccoli* ('Corrierino') but also in the Catholic *Il Vittorioso* and, after *World War II, in the *Communist *Il Pioniere*. The characters of the 'Corrierino', which included Italino (a patriotic boy) and, more memorably, the perennially lucky Signor Buonaventura and the oafish Sor Pampurio, spoke through rhyming texts, not bubbles (*nuvolette* or *fumetti*) in the American fashion. However, although this tradition persisted, American styles and characters made inroads. *Mondadori produced stories under licence for the Italian version of the *Mickey Mouse Weekly* (*Topolino*) from the 1930s, and in the postwar years this weekly was preferred to the 'Corrierino' by children (or parents) of a modern outlook. Several of the American characters who acquired a following in the interwar years, such as Mandrake the Magician and Tarzan, were forced to undergo cosmetic changes during the war (Tarzan becoming Sigfrido, for example).

After 1945 American influences increased, and new strips, including the Katzenjammer Kids and Superman, arrived; the consequence was an incorporation within the Italian comic tradition of a set of assumptions about comic heroes that was closely linked to American reference points. Tex Willer, Buffalo Bill, and Il grande Blek were all products of this cultural exchange, while even the more obviously Italian characters of later years owed their faces to American and British film stars.

In the 1970s, the cheap comic books were supplemented by satirical and political stories of considerable artistic and cultural ambition. Artists like Andrea Pazienza, Milo Manara, and Guido Crepax came out of an alternative culture that mixed the erotic and the political in a manner that recalled Robert Crumb, creator of Fritz the Cat. The Italian *bande dessinée* was a short-lived affair of the early 1980s, much less successful and and with less official support than the French original. Magazines like *Frigidaire* and *Totem* (both of a counter-culture extraction) and the more mainstream *Orient Express* and *Pilot* were only briefly taken up by educated young adults, and closed within a few years of their foundation. However, they did act as a forging ground of some fine comic artists, such as the Bolognese Vittorio Giardino, whose meticulously drawn mysteries set in central Europe also appeared in the leading French periodical *A suivre*, and they gave rise to a handful of characters who outlived the general downturn of the market. Perhaps the most enduring of these was Hugo *Pratt's creation Corto Maltese, who gave rise to a magazine of the same name. Usually alone, and surrounded by space, he offered young men a romantic source of identification that was less obviously commercialized and sexualized than James Bond.

The 1990s witnessed the invasion of cheap translations of American and Japanese comic books, often produced by computer graphics. Although these left little place for more cultured comic art, the world of Italian comics remained vital and creative. The publisher Sergio Bonelli, who was responsible for the long-running Tex Willer, produced the phenomenally successful Dylan Dog, an investigator of the paranormal who counts Groucho Marx as a sidekick. [See also FOTOROMANZO.]   [SG]

See L. Becciù, *Il fumetto in Italia* (1971).

COMIN, ANTONIO, see ITALIAN WRITERS IN AUSTRALIA.

COMISSO, GIOVANNI (1895–1969). Novelist who spent most of his life in and around his native Treviso. He served in a communications division in *World War I before joining *D'Annunzio in Fiume. His first published work, *Il porto dell'amore* (1924), is based directly on this experience. He became well known in artistic circles in the 1920s and had close contacts with writers such as *Svevo and *Saba. During this period Comisso worked as a correspondent for a number of national newspapers, writing *travel pieces on Italy and North Africa and embarking on a lengthy trip to the Far East in 1929. The money he earnt allowed him to purchase a farm outside Treviso where he lived for many years, taking a great interest in the *peasant culture, whose disappearance he charted in *La mia casa di campagna* (1958). He continued to write prolifically and was awarded the Strega Prize in 1955 for the short stories of *Un gatto attraversa la strada*. Though his work received further recognition in subsequent years, he remained isolated from cultural debates of his time. Little of what he wrote is in print today.

Although he started off writing poetry and later attempted to write for the *theatre, Comisso was primarily a writer of prose. His work is difficult to categorize. It is generally *autobiographical, but blurs the distinctions between fiction, *journalism, and *diaries. He often revised and reused the same episodes more than once, and republished some works under different titles in only slightly amended form. *Cina-Giappone* (1932), a collection of already published travel pieces, reappeared as *Donne gentili* (1958) and was finally integrated into the definitive edition of the autobiographical *Le mie stagioni* (1963). There is also little formal difference between genres. Regarded as an exponent of *prosa d'arte* on account of his early preference for the stylized vignette, Comisso never developed a strong notion of plot. His strength lies in an ability to create a sense of place, and is most effectively demonstrated in the depictions of Europe, Asia, and Italy itself in his travel writing. Comisso's *homosexuality, as well as his interest in peasant culture and non-European civilizations, invites comparison with *Pasolini, though he was not a politically motivated writer, and did not perceive his homosexuality in an ideological light. But his representations of sexuality have an idyllic, sensual quality, beyond conventional time and place. They are an important aspect of his work and offer unfamiliar images of masculinity under *Fascism.   [DD]

See N. Naldini, *Vita di Giovanni Comisso* (1985); R. Esposito, *Invito alla lettura di Comisso* (1990).

Commedia all'italiana, see CINEMA.

Commedia dell'arte. A name given to the Italian drama which flourished from the mid-16th to the early 18th c., and was distinct from the learned literary drama (or *commedia erudita*) of the *courts and *academies by being primarily *improvised by professional players [see also COMEDY; THEATRE, 1]. However, the term was not used until the 18th c., perhaps first by the dramatist Carlo *Goldoni, noted for having effected a shift from improvised to scripted plays. What has come to be called the *commedia dell'arte* was variously called the *commedia all'improvviso* or the *commedia mercenaria* in the 16th c., terms applicable to the work of many kinds of acting company operating at different social and economic levels, from small provincial troupes, like those which flourished in the *Naples region in the early 17th c., to companies welcome at the major courts of Europe, like the Gelosi and the Fedeli. As most of our knowledge is of the major troupes, the term has come to be associated more particularly with their activities.

Professional acting troupes seem to have emerged in Italy in the early to middle decades of the 16th c., perhaps taking on a more developed character only from the early 1560s, when actresses became a feature of performance. The largest companies consisted of some ten to twelve players, and had a well-defined complement of male and female performers, who acted stock type roles. These were characterized by costume, accoutrements, and kinds of stage activity, sometimes reflecting regional traits, and were nearly all handed down in many of their essentials from the 16th to the 18th c. A company complement included two *vecchi* (old men), invariably *Pantalone and the *Dottore; one, two or more *zanni* (servants), among them named figures including *Arlecchino, *Brighella, Truffaldino, and in Southern Italy *Pulcinella; at least one *servetta*, often under the name of *Colombina or Franceschina; two or three pairs of lovers, with names like Flavio, Florinda, Isabella, and Ottavio; and the *Capitano, an independent role, sometimes hero, sometimes villain, occasionally functioning as a second or third lover. Of key importance is the fact that such character types were instantly recognizable by their appearance and their stage actions and movement, although only the more ridiculous figures appear regularly to have worn actual masks.

Performances were made on the basis of scenarios which, at a minimum, gave a plot line, exits and entrances, and some indication of stage business. The demands of the scenarios enabled performers to exploit a wide range of performer skills, drawn from many traditions of both popular and elite performance, according to the role performed; such skills included a retentive memory and aptitude for quick study, and the ability to sing, dance, play musical instruments, and engage in acrobatics. The players took over, and turned to their own purposes, the plots, character types, and some staging techniques of the *commedia erudita*, the influence of which is partly felt too in the fact that the action in most of the scenarios invariably takes place in a piazza, whose stylized streets and houses serves as the microcosm of a city. On this functional stage, the companies acted mainly improvised comedies, but were also capable of devising *pastorals and *operatic dramas.

During their heyday in Italy, the best companies

Commedia erudita

performed not only 'improvised' but also scripted drama. The stage space provided for fluid movement of scenes, often with only two or three characters on stage at once, and most of the scenarios (as in Flaminio *Scala's *Il teatro delle favole rappresentative* of 1611) call for a minimum of basic props, such as ropes, tools, lanterns, swords, and tombs etc.—ideal for companies frequently on the move. The popularity of playing to the audience is indicated in the frequent recourse to set-piece soliloquies: musings on love, war, the player's life; expressions of hunger, misery, or madness; a lover's delight at reciprocated passion or despair at contemptuous rejection. In its comic dimensions this drama is essentially farce, replete with plot improbabilities, confusions of identity, riotous physical imbroglios, the apparition of ghosts, and the hasty arrival of policemen or soldiers or amorous rescuers. It delights in the theatrical, in suspense, night scenes, suggestive dialogue, and stage business, like cross-dressing, that exploits female physical charms. At the centre of many scenes are the *lazzi*, extended passages of verbal and physical stage business.

The novelty of the improvised drama in part accounts for its Europe-wide success in the 17th and 18th c. in countries as various as Portugal, Sweden, and Russia. Given the division of the Italian peninsula into many small states, acting companies regularly toured to find audiences, playing in streets and squares, in rooms and halls, and, later, even in purpose-built theatres. Some companies soon travelled beyond the peninsula, and from the early 1570s troupes are found performing in Paris, the Low Countries, and the German states. Royalty often invited the most prestigious troupes like the *Gelosi*, led by two of the most celebrated performers of the age, Isabella and Francesco *Andreini, the *Confidenti*, possibly with Scala as leader or *capocomico*, and the *Fedeli*, fronted by Francesco's son, Giovan Battista *Andreini. Some companies settled abroad on a permanent or semi-permanent basis, as did the players who made up the Parisian Comédie-Italienne from 1661 until their expulsion in 1697, the troupe under Luigi Riccoboni that returned to Paris in 1716 after nearly twenty years' banishment, and the companies found in Warsaw or Dresden or St Petersburg in the 18th c.

By then, however, performance had become stereotypical, the masks increasingly dominating with attention-catching buffoonery. In the 1740s Goldoni began a slow process of reform that led to the replacement of improvised show by scripted drama, although some fine companies, like that of Antonio Sacchi, flourished in Italy in the second half of the century, and in the South others gradually evolved into the characteristic Neapolitan popular theatres of the early and mid-19th c. Probably via the French fairs, the masks were translated to the English theatre in the early 18th c., as figures in pantomime, and in France too they gradually moved away from their Italian roots to become the white-faced clown of pierrot shows. Modern companies in Italy and elsewhere have attempted to revive the idea of an improvised drama of masks and roles, and books are even written purporting to be guides to *commedia dell'arte* performance. But the improvised drama was of its time and place, and is not recoverable. [KR]

Comici dell'Arte. Corrispondenze, ed. C. Burattelli *et al.* (1993). See A. Nicoll, *Masks, Mimes and Miracles* (1931); K. and L. Richards, *The 'Commedia dell'Arte': A Documentary History* (1990).

Commedia erudita, see COMEDY.

Commedia ridicolosa is the name given by critics to a body of plays published in central Italy in the first half of the 17th c. They are fully scripted texts of complex comic intrigues, in which most of the characters are *commedia dell'arte* masks speaking a range of *dialects. It is thought that they were composed for amateur performers who wanted to reproduce the *commedia dell'arte* experience without having the improvising skill. By recording in print some standard material which was usually transmitted orally, they are an important source for the content and structure of *commedia dell'arte* scenarios. Principal authors were Giovanni Briccio (1579–1645) and Virgilio Verucci (dates unknown). [See also COMEDY.] [RAA]

Commentaries were a foremost part of *university methods of teaching and learning in the *Middle Ages and *Renaissance. A lecturer's task consisted in commenting orally to students on a few chosen texts, mainly in philosophy, natural science, and theology. Written down, these commentaries anticipated the roles that notes and introductions to a text, or *biographies and interpretative monographs, perform today. Commentaries were also part of the study of extracurricular authors, such as *Virgil, *Horace, *Ovid, *Cicero, and Seneca.

Biblical commentaries hallowed the *allegorical four senses of Scripture—literal, allegorical, moral, and anagogical (this last relating to the next life).

The commentator interpreted the images, metaphors, and myths or stories that God had used as suitable for weak human understanding, ideally peeling away their 'outer rind' or 'bark' in order to reveal inner truths that went far beyond those attainable by reason. Allegorical interpretation was also applied to classical poems like Virgil's *Aeneid* and Ovid's *Metamorphoses*, the latter giving rise to the numerous commentaries about deep moral and spiritual truths hidden in the ancient myths.

*Dante's *Divine Comedy* and *Petrarch's *Canzoniere* and *Trionfi* gave rise to waves of commentaries, in Dante's case from the 1320s onwards [see DANTE COMMENTARIES]. Much Dante commentary followed Dante himself (or whoever wrote the letter to Cangrande) in applying the biblical 'four senses' to the *Divine Comedy*, turning Dante into a divinely inspired prophet, and his poem into the supreme example of poetic theology. Commentaries on Petrarch provided a short account of each *sonnet's allegory. The honour of a commentary was later extended to *Ariosto's *Orlando furioso*. Normally the commentary appeared with the text, even surrounding it in early printed books. *Machiavelli's *Discorsi* on *Livy are unusual in that they are, and were, quite separable from Livy's text.

A unique Italian development, and an almost exclusively *Florentine one, is the long philosophical commentary on love poetry. The earliest is the *Convivio*, in which Dante writes in the vernacular about three of his own *canzoni*. Guido *Cavalcanti's abstruse 'Donna me prega' received a Latin commentary from *Dino del Garbo in the early 14th c., which was then followed by many others. In the later 15th c. Lorenzo de' *Medici, like Dante, commented on his own poems, while *Pico della Mirandola gave a wide-ranging exposition of *Neoplatonic doctrines in his commentary on Girolamo *Benivieni's lacklustre 'Amor dalle cui'. In the 16th c. this kind of commentary was continued by Benedetto *Varchi and Francesco de' Vieri, though in content it became interchangeable with Neoplatonic love *dialogues. The *Counter-Reformation gave rise to more spiritual commentaries, such as that by Lucrezia *Marinella on Luigi *Tansillo's *Lagrime*.

Nowadays, the commentary tradition is continued most visibly in editions of Dante, but has been extended to editions of modern poets such as *Montale. [LAP]

See O. Besomi and C. Caruso (eds.), *Il commento ai testi* (1992).

Communes. The commune (Italian *comune*) was a self-governing, quasi-republican city. As an institutional form it became common in the 10th to 11th c., particularly in Northern and Central Italy, less in the South and the extreme North-East. The reason for the rise of the commune was essentially the ineffectiveness of monarchical control, and the weakness of the German kings and lack of centralization because of the division between Empire and *papacy. The rise of the commune was in a sense a return to the city-state, but communes were totally different from the cities controlled by the emperor of the Roman imperial period and from the cities controlled in the early *Middle Ages by Lombard kings and the agents of Byzantine emperors. Absence of external force made it possible for the city to be governed by the more influential families who actually lived within it. The commune might be enforced by popular assemblies, and might have councils chosen from the major citizens, and officials such as a *podestà or chancellor, to conduct judicial or administrative business, but it was in practical terms government by the wealthier citizens who lived in the city.

In the early 13th c. the number of communes, ranging from large communities such as *Milan to small ones such as San Miniato, was very large. In the course of the century the traditional commune was affected by powerful social forces. First, the rapid increase of population tended to create a large underclass of unprivileged and poor, hostile to the oligarchs. Second, the expansion of industry and trade led to the existence of *guilds (*arti*), which wished for political power, and to the emergence of wealthy classes which were outside the established groups which had monopolized status and office. Therefore the late 13th and early 14th c. witnessed many conflicts between the *populus* and the *anziani* or magnates. These were in part conflicts between landed wealth and commercial or industrial wealth. They led to the elaboration of even more complicated constitutions, in which power was divided between numerous committees, and in which a larger proportion of the population could participate. The typical commune might be described as 'republican', in the sense that a large number of citizens might participate in some aspect of government during their lifetimes. On the other hand, there was often an important oligarchical element, such as the government of the 'Nine' at *Siena.

At the same time, other tendencies had become prominent during the 13th c., which were to limit the survival of communal regimes in many places.

Communism

Larger cities extended their power by incorporating smaller places in the surrounding *contado*. Thus places such as Pavia, taken over by the *Visconti of nearby Milan, or *Padua, conquered by *Venice, ceased to be self-governing, though they might retain some communal institutions with more local reponsibilities. All cities, large and small, showed a tendency to fall under the sway of despots, who might be local notables, like the Guinigi at Lucca, or nobles, like the *Montefeltro at *Urbino [see SIG-NORIA]. The main reason for this tendency was the danger of leaving the conduct of affairs in the hands of rather directionless committees, especially when war was threatened. By the end of the 14th c. the commune had become a much rarer type than it had been 200 years earlier. Despots were more common, and Italy was split into larger states, such as those of *Florence and Venice. Some communes, such as Lucca after the expulsion of the Guinigi, were to survive into the age of modern republicanism, but they were not many.   [GH]

See J. K. Hyde, *Society and Politics in Medieval Italy: The Evolution of Civil Life, 1000–1350* (1973); P. Jones, *The Italian City-State From Commune to Signoria* (1997).

Communism enjoyed a long-lasting and, in some ways, original influence in Italy. Born of a left split in the Italian *Socialist Party in 1921, the Partito Comunista d'Italia (as it was called) was first led by the intransigent *Neapolitan Amedeo Bordiga before a new leadership under Antonio *Gramsci was installed in 1924. In 1926 the party was suppressed and its members forced underground or into *exile, while Gramsci himself was arrested. For the next four decades the party was led by Palmiro *Togliatti, Gramsci's collaborator and pupil, who sought to develop an original strategy based on the popular front line which he championed at the seventh congress of the Communist International in 1935. On returning to Italy in 1944, he opened the party to all who accepted its programme, and sought to extend Communist influence within the context of a coalition including all the democratic parties.

Due largely to the leading role it played in the *Resistance in the Centre and North, the Partito Comunista Italiano (PCI) became a mass party of between 1.5 and 2 million members. Between 1948 and the 1980s, it represented a powerful presence on the political scene, commanding an electoral following which reached an all-time high of 34.4 per cent in 1976. In keeping with Togliatti's alliance strategy, the party always paid great attention to intellectuals. In the field of high culture, including *cinema, the PCI was very influential, although this resulted in more prestige than power. At the grass roots, the party gave rise to a rich and varied subculture which, in Emilia-Romagna and *Tuscany especially, was a central part of community life. In many parts of the country, the annual *feste de L'Unità* were very popular events.

The PCI built up its organization and subculture during the 1950s. Excluded from power, it turned itself into a disciplined and articulated presence that could mobilize thousands of people at a moment's notice. Even though the economic growth and prosperity of the boom years of the late 1950s and 1960s undermined its organization, the PCI retained a capacity to interpret and lead demands for social and political change. This it proved in the 1970s when, under the enlightened leadership of its most popular secretary, Enrico Berlinguer, it absorbed many of those who had participated in the protest movements of 1968–73, and advanced a controversial proposal for a 'Historic Compromise' (*Compromesso storico*) between Communists, Catholics, and Socialists.

Although the PCI did much to 'Italianize' itself, it remained ideologically and organizationally linked to the Soviet Union, the socialist homeland for Communists. That this link was still in force, despite the Eurocommunism of the 1970s and the breach with the USSR over the latter's invasion of Afghanistan in 1979 and suppression of the Solidarity movement in Poland, was apparent in the response to the fall of the Berlin Wall in 1989. In an attempt to save the PCI from being dragged down with Soviet Communism, the then party leader, Achille Occhetto, called on the party to dissolve itself and found a new force that would carry on its best traditions. After a lengthy internal dispute, the Democratic Party of the Left (PDS) was founded in 1991. Hardliners and radicals unwilling to abandon the Communist idea formed a second party, Rifondazione comunista.

The PCI was an unusual party, which was much admired by foreign leftists in the 1970s for its intelligent leadership, mass support, enviable local government record, and critical attitude towards the Soviet Union. But it was never able to become a governing party. Even after its successes in the mid-1970s, when it collaborated with the *Christian Democrats to deal with the economic crisis and the terrorist emergency, it only entered the government majority in Parliament, whilst remaining outside the government proper. In part this was because it lacked legitimacy. No centre party was willing to enter a formal alliance with it, and the United States vetoed its entry into government. But its exclusion was also the result of a cultural gap. As a party which had renounced revolution in practice, but not ideologically, the PCI was unable to develop practical policies. It always assumed that the accession of the party itself to power was the goal, rather than the means to the achievement of specific improvements and reforms.

For most of the 20th c., Communism appealed because Italian political and economic elites proved unable or unwilling to take full account of the legitimate desires of the lower classes. The experience of *Fascism gave revolutionaries opportunities to acquire credibility and win support that they would not have had in a democracy. In particular, the Resistance tradition allowed the PCI to take up, to some extent, the banner of the national interest. Before the economic boom, the USSR offered a plausible model of rapid development, apparently combined with equality and workers' power. Later, in a political context marked by a failure to deliver reform and by corruption, the idea of Communism remained attractive as a radical alternative unsullied by compromise. By the 1980s, it had become a necessary anchor for those who wished to resist political integration and to express their opposition to commodification. The ideas of *Marx, Lenin, and Gramsci had been substituted by attitudes of hostility towards commercial *television, *advertising, and conspicuous consumption.   [SG]

See D. Sassoon, *The Strategy of the Italian Communist Party* (1981); S. Gundle, *Between Hollywood and Moscow: The Italian Communists and the Challenge of Mass Culture (1943–91)* (2000).

COMPAGNETTO DA PRATO (13th c.). Perhaps a *giullare*. Two *canzoni* survive, both humorous dialogues in *ottonari* [see VERSIFICATION]. Unusually in one a woman asks a man for love, and he concedes. The other is a complaint dialogue in the *malmaritata* tradition, with the woman committing adultery out of revenge.   [JU]

COMPAGNI, DINO (*c.*1246/7–1324). *Florentine *merchant and White *Guelf politician [see BLACKS AND WHITES] who wrote an important *chronicle of *Dante's Florence, the *Cronica delle cose occorrenti ne' tempi suoi*. Compagni was much better-educated than most merchants. He was a member of the Silk *Guild by 1269 and served as a consul of that body six times between 1282 and 1299. At the same time he served the *commune as a member of various councils, and in 1282 and 1294 contributed to the reform of the Florentine constitution; he was tried and acquitted after the expulsion of Giano della Bella (1295), whom he had supported unwaveringly. He was one of the priors in 1289, *gonfaloniere di giustizia* in 1293, and in 1301 a member of the last White priorate. When Corso *Donati took over the city with *papal protection (1301), Compagni left public life both at city-state level and within his guild. He was fortunate in avoiding *exile (unlike Dante), partly at least because of a law exempting recent priors from prosecution.

The *Cronica*, evidently written between 1310 and 1312, focuses on the period 1280–1312 and is a rich source of illumination on people and events alluded to by Dante. It was presumably intended for semi-clandestine circulation, though the Anonimo Fiorentino commentator on the *Divine Comedy (c.*1400) certainly read it [see also DANTE COMMENTARIES]. In one respect Compagni's outlook diverges radically from Dante's: whereas Dante sees the omens of a Florentine decline in the territorial and economic expansion of the 13th c., Compagni is with the majority in understanding the city's development throughout that century as a success story. Otherwise, to a large extent the two writers, who had much in common and must have known each other, see events from the same viewpoint, though Compagni, writing before Dante became famous, mentions him only once, fleetingly (2.25). The *Cronica* has been called a diary of the White Guelf defeat. Rather than identifying broad historical forces, it somewhat naïvely sees the course of events as propelled by wicked, overbearing individuals, abetted by the cowardice and weakness of those who had an interest in obstructing them. With *Henry VII (apparently, at the time of writing) on the point of extinguishing Florence's independence, it reads like a parable about what happens to a free, happy city when it gives in to unwholesome interests.

A small number of *lyric poems by Compagni have also survived. They have a *Guittonian air and show a notable concern with literary and ethical issues.   [JCB]

See I. Del Lungo, *Dino Compagni e la sua 'Cronica'* (3 vols., 1879–87).

Compagnia di Venezia, see PRINTING.

COMPARETTI, DOMENICO, see FOLK AND POPULAR LITERATURE; LITERARY CRITICISM; LITERARY THEORY, 5; POSITIVISM.

COMPIUTA DONZELLA DI FIRENZE

(13th c.). Famous as the first woman poet of Italian literature, she has had her existence doubted by some scholars. But a certain Mastro Torrigiano addresses two *sonnets to her, and *Guittone one of his letters. Her name ('the Accomplished Maid of Florence') is, however, almost certainly a pseudonym. Her three surviving sonnets are in the *Siculo-Tuscan idiom. Two of them suggest a forced marriage and the frustrated desire to retire to a convent, but are as likely to be conventional as autobiographical.   [PH]

Comuni, see COMMUNES.

Comunismo, see COMMUNISM.

Comunità, see OLIVETTI, ADRIANO.

CONCAS, LINO, see ITALIAN WRITERS IN AUSTRALIA.

Concettismo. The dominant poetic style of the 17th c., in both verse and prose, which found equivalents and imitations throughout Europe (e.g. *cultismo* in *Spain, metaphysical wit in England). It deployed complex, far-fetched comparisons, paradoxes, and paralogical statements (*acutezze*) in order to exhibit the writer's genius and ingenuity (*ingegno*), and provoke wonder (*meraviglia*) in the reader. The term derives from *concetto* (from the Latin *concipere*, 'to conceive'), which had been used since *Petrarch to denote the idea behind a work of art. Increasingly in late *Renaissance poetics, and most notably in Camillo *Pellegrino's *Del concetto poetico* of about 1592, it indicated a novel insight into the nature of things and the hidden relation between them, particularly as captured by expanded metaphors or chains of metaphors. The theory of the *concetto* thus promised to resolve the conflicting claims of ornament and edification, which was also increasingly a conflict between individuality of expression and adherence to the cultural norms of the day.

The actual practice originates in stylistic traits found in Petrarch. These were played down by Pietro *Bembo and his followers, then rediscovered and developed in the commercialized, competitive climate of late 16th-c. letters. Some scholars assign a pivotal role to Luigi *Tansillo, or, more frequently, to Torquato *Tasso, while others emphasize the influence of *Counter-Reformation church oratory. In any event, by the 1590s poets like Guido *Casoni and Cesare *Rinaldi were producing verse characterized by extended metaphors which went well beyond the orthodox *Petrarchist canon. They were rapidly followed (in some cases parodied) by poets of the next generation, most notably Tommaso *Stigliani and Giovanbattista *Marino. The success of the latter's *Rime* (1602, with over thirty further editions in the next seventy years) led to his identification as the leader of the new poetic style, which has consequently been dubbed *marinismo,* a term unknown in the 17th c., though Stigliani derogatively described his rival's supporters as 'marineschi'. Marino's importance should not be underestimated, particularly his role in fostering a new self-consciousness among writers, but recent studies have suggested that far from being the inventor of the new style, he may not even be its most representative exponent, and that the term *marinista* is probably best reserved for a restricted group of partisans and imitators of his peculiar combination of rhetorical moderation and ideological radicalism. In fact, by the 1620s *concettismo* involved ever more complex, far-fetched metaphors, as well as a use of antithesis, oxymoron, paronomasia, and chiasmus far more elaborate than anything Marino had produced.

These formal excesses prompted a wave of criticism, as well as attempts, notably by the poet Girolamo *Preti and the theorist Matteo *Peregrini, to tread a safer middle ground. A greater challenge came from the *Jesuits, who were once mistakenly seen as the promoters or even the originators of *concettismo*. From 1623 the censors of the order, to whom all members had to submit their work, were instructed to refuse permission to publish for reasons of convoluted style, as well as content. In the years following the reaction to *concettismo* gained further momentum thanks to official encouragement by Pope *Urban VIII of an alternative, grandiloquently classical manner, often designated *Baroque *classicism. The issues at stake were as much political as stylistic, with classicism increasingly the expression of religious and political absolutism, while many practitioners of *concettismo,* especially in its more full-blooded forms, were variously identified with religious heterodoxy, republicanism, opposition to Spanish hegemony in Italy, and the interests and aspirations of the provincial petty nobility and professional middle classes. By the 1650s *concettismo* was no longer the dominant literary style, and, though it continued to be practised in provincial literary circles, it had lost almost all its initial radical charge. Paradoxically, in view of its heterodox origins, it survived longest in the precious, erudite verse of late 17th-c. conservative-aristocratic *Naples, and the elaborate homilies of Jesuit preachers like Giacomo *Lubrano.   [MPS]

See F. Croce, *Tre momenti del barocco letterario* (1966); O. Besomi, *Ricerche intorno alla 'Lira' di G. B. Marino* (1969).

Concetto, see CONCETTISMO; MARINISMO.

Conciliatore, Il (1818–19) was published twice weekly in *Milan, and was perceived as the organ of *Romanticism, though its name was intended to suggest reconciliation of the old with the new and a non-partisan internationalism. Edited by Silvio *Pellico and Ludovico *Di Breme, it attracted contributions from leading *liberals on economics, *education, social issues, and science. Its literature articles paid particular attention to history and the *theatre, and included contributions by *Berchet, *Borsieri, *Niccolini, and Ermes *Visconti. Earnestly pedagogical in spirit, the 'foglio azzurro' (so called from the colour of its paper) was in trouble from the start with polemical rivals and the *censors, who eventually closed it down.   [MPC]

CONCINA, DANIELE, see BIANCHI, GIOVANNI ANTONIO.

Concordat. Part of the Lateran pacts (signed 11 February 1929), the concordat regulates Church–State relations. It was the product of intense negotiations between representatives of *Mussolini's *Fascist government and the Holy See, and, along with a financial convention and a political treaty, helped rebuild bridges after the schism between Church and State following *Unification. Many were surprised when the 1948 constitution maintained the 1929 agreements, though there have been subsequent amendments—for instance, as regards the provisions for religious *education in schools. [See also PAPACY AND THE CATHOLIC CHURCH.]   [PC]

CONDIVI, ASCANIO (1525–74). Assistant of *Michelangelo, and author of the *Vita di Michelangelo Buonarroti* (1553). This was written in response to *Vasari's first *biography of the artist (1550), which Michelangelo considered misrepre-

sented him. It presents a more flattering view of its subject, emphasizing Michelangelo's noble ancestry and the lack of influence of other artists on his development. The erudite style of the biography has often been attributed to Annibale *Caro, to whom Condivi was related by marriage. Much of the information in the *Vita* was subsequently absorbed by Vasari in his revised and expanded biography in the second edition of his work (1568).   [CR]

Condottieri were military leaders who held *condotte*, mercenary contracts, for the raising of armed forces. They grew in importance as the mainly defensive civic militias of the Italian *communes were superseded towards the end of the 13th c. This was a consequence both of the expansionist policies of the *signori* and remaining republics and of the attempt by the *Avignon popes to regain control over the *Papal States. Greater economic affluence within the peninsula created the capital to pay for hired forces to facilitate such territorial aggrandizement, and, in the period before permanent standing armies, the *condottieri* played an increasingly significant role in shaping the political landscape of the 14th and 15th c., gaining fame and notoriety in their own right.

Initially the military companies were mainly composed of foreign troops and led by foreign commanders, but as the increasingly powerful states of Italy sought to establish permanent defensive and offensive military capabilities, the nature of the *condotte* altered and contracts were issued for longer than the traditional three months. By the 15th c. the *Venetians were securing *condottieri* for two-year periods with an additional year's option, effectively keeping them in permanent service to the Republic; Bartolomeo Colleoni served as Venetian commander from 1455 to 1475. The *Milanese experience typified the expansionist need for continuous military provision, with Giangaleazzo *Visconti employing Iacopo dal Verme (b. *c.*1350), Alberigo da Barbiano, and Facino Cane (d.1412) in his conquest of Northern and central Italy. After Giangaleazzo's death the political vacuum in central Italy benefited many *condottieri*, the *Orsini, *Gonzaga, *Sforza, Bentivoglio, *Montefeltro, *Malatesta, and *Este families all providing instances of *condottieri* princes.

Both *Machiavelli and *Guicciardini somewhat unfairly held the deficiencies of the *condottieri* and the mercenary system responsible for the ease with which Charles VIII of France invaded Italy in

1494; in reality Machiavelli's insistence on the organization and coordination of national armies reflected broader developments in the conduct of warfare beyond the Alps.   [SJM]

See M. Mallett, *Mercenaries and their Masters: Warfare in Renaissance Italy* (1974).

Confessioni di un italiano, Le. Novel by Ippolito *Nievo, written in 1857–8, and posthumously published in 1867 as *Le confessioni di un ottuagenario*. Through the adventures of the narrator and protagonist, Carlino Altoviti, Nievo creates a huge fresco of Italian history from 1775 to 1855. The earlier chapters describe Carlino's happy youth in the Venetian Friuli, and his strange relationship with Pisana (one of the most original characters in Italian fiction), who becomes his guardian angel throughout his dangerous life. Subsequently Carlino takes an active part in the main events of the *Risorgimento, and experiences war, prison, and *exile in London.   [FD'I]

Confidenti, see COMMEDIA DELL'ARTE.

Confino, see EXILE.

Congedo, see CANZONE; SESTINA.

Con gli occhi chiusi, see TOZZI, FEDERIGO.

Congrega dei rozzi. In *Siena in 1531 there was founded a cultural club of artisans which designated itself as a 'Society of Roughnecks', in opposition to the more aristocratic Accademia degli *Intronati; one qualification for membership was not to have learnt any Latin. The Rozzi are associated with a substantial body of plays and sketches, many involving mockery of the *peasant class and using formats also found in other parts of Italy. However, both before and after 1531, the so-called 'Pre-Rozzi' authors, such as Niccolò Campani ('Strascino') and Mariano Manescalco, wrote and performed in a wider range of comic and *epic drama which mingled popular and learned elements, and was not yet subjected to the rigours of strict classical imitation. [See also CLASSICISM; COMEDY.]   [RAA]

CONSOLO, VINCENZO (1933–). *Sicilian novelist. With Gesualdo *Bufalino he made a major contribution to the resurgence of Sicilian fiction in the later 20th c. He has lived mostly in *Milan, where he went to study law in the early 1960s. His

production has not been large. His most successful novel was his second, *Il sorriso dell'ignoto marinaio* (1976), which is centred on the brutal suppression of the uprising at Bronte in Sicily in 1860, and uses a hybrid mixture of narrative techniques and registers that led to comparisons with *Gadda. He can be more playful, for instance in the short but *Baroque *Retablo* (1987), but his work as a whole returns repeatedly to issues of memory, history, and language, particularly the abuse of language as an instrument of power in the Sicilian context. The moral pugnacity of his writing is comparable with that of *Sciascia, as is his sense that the past and present of Sicily can only be understood in dialectic relationship to each other. The complexities and commitment of his writing are especially evident in *Lo spasimo di Palermo* (1998), which is partly *autobiographical, and sets childhood in wartime Palermo against more recent terrorism in the North.   [AWM]

CONTARINI, AMBROGIO (1429–c.1500). *Venetian nobleman, *merchant, and sea captain, who went on an embassy to Persia (1474), where he met Giosaphat *Barbaro. The outward journey took in Austria, Poland, the Caucasus, the homeward Russia and Germany. The account (1487) of his travels is collected in *Ramusio's *Navigationi et viaggi*. [See also TRAVEL WRITING.]   [LL]

CONTARINI, NICOLÒ (1553–1631). *Venetian politician and *historian. He studied philosophy at *Padua and then had a distinguished political career, becoming a member of the Council of Ten and eventually Doge (1630). During the Interdict he supported Paolo *Sarpi against the Pope. He also tried unsuccessfully to extend trading rights to Protestant foreigners and to allow them access to Padua *University. During the Thirty Years War he was responsible for the frontier with *Milan. In 1620 he was nominated public historian. His *Historie venetiane* cover a limited period (1597–1604), but set Venetian events in a European context, ranging from Ireland to Turkey, and include accounts of the political, economic, and religious structures of different countries.   [FC]

CONTE, GIUSEPPE (1945–). Poet, novelist and literary journalist, born in Imperia and a literature graduate of *Milan University. His two outstanding collections so far, *L'oceano e il ragazzo* (1988) and *Dialogo del poeta e del messaggero* (1992), attempt to restore to Italian poetry the clarity and mythic force which he feels it has lost since *Pascoli. [PH]

Conte di Carmagnola, Il (1820, first performed 1828). *Manzoni's first historical *tragedy. The protagonist, a *Renaissance *condottiere, is falsely accused of betrayal, condemned to death, and executed. Though written in verse, it follows *Romantic canons, disregarding the Aristotelian unities and including choruses with the function of commenting on the action, as had been theorized by the German Romantic A. W. Schlegel. [VRJ]

Contemporaneo, Il, founded in 1954 and jointly edited by Carlo Salinari (at the time the *Communist Party's cultural chief) and Antonello Trombadori, was a left-wing version of Mario Pannunzio's liberal journal *Il *Mondo. It hosted a number of important debates, for example on *realism, before becoming a supplement to *Rinascita in 1958. [SG]

CONTESSA LARA (pseudonym of Evelina Cattermole) (1849–96). Born in *Florence to an English father and Russian mother, she lived a colourful life and was eventually shot by a lover. Encouraged by Mario *Rapisardi, she had great success with a book of verses and drawings in 1883. Much censured in their time, novels such as *L'innamorata* (1893) contain interesting celebrations of the female *erotic. [UJF]

CONTI, ANTONIO (1677–1749) was born and educated in the Veneto, where he studied philosophy, mathematics, medicine, and natural science. Under the influence of Locke's *Essay Concerning Human Understanding* he came to a cautious acceptance of the irreconcilability of scientific knowledge and theology, which led him to work with the biologist Vallisnieri on the infinitesimal calculus and numerous other physical and mathematical problems. A cosmopolitan by nature, he lived outside Italy between 1713 and 1726, coming into contact with the greatest philosophers and scientists of the time. In France he expounded to Malebranche, who had influenced him from an early age, his views on the irreconcilability of science and theology; and he attended the Académie des Sciences. In England (1715–18) he knew Newton and the most prominent members of the Royal Society, of which he became a member, he made friendships in Whig circles, and he began a poem on Newtonian physics. Back in Italy from 1726, he was recognized

for the prestige he had acquired abroad; but, then and throughout his life, the very breadth of his interests, and the problematic nature of his philosophical position, prevented him from producing any work of a truly systematic character. All we have are a few *tragedies written in his last years, a famous *translation (published in London in 1751) of Pope's *Rape of the Lock*, and numerous dissertations on aesthetic, scientific, and philosophical topics, which were partly collected during his life in the first volume of his *Prose e poesie* (1739) [see also ENGLISH INFLUENCES]. [SC]

CONTI, GIUSTO DE' (c.1390–1449). *Lyric poet born in *Rome, possibly into the family of the Counts of Valmontone. Little is known of his life; his early years were spent in Rome, his presence is recorded in *Bologna in 1409, and the later part of his life was passed at the *court of the *Malatesta in Rimini. He composed one of the most important *Petrarchan *canzonieri of the 15th c., *La bella mano*, completed in 1440, first published c.1472, and dedicated to a lady named Elisabetta or Isabetta di Bologna. Comprising 150 poems, mainly *sonnets, the *canzoniere* was very popular in the 15th and 16th c. An easy if mannered Petrarchan poet, imitated by his younger peers including *Boiardo, Giusto's diction found favour with the Accademia della *Crusca in the 16th c., assuring his poems a lasting fame, and giving him a reputation, probably exaggerated, as the greatest lyric poet of his period. [See also PETRARCHISM.] [JEE]

CONTI, NICCOLÒ DE' (c.1395–1469). *Venetian traveller to the Middle East and India, whose important account of his voyage (and apology for having converted to Islam) to Pope Eugene IV was inserted into Poggio *Bracciolini's *Historiae de varietate fortunae* (1447), and then into *Ramusio's *Navigationi et viaggi*. [See also TRAVEL WRITING.] [LL]

CONTI, PRIMO (1900–88). Painter and poet. He was prominent in *Florentine *Futurism, founding *Il Centone* with Corrado *Pavolini in 1919. After European success as a painter, he taught art in Florence. He established an important archive of avant-garde material bearing his name in Fiesole. [JJ]

CONTI, SIGISMONDO DE' (1432–1512). Of noble birth, he was educated in Foligno by his father and then in *Rome, where he moved c.1460. From 1476, he was closely associated with such major literary figures as Pietro *Bembo, *Sadoleto, and Filippo *Beroaldo the Elder. Under Pope Julius II he became an apostolic secretary, a post which he held until his death. Besides the *humanist poetry of his early years, he is also the author of a *Historia suorum temporum* and of an elegy on *Platina's death. [LB]

CONTILE, LUCA (1510–74) was a much-travelled polygraph [see POLIGRAFI] who served as secretary to various powerful lords. His writings include religious and moral poems and *dialogues; and three stage *comedies, which contain exemplary and even *allegorical elements not usually found in the *humanist *commedia erudita.* [RAA]

CONTINI, GIANFRANCO (1912–90) is considered by many one of the greatest Italian textual and *literary critics of the 20th c. Born in Domodossola, he taught at the Scuola Normale Superiore in *Pisa, and in Freiburg and *Florence. His interests embraced French, German, Italian, Provençal, and Spanish literature and the theory of *textual criticism, and he combined in his scholarship philological rigour and penetrating critical intuitions. He produced fundamental editions of *Dante's *Rime* (1939) and *Petrarch's *Canzoniere* (1964) and of 13th-c. vernacular poetry, particularly *Poeti del Duecento* (1960). His critical essays on contemporary Italian literature include seminal essays on *Gadda and *Montale, whilst as a literary historian he stressed the importance of *expressionist *plurilingual writing in Italian which originated in Dante. He is particularly associated with the so-called *critica delle varianti,* the interpretation of authorial variants. His attempts to establish the Dantean authorship of the *Detto d'amore* and the *Fiore* stand as a monument to the ways in which philology and criticism can successfully interact. [See also FILOLOGIA.] [DG]

Contrapasso, see DIVINE COMEDY; INFERNO.

Contrasto. Term used for a type of dialogue poem common in the *Middle Ages. The participants may be symbolic abstractions, but can be human, as in the comic *contrasti* of *Raimbaut de Vaqueiras and *Cielo d'Alcamo. The metrical form is commonly a *canzone or *ballata, and the poems often have an oral, popular air. [PH]

CONVENEVOLE DA PRATO (d.?1338). Notary who was exiled from Prato, and taught

grammar at Carpentras in Provence, where *Petrarch was one of his pupils. He later returned to Prato to teach rhetoric and lecture on *Cicero. He is possibly the author of a Latin polymetric poem, dedicated to Robert of *Anjou, in which Italian cities beg for deliverance. [JU]

Conversazione in Sicilia (1941). First published as *Nome e lagrime,* *Vittorini's most famous and successful novel is an account of a man's meetings with a series of emblematic figures in the course of a return to his native *Sicily after years of absence. Written in an intensely poetic style influenced by Faulkner, the novel is an essay on memory and dormant values, with a strong symbolic code and an insistent but poetically disguised warning about ideological simplifications (only incidentally *Fascism). The play with time is particularly adventurous, leading to conflations between mothers and wives, fathers and husbands—devices which help to reinforce a message of primal identities escaping historical definitions. [JU]

CONVERSINO, GIOVANNI, see GIOVANNI CONVERSINO.

Convitato di pietra, Il, see BERTATI, GIOVANNI; CICOGNINI, GIACINTO ANDREA; PERUCCI, ANDREA.

Convito, Il, see DE BOSIS, ADOLFO; PERIODICALS, 1.

Convivio (*Convito*). Unfinished treatise (the title means 'banquet') in Italian by *Dante, probably compiled in 1304–7 but largely unknown until its first printing in 1490. Of the planned fifteen 'trattati' ('books'), only four were completed. In book 1, starting from the *Aristotelian principle that all humans naturally desire to know, Dante defines the work as the meat (poems) and bread (accompanying prose expositions) of the banquet of knowledge; he explains his motive for writing it as the disgrace of *exile and justifies its composition in the vernacular rather than in Latin. In books 2 and 3 he provides first literal and then *allegorical expositions of two of his *canzoni* from the mid-1290s, presenting the *Donna gentile* of *Vita nova* 35–8 as, allegorically, the beautiful Lady Filosofia ('love of wisdom'). In book 4, the poem and commentary attack the definition of nobility as derived from lineage and wealth, rather than as the seed of virtue and happiness sown providentially in the human soul; chapters 4 and 5 outline arguments later developed in *Monarchia,* books 1 and 2. Citing many sources, including the *Bible, Aristotle and his Arab commentators, *Virgil, *Boethius, Albertus Magnus, and *Aquinas, the *Convivio* demonstrates Dante's wide reading and the clarity of his reasoning, in a style that permits also some discursive freedom, vivid exemplifications, and occasional passages of polemic. [See also SCHOLASTICISM.] [PA]

Cookery Books. The first book of gastronomy to have been printed in Italy was *De honesta voluptate et valetudine* by Bartolomeo Sacchi, Il *Platina. It was published first in Latin in *Rome in 1474, then in Italian, French (it became a best-seller in Paris), and German. More than just a cookery book it was, in effect, a synthesis of the gastronomic knowledge of the 15th c. The book incorporates Platina's adaptation of the recipes contained in the *Libri de arte coquinaria* by Maestro Martino, chef to the Patriarch of Aquileia, and the first cook to break away from medieval traditions to found a new type of cooking based on original techniques and creations. In Platina's book, Martino is the creative talent, while Platina is the *humanist, concerned with food hygiene, diet, the ethics of the pleasures of the table, as governed by moderation and a concern for balanced nourishment.

In 1549 an important book was published by Cristoforo di Messisburgo (c.1490–1548), steward to Cardinal Ippolito d'*Este of *Ferrara, and considered the founder of the great tradition of Italian *haute cuisine*. The book, usually known as *Libro novo*, has a long title that explains its content: 'The New Book which teaches how to make all sorts of food according to the season, both meat and fish, and how to arrange banquets, lay tables, furnish palaces and decorate rooms for every great Prince.' The next important book to appear—in 1570—was the *Opera dell'arte di cucinare*, the most comprehensive cookery book of the *Renaissance. Its author, Bartolomeo Scappi (d.1575), concluded his successful career by becoming chef to Popes Paul III and Pius V. The large volume, in which everything is dealt with in great detail, is divided into six books. The first concerns the chef, his kitchen and equipment; the second, meat and poultry and how to make sauces; the third, fish, eggs and soups; the fourth lists foods according to the seasons; the fifth deals with the making of tarts, pies, and cakes; and the sixth with food for the sick and the convalescent.

A century later, in 1662, *L'arte di ben cucinare* was published in *Mantua by the Bolognese Bartolomeo Stefani, chef to the *Gonzaga family. It is the first book in which recipes for ordinary people appear, alongside a section dedicated to princely banquets, including a description of a banquet given by the Gonzagas for *Christina, Queen of Sweden. The description of the table decorations, all made of jelly and sugar, gives a fascinating glimpse into the *court life of the period. At the end of the following century came two significant books, both from Southern Italy: *Il cuoco galante* (1773) by Vincenzo Corrado (1734–1831), and *Apicio moderno* (1790) by Francesco Leonardi. *Il cuoco galante* is written in a simple style and, in spite of using some terms from French (by then the culinary language of Europe), it remains faithful to local traditions. A section is devoted to vegetarian food, where most of the recipes would hold good today. Leonardi's book, in six volumes, reflects his wide knowledge of European cuisines (he eventually became chef to Catherine the Great), while at the same time it emphasizes the importance of regional cooking.

19th-c. Italian cookery books tend to use very stilted language, with many Italianized French words. *Il trattato di cucina, pasticceria moderna* (1854) is the classic example of this style; the author, Giovanni Vialardi, was chef to the King of Savoy, later King of Italy. But in 1891 a book was published that became a classic and, a century later, is still a best-seller. Its title, *La scienza in cucina e l'arte di mangiar bene*, does little to indicate the liveliness of the text and the colloquial, natural style of the prose. The author, Pellegrino Artusi (1820–1911), compiled a collection of 790 recipes, all tested by himself with the help of two faithful servants, and punctuated with anecdotes and supplementary historical information. The first cookery book to be published after the *Unification of Italy, it contains a number of recipes from the South, although most have a definite Tuscan and Emilian flavour.

In 1927 a book was published that became the manual of every middle-class housewife, *Il talismano della felicità* by Ada Boni (1881–1973). The book, still in print, includes some 1,000 recipes, many of French origin. The style is rather flat, but the recipes are excellent and totally reliable. In contrast *La cucina futurista* (1932), by the *Futurists *Marinetti and *Fillia, is much more remarkable for the originality of its recipes. The second half of the century saw two significant histories of Italian cooking, *La storia del pranzo all'italiana* (1963) and *La storia della cucina italiana* (1991) by Massimo Alberini. Recipe books became regional, the most comprehensive being *Le ricette regionali italiane*

(1967) by Anna Gossetti della Salda; a series published by Franco Muzzio includes *La cucina del Piemonte* (1990) by Giovanni Goria and *La cucina veronese* (1987) by Giovanni Capnist. Of modern writers who have celebrated Italian cooking, one of the most successful is the *journalist *Paolo Monelli, whose *Il ghiottone errante* is a fascinating account, several times reprinted, of a culinary journey through Italy.   [ADelC & NL]

CORAZZINI, SERGIO (1886–1907). One of the most interesting poets among the *Crepuscolari*. The son of a *Roman tabacconist, he was unable to complete his education and joined an insurance firm. After publishing three collections of poems—*Dolcezze* (1904), *L'amaro calice*, and *Le aureole* (1905)—he was forced to enter a sanatorium for consumptives in 1906. That same year he published *Poemetti in prosa* and three books of verse—*Piccolo libro inutile* (written jointly with his friend, Alberto Tarchiani), *Elegie*, and *Libro per la sera della domenica*. He was just 21 when he died in Rome.

Corazzini identifies his poetry and his illness, making the latter a metaphor for the uselessness of poetry in the modern world. His unemphatic, wilfully plaintive, and weary tone is a polemical reaction against the loftiness of *D'Annunzio, with explicit representations of himself not as a poet, but as 'un piccolo fanciullo che piange', as he waits resignedly for death. But affection for simple things does not mean poeticizing everyday reality in the manner of *Pascoli. Corazzini rejects the mysteries of *symbolism, and what religious feeling he has is bleakly unconsoling. Everything is overshadowed by a lucid awareness of poetry's marginality. Metrically, his deliberate prosiness leads to an almost avant-garde use of *free verse.   [RD]

Corbaccio (c.1365). Short prose work by *Boccaccio, in which he represents himself as in love with a greedy, sensual widow. He has a dream in which he meets the soul of her husband, who pitilessly exposes the wiles and faults of women in general and of the widow in particular, and cures him completely of his passion. The work draws on a *misogynistic tradition going back to St Jerome, but also has some of the immediacy of a realistic *novella. Its extraordinary biliousness may have also a biographical basis. The title is possibly from *corbo* (crow), a bird of ill omen which pecks out eyes and brains (like Love), or from *corbacchiare* (to trick), or from a word meaning 'lash', connected with the Spanish *corbacho*.   [VB]

CORBINELLI, IACOPO (1535–c.1590). Scholar who was exiled from *Florence in 1562, and spent much of his later life in France. There he edited works including *Boccaccio's *Corbaccio* (1569) and *Dante's *De vulgari eloquentia* (1577). Unusually for his time, and in contrast with *Salviati, Corbinelli believed that editors should not alter the form of earlier texts. [See also TEXTUAL CRITICISM.]   [BR]

CORDARA, GIULIO CESARE (1704–85). Noted *Latinist of *Piedmontese origin, who taught at *Jesuit colleges and Macerata University before being appointed the Jesuits' official historian. He *satirized fashionable learning in his witty, controversial *Sermones* (1737) and wrote a Latin account of the 1745 Jacobite rebellion, *Caroli Odoardi Stuartii expeditio in Scotiam*, published after his death.   [JMAL]

CORDELLI, FRANCO (1943–). *Journalist and *novelist, who is active in public cultural debates as a proponent of the vital social role of literature. His novels, which begin with *Procida* (1973), are experimental, combining different registers and meta-narrative elements.   [JEB]

CORDERO, FRANCO (1928–). Law professor and *novelist. He was forced by ecclesiastical interdiction in 1970 to suspend a controversial course of lectures on philosophy of law at the Catholic University of *Milan. As well as philosophical *novels, notably *Viene il re* (1973), he has written *La fabbrica della peste* (1984), a spirited defence of the magistrates accused by *Manzoni in *Storia della colonna infame*.   [DF]

Cordiglieri, see FRANCISCANS.

CORENO, MARIANO, see ITALIAN WRITERS IN AUSTRALIA.

CORILLA OLIMPICA, see MORELLI FERNANDEZ, MARIA MADDALENA.

CORIO, BERNARDINO (1459–c.1519). *Milanese *historian, who held various offices under the *Sforza and then Ludovico il Moro. He published his major work, the Italian *Historia patria*, at his own expense in 1503. It is a monumental but wholly uncritical history of Milan from its origins to Ludovico il Moro's escape to Germany in 1499.   [DieZ]

CORNAZZANO, ANTONIO (*c.*1432–84). Polymath, born in Piacenza, who lived mainly at the *courts of *Milan (*c.*1455–66) and *Ferrara (1475–84). He was briefly in *Rome in 1450, and probably wrote the Terentian *comedy *Fraudiphila* there. He wrote an *Arte del danzare* in 1455 and a *Vita di Nostra Donna* in *terza rima* (his favourite form), which was to enjoy great popularity after its publication in 1472. His scurrilous *De proverbiorum origine* (1464) was the basis for his more popular vernacular *Proverbi in facezie.* In 1459 he finished a still unpublished *epic on the life and deeds of Francesco *Sforza.

After 1466 he spent some time in the *Venetian Republic in the service of Bartolomeo Colleoni [see CONDOTTIERI], of whom he wrote a Latin *biography. In Venice he published a didactic life of Christ in *terza rima.* In Ferrara he wrote *Dell'integrità della militare arte,* a prose treatise which he later turned into *terza rima* with the Latin title *De re militari.* This enjoyed considerable popularity and may have been used by *Machiavelli. He also dedicated a work on government to the wife of Ercole d' *Este and numerous occasional poems to friends and members of the court. His *Canzoniere* (1502) was highly rated by *Calmeta for its rhetorical ability. [See also MISOGYNY.]   [DieZ]

CORNELIO, TOMMASO, see INVESTIGANTI, ACCADEMIA DEGLI.

CORNER, ALVISE (or Cornaro) (*c.*1475–1566), a polymath based in *Padua, was an expert on hydraulics and architecture, and pioneered land reform. A health fanatic, he wrote an international best-seller on dieting, *Trattato de la vita sobria* (1558). Patron of the playwright *Ruzante, he built probably the first permanent *theatre in *Renaissance Italy, the *loggia* in his Paduan residence.
[RGF]

Cornice ('framework'), used, for example, of the narrative within which the stories of the *Decameron* are framed.

CORNOLDI CAMINER, GIOSEFFA, see WOMEN WRITERS, 2.

Corpus hermeticum, see HERMETICISM.

CORRA, BRUNO, see FUTURISM.

CORRADINI, ENRICO (1865–1931). *Florentine dramatist, *novelist, and militant *journalist. He was editor of the *Marzocco* (1897–1900), and founded *Il regno* (1903). His early plays and novels had been *D'Annunzian in manner and focused on *existential concerns. In the new social climate of the *Giolittian era, his creative writing took a strongly *nationalist turn. His last two, and best-known, literary works, the novels *La patria lontana* (1910) and *La guerra lontana* (1911), are vehicles for a vitalist, anti-democratic and imperialist ideology. He founded the weekly *L'idea nazionale* in 1911 and led the Associazione Nazionalista Italiana (1910–23). He went on to hold several minor government posts under *Fascism.   [JD]

CORRADO, VINCENZO, see COOKERY BOOKS.

Corrente, see TRECCANI, ERNESTO.

CORRENTI, CESARE (1815–88). *Milanese patriotic writer, active in the events of *1848 in Milan and the author of various political pamphlets. In 1846 he published in the *Rivista europea* a public letter to Giulio *Carcano, entitled 'Della letteratura rusticale', calling for more *realistic representation of the *peasantry in literature. The resulting *letteratura rusticale* of the next few decades leads directly into *verismo.   [PH]

Corriere della sera, Il (1876–). *Milanese daily paper. Under the editorship of Luigi Albertini (1900–25) it set the standard in Italy for modern techniques of production and distribution, and established itself as the authoritative voice of conservative *liberalism. By 1920 it was achieving a print run of 600,000. Having first connived at *Fascist violence, Albertini spoke out against the murder of Matteotti in 1924 and found himself dismissed. Forced into conformism until the end of *World War II, the paper subsequently reacquired its conservative liberal voice and much of its authority. A new flexibility was introduced by Piero Ottone, editor from 1972 to 1977, who included the notoriously anti-establishment *Pasolini among his correspondents. [See also JOURNALISM.]   [PH]

Corriero svaligiato, Il, see PALLAVICINO, FERRANTE.

CORSINI, BARTOLOMEO (1606–73). *Tuscan writer. He studied philosophy and *medicine at *Pisa and thereafter devoted himself to literature and music. His *mock-heroic poem, *Il torracchione desolato* (probably written around 1660, but not published until 1768), was inspired by Lorenzo *Lippi's *Malmantile,* and contains parodies of Homer, *Ovid, and Torquato *Tasso. He also wrote *religious poetry and a chronicle of his home town, Barberino, between 1638 and 1646, and translated Anacreon. [FC]

Cortegiano, Il, see CASTIGLIONE, BALDASSARRE.

CORTESE, GIULIO CESARE (c.1570–1624/7). *Neapolitan *dialect poet. He was a member of the city's middle class, like G. B. *Basile, his friend and the other prime mover of Neapolitan dialect literature [see DIALECT WRITING]. He graduated in *law in 1597 and visited Spain in 1601–2, also spending some time in *Florence. It was apparently the snubs inflicted on him by Florentine society that provoked *La vaiasseide* (1612), his *mock-heroic epic in *ottava rima.* But the narration soon turns into an account of the rebellious nature of Neapolitan maids (*vaiasse*) amidst vivid pictures of the noisy and colourful life of the city. His *Viaggio di Parnaso* (1621), telling, again in *ottava rima,* of his meetings with the great poets, is essentially a vigorous defence of dialect poetry, which is seen as innovative and popular, in contrast to the stuffy literature written in Tuscan. He also wrote a *comedy, *La rosa.* He may be the author of *De la tiorba a taccone* (1640), a dialect *parody of contemporary *lyric poetry, published under the name of Felippo *Sgruttendio de Scafato. [DieZ]

CORTESI, PAOLO (1465–1510). *Tuscan *humanist, who spent most of his life in *Rome, first coming to prominence in the 1480s as *Poliziano's opponent in a famous dispute on *imitation (1485), where Cortesi upheld the *Ciceronian cause against Poliziano's eclecticism. His *dialogue, *De hominibus doctis* (c.1489), is the first detailed literary critique of 15th-c. humanist Latin: the terminology used and its silence on the *Florentine humanism of Poliziano and *Ficino show that Cortesi still retained his Ciceronian criteria. In the 1490s he displayed a keen interest in the vernacular, being friendly with the *improviser poets Bernardo Accolti (the 'Unico aretino') and *Serafino Aquilano, and this interest, as well as a now almost Apuleian Latin, is reflected in his final work, the encyclopedic advice book for cardinals, *De cardinalatu* (1510), showing how much Cortesi

had evolved from the callow Ciceronianism of the 1485 polemic. [See also CLASSICISM; LATIN INFLUENCES; LATIN PROSE IN ITALY.] [MMcL]

Cortesia. The equivalent in early Italian literature of the French 'courtoisie', though not so present or important as a term or as an idea, since less Italian literature of the 13th and 14th c. relates to idealized aristocratic *court life. In 13th-c. poetry the term carries connotations of honour, probity, nobility, and good sense. While it can also indicate courtesy in the English sense of good manners, it often also suggests graciousness and generosity. With *Dante especially, it tends to acquire moral weight. In the *Convivio* he identifies it with honourable conduct (2.6). In *Inferno* (33.150) the apparent brutality shown by Dante to the traitor Branca Doria is paradoxically true *cortesia.* Elsewhere in the *Divine Comedy* (e.g. *Inf.* 16.67–9; *Purg.* 14.109–11) the word may be used somewhat nostalgically to invoke a supposedly more honourable past, largely vanished from the money-making present. By the mid-14th c., with *Petrarch, the word occurs relatively infrequently and loses much of its original force. In *Boccaccio it often appears in contexts which invoke or recall the aristocratic values of the past. [See also CHIVALRY.] [JP & JMS]

CORTI, MARIA (1915–2002). Scholar and *novelist. Born in *Milan, where she took degrees in classics and philosophy, she eventually became professor of the history of Italian at Pavia. Her academic *literary criticism focused on problems in both modern and medieval literature. She discusses *Dante and his contemporaries in *Dante ad un nuovo crocevia* (1981) and *La felicità mentale* (1983), and literary *semiotics in *Principi di comunicazione letteraria* (1976) and, partly, *Il viaggio testuale* (1978). Other essays are collected in *Metodi e fantasmi* (1969). Her creative writing includes the outstanding *L'ora di tutti* (1962), which deals with the fall of Otranto to the Turks in 1480, *Il ballo dei sapienti* (1966), an ironic account of Italian school and *university life, *Voci dal Nord Est* (1986), on her experience in the United States, and *Il canto delle sirene* (1989), a collection of short stories which is also a scholarly introduction to the notion of sirens. *Ombre dal fondo* (1997) is a personal memoir of the birth and growth of the centre for *manuscripts of modern authors in Pavia, of which she was the first director. [DieZ]

Cortigiana, see ARETINO, PIETRO.

Cortigiane, see COURTESANS.

CORTO MALTESE, see PRATT, HUGO.

Coryciana (1524). Collection of 399 Latin poems entirely devoted to the praise of a statue of St Anne, the Virgin and Child by Andrea *Sansovino, and of an adjoining picture of the prophet Isaiah by *Raphael, both commissioned in 1510 by the Luxembourg antiquarian Janus Corycius (Hans Goritz) and housed in the church of St *Augustine in *Rome. From 1512, on the feast of St Anne (26th July), Corycius held a celebration in his home, during which the poems were read out. He eventually provided for their publication, and they were edited by Blosius Palladius. Writers included Pietro *Bembo, *Castiglione, *Colocci, *Giovio, and *Sadoleto. The poems document contemporary *humanist interest in the classical topos of poetry paralleling the visual arts. [NC]

Coscienza di Zeno, La (1923). Italo *Svevo's third novel consists of the revealingly unreliable memoirs which the idle, well-off Zeno Cosini writes for his *psychoanalyst, Dr S. Playing hide-and-seek with his own conscience and consciousness, the psychoanalyst, and the reader, Zeno recounts his battles with smoking, with his father, with his rival, Guido Speier, with his wife, Augusta, and his mistress, Carla, his unconscious showing through despite himself. At the height of *World War I, having shaken off all his antagonists, he derisively abandons psychoanalysis and declares himself cured by his success as a wartime speculator, while prophesying the self-destruction of the sick human race. [JG-R]

Così è (se vi pare) (1917) displays *Pirandello's ideas on knowledge and identity in a challenge to the tradition of the well-made play. 'Who is Signora Ponza?' is the insistent question of the inhabitants of the town where Signor Ponza, his wife, and his mother-in-law, victims of an earthquake, seek a new life. Pirandello's skill lies in maintaining interest, but refusing to give an answer. [See also THEATRE, 2.] [JAL]

COSMICO, NICCOLÒ LELIO (*c.*1420–1500). Scholar and poet, born in *Padua, but active also in *Rome, *Mantua, and *Florence. He was a schoolteacher and cultivated both vernacular and Latin poetry, but was notorious for his worldly, dissolute life. His poetry was known for its facile

fluency. His *Canzonete* (1478) are in fact *capitoli* in *terza rima* [see CANTO], containing numerous *Petrarchist clichés and reminiscences of *Dante.
[DieZ]

Cosmology differs from astronomical writings in that the latter deal with predicting and determining planetary and stellar positions using geometry and arithmetic, whereas natural philosophers and cosmologists describe the nature and properties of the heavens and the causes of the various motions. Medieval and *Renaissance cosmology was based on the natural philosophy of *Aristotle, who distinguished between the celestial region, from the moon to the outermost limit of the world, and the sublunar or terrestrial region which included all matter and activities below the moon. This geocentric cosmology relied on Greco-Arabic treatises translated into Latin together with the writings of the *Church Fathers on the six days of creation.

Though the Aristotelian view dominated until the age of *Galileo, Johannes Kepler, and Isaac Newton, many cosmological theories were put forward. *Nicholas of Cusa used the principle of the coincidences of opposites to conclude that there can be neither a fixed centre nor a fixed periphery to the universe, and that the Earth cannot therefore occupy its centre. Domenico Scandella (1532–*c.*1599), who was tried for heresy and condemned to death, believed in pantheism: all things including God and the angels were spontaneously generated from a primordial chaos as worms are from a cheese. Francesco *Patrizi the Younger asserted the infinite nature of the universe. Bernardino *Telesio criticised Aristotelian cosmology and saw the principles of heat and cold as the causes of all terrestrial physical processes. Giordano *Bruno insisted that the infinity of the universe was linked to God's omnipotence, and asserted the coincidence of matter and divinity. [See also ASTROLOGY.] [PLR]

COSSA, PIETRO (1830–81), Author of some fifteen plays and a *lyric poet. He succeeded, with a much less prolific output than many of his contemporaries, in becoming a leading force in the development of 19th-c. Italian *theatre, balancing the influence of French dramatists such as Scribe and Dumas with a knowledge of classical drama and a respect for *Alfieri's plays. His *tragedy *Nerone* (1871) shows impressive stagecraft: the character of Nero is represented less through direct characterization than through the reaction of the people to him. *Messalina* (1876), considered his best work by some, avoids the cliché of the lustful woman, and makes of Messalina a *Romantic heroine assailed by the tragic force of passion. His most innovative play, *I napolitani* (1881), moves close to *verismo* in its colourful depiction of a prison and its scenes of popular life, while at the same time endorsing *Risorgimento ideals.

Cossa himself participated in the first uprisings for independence. He went to the USA in 1851 and to Peru and Chile in 1854, not returning to Italy until 1857, and earned his living while abroad as an *opera singer.   [JAL]

COSTA, PAOLO (1771–1836). Poet and patriot from Ravenna, who was a pupil of *Cesarotti and a friend of *Foscolo in *Padua, resembling the latter in his early verse and revolutionary involvement. Under *Napoleon he taught philosophy in *Bologna, where he later ran a private school. As a ringleader in the 1831 insurrection he briefly fled to Corfu. He combined rationalism with *purism (coediting the 1819–26 Bologna edition of the *Crusca dictionary) and *Risorgimento *nationalism with anti-*Romanticism. Yet he rejected Greek mythology and borrowed from Goethe and Schiller. He theorized his moderate *classicism in *Dell'arte poetica* (1836). His epic *Cristoforo Colombo* appeared posthumously in 1844. A blank-verse epistle on human progress (1835) may have been an indirect rejoinder to *Leopardi's 'Palinodia'.
                    [JMAL]

COSTETTI, GIUSEPPE (1834–1928). Author of over thirty plays which developed from early *Romantic *comedies to naturalist drama [see REALISM; VERISMO] and engagement with social problems. He is now best remembered for his *theatre criticism. Though sometimes inaccurate, his work contains some lively ideas about the theatre of his times.   [JAL]

COSTO, TOMMASO (d.*c.*1613) wrote various works on the history of his native *Naples and a collection of *novelle*, *Il fuggilozio* (1596), in which a group of friends gather in a house in Naples and exchange witticisms, jokes, and tales in order to cheer up the owner, who suffers from gout.
                    [MC]

COTRONEO, ROBERTO (1961–). *Journalist and writer who has been arts editor for *L'Espresso* since 1987. His literary criticism includes *La*

diffidenza come sistema (1985) on the fiction of Umberto *Eco and *Se una mattina d'estate un bambino* (1994). His first *novel, *Presto con fuoco* (1995), tells the story of a lost manuscript of Chopin. *Otranto* (1997) is a portrayal of the city blending history and myth. *L'età perfetta* (1999) is a novel of rumour and gossip set in *Sicily in 1959.   [MH]

Counter-Reformation. Because the term suggests a narrowly religious and political counteraction to the Protestant *Reformation, it is sometimes replaced by 'Catholic Reformation', which recognizes both its continuity with earlier Catholic reforming movements and the fact that it was more than mere reaction, possessing its own theological developments and intellectual vitality.

From soon after its beginnings in 1517, Luther's theological Reformation was well received by devout Italian *humanists, as well as by figures such as Vittoria *Colonna. In the face of Protestant schism, and despite being suspected of *heresy, they advocated theological reconciliation and Catholic ecclesiastical reforms. Pope Paul III set up a commission to investigate laxity, worldliness, and pastoral weaknesses within the Church. Although its report, *Consilium de emendanda ecclesia* (1537), recommended practical reforms, little was done. *Rome's need, however, was not so much for ecclesiastical reforms as for spiritual renewal and doctrinal definition. Renewal was met by creating flourishing lay fraternities, and orders of *clergy, such as the *Theatines, which mingled piety, charity, and scholarship, producing a new generation of competent priests. In 1540 the *Jesuits were formed, not to combat Protestantism but to give scholarly depth to Catholic piety, and *Benedictines, *Dominicans, *Franciscans, and other established orders reformed themselves. The relative freedom of this early Counter-Reformation allowed Teofilo *Folengo and Juan de Valdés (d.1541) to mingle elements of Protestant and Catholic spirituality in their works.

As the religious divisions of Europe hardened and clandestine Italian Protestant groups formed, mainly in Central and Northern cities, intransigent Catholic reformers declared 'spiritual war' against Protestantism. In 1542 the revived Roman *Inquisition and the *Index of Prohibited Books activated suspicions and repression of critics who advocated reforms. Devout preachers and thinkers still expounded biblical doctrines of repentance and grace: the immensely popular tract, the *Beneficio di Cristo* (1543)—written by Benedetto da Mantova and published anonymously—attempted to reconcile Protestant and Catholic spirituality, but was denounced in Ambrogio Politi's book attacking Lutheran doctrines in Italy.

When the Council of Trent eventually met (1545–7, 1551–2, 1561–3), almost thirty years after 1517, its deliberations, complicated by European politics and Catholic pro-reconciliation factions, defined Catholic doctrines and anathematized Protestant teaching, especially regarding salvation and the Eucharist. It also reformed, centralized, and strengthened papal and episcopal authority, and planned energetic policies to educate the clergy, guide the worship and morals of the laity, and censor artistic, literary, and intellectual life. These changes were observed unfavourably by Pietro *Aretino and others, but some bishops, notably Carlo *Borromeo of *Milan, used Tridentine decrees to introduce penitential civic renewals with considerable pastoral benefit. Between 1555 and 1590 three strong popes completed the process, extending discipline and strengthening curial bureaucracy. Tridentine puritanism (mirrored in Protestant lands) and triumphalism spread throughout Catholic Europe and into the New World.

Later Counter-Reformation piety was characterized by Luigi *Tansillo's poetry of intense repentance, and by Torquato *Tasso's *Gerusalemme liberata (1593), a poem of agonized tension between earthly grandeur and human mortality, and the need of God's mercy for both. From 1600 the Counter-Reformation's pursuit of theological heretics was gradually replaced by the suppression of superstitions and social misbehaviour. Scientific studies flourished amongst the clergy and *censorship was challenged, notably by *Galileo and Paolo *Sarpi, the truculent *Venetian priest whose Protestant sympathies and antipathy to Rome were evident in his Istoria del concilio tridentino (1619). [See also PAPACY AND THE CATHOLIC CHURCH.]

[BC]

See H. Jedin, History of the Council of Trent (1957); J. M. Headley and J. B. Tomaro (eds.), San Carlo Borromeo: Catholic Reform and Ecclesiastical Politics in the Second Half of the Sixteenth Century (1988); J. C. Olin, Catholic Reform from Cardinal Ximenes to the Council of Trent 1495–1563 (1990).

Courtesans (cortigiane). A type of elite prostitute emerged in *Rome towards the end of the 15th c., coinciding with the growth in the city's wealth and prosperity, and the demand from *bankers, *courtiers, and diplomats who worked there for women who could fulfil their physical needs, yet who were cultivated and educated enough to participate in erudite conversation. Music-making, conversational skills, and a familiarity with classical and contemporary literature became the accomplishments deemed necessary for the cortigiana, and, together with her high price, distinguished her from the common puttana or meretrice. Some courtesans, such as *Tullia d'Aragona and Veronica *Franco, were members of notable literary and artistic circles and famous for their poetry. Doubts surrounding the status of Gaspara *Stampa point to the ambiguous position of educated *women writers. Courtesans quickly established themselves throughout the peninsula, but the main centres were Rome and *Venice. They flourished in Venice, with its wealth, relative political stability, and liberal atmosphere, until the early 17th c.

[DomZ]

Courtesy, see CORTESIA.

Courts, traditionally the power base of a prince and the refuge for courtiers, took on what is now judged their characteristic form during the later *Middle Ages and the *Renaissance. Stable political conditions encouraged by the *feudal system created the relative security of such courts as that of *Frederick II (1194–1250) in Palermo, where culture could burgeon and cross-fertilize with that of more northerly societies [see SICILIAN SCHOOL; SICILY]. After 1400, from a literary and cultural point of view the Renaissance court became more and more a place of civilized conversation. Whether informal (the *Medici court in the nominally republican *Florence of the 15th c.) or formal (the contemporary *Sforza court in *Milan), a court received the necessary protection and cultural accoutrements (library facilities, pleasant venues for debates and less formal conversations) from a potentate—as happened in the *Naples of Alfonso I of *Aragon, who offered his library as a venue for the Accademia Antoniana (later *Accademia Pontaniana), or the Medici villa at Careggi, which provided a location for Marsilio *Ficino's *Platonic Academy.

The importance of the court for cultural purposes came into its own when colonial powers (notably France, *Spain, and later *Austria) imposed a dynastic succession in their conquered Italian territories, thus curtailing the anarchy of party intrigues and family competition, and imposing conformity and stability on a society reduced to competing for a patron's favour through literary, artistic, or philosophical excellence. The *papal curia, particularly after the time of Alexander VI, was also one of the major centres of *patronage and cultural dynamism, and continued to give artistic and other commissions. The absolutism of European monarchies was mirrored in the powers assumed by certain dynasties in Italy, notably the *Visconti in Milan (until 1402), and the resurgent Medici (particularly after 1537). After 1500, however, most Italian courts depended as vassals upon the influence of larger European powers, a tendency which continued during the 17th c. It diminished only with the rise of *Enlightenment egalitarian notions, which culminated when the effects of the French Revolution made themselves felt through greater democracy and the reduction of court power. The courtly writing of *Castiglione, *Della Casa, and their ilk was a curious by-product of court society, but thousands of courtly manuals were produced containing advice on ingratiation and self-promotion for potential courtiers and diplomats. [See also CHIVALRY; CORTESIA; LINGUA CORTIGIANA.] [JRW]

See C. Ossola and A. Prosperi (eds.), *La corte e il 'Cortegiano'* (1980); C. Mozzarelli and G. Venturi (eds.), *L'Europa delle corti alla fine dell'antico regime* (1991).

CREMONINI, CESARE (*c.*1550–1631) was a leading *Aristotelian philosopher at *Padua *University during the time of *Galileo and Paolo *Beni, and a friend of Torquato *Tasso, *Pigna, and Francesco *Patrizi the Younger. A sworn Aristotelian in scientific matters, his tenure of the Paduan chair of natural philosophy lasted from 1591 to 1629, when he retired. Cremonini fell foul of the *Roman *Inquisition over his *Disputatio de coelo* (1613). He was accused of contradicting the Church by placing too much importance on man's innate power and by seeming to deny the immortality of the soul. In his defence, he vainly attempted to convince the Church, as did Galileo, of the doctrine of the two verities, philosophical and theological. Unlike Galileo, however, Cremonini was not interested in the application of mathematics and quantifiable measurements to scientific issues, and, when Galileo famously invited Cremonini to look through his newly invented telescope, he flatly refused: *De calido innato, et semine, pro Aristotele adversus Galenum* (1626 and 1634) is a good exam-

ple of his method. A founder-member of the Accademia dei Ricovrati, he took part in the literary life of Padua, publishing many *pastoral poems.
[PBD]

CREPAX, GUIDO, see COMICS.

Crepuscolari. The term, *crepuscolarismo* (from *crepuscolo*, 'twilight') was coined in 1910 by G. A. *Borgese, who identified a number of young poets as sharing the same taste for melancholic and spiritual weariness. They never constituted a movement as such and were active in three quite separate centres—Guido *Gozzano, Carlo Vallini, Nino *Oxilia, and Carlo Chiaves in *Piedmont, especially *Turin; Sergio *Corazzini and Fausto Maria *Martini in *Rome; Corrado *Govoni and Marino *Moretti in Romagna. The temporal limits are effectively 1903, when Govoni published *Armonia in grigio et in silenzio*, and 1911, the year of Gozzano's *Colloqui*.

All these poets rejected the grandeur and aestheticism of the sublime as proposed by *D'Annunzio, and also the impressionism and *symbolism of *Pascoli, which was in fact the sublime in another guise. They were of course influenced by both— D'Annunzio's *Poema paradisiaco* and Pascoli's poetics of 'piccole cose' and the 'fanciullino' in particular. But in general they look more to Baudelaire (without his demonic side), to the music of Verlaine, and to Laforgue, Maeterlinck, Jammes, and other minor French *symbolists. They portray themselves as insignificant members of the bourgeoisie, who are ill, irrelevant, and useless—in other words, as *decadents in a knowingly minor key. Their poetry can take on an ironic, self-mocking tone as in Gozzano, but the inward-looking weariness of Corazzini is more characteristic. In either case, there is an implicit polemic against high rhetoric and an awareness of the inutility of literature. All crepuscular poets focus on everyday life and everyday objects, Govoni in particular creating a poetics of the 'oggetto povero'. A narrative vein is also common, with a de-romanticized provincial setting. Formally, there is a distinct lowering of register towards the prosaic and an adoption of *free verse, though Gozzano deliberately plays off everyday language against high literariness in finely calibrated classic metrical forms.

Crepuscular poetry had considerable success with readers, though critics disliked its apparent undermining of literary values. But *Montale recognized its importance and himself continued

Gozzano's juxtapositions of contrasting registers and Govoni's emphasis on the 'oggetto povero', coming even closer to their deliberate anti-poetry in his own late work. An ironic poetry of things has continued with *Giudici and others; combativeness with regard to the literary institutions reappeared in the work of the *Neoavanguardia.   [RD]
    See L. Baldacci, *I Crepuscolari* (1961); M. Guglielminetti, *La 'scuola dell'ironia': Gozzano e i viciniori* (1984).

Crepuscolo, Il (1850–9). *Milanese weekly founded by Carlo *Tenca. Implicitly anti-*Austrian, it aimed at a wide, inclusive readership, publishing articles on science, economics, and agriculture, as well as on popular culture, the *dialects, and literature [see FOLK AND POPULAR LITERATURE]. Contributors included Melchiorre *Gioia, Carlo *Cattaneo, and Camillo *Boito.   [MPC]

CRESCIMBENI, GIOVANNI MARIO (1663–1728). Critic and poet, born in Macerata, who spent most of his life in *Rome, eventually becoming a priest. He was a founder-member of the Accademia dell'*Arcadia, formulating its programme and remaining its first president until his death. His encouragement of literary affectation, and of *pastoral conventions and ritual, led to the secession of *Gravina and his followers. He edited seven volumes of members' *biographies (1708–27) and twelve volumes of their verse and prose works (1716–22). His *Istoria della volgar poesia* (1698) was the first attempt at a general *history of Italian poetry. His own copious *Rime* (1723) lack distinction. His *Arcadia* (1708) recounts the foundation of the academy as a *romance.   [JMAL]

Crime, see ARMED FORCES AND POLICE; DETECTIVE FICTION.

CRINITO, PIETRO (Pietro Riccio) (1476–1507). A *humanist, he was educated at the school of Ugolino *Verino and, from at least 1491, attended the lectures on rhetoric of *Poliziano. He was a member of Lorenzo de' *Medici's circle of artists and men of letters. His main work is the *Commentarii de honesta disciplina* (1504), a collection in *zibaldone form of erudite notes on language and classical civilization, which he gathered together for his lectures. He also edited Poliziano's Latin writings after his death.   [LB]

CRISPI, FRANCESCO (1818–1901) was the dominant political figure in Italy in the last fifteen years of the 19th c. As a young man he was a follower of *Mazzini, and played a prominent part in the expedition of *Garibaldi's *Mille* (1860). His two administrations (1887–91, 1893–6) were marked by major political, social, and economic reforms, anti-*socialism, and an aggressive foreign policy in Europe and Africa. He fell from power in 1896 after Italy's defeat at the Battle of Adua in Ethiopia. Crispi was reviled by sections of the far Left, who accused him of corruption, but was strongly admired by many for his fervent patriotism. His supporters included Giosue *Carducci, Alfredo *Oriani, and Giuseppe *Verdi. Carlo *Dossi acted as his private secretary. Crispi's authoritarianism, charismatic style of leadership, and militarism led him to be seen by the *Fascists as the 'precursor' of *Mussolini. [See also NATIONALISM.]   [CD]

CRISTALDI, FRANCO, see CINEMA.

CRISTOFANO DI GANO GUIDINI (?1345–1410). A religious writer, born into a humble *Sienese family, who became a notary and subsequently a disciple of St *Caterina, devoting himself to the ascetic life after the loss of most of his family in the *plague of 1390. His writings include a translation of Caterina's *Libro della divina dottrina*, a collection of *laudi, and a book of memoirs written over the last twenty years of his life.   [PH]

Cristoforo, Fra, Capuchin friar in *Manzoni's *I *promessi sposi.*

CRISTOFORO DI MESSISBUGO, see COOKERY BOOKS.

CRISTOFORO FIORENTINO (d.c.1524), called the *Altissimo*, *improviser, entertainer, and narrative poet associated with late 15th- and early 16th-c. *Florence, where he entertained a varied public. His literary work includes narrative and *lyric poetry, displaying an inventive wit, skill in *versification, and a wealth of allusions both learned and popular. His major works are a *romance *epic of ninety-four *canti*, the *Primo libro de' reali* (1534), which derives from the prose compilation of *Andrea da Barberino, and two other narrative poems, *La rotta di Ravenna* (c.1516) and *La grande guerra et rotta del scapigliato.*   [JEE]

Cristo si è fermato a Eboli (1945). Famous account by Carlo *Levi of his internal exile in Lucania under *Fascism. His medical skills win him the trust of the peasants and give him an insight into a world of poverty and subjection into which Christ, history, and the state have not penetrated.

[JD]

Critica, La (1903–44). Review, founded by the *idealist philosophers Benedetto *Croce and Giovanni *Gentile, and published largely at Croce's expense in Bari. Its fundamental aims were to record and promote the newly unified Italy's cultural achievements and to encourage anti-metaphysical rationalist thought. In its pages, Gentile evaluated the previous fifty years of Italian philosophy and Croce carried out a similar literary survey. Gentile's commitment to *Fascism prompted his departure in 1925. Croce continued to produce *La Critica* with the help of various disciples. Its articles were informed by his correspondence with international cultural figures and were not censored, despite the review's critical attitude towards the regime. [DCH]

Critica estetica, see CROCE, BENEDETTO; LITERARY CRITICISM.

Critica fascista (1923–43). Fortnightly *periodical based in *Rome, founded and edited by Giuseppe *Bottai, who attempted to make it the forum for intelligent, up-to-date debate within *Fascism on cultural, educational, and political issues. In practice it was never able either to examine seriously the ill-defined abstractions of Fascist ideology or to distance itself from the policies of the regime. All the same, it does reveal that Fascist thinking was far from monolithic. Berto *Ricci, Massimo *Bontempelli, Curzio *Malaparte, Vasco *Pratolini, and Ardengo *Soffici all contributed at one time or another. [PH]

Criticism, see HISTORIES OF ITALIAN LITERATURE; LITERARY CRITICISM.

CROCE, BENEDETTO (1866–1952) was the most prominent Italian intellectual of his day. His copious *historical writings and *literary criticism were tied to a distinctive *idealist aesthetics and historicist philosophy. He had a profound influence not only on subsequent scholarship in these fields, where his pioneering research continues to command respect, even if few would still agree with his approach, but also on Italian culture more generally, through his explicit linking of his *humanist philosophy to a particular view of *liberalism.

He was born in the Abruzzi into a family of wealthy landowners and never had to pursue an academic career or even obtain a degree. Following the early death of his parents in an earthquake, he lived in *Rome with his uncle, the neo-Hegelian philosopher and right-wing statesman, Silvio Spaventa, but he also came into contact with the *Marxist thinker Antonio *Labriola. However, when he gave up his legal studies at the university, it was to engage in ground-breaking antiquarian investigations into various aspects of southern Italian history between the 16th and 18th c. These culminated in his 1891 study of *Neapolitan *theatre over this period, and also formed the basis of his later books on the Kingdom of Naples and the *Baroque era in Italy, which included studies and editions of *Marino and his contemporaries. His first philosophical essay was 'La storia ridotta sotto il concetto generale dell'arte' (1893), a critique of *positivist approaches to the social sciences. Prompted by Labriola, he followed it up with a number of articles attacking crude quasi-*Darwinian materialist interpretations of Marxism, but then going on to criticize Marx's economic doctrines as well.

Infected by the philosophical bug, he began the composition of the *Filosofia dello spirito*, the first volume being *Estetica come scienza dell'espressione e linguistica generale* (1902). In this he argued that all human activity was orientated towards the Beautiful, the True, the Useful, or the Good. These four ideals were the four aspects of what, following Hegel, he termed 'spirito', or human consciousness. The first two corresponded to the theoretical dimensions of spirit, intuition and logic respectively, the last two to spirit's practical aspects of economic and ethical willing. He contended that these four ideals were 'pure concepts', whose content derived from human thought and action. Against Hegel, he argued that they were 'distinct' moments of spirit, which could not be treated as dialectical moments evolving to some all-encompassing synthesis of human thought and action. He employed this thesis to argue that genuine art always expressed the pure imagination or intuition, and could not be seen as either promoting ideas or social facts—an argument he directed against *verismo* in literature.

In 1903 Croce founded his journal, *La *Critica*. Largely written by himself and Giovanni *Gentile, it aimed to transform the humanities within Italy and promote their own neo-idealist perspective. Up until *World War I, it contained regular series of articles by the two main contributors. Croce's were devoted to continuing *De Sanctis' *Storia della letteratura italiana* from 1861 up to the present and eventually became *La letteratura della nuova Italia* (6 vols., 1914–40). He also completed the *Filosofia dello spirito* with the *Logica come scienza del concetto puro* (1905, revised 1909), on the True, and the *Filosofia della pratica: economica ed etica* (1909), on the Useful and the Good. Influenced by Gentile, he revised his view of Hegel, and adopted a historicist argument according to which all meaning and truth evolved immanently through the historical process. However, he still argued that this occurred via a dialectic of 'distinct' moments rather than through a synthesis of opposites. *Ciò che è vivo e ciò che è morto della filosofia di Hegel* (1907) and *La filosofia di Giambattista Vico* (1911) further elaborated this doctrine, as did a two-volume study of Italian historiography in the 19th c. (1921) and *Teoria e storia della storiografia* (1917), the concluding volume of the *Filosofia dello spirito*. He also revised his aesthetic doctrine, enunciating its 'lyrical' yet 'universal' quality as part of the 'circle of spirit' in his *Breviario di estetica* (1913) and in the essay on 'Il carattere di totalità dell'espressione artistica' (1918).

World War I and the rise of *Fascism produced a further revision of his ideas and a fresh wave of creative activity. A conservative liberal, he served as minister of *education in the last liberal cabinet of *Giolitti of 1920–1. Initially tolerant of Fascism, he broke with it completely when it abolished all other political parties and also with Gentile, who became one of its most prominent spokesmen, penning a famous protest against Gentile's 'Manifesto degli intellettuali fascisti' in 1925. Reviled but tolerated by the regime, he continued to publish as an independent voice thoughout the Fascist years. He now identified his philosophy with liberalism, conceived 'metapolitically' as the freedom and creativity of the human spirit. Whereas previously he had argued that moral judgements were matters of history and that all human action must be conditioned by economic or utilitarian considerations, a view that had led him to praise the *Realpolitik* of the Germans during World War I and of *Mussolini immediately after it, he now contended that human action was 'ethico-political' and involved the continuous transformation of reality to conform to human ideals. A series of histories, and especially the essays collected in *La storia come pensiero e come azione* (1938), reflected this change. Important literary and aesthetic studies, such as *La poesia di Dante* (1920), *Ariosto, Shakespeare and Corneille* (1920), and *La poesia* (1936), continued to be major points

of reference for literary criticism until at least the late 1950s. As a philosopher he was kept in view largely by the critical discussions of his ideas in the posthumous writings of *Gramsci. Outside Italy, his main influence was on the Oxford philosopher R. G. Collingwood.   [RPB]

Opere complete (74 vols., 1906–52). See G. Sasso, *Benedetto Croce: La ricerca della dialettica* (1975); R. Wellek, *Four Critics* (1981); R. Bellamy, *Modern Italian Social Theory* (1987).

CROCE, GIULIO CESARE (1550–1609). Prolific popular poet in both Italian and Bolognese *dialect. Born in San Giovanni in Persiceto, near *Bologna, the son of a blacksmith, he had a gift for *improvisation and *parody, and sang his poems all over Northern Italy to the accompaniment of his *lira*. Over 400 chapbooks containing his works have survived. Among the best are an *autobiography in verse, *Descrizione della vita del Croce*, and lively and culturally revealing exchanges between *peasants, women, and craftsmen. His *comedies, some of which are in dialect, were also successful, although not so original as the *commedia dell'arte*. His most famous work, the *Sottilissime astuzie di Bertoldo*, a reworking of a medieval dialogue between Solomon and Marcolfus, is the story of *Bertoldo, a cunning and ugly peasant, who is invited, on account of his extraordinary wit, to the *court of the Lombard king Alboino, where he ultimately dies because he has severed his links with nature and cannot endure the refined gastronomy. Although Croce has frequently been considered a champion of the poor and underprivileged, he was capable of adulating his wealthy *patrons, and expressed deeply conservative attitudes.   [DieZ]

Cronaca bizantina (1881–6). Fortnightly magazine which became the most important *periodical of its time in Italy. It was published and edited in *Rome by Angelo *Sommaruga. Among its contributors were *Carducci, *Pascoli, and *D'Annunzio. The original aim was to articulate a *positivist aesthetics and an open critique of contemporary Italian society and of its petty bourgeois vulgarity in particular. There was a radical change in 1885, when Sommaruga was arrested and the magazine folded. It was purchased by Prince Maffeo Sciarra and fused with the *Domenica letteraria*; D'Annunzio was made editor. The new series reflected the cult of beauty which characterized Roman aestheticism in the 1880s, but lasted only a few months.

[GP]

Cronaca grigia, see PERIODICALS, 1; SCAPI-GLIATURA.

Cronica delle cose occorrenti ne' tempi suoi, see COMPAGNI, DINO.

Cronica di anonimo romano (1357–60) is a *chronicle of events in *Rome and beyond between 1325 and 1355, which climaxes with the dramatic account of *Cola di Rienzo's activities and bloody death. It has survived in fragmentary form and with the loss of its author's name. Recently, however, he has been identified with Bartolomeo di Iacovo da Valmontone. The chronicle is generally considered one of the major prose works of the 14th c., both for its expressive use of the Roman vernacular and for the distinctive secularizing concreteness of its vision.   [ZB]

CRONICO, see VINCIGUERRA, ANTONIO.

CRUDELI, TOMMASO (1703–45). Poet from Poppi in the Tuscan Casentino. Introduced to masonic ideas by English visitors to whom he was teaching Italian in *Florence, he became the first Italian to be imprisoned for *freemasonry (1739–40). His modest output of original verse and his free *translations from La Fontaine's fables show freshness, grace, and descriptive flair. Diderot used his name as a pseudonym.   [JMAL]

Crusades (11th–13th c.). The Italian cities did not provide substantial military forces for the expeditions to liberate the Holy Lands, but their important logistical, naval, and financial contributions, particularly by the *Genoese and *Venetians, were decisive in extending Italian influence, most notably with the creation of the Latin state of Constantinople in 1204. The crusades do not loom large in early Italian literature, though *Dante makes his ancestor Cacciaguida a crusader (*Para.* 15), and *Petrarch makes a notable appeal for a fresh Crusade in the early 1330s (*Canz.* 28). But the first crusade, led by Geoffrey di Bouillon and Tancred, culminating in the capture of Jerusalem in 1099, provided the material and inspiration for Torquato *Tasso's *Gerusalemme liberata* (1581).   [JU]

Crusca, Accademia della (1582–). *Florentine academy, which was often seen before the 20th c. as the embodiment of *purism. In fact it helped to establish a standard for literary Italian and has played a major part in linguistic studies. Originally a light-hearted association, it was soon given by *Salviati the purpose of promoting good usage based on 14th-c. Florentine: its emblem is the bolting-machine which sifts white flour, removing the bran (*crusca*). In 1584 Salviati and others became involved in controversy over the superiority of *Ariosto to Torquato *Tasso, but from 1591 the academicians devoted their efforts chiefly to their *Vocabolario* and related work. The Crusca was merged with other Florentine *academies between 1783 and 1811. It now publishes critical texts, concordances, other works of linguistic interest, and *journals, including its bulletin, *Studi di filologia italiana* (1927–).   [BR]

CUCCHI, MAURIZIO (1945–). *Milanese poet and *journalist. His first collection, *Il disperso* (1976), combines the projection of a precarious poetic self with strongly prosaic narrative. Later collections, such as *Poesia della fonte* (1993), link the issue of individual identity with the condition of the socially marginalized.   [JJ]

Cultura, La, see PERIODICALS, 1.

CUOCO, VINCENZO (1770–1823). Moderate *historian and thinker. Born in Campobasso, he took part in the *Neapolitan revolution of 1799. His *Saggio storico sulla rivoluzione napoletana* (1801) criticized the *Jacobins for having created a 'passive revolution' which did not reflect local conditions. Exiled to *Milan, he became director of the *Giornale italiano* and campaigned for Italian independence from France. From 1806 he held important positions under Joseph Bonaparte and Murat in Naples.   [EAM]

Cuore (1886). Children's novel by Edmondo *De Amicis, intended to instil civic awareness and social generosity in the young of the newly unified Italy. The structurally complex narrative counterpoints Enrico's diary with the moral tuition of his parents' letters, and the detailed picture of everyday 1880s *Turin with the schoolmaster's dramatic stories of children's heroism in the *Risorgimento. [See also CHILDREN'S LITERATURE.]   [ALL]

Cursus. The modern designation for a key feature of medieval Latin prose, referred to in the *Middle Ages as the *stilus gregorianus* after Pope Gregory VIII, its first theorist. The 'Gregorian style' consists in a rhythmic structure given, for reasons of emphasis, to at least two words at the close of a sentence or at the end of the individual clauses out of which a sentence is constructed. (The medieval term *cursus* referred to the rhythmic structure of the sentence as a whole.) There are four main types of *cursus*: the *planus*, which is generally made up of a polysyllabic and a trisyllabic word both of which are stressed on the penultimate syllable (*víncla perfrégit*); the *tardus*, which normally combines a polysyllabic word stressed on the penultimate syllable and a quadrisyllable stressed on the antepenultimate (*víncla perfrégerat*); the *velox*, which generally brings together a polysyllable stressed on the antepenultimate syllable and a quadrisyllable stressed on the penultimate (*vínculum fregerámus*); and the *trispondaicus*, which is commonly formed by a polysyllabic and quadrisyllabic word both of which are stressed on the penultimate syllable (*ésse videátur*). Although this 'style' had its origins in the mid-11th c. in the bureaucracy of the *papal chancery, between the late 12th and 14th c. its influence spread into every area of Latin and vernacular prose-writing in Italy, thanks largely to its dissemination via the *ars dictaminis*. In addition to the *stilus gregorianus*, medieval prose was characterized by two other 'styles': the *tullianus*, based on the figures of *Ciceronian rhetoric, and the *isidorianus*, which exerted considerable influence on vernacular prose, and which depends on effects of rhyme and on an equal number of syllables in the different clauses of a sentence.   [ZB]

See M. G. Nicolau, *L'Origine du 'cursus' rythmique et les débuts de l'accent d'intensité en latin* (1930); T. Janson, *Prose Rhythm in Medieval Latin from the 9th to the 13th Century* (1975).

CUSANUS, see NICHOLAS OF CUSA.

D

DALLAPICCOLA, LUIGI (1904–75). Composer and pianist. He composed the first of a series of works on liberty, *Canti di prigionia* (1938), while in hiding from the *Fascists. Immediately after *World War II, he wrote criticism for *Il Mondo*, and subsequently many other essays, some of which are collected in *Appunti, incontri, meditazioni* (1970).　　　　　　　　　　　　　　　　　　[RS]

DALL'ONGARO, FRANCESCO (1808–73). Writer. Born near Treviso, and a sometime priest, he was an adjutant to *Garibaldi and deputy in the *Roman Republic of 1849 [see 1848], then, after a decade of *exile, professor of literature in *Naples (1861–72). His varied production includes dramas, essays, *lyric poetry, and the patriotic *Stornelli italiani* (1862).　　　　　　　　　　　　[EAM]

DALMISTRO, ANGELO (1754–1839). *Venetian priest and a friend and admirer of Gasparo *Gozzi. He imitated his Horatian *Sermoni* and posthumously edited his collected works (1818–20). He translated works by Pope and Gray, and fostered new poetry, notably that of *Foscolo, in his yearly *L'anno poetico* (1793–1800).　　　　　　　　　　　　　　　　　　[JMAL]

D'AMBRA, FRANCESCO (1499–1558) was a *Florentine of noble family, consul of the Accademia Fiorentina, and comic dramatist [see ACADEMIES]. His three *comedies, *Il furto* (1544), *I Bernardi* (1547), and *La cofanaria* (1565), show a search for originality and complication in their plot mechanisms, and the usual Florentine enjoyment of vernacular wordplay.　　　　　　[RAA]

D'AMBRA, LUCIO (1880–1939), was a prolific writer, producing over fifty popular novels, some forty plays, and several volumes of *theatre criticism, including *biographies of *Goldoni, *Metastasio, and *Alfieri. He was a theatre manager from 1900, and from 1916 made a major contribution as a film director. His work in *cinema was influential both in Italy and Germany.　　　　　　[JAL]

D'AMICO, SILVIO (1887–1955). Drama critic and *theatre historian, who was the founder and first editor of the monumental *Enciclopedia dello spettacolo*, published in nine volumes between 1954 and 1962. A vigorous champion of fidelity to the author's text and intentions in theatrical productions, he wrote for various newspapers including the *Rome daily *Il Tempo*. He founded and edited two widely read theatrical reviews, *Scenario* in 1932 and *Rivista italiana del teatro* (later *del dramma*) in 1937. In 1935 he established the Accademia dell'Arte Drammatica, which now bears his name. He also wrote the novel *Le finestre di piazza Navona*, published posthumously in 1961.　　　[HMcW]

D'ANCONA, ALESSANDRO, see FOLK AND POPULAR LITERATURE; LITERARY CRITICISM; LITERARY THEORY, 5; POSITIVISM.

DANDOLO, ANDREA (1306–54) became Doge of *Venice in 1343. An acquaintance of *Petrarch, he reformed the chancery, codified Venetian *law, and ordered the *commune's archives. His *chronicle makes an important contribution to Venetian *historiography. A patron of the San Marco basilica, he was the last Doge to be buried there.　　　　　　　　　　　　　　[JEL]

DANDOLO, MILLY (1895–1946). Writer of stories for *children, who also wrote *novels of idealized maternity and frustrated love for a growing female readership, with titles such as *Tempo d'amore* (1929) and *Croce e delizia* (1944). She was widely read in the *Fascist period, but, like other writers of *romanzi rosa* (popular romantic fiction), subsequently much criticised for her superficiality.　　　　　　　　　　　　　　　　　　[SW]

D'ANDRÉ, FABRIZIO, see CANTAUTORI.

Daniele Cortis, see FOGAZZARO, ANTONIO.

DANIELLO, BERNARDINO (*c*.1500–65). *Literary critic and occasional writer of verse in the *Petrarchan mould. He belonged to the circle of young intellectuals around Trifon *Gabriele and Pietro *Bembo in *Padua after 1525. His works, largely derived from Gabriele's teaching, include a *dialogue, *Della poetica* (1536), and *commentaries on Petrarch (1541 and 1549) and *Dante (1568). [See also DANTE COMMENTARIES; LITERARY THEORY, 2; PETRARCH COMMENTARIES.] [LPer]

D'ANNUNZIO, GABRIELE (1863–1938) was born in Pescara, a sleepy fishing village raised in 1927 to the status of provincial capital by *Mussolini's *Fascist government, in implicit recognition of D'Annunzio's literary, political, and military exploits on behalf of the nation.

He published his first collection of poems, *Primo vere* (1879), while still a pupil at the elite (and private) Cicognini school in Prato, where he was forced to practise voice control in order to lose his Abruzzese accent and Tuscanize his language, thus gaining great articulacy and oratorical powers; he also consistently came top of the class. In *Rome in 1881 he enrolled at the university, but was mainly concerned with entering the world of *journalism, acquiring regular columns in *Tribuna* and *Cronaca bizantina*. He also published the poems of *Canto novo* (1882), inspired by his love affair for Giselda Zucconi—the 'novelty' claimed in the title implying a revolution in his poetic approach, and particularly a break with the style of Giosue *Carducci, whose neoclassical *Odi barbare* had heavily influenced the language and style of the first collection of poems. *Canto novo* also shocked society because of its display of open sexuality; the definitive edition (1896) excised the personal element (Giselda's name is eliminated, and the dedication to her removed), as D'Annunzio sought to idealize the love interest and exalt his own position.

Simultaneously with *Canto novo* he was writing realistic short stories, *Terra vergine* (1884) and *San Pantaleone* (1886), later collected with others in the *Novelle della Pescara* (1902). In their style and atmosphere they are superficially similar to Giovanni *Verga's tales of *peasant life, with many of which they share the theme of grinding rural poverty. But D'Annunzio was more concerned with observing human derelicts, depicted through the imagination of an adolescent with a penchant for the grotesque and shocking.

Marriage to Maria Hardouin, Duchess of Gallese, in July 1883, did not curtail his priapism; scandalous affairs with women from high society, including Elvira ('Barbara') Leoni, Maria Gravina, and the actress Eleonora Duse provided him with notoriety, as well as a daughter, Renata, by Maria Gravina—an affair for which both were condemned to a three-month amnestied gaol sentence for adultery. More importantly for his creative writing, the affairs provided much of the subject matter for his decadent novels—notably *Il *piacere* (1889), *L'innocente* (1892), *Trionfo della morte* (1894), *Le vergini delle rocce* (1895)—and for the sensual poetry of *Elegie romane* (1888); while his eight-year romance with Eleonora Duse inspired the semi-fictional account found in *Il fuoco* (1904). The novels of the 1880s and 1890s also display what critics describe as strong Nietzschean undertones; D'Annunzio certainly discovered Nietzsche as a fashionable name at that time, and discussed him (and Wagner) in the columns of *Tribuna* (1893), though the poet's earlier exploits and attitudes mark him out as a natural Nietzschean before his time. Other love affairs, such as that with the Countess Giuseppina Mancini, helped in the inspiration for the novel *Forse che sì forse che no* (1910), with its mania for fast cars and aeroplanes; and later *Solus ad solam* gives a harrowingly particularized account of the affair with Giuseppina and her subsequent madness.

In 1887 D'Annunzio had taken a sailing holiday in the Adriatic with Adolfo *De Bosis. The experience confirmed D'Annunzio in his subsequent ambition to see Italy's power over the Adriatic asserted through strong naval forces, and inspired many articles and poems, notably *L'armata d'Italia* (1888) and *Le odi navali* (1893); the trip also created in him a lifelong infatuation with *Venice. His views strengthened in 1895 when he travelled on Edoardo *Scarfoglio's much grander vessel. This journey is recounted in the imaginative epic *Maia*, subtitled *Laus vitae*, in which the intrepid mariners meet with such heroic figures as Ulysses, *redivivus* as a Greek fisherman, Helen of Troy, reduced to cleaning chamber pots in a Patràs brothel, and a host of others. *Maia* was to form the vast opening to the *Laudi*, to be named after the seven Pleiades; *Elettra*, which followed soon after *Maia*, traced in a series of individual poems the history of Western civilization, from its Greek origins to the glories of *Michelangelo and other cultural giants; *Alcyone*, a

Dante

collection in Shelleyan vein, gives the poet a breathing space to recover his forces after the literary exertions of the earlier pieces and also of his political campaigns of 1897 and 1900. These three were published in 1904. Two additions to the *Laudi* were published later, *Merope* in 1912 and *Asterope* in 1916, both of an occasional nature, and two others were proposed but never written.

Forced to flee to Paris by his creditors in 1910, D'Annunzio took up residence in France, where *Le Martyre de St Sébastien* (1911), with music by Debussy, won him a certain notoriety, and was anathematized by the Archbishop of Paris. In 1915 he returned to Italy to begin a campaign to convince Italians to enter the war on the Allies' side, and gave fiery speeches at Quarto and in Rome. He fought as a volunteer, exploited by the Italians for his propaganda value but also accomplishing various heroic feats, by land, sea, and air. Blinded in his left eye in a flying-boat accident in 1916, he used his lengthy convalescence to chart the experience in *Il notturno*, where his style, necessarily adapted to the need to write on narrow strips of paper, produced a new, uncluttered fashion in Italian prose. Once recovered, he accomplished other daring deeds, ending the war with eighteen medals for valour from the Allies, including an MC from King George V. In 1919, disgusted with the Allies' failure to fulfil their obligations by ceding former Austrian Dalmatia to Italy, D'Annunzio led a force of irregulars to capture Fiume, which he held from September 1919 to January 1921, creating an independent state with a democratic, if idiosyncratic constitution (the *Carta del Carnaro*). Driven out of Fiume, he retired to Gardone Riviera to construct his home-cummuseum and mortuary, the complex known as the Vittoriale degli Italiani.   [JRW]

Tutte le opere, ed. E. Bianchetti (1959–76). See J. R. Woodhouse, *Gabriele D'Annunzio: Defiant Archangel* (1998); M. Ledeen, *The First Duce: D'Annunzio at Fiume* (1977).

DANTE (1265–1321) is a towering figure of worldwide importance. In Italian literature and culture his impact begins in his lifetime and from then on is multifaceted and constant, with his so-called minor works playing almost as important a part as his masterpiece. The articles on him here reflect this richness and diversity. The two that follow cover his biography and the reception of his works. There are separate articles on the *Divine Comedy* and each of its three *cantiche* (*Inferno*, *Purgatorio*, and *Paradiso*); on the *Vita nova*, *De vulgari elo-*

quentia, *Convivio*, *Monarchia*, *Quaestio de aqua et terra*, and *Rime* (or uncollected poems); and on *Dante commentaries. Other articles are concerned with historical figures or fictional characters who appear in his work, such as *Beatrice, *Ulysses, *Virgil, and the poets Guido *Cavalcanti and *Sordello, though some, such as these last three, are also figures of importance in their own right. Dante also features prominently in several general articles, principally the *History of the Italian Language; *Literary Theory, 1; *Middle Ages; and *Questione della lingua.

1. Biography

Dante Alighieri was born in *Florence into a *Guelf family towards the end of May 1265. After receiving an ordinary *education, based on the standard classical and medieval Latin authors, he began to write poetry and came into contact with some of the foremost Florentine poets and intellectuals of the time, such as Brunetto *Latini and Guido *Cavalcanti. It was probably the latter, five years his elder and a member of one of Florence's noblest Guelf families, who initially became his model. In 1285 Dante married Gemma Donati. Two years later the couple had a son, Pietro, who was soon followed by two siblings: Iacopo and Antonia; the existence of a fourth child, Giovanni, is still disputed. Neither Gemma nor any of his children is ever mentioned in Dante's works. The opposite is true of *Beatrice, the love of his life, with whom he hardly had any contact at all. If she actually existed, she is likely to have been the daughter of Folco Portinari, Bice, who was born in 1266, married Simone de' Bardi in 1287, and died in 1290.

From the early 1280s and at least until 1307–8 Dante experimented with poetry, exploring ever more demanding forms and subject matter, from the realistic and the burlesque to the philosophical and the theological. He is widely believed to have written, around 1286, the 232 *sonnets of the *Fiore, a bawdy and brilliant *Tuscan adaptation of the *Roman de la rose*, and the 480 settenari of the *Detto d'amore*. He is also believed to have spent about half of the year 1287 in *Bologna, where he came to know the poetry of Guido *Guinizzelli—whom he was later to acknowledge as the father of the *dolce stil novo* (*Purg.* 26.97–9). Two years later he was involved as a cavalry officer in the battle of Campaldino against Arezzo, and in the siege of the *Pisan castle of Caprona, both episodes later remembered in the *Divine Comedy*. In 1290 Beatrice died, an event which at first drew him to the study of theology and philosophy. Nothing else is known about the period 1290–5, except that in those years he wrote the *Vita nova*, the book which established his reputation as the leader of Italian poetry.

In 1295 Dante entered politics, having joined the *Guild of Doctors and Apothecaries—a normal choice for a poet. Within five years he was elected one of the *priori*, Florence's highest office, for the period June to August 1300. It was a critical moment in the conflict between the Guelf *Blacks and Whites, the former intransigently opposed to any popular participation in public life, the latter more open to cooperation with the lower classes. In an attempt to quell the violence, Dante and his colleagues banished the leaders of both factions, including Guido Cavalcanti, who was to die in exile that summer. However, this move failed to pacify the city. In October 1301 the intervention at the Pope's request of Charles of Valois, brother of Philip, King of France, put the Blacks' leader, Corso Donati, back in control. Dante, who at the time was on a peace mission to *Rome, was charged with corruption in office and sentenced to a heavy fine, two years of exile, and a permanent ban from public office. As he refused to submit, his property was confiscated and the sentence changed to perpetual exile. It was the end of Dante's political career. For two further years he was involved with the Whites in their attempt to regain control of Florence, but he left them, 'making a party unto himself' (*Para.* 17.69), just before they were finally defeated at La Lastra, near Florence, on 20 July 1304.

For the rest of his life Dante wandered from court to court, visiting Bartolomeo *Della Scala in *Verona before 1303–4. After 1304 few details of his movements are known, and these are clouded by later legends. Undoubtedly, it was a period of intense activity and rapid intellectual development. Forced into political inactivity, Dante was seeking to restore his self-confidence and reputation, and to find new and more solid grounds upon which to base his future. In this enterprise he was aided by his extraordinary ability to assimilate and synthesize all sources of knowledge, transforming them into a coherent shape of his own. Besides *Cicero and Boethius, he read St *Augustine's *Confessions* and reread *Virgil's *Aeneid*, now with a new sense of purpose. He studied the *scholastic philosophy and theology of St Thomas *Aquinas, St Albert the Great, and St *Bonaventure, but also the mystics and, perhaps, such heterodox thinkers as Siger of Brabant and the speculative grammarians.

In 1303–4 Dante began working on two ambitious projects. The *Convivio* was to be a synthesis in the vernacular of all current philosophical debates, bringing his own philosophical *canzoni* within reach of a wide Italian audience; the *De vulgari eloquentia* was to demonstrate in Latin the formal dignity of his vernacular poetry, in the context of a universal theory and history of language and literature. His hope was perhaps that works of such significance would compel Florence to recognize his merits and revoke his *exile. In fact he never completed them. Probably in 1307 he started to write the poem which would occupy him for the rest of his life, the *Divine Comedy*. The only other book which Dante wrote while working at his great poem was a Latin treatise on politics, *Monarchia*, though when exactly he wrote it is a much debated question. At least three dates are proposed: 1308, 1311–13, and post-1318, the latter being the most likely. In the overlapping of temporal and spiritual powers Dante saw one of the principal roots of the social and moral corruption afflicting the contemporary world. For this reason, he was keenly opposed to the Church's holding or exercising temporal power—which he thought belonged, in God's design, to the Empire. Inspiring many impassioned invectives in the *Commedia*, this belief is brilliantly argued in the *Monarchia*.

In 1310 the Emperor elect, *Henry VII of Luxemburg, descended into Italy to be crowned Holy Roman Emperor in Rome, and to enforce his authority over the peninsula's endemic factionalism. This was the opportunity Dante had been waiting for, to see an end to both the Italian crisis and his personal exile. In the midst of the political and military upheaval caused by Henry's move, Dante wrote public letters to the Princes of Italy and to the Florentines (*Epistles* 5 and 6), urging them to welcome the Emperor-elect as God's envoy, and to Henry exhorting him to strike immediately at Florence, the heart of Guelf resistance (*Epistles* 7). While Henry hesitated, the Gascon Pope Clement V switched sides, allying himself with Robert of *Anjou, King of *Naples, and with the Black Guelfs. When it was finally mounted, the siege of Florence (September 1312) was a fiasco. Dante left Tuscany before it ended, and once again found refuge at the court of the Della Scala in Verona, now ruled by the young Cangrande. The following year the Emperor died of malaria at Buonconvento, near *Siena (24 August 1313). Dante was left bitterly disappointed, having further compromised his chances of ever returning to

Dante

Florence. Nor did this experience change his attitude. The year after, at the death of Pope Clement, Dante wrote another fiery letter (*Epistles* 11), urging the cardinals to elect an Italian Pope and return the Church to its pristine simplicity. In his *Paradiso* he assigned Henry a seat in the Rose of the Blessed (30.133–8), having already predicted eternal damnation for the Gascon Pope who had 'betrayed' him (*Inf.* 19.82–4).

For Dante the conflict of temporal interests between Church and Empire had deprived humanity of these two guides, both of them essential to its wellbeing on earth and its fulfilment in Heaven. As a consequence greed, the root of all evil, had triumphed everywhere. Possessed by an insatiable craving for material goods and power, contemporary society had become utterly corrupt: everyone was fighting for individual advantage and gratification. Nowhere was this more the case than in Florence, which, under the rule of the 'accursed florin', had become for the poet the true kingdom of greed. In the central cantos of *Paradiso*, using as his mouthpiece his own ancestor Cacciaguida, Dante identifies in 'the mixture of peoples' and in individual enterprise—essentially, the geographical and social mobility brought about by a rapidly evolving economic situation—the roots of the city's moral degeneration. This he contrasted with the social stability, sobriety, and purity of the 12th-c. Florence into which Cacciaguida was born. That old Florence is, for Dante, the ideal of a well-ordered civil society in which private and public morality coincide, and all citizens, free of greed, live and die as good men and women, in peace with their neighbours and with God.

The years Dante spent at the court of Cangrande della Scala between late 1312 and, probably, 1318 were the most tranquil of his exile. This situation perhaps strengthened his resolve when, in 1315, he refused the amnesty which Florence offered him on condition that he pay a light fine and acknowledge his guilt. As he wrote to a friend in Florence, how could he, the poet of justice and rectitude, submit to the indignity of the Florentine pardon without making a mockery of everything he believed in and stood for (*Epistles* 12)? Dante chose instead to stay in Ghibelline Verona and, as if to confirm his choice, he dedicated his *Paradiso* to Cangrande—at least if we believe in the authenticity of his last letter (*Epistles* 13). In 1318—though again the date and the motivation behind this move are uncertain—Dante left Verona and settled in Ravenna as a guest of Guido Novello da Polenta. Here his family

joined him, and he completed the *Paradiso*; between 1319 an 1320 he wrote the *Egloge* to *Giovanni del Virgilio and a short scientific treatise, the *Quaestio de aqua et terra*. In 1321 he went on a mission to *Venice on behalf of Guido Novello, charged with the task of negotiating a reduction of hostilities between the Republic and Ravenna. On his way back, he caught malaria, and died on 13 September 1321 in Ravenna, where he was buried.   [LPer]

See P. Toynbee, *A Dictionary of Proper Names and Notable Matters in the Works of Dante* (1898, 1968); U. Bosco (ed.), *Enciclopedia dantesca* (1970–8); G. Petrocchi, *Vita di Dante* (1983); R. Lansing (ed.), *Dante Encyclopedia* (2000).

2. Reception

Dante's critical fortunes and his influence on thinkers, writers, and artists in other media have always gone hand in hand. As early as the 14th c., alongside numerous *Dante commentaries, lengthy narrative and didactic poems, some in *terza rima*, were being written, such as *Nadal's *Leandreide*, *Frezzi's *Quadriregio*, and the *Dottrinale* of Dante's son Iacopo, while the *Divine Comedy* offered clear precedents in language and theme, though not of course in form, for *Boccaccio's *Decameron*. Soon Dante's work was also visibly influencing non-Italian authors, such as Chaucer, Christine de Pizan, and Juan de Mena, and being satirized by Il Za (Stefano Finiguerri), who blends parody and emulation. Meanwhile, manuscript illustrations launched the long tradition of visual renderings of the *Comedy*'s textual material. [See DIVINE COMEDY: ILLUSTRATIONS.]

By the later 15th c. Dante's reputation was declining among critics, despite Cristoforo *Landino's efforts in his commentary (1481) to promote his fellow *Tuscan author as a cultural and linguistic model for all of Italy. But the visual tradition was extended by painters such as *Botticelli, and in poetry *Michelangelo used a Dantesque style to counterbalance the dominant *Petrarchism.

In the later *Renaissance and the 17th and 18th c. Dante tended to be relegated to the cultural margins, with rare exceptions such as the quotation of 'Lasciate ogni speranza, voi ch'entrate' (*Inf.* 3.9) in the *libretto of *Monteverdi's *Orfeo* (1609). He was seldom commented upon by critics, and less popular than *Petrarch or *Ariosto with readers, both inside and outside Italy, although his continuing appeal to visual artists is shown by the work of Flaxman and Blake.

The emergence of *Romanticism in the early

19th c., with its pervasive interest in medieval culture, restored Dante's work, especially the *Comedy*, to cultural pre-eminence. It was adopted as an icon by Italian *nationalism and then by the nascent Italian state, translated into the major European vernaculars, frequently (if sometimes anachronistically) presented as a master-text of newly defined 'European' and 'Renaissance' traditions, published for the first time in cheap and readily available editions, and drawn upon for moral and religious instruction even in Protestant sectors of the Victorian bourgeoisie, in England and elsewhere. It became a cardinal point of reference in 19th-c. culture for poets (Mickiewicz, Tennyson, the Brownings, Longfellow, Baudelaire), novelists (George Eliot), composers (Liszt, Tchaikovsky, *Verdi, *Puccini), painters (Delacroix, the Pre-Raphaelites, Doré), social philosophers and theologians (Carlyle, Ruskin, Arnold, Newman), critics (Pater), and educators (Barlow, Norton). Even a politician such as Gladstone was influenced by Dante.

In the 20th c. Dante's cultural presence spread still further, sometimes into seemingly improbable quarters. He became a key author for Pound, Joyce, and T. S. Eliot, and for Russian poets such as Ivanov and Mandel'shtam. He inspires sculptors (Rodin) and film-makers (*Pasolini, Greenaway). Several silent-film versions of *Inferno* appeared in Italy before *World War I, most famously Giuseppe Di Liguoro's of 1909. More recently he has supplied narrative frameworks for African-American novelists, such as Leroi Jones in *The System of Dante's Hell* (1965) and Gloria Naylor in *Linden Hills* (1985), and for writers of science fiction such as Larry Niven and Jerry Pournelle in *Inferno* (1976). Alongside this creative outpouring, the number of translations, into almost every conceivable language, like the volume of scholarly studies, never ceases to grow. From the late 19th c. the Italian critical and scholarly tradition is joined by autonomous versions in Germany, Britain, France, and the United States, where *Dante Studies* was founded in 1882 as the *Annual Report of the Dante Society of America*, long before its Italian equivalent, *Studi danteschi*, appeared in 1920. The 1990s saw half-a-dozen new *Comedy* translations into English alone. The possibilities opened up by computer technology and the Internet seem likely to extend Dante's fortunes more widely still in the very near future.   [SNB]

See A. Vallone, *Storia della critica dantesca dal XIV al XX secolo* (1981); M. Caesar (ed.), *Dante.*

The Critical Heritage 1314(?) to 1870 (1989); D. Wallace, 'Dante in English', in R. Jacoff (ed.), *The Cambridge Companion to Dante* (1993).

Dante Commentaries. Commentary on *Dante begins with Dante himself. Both the *Vita nova* and *Convivio* include substantial amounts of self-authored commentary on the early lyrics, whilst the *De vulgari eloquentia* confirms that Dante was deeply concerned with the theory and interpretation of his own creative output. The *Divine Comedy* itself contains many passages of metapoetic reflection, though not, it would seem, enough to do away with the need for further elucidation. The sheer bulk of explication and analysis of the text of the *Comedy* is now enormous, and is embodied in scores of annotated editions and Dante readings (*lecturae Dantis*) in several languages.

The two great ages of Dante commentary—so far—have been the 14th and 20th c. Dante's own son Iacopo composed a set of vernacular glosses (*chiose*) on the *Inferno* shortly after his father's death in 1321; Graziolo de' *Bambaglioli did likewise in Latin (*c.*1324); and between 1324 and 1328 the first commentary on the whole *Comedy* appeared, written by the *Bolognese scholar Iacopo della Lana. Lana established one of the basic techniques of Dante commentary, the introductory summary of each canto followed by detailed annotations of individual lines and words, which has survived unaltered into the present day.

The other basic method, the *lectura Dantis*, that is, analytical expositions of the individual cantos, was devised by *Boccaccio for his public lectures in *Florence in 1373–4 (though he did not live to complete the series), and adopted by *Benvenuto da Imola and *Francesco di Bartolo da Buti (who both did) towards the century's end. By 1400 over twenty commentaries, complete and partial, in Latin and the vernacular, from all over Italy, were in circulation. The most notable include those of Guido da Pisa (*c.*1327–8), Pietro *Alighieri (three extant versions, between 1340 and *c.*1358), and the so-called *Ottimo commento*, often attributed to Andrea *Lancia, and also extant in three versions (between 1330 and *c.*1340), along with many often anonymous sets of *chiose*.

That a modern, vernacular author should have been accorded the type of commentary normally reserved for texts of the ancients is a mark of Dante's stature in the decade following his death. The vogue for Dante commentary faded, however, during the *Renaissance. The emergence of

Dante Da Maiano

*Petrarchan lyric refinement as a stylistic model for poets caused the popularity of Dante's very different approach to decline, and the 15th c. produced only one major commentary, that of Cristoforo *Landino (1481), distinguished by erudition, a Platonizing approach to the *Comedy*, and *Tuscan cultural patriotism.

Thereafter, Dante's masterpiece endured centuries of relative neglect by commentators. Alessandro *Vellutello (1544), Bernardino *Daniello (c.1560, published 1568), and Ludovico *Castelvetro (1570) made the most significant 16th-c. contributions. The 17th and 18th c. were even more parsimonious, with only Pompeo Venturi (1732) and Baldassarre Lombardi (1791) undertaking full-scale textual commentaries. It took the roughly simultaneous emergence of *Romanticism in culture and Italian *nationalism in politics, at the turn of the 18th and 19th c., to restore Dante's work to currency and inspire a fresh wave of Dante commentary.

Lombardi's often-reprinted work was soon followed by dozens of similar efforts, especially after the new Italian state both adopted Dante as a cultural icon (starting with the sixth-centenary celebrations of 1865), and began to have the *Comedy* taught in schools. For the first time, commentaries also began to appear outside Italy itself (though *Giovanni da Serravalle's commentary of 1416–17 had been commissioned by two English bishops), especially north of the Alps. The German philologist Karl Witte (1862) and his Swiss counterpart Giovanni Andrea Scartazzini (1874–90) were leading figures in this development.

The influence of the *positivist approach to history and the consequent increase in scholarly knowledge about the *Middle Ages in general laid the foundations for the many massive triple-decker editions of the late 19th and early 20th c.; those of Tommaso Casini (1889), Giacomo Poletto (1894), and Francesco Torraca (1905), along with Giuseppe Vandelli's reworking of Scartazzini (1903), are outstanding. Edward Moore's critical edition of the text (1894), followed by that sponsored by the Società Dantesca Italiana in 1921, further spurred scholars to produce commentaries. Since *World War II in particular they have poured from the presses, representing every conceivable school of interpretation and critical approach, from Catholic to *Marxist, *Crocean to *structuralist, from the scholarly to the superficial.

Contributions likely to be of enduring value include those of Attilio *Momigliano (1945),

Natalino *Sapegno (1955–7), Giuseppe Giacalone (1968–9), Umberto Bosco and Giovanni Reggio (1979, and the first to appear on CD-ROM, in 1992), and Anna Maria Chiavacci Leonardi (1991–7). Valuable non-Italian commentaries include those of the German Hermann Gmelin (1949–51) and the Americans Charles S. Singleton (1970–5), Robert Durling and Ronald Martinez (1996–), and Robert Hollander (2000–). Many commentaries, from the 14th-c. exemplars onwards, are now available on-line, through the Dante Database maintained by Dartmouth College (USA). At the same time, as part of the ever-expanding universe of late 20th-c. Dante studies, multi-author collections of *lecturae Dantis* have also proliferated: those edited by Giovanni Getto (1955) and Tibor Wlassics (1990–5) are among the most comprehensive. [See also COMMENTARIES; PETRARCH COMMENTARIES.]   [SNB]

See A. Vallone, *Storia della critica dantesca dal XIV al XX secolo* (1981).

DANTE DA MAIANO (late 13th c.). *Siculo-Tuscan *lyric poet much influenced by the *Sicilian School and *Guittone d'Arezzo. He exchanged poems with Chiaro *Davanzati, *Guido Orlandi, and *Dante amongst others. He replied to Dante's appeal for help in interpreting his dream in the first *sonnet of the *Vita nova* ('A ciascun' alma presa') with an interesting sonnet ('Di ciò che stato sei dimandatore'), which refers to contemporary medical lore. His Italian poems (two *canzoni*, five *ballate*, forty-seven sonnets) appeared for the first time in the *Giuntina* anthology of 1527, which gave rise to the no longer accepted view that they were 16th-c. forgeries. He also composed two sonnets in Provençal.   [CK]

DA PONTE, LORENZO (1749–1838) is most famous as a *librettist. He came from a Jewish family, was educated in the Veneto, and converted to Christianity while still an adolescent. A series of tormented love affairs, and his contacts with *libertine circles in *Venice, led to his exile from the city in 1779, under the accusation of adultery and public concubinage. For ten years, from 1781, he lived in Vienna, where he obtained the well-remunerated post of poet of the imperial theatres, composed verses and *comedies, and gained his greatest success with the libretti for Mozart's *Nozze di Figaro* (1786), *Don Giovanni* (1787), and *Così fan tutte* (1790). While it is clear today how much each artist stimulated the expressive gifts of the other, the association did not last long, because in 1791 Da Ponte was expelled from Vienna on both political and moral grounds, and was replaced as imperial poet by his perennial rival *Casti.

At this point his wanderings began, including a period in London, where he composed serious and comic libretti and worked as a bookseller/publisher, and ending, from 1804, in the United States. Here he engaged in a variety of activities, as book-dealer, teacher of Italian, essayist, founder of an Italian theatre in New York, and above all as author of his *Memorie*. Published in 1804, this is one of the best 18th-c. *autobiographies, reflecting in its rapid style Da Ponte's experience of American culture, while mainly dealing with the author's experiences in Europe. [See also AUSTRIA; OPERA.]   [SC]

DA PORTO, LUIGI (1485–1529). *Novelliere* and poet. His family ties to Elizabetta *Gonzaga, Duchess of *Urbino, enabled him to receive an education at the Urbino *court (1503–5). He became a friend of Pietro *Bembo, with whom he exchanged letters, and Matteo *Bandello, who dedicated a *novella to him. Fighting with the *Venetian army between 1509 and 1511, he sustained such serious injuries that he decided to devote his life to study. In 1524 he wrote his most famous work, the story of the love of Romeo and Giulietta (which, in Bandello's version, was the source of *Shakespeare's *Romeo and Juliet*). It was published in 1530–1, with a second version appearing in his *Rime et prosa* of 1539. The story betrays the influence of *Masuccio Salernitano's *Novellino*, but it is Da Porto who makes the setting 14th-c. Verona rather than *Siena, gives the characters their familiar names and develops them psychologically, and creates a dramatic ending, with the death of the lovers after the example of *Ovid's Pyramus and Thisbe. Da Porto also composed conventional *Petrarchist verse, and an important collection of *letters (not fully published until 1832), covering the period 1509–28, which include descriptions of his experiences in the Venetian army.   [PLR]

D'ARCO, CIRO, see TORELLI, GIUSEPPE.

D'ARRIGO, STEFANO (1919–92). Novelist. Born in *Sicily, he fought in *World War II, before moving to *Rome in 1946. He first worked as an art critic and published a collection of poetry, *Codice siciliano* (1957). By then, with the encouragement of Elio *Vittorini, he was at work on the novel that made his name, *Horcynus Orca*, which he only com-

pleted in 1975. The title refers to a mythical giant fish, found in the Straits of Messina. The novel itself, a vast, sprawling work which deploys mixtures of Italian and *dialect in a sophisticated style reminiscent of Joyce, follows the maritime adventures of the sailor 'Ndrja Cambria after he set sail from *Naples for Sicily in 1943. The work, divided into three parts which describe the voyage, the encounter with Sicily, and the appearance of the fearful Orca, is a deft recreation of folk and classical myths of the Mediterranean. D'Arrigo published another novel, *Cima delle nobildonne*, in 1985.   [JF]

Darwinism became an issue in Italy even before *The Origin of Species* of 1859 was translated into Italian by Giovanni Canestrini. Darwinian thought continued the challenge which *positivist science was already presenting to divine revelation. For the rest of the century, Catholic intellectuals and scientists attempted to reconcile scientific knowledge and experimental practice with a theistic perspective, and to get questions of causality and determinism deferred to the metaphysical sphere—as was proposed by the *Jesuit astrophysicist Angelo Secchi in *L'unità delle forze fisiche* (1864). But the debate had also a political dimension, stemming from *papal hostility to the newly created Italian state [see RISORGIMENTO].

Already in 1861, *De Sanctis had appointed Jakob Moleschott, a Dutch physiologist celebrated for his scientific materialism, to a professorship in *Turin. However, still in Turin, Filippo De Filippi's 1864 lecture on 'L'uomo e le scimmie' reconciled evolution with Catholic belief, only to come under attack from positivists. One such attack provoked Niccolò *Tommaseo's *Milan pamphlet, *L'uomo e la scimmia* (1869), which took issue with Darwinian determinism. The Catholic position was resisted by Luigi Bombicci Porta, appointed to the chair of geology in *Bologna in 1860, who posited a common materialist basis to both mineral and organic evolution at the chemical level. But scientifically serious opposition continued, notably from Giovanni Giuseppe Bianconi, whose *La théorie darwinienne et la création indépendante* (1874) posits mechanical rather than genetic explanations for analogies in functional anatomy between man and other animals, rather as Secchi had done earlier. Bianconi's attack on positivism was supported by Pietro Siciliani, professor of theoretical philosophy at *Bologna, in *La critica della filosofia zoologica del XIX secolo*, published in *Naples in 1877.

Herbert Spencer's system of evolutionist thought made its impact from the mid-1880s, even before translations of his work began to appear towards the end of the decade. The debate over social Darwinism from the early 1890s onwards was reflected in the pages of Filippo Turati's *Critica sociale*, in which *socialist intellectuals such as Enrico Ferri and Achille Loria tackled the Spencerian positions of Guglielmo Ferrero, presenting *Marx as the Darwin of social science, or human evolution in terms of the survival of the unfittest. Napoleone Colajanni, however, in the second edition of his *Socialismo* (1898) and in successive writings, deplored the unscientific applications of Darwinism by apologists of the Right and the Left.

Italian literary culture as a whole was unreceptive to the implications of Darwinism, though *Carducci's controversial *Inno a Satana* (1865) generically celebrated human progress. *Verismo* was more attuned to the concept of the struggle for life, as is evident in *Verga's project for *I vinti*, and Italian naturalist *theatre from around 1890 to 1910 largely revolved around social-Darwinist struggles for money as a cause of moral collapse. By the 1880s the spiritually inclined novelist Antonio *Fogazzaro, in the essays he collected in *Ascensioni umane* (1899), championed evolution in theistic terms as the struggle of spirit over flesh, only to provoke the official displeasure of the Vatican, in part because he tried to harmonize evolution and nationalism. His novels pursue the same themes more poetically. More noisily, *Marinetti and the *Futurists acclaimed war as the world's unique hygiene. *Nationalist currents of thought were generally apt to attribute an evolutionary advantage and a civilizing mission to the Italians in the earlier part of the 20th c.

The most serious literary reflection on Darwinism came from Italo *Svevo. He wrote two essays on the subject in 1907-8, both published posthumously—'L'uomo e la teoria darwiniana' and 'La corruzione dell'anima'. *Una vita*, originally entitled *Un inetto*, foregrounds the economic struggle for survival and, like his two subsequent novels, examines psychological survival mechanisms. *La *coscienza di Zeno* concludes with Zeno's pronouncement that a radically diseased humanity was an evolutionary mistake which would erase itself.

Darwinism ceased to be a matter of pressing intellectual concern with *World War I and the rise of *Fascism.   [JG-R]

See R. Vivarelli (ed.), *La cultura italiana tra '800 e '900 e le origini del nazionalismo* (1981);

P. Redondi, 'Cultura e scienza dall'illuminismo al positivismo,' in G. Micheli (ed.), *Scienza e tecnica nella cultura e nella società dal Rinascimento a oggi* (1980).

DATI, AGOSTINO (1420–78). After a *humanist *education, he worked as a teacher, opening a school of rhetoric in *Siena, and becoming the official orator of the Republic. He was a prolific writer on philosophical, rhetorical, and historical matters.   [LB]

DATI, CARLO ROBERTO (1619–76). *Florentine patrician and man of letters, professor of classics at the Florentine *studio* [see UNIVERSITIES, 1], and later librarian to Prince Leopoldo. A pupil of *Galileo, and a member of several *academies, Dati's interests included natural philosophy and the history of art, but he is best known for his concern with language, as secretary of the Accademia della *Crusca and the author of the *Discorso sull'obligo di ben parlare la propria lingua* (1657). [See also QUESTIONE DELLA LINGUA.]   [UPB]

DATI, GREGORIO (or Goro) (1362–1435). *Florentine silk *merchant and public servant, who wrote, in *dialogue form, a vernacular *Istoria di Firenze* narrating events of 1380–1406, with the war between Florence and Giangaleazzo *Visconti as its unifying theme. It marks a transition between 14th-c. *chronicle and *humanist history.   [JCB]

DATI, LEONARDO (1407–72). Educated as a notary in *Florence, he took orders in 1432 and moved to *Rome, where he became a friend of Leon Battista *Alberti. In 1433 he moved back to Florence, and in 1441 took part to the *certame coronario* with a poem called *Scaena*, one of the first examples of the adaptation of Latin quantitative metre to Italian [see VERSIFICATION]. He also wrote poetry in Latin, and a commentary on *Palmieri's *Città di vita*, completed before 1464.   [LB]

DATINI, FRANCESCO (?1335–1410). Self-made *merchant adventurer of Prato, who established a great network of companies in Italy, *Avignon, and Iberia. His business and personal archives, which include 140,000 letters, 11,000 of them private, have survived virtually intact. Besides constituting a unique record of medieval trade they afford a detailed picture of his family's everyday life. Prominent among Datini's correspondents are his wife and his friend Ser Lapo Mazzei, under whose influence he bequeathed his entire fortune to Prato's poor. [JCB]

See Iris Origo, *The Merchant of Prato* (1957).

DAVANZATI, CHIARO, see CHIARO DAVANZATI.

DAVANZATI BOSTICHI, BERNARDO (1529–1606). One of the most important figures in 16th-c. *Florentine cultural life. His main work was his concise and faithful *translation into Italian of Tacitus' *Annals*, which from the *Counter-Reformation onwards began to overtake the works of *Livy in popularity. He also composed a short work on the English Schism from the Church of Rome, and works on economic subjects.

[PBD]

DA VERONA, GUIDO (pseud. of Guido Verona) (1881–1939). A key figure in the development of popular fiction in the early 20th c. He began as a poet with *Frammento di un poema* (1902), but soon turned to fiction. His novels were hugely successful with readers of both sexes. Strongly marked by *D'Annunzio's influence, they have a soft-centred, *libertine *eroticism which reduces the *decadent superman to a seducer of young girls. His first successful novel *Colei che non si deve amare* (1911) was about an incestuous affair. *Mimi Bluette* (1916), about a prostitute redeemed by love, was very popular with soldiers in the trenches. A *Jew from near Modena, he committed suicide in the wake of the *Fascist racial laws. [AHC]

DAVILA, ENRICO CATERINO (1576–1631). Historian of the French wars of religion. Born in *Padua, his parents named him after the King and Queen of France, and he early made favourable impressions on Caterina de' *Medici and on Henri, Duke of Vendôme. His most formative experience came when he witnessed the political and religious crises in France, and met many of the political and cultural leaders of the time, including Montaigne. Returning to Italy in 1599, he spent much of the remainder of his life in trouble, meeting an unfortunate death after a road-rage incident.

His *Storia delle guerre civili di Francia* (1634) covered the period from 1559 to 1598 and was immensely successful. Coherent in content, interpretation and style, the 1,054-page work goes beyond *humanist *historiography, and probes into the causes of events, offering its author's own eyewitness accounts. The depth of Davila's human

interest has been compared to *Guicciardini's. He had previously made his literary debut with *Theatro del mondo* (1598–9), a visionary Creation poem whose subject and style did not evidently suit their author. [PBD]

D'AZEGLIO, CESARE TAPARELLI (1763–1830). *Piedmontese monarchist and officer, who defended the Catholic cause against *Enlightenment ideas. He was a member of the associations *Amicizia cristiana* and *Amicizia cattolica*, and a main contributor to *L'Ape*, the first Catholic journal in Italy. *Manzoni dedicated his *Lettera sul romanticismo* to him. [See also ROMANTICISM.] [EAM]

D'AZEGLIO, MASSIMO TAPARELLI (1798–1866). Writer and politician. Born into the *Turinese nobility, the son of Cesare *D'Azeglio, he lived in *Rome from 1821 to 1829, winning a reputation as a landscape painter as well as writing poems and plays. Moving to *Milan in 1831, he met and married *Manzoni's daughter, Giulia, though his two published *historical novels, *Ettore Fieramosca* (1833) and *Niccolò de' Lapi* (1840), owe more to *Grossi than to his father-in-law. He left a third historical novel, *La lega lombarda*, unfinished. In the 1840s and 1850s he was principally active as a moderate *liberal politician, opposed to *Mazzini's revolutionary republicanism. He summed up his views on social reform through peaceful means in a *Proposta di un programma per l'opinione nazionale italiana* (1847). After serving in Carlo Alberto's army in the war of *1848, he was briefly Prime Minister of *Piedmont in 1849. He then withdrew from politics until 1859, when he went on diplomatic missions to Paris and London and opposed *Cavour's plans to make Rome the capital of Italy. His most readable work is *I miei ricordi* (1867), on which he spent his last years. [See also AUTOBIOGRAPHY.]

[DO'G]

DE AMICIS, EDMONDO (1846–1908) is best known as the author of the *children's novel, *Cuore*. He was born in Oneglia near Imola, and after studying in Cuneo, *Turin, and the military academy in Modena, became an army officer. He fought at the battle of Custoza in 1866 and subsequently edited the army paper, *L'Italia militare*, in *Florence. He also published sketches of army life in *La vita militare* (1868). He left the army in 1870 and travelled widely, though he made his home in Turin in 1875.

De André, Fabrizio

He produced fine *travel-books from his stays in Spain, Holland, London, Morocco, Constantinople, Paris, and South America. In 1891 he became a *socialist and devoted much of his subsequent writing to justifying and expounding the cause. He wrote various moralizing novels, including the improbably titled *Amore e ginnastica* (1892). *L'idioma gentile* (1905) crystallized his teaching on language and society, but *Cuore* (1886) gives fullest expression to his patriotic educational zeal. Its mission was to create a sense of responsible nationhood in the young of disparate regions, and to engender social concern and cohesion across class divisions. The emphasis on the importance of feelings was a deliberate refusal of the detachment of *verismo*. It was adopted as a school text throughout Italy.

[ALL]

DE ANDRÉ, FABRIZIO (1940–99). Born in *Genoa, he emerged in the early 1960s as a *cantautore* of unusual poetic gifts. He was influenced by Georges Brassens and *existentialism, and used an allusive, metaphorical style in his songs to create a world of outcasts, prostitutes, and thieves.

[SG]

DE ANGELIS, AUGUSTO (1888–1944). *Roman *journalist who originally trained as a lawyer and published a series of *detective stories between 1935 and 1942. He was a correspondent for *Il Resto del Carlino* and the *Corriere della sera*. In *World War II he joined the *Resistance and was arrested and killed.

[AHC]

DEBENEDETTI, GIACOMO (1901–67). Important Italian critic who made an original and perceptive use of stylistic and *psychoanalytical approaches. He was particularly attentive to contemporary literature, writing innovative essays on *Saba, *Svevo, *Tozzi, *Pirandello, as well as on Proust, Joyce, and Kafka. His main studies are contained in three series of *Saggi critici* (1929, 1945, and 1959) and *Il romanzo del Novecento* (1971). Various volumes of his *Quaderni* have been published since 1973. His creative writings, *Amedeo e altri racconti* (1926), *Otto ebrei* (1944), and *16 ottobre 1943* (1945), deal with questions of *Jewishness and anti-Semitism.

[LL]

DE BOSIS, ADOLFO (1863–1924), a wealthy lawyer, influential if dilettante essayist, and minor (*D'Annunzian) poet, publishing *Amori ac silentio sacrum* (1900), *Liriche* (1907), and *Rime sparse*

(1924). He founded and edited the opulent journal *Convito* (twelve volumes, from 1895 to 1898), which published, among others, *Pascoli, *Carducci, and (especially) D'Annunzio, and helped publicize pre-Raphaelitism in Italy.

[JRW]

Decadentismo. Term used in Italian criticism primarily to indicate the literary (and often the artistic) culture of late 19th-c. Italy as a whole, not merely a current within it. In this respect it differs from terms in English and French, such as *fin-de-siècle*, art for art's sake, Baudelairianism, and symbolism, though *decadentismo* is often made to overlap with all of these. The emblematic and central figures are hence the most important writers of the time, in particular *Pascoli, *Fogazzaro, and *D'Annunzio.

Inevitably the term has had strong polemical or moralistic implications. It emerges in the context of *Croce's critique of the whole range of contemporary Italian literature. In the essays of *La letteratura della nuova Italia* Croce repeatedly points to deviations from the healthier forms of Italian *Romanticism, implicitly and explicitly drawing comparisons with the blend of *classicism and Romanticism still evident in *Carducci; he criticizes what he sees as a morbid cultivation of insincerity and irrationality, politically cynical with respect to *liberal democracy, and, ultimately, a mere outer display around an inner void.

Subsequent discussions could not but take Croce as their starting point. Francesco *Flora's *Il decadentismo* (1949) is the most powerful expression of a view which extends the Crocean perspective to embrace *modernism as a whole, from *Futurism and *Pirandello through to *hermetic poetry. That approach is also visible in left-wing rejections of modernism associated with *Neorealism, though the most forceful analysis of the phenomenon by a left-wing critic, Carlo Salinari's *Miti e coscienza del decadentismo italiano* (1960), focused on what it saw as the different forms of bourgeois decadence in the canonical trio of Pascoli, Fogazzaro, and D'Annunzio, together with Pirandello.

While in this type of discussion *decadentismo* was often seen as representative of a cultural and social corruption that would lead to *Fascism, other less politicized criticism had already emphasized its productive and interesting innovations. Mario *Praz's *La carne, la morte e il diavolo nella letteratura romantica* (1930; trans. as *The Romantic Agony*, 1933) explored the new eroticism of late 19th-c.

Italian and European literature, and Walter Binni's *La poetica del decadentismo* (1936) the new sense of ineffable mystery which 'decadentist' writers evoked principally through a stress on music and musicality. Current usage is inclined to use the term as a morally neutral label, but the negative connotations stemming from Croce have not completely vanished. [PH]

Decameron, Il. *Boccaccio's masterpiece, composed in 1349–51 and then revised and reworked c.1370–2. It draws much from his earlier work, taking actual stories from the *Filocolo* (10.4 and 5) and the *Ameto* (2.10). A new unity is created, however, through the informing idea of a 'human comedy' and through the use of a structuring frame (*cornice*), perhaps of Eastern derivation. This recounts how a group of three young men and seven young women flee the *plague raging in *Florence in 1348, and find refuge for two weeks below Fiesole. They spend their days on pleasure, with walks, dancing, song and, finally, storytelling. Every afternoon each member of the group in turn tells a *novella*, apart from Fridays and Saturdays, which are given over to religious observance and personal hygiene. Hence a hundred tales are told in all over ten days of storytelling.

The *Decameron* portrays the society of the Italian *communes in the autumnal phase of medieval civilization. The emphasis falls on the resourcefulness and vitality that had led in the 13th c. to Italian economic dominance in Europe and the Mediterranean world. But this extraordinary epic of the mercantile class (to which Boccaccio himself belonged) is depicted according to well-established aesthetic criteria of the time. Not only does Boccaccio employ stylistic refinements such as the *cursus* and rhyming prose, but he gives his highly varied and individual creations an exemplary moral value. The 100 stories represent an ideal human journey, beginning with the reproof of vice in day 1 and ending with the exaltation of virtue in day 10. In between there are confrontations with the three great forces which contemporaries viewed as instruments of Divine Providence in the world— Fortune (days 2 and 3), Love (days 4 and 5), Intelligence (days 6, 7, and 8), with day 9 figuring as a transition to day 10.

Boccaccio recasts the themes which had dominated his earlier writings, giving them now the aura of a sequence of 'triumphs', or a 'legend of Everyman', of universal value and significance. There was no precedent for this in ancient and medieval

story-telling, and the *Decameron* was rapidly recognized as the masterpiece which, for the West, embraces all narrative possibilities. Just a few decades after its composition, it was known in most of Europe either in the original or in translation. No other great work in a modern vernacular enjoyed the same success. [VB]

Decameron, ed. V. Branca (1997). See V. Branca, *Boccaccio medievale* (1997).

DE CARLO, ANDREA (1952–) came to prominence with his first novel, *Treno di panna* (1981), endorsed by *Calvino, who praised the cult of surface consciousness in this account of a young man trying to make it in Los Angeles. His second novel, *Uccelli da gabbia e da voliera* (1982), developed a similar plot, though set in *Milan. After two less successful novels, *Macno* (1984) and *Yucatan* (1986), he produced two ambitious works in *Due di due* (1989), an attempt at providing the novel of the sixties generation, and *Tecniche di seduzione* (1991), a love story containing a critique of contemporary society. *Arco d'amore* and *UTO* were published in 1995. [MMcL]

DECEMBRIO, ANGELO (?1415–after 1467). *Humanist younger brother of Pier Candido *Decembrio, and a pupil of *Guarino da Verona. He was at the court of Leonello d'*Este in *Ferrara from 1441 to 1450. This provided the setting for his best-known work, the fictional *dialogues *Politiae literariae*. The interlocutors, who include Leonello and Guarino, discuss all kinds of literary matters, from building an ideal public library to detecting forgeries and unravelling classical metre. The dialogue promotes classical learning only and dismisses medieval authors, including the vernacular poets and narrators who formed the backbone of *court culture. [LAP]

DECEMBRIO, PIER CANDIDO (c.1392–1477). Eminent *humanist, born in Pavia, who spent much of his career in *Milan, serving first Filippo Maria *Visconti (of whom he wrote an informative *biography) and then the *Sforza. He also spent periods in *Rome, *Naples, and *Ferrara. His historical writings include a panegyric of Milan and of Viscontean princely rule, composed in 1435 in response to Leonardo *Bruni's similar celebration of *Florence and its republicanism. In 1441 he completed the revision of his father Uberto's literal *translation of Plato's *Republic*, which he tried to make into a blueprint for

Christian princes. He translated various other Greek texts into Latin and some Latin into Italian. He also wrote philosophical treatises, letters, and a few compositions in vernacular Lombard. A life of *Petrarch, regularly printed in 16th-c. editions of the *Canzoniere and mistakenly attributed to *Antonio da Tempo, is almost certainly by Decembrio.

[LAP]

DE CESPEDES, ALBA (1911–97). Novelist. The daughter of a Cuban diplomat and an Italian mother, she spent her early life in various countries before returning to live in *Rome where she had been born. Her early stories appeared in *Il Messaggero*, followed by a first collection, *L'anima degli altri*, in 1935, and a collection of poems, *Prigionie*, a year later. Her first novel, *Nessuna torna indietro* (1938), depicts a group of female students living and studying in Rome. It attracted widespread interest, but its forthright *feminist voice meant it fell foul of *Fascist *censorship.

A courageous and politically committed figure, De Cespedes joined the *Resistance and later broadcast from Bari under the pseudonym Clorinda for the clandestine station 'L'Italia combatte'. Her novel *Dalla parte di lei* (1949) looks back to Rome during the German Occupation. In 1944 she founded a mainly literary journal, *Il Mercurio*, and continued to write as a cultural *journalist after it folded in 1948. She is best known for *Quaderno proibito* (1952), the title of which refers to the diary of its 40-year old protagonist, who kicks over her respectable marriage, and *Il rimorso* (1962), which analyses through an exchange of letters and a diary the contradictions and conflicts faced by intellectuals in 1950s Rome.

[AHC]

DE CHIRICO, ANDREA, see SAVINIO, ALBERTO.

DE CHIRICO, GIORGIO (1888–1978). Painter, who studied art in Athens (Greek mythological images recurred in his later work) before moving to Munich (1906–10), Italy, and then Paris (1911–14). In *Ferrara during *World War I he met Carlo *Carrà and together they founded *pittura metafisica*, which aimed to go beyond the limits of conventional reality and whose most significant programmatic statement was *Noi metafisici*, written by De Chirico for their first group show in *Rome in 1919.

[DF]

DE CURTIS, ANTONIO, see TOTÒ.

DE DOMINIS, MARCANTONIO (?1560– 1624) came from a noble Dalmatian family, entered and left the *Jesuit order, was a bishop, and taught at Brescia and *Padua before becoming a Protestant and moving to England. His *De republica ecclesiastica* (1617–22) argues in learned detail and at great length against the primacy of the Church of Rome. In 1619 he edited the first edition of Paolo *Sarpi's *Istoria del Concilio di Trento*, to which he added a preface, and in 1622 he returned to Italy, rejoining the Roman church. He was tried for *heresy in 1624, and died during the proceedings. His body was burned in Rome's Campo de' fiori as though he were a heretic. [See also COUNTER-REFORMATION.]

[PBD]

DE FILIPPI, FILIPPO, see DARWINISM.

DE FILIPPO, EDUARDO (1900–84), playwright and actor-director from *Naples, whose forty plays are rooted in the life and language of his city. His use of *dialect, sometimes mixed with Italian, had nothing to do with folklore, which he detested, and all to do with *realism. His plays depict the working and middle classes; they draw not only on *Pirandellian themes of reality and illusion, mask and face, but also on the popular Neapolitan dramatists Raffaele *Viviani and Eduardo *Scarpetta, and on entertainment forms such as the music hall and vaudeville. The family is the focus of his compassionate vision, and family ties and responsibilities are often presented as the sole thread of certainty in a world of crumbling moral values, most notably in *Filumena Marturano* (1946).

He formed a number of companies with his brother Peppino and sister Titina, and frequently acted in and directed his own plays. The De Filippo companies were among Italy's best loved, and Eduardo gained fame and respect as an actor as well as playwright. Despite the inherent problems of the language of his texts, the warmth of his tragicomic vision has attracted translators: the London production of *Sabato, domenica e lunedì* (1959) won the London drama critics' award in 1973. Eduardo also wrote a volume of poetry and several film scripts, and directed the plays of leading European dramatists, including Pirandello and Molière. [See also DIALECT WRITING; THEATRE, 2.]

[JAL]

Cantata dei giorni pari; Cantata dei giorni dispari (1971–6). See M. Giammusso, *Vita di Eduardo* (1993); A. Barsotti, *Eduardo drammaturgo* (1995).

DE FRANCHI, STEFANO (1714–85). Noble and man of fashion, who was the foremost writer of *Genoese verse of his time. His poems, collected in *Ro chittarin o sae straffoggi dra muza* ('The garblings of the muses', 1772), range from the patriotic to the erotic. With the help of numerous collaborators, he brought out in 1755 a Genoese *translation of Torquato *Tasso's *Gerusalemme liberata.* [JMAL]

DE GAMERRA, GIOVANNI (1743–1803). Prolific author of tearful *comedies, born in Livorno and active in *Milan and Vienna, where he enjoyed the protection of *Metastasio. Some plays border on necrophilia, notably *Luisa e Trifour* (in his *Novo teatro* of 1789), and most imitate foreign models—Diderot in *Il padre di famiglia*, D'Arnaud in *I solitarî* (1770), etc. His *libretto *Lucio Silla* was set to music by Mozart (1772). [FF]

DE GASPERI, ALCIDE (1881–1954). Catholic politician. He became leader of the *Partito popolare* in 1923. A founder of the *Christian Democrat Party, he was Prime Minister in a key phase in the history of the Republic (December 1945–53), taking Italy into NATO and championing a role for her in Europe. [PC]

De gli heroici furori, see BRUNO, GIORDANO.

DE GREGORI, FRANCESCO, see CANTAUTORI.

DE GUBERNATIS, ANGELO (1840–1913). Folklorist, orientalist, and literary historian, who founded and directed the *Rivista europea, Rivista orientale*, and *Rivista delle tradizioni popolari italiane*. He was responsible for a *Dizionario degli scrittori contemporanei* (1879), and a *Storia universale della letteratura* (1883–5). He also wrote historical verse dramas. [See also DICTIONARIES OF ITALIAN LITERATURE; FOLK AND POPULAR LITERATURE; HISTORIES OF ITALIAN LITERATURE.] [PBarn]

DEI, BENEDETTO (1418–92), *Florentine annalist and traveller whose works, including his *Cronica* (1470–80) and *Storia fiorentina* (completed 1490), belong to an older, vernacular, historiographical tradition untouched by *humanism [see CHRONICLES]. From his self-imposed exile in northern Italy after 1480 came the hundreds of newsletters, entertaining still for their obsessive eccentricity, which his contemporaries prized. [FWK]

Dei delitti e delle pene (1764). *Beccaria's celebrated work on penal and judicial reform and a masterpiece of the *Lombard *Enlightenment. It was published anonymously, and placed on the *Index in 1766. But it was immediately acclaimed by the French *philosophes*, and was soon translated into French, English, Spanish, German, Greek, and Russian. [GLCB]

Dei doveri dell'uomo, see MAZZINI, GIUSEPPE.

DEI GASLINI, MARIO, see COLONIAL LITERATURE.

Dei sepolcri (1807). *Foscolo's most famous poem, though only 295 unrhymed *hendecasyllables long, is also his richest and most complex. Occasioned by a *Napoleonic edict prohibiting burial within city limits, it moves from reflections on the imagined bond between individuals and the dead they have loved, to the role of graves as means by which the living preserve the values and achievements of their nation and of humanity as a whole, a role which eventually is taken over by great poetry, as exemplified by Homer's *Iliad*. *Neoclassical in its idiom, but *romantic in its compression, depth of feeling, and unexpected changes of direction, it sets the transforming power of the imagination against materialist rationalism in ways that anticipate and bear comparison with *Leopardi. It is addressed to Ippolito *Pindemonte, and was probably influenced by his unfinished *Cimiteri*. Pindemonte replied with a verse epistle which was published with Foscolo's poem in a second 1807 edition. [PH]

DE JENNARO, PIETRO IACOPO (1436–1508). *Humanist and poet. He was born into the *Neapolitan nobility and, like his peer Giuliano *Perleoni, combined literary activity with administrative and diplomatic posts at the *court of Ferrante of *Aragon. A member of the *Accademia Pontaniana, De Jennaro's humanist interests are developed in his minor vernacular works: the *Clepsimoginon* (c.1470), a poem on the love of Helen and Paris dedicated to Ercole I d'*Este; the *Plutopenia* (1470), a dialogue between Wealth and Poverty; and the *Opera de li huomini illustri* (1504).

De Jennaro's most famous work, his *lyric *canzoniere* for an unknown Bianca, was written between 1464 and 1486, and contains amorous, political, religious, and encomiastic poems. Like his contemporaries, De Jennaro strove to write in a language less influenced by local *dialect than earlier literature, a task in which he was only partially successful. The *Pastorale* (1508), begun in 1482 and preserved in three successive versions, relates the author's loss of a feudal territory, allegorized as the exile of the shepherd Gianuario. De Jennaro's last work, the *Sei etate de la vita humana*, in six sets of *capitoli* [see CANTO] in *terza rima*, is interesting mainly for its portraits of the author's Neapolitan contemporaries.   [ELM]

DE LAURENTIIS, DINO, see CINEMA.

DEL BENE, SENNUCCIO (*c*.1275–1349). *Florentine poet. His White *Guelf politics led to his exile, probably in 1302, but certainly by 1312, when he supported *Henry VII's invasion of Italy. He found employment at the *papal court in *Avignon (1316–26), but was later able to return to Florence. In Avignon he became a close friend of *Petrarch, who addressed several *sonnets to him and composed a lament on his death (*Canz.* 287). Sennuccio himself is a late follower of the *dolce stil novo*. Two of his fourteen surviving poems are on the unusual theme of love in old age. There is also a *canzone* on the death of Henry VII praising the emperor's virtues.   [JP & JMS]

DEL BUONO, ORESTE (1923–). Novelist and *journalist. His early *autobiographical novels, *Racconto d'inverno* (1945) and *La parte difficile* (1947), are impressive accounts of imprisonment in Germany during *World War II and the difficulties of returning afterwards to normal life. A second stage in his career saw a more openly experimental style, much influenced by the French *nouveau roman* in *Né vivere, né morire* (1963), for instance. He has *translated widely from French and English, including Maupassant, Gide, Wilde, and Walpole. He has also played a vigorous part in debates about mass culture and modern history and politics in Italy.   [PC]

D'ELCI, ANGELO MARIA (1754–1824). *Florentine nobleman and satirist. An admirer and imitator of Juvenal, whose themes he echoes in his *satires (1817), he also emulated and attacked *Alfieri and opposed innovation in all forms. His works were edited by his grandson G. B. *Niccolini.   [JMAL]

DELEDDA, GRAZIA (1871–1936). Prolific and important *novelist, who also wrote short stories, essays, plays, and stories for children.

She was born and grew up in *Sardinia, not progressing beyond elementary school but soon beginning to contribute romantic stories to magazines 'per signorine'. She is often seen as a characteristically Sardinian writer, and the island, its traditions, and its people certainly loom large in her work. In 1895 she published a study of the popular traditions of Nuoro, where she was born. But she moved to *Rome in 1900 on marrying a Roman civil servant and lived there for the rest of her life, staying rather on the edge of literary circles but contributing to some reviews and magazines.

Her mature work begins with *Il vecchio della montagna* (1900). Subsequent novels, such as *Elias Portolu* (1904), *Canne al vento* (1913), and *Marianna Sirca* (1916), treat themes of universal significance and have much more than regional interest, even though they portray the archaic society and the desolate landscape of Sardinia with the depth and accuracy of the best Italian *veristi*. Deledda's characters are often isolated beings, at odds with society and their families. Love is characteristically violent and antisocial, though the infringement of social codes leads only to self-punishment or self-destruction. In *L'edera* (1908), for instance, the protagonist, Annesa, commits murder out of a misguided love and lives the rest of her life tormented by guilt. At best characters find solace in conventional religion, or alternatively in something more akin to a philosophical pantheism.

Some works were adapted quite early for the *cinema. In the 1916 film of *Cenere* (1904) Eleonora Duse played the part of the self-sacrificing mother. By this stage Deledda was highly popular, and producing novels almost annually. She was awarded the Nobel prize for literature in 1926 for *La madre* (1920).   [UJF]

See M. Miccinesi, *Grazia Deledda* (1975); A. Dolfi, *Grazia Deledda* (1979).

DELFICO, MELCHIORRE (1744–1835). Intellectual with physiocratic leanings. Born near Teramo, he was active principally in *Naples. With other reformers he attempted, from the 1780s onwards, to break the stanglehold of baronial privilege in the Kingdom of Naples. Sympathetic to the *Napoleonic Parthenopean Republic, he later held important posts under Murat (1808–15) and in subsequent administrations.   [GLCB]

Della Casa, Giovanni

DELFINI, ANTONIO, see SURREALISM.

DELFINO, GIOVANNI (1617–99). *Venetian writer. He was cardinal and patriarch of Aquileia and played an active part in the public life of the Republic. He wrote rather conventional and pedantic *tragedies—*Cleopatra, Medoro* (from the *Orlando furioso*), *Lucrezia*, and *Creso*, this last reflecting his philosophical interests in the nature of the soul. None was published until after his death. He contributed to the controversy over the propriety of rhyme in tragedy, and himself used less rhyme in his later works. He was also a member of the Accademia della *Crusca.

[FC]

DEL GIUDICE, DANIELE (1949–). One of the most interesting and refined of contemporary writers. Born in *Rome, he now lives mainly in *Venice, working as a consultant for *publishers such as *Einaudi, and addicted to travel and the study of science. He came to prominence with his first two novels; *Lo stadio di Wimbledon* (1983) recounts an attempt to reconstruct the figure of a mysterious intellectual of a previous generation (the Triestine Roberto *Bazlen); *Atlante occidentale* (1985) centres on the complex, silent relationship between a famous writer and a young scientist. His easily translatable style, geometrical order, and passion for science mark him as a member of the generation influenced by *Calvino, with traces of the dark elements in Conrad, the irrational of Kafka, and the unreal of Handke.

Difficult to summarize in terms of plot, his novels and short stories centre on the search for new emotional horizons, mapping out a range of feelings that privileges manly friendships on an archetypal father/son model. Del Giudice constantly emphasizes sight, as an organ, an instrument or a metaphor, and its counterpart, blindness, in stories about war and aviation that bring into play the perspective of aerial flight as well as chance, error, and the unexpected, all in the effort to give form to the invisible atoms of which matter is made, to achieve a kind of knowledge that lies beyond normal sight or vision. *Staccando l'ombra da terra* (1994) and *Mania* (1997) successfully fuse the brevity of the *racconto* with some of the qualities of the novel. Here Del Giudice has reached maturity, with a style that is lucid, concise, always focused, but also full of emotion, making him the most assured writer of fiction of his generation [see NOVELLA and RACCONTO, 2].

[AD]

DE LIBERO, LIBERO (1906–81). Poet. His first collection, *Solstizio* (1934), and those that immediately followed show the influence of *Ungaretti, whom he knew in *Rome, though his *hermetic poetry has been felt to have a *surrealist quality. His work as a whole looks back elegiacally to his childhood in Ciociaria, south of Rome, and recalls the history of his family there. A greater civic consciousness, springing from his experience of *World War II, is evident in later collections, such as *Banchetto* (1949), though in *Ascolta la Ciociaria* (1953) he returns to the landscape which originally inspired him.

[JJ]

DELLA CASA, GIOVANNI (1503–56). Poet and author of the famous treatise on manners, *Il Galateo*. He was born into a *Florentine merchant family and received his early *humanist *education in *Rome, before returning to Florence some time after 1510 to continue his studies. From 1524 to 1532 he studied *law at *Bologna and Latin and Greek at *Padua, where he also met Pietro *Bembo and established frendships with Ludovico *Beccadelli, Carlo *Gualteruzzi, and Francesco Maria *Molza. He eventually embarked on a professional career in the Church. In 1544 he became Archbishop of Benevento and was nominated papal nuncio to *Venice, where he tried unsuccessfully in 1549 to establish the basis for literary censorship with a list of *heretical books, which anticipates the official *Index of 1569.

His own literary output, which included pornographic *sonnets, was probably the reason for his failure to obtain the coveted cardinal's hat in 1555. Ironically, his poems were eventually put on the Papal Index of 1590. He is best known for *Il Galateo ovvero dei costumi* (1558), written at the suggestion of Bishop Galeazzo Florimonte, after whom it was named. Cast as a direct address to a young man and enlivened by anecdotes from *Boccaccio, it offers advice on topics such as etiquette, social behaviour, and storytelling. It was aimed at an aristocratic readership and was an immediate international best-seller. Della Casa is also one of the major *lyric poets of the 16th c.: he developed the language, imagery, and style of the *Petrarchan *sonnet and *canzone, with innovations in the use of enjambement and an impressive seriousness of tone (*gravitas*), voicing a sense of worldly vanity that seems closely linked with his own failed aspirations.

[PLR]

See A. Santosuosso, *Vita di Giovanni della Casa* (1979).

179

Della dissimulazione onesta, see ACCETTO, TORQUATO.

Della famiglia, Leon Battista *Alberti's first and most substantial vernacular work, was revolutionary in using the vernacular for a genre, the ethical *dialogue, which had hitherto been the preserve of *humanist Latin (he justifies this in the Proem to book 3). The topics of each book are similar to those treated in other classical and humanist dialogues (book 1: on *education; book 2: on marriage and careers; book 3: on husbandry (*masserizia*); book 4: on friendship). However they are given a contemporary perspective, and offer a synthesis of classical erudition and the practical, often bitter, experience of the Alberti family. Throughout, the work endorses Alberti's insistence on *virtù* in the face of even the harshest *fortuna*.   [MMcL]

DELLA LANA, IACOPO, see DANTE COMMENTARIES.

Della pittura, see ALBERTI, LEON BATTISTA.

DELLA PORTA, GIAMBATTISTA (*c.*1535–1615). Natural philosopher and dramatist. Born into a *Neapolitan noble family, where both his uncle and brother had shown interest in the study of antiquities and the natural world, he spent his life in the study of natural *magic and natural philosophy. His encyclopedic interests led to works on ciphers, mnemonics (*L'arte del ricordare*, 1566), physiognomy (*De humana physiognonomia*, 1586), mathematics (*Elementorum curvilineorum*, 1610), agriculture (*Pomarium*, 1583, and *Olivetum*, 1584), hydraulics, the art of prophecy, chemistry, alchemy, and fortification.

He had a restless personality and made frequent journeys throughout Europe, which were described in the *Villae* (1592). He was twice denounced before the Neapolitan *Inquisition for his interests in *astrology and magic. The planned publication of his *Fisionomia umana* (1592) also brought him to the notice of the Venetian Inquisition. His fame led to an invitation in 1579 by Cardinal Luigi d'*Este to develop his scientific research in *Rome. In his youth he had set up his own Accademia dei Segreti in Naples, in 1610 he was admitted to the Accademia dei *Lincei, and in 1611 he was a founder member of the Accademia degli *Oziosi in Naples. His major work was the *Magia naturalis*, published in 1558 with a further expanded edition in twenty books in 1589. He dedicated and presented this work to King Philip II of Spain along with a book on cryptography, *De furtivis literarum notis vulgo de Ziferis* (1563). He *translated Plautus and wrote fourteen *comedies in the 16th-c. tradition influenced by Plautus and Terence, and several *tragedies. His first play was printed in 1589 and, though many were left unpublished, a number of his comedies were performed both privately and at *court. His contribution to the *theatre lies in his lively style and unusual plots.   [PLR]

See L. G. Clubb, *Giambattista della Porta: Dramatist* (1965).

DELLA SCALA. Also known as the Scaligeri, the Della Scala family were prominent in Verona from the 12th c., acquiring the lordship or *signoria* of the city in 1277. Especially under Cangrande I (1291–1329) they greatly extended their dominions. Following defeat by a rival coalition (1337–9), their rule contracted to Verona and Vicenza, from which they were expelled by Giangaleazzo *Visconti (1387). Their appreciation of magnificence can be seen in the residences and tomb monuments they built in Verona. Confirmed Ghibellines (see GUELFS AND GHIBELLINES), Bartolomeo (d.1304) and Cangrande were held to have provided refuge for *Dante, as celebrated in *Paradiso* 17.70–93. Dante's bond of friendship with Cangrande is attested to by *Boccaccio in his *biography of the poet, although contention still surrounds the possible dedication of the *Paradiso* to the ruler. The dynasty also attracted the praise of lesser writers, though in hostile cities (*Padua, *Florence) their expansionist rule could be identified with tyranny.   [JEL & SJM]

DELLA SETA, LOMBARDO (d.1390). *Paduan *humanist and friend of *Petrarch, who entrusted his writings to him on his death. He transcribed many of them and completed the *De viris illustribus* by adding twelve new lives. We have three of his letters, one of which (entitled *De bono solitudinis*) is on the typically Petrarchan theme of the benefits of solitude.   [MP]

Della tirannide, see ALFIERI, VITTORIO.

DELLA TORRE, GIOVANNI, see ITALIAN WRITERS IN SWITZERLAND.

DELLA VALLE, FEDERICO (*c.*1560–1628) was the greatest tragedian of 17th-c. Italy. Apart from a handful of masterpieces he left behind few clues about his life and activities. In the late 1580s and until the death of Caterina of Savoy in 1597, he worked as administrator at the *Savoy court in *Turin, and then in the service of the Spanish governor. Later he moved to *Milan, where he continued revising his theatrical works, published two funeral orations (one on Philip II of Spain), and eventually ended his days.

His first dramatic work (staged in 1595 but published posthumously in 1629) was the *tragicomedy *Adelonda*, a reworking in blank verse of Euripides' *Iphigenia in Tauris*, beloved of the *Counter-Reformation. The play centres on the Greek prince Mirmirano's search for his shipwrecked fiancée, Adelonda, on an island inhabited and ruled by fierce Amazon women, where any visiting male must be sacrificed to a tyrannical deity. The influence of Torquato *Tasso's and Battista *Guarini's *pastoral modes is evident in the conflicts between pleasure and pain, life and death, divine and human loves, appearance and reality. But the work is shot through with a strong dose of Catholic political thought, not only in the religious totalitarianism implicit in the island's law, but in the reconciliation, influenced by Giovanni *Botero's *Della ragion di stato* (1589), between divine and human religious and political systems.

Political interest takes centre stage in Della Valle's next work, *La Reina di Scotia*, first drafted in 1591, redrafted in 1595, and finally published in a third version in 1628. The beheading of the Catholic Mary Queen of Scots at the insistence of Elizabeth I drew strong reactions from the Catholic world. Della Valle portrays the last hours in prison of a saintly and dignified queen, who gains tragic stature in the course of the play, first hoping for a reprieve and then stoically resigning herself to her fate. Through the subtle alternation of seven-syllable and eleven-syllable lines, the play captures the shift in the queen's feelings, providing an analysis of the inner workings of faith in a hostile environment. Psychological disclosure is facilitated by the presence of the queen's maid as confidante, and a female chorus that reflects the fear and pity of the queen's situation. In a style that looks back to Tasso's *Torrismondo* and forward to Racine's dramatic works, the play is concentrated in subject matter and in linguistic range: through successive versions Della Valle achieved a spare style, limited in lexis, and removed from the everyday, in which certain fundamental images can resonate.

In his two later *tragedies Della Valle continues the motifs of this play, in plots based on biblical

subjects. *Iudit* and *Ester* (both published in 1627) show humanity pitted against the ineluctable and inscrutable forces of divine will. The topsy-turviness of the universe is accentuated in these two works by the fact that it is not the eponymous heroines who are ultimately tragic, but rather their male enemies. And though Della Valle's strong female characters invite a *feminist reading, the women appear as the instruments of a divine power that is in the end absolute. [See also THEATRE, 1.]

[PBD]

Opere, ed. M. G. Stassi (1995). See F. Croce, *Federico della Valle* (1965); L. Sanguineti White, *Dal detto alla figura: le tragedie di Federico della Valle* (1992).

DELLA VALLE, PIETRO (1586–1652). *Roman who dedicated much of his life to travelling, after an early career as poet, musician, and *opera scenery designer. He recounted his twelve-year voyage to the East in his *Viaggi*, in the form of fifty-four letters addressed to the *Neapolitan *humanist and doctor Mario Schipano. Published from 1650 to 1663, the letters contain precious documentation, not only on customs but also on important archaeological matters. Della Valle brought considerable learning to his work. He also wrote a grammar of Turkish in seven books. After returning from his travels, he took up his earlier career as composer and *librettist, writing a theoretical work, *Della musica dell'età nostra* (1640), against the excessive and word-obscuring polyphony of earlier music, and in favour of the new fashion for instrumental solos. In his endless search for knowledge, his restless quest for experience, and his modernism, Della Valle is an exemplary figure of his age [see QUERELLE DES ANCIENS ET DES MODERNES].

[PBD]

DELLA VOLPE, GALVANO (1895–1968). Philosopher who studied at the University of *Bologna and was subsequently professor of the history of philosophy in Messina from 1938 to 1965. He was influenced by *Gentile, but broke with his and *Croce's *idealism in favour of left-wing *Fascist positions in the late 1930s. He joined the *Communist Party in 1944 and published various strongly *Marxist works, including *Logica come scienza positiva* (1950) and *Rousseau e Marx* (1960). During the 1950s and early 1960s, at a time of particularly rich dialogue between intellectuals and the Communist Party, but also of political nervousness about splits and factions, he exerted a shaping

influence on younger thinkers like Lucio Colletti. His importance for aesthetics lies principally in *Critica del gusto* (1960), which proposes a re-evaluation of the semantic aspect of literature based on a firm belief in the rational character of the sign.
[MPC]

DELL'ORO, ERMINIA, see POST-MODERNISM.

Del principe e delle lettere, see ALFIERI, VITTORIO.

Del romanzo storico, see MANZONI, ALESSANDRO.

DE LUCA, GIUSEPPE (1898–1962). Priest and writer on a variety of religious and literary topics. As one of the **Frontespizio* group in the 1930s, he argued fervently against the irreligious-ness of *idealism and bourgeois culture. He was one of the founders of the *Edizioni di storia e letteratura* in 1942, and went on to edit anthologies of early Italian religious writers. [CO'B]

DE MARCHI, EMILIO (1851–1901). Popular *Milanese novelist, who spent most of his life in his native city as a teacher and educational administra-tor. In fiction he was a follower of *Manzoni and French naturalism, and saw literature as a vehicle for moral and spiritual improvement. His narra-tives take as their subject matter the lives of poor and humble people from the petty bourgeoisie and working classes, who regularly meet defeat in a cor-rupt and immoral society. His intention is to repre-sent the psychological reality of individuals who, because of their ignorance of the way society works, are incapable of realizing their desires. De Marchi's fundamentally conservative approach to social reality prevents him from imagining any other form of society than that based on traditional class struc-tures. His benign and condescending humour, reminiscent of Manzoni, conveys the moral and intellectual superiority of someone who believes his judgement to be infallible.

He gained popularity with his first novel, *Il cappello del prete* (1888), the story of a petty aristo-crat whose remorse for having killed a priest leads him to reveal his guilt. His best-known novel, *Demetrio Pianelli* (1890), is the story of an honest office worker who, after the suicide of his corrupt stepbrother, falls in love with his widow. Demetrio is portrayed as a humble hero who fights a losing battle against a suffocating social reality. Following an attempt to defend his sister-in-law's honour

against the advances of his superior, he is forced to move to another city, where, in denial of his own feelings, he arranges the marriage between her and her wealthy cousin. The following novel, *Arabella* (1893), is based on the figure of Demetrio's niece, who is also a victim of the depravity of her milieu. Other novels include *Il redivivo* (1895–6), *Giacomo idealista* (1897) (in which the defeated protagonist is now a young philosophy student), and *Col fuoco non si scherza* (1900). He is recognized as the writer of the first Italian novels to be serialized in daily newspapers. His other works include a respected *translation of La Fontaine's fables. He also edited *La buona parola*, a series of short manuals designed to teach the urban masses their duties and rights, to which he himself contributed twenty-one volumes.
[RSD]

See M. C. Gorria, *Il primo De Marchi fra storia, cronaca e poesia* (1963); V. Spinazzola, *Emilio De Marchi romanziere popolare* (1971).

DE MARTINO, ERNESTO (1908–65). Histor-ian, ethnologist, and *folklorist. Initially influenced by *Croce, De Martino's work spanned a vast array of topics including magic, death, shamanism, and the Apocalypse. His pioneering studies of the South involved extensive fieldwork. He is best known for his work on songs and the 'cult of the tarantula' in Puglia in *La terra del rimorso* (1961), in which he argued that the dance provoked by the (imagined) bite of the spider could only be under-stood in the context of the complex sexual mores of the South. His work has frequently led to compari-sons with Carlo *Levi, though De Martino himself criticized Levi's approach. [PC]

DE MAURO, TULLIO (1932–). Professor of linguistics in *Rome, author of important studies on semantics, including *Introduzione alla semantica* (1965), *Senso e significato* (1971), and *Minisemanti-ca* (1982). His most influential work is the *Storia linguistica dell'Italia unita* (1963), which showed that in 1861 only about 2.5 per cent of the popula-tion could use Italian, and illustrated the dramatic implications of this situation. Another important work is the *Grande dizionario dell'uso* (1999–2000). De Mauro is also committed to questions of *edu-cational policy and has been Minister for Education (2000–1). [GCL]

DE MEIS, ANGELO CAMILLO (1817–91). Quixotic polymath and writer. Born near Chieti, he studied medicine at *Naples University, where he also followed the lectures of *De Sanctis. He became a physiologist and historian of medicine, who tried to reconcile the subject matter, methods, and history of the natural sciences with the Hegelian system. He defended philosophical *idealism against *positivism in the autobiographical *epistolary novel *Dopo la laurea* (1868), and further elaborated his thought in the dialogues of *Deus creavit* (1869). His conservative, monarchical treatise *Il sovrano* (1868) led him into a polemic with the democrats, most notably *Carducci.

[JD]

Demetrio Pianelli, see DE MARCHI, EMILIO.

Democrazia cristiana, see CHRISTIAN DEMOCRATS.

DENINA, CARLO (1731–1813). Italy's foremost exponent of *Enlightenment *historiography. A *Piedmontese, he published his *Discorso sulle vicende d'ogni letteratura* in 1760 in *Turin, where in 1770 his *Storia delle rivoluzioni d'Italia* earned him a university chair, though he soon lost it through outspoken opposition to aristocratic frivolity and clerical indolence. From 1782 he wrote prolifically under the patronage of Frederick II of Prussia, producing among much else a substantial group of works on Germany. His *Réponse à la question: Que doit-on à l'Espagne?* (1786) defends *Spain and its culture. [JMAL]

DE NORES, GIASONE (?1530–90) took part in a dispute with Battista *Guarini over the *Pastor fido*. Influenced by the *Counter-Reformation, he objected in particular to Guarini's mixing of tragic and comic genres. He also wrote commentaries on *Aristotle's *Rhetoric* and *Horace's *Art of Poetry*. [See also COMEDY; LITERARY THEORY, 2; TRAGICOMEDY; TRAGEDY.] [DG]

De otio religioso, see PETRARCH, FRANCESCO.

DEPERO, FORTUNATO (1892–1960) joined the *Futurist movement when he moved to *Rome from Rovereto in 1914, painting brilliantly coloured abstract symbolist canvases based on natural motifs. He designed *theatrical sets, wrote free-word and visual poetry, declaimed at Futurist soirées, and composed, together with the painter Giacomo *Balla, the influential manifesto *Ricostruzione futurista dell'universo* (1915). After *World War I, he moved progressively into applied art (typography, textiles, advertising), while continuing to paint. He produced a volume of *parole in libertà* poems, *Liriche radiofoniche* (1934).

[CGW]

DE PISIS, FILIPPO (1896–1956). Painter and poet. He was born into the *Ferrarese aristocracy, and changed his name (Luigi Filippo Tibertelli) to that of a *condottiere* ancestor. A friend of *Govoni and, through him, of *De Chirico and his circle, he himself first published the *Crepuscular prose poems of *Canti della Croara* (1916). Most of the interwar years were given over to painting and spent outside Italy. Further volumes of now anguished metaphysical poems appeared in 1939–43. A nervous disorder led to his spending his last years in a clinic near Monza. [JJ]

De remediis utriusque fortune. Latin work by *Petrarch, begun in 1354 but completed between 1360 and 1366, on how to deal with both good and bad fortune. The first of its two parts contains 122 *dialogues between Ratio, Gaudium, and Spes, and deals with how one should behave at times of good fortune; the second contains 131 dialogues between Ratio, Dolor, and Timor, and deals with the behaviour appropriate to adverse fortune. It is a practical manual of moral philosophy, and was widely read until the 17th c. Today the full Latin text can only be found in the reprinted 1581 Basle edition of Petrarch's works. [MP]

DE ROBERTIS, GIUSEPPE (1888–1963). Influential *literary critic. Originally from Matera, he attended university in *Florence, and later became editor of *La *Voce* (1914–16). He pioneered a form of aesthetic criticism which was in harmony with the new poetry published in *La Voce* by writers like *Soffici, *Sbarbaro, and *Jahier, and especially with the 'frammenti' of Arturo *Onofri. Sharing *Croce's distinction between 'poesia' and 'non-poesia', but more personal in approach, his art of 'saper leggere' involved focusing on the most vital and lyrically intense parts of a work and experiencing them deeply. Much of his extensive later criticism was devoted to *Leopardi and *Ungaretti. [SV]

DE ROBERTO, FEDERICO (1861–1927) is the author of the *historical novel *I *viceré*, one of the most important works of Italian *verismo. Born in *Naples, he moved as a child with his family to Catania, where he lived practically all of his life, working as a *journalist and writer. Like *Capuana and the young *Verga, he too observed the psychological makeup of his characters in the light of the *positivist science of his times. But in contrast to his older contemporaries, he emphasized less the power of human passions and desires than their relation to an inner world of illusion and deception in which, he believed, they originated. His collections of short stories, *La sorte* (1887), *Documenti umani* (1888), *Processi verbali* (1890), and *L'albero della scienza* (1890), all explore the psychological dimension of his characters' actions. His first novel, *Ermanno Raeli* (1889), is largely autobiographical, while *L'illusione* (1891) is devoted to a female protagonist and her illusion of love.

His masterpiece, *I viceré* (published in *Milan in 1894 in two volumes), tells the story of the Uzeda family, the descendants of an ancient Spanish dynasty of viceroys of *Sicily. Set in the period between 1855 and 1882, which witnessed the passage from *Bourbon rule to *Unification and parliamentary democracy, the novel recounts the strategies and intrigues employed by the landed aristocracy to bring the *Risorgimento's revolutionary impetus under its control so that it could continue to rule in the new Italy. Following the basic tenets of naturalism [see REALISM], De Roberto places the narrator of the story outside the action and historical events recounted. He thus surveys the numerous family members in their personal lives and interrelations, creating a polyphony of voices, each intended to express variations on the novel's themes of greed, violence, and insanity. The Uzedas are depicted, in their will to power, desperation, and cruelty, as representatives of a race that has degenerated into madness. Yet, however delirious and blind to social and political realities, they are capable of adapting to the new order, accommodating their economic interests with those of the bourgeoisie to retain their privileges and capacity to rule. De Roberto's wholly negative message is that history is monotonous repetition; what looks like change is only an illusion: the nobility will always find a way of being in control. It is a message meant to undermine bourgeois belief in social progress by placing the reader before a grotesque world of demented desire. With *I viceré*, De Roberto pushes the scientific induction and determinism of naturalism to their limits. The intensity of his polemic distorts the object under examination, causing the emphasis to fall in the final instance not on the real historical existence of the Sicilian aristocracy, but rather on madness and paradox. For this reason,

the novel influenced *Pirandello's *I *vecchi e i giovani* and Giuseppe *Tomasi di Lampedusa's *Il *gattopardo*.

De Roberto's final novel, *L'imperio*, planned as a sequel to *I viceré*, was not completed. It concentrated on the public and political life of *Rome, viewed through the life of the reactionary Prince Consalvo, who, at the conclusion of *I viceré*, was elected to parliament by popular vote. In *L'imperio*, De Roberto takes his negative perspective to the extreme point of social and political nihilism. [RSD]

See C. A. Madrignani, *Illusione e realtà nell'opera di Federico De Roberto* (1972); N. Tedesco, *La norma del negativo: De Roberto e il realismo critico* (1981).

DE' ROSSI, AZARIAH, see JEWS AND JUDAISM.

DE ROSSI, GIOVANNI GHERARDO (1754–1827). The most versatile writer in *Rome under Pius VI, he became also one of Italy's best writers of *comedy in the period immediately after *Goldoni. He modelled his plays on Molière and Goldoni, and occasionally drew more directly on Roman life, as in *Il calzolajo inglese in Roma*.

[JMAL]

D'ERRICO, EZIO, see DETECTIVE FICTION.

DE SANCTIS, FRANCESCO (1817–83). Literary critic and one of the truly great Italian intellectuals. Born at Morra Irpina, he began his teaching career at *Naples as early as 1835, and took part in the revolution of *1848. Imprisoned from 1850 to 1853, he managed to find refuge as an *exile, first in *Turin, then in Zurich, where he taught Italian literature from 1856 to 1860. An admirer of *Mazzini and *Garibaldi, De Sanctis nevertheless accepted the political situation: as governor of Avellino province (September–October 1860), he encouraged moves towards national unity through the new kingdom of Italy. Minister of *Education no fewer than five times, De Sanctis worked for the creation of adequate schooling in the new nation, as well as for a bipartisan system with an effective parliamentary opposition. A discerning critic of Italian society, he fought for the ideals of the moderate Left, especially the need to provide adequate elementary education before Italy's chief ills could be solved.

De Sanctis was the first great critic and historian of Italian literature, for whom the achievements and failures of Italian culture reflected the moral history of the Italian people. Written at a time when France was defeated by Prussia (1870–1), his celebrated *Storia della letteratura italiana* wrestles with the analogous problem of why Italy, the cultural leader of *Renaissance Europe, had been defeated and oppressed by culturally inferior nations. *Dante is described as the genius who was able to create an artistic masterpiece despite the fact that the world of the *Middle Ages was essentially 'the contrary of art'. There is a clearly *Romantic bias towards the *Inferno*, based on the conviction that the conflict between sin and virtue is essentially dramatic and therefore richer in artistic possibilities. Dante himself is seen as a heroic barbarian, vindictive and passionate. *Francesca da Rimini (not the idealized *Beatrice) is 'the first woman of the modern world'; Hell serves as a pedestal for sinners like Farinata and Brunetto *Latini, whose humanity asserts itself triumphantly in Dante's poem.

Italy's greatest poet was followed by its first great artist, *Petrarch. The latter's conflicting ideals and attraction to earthly beauty created a spiritual conflict and internal weakness in the artist. Without a *patria*, family, or strong political convictions, Petrarch inaugurated a cult of formal beauty that produced both the great exploits and the failures of Italian literature and art. His supreme achievement was to create a poetic language for Italians that remained essentially the same over six centuries. Petrarch's contemporary, *Boccaccio, produced, in the *Decameron*, a human comedy that turns its back on the world of the Middle Ages while mocking its values and ideals. The ensuing movement of *humanism was responsible for a fatal and enduring gulf between the masses and an educated elite. Religious hypocrisy and apathy were reflected in the writers' indifference towards their subject matter: what mattered was 'not what one had to say but how one said it'. *Ariosto, with nothing to affirm and nothing to deny, is emblematic of Italian Renaissance authors who created a world of 'pure' art that ignored contemporary reality: his attitude towards *chivalry is one of amused detachment. At the opposite pole, *Machiavelli, 'Italy's Luther', studied man not as an individual but as a member of a group, class, and society, creating an empirical science of politics based on reality. Instead, *Guicciardini codified Italian decadence where everything was sacrificed to the god of self-interest.

The fatal flaw in Italian culture is already apparent in the antithesis Dante/Petrarch. It was Petrarch's legacy that was to be developed in a society that became increasingly corrupt and shackled by foreign domination. Despite the strivings of *Bruno, *Campanella, and *Galileo, Italian writers remained cut off from the mainstream of modern European thought and culture. Regeneration began with *Goldoni's moderate *realism, *Parini's humanity, and *Alfieri's passionate denunciation of tyranny. Lack of space meant that the *Storia* could not adequately examine the roles played by such writers as *Leopardi and *Manzoni. To redress the balance, from 1872 to 1877, De Sanctis's lectures at *Naples University concentrated on the leading authors and movements in 19th-c. Italian literature (*Storia della letteratura italiana nel secolo XIX*). To the last, he maintained that art was a 'social fact, the result of a nation's life and culture'.

His *Saggi critici* are a further tribute to the beliefs and ideals of the *Risorgimento: in, for example, *La scienza e la vita* (1872), he reminded his contemporaries that knowledge must always be grafted onto vigorous moral, human qualities. He warned against the Italians' persistent tendency to mask reality with wishful thinking. *Universities must not be mere 'factories of lawyers, doctors and architects'. De Sanctis described the neglected world of provincial politics and society in *Un viaggio elettorale* (1875); and in his last public lecture (*Il darwinismo nell'arte*, 1883) he warned that humanity must be on its guard against the excesses of both *idealism and animalism. Eclipsed by the fortunes of *positivism, his posthumous reputation was salvaged by *Croce. [See also HISTORIES OF ITALIAN LITERATURE; LITERARY CRITICISM; LITERARY THEORY, 5.] [JAS]

See E. and A. Croce, *Francesco De Sanctis* (1964); S. Landucci, *Cultura e ideologia in Francesco De Sanctis* (1964); D. Mack Smith, 'Francesco De Sanctis: The Politics of a Literary Critic', in J. A. Davis and P. Ginsborg (eds.), *Society and Politics in the Age of the Risorgimento* (1991).

DE SANTIS, GIUSEPPE, see CINEMA; NEOREALISM.

Deserto dei tartari, Il (1940), *Buzzati's most famous novel, is set in a fortress guarding an unidentified empire's boundary against a putative Tartar threat. Young Giovanni Drogo joins the garrison, passes his life in waiting, and is carried away in a coach, dying with dignity as the Tartars finally approach. [JR]

DE SICA, VITTORIO (1901–74) enjoyed a successful career as a romantic actor before turning to film direction in the early 1940s. In tandem with writer Cesare *Zavattini, he was then responsible for creating some of the most memorable masterpieces of *Neorealism, beginning with *Sciuscià* in 1946 and following on with the much admired *Ladri di biciclette* (1948), *Miracolo a Milano* (1951), and finally *Umberto D.* (1952). With the decline of the Neorealist movement, the partnership with Zavattini broke up and his career faltered. He returned to acting, mostly reprising his 'charmer' roles from the 1930s (e.g. in Max Ophuls' *Madame de . . .* of 1953) but turning in an unexpectedly serious performance in *Rossellini's *Il Generale Della Rovere* in 1959. In 1960 he re-emerged as director with *La ciociara* (from *Moravia's novel), and went on to make a number of *comedies, such as *Ieri, oggi, domani* (1963), with Marcello Mastroianni and Sophia Loren, and a fine adaptation of Giorgio *Bassani's elegiac novel *Il *giardino dei Finzi-Contini* (1970). [See also CINEMA.]

[GN-S]

DE SIO, TERESA, see CANTAUTORI.

DESSÌ, GIUSEPPE (1909–77). *Sardinian novelist. He was brought up near Cagliari in Villacidro, which appears, thinly disguised, as the setting of all his novels. After a disturbed adolescence he took a literature degree at *Pisa University and became a teacher and then an educational administrator, mostly in mainland Italy. He spent the last two decades of his life in *Rome. He was an active anti-*Fascist and always remained a man of the Left.

An intense concern with memory in his first novel, *San Silvano* (1939), led to his being dubbed 'the Sardinian Proust'. The next three novels, *Michele Boschino* (1942), *Introduzione alla vita di Giacomo Scarbo* (1948), and *I passeri* (1953), are experiments in lyrical evocation, though *I passeri* also allows recent history into Sardinia's timeless landscape. The last two novels he finished are his best. Both are *historical novels fundamentally concerned with the problem of justice. The concise *Il disertore* (1958), which displays a notably experimental handling of time, associates Sardinia's emergence from prehistory into history with the rise of Fascism. In the more substantial and structurally more traditional *Paese d'ombre* (1972), an able protagonist's upward social mobility mirrors the evolution of Sardinia in the later 19th c. The unfinished *La scelta* was published posthumously.

[JCB]

De sui ipsius et multorum ignorantia, see PETRARCH, FRANCESCO.

Detective Fiction took time to establish an identity for itself in Italy which was distinct from foreign models, particularly American and English ones. In the early days it existed almost exclusively in *translation, so much so that for a long time detective novels by Italians would appear under American or English pseudonyms and were written in a standardized translationese. *Mondadori long dominated the market, launching in 1929 a series that quickly included S. S. Van Dine, Edgar Wallace, Agatha Christie, Ellery Queen, and Rex Stout. The covers were a distinctive yellow, which gave rise to the use of the word *giallo* to mean a detective story, usually in the classic mould.

Mondadori's success in the 1930s reflected changes in reading interests and culture. Urban Italians were drawn to this up-to-date mystery writing for which there was no precedent in the Italian *novel tradition and which was clearly more accessible and appealing than most native 'popular' fiction. But the success was also a major factor in the modernization of Italian *publishing, which now found itself responding to the demands of a mass market in a way that it had not done before.

The first writer of recognizably Italian detective fiction is often considered to be Alessandro *Varaldo, who was already a successful popular novelist and dramatist when he published eight detective novels between 1931 and 1938. Though in the American manner, they have a *Roman setting and the characters include Italian as well as foreign types. Ezio D'Errico (1892–1972), who was also an abstract painter, produced a string of novels modelled on Simenon in the 1930s and 1940s, starting with *Qualcuno ha bussato alla porta* (1936).

*Fascist *censorship stipulated that the murderer should be a foreigner and there should be no suicides. But the genre was noticeably foreign, and the criticism which American novels regularly voiced of the police and politicians and the glamorous aura with which detective fiction surrounded its villains made it increasingly suspect. In 1943 a complete ban was imposed.

The resurgence of popular American culture in postwar Italy brought a new wave of translations and imitations. The tone was now set by the hard-boiled manner of writers such as Mickey Spillane, who emphasized rapid, violent action, sexual potency, and individual crusades against corruption that blurred the distinction between investigator and criminal. It was from this sort of writing that a distinctively Italian detective fiction emerged in the late 1960s in the four Duca Lamberti novels of Giorgio *Scerbanenco, beginning with *Venere privata* (1966). These offered a gritty depiction of organized crime in *Milan, and an investigator, Lamberti, with a complex personal life; they also introduced more literary qualities into the stylized texture of the genre.

Some of the major writers in 20th-c. Italy had already been drawn to detective fiction. *Gadda had first attempted a crime novel in the mid-1920s in his unfinished *Racconto di ignoto italiano del Novecento*. In *Quer pasticciaccio brutto de via Merulana* (1957) he exploited fully the philosophical and literary potential of a murder investigation. In the early 1960s *Sciascia used detective fiction as a means of bringing *Mafia and political corruption to the attention of a broader readership, whilst Umberto *Eco mixed semiotics and medieval murder mystery in his immensely successful *Il nome della rosa* (1979). A measure of stylistic and intellectual sophistication is now the norm, even with a deliberately popular writer such as Loriano *Macchiavelli, whose down-to-earth *Bologna policeman, Antonio Sarti, has passed easily from fiction to television. In the later 1990s Andrea *Camilleri's stories of his *Sicilian *commissario*, Salvo Montalbano, became best-sellers, largely thanks to their ironic humour and their intelligent mixture of different styles and registers. [See also ARMED FORCES AND POLICE.]   [AWM]

See B. Bini, 'Il poliziesco', in A. Asor Rosa (ed.), *Letteratura italiana: storia e geografia* (1989); L. Rambelli, *Storia del 'giallo' italiano* (1979).

Detto d'amore (late 13th c.). Unfinished *allegorical poem of 480 lines in *settenari baciati* (seven-syllable rhyming couplets), with compound or equivocal rhymes [see VERSIFICATION]. Preserved in a single manuscript, once part of the Montpellier manuscript containing the *Fiore*, it was first published in 1888 with the title taken from the word *detto* ('poem') in lines 3 and 459. Based upon some passages in the *Roman de la rose*, though without the imagery of the actual Rose, its composition may have been influenced by Brunetto *Latini. With the *Fiore*, it has been declared 'attributable' to *Dante and is usually published as an appendix to his works. The *Detto* opens with the protagonist's declaration of loyalty to Love (1–80) and his rejection of the opposing arguments of Reason (81–166). He describes his lady's beauty and graceful demeanour (167–276), but his path to Love is barred by Ricchezza (277–360). There follows a list of rules and instructions for the service of Love (361–458); and the poem breaks off as he is about to consult a trusted friend (459–80).   [PA]

Detto del gatto lupesco (early/middle 13th c.). Anonymous *Florentine beast-fable in 144 couplets of nine- and eight-syllable lines, recounting a journey to the Holy Land by its protagonist and narrator, the wolfish cat. Its cultural context and *allegorical significance are much debated.
                                                      [SNB]

De viris illustribus, see PETRARCH, FRANCESCO.

De vita solitaria. Latin treatise in two books by *Petrarch, first composed in 1346, though revisions and extensions continued until 1371. It describes and defends an ideal of the solitary life which is less that of the hermit than that of the classical *humanist absorbed in study and prayer in the midst of nature's beauties.   [MP]

Devotional Writings, see HAGIOGRAPHY; RELIGIOUS LITERATURE.

De vulgari eloquentia (c.1303–c.1305), *Dante's unfinished Latin treatise, ostensibly on how to compose in the vulgar tongue, in fact ranges widely over many aspects of language. It is the first work in Western culture explicitly to assert the greater 'nobility' of the vernacular in relation to Latin, since the former is older, universal, and natural (1.1.4). In addition, Dante examined the divine origins of language, a faculty which he considered to be specific to humanity; the connections between reason, language, and ethics; language as a system of signs; linguistic change and variety; the relationship between French, Italian, and Provençal; and the character of the Romance and in particular of the Italian literary tradition.

Most famously, he drew a detailed and accurate map of the different languages found in the Italian peninsula and islands, as he endeavoured to describe a supraregional form of Italian, the 'illustrious vernacular' (*vulgare illustre*), which could serve as a sophisticated literary tool. He also began to delineate a theory and practice of vernacular poetry centred on metre, genre, and style. This was based on well-established *Ciceronian and *Horatian rhetorical precepts, and on the example of Latin classical literature, whose superiority over writing in the vernacular he continued, in line with tradition, to assert in the treatise. Dante appears to have abandoned his treatise on account of a growing dissatisfaction with the restrictiveness of medieval poetics, whose conventions he brilliantly subverted in the *Divine Comedy*. But the *De vulgari eloquentia* bears all the hallmarks of Dante at his best: bold originality, a carefully structured yet encyclopedic treatment of a highly complex subject, and a concern to demonstrate the uniqueness of his own artistic achievements. [See also LITERARY THEORY, I; QUESTIONE DELLA LINGUA; VERSIFICATION; VOLGARE AND VOLGARE ILLUSTRE.]   [ZB]

Ed. P. V. Mengaldo (1979). See P. V. Mengaldo, *Linguistica e retorica di Dante* (1978); I. Pagani, *La teoria linguistica di Dante* (1982); M. Shapiro, *'De vulgari eloquentia': Dante's Book of Exile* (1990).

DIACCETO, FRANCESCO CATTANI DA (1466–1522). *Humanist who studied philosophy, Greek, and Latin in *Florence, and in 1492 came into contact with Marsilio *Ficino, who was to be an important influence on his thought and writing. Diacceto had close links with the *Medici, and on the death of Ficino he was the natural successor to the chair of philosophy at the Florentine *studio*. He was a major figure at the meetings at the Orti Oricellari [SEE ACADEMIES; RUCELLAI, BERNARDO], and frequented the Accademia Sacra Fiorentina. His *De amore* (1508) was the first of a series of treatises on love in the 16th c. He also wrote *tragicomedies and a *commentary on Plato's *Symposium*. [See also NEOPLATONISM.]   [PLR]

Dialect. The dialects of Italy are not dialects of Italian: they are neither aspects of Italian, nor are they derived from it, because they existed before the Italian language came into being; they are derived (including Florentine, from which Italian developed) from Vulgar Latin, like the other dialects and languages grouped under the heading of Romance. Dialects are much more widely spoken in Italy than in Britain, even by educated people, and are generally very different both from each other and from the national language. This is because of Italy's long history of political division, which prevented the emergence of a national spoken language before *Unification in 1860; up till then Italian existed as an almost exclusively written language, learnt by literary imitation, and Italians spoke dialect at all levels of society. It is estimated that as late as 1861 only 2.5 per cent of Italians

could actually speak Italian. In contrast, surveys conducted in 1988 suggested that by then roughly 80 per cent could speak Italian, about 40 per cent spoke no dialect, about 60 per cent could still speak dialect, some 40 per cent could use both, and those who knew only dialect were down to something like 20 per cent. So while Italian has expanded tremendously since Unification, the dialects have remained vigorous for all that. How long this will continue is uncertain, however; the separate identity of the dialects is under threat not only from the continuing erosion of the number of speakers, but also from the dialects' growing Italianization through contact with the national language.

The Italian dialects may be classified thus: (1) Northern dialects, the so-called Gallo-Italian dialects of *Piedmont, *Lombardy, Liguria, and Emilia-Romagna, plus those of the Veneto; (2) those of the Centre-South, from the Marche to *Sicily; and (3) those of *Tuscany, geographically and linguistically intermediate between the two main groups. In addition, there are other forms of Romance in Italy too distinctive to be ascribed to these groups: *Sardinian, Friulan, Ladin (spoken in parts of the northern Veneto and Alto Adige), and the Provençal and Franco-Provençal dialects of western Piedmont and the Valle d'Aosta. Some idea of the linguistic diversity of the dialects may be gained from the following features: in Northern dialects (but not in the Veneto), tonic vowels equivalent to the *u* in French *dur* and the *œu* in French *bœuf*, loss of final vowels, voicing of intervocalic plosives, absence of double consonants, use of unstressed subject pronouns (not found in Italian), and of the compound perfect for the past historic; in the Centre-South, widespread metaphony (the change in quality of a stressed vowel due to its assimilation to a final vowel, e.g. *curtu* ('short', metaphonic masculine) versus *corta* (non-metaphonic feminine)), indistinct final vowels, assimilation of medial *mb* to *mm* and *nd* to *nn*, absence of *-mente* adverbs, use of the imperfect subjunctive for the conditional. There are also many lexical differences. [See also DIALECT WRITING; DICTIONARIES; GRAMMARS; LITERACY; QUESTIONE DELLA LINGUA; SLANG; SPOKEN LANGUAGE IN LITERATURE.]

[RABGH]

See G. Rohlfs, *Grammatica storica della lingua italiana e dei suoi dialetti* (1966–9); M. Maiden and M. Parry (eds.), *The Dialects of Italy* (1997).

Dialect Writing. [See also DIALECT.] A firm distinction between dialect and the standard literary language only becomes viable with the success of Pietro *Bembo's programme in the 16th c. Before then, though *Tuscan literature tended to furnish linguistic and stylistic models to writers from other regions, it was quite possible to write in the vernaculars of other regions without any strong sense of writing in a subordinate language. After the codification of Tuscan as the standard written form of Italian, the local languages of Italy remained the only medium for spoken communication, and also continued to be used in writing. For cultured writers the decision to write in dialect is always a conscious choice, and one based on the recognition of the inferior status of the language adopted. Conversely, *folk literature, although often in dialect, frequently attempts to approximate to the modes of the national language.

The rationales vary enormously, but the one unifying element behind all dialect literature is an allusion, explicit or implicit, to the national literature. Dialect writing tends to proclaim either its ability to reach as high as the national literature, as in the case of the 18th-c. *Sicilian poet Giovanni *Meli, or, more frequently, to treat lowly topics that the national literature cannot treat. Sometimes, paradoxically, it claims to do both at once. Carlo *Porta, for instance, constantly extols the poetic wisdom of the uncultured, but, picking up the actual words of earlier *Milanese poets, he also asserts the power of his language to deal with weighty matters ('coss de sustanzia'). Not infrequently, dialect-writing offers an explicit parody of the national literature, as when Porta begins his last poem, 'La guerra di pret', with an overt parody of the opening line of Torquato *Tasso's *Gerusalemme liberata. *Parody may then become *expressionism, especially if various dialects and the national language are juxtaposed, as occurs in the *commedia dell'arte.

Much dialect literature in the 19th c. was written in the belief (particularly evident in *Lombard literature) that dialect had a unique relationship with the lower classes and a unique capacity to express their earthy, spontaneous wisdom. But, as *Belli above all demonstrates in his *Roman poetry, writing in dialect could also be adopted as a way of reproducing and preserving the culture of the lower classes, which in Italy has always been regional and hence dialectal.

Only a minority of dialect writers, however, have aimed at communicating directly with the lower classes. Tentative suggestions to this effect came from Lombard *Romantics, such as *Borsieri, who wrote in defence of dialect after *Giordani's attacks

in 1816. But this aim was most clearly and coherently expressed by certain *Jacobin writers, most notably Eleonora *Fonseca Pimentel, as part of their political programme. In fact dialect writings have never appealed to a mass readership, with the exception of dialect *theatre, which could be seen and heard without being read. When uncultured dialect speakers have begun to master the written word, they have read material written in the national language.

In the 20th c. dialect has been the medium of various poets opposed to the dominant *hermetic current, notably Giacomo *Noventa, Delio *Tessa, Albino *Pierro, and Biagio *Marin. But the decline in dialect usage and the transformations of traditional culture have rendered obsolete virtually all the traditional motives for writing dialect literature, though these can still be seen to be active in the work of a poet such as Franco *Loi. Other present-day dialect poets—the so-called *neodialettali*, such as Franca *Grisoni and Franco *Scataglini—tend to use dialect as a way of exploring alternative inner or imaginative worlds rather than the concrete world of everyday life. Significantly, they always provide glossaries or translations. [See also LITERACY; QUESTIONE DELLA LINGUA; SLANG; SPOKEN LANGUAGE IN LITERATURE.]   [VRJ]

La poesia in dialetto: storia e testi dalle origini al Novecento, ed. F. Brevini (1999). See G. L. Beccaria (ed.), *Letteratura e dialetto* (1975); M. Chiesa and G. Tesio (eds.), *Il dialetto da lingua della realtà a lingua della poesia* (1978).

Dialoghi con Leucò (1947). A collection of *dialogues by *Pavese. The interlocutors are classical gods and heroes, with Ulysses as the main representative of human endeavour. The main themes are the conflict between instinct and rationality and the interrelationships between myth, history, and destiny. It was Pavese's own favourite amongst his books.   [NMS]

Dialogues, Renaissance. As a genre the dialogue's status was uncertain, since there existed no classical theoretical discussion of the form. It was not until the second half of the 16th c. that a series of tracts appeared which addressed the literary nature of the genre, notably Carlo *Sigonio's *De dialogo liber* (1561), Ludovico *Castelvetro's *La Poetica d'Aristotele vulgarizzata et sposta* (1567), Sperone *Speroni's *Apologia dei dialoghi* (1574), and Torquato *Tasso's *Discorso dell'arte del dialogo* (1585). Yet prior to these works the popularity of

Diaries

the genre in Italy is witnessed by the numerous dialogues addressing a startlingly wide range of subjects, from courtiership to fortification and the art of war. Its popularity was due in part to the fact that it presented writers with a form which did not demand the sort of detailed technical knowledge required in the composition of genres such as the treatise, and in part to the flexibility it afforded in representing discussions specific to a particular time and place and peopled by known interlocutors, thereby reflecting the oral culture of the age.

There were three principal forms derived from classical practice: the dialectical Platonic model, the Lucianic *satirical form, and the *Ciceronian model of a *disputatio* or free discussion, in which all opinions were entertained with the aim of securing consensus through reasoned persuasion. Beginning with the first volume of Leonardo *Bruni's *Dialogi ad Petrum Histrum* (1401), the erudite *humanist dialogues of the 15th c. were mostly in Latin, from Poggio *Bracciolini's *De avaritia* (1428) to Lorenzo *Valla's *De vero falsoque bono, De libero arbitrio*, and *De professione religiosorum*, all written between 1431 and 1442, and to Giovanni *Pontano's five dialogues set in the context of the *Naples *Academy between 1467 and 1501.

The 16th c., however, saw the flowering of the vernacular dialogue first adopted by Leon Battista *Alberti in his *Della famiglia* in the mid-15th c. Foremost within the genre were the self-conscious *courtly dialogues of Northern Italy written in the Ciceronian style. Addressed to a far wider audience and best exemplified by *Castiglione's *Cortegiano*, first published in 1528, Giovanni *Della Casa's *Galateo* (1558), and Stefano *Guazzo's *La civil conversatione* (1574), such courtesy textbooks enjoyed a European popularity on account of their nonchalant instruction in the subtleties of social comportment in court circles. Through the assumption of an open dialogical form, the onus in judging the merits of the various opinions put forward was clearly placed with the reader. Such dialogues were suited to the elitist social milieu of the Italian courts, enabling the author to secure a voice without disrupting the carefully constructed etiquette of courtly address through assuming too strident an educative tone. The Lucianic satirical form allowed authors to exploit the deliberate ambiguity of the genre to launch polemics with less fear of retribution from the authorities, secular or ecclesiastical. The latter part of the 16th c. saw the move to a closed dialogic form in texts such as Battista *Guarini's *Il segretario* (1594). More akin to the treatise,

such monological pieces were far more didactic and authoritarian than their open and discursive Ciceronian predecessors, reflecting fundamental changes in the political and literary culture of post-Tridentine Italy, brought on by the demise of republican regimes and the advent of *printing [see also CORTESIA; COUNTER-REFORMATION].   [SJM]

See D. Marsh, *The Quattrocento Dialogue* (1980);
V. Cox, *The Renaissance Dialogue* (1992).

Diaries. As hybrid works that include elements of meditation and philosophy, diaries do not lend themselves easily to modern methods of analysis, whose interest lies more in plot and invention. Characterized by an almost total identification of writer, reader, and the person written about, their fundamental requirement is to be updated on a regular if not daily basis, and a commitment to telling the truth, to oneself and to possible readers. In earlier centuries, autobiographical works (e.g. those of *Cellini and Pontormo) were more concerned to create an objective record of events, with little prominence given to individual experience and awareness. The prototype of the 19th- and 20-c. diary is a closed, repetitive work spread over a long period of time, and both nourished and consumed by a pathological sensibility, as exemplified in the monumental diary of the French writer Henri Frédéric Amiel. Strongly conditioned by the time in which they are written, diaries are often the product of particular historical or biographical experiences, such as war and adolescence, and are interrupted when these come to an end. When the writing stands out for its quality, and when there is also a degree of reflection on the organization and meaning of the project, the diary can offer itself as a literary work. In these cases it may be conceived as a cure for the grief and melancholia that often lie at its origins, as happens with *Gadda and *Landolfi and, earlier, with the brief, youthful *Memorie del primo amore* of *Leopardi.

Unlike other countries, where the production of diaries has often been enormous, Italy's contribution to the genre has been limited. The country lacked the large educated class that could dedicate itself to private writing, and also suffered from a degree of political and religious control that discouraged such activity. Given the formality of literary Italian, it is not surprising that in the 18th and 19th c. intimate journals and memoirs (e.g. those of *Alfieri, Carlo *Gozzi, Carlo *Goldoni, *Casanova, and *Cavour) were often written in French. Notable in the modest revival of the diary in Italian

are the *Zibaldone of Leopardi, a singular kind of philosophical journal; the Diario intimo of *Tommaseo; the Diario and Noterelle of Giuseppe Cesare *Abba; *D'Annunzio's not-so-intimate Tacquini; *Svevo's few pages of diary and that of his brother Elio Schmitz, a disturbing document of a generation in crisis; the more limited Colloqui of Giani *Stuparich; and the much more extensive diaries of Sibilla *Aleramo. In the 20th c. there are also writings by *Zavattini, *Flaiano, *Buzzati, *Ottieri, *Comisso, *Dessì, *Bigongiari, *Jacobbi, where, as generally happens with the genre, it is difficult to distinguish between diaries, memoirs, or autobiographical notes. *Gadda wrote a Diario di guerra e di prigionia, as well as his Meditazioni milanesi, *Soffici a Diario di bordo, *Serra a Diario di trincea, as well as his Esame di coscienza di un letterato, and there are diaries by *Alvaro. But the most significant and famous example of the genre is, without doubt, the posthumously published Mestiere di vivere of *Pavese. [See also AUTOBIOGRAPHY; BIOGRAPHY.]
[AD]
See A. Dolfi (ed.), 'Journal intime' e letteratura moderna (1989).

DIAS, WILLY (pseud. of Fortuna Morpurgo) (1872–1956). *Triestine writer of mainly romantic fiction, often with titles such as Romanzo di un cuore (1923) and L'amore più grande (1934). As well as forty-five *novels she wrote an *autobiography, Viaggio nel tempo (1958). After *World War II she joined the *Communist Party and wrote for L'Unità.
[KP]

DI BANZOLE, OTTONE, see ORIANI, AFREDO.

DI BLASI, FRANCESCO PAOLO, see SICILY.

DI BREME, LUDOVICO (1780–1820). Writer and critic. A younger son in an aristocratic *Piedmontese family in *Turin, Ludovico Pietro Arborio Gattinara Di Breme was propelled into an ecclesiastical career. Moving to *Milan, he held various offices in the court of Eugène Beauharnais and kept up a busy social life, remaining there after the *Austrians returned in 1814. His friendship with Mme de Staël and an intellectual affinity with her caused him to rush to her defence in the 1816 polemics over *Romanticism. In Intorno all'ingiustizia di alcuni giudizi letterari italiani, published in Milan in 1816, and a Grand commentaire sur un petit article, which appeared in Geneva the next year, he

extended her arguments in favour of modern rather than classical models and reiterated her warnings against excessive reliance on past cultural achievements. A series of Osservazioni on Byron's Giaour (1818) explored the nature of modern poetry, which he located in the 'pathetic', by which he meant not melancholy but 'depth and vastness of feeling'. He returned to polemic on Romanticism in general in a dispute with *Londonio (1818), and was one of the principal founders of Il *Conciliatore, to which he contributed essays and satirical sketches.
[MPC]

DI CAPUA, LIONARDO (1617–95). Influential physician and man of letters in *Naples. He brought the sceptical experimental principles of *Galileo to bear on *medicine, developing in his Parere (published in 1681 and reprinted many times) the thesis that *Aristotle's natural philosophy is practically useless, and that the medical sciences, like all science, are subject to trial and error. In this he was wholly a modernist [see QUERELLE DES ANCIENS ET DES MODERNES]. He was a founder member of the Accademia degli *Investiganti. His many *sonnets draw on *Petrarchan models and reflect the growing dissatisfaction with *Marinismo shared by the Accademia dell'*Arcadia. He gave his name to the term capuismo, referring to a return to the classical purity of Petrarch. He also influenced the young Giambattista *Vico.
[PBD]

Dictionaries involving the vernacular were chiefly Latin-Italian until, in the 16th c., the flourishing of vernacular literature and *printing encouraged the lexicography of Italian. At first their focus was on approved authors rather than on technical, scientific, domestic, and regional usage. Glossaries between c.1520 and 1540 explained the usage of the 14th-c. *Florentine literary canon, and this remained the basis of dictionaries throughout the 16th and 17th c., though there was some interest in contemporary non-*Tuscan and substandard usage in Acarisio's well-organized Vocabolario and Alunno's Ricchezze della lingua volgare (both 1543), and in Pergamini's Memoriale (1602). The most influential dictionary, the *Vocabolario della Crusca, rigorously promoted a *purism based on 14th-c. Florentine, especially in its first edition (1612). [See also GRAMMARS; QUESTIONE DELLA LINGUA.]

Dictionaries in the 18th c. became less narrow and prescriptive. Technical terminology appeared in e.g. Bergantini's Voci italiane (1745) and especially Francesco D'Alberti di Villanuova's

Dictionaries of Italian Literature

Dizionario universale (1797–1805), based partly on fieldwork. This trend continued during and after the *Risorgimento, as the functions and contacts of Italian expanded and the status of the living language rose. The widely used *Vocabolario universale* of the Tramater company (1829–40) adopted a balance between purism and openness to neologisms. Practical needs were also served by 'methodical' dictionaries which grouped words by subject. In these the problem of whether to include regional terminology was particularly acute, and one, Carena's *Prontuario* (1846–60), was criticized by *Manzoni for not restricting itself to living Florentine usage. Manzoni's advocacy of contemporary Florentine lay behind Giorgini and Broglio's *Novo vocabolario* (1870–97), itself criticized by *Ascoli, and Petrocchi's *Nòvo Dizionàrio* (1887). Neologisms and foreign borrowings were censured by e.g. Fanfani and Arlìa, but purist attitudes were gradually abandoned in early 20th-c. dictionaries such as Panzini's *Dizionario moderno* (1905) and Zingarelli's *Vocabolario* (1917). The first major historical dictionary of united Italy was that of *Tommaseo and *Bellini (1861–79). Notable dictionaries of the later 20th c. include the *Grande dizionario* directed initially by Battaglia (1961–), the *Vocabolario* of the Istituto della *Enciclopedia Italiana (1986–94), the *Dizionario Palazzi Folena* (revised 1992), the *Dizionario Italiano Sabatini Coletti* (1997), and Tullio *De Mauro's *Grande dizionario italiano dell'uso* (1999). [See also SPELLING.]

Both the spread of Italian and the study of *dialects have been served, especially since the 18th c., by dialect-Italian dictionaries such as Cherubini's of *Milanese (1814) and Boerio's of *Venetian (1829). [BR]

See V. Della Valle, 'La lessicografia', in L. Serianni and P. Trifone (eds.), *Storia della lingua italiana*, i (1993).

Dictionaries of Italian Literature. Until recently, Italian culture preferred large-scale discursive histories rather than dictionaries of literature. Convenient works in dictionary form published since the 1960s include: G. Petronio, *Dizionario enciclopedico della letteratura italiana* (1966–70); E. Bonora (ed.), *Dizionario della letteratura italiana* (2 vols., 1976, but updated at various times since); V. *Branca (ed.), *Dizionario critico della letteratura italiana* (3 vols., 1976: rev. 1986); S. Jacomuzzi (ed.), *Dizionario della letteratura italiana: le opere* (1989); Peter Bondanella *et al.* (eds.),

Dictionary of Italian Literature (1996); R. Russell (ed.), *Italian Women Writers. A Bio-bibliographical Sourcebook* (1994), and *The Feminist Encyclopedia of Italian Literature* (1997). Specialized 20th-c. dictionaries are A. *Asor Rosa (ed.), *Dizionario della letteratura italiana del Novecento* (1992), and E. Ghidetti (ed.), *Dizionario critico della letteratura italiana del Novecento* (1997). Some of the most convenient and useful dictionaries are in effect appendices to longer histories, in particular: *Dizionario bio-bibliografico* (2 vols., 1990), which is part of A. Asor Rosa (ed.), *Storia della letteratura italiana* (16 vols., 1984–96); and *Dizionario: cronologia* (2 vols.), appended to G. Bàrberi Squarotti (ed.), *Storia della civiltà letteraria in Italia* (1990–6). The *Enciclopedia dantesca*, ed. U. Bosco (6 vols., 1970–8: rev. 1984), is devoted entirely to *Dante. [See also BIBLIOGRAPHIES OF ITALIAN LITERATURE; HISTORIES OF ITALIAN LITERATURE.]
[NMS]

Didimo Chierico, see FOSCOLO, UGO.

DI GIACOMO, SALVATORE (1860–1934). The major *Neapolitan-*dialect poet of the late 19th c. Abandoning medical studies to devote himself to *journalism and literature, he first wrote short stories in the *veristic manner (collected in 1893 in *Pipa e boccale*), but soon turned to poetry. His numerous collections of poems—*Sunette antiche* (1884), *'O fùnneco verde* (1886), *Mattinate napoletane* (1886), *A San Francisco* (1895), *Ariette e sunette* (1898)—and the longer compositions *'O munasterio* (1887) and *Zi' munacella* (1888), paint a picture of contemporary Naples, with some characters aspiring to improve their social position and others devising different stratagems for survival in increasingly squalid conditions. However, Di Giacomo does not aim so much at social criticism as at exploring in depth the character of the city and its inhabitants. This gives to his verse its intense musicality and *lyricism. Equally lyrical are the plays *O' voto* (1899), *O' mese mariano* (1900), and *Assunta Spina* (1909). He had *antiquarian interests which intensified on his appointment as librarian in the Naples national *library in 1893, and led to *Taverne famose napoletane* (1899) and *Napoli: figure e paesi* (1909). He also wrote some of the most famous Neapolitan songs, such as 'A Marechiare', 'Era de maggio', and 'Tiempe d'ammore'. [AC]

DI GIOVANNI, ALESSIO, see SICILY.

DI MICHELE, GRAZIA, see CANTAUTORI.

DINO DEL GARBO (d.1327). *Florentine doctor and *medical writer who graduated at *Bologna and then taught in various cities, including Florence. His works include a digest of Avicenna, and a Latin *commentary on *Cavalcanti's *canzone on the nature of love, 'Donna me prega'.

[JP & JMS]

DIODATI, GIOVANNI, see BIBLE; RELIGIOUS LITERATURE.

DIONIGI DA BORGO SAN SEPOLCRO (?1300–42). *Humanist friend of *Petrarch and *Boccaccio. He was an Augustinian monk who studied and taught theology in Paris and then in *Avignon, where he met Petrarch in about 1333, presenting him with a minute copy of St *Augustine's *Confessions* which he was never without thereafter. Dionigi met Boccaccio at Robert of *Anjou's *court in *Naples. He wrote *commentaries on classical authors, the most read being that on Valerius Maximus. [MP]

DIONISOTTI, CARLO (1908–98). One of the most influential *historians of Italian literature. He studied in *Turin, moved to Oxford in 1947, and then to a chair of Italian in London in 1949. He was an eminent specialist of the 15th and 16th c. Among his main books are the editions of Pietro *Bembo's works (1931–2), *Gli umanisti e il volgare fra Quattrocento e Cinquecento* (1968), and the three collections, *Geografia e storia della letteratura italiana* (1967), *Machiavellerie* (1980), and *Appunti sui moderni* (1988). He was unequalled in his ability to use the most exacting erudition as a tool for enlightening historical understanding. The recognition of the historical and geographical specificity of different traditions in Italian culture is the best-known legacy he bequeathed to Italian studies. [LL]

Discordo. Metrical form of *troubadour origin adopted by the *Sicilian School. As the name indicates, it served to express inner discord, in its best-known example by the Provençal poet *Raimbaut de Vaqueiras through the juxtaposition of different languages in the same text. [See also GIACOMINO PUGLIESE; GIACOMO DA LENTINI.] [DR]

Discorsi, I, see MACHIAVELLI, NICCOLÒ.

Discorsi dell'arte poetica, see TASSO, TORQUATO.

Discorsi del poema eroico, see TASSO, TORQUATO.

Disperata. Poem expressing complete despair at life or love, originally of popular origin. *Disperate* were cultivated in variety of metres from the 14th to the 16th c. [See also VERSIFICATION.] [PH]

Disputationes camaldulenses, see LANDINO, CRISTOFORO.

DI STEFANO, ENOE, see ITALIAN WRITERS IN AUSTRALIA.

Dittamondo, see UBERTI, FAZIO DEGLI.

Divine Comedy (?1307–20). *Dante's poem is one of the greatest works of world literature. Many things account both for its greatness and for its success in finding new readers through the ages and around the world: its encompassing vision of human life seen under the aspect of eternity; its way of involving the reader as a partner, both in the journey and in the interpretation of the poem that represents it; its previously unmatched blend of sources in earlier literatures, including the Latin *Bible, classical authors, and recent vernacular writing; its equally unexampled range of stylistic registers, from the language of the streets and the countryside to that of scholastic argumentation and mystical exuberance; and, perhaps most of all, its bravura performance as an extended piece of poetic daring. Perhaps no single poem has ever attempted so much, and so nearly succeeded in all its ambitions.

The *Comedy* (first referred to as 'La Divina Commedia' in a Venetian printing of 1555) is arranged in three *cantiche* (or 'canticles': *Inferno, *Purgatorio, and *Paradiso), a word not used before in reference to the parts of a poem, and one that suggests a certain biblical resonance. These are in turn divided into 100 *canti (or 'songs'), another term not previously encountered indicating the divisions of a poem. These range in length from 115 to 160 lines of verse, and there are 14,233 lines in all. What is remarkable is that, since the earliest days of the poems's dissemination, there has been hardly any disagreement about these basic elements of its composition as this has been transmitted through scribal reproduction and, at times, invention. When one thinks of the disputes concerning the shape and content of other major medieval or *Renaissance works, one is struck by the relatively stable nature of Dante's text during its nearly seven centuries of life. Particular words may be problematic in the *manuscript tradition, the inevitable result of the fact that we do not possess an autograph. Nonetheless, the poem has not moved all that far from its creator's version of it. As for its proximity to a contemporary reader, we should be aware that Dante wrote in a tongue closer to present-day Italian than, say, *Shakespeare's language is to current English. [See also TERZA RIMA.]

The *Comedy* relates Dante's voyage through the ten circles of Hell; through Antepurgatory, through seven terraces where souls purge themselves on their way to Heaven, and then into the Earthly Paradise, the first home of the human race; through the nine heavenly spheres and, finally, beyond the physical space of God's creation, into the Empyrean, the only place rightly considered Paradise, where all saved souls dwell in the presence of God, beyond space and time, as though already residing in Eternity [for fuller accounts, see INFERNO, PURGATORIO, PARADISO]. This journey through the afterworld is presented as having taken place in 1300, but rather disconcertingly as occurring both in Easter week (Good Friday fell on 8 April in that year) and two weeks earlier, starting on Friday, 25 March, the anniversary, according to medieval lore, of the Creation, as well as of the Annunciation. The star charts that Dante probably consulted (of one Prophacius Judaeus (*c.*1236–1304)) may not have given the positions of the Sun and Venus for the spring of 1300, but only for that season in 1301. In any event, Dante apparently chose to use the charts for 25 March–2 April 1301 for his poem, a tactic that further confuses the issue. In these particulars, as in many others, we are forced to conclude that Dante managed the details of his poem exactly as he wanted them, paying little heed to a certain kind of reader's desire to have everything 'add up'. For instance, it is an unremitting physical law of Dante's universe that the spirits of the dead have no corporality and thus cannot interact with material things; nonetheless, *Virgil is able to pick up Dante and carry him (e.g. *Inf.* 19 and 23). Such contradictions are clearly deliberate and meant to test us as readers. We are asked to give over our only reasonable hesitations and accede to the fact that we are reading a poem, one made by a writer who amply insists on his authorial independence, while at other times obeying his own laws and conventions. And throughout the poem the reader, addressed some twenty times by the poet, is asked

to concede that this text is to be taken as a truthful record of an actual journey.

The first guide in the poem is the Roman poet Virgil (70–19 BC). While some medieval writers chose to believe that Virgil was in fact a pagan who had experienced, in some miraculous way, the truth of Christianity and was consequently saved, Dante's text makes it clear that he did not share this view. Virgil is damned eternally to Limbo, the best place in Hell, but Hell all the same. This makes Dante's choice of him as the guide to the Christian precincts of Hell and Purgatory all the more surprising and intimidating. Sooner or later one realizes that this choice was an intensely personal one. It has surprised many readers, and even caused a good number of Dante's earliest commentators to decide that Virgil is an *'allegory' of human Reason rather than the historical being he is so clearly meant to be. It seems likely that Dante's decision to cast Virgil as his guide mirrors choices that he had made in his life. Perhaps the most noteworthy of these was to turn from writing prose about poetry (*Vita nova*, *Convivio*, *De vulgari eloquentia*, the latter two left unfinished once he began the *Comedy*) to writing an *'epic' poem that owes much to the example of Virgil.

Virgil's role as guide in the *Comedy* is not limited to Hell, as one might have expected, but continues nearly to the end of Purgatory. He thus presides over, in one possible formulation, the correction and then the perfection of the protagonist's will, the inner subject of the first two *cantiche*. Dante has structured his work in such a way as to give it two basic subjects, the first the drama that occurs as the protagonist (and we) observe the condition of the damned and then of the saved; the second, the inner changes of the protagonist as he develops, first in learning how to respond correctly to sin (by loathing it), and then in coming to reject sin for the love of God, following the example of those on the seven terraces (at last understanding the dangers and false attractions of the world as they now learn to see them). Each terrace is devoted to the purgation of a particular mortal sin: Pride, Envy, Wrath, Sloth, Avarice (and Prodigality), Gluttony, Lust. From the protagonist's reactions on the various terraces, it is clear that he feels himself most vulnerable to the sins of pride, anger, and lust. Improvement is a slow process, one in which we observe him making many mistakes, as when he faints from fear at the conclusion of *Inferno* 3 and from pity at the conclusion of *Inferno* 5. All through the *Inferno* these two emotions will be seen repeated in him, but with successively less damaging results, until, for instance, he is firm against the entreaties made for his pity by Ugolino (*Inf.* 33).

In Purgatory his moral education is more positive. Even though in this realm Virgil has not had the previous experience that he had had of the underworld (*Inf.* 9.22–7, 12.34–6), he is able to guide Dante with respect to the moral virtues (justice, temperance, fortitude, and prudence), if not the theological ones (faith, hope, and charity). Virgil several times in *Inferno* has been shown to be out of his depth: e.g. his inability to deal with the rebellious keepers of the gates of Dis (*Inf.* 8–9), and his utter failure to interpret the evil designs of the Malebranche (*Inf.* 21–3), the devils of the fifth *bolgia* (as the divisions of the circle of the fraudulent are termed). In *Purgatorio* he is often portrayed as the pagan who might have known better, but lacked the necessary faith. Passages in each of the first six cantos show him in such light, and the scene with *Statius (*Purg.* 20–23), the later Roman poet saved (in Dante's eccentric view) by reading Virgil, is intrinsically hard on the earlier poet, damned despite his salvific influence on another pagan.

The second of the poem's three guides connects the *Comedy* to the *Vita nova*, that remarkable early work (1293/4) that makes of *Beatrice a lady beyond the scope of all other poets. The secret of her specialness, as the prose of the work, far more than the verse, makes plain, is her particular relation to the true God, and not the god of Love 'worshipped' by most previous Provençal and Italian *lyric poets [see DOLCE STIL NOVO]. It is revealed that Beatrice has instigated Virgil's mission to guide Dante through the afterworld and, finally, back to her (*Inf.* 2). When she first appears to Dante, uttering as her first word his name (*Purg.* 30.55), it is, within the fiction, nearly ten years since her death (June 1290). Having descended from her seat in Paradise (we will see her there in *Para.* 31–3), she now castigates her former lover-poet for his infidelities to her after she died. The exact nature of these has been a source of debate among scholars; whatever else they involved, it is true that after the early 1290s Dante seems not to have written in unlimited praise of her until he began the *Comedy*, a work that is indelibly marked by her central presence. And in it he confesses his previous abandonment of Beatrice.

Charged with the correction of Dante's intellect, Beatrice leads him through the nine heavens that, in Dante's cosmography, surround the earth in widening circles (those of the Moon, Mercury, Venus, the Sun, Mars, Jupiter, Saturn, the fixed stars, and the crystalline sphere), until she brings him to the Empyrean, where she yields her post as guide to St Bernard, the 12th-c. French theologian, whose responsibility it is to perfect his pupil's intellect in the direct experience of God. Under his tutelage Dante has his final vision of the Trinity. This serves as the culminating moment of the poem, which has recorded this voyage and vision that has lasted precisely a week (Thursday evening to Thursday evening).

A poem centred on the issue of the salvation or damnation of the individual soul, the *Comedy* is also urgently concerned with the question of the political realities and possibilities of Dante's Italy. Born into a Guelf family, Dante developed Ghibelline proclivities early in the 14th c. and eventually became a fervent supporter of the emperor *Henry VII of Luxemburg when the latter descended into Italy in 1310 in order to restore imperial authority [see GUELFS AND GHIBELLINES]. For Dante, that authority descended directly from God, while the more usual political chicanery of the time, which in Dante's eyes opposed the imperial cause in the name of the *Papacy or mere selfish convenience, swept away the possibility of genuine political reform. Dante, who came to see himself as a 'party of one' (*Para.* 17.69), never lost hope in a political resolution to the problems of Italy that would establish a militant imperial city on earth, a community that would parallel the ideal Church militant, currently under the yoke of the corrupt Papacy, but also a part of Dante's implausible yet enduring hope. [See also DANTE COMMENTARIES; DIVINE COMEDY: ILLUSTRATIONS; LITERARY THEORY, I; MIDDLE AGES.] [RH]

La Commedia secondo l'antica vulgata, ed. G. Petrocchi (1966–7). See E. Moore, *Studies in Dante* (1896–1917); C. T. Davis, *Dante and the Idea of Rome* (1957); J. Pépin, *Dante et la tradition de l'allégorie* (1970); P. Boyde, *Dante Philomythes and Philosopher* (1981).

Divine Comedy: Illustrations. The graphic precision and realism of *Dante's poem would seem to invite, or challenge, artists to find pictorial correlatives for its verbal representations. Whilst the responses have been many and varied over the centuries, the beginnings were modest. Illustrations in 14th-c. *manuscripts of the *Divine Comedy* are commonly reserved for the decorated initials and the bottom of the page below the text. The initials may follow general conventions of contemporary illuminations—so, for instance, the initial N of the first line of *Inferno* ('Nel mezzo del cammin di nostra vita') may contain the writer in his study—or they may elaborate an image from the text, as when the P of *Purgatorio* depicts 'la navicella del mio ingegno' (*Purg.* 1.2). The *Pisan artists who co-operated with the commentator Guido da Pisa on the *Inferno* (*c.*1327–8) [see DANTE COMMENTARIES] draw on contemporary panel or fresco painting and introduce a variety of animated figures within the oblong miniatures at the bottom of the page. Many of the early illuminations are in *Florentine manuscripts. Florence also produced monumental paintings. Nardo di Cione's fresco of Hell in S. Maria Novella is based on Dante, whilst Domenico di Michelino's fresco in Florence Cathedral (1465) both celebrates Dante as a hero of civic *humanism and shows the three realms of the afterlife. Elsewhere in the Centre and North, illuminations continued to be produced into the 15th c.

No major artist engages directly with the *Comedy* until Botticelli. The edition of the *Inferno* of Niccolò della Magna (1481) contains nineteen engravings after drawings by him. Then, about 1492, Botticelli began a second series of drawings. They are drawn with stylus and pen upon vellum, occasionally with colour, and fill an entire page. Though self-consciously retrospective in style, they create new definitions of space, and a new visual equivalence for the temporal and spatial elements of the *Comedy*. 16th-c. editions often contain illustrations in the manner of *Michelangelo, who was reputed to have made some Dantesque drawings himself, though none survives.

An emphasis on the heroic is evident in illustrations that accompanied the revival of interest in Dante in the late 18th c. John Flaxman (from 1792) evokes the remote primitivism pursued also in his illustrations for Homer and Aeschylus. William Blake's illustrations (more than 100 in all) clearly recognize Dantean episodes, but are based on his own symbolic interpretations of the universal role of an artist. In the 19th c. Gustav Doré's return to Michelangelesque grandeur is particularly impressive in the *Inferno*, manipulating large but indeterminate scales of perspective, within which the protagonists encounter crowds of tormented heroes. History painting (typified by Reynolds's *Count Hugolino* of 1772) similarly preferred events from the *Inferno* that evoke awe and terror, but the pre-Raphaelites opted for the *Vita nova* and Paolo and *Francesca da Rimini. A 1911 film, *Dante's*

Inferno (1911), returned to grandiose spectacles of human torment. A more *modernist approach, incorporating elements of commentary, is adopted in the television films of canto 1–8 of *Inferno*, made by Peter Greenaway in conjunction with Tom Phillips, who also published a series of modernist illustrations with his translation of the *Inferno* (1985). Many other 20th-c. artists produced illustrations to Dante, but none have yet ousted Doré from his popular pre-eminence. [See also VISUAL ARTS AND LITERATURE.]   [AM]

See P. Brieger, M. Meiss, and C. Singleton, *Illuminated Manuscripts of the Divine Comedy* (1969).

Divisament dou monde, Le, see POLO, MARCO.

Divortio celeste, Il, see PALLAVICINO, FERRANTE.

DOLCE, LUDOVICO (1508–68) spent his life in *Venice, employed by the *publisher Giolito de Ferrari as editor, *translator, and author. In common with other *poligrafi (*Sansovino, *Domenichi, *Ruscelli), he aimed to make classical writers such as *Aristotle, *Cicero, *Horace, and Donatus available to a cultured though not specialist public, and to provide reliable and annotated texts of Italian authors such as *Dante, *Petrarch, *Boccaccio, *Ariosto, Pietro *Bembo, and *Castiglione.

His own literary output was prolific and varied though often unoriginal. The best of his *dialogues on social and artistic subjects is the *Dialogo della pittura* (1557) which deals with the relationship between art and literature and ends with a panegyric on Titian. Also interesting are his views on language in the *Osservazioni sulla volgar lingua* (1550). He wrote lively *comedies in prose and verse, especially *Il ragazzo* (1541) and *La Fabrizia* (1549). The others, *Il capitano* (1545), *Il marito* (1547), and *Il ruffiano* (1551), are derived directly from Plautus. His *tragedies are paraphrases of Seneca and Euripides, though *Didone* (1547) and *Marianna* (1565) are original. His translations include all Seneca's tragedies (1560), the *Aeneid* (1568), and *Ovid's *Metamorphoses* (1553); they were severely criticized by Girolamo Ruscelli.

[ECMR]

Dolce stil novo. The poetic style of *Dante and his closest friends, Guido *Cavalcanti and *Cino da Pistoia, in their love poetry. The phrase is Dante's (*Purg.* 24.57), occurring in a dialogue on poetry with *Bonagiunta da Lucca. The latter contrasts the 'dolce stil novo' with that of *Giacomo da Lentini, *Guittone d'Arezzo, and himself, citing as the first example of the 'nove rime' 'Donne ch'avete intelletto d'amore', the first *canzone in the *Vita nova* (19). Dante asserts for his part that, unlike his more mannered predecessors, he only wishes to be true to the inspiration of love. And, indeed, in general *dolce stil novo* poetry aspires to the status of inspired text: the personal experience of passion of love is a guarantee of truth, but truth of an objective and absolute rather than subjective order. In 'Donne ch'avete' the main innovation is the spontaneous praise of the woman the poet loves as a miraculous creature filled with divine grace. Echoes of liturgical forms and biblical verses create the scriptural aura which is one of the main features of the style, not only in Dante but also in Cavalcanti, who was oriented much more towards natural philosophy and famed as an agnostic intellectual.

Anticipations of this new approach are already visible in the *Bolognese Guido *Guinizzelli, who was a correspondent of Guittone d'Arezzo and, in other respects, a traditionalist. But his *canzone*, 'Al cor gentil', the 'sweetness' of some of his poems, and also, no doubt, a polemical exchange which he had with Bonagiunta all lead Dante to hail him as his own and other poets' lyric 'father' in *Purgatorio* (26.97–9). But the *stil novo* really belonged to *Florence and the next generation of poets. Cavalcanti, if anyone, was the real initiator, as Dante himself suggests when he interprets the name of Cavalcanti's lady, Primavera, as 'Prima verrà' (*VN* 24).

As a school the *dolce stil novo* never extended beyond Dante's immediate circle and did not much outlast the *Vita nova* (?1295). Dante broke with Cavalcanti well before the latter's death in August 1300 and largely abandoned 'dolci rime d'amor', trying out 'stony rhymes' (the 'rime petrose' (1296)) and then committing himself to deliberately harsh-sounding moral *canzoni*. But the imagery, phrasing, and stylistic limpidity of the *stil novo* had a profound impact on the Italian *lyric, in part thanks to the enormous output of Cino, whose lyric career continued after Dante's death.

Some imitators of the *dolce stil novo* are included in modern anthologies alongside the major names—usually Gianni Degli *Alfani, *Lapo Gianni, and Dino *Frescobaldi, but sometimes even *Guido Orlandi and Sennuccio *Del Bene. This extension of the list goes back only to the 19th c., when aesthetes and pre-Raphaelites, with their taste for 'primitive' art, made the *stil novo* into an esoteric

sect of 'Fedeli d'Amore'. About the same time there was a focusing on the idea of the lady-as-angel as a key *stil novo* concept, though it was by no means original, and is to be found in Giacomo da Lentini, Guittone d'Arezzo, and *Dante da Maiano. Dante's *sonnet 'Guido i' vorrei che tu e Lapo ed io'—really an imitation of a Provençal *plazer*—was also given too much weight, to the extent of being deemed a definite poetic manifesto and specifying precisely which poets should be considered members of the circle of practitioners. [GG]

Poeti del dolce stil novo, ed. M. Marti (1969). See also G. Favati, *Inchiesta sul dolce stil novo* (1975).

DOLCI, DANILO (1924–97). Social campaigner and writer. Born in what is now modern Slovenia, Dolci studied architecture in *Trieste. He went to *Sicily in 1952 and devoted himself there to fighting hunger, unemployment, and poverty. His campaign for land reform and improved irrigation techniques brought him into conflict with the landowners and their allies in the *Mafia and politics, causing Dolci to be several times arrested and jailed. His movement attracted worldwide support, and he was described by Aldous Huxley as a secular saint. His early writings, such as *Inchiesta a Palermo* (1956), denouncing living conditions in the Sicilian capital, and *Banditi a Partinico* (1960), an enquiry into the causes of banditry, were companion pieces to his political struggle. He published several series of interviews which allowed ordinary Sicilians to speak for themselves, and also various volumes of poetry. In later years, he placed his faith less in political change and more in the idea of reform through educating the individual to realize his moral potential. [See also MEZZOGIORNO.] [JF]

Domenica del corriere, La (1889–1989) was the first Italian family magazine. A diet of patriotism, short stories, quizzes, and crosswords won it a regular following in its heyday (*c.*1900–50). Its illustrated front and back covers, drawn for nearly fifty years by Achille Beltrame, typically featured a mixture of disasters and curiosities. [See also JOURNALISM.] [SG]

Domenica letteraria, La (1882–5). Weekly paper founded by Ferdinando *Martini in *Rome, after he left the *Fanfulla della domenica. The original aim was to emphasize good taste and moderation, without direct political engagement, and to entertain and inform, especially as regards new books. *Sommaruga became editor in 1883 and introduced new contributors, including some of the best critics of the day, such as *Salvadori and *Scarfoglio. The paper published short stories by *Verga, *Capuana, *Serao, and *D'Annunzio and also poems by *Carducci. When Sommaruga's affairs collapsed in early 1885, the paper was acquired by Prince Maffeo Sciarra and merged with the *Cronaca bizantina. [GP]

DOMENICHI, LODOVICO (1515–64). Born in Piacenza, he was a professional writer, editor and *translator for the *printers Giolito in *Venice (1544–6) and Torrentino in *Florence (from 1547). His prolific output included editions of Luigi *Pulci and *Boiardo, anthologies of *lyric poetry and *facezie, and some mostly derivative works of his own: Rime (1544), Dialoghi (1562), a *comedy, Le due cortegiane (1561), and a verse *tragedy, La Progne (1561). He was imprisoned by the *Inquisition in 1552–3 for translating a work by Calvin. From the late 1550s he was court historian to Cosimo I de' *Medici. [RMD]

DOMENICO DA PRATO (c.1389–c.1433). *Florentine notary who composed love *sonnets and a long patriotic poem praising the Florentine struggle against Filippo Maria *Visconti. He also wrote an invective in defence of 14th-c. vernacular literature and of the *Tuscan vernacular against the *humanist avant-garde and their preference for classical Latin and Greek. [See also VOLGARE AND VOLGARE ILLUSTRE.] [RDB]

DOMENICO DI GIOVANNI, see BURCHIELLO, IL.

Dominicans. Order of friars founded by St Dominic in 1215, to help the Church in its struggles against heresy (in particular the Albigensians), primarily through preaching and the power of their arguments. The order quickly became known for its thinkers and teachers, who included Albertus Magnus and St Thomas *Aquinas. St *Caterina da Siena was a Dominican nun. In the *Divine Comedy *Dante has Aquinas castigate the order for its decadence in the Heaven of the Sun (Para. 11). [PH]

DOMINICI, GIOVANNI (1355/6–1419). *Florentine *Dominican, church reformer and university theologian, who died while attempting unsuccessfully to repress the Hussite *heresy. He is best known for his attack on classical and *humanist learning, Lucula noctis (1405), directed against

*Salutati, and for his treatise on *education, Regola del governo di cura famigliare (1401–3), in which he also condemned the reading of the pagan classics at school. [RDB]

DONATI, FORESE (d.1296). *Florentine friend of *Dante, who meets him on the terrace of the gluttonous in the *Divine Comedy (Purg. 22.37–24.97). A *tenzone of six *sonnets survives, in which he and Dante trade rather obscure and sometimes sexually derogatory insults after the conventions of *poesia giocosa. Some scholars have questioned its authenticity and dated it to the early 15th c. [PA]

Donation of Constantine. The Emperor Constantine was believed to have written to Pope Sylvester granting the *papacy the right to temporal power. Accepted as genuine by *Dante (Inf. 19.115) and by the *Middle Ages as a whole, the donation was exposed as a forgery by Lorenzo *Valla in the 15th c. [PH]

DONDI DALL'OROLOGIO, GIOVANNI (c.1318–89). *Paduan mathematician, astronomer, physician, and professor, who composed moral reflections (in Latin) and some rather uninspiring vernacular poetry. His nickname derives from the extraordinary astronomical timepiece which he designed and built, and which he describes in his Tractatus astrarii. (It was destroyed in the 16th c.) He was a friend and correspondent of *Petrarch. [SNB]

DONI, ANTON FRANCESCO (1513–74). Eccentric prose writer, *satirist, and *publisher, and a typical *poligrafo who lived by his pen. He was born in *Florence, the son of a scissors-maker. After a short period as a Servite monk, he wandered round the courts of Northern Italy, hoping in vain for permanent *patronage. He belonged to three *Academies: the Ortolana (Piacenza), the Accademia Fiorentina, and the Pellegrina (Venice), and knew many *letterati, especially *Domenichi and *Aretino. From 1546/7 he operated a *printing press in Florence before moving to *Venice, where he worked for Giolito de Ferrari.

His most important works are: La libraria (1550) and La seconda libraria (1551), which together form one of the earliest Italian *bibliographies; La zucca (1551), a bizarre anthology of comic sketches, caricatures, and jokes; I mondi (1552/3), a *Dantesque journey through seven imaginary worlds including a description of a Utopian city, based on Platonic ideas; and *I marmi* (1552/3), in which Doni imagines himself as a great bird reporting conversations overheard on the steps of Florence cathedral. His views are often anarchic, his style popular and expressionistic, but behind the humour lies a serious and bitter vein of ironic disillusionment with an unsatisfactory world. He was admired in both Italy and France as a moralist and *humorist. [ECMR]

DONIZETTI, GAETANO (1797–1848) was by the late 1830s the most frequently performed *opera composer in Italy, anticipating *Verdi in his fondness for violent subjects and in the vigour of his style. Besides fine tragic works, *Anna Bolena* (1830), *Lucrezia Borgia* (1833), and *Lucia di Lammermoor* (1835), he produced comic operas, two of which, *L'elisir d'amore* (1832) and *Don Pasquale* (1843), are the best of the kind after *Rossini. For much of his Italian career Donizetti was based in *Naples as Rossini's successor, but he too was drawn by the wealth and artistic freedom offered by Paris, where he composed both *opéra comique* (*La fille du régiment*, 1840) and grand opera (*La favorite*, 1842). [DRBK]

Donna del Vergiù, La, see CANTARI.

'Donna me prega', see CAVALCANTI, GUIDO.

DORIA, PERCIVALLE (d.1264). *Genoese statesman and poet who served at the German court in the South [see FREDERICK II]. Exposed to both the *troubadour and *Sicilian traditions, he composed a *sirventese* in praise of King *Manfredi in Provençal, and two elegant *canzoni* in the Sicilian manner. [JU]

D'ORSO, ANGIOLA. Actress active after 1638 who specialized in the role of the *innamorata*. She contributed to the vogue for Spanish theatre with *Di bene in meglio* (1656) and *Con chi vengo vengo* (1666), both *translations from the Spanish, the second from a work by Calderón. [See also THEATRE, 1.] [FC]

DOSSI, CARLO (1849–1910). The most famous and inventive of the *Scapigliatura novelists. Born into the *Lombard aristocracy and educated in *Milan and Pavia, Carlo Alberto Pisani Dossi began his literary career at 16, when he and his friend Gigi Perelli co-authored two stories published together as *Giannetto pregò un dì la mamma che il lasciasse andare alla scuola*. In 1867 they founded the ambitious journal *Palestra letteraria artistica e scientifica*, whose contributors were to include *Rovani, *Carducci, Francesco *Guerrazzi, and *Settembrini. Perelli brought Dossi into contact with the Milanese *Scapigliatura, and in particular with Giovanni Rovani. Dossi admired him as the equal of *Manzoni and wrote an unfinished study published posthumously as *Rovaniana*. But thanks to his wealth, and his character, he was able to maintain a personal and aesthetic distance from the movement. In 1872 he began a diplomatic career in *Rome, which he abandoned almost immediately, only to resume it in 1877. He married in 1892 and became consul general first in Bogotá and three years later in Athens. Both postings allowed him to pursue a passion for archaeology. He retired upon *Crispi's death in 1901.

In 1868 Dossi published the first of two *autobiographical narratives, *L'Altrieri: nero su bianco*, in which, in a highly creative linguistic pastiche with its main roots in Lombard *dialect, he evokes the golden age of childhood. It was followed by *Vita di Alberto Pisani scritta da Alberto Pisani* (1870), which opens with the defeat of the *Piedmontese at Novara (1849) and his own birth in nearby Zenevredo (Pavia). Like its predecessor it plays memory and storytelling against each other, but now episodes from the past are distinguished linguistically and set apart typographically from the main text; they would later be included as self-standing stories in *Goccie d'inchiostro* (1880). Both volumes were privately published in limited editions of 100 copies each. 1872 saw the publication of the elegy *Elvira*, likewise in a special edition, which included a drawing by the artist Cremona and musical notations by Edwart. Dossi's passion for satirical sketches led to *Ritratti umani, dal calamajo di un medico* (1873), *Ritratti umani. Campionario* (1885), and then to the extended, deeply *misogynistic polemic of *La desinenza in A* (1878), though alongside caricature and *satire came the Rousseauistic utopian vision of the *novel *La colonia felice* (1874). After his death his wife published *Note azzurre* (1912), a selection from the engaging, idiosyncratic notebooks that Dossi continued to write long after he had stopped publishing. A fuller edition appeared in 1964.
[AHC]
See D. Isella, *La lingua e lo stile di Carlo Dossi* (1958).

DOTTI, BARTOLOMEO (1642/51–1713) was the only *satirical poet of the time from the Veneto region. He combined the careers of soldier and man of letters, and led a turbulent life. Accused by the *Venetian authorities of complicity in an assassination attempt, he fled to *Milan, and was imprisoned in Tortona. There he penned his self-defence, much praised at the time. He escaped and returned to Venice, where he distinguished himself in military service, earning a reprieve from his exile. But his troubles pursued him, and he met death at the hand of a hired assassin.

His literary work includes *Rime* and *Sonetti*, published in 1689, and divided like *Marino's *lyrics into the encomiastic, descriptive, and erotic. Dotti does not develop Marino's insistence on nature and the senses; instead he strikes a more moralistic tone that has its roots in a *Lombard poetic tradition later to flourish in the poetry of *Parini and *Alfieri. He is most famous for his *Satire*, published posthumously in 1757, in which he rails against Venetian hypocrisy in a popular and semi-*dialectal Italian.

[PBD]

Dottore, Il. A mask of the *commedia dell'arte* from the late 16th c., the Doctor was a learned or pseudo-learned pedant, invariably a lawyer, and popularly associated with the university town of *Bologna. Given to spouting *macaronic Latin and citing learned authorities, his tended to be the second *vecchio* role (together with *Pantalone), as father to one or more of the young lovers, and often gulled by them or by servants. He was instantly identifiable by a loose-fitting black tunic, belted at the waist, with white ruffs at neck and wrists, black cape, and large black flat cap. [KR]

DOTTORI, CARLO DE' (1618–86). *Paduan poet, dramatist, and novelist, who spent most of his life as a court poet under the *patronage of Eleonora *Gonzaga, *Christina of Sweden, and Leopold of *Austria. His life was turbulent, including in 1641 a brief prison sentence for libelling *Paduan women (see his *satirical poem *Prigione*, written in 1643 and modelled on *Marino's *Camerone*). He was also a leading member of the Accademia del *Cimento and a close friend of *Redi and of *Ciro di Pers, with whom he conducted a fascinating correspondence. His frankness and directness come through in his posthumous *Confessioni*, in which he portrays his intimate life, including his final illness, against the background of a pompous and corrupt society.

His masterpiece is the *tragedy *Aristodemo*, published in 1657. The plot concerns the sacrifice of the virgin Merope by her father, Aristodemo, and the subsequent stoning of her fiancé Policare. With elements taken from Euripides and Sophocles (for the plot), from Seneca (for the thought), and Lucan (for the style), Dottori produced an intensely lyric but also heroic *neoclassical drama. Like those of Federico *Della Valle, it centres on the opposition of victim and victor, but reverses the roles at the end, so that both Merope (an exceptionally strong female portrait) and Aristodemo achieve stoical heroism and tragic annihilation.

The themes of *Aristodemo* also form the basis of his large production of *lyric poetry: from 1643 to 1680 he published collections of *sonnets, *canzoni, and neoclassical sacred and profane odes, with progressively more frequent echoes of the work of Marino and Ciro di Pers. Dottori also wrote poetry in a lighter vein: his *Asino*, published in 1652, is modelled on *Tassoni's *mock-heroic *Secchia rapita* and tells, in ten cantos, of a war between Padua and Vicenza. He wrote a *novel when he was 20 (*Alfenore*, published in 1644), which mixes classical, courtly, Christian, and pagan elements; and several prose dramas. [PBD]

D'OVIDIO, FRANCESCO, see LITERARY THEORY, 5.

DOVIZI, BERNARDO (il Bibbiena) (1470–1520), was a nobleman, politician and eventually cardinal in the service of the *Medici in exile. *Castiglione presents him as an expert on *humour and practical jokes; and he is chiefly remembered as author of the scurrilous *comedy La *Calandra*, first performed in 1513, published in 1521, and the comedy most often reprinted in the 16th c. The impossibly gullible character of Calandro is taken from *Boccaccio's Calandrino; and one feature of this comedy is the effort made to echo the verbal formulas of the *Decameron* as often as possible, perhaps to help an audience link the still unfamiliar performing patterns of *humanist comedy to something they already knew. Calandro is mocked for the audience's benefit in one-off vaudeville routines, related to street theatre and eventually to *commedia dell'arte*. The carnivalesque plot of *beffa* and successful adultery was also familiar from Boccaccio, though humanist comedy eventually preferred more morally acceptable stories ending in marriage. [RAA]

DRAGONCINO, GIOVAN BATTISTA (1497–c.1547). Poet. Born in Fano, little is known of him before 1521, when he is resident in *Venice;

his literary career is wholly associated with the Venetian nobility, and he is mentioned in the correspondence of *Aretino. His poetic works cover several different genres, including *travel pieces, *lyrics in various metres, and encomiastic poems. He is best known for his unfinished *romance *epic, *Marfisa bizarra* (1531), dedicated to Federigo *Gonzaga. Based on the character Marfisa in *Ariosto's *Orlando furioso*, who here goes mad for love, the poem inspired a number of other works about the same character, and continued to be popular into the 17th c.   [JEE]

Drama, see COMEDY; THEATRE; TRAGEDY; TRAGI-COMEDY.

Dramma per musica, see LIBRETTO; MELO-DRAMMA.

DUCCIO DI GANO, see MIRACOLI DELLA VERGINE MARIA, I.

Duchessa di Leyra, La, see VERGA, GIOVANNI.

DURANTI, FRANCESCA (1935–). *Novelist, who uses an accessible style and gripping plots to treat themes such as relationships between mothers and daughters, consumerism, the commercialization of culture, the problems of the woman writer, and the complex interplay between reality and fiction. The first of her eight novels, *La bambina* (1976), recalled her wartime childhood with gentle irony. She gained celebrity with *La casa sul lago della luna* (1984), which explored a translator's growing alienation from reality through identifying himself with the author of the novel he is translating. Alternative realities reappear, with an ironic *science-fiction colouring, in more recent novels: *Progetto Burlamacchi* (1994) concerns an attempt to use a computer program to construct a corruption-free virtual history of Italy, while in *Sogni mancini* (1996) the protagonist analyses her dreams to try to discover her other, left-handed self.   [SV]

DURANTI DA GUALDO, PIETRO (15th–16th c.). Author of a *romance *epic in six-line stanzas entitled *La Leandra* (1508), which enjoyed a notable printing fortune in the 16th c. The theme of the poem is a journey by *Rinaldo to Jerusalem and his adventures there, particularly the wooing of Leandra, the daughter of the Sultan.   [JEE]

DUSE, ELEONORA, see D'ANNUNZIO, GABRIELE; THEATRE, 2.

E

Ecerinis, see MUSSATO, ALBERTINO.

Eclogue, see PASTORAL.

ECO, UMBERTO (1932–). *Semiotician and novelist. Born in Alessandria, he graduated in philosophy from *Turin University with a thesis on the aesthetics of Thomas *Aquinas in 1954. In the 1950s he worked for state *television in *Milan at a particularly creative moment in the city's postwar history and was one of the writers and critics associated with *il *verri,* who later formed the nucleus of the *Gruppo 63. Two books published in the early 1960s made his reputation. *Opera aperta* (1962) sought to establish an aesthetics of indeterminacy in modern art, particularly in music and the visual arts. *Apocalittici e integrati* (1964) was the first sustained attempt in Italy to understand how the messages transmitted by the media of popular culture actually work.

Eco's early aesthetics were strongly influenced by the theory of formativity of his university teacher, Luigi *Pareyson. He now searched for a philosophical discourse which would bring the varied disciplines with which he was concerned within a unified field and progressed through linguistics and information theory to *structuralism and semiotics. He spent much of the period 1967–76 constructing a systematic theory, culminating in *A Theory of Semiotics* (first published in English in 1976). At the same time he wrote extensively for newspapers and magazines, collecting many of his articles in *Il costume di casa* (1973) and *Sette anni di desiderio* (1983), and continued to work on popular culture, with studies such as *Il superuomo di massa* (1976). He was appointed to a specially created chair of semiotics at *Bologna in 1975.

A continuing preoccupation with questions of logic and epistemology is evident in his subsequent work, from *Semiotics and the Philosophy of Language* (1984) to *Kant e l'ornitorinco* (1997), the latter showing a particular concern with recent advances in the cognitive sciences. Text pragmatics and theories of narrativity, especially with reference to the nature, scope, and limits of interpretation also come to the fore in a series of books beginning with *Lector in fabula* (1979). Finally, during the last twenty years of the 20th c., Eco gained worldwide fame as a novelist. *Il *nome della rosa* (1980). *Il pendolo di Foucault* (1988), *L'isola del giorno prima* (1994), and *Baudolino* (2000) pick up the playful, parodistic strain which had been already evident in the short *journalistic pieces of *Diario minimo* (1963), as well as reflecting Eco's interests as a philosopher and semiotician. [MPC]

See R. Cotroneo, *La diffidenza come sistema* (1995); M. Caesar, *Umberto Eco: Philosophy, Semiotics and the Work of Fiction* (1999).

Editori Riuniti, see PUBLISHING.

Education

1. Before 1600

Urbanized Italy had a long tradition of secular schools alongside the monastic, cathedral, and parish schools that were predominant north of the Alps (and which declined dramatically in Italy after 1200). The extent of urban literacy was high, as was the commitment of most towns in the late *Middle Ages to sponsor municipal schooling. Italy was also home to the most significant educational revolution of pre-industrial Europe. From the early days of their heated arguments with the Church over the legitimacy of studying the classics, the *humanists made education a central platform, and it is this professional embodiment of their ideas that became the primary vehicle for the spread of those ideas. The replacement of traditional pedagogical texts, almost all from within the Christian tradition, by classical writers (*Virgil, *Cicero, Terence, *Horace) was accompanied by a belief that education was about the formation of the 'whole' mind and character. Teachers such as *Vittorino da Feltre and *Guarino da Verona put these ideas into practice, while humanists like Leonardo *Bruni and Pier Paolo *Vergerio the Elder publicized the ideas in widely circulated tracts [see also MALATESTA, BATTISTA].

The speed with which the humanist educational agenda, the *studia humanitatis*, took root was spectacular; by the 1440s it is difficult to find a town that was not trying to employ one of the new breed of teachers. Yet the extent to which there was fundamental change is controversial. The persistence of traditional texts at the elementary level can be seen in the history of *manuscripts and *printed books, while scholars have disputed whether the 'moral programme' of the humanists was so distinct from that of their medieval precursors. The elitist agenda of the humanist educators gives the movement particular significance, and helps to explain its spread in and beyond Italy. [See also JESUITS; UNIVERSITIES.]   [PRD]

See P. F. Grendler, *Schooling in Renaissance Italy. Literacy and Learning, 1300–1600* (1989); P. Gehl, *A Moral Art: Grammar, Society, and Culture in Trecento Florence* (1993).

2. 1600–1870

The *Counter-Reformation imposed religious orthodoxy on education as on other aspects of cultural life and discouraged the spirit of enquiry that characterized the *Renaissance. The negative effects were felt particularly in *universities. On the other hand the educational mission of the *Jesuits and other orders resulted in the establishment of new colleges with rigorously organized programmes of study, which could include modern subjects such as algebra and geography and were directed particularly (though not exclusively) at the aristocracy. For the poor there were Sunday schools (Schools of Christian Doctrine) centred on parish churches in the larger cities. These were often staffed by lay confraternities, and aimed to develop elementary reading skills and a basic knowledge of the Bible and the catechism. Carlo *Borromeo was particularly active in promoting schools of this kind in *Milan and other Lombard cities. In *Rome in 1611 there were seventy-eight such schools catering for 10,000 pupils, girls as well as boys.

It is during the *Enlightenment that firm proposals begin to be put forwards for secular state education. These were given a new urgency by the suppression of the Jesuits in 1773. *Habsburg Parma and Milan both tried reformist educational programmes in the later 18th c., whilst in *Naples *Filangieri elaborated a theory of free elementary education for all, the *peasantry included. How narrow and prejudiced education was in practice in the 18th c. can be gauged from the admittedly highly charged account by *Alfieri of his experiences in his *Vita*. But with the absorption of French ideas during the *Napoleonic period it came to be increasingly accepted that elementary education should be free and obligatory for all citizens, and the issue loomed large in *Risorgimento thinking from the *Romantic *manifesti* of 1816 onwards. Nevertheless, even after *Unification, economic, linguistic, and social divisions meant that the high levels of innumeracy and illiteracy were only gradually reduced.   [PH]

3. From 1870

The education system adopted by the Italian State on *Unification was based on the Casati Law (1859). Existing universities were secularized and brought under the control of the Ministry of Education. The major problem of Liberal Italy was illiteracy, and efforts were made in 1877 and in 1911 to reduce this through the extension of primary schools and by taking them out of the control of the local councils who had been so reluctant to fund them. The advent of *Fascism in 1922 brought the philosopher Giovanni *Gentile to the ministry: he reinforced the dominance of classical, humanistic education over technical and vocational development. His successor, Giuseppe *Bottai, tried to redress the balance in his *Carta della scuola* (1939). But this was overtaken by Italy's entry into *World War II.

There were no further major educational reforms until the Gui laws of the 1960s. The result of these was a large increase in numbers in secondary schools and hence in universities, which in part was responsible for the student agitations of 1967 and *1968. Universities remain oversubscribed, understaffed, and (especially in the sciences) underfunded, and the power of professorial *baroni* is still largely intact. But degrees are now being shortened and modernized and the administration decentralized. However, schools and the school exam system are still rigorously controlled from the centre.   [JP]

EGIDIO DA VITERBO (1469–1532). Cardinal, Catholic reformer, linguist, and poet who joined the *Augustinians in 1488. Educated at *Padua, he studied under *Ficino in *Florence, and became an active supporter of the *Accademia Pontaniana in *Naples. His polished rhetoric placed him among the most lionized preachers of his day, but his ablest oration was the appeal for reform which opened the fifth Lateran Council in 1512. His manifold intellectual attainments included a rare knowledge of Arabic and a vernacular poem on *hunting.   [PMcN]

EGIDIO ROMANO, see SCHOLASTICISM.

EGIO, BENEDETTO, see ANTIQUARIANISM.

1848. The most celebrated and widespread of the 19th-c. European revolutions proved also a crucial turning point in the Italian *Risorgimento. Beginning with an insurrection in Palermo in January, revolution spread to *Naples and *Rome, and then, with the overthrow of governments in Paris and Vienna, to Central and Northern Italy. But there were tensions between revolutionaries (amongst whom were *Mazzini, *Garibaldi, Carlo *Cattaneo, Antonio Mordini, and Daniele Manin), between different Italian regions, and between city and countryside. The revolutions veered between extremes and ended in total defeat in the summer of 1849. The ensuing heroic mythology was exploited by Italian *nationalists, but subsequent developments were dominated by moderate *liberals and by *Cavour.   [LR]

Einaudi. *Publishing firm founded in *Turin in 1933 by Giulio Einaudi. Associated from the beginning with dissent from *Fascism, the firm was a fellow-traveller of the *Communist Party (PCI) until the mid-1950s, publishing Il *Politecnico and *Gramsci. It published *translations of major works of American and European literature, history, and social theory, as well as much of the new Italian literature. *Pavese, *Calvino, *Vittorini, Leone *Ginzburg, and Natalia *Ginzburg worked as editors, and were decisive in establishing Einaudi's distinctive identity and prestigious reputation. It nearly collapsed in 1983 after running up heavy bank debts, but was rescued by a semi-merger with *Mondadori.   [DF]

EINAUDI, LUIGI (1874–1961). Politician and economist. He was governor of the Bank of Italy from 1945, a member of the Constituent Assembly, and became President of the Republic in 1948. The postwar economic miracle would not have occurred without his stringent policies.   [PC]

Electronic Resources for Italian Studies, either in the form of commercial publications or accessible through the Internet, are in a constant state of development; in contrast, any information we can give about them on paper is necessarily out of date even before it is published. All that can be provided here, therefore, is a selective account of what is available at the time of writing, and some general indications as to its use. The resources that concern us fall into the following categories: (1) text archives (texts in machine-readable form) and image archives (for instance of specific manuscripts or editions); (2) databases containing bibliographies, catalogues, etc.; (3) websites for research groups or centres, or professional and cultural associations; (4) electronic journals, news groups, and specialist mailing lists.

A number of collections of Italian literary texts are available on CD-ROM or on disk, though their quality is uneven. The best-known and most substantial is the CD-ROM *Letteratura italiana Zanichelli*, edited by Pasquale Stoppelli and Eugenio Picchi, comprising a searchable collection of several hundred texts of Italian literature from the origins to the 20th c. However the major future development of resources is most likely to involve online distribution through the Internet, for a number of reasons: the much greater freedom of access, including in most cases the absence of any financial charge; the ease with which both tools and materials can be updated; the scholarly and educational environment that websites can provide, combining updatable anthologies of texts with information about the criteria of selection and systems of encoding followed. Search engines are also available on the web for the creation of concordances, indices, and word lists and for statistical analysis. In an academic context the question of standards is critical; the scholarly validity of the resources provided needs to be guaranteed through the use of clear and rigorous procedures. Organizations specifically concerned with such standards are the Text Encoding Initiative and the more recently established Scriptoria Nova association.

The largest collection of Italian literary texts has been made available online through a major national initiative, the Biblioteca Italiana Telematica (CIBIT). Broad collections of Italian texts are also accessible in electronic form at a number of sites, of which the most notable are: BAUDHAUS (University of Turin), CRILet (a major venture comprising a wide range of digital resource projects at a variety of centres in Italy), CISADU (University of Rome I 'La Sapienza'), CRAIAT (University of Florence), CRS4 (Sardinia), and LIBER LIBER. Sites of more specific interest include, for *Dante, the Dartmouth and the Princeton Dante Projects (Dartmouth College and Princeton University), DanteNet (Dante Association of America), Tweb Digital Dante Project (Columbia University), Renaissance Dante in Print (University of Notre Dame, The Newberry Library); the website of the Società Dantesca Italiana is particularly interesting because of the facility for linking the text of the *Divine Comedy* to images of its manuscripts. For *Boccaccio there is the *Decameron Web (Brown University), Hyperdecameron (Universities of Lille III, Princeton, Pennsylvania, Zurich, Rome I, and Rome II), Zibaldoni (Rome I, and Rome II); for cultural anthropology the Libri di Famiglia (University of Rome II 'Tor Vergata'); for contemporary literature the Alvaro project (Rome I). Examples of electronic journals are the *Bollettino '900* (University of Bologna), the *Electronic Bulletin* of the Dante Society of America, *Quaderni di Letteratura* (Rome I). Active mailing lists for Italian specialists, with news of publications, meetings, appointments, etc. are Let-it (Rome I), Lettere Italiane (Zurich), and the Italian studies list on the UK JISCmail system.

Web search engines such as Yahoo or Altavista generally allow easy access to most of the sites listed, and in many cases hypertext links help the user to navigate between those of related interest. An invaluable research tool is the online public-access catalogue (OPAC) of the Istituto Centrale per il Catalogo Unico delle Biblioteche Italiane e per le Informazioni Bibliografiche, a union catalogue of Italian libraries. [CC-B]

Elegantiae, see VALLA, LORENZO.

Elegia giudeo-italiana (early 13th c.). A ritual chant (*kina*) of 120 lines, lamenting the dispersion of the *Jews, and praying for the rebuilding of the Temple. It is written in a central Italian *dialect (perhaps that of *Rome or the Marche) in monorhymed tercets. [JU]

Elegie romane, see D'ANNUNZIO, GABRIELE.

Elegy, see LATIN POETRY IN ITALY.

Elettra, see D'ANNUNZIO, GABRIELE.

Elias Portolu, see DELEDDA, GRAZIA.

Emblems. Andrea *Alciato's *Emblematum liber*, published in Augsburg in 1531, inaugurated the genre with a collection of epigrams, each combined with a motto and a picture to yield a neat moral. Alciato's models were essentially literary and classical, above all the poems in the *Greek Anthology*; but his German publisher thought to add the illustrations which made the term *emblema* (literally 'inlaid work') appropriate. Emblems jostled with other symbolic conjunctions of word and image (hieroglyphs, personal devices, *imprese*) for a place in the imagination of *Renaissance Italians. Fostered in the *academies, they tended more to wit than to proverbial wisdom, *concettismo* rather than the didacticism favoured in Northern Europe. [See also ICONOGRAPHY.] [EMcG]

Emigration. Until the mid-19th c. the great majority of Italians lived their lives where they were born. Medieval Italian *merchants and *bankers spent periods away from home, but they commonly returned after relatively short stays. From the *Renaissance onwards Italian artists, musicians, and writers, ranging from Pontormo to *Metastasio and *Goldoni, were invited to foreign *courts and cities, and sometimes remained for years.

Mass emigration developed quite suddenly. Even in 1861 the number of Italians resident abroad was officially calculated to be only 220,000. Earlier waves were predominantly from the rural North, especially the Veneto, and the destinations were the industrial cities of France, Germany, and other Northern European countries. Then North and South America emerged as alternatives, which during the years leading up to *World War I superseded Europe as preferred destinations, especially for Southern Italians. Between 1898 and 1914 an average of a quarter of a million Italians, 70 per cent of them Southerners, crossed the Atlantic each year, though some years saw more than double that figure. By this stage the USA was the favourite destination, whereas Brazil and Argentina had drawn more immigrants in the 1870s and 1880s. Already in 1898 there were more immigrants to the USA from Italy than from any other country. The majority were *peasants driven by rural poverty, whichever part of the country they came from. In the earlier stages it was men rather than families who left. Often they went abroad to work only for short periods, sometimes regularly for a number of years. Most maintained links with their home villages. Particularly in the South these were often reduced to a steadily diminishing population of women, children, and old people, but many emigrants eventually returned if only to die and be buried at home. [See also MEZZOGIORNO.]

The 'safety valve' (as *Nitti first called it) for overpopulation and economic backwardness had its major outlet closed when the USA imposed drastic quotas in the early 1920s, which in 1924 fixed the number for Italy at 4,000 people per annum. Whilst the *Fascist government estimated that there were 9 million Italians living abroad in 1927, that number did not increase again appreciably until after *World War II. The African colonies, gained at great cost from before World War I, never attracted Italians in the numbers that Fascist propaganda projected, though Italians did go to work in French and British possessions. In the 1950s external emigration picked up again as Australia, Canada, and South Africa emerged as new destinations outside Europe, and industrialized Europe again felt the need of southern workers.

But emigration abroad had perhaps less effect on the social fabric of Italy than internal migration. Large numbers of peasants were already moving from the Northern countryside into *Milan, *Genoa, *Turin, and even *Florence by the end of the 19th c. In the 20th c. the haemorrhage increased nationally, until by the later 1960s Italy had changed from a predominantly agricultural to a major industrial country. Though there had been substantial population movements in the 1920s which affected Milan and *Rome in particular, the most dramatic changes came with the postwar economic boom. About 4 million people moved permanently from the South to the North in the 1950s and 1960s, fundamentally altering the social composition and the culture of the towns where they found work.

Italian literature has frequently examined the traumas of postwar internal migration within the context of the modernization of which it is part. Mass emigration abroad has figured much less prominently, though *De Amicis' Sull'oceano (1889) alerted contemporaries to the suffering and exploitation of 19th-c. emigrants, and *Pascoli showed a similar sympathy in some of the Nuovi poemetti (1909). The body of writings by emigrants themselves is considerable and is now being rediscovered, particularly by their descendants in the relevant countries. But Italian or *dialect generally gave way before English, Spanish, and other European languages. Only in the later postwar period is sophisticated work in Italian on any scale produced by Italians working abroad, generally in universities. [See also COLONIAL LITERATURE; EXILE; ITALIAN WRITERS IN AUSTRALIA; ITALIAN WRITERS IN THE UNITED STATES.] [PH]

See F. Durante (ed.), Italoamericana: storia e letteratura degli italiani negli Stati Uniti (1776–1880), vol. i (2001).

EMMEPÌ, see PRAGA, MARCO.

Enciclopedia italiana. Considered the most complete of all Italian *encyclopedias. Apart from obvious political articles, it was remarkably independent of the *Fascist regime under which it was created. It is referred to as the 'Treccani' after Senator Giuseppe *Treccani degli Alfieri, who in collaboration with Giovanni *Gentile helped finance and carry out its organizational plan. With the help of over 1,500 contributors, it was completed in 37 volumes in October 1937, with a supplement for the years 1929–37 appearing in 1938 and the indexes in the following year. In 1948–9 the Treccani Institute brought out an appendix for the period 1938–48, which reflected the social and political concerns of the postwar era. [RSD]

Encyclopedias. It was the *Enlightenment which developed the modern encyclopedia. The first original Italian encyclopedia of note is the Nuovo dizionario scientifico e curioso sacro-profano of Gianfranco Pivati (1689–1764), published in *Venice in ten volumes in 1746–51. But the major English and French encyclopedias were quickly made available in Italian. Chamber's Encyclopedia (1728) appeared in *Venice in 1749 as Dizionario universale delle arti e scienze (9 vols.) and the Italian version of D'Alembert and Diderot's Encyclopédie (1750–72) in 1758–78. The trend to rely particularly on translations from the French continued into the 19th c. A significant exception was Antonio Bazzarini's Dizionario enciclopedico delle scienze, lettere e arti (1830–7), in nine volumes, again published in Venice. Attempts to broaden the availability of knowledge are reflected in the Nuova enciclopedia popolare, published by Giuseppe *Pomba in *Turin in instalments in 1842–3, which was revised and expanded until in its twenty-four-volume sixth edition (1875–88) it could claim to be the equal of its best European counterparts. It was only superseded by the *Enciclopedia italiana (1929–39). [See also ENCYCLOPEDISM.] [NMS]

Encyclopedism. The term 'encyclopedia' is first used by Rabelais, and derives from the Greek 'enkuklios paideia' which appears in Pliny the Elder and Quintilian. However, the notion of an encyclopedia was widespread throughout the *Middle Ages. The 13th c. saw the great Latin encyclopedic projects of Alexander of Neckham, Thomas de Cantimpré, and Vincent of Beauvais, and also the first encyclopedias in the vernacular. Whilst they are inspired by Isidore of Seville's *Etymologiae* and Hugh of Saint Victor's *Didascalicon*, these high medieval encyclopedias are characterized by a greater scientific and practical approach to their material. They are not just concerned with the origin of words, but also with their place in rational discourse, their historical and political significance, and their relationship to objects; they emphasize the importance not merely of knowing the names of things but of discovering their nature and properties. It was requirements such as these that inspired Brunetto *Latini's *Tresor*, which was written in French during the author's *exile in France (between 1260 and 1266), and immediately *translated into Italian by *Bono Giamboni. This is a vast compilation of contemporary knowledge, covering theology, history, ethics, politics, and rhetoric, and is presented to the reader as a basis for his civic and intellectual development. Much the same features are evident in the *Composizione del mondo*, the cosmological treatise written by *Restoro d'Arezzo before 1282.

The encyclopedic cast of mind soon showed itself also in the literary sphere. Brunetto again pointed the way. In his verse *Tesoretto* he used poetic language and *allegory to present an array of theological, philosophical, psychological, and cosmological notions. He was immediately followed by his pupil *Dante, who attempted encyclopedias of linguistics (*De vulgari eloquentia*) and philosophy (*Convivio*), but did not complete either. He then finally fashioned in the *Divine Comedy* the one true encyclopedia of style and poetry that was created in the Middle Ages. Dante's masterpiece provided the model for 14th-c. didactic poetry with encyclopedic aims, such as *Cecco d'Ascoli's *Acerba* and Fazio degli *Uberti's *Dittamondo*. But the great collections of *novelle* also came into being in the same period, starting with *Boccaccio's *Decameron*, whose title alludes to an organizing stucture typical of the medieval encyclopedia.

[See also ENCYCLOPEDIAS for the modern period.] [MP]
See M. Picone (ed.), *L'enciclopedismo medievale* (1993).

Endecasillabi, see HENDECASYLLABLE.

ENDRIGO, SERGIO, see CANTAUTORI.

English Influences did not play a major role in Italian literature until the 20th c., partly because French took precedence as a second language until at least the 1960s. As part of the European audience of English literature, Italians began to admire and produce *Shakespeare's plays in the 18th c., and were taken by the vogue of Richardson; *Goldoni adapted *Pamela* for the *theatre; *Casanova followed the example of the fictional Lovelace. *Foscolo translated Sterne's *Sentimental Journey* and added, in Sterne's style, his humorous self-portrait as Didimo Chierico. Traces of Sterne's manner may be found in the narrators of I *promessi sposi* and *Nievo's *Confessioni*, and survive as late as the *Scapigliatura and *Tozzi. *Manzoni and other authors of *historical novels learned much from Scott; Manzoni's *Fermo e Lucia* also has discernible antecedents in the Gothic novel. The Italianate Byron enjoyed a great vogue and had many imitators, among them *Leopardi in 'Consalvo'. Shelley became a major presence in the late 19th c., partly because of his revolutionary politics, and was echoed and celebrated by *Carducci and *D'Annunzio. He was translated by Adolfo *De Bosis. His urn in *Rome is also evoked in *Pasolini's 'Le ceneri di Gramsci'.

D'Annunzio imitated Wilde, Swinburne, and Pater, as was first demonstrated by Mario *Praz, whose classic study, *The Romantic Agony*, is largely devoted to English Decadence. Praz was the major Italian Anglicist of his time and an outstanding essayist in the tradition of Charles Lamb, whom he translated. He borrowed from Rossetti the title of his extraordinary self-portrait as a collector, *The House of Life*. Emilio *Cecchi, who was also immensely influential as a critic and essayist, derived his elaborate style and taste from Poe, Coleridge, and Stevenson, and wrote a history of the English Romantics. Italo *Svevo learnt English and some techniques (fictional and dramatic) from Joyce. Both Praz and Cecchi were conservative and suspicious of America. On the other hand, the young rebels of the 1930s took English and American writers as models of democracy. *Pavese and

Enlightenment

*Vittorini translated Joyce and Lawrence and borrowed from them in their novels; *Fenoglio in *Il partigiano Johnny* has his autobiographical hero think in English. Closer to Praz and Cecchi in taste, *Montale translated Eliot (as well as *Hamlet*, Hopkins, and Dylan Thomas) and was stimulated by *The Waste Land* and Pound's *Cantos* to undertake the linguistic and visionary experiments of *Le occasioni* and *La bufera e altro*. His later prosy verse is related to Eliot's *The Cocktail Party*, and his poetry and prose often touch on English subjects.

After 1945, no writer is immune to English influence. James is important for *Bassani and *Tomasi di Lampedusa (who wrote a private history of English Literature), while Joyce's *Ulysses* (translated in 1960) proves an important model for *Gadda and *D'Arrigo. Conrad and Stevenson are revered by *Calvino, and England is mythicized by *Ortese. *Arbasino is the perfect Anglophile, including reports and interviews with the likes of Eliot, Forster, and Compton-Burnett in his *Lettere da Londra* (1997). Some poets, notably Attilio *Bertolucci, *Giudici, and *Conte, specialize in English as critics and translators. Dickinson has been translated by Margherita *Guidacci, Shakespeare by Patrizia *Valduga, and Donne by Patrizia *Cavalli. The highly individual Amelia *Rosselli wrote *feminist experimental verse in a sort of Esperanto English.

Genres particularly associated with England have also been influential: the *diary (*Alfieri to *Landolfi), the thriller (*Eco, *Fruttero e Lucentini), *biography (*Citati, *Vassalli). Humorous fiction, from Carroll to Jerome and Wodehouse, stimulated the wit and sparkle of *Zavattini, *Campanile, *Marotta, *Guareschi, *Flaiano, and *Fellini.

[MB]

See M. Praz, *Storia della letteratura inglese* (1966); A. Lombardo (ed.), *Gli inglesi e l'Italia* (1998).

Enlightenment (*illuminismo*). The term used to describe the cultural movement which spread from France to most of continental Europe in the 18th c. The central figures of the French Enlightenment proclaimed the importance of critical reasoning in opposition to authority, in line with Descartes, Spinoza, and Leibniz in the previous century. They also linked the pursuit of reason with practical avenues which had been opened up at the same time by British empiricists such as Locke, Berkeley, and Hume, alongside the scientific ideas of Isaac Newton.

Given the compact national climate of conservative hostility within which the French Enlightenment thinkers elaborated their ideas, they developed a strong sense of the strategic importance of intellectual pursuits and assumed a position of European leadership in championing the cultural and material aspirations of the emerging forces of opposition to the feudal order. Diderot's *Encyclopédie*, written in seventeen volumes between 1751 and 1772, was intended to present, in non-dogmatic form, the most up-to-date thinking for popular consumption and to stimulate further developments. The *philosophes* as a whole promoted a spirit of emancipation from all forms of political, religious, and cultural servitude to blind tradition. The themes of liberty, equality, and tolerance were linked with new objectives in the arts, new ideas about the nature of society, and a desire to promote the study of all branches of knowledge which would transform society and secure happiness for all.

Italian *illuminismo* was conditioned by changes in the peninsula's role in Europe with the advent of the *Habsburgs in *Lombardy and *Tuscany and the *Bourbons in *Naples, *Sicily, and Parma. The unprecedented period of peace between 1748 and 1796, which resulted from the separation of the Italian states from the rival dynasties of Europe, offered the opportunity for reforms. The main, but not exclusive, Enlightenment centres were Lombardy, Tuscany, and Naples. What united all Italian *illuministi* in their different spheres of activity was a shared conviction about the backwardness of Italy compared to other parts of Europe. This view of the plight of the whole peninsula inspired the *journalistic endeavours of individuals like the *Venetian Apostolo *Zeno and the monumental intellectual labours of the Emilian *Muratori, who were concerned in their different ways to shape specifically Italian forms of cultural identity.

In Tuscany the Enlightenment was characterized by harmonious relations between the ruler Peter Leopold (1765–90) and reforming intellectuals like Giovanni Lami, Sallustio Antonio Bandini, and Pompeo Neri, who pioneered changes in cultural, religious, juridical, and economic thinking with a measure of success in terms of practical outcome. These intellectuals did not feel driven to expend their labours in writing great works of reforming zeal, although Ferdinando Paoletti did write in defence of the anti-feudal physiocratic principles of free trade which Peter Leopld was putting into practice.

In Naples the spirit of the Enlightenment found its first expression in *Giannone's historical work in defence of the rights of the secular state against ecclesiastical interference (1723), which became famous in European anti-curialist circles. The arrival in Naples of Charles of Bourbon in 1734 paved the way for changes in Church–state relations as promoted by the resident Tuscan reformer Bernardo *Tanucci. Deeply rooted feudal attitudes, however, impeded political and economic reforms. Ferdinando *Galiani, best known for his economic writings, became a friend of leading French intellectuals during his ten years in Paris (1759–69). In his correspondence with the *philosophes*, after his return to Naples, he discussed many of the philosophical issues of the day, including free will, atheism, materialism, and the existence of God.

A more influential figure in the South was Antonio *Genovesi, who held numerous posts at the University of Naples from 1741. After ecclesiastical hostility to his attempt to replace *scholasticism with a rationalist theology of Cartesian and Lockeian derivation, he turned his attention to promoting an ideal of socially useful learning and *education. His subsequent writings in the field of economics, in which he favoured a combination of free-market and regulatory approaches, inspired two schools of southern disciples. The first, which included Giuseppe Palmieri, Giuseppe *Galanti, and Melchiorre *Delfico, was characterized by a pragmatic desire to apply rational economic ideas of reform to the solution of immediate problems. The second group included the more radical 'utopian' reformers *Filangieri and *Pagano.

The most important centre of Enlightenment thought was *Milan, where many intellectuals managed to gain the confidence of their *Austrian rulers and take an active part in guiding the reforms promoted by Maria Theresa and Joseph II (1740–90). Pietro *Verri took a leading role in organizing groups of intellectuals around the Accademia dei Pugni and the journal *Il *Caffè*, including such figures as Alfonso Longo, Giambattista Biffi, Paolo Frisi, Gianrinaldo *Carli, and Giuseppe *Gorani. The whole range of Enlightenment ideas, including economic, juridical, moral, literary, aesthetic, and linguistic themes, was explored and written about. Cesare *Beccaria, whose *Dei delitti e delle pene* achieved international fame, was invited to Paris by the *philosophes* to promote his ideas, and was offered positions in foreign courts. In an astonishing synthesis of the most advanced ideas of the period,

Beccaria envisaged a modern system of justice based on social theories which drew the admiration also of Thomas Jefferson and Jeremy Bentham. Pietro Verri, in addition to writing on economics and history, wrote works of social philosophy, utilizing the *sensismo* of Condillac and the theories of Maupertuis on pain and pleasure to produce the peninsula's most comprehensive philosophical defence of the idea of historical progress. Verri developed his ideas on pain and pleasure—much admired by Kant—to construct an aesthetic theory based on the artist's manipulation of the 'dolori innominati' of the recipient of the work of art.

The principal achievement of Italian *illuminismo* was to bring the peninsula, albeit with most of its political and social problems still to be resolved, back into the mainstream of European intellectual culture. [See also ACADEMIES.]   [GLCB]

See F. Venturi, *Italy and the Enlightenment* (1972); D. Carpanetto and G. Ricuperati, *Italy in the Age of Reason, 1685–1789* (1987); S. Woolf, *A History of Italy 1700–1860* (2nd edn., 1991).

Enrico IV (1922). *Pirandello's innovatory *tragedy of human aloneness, originally created for the actor Ruggero Ruggeri. It presents an unnamed 20th-c. man who, on falling from his horse during a student cavalcade, remains fixed in his assumed character, the 11th-c. Emperor Henry IV. On regaining his senses twelve years later, he decides to act out his fictional part rather than return to the emptiness of normal life. The tragic outcome is precipitated by the arrival of his former friends intent on 'curing' him of his madness.   [JAL]

Entrée d'Espagne (mid-13th c.). The most impressive work of *Franco-Veneto literature, composed for a *courtly audience, perhaps at *Padua. It is a large *Carolingian *epic dealing with the period building up to Gano's treachery and the battle of Roncesvalle (Roncevaux), but it anticipates *Boiardo and *Ariosto in recounting also Roland's aberrant amorous adventures. [See also ROMANCE.]   [PH]

ENZO, RE, see RE ENZO.

Epic. The term traditionally applies to long narrative poems on historical or legendary events of defining significance for the national, ethnic, or religious community in which they are produced. Their ethos is collective rather than individual, although the narrative focuses on a representative

Epicureanism

hero, and the poet (often anonymous) and his audience are likewise identified with the community to which the narrative refers. *Virgil provides the canonical example from classical antiquity of a self-consciously literary adaptation of the epic genre; Homer, on the other hand, was almost unknown except by reputation in Western Europe before the 16th c. [see also LATIN INFLUENCES; GREEK INFLUENCES].

The indigenous epic of Romance-speaking Europe, of which the 12th-c. French *chansons de geste* are the earliest surviving texts, centres on the legendary exploits of Charlemagne and his Paladins, notably his nephew Roland, in the struggle against Muslim Spain. These narratives circulated in Italy, in both French and *Franco-Veneto versions, in the 13th c., the *Gonzaga library at *Mantua holding an especially notable collection. In the earliest original Carolingian text written in Italy, the *Entrée d'Espagne (*Padua, first half of the 14th c.), Roland has already undergone the decisive change from epic hero to the knight errant of *romance, in a long digression in which he abandons the French army for a series of adventures in the Orient. The *Entrée* and its French antecedents provided the basis for the prose narratives of *Andrea da Barberino and the verse of *La *Spagna*, which for all their warlike subject matter can only loosely be defined as epics. [See also FRENCH INFLUENCES, 1.]

Alongside this elaboration of the Carolingian material, *Dante, *Petrarch, and *Boccaccio all sought in different ways to re-create for their own time the epic which Virgil had provided for imperial Rome. The *Divine Comedy*, while clearly *sui generis*, is nonetheless explicitly presented as a Christian *Aeneid*. Boccaccio's *Teseida* (1339–?41) combines the background material of Statius' *Thebaid* with the love story (reproduced in Chaucer's *Knight's Tale*) of the two suitors of Emilia, the new verse form of *ottava rima* with the twelve-book structure of classical epic. Petrarch's disregard for vernacular epic underlies his attempt to complement the *Aeneid* with his own unfinished poem on ancient Rome, the *Africa* (1338 onwards), relating in Latin hexameters the career of Scipio Africanus, the hero of the Punic wars.

The term 'epic' remains problematic for the *chivalric poems of the *Renaissance. *Ariosto's *Orlando furioso* (1532) has numerous borrowings from Virgil, including the poem's opening and conclusion; but its multiplicity of storylines, the predominance of love as its motive force, and above all the author's ironic distance from his narrative material, prevent it from belonging convincingly to the epic genre. Theoretical objections to this hybrid genre crystallized with the renewed currency of *Aristotle's *Poetics* from the 1540s onwards; an attempt at an epic conforming to Aristotelian norms was *Trissino's *L'Italia liberata dai Goti* (1547–8), in unrhymed *hendecasyllables, on a single historical theme in a uniformly elevated style. The poet who agonized at greatest length over the relationship between the chivalric poems and the requirements of classical epic was Torquato *Tasso; his *Gerusalemme liberata* (1581), with the theoretical underpinning of his *Discorsi dell'arte poetica* (revised for publication as *Discorsi del poema eroico* in 1594), seeks to combine an elevated historical subject—the recapture of Jerusalem in the second *Crusade—with the love interest and enchantments of romance. The result was controversial but hugely popular, providing a model for the Christian epic which greatly influenced Milton. [See also FEUDALISM; LITERARY THEORY, 1, 2.]

[RMD]

See A. Limentani and M. Infurna, *L'Epica* (1986).

Epicureanism was known in the Italian *Middle Ages and early *Renaissance only through the *Stoic writings of *Cicero and Seneca, and dismissed as proposing the unrestrained pursuit of sensual pleasures and the denial of the immortality of the soul (hence *Dante's brief comment in *Inferno 10.14). Lorenzo *Valla initiated a more positive understanding of Epicurean pleasure, linking it to all forms of enjoyment, including beatitude in the next life. The recovery of Lucretius' *De rerum natura* and the translation of Diogenes Laertius' life of Epicurus led to a fuller understanding of ideas of atomism, the infinity of worlds, and gods who take no interest in human behaviour, but at the same time of the sublimity of nature and natural causes without divine intervention. Amongst attempts to refute Lucretius were Aonio Paleario's defence of the immortality of the soul (1536), Torquato *Tasso's *Il mondo creato*, completed in 1594 and published in 1600, and *Murtola's *Della creatione del mondo* of 1608. On the other side were Giordano *Bruno's *De l'infinito universo e mondi* (1584), and his Latin poem *De immenso* (1591). With ever greater censure from the Church, Epicureanism became linked with *libertines (typified by the Accademia degli *Incogniti) and the suspect science of Copernicus and *Galileo.

[LAP]

Epigram, see LATIN POETRY IN ITALY.

Epistolari, see LETTER-WRITING AND EPISTOLARI.

Epistolary Novel. One of the devices used by fiction writers to reduce the implausibility of an omniscient narrator and enhance the *realism of the story by turning the protagonists into narrators who write letters to one another, or leave them for an editor to publish. It is in the latter sense a variant of the 'found manuscript' used by Cervantes, Defoe, and *Manzoni. At the same time it is indebted to the rhetoric of the medieval *ars dictaminis,* as well as to *humanist *epistolari,* both of which used letters edited or composed for effect; to *Renaissance *historiography, with its set speeches attributed to important personages; to the 'dedicatory letters' of *Bandello and other writers of *novelle* witnessing the truth of a story or even including a story; and to didactic *dialogue.

Its beginnings in Italian literaure can be seen in Enea Silvio *Piccolomini's influential and much translated *Historia de duobus amantibus* (1444; Italian *translation 1521). The genre developed fully in literate societies, such as 18th-c. England or France, where letter-writing was a normal occupation and letter-writing primers sold well; most Italian examples of this period are translations. *Foscolo began to write the one significant Italian example of the genre, *Le *ultime lettere di Jacopo Ortis,* some two decades after his model, Goethe's *The Sorrows of Young Werther* (1774), when the need for realism was beginning to be satisfied by *historical novels and the epistolary genre was already in decline. Later noteworthy Italian novels which make extensive use of the device can be reduced to *Tommaseo's *Fede e bellezza* (1840), *Piovene's *Lettere di una novizia* (1941), and Natalia *Ginzburg's *Caro Michele* (1973) and *La città e la casa* (1984). *Verga's *Storia di una capinera* (1871) might be considered an epistolary novel but, like Ortis's one-sided letter-writing, has affinities rather with a pretended *diary. [See also LETTER-WRITING AND EPISTOLARI; NOVEL.] [GC]

See G. F. Singer, *The Epistolary Novel* (1933); L. Versini, *Le Roman épistolaire* (1979).

Epistole metrice, see PETRARCH, FRANCESCO.

EQUICOLA, MARIO (1470–1525) spent most of his life as a courtier, adapting his considerable talents according to necessity. After studying with *Ficino in *Florence, he served the Cantelmo family of Sora, Isabella d'*Este, and Federico *Gonzaga. He was a man of great learning, with a real interest in vernacular culture. His literary works contain more than a small measure of self-publicity. His most famous work was *Il libro de natura de amore* (1525), which owes a great debt to Ficino's *Neoplatonic view of love. In 1541 he wrote a study of Italian metre up to the 15th c. [See also VERSIFICATION.] [PLR]

ERASMO DA VALVASONE (1523–93). Poet and translator. Born in Friuli, he spent almost his whole life there, on his ancestral fief at Valvason. The most notable Friulan writer of the 16th c., he maintained close contacts with many men of letters of the day, including both Bernardo *Tasso and Torquato *Tasso. In the last year of his life he was persuaded to move to the *court at *Mantua. His most important work is the early *La caccia,* on the subject of hunting. The *romance *I primi quattro canti di Lancilotto* (1580) was left unfinished. He also wrote *Le lacrime di Santa Maria Maddalena* (1586), and the *Angeleida* (1590), on the war of the angels in heaven. His *translations, of variable quality, include Sophocles' *Electra* (1588), and the first Italian translation of Statius' *Thebaid,* in *ottava rima* (1570). [JEE]

ERBA, LUCIANO (1922–). *Milanese poet, by profession a lecturer in French at the Università Cattolica. His poetry, which begins with *Linea K* (1951), was quickly associated with the *linea lombarda* [see also RISI, NELO]. It was ironic, urban, up-to-date, autobiographical, and imaginative without being flamboyant. He continued to keep an often polemical distance from both *hermetic poetry and experimentalism, most notably in the 1954 anthology *Quarta generazione,* and in *La giovane poesia* (1945–54), which he edited with Piero *Chiara. *Il nastro di Moebius* (1980), which contains all his previous poetry, shows the consistency of his anti-rhetorical stance. The grace, playfulness, and carefully assumed lightness of tone are if anything heightened in subsequent collections stretching up to *L'ipotesi circense* (1995). [VS-H]

ERIZZO, SEBASTIANO (1525–85). A *Venetian senator and member of the Council of Ten, and a scholar and man of culture. He translated and commented on Plato, publishing the first Italian *translation of his *Timaeus,* and later a collection of his *dialogues. He was also a numismatist, composed *Petrarchist verse, and wrote

Ermes Di Colloredo

a collection of thirty-six tales entitled *Le sei giornate*. [CG]

ERMES DI COLLOREDO (1622–92). A cousin of *Ciro di Pers, he was educated at the *Medici *court and subsequently became a career soldier. He retired in 1658 to his estate, where he wrote copious, mainly occasional, verse in a partially Italianized Friuli *dialect. His poems were published posthumously, beginning in 1785. [MPS]

Ermetismo, see HERMETICISM; HERMETIC POETRY.

Erminia. One of the heroines of Torquato *Tasso's *Gerusalemme liberata.

Eroicomico, see MOCK-HEROIC POETRY.

Eroticism and Pornography. Sex and the body enjoy a distinguished position in Italian literature. From the *poesia giocosa of the 13th and 14th c. to the contemporary *theatre of Dario *Fo, their presence crosses both period and genre. In general terms, however, their representation is closely associated with the comic, a feature normally considered absent from erotic or pornographic writing. Consequently, it is debatable whether many Italian writers who have written about sex (such as *Boccaccio, *Bandello, *Belli, and *Busi), can justifiably be seen as erotic or pornographic. Their overtly comic, and often *satirical, emphasis seems to rob their work of the intention to create some form of excitation in the reader.

In general, distinctions between the erotic and the pornographic, or the sensual and the obscene, and differentiations from other forms of literature that deal with sexual topics, involve judgements of taste and change considerably over time. During the *Renaissance, much as the Internet was to do later, developments in *printing techniques increased accessibility, intensified debates on *censorship, and altered the ways of seeing the links between representations and life.

That the separation of eroticism from pornography revolves primarily round a hierarchy of taste is clear from the erotically charged writing of the Renaissance. Both *Panormita's *Hermaphroditus* (1419–25) and Pietro *Bembo's *Priapus* (?1532) were admired for their elegant and inventive use of Latin in their celebrations of the merits of the penis. *Burchiello, writing in the earlier 15th c., and

Francesco *Berni, some 100 years later, covered much the same ground in Italian, and were considered crude and limited in scope. In general the influence of classical writers such as *Ovid and Petronius on the writing of erotic literature suggests that there was little intention of commenting on sexual mores. Conscious of writing in an illustrious tradition, authors worked within its confines, adopting familiar scenarios and stereotypes of sexual characterization, such as the jealous or elderly husband, to motivate the narrative. Occasionally real social anxieties could make themselves felt, as when the spread of syphilis in the 16th c. added a new theme to the erotic repertory.

The popular *canti carnascialeschi, in which artisans eroticized the various instruments of their different trades, are similarly noteworthy for their verbal inventiveness rather than as indicators of sexual practice. The value given to linguistic virtuosity in inventing new terms and images for familiar activities suggests an element of weariness with the narrative content itself. The high degree of intertextuality may also partly explain the apparent prevalence of *homosexual or bisexual activity in the Renaissance. The pursuit or admiration of young men, rather than women, may simply have offered the possibility of thematic variation in a genre heavily dependent on repetition. Similar difficulties of interpretation relate to the representation of women. In a genre that is devotedly phallocentric, it is unclear whether a writer's *misogyny is an effect of convention or reflects a broader cultural perception of women. The prostitute, or *courtesan, was a recurrent figure, most often the object of virulent attack, as in *La Zaffetta*, Lorenzo *Venier's poem of *c.*1531, which is based on the figure of Angela Zaffetta, a well-known *Venetian courtesan. The work was most likely to be controversial when the conventions of the genre were directed towards recognizable figures. Pietro *Aretino's *Sonetti lussuriosi* (1527), written to accompany a series of drawings by Giulio Romano, strike the modern reader on account of their bold and explicit detailing of a variety of sexual acts. It is, however, probable that they scandalized Aretino's contemporaries as satirical representations of the licentious behaviour of the *papal *court.

The censorship imposed in the wake of the *Counter-Reformation called a halt to what had become a flourishing literary mode in the first half of the 16th c. But some notable works still emerged, such as the famous apology for homosexuality, *Alcibiade fanciullo a scola* (1632), attributed to

212

Ferrante *Pallavicino, which was the subject of great controversy when it was reprinted in Paris in the 19th c. The French capital was also where Giacomo *Casanova wrote his famous (but largely unread) memoirs at the end of the 18th c. His near-contemporaries, the Venetian Giorgio *Baffo and the *Milanese Carlo *Porta, both to some extent protected by the medium of *dialect, develop the bawdiness of Aretino to a remarkable degree. Baffo in particular constructed a distinctive and thought-out form of *libertinism in verse.

Developments in *printing in the 19th c. allowed the creation of a popular pornography dedicated to the depiction of sexual acts without literary pretensions. Such writing has tended to give rise to less controversy than works which combine literariness and sexuality. *Marinetti and *Tondelli were both the subject of court cases on account of the alleged indecency of their work. *D'Annunzio and *Moravia have been condemned as pornographers. But largely thanks to *psychoanalysis new ways of understanding desire were articulated during the 20th c. and given expression in eroticized writing. *Feminists too attempted to write about sexuality in new ways. Rather than advocating stricter censorship of sexually explicit material, Italian feminists have preferred to use so-called pornography to test the limits of representation, and to illustrate the power of the body to resist confinement in its codes. They have also explored the difficulties encountered by women when writing of their experience of the erotic in male-centred linguistic and stylistic registers.   [DD]

See P. Lorenzoni, *Erotismo e pornografia nella letteratura italiana* (1976); N. Borsellino, *La tradizione del comico: l'eros, l'osceno, la beffa nella letteratura italiana da Dante a Belli* (1989).

ERRICO, SCIPIONE (1592–1670) made his literary debut while still a student of theology in his native Messina, with *Endimione* and *Arianna* (1611), two poems in the new genre of the mythological idyll [see PASTORAL]. His ecclesiastical career later took him to *Rome and *Venice. His mainly amatory *Rime* (1619), which enjoyed considerable success, combine graceful musicality and even more far-fetched and ingenious comparisons than was customary in the *concettismo of those years. Errico's defence of *Marino's *Adone, in a *dialogue entitled *L'occhiale appannato* (1629), argued that the poem should be compared not with classical *epic but with its true progenitor, *Ovid's *Metamorphoses*. His two *comedies, *Le rivolte di*

Parnaso (1625) and *Le liti di Pindo* (1634), also touch on controversy over Marino.   [MPS]

ESTE. Ruling house of *Ferrara, and *patrons of the arts and letters. It was founded by Alberto Azzo II (996–1097), who was invested with the town of Este, near *Padua, as a fief of the Holy Roman Empire. In *c.*1240 Azzo VII (d.1264) became *podestà of Ferrara, beginning the Este rule of the city. Obizzo II (d.1293) extended it to Modena (1288) and Reggio (1289); both he and his son Azzo VIII (d.1308) are mentioned by *Dante in *Inferno 12.111–12, and *Purgatorio 5.77–8. In 1309 Ferrara became a *papal territory, and was governed by the Este family as a papal fief from 1332 onwards.

The foundation of the *university (1391), and Este patronage during the reigns of the Marquis Leonello (1441–50) (who was taught by *Guarino da Verona), Duke Borso (1450–71), and Duke Ercole I (1471–1505), turned Ferrara into one of the most innovative cultural centres of the *Renaissance, represented in literature by Tito Vespasiano *Strozzi, *Boiardo, and *Tebaldeo. The high point came under Duke Alfonso I (1505–34), Lucrezia *Borgia's husband, whose brother, Cardinal Ippolito I, is the dedicatee of *Ariosto's *Orlando furioso*. Duke Ercole II (1534–59) was the patron of *Giraldi Cinzio, while Battista *Guarini and Torquato *Tasso were courtiers under Duke Alfonso II (1559–97). The latter had no legitimate son, and on his death Ferrara was reclaimed by the papacy. A branch of the Este family continued to govern Modena and Reggio until 1803, when its dynastic rights passed to the Austrian Este line which became extinct in 1875.   [MGD]

Estetica, see CROCE, BENEDETTO.

Ettore Fieramosca, see D'AZEGLIO, MASSIMO.

EURIALO D'ASCOLI (1485/90–1554) was the *humanist name taken by Aurello Morani dei Guiderocchi, a vernacular poet who wrote mainly in *ottava rima. After a period in *Siena, where he produced epigrams, Eurialo spent most of his life in *Rome. A friend of *Cellini and *Aretino, he wrote *laudi as well as amorous and autobiographical verse.   [GPTW]

EUTICHIO, see NIFO, AGOSTINO.

Eva (1873). Early novel by Giovanni *Verga, written in *Florence and then revised in *Milan. Set in

Florence, the story tells of the love of a *Sicilian painter, Enrico Lanti, for a dancer, Eva. Their love does not withstand the pressures of poverty and Enrico returns a broken man to die in Sicily.

[RL]

EVANGELISTI, VALERIO, see SCIENCE FICTION.

EVOLA, JULIUS (1898–1974) began his career as a painter close to the *Futurists, but became a leading theorist of right-wing *Fascism, with doctrines centred on ideas of tradition and race. His best-known book is *Rivolta contro il mondo moderno* (1934). His postwar writings on occultism and Oriental disciplines influenced neo-Fascist youth groups in the 1970s and 1980s. [LChe]

Exegesis, see ALLEGORY; COMMENTARIES; LITERARY THEORY, I.

Exemplum. Medieval narrative genre, used particularly in *sermon-writing to illustrate moral and religious truths. The 'examples' are of noteworthy actions or behaviour, and are usually drawn from history or the *Bible, but also from saints' lives [see HAGIOGRAPHY] or sometimes fables. The great medieval Latin collections of the 12th and 13th c. inspired 14th-c. vernacular preachers, such as the *Dominicans *Giordano da Pisa, Domenico *Cavalca, and Iacopo *Passavanti, and also *novella*-writers, from the author of the *Novellino* to *Boccaccio, *Sacchetti, and Giovanni di Sercambi [see NOVELLA AND RACCONTO]. The high point of vernacular preaching and hence of the use of the *exemplum* is attained in the early 14th c. in the *Quaresimali* of the *Franciscan *Bernardino da Siena. [MP]

Exile. Throughout the *Middle Ages and *Renaissance banishment was a common means of disempowering political rivals or troublesome subjects. The most famous example in Italy is *Dante, who wrote most of his works during his twenty years as an 'undeserving exile' from *Florence, mostly in Northern Italian *courts. He had been preceded by *Guittone d'Arezzo and Brunetto *Latini. He was followed by *Petrarch's father, then by Leon Battista *Alberti, and the *Medici. With the *Counter-Reformation, Italian Protestants were forced into exile in Northern European countries for their beliefs. But in national *historiography the heroic period of exile came after the *Napoleonic wars. Long- and short-term sufferers included most of

the heroes of the *Risorgimento, from *Foscolo to *Garibaldi. All those who survived were able to return to the newly united country after 1871, though *Mazzini had to remain incognito.

Political exile then returned with *Fascism. The number of those who were forced to live abroad or who chose to do so because of their political beliefs or affiliations was not large, though it included some of the most significant intellectuals of the 20th c., such as *Silone, *Borgese, and *Salvemini. The liberals found refuge in the USA, the communists in Soviet Russia. *Mussolini also used internal exile (*confino*) as a way of dealing with dissident intellectuals within the country, the most famous victims being *Pavese, who spent a year in Calabria as a result of complicity with the *Giustizia e libertà* group in *Turin, and Carlo *Levi. Though *Ungaretti made much of exile as the spiritual condition of modern man in his work, no large body of exile literature came into being during the Fascist years, nor was there a literature of 'inner exile' comparable with that created by German writers under Nazism. Attempts to see *hermetic poetry in this way now seem unconvincing. [See also EMIGRATION.] [PH]

Existentialism had relatively little impact in Italy, at least as it developed in France in the postwar years in the writings of Sartre and Camus. Italian writers and intellectuals were of course aware of their work, but the culture of *Neorealism and *impegno* found the emphasis on isolation and meaninglessness relatively alien except when it became an intellectual commitment to authenticity and social responsibility. In philosophy, the first Italian thinker to develop existentialist themes was Nicola Abbagnano (1901–90), whose work brings together existentialism and Anglo-American pragmatism. Abbagnano developed the concept of 'positive existentialism', which juxtaposes the notion of the possibility of being with the nihilism of Heidegger and the early Sartre. His most important books in this regard are *Introduzione all'esistenzialismo* (1942) and *Esistenzialismo positivo* (1948). On the whole, however, Heidegger would become important in Italian intellectual culture only in the 1970s.

In Italian literature, existentialist motifs, particularly regarding the need to make choices, can be traced in the fiction of *Pratolini, *Pavese, and *Vittorini, as well as in the postwar poetry of *Quasimodo and *Sereni. The one notable writer who consistently shows an existentialist cast of mind (at least in his earlier work) is Alberto *Moravia. His first novel, *Gli *indifferenti* (1929), seems to anticipate Sartre's concerns in *La Nausée* (1938) in its depiction of bourgeois existence and its protagonist's state of impasse. In much of his postwar fiction the existential thinking is overt, especially in *La *noia* (1960), in which the protagonist, Dino, confronts the absurdity of a life of indifference and boredom, but finally reverts to living according to the rules of possession at the base of the capitalist society from which he feels estranged.　　　[RSD]

Expressionism (*espressionismo*). Term frequently used in Italian *literary criticism to indicate writing in prose and verse which goes against the historically prevalent ethos of *classicism, balance, clarity, and restraint, and cultivates (usually self-consciously) linguistic and stylistic excess, often with inroads into *dialect or other non-standard areas of language, and with a thematic emphasis on eccentricity, anomaly, and distortion. Modern expressionism is particularly associated with *Gadda and other *Lombard writers from the 19th c. onwards, but the term is also applied to *macaronic poetry, *poesia giocosa*, and, because of its *plurilingual features, the *Divine Comedy*.　　　[PH]

F

FAÀ GONZAGA, CAMILLA, see NUNS.

FABA, GUIDO, see ARS DICTAMINIS; LETTER-WRITING AND EPISTOLARI, I.

FABBRI, DIEGO (1911–80). Dramatist, who graduated in law in 1936, and used his knowledge of legal procedures in his plays. The title of his most notable play, *Processo a Gesù* (1955), indicates the nature of his work as a probing, challenging inquiry into mid-20th-c. Christianity. Fabbri once said that all of his work could be seen in terms of a *processo* ('trial'). His preoccupations are also evident in his important collection of essays *Ambiguità cristiane* (1954). His plays can be divided into different types: those concerning individual conscience (e.g. *Inquisizione,* 1950), plays concerning Catholicism (e.g. *Processo a Gesù*), family dramas (e.g. *Processo in famiglia,* 1953), and lighter boulevard pieces (e.g. *Il seduttore,* 1951). But it is more important to see the underlying Catholic preoccupations in all his work from the early 'intimist' dramas of the 1930s to the plays of the late 1970s. Clearly influenced by *Pirandello's *theatre plays in his dramatic construction, Fabbri is more often compared to Ugo *Betti, whose religious concerns he shares. Fabbri also adapted novels for the stage, screen and *television. [JAL]

FABRIZI DELL'ACQUAPENDENTE, GIROLAMO, see MEDICINE.

FABRONI, ANGELO (1732–1803). *Florentine who became Dean of *Pisa University, and a scholar and *publisher. From a press set up in his house he brought out a *Giornale dei letterati* (1771–96) and his own mainly *biographical works, including the fourteen-volume *Vitae italorum* (1778–85), written in elegant Latin. He also translated parts of Gibbon (1779–86). [JMAL]

FACCIO, RINA, see ALERAMO, SIBILLA.

Facezie (also *motti* or *burle*) are jokes, quips, and witty retorts. In medieval and *Renaissance Italy they gave rise to a well-defined and popular subgenre of *novella,* cultivated particularly in *Florence. *Boccaccio's *Decameron* Day 6, whose protagonists include cooks and bakers as well as Guido *Cavalcanti and *Giotto, was particularly influential, though the popularizing possibilities are more exploited in, for example, the 15th-c. *Motti e facezie del piovano Arlotto.* Conversely, there is the salacious Latin *Liber facetiarum* of the Florentine Poggio *Bracciolini, which he composed at the *Roman Curia.

Outside *Tuscany, Antonio *Cornazzano composed *Proverbi in facezie,* making *facezie* into amusing anecdotes to explain obscure proverbs. The outstanding collection of the 16th c. is again Florentine—Lodovico *Domenichi's *Facezie, motti e burle,* which went through at least a dozen ever-expanding editions from 1548 to 1599 and which elevates Florentine wit to the level of making it desirable in a great and wise ruler. *Castiglione has Bibbiena (Bernardo *Dovizi) lead a discussion in *Il cortegiano* (book 2) on the kind of *facezie* appropriate for a courtier to tell. [See also BEFFA.] [LAP]

FACIO, BARTOLOMEO (or Fazio) (c.1400–57). *Humanist who studied with *Guarino da Verona at Verona, before moving to *Florence in 1429, and then to *Genoa in 1430. He was sent as ambassador of the Republic of Genoa to *Naples, whence he moved in 1445 as secretary and official historian to Alfonso of *Aragon. His output includes works on grammar, two treatises on moral philosophy, a Latin *novella* (based on the *Pecorone*), letters (mostly lost), four invectives against Lorenzo *Valla, and the *De viris illustribus,* a series of lives of famous men, whose importance lies in

the light it sheds on humanist historical methodology. [See also HISTORIOGRAPHY.]   [PLR]

FAGIUOLI, GIOVANNI BATTISTA (1660–
1742). *Florentine playwright who wrote facetious
Rime (1729–34), *capitoli* [see CANTO], and nineteen
*comedies in Florentine vernacular. These were
widely performed in *academies and aristocratic
houses. Fagiuoli's bland *satire of contemporary
manners is always respectful of the cultural and
religious bigotry reigning in the *Tuscan grand
duchy under Cosimo III de' *Medici. Still,
*Goldoni may have been inspired by his best char-
acters, like the old miser (in *Il cicisbeo consolato*,
L'avaro punito, etc.) and the Tuscan *peasant
Ciapo (in *Il marito alla moda*, *Il podestà di Capraia*,
etc.), who counters his master's, or the government's, persecutions with rustic common sense
and colourful sayings.   [FF]

Fairy Tales, see FOLK AND POPULAR LITERATURE.

FAITINELLI, PIETRO DE' (1280/90–1349).
Aristocratic author of some nineteen bitterly
effective *sonnets treating political themes from a
*Guelf perspective. They were written during his
*exile from Lucca (1310–31), which he spent in
various *courts in the Veneto.   [SNB]

FALDELLA, GIOVANNI (1846–1928). *Piedmontese *journalist, politician, and writer. As a journalist he wrote for various papers and *periodicals
in *Turin and *Rome, often under pseudonyms
(Spartivento, Cimbro, and others). As a writer of
fiction, he cultivated the aesthetic *expressionism
characteristic of the Piedmontese *Scapigliatura in
narratives such as *Una serenata ai morti* (1884),
Tota nerina (1887), and *Madonna di fuoco e madonna
di neve* (1888). He became a moderate Left deputy
in 1881 and a senator in 1896. *Un viaggio a Roma
senza vedere il papa* (1880) and *Roma borghese*
(1882) present dispassionate portraits of the new
capital.   [AHC]

FALLACARA, LUIGI (1890–1963). Catholic
*hermetic poet. Though he was from Bari, his focus
was *Florence, where he contributed briefly
to *Lacerba* and later more extensively to *Il
Frontespizio. He converted to Catholicism in 1925,
and his poetry attempts to combine *modernism
and Christian spirituality. In later years he
edited and *translated various medieval mystics.
          [JJ]

FALLACI, ORIANA (1930–). Outstanding
*journalist and best-selling *novelist, who equivo-
cates brilliantly (or, many say, disastrously)
between fiction and first-person reportage or *autobiography, with self-incriminating *existential
urgency. *Niente e così sia* (1969) dramatizes the
moral dilemma of the Vietnam war; *Intervista con
la storia* (1974) contains interviews with political
leaders; *Lettera a un bambino mai nato* (1975) is
written by a mother to the child in her womb; *Un
uomo* (1979) addresses Fallaci's dead companion,
the Greek freedom fighter Alekos Panagoulis; and
the massive and ambitious novel *InsciAllah* (1990)
is centred on the embattled Italian peace-keeping
force in the war-torn Beirut of 1983.   [JG-R]

FALLOPPIA, GABRIELE, see MEDICINE.

FALQUI, ENRICO (1901–74). *Literary critic
and scholar with European as well as Italian
interests. His criticism, for example, in *Ricerche di
stile* (1939), emphasized literary style, which he distinguished from technique. In 1939 he published,
with *Vittorini, *Scrittori nuovi*, a (for the time)
controversial *anthology of contemporary Italian
writers. He gives the measure of the literary culture
of the period in *La letteratura del ventennio nero*
(1947), *D'Annunzio e noi* (1947), and the several
volumes of *Novecento letterario*, published during
the 1950s. He was the husband of the novelist
Gianna *Manzini.   [RSD]

Fanciullino, Il, see PASCOLI, GIOVANNI.

Fanfulla della domenica, Il (1879–1919).
Weekly literary supplement of the *Rome newspaper *Il Fanfulla* (the name of a patriotic soldier in
the historical novels of Massimo *D'Azeglio). The
programme of its first editor, Ferdinando *Martini,
was to promote cultural unification and to extend
learning beyond traditional élites. Contributors
included *Carducci, *Verga, *Capuana, *De
Marchi, *Serao, and *Bersezio.   [DF]

Fantastic. As in other languages, the terms
'fantastico' or 'letteratura fantastica' are used to refer
mainly to short stories or *novels characterized by
an ambiguous relationship between *realism and
anti-realism, reality and dream, natural order and
the supernatural dimension, with implications of
unease and disorientation in both the protagonists
and the reader. The genre flourished generally in
Europe during the 19th c., its acknowledged

masters being Poe and Hoffmann. It becomes significant in Italy in the later decades of the century, being cultivated particularly by *Scapigliati such as *Tarchetti, *Faldella, and the *Boito brothers. It continues in some of the work of *Verga and *Capuana, who are best known as *veristi, and also in parts of the production of *De Marchi, Remigio *Zena, and *Fogazzaro.

For much of the 20th c. the fantastic has tended to be seen as a secondary trend, but figures such as *Savinio, *Landolfi, and *Buzzati have received increasing attention in recent years. *Calvino's work in particular has led to a revision of the critical map. Overall, Italian fantastic literature has followed the general trend away from the spectacular (the 'visionary' approach in Calvino's term) towards more psychologically oriented writing, with a greater sensitivity to the revelatory power of eruptions from the unconscious. [NG]

See N. Bonifazi, *Teoria del fantastico e il racconto fantastico in Italia* (1982).

FANTONI, GIOVANNI (1755–1807). Poet from Fivizzano near Massa. He studied in the *Benedictine convent of Subiaco, and in 1776 became a member of the *Arcadia academy as Labindo Arsinoetico. He was appointed to the chair of eloquence at *Pisa in 1800, but was dismissed as a result of joining the *Jacobins. His *neoclassical poems, published as *Odi* (1782) and then posthumously as *Poesie* (1823), use a large number of classical, mostly *Horatian, metres. He is the most important predecessor of *Carducci's *poesia barbara* [see also VERSIFICATION]. [CCa]

Farce, see BEFFA; COMEDY; FO, DARIO.

Farfalla, La, see PERIODICALS, 1.

Farfalle, Le, see GOZZANO, GUIDO.

FARINA, SALVATORE (1846–1918). *Journalist, playwright, and *novelist who enjoyed great success with novels such as *Il tesoro di Donnina* (1873), *Amore bendato* (1875), and *Capelli biondi* (1876). A *Sardinian by birth, he graduated in law at *Turin University before moving to *Milan, where he became closely associated with the *Scapigliatura, and wrote for the *Rivista minima* and *Nuova antologia* and edited the *Gazzetta musicale*. He wrote a chapter of *Tarchetti's *Fosca* (1869) to ensure that his dying and destitute friend was paid for its serialization. He suffered from a long period of amnesia, subsequently reconstructing his life in three volumes of *autobiography (1910–15). [AHC]

FARINACCI, PROSPERO, see LAW.

FARINACCI, ROBERTO (1892–1945). *Fascist leader, with his power base in Cremona. An extremist often at odds with *Mussolini, he became a fervent anti-Semite and Nazi enthusiast. He founded and edited *Regime fascista*, established the literary *Premio Cremona* [see LITERARY PRIZES], and published various accounts of the rise of Fascism, including his diary, *Squadrismo* (1933). In 1945 he was captured and shot by partisans. [PH]

Farinata. Ghibelline leader from the *Florentine Uberti family in the circle of the Heretics in *Dante's *Inferno*.

FARNESE. Dukes of Parma and Piacenza (1545–1731). The family had their fortunes transformed by the election of Alessandro Farnese as Pope Paul III (1534–49). A prodigious *patron of the arts, he also invested his illegitimate son, Pier Luigi, as first Duke of Parma and Piacenza in 1545. The Duke employed as secretaries Claudio *Tolomei and Annibale *Caro, who soon after his assassination in 1547 passed into the service of his son, Cardinal Alessandro (1520–89). The latter presided over the golden age of his family's literary patronage, employing (besides Caro and Tolomei), Paolo *Giovio, Fulvio *Orsini, and Onofrio Panvinio [see ANTIQUARIANISM]. [SD]

Farse cavaiole were a form of *carnival stage *comedy performed in Southern Italy in the 15th–17th c. They gained their name from exploiting the *dialect and the reputation for stupidity of the town of Cava dei Tirreni near Salerno. They used a range of character stereotypes sometimes rather different from other theatrical masks, and are seen as having an effect on the mainstream *theatre comedy of 17th-c. *Naples. [RAA]

Fascism. Political movement founded in *Milan on 23 March 1919 as *Fasci di combattimento*, the term *fascio* (from the Latin *fascis* ('bundle'), the symbol of the Roman magistrates, the *lictores*) having been used by various extraparliamentary groups since the 1890s. Fascism initially took the form of armed reaction against organized labour in rural areas and northern cities. In November 1921 it became a political party, on 28 October 1922 it seized state power and in 1924 won a rigged election. By the end of 1926 it had suppressed free trade unions, elective local assemblies, and opposition parties. From then on its leader *Mussolini sought to consolidate what he himself called a totalitarian state. In 1928 parliament was subordinated to a Grand Council which he controlled; corporations and mass organizations were set up; the state increasingly intervened in the economy; party membership became obligatory for public-sector employees; surveillance and arrests were used to silence dissent. In 1929 the Lateran Pacts [see CONCORDAT] normalized relations with the *papacy and gave Catholic organizations a margin of autonomy. In the 1930s Fascist foreign policy aimed increasingly at expanding Italian possessions and influence in East Africa and the Balkans.

In 1938–9 an alliance was concluded with Nazi Germany; anti-Semitic legislation was introduced and Italy intervened alongside Germany in support of General Franco in the Spanish Civil War and then (June 1940) in *World War II. From late 1942 the disastrous conduct of the war fuelled internal dissent and ultimately opposition from military leaders. After the Allied landings in *Sicily in July 1943 Mussolini was voted out of office by the Grand Council (25 July) and arrested. Subsequently rescued by the Germans (September 1943), he headed a reconstituted Fascist government, the Repubblica Sociale Italiana, in Northern Italy and continued the war alongside the occupying German army until their final defeat by the Allies and partisans on 25 April 1945. [See also RESISTANCE.]

The relations between Fascism and literature may be divided into four types. The first is the relation of writers to Fascism. In its 'movement' phase (1919–24), when it presented itself as a radical force of national regeneration, Fascism attracted the support of many writers, including *Marinetti, *Ungaretti, *Papini, and *Pirandello. As a regime (1925–43) it was ideologically less fanatical than the Nazi regime in Germany and did not drive writers into *exile or 'inner exile' to the same extent. *Silone, anti-Fascist and ex-Communist, wrote from abroad out of necessity. In the late 1930s, however, with its increasing conservatism, imperialism, and alliance with Nazi Germany, Fascism lost much of its appeal, particularly for younger writers, such as *Vittorini and *Pratolini, who either sought to push it back to its supposedly radical origins or crossed over to anti-Fascism. But there were writers who supported Fascism to the end.

Second, Fascism influenced literature by using the machinery of the state to curtail the activities of oppositional or dissident publishers, suppressing them or forcing them to change identity, and then to control the circulation of texts and the performance of plays through *censorship. *Jewish authors, both Italian and foreign, were banned after 1938. During the war there was censorship of books and plays from enemy countries.

Third, through its control of the press, the school curriculum, and, less directly, *universities and *publishing, Fascism influenced *literary criticism, the teaching of Italian literature and literary history. Examples were the promotion of a cult of *Dante as national poet and Mussolini's personal underwriting of the national edition of the works of *D'Annunzio, published by *Mondadori in forty-nine volumes. This influence was never total, however; the prestige of the *liberal *Croce, in particular, ensured that literary criticism remained partly insulated from Fascism.

Fourth, there is the question of how far Fascism influenced literary production. Fascist intellectuals repeatedly appealed for a wholesale cultural renewal, and mutually opposed movements like *strapaese (led by *Maccari and *Malaparte) and *900 (Novecento) or stracittà (led by *Bontempelli) both claimed to represent Fascist ideology. Yet despite Fascism's pretensions to totalitarianism it did not enforce strict cultural uniformity, and writers who Fascistized their work did so more or less voluntarily. *Gramsci gave the polemical label brescianesimo (after the Catholic *journalist Padre *Bresciani Borsa) to writers who aligned themselves with political reaction after 1918. Conversely, *hermetic poetry has been seen by some as resulting from the Fascist curtailment of free speech, though such a monocausal explanation is almost certainly inadequate.   [DF]

See R. Ben-Ghiat, *Fascist Modernities: Italy 1922–1945* (2001).

FASCITELLI, ONORATO (1502–64). *Humanist and *Benedictine monk, with contacts in the literary circles of *Rome and *Naples. With Paolo Manuzio [see MANUZIO, ALDO] he edited collections of Latin and Italian texts, notably the Aldine edition of *Petrarch of 1546. His Latin poems include almost literal *translations of Petrarch's *Canzoniere, as well as verses dedicated to friends.   [SR]

Fashion

Fashion emerges with the early phases of capitalism, the expansion of trade, and the growth of cities. Its beginnings can be traced back to the 14th c. with the breakdown of hierarchical relationships among the classes and the increase in the power of the bourgeoisie. During the high *Renaissance, bourgeois culture first displayed a self-awareness about the fashioning of the human subject as a controllable and artful process. In this context, dress became a powerful vehicle for sending ideologically connoted messages. Highly considered and much read from the 16th c. onwards in the *courts of Italy and Europe, *Castiglione's *Cortegiano* offered readers a key to understanding the symbolic and political charge of appearances; it shows how courtly society was aware of fashion, and exploited its function as creator of the public image. At the same time, during the Renaissance, the numerous sumptuary laws were a way for the ruling classes and the church to exercise social control over the lower classes and women. Interestingly enough, these laws were unfailingly transgressed.

After the 16th c., *Spanish and above all French fashion held an hegemonic position in Italy and Europe. Most men and women of the nobility bought their clothes and accessories in Paris, those who could afford it employing a French tailor. A pungent portrait of the tastes of a Milanese 'giovin signore' is offered in Giuseppe *Parini's *Il giorno* (1763), originally dedicated to the goddess Fashion. As a reaction to foreign influences, and spurred on by the struggle for unification, attempts were made in the fashion world to create a more independent way of dressing. Among other things this involved renaming colours; society ladies started to dress in red, after Garibaldi's redshirts, and called their colours *magenta* or *solferino*, with reference to the victorious battles of the *Unification campaign. However, this *nationalistic impetus did not last long, since French fashion always exercised a stronger appeal. The Italian fascination with Parisian couture survived even during *Fascism, necessitating several initiatives by *Mussolini's regime to ban foreign influences in fashion, as well as prohibiting any use of foreign terms to describe outfits or style. The regime's push to Italianize daily life can be seen in the support it gave to the organization of the first fashion exhibition in *Turin (1933), and the promotion of the Ente Nazionale della Moda (1935).

The development of an authentic Italian style occurred only after *World War II in the context of a new international fashion system. In the 1950s Italian designers such as the Sorelle Fontana, Emilio Pucci, and Shubert started to make their names in foreign markets, above all in America. In the *cinema, American films about Italy gave the country a romantic allure through an intimate link between fashion and art; some of Hollywood's most famous actresses wore dresses by Italian designers. Later on, in the 1960s, the emergence of ready-to-wear fashions revolutionized and democratized the fashion world. But it was not until the 1980s that the 'made in Italy' look burst onto the international scene on a grand scale. *Milan became one of the world capitals of fashion, and designers such as Armani, Valentino, Versace, Ferrè, Krizia, Biagiotti, Moschino, and others created and established the 'Italian look'. Since then the fashion scene has witnessed not only the continued activity of designers of the older generation, but also the emergence of fresh ideas and experiments with fabrics, styles, and art, associated with Gigli, Dolce and Gabbana, Prada, etc. [EP]

See R. Levi Pisetzky, *Storia del costume in Italia* (1964–9); G. Bianchino, G. Buttazzi, A. Mottola Molfino, and A. C. Quintavalle (eds.), *Italian Fashion* (1985).

Fatti di Cesare, I, see CANTARI.

FAUSTINI, GIOVANNI (1615–51). *Venetian *librettist and impresario, who worked mostly with Francesco Cavalli. His settings are often foreign lands and his plots involve the misadventures of noble lovers, who are set against other characters from contrasting social classes, with borrowings from *Spanish drama, *pastoral theatre, and ancient Roman comedy. He uses *hendecasyllables and *settenari* [see VERSIFICATION] for recitatives and closed, usually strophic, regular forms for lyric pieces. [FC]

FAVA, GUIDO, see GUIDO FAVA.

Febus, see CANTARI.

Fede e bellezza, see TOMMASEO, NICCOLÒ.

FEDELE, CASSANDRA (1465–1558) was born in *Venice and educated by men, first by her father. She was invited to the *Spanish court between 1487 and 1494, but was not allowed to leave Venice. She was active among *Paduan *humanists between 1487 and 1497, and praised by Angelo *Poliziano. She married in 1498; her husband died in 1520. She left behind Latin *letters, including a number to well-known humanists, and orations, two of which she delivered in public at the ages of 21 (1487) and 91 (1556). She lacks the inventiveness and originality of her contemporary, Laura *Cereta, and distances herself from women generally. [See also WOMEN WRITERS, 1.] [AR]

Fedeli, see COMMEDIA DELL'ARTE.

FEDELI, AURELIA (pseud. of Brigida Fedeli), an actress working in Italy and then France from c.1640. She published a volume of poetry, *I rifiuti di Pindo* (1666), dedicated to Louis XIII, which contains *sonnets, *madrigals, *canzoni*, and *dialogues to be set to music. [FC]

FEDERICI, CAMILLO (pseud. of Giambattista Viassolo) (1749–1802). Prolific actor-playwright of *Piedmontese origin, active (especially 1786–91) in *Venice and *Padua. He wrote *Goldonian *comedies of character, but cultivated pathos. He excelled at adapting foreign novelties, and was influenced by Iffland, Kotzebue, and the 'comédie larmoyante'. [JMAL]

FEDERICO II, see FREDERICK II.

FEDERIGO DA MONTEFELTRO (1422–82) was ruler of *Urbino from 1444 till his death. A former pupil of *Vittorino da Feltre's *humanist school in *Mantua, he invested a large proportion of his substantial earnings as a *condottiere* in *patronage, building his remarkable palace and turning Urbino into a leading humanist and artistic centre. His library, containing over 1,000 *manuscripts, was one of the most wide-ranging of his time. [See also MONTEFELTRO.] [LChe]

FEDERZONI, LUIGI (1878–1967). Writer, *journalist and politician from *Bologna. He became a *nationalist deputy in 1913, and later a *Fascist minister and a member of the *Accademia d'Italia. He edited the *Nuova antologia* (1931–43), making it much more of an organ for the regime. [PH]

FELICIANO, FELICE (1433–after 1479). Veronese numismatist and epigraphist, his *Alphabetum romanum* revived Roman lapidary writing in the age of *humanism. He also devoted himself to archaeology and alchemy, and his alchemical misadventures inspired two of the tales

of Sabadino degli *Arienti. He composed poems and *novelle* (including a vernacular *Gallica historia di Drusillo intitulata Iusta Victoria*). Francesco *Colonna's *Hypnerotomachia Poliphili* was erroneously attributed to him. [CG]

FELLINI, FEDERICO (1920–94) began his career as a film-maker under the shadow of *Neorealism, but already in *La strada* (1954) affirmed a distinctive poetic streak. *La dolce vita*, which won the *Palme d'or* at Cannes in 1960, was a beacon of the new art cinema of the 1960s. But it was his next film, *Otto e mezzo*, a barely disguised *autobiography about a film director undergoing a creative crisis, which definitively created the Fellini trademark. Subsequent films have often had his name added to the title (as in *Fellini-Satyricon*, 1969) or have had the director appear in them himself as a master of ceremonies (*Intervista*, 1987). All his films display, or are about, showmanship, and the showman often doubles as thaumaturge, calling forth the healing power of memory. [See also CINEMA.] [GN-S]

FELTRINELLI, GIAN GIACOMO (1926–72). *Publisher. In 1947 he joined the Italian *Communist Party, with whose encouragement he established in *Milan in 1951 a library and archive of the international labour movement and in 1952 a book-publishing and distribution operation, the Cooperativa del Libro Popolare. In 1955, with money from the family timber business, he founded Feltrinelli Editore, and set up a chain of bookstores. He left the party in 1957. In the same year his firm achieved renown with the first world publication of Pasternak's *Doctor Zhivago*, then banned in the Soviet Union. Another early success was *Il *gattopardo* (1958). The firm subsequently published historians, novelists, and poets, including the *Gruppo 63. In the 1960s Feltrinelli supported Third World revolution and from 1968 advocated armed struggle in Italy. In March 1972 he was found blown up by a bomb, apparently by his own hand, next to an electricity pylon near Milan.
[DF]

Feminism. Of all the social and civil movements which swept across Italy in the late 1960s and 1970s, it was feminism which had the greatest long-term impact on personal, family, economic, and political life. Refusing to separate personal experience from wider political strategy, feminism challenged important legal, economic, psychological,

Feminism

and cultural aspects of women's lives, sweeping aside traditional forms of politics in its appeal to a constituency undefined by age or class. This new feminism also differed from previous waves of feminist organization, such as the suffrage movement at the turn of the century or the reformist, emancipationist movements after *World War II, which had sought accommodation on equal terms within existing forms of civic politics. Earlier demands for women's rights had recognized implicitly the legitimacy of the state, and wanted women to participate in the political process as equal partners. 19th-c. activists such as Anna Kuliscioff (from the fledgling *Socialist party) and Anna Maria Mozzoni (an independent Republican and *Mazzinian) sought to improve the material conditions of women's lives, and to better their position within the institutions of the new Italian State [see UNIFICATION]. The new feminism similarly campaigned vigorously for reform, but came to see in emancipation not an ideal but a further erasure of sexual difference. While remaining rooted in political activism, demanding equality in family law, and fighting for divorce and the right to abortion, feminists also sought to understand ways in which women remained oppressed by linguistic structures and philosophical categories as well as by religious ideology and patriarchal legislation.

Feminist groups began to emerge in the larger cities in the early 1970s. Influenced by the American experience, women began to practise their own form of consciousness-raising, or 'autocoscienza'. Repressive Catholic ideology was explored and rejected, particularly as projected onto the ambivalent figure of the mother. Even more significant were the accusations against the Italian Left that it replicated traditional patriarchal structures, privileged class analysis, and consistently set aside women's specific issues. Women now sought independence from orthodox politics and organized themselves in local and regional groups with a loose federal structure, pursuing distinctive social and cultural agendas and elaborating a new politics based on the analysis of everyday social relations both with men and with other women. Autonomous women's research and study centres were set up, such as the Centro Culturale Virginia Woolf in *Rome, and numerous feminist journals and magazines appeared (such as *Diotima, Donnawomanfemme,* and *Memoria*), often published by women (Edizione delle Donne, Tartaruga Edizioni, Essedue Edizioni, etc.) and sold in the 'librerie delle donne' which were established in many cities.

In the 1970s a wave of reforming legislation transformed family and personal life. The Movimento di liberazione della donna (MLD), affiliated to the Radical party, demanded contraception, abortion, free medical services, full legal equality, the end of economic exploitation, and the end of discrimination on grounds of sex. In 1970 women were decisive in ensuring the passage of a divorce bill through parliament and the defeat of the 1974 referendum aimed at its repeal introduced by the *Christian Democrats. In 1975 the Christian Democrats and the *Communists united to pass a reform of family law which finally abolished adultery (by women) as a criminal offence, and ended discrimination against illegitimate children. All the disparate women's groups united in the campaign to legalize abortion, which was finally achieved in 1978 and upheld overwhelmingly by referendum three years later. These major pieces of legislation achieved, the women's movement returned largely to its former loose, fragmented, and local forms of organization.

As well as achieving significant legal reform, feminists explored cultural and literary issues. The feminist presses published new work by women and translated key foreign texts, while the study and research centres produced theoretical tracts on philosophy, psychoanalysis, and literature. Much attention was given to developing theories of sexual difference and elaborating new forms of social relations. Women now wrote in greater numbers than ever before, and some became highly successful in the literary marketplace—notable instances being Dacia *Maraini, Gina *Lagorio, Fabrizia *Ramondino, Francesca *Sanvitale, and, among younger writers, Susanna *Tamaro and Silvia *Ballestra.

As with other fragmenting grassroots movements in Italy after a decade of intense political activism, feminism was no longer to mobilize on a mass scale in the 1980s. With major changes achieved in family law and equal economic opportunity, there was no single issue capable of rousing an ideology-weary nation. The 1980s saw feminists shift from demanding radical legal and political change to a more reflective theoretical and political consideration of questions of sexual difference. Influenced in its early conscious-raising days by American militant radicalism, more recent Italian feminist theory is marked by contact with the philosophical and theoretical traditions of France, especially the work of Luce Irigaray. As a whole Italian feminism has been singularly successful in bridging the gap between theory and practice, between a rigorously academic, theoretical analysis, and a more pragmatic engagement with issues which affect all women.

Three decades after the first feminist groups appeared, Italian women are active in all areas of work, political, and particularly cultural life, but still in a minority. Since women first achieved the vote in 1946 their number in parliament has not risen above 10 per cent. At the end of the 20th c. feminism found itself somewhat adrift politically, with few clear and tangible objectives in pursuit of which women could come together. Even the collapse of the First Republic found women largely silent spectators. Nonetheless the tangible achievements of feminist activism remain, and there has been a permanent transformation of women's personal and family lives not registered by orthodox politics. [See also 1968; MISOGYNY; WOMEN WRITERS.]   [SW]

See Y. Ergas, *Nelle maglie della politica: femminismo, istituzioni e politiche sociali nell'Italia degli anni '70* (1986); P. Bono and S. Kemp, *Italian Feminism* (1990); G. Kaplan, *Contemporary Western European Feminism* (1992).

FENOGLIO, BEPPE (1922–63). *Novelist responsible for the most successful and convincing Italian literary representations of the *Resistance. He was born in Alba, a market town in the Langhe region of *Piedmont, and spent most of his life there. At the *liceo* he cultivated his interest in English literature and came under the influence of the philosopher Pietro Chiodi [see RESISTANCE]. An unremarkable university career was interrupted by officer training; he was in *Rome when the armistice was declared on 8 September 1943. His partisan career, details of which are sketchy and often confused by his subsequent writings, was spent with monarchist brigades in the Langhe. After the war he worked for a wine firm, but concentrated on writing. He was signed up by *Einaudi, and in Elio *Vittorini and Italo *Calvino had editors who had themselves written about the Resistance.

His first published volume, *I ventitré giorni della città di Alba* (1952), contains a mixture of Resistance stories and stories of *peasant life. The best Resistance stories offer a welcome alternative to what was then the official version of the partisan struggle. Fenoglio's partisans are often weak and cowardly and singularly unprepared for the harshness of warfare. The peasant stories are less compelling, suggesting that at this early stage in his career Fenoglio was more comfortable with

narrative situations drawn from his own experience. By the time he published *La malora* (1954), he had overcome this problem. This short novel, narrated by its peasant protagonist, Agostino, presents a desperate picture of the bleakness of peasant life in the Langhe in the early part of the 20th c. *Verga may well have influenced Fenoglio's blend of *dialect and literary Italian, but the unremitting gloom and despair owe more to Maupassant and Zola.

In the mid-1950s Fenoglio published a number of *translations of English literature (including a much-praised version of Coleridge's *Ancient Mariner*). As well as stories, he also completed a novel, *Primavera di bellezza* (1959). Though lacking some of the drama of his other writings, this is notable for its savagely ironic indictment of the Italian army, especially its high-ranking officers, and for the *expressionism of the writing, which led *Contini to invoke comparions with *Gadda. But his energies were now concentrated on a large-scale account of his partisan experiences. This was still unfinished at the time of his death from a smoking-related illness. It was eventually published as *Il partigiano Johnny* in 1968, though subsequent scholarly editions have changed that text radically, without, however, resolving all the problems raised by the manuscripts. It is the language of *Il partigiano Johnny* which is immediately striking: some sections are in an idiosyncratic form of English, others are in a blend of Italian and English, others again in Italian. Critics have tended to home in on the linguistic curiosities and problems, some seeing evidence of an Italian Joyce in the making. But Fenoglio's narrative power and skill are at least as important, with compelling descriptions of violence and suffering on the Langhe hills.

Still powerful, but more accessible, is *Una questione privata* (1963), the story of a partisan, Milton, who abandons the struggle to discover the truth about his lover whom he suspects of having an affair with his best friend. Both this work and *La malora* have been turned into reasonably accomplished films for *television.   [PC]

See R. Bigazzi, *Fenoglio: personaggi e narratori* (1983); P. Cooke, *Fenoglio's Binoculars, Johnny's Eyes* (2000).

Fermo e Lucia, see MANZONI, ALESSANDRO.

Ferrara. City at the head of the Po delta in Northern Italy. Of medieval origins, it attained strategic and economic prominence through its location at the intersection of a network of waterways. In 1309 it became part of the *Papal States, and as a papal fief it was governed by the *Este family from 1332 to 1558. Following the foundation of the *university in 1391, it rose to prominence as a centre of *humanism, attracting figures like *Guarino da Verona and Pietro *Bembo, and fostering local writers such as Tito Vespasiano *Strozzi, *Boiardo, and *Tebaldeo. In 1492 Duke Ercole I ordered an expansion of the city known as *Addizione Erculea*; supervised by the local architect Biagio Rossetti, the project doubled the area of the city, introducing into its northern part an airy, geometric spaciousness, which prompted Jacob *Burckhardt famously to declare Ferrara 'the first modern city of Europe'. *Ariosto moved into this urban enlargement in 1529 when he bought a house in Contrada Mirasole (presently Via Ariosto). The *court of Alfonso II was the focal point for poets like Torquato *Tasso and Battista *Guarini, and a refuge for unorthodox religious figures like Vittoria *Colonna.

When the city was finally reclaimed by the papacy in 1598, the court moved to Modena, while Ferrara gradually fell into decline. In the 20th c. it became a centre for the most important 'metaphysical' painters and writers—*De Chirico, *Carrà, *Savinio, and *De Pisis. The experiences of the city's *Jewish community in the 1930s and 1940s is the subject of Giorgio *Bassani's cycle of novels and stories *Il romanzo di Ferrara* (1956–74).

[MGD]

FERRARI, BENEDETTO (?1603–81). Composer, *librettist and impresario, who was born in Reggio Emilia and worked principally in *Venice and Modena, with two years in Vienna (1651–3). His *Andromeda* (1637) introduced public *opera to Venice, while his *Inganno d'amore* (1653) introduced Italian opera to the *Austrian imperial court. His plots are derived from Greek mythology and *chivalric *epic, with subplots and comic scenes typical of Venetian opera. His three books of *Musiche varie* include settings of his own poetry.

[FC]

FERRARI, GIUSEPPE (1811–76). *Milanese philosopher and politician with republican ideals, who believed in a federalist solution for Italy and drew on the ideas of *Romagnosi and *Vico. He spent some years in *exile in France, and wrote polemically on Italian history and culture in both French and Italian.

[EAM]

FERRARI, PAOLO (1822–89). Playwright from Modena who advocated a return to the techniques of Carlo *Goldoni tempered by the *theatrical effects of the contemporary French stage. Influenced by Dumas père, after *Unification he adopted the form of the thesis play in, for example, *Il duello* (1868), *Cause ed effetti* (1871), and *Il suicidio* (1875). His conservative-minded plays provide an index to the attitudes of the bourgeoisie of post-*Risorgimento Italy. He became more outspoken in his themes after unification. His *Goldoni e le sue sedici commedie nuove* (1851) was revived by *Strehler in 1957.   [JAL]

FERRARI, SEVERINO (1856–1905). Poet and university teacher, and a disciple and lifelong friend of *Carducci. His early *Il mago* (1884) was modelled on Heine's *Atta Troll*. The odd title *Bordatini* ('Gingham') for his next two volumes (1885 and 1886) points to his *Romantic aspiration to popular poetry, that is, poetry favoured or produced by the people. He ended by drawing inspiration from the most sophisticated poetic tradition as represented by *Petrarch and *Poliziano. Had he lived longer, he might have become a protagonist of *decadentismo. He is now remembered for editing Petrarch (with Carducci) [see PETRARCH COMMENTARIES] and Il *Pistoia (with A. Cappelli), and for an *Antologia della lirica moderna italiana* (1898).   [GC]

FERRARINO DA FERRARA, see TROUBADOURS.

FERRARIS, MAURIZIO, see STRUCTURALISM AND POST-STRUCTURALISM.

FERRAZZI, CECILIA (1609–84). *Venetian famous for the *autobiography that forms part of the papers of her trial for *heresy. She had experienced ecstatic visions from an early age, and suffered an eating disorder whereby she seemed to exist only on communion loaves. Denounced in 1637 by her father confessor as possessed by the Devil, she led a wandering existence, eventually running homes for female orphans and abused girls. She was brought to trial for refusing to release the girls, accused of feigning the signs of saintliness, and imprisoned for seven years. Her work was not published until 1990.   [PBD]

FERRERO, GUGLIELMO, see DARWINISM.

FERRERO, LEO (1903–33). *Journalist and writer, who associated with Piero *Gobetti in

*Turin and the *_Solaria_ group in *Florence. As a result of questioning *Fascism's narrowly *nationalistic views of culture, he was forced into *exile and worked as a correspondent in France and America. He died in New Mexico. [SVM]

FERRETI, FERRETO DE' (1294?–1337), a notary from Vicenza, who wrote Latin poems (including one on the death of *Dante) and *historical works. His _Historia rerum in Italia gestarum_ follows the model of Albertino *Mussato. [MP]

FERRETTI, IACOPO (1784–1852). One of the best-known 19th-c. *librettists, who collaborated with *Rossini on _La Cenerentola_ and _Matilde di Shabran_, and with *Donizetti on _L'ajo nell'imbarazzo_ and _Torquato Tasso_, as well as with Mercadante and other composers. A *Roman by birth, he was professor at the Collegio Romano, and a friend of *Belli. He also wrote occasional and *satirical verse. [FD'I]

FERRI, GIUSTINO (1857–1913) wrote successful *_romanzi d'appendice_ satirizing *Roman high society based on his experience as a gossip columnist for the *_Cronaca bizantina_. Chief editor of the journals _Il_ *_Fanfulla della domenica_ and *_Capitan Fracassa_, he produced a coruscating attack on *D'Annunzio's cult of the superman in the novel _Il capolavoro_ (1901). [PBarn]

FERRIGNI, PIETRO FRANCESCO LEOPOLDO COCCOLUTO, see YORICK.

Festivals. Numerous local popular festivals are recorded in medieval Italy, including rowdy charivari and feasts of patron saints like San Gennaro in *Naples or San Giovanni in *Florence. The best known is the early form of *carnival in *Rome, involving pigs in barrels at Testaccio, races of animals, races of *Jews, bullfights, and feasting; in Florence with masks, balls, jousts, battles of stones, *_canti carnascialeschi_ (like Lorenzo de' *Medici's 'Canzona a Bacco'), and football; or in *Venice with dancing *_zanni_, the execution of pigs and a bull, acrobatics, and pantomimes. Gradually these ceremonies were politicized, passing into the control of local authorities. The Roman carnival became overlaid with *humanist themes, especially in the pageants of Piazza Navona, which popes from Julius II onwards turned into Roman triumphs, celebrating the successes of *papal policy.

The carnival was revived after the 1527 *Sack of Rome, the most striking one being that of 1545, widely known through contemporary albums, where the last Testaccio festival to be held (before 60,000 spectators) was eclipsed by the procession of thirteen ornate floats celebrating Paul III's victory over *heresy. The Florentine carnival, which contained an important theatrical element in the plays of Giovanni Maria *Cecchi, also became closely identified with the *Medici family: in 1566 it lasted several months, and was used to celebrate the marriage of Francesco de' Medici to Joanna of Austria, including an *allegorical cavalcade for Candelmas, _Trionfo de' Sogni_, and for _giovedì grasso_ the enormous _Mascherata della genealogia degli Dei_ designed by *Vasari, *Bronzino, and Giambologna. *Theatre also played an important role in Venice, where the plays of *Ruzante were performed, and where in 1542 *Aretino's _Talanta_ was put on in a magnificent set designed by Vasari. The government tried to control the disorder of carnival, particularly the element of status reversal in which citizens mimicked the Doge and Signoria, and finally took it over from 1550, turning it from a violent popular festival into an assertion of the régime's authority, and of the erudition and wealth of the republic.

Other festivals persisted, however, in Venice, including Corpus Domini, battles on bridges with fists or sticks, winter games on the ice, and elaborate regattas, but their representations by Canaletto and Guardi show how closely they were identified with the state. Some festivals had a *chivalric flavour, including the jousts in Florence immortalized by *Poliziano, or the great Belvedere tournament of 1565. These involved carousels, or even elaborate mock battles with a siege and artillery, sometimes staged on the river, as for the 1661 marriage of Cosimo III and Marguerite-Louise d'Orléans. Fireworks played an increasingly important role, especially in the festivals of Cosimo II recorded by Jacques Callot (1615–21).

Triumphs became an essential element of public festivals, involving a procession with floats (and sometimes machines) and music along a route decorated with architectural _apparati_, and punctuated by performances of playlets or harangues. The earliest recorded triumph is in Naples for Alfonso of *Aragon, and it remained the standard pattern for the reception of dignitaries for four centuries, notable examples being those for Leo X (1515, designed by Del Sarto, Pontormo, and Rosso), for Charles V (1529–33, 1536), and for *Christina of

Sweden (1656), for which albums were published. Similar allegorical spectacles also marked marriage celebrations, especially those of Cosimo I and Eleanor of Toledo (1539), and that of Ferdinando de' Medici to Christine de Lorraine (1589), whilst elaborate machines in Piazza Navona marked the marriage of Louis XIV, and ornate rituals were developed around the catafalque at funerals, such as that for Cosimo I (1574). *Baroque ceremonial was particularly developed at court festivals of *Ferrara and *Savoy, involving music, ballet, and showy costume and decoration. What had started as popular festivals had become part of the apparatus of the state, as witness Shrove Tuesday in Rome in 1650, when Count Soderini was executed in the Piazza del Popolo by a hangman dressed as Pulcinello. [RAC]

See S. D'Amico (ed.), *Enciclopedia dello spettacolo* (1954–66); A. M. Nagler, *Theatre Festivals of the Medici (1539–1637)* (1964); R. Strong, *Splendour at Court* (1973); M. Chiabò and F. Doglio (eds.), *Il Carnevale: dalla tradizione arcaica alla traduzione colta del Rinascimento* (1989).

Feudalism. Though the significance and utility of the term is much disputed, it is commonly used of the land-based hierarchical organization of society prevalent in much of medieval Europe from about AD 1000. The basis was an oath of fidelity sworn by a vassal to his lord. In return for loyalty, the vassal would receive protection and material benefit in the form of a fief, normally land worked by *peasants. The growth of the *communes from the 12th c. onwards and the extension of their jurisdiction over the surrounding countryside largely checked the development of feudalism in Northern and Central Italy. In the South, with its succession of Norman, German, and *Anjou rulers, a feudal system is much more clearly identifiable. Some of the vocabulary and imagery of feudal service appears in medieval Italian love literature—in *lyric poetry and in some parts of the *Decameron, for instance. But *French *romances and the *troubadour lyric probably had more influence than social reality. A feudal narrative literature that is purely native to Italy is impossible to find. [See also CHIVALRY; EPIC; SIGNORIA.] [CEH]

Fiabe, see FOLK AND POPULAR LITERATURE; CALVINO, ITALO.

FIACCHI, ANTONIO (1842–1907). *Bolognese writer. In the earlier part of his career he wrote plays in Italian and *dialect. In 1880 he co-founded with Alfredo *Testoni the journal *Ehi ch'al scusa* ('Oh, excuse me …'), to which he contributed caricatures of Bolognese types. These were redeployed in *Bologna d'una volta* (1892), his fictionalized memoirs as 'Sgner Perein'. [PBarn]

FIACCHI, LUIGI (1754–1825). Born in the Mugello, he became a priest, and taught mathematics and philosophy in *Florence, but also cultivated poetry and belonged to the Accademia della *Crusca. He is best known for verse fables modelled on La Fontaine, of which the first complete edition appeared in 1807. He also edited Lorenzo de' *Medici (1825) and other *Renaissance writers. [JMAL]

FIAMMA, CARLO, see GAREGGIAMENTO POETICO, IL.

Fiammetta (*Elegia di Madonna Fiammetta*) (1343–4). Prose *romance by *Boccaccio, which reverses the usual relationship between lovers in medieval literature and in Boccaccio's own early works. The setting is *Naples and the narrator is Fiammetta, who tells of her love for a young *Florentine *merchant, dwelling for the most part on his abandonment and betrayal of her. The result is the first example in fiction of modern psychological *realism based entirely on bourgeois characters, though there are few concessions to the representation of social life, and the narrative texture echoes and reworks the classics (*Ovid and Seneca especially) and *Dante, sometimes to excess. [VB]

FICINO, MARSILIO (1433–99). The great *Florentine Platonist and one of the most learned and influential thinkers of the *Renaissance. He was ordained in 1473 and elected a canon of Florence's cathedral in 1487. Destined for a medical career by his father, a doctor in the service of the *Medici family, he acquired, in addition to much medical learning, a rare mastery of Plato, *Aristotle, and later Greek philosophy. Under the *patronage of Cosimo de' Medici, who gave him a villa at Careggi, he undertook to render all of Plato's dialogues into Latin, though he interrupted this almost immediately in order first to translate the *Corpus *hermeticum* under the title of the *Pimander* [see also BENCI, TOMMASO]. With financing from Filippo Valori and other admirers, and having selectively consulted the renderings of some of the dialogues by such *humanist predecessors as Leonardo

*Bruni, Ficino published his complete Plato in 1484 (a date selected perhaps for astrological reasons) and dedicated it to Lorenzo de' *Medici (who had not contributed to the financing). He included prefaces (*argumenta*) for each dialogue and a long commentary he had written by 1469 on the *Symposium* subtitled the *De amore* (a vernacular version of which he also prepared). This became the seminal text of Renaissance love theory. Cosimo had Ficino's versions of Plato's *Parmenides* and *Philebus* read to him on his deathbed in 1464.

Over the years he composed other magisterial Plato commentaries, some incomplete, on the *Timaeus*, *Philebus* (the subject too of a public lecture series), *Parmenides*, *Phaedrus*, *Sophist*, and the passage on the Nuptial Number in the *Republic* 8. While continually revising his Plato during the 1470s and publishing his *De christiana religione* in 1476, Ficino compiled his most important original work, a huge eighteen-book *summa* on the immortality of the soul which he published in 1482. Indebted to *Augustine and *Aquinas, it was the fruit of his conviction that Platonism (for us *Neoplatonism, since he regarded Plotinus as Plato's most profound interpreter) was reconcilable with Christianity. He called it, significantly, his *Theologia platonica*—borrowing the title from Proclus whom he much admired and was often indebted to—and then subtitled it, following Augustine, *De immortalitate animorum*. In the 1480s he turned to Plotinus, with whom he had been familiar since the 1460s, and rendered the *Enneads* into Latin. For these he also wrote extensive *commentaries and notes, publishing the whole in 1492 and again dedicating it to Lorenzo.

In 1489 (and some scholars have argued it was a spin-off from his Plotinus project) Ficino published a three-book treatise on prolonging health entitled the *De vita*, a work packed with encyclopedic pharmacological and other learning and combining philosophical, astrological, magical, and psychiatric speculations. The third book in particular is a remarkable treatise on scholarly melancholy and deals *inter alia* with amulets, talismans, star and demon magic, regimen, mood elevation, and holistic medicine. When confronted with the threat of a curial investigation into its unorthodoxy, Ficino defended himself on the problematic grounds that he was presenting ancient views rather than his own. It remains the key to Renaissance magic theory and Jungians have heralded it as a founding text in psychotherapy and depth psychology.

In the last few years of his life he published *translations of other Neoplatonic authors, including Iamblichus, Porphyry, Proclus, and Synesius; translated and commented on the works of the (Pseudo-)Areopagite; embarked on a series of commentaries on St Paul; and first supported and then vehemently attacked *Savonarola.

Unlike most scholars, Ficino was able to exert a formative influence on his own and two subsequent centuries for several reasons. First, there was the intellectual fascination and novelty, bordering on unorthodoxy, of his revival of Neoplatonism, and the unfamiliar nature of what he had to say about the complementary roles of religion and philosophy in nurturing the spiritual life. His ecumenism, his delight in the notion that worship is natural and inherently various, and his diverse interests would even today align him with the liberal wing of Christian theologians. Second, a revered teacher of the *signori* and their sons, he cultivated and sustained a learned and pastoral correspondence with well over 100 pupils, friends, and admirers, many of them, including Lorenzo and various cardinals, in the highest offices of church and state, in Italy and abroad (his *Platonic Academy). His twelve books of Latin letters (and there are others besides) range from elegant thank-you notes and witty compliments to philosophical treatises. Third, he was one of the first early modern intellectuals to enjoy the accelerated Europe-wide exposure made possible by the invention of the *printing press. His works are now among the most splendid and valuable of the incunabula, and the *De amore* and *De vita*, along with the *Pimander* and Plato translations and a medical treatise on the *plague, became best-sellers.

Though he had a humanist training and freely quoted the Roman poets, and though a pious philosopher-scholar-apologist-priest with a missionary goal, he was also the first of the Renaissance mages dedicated to the notion of a world spirit and a world soul. His interests embraced mythology (for him, poetic theology), *astrology, *magic, *numerology, demonology and the occult, music and musical therapy—interests which he found in Plato and thus saw as authentic aspects of the Platonic tradition. While the depth of his technical understanding of later Platonism has rarely been equalled (his works of translation and interpretation bear witness to an enlightened and dedicated scholarship), his original philosophical, theological, and magical speculations constitute one of the great monuments of Renaissance thought and were enormously and diversely influential. [MA]

Opera omnia (1576 and 1962). See P. O. Kristeller, *The Philosophy of Marsilio Ficino* (1943); M. Allen, *The Platonism of Marsilio Ficino* (1984).

Fidenziana, see SCROFFA, CAMILLO.

Fiera letteraria, La (1925–36 and 1946–77) was a weekly magazine founded in *Milan in 1925 by Umberto Fracchia with the purpose of creating a forum for the free exchange of literary and cultural ideas along the lines of the French review *Les Nouvelles littéraires*. In 1929, it changed its editorial resi-dence to *Rome and its name to *Italia letteraria*, as it became more and more involved with *Fascist political culture. In 1936 it became *Meridiano di Roma*. From 1946 to 1977 it returned to its original name and purpose under the directorships of Enrico *Falqui, G. B. *Angioletti, Vincenzo *Cardarelli, and Diego *Fabbri.
[RSD]

FIESCHI ADORNO, CATERINA (St Caterina of Genoa) (1447–1510). Member of a noble family of *Genoa, where she spent her whole life exercising her talents for spiritual leadership, the organization of works of charity that attracted lay and clergy, and the composition of a body of works collectively entitled the *Opus cathariniarum* (published in 1551). Some parts were written by herself, and others by her confessor and followers under the inspiration of her oral teachings. [LAP]

Figaro (1862–69). The most ambitious and interesting of various 19th-c. Italian *periodicals with this title was the *Milanese review, originating mainly with Antonio *Ghislanzoni and aiming to publicize modern, principally French, ideas of literature and art. In 1864, under the editorship of Emilio *Praga and Arrigo *Boito, it became briefly an important forum for the *Scapigliati.
[GP]

FILANGIERI, GAETANO (1752–88). Reforming nobleman, and one of the group of *Neapolitan *Enlightenment thinkers who came to prominence in the 1770s. He himself was called, not long before his untimely death, to serve on the Neapolitan Supreme Council for Finance in 1787.

His major work—preceded by two lesser studies of 1771 and 1774 respectively—is *La scienza della legislazione*, written between 1780 and 1783 and consisting of five books, the last incomplete. It has a remarkable unity of intent. Filangieri proposes a framework of legislation as the foundation for a comprehensive model of a reformed society. He combined his use of *Vico, Montesquieu, Rousseau, and other reformist sources with a profound understanding of changes afoot throughout Europe and beyond. Thus, his anti-*feudal stance was supported by references to the American Revolution as the focus of the new spirit of liberty and democracy. Under the influence of *freemasonry, he advocated the transformation of Catholicism into a civic religion, and he proposed a socially stratified system of *education which would benefit the state. His work made an impact in Europe and beyond, initiating a friendship between him and Benjamin Franklin. [GLCB]

FILARETE, FRANCESCO (*c*.1400–*c*.1469), whose real name was Antonio di Pietro Averlino, began his career as architect and architectural theorist when he moved to *Milan at the invitation of Duke Francesco *Sforza. His great contribution to architectural theory is his *Trattato di architettura* in twenty-five books (1461–4), the first to be written in the vernacular and illustrated with drawings.
[PLR]

FILELFO, FRANCESCO (1398–1481). *Humanist and probably the most accomplished Greek scholar of his generation. He was taught by *Chrysoloras, whose daughter he married, and spent seven years in Constantinople (1420–7) collecting manuscripts. He brought to Italy the works of Sextus Empiricus, which contained the most complete account of ancient scepticism. He taught Greek at *Florence (1429–33) and *Siena (1434–8). He was called to *Milan in 1439 at the end of the *Visconti regime, and remained to become the official court historian for Francesco *Sforza and Lodovico Il Moro, writing a massive poem glorifying his masters, the *Sforziade*, which occupied him for twenty years. His other writings include an incomplete but interestingly disparaging *commentary on *Petrarch's *Canzoniere*, a treatise on moral philosophy, drawing mainly on *Aristotelian teaching (though he was also sympathetic to *Epicureanism), *dialogues, and *letters and poems in Greek and Latin. His *translations from Greek include texts by Hippocrates, Plutarch, and Xenophon. [See also CLASSICAL SCHOLARSHIP; PETRARCH COMMENTARIES.] [LAP]

FILELFO, GIOVAN MARIO (1426–80). Son of the *humanist Francesco *Filelfo and his *Byzantine wife, he excelled in Greek and in learned *improvisation, which earned him teaching positions throughout Italy. Apart from his considerable production of *Latin poetry and prose, he wrote an Italian *romance (*Glicefila*) and an uninspired *Vita di *Dante*.　　　　　[JK]

FILEREMO, see FREGOSO, ANTONIO FILEREMO.

FILETICO, MARTINO (*c.*1430–*c.*1490). *Humanist *educator, who taught the children of *Federigo da *Montefeltro in *Urbino, of Alessandro *Sforza in Rimini, and of Antonio *Colonna in *Rome. He *translated Theocritus and Isocrates into Latin, wrote *commentaries on *Cicero, Persius, and Juvenal, and lectured on rhetoric and Greek at the University of Rome.　　　[JK]

FILICAIA, VINCENZO DA (1642–1707). One of the earliest exponents of the pre-*Enlightenment poetics of the late 17th c. Born into the lesser *Florentine nobility and educated by the *Jesuits, he became a doctor of law at the University of *Pisa. He was elected to the Accademia della *Crusca at 22 and became a friend of Francesco *Redi and Lorenzo *Magalotti. Modest means forced him into rural retirement, broken only after 1684 when the publication of five *canzoni* celebrating the liberation of Vienna brought him fame, and the *patronage of Queen *Christina of Sweden. Cosimo III of *Tuscany then made him a senator and entrusted him with a series of increasingly important offices.

Among the early members of the Accademia dell'*Arcadia, he was a defender of *Dante, *Petrarch, and the literary tradition of Florence, which he saw himself as continuing and renewing in his own poetry. This was almost exclusively political, philosophical, and religious, but the combination of serious subject matter and simple but elevated diction does not in fact amount to a forward-looking poetic reform. Filicaia was essentially a conservative, whose style was shaped by *Petrarchism, his traditionalist views, and contemporary *classicism, rather than an innovator pointing the way to the rationalist literary reforms which would be advocated towards the end of his life by younger critics such as *Muratori and *Gravina. He collected and revised his Italian poems shortly before his death. They were partly published by his son as *Poesie toscane* (1707). Much of his Latin and some vernacular verse remains in manuscript.　　　　[MPS]

See W. Binni, *L'Arcadia e il Metastasio* (1963).

Filippo, see ALFIERI, VITTORIO.

FILLIA (pseud. of Luigi Colombo) (1904–36). *Futurist poet, painter, narrator, dramatist, and theorist. He was the leader of the *Turinese *Secondo Futurismo* in the 1920s and 1930s, exhibiting paintings, and involved in applied design projects for objects such as furniture and ceramics. He was also a dramatist of 'mechanical' sensuality, with works like *Lussuria radioelettrica, sensualità* (1925) and *L'uomo senza sesso* (1927).　　[CGW]

Film, see CINEMA.

Filocolo (*c.*1336–8). Prose *romance in five books by *Boccaccio and his first work for *Fiammetta. The title is rough-and-ready Greek for the 'labour of love', and the work is the first Italian prose version of the famous (originally Byzantine) story of Fiorio and Biancifiore—their childhood love, separation, tribulations, eventual reunion, marriage, Christian conversion, and return home. But Boccaccio embellishes what had been a slender account in French prose (drawing also perhaps on a previous Italian verse version) with erudite digressions and autobiographical allusions, some more fantastic than others. During his search for Biancifiore, Florio joins an aristocratic band of young men and women in a beautiful garden in *Naples, who illustrate their discussions of 'questioni d'amore' with what are in effect *novelle*. Two of these anticipate stories in the *Decameron* (10.4 and 5), and the whole episode has sometimes been deemed a *Decameron* in miniature.　　　　[VB]

Filologia is derived from Latin *philologia*, at first 'love of learning or letters', then 'explanation of the writings of others'. *Filologia* was used from the 17th c. to denote literary studies, or historical studies as opposed to philosophy. Since the early 19th c. it has acquired the more specialized sense of the study of texts with particular reference to their tradition and transmission [see TEXTUAL CRITICISM], their language, and their interpretation. The term may refer predominantly to linguistic history, as does modern English 'philology', in contexts such as *filologia comparata*, the comparative study of languages, or *filologia romanza*, the study of the history of the Romance languages; but a close association between *filologia* and textual studies was established in the 19th c. when, particularly through the influence of *Ascoli, historical linguistics was seen as more properly the province of *glottologia* than of *filologia*. Michele *Barbi's *nuova filologia* aimed to integrate the study of the full tradition of a text with knowledge of the culture and language of the author and of those who transmitted the text, thus treating the text as a living thing.   [BR]

Filostrato (*c*.1335). Verse *romance in nine parts in *ottava rima* by *Boccaccio, who intended the Greek name to mean 'vanquished by love' and dedicated the work to a distant love named Filomena. The story, taken up by Chaucer and *Shakespeare, is that of Troilo and Creseida, who are brought together through Pandaro, but thrown into crisis when Creseida leaves Troilo for Diomede, Troilo being finally killed by Achille whilst seeking to take vengeance on Diomede. What had been a secondary episode in medieval romances such as Benoît de Sainte-Maure's *Roman de Troie* and *Guido delle Colonne *Historia troiana* is revitalized in the light of the *dolce stil novo* and the *Divine Comedy*. In particular the *ottava rima* introduced a form that would be decisive for later Italian verse narrative, though Boccaccio's treatment of it here is dependent more on the less exalted *sirventesi* and *cantari*.   [VB]

FINARDI, EUGENIO, see CANTAUTORI.

FINIGUERRI, STEFANO, see DANTE, 2.

FIOCCHI, ANDREA (Andrea da Firenze) (1400–52) was employed at the Roman Curia, where he developed an extensive knowledge of antiquities. He wrote a *De magistratibus romanorum* (*c*.1425), and took part in the *humanist debate on the language of Ancient Rome, defending the thesis of Flavio *Biondo that the vernacular had grown out of Latin.   [LB]

Fiore, Il. The title given to a late 13th-c. (probably *c*.1285–90) *Tuscan, almost certainly *Florentine, narrative poem made up of 232 *sonnets and based on the *Roman de la rose* (1225–30 and 1268–82). The poem, which survives in a single manuscript (H 438 of the Inter-university Library of Montpellier), was first published in 1881. Originally the manuscript also contained the *Detto d'amore*, an even older Tuscan adaptation of the *Rose*. Although the *Fiore* follows the basic narrative structure of its source (the Lover's attempts to conquer the 'flower', standing for the female object of his desire), it is much more than an abbreviated translation. It creatively synthesizes Guillaume de Lorris's and Jean de Meun's parts of the *Rose* into a radically new and unified text, not least by eliminating Jean's lengthy encyclopedic and doctrinal passages. However, the *Fiore*'s main novelty lies in its use of a lyric form, the sonnet, for narrative ends and in its colourful style and language, most notably its interplay between French and Italian forms.

Rather than for its literary achievements, the *Fiore* continues to be best known for the fact that considerable circumstantial evidence exists for its having been written by *Dante. The name Durante, which appears twice in the poem and of which Dante is the form of endearment, provides the main basis of this attribution; though significant additional support comes from the many ideological, literary and formal elements which the *Fiore* shares with the poet's work. [See also FRENCH INFLUENCES, 1.]   [ZB]

Ed. G. Contini (1984). See Z. G. Baranski and P. Boyde (eds.), *The Fiore in Context* (1997).

Fiore di virtù. Moralizing work in thirty-five chapters on the vices and virtues, written in the early 14th c. by one 'Frate Tommaso', probably Tommaso Gozzadini, a *Bolognese notary. Each chapter comprises a definition, a comparison with the animal world, the morals to be drawn, and a concluding *exemplum*.   [MP]

FIORETTI, BENEDETTO (pseud. Udeno Nisiely) (1579–1642). A *Tuscan whose main work is the unexpectedly lively and engaging *Proginnasmi poetici*, published from 1620 to 1639 in five volumes, conceived as a survey of all the best Greek, Latin, and Italian writers with the purpose of teaching everything necessary to the disciplines of poetry, rhetoric, criticism, and morality. Much of his writing is humorous, particularly in barbed comments on the canonical Greek and Latin authors and on certain contemporaries. However, he takes literature seriously, valuing more its usefulness than its delightfulness, and tends to disagree with *Aristotle's *Poetics* when they conflict with Christian morality.

His work is an attempt to pursue a more historical, less theoretical analysis of the texts at his disposal. However, his freedom is limited by a certain fondness for *Renaissance rhetorical categories, and by a tendency, entertaining though it is, to be quirkily judgemental in his analyses. He is keenly aware of issues of language and style, and he takes a strong position in the *Questione della lingua regarding the *Vocabolario della Crusca. In reply to *Beni's anti-Florentine and anti-archaic views, Fioretti, like Lionardo *Salviati, maintains the excellence of the *Florentine language, which for him was proven by the close similarities between contemporary Florentine and the language of *Dante and *Petrarch. Fioretti's Esercizi morali (1633) repeat his ideal of poetry as a source of virtue; his Osservazioni di creanze (1633) contain 203 precepts on moral, literary, and grammatical topics.   [PBD]

Fioretti di San Francesco. An anonymous collection of stories in Italian mainly about St *Francis of Assisi and his companions. Its source (now lost) was the Latin Actus Beati Francisci et sociorum eius, composed before 1330 probably by Fra Ugolino da Monteregio with the help of his nephew, Fra Ugolino da Sormano; fifty-three chapters of this book were translated into Italian and called Fioretti in the second half of the 14th c. by a *Tuscan friar, who may have been the *Florentine Fra Giovanni de' Marignolli. The collection contains enchanting accounts of Francis preaching to the birds, converting the 'ferocissimo lupo' of Gubbio, and explaining to Frate Lione the true nature of perfect joy; it also includes some other cognate stories, notably of St Anthony of Padua preaching to the fishes, while three narratives focus on St Clare (Chiara di Assisi), the founder of the Order of Poor Clares. Divine apparitions, the supernatural, and the miraculous loom large in this world of faith, piety and voluntary self-abnegation. Whatever its historical value may be, the collection (first printed in Vicenza in 1476) has a compelling naïvety which seems to distil the authentic spirit of *Franciscanism.   [PMcN]

FIORILLO, SILVIO, see PULCINELLA.

Fiorio e Biancifiore, see CANTARI; FILOCOLO.

FIRENZUOLA, AGNOLO (1493–1543). Writer best known for his *novelle. He studied at *Siena and *Perugia before entering the Vallombrosan order in 1517. From 1518 to 1522 he held the position of procuratore at the *papal curia under the *Medici Pope Leo X, and was acquainted with literati at court such as Pietro *Aretino, Pietro

*Bembo, Annibale *Caro, Giovanni *Della Casa, and Francesco Maria *Molza. In 1524, in the hope of further Medici *patronage, he wrote a treatise defending the Tuscan language and criticizing the spelling proposed by Giangiorgio *Trissino. In 1526, after a series of personal disasters, he left the Vallombrosan order. On the death of Clement VII, and the end of *Florentine influence in *Rome, he returned to *Tuscany. He later became abbot of San Salvatore at Prato and founded the Accademia dell'Addiaccio.

Although few of his writings were published during his lifetime, they circulated widely in manuscript. His incomplete collection of novelle, written in 1525 for Costanza Amaretta, looks back to the *Decameron, though there is a stronger sense of morality and a refinement of style in accordance with 16th-c. tastes: the setting is in a villa near Florence during April 1523, and the stories are delivered by three women and three men over a period of six days. Firenzuola's preoccupation with rhetoric and the writing of elegant prose led him in the same year to translate the Metamorphoses of Apuleius, with the title Asino d'oro. He wrote two popular prose *comedies (both published in 1549), La Trinunzia, which has echoes of Bernardo *Dovizi's Calandra, and I lucidi, after Plautus. His La prima parte dei discorsi degli animali (published in 1548) introduced, with strong moral overtones, a series of Indian tales (Panciatantra) which had first appeared in Europe in the 13th c. and had been translated into Spanish in 1493. A contribution to the contemporary debate on the nature of women, his Epistola in lode delle donne (1525) proposes the equality of the sexes, while the Dialogo delle bellezze delle donne (1542) comprises two *dialogues on beauty and the ideal woman. His poetry has strong echoes of *Poliziano and Lorenzo de' *Medici, and includes a collection of *Petrarchan lyrics published in 1549; but his importance lies more in his determination to show that a refined prose style could be achieved in the vernacular. [See also FEMINISM; QUESTIONE DELLA LINGUA.]   [PLR]

Opere, ed. D. Maestri (1977).

FIRPO, EDOARDO (1889–1957). *Genoese *dialect poet and a piano-tuner by trade. His first collection, O grillo cantadö (The singing cricket), appeared in 1931. His gently melancholic poems are closely bound up with the life and landscape of his region. Imprisoned by the Germans during the war, he was later active in the *Communist Party.

[JJ]

Fiume

FIUME (Rijeka, Croatia). See D'ANNUNZIO, GABRIELE.

FLAIANO, ENNIO (1910–72). Prolific, multi-faceted writer who became a legendary figure in *café society of 1950s *Rome. He wrote one novel, *Tempo di uccidere* (1947), and then various volumes of short stories. He provided screenplays for *Rossellini, *Antonioni, and above all *Fellini, from *I vitelloni* (1953) onwards. As a critic he was interested mostly in experimental *theatre. The diaristic writings of his later years vividly satirize the vulgarity of contemporary affluence. [JEB]

FLAMINIO, MARCANTONIO, see LATIN POETRY IN ITALY.

FLERES, UGO (1857–1939) wrote for *Capitan Fracassa* and *Cronaca bizantina* and published two volumes of poetry, as well as *realist stories and novels. Like his friend *Pirandello, he was strongly opposed to *D'Annunzio. He was director of the Galleria dell'Arte Moderna in *Rome (1908–33) and was himself a talented caricaturist. [AHC]

FLORA, FRANCESCO (1891–1962). Influential critic and editor, who was professor at *Milan's Bocconi University, then at *Bologna. He was a disciple of *Croce and chief editor of *La *Critica*. He also founded *Aretusa* (1944) and *La Rassegna d'Italia* (1946). Consistently in the forefront of critical debate, he concentrated on contemporary issues, and published twenty-five major studies, including *Dal romanticismo al futurismo* (1921), *D'Annunzio* (1926), *Benedetto Croce* (1927), *La poesia ermetica* (1936), and *Orfismo della parola* (1954). His novel ideas were often obscured by an opaque critical style. [See also HERMETICISM.]

[JRW]

Florence

1. Before 1532

Florence (Firenze) was a minor Roman colony founded in the late republican period, not, as was commonly believed in the *Middle Ages, by Caesar, and was at first inferior to nearby Fiesole. The medieval attachment to the legendary imperial connection of early Florence was converted in the 15th c., partly for reasons of propaganda, into a republican origin, which was in fact more correct. The medieval *commune, including the election of consuls, dates from the 12th c., when Florence was still

a city with little control over the surrounding countryside. It has not much in the way of material relics of its Roman origin. Its most striking early buildings, both dating from the 11th and 12th c., are the baptistery, at the centre of the city, and the church of S. Miniato, overlooking the city from the south side of the Arno. During the late 12th and early 13th c. Florence was repeatedly involved in the *Guelf/Ghibelline struggles of Empire and *papacy. Florence was generally on the Guelf, or papal, side. A brief period of Ghibelline ascendancy, resulting from the battle of Montaperti in 1260, was ended by the Guelfs' return in 1266 and the expulsion of many Ghibelline families, after which Guelfism remained a Florentine orthodoxy.

Florence's pre-eminence in Western Europe might be said to date from the minting of the gold florin, the first gold currency in the West, in 1252. During the 13th and 14th c. Florence was an extremely important industrial and commercial city. This importance was partly based on the woollen cloth industry, carried on in a large number of workshops, using wool imported from England, France, and Spain. It also depended on Florence's unique role in the European world of international finance. This was assisted by the participation of Florentine *merchants in the taxation and finance of the papal court, which involved the transfer of large sums of money from all parts of Europe to Rome, the link with the papacy being assisted, of course, by Florence's political Guelfism. The Florentine dealer in foreign currencies became a characteristic figure in European commerce, and this elaborate handling of money was the source of the wealth of the *Bardi and Peruzzi, the *Alberti, the *Medici, and many other great families. Guelfism, cloth, and money fitted together to propel the city into great wealth.

On the basis of wealth, Florence became, from the late 13th c., a major artistic and literary centre, already the home of *Dante and *Giotto around 1300. The city's international economic importance began to decline in the late 13th c., but this was compensated to some extent by the conquest of a state, the *contado*, outside the walls. Arezzo became a subject city in 1377, *Pisa in 1406. Florentines remained capable of great expenditure on literature and art in the age of the *Renaissance, when they patronized Leonardo *Bruni, *Brunelleschi, Masaccio, *Leonardo da Vinci, and *Machiavelli. During this period, the 15th and early 16th centuries, however, Florence was gradually transformed from a self-consciously republican commune, ruled by elected priors, into the despotism of the Medici. Lorenzo de' *Medici's death in 1492 was followed by a brief revival of the republic, but, from the 1530s, Florence was the capital of Duke Cosimo's Grand Duchy of *Tuscany.   [GH]

   See F. Schevill, *History of Florence* (1936); E. Borsook, *The Companion Guide to Florence* (1997).

2. 1532 onwards

The return of the *Medici in 1532 under *Spanish *patronage established a dynasty that was to rule over the city and soon over the whole of *Tuscany for 200 years. Almost from the beginning the Medici dukes (Grand Dukes from 1569) were organized and tolerant, and took pride in encouraging the arts and sciences. Though Florence ceased to be the leading intellectual and economic city in Europe, its primacy was almost unquestioned within Italy. That the *Vocabolario della Crusca* (1612) was a Florentine product was a sign not just of a glorious linguistic past but of prestige in the present. Only as the 17th c. progressed was the city afflicted by the stagnation and regressiveness evident in much of the peninsula.

   After the death of the last Medici in 1737, rule passed to the House of Lorraine. Pietro Leopoldo, Grand Duke from 1765 to 1790, when he unwillingly became Emperor Leopold I of Austria, was one of the most advanced of *Enlightenment rulers, and his legal reforms included the abolition of the death penalty. The city continued to be a centre for progressive writing and thought—typified by *Vieusseux's *Antologia* (1821)—under Ferdinando III, who, with remarkably bloodless interruptions during the *Napoleonic periods and the revolutions of *1848, was Grand Duke until the wars of 1859 brought about national *Unification.

   Florence was the political capital from 1865 to 1870 but remained cultural capital for much longer. Though *Manzoni's attempts to make contemporary spoken Florentine the national language came to nothing, the city produced or drew to itself most of the important writers and artists of subsequent decades (including *Papini, *Prezzolini, *Pratolini, *Vittorini, *Betocchi, *Montale, *Luzi, and *Rosai). In the first fifty years of the 20th c. it generated a host of *modernist reviews, of which the best known are *Leonardo, La *Voce,* and *Solaria,* and was at the centre of *hermetic poetry in the 1930s. It was also a centre of the modernizing trend within *Fascism.

   With the end of *World War II (which caused less damage to the centre than the Arno flood of 1966), cultural primacy passed to *Milan and *Rome, to which most of the figures just listed now moved. Today Florence is a thriving provincial centre, dependent on cultural tourism, artisanal products, and to a certain extent manufacturing industry. It has had a full *university restored to it only since 1923, the original foundation having been moved to *Pisa by the Medici in 1472.   [PH]

   See E. Cochrane, *Florence in the Forgotten Centuries (1527–1800)* (1973).

FLORIDI, ACCADEMIA DEI, see BANCHIERI, ADRIANO.

FLORIO, JOHN (1553–1625), son of a *Florentine Protestant exiled in England, was an influential teacher of Italian to the nobility and royalty from 1576 to his death. His *First Fruites* (1578) and *Second Fruites* (1591) included essays on the English and Italian languages and *dialogues in both languages written for didactic purposes. His *Giardino di ricreatione* (1591) was a collection of 6,150 Italian proverbs. In 1598 he brought out his masterpiece, *A Worlde of Wordes: a Most Copious Dictionarie in Italian and English.*   [PBD]

FO, DARIO (1926–). Performer, dramatist, stage designer, director, *theatre historian, and political activist, with an ambivalent position in Italian 20th-c. culture as both radical iconoclast and major cultural export. He began his theatrical career in 1952 with *Poer nano* (Poor Dwarf), a series of sketches for *radio involving a sympathetic simpleton who bungles the telling of well-known stories from established culture, thus allowing an alternative version to be heard. The truth-telling fool was to appear in various guises in Fo's theatre, and has provided him with a powerful and lively vehicle for subversion.

   Fo's work constitutes a series of challenges to Italian politics, letters, and society. He endorsed a form of *socialism to the left of the Italian *Communist Party, while his theatrical practice and writings on theatre show him as a leading proponent of popular culture, as do his views on *dialect and its use. His plays have vindicated the power of farce, often considered an inferior genre, as a medium for incisive thought and unnerving humour. Early farces include *I cadaveri si spediscono e le donne si spogliano* (1957), a skit on a do-it-yourself divorce in a country where divorce was not yet legal; later farces, such as *Morte accidentale di un anarchico* (1970),

Fogazzaro, Antonio

Non si paga, non si paga (1974), *Il Fanfani rapito* (1975), and *Clacson, trombette e pernacchie* (1981), are more potent, and clearly reveal Fo's reading of *Marx, Lenin, *Gramsci, and Brecht. Acclaimed for these plays and for his one-man show, *Mistero buffo*, comprising alternative versions of stories from the Bible, ecclesiastical legend, and history, Fo knows as a consummate performer how to seize the moment and adopt a satirical stance towards icons of contemporary culture. He creates characters to be played by himself and his wife and partner, Franca *Rame, and his plays are full of the specifics of Italian culture and politics; yet they have been widely adapted and successfully performed in many countries. He was awarded the Nobel prize for literature in 1997. [See also COMEDY.]   [JAL]

Le commedie (1966–). See D. L. Hirst, *Dario Fo and Franca Rame* (1989); T. Behan, *Dario Fo: Revolutionary Theatre* (2000).

FOGAZZARO, ANTONIO (1841–1911). Catholic novelist and poet, who was both successful and controversial in his own lifetime. Born in the Catholic stronghold of Vicenza, he was initially educated at home, partly under the tutorship of Giacomo *Zanella, and then studied law in *Turin. He moved to *Milan until his marriage in 1866, when he returned to Vicenza, which remained his principal residence for the rest of his life. In 1873 he regained the religious faith he had lost in his youth. His work is strongly autobiographical, drawing on his family and friends for his characters, and, for his settings, on stays from his childhood onwards in the rural Valsolda. More importantly, Fogazzaro represents the psychological and spiritual conflicts and aspirations of the Northern Italian Catholic middle and upper classes, to which he belonged, caught between *nationalist enthusiasm and the Church's condemnation of the new Italy, and between traditional beliefs and the desire for modernization. From the early 1890s onwards he concerned himself particularly with *Darwinian ideas of evolution. For most of his career he struggled to harmonize the irreconcilable, both in his fiction and in the essays and talks for which he also became famous. The latter are gathered principally in *Ascensioni umane* (1899).

After some early poetry—the epistolary *Miranda* (1874) and the lyrics of *Valsolda* (1876)—he published a first novel *Malombra* in 1881. It is a remarkable exercise in late romantic horror, telling of the love of a feeble aesthete (in effect a self-representation) for the beautiful, passionate, and ultimately deranged and evil Marina di Malombra. Subsequent novels were in a more *realistic mode, though Fogazzaro was opposed to what he saw as the aesthetic ugliness and *socialist implications of *verismo proper. *Daniele Cortis* (1885) uses a politician protagonist to voice ideas on the need to separate Church and state, with at the same time the moral authority of the Church being preserved as a force for order and as a protection against socialism. The novel was a success, no doubt mostly because it also represents the torments of its hero as lover, forced by his own morality to renounce (or postpone) the love he feels on this earth for the married Elena. The demands of love and morality, shorn of the political dimension, are taken up in *Il mistero del poeta* (1888). Both areas of concern return in *Piccolo mondo antico* (1895). This, the most successful of Fogazzaro's novels with critics and public alike, recreates the Valsolda of the 1850s as simultaneously both an idyllic backwater and the theatre for the personal drama of Franco and Luisa Maironi, its husband and wife protagonists (based on Fogazzaro's parents). The eventual (evolutionary) outcome is religious and political awareness in the husband, submission in the wife, and the prospective birth of a new child and a new Italy.

Fogazzaro never re-created the novel's richness of character, tone, and style (its humorous but tender use of *dialect, for instance) in his later novels. All the same, these develop rather than repeat his established themes and situations. *Piccolo mondo moderno* (1900), whose protagonist is Franco and Luisa's son, Piero, centres on the problems of modern Catholicism and the temptations of passion. *Il *santo* (1905), again concerned with Piero Maironi, who has now committed himself fully to the Christian life, explores the difficulties of being saintly in the modern world, and discusses more openly than in previous novels the need to reform both relations between Church and state in Italy and the Church's attitude to science. The novel was an international success, but to Fogazzaro's horror its plainly progressive stance led to its being placed on the *Index in 1907. He was unable to take his debate further forward in his last, rather tired novel, *Leila* (1911).

Fogazzaro was pigeonholed as a *decadentist writer for most of the 20th c., but his writing engages with important issues and has certain psychological and technical riches not to be found in *D'Annunzio or *Verga.   [AM]

See T. Gallarati Scotti, *La vita di Antonio Fogaz-zaro* (1920); P. Nardi, *Antonio Fogazzaro* (1928).

FOGLIETTA, PAOLO, see GENOA.

FOLCACCHIERI, FOLCACCHIERO DEI, see SICULO-TUSCAN POETS.

FOLCHETTO DI MARSIGLIA (Folquet de Marselha) (*c*.1160–1231). Provençal *troubadour, later Bishop of Toulouse and fierce adversary of the Albigensians. His 'A vos, midontç, voill retrair' en cantan' inspired *Giacomo da Lentini's 'Madonna dir vo voglio', and his 'Tan m'abellis' is mentioned approvingly by *Dante (*DVE* 2.6). Dante assigns him a long speech in *Paradiso* 9, reflecting both the love-poet and the churchman. [JU]

FOLENA, GIANFRANCO (1920–92). Out-standing philologist and *historian of the Italian language who was professor at *Padua University. His philological mastery is evident from *La crisi linguistica del Quattrocento e l''Arcadia' di I. San-nazaro* (1952) onwards. His main areas of scholar-ly interest remained *medieval and *Renaissance texts. He was particularly concerned with the Ven-eto, as he showed in *Culture e lingue nel Veneto medievale* (1990). [See also FILOLOGIA.] [LL]

FOLENGO, TEOFILO (1491–1544). The most important *macaronic poet of the Italian *Renaissance. Born in *Mantua into a family origin-ating from Parma, he was originally named Gero-lamo, adopting the name Teofilo when he became a monk. He studied in the *Benedictine monastery of S. Eufemia in Brescia, where he was ordained in 1508. Between 1513 and 1516 he was in *Padua, where he became acquainted with the *Nobile Vigonze opus* and other macaronic Latin works by writers such as Tifi *Odasi.

In 1517, under the pseudonym Merlin Cocai, he published the first edition of his *Maccheronee*. He continued to revise and expand these poems throughout his life, producing four subsequent edi-tions. He is most famous for the *mock-heroic *epic *Baldus*, but his work in macaronic Latin also includes epigrams and other short poems, a mock-heroic poem, the *Moscheide*, on the war between flies and ants, and an effective *parody of *Virgilian eclogues in the *Zanitonella*, which represents the unrequited passion of the peasant Tonello for the peasant maid Zanina, and his subsequent return to sanity. He also used Italian and macaronic, and a

mixture of verse and prose, in the partly allegorical *Caos del tri per uno* (1526), and Italian only in the *Orlandino* (1526), a *chivalric poem in *ottava rima, which shows remarkable stylistic versatility and a keen interest in expressive language. In 1525, for unknown reasons, he was expelled from his monas-tic order, though some time after 1530 he followed his brother Giambattista, also a Benedictine monk, on a journey to Central and Southern Italy, during which he had contacts with Vittoria *Colonna. In 1533 he published *La umanità del Figliuolo di Dio*, a religious poem in *ottava rima*. In 1534 he was re-admitted to the Benedictines and sent to *Sicily. He returned to Northern Italy in 1542, and stayed in a Benedictine house near Bassano del Grappa until his death.

The *Baldus*, in twenty-five books of hexameters in the final version, is one of the masterpieces of Italian comic literature. It tells the story of Baldus, the son of the King of France's daughter and of a French baron, but born in a peasant's hovel in the village of Cipada near Mantua. Raised by the locals, he becomes a thug, constantly in trouble with the law and abetted by a cunning, amoral gypsy figure, Cingar. After violently taking his revenge on the poor of the village for sending him to prison, he embarks on a series of picaresque and fantastic journeys, which end in the afterworld. Folengo's linguistic revolt reaches its culmination in this poem. It has been seen as a rebellion against con-temporary social inequality. It is certainly a rejec-tion of the idealized *pastoral and *Petrarchan worlds that were the norm in Italian literature. [DieZ]

See E. Bonora and M. Chiesa (eds.), *Cultura let-teraria e tradizione popolare in Teofilo Folengo* (1979); G. Bernardi Perini (ed.), *Teofilo Folengo: nel quinto centenario della nascita* (1993).

FOLGORE, LUCIANO (pseud. of Omero Vec-chi) (1888–1966). *Futurist poet, whose *Il canto dei motori* (1912) sang the modern world of machines, but in a traditional, *decadent language. His next volume, *Ponti sull'oceano* (1914), went even further than *Marinetti's manifestos in the destruction of syntax, by altogether abolishing verbs, even in the infinitive, and staying much closer to the harsh human experience of the industrial world than Marinetti's erotic-idealist rhetoric. After *Città veloce* (1919) Folgore turned to the critical, anti-literary, deflating strategy of *parody in *Poeti con-troluce* (1922) and *Poeti allo specchio* (1924). [CGW]

Folgore Da Sangimignano

FOLGORE DA SANGIMIGNANO (before 1280–before 1332). The nickname of Giacomo di Michele; *folgore* ('splendour') aptly captures the quality evoked in his poems. He is named as doing military service for *Siena in 1295 and for his native commune of Sangimignano in 1305–6, and with the title of knight in a posthumous document of 1332.

The author of two cycles of *sonnets, respectively on the days of the week and on the months of the year, he describes an idealized aristocratic life of feasting, jousting, and *hunting. The quality most insistently praised is liberality, and the tradition identifying Folgore's 'brigata nobile e cortese' with the 'spendthrift company' condemned by *Dante in *Inferno* 29, although unfounded, is an understandable deduction from the ethos of the sonnets. Five sonnets have survived from a cycle on the arming of a knight and four expressing indignation at the weakness and disunity of the *Tuscan *Guelfs in 1313–15. The cycle on the months was the subject of a low-style *parody by *Cenne dalla Chitarra of Arezzo.   [RMD]

Folk and Popular Literature. It was the *Romantic movement, with its preoccupations with questions of nationality and ethnicity and its polemical attitude towards established literary tradition, which first constructed an idea of an Italian *popolo* and began to explore its customs and beliefs and to value its stories and poems. The political dimensions already evident in 19th-c. debates came to the fore with *Gramsci's assertion that Italian literature had always been elitist and that a new national-popular literature needed to be forged as part of the revolutionary project. Conversely in the later 20th c. fundamental terms such as *popolo* and *letteratura* came to seem increasingly porous. The *popolo* were never homogeneous culturally and linguistically, nor as a political and social class, and *letteratura* seemed an inappropriate term for oral, *dialect production, though the phrase *letteratura popolare* still seemed applicable to works produced by individuals which were intended to have broad appeal. Overall it now seems appropriate to use the term 'popular' and 'folk' to designate a loosely defined body of texts which stylistically situate themselves on what is felt to be a 'lower' or 'simpler' level than that of the literary canon as normally envisaged, and which were apparently composed for oral performance to members of the *peasantry or the urban lower classes, though the actual audience may have been wider and the oral versions are

mostly phantoms behind the written texts of often named, literate authors.

Whatever the region, the stories which Italian peasants told were undoubtedly traditional and told in dialect. Some at least are well known outside Italy. A few stories in the *Novellino* and *Boccaccio may well be of peasant origin, but the earliest convincing examples are in the *Piacevoli notti* of the 16th-c. *Venetian, Giovan Francesco *Straparola (who has the earliest known version of the Puss-in-boots story), and the *Pentamerone* of the *Neapolitan *Basile early the next century. Collections of folk tales began to be made only in the second half of the 19th c. Most were regional, one of the most important being Giuseppe *Pitrè's four-volume *Fiabe, novelle e racconti popolari siciliani* (1875), which, unlike most other contemporary collections, made every effort to preserve the dialect of the originals. Though Domenico Comparetti attempted a general collection in his *Novelline popolari italiane* (1875), the first broad-ranging anthology to gain a wide readership was *Calvino's *Fiabe italiane* (1956), which retold the stories—as its title suggests, all of a more or less fabulous kind—with the teller's characteristic brilliance. Calvino himself notes in his introduction that, if Italian folk stories have a distinguishing feature, it is a relative lack of interest in violence and a relatively strong emphasis on love with respect to other European traditions.

Collections of folk songs begin to be made somewhat earlier in the 19th c. Two of the earliest were by Germans, Wilhelm Müller and Bernard Wolff (1829) and August Kopisch (1838). The most powerful was *Tommaseo's *Canti popolari toscani corsi illirici e greci* (1841–2), though the result is in many ways a projection of Tommaseo's own tensions and energies onto the *popolo*. In 1877, in his *Poesia popolare italiana*, Alessandro D'Ancona proposed a theory that would be much built on in subsequent decades—namely that the *Sicilian *strambotto* furnished the model for the *Tuscan *stornello*, which in its turn conditioned other forms of Italian folk song, a radical change coming in the North from the encounter with a Celtic substrate which led to the development there of narrative as against lyric genres. That theory has now collapsed, as has *Croce's aestheticizing approach in *Poesia popolare e poesia d'arte* (1929), which distinguished popular from high poetry solely on the grounds of greater emotional and aesthetic simplicity, whatever the real social origins. However the difficulties to which both approaches were responding remain: the tradition of popular, or popularizing, narrative verse built round stories of French origin is indeed stronger in the North [see FRANCO-VENETO LITERATURE] and Centre [see CANTARI] than in the South; and the origins of the popular *lyric are inextricably tangled with the origins of the more courtly lyric, the earliest texts of both dating to the 13th c. or earlier and some degree of mutual contamination being evident at various times subsequently. In particular popular songs from at least the 19th c., especially ones on political or social themes, often aspire to the national language even if they are affected by local usage.

An important, polemical collection of 'popular' poetry was published by *Pasolini as *Canzoniere italiano* (1955), in which he includes soldiers' songs from *World War I and songs of the *Resistance as well as much older material. [See also CHILDREN'S LITERATURE; DIALECT; DIALECT WRITING; POPULAR SONG.] [PH]

FONSECA PIMENTEL, ELEONORA (1752–99). Poet and *journalist. Born into a noble Portuguese family established in *Naples, she was admitted at a young age to the *Arcadia Academy and wrote occasional epithalamia, cantatas, and *libretti for the Neapolitan court. She became an active republican and was imprisoned in 1798. Released by the French, she edited the *Jacobin paper, *Il monitore napoletano* (1799). On the return of the Bourbons she was re-arrested and executed [see RESTORATION]. [CCa]

Fontamara (1949, first version 1933) was Ignazio *Silone's first and best known novel. *Fascism adds to abuses already suffered by the *peasants in an Abruzzo village, when a developer nominated *podestà by Rome takes away their water and grazing rights. Berardo Viola is their leader; seeking work in *Rome, he ends up in prison, learns about *Communist ideals, confesses falsely to being the unknown suspect of various attacks on Fascism, and dies. His two friends, one of whom is the real culprit, return to Fontamara and set up a clandestine newspaper. The village is attacked; three survivors make for Switzerland and tell their tale to Silone. [JR]

FONTANA, FERDINANDO (1850–1919). *Milanese writer and *journalist, whose copious production includes *dialect verse and plays, *libretti (for *Puccini's *Le Villi*, for example), *travel books, and *socialist polemic. His contributions to two documentary volumes, *Milano 1881*,

Mediolanum (1881) and *Il ventre di Milano* (1888), helped promote the idea of Milan as Italy's moral capital. As a critic, he staunchly defended *verismo. [PBarn]

FONTANELLA, GIROLAMO (*c.*1612–43/4). Little is known of this *Neapolitan poet, thought by many to be the finest writer of *pastoral verse of the 17th c. He is partly indebted to *Marino, especially in the *Ode* (1633, revised and expanded 1638), but he also draws directly on the earlier Neapolitan pastoral tradition, particularly *Sannazaro. His *Nove cieli* (1646) uses the conventions of *concettismo to create graceful miniature portraits, frequently incorporating mild-mannered moral dicta, while the *Elegie* (1645) turn to declamatory pathos. [MPS]

FONTE, MODERATA (pseud. of Modesta Pozzo de' Zorzi) (1555–92). *Venetian poetess and writer. Orphaned in 1556, she went to live with her uncle, who ensured her *education. In 1581 she published *I tredici canti del Floridoro*, an unfinished *epic poem with echoes of *Ariosto. Her most famous work is *Il merito delle donne*, which criticizes contemporary patriarchal social structures and male attitudes, and was published posthumously in 1600 by her daughter Cecilia. [See also FEMINISM; WOMEN WRITERS, 1.] [PLR]

FONZIO, BARTOLOMEO (Bartolomeo della Fonte) (1446/9–1513). *Humanist who succeeded Francesco *Filelfo in the chair of rhetoric at *Florence in 1481, and who, despite being the recipient of an important Latin elegy by *Poliziano, later quarrelled with his famous colleague. For a brief spell (1489) he was Matthias Corvinus' librarian in Budapest, gathering important *manuscripts for the Hungarian king. In 1493 he became parish priest at Montemurlo, where he died in 1513. He is mostly known for six introductory orations for lecture courses on Latin authors, which amount to his own (rather unoriginal) poetics; but he also carried out important textual work on the first editions of Celsus (1478) and Persius (1480). [MMcL]

Food, see CAFÉS; COOKERY BOOKS.

FORESTI, IACOPO FILIPPO, DA BERGAMO (1434–1520). Augustinian friar resident for most of his career at the convent of S. Agostino in Bergamo. He is best known for his *Supplementum chronicarum* (1483), a history of the world from the

Creation to 1434, a continuous best-seller from its first printing right through the 16th c. It was *translated into Italian in 1488, and frequently updated. Another *encyclopedic work, *De plurimis claris selectisque mulieribus christianis* (1494), is dedicated to the women of the *court of *Ferrara. Foresti was also prior of the convents at Imola (1494) and Forlì (1496). [See also CHRONICLES.]   [JEE]

FORMIGGINI, ANGELO FORTUNATO (1878–1938). *Publisher. From an old *Jewish family in Modena, he was active at the turn of the century in *socialist and *positivist circles. He remained committed to publishing as a channel of popular *education. He founded his firm in *Bologna in 1908, then moved it to Modena (1909), *Genoa (1911), and *Rome (from 1916). He published various series, including *biographies (*Profili*) and *Classici del ridere*, and from 1918 the monthly literary review *L'Italia che scrive*. He had initially supported *Fascism, but in November 1938 he committed suicide by jumping from the bell tower of Modena cathedral in protest against the anti-Semitic laws.   [DF]

Formula di confessione umbra. Confessional formula written near Norcia in 1065, offering the earliest surviving examples of a typical central Italian *dialect. It uses Latin to address God and saints, and the vernacular in those parts specifying penitences and sins.   [MM]

Forse che sì forse che no, see D'ANNUNZIO, GABRIELE.

FORTEGUERRI, NICCOLÒ (1674–1735). Born in Pistoia, he lived mainly in *Rome as a curia official. He contributed to anthologies of *Arcadian *lyric poetry and published fables and *satires, but he is remembered for *Ricciardetto* (written 1716–25), a *mock-heroic *chivalric narrative in thirty cantos, with some elements of satire. Partial English translations were made by J. H. Merivale (1820) and Lord Glenbervie (1821).   [JMAL]

FORTINI, FRANCO (pseud. of Franco Lattes) (1917–94). Poet, critic, and essayist. He wrote his first poetry around 1937 while at the University of *Florence, where he graduated in 1940 in literature and philosophy, and where he was influenced by Giacomo *Noventa. Subsequent influences were Paul Éluard and Bertolt Brecht, both of whom he

would also translate. Conscripted in 1941, after the armistice he escaped to Switzerland, where he met Italian anti-*Fascists and joined the clandestine *Socialist Party (PSI); in 1944–5 he served in a partisan brigade in the Val d'Ossola.

After the Liberation he settled in *Milan. He worked on *Il *Politecnico* (1945–6) and *Avanti!* (1946–7) and published his first collection of verse, *Foglio di via* (1946), and the novel *Agonia di Natale* (1948). He worked in publicity for Olivetti (1947–53), as a consultant to various publishers (from 1959), and as a schoolteacher (1964–71). With other left-wing Socialists he edited the *periodical *Ragionamenti* (1955–7). His first collection of cultural-political essays, *Dieci inverni*, appeared in 1957; later that year he left the PSI after its turn to social democracy and became a prominent voice of the new Left, through the periodicals *Officina* (1958–9), *Quaderni rossi*, and *Quaderni piacentini* and the essays collected in *Verifica dei poteri* (1965). He went on to publish four further collections of his own verse (1959, 1963, 1973, and 1984), a volume of verse *translations (1982), and other literary translations, including notable versions of Proust's *Albertine disparue* and (with his wife Ruth Leiser) of Goethe's *Faust*.

From 1971 until retirement in 1986 he taught *literary criticism at the University of *Siena. He continued to produce political and polemical essays and *journalism, but, despite his considerable influence as a dissident Left intellectual and cultural critic (he consistently opposed both the *Communist Party (PCI) and mass culture from the late 1940s), he saw himself primarily as a poet. His poetry was rarely explicitly political. He saw the political force of poetic language as lying rather in its ability to resist a reified and inauthentic reality.   [DF]

See R. Luperini, *La lotta mentale: per un profilo di Franco Fortini* (1986).

FORTUNATO, MARIO, see IMMIGRANT LITERATURE.

FORZANO, GIOVACCHINO (1884–1970). Author of numerous *libretti and popular dramas, who collaborated with *Mussolini on three plays, *Campo di maggio* (1930), *Villafranca* (1931), and *Cesare* (1939). He also wrote and directed the propagandistic film *Camicia nera* (1933). He was often perceived as a self-serving supporter of *Fascism, and his artistic reputation did not survive its collapse.   [CEJG]

Fosca, see TARCHETTI, IGINIO UGO.

FOSCOLO, UGO (1778–1827). Poet and patriot, now perceived as the major literary figure in *Napoleonic Italy and generally rated one of the greatest Italian authors since the *Renaissance. He was born to a Greek mother and a doctor of Venetian descent on the Ionian (then Venetian) Island of Zante (Gr. Zakinthos) and was first educated there and at Split. His father died in 1788, and in 1793 his future Italian orientation, and what his poetry mythicizes as his destiny as an *exile, were determined when he left Zante never to return and was brought to *Venice. Here his precocious talent was recognized by *Cesarotti and others. An outsider in Venetian society, he made a boast of poverty and cultivated romantic and revolutionary personae, with that of the 'liber'uomo', or modern republican on the ancient model, most marking his writing after the invasion of Italy by French armies under Bonaparte (1796). His career took off with the *Alfierian *tragedy *Tieste,* staged in Venice in January 1797, and the ode 'A Bonaparte liberatore', in which, having enrolled in the advancing revolutionary forces in *Bologna in April 1797, he now hailed their victorious general. Returning to Venice, during the short-lived municipality that followed the demise of the aristocratic republic, he distinguished himself by his extremist oratory in the open debates of the Società di Pubblica Istruzione, only then to see the 'liberator' hand the city and most of its territory to *Austria by the Treaty of Campoformio (October 1797).

A refugee in *Milan, the capital of the French-controlled Cisalpine Republic, he engaged in revolutionary *journalism and became a friend of *Napoleon's laureate-to-be Vincenzo *Monti. In 1799–1800, with Bonaparte absent and the French hard-pressed in Italy by an Austro-Russian counter-offensive, he fought gallantly in the republican cause, reaching the rank of captain, which he retained after Bonaparte's victory at Marengo (June 1800) had re-established French power. But any prospect of further advancement in the army was jeopardized by his outspoken assertion of Italian interests, which made him politically suspect in French eyes. At the news of Bonaparte's return from Egypt and his *coup d'état* of November 1799, he had reissued 'A Bonaparte liberatore' with a dedication inviting the general to erase the memory of Campoformio by restoring Italian liberty, and warning him against the temptation of absolutism. His disenchantment was confirmed under the cor-

rupt second Cisalpine Republic. In his *Orazione a Bonaparte* (1802), on behalf of delegates summoned to meet Bonaparte at Lyons, he denounced the very administration which had commissioned him to speak, and called upon Bonaparte (this once with flattery) to regenerate the republic. In 1801–2 he also completed *Ultime lettere di Jacopo Ortis,* a partial edition of which had been published in Bologna in 1798. Venting his accumulated disillusionment, he now recast it as a work of political protest and published it in Milan in 1802.

The *Ortis* is a landmark in the emergence of romantic sensibility and the *novel form in Italy, and reflects Foscolo's retreat from revolutionary idealism. So too do the *Poesie,* published in Milan in 1803, in which, repudiating his juvenilia, he gathers poems written since 1798: two *neoclassical odes, 'A Luigia Pallavicini caduta da cavallo' and 'All'amica risanata', and a dozen *sonnets. The former vie with *Parini's late odes in exquisite craftsmanship and apt handling of Greek mythology. The sonnets are marked by the influence of *Petrarch and Alfieri, but taken as a whole represent, in their often unrestrained subjectivism, a counterpart to the 1802 *Ortis*: three of exceptional intensity ('Alla sera', 'A Zacinto', and 'In morte del fratello Giovanni') rate among the finest in Italian. The second ode and the sonnets, like the novel, anticipate themes that come to the fore in Foscolo's later poetry: exile, death, the tomb, commemoration, immortality through poetry, and the restorative function of beauty.

Also important at this stage for the subsequent development of his poetics and poetry was his study of classical poets and of *Vico. The influence of Lucretius' *De rerum natura,* already detectable in the sonnets, clearly showed itself later on in *Dei sepolcri* and *Le grazie,* and in the projected series of 'carmi', didactic lyrics in blank verse, to which the two works relate. Vico's thought, propagated in Milan by *Neapolitan exiles, provided a vision of primitive times that determines the image of prehistory in *Dei sepolcri* and of medieval history in the essays on *Dante. 1803 saw the publication of *La chioma di Berenice,* a learned commentary on Catullus' *Coma Berenices,* together with an Italian *translation of the poem. Among other things, this enhanced his command of blank verse, the metre of *Dei sepolcri* and *Le grazie,* as did a translation of Homer's *Iliad* 1 and 3, carried out in 1804–6, when he was posted to the army assembled on the French coast in readiness for Napoleon's planned invasion of England. Here he also began translating Sterne's

Foscolo, Ugo

Sentimental Journey while in contact with English nationals held under surveillance. Amongst them was the young woman (perhaps Sophia Hamilton) who bore him Floriana, the daughter at his side during his last years in England. After his return to Milan (March 1806) he escaped further involvement in Napoleon's military adventures, and understanding superiors left him free to pursue literary projects. These bore fruit in April 1807 when he published his translation of *Iliad* 1 and, to immediate acclaim, *Dei sepolcri*, which had taken shape the previous summer. Subsequently, to foster martial spirit and military awareness, he edited in 1808–9 the works of Raimondo *Montecuccoli, who, as Austrian field marshal, had been the most successful European commander of his day.

Bonaparte's self-proclamation in May 1804 as Emperor, and King of Italy, ushered in a decade of conformism, which, as his regime consolidated itself, was marked by growing regimentation of intellectuals and intolerance of dissent. Putting principle before profit, Foscolo disdained to become a professional writer within the cultural establishment and indeed became its scourge, though professionally he remained a soldier, as he was fond of asserting in order to distance himself from salaried intellectuals. With Napoleon at the summit of power and prestige after stunning victories at Austerlitz and Jena, *Dei sepolcri*, far from indulging in the adulation of the Emperor and the anti-British abuse then customary among Italian poets, takes issue with a Napoleonic decree regulating burial, pours scorn on his 'bello italo regno' and its capital, celebrates Italian glories centred on *Florence, and, to remind Italians that Napoleon is not invincible, hails the victor of Trafalgar (1805) as hero. When, despite this, Foscolo briefly holds the chair of eloquence at Pavia, his inaugural lecture, *Dell'origine e dell'ufficio della letteratura*, of January 1809, dares to omit all praise of the Emperor. Without naming Alfieri, Foscolo reaffirms his doctrine of the writer's independent civil mission in implicit contrast to the acquiescence advocated by government panegyrists such as *Giordani. Delivered to a crowded audience and seen as an event at the time, the lecture made a profound impression on young admirers such as the *Pellico brothers, *Borsieri, and *Di Breme, who were soon to become the standard-bearers of Italian *Romanticism.

Tensions between Foscolo and the literary establishment erupted into open feuding, and ended his friendship with Monti, when in 1810 he attacked individuals and provoked a campaign aimed at

intellectuals who did not toe the line. At the end of 1811 the première of his tragedy *Ajace* at La Scala was turned into a fiasco by a cabal of establishment enemies, and the *censors banned the play, which was in any case interpreted as covert satire of Napoleonic tyranny. Granted long leave outside the Kingdom of Italy, in the summer of 1812 he withdrew to *Tuscany (then a French *département*). There he published the translation of *A Sentimental Journey*, accompanied by *Notizia intorno a Didimo Chierico*, a whimsical portrait of the pseudonymous translator, and wrote a third tragedy, *Ricciarda* (published in London in 1821), set in medieval Italy. From April 1813, in the seclusion of Bellosguardo above Florence, he devoted himself to *Le grazie*, which subsumed parts of the earlier scheme for a series of 'carmi'. Here the contemporary world has largely receded from view, yet the topical allusions (notably to Italy's heavy losses in Napoleon's Russian campaign), rather than merely providing a foil for serene mythological fantasy, contextualize the poem's theme of the humanizing power of beauty and art, in relation to the inhumanity of the time and to an official education policy that favoured science and technology at the expense of the humanities. Moreover, in Florence he continued work on the *Hypercalypsis* (or *Didymi clerici prophetae minimi Hypercalypseos liber singularis*), an esoteric *satire on the Milanese cultural establishment written in biblical Latin and in the style of Old Testament prophecy and the Apocalypse. Significantly, Foscolo himself figures in it as a 'vir militaris' as well as writing under the guise of Didymus.

Returning to Milan after Napoleon's defeat at Leipzig (October 1813), he worked for the survival of the Kingdom of Italy as an independent state, but the Emperor's abdication in April 1814 was quickly followed by *Austria's reoccupation of *Lombardy. As the foremost anti-Napoleonic intellectual he was invited to edit a government-run journal, but when Napoleon returned to power in March 1815, and officers of the disbanded Italian army were required to swear allegiance to Vienna, he slipped away into a self-imposed exile from which he never returned. Living in poverty near Zurich for more than a year, he drafted long passages of *Della servitù d'Italia* to demonstrate the impossibility of Italian freedom, republished *Ortis* (1816), with a critically important 'Notizia bibliografica' and a damning indictment of Napoleon, and completed and published the *Hypercalypsis*.

He reached London in September 1817 to be fêted by the mainly Whig aristocracy as the real

Jacopo Ortis (whence the immediate republication of the novel) and as one who had defied the dreaded Napoleon. He impressed by his conversation and learning, his Graeco-Italian origins making him appear a unique embodiment of the dual classical tradition. But England was not conducive to literary creativity. A projected volume of semi-fictional *Lettere scritte dall'Inghilterra*, fixing his impressions of English society and culture, was soon abandoned. Fragments of *Le grazie* were revised and published (1822), yet the work as a whole remained far from complete, as did the translation of the *Iliad*. Lacking any other livelihood, he wrote for the periodical press and interpreted the Italian classics for a sophisticated English readership in essays which inaugurated modern Italian criticism. He made his debut with Dante articles for the *Edinburgh Review* (1818) and 'Narrative and Romantic Poems of the Italians' for the *Quarterly Review* (1819), and went on to write for various other journals. An incomplete essay attacking *Manzoni's historical *realism ('Della nuova scuola drammatica italiana'), undertaken in 1826 for the *Westminster Review*, remained unpublished until 1850. *Essays on Petrarch*, his critical masterpiece, appeared in volume form in 1821 and 1823.

He made sizeable earnings but lived beyond his means, to the despair of generous friends who supported him. In 1821, after the death of her grandmother, Floriana entered his life with a legacy which he lavished on 'Digamma Cottage', a modest villa leased in 1822. From 1823 his biography becomes a story of social eclipse and literary drudgery, mainly for William Pickering, who published a *Decameron* (1825) with his introductory 'Discorso' and the epoch-making 'Discorso sul testo della "Commedia" di Dante' (1826), intended for an edition of Dante. His last ambition, to be professor of Italian at the new London University, was overtaken by the illness from which he died at Turnham Green on 10 September 1827. Buried in Chiswick churchyard, in 1871 his remains were reinterred in the Florentine church of S. Croce, which in *Dei sepolcri* he had identified as the nation's pantheon.

As the figure who best articulated the evolution of Italian national awareness under Napoleon, Foscolo became one of the guiding lights of the *Risorgimento generations and was subsequently venerated after Italian *Unification. As a writer he was chiefly admired for *Ortis* and *Dei sepolcri*. During the 20th c. there was a reappraisal of *Le grazie* and the discovery of the 'Didymean' component of

his œuvre. His personality and many aspects of his writing are now perceived as representing romanticism in all but name well before the term was first promoted in Italy in 1816. [JMAL]

Edizione Nazionale delle Opere di Ugo Foscolo, ed. M. Fubini *et al*. (23 vols., 1933–). See G. Chiarini, *La vita di Ugo Foscolo* (1910); M. Fubini, *Ugo Foscolo saggi, studi, note* (1978); G. Cambon, *Ugo Foscolo, Poet of Exile* (1980).

FOSSA DA CREMONA, see MACARONIC LITERATURE.

FOSSATI, GIUSEPPE, see ITALIAN WRITERS IN SWITZERLAND.

Fotoromanzo. Term designating the *photographed stories which were pioneered in the postwar years by magazines like *Bolero-film* and *Grand Hotel*. The latter was (and is) the most successful of the type. Initially it employed artists such as Walter Molino, who created a cast of glamorous heroines and handsome heroes, going through trials and tribulations that owed much to the 19th-c. *feuilleton*. As photographs replaced drawings, and the *fotoromanzo* became distinct from the *fumetto* [see COMICS], a sort of sub-star system came into being, which included the future film stars Gina Lollobrigida and Sophia Loren, the singer Achille Togliani, and the *television presenter Mike Bongiorno. *Fotoromanzi* were a sort of pocket cinema that enjoyed enormous popularity among lower-class women, who regularly passed old copies from hand to hand. Despised by intellectuals and satirized by film directors, including *Antonioni and *Fellini (in *L'amorosa menzogna* and *Lo sciecco bianco* respectively), they continued to prosper in the 1980s and 1990s and were long the only Italian equivalent of the television soap opera. They found a ready export market in Germany and the Middle East. [SG]

FRABOTTA, BIANCA MARIA (1946–). Poet and professor of Italian literature at *Rome University. She has promoted the study and importance of *women writers, particularly with *Donne in poesia* (1976) and *Letteratura al femminile* (1980). Her own poetry, beginning with *Il rumore bianco* (1982), highlights themes of silence, absence, and travel. [CO'B]

FRACASTORO, GIROLAMO (*c*.1476–1553). Physician, philosopher, and Latin poet.

After teaching for some years at the University of *Padua, he returned to his native Verona to practise medicine. His medical epic *Syphilis* (1530) gave its name to the disease whose first victim, according to Fracastoro's own myth, was the shepherd Syphilus. His influential *Naugerius, sive de poetica dialogus* (1533) argues that what ultimately distinguishes poetry is not subject matter or objectives like pleasure or instruction, but the cultivation of absolute beauty of expression. The *dialogue in effect defends *Renaissance poetic practice, to which it stands in closer relation than other 16th-c. discussions of poetics. [See also LATIN POETRY IN ITALY; LITERARY THEORY, 2; MEDICINE.]

[SPC]

FRACCHIA, UMBERTO, see FIERA LETTER-ARIA, LA.

FRACHETTA, GIROLAMO (1558–1620). Philosopher and political writer who served Luigi d'*Este, Scipione *Gonzaga, and the Spanish embassy in *Rome, but later moved to *Naples. He displayed literary-philosophical interests in *Dialogo del furore poetico* (1581), but turned to issues of morality and civic responsibility in *Il prencipe* (1597) and *Della ragione di stato* (1623). He proposed taxation of the nobility, believing it contributed to social order and tranquility, and, following many of his contemporaries, thought that political problems should be dealt with pragmatically, not dogmatically. [See also POLITICAL THOUGHT; RAGION DI STATO.] [FC]

Fra Cipolla. Clever and deceitful monk in *Boccaccio's *Decameron* (6.10).

France, see FRENCH INFLUENCES.

FRANCESCA DA RIMINI (d.1283/6). Born in Ravenna, she was married to Gianciotto *Malatesta of Rimini, who killed her and her lover, his brother Paolo. *Dante meets her among the lustful in Hell (*Inf.* 5.73–142), in an episode which appealed particularly to *Romantic sensibilities, inspiring poems (Leigh Hunt's *The Story of Rimini*), paintings (Dante Gabriel Rossetti), *tragedies (*Pellico, *D'Annunzio), *operas (Rachmaninov), and an overture (Tchaikovsky). In Dante's text she is more ambiguous, deflecting responsibility from herself and blaming Love, Paolo, and the writer of the *romance of Lancelot for her adultery. The episode is part of Dante's critique of the potential moral dangers of love literature, including *Guinizzelli's poetry and his own. [PA]

Franceschina, see ZANNI.

FRANCESCO CIECO DA FERRARA (mid-15th c.–1506). Narrative poet. His place of birth and family background are unknown, and there is no evidence to support the surname Bello by which he has often been known, or his identification with the *Florentine poet Francesco d'Antonio. His name indicates that he was blind. In the 1490s he was attached, as poet and entertainer, to the *courts of *Mantua and Bozzolo, enjoying the *patronage of Isabella d'*Este and Antonia del Balzo. His principal work, *Il Mambriano* (1509), was begun in this period. At the end of his life Cieco was resident in *Ferrara under the patronage of Ippolito d'Este, and died there. *Il Mambriano* tells the story of the campaigns of Mambriano against Charlemagne and *Rinaldo, and the adventures of *Orlando and Astolfo in North Africa. The last section of the poem narrates the liberation by Orlando of the pilgrim route to Compostella. The poem also contains seven humorous *novelle within the narrative. It won the appreciation of contemporary critics and poets, including *Ariosto and Torquato *Tasso, and its popularity is attested by many 16th-c. editions. Francesco is also the author of a *pastoral play, the *Comedia di malprattico*, which links him to the burgeoning dramatic traditions of Ferrara and Mantua. [JEE]

FRANCESCO DA BARBERINO (1264–1348) (Francesco di Neri di Ranuccio) practised in *Florence as a civil and canon lawyer from 1297 but left the city in 1303, probably for political reasons. He travelled in Northern Italy and France until 1313, when he returned to Florence. He held numerous public offices until his death in the *plague.

His two surviving literary works, both written during his *exile, are compilations of ethical and social instruction. The *Documenti d'amore*—'amore' being understood in a spiritual sense—are in twelve unequal parts, each embodying the teaching of a particular virtue. The vernacular text, in a variety of verse forms, is accompanied by a Latin prose *translation and a copious Latin commentary; typically, the verse gives precepts for good behaviour, which the commentary amplifies with anecdotes and citations. The *Reggimento e costumi di donna* is an etiquette book for women, without the

Latin superstructure of the *Documenti*. Written in rhythmic prose interspersed with verse, it contains narrative passages, such as the account of a princess's wedding in part 5, which have a sensual charm similar to that of some *cantari*.   [RMD]

FRANCESCO DA CASTIGLIONE, see VIT-TORINO DA FELTRE.

FRANCESCO DA FIANO (*c*.1350–*c*.1420). Employed by the *Roman Curia, his main work was the invective *Contra ridiculos oblocutores et fellitos detractores poetarum*, in which he defends classical poetry, using a mode of *allegorical interpretation which derives immediately from *Petrarch, with whom he corresponded, and *Boccaccio, and which is also to be found in the same period in *Salutati's *De laboribus Herculis*.   [LB]

FRANCESCO DA FIRENZE, MASTRO, see SICULO-TUSCAN POETS.

FRANCESCO DEGLI STABILI, see CECCO D'ASCOLI.

FRANCESCO DI BARTOLO DA BUTI (1324–1405). Author of a vernacular *commentary on *Dante's *Divine Comedy*, based on lectures given in *Pisa in about 1385. The written version, dating from the mid-1390s, survives in over thirty manuscripts. He also wrote Latin commentaries on *Horace and Persius, and a manual of rhetoric. [See also DANTE COMMENTARIES.]   [SNB]

FRANCESCO DI VANNOZZO (*c*.1340–after 1389). *Lyric poet and musician. He was born in *Padua into a family of émigrés from Arezzo, but spent his life as *court poet in several Northern Italian cities—Padua, Verona, *Venice, *Bologna, and *Milan, where the last known reference to him shows him working for the *Visconti. He was skilful and prolific, and turned his hand to many genres, including *dialect *frottole. He was a typical poet-for-hire of the second half of the 14th c. *Petrarch, whose poetry had a strong influence on him, mentions his talents as a musician.   [SNB]

Franciscans (also called *Cordiglieri, Frati minori*, and *Frati bigi*). Followers of St *Francis of Assisi, whose rule insisted on total poverty not only for every friar but also for the corporate order. More than 5,000 were present at one Chapter General before Francis died, and there were about 1,250 in England alone by 1250. With this phenomenally rapid spread and the consequent need for practical organization, the ideal poverty soon proved impractical, and two factions developed within decades of the order's foundation: the Spirituals, who insisted on fidelity to the founder's wishes, and the Conventuals, who wished to relax the rule to allow corporate ownership of property. In 1317–18 Pope John XXII judged in favour of the Conventuals.

From early times Franciscans distinguished themselves in theological scholarship, and in their first century could count among their members thinkers such as Robert Grosseteste, Roger Bacon, St *Bonaventure, and Duns Scotus. They also devoted themselves to worldwide missions, reaching China by 1294 and pioneering in India and the Americas. Today they preach in every mission field on earth. They have also fostered several popular devotions, such as the Christmas Crib and Sacred Heart. Franciscans figure vividly in Italian literature from *Dante to *Manzoni. The *Cappuccini* are a 16th-c. offshoot, founded by Fra Matteo da Bascio.   [PMcN]

FRANCIS OF ASSISI, ST (San Francesco d'Assisi) (1182–1226). Religious leader, founder of the *Franciscan order, missionary, and poet whose example profoundly affected the course of Christendom. Converted to Christ in his 20s, he rejected the lifestyle of his father, a rich *merchant of Assisi, and embraced the evangelical ideal of poverty and preaching. He soon attracted disciples, who begged from the rich and ministered to the poor and sick. In 1210 their way of life won approval from Innocent III, and was confirmed by Honorius III in 1223. Francis preached charismatically in Central Italy, and went abroad to evangelize Muslims (Syria 1212, Morocco 1213–14, Egypt 1219). Not long before he died, he expressed his sense of kinship with all creation in his biblically inspired 'Cantico di frate sole', now seen as the first milestone of Italian literature. He is believed to have received the stigmata in 1224. He was canonized in 1228. [See also FIORETTI DI SAN FRANCESCO.]   [PMcN]

FRANCO, MATTEO (1448–94). *Florentine priest and *Medici protegé, who was a good friend of *Ficino and *Poliziano, and, for a while, of Luigi *Pulci, with whom he subsequently exchanged violent but entertaining *sonnets. Many of his lively and witty *letters to Lorenzo de' *Medici and his circle have survived.   [DieZ]

Franco, Niccolò

FRANCO, NICCOLÒ (1515–70). *Poligrafo*, born in Benevento, who moved to *Naples in about 1535 and then to *Venice, where he became secretary to Pietro *Aretino. The extremely violent rupture between them led to his scurrilous *Rime contro l'Aretino*, which, together with his *Priapea*, were put on the *Index. His *Pistole vulgari* (1539) is a varied collection of letters, whose addressees include notable contemporaries, *Petrarch, and *puttane*. As well as ten *Dialoghi piacevoli*, he published *Il petrarchista* (1539), a *dialogue satirizing *Petrarchism, and a *novel, *La Philena* (1547). Franco left Venice in 1539 and spent periods in *Piedmont, *Mantua, Basle, and Naples. In his later years he was in *Rome with Cardinal Morone. His anticlerical *satires offended Pope Paul IV, and he was arrested, tried by the *Inquisition, and hanged.

[DieZ]

FRANCO, VERONICA (1546–91). *Venetian poet and high-ranking *courtesan, famous in her day for her intellectual and artistic accomplishments. She was eagerly sought by noblemen and royalty, painted by Tintoretto, and visited by Henry III of France. Married to a doctor but, despite this, uninhibited concerning her profession, she wrote letters and poems to various men of letters, including Domenico *Venier, who emended her poems (all in *terza rima*) for her prior to their publication in 1575. Her verse is essentially *Petrarchist in style, but shows an untypically independent spirit. She frequently plays the dominant part in amorous discourse, and distinguishes between emotional involvement and sexual availability, describing the pleasures of physical love in ways that transcend Petrarchist conventions. Her belief in the importance of *education led her to profess openly a preference for literary personalities. She stressed her own erudition when slighted and defended her ability to make use of different poetic registers. She was indicted by the *Inquisition in 1580 and, on being declared innocent, devoted the remainder of her life to penitence and good works.

[ABu]

Franco-Veneto Literature. The term designates a series of texts, mostly narrative poems, written in French or in a hybrid literary language compounded from French and Veneto *dialect in the 13th and 14th c. in North-East Italy, especially around Verona, Treviso, *Padua, and *Ferrara. French literature enjoyed high prestige in much of Europe during this period. *Dante, Brunetto *Latini, and others considered French an easy, pleasurable language; Dante thought it was especially suitable for prose narrative. The Veneto had had close connections with France from at least the Fourth *Crusade (1202–4). Original French narratives were composed there such as the *chronicle of Martino da Canal and the *Milione* of *Marco Polo. [See FRENCH INFLUENCES.]

The numerous linguistically hybrid narrative poems rework *chansons de geste*—that is, the French *epic poems centring on Charlemagne and his knights, with the *Chanson de Roland* at their head. Much of the original material is retained, though there are definite shifts of emphasis. The *Geste Francor*, for instance, concentrates on family intrigues and treachery, whilst the *Entrée d'Espagne* is an original elaboration of events preceding Ganelon's treachery and the battle of Roncesvalle. The poems are generally written in lines of eight, ten, or twelve syllables, and, like the French originals, usually in monorhymed *laisses*. They were presumably sung or recited, initially at least to popular audiences. From the beginning recitals were probably based on written texts, though all surviving manuscripts date from the 14th c. The only poets we know by name are *Niccolò da Verona and *Niccolò da Casola. Presumably the introduction of Veneto dialect into what aspired to be French was initially intended to make the poems accessible to an uneducated public. But later poems, which were aimed at a more cultured audience, follow actual French usage more closely, though oddly enough often that of the earlier 13th c.

[PH]

Le origini, ed. A. Viscardi *et al.* (1956). See A. Roncaglia, 'La letteratura franco-veneta', in E. Cecchi and N. Sapegno (eds.), *Storia della letteratura italiana*, vol. ii (1965).

Frati godenti ('Jovial Friars'). The popular name given to the Cavalieri di Santa Maria ('Ordo militiae beatae Mariae'), an order which included lay and clerical members. Its Rule was approved in 1261 with the aim of reconciling the factions in the Italian *communes.

[PA]

Frati minori, see FRANCISCANS.

FREDERICK II (1194–1250). King of *Sicily from 1198, and Emperor from 1220, Frederick (Federico) was the grandson of Frederick I Barbarossa and the son of Henry VI and Constance, the daughter of the Norman king Roger II. He spent much of his life struggling with the *papacy, the *Guelf cities of central Italy, and the *Lombard League in the North, as well as with other German princes. In the South his power was unquestioned. He founded the *University of *Naples (1224), built cities and castles, promulgated a *law code, the *Liber augustalis*, and maintained an intellectually and culturally outstanding *court. For contemporaries he was, as Matthew Paris called him, the 'Stupor Mundi', 'the wonder of the world'. *Dante spoke well of him in the *De vulgari eloquentia* (1.12), but questioned his authority in *Convivio* book 4 and then damned him as a heretic (*Inf.* 10.119).

The court drew writers and thinkers from diverse cultures and languages (Latin, German, Byzantine, and Muslim). Among them were the astrologer Michael Scot (whose *translations helped spread knowledge of Arabo-Aristotelian philosophy in the West), the philosopher Theodore of Antioch, the mathematician Leonardo Fibonacci of Pisa, and numerous notaries and jurists trained in law, grammar, and rhetoric at the University of *Bologna. There were also German *Minnesinger* and Provençal *troubadours. It was in this climate that between 1220 and 1250 the *Sicilian School, the first coherent group of poets writing in an Italian vernacular, came into being and flourished. We have three poems by Frederick himself—two love *canzoni* and and a moralizing *sonnet, all reflecting the general themes and conventions of the school. He also composed a technical treatise on falconry, *De arte venandi cum avibus* [see also HUNTING AND FALCONRY].

After Frederick's death German power in Southern Italy soon came to an end, when the French under Charles of *Anjou defeated and killed his natural son *Manfredi in 1266 and his grandson Conradin in 1268.   [CK]

See E. H. Kantorowicz, *Frederick II* (1931); D. Abulafia, *Frederick II: A Medieval Emperor* (1988).

Free Indirect Speech. A narrative device (in Italian generally known as 'stile' or 'discorso indiretto libero', on the model of the French 'style indirect libre'; in German as 'erlebte Rede'), which allows the words of a character to be presented as if they were attributed to the narrator. For example: 'He complained: "They hate me"' (Direct Speech), corresponds to: 'He complained that they hated him' (Indirect Speech), and to: 'He complained. They hated him' (Free Indirect Speech). The device is commonly used in 19th and 20th c. novels.

Among representative exponents we have Giovanni *Verga and Giorgio *Bassani.   [LL & GCL]

Freemasonry (*Massoneria*), with its esoteric ritual, cosmopolitan outlook, and faith in reason and progress, reached Italy with the *Enlightenment. In the 19th c. it became radically anticlerical, attracting support from wide sectors of the *liberal establishment under *Crispi and *Giolitti. Anathematized successively by the *papacy, the Italian *Nationalist Association, and the *Socialist Party, it was suppressed by the *Fascist government in 1925. Reconstituted after *World War II, it abandoned much of its anticlericalism and some of its secrecy, but remained influential behind the scenes as the cement of the bureaucratic caste. Since 1964 it has been suspected of backing organized crime, neo-Fascist terrorism, and attempted *coups d'état*, most notoriously through its P2 lodge.

[RAbs]

Free Verse. The notion of the *verso libero* (as opposed to *endecasillabi sciolti*, the Italian equivalent of blank verse) emerges in Italy at the very end of the 19th c., an aggressive formulation being given by Gian Pietro *Lucini in *Ragion poetica e programma del verso libero* (1908). But there were already clear pointers in *Carducci's *Odi barbare*, *Pascoli's metrical experiments, and the free strophes of *D'Annunzio. Rejection of metrical regularity quickly reached an extreme point with *Marinetti's *parole in libertà*. Subsequently standard prose syntax and rhythms became the more common model for free verse, even with avant-garde poems such as *Soffici's *Chimismi lirici* (1915), though more adventurous disruptions of normal language are then practised again by the *Neoavanguardia* of the 1960s, most successfully by *Sanguineti.

In general, 20th-c. Italian poetry moves away from pre-determined patterns. But traditional metres often make themselves felt beneath the ostensible freedom, for instance in the earlier poems of *Ungaretti and *Montale; or a more or less regular pulse emerges, as in *Pavese's *Lavorare stanca* and Attilio *Bertolucci's *Camera da letto*. At the same time poets as different as *Saba, *Zanzotto, and *Valduga also show the resilience of strict forms. [See also LYRIC POETRY; VERSIFICATION.]

[PH]

FREGOSO, ANTONIO FILEREMO (*c.*1460–*c.*1530). Poet born into the noble

French Influences

*Genoese family ruling Carrara. He was linked with the *Sforza of *Milan, but withdrew to the country, taking the name Fileremo. He wrote *terza rima* poems, such as *Riso di Democrito* (1506), which were widely esteemed for their philosophical content.   [ABu]

French Influences

1. Before 1600

There was extensive interaction between France and Italy throughout the *Middle Ages and the *Renaissance. Until *humanism and *Petrarchism established themselves as the foremost movements in European culture, the influence was mostly one way. Though Italian *merchants and *bankers were active in the major French centres from at least the 13th c., French culture had the greater prestige. It was also associated with the stronger political power, as was demonstrated repeatedly. The Normans became rulers of *Sicily in the 12th c., the Angevins rulers of Sicily and *Naples in the 13th [see ANJOU], and in the 14th c. the *papacy was exiled (as Italians saw it) to *Avignon. It was Charles VIII's invasion in 1494 which led to the struggle of France and Spain for control of Italy in the first half of the 16th c.

During the 13th and 14th c. Latin, French, Provençal, and various Italian *dialects competed for linguistic and cultural hegemony in the Italian peninsula. Each of these languages had certain characteristics ascribed to it. For example, authors such as the *Florentine Brunetto *Latini wrote in French both for its status as a prestigious language shared by many literate people and for its association with the entertaining tales of knights' adventures. From the 13th to the early 15th c., Northern and Central Italians created versions of French works in their own dialects, such as the 14th-c. *Tuscan *Tristano riccardiano* and the late 13th-c. *Fiore*, a reduced version of the *Roman de la rose* now commonly ascribed to *Dante. They also created original texts in French, such as Brunetto Latini's *Li Livres dou tresor* (1268) and Marco *Polo's *Il Milione* (1300), and others in a hybrid language known as *Franco-Veneto. The most famous examples of the latter are a compilation of Carolingian tales known as the *Geste Francor* and an original Carolingian *epic, the *Entrée d'Espagne* (both early 14th c.).

The *chivalric epics of the Emperor Charlemagne and his nephew Roland served as the most popular literary vehicle for the diffusion of French cultural models in Italy. Their appeal surpassed that of all other genres, including the courtly *romance, which was also devoted to the adventures of knights. However, as Ruggero Ruggieri's term 'chivalric humanism' suggests, the *translation and creation of French texts in late medieval Italy not only indicates an identification of the French language with the chivalric cultural model, but also paralleled (and often overlapped with) the absorption of Latin literature, especially, so far as narrative poetry was concerned, *Ovid and *Virgil.

While the Carolingian material appealed to different social groups throughout the Italian peninsula, the chivalric epic gained its greatest popularity in the cities of the Veneto in the early 14th c., and then in Tuscany at the end of the same century. As its production moved to central Italy, the genre lost its French veneer. In the 15th and 16th c. Italians rewrote the Carolingian tales in distinctively Italian form, and established their own Renaissance epic tradition in *ottava rima*. But the stories of Charlemagne and Roland survive in recognizable form in the epics of Luigi *Pulci, *Boiardo, and *Ariosto, and constitute the most influential legacy bequeathed by the French to Renaissance Italian literature. [See also MOCK-HEROIC POETRY; TROUBADOURS.]   [JV]

See R. Ruggieri, *L'umanesimo cavalleresco italiano* (1977); H. Krauss, *Epica feudale e pubblico borghese* (1980).

2. From 1600

Italy's cultural dominance faded generally in Europe towards the end of the 16th c. From then on, as in the *Middle Ages, French literature influenced Italian, rather than vice versa, and with almost unbroken intensity.

French was the first language of educated *Piedmontese, as well as being the principal language of high culture in Europe. Most Italian writers have read and spoken French and many have composed French works. Some have lived in France, for personal, professional, or political reasons. *Marino spent the years 1615–23 at the French court under Maria de' *Medici's *patronage. *Goldoni directed the Comédie-Italienne in Paris in the 1760s and 1770s. *Mazzini found refuge in France, as well as England, in the mid-19th c. And *Ungaretti studied at the Sorbonne during the *belle époque*.

France has often provided models and images of modernity, though at times these have been polemically rejected. Ronsard's form of *Petrarchism led Marino to *Baroque poetry, and his metrical experiments produced *Chiabrera's *canzonetta* [see VERSIFICATION], whilst the Italian *novel followed the fashion started by Honoré d'Urfé's *L'Astrée*. In the 18th c. *Metastasio's *libretti drew on the plots of French classical *tragedy, and Goldoni's *comedies of character in emulation of Molière outshone his more original realistic plays in *Venetian *dialect. The Italian *Enlightenment was greatly influenced by the French. The *Encyclopédie* was published in Lucca (1758–71) and Livorno (1769–79), and Montesquieu, Voltaire, Diderot, and Rousseau were swiftly translated. *Milanese intellectuals, such as Pietro *Verri and Cesare *Beccaria, were in touch with the *philosophes*, and drew on their ideas for their debates on modernization in *Il*Caffè*. French rationalism and *classicism shaped *Parini's satire of the nobility in *Il giorno*. Parini and Verri were subsequently members of Milan's short-lived republican government following the 1796 French invasion. But *Alfieri, whose enlightenment ideals are evident in *Della tirannide* (1777) and his tragedies, whose *autobiography was stimulated by Rousseau's *Confessions*, and who celebrated the French Revolution, turned reactionary after 1792, and castigated everything French in *Il misogallo* (1793–8). In contrast, Vincenzo *Monti's poetry both celebrated *Napoleonic rule and called for Italian *Unification.

Italian *Romanticism owed much to its French counterpart, though it was intertwined with *Risorgimento patriotism and less concerned to subvert purely literary conventions. Rousseau's sentimental introspection in *La Nouvelle Héloïse* influenced *Foscolo's *Ultime lettere di Jacopo Ortis* (1817), while his ideas on nature influenced *Leopardi. Madame de Staël's *De l'Allemagne* (1813) popularized German Romanticism, and her 1816 article encouraging Italians to read foreign literature prompted much discussion. *Manzoni's use of the *historical novel was inspired not only by Sir Walter Scott but also by the French historian Augustin Thierry.

After Unification Italy drew both on *positivism and the gradual reaction against it. *Verga and *Capuana's *verismo* was stimulated by Flaubert and Zola, and led to the subsequent general vogue for *realist fiction and drama. Then *D'Annunzio's *decadent aestheticism exploited motifs and techniques from Verlaine and lesser *symbolists, while the *Crepuscolari* subsequently took up the latter as part of their challenge to D'Annunzio's heroic conception of the poet. In the early 20th c. ideas flowed in both directions between the closely connected

Italian and French avant-gardes. Once a *Futurist, *Marinetti repudiated his earlier French symbolism; but French currents also encouraged his celebration of the industrial world. Apollinaire's *modernism and the associated rediscovery of Mallarmé and Rimbaud influenced the *Lacerba* group and *Ungaretti's poetry, preparing the way for interwar *hermeticism.

*Moravia's *existentialism and *Calvino's *structuralism are indicative of the important role that French culture has continued to play since *World War II. But since the late 1970s literature, like *feminism and philosophy, has treated French culture as just one in a number of external reference-points. [SV]

See F. Livi, *Dai simbolisti ai crepuscolari* (1974); P. Milza, *Français et italiens à la fin du XIXe siècle* (1981).

FRESCOBALDI, DINO (*c.*1271–*c.*1316). *Florentine *banker and poet, from one of the most important families in the city. He was active in *Black *Guelf politics, and was a wholehearted supporter of Charles of Valois when he invaded in 1301. As a poet he attempted to liberate the *dolce stil novo* from slavish copying of *Cavalcanti and *Dante, though a real breakthrough would only be achieved by *Cino da Pistoia. The most famous of his twenty-one surviving poems is the *canzone* 'Morte avversara', an anguished search for death in the face of amorous rejection. In his *Trattatello* *Boccaccio claims that it was Frescobaldi who returned the first seven *canti* of the *Inferno* to Dante in *exile, and encouraged him to continue with the poem. This claim has been very influential in the debate about the interrupted composition of the *Divine Comedy*. [JU]

FRESCOBALDI, MATTEO (*c.*1297–1348). Son of the poet Dino *Frescobaldi. His own twenty-three surviving poems mostly follow in his father's stylistic footsteps. He also wrote anguished political and moral *lyrics in *Dante's manner, responding to developments in his native *Florence. [SNB]

FREUD, SIGMUND, see PSYCHOANALYSIS.

FREZZI, FEDERICO (*c.*1350–1416). Born in Foligno, he taught theology and travelled widely, dying in Constance during the Council. Between 1394 and 1403 he wrote his *Quadriregio*, in 74 *canti* of *terza rima*, describing—clearly under

*Dante's influence—the journey from sin to salvation through the realms of Love, Satan, the Vices and the Virtues, under the guidance of Cupid and then Minerva.   [SNB]

FRISI, PAOLO, see ENLIGHTENMENT.

Frontespizio, Il (1929–40). *Florentine Catholic periodical, edited mainly by Piero *Bargellini. Contributors included Carlo *Betocchi, Giovanni *Papini, Nicola *Lisi, and Carlo *Bo. It combined religious traditionalism, expressed particularly by Giuseppe *De Luca, with a keen interest in modern cultural developments, publishing poetry and fiction, exploring recent Catholic writing, and defending modern Italian painters. Bo, sometimes in disagreement with other contributors, promoted the French *symbolist heritage. Having crystallized his views in 'Letteratura come vita' (1938), he left, along with Mario *Luzi and other younger writers, who for a while had made the journal an important centre of the *hermetic movement.
                                                          [SV]

Frottola. A very free metric form, with lines of varying lengths, mainly short, in rhyming couplets (AABB), triplets (AAA BBB), or variable groups (AAA BB CCCC), with a sentements content, somewhere between nonsense and moral and political argument, and with frequent use of mnemonic rhyme (where a rhyme at the end of one sentence is also the first rhyme in the next). It is in use from the early 1300s up until the first half of the 16th c. A variant is the *endecasillabo frottolato*, a series of *hendecasyllables all with internal rhymes. [See also VERSIFICATION.]   [PGB]

FRUGONI, CARLO INNOCENZO (1692–1768). Poet belonging to the second generation of Arcadians. Born into a noble *Genoese family, he was educated by the Somaschi order, for which he taught until leaving it at the age of 39. He was a member of the *Arcadia Academy (as Comante Eginetico), and became *court poet at Parma, under the *Farnese, and, from 1749, under the *Bourbons. He also served as director of the theatre and Secretary of the Accademia di Belle Arti. His joint volume with Francesco *Algarotti and Saverio *Bettinelli, *Versi sciolti di tre eccellenti autori* (1758), launched the vogue for *endecasillabi sciolti* (unrhyming *hendecasyllables [see also VERSIFICATION]). His prolific poetic output, encompassing *lyric, narrative, and dramatic

verse, was collected in the posthumous *Opere poetiche* (10 vols., 1779).
                                                          [CCa]

FRUGONI, FRANCESCO FULVIO (*c.*1620–86). Born in *Genoa, he served several of the city's leading families, before and after becoming a Friar Minim. He was one of the most widely travelled of 17th-c. writers, studying theology at Alcalà and Salamanca, and touring Europe in the service of the statesman and novelist Anton Giulio *Brignole Sale. He was sharply critical of almost every aspect of his society, from ladies' attire (the subject of a youthful poem) to literary style, but nevertheless shared many of its obsessions and vices, regularly antagonizing his religious superiors, the Genoese authorities, and his *patrons. A poet, novelist, essayist, *satirist, and *hagiographer, he was above all one of the most copious of *Baroque prose writers. His major work is the multi-volume *Cane di Diogene* (1687–9), a satire on the fashions and literary culture of the day which takes its name from its supposed narrator (and observer of human follies), the dog of the Cynic philosopher Diogenes. Its seven books, dubbed *latrati* ('howls'), are subdivided into twelve episodes which display many of the characteristics of the 17th-c. prose *romance, but also carry intimations of the 18th-c. *conte philosophique*.
                                                          [MPS]

Frusta letteraria, La. Fortnightly review written and published by Giuseppe *Baretti in *Venice, between October 1763 and January 1765. After twenty-five issues, falsely dated from Rovereto, it was forbidden by the Venetian *censorship, and continued from near Ancona for eight more numbers, which contain Baretti's *Discorsi* against a detractor, Padre Buonafede. Following the example of much-admired English papers, from *The Spectator* on, Baretti assumed the identity of a retired adventurer, the irascible Aristarco Scannabue ('dunce-killer'), who registers in the *Frusta* ('scourge') his mostly indignant reactions to the books lent him by a neighbouring priest. Politically a conservative, he attacks the Frenchified ('infranciosato') *Enlightenment of Pietro *Verri, and the (to him) immoral *theatre of *Goldoni. Even more effectively he blasts old-fashioned poets and scholars—mawkish *Arcadians, pedantic members of the *Crusca, beastly *antiquarians. In this battle against frivolous and out-dated literature, as well as in his taste for lively, concrete language (like that of *Cellini), and in his approval of useful books on health, agriculture, and economics, Baretti appears closer to his time than he cared to admit. The idiosyncratic *Frusta* failed to rally public opinion but ranks among the most original and entertaining *periodicals of the 18th c. [FF]

FRUTTERO E LUCENTINI. Carlo Fruttero (1926–) and Franco Lucentini (1920–) are writers, *translators, and *journalists who have worked together on *science fiction (as editors of the *Urania* series), *comic books (as editors of the magazine *Il Mago*), poetry, *theatre, and *satire. However, their popularity is due to their collaborative *detective novels, the first of which was *La donna della domenica* (1972). In *La verità sul caso D.* (1989) they completed Dickens's unfinished *The Mystery of Edwin Drood*. Lucentini was a member of the *Gruppo 63 and Fruttero co-edited, with Sergio *Solmi, an anthology of science fiction in 1959. [AWM]

FUCINI, RENATO (1843–1921). *Tuscan writer who first came to prominence with his *Cento sonetti* (1872), comic verse in *Pisan *dialect published under the anagrammatical pseudonym Neri Tanfucio. On Pasquale Villari's suggestion [see GIORNALE STORICO DELLA LETTERATURA ITALIANA], he visited *Naples and published his impressions of popular life there as *Napoli ad occhio nudo* (1877). From now onwards he specialized in the prose sketch, or *bozzetto* [see NOVELLA AND RACCONTO]. First published in the *Rassegna settimanale*, his *bozzetti* of rural Tuscany were gathered in the much reprinted *Le veglie di Neri* (1882). A second collection, *All'aria aperta*, did not appear until 1897.

Fucini's verbal sketches have frequently been compared to the impressionistic paintings of the *Macchiaioli, whom he frequented. He was much anthologized and imitated by writers like Ferdinando *Paolieri, but his importance was subsequently questioned. *Marxist critics argued that he portrayed *peasants as unintelligent and self-interested, and lacked the moral and political commitment of true *veristi. This, however, is to overlook his moderate reformism and genuine compassion for suffering. His best *bozzetti*, such as 'Il matto delle giuncaie', convey an authentically tragic worldview, and others—'Scampagnata', for example—mock the parochialism of the country bourgeoisie. [PBarn]

FULVIO, ANDREA, see ANTIQUARIANISM.

Fu Mattia Pascal, Il (1904), *Pirandello's best-known novel, was his first extensive treatment of the mask theme. Wrongly identified as dead, Mattia Pascal creates a new life in *Rome, but cannot maintain his fictional identity. Returning home, he finds his wife remarried, forcing him to remain the 'late' Mattia Pascal. [DR]

Fumetti, see COMICS.

Fuoco, Il, see D'ANNUNZIO, GABRIELE.

Furbesco, see SLANG.

FUSINATO, ARNALDO (1817–88). Patriot and poet. Born near Vicenza, he fought in *Venice in *1848–9, writing 'A Venezia' (1849), which became one of the most popular poems of the *Risorgimento. His poems are generally similar in style to those of *Guadagnoli and *Giusti. [EAM]

Futurism, founded in 1909 by Filippo Tommaso *Marinetti, was the first 20th-c. avant-garde movement. It considerably influenced European movements like Dadaism and *surrealism. The iconoclastic proclamations of Marinetti's initial manifesto, published in the Parisian newspaper *Le Figaro*, to attract maximum attention and imply that Italian culture was once more becoming a force to be reckoned with, could be applied to the arts in general. Art was to reject tradition, and the inner world of *Romanticism and *symbolism, reflecting instead the dynamism of the modern industrial age, and celebrating machines, speed, and even war. Futurism's base was *Milan, and initially it was centred around the group associated with Marinetti's magazine *Poesia* (which included Paolo *Buzzi). It quickly attracted other writers seeking to break away from the past, like Aldo *Palazzeschi, who did not entirely share Marinetti's poetics. Noisy, provocative recitations of Futurist compositions and various publicity-seeking stunts soon gained widespread attention.

Futurism's anti-academic ideas soon spread to painting. The signatories of the two 1910 manifestos on Futurist painting, Umberto *Boccioni, Carlo *Carrà, Luigi *Russolo, Giacomo *Balla, and Gino Severini, painted *modernist subjects, attempting to capture universal dynamism through vivid contrasts of colour. But it was only after they had taken account of recent Cubist advances, through the agency of the Paris-based Severini, that they began to make an international impact. The

Futurism

aesthetics explained in the catalogue of their 1912 Paris exhibition centred on 'simultaneità'—the fusion of sensation and memory, and the bringing together of the dynamic forces within objects with those of the outer world. This exhibition was the first of many in European capitals, which brought the Futurists into closer contact with other experimental artists. Boccioni also endeavoured to translate the rejection of the sublime and the fusion of objects with their environment into Futurist sculpture, while Russolo and Francesco Balilla Pratella challenged conventional notions of harmony in their Futurist music. The architect Antonio *Sant'Elia envisaged a functional, anti-decorative Futurist city.

Early Futurist literature used *free verse, for which Marinetti (who was influenced by recent French poetry) and Gian Pietro *Lucini had campaigned even before 1909. But Marinetti's 1912 *Manifesto tecnico della letteratura futurista* announced that *parole in libertà* were the means of expressing Futurism's dynamic vision, and this radical innovation put the movement at the forefront of international literary developments. 'Freed' from traditional syntax, punctuation, and parts of speech like adjectives, which were seen as slowing down communication, nouns were linked to each other directly, by analogies, so as to present simultaneous sensory experiences in a non-hierarchical manner. Verbs were used in the infinitive to escape subjectivity, while mathematical signs and other typographical devices created special effects. Literary and visual experimentation then came together in the daring 'tavole parolibere', or 'free-word paintings', produced by both writers and artists, which later influenced concrete poetry. Many appeared in the *Florentine periodical *Lacerba*, which in 1913 also published a free-word Futurist manifesto by Guillaume Apollinaire.

After the *Lacerba* group left the movement, Futurism continued to be active in various cities. One important younger group was based in Florence and centred on the periodical *L'Italia futurista* (1916–18). Their works, like Bruno Corra's novel *Sam Dunn è morto* (1915) and Mario *Carli's poems *Notti filtrate* (1918) show occultist, pre-surrealist characteristics. Carli and Emilio Settimelli took up Marinetti's ideas on Futurist drama and the potential of the music hall, and worked with him to develop the *Teatro sintetico*—brief, satirical, witty, or absurd sketches which claimed to sum up, in a few moments, the complexities of the conventional three-act play. 'Syntheses' by many Futurists, including Francesco *Cangiullo, were performed throughout Italy in 1915–16. The group also experimented with Futurist *cinema. The presence of a significant number of women in this group, like Maria Ginanni, Irma Valeria, and Rosa Rosà, tempered the movement's fundamental and quite explicit *misogyny.

Futurist ideology had strong political aspects from the start. It rejected Italian (and other) cultural traditions, but it was as *nationalistic as it was revolutionary. Making varying alliances on both Right and Left, the movement campaigned for *irredentism, anticlericalism, the Libyan War, and intervention in *World War I, in which various Futurists, including Boccioni, lost their lives. In the period of upheaval which followed, Marinetti, Carli, and Settimelli were extensively involved in political activism alongside ex-combatants' organizations, especially in early *Fascism, with whose revolutionary elements they sympathized. Under Fascism, Futurism survived as a purely artistic movement embodying modernistic values which at least part of the regime was keen to promote. Younger members, including Marinetti's wife, Benedetta, replaced those who had left or been killed in the war. During this period the movement was particularly active in literature, *theatre, painting, architecture, *photography, and the decorative arts. Among its most significant achievements were Fortunato *Depero's typographical innovations and Enrico *Prampolini's continuing experiments in new dramatic forms and stage design.   [SV]

See M. W. Martin, *Futurist Art and Theory* (1968); C. Salaris, *Storia del futurismo* (1985); L. De Maria (ed.), *Marinetti e i futuristi* (1994).

G

GABRIELE, TRIFON (1470–1549). *Venetian, venerated by his contemporaries as a major literary figure and a model of integrity, who was Pietro *Bembo's closest friend and adviser, and beloved mentor of many young intellectuals from the Veneto and beyond. His interests were mainly in rhetoric and poetics. His *commentaries on *Dante and *Petrarch were the first in which the analysis of language and style took precedence over philosophical and moral discourse. He never wrote anything for publication, instead letting his students (among them Bernardino *Daniello, Giasone *De Nores, and Vettor Soranzo) develop and publish his ideas under their own names. For this reason he was known as the 'Venetian Socrates'. [See also DANTE COMMENTARIES; LITERARY THEORY, 2; PETRARCH COMMENTARIES.]   [LPer]

GADDA, CARLO EMILIO (1893–1973) is one of the greatest figures in 20th-c. Italian literature. His work is not readily classifiable, nor easy for the casual reader. But the linguistic and stylistic eccentricity of his prose and the unpredictable vitality of his intelligence makes it both immediately recognizable and highly enjoyable.

He was born in *Milan into a middle-class family with remote aristocratic connections. Following his father's premature death and the deterioration of the family's financial circumstances, he had temporarily to renounce his literary ambitions in order to pursue a career in industrial engineering. He took part enthusiastically in *World War I, but was captured during the Italian defeat at Caporetto in October 1917 and spent over a year in a German prison camp. On returning to Milan he learnt of his beloved brother's death in the war. These tragic events are reflected in the *diaries of *Giornale di guerra e di prigionia* (first published in part in 1955) and underlie much of his later writing. Between the wars he worked as an engineer for several chemical companies in Italy and abroad, including one year

in Argentina and a later spell working on the central heating system of the Vatican. But he never gave up his literary and philosophical interests.

In 1924–6 he wrote substantial fragments of a novel, *Racconto italiano di ignoto del Novecento* (published only in 1983, with Gadda's commentaries and working notes). He also studied philosophy for a while at Milan University, one fruit of which was a highly individual treatise *Meditazione milanese* (published in 1974). He was publishing technical articles in the 1920s, but helped by his wartime friends Bonaventura *Tecchi and Ugo *Betti, he also found openings for some literary reviewing. After moving to *Florence, he became close to the *Solaria group. He contributed to the review, and his first books to be published appeared under its imprint, namely *La Madonna dei filosofi* (1931) and *Il castello di Udine* (1934). They were well received by sympathetic critics, but his name remained generally unknown until the late 1950s. He had moved to *Rome during *World War II. In 1957 he published the book version of *Quer pasticciaccio brutto de via Merulana*, an idiosyncratic *detective story set in *Fascist Rome, which had wider success. Then in 1963 came the first edition of his masterpiece, *La *cognizione del dolore*, most chapters of which had appeared in *Letteratura* in 1938–41, and which would be republished in augmented form in 1970.

This novel confirmed Gadda's stature. With its thin disguise of an imaginary South American setting and the more formidable linguistic carapace (mixing standard Italian with archaic literary forms, contemporary *dialects, and foreign languages), it is a cathartic attempt to dispose of an intractable autobiographical burden by means of an extremely skilful process of aesthetic and narrative elaboration. Like *Quer pasticciaccio*, it has an apparent incompleteness and openness and was quickly taken up by the *Neoavanguardia. But Gadda's intentions and practice are clearly quite different;

he never aims at subverting existing models, and the novelty of his writing is the outcome of the impossibility of achieving the traditional narrative, ethical, and gnoseological aims of making literature embrace the whole of life. The impasse is already plain in the reflexive parts of the *Racconto di ignoto italiano* and is then reaffirmed in the far more mature but still personal essays on literary issues of *I viaggi la morte* (1958).

Incompleteness is for Gadda not an abstract concept or a statement of poetics, rather an existential condition that translates itself into his fragmentary but strangely homogeneous œuvre. Not just the novels but almost all his other narrative works (*Accoppiamenti giudiziosi*, *L'*Adalgisa*, *Le meraviglie d'Italia*, *Novelle dal ducato in fiamme*, *Novella seconda*, *Verso la Certosa*) are visibly in an unfinished state, and were published either after his death or almost in spite of him. But they form part of the same infinite narrative flow that endlessly approaches autobiographical truth only to produce a system in permanent disintegration, in which the final synthesis never materializes. Recent research has shown how textual exchanges occur between different parts of this large body of texts, often for practical reasons, but also because most of the scattered fragments of his narrative universe have an affinity with each other. The energy contained in the frustrated attempts at personal salvation and artistic accomplishment then finds almost sexual release in the extraordinary explosion of Gadda's uncontrollable but also skilfully crafted language. This energy is evident also in the few works that stand apart from the central galaxy of his writing. *Eros e Priapo* (published in 1967, but written probably during the war years) is a savagely satirical essay on Fascism, in which the author, with symptomatic verbal violence, implicitly retracts his youthful sympathies for *Mussolini. In the comic radiophonic conversation *Il guerriero, l'amazzone, lo spirito della poesia nel verso immortale del *Foscolo* (broadcast in 1958, when he was working for the Italian state *television), Gadda has iconoclastic fun at Foscolo's expense, whilst *I Luigi di Francia* (1964) is a light-hearted account of the history of the French monarchy.

For years Gadda was an outsider, in the postwar years partly because of his hostility to the literary and political ideology of *Neorealism. However he enjoyed considerable fame towards the end of his life, and also the friendship of younger writers, such as *Manganelli and *Pasolini. But he remained a solitary and unique figure in the landscape of Italian

letters. Though critics such as Gianfranco *Contini had always valued his work highly, it was only in the 1980s and 1990s that critical study of his work was undertaken in depth and a reliable edition was published. [GS]

Opere, ed. D. Isella *et al.* (5 vols., 1991–3). See G. Roscioni, *La disarmonia prestabilita* (2nd edn., 1975); G. Contini, *Quarant'anni di amicizia* (1989); M. Bertone and R. S. Dombroski (eds.), *Carlo Emilio Gadda* (1997).

GADDA CONTI, PIERO (1902–). *Milanese *novelist who was quite well known in the 1920s and 1930s. His earlier fiction, beginning with the stories of *L'entusiastica estate* (1924), privileges romantic evocation of the pains and pleasures of bourgeois adolescence. He later turned to *historical fiction. *Adamira* (1956) follows the adventures of a female actor against the background of a colourful version of 17th-c. *Tuscany. *La paura* (1970) centres on the brutal suppression of Milanese workers by General Bava Beccaris in 1898. In 1974 he published a tantalizing collection of extracts of letters from his now much more famous cousin as *Le confessioni di Carlo Emilio *Gadda* (1974). [PBart]

GAETA, FRANCESCO (1879–1927). *Journalist, poet, and short-story writer. He lived for most of his life in his native city of *Naples. His best work, highly rated by his friend Benedetto *Croce, appears in *Sonetti voluttuosi ed altre poesie* (1906) and *Poesie d'amore* (1920), which combines visual sensitivity with a high degree of musicality. [CFB]

GAGLIARDI, FERDINANDO, see ITALIAN WRITERS IN AUSTRALIA.

GALANTI, GIUSEPPE MARIA (1743–1806). *Neapolitan economist and reformer. A pupil of Antonio *Genovesi, he carried out an official survey of the Kingdom of Naples, *Nuova descrizione storica e geografica delle Sicilie* (1786–90), that exposed the injustices of *feudalism, but abandoned work on a second, expanded edition in 1794 for political reasons. [JMAL]

GALATEO, IL (1) (Antonio de Ferrariis) (1444–1516/17) graduated in *medicine at *Ferrara in 1474, then lived in *Venice, *Padua, and *Naples, where he became a member of the *Accademia Pontaniana. He wrote on a wide variety of topics, including natural philosophy, philology, *education, religion, history, and morals. He disagreed with Lorenzo *Valla in the debate concerning the *Donation of Constantine. [PLR]

Galateo, Il (2), see DELLA CASA, GIOVANNI.

GALEANI NAPIONE, COUNT GIAN-FRANCESCO (1748–1839). A *Piedmontese senior civil servant who worked for both the House of *Savoy and *Napoleon, he wrote prolifically on the most diverse subjects throughout his long life. He is chiefly remembered for his *Dell'uso e dei pregi della lingua italiana libri III* (1791), in which he champions Italian (and its use throughout Italy, Piedmont included) against French and opposes the Gallicizing tendencies represented by *Cesarotti. As early as 1780, and at intervals later, he mooted the idea of a federation of Italian states under the *papacy, foreshadowing the neo-Guelfism of *Gioberti. [JMAL]

GALEAZZO DI TARSIA (*c.*1520–53) *Petrarchist poet. He was Baron of Belmonte in Calabria and infamous for his cruelty and violence to his subjects, for which he was more than once arraigned. He was eventually killed in mysterious circumstances in *Naples. He collected fifty of his poems (mostly *sonnets) in a *canzoniere*, which was only published in 1758. Many of the poems are dedicated to his wife, others to Vittoria *Colonna. His Petrarchism is traditional in its themes, but his original treatment of the sonnet form influenced *Foscolo. [NC]

GALEOTTO DEL CARRETTO (1455/60–1530). *Court poet and dramatist. From the family of the Marquesses di Savona, he was associated with the courts of Monferrato, *Milan, and *Mantua, and enjoyed the *patronage of Isabella d'*Este, to whom a number of his works are dedicated. He wrote *lyric poems in a range of metres, some of which were set to music by contemporary composers. His dramatic pieces remain poised between medieval dramatic modes and the new *theatre based on classical models—the *Comedia di Timon greco* (1497/98), in *ottava rima*, derived, like *Boiardo's *Timone*, from Lucian; a *tragedy *Sofonisba* (1502); the *Nozze di Psiche e Cupidine* (1502), a poor adaptation of Apuleius; *Tempio d'amore*, a dramatic *allegory (1504); and a bawdy *comedy, *Li sei contenti* (?1499/1500). Most of these plays were published posthumously. [JEE]

GALIANI, FERDINANDO (1728–87). Diplomat and gifted intellectual who was born in Chieti but lived and worked principally in *Naples. He is principally remembered for his writings on political economy, dealing with the theory of value in *Della moneta* (1751), and attacking *laissez-faire* thinking in *Dialogues sur le commerce des bleds* (1770). During his period in Paris (1759–69) as secretary to the Neapolitan Ambassador, he became a friend of leading intellectuals, including Madame d'Épinay, Diderot, and d'Alembert. The correspondence, in French, which he began with them on his return to Naples, has literary merit and interest, as well as being a significant document of Franco-Italian intellectual relations. He also left writings on *Horace (1765), the Neapolitan *dialect (1779), and the duties of princes (1782). [GLCB]

GALILEI, VINCENZO (1520–91). Music theorist, composer, and father of Galileo *Galilei. He trained in *Venice with Gioseffo *Zarlino (with whom he later disagreed over the interpretation of ancient musical sources). He then became a major figure in the *Camerata de' Bardi in *Florence, attempting to revive the union between music and poetry characteristic of ancient Greek tragedy, and writing 'monodic' compositions with simple harmonies, as theorized in his *Dialogo della musica antica e moderna* (1581). [FC]

GALILEO GALILEI (1564–1642). Astronomer and scientific writer, who was professor of mathematics in *Pisa (1589–92) and *Padua (1592–1610). Using a powerful telescope, he observed that the Moon has mountains and that four satellites revolve around Jupiter, thus disproving the Ptolemaic system of the universe. After he published these discoveries in the *Sidereus nuncius* (1610), he was appointed mathematician to the Grand Duke Cosimo II in *Florence and became a member of the Accademia dei *Lincei. His letters on sunspots (1612) and the letter to Christine of Lorraine, on reconciling God's two books, nature and the *Bible (1615), made him a prominent supporter of Copernicus' model of a heliocentric world system. In 1616 he was summoned to *Rome and questioned by Cardinal Bellarmino, but was unable to prevent the suspension of Copernicus' book. In a controversy on comets, a *Jesuit, Orazio Grassi, published his *Libra astronomica et philosophica*, to which Galileo replied with a point-by-point demolition of Grassi's arguments in *Il saggiatore* ('The Assayer', 1623).

The election of Pope *Urban VIII encouraged him to write his *Dialogo sopra i due massimi sistemi del mondo*, in which his friend Filippo Salviati argues the case for Copernicanism against the *Aristotelian Simplicio in the presence of an 'impartial' judge, another friend, Giovan Francesco Sagredo. Published in 1632, the book's clear bias towards Copernicanism raised again the problem of reconciling the new astronomy with the Bible, and Galileo was summoned to Rome, examined by the Holy Office, and required to recant and swear that he believed that the earth is stationary and that the sun revolves around it (22 June 1633). It is not known for certain whether after the trial he really did say, 'Eppur si muove'. Sentenced to house confinement in his villa at Arcetri (then just outside Florence), he continued to work, and his *Discorsi intorno a due nuove scienze* on mechanics and local motion were published in Holland (1638). His experimental method of observation and testing was carried on by his pupils, Vincenzo *Viviani and *Torricelli, and by the Accademia del *Cimento.

Galileo's literary interests included some poetry (a *capitolo* in *terza rima [see CANTO], six *sonnets, and two *canzoni*), a draft for a *comedy, and two lectures on *Dante to the Accademia Fiorentina (1588). He annotated *Petrarch, *Ariosto (whom he admired), and Torquato *Tasso's *Gerusalemme liberata*, which he criticized severely for its poor characterization and often empty style. By writing in Italian, Galileo aimed to spread Copernican *cosmology and the new sciences to a wide lay reading public; and his own prose style, whilst showing touches of *Baroque rhetoric and discursiveness, is vividly dynamic and persuasive in its argumentation, its presentation of the wonders of the natural world, and its passages of what proved to be dangerously sarcastic polemic directed against his opponents. [PA]

See G. Varanini, *Galileo critico e prosatore* (1967); T. Wlassics, *Galilei critico letterario* (1974); S. Drake, *Galileo* (1980).

GALIZIANI, TIBERTO, see SICULO-TUSCAN POETS.

GALLARATI SCOTTI, TOMMASO (1878–1966). *Novelist and *biographer. An aristocrat born in *Milan, he studied at *Genoa University and became active in the modernizing current within the Catholic Church [see PAPACY AND THE CATHOLIC CHURCH]. His experiences are reflected in the early stories of *Storie dell'amor sacro e dell'amor profano* (1911) and in his *biography of his close friend *Fogazzaro (1920), both of which were put on the *Index. After serving in *World War I, he became an active anti-*Fascist, and was kept under regular police surveillance. At the end of *World War II he became Ambassador to Spain and then to England. As well as novels, he wrote a biography of *Dante (1922) and a study of the young *Manzoni (1969). [PH]

GALLETTO (late 13th c.). *Pisan judge, mentioned as one of the 'municipal' poets in *Dante's *De vulgari eloquentia* (1.17). Two *canzoni survive, one very much in the *Sicilian tradition, with an elaborate rhyme scheme, and the other more *Guittonian, using forced, equivocal rhymes. [JU]

GALLIAN, MARCELLO (1902–68). Roman *novelist and *journalist, who strongly supported *Fascism as a revolutionary movement. His fiction, which was influenced by the *realismo magico* of *Bontempelli and the *900 (Novecento) group, has dropped out of favour since Fascism's fall. [SVM]

GALLINA, GIACINTO (1852–97). *Venetian dramatist, who wrote mostly in *dialect. His early plays are influenced by *Goldoni but exaggerate his sentimental and moralistic tendencies. Nonetheless, the trilogy *Una famegia in rovina*, *Le barufe in famegia* (both 1872), and *Zente refada* (1875) is a moving representation of the decline of the traditional Venetian bourgeoisie and the erosion of patriarchal values. An artistic crisis led to a decade's silence and then to a second trilogy which is perhaps the greatest achievement of *theatrical *verismo. La famegia del santolo*, *Serenissima* (both 1891), and *La base de tuto* (1894) chart the defeated aspirations of a petty bourgeois family in a society founded on financial self-interest. [PBarn]

GALLO, FILENIO (d. 1503) from *Siena was an Augustinian friar and author of *lyric poetry and dramatic eclogues, composed during his sojourns in *Venice and *Padua. The eclogues achieved extraordinary success during the 16th c., and played an important role in the diffusion of the genre in Northern Italy and *Naples. [See also PASTORAL.] [ELM]

GALT, WILLIAM, see NATOLI, LUIGI.

GAMBARA, VERONICA (1485–1550). Aristocratic and learned poetess, well versed in the classics, philosophy, and theology. Born near Brescia, she was married in 1508 to Gilberto, lord of Correggio, thereby gaining a privileged status which enabled her to develop her poetic skills. She succeeded her husband on his death in 1518 and proved an active ruler, receiving Charles V after his coronation as Holy Roman Emperor in *Bologna in 1530, and successfully resisting an invasion by Galeotto Pico della Mirandola in 1538.

Similarly active in the world of letters, she exchanged verses and letters with Pietro *Aretino, Pietro *Bembo, Vittoria *Colonna, and others, and produced a sizeable body of essentially *Petrarchist verse. Her love poems include impassioned youthful laments over frustrated or unrequited love and more mature expressions of conjugal bliss. Other poems offer bucolic descriptions of nature interspersed with praises of her peers, encouragements to the Emperor in his military campaigns, and outpourings of religious piety. She has often been judged to put elegance before emotional engagement, but consideration of her full body of work (only recently published) suggests that some reassessment is due. [ABu]

GANDOLIN, see VASSALLO, LUIGI ARNALDO.

Gareggiamento poetico, Il ('the poetic contest'). An *anthology of madrigals edited by Carlo Fiamma and published in *Venice in 1611, organized thematically into a kind of *encyclopedia, or pattern-book. It contains compositions by leading contemporary poets of all persuasions, including Torquato *Tasso, Guido *Casoni, Battista *Guarini, Cesare *Rinaldi, Giovanbattista *Marino, Gaspare *Murtola, Gabriello *Chiabrera, and Giovan Battista *Strozzi. The fact that it was evidently intended to provide models to be imitated has generated considerable modern interest, but the collection was never reprinted, and does not figure in the literary discussions of the day. [MPS]

GARETH, BENEDETTO, see CARITEO, IL.

GARGIULO, ALFREDO (1876–1949). *Literary critic, originally from *Naples, who contributed regularly to La *Critica and La *Ronda. Following *Croce, he emphasized the lyricism of the work of art and held to the distinction between 'poesia' and 'non-poesia'. Unlike Croce, he was receptive to contemporary verse (notably *Ungaretti, for whom

he wrote a preface to *Sentimento del tempo*) and prose (notably *Cecchi), though he was hostile to more avant-garde writers such as *Palazzeschi. His principal books are *Gabriele D'Annunzio* (1912), *Letteratura italiana del Novecento* (1940), and *Scritti di estetica* (1952). [RSD]

GARIBALDI, GIUSEPPE (1807–82) rose from humble beginnings in Nice (then part of *Piedmont) to become a national hero. Thanks to new developments in communications, he was probably the first revolutionary leader to enjoy worldwide adulation. He learnt his military and political skills in Brazil and Uruguay, after taking part in *Mazzini's uprising of 1834, and returned to win spectacular successes defending the Roman Republic against France in 1849 [see 1848]. The high point of his career was the expedition of the Thousand (*Mille*) to liberate *Sicily in 1860, but his defeats (at the hands of *Cavour in 1860–1, Aspromonte in 1862, and Mentana in 1867) merely cemented his reputation. His retirement home on Caprera was a place of pilgrimage for followers and admirers, and his name became a fundamental reference point for both Left and Right in 20th-c. Italy. [See also RISORGIMENTO; UNIFICATION.] [LR]

GARIN, EUGENIO (1909–). Intellectual historian and philosopher who taught at the University of *Florence and then the Scuola Normale in *Pisa. Mainly known for his work on Italian *Renaissance thought, he was the most influential proponent of the idea of 'civic' *humanism, particularly in his work on Renaissance *education. But his vast range of works also includes important studies of modern thinkers. [DR]

GAROGLIO, DIEGO (1866–1933). Writer from *Piedmont who was among the founders of *Vita nova* and *Il* *Marzocco* in *Florence. He was a defender of *D'Annunzio, *Pascoli, and European *symbolism, and attempted in his own verse to reconcile aestheticism and social commitment. Originally a staunch *Socialist, he supported Italian intervention in *World War I, and later had special responsibilities for culture within the *Fascist party. [PBarn]

Garzanti. *Milanese *publisher. Originally Fratelli Treves (founded 1861), it was renamed Aldo Garzanti Editore in 1939 as an effect of the *Fascist anti-Semitic legislation. Its headquarters were destroyed by the Allied bombing of March 1943. After the war it published *Pasolini and *Fenoglio among others, the literary magazine *Nuovi argomenti*, and low-cost *encyclopedias and dictionaries. [DF]

GARZONI, TOMMASO (1549–89). Erudite writer. He studied *law at *Ferrara and *Siena, and then entered the monastery of Santa Maria del Porto in Ravenna. He spent most of his life there, though he had contacts with literary circles and was elected to the Accademia degli Informi [see ACADEMIES] in Ravenna just before his death. His interests ranged from natural philosophy to manual trades. He is best known for *La piazza universale di tutte le professioni del mondo* (1585), which, with its descriptions of unusual professions, shows a fascination with taxonomy and encyclopedic listings evident also in other writings. Many of his writings were aimed at confuting the occult philosophy of Cornelius Agrippa von Nettesheim. [PLR]

GASSMAN, VITTORIO (1922–2000). Classical actor who became best known for his *cinema roles in films such as *Riso amaro* (1948), *I soliti ignoti* (1958), and *Il sorpasso* (1962). He published poetry and fiction, as well as writing extensively on the *theatre. [SG]

GATTO, ALFONSO (1909–76). Poet and *journalist. Born in Salerno, he studied literature for a while at *Naples University before leaving for *Milan, where he was briefly arrested for anti-*Fascist behaviour in 1936. Moving to *Florence, he became part of the *hermetic tendency and wrote for various journals and reviews, including *Il *Bargello*. In 1939 he and Vasco *Pratolini founded the journal *Campo di Marte*, which attempted to give hermetic thinking a more social dimension. Like all Gatto's poetry, even his hermetic work (gathered with his early verse in *Poesie*, 1939) returns constantly to the landscape of the south of Italy and to the simple pleasures and wonders of sensory experience.

Gatto took part in the *Resistance as a member of the *Communist Party and wrote regularly for *L'Unità* until he left the party in 1951. The war and the Resistance led to a more realistic manner and a focusing on themes of social injustice, particularly in the collections later brought together in *La storia delle vittime* (1966). His work overall has *surreal features as much as hermetic ones, deriving much of its force from creating contrasts between intense

musical rhythm and visual seductiveness and obsessive reflection on the mystery of death. This was the explicit subject of the last poem he wrote before he was killed in a car crash near Grosseto. [CO'B]

See R. Aymone, *L'età delle rose* (1982).

Gattopardo, Il (1958). *Novel by *Tomasi di Lampedusa, which explores themes of death and transience in densely evocative language. It begins as *Garibaldi lands in *Sicily in May 1860. Don Fabrizio Corbera, Prince of Salina, whose family emblem is a leopard rampant, lives out the passing of the old aristocratic order with resignation, aware of the underlying inertia of Sicilian life. Tancredi Falconeri, his nephew and adoptive son, joins Garibaldi with an ambiguous attitude to the changes in progress. Cynical career ambitions lead him to marry Angelica, the daughter of wealthy parvenu Calogero Sedàra. After Don Fabrizio's death in 1883, the family falls apart.

When it was eventually published, the novel met with favourable reviews and remarkable commercial success, both in Italy and abroad, and Luchino *Visconti made it into a film in 1963. But its pessimistic view of Sicilian history and of the *Risorgimento in particular was the subject of fierce critical debate. A revised version of the text was published in 1969. [JD]

GAUDENZIO, PAGANINO, see ITALIAN WRITERS IN SWITZERLAND.

Gay Writing, see HOMOSEXUALITY.

GAZA, THEODORE (*c.*1400–1475/6) arrived in Italy from *Byzantium before 1440. After studying Latin in *Mantua, he taught Greek in *Ferrara, *Rome, and *Naples. His Latin *translations of *Aristotle's scientific works were influential, as was his Greek grammar. Like his patron Cardinal *Bessarion, he promoted Greek studies among Italian *humanists. [See also GREEK INFLUENCES; GREEK WRITING IN ITALY.] [JK]

Gazzetta letteraria, La (1877–1902). Weekly review, initially a supplement of the *Turinese *Gazzetta piemontese* (1867–94), but later independent. It was founded and initially edited by Vittorio *Bersezio, who aimed to make it an up-to-date cultural journal voicing the ideals of post-*Unification Italy. It attracted virtually all the most important *journalists of the time and included discussions of literary events in Italy and abroad as well as essays and reviews. It also published stories, poems and *travel writing by authors such as *Aleardi, *De Amicis, *De Gubernatis, *Di Giacomo, *Faldella, *Fleres, Marco *Praga, *Serao, and *Verga. In later years it tended to express more rigidly moralizing views. [See also PERIODICALS, I.]   [FD'I]

Gazzetta veneta, see PERIODICALS, I.

Gelati, Accademia dei. One of the most important 17th-c. academies, named after the frozen wood in its emblem, it was founded in *Bologna in 1588 by a group of young gentlemen associated with the *university. Influenced by the example of Bologna's senior poet, Cesare *Rinaldi, the Gelati quickly published two verse *anthologies, *Ricreazioni amorose* (1590) and *Rime* (1597), which were early landmarks in the transition from *Petrarchism to *concettismo*. Subsequently, led by Claudio *Achillini and Ridolfo *Campeggi, they championed the poetry of *Marino. Their own later production included much religious verse and tended to the moderate *Baroque style typified by another academician, Girolamo *Preti. They published *biographies of their leading members as *Memorie* (1670), and were also involved as theorists in the development of Bolognese Baroque painting. [See also ACADEMIES.]   [MPS]

GELLI, GIOVAN BATTISTA (1498–1563). From a humble background (he was a shoemaker), he studied literature and philosophy, and attended the meetings in the Orti Oricellari in Florence [see RUCELLAI, BERNARDO]. His support for the *Medici eventually secured him employment in minor administrative posts. In 1540 he entered the Accademia degli Umidi, where he held the title of Consul [see ACADEMIES]. When this institution was transformed into the Accademia Fiorentina in 1541 he held a series of readings on *Dante and *Petrarch, which were published in 1551; further Dante lectures were published after 1553.

Gelli's main concern was to further the cause of the living vernacular and to make culture available to all [see QUESTIONE DELLA LINGUA]. He wanted classical works *translated into contemporary Tuscan, which could then be raised to the status of a literary language. To this end he translated contemporary texts written in Latin, including works by Paolo *Giovio, as well as plays by Euripides. His output for the *theatre included *La sporta* (1543) and *Lo errore* (1556). His erudition is evi-

dent in *La Circe* (1549), in which Greek, Latin, and contemporary poets and philosophers appear in a series of conversations on the importance of reason. His *Capricci del bottaio* (1546, first complete edition 1548), which consists of ten conversations between a cooper and his soul on the importance of reason, was placed on the *Index in 1562 for its *satirical content.   [PLR]

See A. L. De Gaetano, *Giambattista Gelli and the Florentine Academy* (1976).

Gelosi, see COMMEDIA DELL'ARTE.

Genealogiae deorum gentilium. Treatise in fifteen books by *Boccaccio, in which he brings together all that he had learnt in forty years of study of the myths, heroes, and epic achievements of antiquity, and also (in books 14 and 15) presents an important defence of poetry. Begun before 1350 at the invitation of its dedicatee, Hugh IV of Lusignan, King of Cyprus, it was drafted by 1360, but continually revised thereafter up until Boccaccio's death. It stands out from contemporary treatises for its methodological coherence and its adherence to its sources, whilst also impressing with its imagery, narrative verve, and *allegorical interpretations. Along with the *De casibus* and *De mulieribus* it created the 14th- and 15th-c. image of Boccaccio as primarily a moralist and a master of erudite learning. Translated into the major European languages and continually republished, it was widely used as a reference book up to the 19th c., particularly by figurative artists.   [VB]

GENNARI ALESSANDRO, see RESISTANCE.

Genoa (Genova) was an important port for Cisalpine Gaul in Roman times. It became effectively an autonomous state with the granting of significant privileges by Berengarius II in 958 and the development of a form of consular government. Commercial growth followed. Antioch was the first of a number of colonies to be conquered in the Middle East (1098), leading to prolonged struggles with *Pisa and *Venice. In the 16th c. the admiral Andrea Doria aligned the city with Charles V of *Spain. The city now entered another phase of commercial prosperity and played a significant role in European politics well into the 17th c. The old aristocratic republic became the Ligurian Republic in the wake of the French Revolution [see NAPOLEON AND THE FRENCH REVOLUTION], and the city was eventually absorbed into the Kingdom of

Genora, Giacomo

*Piedmont in 1815. *Unification in 1860 led to industrialization, with the development of the Ansaldo naval dockyards and the ironworks. Genoa's working class first showed its strength by organizing the first-ever strike in an Italian city (1900). It was firm in its opposition to *Fascism and continued to have an impact on national politics in the postwar years.

Whilst modern Genoa has two outstanding authors in Eugenio *Montale and Edoardo *Sanguineti, earlier names of note are more rare. There is the *dialect poetry of the *Anonimo Genovese (late 13th c.), Paolo Foglietta (16th c.), and Gian Giacomo *Cavalli (17th c.). Then come Ansaldo *Cebà, Gian Vincenzo *Imperiale, Anton Giulio *Brignole Sale, Francesco Fulvio *Frugoni, and the *novelist Giovanni Ambrosio *Marini. In the 19th c., apart from Giuseppe *Mazzini, there are the novelists Giovanni *Ruffini and Remigio *Zena.   [LS]

GENORA, GIACOMO, see ITALIAN WRITERS IN SWITZERLAND.

GENOVESI, ANTONIO (1713–69). Philosopher and economist, who was an important figure in Southern *Enlightenment thought. Ordained in 1737, he obtained the chair of metaphysics at the University of *Naples in 1741. The publication in 1743 of his *Elementi di metafisica* brought upon him the suspicion of heterodoxy, and he moved to the chair of ethics in 1745. But once again his writings stirred up ecclesiastical opposition and from this point he reorientated his intellectual pursuits. In his *Vero fine delle lettere e delle scienze* (1753), and also in subsequent philosophical and ethical writings, he championed the ideal of a socially conscious approach to learning favouring the lower classes.

In 1754 the university appointed him to the first chair of political economy to be established in Europe, and his lectures provided the core of the *Lezioni di commercio o sia di economia civile* (1765), for which he is best known. This influential work combines a protectionist international approach for promoting the national economy with a more free-market domestic approach favouring free exchange and the creation of a productive and dynamic middle class. Genovesi has been seen as a precursor of Adam Smith in connection with the labour theory of value.   [GLCB]

GENTILE, GIOVANNI (1875–1944). *Idealist philosopher. Born near Trapani but taking his degree at the Scuola Normale of *Pisa, Gentile became a friend and associate of *Croce, with whom he founded *La *Critica* in 1902. But the two parted company philosophically with Gentile's elaboration of his particular version of idealism, Actualism (*attualismo*). Political disagreement followed. Gentile became a prominent figure in the *Fascist party and his *Manifesto degli intellettuali fascisti* (1925) led to a counter-manifesto promoted by Croce. Gentile became a senator in 1922 and as minister for *education was responsible for a significant school reform. He went on to direct the *Enciclopedia italiana*, but was a much less important figure in the 1930s. After the fall of *Mussolini he gave his support to the Fascist Repubblica Sociale Italiana. In April 1944 he was captured and shot by *Communist partisans.

Gentile's Actualism brought *Mazzinian *nationalism and philosophical idealism together. It rejected Croce's divisions of Spirit into the beautiful, the true, the good, and the useful and also his view of the inevitable discrepancy between the concepts of spirit and actual social and political institutions. In works such as *Teoria generale dello spirito come atto puro* (1916), Gentile argued that the real and the ideal were joined in what he saw as the pure act. Politically this meant turning *liberal values inside out. Freedom was only truly possible if other individuals represented the condition of our liberty rather than a restriction on it. This in turn was only possible if the state was experienced not as a restriction upon liberty but rather as the very substance of liberty itself. In a truly democratic society the state did not exist apart from its citizens but within them. This conception of the state as inseparable from the individual runs through all of Gentile's mature writings. It was fundamental to his adherence to Fascism, within which he was the one thinker of intellectual importance.   [DS]

See Gabriele Turi, *Giovanni Gentile* (1995).

GENTILE DA CINGOLI (13th–14th c.). After medical studies in Paris, he held a chair in philosophy at *Bologna (1292–1318), and was instrumental in the fruitful Bolognese encounter between Averroism and speculative grammar. He was a radical *Aristotelian influence on *Dante. [See also SCHOLASTICISM.]   [JU]

Gergo, see SLANG.

GERI D'AREZZO (*c.*1270–1339). Notary from Arezzo who studied at *Bologna and then worked in *Florence. His *humanist interests looked forwards to *Petrarch. He studied *Statius, made a collection of his own *letters, and wrote a *dialogue on love dedicated to *Francesco da Barberino. A verse letter also survives.   [PH]

German Influences. For a mixture of political and cultural reasons Italian writers have always looked more towards France and, in recent times, towards English-speaking countries than towards Germany and *Austria. All the same, it was at the Southern Italian court of a German Emperor, *Frederick II, that the first substantial body of *lyric poetry in Italian was written by the poets of the *Sicilian School, though the poetry itself owed much more to the *troubadours than to the Minnesingers. From then until the 16th c., Italian writers, especially the *humanists, follow classical precedents, and adopt attitudes of indifference, hostility, and superiority in such pronouncements as they make about the Germans. Lutheranism, however, had a serious impact, leading first to the production of a certain amount of *heretical material and then, by reaction, to the *Counter-Reformation, which had a decisive influence on all aspects of Italian culture.

The newly emerging German literature of the 18th c. was admired by Gasparo *Gozzi, and the *classicism of Winckelmann naturally found general approval. Aurelio *Bertola de' Giorgi published his *Idea della bella letteratura alemanna* as early as 1784. But culturally Italy was still more oriented towards France. Austria was now ruling *Lombardy and the North and provided a context in which French *Enlightenment thought (shorn of its revolutionary implications) could flourish. With the rise of *Romantic sensibilities, Italian writers began also to look to Schlegel, Schiller, and Herder as well as to Rousseau and Mme De Staël. *Foscolo rewrote, with a political twist, Goethe's *The Sorrows of Young Werther* in his *Ultime lettere di Jacopo Ortis*. Giovanni *Berchet translated Bürger's ballads into prose. Other poets of the 19th c., from *Manzoni to *Carducci, took lessons from Heine, Goethe, and von Platen, particularly as regards historical ballads and ironic love lyrics.

German idealist thought became increasingly important from the *Risorgimento onwards. Whilst politically the Austrians (often blurred with Germans) are their perceived enemy after the *Restoration, Hegel is enthusiastically embraced by Risorgimento thinkers and activists, especially in

*Naples. Imprisoned for political reasons, *De Sanctis and Silvio Spaventa translate Hegel's *Logic* and his *Phenomenology of the Spirit* respectively [see IDEALISM]. After them *Croce rethinks Hegel in depth. Even *Marx tends to be read in an idealist vein up to and including *Gramsci. On the other hand, Italian literary scholarship draws deeply on the rigorous textual methodology of Lachmann [see also TEXTUAL CRITICISM], and linguistic studies on the tradition going back to von Humboldt.

German and Austrian influences were particularly strong in the North-East, especially *Trieste, which was Austria's main port until 1918. *Svevo reads and digests Schopenhauer better than Marx, and is the first Italian author of note to absorb Freud into fiction. *Saba performed a similar operation in poetry. Their sophistication contrasts with the trivialization of the Nietzschean *Übermensch* in the *superuomo* figures of *D'Annunzio's novels. Though Rilke was known and respected, the generation of poets which emerged from *World War I felt itself more closely allied with Baudelaire, Mallarmé, and their successors. The novelists too, never given to the long novel, were largely indifferent to the *Bildungsroman* as a practical proposition. The programmatic hostility of Nazism to *modernism had no counterpart in *Fascist Italy, and in cultural terms the alliance between the two regimes remained largely propagandistic, though there were enthusiasts for the new Germany, such as Giovanni *Papini, who attended the Weimar conference of the Nazi European Writers' Union in 1942 as the Italian representative.

Since the end of *World War II literature in German has been just one of the various foreign resources on which Italian writers have drawn from time to time. The 'Gruppe 47' provided a name and some ideas for the *Gruppo 63 and the *Neoavanguardia* as a whole. Franco *Fortini's poetry is affected by that of Brecht, whom he translated. Dino *Buzzati and more recently Paola *Capriolo have recreated something of Kafkian *unheimlichkeit* in Italian, whilst Trieste's links with Middle European culture have been given new literary life by Claudio *Magris.   [PH]

See B. Croce, 'Per la storia del pensiero tedesco in Italia', in *Aneddoti di varia letteratura*, vol. iii (1942).

Gertrude, see MONACA DI MONZA.

Gerusalemme conquistata, see TASSO, TORQUATO.

Gerusalemme liberata (1581). *Epic poem in twenty *cantos by Torquato *Tasso, based on the conquest of Jerusalem by the *Crusaders in 1099. It describes successive stages of the siege, including the election of the leader Goffredo (the historical Godefroy de Bouillon) and the arrival of the Christian forces before the city, the expedition to an enchanted wood to cut timber for a siege-tower, which is set on fire by the defenders, and the final successful assault. A variety of episodes, mainly of an amorous nature, complement the military action. The best-known of these, which inspired many subsequent writers and artists, are the narrow escape from death at the stake of the Christian pair Olindo and Sofronia (canto 2); the unrequited love of the pagan Erminia for the Christian knight Tancredi, and her taking refuge with shepherds from the horrors of the battlefield (7); the unwitting killing of the pagan warrior Clorinda by her Christian lover, Tancredi (12); and the imprisonment of the Christian champion, Rinaldo, by the enemy princess, Armida, in her enchanted garden (14). This last event is crucial to the development of the plot, since Rinaldo must be rescued from his imprisonment before the siege of Jerusalem can proceed to its successful conclusion. [CPB]

Geste Francor. A group of seven anonymous poems written in the hybrid language characteristic of 13–14th c. *Franco-Veneto literature. They are contained in a single manuscript and were given their title ('Deeds of the Franks') by its editor, Pio *Rajna. They constitute an attempt to rework as one unitary cycle various French narratives dealing with the complex intrigues within Charlemagne's family. [See also EPIC.] [PH]

GHERARDINI, GIOVANNI (1778–1861). *Milanese philologist and lexicographer, who played a part in the debate over *Romanticism with his translation (from the French) of A. W. Schlegel's *Corso di letteratura drammatica* (1817), though the notes reflect his own eclectic stance. He also wrote *libretti, including that for *Rossini's *La gazza ladra* (1817). [MPC]

GHERARDO DA CREMONA (d.1187). Prolific translator of Arabic scientific texts into Latin. He went to Toledo precisely for the purpose of studying at first hand the Ptolemaic *Almagest*, completing his translation of it in 1175. His other seventy or so *translations included texts on arithmetic, algebra, geometry, philosophy, and *medicine. [JT]

Ghibellines, see GUELFS AND GHIBELLINES.

GHIBERTI, LORENZO (1378–1455). *Florentine sculptor and goldsmith. His *Commentarii* collect historical and scientific information about the figurative arts, the theory of vision, and anatomy, and include *biographies of artists from *Giotto to Ghiberti himself. [LB]

GHISLANZONI, ANTONIO (1824–93). Multi-talented *Lombard. An active patriot and a highly successful baritone until illness curtailed his career, he became a poet, popular novelist, *librettist (notably of *Verdi's *Aida*), critic, polemicist, *Scapigliato, and founding editor of the *Rivista minima*. He is best known for his *fantastic tales. His *Abrakadabra* (1884) is an early experiment in *science fiction. [PBarn]

GHISLERI, GUIDO (13th c.). *Bolognese poet mentioned approvingly by *Dante, who twice cites the opening line of his *canzone 'Donna lo fermo core' (*DVE* 1.15 and 2.12). Nothing else of his survives. [JP & JMS]

Giacinta (1879). Luigi *Capuana's first *novel, and the one most inspired by the naturalist tenets of heredity and environment. Raped at the age of 14 Giacinta defies the injustice of a social code that has made her an outcast. Her act of defiance leads her to madness and suicide. [RSD]

GIACOBBE, MARIA, see SARDINIA.

GIACOMINO DA VERONA (13th c.). *Franciscan by whom we have two eschatological poems, *De Jerusalem caelesti* and *De Babylonia civitate infernali*, which describe Heaven and Hell after the model of the *Apocalypse* in a way that resembles *Bonvesin de la Riva rather than *Dante. The language is largely Veronese and the metre alexandrines in monorhymed, often assonancing quatrains. [JU]

GIACOMINO PUGLIESE (early 13th c.). Poet of the *Sicilian School, whose *lyrics (seven *canzoni, one *discordo) have often been thought to have a distinctively popular or realistic quality. Except for the elegant *canzone* on the death of his lady, 'Morte, perché m'ài fatta sì gran guerra', they use shorter metres and often contain dialogue, whilst their preferred theme is the remembrance of the alternate joy and anguish of sensual passion.

Overall they represent a dramatic departure from the impersonal and highly stylized conventions of the *troubadour tradition.   [CK]

GIACOMO DA LENTINI (Iacopo da Lentini) (early 13th c.). A notary at the *court of *Frederick II (and sometimes referred to as 'il Notaio' by *Dante and others), he is generally considered to have been the leader of the *Sicilian School and was certainly its most prolific, influential, and inventive member. His verse (at least sixteen *canzoni*, one *discordo*, and nineteen *sonnets) draws heavily on the *troubadour tradition, but is novel in its use of natural and artistic images, *scholastic language, and local allusions, and shows a distinctive concern with the condition, function, and craft of poetry. Dissatisfaction with the limitations of troubadour modes is central to the *canzone* 'Amor non vole ch'io clami', which expresses the double desire to avoid stylized amorous conventions and to shape poetry along more innovative lines. Giacomo may have best realized this desire by inventing the sonnet, which he quickly made a powerful vehicle for the intellectually refined expression of a range of amorous and ethical sentiments. For example, 'Io m'aggio posto in core a Dio servire' attempts to harmonize courtly sentiments with religious ideals, and to reconcile profane and sacred love.

Dante praises Giacomo's *canzone* 'Madonna, dir vi voglio' (*DVE* 1.12) but then dismisses him as old-fashioned (*Purg.* 24.56–7).   [CK]

GIACOMO DI MICHELE, see FOLGORE DA SANGIMIGNANO.

GIACOSA, GIUSEPPE (1847–1906). One of the best-known playwrights of his time. After university in *Turin, he began to practise law there but was drawn to the *theatre after the success of *Una partita a scacchi* (1873), a romantic verse play with a medieval setting. Other highly successful verse plays followed (published in six volumes between 1875 and 1890), and also the regional stories of *Novelle e paesi valdostani* (1886). He was appointed director of the Drama Academy in *Milan in 1888.

He had enormous success with the historical drama *La Signora di Challant* (1891), which was performed by Eleonora Duse in Italy and Sarah Bernhardt in the United States. But he concentrated on developing *realistic prose drama in Italy, now putting love stories in a bourgeois setting. *Tristi amori* (1888) blazed the way, followed by I

diritti dell'anima (1894) and, more impressively, *Come le foglie* (1900), which offers an uneasy vision of bourgeois values in crisis and delineates psychological tensions with some of the intensity of Ibsen's dramas. Giacosa also wrote the *libretti for *Puccini's *Manon Lescaut* (1893), *La Bohème* (1896), *Tosca* (1899), and *Madama Butterfly* (1904), the first of these with Emilio *Praga and the others with Luigi Illica.   [AC]

Giallo, see DETECTIVE FICTION.

GIAMBATTISTA DA MONTE, see MEDICINE.

GIAMBONI, BONO, see BONO GIAMBONI.

GIAMBULLARI, BERNARDO (*c.*1450–?1525) was a court poet of Lorenzo de' *Medici, and Pope Leo X. He composed numerous *laudi* as well as *canti carnascialeschi*. *Nencia da Barberino*, thought to be by Lorenzo, has also tentatively been attributed to him. Bernardo completed Luca and Luigi *Pulci's *Ciriffo Calvaneo*.   [GPTW]

GIAMBULLARI, PIER FRANCESCO (1495–1555) was a staunch if somewhat eccentric supporter of the primacy of *Florentine culture and language. A member of the Accademia Fiorentina [see ACADEMIES], he studied *Dante and wrote a treatise on the dimensions of *Inferno*, which was printed in 1544 with an alphabet designed to teach Florentine pronunciation, and justified in the *Osservazioni* (1544) of 'Neri Dortelata', probably a pseudonym of Giambullari himself. In the *dialogue *Il Gello* (1546), Giambullari claimed that Florentine was not corrupted Latin but descended from Aramaic via Etruscan. His grammar, the first by a Tuscan since Leon Battista *Alberti's, printed as *De la lingua che si parla e si scrive in Firenze* (1552), asserted the importance of contemporary educated Florentine but failed to counter the dominance of Pietro *Bembo and other Northern Italians [see GRAMMARS; QUESTIONE DELLA LINGUA]. He also wrote a *Historia dell'Europa* (1566) covering the period 800–947.   [BR]

GIANCARLI, GIGIO ARTEMIO (d. before 1561) was born in Rovigo, but it was in *Venice that he composed and performed in his complex scurrilous *comedies: his two surviving titles are *La capraria* (1544) and *La zingana* (1545). In his professionalism, and his use of multiple *dialects, he can be seen as a precursor of *commedia dell'arte. [See also POLYGLOT THEATRE]. [RAA]

GIAN DAULI (1884–1945) (pseud. of G. Ugo Nalato). *Novelist, *translator (of English literature), and *publisher. In the period 1928–33 he was one of the first to bring the new *American literature to the attention of the Italians. His two important novels, *La rua* (1932) and *Cabala bianca* (1944), still await due critical recognition. [MD]

GIANNINI BELOTTI, ELENA, see PSYCHOANALYSIS.

GIANNONE, PIETRO (1) (1676–1748). Practising lawyer and *historian, who spent his early career in *Naples until excommunicated for his *Historia civile del Regno di Napoli* (1723), a history which was also a theoretical defence of the rights of the secular state against ecclesiastical interference. Giannone fled Naples for Vienna, and his work was placed on the *Index (1724), though it became famous in Italian and European anti-curialist circles. In Vienna he prepared a treatise, the *Triregno* (not published until 1895), which periodized religious development in history. Returning to Italy, he was arrested in *Savoy in 1736. He died in prison, but not before completing an *autobiography, also published posthumously. [GLCB]

GIANNONE, PIETRO (2) (1792–1872). Poet and patriot. After serving in the army during the *Napoleonic period, he became a *carbonaro and subsequently spent much of his life in *exile in Paris and London. His best-known work is *L'esule* (1829), a patriotic *autobiographical poem in fifteen *cantos, indebted to Byron, *Berchet, and *Prati. [DO'G]

GIANNOTTI, DONATO (1492–1573). *Florentine *humanist and constitutional *historian, who was secretary to the Republic's Council of Ten (1527–30), then exiled by the *Medici. His most important treatises, *Repubblica dei viniziani* (written in 1525/6, published in 1540) and *Della repubblica fiorentina* (written in 1531, published in 1721), advocate a mixed government based on *Aristotelian theory and *Venetian practice. [ECMR]

GIARDINO, VITTORIO, see COMICS.

Giardino dei Finzi-Contini, Il (1962). Giorgio *Bassani's most famous *novel is the story of a Ferrarese *Jewish family that disappears in the deportations to Germany in the autumn of 1943. The narrator reconstructs the distant years of his youth in 1930s *Ferrara, filled with intimations of war, love (in particular for the almost mythical figure of Micòl Finzi-Contini), and games of tennis, and all coloured by his awareness of the subsequent historical tragedy. [AD]

GIGLI, GIROLAMO (1660–1722). Dramatist and scholar, who had to give up his chair of languages in *Siena and move to *Rome because of the scandal caused by his *comedy *Don Pilone, ovvero il bacchettone falso* (1711), in which, imitating Molière's *Tartuffe*, he exposed the hypocrisy of his fellow Sienese. Early plays such as *Don Chisciotte* depended on the *commedia dell'arte and *Spanish theatre, but from about 1704 on he mostly followed *French models, from Corneille to Montfleury. Among the best are *Il Gorgoleo* (from Molière's *Pourceaugnac*), *La Dirindina o il maestro di cappella* (1715), which features a *virtuosa* and an *impresario* and is the earliest example of *satirical meta-*libretto, and *La sorellina di Don Pilone* (1712), which pokes fun at his own stingy and shrewish wife, and was admired by *Goldoni.

As a linguist, Gigli tried to prove the superiority of Sienese over *Florentine Italian in a polemical *Vocabolario cateriniano* (published in 1717 with the works of St *Caterina of Siena). No less stinging and idiosyncratic are his collections of fictional *letters, such as *Il gazzettino* (1712–14), in which the arrival in Europe of Chinese Amazons looking for husbands is the pretext for satirizing the *Jesuits, the *Crusca, the *Arcadia, etc. [FF]

GIGLI, GIUSEPPE (1862–1921). Critic and scholar who dealt primarily with the Italian *novella* but studied too the folklore of the area around Otranto where he was born, publishing *Superstizioni, pregiudizi, e tradizioni d'Otranto* (1893). He also published several collections of verse. [PBarn]

GIMMA, GIACINTO (1668–1735). Lawyer and polymath from Bari, who made the first attempt (preceding *Quadrio by a decade) to write a history of Italian literary culture in his *Idea della storia dell'Italia letteraria* (1723), a work marked by *Arcadian concern to defend the Italian tradition against foreign strictures. [JMAL]

GINANNI, MARIA, see FUTURISM; WOMEN
WRITERS, 3.

Ginestra, La, see LEOPARDI, GIACOMO.

GINZBURG, CARLO (1939–). Son of Leone
*Ginzburg and Natalia *Ginzburg, and one of the
most original Italian historians of his generation.
Through his analysis of unpublished accounts of
trials of witches and *heretics he has developed new
ideas on the relation between high and popular culture. Among his main works are *I Benandanti*
(1966), *Il formaggio e i vermi* (1976), *Storia nottur-
na: una decifrazione del sabba* (1989), and *Occhiacci
di legno* (1998). [LL]

GINZBURG, LEONE (1909–44). Born in
Odessa, he grew up mainly in Italy and studied in
*Turin, where he emerged as one of the leaders of
the anti-*Fascists inspired by *Croce and *Gobetti.
He married Natalia *Ginzburg in 1938, and was
one of the forces behind the foundation of the *Einaudi publishing house. Arrested in *Rome in 1943,
he was tortured and died in prison. His writings on
Russian literature, on philological questions on
*Ariosto and *Leopardi, and on political issues, all
revealing his moral commitment and learning, are
collected in the posthumous *Scritti* (1964). [LL]

GINZBURG, NATALIA (1916–91). *Novelist
and playwright. She was born in *Turin into the
intellectual Levi family which was already involved
in anti-*Fascist activity before *World War II. She
began writing early, publishing her first story (as
Natalia Levi) in *Solaria* in 1933. She married
Leone *Ginzburg in 1938. After his death in prison
in 1944, she eventually took up work with the
publishers *Einaudi in Turin, where she became a
friend of *Pavese and other writers. In 1950 she
married the professor of English, Gabriele Baldini.
Brought up a *Socialist, she was elected to parliament as an independent left-wing deputy in 1983
and re-elected in 1987.

Ginzburg's early stories such as *La strada che va
in città* (first published under the pseudonym
Alessandra Tornimparte in 1942) and *È stato così*
(1947), while verging on melodrama, show women
failing to realize themselves, and their men failing to
offer more than superficial contact, while the short
story 'La madre' shows the tragically limited choices
available to women in the postwar period. Her first
full-length novel, *Tutti i nostri ieri* (1952), recounts
the intertwining destinies of two bourgeois

Northern families in the context of Fascism,
*World War II, and the *Resistance. There is, how-
ever, no historical sweep in this novel; the characters barely comprehend their own lives, let alone
larger events around them, as Ginzburg offers an
oblique, complex view of human behaviour and
motivation. With later novels she sheds her previous distaste for *autobiography and draws increasingly on her own experience.

Early fears of being tainted with the narcissistic
sentimentalism of much *women's writing had
led her to reject a personal voice and adopt a
rhetorical style which was spare and devoid of
description. While *Le voci della sera* (1961) marks
this shift, it is with *Lessico famigliare* (1963) that she
moves to a direct representation of her own family.
Snatches of dialogue, stories, rhymes, and sayings
that are peculiar to the family signify internal cohesion and mutual understanding. The absence of
sentimentalism becomes all the more striking in the
description of her marriage to Leone and his
imprisonment and death. Here she achieves
poignantly dramatic effects by dramatic understatement. Her later novels, notably *Caro Michele*
(1973) and *Famiglia* (1977), attempt to confront
the Italy of terrorism, social collapse, and moral relativism, and the destruction it seemed to be inflicting
on the family unit. Significantly, her last book,
Serena Cruz o la vera giustizia (1990), was an
account of her struggle to prevent a child being
wrenched from her adoptive family by an authoritarian legal system.

Ginzburg turned to the *theatre in the 1960s.
Plays such as *L'inserzione* (1965), *Paese di mare*
(1968), and *La porta sbagliata* (1968) explore the
dramatic changes in social structure and behaviour
taking place in Italy. Her female characters are no
longer passive victims, but have become neurotic
and aimless, their men treacherous and aggressive,
their parents increasingly irrelevant to their lives.
But *Ti ho sposato per allegria* (1966) remains one of
the most optimistic of her works, as the couple,
married almost by chance, decide to stay together.

Ginzburg's focus on the family includes an
attention to the larger social context, whether of
Fascism or the changing Italy of the postwar years,
but she puts the minutiae of everyday life centre
stage. Like the *Neorealists with whom she was
once associated, she represents a move away from
high culture in literature. But her touch is lighter,
her clear and simple prose carefully achieved. Nor
does she beat a sectarian drum, whether *Jewish,
*feminist, or revolutionary. She looks on her

protagonists sympathetically and untangles their foibles with melancholic humour and pessimistic irony. [SW]

See M. A. Grignani and others, *Natalia Ginzburg: la narratrice e i suoi testi* (1986); A. Bullock, *Natalia Ginzburg: Human Relationships in a Changing World* (1991).

GIOACHINO DA FIORE (*c.*1130–1202). Calabrian monk, whose principal works were the *Concordia Veteris et Novi Testamenti* and the *Expositio in Apocalypsim*. He divided history into three ages, associated with the Father (the Law), the Son (the Gospels), and the Holy Spirit (the imminent age of church reform and monastic contemplation in preparation for the end of the world). His millenarian doctrines inspired many later 'Joachimite' prophecies, predicting the election of an angelic Pope, a renewed spiritual Church, and sometimes the advent of an ideal king or emperor. They influenced religious protesters and reformers, particularly the Spiritual *Franciscans. *Dante describes him as 'di spirito profetico dotato' (*Para.* 12.140–1). [PA]

GIOBERTI, VINCENZO (1801–52). *Turinese philosopher, priest, and politician. His republican sympathies brought him into conflict with the *Piedmontese authorities; he was imprisoned, erroneously suspected of being a member of *Mazzini's *Giovine Italia*, and *exiled (1833). He settled in Brussels (1834–45), where he published his influential *Del primato morale e civile degli italiani* (1843) proposing that Italy's future lay in a neo-Guelf federation of states under the presidency of the *papacy and backed by the military power of Piedmont. At the basis of his thought was a distinctive reformism which identified religion with civilization, and saw the Church as the custodian of Italy's moral and social values. On the apparently auspicious election of Pius IX, in 1847 Gioberti was elected minister and then president of the Piedmontese Chamber of Deputies. The accession of *Vittorio Emanuele II in March 1849 put an end to his active political career, and he returned to live in Paris. Under the influence of Hegel he moved towards an almost pantheistic vision in *Rinnovamento civile d'Italia* (1851), whilst his neo-Guelfism became a belief that Piedmont should assume the political leadership of a united Italy. [EAM]

GIOIA, MELCHIORRE (1767–1829). Economist and *political writer from Piacenza. He was a follower of Locke and Condillac, and a supporter of the French Revolution until disillusioned by the Treaty of Campoformio [see NAPOLEON AND THE FRENCH REVOLUTION]. In *Quale dei governi liberi meglio convenga alla felicità dell'Italia?* (1796) he argued that for religious and cultural reasons Italy should become a single republic. He founded, or co-founded, various short-lived papers criticizing Napoleonic rule, beginning with the *Monitore italiano*, co-founded with Pietro Custodi and *Foscolo in 1798. After Napoleon's victory at Marengo in 1800 he was appointed *historiographer of the Cisalpine Republic. His major economic treatises were written after the *Restoration. [EAM]

GIOLITTI, GIOVANNI (1842–1928). Politician who gave his name to the 'era' before 1914, during which he was frequently prime minister, presiding over great economic growth and many important social reforms. A master at creating majorities, he adopted a less repressive attitude to labour disputes than his predecessors and sought cooperation with moderates of both Left and Right. But he systematically used patronage and the prefectural system to sustain his local power bases, particularly in the South. Despite the invasion of Libya in 1911, he came to be loathed by the anti-establishment Right, particularly when he opposed Italian intervention in *World War I. In his last premiership in 1920–1 he successfully thwarted *Socialist revolutionaries but opened the way for the *Fascists to take power. [JD]

GIORDANI, PIETRO (1774–1848). Critic and essayist. Born in Piacenza, he studied in Parma, and was for three years a *Benedictine monk, subsequently moving restlessly between various Northern cities. He was one of the founders of *Biblioteca italiana* in *Milan and was later associated with *Vieusseux's *Antologia* in *Florence. Whilst politically anti-*Austrian, he held moderately conservative views as a critic, fighting the use of *dialect, for instance. His extensive writings on art, notably on *Canova and Tenerani, were similarly based on *classicist aesthetics. He was a friend of *Leopardi and is particularly known for having been the first critic of note to recognize his genius. [FD'I]

GIORDANO DA PISA (*c.*1260–1311). *Dominican friar and celebrated preacher. In 1305–6 he preached at S. Maria Novella in *Florence sometimes several times a day. About 700 *sermons, some in Latin but more often in the vernacular, have survived as they were taken down by listeners. They have a practical, informative, moral emphasis. [JP & JMS]

GIORGIO, FRANCESCO, see NUMEROLOGY.

GIORGIO DI GALLIPOLI, see GREEK WRITING IN ITALY.

Giornale de' letterati, see PERIODICALS; ROME.

Giornale de' letterati d'Italia, see MAFFEI, SCIPIONE.

Giornale storico della letteratura italiana (1883–). The most important journal to emerge from *positivist historical *literary criticism in Italy. The initial idea came from the historian Pasquale Villari (1826–1917), and the first editors were Arturo *Graf, Rodolfo Renier, and Francesco Novati. The aims were to study Italian literature in relation to classical literatures, to present bibliographical and archive source material, and to reconstruct the cultural, political, and linguistic context of works of literature. This was seen as groundwork for an eventual *history of Italian literature, existing histories being judged impressionistic and rhetorical.

As positivism entered into crisis, the journal adopted an essentially linguistic and philological bent, largely through the contributions of Ernesto Giacomo *Parodi and Pio *Rajna. In the new century, it began to include considerations of contemporary literature. Under Vittorio Cian's editorship (1918–38), it polemicized with *Croce, who criticized its neglect of aesthetic questions and resistance to a global conception of history. Between the wars, Michele *Barbi became increasingly influential as an advocate of the 'nuova *filologia' which sought to piece together a work's original linguistic context. It remains the most authoritative forum for philological research in Italy. It has always been published by Loescher in *Turin. [See also PERIODICALS, 2.] [PBarn]

Giornale veneto de' letterati, see PERIODICALS, 1.

Giorno, Il (1763), Giuseppe *Parini's four-part mock-heroic *satire in unrhyming *hendecasyllables, in which the narrator advises an effete young nobleman on the organization of his day, from his rising in the morning (*Il mattino*) to his

afternoon activities (*Il mezzogiorno*), the evening and the night (*Vespro* and *Notte*); the last two were published posthumously. [JRW]

Giorno della civetta, Il (1961). Leonardo *Sciascia's first novel was also the first critical portrayal of the *Mafia in Italian fiction. The investigation into a murder in a small town in *Sicily begins with local petty criminals but widens to take in holders of political office in *Rome, exposing collusion between organized crime and political power. [See also DETECTIVE FICTION.] [JF]

GIOTTI, VIRGILIO (pseud. of Virgilio Schönbeck) (1885–1957). Probably the best *Triestine *dialect poet. Born in Trieste, he moved in 1907 to *Florence, where he associated with writers of *La *Voce* and published his first collection, *Piccolo canzoniere in dialetto triestino* (1914). He later contributed to *Solaria*, though he returned to Trieste in 1919. His entire production in dialect was collected posthumously in *Colori* (1957). He has been compared to Greek *lyric poets for celebrating in terse and refined language the dignity of everyday life. Giotti was an effective and esteemed painter, and his verse also has vivid pictorial qualities. [KP]

GIOTTO DI BONDONE (*c.*1267–1337). *Florentine artist, whose major achievements are the frescoes in the Arena chapel in *Padua and in the *Bardi chapel in S. Croce in Florence. He also designed the bell tower of Florence cathedral. The frescoes of the life of St *Francis in the Basilica Superiore at Assisi may be one of his earlier works. *Dante already sees him as having eclipsed Cimabue (*Purg.* 11.94–6). He dominates 14th-c. Italian painting, and from the *Renaissance onwards is seen as the inventor of dramatic and natural representation in modern art. [CEH]

GIOVANNI BALBO DA GENOVA (d.?1298). *Dominican friar, who wrote the *Catholicon* (1286), based upon *Uguccione da Pisa's *Derivationes*. It contains a 'Prosodia', or handbook of Latin grammar and rhetorical terms, followed by an alphabetically arranged lexicon of words with their meanings and etymologies. Used by scholars such as *Petrarch and *Boccaccio, it was one of the earliest books to be printed (Mainz, 1460). [PA]

GIOVANNI CONVERSINO (Giovanni da Ravenna) (1343–1408), schoolmaster, *humanist,

Giovanni Da Prato

and statesman, was born in Buda, where his father was physician to King Louis of Hungary, but raised in Ravenna. Educated in *Ferrara and at the *Universities of *Bologna and *Padua, Conversino first pursued the career of schoolmaster at Belluno before entering service at the Carrara *court in Padua as courtier and notary from 1379 to 1383 and again from 1393 to 1404. He held the post of chief notary of Ragusa (Dubrovnik) (1384–7), schoolmaster at Udine (1389–92), and tutor to Francesco *Barbaro in *Venice (1405–7). His works, closely linked to the Carrara family, include three treatises on court life and a *dialogue on the preferable way to live (*Dragmalogia*), upholding the glories of *signorial rule. His letters and *autobiography, *Rationarium vite* ('Account Book of Life'), provide an arresting portrait of 14th-c. Italy as well as of the author's troubled and fascinating personality.   [BK]

GIOVANNI DA PRATO (Giovanni Gherardi) (*c*.1367–*c*.1446) played a significant role in the promotion of the vernacular in the early 15th c. After studying *law in *Padua, he practised as a notary and architect in *Florence, and lectured on *Dante (1417–25) in the *university. Like Cino *Rinuccini and *Domenico da Prato, he defended the vernacular from *humanist attacks, and is best known for his incomplete prose work, *Il paradiso degli Alberti*. Probably written in the 1420s, it follows the structure of the *Decameron*, containing a frame tale, mainly set in the Alberti family's villa and grounds (hence the title), and nine rather digressive *novelle* [see also ALBERTI, ANTONIO DEGLI; ALBERTI, FRANCESCO D'ALTOBIANCO; ALBERTI, LEON BATTISTA].   [MMcL]

GIOVANNI DA RAVENNA, see GIOVANNI CONVERSINO.

GIOVANNI DA SERRAVALLE, see DANTE COMMENTARIES.

GIOVANNI DA VITERBO (13th c.). Judge who, whilst employed in the 1240s in *Florence, composed a *De regimine civitatum* on the duties of the *podestà*. The work was used by Brunetto *Latini in his *Tresor*. Its claims for the divine origin of imperial authority anticipate *Dante.
                                    [JP & JMS]

GIOVANNI DELLE CELLE (1310–*c*.1396) was a Vallombrosan *Benedictine monk, first in

*Florence and then at the 'Celle' or hermitage of Vallombrosa. His writings include *sermons, *hagiography, *translations, and *letters in both Latin and Italian. The letters reveal a wide classical and patristic learning and an outspokenness about his own times.   [JP & JMS]

GIOVANNI DEL VIRGILIO (late 13th c.–*c*.1327). Early *humanist scholar. Although his family was originally from *Padua, he was born in *Bologna and taught at the *university there from at least 1321. He held courses on *Virgil, *Statius, Lucan, and *Ovid, and may owe his surname to his fame as a scholar and admirer of Virgil. *Petrarch may have been among his students. He is best known for the *allegorical Latin eclogues which he exchanged with *Dante in 1319–20 and which clearly reveal his elitist thinking. In a thinly veiled attack on the *Divine Comedy*, he invites Dante to write a Latin poem on an *epic theme which will reveal his true poetic worth and raise him above the uncultured audience for the vernacular poetry which he had previously written. To Dante's polite yet trenchant rebuttal, Giovanni can only reply with praise for his interlocutor and an invitation to Bologna. This invitation is turned down in Dante's second eclogue, which closes the correspondence. Among Giovanni's more academic works are a *commentary on Ovid's *Metamorphoses*, a short *Ars dictaminis*, and various grammatical treatises. His final work seems to have been another eclogue, sent to Albertino *Mussato in 1327.   [CEH]

GIOVANNI GRASSO, see GREEK WRITING IN ITALY.

GIOVANNITTI, ARTURO, see ITALIAN WRITERS IN THE UNITED STATES.

Giovine Italia, La, see MAZZINI, GIUSEPPE.

GIOVIO, PAOLO (1486–1552). Scholar and *historian. After training as a physician in *Padua and Pavia, he practised *medicine in his native Como before moving to *Rome in 1512. Here he taught, continued to practise medicine, and enjoyed the *patronage of Popes Julius II, Leo X, and Clement VII. He was present during the *Sack of Rome in 1527. He travelled widely on diplomatic missions with Ippolito de' Medici, from which came such works as an account of Turkish affairs in Italian (1538) and a description of the British Isles in Latin (1548). He also wrote works on medicine and natural history. He left Rome in 1549 and moved to *Florence, living at the *court of Duke Cosimo I until his death.

Giovio was fascinated by the great and powerful; he wrote two series of celebrations (*Elogia*) of great men of his time (1546 and 1551) and a series of *biographies (1549), and built a villa (which he called the Museum) at Borgo Vico on Lake Como to house his collection of their portraits. His privileged access to the information that flooded into Rome from Europe and beyond, as well as his deep interest in contemporary events, makes *Historiarum sui temporis libri* (1550–2 and soon translated by Ludovico *Domenichi) one of the most valuable and anecdotally rich *Renaissance histories [see HISTORIOGRAPHY], though methodologically it follows in the *humanist tradition and looks back to *Livy and Polybius as its models. Giovio's influential *Dialogo dell'imprese militari e amorose* (published posthumously in 1555) is the first comprehensive study of *imprese*. [PLR]
See T. C. Price Zimmerman, *Paolo Giovio* (1995).

GIRALDI CINZIO, GIAMBATTISTA (1504–73). *Novelliere* and dramatist, who lived and wrote mainly in his native *Ferrara, where he held a chair of literature. For most of his life he was engaged in composing his *novelle*, or *Hecatommithi* (1565), whose plots became an important European source. However, his most important work was as a dramatist and dramatic theorist. His *Orbecche* was the first original *tragedy in classical style to be performed in Italy, in 1541: its plot related to *Decameron* 4.1, but its theatrical inspiration was the bloodthirsty tragedies of Seneca.

After two more plays, Giraldi began to put theoretical ideas on paper, and his *Discorsi intorno al comporre dei romanzi, delle comedie, e delle tragedie* were published in 1554. In this work, and in most of his nine tragedies, he struck a balance between *Aristotelian precepts and contemporary requirements. His most striking decision was that the ferocious Senecan catastrophe should be replaced by something more emotionally and morally satisfying; so his plays after *Orbecche* are tragedies with happy endings, in which virtuous heroes and heroines, although severely threatened, emerge unscathed, and lurid punishments are reserved for the villains who deserve them. In this way Giraldi reconciled classical catharsis with Christian poetic justice, and paved the way for the genre designated as *tragicomedy. His views

inevitably aroused opposition, particularly from the rival tragedian Sperone *Speroni, with whom he conducted a partially anonymous debate. Giraldi also mounted a 'satyr play', *Egle*, in 1545; but his chosen formats (based on Euripides) were not those ultimately canonized for the *pastoral genre. [See also LITERARY THEORY, 2; THEATRE, 1.]
[RAA]
See P. Horne, *The Tragedies of Giambattista Cinthio Giraldi* (1962).

GIRARD PATEG (*c*.1180–*c*.1260). Cremonese lawyer who wrote a pedantic *Splanamento de li Proverbii de Salamone* in alexandrine distichs, and the *Noie*, a lively *frottola cataloguing his dislikes in the manner of the *troubadour complaint (*enueg*). The language of both is a form of *Lombard. [JU]

GIRAUD, GIOVANNI (1776–1834). Playwright, born in *Rome into a noble family originally from France. He was one of *Goldoni's most talented and prolific imitators. He begins with farce in *Il merlo al vischio* (1797), but quickly progresses to social *satire, as in *L'aio nell'imbarazzo* (1807). His last play, *Il galantuomo per transizione* (1833), is an acute observation of hypocrisy in high places.
[DO'G]

Giubbe Rosse, see CAFÉS.

Giudecca, the bottom of *Dante's *Inferno*, where the souls of the Traitors to their lords are punished.

GIUDICI, GIOVANNI (1924–). Poet whose importance is being increasingly recognized. Born near La Spezia, he has worked for much of his life in public relations for Olivetti in *Turin and *Milan. His œuvre as a whole constitutes a kind of *autobiography, written in a series of largely ironic, non-lyrical idioms, which may also distance themselves at times from normal prose usage. *La vita in versi* (1965), *Autobiologia* (1969), and *Il male dei creditori* (1977) centre on threats from the mechanized modern world. In *Il ristorante dei morti* (1981) and *Lume dei tuoi misteri* (1984) different personae are used to give different perspectives on everyday reality. The problem of high poetry, raised particularly in *O beatrice* (1972), then becomes a reworking of *troubadour techniques in *Salutz* (1986). A more relaxed but melancholic tone is then struck in *Quanto spera di campare Giovanni* (1993) and *Eresia della sera* (1999). [JJ]

GIUFREDDI, ARGISTO, see SICILY.

GIUGLARIS, LUIGI (1607–53) was a *Jesuit and an outstanding orator and preacher in the style of *concettismo. His most important works include *Scuola della verità aperta a' prencipi* (1650); *Quaresimale,* a collection of Lenten *sermons published in 1665; and *Teatro dell'eloquenza* (1672). [PBD]

GIULIANI, ALFREDO (1924–). Critic and poet. Born near Pesaro, he took a degree at *Rome University and has pursued an academic career as professor of contemporary literature. He has published various collections of critical essays, dealing with theoretical and historical issues particularly in relation to European poetry, including notably *Le droghe di Marsiglia* (1977). The first of several collections of poetry was *Il cuore zoppo* (1955). He has also written an experimental *novel, *Il giovane Max* (1972). After being the poetry editor of *il *verri* in the late 1950s, he edited and introduced the anthology *I novissimi* (1961) which included essays and poems by himself, *Balestrini, *Pagliarani, *Porta, and *Sanguineti, and acted as a kind of poetic manifesto for the *Neoavanguardia. He was the first editor (1967–8) of *Quindici*. [MPC]

GIULIANI, VERONICA, see NUNS; WOMEN WRITERS, 2.

GIULIOTTI, DOMENICO (1877–1956). Controversial *Tuscan writer and poet, who founded the journal *La Torre* with his friend Federigo *Tozzi in 1913 and used it to express deeply reactionary Catholic views. He later wrote for *Il *Frontespizio*. His verse, published in the 1930s, moved from initial pessimism to later optimism. [CO'B]

Giullari. The term *giullare* derives from *joglar,* the Provençal version of Latin *ioculator,* and is similarly used of wandering jesters or minstrels from at least the early 13th c. (in French *jongleurs*), though presumably the phenomenon closely follows its emergence in France, where their influence and presence is perceptible in *chansons de geste, fabliaux,* and *troubadour poetry. Some troubadours active in Italy were in effect *giullari,* such as *Raimbaut de Vaqueiras, one of whose poems is a dialogue between a disreputable *giullare,* speaking Provençal, and a well-off girl speaking Genoese. Though *giullari* (such as *Ruggieri Apugliese) are

commonly associated with oral production and performance, some early popular devotional compositions, such as the early 13th-c. *Ritmo su Sant'Alessio* [see HAGIOGRAPHY], probably originate with them, whilst the poem 'Salv'a lo vescovo senato', which praises a bishop whilst begging the gift of a horse, has the air of a typical *giullare* composition. The cultural space occupied by the *giullari* was subject to encroachment both by religious *laudi and by secular *cantari in the 14th c., but stylistic elements of the oral *giullare* tradition are transmitted via *cantari* to the *epics of Luigi *Pulci, *Boiardo, and *Ariosto. [See also CANTASTORIE.] [JU]

GIUNTI. A mercantile family of *Florentine origin active as booksellers, *publishers, and *printers throughout the *Renaissance in both Florence and *Venice. In Florence, Filippo and his son Bernardo, active between 1497 and 1551, filled a leading role, publishing important works of Florentine writers and scholars. From the freedom of another state, they also pirated successful Venetian publications, such as the Aldine octavos [see MANUZIO, ALDO]. The family's Venetian operations, though substantial, were less significant. By the second half of the 16th c. the Giunti were major international booksellers, with branches throughout Western Europe, and publishing enterprises in both France and Spain. [CF]

Giuntina di rime antiche. The title usually given to the *Sonetti e canzoni di diversi antichi autori toscani,* edited by Bardo Segni and published by *Giunti in *Florence in 1527. It contains *Dante's *Vita nova* (minus the prose), his fifteen *canzoni, poems by *Cino da Pistoia, Guido *Cavalcanti, *Dante da Maiano, *Guittone, and others ranging from the *Sicilians to 14th-c. Florentines. For some of the poems it is the only extant source. It has been interpreted as a polemical Florentine riposte to Pietro *Bembo's *Prose*. More recently it has been seen as an attempt to demonstrate that early Florentine literature, which Bembo excluded from the canon, should be given a place, as it constituted a necessary prelude to *Petrarch. [NC]

Giuoco delle parti, Il (1918). A play by *Pirandello which revisits the adultery theme with dark humour and grotesque *tragedy. The cerebral protagonist, Leone Gala, outwits his wife and her lover in their game to rid themselves of him, only to remain tragically alone after his hollow triumph. [JAL]

GIURLANI, ALDO, see PALAZZESCHI, ALDO.

GIUSTI, GIUSEPPE (1809–50). *Tuscan poet, best known as a *satirist. Born at Monsummano near Pistoia, he studied law at *Pisa and became known to the police for his republicanism and poems such as the anti-*Austrian 'La guigliottina a vapore' (1833). Graduating in 1834, he moved to *Florence, entering the *studio* of Cesare Capoquadri and winning the friendship of Gino *Capponi. The poems he was now writing (which he called 'scherzi') were mostly telling moral and social satires in pungent, ostensibly colloquial Tuscan, targeting profiteers and turncoats ('Il brindisi di Girella'), social climbers ('Gingillino'), and the *nouveaux riches* ('La vestizione'), as well as the police, nobility, clergy, and the Austrians. They were read widely in manuscript, inside and outside Tuscany. After an unauthorized Swiss edition of 1844, Giusti published a first collection as *Versi* in 1845.

Friendship with *Manzoni and several other *Lombard writers in *Milan in 1845 led Giusti to moderate his political views. In 'L'Arruffapopoli' and 'I più tirano i meno' he attacked Francesco *Guerrazzi and other democratic extremists. He also wrote a few sentimental poems, the most elegant of which were 'La fiducia in Dio' and 'Affetti di una madre'. In 'Sant'Ambrogio' (1846) he combined a profound level of reflection and compassion with humour and patriotism to produce a hymn to the brotherhood of man worthy of *Manzoni himself. In *1848 he served as a major in the National Guard, and sat as a *liberal deputy in the Tuscan legislative assembly. When the Grand Duke Leopold II returned to Florence, supported by the Austrian militia, Giusti, who in his 'Delenda Carthago' had written 'non vogliamo tedeschi', withdrew reluctantly from public life and retired to the house of Gino *Capponi.

Giusti was a shrewd witness of the society of his time, and was able to interpret accurately the moderately revolutionary attitudes of the man in the street who had grown up in the Tuscany of the Grand Dukes Ferdinand III and Leopold II. His poems continued to be popular throughout the century, in part because of the vitality of their language. He also left a rich *Epistolario* and a book of memoirs published in 1890 as *Memorie inedite (1845–9)*.

[EAM]

See M. Bossi and M. Branca (eds.), *Giuseppe Giusti: il tempo e i luoghi* (1999).

GIUSTINIAN, BERNARDO (1408–89). *Venetian politician and historian, the son of Leonardo *Giustinian. With Bernardo *Bembo and others, he attended the schools of *Guarino da Verona, Francesco *Filelfo, and *Trapezuntios. His *De origine urbis Venetiarum rebusque ab ipsa gestis historia* deals with Venetian history up to the year 809, and marks a move in Venetian *historiography away from the popular tradition. He also wrote a biography of his uncle, St Lorenzo Giustinian. [CG]

GIUSTINIAN, LEONARDO (*c*.1385–1446). *Venetian poet and *humanist, from an illustrious senatorial family. His brother was St Lorenzo, bishop of Castello and patriarch of Venice, another brother, Marco, made a brilliant political career, and his son Bernardo *Giustinian was a renowned historian. Educated in Venice at the school of Giovanni *Conversino, he then studied natural philosophy at *Padua.

He held many public offices and was a friend and correspondent of Francesco *Filelfo, Ambrogio *Traversari, *Guarino da Verona, and *Ciriaco d'Ancona. He collected a rich library of works in Greek, Latin and the vernacular. His ostensibly simple vernacular poems blend Venetian and literary *Tuscan and exploit popular *canzonetta* [see VERSIFICATION] and *strambotto* forms. He set some to music himself. His style was much imitated in subsequent *poesie giustiniane*, which are often not easily distinguishable from his own work. Besides his poetical production, Giustinian left some Latin epistles and an oration on the death of the statesman Carlo Zeno. [CG]

GIUSTINIAN, PAOLO (1476–1529). *Humanist with close links to the *papal court. Together with Piero *Quirini, he wrote a work on the reform of Church which was presented to Pope Leo X at the Fifth Lateran Council. The importance of this work for the history of humanism lies in its pointing to the dangers inherent in the study of ancient philosophy and literature which, according to the authors, should only be used for religious study. [See also COUNTER-REFORMATION.] [PLR]

Giustizia e libertà. Anti-*Fascist movement which developed around the newspaper of the same name founded in 1929 by Carlo and Nello Rosselli in Paris [see also ROSSELLI, AMELIA]. It attempted to unite Republicans, *Socialists, and democrats, and drew most support from

Glottocrisio Ludimagistro Fidenzio

intellectuals. Its most famous nucleus was in *Turin and included Carlo *Levi and Leone *Ginzburg. It took a more leftward turn in 1942 and was renamed the *Partito d'Azione, though the original name was kept for its partisan bands [see RESISTANCE]. [PH]

GLOTTOCRISIO LUDIMAGISTRO FID-ENZIO, see SCROFFA, CAMILLO.

GNOLI, DOMENICO (1838–1915). *Roman poet, whose early verse belongs to the *neoclassical *Scuola romana*. He then turned to *Carduccian patriotic odes. His later poems, published under the pseudonym Giulio Orsini, are formally innovative and anticipate the tone of the *Crepuscolari. Gnoli was a successful librarian, who headed the national and other *libraries in Rome. [PBarn]

GOBETTI, PIERO (1901–26). *Journalist and writer. He founded, aged 17, in *Turin the magazine *Energie nove* (1918–20). Influenced by political events in Russia and Italy, he adopted a distinctive *liberal-*socialist stance, arguing that the *Risorgimento had been a failed revolution and that a modern revolutionary movement must be based on workers and *peasants led by a radical political elite. He went on to become *theatre critic for L'*Ordine nuovo and founded the *periodicals *Rivoluzione liberale* (1922) and the more literary Il *Baretti (1924). In 1923 he set up a *publishing house which produced political and literary texts, including the first edition of *Montale's *Ossi di seppia* (1925). After being harassed by police and beaten up by *Fascists he left for Paris in February 1926. He died of acute bronchitis two days after arriving. [DF]

Goffredo. The leader of the *Crusader army in Torquato *Tasso's *Gerusalemme liberata.

GOFFREDO DA VITERBO (1133–91). Author of *encyclopedic and historical works in Latin, notably the *Speculum regum, Memoria seculorum* and *Pantheon*. He was a chaplain and notary to the *Hohenstaufen emperors, Conrad III, Frederick I, and Henry VI, and undertook diplomatic visits all over Europe on their behalf. [CEH]

Golden Age, see PASTORAL.

GOLDONI, CARLO (1707–93). The most important Italian playwright of the 18th c. A *Venetian, he wrote about 150 *comedies, in Italian, Venetian *dialect, and, in two instances, French, and some fifty *libretti and shorter intermezzi, which were set to music by composers such as Paisiello, Galuppi, Piccinni, Cimarosa, Haydn, and Mozart.

The son of a doctor, Goldoni advanced erratically towards a legal career, finally taking a law degree in *Padua in 1731. But in the mid-1730s he began providing Venetian actors (the Imer Company, at the San Samuele theatre) with *tragicomedies, starting with *Belisario* (1734), and *commedia dell'arte scenarios. In some of the latter, such as *Momolo cortesan* of 1738 and the slightly later *Il mercante fallito*, he wrote out the role of the main character in full, word by word, for a promising actor, F. Golinetti. Through the figure of Momolo, a young Venetian bourgeois, the observation of everyday life began to enter a *theatre dominated till then by the farcical, stereotyped jokes of the *commedia dell'arte*. From 1745 to 1748 Goldoni lived in *Pisa, successfully practising law, but not breaking with literature—he was received in the local *Arcadia in 1745 as Polisseno Fegejo—or with the theatre. But in that year, at the request of Antonio Sacchi, the greatest actor of the time in the masked role of Truffaldino, he wrote the scenario *Il servitore di due padroni*, which was destined to become one of the greatest hits of the 20th c., in the *mise-en-scène* of directors such as Max Reinhardt and Giorgio *Strehler.

Goldoni returned to Venice in 1748, with a contract binding him to write and stage eight plays a year for five years for the company of Gerolamo Medebach, performing at the theatre of Sant' Angelo. Between 1748 and 1753 he composed for the Sant'Angelo more than forty comedies, among them some of his best and most famous plays—*La vedova scaltra, La famiglia dell'antiquario, Il *teatro comico, Pamela* (derived from Richardson's novel, and his first comedy without masked stock characters or *maschere), Il bugiardo* (inspired by Corneille), *La bottega del caffè*, and *La *locandiera*.

These were the years of his 'reform of the theatre', during which he brought to the Venetian stage a new type of comedy, one no longer improvised by the actors on the basis of a sketchy scenario, like those of the *commedia dell'arte*, but completely *premeditata*, as he put it, that is, entirely written down by the author and committed to memory by the actors, dialogue by dialogue, speech by speech. The plays were no longer based on the often obscene *lazzi* (gags or slapstick) of the traditional masks—the two old men, *Pantalone and the

*Dottore, the two *zanni*, *Brighella and *Arlecchino, and so on—but presented characters taken, like Momolo in 1738, from the everyday life of Venice: merchants and housewives, middle-class young people of both sexes, gondoliers, and the like. They were no longer, in a word, designed solely to keep the audience entertained at all costs, but were also calculated to make them laugh at themselves and their own foibles, that is, to make them think. Especially remarkable among the plays written for Medebach are those in Venetian *dialect, like *La putta onorata* or *I pettegolezzi delle donne*, in which the life and language of common people explode on the stage in all their colour and intensity. In other comedies, such as *Il cavaliere e la dama* and *Le femmine puntigliose*, he satirizes impoverished noblemen, too lazy and proud to work, but not above borrowing money and taking advantage of the hard-working merchants whom they despise.

From 1753 to 1762 Goldoni was employed by the noble Vendramin brothers, at their San Luca theatre. Here he was forced to come to grips with and resolve a series of problems: actors unaccustomed to performing fully written texts committed to memory, a stage too large for the middle-class interior settings he favoured, and the competition from his former employers at the Teatro Sant' Angelo, where a clever and prolific abbé, Pietro *Chiari, was enjoying considerable success imitating and popularizing Goldoni's own inventions. In the early 1760s there was also competition from Carlo *Gozzi and his *Fiabe*. For several years, Goldoni struggled to find his way, experimenting with historical comedies, such as *Terenzio* and *Torquato Tasso*, and exotic *tragicomedies, such as *La sposa persiana* (which was so successful that it was followed by two other plays with the same heroine), *La peruviana*, and *La bella selvaggia*. There were also brilliant sketches of popular life in Venice in dialect verse, to be performed in the closing days of the *carnival, like *Le massere*, *Le donne de casa soa*, *Il campiello*, as well as penetrating character studies, especially of young women, whose uneasiness seems to reflect that of an entire society confronting the decline of the *ancien régime*, notably *La donna sola*, *La donna forte*, and *La donna di maneggio*.

In 1759 Goldoni spent an unsuccessful period of several months in *Rome as director of the Tordinona theatre. He then returned to Venice, and in his last stay there he composed one after another for the Teatro San Luca what are now considered his major masterpieces: *Gl'innamorati* in 1759, *I rusteghi*, *La casa nova*, *La guerra* in 1760, the trilogy *Le smanie per la villeggiatura*, *Le avventure della villeggiatura*, and *Il ritorno dalla villeggiatura* in 1761, *Sior Todero brontolon* and *Le baruffe chiozzotte* in 1762. This last is a remarkable fresco of popular life set among the fishermen of the little town of Chioggia, then part of Venice's mainland territories. The other plays of the 1759–62 period bring to the stage the Venetian middle-class world, which had been Goldoni's main focus in the late 1740s and early 1750s. In the works produced then he had been wholly sympathetic to his merchants and confident of their ability to adapt to the new culture of the *Enlightenment and to detach themselves from the superannuated authoritarianism of the Venetian patriciate. The middle-class characters of his final Venetian comedies are victims of a crisis of values, the older generation narrow-minded and insular despots within the family and suspicious of everyone outside it, and the young men and women overfrivolous, imprudent, and headstrong.

This uncertainty over the status and future of his own class on the part of the bourgeois Goldoni is more than made up for by an extraordinary refinement in his art as a writer. Following the example of French playwrights, chiefly Molière, the earlier plays had been centred on the construction of characters—the liar, the gambler, the backbiter, the miser, and so on. Developing in a way that was being contemporaneously championed by Diderot, his later plays expand their horizons to take in the representation of family or professional groups, where each individual character conditions and is conditioned by all the others. The social group that constitutes the play's initial given is galvanized into action by some specific or recurring event that puts its resources to the test—the temptations of carnival for the young wives and daughters of *I rusteghi*, a costly removal from one apartment to another for the snobbish bourgeois and his family in *La casa nova*, the moment of uncertainty between the cease-fire and the resumption of hostilities for the officers of *La guerra*, the departure in the *Villeggiatura* trilogy for country holidays in family-owned or rented villas in conformity with the fashion that Goldoni considered to have become a mania.

In 1762 he left for Paris, intending to stay for two years as resident playwright at the Théâtre Italien, but, as things turned out, spending the rest of his life in France. He was soon disappointed with the Italian Comedians, who expected scenarios on which to improvise, in the tradition of the *commedia* *dell'arte*, and gradually withdrew from the theatre, becoming Italian tutor at Versailles, first to the daughter of Louis XV (1765–9) and then to the sisters of Louis XVI (1770–80). But he wrote a few more notable comedies, including the sentimental trilogy of *Zelinda e Lindoro* (1763), the dazzling *Il ventaglio* (which was performed in Venice in 1765), and, in French, *Le bourru bienfaisant*, which is closer to Molière's elegant regularity, and was performed in 1771 at the Comédie Française. In 1787 he published his *Mémoires pour servir à l'histoire de sa vie, et à celle de son théâtre*, which he dedicated to Louis XVI. Gibbon remarked that they were 'more truly dramatic than his Italian comedies', but they are a precious, if not wholly reliable, record of his theatrical career, and among the most entertaining and typical of 18th-c. *autobiographies, in their blend of picaresque verve, candour, and malice. Goldoni died at the height of the French Revolution, ailing and deprived of his royal pension by the revolutionary government. [FF]

> *Tutte le opere*, ed. G. Ortolani (14 vols., 1935–56). See T. Holme, *A Servant of Many Masters: The Life and Times of Carlo Goldoni* (1976); F. Fido, *Guida a Goldoni: teatro e società nel Settecento* (1977); F. Angelini, *Vita di Goldoni* (1993).

GOLDONI, LUCA (1928–). Newspaper commentator and *humorist who has published several collections of articles, such as the popular *Dal nostro inviato* (1968). He has also published popularizing *biographies of *Mussolini, *Casanova, and other famous Italians. His creative narrative writings consist mostly of humorous anecdotes and sketches of Italian life. [GUB]

GONZAGA. The ruling dynasty of *Mantua from 1328 to 1708. From humble origins, they established their reputation through military leadership and advantageous marriage alliances to the neighbouring *Malatesta, *Montefeltro, and *Este dynasties. As a result of strong links with Northern Europe, Gianfrancesco Gonzaga (1395–1444) was created Marquis by the Emperor Sigismund in 1433, Federico Gonzaga (1500–40) becoming Duke in 1530. The family undertook extensive building work and the *court was famous for its magnificence, attracting *humanists and artists such as *Vittorino da Feltre, Leon Battista *Alberti, Mantegna, and Giulio Romano under the *patronage of Ludovico (1412–78) and Francesco Gonzaga's wife, Isabella d'Este (1474–1539). [SJM]

GORANI, GIUSEPPE (1740–1819). *Milanese nobleman, indefatigable traveller, and political adventurer, who sampled careers in the military and diplomatic services, and travelled to Paris to support the Girondists during the French Revolution. His writings include *Il vero dispotismo* (1769), which attempts to reconcile contractualism with enlightened despotism, and the historically valuable *Mémoires pour servir à l'histoire de ma vie*. [GLCB]

GORIA, GIOVANNI, see COOKERY BOOKS.

GORRIO, TOBIA, see BOITO, ARRIGO.

GOSSETTI DELLA SALDA, ANNA, see COOKERY BOOKS.

GOTTA, SALVATORE (1887–1980). Prolific popular novelist from *Piedmont, who also wrote *biographies, plays, and children's books. He is best known for a three-volume cycle of *novels begun in 1917, *La saga dei Vela* (1954), which charts the story of the Vela family through a century of Italian history. [SVM]

GOVERNI, GIANCARLO, see RESISTANCE.

GOVONI, CORRADO (1884–1965). Poet of considerable importance, and also a novelist. He was born near *Ferrara into a prosperous farming family, though, following the disposal of the family property, he spent much of his life in various temporary posts. His early verse, beginning with *Le fiale* (1903), which contained the erotic *sonnet sequence *Vas luxuriae*, displayed both *decadent and *crepuscolare features. Subsequent collections led into *Futurism, notably *Rarefazioni e parole in libertà* (1915). He left Ferrara for *Rome in 1919, eventually becoming secretary of the *Fascist Sindacato Nazionale Scrittori e Autori. His narrative production was particularly intense between the wars, though he continued to publish poetry until the end of his life.

His work as a whole is characterized by a free and rich outpouring of imagery which has been drawn on by other poets, including *Ungaretti and *Montale. Whilst undoubtedly modern in manner, it is not closely bound up with any one movement or tendency. The poems of *Aladino* (1946), written for his son who was amongst those killed by the Germans at the Fosse Ardeatine in 1944, are amongst his most direct. [CO'B]

GOZZADINI, TOMMASO, see FIORE DI VIRTÙ.

GOZZANO, GUIDO (1883–1916). The most important of the *crepuscolari* poets and an author who had a decisive influence on subsequent 20th-c. Italian poetry. Born into a well-off middle-class family in *Turin, he studied law at university but went to more literary lectures, and entered the city's literary circles. From 1904 onwards he was identified as suffering from tubercolosis, and spent various periods of convalescence in the country or on the Ligurian coast. Largely for reasons of health, he made a three-month voyage to India in 1912–13, out of which came a series of newspaper articles, posthumously republished as *Verso la cuna del mondo* (1917).

His first book of poems, *La via del rifugio* (1907), was well received by both critics and public. His most important collection, *I colloqui*, followed in 1911, and enjoyed even greater success. During these years he had a complicated relationship with Amalia *Guglielminetti, which caused something of a scandal at the time. It had originally begun with his letters to her: their correspondence was eventually published in 1951 as *Lettere d'amore*. When Gozzano died of his illness during *World War I, he left some impressive uncollected poems and an unfinished third volume. This was *Le farfalle*, an attempt to resuscitate didactic verse with a series of longish blank verse poems on butterflies. He had also published stories and fables in newpapers and *periodicals. Apart from the six fables of *I tre talismani* (1914), all of these were published posthumously, as *La principessa si sposa* (1917), *L'altare del passato* (1918), and *L'ultima traccia* (1919).

Gozzano's literary roots lie in *symbolist poetry, especially Jammes, Maeterlinck, and Verhaeren, though he also learnt crucial lessons from Baudelaire. He was also intensely aware of contemporary Italian poetry. From *Pascoli he derives an interest in day-to-day reality, a willingness to inject new life into traditional forms with metrical and linguistic experiments, and a sense of the possibilities offered by the longer poem. But he was much more influenced by *D'Annunzio, whom he first imitated and then decisively rejected. For a while, with all the admiration of a member of the provincial bourgeoisie sensitive to his inferiority and his own physical and emotional feebleness, Gozzano looked up to D'Annunzio as an aesthete, a poet in the grand style, flamboyantly present in high society and on the public stage. But the rejection which followed

turned ineptitude and illness into a means to a superior ironic awareness. Gozzano becomes an anti-D'Annunzio.

Especially in the *Colloqui* he creates for himself a quite different persona—the poet who worships literature as much as D'Annunzio but who is aware of its uselessness. Scenes of luxury, grand deeds, and passions are set against provincial life, a prosaic everydayness characterized by the ageing, unpretentious relics of 'L'amica di nonna Speranza', the attractions of chambermaids of 'Elogio degli amori ancillari', and the all-too-sentimental passions of unmarried, not so attractive country girls represented by 'La Signorina Felicita, ovvero la felicità'. Instead of a tone of all-pervasive sublimity Gozzano creates a tension between language and situations that are quite prosaic, and style and forms that go back to *Dante and *Petrarch. Lyric outpourings and self-indulgence are replaced by narrative detachment from the self's history. Irony becomes the key. In *Via del rifugio* it centres on the clash between easy metrical forms, almost nursery rhymes, and philosophical reflection. More commonly it is a clash between anti-heroic subject matter and an extreme stylistic refinement that tends to conceal itself. Difficult rhymes are hidden in the middle of long lines, or set in patches of normal bourgeois conversation, which in some poems is in Turinese *dialect. Or else there is self-irony, through ostensible shame at the uselessness of poetry being set against the cultivation of poetic form, and there is a highly conscious display of the insignificance of the spineless, arid figure of the poet-persona. D'Annunzio's aestheticism persists only in *parody form, with celebrations of what Gozzano affectionately but mockingly terms the 'buone cose di pessimo gusto' and the dusty residues of a conventionally romantic past.

The *Colloqui* constituted a founding act for the language and tone of 20th-c. Italian poetry, and the varied impact of the collection is evident from *Montale to *Giudici and beyond. [RD]

Tutte le poesie, ed. A. Rocca (1980). See E. Montale, 'Gozzano dopo trent'anni' (1951), in *Sulla poesia* (1976); E. Sanguineti, *Guido Gozzano: indagini e letture* (1966).

GOZZI, CARLO (1720–1806). *Venetian playwright, and younger brother of Gasparo *Gozzi. Owing to the family's precarious finances (they owned land in Friuli) he was self-taught, though avidly cultured and particularly interested in 15th and 16th-c. *Tuscan literature, including the burlesque (Luigi *Pulci, *Burchiello, *Berni). After three years in Dalmatia in the Venetian military, he returned to Venice in 1744 and in 1747 founded, along with his brother and some friends, the *Accademia dei Granelleschi, whose output, significant but often anonymous, was mainly poetry in burlesque mode. Extremely polemical in style, the Accademia highlighted *Dante's role within the national literary tradition, but took up a retrograde stance regarding ideological, cultural, and linguistic innovations from outside Italy. The satirical operetta *La tartana degli influssi invisibili* (1757), a fantasy in *ottava rima*, *sonnets, and *terza rima*, marks the opening of a vigorous polemic over the plays of *Chiari and *Goldoni, who were accused of corrupting public taste and morals, by importing character types from France (particularly female characters), and reflecting behaviour and ways of thought that were considered a social peril. These polemical works, which Goldoni countered in the late 1750s and early 1760s with further arguments, resemble Gozzi's *satirical poem in twelve *canti*, *La Marfisa bizzarra* (1761–8), in having the character of anti-*Enlightenment pamphlets, in which *theatre becomes a metaphor for a general decline in moral values, capable of destabilizing the order inherent in the system of distinct social classes.

Working with the famous actor-director Antonio Sacchi, who had restored the fortunes of the Teatro S. Samuele, where the repertoire of the traditional *commedia dell'arte* and theatre of masks were still thriving, Gozzi devised the satirical, *allegorical fable, *L'amore delle tre melarance*. It was produced as a kind of improvisation and first staged on 21 January 1761, and its success led to the subsequent writing of ten more fables (*Il corvo, Il re cervo, Turandot, La donna serpente, Zobeide, I pitocchi fortunati, Il mostro turchino, L'augellino belverde, Zeim re de' Geni*). This cycle concluded in 1765 and, at a volatile time for the Venetian theatre (in 1762 Goldoni had abandoned Venice for Paris), created a kind of theatre in which the fairy-tale element combined with strong allegorical motifs. The stage became a meta-theatrical medium, whilst the mask was used to suggest a modern theme, the self in conflict, divided and multiplied. The interest which Gozzi's experimentalism aroused in the German literary world, from Goethe to Schiller, Schlegel, Jean Paul, and Hoffmann, can be accounted for by this theoretical strand. His *Memorie inutili* (1797) are of notable interest as an *autobiography in which the author-protagonist maintains an ironic balance, using theatre to support and prove his argument. [See also FOLK AND POPULAR LITERATURE.]   [IC]

Opere edite e inedite (1801–3); *Fiabe teatrali*, ed. A. Beniscelli (1994). See G. Luciani, *Carlo Gozzi (1720–1806): l'homme et l'œuvre* (1977); P. Bosisio, *Carlo Gozzi e Goldoni* (1979); C. Alberti (ed.), *Carlo Gozzi scrittore di teatro* (1996).

GOZZI, GASPARO (1713–86). A *Venetian of noble birth, elder brother of Carlo *Gozzi and husband of Luisa *Bergalli, he was a prime example of a prolific writer who had to combat financial difficulty through his own intellectual endeavours. He *translated from Latin and French and was active from 1747 in the traditionalist environment of the *Accademia dei Granelleschi, where he distinguished himself as the champion of the renewed reputation of *Dante. With precarious financial results, he attempted in that same year to manage the Teatro S. Angelo with his wife's help, offering a French repertoire based on the literary canon (Boursault, Destouches, Voltaire). His *Lettere diverse*, the first volume of which came out in 1750, reveal an elegant and ironic writer of prose. As one of the first true *journalists of the 1760s (writing for the *Gazzetta veneta, Osservatore veneto*, and *Sognatore italiano*), he had a broad range of literary expression, ready to seize on and respond to the demands of a newly widened readership.   [IC]

GRAF, ARTURO (1848–1913). Poet and (in his time) an influential *literary critic. His father was German and he was born in Athens. For a time he studied in Romania, but spent most of his adult life in *Turin, where he taught Italian literature at the university from 1882, Guido *Gozzano being one of his students. His academic writings show a highly aware engagement with contemporary intellectual issues. In *Preraffaelliti, simbolisti ed esteti* (1897), for example, he recognized the strength of the *idealistic reaction to *positivist thinking, while contending that positivism could profitably acknowledge its inability to penetrate certain areas of the unknown. In other works of criticism, in particular *Dello spirito poetico de' tempi nostri* (1877) and *Crisi letteraria* (1888), he argued that poetry was not threatened by advances in scientific knowledge but that it could adapt to them. He suggested further that the relationship between art and science should be symbiotic rather than antagonistic. Many critics have noted that Graf's verse bears little relation to his theory of poetry and reflects instead the interest in medieval culture demonstrated in *Miti, leggende e superstizioni del medioevo* (1892). The lyrics of his best-known collection of verse, *Medusa* (1880), are often melancholy in tone and rely upon imagery drawn from a *symbolist repertory.   [CFB]

GRAMIGNA, GIULIANO (1920–). *Bolognese *literary critic, poet, and *novelist. His criticism, appearing in reviews such as *il *verri* and *Aut-Aut*, displays a strong interest in *psychoanalysis and linguistics. After a *hermetic start as a poet with *Taccuino* (1948), his creative work has constantly explored modern and *post-modern questionings of literary structure and personal identity.   [JJ]

Grammars. The first vernacular grammar was written exceptionally early (1437–41) by *Alberti. He wished to show that contemporary cultured *Florentine could be analysed in the same way as Latin, but his Latin-based scheme made it hard to deal with vernacular innovations. The main tradition of grammars began only in the 16th c., together with the rise of imitation of 14th-c. Florentine and the advent of *printing; as with *dictionaries, approved literary usage, presented prescriptively, rather than regional or colloquial usage, remained for long their principal basis. The first steps were taken outside *Tuscany, where need for guidance was strongest, and by men from *Venetian territory, whose lack of a strong local vernacular literary tradition made them relatively immune to linguistic chauvinism. Gianfrancesco Fortunio's *Regole grammaticali* (1516) used 14th-c. texts to teach morphology and spelling, but it was above all Pietro *Bembo's *Prose della volgar lingua* (1525) which established *Petrarch and *Boccaccio as models for verse and prose. Contemporary Florentine influence was felt primarily through the pro-Bembist *Salviati's *Avvertimenti*; Pier Francesco *Giambullari's grammar (1552), which discussed both contemporary and earlier usage and treated syntax fully, had limited influence even in Tuscany.

The major 17th-c. grammar, Buonmattei's *Della lingua toscana* (complete edition 1643), followed Bembo's norm but tolerated some variation, and attempted to apply *Aristotelian thought to language. Corticelli's *Regole ed osservazioni della lingua toscana* (1745, republished for over a century) were based more strictly on the authority of good writers. *Soave's *Grammatica ragionata della lingua italiana* (1770) was similarly traditional, in spite of the links

with French *Enlightenment grammatical thought which its title suggested. *Purism based on 14th-c. usage continued to dominate into the 19th c., particularly in *Puoti's *Regole elementari* (1833). Moise's detailed *Regole ed osservazioni* for young people (1878) were based on the literary tradition. Fornaciari, who gave ample attention to syntax in his complementary *Grammatica* (1879) and *Sintassi italiana dell'uso moderno* (1881), studied both contemporary and older written usage: the foundation of his 'modern usage' lay in the Tuscan people, but writers provided its definitive testimony. On the other hand, the influence of *Manzoni's linguistic thought and writings led grammarians such as Boni (1883), Petrocchi (1887), and Morandi and Cappuccini (1894) to codify contemporary Tuscan usage, including forms which were strongly regionally marked.

*Croce's neo-idealism discouraged the serious study of grammar, and there was little innovation in the first half of the 20th c., when grammars were produced principally for the classroom. Goidànich (1918) taught a formal Italian but also discussed familiar and archaic usage. The grammars of Trabalza and Allodoli (1934) and of Battaglia and Pernicone (1951) favoured literary rather than living usage. Only later did a new approach emerge in Serianni's *Grammatica italiana* (1988), which focused mainly though not exclusively on modern Italian, spoken as well as written, non-literary as well as literary, and above all in the *Grande grammatica* (1988–95) of Renzi and others, which used in part the methods of generative grammar and discussed all forms in use, 'correct' or not.

The principal modern historical grammar is the *Grammatica storica della lingua italiana e dei suoi dialetti* (1966–9) by Rohlfs, although Castellani's *Grammatica storica* (2000–), based on Tuscan, has recently started to appear. Study of the historical grammar of *dialects, which offered a subject more suitable than the artificially codified literary language, was cultivated from the mid-19th c. Only exceptionally were descriptive dialect grammars written in the 18th and 19th c.; but, as both the use of dialects and purist attitudes declined, several were produced towards the end of the 20th c. [See also QUESTIONE DELLA LINGUA and HISTORY OF THE ITALIAN LANGUAGE.]
                                                                                     [BR]
See C. Trabalza, *Storia della grammatica italiana* (1908); G. Patota, 'I percorsi grammaticali', in L. Serianni and P. Trifone (eds.), *Storia della lingua italiana*, vol. i (1993).

Gramsci, Antonio

GRAMSCI, ANTONIO (1891–1937). *Communist leader and *Marxist theoretician. Born in Ales, *Sardinia, he attended secondary school in Cagliari, and university in *Turin. He planned to write a thesis on historical linguistics but never graduated. Instead he became increasingly active in the Italian *Socialist Party, and from 1915 worked full-time as a *journalist for the party newspapers, *Il Grido del popolo* and *Avanti!* After the Bolshevik Revolution he moved to the Left of the party, cofounding in 1919 *L'*Ordine nuovo* and in 1921 the Communist Party of Italy. In 1924 he was elected to parliament and became general secretary of the party, leading its opposition to *Fascism after the assassination of Giacomo Matteotti. Arrested in November 1926, he was sentenced in 1928 to twenty years in jail. He was sent, because of ill-health, to the Casa Penale Speciale di Turi, near Bari, where he spent five years; he was then moved to guarded clinics. Released in April 1937, he died of a cerebral haemorrhage a few days later in *Rome.

During his incarceration Gramsci wrote notes in twenty-seven school exercise books, first published posthumously in six volumes from 1948 to 1951 under the general title *Quaderni del carcere*, as well as numerous letters, published as *Lettere dal carcere* (three main Italian editions: 1947, 1965, 1996). It is on these two publications that his international reputation largely rests, though many of his pre-prison writings are also of considerable interest. His *theatre reviews, written in 1915–18 for the Turin edition of *Avanti!*, include opinions on *Pirandello later developed in the *Quaderni*.

The *Quaderni* contain notes on many subjects, from Italian history to popular literature, linguistics, Catholicism, and philosophy. Gramsci's starting point, and his central concern as a Marxist and political activist, was to understand why the success of the Russian Revolution of 1917 had failed to be repeated in the West, despite the acute social crisis at the end of *World War I, and why the forces of conservatism or reaction had triumphed instead. He was thus equally concerned to make sense of Fascism, its social base and the reasons for its success. These inquiries led him to make an excursus into Italian history, in which he saw the tenacity of local civic traditions, the lack of a Protestant *Reformation, the late development of the nation-state, the incomplete transition from *feudalism to capitalism, and the absence of a popular revolution of the French type as having prevented a full development of the Italian state and economy both before and after *Unification. Behind these were other causes, notably the entrenched tendency of Italian intellectuals to constitute a priest-like caste detached from the mass of the people.

Among Gramsci's most influential concepts has been that of hegemony (*egemonia*), a term he borrowed from the Russian Marxists but redefined in the *Quaderni* to include a component of 'intellectual and moral leadership', without which political power could not be secure. Intellectuals (a category which for Gramsci included political activists as well as opinion leaders) exercised hegemony by cementing disparate social actors into an alliance and directing them towards a common goal. Fascism had attained a repressive form of hegemony; Communism had to strive to attain an expansive, liberating form. The originality of this view within a largely materialist and sometimes determinist tradition of Marxist thought lay both in the importance it gave to culture and ideas and in its emphasis on the need to win allies and actively build consent in order to effect lasting political change. Many of Gramsci's other key concepts, such as 'war of position', 'historical bloc' (*blocco storico*), 'Jacobinism', and 'intellectual and moral reformation', are closely connected to that of hegemony, as are his writings on linguistics, philosophy, and 'common sense'.

The notes on literature in the *Quaderni* share these preoccupations. In Gramsci's analysis, the 'non-national-popular' character of Italian literature (exemplified by many writers, from *Manzoni to *Ungaretti) and the preference of the mass reading public for *detective stories imported from France or England were symptoms of the detachment of Italian intellectuals from the people. These ideas, sometimes misinterpreted or taken out of context, were highly influential in Italy from 1947 to the 1960s, particularly in the orbit of the Communist Party (PCI). Gramsci's huge influence outside Italy, which dates from the mid-1950s with the first translations, is attributable largely, though not exclusively, to his creative rethinking of political strategy for the Left in response to contemporary events and conditions. [See also LITERARY THEORY, 6; POLITICAL THOUGHT.] [DF]

See C. Mouffe (ed.), *Gramsci and Marxist Theory* (1979); J. V. Femia, *Gramsci's Political Thought* (1981).

GRANDE, ADRIANO (1897–1972). *Genoese poet, who was one of the founders of the literary review *Circoli* (1931–6). He was a volunteer in the Ethiopian war, from which sprang his *Poesie in*

Africa (1938). His highly literary poetry often uses imagery from the Ligurian landscape to express strong religious feeling. [JJ]

GRANDI, ASCANIO (1567–1647) is best known for his *epic poems, *I fasti grandi* and *Il Tancredi*, published in 1635 and 1636. [PBD]

GRANDI, DINO (1895–1988). One of the most important *Fascist leaders. He moved from the foreign ministry to become Italian Ambassador in London and then minister of justice in 1939. On 25 July 1943 he successfully presented a motion to the Fascist Grand Council calling for *Mussolini to resign and hand power to the king. He was sentenced to death for this act, but found refuge in Portugal. In 1983 he published his memoirs as *Mio paese: ricordi autobiografici*. [PC]

Grand Tour, see TRAVELLERS IN ITALY.

GRANELLI, GIOVANNI (1703–70). *Jesuit *tragedian. A native of *Genoa, he won early admiration with *Sedecia, Manasse*, and *Dione*, which were performed in *Bologna and Parma at the Jesuit colleges. The third, which dramatizes the death of Dion of Syracuse, is generally considered the finest. Subsequently, Granelli devoted all his energies to preaching. [JMAL]

GRASSI, ORAZIO, see GALILEO GALILEI.

GRASSI, PAOLO, see STREHLER, GIORGIO; THEATRE, 3.

GRATIAN, see LAW; TWELFTH-CENTURY RENAISSANCE.

GRAVINA, GIAN VINCENZO (1664–1718). Calabrian author of numerous works on law and *literary theory. He spent the years 1680–9 in *Naples before moving to *Rome, where he became a founder member of the Accademia dell' *Arcadia (1690). His *Origines iuris civilis* (1708), which brought him European fame, was based on the view that the function of the jurist, as of the intellectual and poet, was to create a civil society based on the force of law against the tyranny of regal absolutism. The thrust of *La tragedia* (1715), his treatise on the nature of *tragedy, and of the five tragedies he wrote, was to illustrate the suitability of the genre for this purpose. Such concerns led him in 1711 to leave the Arcadia, whose *classicism had

lost its regenerative impulse, and they underly his most famous and most important work, *Della ragion poetica* (1708), in which he defines poetry as an intuitive and imaginative form of knowledge with the power to inspire civic renewal. Although the theoretical affinities critics have claimed for him with *Vico are more apparent than real, both thinkers produced powerful and influential reappraisals of the moral and civic significance of the poetry of Homer and *Dante. [GLCB]

GRAZIANI, GIROLAMO (1604–75). *Baroque *epic poet at the *Este *court. After several years as Estense ambassador in Paris, he returned to Modena and was nominated Secretary of State. He wrote panegyrics and epic poems, of which the greatest was *Il conquisto di Granata* (1650), on Ferdinand the Catholic's assault on the Turks in 1492. In its observance of *Aristotelian rules and its religious and moral orthodoxy, the work recalls Torquato *Tasso, although more space is given to love themes and to adventurous digressions, such as that on Columbus's discovery of the New World. His use of metaphors and *concetti* is typical of Baroque poetry. [PBert]

Grazie, Le, see FOSCOLO, UGO.

GRAZZINI, ANTON FRANCESCO (Il Lasca) (1503–84). Versatile vernacular author. He was an active figure in *Florentine literary life, and in 1540 was responsible with others for setting up the Accademia degli Umidi, where he took the name Il Lasca ('The Roach') [see also ACADEMIES]. For his unwillingness to conform to the Umidi's increasingly dogmatic rules, he was expelled in 1547 for 20 years. A persistent critic of *humanist pedantry and of formal literary conventions, he shows in his own work a profound understanding of, and a willingness to experiment with, a wide range of forms, including prose and verse *comedies, serious and comic verse, and vigorous *novelle. He edited collections of poetry by Francesco *Berni, Il *Burchiello, Agnolo *Firenzuola, and Benedetto *Varchi. He was re-admitted to the Accademia in 1566, and in 1582 was one of the founders of the Accademia della *Crusca. [PLR]

Greek Influences. Greek literature first became accessible in Italy when in 1397–1400 the *Byzantine scholar *Chrysoloras came to teach young *humanists such as Leonardo *Bruni and the elder *Vergerio in *Florence. In the first half of the 15th c.

Greek Writing in Italy

scholars like *Guarino da Verona, Francesco *Filelfo, and *Aurispa were responsible for bringing many Greek codices to Italy from the East. This first generation of Greek-reading humanists made Latin versions of major texts by Aristotle, Plato, and Plutarch, particularly works which nourished the ideals of 'civic' humanism. In mid-century the interest in Greek was stimulated by two further influxes of scholars: first those such as *Pletho and George *Trapezuntios, who attended the Council for the Union of the Eastern and Western Churches in *Ferrara and Florence (1438–9); and second, the later diaspora of Byzantine scholars, such as *Gaza and *Bessarion, who fled to Italy after the sack of Constantinople (1453).

After the civic interests of the first half of the 15th c., the emphasis shifted to Plato's more contemplative works; the entire Platonic and Neoplatonic corpus was translated into Latin by *Ficino and published in the new medium of *print by 1492, becoming the main source for *Renaissance *Neoplatonism. Florence was the centre not just of these Platonic studies, but also of *Aristotelian scholarship under teachers like *Argyropoulos, while Demetrios Chalcondylas (1423/4–1511) supervised the production of the first printed edition of Homer in 1488. The myth of Florence as a new Athens stems from these interests, and *Machiavelli's cult of Roman history can be seen as a reaction against the philhellenic culture of Lorenzo de' *Medici's circle. This increased knowledge of Greek, a classical language which also had dialects, enhanced the status of the *volgare, which no longer faced a direct, inevitably detrimental, comparison with Latin.

The greatest Greek scholar of the time, *Poliziano, incorporated a Platonic ascent in his *Stanze per la giostra (1475–8), but typically he also sought out more recondite sources; the protagonist of the Stanze is modelled on Euripides' Hippolytus, while Poliziano's *Orfeo owes something to ancient Greek satyr plays. Greek texts became ever more accessible through the increasing number of Latin *translations in the late 15th c. and, in the 16th c., through printed editions of original Greek texts, notably those produced by Aldo *Manuzio in *Venice between 1494 and 1515: by 1518 all the major Greek literary texts available today had already been printed in Italy. Aristotle's Poetics, the most influential Greek work in the 16th c., had been translated into Latin by Giorgio Valla (1498) before its first Greek edition appeared in Manuzio's Rhetores Graeci (1508).

Aristotle's ideas on the unities of time, place, and plot were first exploited by *Trissino in the preface to his Sofonisba, but the full impact of those ideas was only felt after *Robortello's commentary appeared in 1548. The most obvious example of their influence is to be found both in Torquato *Tasso's theoretical works on the *epic, the Discorsi dell'arte poetica and Discorsi del poema eroico, and in his practice as an epic poet in the *Gerusalemme liberata. Tasso's poem was also shaped by his reading of Homer, whose poems were by now in circulation in Italy, while his *pastoral drama, Aminta, owed as much to Greek as to Latin sources. Another index of the strength of Greek influence on the vernacular by the end of the 16th c. was Battista *Guarini's *Pastor fido, which is indebted not only to Greek and Latin pastorals but also to Sophocles' Oedipus Rex and to a less predictable source, Pausanias. But this period was the apogee of Greek influence on Italian writers, which subsequently declined with the demise of humanism in its Renaissance form: despite the appeal Greek culture held for writers such as *Foscolo, *Leopardi, and *D'Annunzio, it was never as pervasive as the Latin influences. [See also ANTIQUARIANISM; CLASSICAL SCHOLARSHIP; CLASSICISM; GREEK WRITING IN ITALY; IMITATION; LATIN INFLUENCES; LATIN POETRY IN ITALY; LATIN PROSE IN ITALY.]   [MMcL]

See R. Weiss, *Medieval and Humanist Greek* (1977); J. Hankins, *Plato in the Italian Renaissance* (1990); N. G. Wilson, *From Byzantium to Italy: Greek Studies in the Italian Renaissance* (1992).

Greek Writing in Italy. In the 13th c. a group of poets from the Italo-Greek communities of the Terra d'Otranto produced a body of Greek poetry in *Byzantine dodecasyllables, a form of iambic trimeter. Drawing on Greek *manuscripts in the Basilian monastery of S. Niccolò di Casole, these poets combined classical and Christian themes; in addition, Giovanni Grasso and Giorgio di Gallipoli wrote celebrations of Emperor *Frederick II, echoing the Ghibelline conceits of *Pier della Vigna and his circle. The 14th-c. Calabrian monk Barlaam, known as the Greek teacher of *Petrarch, wrote many theological, philosophical, mathematical, and astronomical treatises. The Byzantine scholars who emigrated to Italy before and after the fall of Constantinople (1453) continued to compose learned works in their native tongue, as well as *grammars for Italian students. A few Italian *humanists, notably Francesco *Filelfo and Angelo

*Poliziano, achieved sufficient proficiency to write letters and poems in Greek. Crete under *Venetian rule produced a substantial amount of Greek literature: from the didactic, religious, and love poems of Marino Falier in the 15th c. to Ioannes Andreas Troïlos's verse tragedy *King Rodolinos*, based on Torquato *Tasso's *Il re Torrismondo* and published in *Venice in 1647 soon after the Turkish invasion of the island. [See also CLASSICAL SCHOLARSHIP; CLASSICISM; GREEK INFLUENCES.]   [JK]

Gregorian Style, see CURSUS.

GRIFFO, FRANCESCO, see MANUZIO, ALDO.

GRILLO, ANGELO (*c.*1560–1629). A member of an important *Genoese family, he became a *Benedictine at an early age, moving from monastery to monastery across Italy, and rising to be abbot of several, including S. Paolo-fuori-le-Mura in Rome, where he was one of the original members of the Accademia degli *Umoristi. Monastic rules did not prevent him from taking full part in the literary life of the day. His extensive religious verse hovers between *Petrarchism and *concettismo*, with substantial debts to Torquato *Tasso. His *Lettere* (1612), containing correspondence with most of the major writers of the day, give a detailed picture of contemporary literary life. He may also have been the author of *erotic verse published under the alias Livio Celano.   [MPS]

GRILLO PAMPHILJ, TERESA (late 17th–early 18th c.) *Genoese poet. As the wife of Prince Doria Pamphilj, she held an important literary salon in *Rome. She was a disciple of Alessandro *Guidi, and a member of the *Arcadia (as Irene Pamisia). Poems by her were included in *Rime degli Arcadi* (1716) and other 18th-c. anthologies.   [CCa]

Grinzane Cavour, see LITERARY PRIZES.

Griselda. The heroine of the last story in *Boccaccio's *Decameron*. Griselda is a poor shepherdess, chosen as his wife by Gualtieri, the Marquis of Saluzzo, who subjects her to a series of appalling trials, culminating in the apparent murder of their son and daughter. In the end overcome by her gentleness, submissiveness, and powers of self-denial, he restores her to wifely splendour and is himself transformed. Thus Griselda has triumphed over the three forces that rule the world of the

Decameron—fortune, sexual love, and human intelligence, here demonstrated in its most perverse form by Gualtieri. This stylized ideal figure, which owes much to images of the Virgin, had European appeal. The story became known to the learned through *Petrarch's Latin translation; but literary and popular versions in prose and verse, as well as theatrical, musical, and pictorial reworkings, are known as far afield as Iceland.   [VB]

GRISMONDI SECCO SUARDI, PAOLINA (1746–1801). Poet from Bergamo who studied in Verona under Gerolamo *Pompei and entered the *Arcadia as Lesbia Cidonia. She was admired and praised in Italy and France for her outstanding culture and beauty. Lorenzo *Mascheroni dedicated to her *L'invito a Lesbia Cidonia* (1793).   [CCa]

GRISONI, FRANCA (1945–). Poet who writes in the *dialect of Sirmione on Lake Garda where she lives. Beginning with *La böba* ('The Hoopoe', 1986), she has created from simple language an intellectually complex, musically distinctive voice focused largely on love relations. Her third book (1988) is significantly entitled *L'oter* ('The Other').   [PH]

GROSSI, TOMMASO (1790–1853). Poet. Born near Como, he studied law at Pavia and then lived in *Milan, where he was active politically and in *Romantic circles. He became a friend of *Porta, with whom he collaborated, and *Manzoni, in whose household he lived for some time in the 1820s. His early works were principally in Milanese *dialect. They included the satirical *La prineide* (1815), which led to trouble with the police, and the *novella in versi La fuggitiva* (1816), which he later translated into Italian. Works that followed were written in Italian and tended to be on medieval subjects, notably the narrative poem *Ildegonda* (1820), the heroic poem *I lombardi alla prima crociata* (1826), and the *historical novel *Marco Visconti* (1834).   [DO'G]

GROTO, LUIGI (Il Cieco di Adria) (1541–85), despite his blindness, had a rich career as musician, teacher, diplomat, and even actor (playing the part of blind Tiresias in Sophocles). His extensive writings include *letters, orations, *dialogues, *translations, *astrological almanacs, and up to a dozen *theatre works of various genres, some of which have not survived. His *pastoral play *Calisto* (1561) was one of the earliest regular plays in the genre; his *comedies have touches of originality in terms of social and psychological *realism; and his *tragedy *Adriana* is an early stage version of the Romeo and Juliet story. [See also DA PORTO, LUIGI.]   [RAA]

Grotteschi. The name of a group of playwrights of the early 20th c. (also *teatro grottesco*), after the subtitle of 'grottesco in tre atti' ('grotesque in three acts') given by Luigi *Chiarelli to his play *La maschera e il volto* (1916). The group also included Luigi *Antonelli, Enrico *Cavacchioli, and *Rosso di San Secondo. *Grottesco*, a term used in art criticism for an ornamental style of the *Renaissance, in this theatrical context carries notions of strangeness and estrangement, lack of autonomy and the divided self. Postwar disillusionment was an important factor behind the elaboration of these notions. *Pirandello's views, as expressed, for instance, in *Il fu Mattia Pascal* (1904), were an inspiration for the group, and some of his plays have much in common with their work, for instance *Così è (se vi pare)* (1917) and *Il *giuoco delle parti* (1918). Formally, their writings were parodies or rejections of the 19th-c. well-made play, and contributed to the *theatrical revival of the early 20th c.   [JAL]

Gruppo 63 was the name adopted (in a deliberate echo of the German Gruppe 47) by a group of writers of the *Neoavanguardia who met in Palermo from 3 to 8 June 1963, to discuss cultural matters such as the function of intellectuals in contemporary society, the role of literature, and what it is that a writer should be doing. Further meetings were held in 1964 and in 1965, the latter to discuss the experimental *novel. Anthologies of critical and theoretical writings and the works of participants were published, mainly in the series *Materiali* of the *Milanese publisher *Feltrinelli, in the same publisher's periodical il *verri, and then in *Quindici. The decision to close the latter brought the group to its end in July 1969.   [CGW]

GUADAGNOLI, ANTONIO (1798–1858). Aretine teacher who wrote burlesque poetry. His heart was in the *Arcadia, though he had liberal tendencies. Appointed *gonfaloniere* of Arezzo in 1849, he refused *Garibaldi entrance to the town when he was returning from *Rome in 1849.   [EAM]

GUALDO, LUIGI (1847–98). *Novelist. Born into a wealthy family in *Milan, he was educated in Paris and lived most of his life between the two cities, frequenting the literary salons of both. He wrote novels in both French and Italian, treating principally the psychology of love, often with *decadent inflections. They include *Une ressemblance* (1874), *Un mariage excentrique* (1879), and *Decadenza* (1892). This last shows much more attention to plot and style than the rest of his work. Among his friends he counted Gautier, Bourget, *Verga, *Capuana, and *D'Annunzio.   [AHC]

GUALTERUZZI, CARLO (1500–77) studied *law at *Bologna and later philosophy and literature. After a period in the retinue of Goro Gheri, Bishop of Fano, he moved to *Rome in 1527. He corresponded with a wide circle of literati and learned men, including Ludovico *Beccadelli, Giovanni *della Casa, and Pietro *Bembo. He edited the *Novellino* and the works of Bembo.   [PLR]

GUARAGNA GALLUPPO, BIAGIO (c.1620–after 1679). Born near Cosenza, he studied in *Naples and served as a government official in various Southern cities. His only published collection of poems, *Poesie* (1679–80), is predominantly in the *Baroque classical style but includes a small appendix of verse imitating *Marino.   [MPS]

GUARDATI, TOMMASO, see MASUCCIO SALERNITANO.

GUARESCHI, GIOVANNI (1908–68). Emilian *novelist and *journalist. He won international popularity with his Don Camillo books. These derive from a column he wrote for *Candido*, a *nationalist weekly, both anti-*Communist and anti-NATO, which he founded with Giovanni Mosca in 1945. From *Mondo piccolo: Don Camillo* (1948) onwards, they present the political strife of postwar Italy in microcosm. Don Camillo, the parish priest of a small country town on the lower Po, is forever sparring, politically and physically, with the Communist mayor, Peppone, but, under the surface, the two are brother Italians whose good sense prevents serious conflict and who help each other out of trouble. The voice of the crucified Christ who talks to Don Camillo transcends politics. In *Il compagno Don Camillo* (1963), Guareschi's hero visits the USSR and sees the failure of the Soviet system.

However, though often seen as successful anti-Communist propaganda, most of the Don Camillo books anticipate modern consumerist Italy and the Catholic–Communist historic compromise mooted in the 1970s, as is evident in the posthumous *Don Camillo e i giovani d'oggi* (1969). Guareschi also wrote other humorous works, including his prisoner-of-war memoirs, *Diario clandestino (1943–5)* (1949), and *diaristic sit-coms of his own family life. [JG-R]

GUARINI, ALESSANDRO (*c.*1565–*c.*1636). *Ferrarese man of letters and son of Battista *Guarini. He is famous for his *Il farnetico savio overo il Tasso*, (1610); its thesis is that Torquato *Tasso feigned his madness as a noble self-defence mechanism, in order to give a hostile and unfair world an excuse for not recognizing his poetic talent. Such a view appears feasible, not only because of our knowledge of Tasso's letters, but also because of the evidence of mental lucidity demonstrated by the *dialogues Tasso produced while 'mad'. It may be related to the theme, best represented by Torquato *Accetto's works and in *Quietism, of honest dissembling for self-protective reasons. Guarini is also known as an often naïve and certainly most enthusiastic supporter of *Dante in an age not given to such support. He wrote military historical works and a treatise on the Catholic faith.
[PBD]

GUARINI, BATTISTA (1538–1612) is best known as a *pastoral dramatist. Born in *Ferrara, he studied at *Padua and then served as a courtier and diplomat, principally with Alfonso d'*Este in his home-city. In this capacity he composed various Latin orations. Unlike his younger rival Torquato *Tasso, he seems to have had few difficulties in withstanding the pressures of *courtly life. Although his masterpiece, *Il *pastor fido* (published in 1590), was completed during a prolonged absence from the Este court, it is generally supportive of existing social structures. His other works include *lyric verse, a *dialogue on liberty and the *comedy *Idropica* (1584), which aimed to bring a sense of dignity both of a moral and artistic nature back to the genre but is more noteworthy as an example of the popular *theatre of the time. His treatises, *Il Verato* (1588) and *Il Verato secondo* (1593), written in defence of his pastoral drama and subsequently reworked in the *Compendio della poesia tragicomica* (1601), are interesting efforts to justify the legitimacy of the hybrid genre, *tragicomedy, which he argued was more in keeping with the aspirations and tastes of the contemporary world than either comedy or *tragedy alone.
[CEJG]

GUARINO, BATTISTA (1435–1503). Son of *Guarino da Verona, and his successor as head of the court school in *Ferrara, he is mainly known as the author of a pedagogical treatise based on his father's practice and written in 1459, the *De ordine docendi ac studendi*. The order of teaching proceeds from the study of Latin and Greek grammar to the classical poets, historians, orators, and moral philosophers. The method of study involves the close reading, including reading aloud, of the best authors, with constant revision and memorization. The treatise provides probably the best summary of *humanist *education in the 15th c. [DR]

GUARINO DA VERONA (Guarino Guarini) (1374–1460). *Humanist *educator. Born in Verona, he studied under *Giovanni Conversino in *Padua, where he knew the elder *Vergerio. In 1403 he went to Constantinople to study Greek with *Chrysoloras, returning to Italy in 1408, and in the following years taught in *Florence, *Venice, and Verona, before settling in 1429 in *Ferrara, where he remained for the rest of his life. Here he established a private school, then in 1431 was employed as *court tutor by the ruling *Este family, at the same time running a school for boarders; he later also taught at the newly instituted *university.

Deeply influenced by Chrysoloras, his teaching centred on the direct and detailed reading of major classical texts; it is described in detail in the *De ordine docendi* of his son and successor, Battista *Guarino. His curriculum and method had much in common with the practice of *Vittorino da Feltre and the treatise of Vergerio, but with a much greater concentration on the humanist disciplines of grammar, history, poetry, moral philosophy, and rhetoric. His works included a popular Latin grammar (the *Regulae*), a large number of Latin *letters and orations of a strongly classicizing character, and a Latin *translation of an educational treatise by Plutarch widely circulated under the title *De liberis educandis*. With a large number of distinguished pupils, and closely connected to many of the leading humanists of his day, he played a major part in the establishment of the humanist Latin and Greek curriculum as the norm for secondary education
[DR]

GUARNIERI, SILVIO (1910–92). Novelist and left-wing *literary critic, whose studies include *Cinquant'anni di narrativa in Italia* (1955) and *Condizione della letteratura* (1975). Among his *autobiographical writings is *L'ultimo testimone* (1989), an important memoir of the attitudes of *Montale and other writers towards *Fascism in 1930s *Florence. [JJ]

GUAZZO, MARCO (1480/5–1556). Soldier, *cantastorie*, and versifier, born in *Padua, but chiefly associated with the *Gonzaga of *Mantua in the early 16th c., he is the author of a number of *romance *epics: *Belisardo fratello del conte Orlando* (1525), in three books, followed by a fourth entitled *La fede* (1528); *Astolfo borioso* (1531–3); several works of history, including one on the invasion of Charles VIII (1547); and two companion pieces for the *theatre, *Comedia intitolata Errori d'amore* (1525), and *Tragedia intitolata Discordi d'amore* (1526). [JEE]

GUAZZO, STEFANO (1530–93) studied *law and spent most of his life in the service of the *Gonzaga family. He set up the Accademia degli Illustrati in Casale Monferato in 1561. Amongst other works he wrote the treatise in four books *La civil conversatione* (1574), which deals with manners, proper behaviour, and the nature and duties of the courtier. [See also ACADEMIES; COURTS.] [PLR]

GUCCINI, FRANCESCO, see CANTAUTORI.

Guelfs and Ghibellines. The two factions whose struggles dominated politics in the Italian *communes during the 13th c. The names derived from German *Welf*, a family name of the Dukes of Bavaria, and *Waiblingen*, a castle of the *Hohenstaufen. The Guelfs were associated with the *papacy and the Ghibellines with the Empire. Though the conflicts between them were often merely superimposed onto pre-existing rivalries between noble families (such as that between Buondelmonti and the Amadei in *Florence), all the same the Guelf party was more commercial and up to a point more republican. Whilst sudden fluctuations did occur, some cities (such as Florence and *Milan) were traditionally Guelf, whereas others (such as *Siena and *Pisa) were traditionally Ghibelline. By 1300 the Guelfs in *Tuscany had become further divided into *Black and White factions. Florence became definitively Guelf with the expulsion of the Whites in 1301. [CEH]

GUERRA, TONINO (1920–). *Dialect-poet, *novelist, and screen-writer. Born in Santarcangelo in Romagna, he became a primary schoolteacher. During *World War II he was deported to Germany. He later graduated at the University of *Urbino. Though he has published extensively as a novelist, he is known most for his work with *Antonioni, *Fellini, and *Rosi, and for his poetry in Romagnolo dialect. His most important poems, mostly published during the *Neorealist years, beginning with *I scarabócc* ('Scribbles', 1946) and followed by *La s-ciuptèda* ('The Shot', 1950) and *E lunèri* ('The Calendar', 1954), were gathered as *I bu* ('Oxen', 1972). They combine lyricism, realism, and political commitment in their evocations of personal memories of the war and urban and rural poverty at home. [DieZ]

GUERRAZZI, FRANCESCO DOMENICO (1804–73) *Historical novelist. Born in Livorno, he studied law at *Pisa, where he met Byron, for whom he wrote *Stanze alla memoria di Lord Byron* (1825). Until 1860 he was frequently arrested for republican *journalism and revolutionary activities. In 1849 he was sentenced to fifteen years in prison, subsequently commuted to *exile.

His novels aim to inspire patriotic ardour with their re-creations of glorious past events, particularly *La battaglia di Benevento* (1827) and *L'assedio di Firenze* (1836), which contain long discursive passages, anti-clerical outbursts, and a measure of black humour and satanism in the Byronic manner. Further historical novels, such as *Veronica Cybo* (1838), *Isabella Orsini* (1844), *Beatrice Cenci* (1853), and *Pasquale Paoli* (1860), attempt to make the portrayals of their protagonists both *realistic and *romantic. But Guerrazzi is at his best as a humourist and fantasist, as in *Serpicina* (1847), *Storia di un moscone* (1858), and the autobiographical *Il buco nero* (1862). He was elected to parliament in 1860, supporting the republican right until he retired in 1870. He continued to produce fiction in his later years, including *L'assedio di Roma* (1863–5), as well as writing on politics and *translating from English and German literature. [DO'G]

GUERRAZZI, VINCENZO (1940–). Working-class writer, based in *Genoa, whose work (mostly produced in the 1970s) attempts to give voice to a disaffected industrial proletariat, which is seeking to appropriate politics to their own needs. He has written *novels, beginning with *La fabbrica del sogno* (1977), as well as sociological studies and accounts of workers' struggles. [JEB]

GUERRINI, OLINDO (1845–1916). Poet and *satirist who wrote under different pseudonyms.

He is best known as the poet Lorenzo Stecchetti, author of a blasphemous, *erotic first collection, *Postuma* (1877). Guerrini's work also includes *dialect verse and tiresome *parodies of women's poetry, *Rime di Argia Sbolenfi* (1897). He was director of *Bologna University Library and a friend of *Carducci.   [AHC]

GUERZONI, GIUSEPPE (1835–86) was actively involved in the *Garibaldian campaigns from 1859 to the late 1860s as combatant, secretary, and *journalist. He subsequently became a professor of literature and published academic works, such as *Il primo rinascimento* (1878), and *biographies of Nino Bixio (1875) and Garibaldi (1882).
                                                        [MPC]

GUGLIELMINETTI, AMALIA (1881–1941). Born into a wealthy family, she entered *Turinese literary circles after publishing a first collection of verse, *Voci di giovinezza* (1903). Her notorious relationship with *Gozzano—their letters were published in 1951 as *Lettere d'amore*—was followed later by an equally tormented and tormenting one with the much younger *Pitigrilli. Her novels of passion, beginning with *Gli occhi cerchiati d'azzurro* (1918) and *La rivincita del maschio* (1923), sold well. She was an active *feminist, but one who enjoyed dramatic scandals and whose public persona owed much to the female figures created by *D'Annunzio and Swinburne.   [RD]

GUICCIARDINI, FRANCESCO (1483–1540). Major *Renaissance historian and *political thinker. He was a member of a prominent *merchant family in *Florence and a practising civil *lawyer (he took his doctorate in 1505). His marriage in 1508 to Maria, daughter of the leading citizen Alamanno Salviati, was followed by his first writings: *autobiographical memoirs or *Ricordanze*, some family memoirs, and a history of Florence. These were followed in 1512, after his election as Ambassador to Spain aged only 28, by the first of several blueprints for reforming Florence's government, the Logrogno *Discorso*, dated 27 August 1512, three days before the fall of Piero Soderini's republican regime and the restoration of the *Medici. In the same year he wrote the first of three versions of his reflective *Ricordi*. His return to Florence in 1514 and first experience of political office stimulated two other blueprints for reform, one on the government of Florence after the Medici restoration in 1512, and the other on how the Medici family

should secure power. Both of these texts realistically accept the Medici's need to base their power on partisans who would be supported from *Rome, not Florence, and motivated by self-interest or necessity; the digression on 'new' states in the second (1516) shows the early influence of *Machiavelli's *Principe*. Guicciardini's first horoscope in 1515 seemed to predict correctly his growing power and wealth in *papal service, since he was shortly afterwards appointed consistorial advocate by the Medici Pope Leo X; in 1516 papal Governor of Modena and in 1517 also of Reggio; in 1521 papal Commissary General in the war against the French; in 1525 Governor of the Romagna under the new Pope Clement VII, the former Cardinal Giulio de' Medici; and in 1526 papal Lieutenant-General in the War of the League of Cognac.

The *Dialogo sul reggimento di Firenze* (composed between October/November 1521 and April 1524 or later) belongs to this period of papal service, but was probably intended as a realistic and publishable plan for republican reform in Florence—the scheme in book 2 more closely resembles that of the 1512 Logrogno discourse than the two blueprints for Florence which followed, although overall it shares their political realism. It may have been a response, like the discourse of Machiavelli on the same subject, to Cardinal Giulio's invitation to address the problems created by the death in May 1519 of Lorenzo, Duke of Urbino, the city's Captain General and, with Leo X (who died in December 1521), the last legitimate descendant of Lorenzo de' *Medici. A failed conspiracy against Cardinal Giulio in 1522, and the latter's subsequent election to the papacy in December 1523, simultaneously increased Medici power in Rome and the danger of revolution in Florence. Fearful of alienating his Roman patrons and his Florentine compatriots, Guicciardini doubtless intended the *dialogue to be ambiguous, in its final preface disclaiming that it had any political relevance or that he intended to publish it. But despite its apparent republicanism, it transforms the traditional classification of good and bad governments and offers a new empirical justification for restrictive or one-man government.

Losing his position as Lieutenant-General of the papal army in May 1527, following the *Sack of Rome by imperial troops and the collapse of the Medici regime in Florence, Guicciardini embarked on another period of writing in his villa outside the city: two orations, the *Accusatoria* and *Defensoria* (which anticipated the charges of contumacy brought against him two years later, when he was exiled as a rebel after fleeing the city); his second (unfinished) history of Florence, the *Cose fiorentine*; a third version of the *Ricordi*; and his *Considerazioni* on the *Discorsi* of Machiavelli, written en route to *exile in Rome. He was largely absent from Florence during the momentous events from the Treaty of Barcelona in 1529 to the Medici's final restoration in August 1530, and again from 1531 to 1534, as Vice-Legate and Governor of *Bologna; but he retained a political role in the city as papal mediator and emissary in 1529 and 1530 and, in 1532, as one of twelve Reformers appointed by the *balia*, or extraordinary council, which he had himself proposed in another advisory address to the Medici (30 January 1532). In this capacity he was partly responsible for making Alessandro de' Medici (the illegitimate last descendant of the elder line) Duke of Florence three months later, subsequently becoming one of his closest advisers. His defence of Alessandro against the Florentine exiles' charges of tyranny in 1535–6 challenged traditional republican ideology, but it was entirely consistent with the political pragmatism expressed in the *Dialogo*. He retired to Florence on the death of Clement VII in 1534 and, after writing a preliminary commentary on the years 1525–7, devoted the last years of his life to writing his longest work, the meditative *Storia d'Italia*, which, it has been said, finds no lesson in its subject 'except the mutability of history and the selfishness of power'. Like all his works, it was not published until after his death, the first sixteen books appearing in 1561, the last four in 1564.

Although politics played an all-important role in Guicciardini's writings, other influences helped to mould his outlook, especially the mercantile tradition of scrupulous record-keeping and the legal tradition of arguing *pro et contra*. Despite learning Greek and Latin as a boy and having Marsilio *Ficino as a godparent, he always wrote in colloquial Italian and combined an appraising and often sceptical attitude to life with an interest in prophecies (he collected all of *Savonarola's), in horoscopes, and in *astrology. His originality consists in the detached and often ironic attitude to life expressed both in his *Ricordi* and in his final history of Italy. [See also HISTORIOGRAPHY.]

[ABr]

Opere, ed. E. L. Scarano (1970); *Selected Writings*, trans. M. Grayson (1965). See R. Ridolfi, *Vita di Francesco Guicciardini* (1960), trans. C. Grayson (1967); M. Phillips, *Francesco Guicciardini: The Historian's Craft* (1977).

GUIDACCI, MARGHERITA (1921–92). Highly *religious poet. After some early *hermetic verse, she made simplicity and clarity of meaning a central feature of her mature work, even in collections such as *Neurosuite* (1970), which explored her experience in a psychiatric institution after a mental breakdown, and *L'orologio di Bologna* (1981), which was a response to terrorist outrage. But poems of later collections such as *Inno alla gioia* (1983) characteristically celebrate joy and love.

[SW]

GUIDEROCCHI, AURELLO MORANI DEI, see EURIALO D'ASCOLI.

GUIDI, ALESSANDRO (1650–1712). Poet. Born in Pavia, he served *Christina of Sweden in *Rome from 1685 to her death. In 1691 he entered *Arcadia and became its foremost *lyric poet and chief representative of an early Pindarizing current based on imitation of *Chiabrera as second only to *Petrarch in Italian poetry. He was extolled by both *Gravina and *Crescimbeni, who edited his poetry (1726), and imitated by *Parini. *Alfieri attributed his own self-discovery to the power of Guidi's verse. *Leopardi dismissed his Pindaric aspirations, but Guidi's *canzone a selva* (that is, free *canzone*) is the closest metrical precedent for his own *canzone libera*. [JMAL]

GUIDICCIONI, GIOVANNI (1500–41). Poet from Lucca, who had a distinguished political and ecclesiastical career under the *papacy of Paul III, becoming Governor of *Rome, of the Romagna, and later Bishop of Fossombrone. A friend of Pietro *Bembo, Trifon *Gabriele, and Annibale *Caro, he was the author of an oration to the republic of Lucca following popular riots, and a substantial collection of *letters. His *canzoniere*, mainly composed of *sonnets, is of note for the importance given to religious and political themes, as exemplified in a sonnet sequence on the *Sack of Rome. [ELM]

GUIDICCIONI, LAURA (1550–99) left her native Lucca for *Florence in 1588 with her husband, Orazio Lucchesini, where she collaborated on *theatrical projects with the composer Emilio de' Cavalieri. She was an accomplished poetess in the *Petrarchan mould, though only two *sonnets and two *pastoral dramas survive. [ELM]

GUIDO DA PISA, see DANTE COMMENTARIES; LITERARY THEORY, I.

GUIDO DELLE COLONNE (c.1210–after ?1287). Important member of the *Sicilian School. Probably from Messina, he was active as a *lawyer, judge, and *court functionary between 1243 and 1280. He is often identified with a Guido de Columnis, the author of a Latin prose *Historia destructionis Troiae*, modelled on the *Roman de Troie* of Benoît de Sainte-Maure (begun and interrupted in 1272 and finished in 1287). His surviving poems amount to five *canzoni*, one of these being of uncertain attribution.

Guido was probably a later member of the school. He draws extensively on his predecessors, developing the topics of the lover's happiness or distress, pleas to the lady, and analyses of the workings of love. But his poems are closely knit, and show technical and rhetorical skill. Whilst some of his similes draw on the usual Sicilian repertory of natural phenomena and the marvellous, others (especially in his famous 'Ancor che l'aigua per lo foco lassi') are developed into intellectually complex analogies between the workings of nature and of love, in a way that looks forwards to Guido *Guinizzelli. In the *De vulgari eloquentia* (1.12 and 2.6) *Dante singles him out among the Sicilian poets, and praises his excellence in the construction of verse periods.   [JP & JMS]

GUIDO FAVA (or Faba) (before 1190–after 1243) taught grammar at *Bologna and wrote treatises on the *ars dictaminis*. His importance for Italian rests with his *Gemma purpurea*, containing model *letters in the vernacular, and his *Parlamenti et epistulae*, which reworks in Latin a series of invented vernacular speeches and letters, offering in each instance three Latin versions of increasing rhetorical complexity.   [JU]

GUIDO ORLANDI (late 13th c.–early 14th c.). *Florentine poet writing in the *Siculo-Tuscan manner, whose style shows nevertheless some influence of the *dolce stil novo*. He took part in poetic exchanges with Guido *Cavalcanti.   [JU]

GUIDUCCI, ARMANDA (1923–92). *Neapolitan critic and *feminist writer. Early work included academic studies of Cesare *Pavese (1967) and of the relationship between contemporary culture and *Marxist aesthetics in *Dallo zdanovismo allo strutturalismo* (1967). Later she directed cultural programming for Swiss television. Her feminist works, however, had the widest influence. *La mela e il serpente* (1974) is an analysis of

female psychological and social development, filtering the narrator's life through her experience of gender. *Due donne da buttare* (1976), *La donna non è gente* (1977), and *All'ombra di Kalì* (1979) examine gender definition through social history and cultural anthropology.   [SW]

Guilds (*arti*). Associations of *merchants and artisans which came into being in the late 12th c. and combined social and religious functions with the regulation of crafts and professions. During the 13th c. they were active in campaigns for a broader distribution of power within the *communes, and membership became a prerequisite for participation in civic government. However, they were often manipulated by leaders who were members of the nobility. In *Florence the merchant-aristocratic guilds (*arti maggiori*) and the craft guilds (*arti minori*) were commonly at loggerheads, leading in 1378 to the revolt of the *ciompi* (wool-combers). The political power of the guilds declined steeply in the 15th c.   [CEH]

GUINIZZELLI, GUIDO (13th c.). *Bolognese poet, who was an important precursor of the *dolce stil novo*. We have five *canzoni and fifteen *sonnets which are definitely his, plus fragments of two other poems. His precise identity is uncertain, but he may have been Guido di Guinizzello di Magnano, exiled from Bologna with the Lambertazzi Ghibellines in 1274 and dying in Monselice about two years later [see GUELFS AND GHIBELLINES]. He corresponded with *Guittone d'Arezzo, whom he respectfully addressed as 'caro padre meo' and by whom he was called in return 'figlio dilettoso'. Assuming the sonnet in question is indeed addressed to him, he was later accused by Guittone of the 'laido errore' of wishing to praise his lady using ideas and terms from natural philosophy. *Bonagiunta da Lucca also charged him with making love poetry obscure through his philosophical importations. But these were the very reasons for which *Dante admired him, and increasingly so as time went by. He already terms him a 'saggio' in the *Vita nova* (20) for his profound and innovative *canzone*, 'Al cor gentil rempaira sempre Amore'. He calls him 'nobile' in the *Convivio* (4.20) and the 'greatest' of the illustrious Bolognese poets in the *De vulgari eloquentia* (1.15), praising his exceptional skill in the art of the *canzone*. This exaltation of Guinizzelli (which perhaps continues in *Purg.* 11.97–9) is polemical, given the disdain shown in the *Divine Comedy* for Dante's former friend

Guittone D'Arezzo

Guido *Cavalcanti. It culminates in the meeting on the terrace of the lustful (*Purg.* 26) where Dante calls him his poetic father and the father of all those who 'rime d'amor usar dolci e leggiadre', one whose fame will last as long as does modern poetry. Perhaps Guido has been placed amongst the lustful because in the sonnet 'Chi vedesse a Lucia un var capuzzo' he wanted to take forcible hold of his lady and kiss her mouth and face, though the conclusion of the poem already expresses repentance for this immoderate desire.

In the first stanza of 'Al cor gentil' some see a rewriting of the prologue of the gospel of St John and therefore a deliberate assumption of a scriptural style which looks forwards to the *dolce stil novo* proper. The sonnets too display motifs which will reappear in Cavalcanti and Dante, such as the lady's salvific greeting ('saluto'), the use of natural imagery to praise her (recalling the *Song of Songs*), and the idea of love as a passion that carries all before it, though a poem such as 'Vedut'ho la lucente stella diana' actually fuses together new and old styles.   [GG]

M. Marti, *Poeti del dolce stil nuovo* (1969). See G. Favati, *Inchiesta sul dolce stil nuovo* (1975).

GUITTONE D'AREZZO (*c*.1230–94). The most prolific and influential Italian vernacular poet and prose writer before *Dante, dominating Italian letters from the demise of the *Sicilian School until the *Florentine *dolce stil novo* became an established lyric mode. He was the first poetic voice of the *communes and the first Italian poet to write on moral and political themes in the high *lyric style. All his work has the stamp of an original and powerful mind.

His surviving work comprises forty *letters and some 300 poems, these dividing evenly between about 140 courtly poems (*c*.1250–*c*.1263), and the moral writing, in verse and prose, that accompanied and followed his conversion (*c*.1265). The entire corpus is unified by his inherent sobriety, didactic sententiousness, and stylistic virtuosity. A conflict between the inherited Romance tradition and his learned civic formation and logical, moral temper is already apparent in the 120 *courtly *sonnets, most of which he links, for the first time in the history of the sonnet, into cycles (five in all, three of them narrative), to probe the moral inconsistencies of the conventional love ethos. The 20 courtly *canzoni* display a pioneering grasp of the difficult style of the Provençal *troubadours (*trobar clus*).

The *Guelf defeat at Montaperti (1260) and his self-*exile from Arezzo precipitated Guittone's conversion in the mid-1260s, when he left his wife and three children to join the Milites Beatae Virginis Mariae (or *frati godenti*), a new lay order founded (1261) to promote civic harmony, and whose spokesman he became. A series of palinodes announce a muscular new assertion of the moral will, abandoning Love and embracing Christian ethics. They introduce a body of mature work, much of it in correspondence form, in which he preached an austere code of practical civic conduct to all ranks of contemporary central Italian society. This blunt and sober writing of his maturity is marked by formal inventiveness. The prose letters, without precedent in Italian, furnish an anthology of models for *sermons and political speeches. He invented the double sonnet and perfected the *lauda-*ballata; he addressed the communes of Arezzo, *Pisa, and Florence, and leading political figures like Nino Visconti and Corso Donati; and his exchanges with poets like Chiaro *Davanzati, Guido *Guinizzelli, and Guido *Cavalcanti point to a looming crisis of allegiances and styles in which Guittone's prosaic moralizing and dense style were to be the anti-model of the *Tuscan lyric avant-garde. In spite of recent reappraisals his work is still struggling to recover from Dante's brief but deadly dismissals (above all *DVE* 2.13 and *Purg.* 24.56).

Guittone willed his estate to build the Camoldolese monastery near Florence.   [VBM]

Lettere, ed. C. Margueron (1990); *Le rime di Guittone d'Arezzo*, ed. F. Egidi (1940). See C. Margueron, *Recherches sur Guittone d'Arezzo* (1966); V. Moleta, *The Early Poetry of Guittone d'Arezzo* (1976).

H

HABSBURG. Family dynasty of South German origin which ruled *Austria from the 15th c. to the end of *World War I. Habsburg involvement in Italy varied, depending on the state of the complex diplomatic and marriage alliances that were their trade mark. It began effectively with the occupation of *Trieste in 1466 and reached a peak with the establishment of *Spanish domination under the Emperor Charles V in the mid-16th c. But subsequently, at one time or another, *Mantua, Parma, Piacenza, *Sardinia, and *Sicily all had Habsburg rulers. During the 18th c. Habsburg (i.e. Austrian) control was firmly established over *Lombardy, whilst *Tuscany was ruled by the Habsburg-Lorraine branch of the family. For patriots of the *Risorgimento period the Habsburgs were synonymous with repressive Austrian power.

[PH]

Hagiography, the writing (and writings) of the lives of the saints, is definable more by content than by its forms, which are as various as its uses. One of the earliest surviving vernacular texts, the incomplete *Ritmo su S. Alessio* (late 12th or early 13th c.), is representative of medieval hagiography in general, both in its dependence on non-vernacular originals and in its paraliturgical role (in this case as a text to be sung). Similarly, the widely disseminated *translations from the 6th-c. *Lives of the Fathers* and the *Dialogues* of Gregory the Great, overseen in the early 14th c. by Domenico *Cavalca, served as a reservoir of *exempla* for *sermons, as evinced in the *Specchio della vera penitenzia*, compiled by Iacopo *Passavanti. Saints' lives also provided material for sung *laude*, *sacre rappresentazioni*, and iconography.

The effectiveness of *humanist censure of miracle-laden stories was limited by the difficulty of applying historical criteria when writing the lives of people about whom frequently not much was known. Moreover, the secular, *biographical conventions which privileged cause, event, place, and time were inappropriate to evoke lives which were, by definition, miraculous and other-worldly. This is testified by the continuing appeal of the 13th-c. *Legenda aurea* of *Iacopo da Varagine, which enjoyed several vernacular translations down to the early 17th c. In the wake of the Protestant and Catholic *Reformations, attitudes to the cult of saints provided perhaps the most visible boundary which marked the confessional divide [see also COUNTER-REFORMATION]. Hagiography therefore assumed renewed importance as a defining feature of reformed Roman Catholicism.

The introduction of the revised Roman Breviary in 1568, with its pruned saints' calendar and rewritten hagiographical readings at Matins, had the effect of forcing hagiographers to refurbish their local cults, whose practices and even legitimacy were now closely examined by *Rome. The result was a renaissance in ecclesiastical erudition (c.1550–1750), as authors sought to celebrate the traditions of their local churches. Hagiography should therefore be viewed in relation to the genres of civic *history, *biography, *chronicle, episcopal calendar, and topographical description as demonstrated, typically, by Pietro Maria Campi's three-volume *Historia ecclesiastica di Piacenza* (1651–62), in which lives of his city's saints were to be found anchored securely in his chronological narrative. The concomitant tightening up of the canonization process under close *papal supervision (completed by 1634), also had considerable influence on the content and structure of works designed to promote their subjects' candidacy for sainthood. Even considered more narrowly, hagiography enjoyed considerable popularity, as can be seen in the Kingdom of *Naples for the period 1500–1750, when no fewer than 279 *Vite* were published in 327 editions. In the 17th c. hagiographical subject matter also engaged the attentions of writers of *romances such as G. B. *Manzini, who wrote a *Vita di*

S. Eustachio (1631). It was also adapted by A. G. *Brignole Sale into the popular *romanzo sacro*, as in his *Maria Maddalena peccatrice e convertita* (1636).

Subsequently the fortunes of hagiography have been influenced, on the one hand, by papal canonization policy and, on the other, by the devotional preferences of the faithful. The former, particularly since the publication of *Rerum novarum* (1891), has seen a greater social inclusiveness, which has led to a higher proportion of works dedicated to laymen and women from the professional and working classes, who have also sometimes been celebrated in film—for example, Maria Goretti in *Cielo sulla palude* (1949). The latter has ensured a steady publication (and reprinting) of works devoted to figures, ancient and modern, who continue to inspire their devotees, both in the world and within religious communities, where refectory readings are still widespread. [SD]

See S. Ditchfield, 'Sanctity in Early Modern Italy', *Journal of Ecclesiastical History*, 47 (1996); *Sanctorum: bollettino dell'associazione italiana per lo studio della santità, dei culti e dell'agiografia* (1996–).

Hecatommithi, see GIRALDI CINZIO, GIAMBATTISTA.

Hendecasyllable (*endecasillabo*). The most common type of verse line in Italian typified by *Dante's 'Nel mezzo del cammin di nostra vita', which opens the *Divine Comedy*. The last accented syllable is the tenth, and there are eleven syllables in the *piano* type. Normally the fourth or sixth syllable is accented, or both, a structure which derives from the model of the Provençal *décasyllabe*, whose division into two parts it reflects. For both the fourth and sixth syllables to be unaccented is rare in the 13th c., marginal thereafter, but relatively frequent in the 20th c. When the fourth is accented, there is normally an accent on the eighth or the seventh, the latter being less favoured by the *Petrarchan tradition. *Endecasillabi sciolti* are unrhyming hendecasyllables. [See also VERSIFICATION.] [PGB]

HENRY VII OF LUXEMBURG (?1274–1313). Elected Emperor in 1308, he led a campaign in Italy (1310–13), where *Dante hoped he would re-establish imperial justice and peace (*Epistles* 5–7; *Para.* 30.133–8). His death is the subject of a *canzone* by *Cino da Pistoia. [PA]

Heresies, as defined by the Catholic Church, were originally ecclesiastical offences, but from 1139 also received secular punishments, later including death by burning. After 1231, in Northern and Central Italy, *Waldensians and other heretics disdaining the sacraments and priesthood were investigated by the *Inquisition, whose net also gathered in Pelagian heresies (salvation is earned by good works), protesters against clerical abuses, and scholars asserting that Councils are superior to Popes. After 1520, *Reformation teaching was sympathetically received by devout Italian *humanists, both clergy and laity, especially in *Ferrara, but from 1542 the *Counter-Reformation pursued and vigorously attacked Protestant ideas throughout Italy, scrutinizing even the poems of Vittoria *Colonna. Persecution encouraged Nicodemism (outward orthodoxy cloaking secret heresy), but those who openly professed Lutheranism, a radical Reformation, or Pelagianism were prosecuted.

After 1600, theological heresies declined in importance, and were gradually replaced by social misdemeanours and superstitions, mainly punished by church excommunication only. Heresy charges therefore became less an instrument of religious and social control, although heresy itself remained a vehicle for social and political dissent. 18th-c. Italian heterodoxies derived mainly from *Jansenist controversies, the *Enlightenment, or secular *nationalism, and more recently from exaggerated emphasis upon faith, *Marxism, and rationalism in theological and biblical criticism. [See also PAPACY AND THE CATHOLIC CHURCH.] [BC]

Hermaphroditus, see EROTICISM AND PORNOGRAPHY; PANORMITA, IL.

Hermes, see PERIODICALS, I.

Hermeticism. When Marsilio *Ficino was engaged in his *translation of Plato in 1463, Cosimo de' *Medici asked him to interrupt his work in order to translate a new corpus of Greek texts that had just been brought to *Florence. His Latin translation of these comprised the first fourteen treatises of what is known as the *Corpus hermeticum*; Ficino named them *Pimander*, after the title of the first treatise, and they were printed in 1471. Another text called *Asclepius* (probably translated into Latin by Apuleius in the 2nd c. AD) had been known in the *Middle Ages and was printed in 1469. During the *Renaissance these texts were thought to have been written originally in Egyptian by the quasi-biblical figure Hermes Trismegistus, or Mercurius Trismegistus (sometimes also equated with the god Thoth), a supposed contemporary of Moses. Despite the fact that in 1614 Isaac Casaubon, after a meticulous analysis of the texts, had indicated that they had actually been composed very much later, they continued to exert a profound influence on European theological, mystical, and Neoplatonic writings until the 18th c.

The intellectual provenance of the hermetic corpus is still a matter of debate. They were first thought to have emerged from the *Neoplatonic tradition of Greek philosophy, whereas recent research now points towards Egyptian as well as Greek philosophical developments during the Ptolemaic, Roman and early Christian eras. The texts circulated widely in late antiquity and were condemned by St *Augustine. The terms hermetic and hermeticism are often related in error to Renaissance ideas on *magic and the occult; the texts of the *Corpus hermeticum* have very little to offer on such topics, although some passages are important for the development of Renaissance occultism. It is of course possible that the magical elements had been deliberately excised in *Byzantium, when the collection was put together. As we have them, they deal mainly with spiritual and theological matters, and they had a real impact on the debates on such important religious issues as the divine creation and the immortality of the soul.

For Marsilio Ficino, Hermes Trismegistus provided a link between Plato and the Old Testament; he helped him to see Plato as a Christian philosopher, and to incorporate his theories into a new theological system. In this sense, it has been said, the importance of Hermes lies more in his great age than in what he writes. A distinction has also been made between two strands of hermetic writings: the theoretical *Hermetica*, the main thrust of which is spiritual and theological, and which include the texts translated by Ficino and Ludovico *Lazzarelli (who added three more treatises to the translation of the *Corpus hermeticum*), the *Asclepius*, and the fragments of Stobaeus; and on the other hand the technical *Hermetica*, which have no coherent doctrines and contain material on *medicine, magic, alchemy, *astrology, and natural philosophy. There are, however, themes that belong to both, and it is difficult at times to make a clear distinction between the two strands.

Ficino's translation achieved great popularity and circulated widely, with translations into Italian (Tommaso *Benci, 1463), French, Spanish, and Dutch. Hermeticism, sometimes mingled with other Neoplatonic and cabalistic themes, permeated the writings of philosophers such as Giovanni *Pico della Mirandola's *conclusiones*, Francesco *Patrizi the Younger's *Nova de universis philosophia*, Agostino Steuco's *De perenni philosophia*, Francesco Giorgi's *De harmonia mundi*, as well as works by Giordano *Bruno, *Nicholas of Cusa, Agostino *Nifo, and Lefèvre d'Étaples. It became part of an arcane language of symbols, and must be taken into account in all its manifestations if one is to understand the meaning and intent of a large body of Renaissance art, literature, and philosophy. [PLR]

See F. Yates, *Giordano Bruno and the Hermetic Tradition* (1964); G. Fowden, *The Egyptian Hermes: A Historical Approach to the Late Pagan Mind* (1986); B. Copenhaver, *Hermetica: The Greek Corpus Hermeticum and the Latin Asclepius in a New English Translation* (1992).

Hermetic Poetry (*ermetismo*) was the dominant current in Italian poetry and *literary criticism in the 1930s and early 1940s. The poetry was dubbed hermetic, that is, accessible only to initiates, since it displays features, such as concision, allusiveness, and personal symbolism, that render its immediate comprehension difficult.

This form of hermeticism is only loosely related to the *Renaissance *hermeticism discussed in the previous entry. It has its roots in 19th-c. *Orphism and French *symbolism. The post-symbolist poet, impatient with the discursive uses of language, was eager to exploit its original creative power and its capacity for expression beyond the limits of ordinary logic. This approach is discernible in the *expressionism of Arturo *Onofri, *Rebora, and *Campana, but becomes the essence of the poetic act in *Ungaretti, whose *Porto sepolto* (1916) uses words to evoke rather than describe experience, endowing them, by analogy, with additional density of meaning. 'Analogy' denotes a metaphorical procedure which substitutes identity for comparison and, in a unitary image, establishes a correspondence between disparate orders of human experience. It was in view of the obscurity of bold analogies that the epithet *ermetico* was first applied, in a pejorative sense, to the poetry of Ungaretti, *Montale, and *Quasimodo by the critic Francesco *Flora in *La poesia ermetica* (1936). However, like many others, Flora came later to recognize their importance.

Historical Novel

The symbolism which Ungaretti and Montale deployed defensively against the contingency of existence and the ravages of time was cultivated by the younger generation of poets as a positive means to grasp hold of reality. This development, along with the predilection for analogy, is a defining characteristic of hermeticism as a movement. At its heart were the *Florentines *Luzi, *Bigongiari, and *Parronchi, and three Southern poets, Quasimodo, *Gatto, and *Sinisgalli, who moved North and wrote poetry that gives thematic importance to their landscapes of origin. But the landscape to which hermetic poets primarily responded is an inner one, their purpose being to fashion poetic objects that would embody their inner experience or lyrical intuitions. Alongside the poets worked critics who helped to shape the ideology of hermeticism, chief among them *Bo and *Macrì, with Florentine *periodicals like *Solaria, Il *Frontespizio, Il *Bargello, and *Campo di Marte debating the issues in subtle and largely sympathetic terms.

The sense of absence, of waiting upon events, that hermetic poetry frequently conveys has been linked with the repressive climate of Italy under *Fascism. Certainly by the late 1930s the rhetoric and pretensions of the regime had become completely antithetical to hermetic ideals. These were summed up in Bo's essay 'Letteratura come vita' (1938), which saw in literature the 'greater life' of the spirit: a watchfulness on behalf of authentic being in the face of materialism, depersonalization, and the threat of oblivion. This attitude—clearly spiritual, and often implicitly or explicitly religious—betrays an affinity with the philosophical *existentialism of Jaspers and Heidegger. It was also an overt link with *Petrarch, *Leopardi, and a tradition in Italian poetry which gave priority to the power of memory and of the past in the present. With the fall of Fascism absence was reinterpreted in political rather than spiritual terms. *Neorealism, which emerged as the dominant current in Italian culture, replaced it with the presence of the democratic masses in history and passed negative judgements on the hermetics' rejection of history and abstract intellectualism. But hermeticism achieved much: it opened 20th c. Italian literature to the European mainstream, renewed the language of poetry, prepared Italian critics to embrace *structuralism and *semiotics, and preserved poetry, under difficult circumstances, as an index of humanity and personal integrity. [SPC]

See S. Ramat, L'ermetismo (1969); D. Valli, Storia degli ermetici (1978); F. Di Carlo, Letteratura e ideologia dell'ermetismo (1981).

Historical Novel. The Italian historical novel is often considered to have been born in 1827 with the publication of *Manzoni's I *promessi sposi and Francesco Domenico *Guerrazzi's La battaglia di Benevento. However, beginning with Vincenzo *Cuoco's Platone in Italia (1806), the two preceding decades had seen a stream of narrative works dealing in various ways with historical characters and events. There had also been a heated debate on the legitimacy of mixing history and fiction, which Paride *Zajotti, for instance, had condemned as monstrous in the *Biblioteca italiana. The 1830s and 40s saw novels by G. B. *Bazzoni, Carlo *Varese, Davide *Bertolotti, and others, which were clearly influenced by Scott, whose Kenilworth was translated by 1827. But Manzoni's influence was enormous. Giovanni *Rosini and Cletto *Arrighi borrowed his characters; Ignazio *Cantù, Cesare *Balbo, Niccolò *Tommaseo, and Massimo *D'Azeglio adopted his Christian and conciliatory ideology, D'Azeglio's Ettore Fieramosca (1833) proving a best-seller.

Notwithstanding Manzoni's own disavowal in Del romanzo storico (1845), the genre was taken up by *Rovani, *Nievo, *Verga, *Fogazzaro, and subsequently *Bacchelli. Its capacity to voice political and social criticism, already evident in *Pirandello's I *vecchi e i giovani, was exploited by *Neorealists such as Francesco *Jovine and Vasco *Pratolini, and continued from different ideological perspectives by *Tomasi di Lampedusa, *Sciascia, and *Morante. Lampedusa's Il *gattopardo (1958) and Morante's La *storia (1974) were both best-sellers, as was *Eco's Il *nome della rosa (1980), which marked a shift towards historical *detective fiction. A variety of approaches, ranging from the politically charged to the playful, are displayed in historical novels of the later 20th c., as evidenced by the work of *Consolo, *Malerba, *Vassalli, Roberto *Pazzi, and Rosetta *Loy. [FD'I]

See G. Petrocchi, Il romanzo storico nell'Ottocento italiano (1967); G. De Donato, Gli archivi del silenzio (1995).

Histories of Italian Literature. Literary historiography in Italy begins with *Dante. In fact the *De vulgari eloquentia, at the beginning of the 14th c., presents an extraordinarily sharp and committed view of the origins of Italian literature, which has not only marked subsequent interpretations but is also impossible for us to disregard, even now, in our evaluation of those beginnings. Histories of Italian literature, however, in a sense which is more germane to that in which we use this label, make their first appearance in the 18th c. After the work of scholars such as *Crescimbeni (1698), *Gravina (1696–1708), *Muratori (1706), *Gimma (1723), *Quadrio (1739–52), *Mazzuchelli (*Scrittori d'Italia*, 1753–63), and others, we find the formidably erudite, comprehensive *Storia della letteratura italiana* (1772–82) by *Tiraboschi, which, for its richness of information, is still valuable.

In the 19th c. the presentation of Italian literary history was naturally linked with *Risorgimento ideals and coloured by ideological assumptions concerning the Italian national tradition. Relevant in this context are the works by *Foscolo and *Mazzini, P. Emiliani Giudici (1844, 1855), Cesare *Cantù (1851), and *Settembrini (1866–72), up to that masterpiece which is *De Sanctis' *Storia della letteratura italiana* (1870). This can still be read with interest and pleasure, for what it says about Italian literature from the viewpoint of a forceful critic inspired by philosophical *idealism and interested in aesthetic appreciation, rather than in the philological interpretation of texts. After De Sanctis we have the fundamental contribution made to Italian literary studies by *Croce, which takes the shape not of a self-contained history of Italian literature, but of monographic studies such as those devoted to Dante (1921), poetry from the 14th to the 16th c. (1933), *Ariosto (1910), the *Renaissance (1945–52), the 17th c. (1911, 1931), *Manzoni (1930), and the *Letteratura della nuova Italia* (1914–15).

In the post-*Unification period an attitude favourable to a scholarly and philological approach becomes prevalent. There is the influential collective history published by Vallardi in *Milan. The first series had six volumes (1874–80) under the title *Storia letteraria d'Italia scritta da una società d'amici sotto la direzione di Pasquale Villari*; this includes, as volume ii, A. Bartoli's impressive *I primi due secoli della letteratura italiana* (1880), which was reshaped into a *Storia della letteratura italiana* in eight volumes (1878–89), still devoted to the first two centuries. There were two subsequent editions with the title *Storia letteraria d'Italia scritta da una società di professori*; some volumes were rewritten, others updated, but without always superseding the previous ones. The collection also includes volumes devoted to genres (*La satira*, *La commedia*, etc.). The current edition is published by Piccin

Nuova libraria (1981–) under the direction of A. Balduino.

Among important post-1945 multi-volume works are the series published by Marzorati: *Problemi e orientamenti critici* (1948–9), divided into *Le correnti, I maggiori, I minori, I contemporanei*, and *I critici* (1956–74); and the histories of literature edited by *Cecchi and *Sapegno for *Garzanti (1965–9); by C. Muscetta for *Laterza (1970–80); by *Asor Rosa for *Einaudi (1982–96); by G. Barberi Squarotti for UTET (1990–); by R. Ceserani and L. De Federicis for Loescher (1991–3); by F. Brioschi and C. Di Girolamo for Bollati Boringhieri (1993–); and by E. Malato for Salerno (1995–). There are numerous works written by individual authors, many of them interesting and also influential, particularly through being used as school textbooks. Among the most notable are those by Vittorio Rossi (1903–4); Eugenio Donadoni (1923); Attilio *Momigliano (1933–5); Francesco *Flora (1940–1); Sapegno's three-volume *Compendio* (1936–47) and his more compact and ideologically committed one-volume *Disegno storico* (1949); G. Ferroni (1991). The introductions to various authors and texts in *Contini's anthologies (1968–) offer a brilliant, synthetic history of Italian literature.

Among those in English it is worth recalling the works by R. Garnett (1898), E. H. Wilkins (1954, updated in 1974 by T. G. Bergin, who also added a chapter on the post-1945 years), and J. H. Whitfield (1960, and in 1980 with a new chapter by J. R. Woodhouse for the period after 1922). An authoritative volume was edited by P. Brand and L. Pertile for Cambridge University Press (1996), which includes forty-four sections (of which three are devoted to opera), written by nineteen authors. [See also BIBLIOGRAPHIES OF ITALIAN LITERATURE; DICTIONARIES OF ITALIAN LITERATURE; LITERARY CRITICISM.]   [LL & GCL]

See G. Getto, *Storia delle storie letterarie* (1942).

Historiography

1. The Renaissance

The *Middle Ages wrote history principally in the form of *chronicles. *Humanist historiography, like humanist Latin prose, seems to spring fully formed from the pen of Leonardo *Bruni in the early 15th c. *Petrarch's interest in *Livy and other classical historians had re-established the importance of the discipline within *humanism, but his own historical works, *De viris illustribus* and *Rerum*

Historiography

memorandarum libri, were medieval in genre, even though they first adumbrated major problems such as irreconcilable sources and the ancient–medieval–modern periodization. Bruni's *Historiae florentini populi libri XII* (*c*.1444) combined this cult of historiography with the local patriotism that had produced the earlier chronicles, setting a new standard for future histories of Italian cities. Charting the history of *Florence *ab urbe condita* ('from the city's foundation'), the work was modelled largely on Livy, notably in its use of Latin, its concentration on one city's history, its chronological order, its division into books, and the use of imagined speeches (though in Bruni the speeches were often based on archival documents).

The main achievements of this kind of historiography included a critical attitude to predecessors, the use of archive sources, and an insistence on natural causes rather than the divine providence often invoked in chronicles. Amongst its limitations were the fact that the elegant classical Latin often disguised or ignored the most distinguishing features of the contemporary city-state: Bruni says little or nothing about the importance of the *guilds, or the shift in Florence from a guild-dominated republic to a de facto principate under Cosimo de' *Medici. The Brunian model was followed both in Florence (by Poggio *Bracciolini and Bartolomeo *Scala) and elsewhere (Simonetta for *Milan, *Sabellico and Pietro *Bembo for *Venice).

Bruni also first pioneered the more personal commentary on his own times (1440), a form modelled on Caesar's commentaries and popular with other humanists, most notably Enea Silvio *Piccolomini. The *biography, modelled on Plutarch, was another genre destined for longevity, again pioneered by Bruni with his lives of *Cicero, *Dante, and Petrarch (but see also Antonio *Manetti, Benedetto *Accolti, and *Vespasiano da Bisticci). Bruni also pioneered the account of a single conspiracy or war, modelled on Sallust's works (later exemplified by *Poliziano's account of the *Pazzi conspiracy of 1478, Bernardo *Rucellai's *De bello italico* on the French invasions of the 1490s). One other important genre was the broad history that embraced more than one city, like Flavio *Biondo's history of the decline of the Roman Empire (*c*.1450), a vast work in Livian decads that covered the millennium from the Sack of Rome (AD 410) to Biondo's own time.

Important as a progenitor of Gibbon's account, Biondo's work nevertheless revealed the long-term problems of Latin historiography: as he came closer to his own time he, like *Valla in his *Gesta Regis Ferdinandi*, had to use neologisms for modern inventions such as cannons or compasses, in order to avoid long periphrases. In the long run the more contemporary the history, the more convenient it would become to use the vernacular or *volgare* [see also QUESTIONE DELLA LINGUA]. Though Latin continued to be used in the 16th c. for important historical works by the likes of Paolo *Giovio and *Sigonio, it was the vernacular histories by *Machiavelli, and more importantly *Guicciardini, that made the more incisive contribution to the discipline—even though these two historians would never have written in the way they did about individual psychology and causality without the achievements of their humanist predecessors. Humanist Latin historiography ran out of steam by 1600: the very use of classical but rather ambiguous Latin was emblematic of its inability to reflect contemporary historical and cultural change. Even in the vernacular the discipline was hampered by the tendency to perceive historiography as literature or rhetoric, as well as by *Counter-Reformation *censorship; the texts and legacy of humanist historiography were only rediscovered in the early 18th c. by *Muratori. [MMcL]

See D. J. Wilcox, *The Development of Florentine Humanist Historiography in the Fifteenth Century* (1969); E. Cochrane, *Historians and Historiography in the Italian Renaissance* (1981).

2. After the Renaissance

The international prominence of *Machiavelli and *Guicciardini in the 16th c. was not matched until a number of 18th-c. Italian historians, writing under the influence of the French encyclopedists, gained wider recognition. The 'father of Italian history' was Lodovico Antonio *Muratori, who brought the social history of the medieval *communes into the scientific domain. Muratori's *Neapolitan contemporary, the elder Pietro *Giannone, wrote an anticlerical history of the Kingdom of Naples, translated into English in 1729, which brought him into conflict with the *Inquisition. The most original contribution to *Enlightenment historiography was undoubtedly that of Giambattista *Vico, whose *Principi di una scienza nuova* (1725) remains an influential historiographical speculation about the dialectic between consciousness and nature. Similarly resonant for later historians was the work of Vincenzo *Cuoco, whose participation in the Parthenopean Republic [see NAPOLEON AND THE FRENCH REVOLUTION] and consequent persecution and *exile led him to write the *Saggio storico sulla rivoluzione napoletana* (1801), in which he formulated the concept of a 'passive revolution' failing to meet the concrete needs of the people.

The travails of the *Risorgimento period fostered the federalist current in Italian historiography. Vincenzo *Gioberti was influential in arousing belief in an Italian national destiny under the aegis of the *papacy. Carlo *Cattaneo argued in various essays for a federation of democratic republics in Italy and published important collections of documents on the wars of 1848–9 during his self-imposed exile in Switzerland. His collaborator in this work was Giuseppe *Ferrari, whose *La federazione repubblicana* (1851) and *Histoire des révolutions d'Italie* (1856–8) provided intellectual cornerstones for the radical opposition in *liberal Italy.

The two most illustrious Italian historians of the period after *Unification were Francesco *De Sanctis and Benedetto *Croce, both of whom were committed to the post-Risorgimento settlement. De Sanctis, like others amongs his Neapolitan contemporaries, had eagerly assimilated Hegelian *idealism as a young man, and brought a Hegelian vision to bear on the evolution of Italian literature in his *Storia della letteratura italiana* (1870–1) and in his various essays on Italian history. His disciple, Croce, was a historian and historiographer as well as a *liberal philosopher; his *Storia d'Italia dal 1871 al 1915* (1928) and *Storia d'Europa nel secolo XIX* (1929) are classics of neo-Hegelian thought, which, in pointed opposition to *Fascist ideology, see history as the study of the idea of freedom becoming manifest in human activity. Fascist historiography, on the other hand, as articulated by *Gentile and *Volpe in particular, saw *Mussolini's revolution as the continuation and culmination of the dynamics of the Risorgimento.

The post-Fascist period in Italian historiography has been dominated by the debate about the origins and outcomes of Fascism. This set *Marxist and *marxisant* historians against those still faithful to the Crocean heritage and against those who found their models in Anglo-Saxon and German historical work. The most influential figure in the Marxist camp was Antonio *Gramsci, whose *Quaderni del carcere* included searching analyses of Italian history, in which he developed Cuoco's concept of the 'passive revolution', alongside elaborations of Leninist ideas about 'hegemony'. His most prominent legatees, such as Ernesto *De Martino, Ernesto Ragionieri, Guido Quazza, and Paolo

Spriano, contributed notably to the development of Italian social and economic history. The representatives of the liberal tradition, such as Gaetano *Salvemini, Federico Chabod, Rosario Romeo, and Nino *Valeri elaborated a powerfully anti-authoritarian critique within the same framework of debate. Somewhat apart, but more controversial, was the work of Renzo De Felice, whose multi-volume political *biography of Mussolini (1965–97) fuelled re-evaluation of the Fascist regime and ideology.

Postwar Italian historiography may lack the world resonance of the *Kulturstreit* in Germany and the social-scientific diversification of English-speaking historians, but it remains a vital component of the country's academic culture. [RAbs]

See D. D. Roberts, *Benedetto Croce and the Uses of Historicism* (1987).

History of the Italian Language. The language originated in medieval *Tuscan *dialect, and particularly *Florentine, which was until the late *Middle Ages fairly insignificant among the profoundly divergent Romance dialects of Italy. Lack of Italian political unity, compounded by the rise of many (sometimes linguistically prestigious) municipal centres, disfavoured the emergence of an 'Italian language', though the earliest surviving allusion to an 'Italian' language dates from the 15th c. The linguistic pre-eminence of Florentine in the 14th c. arose from its use by such writers as *Dante, *Boccaccio, and *Petrarch, but also from Tuscan (and particularly Florentine) commercial ascend-ance. The oldest surviving Tuscan text is a *Pisan naval account book (late 11th or early 12th c.), followed by part of a Florentine *banker's book (1211); from the mid-13th c. most Tuscan texts are from Florence, *Siena, and Arezzo, and by 1375 eight-ninths of vernacular texts in Italy were Tuscan. The economic and cultural rise of Tuscany was accompanied by an explosion of vernacular literacy, even in rural communities, and an increasingly negative evaluation of other dialects.

Only in the early 16th c., however, did it become widely accepted that some form of the indigenous spoken language of Italy (as opposed to Latin) should form the medium of written cultural discourse. The *Questione della lingua*, the debate about which form of the 'lingua volgare' should be employed for this purpose, was a complex one which continued well into the 19th c. The case for 14th-c. literary Florentine was successfully argued by the *Venetian Pietro *Bembo in his *Prose della*

Hoepli

volgar lingua (1525). The result was an enduring gulf between an already archaic and almost exclusively written cultural language which was ill-equipped for use in everyday discourse, and the speech of the Italians, only a minute proportion of whom were functionally literate and therefore able to know Italian. Even for the 1860s estimates of knowledge of Italian range between 2.5% and 12% of the population.

In the 19th c. Alessandro *Manzoni envisaged the *Questione della lingua* as no longer an exclusively literary question, but rather one regarding the best means of extending knowledge of Italian to the Italians at large. Manzoni proposed contemporary spoken Florentine as the basis of the national language. In his 1868 report on the unity of the language and the means of diffusing it, he proposed that Florentine should be taught in schools, and a modern Florentine *dictionary published. In response *Ascoli cogently argued that overturning the established linguistic tradition for a variety of Florentine, much of whose structure was unfamiliar to the majority of educated people, would simply reinforce the historical gulf. In the event, a major role in the popularization of 'traditional' literary Italian was played in the newly united Italy by such factors as migration, military service, the *educational system, and the mass media. But in consequence the once remote and relatively homogeneous literary language began to show systematic variation according to region, social group, topic, register, context of discourse, and so forth.

In the year 2000 the overwhelming majority of Italians understood and used Italian, although in ways often divergent from the literary standard language. Over 35 per cent of the population uses exclusively Italian, even at home (the domain of discourse historically most resistant to Italian). While the remainder continue to use dialect at least with some members of their families, the proportion employing Italian at home at least some of the time is well over 60 per cent. [See also DICTIONARIES; GRAMMARS; LINGUA CORTIGIANA; PURISM; VOLGARE AND VOLGARE ILLUSTRE.] [MM]

See T. De Mauro, *Storia linguistica dell'Italia unita* (1976); B. Migliorini and T. G. Griffith, *The Italian Language* (1984); F. Bruni, *L'italiano* (1987).

Hoepli, see PUBLISHING.

HOHENSTAUFEN. German dynasty from Swabia, which furnished a succession of Holy Roman Emperors, and played a major part in the affairs of medieval Italy. In the later 12th c. Frederick I Barbarossa (Emperor 1152–90) attempted repeatedly to subdue the Northern Italian *communes, but was eventually defeated at Legnano by the *Lega lombarda* (1176). His grandson *Frederick II, who was King of *Sicily from 1212 and Emperor from 1220 until his death in 1250, kept a splendid and cultured court in the South of Italy and Sicily. The dynasty came to an end with the invasion of Charles of *Anjou. Frederick's natural son, *Manfredi, was defeated and killed at Benevento (1266), and his grandson, Conradin, was defeated at Tagliacozzo (1268), and captured and beheaded in *Naples a few months later.

[PH]

Homosexuality. *Dante's association of sodomitical behaviour with political instability in the *Divine Comedy (Inf. 16)* established a strong model for the subsequent representation of homosexuality. Italian literature has shown less interest in the figure of the individual homosexual than in the potentially disruptive nature of the diffusion of alternative sexual practices. The accusation of sodomy in the *Middle Ages and *Renaissance was often used to discredit political opponents, and the same tactic was still found in the 20th c. Both *Fascists and anti-Fascists deployed a homophobic rhetoric to invalidate the political authority of their rivals. Conversely, there is also a tradition of celebrating homosexuality's radical potential.

The practice of sodomy was roundly condemned by the Catholic Church. All the same some homosexual love poetry was written in the manner of *poesia giocosa* in the 14th c., particularly in *Perugia, and a learned tradition of comic homosexual verse would continue with figures such as Camillo *Scroffa. Nor does religious injunction hang heavy over the sodomitical protagonists of *Boccaccio's and *Bandello's stories. *Aretino, in *Il marescalco* (1532), makes the homosexual stablemaster the butt of a malicious *beffa*, but the play can also be read as an extended and humorous critique of the institution of marriage. Homoerotic elements appear in the work of *Ariosto, Torquato *Tasso, and *Poliziano, although the poetry of *Michelangelo constitutes the most important homosexual document of the period. The fact that the poet's desire is expressed in terms of heterosexual lyric conventions, and is bound up with the politics of *patronage, makes it difficult to assess accurately what this form of love between men entailed. *Ficino's *Neoplatonic validation of male friendship is similarly difficult to interpret. Further complexities are manifest in the activities of the *Florentine *Academies, where networks of patronage and power are expressed through the language of homoeroticism, or vice versa through accusations of sodomy.

Homosexuality became increasingly associated with ancient Greece. In *Dei delitti e delle pene* (1764) Cesare *Beccaria argued that 'la greca libidine' was a clear sign of a decadent society. Luigi *Settembrini's *novella*, 'I neoplatonici', remained unpublished until 1977, in spite of being presented as a translation from the Greek. An element of homoeroticism runs through the work of *Marinetti and *D'Annunzio, but generally homosexuality in 20th-c. literature is used to signal a state of social and political corruption. This trend is clearest in the work of left-wing writers such as *Pratolini, *Morante, and Natalia *Ginzburg. Giorgio *Bassani's *Gli occhiali d'oro* (1958) offers a more sympathetic and complex representation of a middle-class homosexual forced to commit suicide because of Fascist society's disapproval. In this period homosexuality often involves the transgression of class boundaries, and in its more affirmative representations, the construction of an Arcadian myth of the Italian people. This emerges most notably in the poetry of Sandro *Penna, and more problematically in the work of *Pasolini, who follows his pastoral fantasy from Friuli, to *Rome, and then to the Third World. It is significant that Pasolini again associates homosexuality and political critique.

In the 1980s Italy has produced a number of writers who explore aspects of homosexuality in contemporary settings. Aldo *Busi and Pier Vittorio *Tondelli are the most significant. Neither accepts the label of 'gay writer', but in each there is a positive sense of homosexuality as a position of social dissidence, and on a literary level, as an innovative linguistic and narrative resource. On the other hand, whilst male homosexuality has a strong, if uneven presence, in Italian literature, lesbianism is notable for its almost complete absence. In *erotic literature, lesbianism appears only sporadically. Otherwise lesbians are represented again as agents of political corruption, as in Pratolini's *Cronache di poveri amanti* (1947). Singular examples of lesbian self-representation are Sibilla *Aleramo's *Il passaggio* (1919), Dacia *Maraini's *Lettere a Marina* (1981), and Pina Mandolfo's *Desiderio* (1995).   [DD]

See M. Mieli, *Elementi di critica omosessuale* (1977); F. Gnerre, *L'eroe negato* (1981).

HORACE. Quintus Horatius Flaccus (65–8 BC), one of the greatest Roman poets, whose skilful mastery of a rich variety of lyric forms is matched both by the wealth of his subject matter—ranging from politics to love, from poetry to ethics, and from everyday life to autobiography—and by the diversity of his tones, which shift from irony to didacticism and from affection to invective. During the *Middle Ages, the *Renaissance, and as far as the *Enlightenment, his influence in Italy and elsewhere was all-pervasive. He enjoyed a major reputation as a moralist (his *Satires* are the major source for *Ariosto's poems of the same name); and, thanks to his *Ars poetica*, he was considered the major authority on the composition of poetry. Although the 19th-c. *Romantics showed limited regard for him, his vital role in Italian literature was reaffirmed by *Pascoli in his Italian and Latin verse.   [ZB]

Horcynus Orca, see D'ARRIGO, STEFANO.

Household Treatises, or *libri domestici*, began as marginal notes on family matters made on 14th-c. *Florentine *merchants' ledgers. These developed into more detailed records of family life as the mercantile class grew in importance in Florence. In the 15th c. the two strands of business and family were integrated into single *ricordi* or *ricordanze*. Political and social comments were added, but only as many as were relevant to the family's economic situation. These *ricordi* were normally in vernacular prose, with little literary merit or aspirations. Among the fuller accounts are those of Donato Velluti, Giovanni *Morelli, Lapo Niccolini, and Bonaccorso Neri. [See also ALBERTI, LEON BATTISTA.]   [GPTW]

Humanism was the major intellectual movement of the Italian *Renaissance. Its programme was largely initiated by *Petrarch, who found in *Cicero's *Pro Archia*, a text he discovered in Liège in 1333, the key term *studia humanitatis*, referring to poetry and those subjects that have affinities with it, namely grammar, rhetoric, moral philosophy, and history—a list which is linked both etymologically and in substance to the modern concept of the humanities. In Renaissance Latin the term *humanista* designated one who taught these five subjects, in Latin and often in Greek, and it is on this term that the meaning of the word 'humanism', in its Renaissance sense, is based. Petrarch's and the humanists' preference for these subjects also implied a rejection of those associated with *Aristotelian *Scholasticism: logic, physics, and metaphysics.

In addition to this list of academic preferences, the humanist movement was distinguished by important new attitudes and concerns. The foremost of these was the search for lost classical texts, epitomized by Petrarch's find in Liège and his even more important discovery of Cicero's *Letters to Atticus* in the Verona cathedral library in 1345. Petrarch was followed by other famous humanist *manuscript hunters such as Poggio *Bracciolini. A second strand in the new mentality was the development of a critical sense, regarding the authenticity both of texts and of their readings: thus Petrarch was able (in *Seniles* 16.5) to prove, by examining the vocabulary of the document, that an Austrian tax privilege, purporting to date from Julius Caesar's time, was in fact a recent forgery. Using similar philological techniques, Lorenzo *Valla later showed that the so-called '*Donation of Constantine' could not have been written by the 4th-c. Emperor.

A third, related element was the emergence of a new historical awareness and avoidance of anachronism: Petrarch and his successors acquired a more and more accurate historical knowledge not just of the ancient world, but also of the medieval period, leading to a proliferation of *historiographical work from Leonardo *Bruni's to *Guicciardini's. Another innovation was the belief, proclaimed in many places by Petrarch, that Latin was superior to the vernacular and that works written in the latter, even those by *Dante, *Boccaccio, and Petrarch himself, were of questionable importance: it was this kind of attitude that led to the temporary decline of the vernacular in the century that followed Petrarch's death, the 'century without poetry', as Italian critics have called it. It also led to the belief that all worthwhile literature, whether in Latin or the vernacular, should be informed by *imitation of classical models.

In the 15th c. humanism mainly refined these attitudes, but there were two major developments. First a 'civic' strain of humanism emerged, mostly in *Florence, championing active participation in society over Petrarch's contemplative ideal, a tendency epitomized by the two influential Florentine chancellors in the early part of the century, *Salutati and Leonardo Bruni. Such a preference also involved a celebration both of Florentine republican ideology, emphasized during the wars with Giangaleazzo *Visconti, and of the vernacular

literary achievements of Dante, Petrarch, and Boccaccio. Secondly, the language and learning of ancient Greece was revived in the late 1390s, when Salutati invited *Chrysoloras to Florence; this eventually led to a series of important translations from Greek into Latin, the most influential of which was Marsilio *Ficino's version of the whole of Plato (1484), the chief source for Renaissance *Neoplatonism, and the major initiative associated with the Florentine *Platonic Academy.

Humanism had begun outside the *universities with figures such as Petrarch and Bruni; by the end of the 15th c. many of its values, notably the establishment of accurate primary texts, had become academic norms, with figures such as *Poliziano, Filippo *Beroaldo, and Domizio *Calderini. By the start of the 16th c., humanism was firmly established in schools and universities. Its values and attitudes now passed more firmly into the vernacular, and are a fundamental constituent of the works of High Renaissance authors such as *Machiavelli, Pietro *Bembo, and *Ariosto. [See also ACADEMIES; ANTIQUARIANISM; CLASSICAL SCHOLARSHIP; CLASSICISM; GREEK INFLUENCES; GREEK WRITING IN ITALY; LATIN INFLUENCES; LATIN POETRY IN ITALY; LATIN PROSE IN ITALY; LITERARY THEORY, 2; WOMEN WRITERS, 1.]   [MMcL]

See A. Rabil (ed.), *Renaissance Humanism: Foundations, Forms and Legacy* (1988); J. Kraye (ed.), *The Cambridge Companion to Renaissance Humanism* (1996).

Humour and Irony. According to Gérard Genette the ironic function can be placed between the ludic and the *satirical, and the humorous between the ludic and the serious [see PARODY AND PASTICHE]. Freud thought that a joke (*Witz*), is a contribution made to the comic by the unconscious; its root is in the region of the Id, bringing out the unpleasant latent substance hidden under an apparently innocuous surface, whereas humour is a contribution made to the comic through the agency of the Superego, exerting a more protective, parental function, suggesting that what lies behind a menacing aspect may after all not be as threatening as one feared. Irony may be derisive, and if it is bitter rather than humorous, it is called 'sarcasm'. But sarcasm, as a biting form of mockery, need not be ironic. Irony may be just humorous and not derisive. It is clear that humour and irony can exist quite independently. In irony it may be useful to distinguish two aspects, one related to the figure of speech, the other associated with a more pervading attitude which may not be specifically manifested in any individual passage.

As a figure of speech, irony is seen at work in statements whose intended meaning is the opposite of the literal one. Saying 'good' to mean 'bad' (or, less commonly, 'bad' to mean 'good') is a form of irony. Irony needs to be distinguished from other devices with which it can be associated, such as litotes (*meiosis* or *deminutio*, especially *antenantiosis*, i.e. the denial of the opposite), which can be employed as forms of ironic understatement (e.g. saying 'passable' or 'not bad' meaning 'good' or even 'excellent'). It is also separate from euphemism, i.e. the replacement of a forbidden term or notion by a more acceptable, sometimes opposite one (this is called 'antiphrasis' if the meaning-reversal is occasional, suggested by the context, as in 'blessed' for 'cursed'; and 'enantiosemy' if the expression is in itself ambiguous, as in the Italian 'incurvabile', used to designate something that can or cannot be bent). If irony is not perceived the statement may be considered misleading, or mistaken, or false. Medieval and *Renaissance treatises on rhetoric offer complex analyses of irony.

In a more general sense the notion of irony has been used to characterize the attitude of authors such as *Ariosto and *Manzoni. For Ariosto this involves a smiling, sceptical attitude towards his themes, and even, ambiguously, towards his *patrons. In Manzoni irony is not only a textual device (for instance, when we are informed that Spanish soldiers in Lecco 'teach modesty to the girls and women of the area'), but seems to introduce a more subtle disenchantment which makes his religious and political commitment less solemn and therefore more appealing and effective: see, for example, the mention of his 'twenty-five readers', or the reflection that, in order to explain certain aspects of his book, another one would be needed, but 'of books, one at a time is enough, if even that is not one too many'.

Quite separate from the rhetorical device is the notion of irony which suggests a conflictual attitude, a contradiction between expression and content, a difference of viewpoints, and, in a still more general way, the sense of estrangement which has been deemed to characterize the position of the artist in bourgeois society. 'Dramatic irony' has been used to refer to different assumptions which allow the audience of a play to interpret the words of a character differently from other characters. Generally the polyphonic aspect of the modern novel (analysed by Bakhtin) illustrates this notion of irony. Among modern authors for whose characterization the notion of irony has frequently been used are *Pirandello, *Svevo, *Gadda, and *Calvino. The notion of *umorismo, analysed as the 'sentimento del contrario' in a well-known essay by Pirandello (1908), and of *grottesco, have also been brought into play, in connection with that of irony, to define certain aspects of 20th-c. Italian culture.

[LL & GCL]

See G. Guglielmi, *L'ironia*, in A. Asor Rosa (ed.), *Letteratura italiana*, vol. v (1986); D. Knox, *Ironia: Medieval and Renaissance Ideas on Irony* (1989).

Hunting and Falconry. After conquering the *Sicilian *court of Emperor *Frederick II, himself the author of the unsurpassed treatise *De arte venandi cum avibus* (*c.*1236), hunting, and especially falconry, becomes a favourite subject for poetic expression. It inspires some remarkable metaphors and similes in *Dante's *Divine Comedy, where God is the falconer, and the heavenly vault the lure of human desire. Dante's contemporary *Folgore da Sangimignano devotes to the theme of hunting some of his best *sonnets, while *Boccaccio's first work of fiction is the *Caccia di Diana, a poem in *terza rima that mixes pagan imagery with Christian *allegory. In the late 15th c. Lorenzo de' *Medici composes *L'uccellagione di starne*, a tale of a partridge hunt in *ottava rima, better known as the *Caccia col falcone*; while his friend *Poliziano in the *Stanze per la giostra* (1471) portrays Lorenzo's brother, Giuliano, as a fierce hunter who, faced with the beauty of a silvan nymph, becomes her helpless prey. In the 16th c. the great variety of manuals and treatises on hunting is hardly matched by works of poetic quality. Although there still are men of letters, like *Erasmo da Valvasone (*La caccia* of 1591), and genuine poets, like Gabriello *Chiabrera, who write on the subject with gusto, the 'heroic' age of hunting seems all but over.

[LPer]

Hypnerotomachia Poliphili, see COLONNA, FRANCESCO.

IACOPO DA LENTINI, see GIACOMO DA LENTINI.

IACOPO DA LEONA (mid-13th c.). *Tuscan magistrate, notary, and poet in the Guittonian tradition. His eight surviving *sonnets are mediocre, but his skill is praised in *Guittone d'Arezzo's moving *canzone on his death, 'Comune perta fa comun dolore'. [JU]

IACOPO DA VARAGINE (Varazze) (1228/30–98). *Dominican friar, later bishop of *Genoa. His *Legenda aurea* ('Golden Readings'), containing *sermons on major feasts and the lives of saints, provided picturesque and exemplary material for artists and writers of *novelle up to the *Renaissance. It was translated into English by Caxton (1483). [PA]

IACOPO MOSTACCI (13th c.). Falconer to *Frederick II and *Manfredi, and a minor member of the *Sicilian School. As a young man he took part in a *tenzone with *Giacomo da Lentini and *Pier della Vigna about the nature of love, reproducing merely conventional motifs. [JU]

IACOPONE DA TODI (1236–1306). *Umbrian poet and mystic. Destined for the law, he is said to have undergone a conversion in 1268 when his wife died and was found to be wearing a hair-shirt beneath her fancy outer clothes. He lived as a 'bizzocone' (a kind of tertiary) before entering the *Franciscan order as a lay brother in 1278. He was part of the Spiritual wing of the order, led by Giovanni da Parma, Pier Gianni Olivi, and *Ubertino da Casale, this, therefore, providing him with the institutional context for his at times fiercely anarchic brand of Christianity. In 1294 he addressed a poem (74) to the newly elected *Celestine V exhorting him to maintain the ascetic ideal during his *papacy, and was subsequently part of a delega-

tion to the Pope seeking official recognition for the Spiritual cause. In 1297 he signed the Lunghezza manifesto declaring that *Boniface VIII, Celestine's successor, was no longer Pope and calling upon the cardinals to end the Church's decadence. Captured in the wake of Boniface's siege of Palestrina in 1298, he was tried and imprisoned. One poem (53) shows him accepting almost masochistically the squalor of prison, but in another (55) he begs Boniface to lift the excommunication now weighing on him. He greeted the prospect of death with righteous satisfaction (83), and was restored to freedom and the communion of the Church in 1303 by Benedict XI.

Two Latin tracts and the *Stabat mater* have been attributed to him. But he is known principally as a writer of some ninety-two *laudi—many more than we have by any other single individual in the 13th c. Marked throughout by a distinctive blend of irony, energy, and mysticism, they are moved in their more confessional moments by a sometimes self-annihilating yearning to live out at first hand the suffering of Christ. But anguished meditation on the perennial truths of death and decay give way from time to time to a satirical, even scabrous denunciation of the egotistic worldliness and hollow intellectualism of his contemporaries. The style and tone of his ostensibly primitive Umbrian *dialect is correspondingly popular and anti-intellectual, but the incantatory rhythms are carefully structured and an acquaintance with the high *lyric tradition of the *Sicilian School and the perhaps of the *dolce stil novo is evident just below the surface. [JT]

Laude, ed. F. Mancini (1977). See *Jacopone e il suo tempo* (1959); F. Suitner, *Jacopone da Todi* (1999).

Iconography. Directly or indirectly, all sorts of literary works can be connected with iconographic invention. *Dante's *Inferno* was plundered by late medieval artists for details of Hell, while *Petrarch's

Trionfi was not only extensively illustrated, but also encouraged the fabrication of *allegorical imagery. However, the iconographic handbook, a text intended as a guide to the proper depiction of themes and figures, was essentially a *Renaissance creation, connected to the revival of classical antiquity. Vincenzo *Cartari's *Imagini de i dei degli antichi*, published in *Venice in 1556 and republished with additions and illustrations in 1571, was the crucial work for mythology, exploiting a market prepared by the Italian *translation (1547) of *Boccaccio's *Genealogiae deorum*. Cesare *Ripa's *Iconologia* (1593), a dictionary of personifications from *Abundantia* to *Zelo*, was even more influential. Although addressed primarily to literary men—poets, academicians, and so on—it had its greatest effect on artists, especially after the publication of the expanded and illustrated edition of 1603 (and many others followed). Cartari and Ripa had an immediate impact on programmes for *festivals and on the publications associated with them, the accounts of pageantry that proliferated during the 16th and 17th c. These latter themselves often served as iconographic compendia. [See also EMBLEMS; VISUAL ARTS AND LITERATURE.] [EMcG]

Idealism. In modern Italian culture idealism has tended to mean not just the primacy of mind or spirit over matter, or the struggle of ideals or principles against *Machiavellianism, but rather the current of thought deriving from Friedrich Hegel, whose work became known in Italy in the early 19th c. [see GERMAN INFLUENCES]. Much as they drew imaginative nourishment from the poetry of *Foscolo and *Leopardi, activists and intellectuals took up Hegelian idealism in an attempt to provide the philosophical justification for Italian *Unification. Particularly notable were *Neapolitan Hegelians such as Bertrando and Silvio Spaventa and *De Sanctis. Hegelian thought was then developed in much greater depth by *Croce and *Gentile. Though they eventually arrived at opposed interpretations of Hegel's *Geist* (rendered in Italian as 'spirito'), they were united in rejecting *positivist methodology and traditional metaphysics. Like Hegel, they believed that human spirit had to be understood as the unfolding in history of a succession of ever higher stages of human freedom. For them one stage of this process was Italian Unification. But where Gentile's attempt to abolish Hegelian distinctions led him to *Fascism, Croce maintained his *liberal idealism as an oppositional stance throughout the Fascist years. The political

and cultural importance of idealism waned rapidly after Croce's death in 1952. [DS]

Idylls (Idilli), see LEOPARDI, GIACOMO; PASTORAL; PRETI, GIROLAMO.

ILICINO, BERNARDO, see PETRARCH COMMENTARIES.

ILLICA, LUIGI, see LIBRETTO; PUCCINI, GIACOMO.

Illuminismo, see ENLIGHTENMENT.

IMBRIANI, VITTORIO (1840–86). *Neapolitan writer. Exiled with his father, he later fought with *Garibaldi, though he then became a fervent monarchist. In his fiction, like *Dossi and *Faldella, he foreshadows *Gadda, with determinedly anti-*Manzonian prose and the grotesque social *satire of novels like *Dio ne scampi dagli Orsenigo* (1876). He is equally fierce in his extensive *literary criticism, especially *Fame usurpate* (1877). [PBarn]

Imitation. The question of literary imitation was one of the most debated topics in *literary theory in Italy between 1400 and 1600. Although *Dante's *De vulgari eloquentia* (2.6) showed some inkling of the classical concept of *imitatio*, it was *Petrarch who first articulated imitation theory in clear terms, notably in three important letters (*Familiares* 1.8, 22.2, 23.19). His main theme was the preference for *similitudo* over *identitas*, namely the production of texts which hinted at, but did not reproduce verbatim, classical models lying beneath the surface. The increased use of Latin in the age of *humanism, and particularly the works of Lorenzo *Valla, inculcated a greater sensitivity to classical vocabulary and syntax, and led eventually in the late 15th c. to the rise of *Ciceronianism (and an antagonistic 'Apuleianism').

The debate came to a head in three polemics of the late 15th and early 16th c., which saw three Ciceronians (Paolo *Cortesi, the younger Ermolao *Barbaro, and Pietro *Bembo) pitted against three eclectics (*Poliziano, Giovanni *Pico della Mirandola, and Giovanfrancesco *Pico). An analogous development in the vernacular prose of the time saw the brief emergence of a highly Latinate, 'Apuleian' vernacular in Francesco *Colonna's *Hypnerotomachia Poliphili* (1499). But the theoretical debate was settled in both languages by Bembo, who in the early 16th c. reasserted the superiority of Ciceronian Latin and, in his *Prose della volgar lingua* (1525), established Petrarch as the canonical model for vernacular poetry, and *Boccaccio for prose. [See also HISTORY OF THE ITALIAN LANGUAGE; QUESTIONE DELLA LINGUA.]   [MMcL]

IMMANUEL ROMANO (*c.*1265–*c.*1329), also known as Manoello Giudeo or Ebreo, is the only *Jewish author known to have written in an Italian vernacular during the *Middle Ages. Alongside a significant literary output in Hebrew, five Italian *sonnets survive, one of them part of an exchange of laments with *Bosone da Gubbio on the death of *Dante. The others include witty expressions of religious indifference that contrast with the devotional nature of his Hebrew writing. He also wrote a *frottola* on life at the *court of Cangrande *della Scala which makes remarkable use of onomatopoeia.   [SNB]

Immigrant Literature, that is, writing by immigrants, is a recent, inchoate phenomenon in Italy. The 1980s and early 1990s witnessed an unprecedented influx of predominantly North and West Africans into Italy, followed by East Europeans. So far, it is the former who have narrated their experiences, though their works are few in number and distributed by marginal publishers. Almost without exception, the texts are collaborations between an immigrant and a native Italian speaker, who translates, transcribes, or edits the original stories. Interventions of this sort influence their generic identity. For example, the involvement of the *journalist Oreste Pivetta in the writing of Pap Khouma's *Io venditore di elefanti* (1990) results in a chronicle with polemical overtones; and the sociologist Giuliano Carlini headed a project collecting the testimonies of immigrants in *Genoa for *La terra in faccia: gli immigrati raccontano* (1991), which became in effect a case study or an educational resource. What unites the diverse works is the story they recount, of travelling through Italy from south to north in a journey which progressively erodes the myth of Western opulence, which drew the immigrants away from their native countries, and reduces their existence to subsistence. The best are shifting, uncomfortable narratives which express the physical and psychological difficulties of immigration. As literary works, two of the most interesting are novels: *Immigrato*, by Mario Fortunato and Salah Methnani (1990), and Mohsen Melliti's first work, *Pantanella* (1993).   [JEB]

Impegno came to be widely used in modern Italian in the sense of 'political commitment' or 'engagement' in the years from 1945 to 1956, when there was a widespread belief that *intellectuals and writers should be actively engaged in the emancipation of the working masses. Questions related to the intellectual's social mission were discussed regularly in the pages of the best-known political and cultural journals of the period, such as *Belfagor*, *Società*, *Il *Ponte*, *La Nuova Europa*, and, most importantly, *Il *Politecnico*. The principal issue in the debate was the relation of culture and politics. *Impegno* thus became the concept at the base of the general struggle for the renewal of Italian society, influencing the formation of an ideological bloc drawn from different classes and social groups. With a definite articulation to the left, the culture of *impegno* prevailed in the *universities and in the reviews and journals of the time; it was disseminated by well-known literary intellectuals such as *Calvino, *Vittorini, and *Fortini; and its extensive appeal made it synonymous with culture itself. As a result of the ideological alliance, the battle for a culture that would be at once national and popular was not limited to strictly *Marxist domains, although writers affiliated with the *Communist Party played significant roles, particularly in debates on the relation of intellectual freedom and social commitment.

The most dogmatic inflection of *impegno* came in the form of Zhdanovism (named after the Stalinist cultural theorist Andrej A. Zhdanov), which pushed the principle of commitment to its extreme limits. To be 'progressive' meant embracing socialist *realism and the belief that all literature was the expression of a political philosophy. As a form of Communist cultural idealism, Zhdanovism was incapable of understanding the more negative and experimental narratives and *theatre of 20th-c. Marxist writers. However, numerous Communist and *Socialist intellectuals resisted the Communist Party's official definition of *impegno*, and, after the Hungarian revolution of 1956, many were forced by both circumstance and conviction to abandon the Party. At the end of the 1950s, across a wide spectrum of culture on the left, there began a strong re-evaluation of the notion of *impegno* in relation to the demands of modern bourgeois culture and orthodox Marxism. Two tendencies emerged: a revolutionary viewpoint, according to which commitment was directed toward the overthrow of the capitalist mode of production; and a reformist position, according to which the new technological rationality developed by capitalism could be put to the service of socially progressive ends.

Compared to the French concept of *engagement*, especially as developed by Jean-Paul Sartre, the culture of *impegno* embraced *populism uncritically, as *Asor Rosa argued in particular, and made no concentrated attempt to question the institution of culture and the class privileges of intellectual groups. Moreover, in contrast to Sartre's brand of commitment, *impegno* harboured a traditional, *humanist-intellectualist concept of culture, not significantly different from the one held by writers and thinkers of the previous generation who were committed to *Fascism. The majority of Italian intellectuals of the time had fought in the *Resistance, and for them culture was an unproblematic concept, essentially practical in nature, aimed, as Vittorini put it in the first editorial of *Il Politecnico*, to defend against and combat suffering. After 1956, without a new concept of culture to sustain it, the notion of *impegno* became, for large groups of Italian intellectuals, an obstacle that prevented them from going beyond their ideology to interrogate the institutional role played by the cultured classes. [RSD]

See A. Asor Rosa, *Intellettuali e classe operaia* (1973); S. Chemotti (ed.), *Gli intellettuali in trincea: politica e cultura negli intellettuali del dopoguerra* (1977).

IMPERIALE, GIAN VINCENZO (1582–1648). Hedonistic and elegant *Genoese nobleman, art collector, and man of letters. His literary works include the 'argomenti' of the 1604 Genoese edition of Torquato *Tasso's *Gerusalemme liberata*. The *Stato rustico* (1607) is a didactic poem in blank verse which describes an imaginary journey from Genoa to Greece, where the semi-autobiographical poet-shepherd Clizio is welcomed on Mount Helicon by Apollo and the Muses. The work caught the imagination of *Marino, who introduced the character of Clizio into canto 1 of the *Adone*. Imperiale also published a *canzoniere and *hagiographic verses on St Theresa. More interesting, for their documentary value, are two works, *Viaggi* and *Giornali*, which record for private consumption some of the trips he made across the length and breadth of Italy, during which he met leading men and women of the time. His work as an art connoisseur and collector has recently begun to attract critical attention in Italy. [PBD]

Imperio, L', see DE ROBERTO, FEDERICO.

Impresa. The *Renaissance vogue for *imprese*, combinations of word and image which expressed a personal meaning, developed, with much refinement and literary elaboration, from *chivalric and *courtly traditions of heraldry. The publication of Horapollo's 'key' to the Egyptian hieroglyphs in Venice in 1505 provided a *humanist impetus; and the genre was effectively codified in Paolo *Giovio's *Dialogo dell'imprese militari e amorose* (1555). *Imprese thereafter properly involved a non-human image of an intriguing kind, a short motto in Latin or a foreign vernacular, and an air of mystery. Giovio's treatise, and those which followed (by Girolamo *Ruscelli, for example), encouraged ingenuity in devising *imprese*, which, unlike *emblems, dealt not in moral generalities, but in private aims and messages. [See also ICONOGRAPHY.] [EMcG]

Improvised poetry occupied a distinctive place in educated Italian culture from the late 15th to the mid-19th c. The famous Renaissance improviser, Bernardo Accolti, known as the 'Unico aretino' (1458–1535), features in *Castiglione's *Cortegiano*. Especially in the 18th c., improvised poetry contributed to the myth that the Italians were gifted by nature with inspired spontaneity and an inherently musical language. There was (and to some extent still is) a popular tradition of extempore verse, mainly in *ottava rima* [see also FOLK AND POPULAR LITERATURE]. But Italy was unusual in cultivating and celebrating skilled improvisers working with the language, idiom and forms of the literary *lyric—though the borders with popular improvisation were uncertain, as they were with literary poetry. In 1725 the Sienese improviser Bernardino *Perfetti became the first poet since *Petrarch to receive the laurel crown on the Capitol in *Rome. The coronation signalled the arrival of learned improvisation in *academies and salons. By the turn of the century, improvisations were performed to a paying public in halls and theatres. Improvised poetry generally had an instrumental accompaniment and was in some measure 'sung'. As Saverio *Bettinelli describes in his *Dell'entusiasmo* (1769), the virtuoso professionals gave every sign of entering states of poetic ecstasy, delivering odes, narrative poems, *canzonette* [see VERSIFICATION], and *sonnets with a fluency and power that amazed their audiences, who suggested themes and very often rhymes and metres. Some improvisers such as Tommaso Sgricci (1788–1836) specialized in full-length verse *tragedies. Like the heroine of De Staël's *Corinne ou l'Italie* (1807), many of the most famous performers were women, such as Maria Maddalena *Morelli Fernandez (Corilla Olimpica) and Teresa *Bandettini. Though Perfetti and others actively discouraged transcription, a very large number of improvisations were recorded in some form. Later dismissed as frivolous or trivial, the whole phenomenon has recently begun to re-engage scholarly interest. [MPC]

See A. Di Ricco, '*L'inutile e meraviglioso mestiere':* poeti improvvisatori di fine Settecento* (1990).

Incogniti, Accademia degli. Founded in 1627 by Gian Francesco *Loredan, and lasting until his death in 1661, this academy drew to itself the main literary figures of *Venice and others from outside who were sympathetic to a *libertine programme and to Venice's political and cultural independence, such as Girolamo *Brusoni, Ferrante *Pallavicino, Angelico *Aprosio, Pietro *Michiel, and Francesco *Pona. The name 'Incogniti' alludes to members' use of subterfuges like paradox, *allegory, and irony in order to deflect censure.

The academy nurtured the political and cultural values of Traiano *Boccalini, as expressed in his *Ragguagli di Parnaso* (1612–15). Its libertinism was fortified by the *Aristotelian naturalism (linked with sceptical and *Epicurean currents) taught at the University of *Padua, which was attended by the Venetian upper classes. Its general philosophy was that nothing is knowable beyond the world of nature to which we have access by reason alone, that the soul is mortal, and that the pleasures of the senses and the satisfaction of sexual instincts are part of natural life. *Machiavelli was an influence through formulating a view of religion as a product of human history rather than divine revelation, exercised by an elite for the purpose of social control. Hardly surprisingly, the censors often placed *Incogniti* works on the *Index.

These works included *satirical prose and verse compositions imitating *pasquinate*, *biblical stories turned into *erotic adventure *romances, collections of *novelle* praising natural instincts and pleasure, historical narratives (often anti-Spanish or anti-*papal), and an array of often hybrid genres, mixing historical, allegorical, *epistolary, and picaresque elements. Continuing a practice set by *Aretino and the *poligrafi* in the mid-16th c., *Incogniti* authors wrote in a lively, contemporary idiom, usually bereft of classical baggage and archaic vocabulary. They wrote quickly on themes of contemporary interest for as wide a readership as possible. Many of their satirical writings were anonymous, with false dates and places of publication, and hence knowingly clandestine.

The academy's historical writings were inspired by Paolo *Sarpi, as well as Machiavelli and *Guicciardini, all of whom were viewed as exposing the workings of tyranny, and so as alerting readers to the abuses of power, both political and religious. [See also ACADEMIES.] [LAP]

See T. Gregory *et al.*, *Ricerche sulla letteratura libertina e letteratura clandestina nel Seicento* (1981).

Incunables, see PRINTING.

Index Librorum Prohibitorum. The official list of books which Catholics are forbidden to read or possess. The Church has always claimed a pastoral duty to review books and where necessary condemn them, but the first official indices in Italy were issued in the 16th c. by secular governments (Milan 1538, Lucca 1545, Siena 1548, Venice 1549). In 1542 the Congregation of the Holy Office was given responsibility for supervising publications, but it was only in 1559, after a number of false starts, that the first Roman Index was published. This list banned all books (even those not published) by certain Protestant authors and *printers; it also condemned the complete works of *Aretino and *Machiavelli, and *Boccaccio's *Decameron*. The revised Tridentine Index of 1564 included books judged immoral as well as *heretical (including unauthorized translations of the *Bible), and imposed a penalty of excommunication on those who read them. It did, however, allow for corrected editions of books to be published, and permitted the granting of licences to read prohibited books. In 1571 Pius V established a new Congregation to take responsibility for the Index, and subsequent versions incorporated old and new titles.

Initially, books were examined only after publication on receipt of a denunciation against them, and the lists were therefore never up to date. Furthermore, recent research suggests that the work of the Congregation of the Index was characterized by frequent disagreements and policy changes. In the 18th c. governments of various Italian states increasingly restricted the activities of clerical censors, and in 1897 Leo XIII entrusted responsibility for the control of literature more fully to diocesan bishops. In 1917 the duties of the Congregation of the Index were finally transferred back to the Holy

Office. The last Index was published in 1948, and in 1966 the decision was taken not to publish any further lists. The Index now has no legally binding authority, and the new code of canon law issued in 1983 makes no reference to it. The archives of the Index were opened to scholars in 1998. [See also CENSORSHIP; COUNTER-REFORMATION; INQUISITION; PAPACY AND THE CATHOLIC CHURCH.]
[NSD]

INDIA, FRANCESCO (16th–17th c.). Veronese doctor who wrote treatises on scientific, literary, and philosophical subjects. These include *Discorsi della bellezza e della grazia* (1597), another *discorso* on *Della Casa's *sonnet 'Questa vita mortal' (1602), and *L'heroe overo della virtù heroica* (1591), which defines a hero as anybody who has excelled in his own field, and gives as an example another Veronese doctor, Marc'Antonio Della Torre. [FC]

Indifferenti, Gli (1929), *Moravia's debut *novel, marked him as one of the most promising writers of his generation. It is a psychological study of the moral apathy of a middle-class family. The mother, Mariagrazia, her daughter, Carla, and her son, Michele, all passively accept the selfish scheming of Mariagrazia's lover, Leo. The novel, because of its critical portrait of middle-class Italy, has been considered inherently anti-*Fascist. [GUB]

Indovinello veronese. A fourteen-word riddle, probably from late 8th-c. Verona, which seems to represent fingers writing in black with a quill on parchment as oxen pulling a white ploughshare and sowing black seed. It is generally considered the earliest Italo-Romance document, though it has been argued that the language is Latin influenced (deliberately?) by the vernacular. A recent analysis of the opening word ('Se'), not as a Latin reflexive pronoun, but as a characteristically Romance presentative marker, strengthens the riddle's claim to be the earliest Italo-Romance document. [MM]

Inferno. The first of the three *cantiche* of *Dante's *Divine Comedy. Dante emerges from a dark wood and meets the shade of *Virgil, who guides him down through Hell. This is imagined as a funnel-shaped pit broad at the top but narrowing to the centre of the earth directly below Jerusalem. After a vestibule containing the souls of the moral cowards (*vili*), the pit is divided into nine circles each given over to a particular class of sin: (1) Limbo (virtuous

pagans and unbaptized children, all guilty of original sin); (2) lustful; (3) gluttons; (4) misers and spendthrifts; (5) wrathful; (6) heretics (specifically those who do not believe in the immortality of the soul); (7) violent, subdivided in three sub-circles (*gironi*), containing (i) the violent against others and their property, (ii) the violent against themselves (suicides) and their property (squanderers), and (iii) the violent against God (blasphemers) and his property, nature (sodomites and usurers); (8) fraudulent, divided in the ten sub-circles (*bolge*) of *Malebolge* into (i) panders and seducers, (ii) flatterers, (iii) simoniacs (corrupt clergy), (iv) sorcerers and astrologers, (v) *barattieri* (corrupt holders of public office), (vi) hypocrites, (vii) thieves, (viii) false counsellors, (ix) sowers of discord, (x) falsifiers; (9) traitors, divided into four groups—traitors against their family, country, guests, and lords.

Dante and Virgil meet and converse with the souls of numerous sinners as they descend. All are suffering what appear as physical punishments, each of which is appropriate to the crime committed—the principle of *contrapasso*. The further down the sin, the worse it is and the worse the punishment, though the moral issues that are raised are often by no means clear-cut, most famously in the cases of *Francesca da Rimini and *Ulysses. The bottom-most and basest sinner is Lucifer, a frozen three-headed monster, chewing forever on the souls of Judas, Brutus, and Cassius. Dante and Virgil climb up Lucifer and, via a narrow passage, emerge on the other side of the globe on the shore of Mount Purgatory. [PH]

Ingannati, Gli (1532) was the first influential *comedy of the Accademia degli *Intronati. Lelia serves her beloved Flamminio as a pageboy, and attracts the attentions of his current love-object, Isabella. Lelia's twin brother then appears to complicate the plot, which ends in *carnival solutions much bawdier than those of Shakespeare's *Twelfth Night* (a clear if indirect derivative). [RAA]

INGEGNERI, ANGELO (1550–after 1613) was a *Venetian man of letters and *academician. He is most remembered as an organizer of *theatre spectacle. On the strength of his experience he wrote a treatise, *Della poesia rappresentativa*, on literature for performance (1598), which is an important source of information on both dramaturgical theory and stage practice. [See also LITERARY THEORY, 2.] [RAA]

INGENHEIM, LUCIANO VON, see ZUCCOLI, LUCIANO.

INGHILFREDI (13th c.). The author of seven *canzoni* of markedly Provençal inspiration. He was originally thought to be Sicilian because some of his poems are included in manuscripts containing poetry of the *Sicilian School. His real origins may be in Lucca. [JU]

Inni sacri. Sequence of five poems by *Manzoni, celebrating the major events of the Catholic calendar: the Resurrection, Mary's name-day, Christmas, the Passion, and Pentecost. Composed between 1812 and 1822, they were the first poems Manzoni wrote after embracing Christianity, and mark his repudiation of *neoclassical poetry. [VRJ]

Innocente, L', see D'ANNUNZIO, GABRIELE.

INNOCENT III (Lotario dei Conti di Segni) (1160–1216) wrote *De miseria humane conditionis* (1195) on the sufferings of life and the inevitability of death. As Pope (1198–1216), he launched the *Crusade against the Albigensian heretics in France (1208) and encouraged the foundation of the *Franciscan and *Dominican orders. [PA]

Innominato, L'. Powerful and wicked lord in *Manzoni's *Promessi sposi*, who undergoes a religious conversion.

Inquisition, a body of ecclesiastical tribunals using inquisitorial procedures, first established in the 13th c. to prosecute Catholics suspected of *heresy and other serious religious offences. In 1542 they were supplemented by the Sacred Congregation of the Roman and Universal Inquisition or Holy Office, created by Pope Paul III to counter the threat of Protestantism. The Congregation gradually established control over the existing Italian tribunals (except those in *Sicily and *Sardinia, subject to the *Spanish Inquisition). The Inquisition was not usually concerned with literary works, though a number of Italian writers were investigated for their beliefs, and some (most notably Giordano *Bruno) were executed.

The impact of the Inquisition in Italy remains a matter of debate, though it undoubtedly exercised a deterrent effect on writers from the mid-16th c. The Italian tribunals were suppressed in the 18th c.,

but the Congregation survived, and in 1965 was renamed the Congregation for the Doctrine of the Faith. In recent years, Pope John Paul II has sought to distance the Church from elements in the history of the Inquisition (the condemnation of *Galileo was recognized as an error in 1992, for example). In 1998, the Archives of the Congregation in *Rome were formally opened to scholars. [See also CENSORSHIP; COUNTER-REFORMATION; INDEX LIBRORUM PROHIBITORUM; PAPACY AND THE CATHOLIC CHURCH, 1.] [NSD]

INSANA, JOLANDA (1937–). Poet born in Messina who lives and works in *Rome. She established her name and voice with her second collection, *Fendenti fonici* (1982)—brief poems of considerable emotional and linguistic violence, often mixing Latin, *Sicilian, and older poetic Italian. Later collections, notably *L'occhio dormiente* (1997), draw on images of *peasant life, but also look outwards to Arab culture in a way unusual in Italian poetry. She has *translated Sappho, and *Andreas Capellanus' *De amore*. [PH]

Intellectuals, see GRAMSCI, ANTONIO; IMPEGNO; LETTERATO.

Intelligenza, L' (early 14th c.). Anonymous didactic poem in 309 nine-line stanzas, whose detailed description of a lady's features, dress, jewellery, and palace is an *allegory of the intellect's role in the human soul, whilst the various parts of the palace correspond to the organs of the body. The poem draws on Italian and Provençal lyric practice, as well as on French *romances, including the *Roman de la rose*, and on Latin *encyclopedias. [JU]

INTERLANDI, TELESIO (1894–1965). Leading *Fascist *journalist and writer. He edited the daily *Il Tevere*, the review *Il *Quadrivio* (1933–43), and the *La Difesa della razza*, a fortnightly paper he founded in 1938, the purpose of which was to establish a 'scientific' basis for the regime's anti-Semitic propaganda [see JEWS AND JUDAISM]. He *translated works by Chekhov and Andreev, and, with Corrado *Pavolini, co-authored a play, *La croce del sud* (1927). He published collections of his articles as *I nostri amici inglesi* (1935), *La condizione dell'arte* (1940), and *Pane bigio* (1972). [RSD]

Intermedi, see MUSIC.

Intronati, Accademia degli. The educated aristocrats of *Siena formed one of the first literary and cultural clubs in Italy around 1525; and the Academy of the 'Deaf and Daft' (as 'Intronati' might be translated) became an influential model—both in its constitution, with its self-deprecating nicknames and rituals, and in its production of dramatic literature and of social games. Their anonymous play *Gli *ingannati* (1532) was a turning point in comic dramaturgy, in its use of *romance elements alongside the more scurrilous material of earlier *humanistic *comedy, and in its cautious but unmistakable foregrounding of female characters alongside the male ones. *Alessandro* and *L'amor costante* were attributed to Alessandro *Piccolomini, who was certainly a coordinating figure; but it is probable that all Intronati dramaturgy was the result of teamwork. This is also true of *La pellegrina*, ostensibly by Girolamo Bargagli, composed in the 1560s but finally produced for the very prestigious *Florentine wedding festivities of 1589.

The Intronati were also renowned for their 'Sienese evenings' (*veglie senesi*), in which cultured word-games were a focus for interchange between men and women. Girolamo Bargagli's *dialogue about games, *Dialogo de' giuochi* (1572), and his brother Scipione *Bargagli's *Trattenimenti* ('Pastimes') (1587), were attempts to set some of these down for posterity. The Intronati and their rivals, the *Congrega dei rozzi, survive as institutions in Siena to this day, each with its own *theatre. [See also ACADEMIES.] [RAA]

INVERNIZIO, CAROLINA (1851–1916). Prolific *novelist who was immensely popular in her lifetime. She addressed herself largely to a female readership with melodramatic tales of crime and passion, many of them first serialized in newspapers, with titles such as *Il bacio di una morta* (1889) and *I drammi dell'adulterio* (1898). She herself was born near Pavia into a well-off family and later lived a placid bourgeois existence as an officer's wife in *Florence. Much denigrated by critics after her death as trivial *romanzi d'appendice*, her novels have been recently reassessed as both culturally and sociologically significant. [UJF]

Investiganti, Accademia degli. Established in *Naples in 1650 by the physician Tommaso Cornelio, this was one of the longest-lived of the early Italian scientific *academies, continuing (with various interruptions) until 1737. Its most important activities date from the first forty years of its existence. It was more notable for introducing foreign ideas—notably those of Pierre Gassendi—than original research, but its anti-*Aristotelian and strongly experimental approach to natural philosophy served as the main focus of a group of Southern doctors and philosophers, who described themselves as the 'neoterici' (i.e. supporters of new scientific and medical ideas). It also had an interest in literary matters, criticizing *concettismo and championing a return to the purity of *Petrarch. [MPS]

INVREA, GASPARE, see ZENA, REMIGIO.

Io cerco moglie!, see PANZINI, ALFREDO.

IRNERIUS, see LAW; TWELFTH-CENTURY RENAISSANCE.

Irony, see HUMOUR AND IRONY.

Irredentism (*irredentismo*). The movement to bring about the integration in the newly unified Italy of those borderline territories which had been omitted from the *Unification settlement. The 'unredeemed' lands were identified particularly with *Trieste, Venezia Giulia, and the Istrian peninsula. Irredentism was a major factor in Italy's decision to join in *World War I in 1915. It was the failure to 'redeem' Istria at the end of the war which led to *D'Annunzio's Fiume expedition. [PH]

ISELLA, DANTE, see STRUMENTI CRITICI.

Isola di Arturo, L', see MORANTE, ELSA.

Istoria di Altobello e di re troiano suo fratello. A narrative poem which introduces a new campaign and numerous extra episodes into the framework of the Carolingian *romances. First printed in 1476, it was one of several such poems which provided material for *Boiardo's *Orlando Innamorato*. [RMD]

Istorie fiorentine, see MACHIAVELLI, NICCOLÒ.

Italia letteraria, see FIERA LETTERARIA, LA; PERIODICALS, I.

Italia liberata da' Goti, see TRISSINO, GIANGIORGIO.

Italian Book and Manuscript Collections outside Italy

Italian Book and Manuscript Collections outside Italy. The most important are in Great Britain, Germany, and the USA. In London the British Library has some 4,500 Italian incunabula, some 15,000 16th-c., some 20,000 17th-c., and probably an even larger number of 18th-c. printed books. In the Department of Printed Books the most important single Italian collection is probably that donated in 1825 by Sir Richard Colt Hoare (1758–1838), consisting of several hundred works on Italian local history. There can scarcely be an Italian town not represented here, with books printed mostly in the 17th and 18th c. The British Library also has an impressive number of printed Italian city statutes and owns many very valuable Italian *manuscripts, although no named collection. University College London holds the Barlow *Dante Library, which includes letters from other eminent Dantists and was bequeathed by Henry Clark Barlow (1806–76).

The Bodleian Library acquired in 1817 about 300 Italian manuscripts collected by the *Jesuit Matteo Luigi Canonici (1727–1805). An elaborate catalogue of this collection (published only in 1864) was compiled by Count Alessandro Mortara, a *Tuscan who lived for ten years in Oxford, dying in *Florence in 1855. In 1852 the Bodleian also acquired his library of some 1,400 volumes. Cambridge University Library received the Acton Collection from Lord Morley in 1903. Originally amounting to some 59,000 volumes, it was assembled at Aldenham Hall, Shropshire, by John, first Baron Acton (1834–1902), who became regius professor of modern history at Cambridge in 1895. It includes a number of important works of Italian history which are not in the British Library. The Bute collection was acquired by the University Library in 1949. There are some 900 volumes in all, containing over 1,500 items, mainly plays: about 650 printed before 1600, 588 in the 17th c., and about 300 printed after 1700. The origin of the collection is obscure, but the books may have been bought by John Stuart, first Marquess of Bute (1744–1814), who from 1779 to 1783 was Envoy to *Turin. The John Rylands University Library in Manchester has one of the best collections of Aldine editions in the world [see MANUZIO, ALDO]. The university library has also the largely 16th-c. collection of Richard Copley Christie (1830–1901), and the bequest of Professor Walter Llewellyn Bullock (1890–1944). This collection of over 5,000 books and several hundred pamphlets includes over 2,600 volumes printed between 1500

and c.1625 and important critical editions of Dante, *Petrarch, *Boccaccio, *Ariosto, and Torquato *Tasso, as well as many works on the *questione della lingua.

In *Germany the two most important centres for early Italian books are probably Stuttgart and Erlangen University Library, followed by Munich and Wolfenbüttel. The Württembergische Landesbibliothek in Stuttgart has a rich collection of *Savonarola, and Erlangen has many popular works of vernacular literature, a number of them unique copies. In *Spain the Colombina Library, Seville, has recently published a catalogue of its Italian-language books, many of which were acquired in various European cities by Fernando Colón, the natural son of Christopher Columbus. In Russia the Saltykov-Shchedrin Public Library in St Petersburg now contains some 900 Aldines, which makes it compare very favourably with the great collections of Britain and America.

In the USA certain libraries are rich in Italian plays—the Folger Shakespeare Library in Washington, DC; the University Library at Chicago (Joseph G. Regenstein Library); and the University of Illinois Library at Urbana. Cornell University holds the large collections of Dante and of Petrarch formed by Willard Fiske (1831–1904). The Newberry Library, Chicago, has a splendid collection of Italian printed books from the 15th to the 17th c. An important collection of works printed by Manuzio and his heirs is the Ahmanson-Murphy collection at the University of California, Los Angeles. There are important Dante collections in Harvard University Library and Boston Public Library. [See also ELECTRONIC RESOURCES FOR ITALIAN STUDIES; LIBRARIES.] [DER]

Italian Influences on English Literature, see RECEPTION OF ITALIAN LITERATURE IN BRITAIN.

Italian Language, see HISTORY OF THE ITALIAN LANGUAGE; LITERACY; QUESTIONE DELLA LINGUA; SPOKEN LANGUAGE IN LITERATURE.

Italiano, L' (1926–42). Founded in *Bologna by Leo *Longanesi as a *satirical *Fascist weekly continuing the *strapaese manner of Il *Selvaggio, it published articles by quite diverse writers, who included *Maccari, *Moravia, *Soffici, and *Ungaretti. It was a forum for criticism of bourgeois conformity within Fascism and contributed to a gradual erosion of intellectual support for *Mussolini through the ironic and analytical writing it promoted. It thus provided younger Fascists with the beginnings of what would become more radical criticism of the regime during *World War II. [DCH]

Italian Writers in Australia. Until relatively recently, writing in Italian about Australia was sparse and not especially literary. The Spanish missionary Rudesindo Salvado wrote some engaging *Memorie storiche* (1851) of his experiences in Western Australia; and the *journalist Ferdinando Gagliardi provided an observant picture of Melbourne and colonial social life in his *Australia: lettere alla Gazzetta d'Italia* (1881). But an eccentric patriot, Raffaello Carboni, did compose *Gilburnia*, a melodramatic narrative poem on the clash between whites and blacks, published privately in *Rome in 1872. Gino Nibbi writes of early 20th-c. migrant experience in the short stories of *Il volto degli emigranti* (1937), though he allows whimsical dissatisfaction with the perceived values of Australian society to dominate the stories. His *Cocktails d'Australia* (1965) is less dismissive.

Large-scale Italian immigration after *World War II found literary representation (though not for some years) in novels such as Rosa Cappiello's well-received *Paese fortunato* (1981), which emphasizes violent emotion and sexuality, and the less spectacular collection of short stories *Australia cane* (1971) by Pino Bosi. Vincenzo Papandrea's *La quercia grande* (1996) and Enoe Di Stefano's *L'avventura australiana* (1996) are more autobiographical. The migrant experience has also been expressed in the subdued verse of Luigi Strano, and in more emotive vein by Mariano Coreno, who, like Mary Ceravolo and Sergio Ubaldi, has published verse in both Italian and English. Lino Concas has written poetry with a more forceful and metaphysical character. While *theatre performance has thrived, few texts have been published, one example being *La luna e la ginestra* (1988) of Antonio Comin. In Melbourne, Nino Randazzo polemically rebutted *Mafia allegations against the Italian community in his *Victoria Market* (1992). [See also EMIGRATION.] [ADP]

See G. Rando, 'Narrating the Migration Experience', in S. Casles, C. Alcorso, G. Rando, and E. Vasta (eds.), *Australia's Italians: Culture and Community in a Changing Society* (1992).

Italian Writers in Switzerland. The complex linguistic and cultural reality of Italian-speaking Switzerland, primarily Canton Ticino and Canton

Grigioni, has long included a literary dialogue with Italy proper, as well as an autonomous tradition of Italian writing. Literary magazines go back to the *Piccola rivista ticinese*, founded by Francesco *Chiesa in Lugano (1896–1901), and *Pagine libere* (1906–12), whilst *Bloc notes, Idra*, and *L'Almanacco* are amongst the most interesting of current poetry magazines in Italian.

The earliest Swiss literature in Italian consists of four *sonnets dated 1536 and attributed to Giovanni Della Torre, or Torriani (1512–71). The first recorded poets are Paganino Gaudenzio (1595–1649), from the Grigioni, who lived and worked in *Florence, and the priest Giacomo Genora (?1659–1731) who wrote Latin hexameters in praise of rustic culinary arts. The 18th c. boasts equally few names of note—Giuseppe Fossati (1759–1811), from the Ticino, a minor poet but an excellent *translator, Gian Menico Cetti (1780–1817), and Diego Girolamo Maderni (d.1761). More interesting are slightly later *historians and pedagogic writers, such as Francesco *Soave (1743–1806), who became *Manzoni's tutor and wrote a *Galateo o trattato elementare dei doveri dell'uomo*, and Girolamo Ruggia, the author of a long poem in the Manzonian manner, *Genio eminente di Napoleone*. The influence of northern *Romanticism produced interesting writers with naturalist interests, such as Luigi Lavizzari (1815–75), author of *Escursioni nel Cantone Ticino*, and Silvio Calloni (1850–1931), whose *Noterelle entomologiche* (1885) combine literary and scientific prose.

The 20th c. has been much richer. Francesco Chiesa (1871–1973) first became well known for his *Bildungsroman, Tempo di marzo* (1925); his major achievement in poetry is to be found in the late *Sonetti di San Silvestro* (1971). Almost as popular was Giuseppe Zoppi (1896–1952), whose poetry and fiction grew out of his first success, *Il libro dell'alpe* (1922), a collection of short prose pieces celebrating Alpine life. Currently the best-known writer in Italian is Grytzko Mascioni (1936–), who has published various novels, notably *La notte di Apollo* (1990), while his poems (a collected edition appeared in 1984) combine erudition and *expressionism. Fleur Jaeggy (1940–), who has now moved from Lugano to *Milan, returns to her experiences in a Swiss boarding school in *I beati anni del castigo* (1989), though she shows a wider range in other novels.

Three modern poets are particularly worthy of note. From his first collection *Né bianco né viola*

Italian Writers in the United States

(1944), Giorgio Orelli (1921–), from the Ticino, has followed an un-*hermetic itinerary which has all the same absorbed the lessons of his major Italian contemporaries, in particular *Montale. *Sinopie* (1977) moves towards narrative and stylistic freedom, and *Spiracoli* (1989) takes the further step towards poetic prose. Fabio Pusterla (1957–), who has been publishing since the 1980s and who has also translated Philippe Jaccottet, is a more restrained explorer of what imaginative residues he can find in a reduced and painful present. Dubravko Pusek, born in Croatia in 1956, came to the Ticino as a young boy and has published numerous collections of poetry, with at their core a sense of the resistance of the world to comprehension and at the same time a conviction of the value of poetic form. He has also translated extensively from Croatian.

Neutrality and tolerance made Italian Switzerland a haven for political *exiles from the 19th c. onwards. During the *Risorgimento Carlo *Cattaneo was published by the Edizioni Capolago, which was established in the 1850s in Lugano. So too were Carlo and Nello Rosselli [see GIUSTIZIA E LIBERTÀ] when the firm was revived in the 1930s. *Fontamara* was written during *Silone's exile in Zurich. 'Finisterre', the first section of what was to become Montale's *Bufera e altro*, was published in Lugano in 1943, and *Saba's *Ultime cose* in 1944.　　[ET]

　　See G. Orelli, *Svizzera italiana* (1986); G. Bonalumi, R. Martinoni, and P. V. Mengaldo (eds.), *Cento anni di poesia nella Svizzera italiana* (1997).

Italian Writers in the United States. Writing in Italian in the USA began with the waves of immigrants of the late 19th c. and was conditioned by the status and culture of its practitioners until at least the end of *World War II. Until then, most focused on their immediate experiences of abandoning Italy and the difficulties of adapting to life in America. Generally not highly literate, they faced in acute form problems of language plurality, having to choose between or combine standard Italian usage, *dialect usage (the spoken norm for the vast majority of immigrants), and the dominant American English, which itself had many varieties and was usually imperfectly mastered by first-generation immigrants. The great majority of those immigrants who wrote in Italian remained inevitably on the literary margins. They include Bernardo Ciambelli, whose *I misteri di Mulberry* (1893) is one of the first documented Italian texts written in the United States, and the better-known Emanuele Carnevali (1897–1944) and Arturo Giovannitti (1884–1959), both of whom wrote poetry on their experiences as immigrants in both Italian and English.

Figures of this type are obviously quite different from the Italian writers who came for long or short periods to America during the first half of the century. Emilio *Cecchi's *America amara* (1939) typifies the horror and fascination that America awoke in many Italian intellectuals of the 1930s. [See also AMERICAN INFLUENCES.] Other figures who spent longer there, sometimes to escape *Fascism, like G. A. *Borgese or Giuseppe *Prezzolini, still looked primarily to Italy and were very rarely assimilated to Anglophone literary culture. But after World War II a new type of Italo-American immigrant writer emerges, of whom Joseph Tusiani (1922–) is an early example. Already educated to high-school or university level in Italy, these writers often become scholars and critics of Italian literature in American universities, and prove able, particularly in poetry, to draw on both Italian and Anglophone traditions. Their names include Giovanni Cecchetti, Pier Maria *Pasinetti, Franco Ferrucci, Giose Rimanelli, Paolo Valesio, Peter Carravetta, and many others.

Perhaps not surprisingly, the most successful writers of Italian origin born in the USA have opted to write in English, even if, like Mario Puzo, they have written on forms of the Italian experience of America. Younger poets, like Dana Gioia and Daniela Gioseffi, are to all intents and purposes American poets, but with an intense interest in the Italian tradition. [See also EMIGRATION.]　　[AJT]

　　See J.-J. Marchand, *La letteratura dell'emigrazione* (1991); P. A. Giordano and A. J. Tamburri (eds.), *Beyond the Margin: Readings in Italian Americana* (1998).

J

JACOBBI, RUGGERO (1920–81). Born in *Venice, and already active as a critic and director before *World War II, he spent the years 1946–60 in Brazil working in *cinema, *theatre, and *television. On his return he taught Brazilian and then Italian literature at *Rome University. His notes on modern Italian literature were edited as *L'avventura del Novecento* (1981). [PH]

Jacobinism acquired its name from the radical democratic club established in the St Jacques monastery in Paris in 1789. It developed in Italy as it became clear that the cooperation between reformers and enlightened sovereigns, typical of the *Enlightenment period, was no longer possible after the French Revolution. Inspired by a radical ideology of democracy and equality, largely modelled on the French constitution of 1793, Italian Jacobins hailed the French armies that began occupying Italy in 1796 as liberators, and took part enthusiastically in the republics that were set up under French protection all over Italy. They believed in the need to free the people from tyranny and in universal *education, with the aim of overcoming ignorance and popular antagonism to their cause. They set up debating clubs, which saw some participation from women, and produced journals and ideologically driven *theatrical pieces. One distinguished Jacobin poet was Edoardo *Calvo. In 1799 all Italian Jacobin republics were defeated, the old regimes restored, and many Jacobins forced into *exile. Some were executed, including the *Neapolitan *journalist Eleonora *Fonseca Pimentel. [See also NAPOLEON AND THE FRENCH REVOLUTION.] [VRJ]

JAEGGY, FLEUR, see ITALIAN WRITERS IN SWITZERLAND.

JAHIER, PIERO (1884–1966). Poet and *novelist. Born into a *Genoese *Waldensian family, and always religiously inspired, he worked for much of his life for the railways, partly because his opposition to *Fascism allowed him few other openings. As a young man he wrote extensively for the *Florentine review, *La *Voce*, becoming its editor from 1911 to 1913. He also wrote for *Lacerba* and *Riviera ligure*. He was a volunteer in *World War I and edited *L'Astico* (1918), the trench newspaper. His *Resultanze in merito alla vita e al carattere di Gino Bianchi* (1915) satirizes Italian bureaucracy, but he is best known for the lyrically autobiographical *Con me e con gli alpini* (1920). [ES]

Jansenism questioned the doctrines of the Council of Trent on divine grace and human free will [see COUNTER-REFORMATION]. It took its name from Cornelius Jansen, author of *Augustinus* (1640). The Jansenists were accused of coming close to the Calvinists' denial of free will. The dispute became entangled with political issues, especially in France, where the Jansenists became identified with the convent of Port-Royal. Three years after the *papal condemnation of their doctrines, Pascal's *Lettres provinciales* (1656) upheld the superiority of their severe ethical positions over the casuistry of the *Jesuits. The most famous Italian to be influenced by Jansenism was *Manzoni. [VRJ]

JANUS NICIUS ERYTHRAEUS, see ROSSI, GIAN VITTORIO.

JARRE, MARINA (1925–). *Novelist born in Riga of a *Waldensian mother and a Latvian Jewish father, who moved to Torre Pellice in the Waldensian valleys at the age of 10, and later to *Turin. Her most significant novels include *Ascanio e Margherita* (1990), which tells the story of the love between a Waldensian woman and a Catholic man during the 17th-c. persecutions of the Waldensians by the Duke of *Savoy, and *I padri lontani* (1995), which examines her own dual roots. [VRJ]

Jesuits. Members of the Society of Jesus. The origins of the Society can be traced to the commitment of Ignatius Loyola and six companions in Paris in 1534 to devote themselves to a life of poverty and service. The group subsequently travelled to *Venice, where they worked in local hospitals and were ordained as priests. Their intention was to continue their voyage to Jerusalem, but they were unable to secure a passage, and therefore dispersed to other Italian towns before assembling again in *Rome in 1538. In 1540 Pope Paul III issued a bull instituting the Society and authorizing Ignatius and his companions (now numbering nine) to accept recruits. Their aim was to live as itinerant preachers, and members of the Society took an oath to travel wherever the Pope might order them. The unusual organization of the Society was designed to facilitate this. Although it was structured into provinces (there were eventually five in Italy), Jesuits were not required to wear any distinguishing habit (in Italy, they generally wore a simple priest's cassock), and the daily administration of the Society was entrusted to a General, elected for life by a representative General Congregation and resident in Rome. Members of the Society were relieved of duties that would interfere with their ministry, such as the obligation to recite the liturgical Hours in common, and they were prohibited from accepting any beneficed cure of souls that would restrict them to one location, except at the Pope's specific orders.

The Society grew rapidly in its early years, especially in Italy, but despite their commitment to preaching, the Jesuits became increasingly involved in *education. Ignatius had not initially considered this a part of the Society's mission; but in the 1540s he authorized the creation of Jesuit schools that would educate lay pupils as well as the Society's own novices. The first Jesuit school in Italy was founded at Messina in 1548; by 1565, there were thirty in Italy. In many cities, these schools were immensely popular—not least, perhaps, because the Society charged no tuition fees. The schools' *humanist curriculum was carefully constructed, and allowed time for rest and recreation, as well as religious development. The Jesuits also established their own colleges attached to *universities. The Society's Roman College (the Collegio Romano), which opened in 1551, took pupils up to university level, though it did not at first adopt the title of University.

The commitment to education established the Society's association with secular culture. Jesuit authors have contributed to all areas of literature, drama, and scholarship, including the sciences. In the schools, Jesuits and their pupils frequently adapted the dramatic texts of other authors, or composed their own, for presentation in public, often setting the words to music as well. The Society also engaged actively in doctrinal disputes. Even within the Roman Catholic Church, however, it was the object of increasing suspicion, and in the second half of the 18th c. the Jesuits were expelled from several Catholic states, including *Naples, *Sicily, and Parma. In 1773, after years of pressure from the rulers of Spain and France, the Society was reluctantly suppressed by Pope Clement XIV. Jesuits continued to operate in non-Catholic states, and in new positions within the Church, until the Society was restored by Pope Pius VII in 1814. Since then, Jesuits have re-established themselves throughout the Catholic world. In Rome, they are responsible for the administration of several important institutions, including the Gregorian University and the Vatican Radio Station. [See also BARTOLI, DANIELLO; CLERGY; PAPACY AND THE CATHOLIC CHURCH.]   [NSD]

See W. V. Bangert, *A History of the Society of Jesus*, 2nd edn. (1986); J. W. O'Malley, *The First Jesuits* (1993).

Jews and Judaism. The small Jewish community in Italy, consistently numbering between 30,000 and 50,000 people, can claim to be the longest-standing such community in Europe. Records exist of a Jewish presence in *Rome from 161 BC, and Roman, Jewish, and early Christian history are closely intertwined after the colonization of Judaea by Pompey in 63 BC. Restrictions on Jewish life under the Romans began with the Christianization of the Empire under Constantine, but the community retained a presence under *Byzantine and Longobard rule. Nuclei existed also in the South and on the islands in the 6th and 7th c., and Jews especially prospered in *Sicily (as in Spain) under Muslim rule (827–1061). There is evidence that the Talmud entered and spread through Europe via Bari, Rome, and Pavia in the 10th c.

Throughout the *Middle Ages and the *Renaissance, in each city-state or kingdom where Jews settled they were received and accomodated according to shifting local politics and theology. They tended to settle into certain commercial niches, such as usury (after the Church proscribed it for Christians), *banking, and jewelling. Their status was often subject to sudden changes. In medieval controversies surrounding *heresies and the *Crusades, or Church and Empire, the question of the Jews and of deicide was often a bone of contention, and the subject of *papal pronouncements. In 1236, for example, Pope Gregory IX condemned the Talmud; in 1257 an edict forced Jews in Rome to wear yellow circles and other such badges. At times throughout this period, both *Dominicans and *Franciscans carried out anti-Jewish preaching, and accusations of child sacrifice and host desecration were not uncommon (e.g. in Trento in 1475). Expulsions from cities occurred at several points in the 15th and 16th c. *Venice established the first ghetto in 1516, and was followed by almost all other centres of Jewish population at varying points of the 16th and 17th c. The Church became even more hostile and bent on conversion and restriction after the Council of Trent (1542) [see COUNTER-REFORMATION] and Paul IV's *Cum nimis absurdum* (1555), and was still issuing hostile edicts under Pius VI in 1775.

The makeup of the Italian-Jewish population was substantially altered in the 14th and 15th c. by three waves of immigration. The first two were from German, 'Ashkenazi' communities into *Lombardy and the Veneto after 1348, and from Provence into *Piedmont after expulsions in 1306 and 1394. The third and greatest wave was of so-called Marranos, Spanish and Portuguese 'Sephardic' Jews, expelled in 1492 and 1497 respectively, destined particularly for Livorno, Venice, and *Ferrara. Each wave brought with it different rituals and traditions, which were, on the whole, preserved separately once in Italy. Despite uneasy relations with many host states, small city communities survived and often flourished, especially *Medici Livorno, the only main Jewish centre never to institute a ghetto, and to accord freedom of religion, commerce, and other rights (under Ferdinand I's 1593 constitution).

Jewish intellectuals took part in varied aspects of cultural life in late medieval and Renaissance Italy: *Immanuel Romano admired *Dante's work and wrote poetry himself; there were several Jewish papal doctors, such as Isaac ben Mordechai; several Jewish writers absorbed and contributed to *humanist culture, such as *Leone Ebreo, Azariah de' Rossi, and Leone Modena; Jewish *printers, in Venice and elsewhere, played a significant role in the spread of the printed book (e.g. the Soncino family). Conversely, important humanists became interested in reading and printing Hebrew (e.g. Daniel Bomberg in Venice) and in the Jewish mystic tradition of Kabbalah, most notably *Pico della Mirandola. A certain amount of *Enlightenment tolerance with regard to the Jews filtered through to Italy from northern Europe in the 18th c., but the real modern emancipation of Italian Jewry coincided precisely with the *Risorgimento. It began with the *Napoleonic invasion of the peninsula in 1796, suffered a setback after *Restoration in 1815, but took a significant step towards freedom with Carlo Alberto's 1848 *Statuto*, and again with the founding of the Italian nation-state in 1861. The Roman ghetto was finally closed on the liberation of Rome in 1870. Several important Risorgimento figures, such as *Mazzini, Massimo *D'Azeglio, and *Cattaneo, supported emancipation.

Many Jews fought for Italian unity, and prospered on *Unification, remaining fervent *nationalists into the 20th c. Success also led to widespread assimilation and the loss of religious faith and customs. Ingrained Catholic anti-Semitism remained commonplace, however, as is evident in popular novels of the period, such as Antonio Bresciani's *L'ebreo di Verona* (1850–1). Some of the vitality of Jewish-Roman life in this period is recorded in G. G. *Belli's poetry. Patriotic pride meant that, alongside notable Jewish anti-Fascists, such as Claudio Treves, Giuseppe Emanuele Modigliani, and the Rosselli brothers [see ROSSELLI, AMELIA], many Jews supported *Fascism. Although elements of the 1929 *Concordat between the Fascist state and the Church restrained Jewish life, there was little state-led anti-Semitism until the race campaigns of 1937 and the severely restrictive Race Laws of 1938, clearly modelled on Hitler's Nuremberg Laws. Some prominent Jews emigrated following 1938, but during the first part of the war Italy remained a safer haven for Jewish refugees than any other Axis territory. Following *Mussolini's Fall and the 1943 Armistice, the Nazi-Fascist Salò Republic began deportations to concentration camps from Italy (and the establishment of holding camps and one actual death camp in Italy itself, at San Sabba, near Trieste), aided in their task by the records of Jews in Italy compiled under the 1938 laws. Approximately 7,500 Italian Jews died in the Holocaust.

Under the republic, Jews have enjoyed full equality of rights and citizenship. In Italian literary and intellectual life of the 20th c., writers of Jewish origin (although very few of them have been practising Jews) have been particularly prominent, leading the historian H. Stuart Hughes to label this a 'silver age' of Italian-Jewish writing—e.g. *Bassani,

Journalism

*Debenedetti, *Fortini, Natalia and Carlo *Ginzburg, Primo *Levi, Carlo *Levi, Attilio and Arnaldo *Momigliano, *Moravia, *Pressburger, *Saba, and *Svevo.   [RSCG]

See H. S. Hughes, *Prisoners of Hope: The Silver Age of the Italian Jews* (1983); R. Bonfil, *Jewish Life in Renaissance Italy* (1994); C. Vivanti (ed.), *Gli ebrei in Italia* (1997).

Journalism. The first gazettes, which appeared in Italy in the second half of the 17th c., were mostly official government organs of information. Newspapers became politicized as a result of the French Revolution and played an important role in the *Risorgimento. But it was the formation of a national political class and then urbanization and industrialization between 1860 and 1914 that created the conditions for the emergence of daily papers like *Il Secolo* (1866), *Il *Corriere della sera* (1876), and *La Stampa* (1894), and of the illustrated weeklies, notably *Illustrazione italiana* (1875). By the early 20th c. the main characteristics of the Italian press were already established.

Contemporary journalism is often seen by the public in Italy as coterminous with the writings of leading journalists—the so-called 'grandi firme' such as Indro *Montanelli, Enzo *Biagi, and Oriana *Fallaci. These personalities not only contribute to newspapers and periodicals but write books of fiction, *biography, and history. Indeed, the genre is cannibalistic by nature and defies clear lines of demarcation. On the one hand, it includes the work of external collaborators—writers and intellectuals grace the *terza pagina* (the cultural page) that *D'Annunzio is said to have inaugurated; on the other, there is a proliferation of specialist pages, each with its own particular language. The sports press has long been a strong presence in Italy, but *Il *Giorno* introduced the first financial pages in 1956, while more recently computing has called a whole new form of coverage into being. The growth of new media, notably *television, and their related forms of journalism has further complicated the picture. Print journalism nonetheless represents the archetypal form. A journalist in Italy is, in law, a member of a profession and has to be accredited by the Ordine dei Giornalisti, a corporate body with origins in the *Fascist period. Training, ethos, career structure, and the attribution of social status still privilege the journalist writing for one of the major daily newspapers.

Many of the features of Italian journalism have remained constant over the 20th c. There is little or no popular journalism comparable to that found in the USA, Britain, or Germany. Readership of newspapers has hardly risen above the 5 million mark since 1915, though journalistic prose has lost much of its literary and academic aura in emulation of a rather unreal 'Anglo-Saxon' model. The influx of English words in the press is but one indication of this influence. Yet it is still common to have an article by Claudio *Magris or the sociologist Francesco Alberoni on the front page. Finally, journalism has continued to echo the strength of regionalism. *La Stampa* and *Il Corriere della sera* are still closely identified with *Turin and *Milan respectively, while *La Repubblica* includes local pages in its editions depending on where copies are sold. The imbalance between the North and Centre and the South is still striking in terms of the production and consumption of the press.

To some extent the role of a popular press has been played by weekly magazines. In the 1950s magazines began to reach new readers, notably women, the inhabitants of predominantly rural areas, and those with limited reading competence. *Famiglia cristiana*, the Catholic weekly, sold over 1 million copies, while the newly launched *Gente* and *Epoca* appealed to the widespread fascination with Hollywood film stars and European royalty. Their combination of photographs, often in colour, and simplified, less dense text made them more accessible than the newspapers with their difficult language, small print, and lack of illustrations. The use of *photography spread to the new upmarket current affairs magazines, such as *L'Espresso* and *Panorama*, in the 1960s, partly in the wake of the photojournalism pioneered in the United States by *Life* and *Look*.

The 1980s saw more profound changes, many of which occurred also in other countries. First, there was a remarkable growth in the number of women journalists, mainly working for magazines. Secondly, social and cultural issues occupied more space, sometimes being given more prominence than political news. One notable feature of 'settimanalizzazione' (as it was called) was the colour supplement, though the whole phenomenon has been held to show the press's increasing subjection to the values and methods of television. Thirdly, notions of objective reporting, already contested by commentators such as Umberto *Eco, were frequently abandoned in favour of a more subjective mode. Finally, and perhaps most significantly, technological developments reduced the role of the journalist as news-gatherer and author and gave greater powers to the copy editor. Overall, there was a widespread feeling in the profession, especially among its father figures, that journalism was being debased. Certainly the supremacy of the printed word was no longer unquestioned. [See also PERIODICALS.]

[REL]

See P. Murialdi, *Storia del giornalismo italiano* (1986); V. Castronovo and N. Tranfaglia (eds.), *La stampa italiana nell'età della televisione, 1975–94* (1994); R. Lumley, *Italian Journalism: A Critical Anthology* (1996).

Journals, see JOURNALISM; PERIODICALS.

JOVINE, FRANCESCO (1902–50). *Neorealist *novelist and short-story writer. His fiction is set in his native Molise and influenced by 19th-c. *veristi*, particularly *Verga. He trained as a primary school teacher and then took a degree in philosophy at *Rome University. During the 1930s, tired of *Fascist Italy, he worked in Italian schools in North Africa. He returned to Italy at the start of the war and became an active participant in the *Resistance in 1943. He joined the *Communist Party in 1948 and played an active part in the debates about politics and culture in the immediate postwar years [see IMPEGNO].

Apart from *journalism and a children's story, *Berluè* (1929), his first published work was *Un uomo provvisorio* (1934), a novel about a young doctor who leaves Molise to become a specialist in the big city, but finds only listlessness and indifference. When he returns to his village, he discovers a sense of purpose through saving a child's life. *Signora Ava* (1942) portrays the rural South at the end of *Bourbon rule. It is suffused both with a certain wistful, indulgent irony and with a sense of injustice at the failures of the *Risorgimento. The essay 'Del brigantaggio meridionale' (1970) reveals much of the historical research that went into the novel. [See also MEZZOGIORNO.]

Jovine's last and most famous work, the posthumously published *Le terre del sacramento* (1950), is an emblematic Neorealist novel. Set in Molise in 1921–2, it gives its powerful ethical themes an epic colouring. It recounts the tragic failure of the *peasants' struggle for land, and the death at the hands of the Fascists of the student, Luca Marano, who becomes their leader. All the same the story gives hope for moral regeneration and social transformation in the countryside.

Jovine published four volumes of short stories which were later gathered in *Racconti* (1960). Some of his journalism was later published in *Viaggio nel Molise* (1967). [JD]

See A. Procaccini, *Francesco Jovine: The Quest for Realism* (1986).

Judaism, see JEWS AND JUDAISM.

K

KHOUMA, PAP, see IMMIGRANT LITERATURE.   KULISCIOFF, ANNA, see FEMINISM.

L

LABRIOLA, ANTONIO (1843–1904). Philosopher and founder of theoretical *Marxism in Italy. His early training was in the Hegelianism of the *Neapolitan school [see GERMAN INFLUENCES]. From 1871 he taught philosophy at *Rome and also published on Socrates and ethics. His favourite pupil, Benedetto *Croce, edited his three important essays on historical materialism.   [JD]

LA CAPRIA, RAFFAELE (1922–). *Neapolitan novelist and critic. Though he spent periods abroad after taking his law degree in Naples, his meticulously crafted and densely detailed *novels are centred on his native city. The early Un giorno d'impazienza (1952) and the autobiographical Ferito a morte (1961) focus on psychological responses to problems of industrialization and cultural change. L'armonia perduta (1986) is a collection of imaginative discussions of the city's identity.   [JEB]

Lacerba (1914–16). Important *Florentine avant-garde magazine founded by Giovanni *Papini and Ardengo *Soffici after they left La *Voce to concentrate on the arts. During their alliance with *Marinetti's *Futurism, Lacerba became the movement's showcase, publishing many manifestos and experimental poems. Soffici's Parisian contacts brought contributions from Apollinaire and Max Jacob, including Apollinaire's Futurist manifesto. The editors promoted interest in Mallarmé, Lautréamont, and Laforgue, polemically claiming them as predecessors when they broke with Marinetti. Lacerba also published important work by *Palazzeschi and early texts by *Ungaretti, *Sbarbaro, and *Campana. From September 1914 it campaigned violently for intervention in *World War I.   [SV]

LAGORIO, GINA (1930–). *Piedmontese *novelist, who has taught, worked in *publishing, and been an independent left-wing member of parliament (1987–92). Piedmont is central to her fiction, which depicts a variety of unheroic characters in a spare but readable style. La spiaggia del lupo (1977) has its female protagonist achieving the strength to pursue an artistic vocation. But *Tosca dei gatti* (1983) explores the failure of a writer to penetrate the isolation and despair of a lonely janitor in an out of season seaside condominium. *Il bastardo* (1996) is a *historical novel, portraying 17th-c. Piedmont through reconstructing the life of Don Emanuel di Savoia. [SW]

LAJOLO, DAVIDE (1912–84). Born near Asti, he was involved in the *Resistance movement, became director of the *Communist newspaper *L'Unità*, and in 1958 a parliamentary deputy for the Communist Party. He is the author of several volumes of narrative, poetry, and essays focusing mainly on the history and culture of postwar Italy. The reliability of some parts of his best-known work, a *biography of Cesare *Pavese (*Il 'vizio assurdo'* of 1960), was seriously questioned after the publication of Pavese's original correspondence in 1966. [LPer]

LALLI, GIOVAN BATTISTA (1572–1637). Poet and lawyer who became Governor of Parma for the *Farnese family. His *mock-heroic poems, *La moscheide* (1614) and *La franceide* (1629)—the latter on venereal disease—adapted *Marinist *concettismo* to the comic repertory. He parodied *Virgil in *L'Eneide travestita* (1633), but attempted serious imitation of Torquato *Tasso in *Tito Vespasiano ovvero Gerusalemme desolata* (1635). [FC]

LA LUMIA, ISIDORO, see SICILY.

LAMARQUE, VIVIAN (1946–). Poet born near Trento who has spent most of her life as a schoolteacher in *Milan. Her ostensibly childlike poetry, beginning with *Teresino* (1981), is directly concerned with her personal life, and, in *Il signore d'oro* (1986) and the two subsequent volumes, with her experience of *psychoanalysis. [PH]

LAMBERTAZZI, FABRUZZO DE' (*c*.1240–?1300). Poet and *banker. He belonged to a noble family of *Bologna and was exiled in 1274. *Dante cites him in the *De vulgari eloquentia* (1.15) as one of the illustrious *Bolognese poets who do not limit themselves to the local *dialect. Only one moralizing didactic *sonnet survives. [JP & JMS]

LAMBRUSCHINI, RAFFAELLO (1788–1873). *Genoese reformer, a priest in his youth, who campaigned for *educational reform, publishing *Sulla educazione* (1850). He also campaigned for the improvement of rural conditions and was one of the founders of the *Giornale agrario toscano* (1827). He was elected to the Senate after *Unification. [MPC]

Lamento di Cecco di Varlungo, see BALDOVINI, FRANCESCO.

LAMI, GIOVANNI, see ENLIGHTENMENT.

LAMPEDUSA, GIUSEPPE TOMASI DI, see TOMASI DI LAMPEDUSA, GIUSEPPE.

LANCELLOTTI, SECONDO (1583–1643) was one of the leading figures in the Italian *Querelle des anciens et des modernes*. Born in *Perugia, he became an Olivetan monk and preacher, but in 1611 left the order and began a life of wandering around Europe. He is known for the modernism announced by the title of his main work, *L'hoggidì, overo il mondo non peggiore né più calamitoso del passato* (1623). Like *Beni and *Tassoni, he does not dismiss the ancients out of hand, but weighs up the relative merits of ancients and moderns and comes to the conclusion that modern Italian achievements in the humanities and sciences outstrip those of the past, thus signalling the end of the *humanistic project that had started in the 14th c. In 1636 he renewed his modernist thesis with *I farfalloni degli antichi historici notati*. His work on the fallibility of human wisdom, *Chi l'indovina è savio*, was published in 1640. [PBD]

LANCIA, ANDREA (d.*c*.1360). *Florentine notary and author of many *translations into Italian of Latin classics, including *Virgil's *Aeneid* and *Ovid's *Remedia amoris*. The mid-14th-c. *commentary on the *Divine Comedy* known as the *Ottimo commento* has been persuasively attributed to him, partly on the basis of the initials A.L.N.F. (plausibly 'Andrea Lancia, notaio fiorentino') that appear in several manuscripts. [See DANTE COMMENTARIES.] [SNB]

LANDINI, FRANCESCO, see ARS NOVA.

LANDINO, CRISTOFORO (1425–98) was a poet, scholar (though he never mastered Greek), tutor of Giuliano and Lorenzo de' *Medici, older friend and admirer of *Ficino, and champion of *Virgil, *Dante, and the vernacular. In 1458, after a long-contested election, he succeeded Carlo *Marsuppini in the chair of rhetoric and poetry at the *studio* [see UNIVERSITIES, 1] in *Florence, and lectured philosophically on *Cicero, *Horace, Juvenal, Persius, Virgil, *Petrarch, and Dante. In 1465 he became *cancelliere* (general secretary) of the *Guelf party, and later *scriptor* (writer of official letters) for the Florentine government.

Apart from three books of youthful Latin elegies entitled *Xandra* and initially dedicated to Leon Battista *Alberti, he composed three philosophical *dialogues: *De anima* (c.1471), *De vera nobilitate* (written in the 1480s), and in between his best-known original work, the *Disputationes camaldulenses* (c.1472). Here he imagines four days of Platonizing conversations between Lorenzo, Donato *Acciaiuoli, Alberti, Ficino, and others, in the setting of the great monastery of Camaldoli in the summer of 1468. In the first book, Alberti and Lorenzo debate the virtues of the active and contemplative lives, awarding primacy to the contemplative; in the second, Alberti and Ficino discuss the highest good; and in books 3 and 4, Alberti interprets books 1–6 of the *Aeneid* *Neoplatonically, as the story of the hero's arrival at contemplative perfection (Italy), having conquered the vices and passions of the *vita voluptuosa* (Troy) and the *vita activa* (Carthage). Landino was variously indebted here to Ficino and *Aquinas, to the ancient Virgil commentators Servius and Fulgentius, and to *Salutati's *De laboribus Herculis*. He also follows Ficino in deriving a doctrine of inspiration from Plato's *Phaedrus* and *Ion*, and conceives of true poetry as resulting from divine inspiration and therefore as veiling divine secrets.

He published *commentaries on Horace and on Virgil's *Aeneid* (1488). But his most famous commentary is on Dante's *Divine Comedy* (1481), memorably illustrated by *Botticelli. This dwells on the poet's debt to Virgil and therefore to Plato, while acknowledging the *Comedy*'s *Aristotelian elements. It did much to revive interest in Dante, and made Landino into one of the most influential literary critics of the Florentine 15th c. [see also DANTE COMMENTARIES]. He also *translated into Italian Pliny's *Natural History* (1473) and Giovanni Simonetta's history, *Rerum gestarum Francisci Sfortiae* (1489). His pupils included two distinguished English *humanists, William Grocyn and Thomas Linacre. [MA]

Scritti critici e teorici, ed. R. Cardini (1974);
Disputationes camaldulenses, ed. P. Lohe (1980).
See R. Cardini, *La critica del Landino* (1973);

A. Field, *The Origins of the Platonic Academy* (1988).

LANDO, ORTENSIO (c.1505–c.1555) was the author of three Latin and several Italian prose works which all show, in different ways and to different degrees, his learning, love of paradox, and disrespect for established reputations and institutions. Born in *Milan, he entered the Augustinian order, but left about 1535, and travelled extensively for several years in Italy, Germany, and France, before settling in *Venice in 1545. His most successful work, the *Paradossi*, first published in Lyons in 1543, humourously subverts accepted truths. In 1548 he published the first Italian *translation of More's *Utopia*, and a tongue-in-cheek *travel work, *Commentario delle cose d'Italia*. His religious views are difficult to determine, but they were always suspect to the authorities, and all his works were put on the *Index in 1564 [see COUNTER-REFORMATION].
[CF]

LANDOLFI, TOMMASO (1908–79). One of most interesting *novelists of the generation of *Bilenchi, *Pratolini, and *Vittorini, and one the few Italian authors (along with *Savinio, *Loria, *Buzzati, and *Bontempelli) who can be spoken of in terms of the *fantastic and of *surrealism. Born near *Rome, his literary formation was in *Florence, where he entered into contact with *hermetic circles and contributed to *Campo di Marte* and *Letteratura*. He writes in a refined 19th-c. style modelled on *Leopardi's *Operette morali*, which, together with the oddity of his 'lunar' stories, inspired by Northern models such as Poe, Dostoevsky, and Gogol, and his taste for ironic citation and collage, helps account for the attraction he exercised over critics.

Obsessed by a passion for gambling, Landolfi played a deadly game of dissipation and sacrilege with both literature and life. The themes of his novels and stories are those of the error, the pointless challenge, surrender, defeat, and self-destruction; and the sin which, while it could be the prelude to art, leads instead to the negation of life. The French title which Landolfi gave to one of his works is a characteristically ambiguous reference to sin and death: *La biere du pecheur* can be translated either as 'The Fisherman's Beer' or as 'The Sinner's Coffin'. Even judging by his biography, we can see how from childhood onwards words are for him a surrogate for love, and love is linked to death, so that from the beginning writing is the desire for dissolution, at the same time pleasure and suicide, enjoyment and crime. Starting with the *Dialogo dei massimi sistemi* (1937), his first collection of stories, *Pietra lunare* (1937), a novel of metamorphoses whose young protagonist falls in love with a woman-goat, and *Mar delle blatte* (1939), Landolfi brings into play the processes of approach and desire, the wager, loss, and violence, that characterize relationships with women throughout his work, both in the novels and in the short stories. His fiction tends to a highly self-conscious form of ostensibly autobiographical fantasy, which becomes particularly marked in the pseudo-diaries *Rien va* (1963) and *Des mois* (1967). Landolfi also published experimental verse, notably *Viola di morte* (1972) and *Il tradimento* (1977), as well as essays and *translations, especially of Russian literature. [AD]

See O. Macrì, *Tommaso Landolfi narratore poeta critico artefice della lingua* (1990).

LANZI, LUIGI ANTONIO (1732–1810). *Jesuit who became keeper of antiquities at the Uffizi in *Florence. He was a pioneer in Etruscan archeology and philology, but he is remembered more for *Storia pittorica della Italia* (definitive edn. in 6 vols., 1809), the first systematic treatment of the history of Italian painting. [JMAL]

LAPINI DA MONTALCINO, PIETRO, see PETRARCH COMMENTARIES.

LAPO DA CASTIGLIONCHIO (THE ELDER) (d.1381), from a noble *Florentine family, was an eminent canon-*law scholar, leading the Florentine *Guelf party's struggle to maintain supremacy in *communal politics. A friend of *Petrarch's, he was an enthusiastic amateur of classical Latin authors, especially *Cicero and Quintilian; his best-known vernacular work is a moralizing letter to his son. [RDB]

LAPO DA CASTIGLIONCHIO (THE YOUNGER) (1405/6–38) was employed in various administrative posts around Italy. In his *dialogue *De curiae romanae commodis* (1438), he defended the *papacy's opulence, claiming that it was not in conflict with the spirit of the Gospel and was needed to guarantee the Church's well-being. [LB]

LAPO GIANNI (late 13th or early 14th c.). *Florentine poet usually considered an adherent of the

dolce stil novo. We know that he was a notary since manuscripts refer to him as 'ser'. But he may have been any one of several individuals of the same name. He is the author of eleven *ballate*, three substantial *canzoni* (one of which rails against love), two independent *canzone* stanzas, and the famous extended double *sonnet, 'Amor, eo chero mia donna in domìno'. The preference for *ballate* links him with *Cavalcanti and Gianni degli *Alfani. Otherwise he reworks *dolce stil novo* language and imagery in an 'international Gothic style', looking backwards in some ways and forwards to the 14th c. in others.

Modern scholars have serious doubts whether he can really be considered one of the founders of the *dolce stil novo* alongside Cavalcanti, *Dante, and *Cino. The presumed indirect references to him in poems by the first two are ambiguous, and there are good philological grounds for thinking that 'Lippo' (i.e. Lippo Pasci de' *Bardi) should replace 'Lapo' in Dante's sonnet 'Guido i' vorrei che tu e Lapo ed io', and that the figure praised for achieving excellence in the vernacular in the *De vulgari eloquentia* (1.13) is not 'Lapus' but 'Lupus' (perhaps Lupo degli Uberti who had family connections with Cavalcanti and by whom we have a small number of poems). [GG]

See G. Gorni, *Il nodo della lingua e il verbo d'amore: studi su Dante e altri duecentisti* (1980).

LASCA, IL, see GRAZZINI, ANTON FRANCESCO.

LASCARIS, CONSTANTINUS (1434–1501) left Constantinople after its capture by the Turks in 1453, eventually finding employment as a professor of Greek in *Milan from 1458 to 1465, followed by a year in *Naples. From 1466 until his death he lived and taught in Messina; among his pupils was Pietro *Bembo. His grammar textbook, *Erotemata* (*Questions*), published in Milan in 1476, was the first Greek book printed in the West. He possessed a valuable library of Greek *manuscripts, some copied in his own elegant hand. [See also BYZANTIUM; GREEK INFLUENCES; GREEK WRITING IN ITALY.] [JK]

LASCARIS, JANUS (1445–1534) entered the service of Cardinal *Bessarion after the fall of Constantinople. He moved to *Florence, from where he went on journeys in search of Greek *manuscripts for Lorenzo de' *Medici, and taught Greek in the Florentine *studio*. He was an important editor and *printer both in Florence and *Rome.

Lateran Pacts

[See also BYZANTIUM; GREEK INFLUENCES; GREEK WRITING IN ITALY.] [PLR]

Lateran Pacts, see CONCORDAT.

Laterza, founded in 1885 as a printing firm, began publishing in Bari in 1901 and became one of Italy's most prestigious *publishers. Central to its success was the collaboration between Giovanni Laterza and his editorial adviser Benedetto *Croce, the sales of whose many books gave the firm a solid financial basis. Its head office is still in Bari but the editorial office is now in *Rome. [DF]

LATINI, BRUNETTO (*c.*1220–?1294). *Florentine writer. He was a notary and served Florence as an official scribe and negotiator in the 1250s. Returning from an embassy to Castile, he learned of the Ghibelline victory at Montaperti (1260), and lived in exile in France until the restoration of the *Guelfs enabled him to return to Florence (1267). He then resumed public service as scribe, member of councils, and Prior (1287).

His *Tresor* was written in French, mostly during his *exile [see FRENCH INFLUENCES]; an Italian version has been attributed to *Bono Giamboni. A compendium of philosophy in a vernacular tongue, and thus an antecedent of *Dante's *Convivio, it is a 'treasure' of wisdom in three books: the 'small change' of theology, history, and natural science, the 'jewels' of moral instruction; and the 'gold', the arts of rhetoric and government. The *Rettorica*, an Italian *translation and exposition of *Cicero's *De inventione*, chapters 1–17, is also concerned with fostering the *ars dictaminis in the *commune. The *Tesoretto*, an unfinished narrative poem in *settenari baciati* [see VERSIFICATION], describes how the newly exiled Brunetto strayed into a strange forest, from which he travelled to receive instruction from Lady Natura, the attendants of the Empress Virtù, *Ovid, and Ptolemy; it includes an account of his confession and a discourse on the seven deadly sins. The *Favolello*, also in *settenari baciati*, composed in response to a poem (now lost) by *Rustico Filippi, discusses true friendship along the lines of Cicero's *De amicitia.*

Brunetto was the leading promoter of pre-*humanist culture, civic values, and rhetorical skills in late 13th-c. Florence. He was, probably informally, Dante's teacher, perhaps in moral or political philosophy or in rhetoric and versification. He is the subject of an episode in the *Inferno*, where he is placed among the sodomites, although some

critics dispute whether his sin is to be interpreted as sexual (*Inf.* 15.22–124). [PA]

See B. Ceva, *Brunetto Latini, l'uomo e l'opera* (1965); J. Bolton Holloway, *Twice-Told Tales: Brunetto Latino and Dante* (1993).

Latin Influences. Vernacular writing of the 13th and 14th c. is heavily indebted to medieval Latin traditions, from *scholastic philosophy to medical, legal, and rhetorical treatises. It is the *Divine Comedy* which, without denying these traditions, first gives what we consider to be classical texts a comparable importance. *Dante takes his fundamental notion of a journey to the underworld from *Virgil's *Aeneid* and makes Virgil himself one of the main characters of his poem, incorporating in it many intertextual echoes of the Latin poet (as well as of *Ovid, Lucan, *Statius, and others). In the age of *humanism it was natural to look back to classical models for genres, motifs, and language: so *Petrarch's *Canzoniere* is also haunted by myths, particularly that of Daphne, drawn from Ovid and Virgil, and his debt to Propertius is now clearly established; while *Boccaccio turns to Apuleius for at least two of his *Decameron* stories, and for some of his language. The importance of *Cicero for humanist prose in Latin and the vernacular is indisputable, while *Poliziano was inspired for his works in both languages by 'minor' models such as Sallust, Statius, and Claudian. Apuleius was a crucial ingredient in the bizarre style of Francesco *Colonna's *Hypnerotomachia Poliphili*, while Poliziano's *Orfeo*, *Sannazaro's *Arcadia* and Torquato *Tasso's *Aminta* all look back to classical *pastoral poetry. Even the *epic *romances of *Ariosto and Tasso, so medieval in their historical sources and Christian in content, are shot through with deliberate classical echoes of motifs, images, and phrasing—notably the rescue of Angelica and Olimpia in the *Orlando furioso*, which is modelled on Ovid's account of Perseus rescuing Andromeda, while from the first line onwards the *Gerusalemme liberata* echoes Virgil's *Aeneid*. Similarly in prose, *Castiglione's *Cortegiano* was originally in three books, a structure modelled on Cicero's *De Oratore*, in which there is also a discussion of wit in book 2. *Machiavelli is particularly indebted to the historical examples he finds in *Livy for his political theories. For his *Mandragola* he is indebted to Livy's account of the rape of Lucretia, though, like other *Renaissance writers of *comedy, he finds his literary models in Plautus and Terence.

After the Renaissance, once humanism retreats

into the *universities and *academies and no longer interacts with creative literature, the weight of the Latin literary tradition is still felt, though not in so prominent a fashion. *Marino's *Adone is inspired by the Adonis episode in Ovid's *Metamorphoses*, while the source of *Metastasio's *Didone abbandonata* is clearly Virgil. Even in the *Romantic age, Italian writers still looked back to Latin texts: *Alfieri's *Mirra* is based on Ovid once more, while the poetry of *Leopardi and *Foscolo also drew heavily on classical, especially Latin, texts. At the end of the 19th c. *Carducci in his *Giambi ed epodi* and *Odi barbare* tried to graft classical metres as well as subject matter onto the stock of Italian poetry. In the 20th c. Italian writers remained remarkably aware of classical Latin literature, not least because many were educated in classical *licei*. So even a *post-modern writer like *Calvino can set at the core of Le *città invisibili* the city of Bauci, modelled on the central tale of Baucis in the middle book of Ovid's *Metamorphoses*, while the speculations on life and death in his *Palomar* owe something to the ruminations of the Elder Pliny. But Latin literature has rarely furnished fundamental models and points of reference. [See also ANTIQUARIANISM; CLASSICAL SCHOLARSHIP; CLASSICISM; GREEK INFLUENCES; IMITATION; LATIN POETRY IN ITALY; LATIN PROSE IN ITALY; MIDDLE AGES; VERSIFICATION.]

[MMcL]

See T. M. Greene, *The Light in Troy: Imitation and Discovery in Renaissance Poetry* (1982); M. L. McLaughlin, *Literary Imitation in the Italian Renaissance: The Theory and Practice of Literary Imitation in Italy from Dante to Bembo* (1995).

Latin Poetry in Italy. The Italian tradition of Latin poetry compares itself directly with classical models in a continual tension of *imitation and emulation. The first medieval examples include a large array of *epic or historical poems, alongside works as diverse as *Arrigo da Settimello's *Elegia de diversitate fortunae*, the well-known *Dies irae*, and Thomas *Aquinas' eucharistic hymns. In the early 14th century, the *Paduan pre-*humanists laid the foundations for a new kind of Latin poetry, with the discovery of Seneca and Catullus and with Albertino *Mussato's experiment with *tragedy, the *Ecerinis* of 1315. *Dante, inspired by *Giovanni del Virgilio, revived the *pastoral (c.1320), a genre subsequently attempted by *Petrarch and *Boccaccio. Petrarch's *Bucolicum carmen* (c.1346–66) and his unfinished epic poem *Africa* (after 1338) are both based on *Virgilian models.

However, it was in the 15th c. that Latin poetry really flourished in the Italian courts. The *Hermaphroditus* (1425) by *Panormita opens the way to numerous collections of epigrams, a genre whose characteristics helped the humanists achieve the integration of the classical world with contemporary reality to which they all aspired. Apart from the epigram, the other major genre is the elegy. In the collections by Giovanni *Marrasio, Enea Silvio *Piccolomini, *Basinio da Parma, Cristoforo *Landino, echoes of Tibullus, Propertius, and *Ovid can be discerned, but there is an equally strong tendency towards experimentation, the best examples of which can be found in *Poliziano and *Pontano. Of the former's work, the most memorable are *Sylva in scabiem* (c.1475–8) and the four *praelectiones*, or verse lectures, entitled *Silvae* (1482–6). The prolific Pontano, in spite of his determination to be a true continuer of the classical tradition, also attempts new genres, for example in his nursery songs (*Neniae*), and his poems to dead friends and relatives (*Tumuli*).

In spite of *Sannazaro's *Eclogae piscatoriae* and *De partu Virginis* Italian poetry triumphs over Latin in the 16th c., though the latter remains part of the humanist apprenticeship of major Italian writers such as Pietro *Bembo, *Ariosto, and *Castiglione. Nevertheless, in some cases Latin is deliberately chosen to express new ideas and feelings in established genres, for instance by the humanist Marcantonio *Flaminio (1498–1550), or as a way of exploring new and different directions, as in the case of the *Syphilis* by Girolamo *Fracastoro or *Scacchi ludus* by Marco Girolamo *Vida. In the *Baroque era there is then a reaction against the classics; Latin poetry is relegated to school exercises, particularly in the teaching of the *Jesuit colleges. The last major creative exponent of Latin poetry is *Pascoli, with his *Carmina*, especially the *Poemata christiana*, written between 1891 and 1911.

[SR]

Renaissance Latin Verse: An Anthology, ed. A. Perosa and J. Sparrow (1979).

Latin Prose in Italy. Latin prose was written by Italian authors from at least the time of the earliest vernacular texts, most writers from the 13th to the early 16th c. composing works in both languages. *Dante wrote two important theoretical works in Latin (*De vulgari eloquentia* and *Monarchia*), but it was *Petrarch who established the more influential intellectual paradigm when he wrote the majority of his works in the learned language, and proclaimed Latin's canonical superiority over the *volgare*. After meeting Petrarch, *Boccaccio largely abandoned the vernacular for works in Latin, and the prestige of the language in the age of *humanism was such that most intellectual energy was channelled away from the *volgare* into Latin during the century that followed Petrarch's death.

Some 15th-c. writers, such as Leon Battista *Alberti, Leonardo *Bruni, *Landino, *Pico della Mirandola, and *Poliziano, did use both languages, but the majority of their works were in Latin, and many of the most important humanists wrote only in the classical tongue, notably *Salutati, Poggio *Bracciolini, *Valla, and the younger Ermolao *Barbaro. By 1500 Italian humanists had achieved an almost perfect copy of classical Latin prose, the chief model being *Cicero, while the debate over literary *imitation was a key topic in *literary theory between 1400 and 1600.

Apart from *dialogues, the main prose genres in these two centuries were orations, *letter-writing, *biographies, *historiography (Bruni, Poggio Bracciolini, Bartolomeo *Scala, Pietro *Bembo) and treatises on philosophy (*Ficino, Pico della Mirandola, *Pomponazzi) and poetics (G. C. *Scaligero). The liveliest, if not the most classical, Latin prose was probably that used by Poggio for his collection of bawdy tales, the *Facetiae* (1438–52) [see FACEZIE], and by Enea Silvio *Piccolomini (Pius II) for his *autobiographical and historical *Commentarii* and his *Historia de duobus amantibus*. Alberti's Latin is also quite distinctive, but the greatest Latin stylist of the century was Poliziano, a scholarly and creative genius who was sensitive to the riches of the language, and an individualist who, in a famous polemic on literary imitation with Paolo *Cortesi, championed his right to depart from the prevailing Ciceronian norm in order to express his own distinctive sense of style. The dominant Ciceronianism spawned an even more extreme reaction in those, such as Filippo *Beroaldo and Giovan Battista Pio (*c.*1460–1540), who imitated the extravagant Latin of both archaic and late Latin writers, particularly Apuleius, a style replete with lexical rarities, unusual diminutives, and *Baroque wordplay. This experimental phase would eventually lead to the humorous *macaronic Latin poetry of *Folengo, but Bembo's intervention in the 1512 debate with Giovanfrancesco *Pico proved decisive in reinstating Ciceronianism as the norm for writing in Latin in the 16th c. After 1530, when humanism became part of the academic establishment, Latin was less frequently the medium for

creative writing, and although humanists such as Bembo continued to write substantially in both Latin and the vernacular, most Italian authors now wrote mainly in the latter.

Latin continued to be used both for *translations of key vernacular works (by *Machiavelli, *Castiglione, *Della Casa) to allow them to reach an international reading public, and for scientific treatises (*Galileo's *Sidereus nuncius*), legal, medical, and theological works, and academic dissertations, right down to 1800 and beyond. Nowadays original Latin prose is composed only on ceremonial occasions, and for the originals of *papal encyclicals and related documents. [See also ANTIQUARIANISM; CLASSICAL SCHOLARSHIP; CLASSICISM; LATIN POETRY IN ITALY.]   [MMcL]

See P. Van Tieghem, *La Littérature latine de la Renaissance* (1944); J. IJsewijn, *Companion to Neo-Latin Studies* (1990–8).

LATTANZI, CAROLINA (d.1818) delivered the oration *Schiavitù delle donne* at a *Jacobin academy in *Mantua in 1797. In 1804 in *Milan she founded the *Corriere delle dame*, a very successful weekly *journal which she ran until her death. It covered fashion, politics and current affairs, medical discoveries, scientific inventions, and theatrical reviews. [See also FEMINISM.]   [VRJ]

LATTES, FRANCO, see FORTINI, FRANCO.

LATTUADA, ALBERTO (1914–). Film director who showed a preference for literary adaptations, among them Riccardo *Bacchelli's *Il mulino del Po* (1949), and Gogol's *Il cappotto* (1952). He also made forays into *Neorealism with *Il bandito* (1946) and *Senza pietà* (1948), and then into big productions for *television, such as *Cristoforo Colombo* (1984).   [CGW]

Laudario di Cortona, see LAUDI; PASSIONE.

Laudi. *Religious poems, metrically normally *ballate*, with a strongly popular basis. They flourished particularly in 13th-c. Umbria, with its powerful *Franciscan traditions, but were composed and sung in Central Italy generally until at least the 16th c. Most *laudi* are anonymous, being preserved in collections such as the *Laudario di Cortona* of the 1270s. A major exception from the end of the 13th c. is the extensive and distinctive body of work by *Iacopone da Todi.

The origins of the *laudi* probably lie in the Latin

liturgy and more particularly in the praise psalms used in the Morning Office. Formally, the earliest *laude* (from Latin *laudes,* 'praises') probably consisted of little more than an invocation and collective response. For instance, 'Laudato et benedettó et glorificato sia lo Padre' might be pronounced by the preacher and repeated by the crowd with the progressive substitution of 'sia lo Filio' and 'sia lo Spiritu Santo'. Subsequently there was some theatricalization of the genre, with extended monologues and dialogues. The manner was always popular and regional, but devices and imagery from secular *lyric poetry appear already in the *Laudario di Cortona* and are subsequently used freely and often with some sophistication. As a means of giving public expression to deep feelings, the *laudi* often became vehicles of spiritual or social protest.   [JT]

See V. De Bartholomaeis, *Le origini della poesia drammatica italiana* (1953).

Laura. The female figure at the centre of almost all *Petrarch's Italian poetry, though she has a much smaller part in his Latin works. Attempts to identify a historical woman have so far been fruitless. The only information we have comes from Petrarch, who says that he first saw her in *Avignon in the church of St Clare on 6 April 1327, and that she died twenty-one years later to the day in the *plague of 1348. Her name appears as Laureta in the acrostic of *Canzoniere 5. According to two later *sonnets (*Canz.* 77 and 78) Simone Martini painted a portrait of her, almost certainly a miniature.   [MP]

Laurenziana, Biblioteca, see LIBRARIES.

LAVAGETTO, MARIO, see LITERARY CRITICISM.

LAVIZZARI, LUIGI, see ITALIAN WRITERS IN SWITZERLAND.

Lavorare stanca, see PAVESE, CESARE.

Lavoro critico, see PERIODICALS, I.

Law. Italy played a dominant role in the elaboration of civil law from early medieval times to the end of the *Renaissance. *Bologna was the birthplace of the mode of teaching and organizing law based on the Roman compilations of Justinian; in the late 11th c., Irnerius produced there a framework of juridical concepts which made it possible to provide rational legal solutions to conflicts of interest in society in place of solutions based on force or custom. He also allied *scholastic logic to legal teaching, and thereby systematized the disparate materials of the Roman law, for which he supplied an extensive gloss. This was later superseded by the 'great' gloss of *Accursius, which remained authoritative until the 17th c. The two towering figures in Italian law in the medieval period were *Bartolo da Sassoferrato and Baldo degli Ubaldi (1327–1400); the former writing an extensive *commentary in the form of a gloss on the whole corpus of civil law, the latter being responsible for the development of *opinio communis,* a means of settling legal points which combined argument with the citation of authorities. Early Italian lawyers were prominent in politics (notably in the negotiations between Pope and Emperor and in municipal legislation), and were well known to literary circles. *Dante even gave Gratian (*fl.*1140), the author of the first authoritative compilation of canon law known as the *Decretum,* a place in his Paradise, and a later professor of law, *Cino da Pistoia, was a poet and close friend of both Dante and *Petrarch.

In the 15th and 16th c., legal studies were transformed by the *humanist movement. The lost texts of forensic rhetoric by *Cicero and Quintilian, rediscovered by Poggio *Bracciolini in the early years of the 15th c., were used to revise the legal curriculum and make it more sensitive to linguistic issues. Lorenzo *Valla, whose legal disciples were known as *i culti,* successfully applied to Roman and canon law the principles of historicity, philology, and linguistic elegance. His spiritual heirs were Angelo *Poliziano, who practised his philological skills on the *Florentine manuscript of Justinian's compilation of Roman law and on Theophilus's Greek *Paraphrasis* of the Code; and Andrea *Alciato, who as well as being the author of the *Emblemata* (1531) introduced the criterion of elegance into legal commentary and sought to reconcile history and law in a humanist way. In spite of these Italian contributions to the new form of legal study, it came to be known as the *mos gallicus* (the French mode) because it was said to derive from the philological work of the French scholar Guillaume Budé (1467/8–1540). The *mos italicus,* which was associated with the outmoded scholasticism, was contrasted unfavourably with the *mos gallicus.* This latter gave rise in France to a school of historical legal studies, which is associated with the birth of history as an academic subject;

whereas in Italy, the conservative effect of the *Counter-Reformation was to reinforce the traditional use and study of Roman and canon law. There were, however, a number of impressive jurists who wrote influential monographs on forward-looking topics at the end of the 16th c., notably Alessandro Turamini (?1556–1605) on legal interpretation, Iacopo Menochio (1532–1607) on presumption, and Prospero Farinacci (1554–1618) on testimony, and foreign students continued to flock to Italian *universities to study law until the outbreak of the Thirty Years War.

[IWFM]

See O. F. Robinson, T. D. Fergus, and W. M. Gordon, *An Introduction to European Legal History* (1985); I. Maclean, *Interpretation and Meaning in the Renaissance: The Case of Law* (1992).

LAZZARELLI, LUDOVICO, see HERMETICISM.

LAZZARINI, DOMENICO (1668–1734). Founder member of the Accademia dell' *Arcadia and from 1711 professor of classics at *Padua. He championed the Greek model in *tragedy. *Ulisse il giovane* (1719), his adaptation of the Oedipus myth, has Ulysses murder his son and commit incest with his daughter. [JMAL]

Leandreide, see NADAL, GIOVANNI GIROLAMO.

LEDDA, GAVINO (1938–). *Sardinian writer. He was an illiterate shepherd until starting his military service in 1958. He subsequently took a literature degree at *Rome, and became a lecturer in Romance philology at Sassari University. His first book, *Padre padrone: l'educazione di un pastore* (1975), gives a powerful and passionate account of his struggle against an authoritarian father, and against poverty, ignorance, and isolation. The divisions created by different forms of *education and upbringing, and the struggle to preserve Sardinian culture in the modern world, are at the centre of much of his subsequent narrative and essays, including *Lingua di falce* (1977), *Dopo Padre padrone* (1978), *Le canne amiche del mare* (1978), and *I cimenti dell'agnello/Sos chimentos de s'anzóne* (1995). [DieZ]

Leggenda di Santo Giosafà, La, see CANTARI.

Leila, see FOGAZZARO, ANTONIO.

LEMENE, FRANCESCO DE (1634–1704). Poet from Lodi, best known for his poems for music, especially his *canzonette* [see VERSIFICATION]. He also wrote a *dialect play in the same vein as those of his friend Carlo Maria *Maggi, and a mock *epic on the history of macaroni. He belonged to the Accademia dell'*Arcadia, and thought of himself as a literary reformer, though his verse remained too close to *concettismo* for *Enlightenment and *Romantic taste. [MPS]

Le Monnier. *Florentine *publishers, originally a printing firm acquired in 1832 by Felice Le Monnier (1806–84). He was a fervent Italian *nationalist and made the firm a major publisher of *Risorgimento literature, beginning with *Niccolini's *Arnaldo di Brescia* (1837). Then came series such as the *Biblioteca nazionale italiana*, launched in 1843. It now publishes principally schoolbooks. [MPC]

LEONARDI, FRANCESCO, see COOKERY BOOKS.

Leonardo. *Periodical published in *Florence in three series (1903–7) and edited by *Papini and *Prezzolini. Their programmatic statement in the first issue emphasized their combination of youth and elevated intellectual aspirations. The precursor of the subsequent Florentine reviews *La *Voce* and *Lacerba*, it gave particular emphasis to contemporary philosophy and religion. In response to the late 19th-c. crisis of rationalist and *positivist thought and against the *idealism of *Croce, it promoted the philosophy of Bergson and the pragmatism of William James. [DF]

LEONARDO ARETINO, see BRUNI, LEONARDO.

LEONARDO DA VINCI (1452–1519) left one of the most extensive bodies of writings of any artist on record: some 6,500 pages of notes on a variety of scientific and artistic topics, containing over 100,000 drawings. His autograph *manuscripts were first published in the 20th c. They range from unbound pages to small pocket notebooks that record observations to drafts for treatises: for instance the early Manuscript C on optics (c.1490); Madrid Manuscript I, containing beautiful drawings of machinery, from the late 1490s; and the Codex Leicester on the dynamics of water (c.1508–10). Only in the 20th c. has scholarship reached the point of ordering these diverse and fragmentary writings chronologically, so that developmental aspects of his thought can be glimpsed. As an artist, although he had an unprecedentedly privileged career, his access to knowledge was limited by social status. But current research is revising long-standing views of Leonardo as a writer incapable of synthesizing ideas. His habits of observation and experimentation are grounded in *Aristotelian principles. *Print technology was, moreover, beginning to provide widespread access to learned culture. His most advanced treatises indicate his intention to contribute to this information revolution through the publication of illustrated scientific texts with practical applications.

Leonardo's most important literary contribution was his approach to painting as a natural science, grounded in geometry and direct observation of natural phenomena. Through the *Trattato della pittura* that his student Francesco Melzi compiled (*c.*1550) from eighteen notebooks—two main sections of which were published simultaneously in French and Italian in 1651 and soon translated into the major European languages—Leonardo's ideas formed the core of academic artistic instruction for three centuries in many institutional settings. Over time, these ideas were disseminated so widely that their source was no longer recognized. In the late 18th c. engravings after his inaccessible work reestablished his artistic reputation. Ironically, further publications of his writings since the late 19th c. encouraged modern artists to reject the academic tradition that Leonardo's literary legacy helped to establish.

Leonardo was born near Vinci, the illegitimate son of a notary, and apprenticed with the leading *Florentine artist Verrocchio until 1476, collaborating on paintings and probably a variety of other projects, including sculptures, architecture, and engineering consultations, records of which do not survive but which certainly shaped his career. From about 1482, he spent two decades at the *Sforza court in *Milan. His earliest writings cover a wide variety of subjects related to *court activities, including military engineering and architecture; his first important notes on optics and painting immediately precede the monumental mural of the Last Supper (*c.*1495–7); and his witty, polemical arguments in defence of painting against poetry, music, and sculpture are the first important contribution to modern comparisons of the arts. The literary forms and arguments are varied, their sources ranging from medieval *contrasti* and *tenzoni* to *Petrarchan poetry and classical and *scholastic texts.

After the French invasion forced him to leave Milan in 1499, he went with his friend and occasional collaborator, the mathematician Luca *Pacioli, first briefly to *Venice and then to *Florence, where he enjoyed six very productive years. He fell out with the new republican government over the completion of a second colossal mural, the *Battaglia di Anghiari*, abandoned in 1506 when he returned to Milan. These experiences also yielded many new writings on painting, optics, anatomy, geology, geometry, and such specialized topics as the flight of birds and the physiology of the eye. After a peripatetic decade between Milan, Florence, and *Rome, in 1516 Leonardo accepted an invitation from the French king Francis I. In his final three years, spent on French soil, he continued to write. [CJF]

Treatise on Painting, ed. and trans. A. P. McMahon (1956); *Edizione nazionale dei manoscritti e dei disegni di Leonardo da Vinci*, ed. A. Marinoni (1987–). See M. Kemp, *Leonardo da Vinci* (1981).

LEONARDO FIBONACCI, see FREDERICK II.

LEONE, SERGIO, see CINEMA.

LEONE EBREO (1460/?65–after 1523) (pseud. of Yehudah Abravanel). Physician and poet, whose *Dialoghi d'amore* became one of the most influential philosophical works of the European *Renaissance. Born in Lisbon, he lived in Spain from 1483 until the expulsion of the *Jews in 1492, when he settled in *Naples with his father, perhaps moving elsewhere in 1521. His writings included a lost *De coeli harmonia*, apparently dedicated to *Pico della Mirandola, and several poems in Hebrew, of which *Telunah 'al ha-zeman* (A Complaint against Time), written probably in 1503–4, is the most important. The three *Dialoghi d'amore* of about 1512 combine *Neoplatonic and *Aristotelian philosophy with Maimonides, ibn Gabirol, and the *Cabbalah*. The two speakers, Philone and Sophia, range freely over the whole field of human knowledge, but Leone's central theme is the idea of love as a universal force, its ultimate end being union with God, who has made love the covenant between Himself and creation. Though there has been debate about its original language, it first appeared in Italian in 1535. Many other editions followed and it was quickly translated into French, Spanish, Latin, and Hebrew. [BG]

LEONETTI, FRANCESCO (1924–). Militant intellectual, poet, and novelist, associated with several important literary *periodicals since the 1950s. As a student in *Bologna, Leonetti published his first book of poetry, *Sopra una perduta estate* (1942), alongside those of his friends, *Pasolini, Roberto *Roversi, and Luciano Serra. Over a decade later, the group re-formed to launch the journal *Officina* (1955–9), which attempted to find a third way for poetry and for the literary intellectual between apolitical *hermetic writing and stale *Neorealism. When *Officina* collapsed, Leonetti moved closer to *Vittorini and the *Neoavanguardia in the 1960s, collaborating on *Il *Menabò di letteratura* and publishing experimental novels such as *Conoscenza per errore* (1961), *L'incompleto* (1964), and *Tappeto volante* (1967). He was associated with the far Left politics of the later 1960s, working on journals such as *Che fare* and *Voce operaia*. He published essays and a long narrative poem, *Percorso logico del 1960–75*, in the following decade. In 1979, he helped Nanni *Balestrini co-found the eclectic magazine *Alfabeta*, alongside Umberto *Eco and Paolo *Volponi among others. In 1994, he and Volponi published a reflective dialogue, *Il leone e la volpe*, on the problems of the old-style intellectuals in contemporary Italy. His is the crow's voice in Pasolini's film *Uccellacci e uccellini* (1966). [RSCG]

LEONI, MICHELE (1776–1858) established his reputation as a *translator, especially from English. In the years 1811–22 he translated *Ossian, *Shakespeare's *tragedies, Milton, Goldsmith, Pope, and others. Though criticized by some for his wordiness and fear of using concrete terms, he gave a major impetus to the knowledge of these writers in Italy. [MPC]

LEONICENO, NICCOLÒ, see MEDICINE.

LEONZIO PILATO (d.1364), a scholar from Calabria, belonged to the Italo-Greek community of Southern Italy [see also BYZANTIUM; GREEK INFLUENCES; GREEK WRITING IN ITALY] and was more at home in Greek culture than in Latin. He met *Petrarch in *Padua in January 1359 and translated a selection from Homer into Latin for him. Petrarch convinced *Boccaccio to arrange for Pilato to give public lectures in *Florence on Greek

from 1360 to 1362. During this period he lived in Boccaccio's house and produced a complete Latin *translation of the *Iliad* and *Odyssey*, which was later sent to Petrarch. Pilato's poor command of Latin and adoption of the medieval method of rendering Greek word for word made his translations unidiomatic, plodding, and literal; but they were nevertheless carefully studied by Petrarch and also by Boccaccio, who in his *Genealogiae deorum gentilium* used material concerning classical mythology taken from Pilato's explanatory notes. In addition to Homer, Pilato lectured on Euripides' *Hecuba* and translated 466 lines of the text. He also produced Latin translations of the Greek passages in the *Digest* of Justinian, the fundamental document for the medieval and *Renaissance study of Roman *law. He died at sea in the Adriatic. [JK]

LEOPARDI, GIACOMO (1798–1837). The major Italian poet of the 19th c., who is at least as important as a voice of European pessimism. He emerged from and was deeply marked by an inauspicious provincial environment. He was born at Recanati, near Ancona in the Marche, the eldest son of Count Monaldo Leopardi and Adelaide Antici. For centuries the family had been among the leading landowners of the region, and closely connected with the Church (throughout Leopardi's lifetime Recanati was part of the *Papal States). By 1803 family finances were in a catastrophic state, and Leopardi grew up in a household, largely administered by his mother, struggling to maintain aristocratic standards and simultaneously to economize.

Leopardi, his brother Carlo (b.1799), and his sister Paolina (b.1800), the two siblings to whom he was closest, were educated at home by private tutors on the *Jesuit model, following courses of study with annual exams which were held first in the presence of the family, and later before a wider public. He began to write verse at a remarkably early age. The *sonnet 'La morte di Ettore' of 1809 opens a long series of poems and *translations written over the next two years. In 1811–12 he composed two *tragedies, *La virtù indiana* and *Pompeo in Egitto*. In 1810 he began to study philosophy and wrote the *Dissertazioni filosofiche*, again in 1811–12.

Leopardi's formal studies came to an end in 1812. Apart from his tutor Sanchini he had already come into contact with Canon G. A. Vogel, an Alsatian exile, who perhaps suggested to him the idea of keeping a commonplace book, a *zibaldone, and he was already accustomed to studying on his own in the 16,000-volume family library, much of it accumulated by his father. This library now virtually became his home as he began to dedicate himself to what he later called 'sette anni di studio matto e disperatissimo'. In 1813 he began to teach himself Greek, then Hebrew, received permission to read books on the *Index, and composed a *Storia dell'astronomia*. During this period he laid the foundations of his reputation as one of the outstanding philologists of his generation in Italy: among his most important contributions in 1815–16 were *In Iulium Africanum* and *Discorso sopra la vita e le opere di M. Cornelio Frontone* as well as several translations. His *Saggio sopra gli errori popolari degli antichi* combines *Enlightenment suspicion of superstition with creative rewriting of those same myths and 'errors', while the *Orazione agli Italiani in occasione della liberazione del Piceno* continues to reflect his father's reactionary political ideas.

1816 also saw him turn to more obviously creative writing. He wrote original poems in Greek, with Latin translations, and, in Italian, 'Le rimembranze', 'Appressamento della morte' (a fragment of which he included in the last edition of the *Canti* as 'Spento il diurno raggio'), the unfinished tragedy *Maria Antonietta,* and a series of *satirical poems, 'Sonetti in persona di Ser Pecora fiorentino beccaio'. The following year he made his first entries in the series of notebooks which he later called his *Zibaldone di pensieri*. At the end of 1817 a visit by his cousin Geltrude Cassi Lazzari to Recanati gave rise to the acute self-analysis of the *Diario del primo amore* and its poetic elaboration in 'Il primo amore'.

By this stage the young scholar was taking more than a passing interest in the debates surrounding *Romanticism. In 1818 he drafted his most extended reflections on the subject, and indeed on poetics in general, the *Discorso di un italiano intorno alla poesia romantica* (not published until 1906), and wrote the first two *canzoni* which he included in the *Canti*, both of them on patriotic themes, 'All'Italia' and 'Sopra il monumento di Dante'. The poems seem to confirm the *classicism of the *Discorso* and its hostility to the extravagances, as he perceives them, of the Romantics, though Leopardi's search for a poetic language founded in nature brings him closer to the ambitions of a wider European Romanticism than he realizes.

When he was 21, Leopardi's eyesight and general health were already ruined by the continuous application to study. Psychologically he was oppressed by the petty restrictions of his home, which he made a failed attempt to flee. He later saw himself as having turned at this point from literature to philosophy, following the same pattern as the human spirit in its journey from antiquity to modernity. Even so, a new poetry begins to emerge, in the form of short, nature-centred lyrics (or *idilli*), more intimate in tone than the *canzoni*, which were addressed to a political or at any rate public audience. 'L'infinito' of 1819 is the first of the *idilli* written between 1819 and 1821, which include 'Alla luna', 'La sera del dì di festa', 'Il sogno', and 'La vita solitaria'. In 1820 his philological interests and continuing need to call on the Italian people to waken from their slumbers combined in the *canzone* 'Ad Angelo *Mai'.

From this point on his personal and intellectual life begin to take on a certain pattern. From 1821 until it peters out in 1832, the *Zibaldone* is the instrument which he uses to study, refine, and define his philosophical ideas in the broad sense. It is here that he explores the relation between nature and reason and the structures of contemporary society, establishes the foundations of his pessimism in the mid-1820s, and develops it into a more radical materialism in subsequent years. Throughout he includes philological notes and occasional personal reflections.

With his first journey away from home in November 1822 to stay with the Antici family in *Rome, Leopardi initiates a cycle of departures and returns which continues until he leaves Palazzo Leopardi for the last time in 1830. The first journey proved a considerable disappointment. Subsequent ones are invariably the source of powerful mixed feelings, and are often connected with the hope of finding a post or at least with the need to fulfil some work commitment.

His creative writing seems similarly to have come in spurts. The first led to a new series of *canzoni*, written between October 1821 and July 1822, comprising 'Nelle nozze della sorella Paolina', 'A un vincitore nel pallone', 'Bruto minore', 'Alla primavera, o delle favole antiche', and 'Ultimo canto di Saffo', as well as the first of a projected series of sacred hymns, 'Inno ai patriarchi'. While they carry forward the earlier polemic against the decadence of the moderns, 'Ultimo canto di Saffo' in particular seems to open the way towards the denunciation of a more universal suffering, and makes space for a reflective, 'pathetic' voice more reminiscent of the *idilli* than of the other *canzoni*: it is an essential stage on Leopardi's path towards the creation of a

Leopardi, Giacomo

distinctive voice within an increasingly (and quite original) free strophe structure. This takes another step with the composition of 'Alla sua donna' in September 1823. After his return from Rome, however, Leopardi's major creative effort is directed towards the writing of the moral essays and *dialogues in prose of the *Operette morali, twenty of which were composed during 1824. This extraordinarily productive year also saw the drafting of the *Discorso sopra lo stato presente dei costumi degl'Italiani* (published posthumously). The only poem which he wrote between 1823 and 1828, 'Al conte Carlo *Pepoli' of 1826, pushed the humour and irony of the *Operette* almost to the point of sarcasm, and was not much to the taste of its recipient.

Leopardi went to *Milan in July 1825 to work on an edition of *Cicero (quickly abandoned) for the *publisher A. F. *Stella. In September he moved to *Bologna, where he completed a commentary on *Petrarch's *Canzoniere* (1826). After wintering in Recanati, he returned to Bologna in April 1827 and in June transferred to *Florence, where he continued to work on commissions for Stella. His *anthology of Italian prose, the *Crestomazia italiana della prosa* was published in 1827, followed by the *Crestomazia italiana poetica* in 1828. He published an edition of his *canzoni*, with a provocative preface and notes in Bologna in 1824. The *idilli* appeared subsequently as *Versi* (1826). Three of the *operette* were published in *Antologia* and then in the Milanese *Il Nuovo ricoglitore* in 1826; Stella produced the first edition in book form in the summer of 1827. These were busy years: in Bologna, Leopardi was well received in cultural and aristocratic milieux, in Florence he was in close contact with the *Vieusseux circle, he was being published, and was leading a surprisingly active social life. But there is a sense also in which he was living on intellectual and creative capital, enjoying the fruits of labours which to a considerable extent had been completed two or three years earlier, even though in Florence he did write two further *operette*. What he had to do in the present, particularly the commissions for Stella, he found irksome and wearying.

He spent the winter of 1827–8 in *Pisa, where he found a climate more conducive to his health, as well as a welcoming social ambience. From here he wrote to his sister in May 1828 that he had written some poems 'all'antica'. It was the beginning of another great cycle of lyrics, written between April 1828 and April 1830, in Pisa and then in Recanati. The *idilli*, 'A Silvia', 'Le ricordanze', 'La quiete

dopo la tempesta', 'Il sabato del villaggio', and 'Canto notturno di un pastore errante dell'Asia' have a musicality and purity of diction which are only partly prepared for by earlier compositions. They also have a new kind of metrical freedom which will continue in subsequent poems.

In 1830 he returned to Florence, where a new friend, Antonio *Ranieri, oversaw the publication of the poems, under Leopardi's direction, with their now definitive title, *Canti* (1831). In the winter of 1831–2 he and Ranieri paid a rather hectic visit to Rome. But by now Leopardi was caught up in a doomed infatuation with the society beauty Fanny Targioni Tozzetti, from which came the poems of the so-called Aspasia cycle, composed probably between 1832 and 1835. These—'Il pensiero dominante', 'Amore e morte', 'Consalvo', 'A se stesso', and 'Aspasia'—have a new bleakness of tone, though at least the first two have also the same majestic simplicity of the unfinished hymn 'Ad Arimane' (probably written in 1833) and the two sepulchral poems written between 1831 and 1835, 'Sopra un basso rilievo antico' and 'Sopra il ritratto di una bella donna'. These poems overall, however, evidence a desperate form of personal self-assertion of a kind which Leopardi had not displayed in his writings since the early 1820s. This 1830s titanism (as it is generally called) intersects with an increasingly concerned and increasingly trenchant criticism of contemporary thinking and behaviour. Such criticism partly continues the thinking of the *operette*, the last two of which are written in 1832. Since 1827 Leopardi had also been working on a systematic reduction of his thought in the *Operette* in what takes shape in the 1830s as the *Centoundici pensieri*, designed for public consumption, but not published during his lifetime. In verse he produced some overtly *satirical or *parodistic compositions, including the 'Palinodia al marchese Gino Capponi' and 'I nuovi credenti', which lampooned the new spiritualism. Both these poems were probably written in 1835. In 1831 he began the 'Paralipomeni della Batracomiomachia', a *mock-heroic satire in *ottava rima* on *liberal politics of the time, which he continued working on until his death.

He spent the last years of his life in *Naples in the company of Ranieri and his sister. Here, with Ranieri's help, he undertook an edition of his complete works in six volumes, to be published by Starita. The volume containing the poems appeared in 1835, but the entire project was blocked by the *Bourbon censorship on the publication of the first thirteen *operette*. His last poems, 'La ginestra' and 'Il tramonto della luna', were probably written while he was staying during the second half of 1836 and the winter of 1836–7 at Villa Ferrigni on the slopes of Vesuvius. The mountain's volcanic landscape features particularly in 'La ginestra', which, with its call for human solidarity against the destructiveness of nature, is often read as Leopardi's poetic testament. On his return to Naples in February 1837 his health declined rapidly, and he died on 14 June. [See also LYRIC POETRY; VERSIFICATION.] [MPC]

   Poesie e prose, ed. R. Damiani and M. A. Rigoni, 2 vols. (1988–9); *Zibaldone*, ed. R. Damiani, 3 vols. (1997). See J. H. Whitfield, *Giacomo Leopardi* (1954); A. Prete, *Il pensiero poetante: saggio su Leopardi* (1980).

LEPOREO, LUDOVICO (1582–*c*.1655). Poet, born near Pordenone, who studied at *Padua and then moved to *Rome. He wrote poems for music and took *concettismo* to extremes in his *leporeambi*, fourteen-line poems distinguished by complicated rhymes and word-play, of which he published various collections. His *Prosa rimata curiosa* (1652) is another experiment in stylistic virtuosity. [FC]

LESBIA CIDONIA, see GRISMONDI SECCO SUARDI, PAOLINA.

LETI, GREGORIO (1630–1701) was a prolific and unscrupulous historian and scourge of the Catholic Church. His adventurous life resembles that of many Italian *libertines of the time: born in *Milan, he was forced by a quarrel to leave Italy for France, but he stopped at Geneva, married, and converted to Calvinism. Short of money, he went to France in 1679, but rejecting efforts to lead him back to the Catholic Church, he came to London, where he remained under the *patronage of Charles II from 1680 to 1683. His *Teatro britannico* (1684) insulted English Catholicism and led to his exile in Holland, where, as official historian, he remained until his death.

   Earning his living by his pen, he thought little of plagiarizing or attributing his works to others. He was fiercely outspoken and frequently obscene in his criticism of the Church and of Europe's principal states. His first-hand knowledge of the statesmen of Europe allowed many valuable historical insights, but these were laced with strong doses of vitriol and wit. *Il nipotismo di Roma* (1667) lays bare the nature of *papal family ties, while *Li precipitii*

della sede apostolica (1672), *Il Vaticano languente* (1677), and *L'Inquisizione processata* (1681) form a notable series of attacks on the evils of the *Inquisition. His *biographies of Popes and rulers are part fact part fiction and immensely readable, perceptive but unreliable. He also wrote larger-scale histories, historical and political *dialogues, a critique of lotteries, and a series of works, purportedly based on the words of 'political confessors', that reveal the 'secrets' of the leaders of Europe. [PBD]

   See L. Fassò, *Avventurieri della penna del Seicento* (1923); G. Spini, *Ricerca dei libertini: la teoria dell'impostura delle religioni nel Seicento italiano* (1950).

LETO, GIULIO POMPONIO (1428–98). *Humanist *antiquarian. The illegitimate son of the count of Sanseverino, he moved in the 1450s to *Rome, where he founded the *Accademia Romana, a group of humanists devoted to the study of antiquity. Around 1465 he began teaching rhetoric at the *University of Rome, but left for *Venice two years later, planning to travel to the East. In 1468, however, members of the Accademia were accused of conspiracy against Pope Paul II and Leto was extradited to Rome, where he was imprisoned for several months and tortured. In 1470 he resumed teaching at the university. His main interest was Roman antiquities, including numismatics, epigraphy, topography, and agriculture. He produced editions of ancient Latin grammarians, as well as a history of Roman and Byzantine emperors. [JK]

Lettera semiseria di Grisostomo al suo figlio, see BERCHET, GIOVANNI; ROMANTICISM.

Letterato (from Latin *litteratus*) referred in medieval usage to a person who knew how to read and write, as opposed to someone illiterate. In its current meaning, it designates someone who cultivates literature largely at the professional or academic levels and who is well informed and educated. It is sometimes used to indicate a cultural and intellectual orientation that is wholly erudite and technical in nature. *Marxist writing has often seen the 'letterati' as a caste who tried to abstract themselves from the social and political realities of Italy. [See also GRAMSCI, ANTONIO.] [RSD]

Letteratura (1) (or Latin 'litteratura') was used in Italy up to the 17th c. in the senses that Quintilian

Letteratura (2)

had given the term in the 1st c. AD, that is, to mean 'alphabet', 'writing', but also, secondarily, 'philology'. But then a meaning emerges that is closer to that in common use today, that is, a body of written texts belonging to a particular culture which are characterized by aesthetic value and/or intent. From the 19th c. onwards definitions have been proposed which either include every form of writing aimed at an audience (prose and verse, high and popular writing, *lyric, narrative, and *theatrical works, historical and scientific works, whether imaginative or not), or exclude one or more of these categories. In the first half of the 20th c. *Croce's distinction between 'poesia' and 'letteratura' (or 'non poesia') offered an *idealist solution, identifying the second term in each case with all the components of a text which have no aesthetic value, even if they do have value on a structural, historical, cultural, or philosophical level. In the postwar period attempts to define the concept of literature tried to identify the literary features of a text in more precise detail, but did not resolve the debate over the boundaries between the literary and the non-literary. The tendency currently prevalent in Italy, and subscribed to both by sociological historicists of *Marxist extraction and by *semioticians, is to embrace within literature all the written products of a particular culture, including popular and commercial texts. [See also LITERARY THEORY, 6.]

[NG]

Letteratura (2) (1937–68). *Florentine review, founded by Alessandro *Bonsanti, which attracted both former contributors to *Solaria, such as *Gadda, *Vittorini, and *Montale, and the more *hermetic wing of the *Frontespizio group, including *Betocchi, *Bo, and *Luzi. Bonsanti aimed to create an exclusively literary review, but the dissonance with respect to the increasingly authoritarian *Fascist regime was evident. Most notable Italian writers contributed at some point in the review's history. After *World War II the scope was extended to include more *literary criticism and articles on the visual arts. The review moved to *Rome in 1953. After its demise as *Letteratura*, it continued until 1971 as *Arte e poesia*. [DCH]

Letter-Writing and *Epistolari*

1. Before 1800

In the *Middle Ages, Italian letter-writing as a literary activity—whether in Latin or the vernacular, prose or verse—was deeply influenced by the works of classical, early Christian, and later authors. Compositional rules devised for Latin letter-writing appeared in the *ars dictaminis of the 11th–12th c., while style and elocution followed the rhythmical prose rules of the *cursus. The teachings of *Alberico da Montecassino, *Boncompagno da Signa, and *Bene da Firenze were adopted by chancellors, notaries, and lawyers, among them *Pier della Vigna, Chancellor of the emperor *Frederick II. *Guido Fava produced around 1220 a rudimentary set of epistolary formulae in the vernacular. Later in the 13th c. *Guittone d'Arezzo wrote letters in a highly elaborate, sermon-like style. During the 14th c. the vernacular was adopted for official correspondence by *communal chanceries and members of religious communities, notably by St *Caterina of *Siena.

It was *Petrarch who revived classical epistolography in his compendious and varied collections of letters. He had rediscovered *Cicero's letters to Atticus in 1345. Following in his footsteps, Coluccio *Salutati discovered a complete manuscript of Cicero's *Ad familiares*. But whereas Petrarch's attention to moral teachings in a *stilus familiaris* led him to prefer Seneca over Cicero, 15th-c. *Florentine *humanist chancellors—Salutati, Leonardo *Bruni, and Poggio *Bracciolini—looked rather to Cicero for a political eloquence which they saw as more relevant to their civic concerns. Later Iacopo *Sadoleto and Pietro *Bembo, appointed *segretari ai brevi* by Pope Leo X in 1513, secured the dominance of Ciceronianism in the correspondence of the *papal curia, and set the European standard for Latin epistolary style. Latin letter-writing also developed a narrative vein: *Boccaccio's tale of Griselda (*Decameron* 10.10) was *translated into Latin by Petrarch and inserted into his *Seniles* (17.3); Enea Silvio *Piccolomini's *Historia de duobus amantibus* is recounted in one of his letters. Humanist scholarly correspondence entered print with Aldo *Manuzio's edition of *Poliziano's *Epistolae* (1494), which included the letters of his correspondents. [See also LATIN PROSE IN ITALY.]

Vernacular epistolography did not attain a comparable status until the 16th c., when it was re-established in most Italian chanceries and *courts. Pietro *Aretino's *Lettere* (1537–56) made letter-writing the fashionable genre of the day. Letters by prominent writers such as Bembo, Bernardo *Tasso, Annibale *Caro, and Torquato *Tasso were published along with their major works. Handbooks of letter-writing, such as Francesco *Sansovino's *Secretario* (1564), devised for the thriving occupation of court secretary, enjoyed enormous success. Gabriello *Chiabrera in his *Sermoni* (1624–32) imitated the *Horatian epistle in verse. Remigio *Nannini's translation of *Ovid's *Heroides* (1555) was likewise successful, prompting further imitations by Giovanbattista *Marino in *Lettera di Rodomonte a Doralice* (1619) and Antonio *Bruni in *Epistole heroiche* (1627). The literary letter, both in Latin and in the vernacular, was the genre favoured by women from the 15th to the 17th c. [see WOMEN WRITERS, 1].

Letter-writing came to exercise a remarkable influence over the Italian literary world. The different types included letters by statesmen and politicians, *travel letters (first collected in Giovanni Battista *Ramusio's *Le navigationi et viaggi*, 1550–9), letters from *Jesuit missions, pastoral letters, which were usually disseminated from the pulpit to huge audiences, and letters on scientific subjects, such as *Galileo Galilei's *Il saggiatore* (1623). In the 18th c. erudite correspondence was intensively exchanged and propagated in literary *periodicals. Montesquieu's fictional *Lettres persanes* (1721) led to pamphlet-like *satires such as Saverio *Bettinelli's *Lettere virgiliane* (1758), whilst the *epistolary novel inspired Ugo *Foscolo's *Le ultime lettere di Jacopo Ortis* (1798). After Boileau and Pope the Horatian verse epistle enjoyed great popularity; merging with didactic poetry in the *Versi sciolti di tre eccellenti autori* of C. I. *Frugoni, Bettinelli, and *Algarotti (1758), it led to Lorenzo *Mascheroni's masterpiece, *Invito a Lesbia Cidonia* (1793). [CCa]

See J. Basso, *Le genre épistolaire en langue italienne (1538–1662)* (1990).

2. 1800 onwards

In contrast to earlier times, when letters were often conceived as treatises, or to be read in the presence of others (as in the case of *Petrarch), in the early 19th c. the personal, subjective element comes much more to the forc. Even the letters of *Foscolo, *Leopardi, and *Manzoni are read with this in view, for all their literary importance. The emphasis on the private becomes progressively more marked from the 19th to the 20th c., even if the possibility remains of the self-conscious artist writing with an eye to posterity, using all the devices that such a purpose might require. By definition the history of a dialogue made necessary by distance (though there is also the alternative form of the family letter), letter-writing now leads back into the labyrinth of the self, opens up the folds of neurosis, as in the

letters of *Svevo to his wife, *Quasimodo's letters to Sibilla and Maria Cumani, the love letters of *Pavese; absence is compensated by a game of seduction that idealizes or denigrates the self or the other according to the needs of the moment. Thus we have a whole typology of letters: faithful or unfaithful, true or fictitious (*Pasolini's *Lettere luterane* are a case of the latter), sincere or mendacious, three-sided or direct, immediate or delayed, letters to be destroyed, or not to be sent, to be read or reread, or written and rewritten in order to construct an alternative self. More striking still, when we analyse the texts, are the points at which the writer both reveals and conceals himself, displaying to the gaze of the other the elements of a total game that includes, in literary guise, both life and death.

The recurrent defining features of the letter as a genre are the fact of being directed to an individual or a clearly limited group, the addressses of the sender and receiver, the date (which may have to be inferred, when it is missing, from elements internal or external to the text), the opening, the conclusion, and the signature. These features are often expressed in formulae and vary according to fashion: the opening or conclusion, for instance, is extended and effusive in the 19th c., polite and detached in the early 20th c., and nowadays friendly and concise. Their significance is evident from the effect of even the slightest variations in the forms of address, not to mention the difference between the alternative uses of the second person: *Lei, voi,* or *tu.*

Like *diaries, letters were long considered minor, non-literary forms of writing, and used even in the case of major authors as a source of biographical information or as background to other texts. Only recently have they become important objects of study in terms of literary history and style. They can be essential for the reconstruction of particular historical events (*Ungaretti's letters from the front in *World War I, *Gramsci's letters from prison, letters from condemned prisoners in the *Resistance); of literary movements (letters to publishers or to editors of journals, or those between *Verga and *Capuana, a major source for understanding the first stages of *verismo*); or of friendships (the letters of the *hermetic generation, notably critics like *Jacobbi and Macrì). Or they can be studied as deviations from the norms of a conventional genre, for instance the letters of *Saba and *Gadda, or in a different way those of Cristina *Campo, for a long time almost the only known work by this writer. [See also EPISTOLARY NOVEL.] [AD]

Levi, Carlo

See A. Dolfi (ed.), 'Frammenti di un discorso amoroso' nella scrittura epistolare moderna (1992).

LEVI, CARLO (1902–75). Writer, painter, doctor, and *journalist from *Turin who dealt with *existential and social themes in his writing and became what *Calvino called an ambassador for the *peasant world.

Though he took a degree in medicine, he was already known as an expressionist painter in the 1920s. After the death of his friend Piero *Gobetti, he joined the *Giustizia e libertà group in Turin. He was arrested and eventually sent into internal exile in Lucania (1935–6). In 1939 he fled to France, where he wrote his first book, Paura della libertà (1946), a series of meditations on the crisis in Western civilization and its roots in the human sense of the sacred. He returned to Italy during the war, and wrote *Cristo si è fermato a Eboli during the German occupation in *Florence in 1943–4, at the same time as he was working with the *Resistance movement in the city. After its liberation he edited La Nazione del popolo on behalf of the Comitato di Liberazione Nazionale. Cristo si è fermato a Eboli met with immediate success on publication in 1945 and made its author a public figure.

Whilst he re-established himself as a painter after the war, Levi was now writing extensively. His third book, L'orologio (1950), evokes the state of Italy in 1945, taking off from his experience as editor of L'Italia libera, the *Rome newspaper of the *Partito d'azione. His remaining books are investigative and committed *travel writings. Le parole sono pietre (1955) focuses on the struggles of *Sicilian sulphur-miners and peasants. He then turns to the Soviet Union in Il futuro ha un cuore antico (1956), West Germany in La doppia notte dei tigli (1959), and *Sardinia in Tutto il miele è finito (1964). In 1963 Levi was elected to the Senate as an independent standing on the *Communist Party's list. [JD]

See G. De Donato, Saggio su Carlo Levi (1974).

LEVI, NATALIA, see GINZBURG, NATALIA.

LEVI, PRIMO (1919–87). The most important Italian-Jewish writer of the 20th c. and one of the most powerful voices to emerge as a witness to the Nazi Holocaust. He is also significant as a bridge between the 'two cultures' of science and literature. Until very recently his work, although studied in schools, suffered from a certain critical neglect in Italy, and Levi was admired for his status as a survivor rather than as a writer of literature. In fact he is a fine essayist, short-story writer, and moralist. Like Italo *Calvino, he combines a rationalist and at times rather conservative pragmatism with a richly ironic and comic vein, both aspects being related to his *Piedmontese roots. Whilst his work has been conventionally praised for an almost styleless lucidity and statuesque calm in the face of horror, in fact the calm language and pre-modern values constantly give way to traumatic, fragmented language, to probing moral enquiry, or to exuberant sentiment, creating a highly varied and inspiring whole. In his confrontation with the catastrophic events of modernity—the Holocaust, but also the excesses of science—Levi is always more Pascal's thinking reed than the statue. His work is also enriched by his eclectic intellectual curiosity, including his fascination with languages and sign systems of all kinds.

Born into the small and largely assimilated Jewish community in *Turin [see JEWS AND JUDAISM] which he depicted in Il sistema periodico (1975), Levi attended the Liceo Massimo D'Azeglio, a former centre of liberal anti-*Fascist views. He read widely and eclectically, but in keeping with his father's *positivist outlook, he rejected his *humanist *education and chose to study chemistry at *university. He managed to graduate despite the 1938 race laws. Following the armistice in September 1943, he joined the *Resistance, but was betrayed and captured almost immediately. Preferring to declare himself a Jew rather than risk execution as a partisan, he was imprisoned at the concentration camp at Fossoli, from where, in February 1944, he was deported to Auschwitz. He remained there until its liberation by the Red Army in January 1945. He reached Turin again in October 1945. On his return, he started a career as an industrial chemist and manager which would last thirty years. He also wrote a number of stories and poems about his time in Auschwitz, and a medical report with doctor and fellow deportee Leonardo Debenedetti, on camp conditions. The stories were published in book form as *Se questo è un uomo in 1947, by De Silva, having been rejected by *Einaudi. The book was praised by a small number of reviewers (including Calvino), but had little impact.

In 1958, with interest in the Holocaust growing, Einaudi republished Se questo è un uomo in a slightly revised edition, to much greater acclaim. This success persuaded Levi to write more, and in 1963 he published La tregua, the picaresque account of his ten-month journey home from Auschwitz to

Turin in 1945. His public intellectual life of inter- views, articles for *La Stampa* and *literary prizes begins with *La tregua*. In 1966 and 1971 respective- ly, he published two collections of stories blending science and fantasy. *Storie naturali* (initially under a pseudonym, Damiano Malabaila) and *Vizio di forma*. These witty but often dark inventions have grown in stature as both their subterranean links with his Holocaust work and their own literary qualities have become more evident. Along with Calvino's *Cosmicomiche*, they represent important moments in the relationship between science and literature in Italy. In 1975 came *Il sistema periodico*, an *autobiography loosely structured according to chemical elements. Each chapter centres on a real, fictional, or metaphorical encounter with an element at a certain time of Levi's life. The book was hailed in America especially—Saul Bellow called it 'a necessary book' in 1984—and Levi's immense international reputation stems from this reception. His next work, *La chiave a stella* (1978), was, by contrast, very local in its style and theme: it consists of the work stories of a industrial rigger, Libertino Faussone, who, in his odd mixture of Piedmontese *dialect and technical jargon, tells of his epic and intimate struggles with bridges, dams, and the like.

Levi's only fully fledged work of fiction, *Se non ora, quando?*, the story of a Jewish partisan band in *World War II, appeared in 1982, winning both the Viareggio and the Campiello literary prizes. 1985 saw the collection of articles, *L'altrui mestiere*, which illustrates better than any other work what Calvino called Levi's 'encyclopedic curiosity'. His final and, for many, most striking book was *I som- mersi e i salvati* (1986), in which he revisits many of the moral and historical questions thrown up by the Holocaust. The essays on memory, communica- tion, the shame of the survivor, the Nazis' 'useless' violence, and on the 'grey zone' of moral ambiguity between victim and oppressor are models in humane, ethical meditation. Levi published his poetry as *Ad ora incerta* (1984), as well as other stories and essays—*Lilìt* (1981), *Racconti e saggi* (1986), an anthology of favourite books entitled *La ricerca delle radici* (1981). He also made several *translations, including works by Kafka and Claude Lévi-Strauss. He committed suicide in April 1987.
[RSCG]
See M. Cicioni, *Primo Levi: Bridges of Knowledge* (1995); M. Belpoliti (ed.), *Primo Levi* (1997); E. Ferrero (ed.), *Primo Levi: un'antologia critica* (1997).

Lexicography, see DICTIONARIES.

LIALA (pseud. of Amaliana Cambiasi Negretti) (1897–1995). Successful author of popular roman- tic fiction (*romanzi rosa*) who continues to be wide- ly read today. Born in Carate di Lario near Como, she began publishing stories in newspapers and magazines at an early age. After her marriage to the Marquis Cambiasi, a naval officer, she had a pas- sionate affair with an aviator who died in a flying competition. Many of her seventy or so *novels, which began with *Signorsì* (1931), have an aviator protagonist. Amongst the most successful were 'the Lalla cycle'—*Dormire e non sognare* (1944), *Lalla che torna* (1945), and *Il velo sulla fronte* (1946). She published her last novel, *Frantumi di arcobaleno*, in 1985. [AHC]

Liberal Arts. Seven in number, the liberal arts constituted the core of the medieval arts syllabus and enshrined the *encyclopedic ideal of medieval and *Renaissance pedagogy. They were divided between the arts of discourse, the so-called *trivium* of grammar (which embraced both grammar in the modern sense and the study of literary texts), rhetoric and dialectic, and the more advanced mathematical or philosophical *quadrivium* of arith- metic, geometry, music, and astronomy. Vocation- ally tailored to produce clerics and notaries, the domination of dialectic and *scholastic logic in the 13th-c. *university curriculum was increasingly challenged by *humanists in the late 14th c., who developed a revised educational programme, the *studia humanitatis*, which favoured a philological approach to classical texts and the study of rhetoric over logic. [See also EDUCATION, I; LITERARY THEORY; MIDDLE AGES.] [SJM]

Liberalism dominated Italian political life after the *Risorgimento, its major exponents being Giuseppe Zanardelli and Giovanni *Giolitti. Italian Liberals favoured constitutional *monarchy, secu- larism, social conservatism, administrative central- ization, and balanced budgets. From 1876 they promoted enlarged suffrage and experimented with social reform and *colonialism. In foreign policies they aimed to advance national interests within a European balance of power. But public perceptions of the Liberals' ineffectiveness and corruption, and their own lack of resolve, did much to open the way to *Fascism. Liberal thought was most impressively articulated by Benedetto *Croce, who continued to publish throughout the Fascist period. The reconstituted Liberal Party (PLI) has had limited support since *World War II. However, whilst most intellectuals and writers have been drawn more to the left, Liberal thinking has remained fundamental to economic and administrative policy and practice.

[RAbs]

Liber pontificalis ('*papal book'). A compilation of *biographies of the Popes which, in their original form, extend to 870. They were continued in a different style down to the 15th c., notably by Bartolomeo Sacchi (il *Platina). [SD]

Libertines and Libertinism. The terms refer to a heterogeneous group of free thinkers in religious matters in 17th-c. Italy. From the 17th c. 'libertine' was synonymous with 'atheist', though in practice libertine views ranged from all-out atheism to religious tolerance. The most fertile area for libertinism was, from the 1630s onwards, *Venice and its *university in *Padua, both of which were celebrated as centres of freedom by the philosopher Cesare *Cremonini. Other important centres were *Rome during the pontificates of *Urban VIII and Innocent X, and *Florence, with its university in *Pisa. The *Spanish territories of Italy (*Milan, *Genoa, *Naples, Palermo), *Turin, and the courts of the *Este at *Ferrara and the *Gonzaga at *Mantua were hardly touched by libertinism.

The first Italian libertines were Giordano *Bruno and Tommaso *Campanella, though both writers vacillated between a *Neoplatonic-idealistic view of the universe and an *Aristotelian-realist approach to religious questions, as is clear from Bruno's *Spaccio de la bestia trionfante* and Campanella's *Atheismus triumphatus* (ch. 2). However, both plainly held religion to be a man-made *lex* (law), variable from continent to continent, and hence were drawn to question the absolute authority of the Roman Church. Indeed, like later libertines, they concluded that religious truth was at best relative, and religious tolerance was paramount, though they did not believe that religion should be abandoned because man-made: rather, it should become a natural branch in essential law-making processes. However, they did call into question the role of Christ as divine Son of God; since man is wholly natural, and religion man-made, Christ is merely a mage or magician, and at worst a trickster.

The first out-and-out Italian libertine was Giulio Cesare *Vanini, who in effect demolished the supernatural in religion, leaving no room for belief in the immortality of the soul or in the existence of a personal God, and exalting the role of the passions, especially the libido, which he saw as legitimately permitted to vent itself in previously prohibited acts. Equating man with other animals, Vanini taught that both were products of nature, arriving at the pre-Darwinian thesis that man was descended from the apes. He was highly influential within Italy and abroad, and his sorry death at the stake in Toulouse ensured his future reputation amongst French libertines. After Vanini, libertine activity in Italy moved to the Venetian Accademia degli *Incogniti from 1630 to around 1660. The Incogniti, most of whose writings were put on the *Index, brought libertine ideas into literary works, including the *novel and the *novella*. Foremost amongst them was Ferrante *Pallavicino, who, along with Gregorio *Leti, played a crucial role in the diffusion of libertine ideas throughout Europe, both with his novels and with his unsparing, often obscene prose *satire on the Catholic Church. His fame and influence lived on after his death, thanks to the anonymous *L'anima di Ferrante Pallavicino* (perhaps by Gian Francesco *Loredan). His death by decapitation, preceded by disfiguring torture, helped to fuel the myth of the outrageous free thinker throughout the second half of the 17th c. [PBD]

See G. Spini, *Ricerca dei libertini: la teoria dell'impostura delle religioni nel Seicento italiano* (1950); T. Gregory *et al.* (eds.), *Ricerche su letteratura libertina e letteratura clandestina nel Seicento* (1981).

Libraries are an essential feature of intellectual life, always present in a civilization with a developed culture. In the *Middle Ages, libraries were found primarily in religious institutions: the oldest surviving library in Italy is that of the cathedral chapter of Verona, the Biblioteca Capitolare, already in existence in the 9th c. It was above all in monastic libraries, on both sides of the Alps, that Italian *humanists searched for the lost masterpieces of classical literature. Under the influence of humanism, new library patterns emerged in Italy in the 15th c. Wealthy individuals, some of them laymen, began to amass books in pursuit of private cultural programmes; rulers of states built up libraries for reasons of prestige. The two patterns could converge. The public library established by Cosimo de' *Medici in 1441, in a purpose-built room in the convent of S. Marco in *Florence, began with some 800 books from the private collection of the humanist Niccolò *Niccoli. Much of this collection is now in the Florentine Biblioteca Laurenziana. Equally, the magnificent collection of illuminated *manuscripts put together in the second half of the century by *Federigo da Montefeltro, Duke of *Urbino, owed much to his *education in the famous humanist school of *Vittorino da Feltre in *Mantua. The *Vatican library, founded by Pope Nicholas V in 1450, comes into the category of a ruler's library; but, like the library of S. Marco, it was intended to serve wider interests, and to be used by others than the founder. Architectonically the most perfect of these 15th c. libraries is the Biblioteca Malatestiana established in Cesena by its ruler, Malatesta Novello, and built in 1447–52; its reading room, with its chained manuscripts, is still exactly as planned. The 15th c. also saw the beginning of the first civic library in Italy, the Biblioteca Marciana of *Venice. In 1468 Cardinal *Bessarion left to the Republic 476 Greek and 263 Latin manuscripts. It took Venice almost 100 years to house them adequately; the building then constructed in the Piazzetta di San Marco, to a design by Francesco *Sansovino, is still in use today.

The advent of *printing led to a vast increase in the numbers and availability of books, which by the 16th c. were within the price range of most literate Italians. At the same time the religious differences which split Christendom underlined the importance of the printed word in the battle for men's minds and souls. These influences led to the founding of numerous libraries in Italy, many at the instigation of churchmen, all open in varying degrees to the public, and most still in existence today. One of the first and most important was the Biblioteca Ambrosiana, a purpose-built library of modern design founded by Cardinal Federico *Borromeo in *Milan, which opened its doors in 1609. This was followed by the Vallicelliana, the Angelica, and the Alessandrina (the university library), all in *Rome, and by libraries in *Naples, Florence, and many other cities of Central and Northern Italy. Architecturally, these libraries broke away from the monastic model of a vaulted room with frescoed walls and ceilings, and books in low *plutei* or cupboards, in favour of functional, well-lit reading rooms with books lining the walls, arranged in cupboards or on bookshelves. Further libraries were founded in the 18th c., by the end of which few Italian cities of any size lacked a civic library open to the public. In the second half of the century many were substantially enriched by manuscripts and books from the libraries of religious houses suppressed by the

policies of the *Habsburg Empire, policies largely imitated in the Italian states. This process continued during the *Napoleonic period.

This rich and complex pattern of libraries was inherited by the new Italian state in 1860, and has proved difficult to handle. Leaving aside the libraries of religious foundations, such as the Vatican, the Ambrosiana, and the Capitolare of Verona, which continued (and continue) to be administered by the founding body with little help from the state, Italian libraries open to the public are divided into two groups: those administered by the state and those run by the commune. At the head of the state library system come the seven national libraries (at Rome, Florence, Venice, Milan, *Turin, Naples, and Bari), incorporating pre-existing collections and libraries, mainly of former ruling families; there are also about thirty other state libraries of varying nature scattered throughout the peninsula, including university libraries (*Bologna, *Pisa). The logic behind the inclusion of libraries in this second group is not always clear, and has undoubtedly sometimes militated against their efficiency. Libraries run by the commune have fared differently according to the goodwill of the local authority. All have faced the same problems: the difficulty of compiling and making available adequate catalogues of their enormous stock of manuscripts and printed books, and the inadequacy of their once trend-setting but now antiquated library buildings to house the explosion of printed matter which has characterized the last fifty years. Both categories of library have also been bedevilled by ambiguities of aim, which have adversely affected their efficiency: almost without exception, they contain important research material; yet all, even the great national libraries, have been required to function as lending libraries as well.

The cataloguing problem can be eased with respect to printed books by the use of modern technological aids. Unfortunately, these have so far been applied in Italy in a haphazard way, though a computerized national library system (SBN) does exist, to which it is hoped that all libraries, whatever their nature, will eventually adhere. There is an ever-growing number of libraries (though not including the largest and most important) with automated catalogues of accessions and even of earlier holdings, and many of these can be consulted on the Internet or the rare books database of the Consortium of European Research Libraries.

[CF]

See E. Bottasso, *Storia della biblioteca in Italia*

Libretto

(1984); W. A. Wiegand and D. G. Davis (eds.), *Encyclopedia of Library History* (1994).

Libretto, literally a small book, denotes both the pocket-sized printing of the literary text of an *opera, and the literary component in the operatic complex. Until about 1900 libretti were offered to the audience, like today's theatre programmes, as an aid to understanding and a memento. Besides the text, the author's name (but not necessarily the composer's), and the date and place of the production, there might be a dedication and prefatory matter, with an *antefatto* explaining the situation before curtain-up, and sometimes a synopsis. Other possible information includes: a list of characters with the names of singers, dancers, choreographer, designer, and engineer; descriptive lists of scenes, machines, and balletic entries; credits for any aristocratic patrons allowing their dependants to participate; the printer's name; a censor's licence.

In the 17th and 18th c. an operatic musical score was normally modified or composed anew for each revival, was rarely published, and may now be lost or unidentified. A libretto is frequently the sole evidence for an opera's production or revival; it also enables the historian to identify the occasion for a surviving manuscript score, and to reconstruct theatrical repertories and the careers of the artists named.

Intended for the ear, not the eye, the words of an Italian opera were sung throughout. A libretto resembles a short play text in format and other literary characteristics, but its art is not self-sufficient. A specimen cobbled together by a hack *theatre poet may deserve critical contempt; but the form has also attracted accomplished writers from earliest times (around 1600), such as Ottavio *Rinuccini and Gabriello *Chiabrera. Rinuccini's libretti are almost indistinguishable from spoken drama: it was the little-known Alessandro *Striggio who first realized, in *Monteverdi's *Orfeo* (1607), the need to reduce the *versi sciolti* (that is, recitative dialogue in the naturalistic time-scale of a spoken play) to make room for the lyric strophes of arias (that is, expanded psychological moments) and for ensembles, choruses, dances, and illustrative *sinfonie*.

After the commercialized sensationalism of *Venetian public opera, the libretto aspired to greater dignity at the Viennese court, and was reformed by the *classicizing *Arcadian Academy. Its prolific librettist Apostolo *Zeno was succeeded as Caesarean poet by Pietro *Metastasio, whose elegant verses were set and reset by innumerable composers. The playwright Carlo *Goldoni wrote innovative comic-opera libretti, but was not alone in concealing his authorship under a pseudonym. Ranieri de' *Calzabigi, however, took pride in his tragic collaborations with Gluck, and Giovanni Battista *Casti and Lorenzo *Da Ponte (Mozart's partner) were equally proud of their *comedies. *Rossini set several excellent comedies, but formed no lasting relationship with a librettist, unlike Vincenzo *Bellini, who worked closely with Felice *Romani. *Donizetti, himself author of *opere buffe*, was able to dictate terms to his librettists. *Verdi's dramatic instincts galvanized the unremarkable Francesco Maria *Piave, among others, into producing serviceable libretti, but his last and finest partner was the inventive metrist Arrigo *Boito. *Puccini's most frequent collaborators, Giuseppe *Giacosa and Luigi Illica (1857–1919), worked as a team.

The increasing personalization of musical style tempted many composers to write their own libretti (Mascagni, Busoni, Pizzetti). As during the *Risorgimento, opera remained sensitive to surrounding influences such as *verismo* and *fin-de-siècle* *decadentismo*: Gabriele *D'Annunzio was himself a librettist (as were *Pascoli and later *Pirandello); like *Carducci, he had at first despised opera but changed his mind. Conservative conformity under *Fascism was challenged by the librettist-composers G. F. Malipiero and *Dallapiccola, but really experimental work did not ensue until c.1960: *Nono assembled his own libretti (a collage of eight authors in *Intolleranza*); Luciano Berio has worked with Edoardo *Sanguineti and Italo *Calvino. [See also MUSIC.]   [BLT]

See E. Istel, *The Art of Writing Opera Librettos* (1922); P. J. Smith, *The Tenth Muse* (1970); A. Cassi Ramelli, *Libretti e librettisti* (1973).

Libri Memorialium, SEE MEMORIALI BOLOGNESI.

Libro dei cinquanta miracoli, SEE MIRACOLI DELLA VERGINE MARIA, I.

LIBURNIO, NICCOLÒ (c.1477–1557) was born in Friuli but lived mostly in *Venice. He himself wrote *Petrarchist verse after the model of Pietro *Bembo, but his *Le vulgari elegantie* (1521) and *Le tre fontane* (1526) advised *imitation of *Dante, as well as *Petrarch and *Boccaccio. Most of his later works, for instance *Le occorrenze humane* (1546), are compilations of learning or moral advice.   [BR]

Liceo, see EDUCATION, 2.

LIGORIO, PIRRO, see ANTIQUARIANISM.

LIGUORI, ST ALFONSO MARIA DE', see RELIGIOUS LITERATURE; SERMONS.

Limbo. First circle of *Dante's *Inferno,* where the souls of unbaptized children and virtuous pagans dwell.

LINATI, CARLO (1878–1949). *Novelist, *translator, and critic. Born in Como, he took a law degree at Parma and, after service in *World War I went to *Milan, where he dedicated himself to literature. He contributed to *Poesia, La *Voce,* and *La *Ronda* and wrote *D'Annunzian *novels—*Barbogeria* (1917), *Due* (1928), and *Cantalupa* (1935). But he revealed his talents as a writer of short prose texts, notably in *I doni della terra* (1915) and *Sulle orme di Renzo* (1919). He also published various collections of *prosa d'arte,* which he first began to write for the *Corriere della sera,* running from *Nuvole e paesi* (1919) to *Milano d'allora* (1946). He wrote extensively on literature in English, collecting his essays in *Scrittori anglo-americani* (1932), and brought James Joyce's work to the attention of the Italian public, translating *Exiles* (1920) and *A Portrait of the Artist as a Young Man* (1950). He also translated works by D. H. Lawrence and Henry James (1934).

[AC]

Lincei, Accademia dei. The first and most famous of the scientific *academies in Italy, founded in 1603 in *Rome by Federico *Cesi, Francesco *Stelluti, Anastasio De Filiis, and Jan Heck, a Flemish doctor. The academy dedicated its activities to the study of the natural and mathematical sciences and to the use of the experimental method associated with *Galileo. Its name refers to the lynx, and its emblem showed that animal at once flaying Cerberus (conquering evil) and gazing towards the sky in the act of enlightened observation. The statutes, drawn up by Cesi, laid down a strict code of ascetic behaviour and excluded from the academy priests, politicians, and anyone caught up in religious and political polemics. The European dimension of the Academy was characteristic of the founders' foresight and perspective: elections were made of foreign corresponding members, a practice that continues to this day.

Members included Claudio *Achillini, Pietro *Della Valle, Galileo (from 1611), Pietro Sforza *Pallavicino, Giambattista *Della Porta (from 1610), and Filippo Salviati. Their work involved the large-scale publishing of scientific results based on direct observation, including Galileo's work on the moon's surface (1610) and his *Saggiatore* (1623). The Academy defended Galileo at his trial in 1616, and played a crucial role in the early diffusion and promotion of his method. With the premature death of Cesi in 1630, the Academy closed, and, despite the best efforts of his friend Stelluti, further work was impossible after Galileo's condemnation by the Church in 1632. The true successor of the Lincei was the Accademia del *Cimento, founded in *Florence in 1657. Though there were earlier attempts, the Accademia dei Lincei was finally revived in 1874, thanks to the *Piedmontese statesman and scientist Quintino *Sella. [See also LITERARY PRIZES.]   [PBD]

See E. Bellini, *Umanisti e lincei: letteratura e scienza a Roma nell'età di Galileo* (1997).

Linea lombarda, see ERBA, LUCIANO; RISI, NELO.

Lingua cortigiana. The argument that the vernacular literary language should be based on *Tuscan but refined through the usage of the *Roman *court was apparently put forward by *Calmeta in his *Della volgar poesia,* written in the second half of the 15th c. This is now lost, but the contents are summarized by Pietro *Bembo and *Castelvetro. Arguments for drawing on the best courtly usage were then advanced by *Colocci in his *Apologia delle rime di Serafino Aquilano* (1503), *Equicola in his *Libro de natura de amore* (1525), and *Castiglione in the *Cortegiano* (1528), although they all refer to a 'lingua commune' rather than a 'lingua cortigiana'. It is not clear that such a language ever existed, although an approximation to it has been identified in Northern Italian court literature of the later 15th c., and in the work of *Boiardo. [See also QUESTIONE DELLA LINGUA.]   [NC]

L'innocente, see D'ANNUNZIO, GABRIELE.

Lipogram. Text in which all words or phrases containing one particular letter have been omitted. A lipogram in -*e* is one in which no *e* appears. There are examples in ancient Greek and medieval Latin. Like Raymond Queneau and Georges Perec in French, Umberto *Eco has composed some modern lipograms in Italian.

[DieZ]

LIPPERINI, GUENDALINA, see REGINA DI LUANTO.

LIPPI, LORENZO (1606–65). *Florentine painter and poet, who was a protégé of Ferdinando II de' *Medici, and the founder, with Salvatore *Rosa, of the Accademia dei Percossi. His *mock-heroic poem *Il Malmantile racquistato*, published posthumously under the anagrammatical name Perlone Zipoli, exploits the comic possibilities of spoken Florentine and contains numerous digressions derived mainly from *novelle* by *Basile. As a painter Lippi followed Caravaggio and Rosa, whose portrait he painted. He also illustrated the *Orlando furioso* and the *Gerusalemme liberata*.

[FC]

LISI, NICOLA (1893–1975). *Tuscan *novelist and *journalist who, with *Bargellini and *Betocchi, was a member of the Catholic *Frontespizio* group from its inception. In his fiction he wrote mostly about daily life in his native Mugello, as in his best-known novel, *Diario di un parroco di campagna* (1942). [DCH]

Literacy. In his esssay on *Perché la letteratura italiana non sia popolare in Italia* (1856), *Manzoni's friend Ruggiero *Bonghi, who was to become minister for *education in 1874–6, omits to mention the main reason why Italian literature was not popular in Italy, i.e. that the majority of Italians could not *read. Statistics for literacy are difficult to establish and notoriously unreliable, particularly for past centuries. According to Grendler (1989) in 1480 *Florence about 30–3 per cent of boys aged 10–13 can be estimated to have been literate. From a *Venetian census of 1587 there is evidence that 23 per cent of children aged 6–15 (33 per cent for boys, 13 per cent for girls) received *education in schools, convents, or at home. This includes all the children in the families of nobles, professionals, and *merchants, constituting about 10 per cent of the population. In what way the residual 13 per cent of literates was distributed among the lower classes, which amounted to 90 per cent of the population, seems impossible to establish. Figures are likely to have been comparable in other affluent *Renaissance cities. By way of comparison, it has been estimated that York in 1530 had 20–25 per cent male literacy and hardly any adult female literacy.

The situation is further complicated by the distinction between Latin and vernacular literacy. For Latin, known only to a minority, literacy was a sine qua non. All those who knew Latin were literate—in fact it was not possible to know Latin and be illiterate. On the other hand everyone had a vernacular mother tongue. What proportion was literate in the vernacular and not in Latin is difficult to ascertain. Generally women were not taught Latin. According to *Dante (*VN* 25.6) the first vernacular poet wrote in order to be understood by women, to whom Latin verses were inaccessible, and in the *Epistle* to Cangrande the vernacular is described as the language in which 'even womenfolk communicate'. Leonardo *Bruni considered 'nurses and womenfolk' incapable of using Latin even in ancient Rome. The great mass of those who read works in the vernacular must have been monolingual literates, according to Petrucci (1995). Less is known about schooling in the vernacular than in Latin. Among the most common Italian books used, apart from alphabet books, were the *Fiore di virtù* and the *Orlando furioso*, and in the 16th c. textbooks are published to satisfy the demand of people who did not know Latin, for instruction (reading, writing, arithmetic) in the vernacular. It seems that in Venice, in 1587, 46 per cent of the pupils attended *humanistic schools (with Latin), and 54 per cent vernacular ones.

For the post-*Unification period we have better information about literacy. Statistics give about 75 per cent illiterates in 1861, 48 per cent in 1901, 13 per cent in 1951, decreasing to 8 per cent in 1961, 5 per cent in 1971, 3 per cent in 1981, 2 per cent in 1991. A peculiarity of the Italian situation, which was dramatically highlighted in a major study by De Mauro (1963), is the link between literacy and knowledge of the national language. This depends on the nature of Italian, which until the mid-20th c. was mainly a written language, and therefore, like Latin since medieval times, only familiar to people who were literate. The spoken language, in Italy, was the *dialect, which differed, sometimes to the point of unintelligibility, from region to region. For the majority of the population this stopped being true in the 1950s, owing mainly to the spread of *television. From then on the link between literacy and familiarity with Italian is effectively severed, and it is possible for people to speak and understand Italian even if they are illiterate or semiliterate (a distinction which is made in the statistics only since 1951). De Mauro's investigations, aimed at establishing how many people were familiar with Italian at the moment of Unification, in fact led him to revise the statistics for literacy, suggesting a percentage of effective illiterates far higher than expected. In many cases elementary teaching was in dialect and did not provide the basis for an ability to read and write. Only for *Tuscany and *Rome can it be assumed that elementary education enabled people to use Italian. For other regions this required secondary education. And the figure for those who had these qualifications was 2.5 per cent. Arrigo Castellani in 1982 endeavoured to revise this figure, but could not push it beyond 10 per cent. This clearly affects the citizens' sense of belonging to a culture whose language was unintelligible to the majority of them, and goes a long way towards explaining certain weaknesses of the Italian national tradition.

A question which is distinct from that of literacy concerns the notion of orality and the fact that literature does not necessarily imply literacy. There are oral traditions, such as those of the *giullari* or *jongleurs*, the *cantastorie*, the preachers, not to speak of the domain of folklore [see FOLK AND POPULAR LITERATURE], including genres such as *proverbs, riddles, counting rhymes, and songs of different kinds, performed and appreciated by audiences which may have been largely or even totally illiterate. But even products which may have enjoyed an oral transmission, once they are fixed in writing, collected, studied, and discussed in their relation to literary texts proper, by the very fact of being an object of scholarly interest are inevitably absorbed into the world of literacy.   [GCL]

See T. De Mauro, *Storia linguistica dell'Italia unita* (1963); P. F. Grendler, *Schooling in Renaissance Italy: Literacy and Learning, 1300–1600* (1989); A. Petrucci, *Writers and Readers in Medieval Italy: Studies in the History of Written Culture* (1995); B. Richardson, *Printing, Writers and Readers in Renaissance Italy* (1999).

Literary Criticism, that is, the interpretation and assessment of literary works and authors, as we understand these activities today, was born in Italy in the second half of the 18th c. Until then reflection on literature and its products preceded rather than followed the work itself, consisting of treatises on poetics and rhetoric which provided the writer with rules to observe and models to imitate, derived from classical literature or from Italian authors of the 14th c. [See LITERARY THEORY.] The only exceptions are the so-called *commentaries, which generally consisted of explanatory notes or illustrations to the most important texts, and were often anonymous or brought together material by several authors. The change comes with *Enlightenment

writers such as *Bettinelli, *Baretti, *Algarotti, and *Cesarotti, who dismiss appeals to tradition and focus on personal judgement and the relationship between literary texts and political and social realities. For them criticism has the important function of aiding the greatest possible number of the people to develop an informed approach to Italian and foreign literature. Italian *Romantic criticism continues along the same lines, though a new emphasis on instinct and spontaneity means that great importance is now assigned to popular poetry [see DIALECT WRITING; FOLK AND POPULAR LITERATURE], whilst passion or inspiration are pronounced necessary for all great art.

The two great authors of the early 19th c., *Manzoni and *Leopardi, are also two of the most innovative critics and theorists of literature. Both are affected by Romantic ideas. In his writings on drama, most notably the *Lettre à M. Chauvet* (1823), Manzoni gives priority to the notion of truth, in the name of which he is able to dismiss the unities of time, place, and action that had long stifled Italian and foreign drama. Leopardi similarly breaks with poets such as *Parini and Vincenzo *Monti in founding his poetics on the expression of individual sentiment. Romantic precepts also provide *De Sanctis with his starting point, but he goes on to enrich them through the assimilation of Hegelian dialectics. For him, the inseparable union of form and content means that neither is analysable or judgeable in isolation from the other and that the individual work is not separable from the concrete reality from which it emerged. His critical essays and his *Storia della letteratura italiana* (1871) construct the history of Italian culture and consciousness via a dialectic of authors and trends, all, however, characterized by their specific individual identities.

The later 19th c. saw the rise of the 'scuola storica' of Alessandro D'Ancona, Domenico Comparetti, Pio *Rajna, Adolfo *Bartoli, and Francesco Torraca, founded on the *positivist admiration for the exact sciences. Rather than formulate judgements, criticism was to develop the correct understanding of literary texts, establish biographical facts and the sources of literary works, and study the evolution of literary genres. Exemplary in this respect is Rajna's *Le fonti dell'*Orlando furioso* (1876), whilst the *Giornale storico della letteratura italiana* (1883–) remains still the major journal of philological and scholarly study in the field of Italian literature.

Attention to aesthetic values is vigorously reborn

at the beginning of the 20th c. with Benedetto *Croce, who follows De Sanctis in going back to Hegel. In his *Estetica come scienza dell'espressione e linguistica generale* (1902) and subsequently in the essays published in *La *Critica* (1903–44), he formulated the idea of art as an autonomous category of the spirit, in which intuition and expression are identified with each other, and each individual work is a unique creation; research into sources and attempts to insert a work in the history of literary genres are therefore misleading. The important critical act is to distinguish between '*poesia' and 'non poesia', that is, poetry and literature ('*letteratura'), or poetry and structure. It was a view of criticism which was extremely influential until at least the late 1950s.

But many critics from the first half of the century developed individual voices often of great intellectual scope and refinement. Giuseppe Antonio *Borgese (the inventor of the term *Crepuscolari* and the discoverer of *Moravia and *Tozzi) brought Croce and De Sanctis together in a richly balanced synthesis. Other notable names, all active on the *terza pagina* (the literary page of newspapers) as well as in literary *journals, are Renato *Serra, Emilio *Cecchi, Pietro *Pancrazi, Enrico *Falqui, and Giacomo *Debenedetti, who was one of the first Italian critics to be interested in *psychoanalysis. Attilio *Momigliano and Luigi Russo both start from Croce, but the former moves towards expressing an ever more refined aesthetic sensibility, whilst the second becomes increasingly attentive to the links between literature and reality. Both exert a profound influence on academic criticism of the 1950s and 1960s.

In the second half of the 20th c. much criticism in Italy, as in the West generally, sought new ideas and methods in non-literary ideologies and disciplines. *Marxist thought of *Gramscian derivation assumes a variety of forms in the work of Carlo Salinari, Carlo Muscetta, *Fortini, Giuseppe Petronio, *Asor Rosa, and Romano Luperini; concepts and methods originating in linguistics, *structuralism, and *semiotics are taken up by Cesare *Segre, *Corti, and *Eco; *psychoanalytic approaches are developed by Francesco Orlando and Mario Lavagetto. But the philological tradition has remained strong; its most illustrious exponents, notably *Dionisotti, Giuseppe Billanovich, and *Branca, are sensitive to the multiple implications of literary texts—geographical, environmental, social—and to a range of other historical factors, including human relations, the circulation of

books, and the relations between the various arts, all of which they insist must be taken into account for a true history of culture to emerge. Romance philology and the *history of the Italian language, most notably the work of Benvenuto Terracini, provided the starting point and the methodological underpinning for the work of the best Italian structuralist and semiotic critics—*Semiotica filologica* is not by chance the title of a work published by Segre in 1979. They also provide the foundations for the immensely influential work of Gianfranco *Contini, especially his innovative development of criticism of authorial variants.

In the 20th c. professional critics frequently played a valuable role in introducing and interpreting major writers; the reception of *Montale and *Gadda is linked in both instances in important ways with Contini's essays on them. Vice versa writers like Montale, *Calvino, *Pasolini, and *Zanzotto have written extensively on literature in general and on specific authors in ways that have proved influential, but which have generally been more independent of schools and tendencies. [See also HISTORIES OF ITALIAN LITERATURE.]   [NG]

See M. Puppo, 'Critica letteraria', in V. Branca (ed.), *Dizionario critico della letteratura italiana* (1986); G. Leonelli, *La critica letteraria in Italia* (1945–94) (1994); P. V. Mengaldo, *Profili di critici del Novecento* (1998).

Literary History, see HISTORIES OF ITALIAN LITERATURE.

Literary Prizes (*premi letterari*) are a characteristic feature of modern literary culture, though there are various precedents in the history of Italian literature. Famous instances are the coronation of *Petrarch on the Campidoglio (1341), the *Certame coronario* organized by Leon Battista *Alberti (1441), and the prize set up by the Accademia della *Crusca in the early 19th c.

The literary prize in its modern form came into being in Italy later than in most other European countries, but its origins and development were similar. With the loss of public interest in purely academic awards, prizes were promoted by critics and readers outside the jurisdiction of official bodies. Financial backing came from sources such as private firms, insurance companies, and banks, and from local or regional government, the end in all cases being more or less explicitly commercial. The first prize of any importance was founded in 1924 by *Mondadori. It was to be an annual prize for unpublished works by unknown authors, the jury being drawn from some of the firm's established authors. In 1927 the writers and artists who frequented the Bagutta restaurant in *Milan founded and financed the Bagutta prize. In 1930 Leonida Repaci and some other writers and critics spending the summer in Versilia established the Viareggio prize.

But it was only after the war that prizes became a significant cultural phenomenon. The Strega prize was founded in 1947 in the salon of the *Bellonci family in *Rome, with a jury of over 300 members drawn from the literary and publishing world. Other notable prizes followed: the Accademia dei *Lincei (1952); the Bancarella (1953), financed by 150 booksellers; the Campiello (1963), with two juries, one made up of readers, the other of critics; the Grinzane Cavour (1982), with a jury of secondary school students; the Alassio (1995), which is unusual in having an international jury. Most prizes are for already published fiction, but others are for poetry (Montale), *journalism (Estense), *children's literature (Andersen), *women's writing (Rapallo), *biographies (Comisso), *translation (Monselice), and unpublished works (Calvino, Montblanc). A 1995 survey gave the total number as 686, though this is probably an underestimate. All have promoted the cause of literature to some degree, but their positive utility is being increasingly undermined not just by their sheer proliferation, but also by the shift in media attention from the books themselves to disputes between panel members.   [GBB]

See M. Bellonci, *Come un racconto: gli anni del premio Strega* (1971); *Catalogo dei premi letterari italiani* (1995).

Literary Theory

1. Before 1400

On the basis of classical (Plato, *Aristotle, *Cicero, *Horace) and patristic sources (*Augustine, Gregory the Great [see also CHURCH FATHERS]), the *Middle Ages developed a highly sophisticated and multifaceted tradition of literary theory and criticism, as well as a variety of analytical tools, ranging from glosses on individual words to *commentaries on complete texts and to critical introductions (*accessus*). A central role was accorded to the *imitation and the interpretation of canonical texts in religious and secular culture, and, specifically, in the *education system. Indeed, *grammar—the first of the *liberal arts—used the works of authori-

tative classical Latin writers (*auctores*) to provide instruction both in writing correctly and in exegesis (*enarratio poetarum*). The analysis of the *auctores*, who were hierarchically categorized according to subject matter, style, and structure, was intended to help imitation (*imitatio*), and, in particular, to ensure that confusion between different genres was avoided and that stylistic propriety was maintained. Rhetoric, which had lost its original links with political and forensic oratory, increasingly provided prescriptive instruction on matters of style and structure (as in the case of the *ars dictaminis*), thereby blurring the boundaries between itself and grammar. The *enarratio poetarum* not only dealt with matters of form, but also provided moral and philosophical interpretations of the classical poets so as to make them acceptable to Christian audiences. It was a commonplace of medieval criticism that behind the fictions of literature lay valuable truths, and that it was on these truths that readers had to focus (modern scholarship has reductively and anachronistically termed this kind of exposition *allegory).

Biblical exegesis too underlined the complexity of meaning lying beyond the literal level of Scripture. However, in order to underline the *Bible's superiority, its divinely inspired account of providential history was deemed to include a greater number of 'senses' than human writing. Scriptural commentators were intent not only on explicating these 'senses', but also on examining the textual and literary character of the Bible. Given the far from dissimilar aims of religious and secular exegesis, from the 12th c. onwards the two interpretive traditions became increasingly intertwined [see TWELFTH-CENTURY RENAISSANCE]. As a result, increased attention was paid to the relative standing of poetry in relation to the other 'sciences'. Thus, Thomas *Aquinas afforded it limited cognitive value, while *Dante claimed that poetry, or at least the poetry of his all-embracing *Divine Comedy*, constituted a uniquely privileged form of knowledge. Both *Petrarch and *Boccaccio followed Dante, as did other proto-*humanists, in recognizing poetry's superiority in relation to the liberal arts, and associated it closely with philosophy and theology.

Medieval Italian reflection on literature established what may be called 'modern' literary theory and criticism. Dante was the first non-classical writer to be treated on a par with the great Greek and Latin *auctores*. In the course of the 14th c., the full weight of contemporary critical practice was

Literary Theory

brought to bear on the *Divine Comedy*, especially in the many detailed commentaries, the variety and subtlety of which is evident from comparing Guido da Pisa, Pietro *Alighieri, and *Benvenuto da Imola [see also DANTE COMMENTARIES]. Strong doubts, however, stemming from Dante's choice of the vernacular, were forthcoming from classicizing proto-humanists such as *Giovanni del Virgilio, and later Petrarch. The issue of the relationship between Latin and vernacular, which had been addressed by Dante in the *De vulgari eloquentia* and the *Convivio*, became increasingly important during the course of the 14th c. So too did the question of the relationship between contemporary writers and their classical forebears, an issue which was at the heart of Petrarch's and Boccaccio's thinking about literature [see also LATIN INFLUENCES].

Dante's 14th-c. reception was conditioned not only by the genius of his poetry, but also by the influence of the constant and careful self-elucidation evident in all his works from the *Vita nova* to the *Divine Comedy*. Metaliterary reflection and debate is characteristic of medieval literature as a whole and is particularly foregrounded in Italian *lyric poetry from the *Sicilian School onwards. It is in Dante, however, that it finds its supreme expression. [ZB]

See G. Ronconi, *Le origini delle dispute umanistiche sulla poesia* (1976); A. J. Minnis and A. B. Scott, *Medieval Literary Theory and Criticism c.1100–1375* (1988); Z. G. Baranski, 'Sole nuovo, luce nuova': saggi sul rinnovamento culturale in Dante* (1996).

2. The Renaissance

Literary theory in Italy developed in two broadly century-long phases during the *Renaissance: in the 15th c. it was largely in Latin and about Latin literature, classical or *humanist; in the 16th c. it was mainly in and about the *volgare. In the 15th c. the first major impetus to literary theory was provided by the 1421 discovery of the Lodi manuscript containing some of *Cicero's then unknown literary critical works: the *Brutus* in particular inspired humanists such as *Polenton, *Sabellico, and *Cortesi to write their own literary histories. There was little *Greek influence, though George *Trapezuntios' *Rhetorica* (?1437) owed something to Dionysius of Halicarnassus's treatise on composition. The most influential Latin work was *Valla's *Elegantiae*, which established rigorous standards of Latinity both in syntax and lexis, but the most innovative critic was *Poliziano, who con-

sistently defended Silver Latin models such as Quintilian and *Statius, as opposed to Cicero and *Virgil. In the letter accompanying the *Raccolta aragonese* he also defended *Cino da Pistoia against *Dante. His antagonist Cortesi, in his *De hominibus doctis*, adopted a Ciceronian standpoint on *imitation, drawing on the *Brutus* for both the structure and the (rather opaque) critical terminology of his survey of 15th-c. Latin. The last great critic of the century was *Pontano, whose *Actius* offered a detailed analysis of alliteration (a term he invented), brevity, and rapidity in Virgil and *Livy.

The 15th-c. humanists revived mainly Latin literary theories (embracing especially the general notion of *imitation, *Horace's contrast of *ars* and *ingenium*, Cicero's doctrine of the three styles, but also Plato's idea of poetic *furor*), and preferred commenting on specific texts and literary histories to works of systematic theory. As for 15th-c. vernacular theory, Dante and *Petrarch were rarely criticized, but *Boccaccio was regularly attacked throughout the century even by Florentines (Filippo *Villani, Matteo *Palmieri, *Landino) for the immorality of the *Decameron*. Lorenzo de' *Medici was the first, in his *Comento*, to defend Boccaccio, though he simply praised the excellence of his vernacular, and did not engage with the moral criticism. The turning point came in Pietro *Bembo's *Prose della volgar lingua* (1525), which pointed out that, although decorum demanded that the style should be appropriate to the subject matter, it is the quality of the former which determines literary value, not the latter. Despite this influential judgement, the *Counter-Reformation once more focused attention on the moral content and the *Decameron* was eventually put on the *Index of banned books.

The 16th c. saw an enormous increase in the number of autonomous theoretical texts (or poetics) in both Latin (*Vida, *Fracastoro, G. C. *Scaligero) and the vernacular (*Trissino, *Daniello, *Speroni). But two major texts with a more practical focus were far more influential in the first half of the century. Bembo's *Prose* (1525) firmly established Petrarch and Boccaccio as the models for vernacular verse and prose. Secondly the 'rediscovery' of *Aristotle's *Poetics* (1536–48), with its emphasis on the unities and on the genres of *epic and *tragedy, shaped all subsequent theoretical and practical criticism. The second half of the century saw attempts to reconcile the *Poetics* with Horace's *Ars poetica*, the writing of new poetics in response to Aristotle, and a new emphasis on genres, with separate treatises appearing dealing with *comedy, *pastoral, *romance, *epic, and the *sonnet. Towards the end of the century, there were a series of 'querelles' over vernacular texts that seemed generically anomalous—the *Divine Comedy, *Orlando furioso, *Gerusalemme liberata, and *Pastor fido. The controversies were further fuelled by the Counter-Reformation demand for justification of secular poetry, the effects of which are evident in Torquato *Tasso's two sets of theoretical Discorsi.

[MMcL]

See B. Weinberg, A History of Literary Criticism in the Renaissance (1961); M. L. McLaughlin, Literary Imitation in the Italian Renaissance (1995); G. Baroni and R. Alhaique Pettinelli (eds.), Storia della critica letteraria in Italia (1997).

3. 1600–1690

Literary theory and criticism in the *Baroque period continued to treat some of the issues of the 16th c. The flood of Latin *commentaries on *Aristotle's Poetics came to an end with Paolo *Beni's examination of the tradition In Aristotelis Poeticam commentarii (1613). His work is remarkable for its scholarship and accuracy, but it does not relate at all directly to the more vital vernacular issues of the time, except to the debate, still current in the first decades of the 17th c., over whether for reasons of credibility Italian drama should be written in verse. The debates over Torquato *Tasso's *Gerusalemme liberata continued, but the issue took on renewed life after the publication in 1612 of the *Vocabolario della Crusca, a linguistic event that also had important literary consequences. The pro-*Florentine, pro-14th-c. bias of the dictionary, which excluded Tasso from its list of modern linguistic authorities, angered many writers, who, like Beni, saw Tasso as the greatest poet ever. After this episode Tasso became more accepted, and imitated, while, conversely, the 16th-c. trend towards devaluation of *Dante grew more acute, his popularity reaching an all-time low.

With the publication in 1623 of *Marino's *Adone, a dispute flared up similar to that caused by the Liberata. Marino's work, with its sensual metaphorical language and its non-*epic structure and morality, stirred up a debate over the rival claims of classical purity and sobriety on the one hand and the excesses of *marinismo on the other. The debate went on until it was finally decided in favour of the classical by the Accademia dell'*Arcadia, whose view of the matter prevailed in Italian

criticism well into the 20th c. But the divisions are misleading, because much anti-Marinist comment came from writers who were not at all immune to Marinism themselves, such as Salvator *Rosa. Connected with marinismo was the 17th-c. explosion of *concettismo, or the theory and practice of metaphorical writing. Taking their cue from Aristotle, theorists such as *Peregrini and *Tesauro published treatises on metaphor and its marvellous possibilities. Another new development in literary theory in the earlier 17th c. was the *Querelle des anciens et des modernes. Writers such as *Beni, *Tassoni, and Secondo *Lancellotti began systematically to celebrate a new modernism, in science or creative arts or both.

During this period the literary *academy continued to flourish, important because it allowed certain freedoms (from the *university, from the *court, from the Church) for men and occasionally women to discuss and exchange ideas and received notions. Along with much that is otiose, one can see in the work of the academies in this period a gradual acclimatization of the idea of progress and cultural development. This change of direction is even more noticeable in the birth of the important scientific academies, those of the *Lincei, the *Cimento, and the *Investiganti. [PBD]

See L. Anceschi, Le poetiche del Barocco (1963); M. Costanzo (ed.), Critica e poetica del primo Seicento (1969–71).

4. 1690–1800

The founding of the Accademia dell' *Arcadia in 1690 inaugurates a period dominated by its objective of restoring good taste after the extravagance of *marinismo and thereby resurrecting Italy's lost pre-eminence in poetry. Around the turn of the century much writing is stimulated by French strictures against Italian poetry, the foremost theorists being P. *Calepio, L. A. *Muratori, G. *Gravina, and A. *Conti, in all of whom aesthetic rationalism and didacticism are tempered by hedonism, appreciation of the role of imagination and poetic language, and a respect for tradition that usually includes the Poetics of *Aristotle and his *Renaissance commentators. The most representative and influential statement of theory is Muratori's Della perfetta poesia italiana (1706), while the Cartesian Gravina, in Della ragion poetica (1708), seeks to pioneer poetics as a science deduced from rational first principles and conceives poetry itself as a rudimentary and imperfect form of cognition through which philosophical truth is transmitted by means of image and emotion. In this and in his preference for the primitive (Homer and *Dante) over the refined (*Virgil and Torquato *Tasso), he points distantly towards *Vico's *Scienza nuova* (1725). For Vico, imagination and poetry are the first, pre-rational form of knowledge, with the Homeric poems (rather than an intentional repository of philosophy) expressing the collective imagination of the youthful Greek nation.

More limited yet significant steps towards *Romanticism are taken after 1750 with the literary utilitarianism and *sensismo* of the *Enlightenment, which inherently tend to aesthetic relativism, and begin to shake (but do not break) the dominance of poetry over prose by opening up the range of poetic subject matter to the prosaic—science, philosophy, and everyday realities—and legitimizing the free use of blank verse, which was originally confined to *tragedy [see also VERSIFICATION]. The most notable theoretical contributions, however, take a psychological approach: in *Ricerche sulla natura dello stile* (1770), *Beccaria purports to found a new rhetoric based on a better understanding of sensation and the association of ideas, while Pietro *Verri, in *Discorso sull'indole del piacere e del dolore* (1773), seeks to define, by analysis of the emotions, the specific nature of aesthetic pleasure.

The closing decades of the 18th c. see sharply contrasting tendencies. In *Del principe e delle lettere* (1778–86) *Alfieri presents a romantic intensification of *sensismo*, seeing poetry as the fruit of divine frenzy and the sublime expression of a sublime soul, radically criticizing literary *patronage, and reconstituting the poet as *vate*, or national bard and prophet of Italy's rebirth. But the triumph of *neoclassicism, with its concept of ideal beauty, in the fine arts, thanks to Winckelmann and his pupils, also ensures its pervasive influence in the literary field, especially during the revolutionary and *Napoleonic period, when it becomes the aesthetic of state art. It left its mark on theory, for example in *Parini's *De' principii generali delle belle lettere* (1773–5), and conditioned the practice of poets from *Savioli Fontana and the late Parini to *Mascheroni, Vincenzo *Monti, *Foscolo, and the early *Manzoni. [JMAL]

See J. G. Robertson, *Studies in the Genesis of Romantic Theory in the Eighteenth Century* (1923); M. Fubini, *Dal Muratori al Baretti* (1968).

5. 1800–1900

The controversy between *Romanticism and *classicism dominated the first two decades of the 19th c. and continued in various forms until its end. It was largely a way of airing, under the cover of literature, a series of contentious political and cultural issues, such as the need for a viable literary language, the democratization of *education, and the freedom of intellectuals from government *patronage and political control. *Pellico declared that 'romantic' meant *'liberal' whereas 'classicist' meant 'reactionary' and 'spy for the *Austrians', and *Botta charged the Romantics with being traitors to their country. But the real situation was more complex. In fact a number of 'liberal' writers (e.g. *Foscolo and *Leopardi) preferred classical or traditional forms to romantic innovations that were destined to become the next establishment clichés. One of the controversy's positive outcomes was that the best contributions to it, many published by the short-lived journal *Il *Conciliatore* (1818–19), provided models of how to argue cultural questions for later *periodicals, the most influential of which were *Vieusseux's *Antologia* (1821–33), *Cattaneo's *Il *Politecnico* (1839–45), and *Tenca's *Il *Crepuscolo* (1850–9).

Foscolo's and Leopardi's extensive critical writings remained mostly unknown to their Italian contemporaries. In his 'Lettre à M. Ch[auvet]' (1823) on *tragedy *Manzoni put paid at last to the pseudo-Aristotelian unities: he was, however, more influential as a practitioner in single-handedly renewing Italian narrative language than he was as a theorist. *Berchet, *Di Breme, *Borsieri, and Ermes *Visconti, on the other hand, are most memorable for their writings in defence of Romanticism. But *Risorgimento intellectuals tended not to appreciate the perceptiveness of classicist stalwarts like *Londonio, *Acerbi, and *Zajotti, and, following the example of *Alfieri, Foscolo, and *Mazzini, idealized literature as an indispensable tool for moral and civil education. In reality the majority of the Italian population was illiterate, or had to choose between bread and books.

Many of the better strands of Romantic criticism were drawn together by *De Sanctis, who combined an *idealist view of form with a text- and context-based understanding of literary genres and contents, and believed that their artistic synthesis generates exemplary aesthetic and moral values. He influenced later critics such as *Croce and *Gramsci more than his contemporaries. *Carducci, for one, disliked his methodology, and became the leader of the so-called historical school of *literary criticism, which combined antiquarian erudition with the new German philological techniques. Its best known representatives were Adolfo *Bartoli, Domenico Comparetti, Alessandro D'Ancona, Francesco D'Ovidio, and Pio *Rajna, and its most impressive forum the *Giornale storico della letteratura italiana (1883–).

The *positivism underlying historical criticism led, in the last thirty years of the century, to the development of theories of *realism, which were elaborated as *verismo by *Capuana and *Verga. These in turn provoked spiritualizing reactions exemplified in the critical writings of *Fogazzaro. Though *decadentismo and *symbolism affirmed themselves as important literary tendencies, it is only in the essays of *Pascoli that they achieve interesting critical formulation. [GC]

See C. Cappuccio (ed.), *Critici dell'età romantica* (1961); G. Grana (ed.) *I critici*, vol. i (1973).

6. 1900 onwards

Despite the iconoclastic incursions of *Futurism, Italian literature and *literary criticism of the first half of the 20th c. were dominated by *De Sanctis' view of Italian literary history evolving organically within the wider history of the nation, and even more by *Croce's *idealism. The latter's *Estetica* (1902) posits the ultimate aim of the literary creation as being absolute poetic beauty, disconnected from the contingencies of life and history, and distinct from technical and rhetorical skill. This perspective subsequently encouraged a sense of aristocratic isolation in both writers and critics, though it also provided strong grounds for asserting the superior autonomy of true art with respect to other disciplines and activities. Though Croce himself disapproved of *modernism, the rarefied poetics of movements such as 1930s *hermetic poetry did not mark a new departure in this respect.

The counter-arguments were voiced particularly in a political context. In hard-line *Fascist and *Communist thinking, literature was seen effectively as propaganda. But the case for commitment (*impegno) was also put more subtly in the period immediately following *World War II, which saw the best efforts to re-seed literary practices in the terrain of real social circumstances and effective political action. In the *populist ideology of *Neorealism the writer was morally committed to the cause of the oppressed, and therefore obliged to give them centre stage in the literary text.

From the 1960s onwards, the two main trends of Crocean idealism and *Marxist commitment, both now academically entrenched, were challenged by a series of important developments that drew heav-ily on new thinking and practices outside Italy (particularly in France). In the 1960s, *structuralism, in the work of D'Arco Silvio *Avalle, Maria *Corti, Cesare *Segre, and others, looked away from the author and context as positive and primary sources of meaning, and focused attention on the literary text itself, down to its minutest details, as an independent system of relations, which did not necessarily embody an idea (or give effect to an intention). At about the same time the *Neoavanguardia briefly resurrected the spirit of Futurism and proclaimed the need for more experimental and innovative literary practices, which would be less subservient to political aims or impalpable dreams, and more rooted in the materiality of language. In the 1970s, structuralism itself was felt to be in thrall to idealist illusions; post-structuralism sought to dispel any systems of thought centred on absolute certainties, and to uncover the essential fragility and incompleteness of any text. But in Italy post-structuralism enjoyed far less success than *semiotics, which had a prime theorist in Umberto *Eco, and which took account of fundamental strengths and weaknesses of alternative approaches. Semiotics focused on language and textuality in the investigation of literary meaning, but recognized the impracticable and finite nature of perfectly closed systems, whilst respecting the specificity and autonomy of each individual mode of signification. It also appreciated the need for a global perspective on the various communicative processes, and, though ready to attend to all types of signifying strategy, from elitist high culture to the mass media, it took account of the inevitable ideological dimension implicitly or explicitly active in any system of signs. That is not to say that it has been universally adopted. On the whole, academic criticism in Italy continues to a large extent to be based on historicist and philological premises. [GS]

See U. Eco, *Opera aperta* (1962); P. Orvieto, *Teorie letterarie e metodologie critiche* (1982).

LIVY (Titus Livius) (59/64 BC–AD 12/17), historian of the Roman Republic from its foundation. Of the original 142 books of his *De urbe condita*, only books 1–10 and 21–45 survive, thanks largely to *Petrarch, who brought together thirty which had been previously scattered in various locations, emended them, and put them in the right order. Petrarch's manuscript was then owned and further emended by Lorenzo *Valla. In the 15th c. Livy became the favourite historian of the Italian republics, especially *Florence, from Leonardo *Bruni onwards.

*Machiavelli treated him as the supreme political scientist in the *Discorsi*, which are cast as a *commentary on the first ten books of his work.

[LAP]

LIZZANI, CARLO (1922–), film director, scriptwriter, and historian. He began scripting *Neorealist films, then directed his own, often about the *Resistance (for example *Achtung! Banditi!* of 1951), or Italian 20th-c. history and politics: *Cronache di poveri amanti* (1953) from *Pratolini's novel, and *Il processo di Verona* (1963). His history *Il cinema italiano* has had many editions (the latest in 1979). [See also CINEMA.]

[CGW]

Locandiera, La (1753). *Comedy in three acts by *Goldoni. The innkeeper Mirandolina, courted in vain by two ridiculous noblemen (a penniless marquis and a recently ennobled upstart) manages to enthrall with her charms and intelligence a third guest, a *misogynist knight, only wisely to marry her butler in the end.

[FF]

LOCCHI, VITTORIO (1889–1917). *Tuscan poet who was an enthusiastic volunteer in *World War I. His best-known poem, *La sagra di Santa Gorizia* (1917), celebrates the taking of Gorizia in a pseudo-popular style. He was drowned when a troopship taking troops to Salonica was sunk. The *Fascists later claimed him as a protomartyr to their cause.

[PBarn]

LOI, FRANCO (1930–). One of the strongest *dialect poets of the later 20th c. Though born in *Genoa, he has lived in *Milan since the age of 7. He has worked in *advertising and for *Mondadori. He was active for many years in the *Communist Party and then moved to the independent Left. He began writing poetry in Milanese dialect in the mid-1960s, publishing a first collection, *I cart* (The Cards), in 1973. Rather than the literary Milanese of Carlo *Porta, Loi adopts the mixed idiom (and the stance) of the urban working class and the ex-*peasants who moved into the city after *World War II. His representations of everyday reality are often grotesquely comic, satirical, or horrific, though he also introduces reflection, irony, and political discussion. The result is a polyphony of conflicting tones and registers which continues the *expressionist tradition of *Lombard writing. His most ambitious work is the long autobiographical narrative *L'angel* (1981).

[GM]

LOMAZZO, GIOVAN PAOLO (1538–1600). Writer and painter, originally from *Milan. His painting career was cut short when he went blind aged 33. His literary compositions include *Rabisch* (1589), written in an invented local *dialect. He wrote a number of works on the *visual arts, including *L'idea del tempio della pittura*, which sets forth an original arrangement of artists and styles based on esoteric ideas.

[PLR]

LOMBARDI, BALDASSARRE, see DANTE COMMENTARIES.

LOMBARDO, NICCOLÒ (1670–1749). *Neapolitan *dialect poet and a lawyer by profession. His *La Ciucceide* (1726), comprising fourteen cantos of *ottava rima in praise of donkeys, is memorable for its wit and refinement as well as its unusual theme.

[JMAL]

LOMBARDO RADICE, MARCO, see RAVERA, LIDIA.

Lombardy. The Northern Italian territory which took its name from the Germanic Lombards (Langobardi), who conquered Northern Italy in the 6th c. Linguistically the Italian *Lombardia*, a syncopated form of *Longobardia* or *Langobardia*, probably followed the model of the name *Romania*, the *Byzantine territory of Italy. Up to the 16th c. it referred to most of Northern Italy from the Apennines to the Alps. In the 13th and 14th c. even writers from Parma considered themselves Lombard, as would people from *Bologna, *Turin, and Treviso, though not those from *Venice. In the 13th c. Lombard was used in Europe as a synonym for Italian. Lombardy became later identified with the state of *Milan.

Since 1948 it has been one of the twenty Italian regions, with Milan as its capital. Lombard *dialects (which include the dialects of the Swiss Ticino) belong to the Gallo-Italic group. Literature in Lombard had its first flowering with the Milanese *Bonvesin de la Riva and the Cremonese *Girard Pateg in the 13th c. In the 16th c. popular poems and *comedies were written in the dialects of Brescia and Bergamo. Milanese dialect poetry flourished in the early 19th c. with Carlo *Porta, Tommaso *Grossi, and others, and has flourished again in the 20th c. in the work of figures such as Delio *Tessa and Franco *Loi. [See also DIALECT WRITING; FOLK AND POPULAR LITERATURE.]

[DieZ]

LOMBROSO, CESARE (1835–1909). Criminologist. Born in Verona, he studied at Pavia and taught psychiatry there and then criminal anthropology at *Turin. His arguments in *L'uomo delinquente* (1876), that certain 'born' criminals are biological throwbacks to an earlier evolutionary stage, profoundly influenced Italian *veristi*, as did his contention, in *La donna delinquente* (1893), that woman is a primitive, latently criminal being. *Decadentismo*, conversely, was much influenced by his *Genio e follia* (1864) and *L'uomo di genio* (1894), in which genius too is classed as a degenerative condition. His studies extended to political crimes and to spiritualist phenomena. He was also a committed and active *Socialist. [PBarn]

LOMONACO, FRANCESCO (1772–1810). Patriotic writer. Born in Lucania, he studied in *Naples, leaving for France after the failure of the 1799 revolution, on which he wrote a *Rapporto al cittadin Carnot* (1800). His *biographies of Italian military leaders led to a chair at the Scuola Militare in Pavia in 1805. He drowned himself when his *Discorsi letterari e filosofici* (1809) were confiscated as overly democratic. [EAM]

LONDONIO, CARLO GIUSEPPE (1780–1845). *Milanese economist whose *classicist leanings in literature led him to attack *Romanticism in a reply to Mme de Staël's essay on *translation in *Biblioteca italiana* (1816). His *Cenni critici sulla poesia romantica* (1817) drew him into polemic with *Di Breme. He translated Lessing's *Laokoon* (1833). [MPC]

LONGANESI, LEO (1905–57). Right-wing *satirical *journalist from Romagna. As a young man he took up *strapaese* ideas and made his name with the supposedly ironic *Vademecum del perfetto fascista* (1926), which first made much of the dictum 'Mussolini ha sempre ragione'. He founded and edited various *periodicals, including *L'*Italiano* (1927–42), *Omnibus* (1937–9), and *Il Borghese* (1950–), and was one of the first Italian editors to exploit *photographs in order to reach a popular market. Although his enthusiasm for *Fascism had cooled by 1936, he became a strenuous defender of *Mussolini after 1945, in particular in *Un morto fra noi* (1952). [SG]

LONGHI, ROBERTO (1890–1970). Influential art historian and critic in the formalist mould who worked at *Bologna and *Florence universities. He wrote seminal works on Piero della Francesca, *Ferrarese art, and Caravaggio, and founded the art and literature journal *Paragone* in 1950. He also collaborated with the *cinema critic Umberto *Barbaro on documentary films on art. In his criticism he used a highly subtle *prosa d'arte* in an attempt to render verbally the aesthetic qualities of the paintings he was writing about. [LChe]

LONGO, ALFONSO, see ENLIGHTENMENT.

LOPRESTI, LUCIA, see BANTI, ANNA.

LOREDAN, GIAN FRANCESCO (1607–61). Gifted *Venetian aristocrat, founder and main motive force of the Accademia degli *Incogniti. His own output includes a partly historical *romance, *La Dianea* (1635), about the Thirty Years War, intertwining favourable presentations of a Swedish Protestant *condottiere, King Gustavus-Adolphus, and an irreligious Austrian Protestant, Albrecht von Wallenstein, with piquant anti-clerical satire and erotic interludes. It was immensely popular. As well as a very large letter-collection, he also wrote a parody of Genesis commentaries, *L'Adamo* (1640), in which Adam enjoys Paradise all by himself until he succumbs to the sensual charms of Eve, cast here as Venus. Loredan protected priests who abandoned their orders and professed irreligious opinions, such as Ferrante *Pallavicino, whom he made his secretary, and Antonio Rocco (1586–1653), whose glowing account of pederast seduction, *L' Alcibiade fanciullo a scola*, he published in 1651, to the instant wrath of the censors. [See also LIBERTINES AND LIBERTINISM.] [LAP]

LORENZI, BARTOLOMEO (1732–1822). Priest from the Valpolicella who was celebrated in his day as a poetic *improviser. He also contributed to the *Enlightenment vogue for georgic verse with *La coltivazione dei monti* (1778), an *ottava rima* poem on hill-farming marked by informed enthusiasm for agriculture and humane attitudes towards the *peasantry. [JMAL]

LORENZI, GIOVANNI BATTISTA (1721–1807). *Neapolitan author of thirty *libretti for *opera buffa*, usually set to music by Paisiello or Cimarosa. Among the most famous are the touching *Nina, o sia la pazza per amore* (with Giuseppe Carpani), and the delightful *Socrate immaginario* (with Ferdinando *Galiani), satirizing the craze for Greek philosophy. [FF]

LORENZINI, CARLO, see COLLODI, CARLO.

LORIA, ARTURO (1902–57). Short-story writer and critic. He was one of the chief contributors to *Solaria* and *Letteratura* in prewar *Florence, though he also spent time in the USA. In 1945 he founded *Il *Mondo* with *Bonsanti and *Montale. His stories were highly acclaimed by the critics of the day. [See also NOVELLA AND RACCONTO.]
[SVM]

LOSCHI, ANTONIO (1365–1441). One of the key *humanists of Leonardo *Bruni's generation. Born in Vicenza, he worked alongside *Salutati in the Florentine chancery, but became the latter's political opponent when, as head of the *Visconti chancery from 1398, he exchanged Latin invectives with him in the war between *Florence and *Milan. Against Florence's republican ideology, Loschi maintained the superiority of a single ruler. Later his humanist skills gained him employment in the *papal curia from 1409 onwards, and attendance at the Council of Constance. Apart from Latin letters and the invectives, his most significant work was a Latin *commentary on eleven of *Cicero's orations.
[MMcL]

LOTARIO DEI CONTI DI SEGNI, see INNO-CENT III.

LOVATI, LOVATO (1241–1309). *Latin poet and pre-*humanist. A notary and judge who associated with like-minded scholars in his native *Padua, he studied classical authors little known at the time, composing a short Latin treatise on metre in Seneca, and four classicizing verse letters (1268–87). He engaged in a poetic exchange with his more famous pupil, Albertino *Mussato, and was highly regarded as a poet by *Petrarch. Some of his works (including Latin poems on the Tristan legend and on the history of Padua) have been lost, or survive only in fragmentary form.
[CEH]

LOY, ROSETTA (1931–). One of the most accomplished of modern Italian writers, who repeatedly returns to the more painful parts of recent Italian history. She herself is from an upper-class *Roman family and her first novel, *La bicicletta* (1974) traces how such a family is forced by circumstances to face up to the unpalatable realities of *World War II. As in her subsequent fiction, Loy criticizes the superficiality of her class, while recognising the lasting impact of early traumatic

experience. Her most famous novel, *Le strade di polvere* (1987), is something of a departure from her customary pattern; set in the *Piedmontese countryside, it traces the history of the Gran Masten family in the *Napoleonic period and the decades that follow, but the surface texture of the work has hints of the magic *realism [see also REAL-ISMO MAGICO] of Garcìa Marquez (whom Loy admires), and the experience of time is circular rather than linear. Her recent work returns to the exploration of the indirect resonances of history on individual and family life, most forcefully in *Cioccolata da Hanselmann* (1995). *La parola ebreo* (1997) is a powerful *autobiographical memoir of the hypocrisy of the Roman middle class towards the *Jews in the the later *Fascist years.
[SW]

LUBRANO, GIACOMO (1619–93). Poet and preacher. He joined the *Jesuit order in 1635, and spent most of his uneventful life in *Naples, though his vast fame as an orator brought invitations to deliver *sermons in *Rome, Palermo, *Venice, and even *Malta (ironically, late in life he was affected by a partial paralysis of the tongue). His copious production in Italian and Latin includes two collections of sacred and moral verse, *Scintille poetiche* (1674) and *Suavidalia epigrammaton libri decem* (1690), as well as homilies, letters, and orations.

Both chronologically and stylistically, his Italian poetry represents one of the most extreme instances of late Neapolitan *concettismo. It is ideologically orthodox, but convoluted and hyper-erudite in form, describing the mysteries of God and nature in a charged, elliptical, clipped language, and rushing jerkily from one metaphor to the next. It was mocked as absurd for over 200 years, but has recently found some favour for those same hallucinatory qualities which previously caused it to be dismissed as demented. It is a style with ideological implications; despite conventional conclusions, a certain restlessness reveals itself here and there in Lubrano's faith, together with a view of the natural world more akin to that of Lucretius or Heraclitus than to the official Jesuit science of his day.
[MPS]
Scintille poetiche, ed. M. Pieri (1982).

LUCARELLI, CARLO (1960–). A member of the 'scuola emiliana' of younger Italian crime writers, who has explored various sub-genres of crime fiction. His novels about Inspector De Luca, such as *L'estate torbida* (1991), provide an intriguing reading of Italian society in the aftermath of the

fall of *Fascism and the years immediately following *World War II. [See also DETECTIVE FICTION.]
[GP]

Lucia. Heroine of *Manzoni's *Promessi sposi.

LUCINI, GIAN PIETRO (1867–1914). *Milanese poet, narrator, and critic. He suffered throughout his life from tuberculosis, but was able to take a degree in the philosophy of law at Pavia in 1892 and to elope with Giuditta Cattaneo the next year. Intellectually insatiable and chaotic, he was drawn to the *Scapigliatura, symptomatically entitling the first story he published 'Spirito ribelle' (1888), and later writing an admiring essay on Carlo *Dossi (1911). The rebellious vein continued with anti-militarist, pro-republican *journalism and with violent attacks on *D'Annunzio for his decadent aestheticism and hedonism, culminating in Antidannunziana (1914). In 1905 he began to contribute verse and prose to Poesia, the review edited by *Marinetti, who published his most characteristic collection of poems, Revolverate, in 1909. In the same year Lucini began to distance himself from *Futurism, as he later described in 'Come ho sorpassato il Futurismo' (published in La *Voce in 1913), dismissing its overblown rhetoric and its wholesale rejection of the past. Polemically discursive as a poet and difficult to read, ideologically eccentric, and philosophically eclectic, he was long forgotten. He was rediscovered in the 1960s as a precursor of the experimentalism of the *Neoavanguardia both in his practice and in his extensive theoretical essays on Italian *free verse. [GS]

LUIGINI, FEDERICO (16th c.) from Udine was the author of a treatise on women, the Libro della bella donna (1564), dedicated to Lucrezia *Gonzaga Manfrona, and giving a physical and moral portrait of the ideal lady. A small quantity of Italian love *lyrics by him were published in 16th-c. *anthologies. [ELM]

Luna e i falò, La (1950). *Pavese's last and densest novel is cast as an account by a successful middle-aged emigrant of his return to his childhood home. His quest for self-knowledge intertwines with a triple narrative that embraces the war years, his life in America, and memories of his youth. Via myth, symbol, and intense evocations of the landscape and traditions of the *Piedmontese Langhe, a counterpoint is created between cyclical natural time and the ravages of history and individual lives.

The story of how the beautiful but treacherous Santa was shot by partisans, and her body burnt, ends the book on a note of destruction, sacrifice, and rebirth. [NMS]

LUNARDO DEL GUALLACCA, see SICULO-TUSCAN POETS.

LUPERINI, ROMANO, see LITERARY CRITICISM.

LUSSU, EMILIO (1890–1975). *Sardinian politician and writer. As a young interventionist he fought in *World War I, and was one of the few intellectuals to record and analyse their experiences with his Un anno sull'altipiano (published in Paris in 1938). In 1920 he founded the democratic and *Socialist Partito Sardo d'Azione, which he represented in Parliament from 1921 to 1926, when he was expelled along with other anti-*Fascists. Imprisoned by the Fascists on Lipari, he escaped in 1929 along with Carlo Rosselli [see ROSSELLI, AMELIA] and Fausto Nitti. In the same year he, Rosselli and Alberto Tarchiani founded the *Giustizia e libertà movement in Paris. Lussu wrote for the movement's Quaderni under the pseudonym Tirreno. He became leader of the radical and revolutionary wing of the *Partito d'Azione that grew from the movement, and took part in the *Resistance in France and Italy. After the party was dissolved in 1946, he became a militant socialist politician. His books are chiefly political memoirs, and written in powerfully ironic style. Marcia su Roma e dintorni (1933) is an account of the rise of Fascism and the consolidation of the regime, while Sul Partito d'Azione e gli altri (1968) analyses the politics of the Resistance and postwar period.
[SVM]

LUZI, MARIO (1914–). Important Catholic poet, *hermetic in his earlier work, but subsequently tracing an impressive path of his own. Born near *Florence, Luzi took a degree in French literature there and after teaching in schools in various cities returned as a professor of French in 1955.

His early collections—La barca (1935), Avvento notturno (1940), Un brindisi (1946), Quaderno gotico (1947)—combine daring analogical transitions and classicism of form in the manner of Mallarmé. Primizie dal deserto (1952) and Onore del vero (1960) confront more directly the problems of man's constitutional weakness and the relationship between poetry and history, time and eternity, with

Lyric Poetry

noticeable influence from T. S. Eliot and *Montale's *Occasioni*. A further phase is evident in *Nel magma* (1963), *Dal fondo delle campagne* (1965), and *Su fondamenti invisibili* (1971), which abandon regular form for freer longer lines, and show a new preference for narrative discourse. In the following collections, *Al fuoco della controversia* (1978), *Per il battesimo dei nostri frammenti* (1985), *Frasi e incisi di un canto salutare* (1990), and *Viaggio terrestre e celeste di Simone Martini* (1994), the emphasis falls more on problems of earthly existence. The verse takes on a broken quality in its search for a musical union of sense and sound. The *symbolist aim for words which speak of eternal values is now directly set against the dramatic inauthenticity of historical events, illuminated only by faith that reality must have a sense and the hope of ultimate Christian reconciliation.

As well as criticism and *translations (particularly of French symbolists), Luzi has written plays, collected as *Teatro* (1993), in which, following the model of Eliot, meditation prevails over action.

[RD]

See L. Rizzoli and G. C. Morelli, *Mario Luzi* (1993).

Lyric Poetry. Until at least the early 20th c. lyric poetry occupied a prime place in Italian literature. It was the linguistic, stylistic, and qualitative reference point for other poetic genres, and the genre in which creative writing was commonly felt to achieve its highest and purest form. Though his theorization of the issue was unique, *Croce expressed widely shared assumptions when he declared that all successful art is fundamentally lyrical. The centrality of lyric poetry is established from the 13th and 14th c. A self-confirming sophisticated tradition emerges with the *Sicilians and evolves through the *dolce stil novo* and *Dante to *Petrarch's *Canzoniere*. It has distinctive poetic forms (principally the *canzone* and *sonnet), distinctive metres (principally the *hendecasyllable and *settenario*), and a distinctive language at no stage the same as prose or spoken usage. Early verse and prose narrative are weak in comparison. Almost inevitably Dante, in the *De vulgari eloquentia*, finds the noblest Italian language in the best lyric poetry, whilst Petrarch simply does not practise any other form of vernacular composition.

Subsequent lyric poetry is written largely in the shadow of Petrarch, though not at first systematically, and always with the possibility of Dantesque interferences (as in *Michelangelo), or of the more

or less ritualized anti-Petrarchan manœuvres of comic poets like *Berni. In the 16th c. Petrarchan imitation in serious poetry is triumphantly formalized by Pietro *Bembo, with the consequence that the idiom of Petrarch's lyric becomes the basis for that of all poetry (including the *epics of *Ariosto and Torquato *Tasso), and hence a resource that almost transcends history. *Petrarchists, *Marinists, *Arcadians and *Enlightenment poets all work with an idiom in slow evolution and, in spite of polemics and and partial changes of direction, with fundamentally the same *humanist assumptions. In their different ways the *neoclassical *Foscolo and Vincenzo *Monti continue and re-affirm traditional practices. Renewal, when it comes with *Leopardi, is achieved not by turning to some phantasmagorical spoken language of ordinary Italians, as the *Romantics proposed, but by re-affirming the stylistic and poetic values of Petrarch. Later in the 19th c. *Carducci, *Pascoli, and *D'Annunzio will attempt further new paths, thematically and formally, but the lyric largely retains its bardic tone, its poetic language, and its traditional metres and forms; and with them it retains a cultural prestige which still tends to place it above prose narrative, especially the *novel.

The perceived coherence of poetry and the poetic tradition is seriously threatened at the start of the 20th c., not so much by the iconoclasm of the *Futurists as by *Ungaretti, *Montale, and the *hermetic poets in general, whose sense of loss and fragmentation is as much poetic as existential. Petrarch remains a touchstone for Ungaretti and, to a lesser extent, Dante for Montale, whilst rebuilding or rediscovering the tradition becomes a paramount concern for critics and poets alike. But the century sees a progressive movement towards the prosaic and the colloquial. *Free verse of one kind or another gradually asserts itself as the norm, and, after a final flurry during the *Fascist period, the bardic stance is largely sidelined as embarrassing. Although hermetic poetry in a broad sense is often seen as the dominant trend in the first part of the 20th c., much poetry moves in other directions, most impressively with *Saba. Since *World War II diversity has been even more apparent. Certain moments can be picked out—notably attempts at a popular or choral poetry in the wake of the *Resistance—and groups have continued to be born and to die, such as the *Officina group and the *Neoavanguardia. However *Zanzotto, *Luzi, Attilio *Bertolucci, *Caproni, and most other poets have followed clearly their individual courses, whilst sharing an intense awareness of the lyric of the past, and a general sense of the problematic nature of poetry and poetic language. Only Montale has been given a prominent public profile, coming to be seen as an emblem for the preservation of personal decency through Fascism, the war, and the social and political turmoils that followed.

The diversity within contemporary poetic practice in Italian is accompanied by a new willingness to take *dialect poetry seriously. Past writers such as Carlo *Porta and *Tessa are now commonly seen as belonging to an independent *Milanese tradition by no means inferior to the national one. In spite of its limited readership, contemporary dialect poetry has also flourished, particularly since the late 1970s. With poets such as *Noventa, *Marin, and *Pierro it can seem paradoxically to achieve the sort of high lyricism that modern poetry in Italian has often declared beyond its reach. [See also DIALECT WRITING; POESIA; VERSIFICATION.] [PH]

See P. V. Mengaldo, *La tradizione del Novecento* (3 vols., 1975–91).

M

Macaronic Literature. The term 'macaronic' derives from *maccaroni* or *maccheroni*, formerly designating humble, coarse dumplings made of flour and bread crumbs, and resembling modern *gnocchi*. From its beginnings *Renaissance macaronic literature cultivates an appropriately 'kitchen' vulgarity of language and content, which it turns to simultaneously ribald and sophisticated ends. In fact it is thoroughly learned and self-aware. Rather than mixing perceptibly distinct languages in the same text, it has an ostensible linguistic unity; it is founded on essentially classical Latin structures (especially those of *Virgilian poetry) but introduces Latinized *dialect and Italian terms with Latin suffixes, though characteristic Latin endings (e.g. the accusative *-m*) may be omitted. The comedy comes partly from the clash between the different elements in the language and partly from the use of high rhetoric to represent deeply mundane contents and concerns.

It was mainly a Northern Italian phenomenon, originating among *university students at *Padua, in the second half of the 15th c., although anticipations have been found in some 13th-c. *sermons. An early practitioner, and the originator of the founding image, if not of the practice of macaronic writing, is the Paduan Tifi *Odasi, the author of an unfinished poem, *Macaronea* (1490), about a carefree gang of bon viveurs and practical jokers called 'macaronei'. He announces that the reader will behold in his work a thousand wounds done to the grammarian Priscian and a new grammar which the whores have taught him ('Aspicies, lector, Prisciani vulnera mille, / gramaticamque novam quam nos docuere putane'). Other early writers of macaronic verse are the anonymous author of the *Nobile Vigonze opus*, on the deeds of a noble Paduan from the Vigonzi family, Bassano da Mantova, Fossa da Cremona, and the *Piedmontese Gian Giorgio *Alione. But the most important macaronic writer is Teofilo *Folengo, who, after the *Maccheronee*,

and the parody of Virgilan eclogues in the *Zanitonella*, published his main work, *Baldus*, under the pseudonym Merlin Cocai. Set in a small village near *Mantua, *Baldus* is essentially a *mock-heroic *epic, with vivid representations of *peasant life, Pantagruelian eating, and extraordinary events. It exerted an important influence on Rabelais, amongst other European writers.

It is doubtful whether macaronic writing can be considered anti-classical, but its disparate linguistic material has led to much of it being labelled *expressionist.   [DieZ]

MACCARI, MINO (1898–1989). *Satirical artist and *journalist, born in *Siena, who founded and edited *Il *Selvaggio* and was one of the main voices of *strapaese* during *Fascism. His satirical verse—collected as *Orgia* (1918) and *Il trastullo di strapaese* (1928)—is easily outshone by his vigorously inventive cartoons and etchings.   [PH]

Macchiaioli (*c.*1855–62). Group of *Tuscan painters, whose work is characterized by strong *chiaroscuro* ('macchia' means 'daub' or 'patch'). Important members were Giovanni Fattori (1825–1908), Telemaco Signorini (1853–1901), Silvestro Lega (1826–95), Raffaello Sernesi (1838–66), and Giuseppe Abbati (1836–68). All were active in the *Risorgimento.   [AM]

MACCHIAVELLI, LORIANO (1934–) is best known for his series of *detective novels about a *Bolognese policeman, Antonio Sarti. He has also written other novels about Bologna and has worked as director and actor in political *theatre there.

[AWM]

MACEDONIO, MARCELLO (late 16th c.– 1620). *Neapolitan nobleman, and one of the earliest Southern imitators of *Marino, though his poetry also remains close to the language and conventions of *Petrarchism. Much of his work is devoted to his unrequited love for Isabella Sanseverino. No less conventionally exemplary was his conversion late in life, when he became a Carmelite friar. [MPS]

MACHIAVELLI, NICCOLÒ (1469–1527). Probably the most famous Italian writer on politics, whose very name later became a byword for duplicity and evil intent. Niccolò di Bernardo Machiavelli's life spanned one of the most tumultuous periods in the peninsula's history. Born in the year that Lorenzo de' *Medici succeeded his father Piero as leader of the *Medici family in *Florence, he died shortly after the *Sack of *Rome in 1527. In the intervening years he witnessed four changes of regime within Florence, the invasion of Italy by both French and then imperial forces, the burning of *Savonarola, and the pre-eminence of the *Borgias in *papal Rome. Although his family was not part of the political elite, Machiavelli received a standard *humanist *education, probably attending lectures at the Florentine *studio*. His father's diary refers to a small family library of classical works, including *Livy, and Machiavelli has been identified as the copyist of a manuscript of Lucretius dated in the 1490s.

Despite being ineligible to hold political office, Machiavelli rose to a position of considerable importance within Florence as a chancery official and diplomat. He secured his first position, as Second Chancellor, in June 1498, shortly after the defeat of the Savonarolans, in the broader-based republic established after the exile of the Medici in 1494. As such he was nominally responsible for the administration of affairs within the Florentine territorial state, which at that time covered large areas of *Tuscany and parts of Umbria. In July 1498 he was granted the additional job within the chancery of serving the Ten of War. Once his patron and protector Piero Soderini was elected Gonfaloniere of Florence for life in 1502, Machiavelli was sent on increasingly important political and diplomatic missions traditionally deemed beyond the scope of a Second Chancellor; in 1507 he was also made Chancellor of the Nine of the Militia. The experiences gathered during the fourteen years of service to the republic provided the basis for his early political writings, which included the *Discorso fatto al magistrato dei dieci sopra le cose di Pisa* (1499), the *Descrizione del modo tenuto dal Duca Valentino nello ammazzare Vitellozzo Vitelli* (1503), *Del modo di trattare i popoli della Valdichiana ribellati* (1503),

Ritratto di Francia (1510), and *Ritratto delle cose della Magna* (1512). The observations and the maxims they contain find their way, in modified form, into all his major works, the time spent in the company of Cesare Borgia in 1502–3 being particularly evident in the *Principe*.

The *Principe* and the *Discorsi*, Machiavelli's most famous works, were completed during the *exile forced on him upon the return of the Medici to Florence in 1512. Machiavelli first mentions the *Principe* in a letter dated 15 December 1513 to his former diplomatic colleague and correspondent Francesco Vettori, referring to the tract as his 'opuscolo *De principatibus*'. The volume is dedicated to Lorenzo de' Medici the younger (1492–1519), who had recently taken possession of the Duchy of *Urbino, but there is no certainty that it even found its way to its dedicatee. As he says in his dedicatory letter, he aims to integrate the knowledge acquired during diplomatic experiences whilst in the employ of the republic between 1496 and 1512 and his reading of the ancients to produce a work of particular use to new princes. His stated aim both in his correspondence with Vettori and implicitly in his dedicatory letter was to regain employment and conquer what he considered the malignity of fortune. His advice is directly addressed to individuals recently come to power, and centres on the strategies to be adopted in order to secure and maintain rulership. This involved a far broader definition of what constituted princely rule than was customary, and specifically excluded hereditary rulers, the traditional recipients of such advice books.

The text is characterized by a series of binary oppositions, the most important of which are *fortuna* and *virtù*, *forma* and *materia*. Machiavelli conceived of the political realm as an arena in which the ordering power of *virtù* was set against the disruptive influence of *fortuna*. The *virtuoso* qualities of the prince were to be deployed in fashioning the acquired territory in such a way as to secure his own rule and prevent others from seizing any opportunity that might arise to conquer it for themselves. To achieve this end conventional moral precepts might periodically have to be sacrificed on the altar of necessity. Consciously rejecting the exemplary rulers imagined in humanist Mirrors of Princes, Machiavelli argued that behaving virtuously could lead to ruin in a world where others were less scrupulous. The prince therefore required a mixture of guile and force: the former was required in order to maintain a reputation for virtue in the eyes

Machiavelli, Niccolò

of his subjects, who provided his surest defence against attack; the latter was required as a means of enforcing obedience when required, and strengthening the otherwise fragile bond of love. In this context Machiavelli's *virtù* differed markedly from classical and Christian notions of virtue, as he made a virtue of necessity, subordinating ethical considerations to practical ones of political survival. It was predominantly on the basis of this one text, first published in 1532, that the figure of the duplicitous Machiavel became increasingly widespread in European literary and dramatic works.

Despite becoming increasingly impatient with his failure to win the trust and *patronage of the Medici family, Machiavelli continued to write. He also frequented the Orti Oricellari group of liberal patricians, which met in the gardens of Bernardo *Rucellai's son Cosimo from 1514 onwards, dedicating his *Discorsi* to two of their number in 1516–17, Cosimo and Zanobi Buondelmonti. This informal circle of young patrician Florentines with literary and political interests, including the historians Jacopo *Nardi and Filippo de' *Nerli and the poet Jacopo da Diacceto, provided Machiavelli with an informed and appreciative audience for his ideas as well as financial support. A *commentary loosely based on the first ten books of *Livy's History of Rome, the *Discorsi* were not published in Machiavelli's own lifetime, and it is unclear whether the present text constitutes the author's final version. Divided into three books, they seek to address the perceived shortcomings in contemporary Florentine republican government through recourse to the exemplary republic of ancient Rome, using Livy's text as a didactic touchstone to consider a range of issues pertinent to the founding and maintenance of a durable and glorious republican polity.

Often seen as the expression of Machiavelli's true political inclinations and the antithesis of the autocratic *Principe*, the *Discorsi* in fact share many characteristics with the other text. Machiavelli repeatedly uses the term *principe* in the *Discorsi* to refer both to individual founders of republics and to those individuals who undertake the reform of corrupted republics by returning them to first principles. In the *Discorsi*, however, such princes seek to transfer their own personal *virtù* into the institutions of a self-governing republic, ensuring its continued liberty and security on their demise. As with the *Principe*, when necessity dictated the moral imperative remained the maintenance of the governmental form, in this instance the safety of the

patria, to the exclusion of any considerations of justice, humanity, or even glory, whilst *fortuna* continued as a malign force to be countermanded by *virtuoso* leaders and dynamic expansion.

Machiavelli showed himself dismissive of humanist conventions in this text, particularly in his functional approach to the political importance of religion, and in his rejection of the traditional consensus view of republican harmony. Defining it as a sect, Machiavelli equally held Christianity responsible for effeminizing Italians, rejecting it in favour of a classical civic religion which focused on action rather than contemplation. In binding citizens to their country and engendering a spirit of self-sacrifice for the maintenance of liberty, Machiavelli praised the founders of religions above the founders of states. He similarly discarded idealized descriptions of the republic as a harmonious body politic with all the parts working in unity towards a commonly held good. Rejecting the essentially defensive and static models of Sparta and Venice, Machiavelli embraced the expansionism and plurality of the Roman Republic, controversially claiming that its disunion was the very source of its greatness. A correctly ordered constitution, which ensured representation for all the constitutive ranks of society, could channel the inevitable social tension to solve the problem of the heterogeneity of ends, only policies which were to the mutual advantage of all parts gaining approval. In this way liberty was secured by the competition between the different social ranks. Social conflict was seen as a small price to pay in securing glorious expansion. Moreover, the mutual suspicion between these social groupings prevented any one sector from seizing undue authority and depriving the others of their liberty. It was in this context that the correct ordering of the institutions of the republic was paramount, for, properly fashioned by a founding prince, they prevented the possibility of particular interests predominating and corrupting the political life of the republic.

In 1518 Machiavelli wrote his black *comedy *Mandragola*, a pessimistic portrayal of the Florentines' inability to regain their ancient virtue. However, on the death in May 1519 of the eventual dedicatee of the *Principe*, Lorenzo di Piero de' Medici, Machiavelli began work upon his *Arte della guerra*, a *dialogue he completed in 1520. Often characterized as the third of the trivium of his major political works, the dialogue deals extensively with themes previously touched upon in both the *Principe* and the *Discorsi*, namely the ordering of military forces as both a bulwark against external aggression and as a means of securing internal peace. For in an age when the classical notion of universal participation in civic assemblies was no longer realizable, the formation of a well-ordered civic militia would, he thought, sustain the participatory ideal through involvement in defending the *patria*.

Finally, in 1520, the Medici's attitude seemed to soften, with Giulio de' Medici, then Pope Clement VII, asking Machiavelli to write a tract on the best form of government for Florence, the result being the *Discursus florentinarum rerum*. Later that year the Pope also commissioned him to write the *Istorie fiorentine*, a commission which placed him in an illustrious tradition of official humanist *historians of Florence from Leonardo *Bruni to Bartolomeo *Scala, and which he completed in 1525. In focusing in particular upon the history of Florence's factional divisions and the city's corruption Machiavelli trod warily, given the Medicean origins of the commission, concentrating on internal affairs prior to the accession of Cosimo de' Medici in 1434, and on foreign affairs during the period of Medicean hegemony. Strategically he chose 1494, the year of Lorenzo de' Medici's death, as the end point of his history. Subsequent to finishing the *Istorie* he finally secured an official position as one of the five officials appointed to oversee the fortification of Florence in 1526. During the same period he wrote another comedy, *Clizia*, and a couple of tracts based on his visit to Lucca in 1520. Ironically, on the restoration of the Florentine Republic in 1527 after the Medici had once again been driven from the city, Machiavelli was unsuccessful in gaining a post in the new regime on account of his links with the Medici. He died shortly afterwards at the age of 58, rejected by the new republicans, his own life a case study in the vagaries of political fortune.

Apart from the works for which he is best known, Machiavelli was also an occasional poet, at his best in his mordant *capitoli* [see CANTO] and his earthy *canti carnascialeschi*. He also wrote an ironic prose fable, *Belfagor*, on the visit of a devil to Florence. It is debated whether he is the author of an important *Discorso o dialogo intorno alla nostra lingua*, not published until 1730, which argues for the essentially Florentine character of the Italian literary language against both Pietro *Bembo and the proponents of the *lingua cortigiana*. [See also POLITICAL THOUGHT.]   [SJM]

Tutte le opere, ed. M. Martelli (1971). See J. R.

Hale, *Machiavelli and Renaissance Italy* (1961); Q. Skinner, *Machiavelli* (1981); M. Viroli, *Machiavelli* (1998).

MACRÌ, ORESTE, see HERMETIC POETRY.

MADERNI, DIEGO GIROLAMO, see ITALIAN WRITERS IN SWITZERLAND.

Madrigal. The 14th-c. madrigal is a form set to polyphonic secular music, made up of tercets (from two to five) followed by couplets (one or two) and/or by an isolated line, with a highly variable rhyme scheme, in *hendecasyllables or in hendeca-syllables and *settenari* [see VERSIFICATION]. The most notable early examples are by *Petrarch. The 16th-c. madrigal, also set to music and normally shorter than the *sonnet, is the free form *par excellence* among the different kinds of short poem; it consists of hendecasyllables and *settenari* that are usually only partly rhymed.   [PGB]

MAFFEI, ANDREA (1798–1885). *Translator and poet. Born in Trento, he studied privately in Italy and in Germany, and translated Milton, Schiller, Goethe—including *Faust* (1866–9)—and other major German and English writers. His own poetry was influenced by Vincenzo *Monti and Lamartine. He also wrote the *libretto for *Verdi's *Masnadieri*.   [FD'I]

MAFFEI, RAFFAELE, see ANTIQUARIANISM.

MAFFEI, SCIPIONE (1675–1755). Veronese writer and scholar. He was one of the founders of the *Giornale de' letterati d'Italia* (1710–40), which was intended to promote an Italian cultural identity in touch with the mainstream of European developments. He wrote on a wide range of topics, making him a representative figure of the early Italian *Enlightenment. He applied new philological and historical methods to reconstructing medieval codices and defending Catholic orthodoxy against *Jansenism (1752). His *Consiglio politico presentato al governo veneto* (1738) promoted the idea of a *Venetian constitution based on the English model, an idea first introduced in his history of Verona (1732). His literary output, influenced by his membership of the Accademia dell'*Arcadia, includes *Rime e prose* (1718) and discussions of literary and *journalistic themes in *Osservazioni letterarie* (1737–40). He wrote a *Discorso storico sul teatro italiano* (1723) as a preface to a selection of Italian

Mafia

*tragedies by various hands, and also a defence of the *theatre against ecclesiastical accusations of immorality (1753). He contributed two *comedies and a melodrama, *La fida ninfa* (1730), to an Arcadia-inspired theatrical reform, but his most successful work remained his tragedy *Merope* (1713), imitated by Voltaire, and still considered to be the model of Italian *neoclassical tragedy before *Alfieri.

[GLCB]

Mafia. A criminal body with a distinctive code of behaviour began to emerge in *Sicily around the middle of the 19th c. The word first appears in written literature in the title of the dialect play *I mafiusi di la Vicaria* (1863), by Gaspare Mosca and Giuseppe Rizzotto. The term does not appear in the text itself, but the play was performed all over Italy and the word entered common currency immediately. The Mafia intrigued and horrified public opinion, and was the subject of several reports, most famously the Franchetti–*Sonnino report into conditions in Sicily (1876). However, setting a trend which was to become common, prominent Sicilians like the writer Luigi *Capuana and the folklorist Giuseppe Pitrè reacted indignantly to what they saw as a slur on the island. The *veristi, in spite of their commitment to examine and expose the more dubious aspects of society, never cast critical light on the Mafia, which was celebrated in popular fiction and in poems by Nino *Martoglio. Only in the 1940s and 1950s did writers such as Leonardo *Sciascia, Danilo *Dolci, and Michele Pantaleone present hostile portrayals of the effects of Mafia activity.   [JF]

MAGALOTTI, LORENZO (1637–1712). Diplomat, man of letters, scientist, essayist, and traveller. Born in *Rome of a noble *Florentine family, he studied with the *Jesuits and, at *Pisa, anatomy and mathematics with followers of *Galileo such as Vincenzo *Viviani. He was made secretary to the Accademia del *Cimento in 1660. He wrote up its experiments from 1662, and published them in 1667 as *Saggi di naturali esperienze*. His scientific prose owes something to Galileo's example, but shows a more conscious search after literary and *classicist effects, in a new, more refined and purist mode. After the break-up of the Cimento Academy in 1667, and throughout the 1670s, Magalotti embarked on a long series of travels throughout Europe, which earned him the title of 'postiglione d'Europa'. The fruits of these were numerous reports, *letters, and *travel writings

which demonstrate his powers of observation of human nature, his inquisitive disposition, and his openness of mind in matters cultural and political.

His best work, the *Lettere sopra le terre odorose d'Europa e d'America dette volgarmente buccheri* (1695), and the *Lettere scientifiche ed erudite*, show a fluency and agility that matches his curiosity and sensitivity in his observations of natural phenomena. His model in these works was Joseph Addison, whose essays he much admired. He left unfinished an important anti-*libertine work, *Lettere familiari contro l'ateismo* (1719), purportedly addressed to a German atheist. In this work, and in his unsuccessful and fleeting career as a monk, Magalotti showed an awareness of the problems, after Galileo's famous condemnation, of reconciling the claims of scientific research and the Catholic faith, an awareness which, however, did not lead him into libertinism. A gifted linguist and a man of deep and wide learning, he wrote some poetry, of which his Anacreontic *Canzoni* are the best examples, *translated parts of Milton's *Paradise Lost* and John Philips' *The Cyder* (1708), and proved himself to be the best Dantist of his age in his *commentary (1665–6) on the first five cantos of *Inferno* [see DANTE; DANTE COMMENTARIES].   [PBD]

Saggi di naturali esperienze, ed. T. Poggi Salani (1976). See G. Güntert, *Un poeta scienziato del Seicento: Lorenzo Magalotti* (1966).

Magazines, see PERIODICALS.

Maggi were popular verse compositions which flourished from the 15th c. in Northern and central Italy, especially in *Tuscany, Emilia, and Liguria, where they were recited during the *Calendimaggio*, the spring festival celebrated on 1 May. Among the earliest is *Poliziano's 'Ben venga maggio'. Many, such as the 15th-c. 'Hor è di maggio' for four voices, were set to *music, usually monotone, and sung by amateur performers. The verse form consisted of quatrains of seven- or eight-syllable lines [see VERSIFICATION]. Historic events and classical, *chivalric, and sacred legends also came to be common themes. *Maggi* flourished well into the modern period.   [GPTW]

MAGGI, CARLO MARIA (1630–99). *Milanese author most famous for his *dialect plays: *Il manco male* (1695), *Il Barone di Birbanza* (1696), *I consigli di Meneghino* (1697), *Il falso filosofo* (1698), and *Concorso de' Meneghini* (?1699). He first gained a reputation as a writer of *libretti. Most of these were never published, and some were later disowned by the author and destroyed. He then wrote religiously oriented poetry, according to the demands of the new *Jesuit-led cultural policy. His *Rime varie* (1688) attracted the approval of *Muratori and other representatives of anti-*Baroque culture. His dialect plays celebrate the special quality of Milanese as a language, which is described in *Concorso de' Meneghini* as clear and unaffected, and which 'seems as if it had been made on purpose just to tell the truth' ('che apposta la pär fä / par dì la verità'). They also construct the long-lasting archetypal Milanese character, Meneghino, the long-suffering, sensible, no-nonsense plebeian servant, and create an image of the 'verzee', the main vegetable market in Milan, which is portrayed in the *Barone di Birbanza* as the place where the most truthful and spontaneous expression of the culture of the Milanese populace is to be found. Later Milanese writers such as *Parini and Carlo *Porta saw him as a seminal figure. [VRJ]

Magic. From *Augustine to *Aquinas and beyond, intellectuals had debated the limits and dangers of magic, seen as the effecting of preternatural control over nature with the assistance of demons. Yet there are great problems in defining magic. It can be linked to *astrology, divination, religion, natural philosophy, and witchcraft. It appeared in erudite writings by philosophers, theologians, lawyers, and men of science. It was seen as a religious rite, and as a means of union with the Almighty. But it also aimed, in necromantic writings, at establishing contact with demons. In the *Renaissance in particular magic needs to be considered in its broad intellectual context. There was a close relationship between traditional magic, experimental science, *Aristotelianism, and Platonism, which gave rise to differing and ever-changing conceptions of nature. The texts of *hermeticism, the revival of *Neoplatonism in 15th-c. *Florence, Giovanni *Pico della Mirandola's studies of the Cabbala, all represent a body of writings that provided both physical and metaphysical support for beliefs in magic, and helped it to play a significant role in the history of science as well as in the lives of ordinary people.
[PLR]
See R. Kieckhefer, *Magic in the Middle Ages* (1989); S. Clark, *Thinking with Demons: The Idea of Witchcraft in Early Modern Europe* (1997).

MAGLIABECHI, ANTONIO (1633–1714). Librarian and scholar. Physically deformed and utterly unsociable, he never travelled beyond his house and library in *Florence, though he corresponded prolifically with many other scholars. He compiled a catalogue of the Arabic, Persian, Turkish, and Hebrew manuscripts in the Biblioteca Laurenziana, and Grand Duke Cosimo III de' *Medici entrusted him with the custody of the Biblioteca Palatina. In 1700 he collaborated with Iacopo Rilli and others on *Notizie letterarie ed istoriche intorno agli uomini illustri dell'Accademia Fiorentina*, of which only the first part was completed. His own very large library, the Biblioteca Magliabechiana, was opened to the public in 1747 and, when amalgamated with the Palatina, formed the foundation of what is now the Biblioteca Nazionale Centrale in Florence. [See also LIBRARIES.] [DER]

MAGNO, CELIO (1536–1602). *Venetian poet and politician who rose to high-ranking office and served on various diplomatic missions abroad. He associated with the circle around Domenico *Venier and wrote verse which is largely *Petrarchist but has a distinctive intensity, particularly in his *canzoni*. [ABu]

MAGRELLI, VALERIO (1957–). *Roman poet whose abstracted, philosophical lyrics have a transparent, geometric quality. His first collection, *Ora serrata retinae* (1980), is centred on relations between the self, the body, looking, and writing. *Nature e venature* (1987) introduces motifs of the 'vita delle cose', of everyday objects and the experience of modern life and technological culture. The 'sentirsi male' that characterizes both collections becomes physical illness in *Esercizi di tiptologia* (1992). In a new departure *Didascalie per la lettura di un giornale* (1999) draws its idiom from newspaper language. [MH]

MAGRIS, CLAUDIO (1939–). *Triestine writer. By profession he is a Germanist at Trieste University and an authority on Central European literature, on which he wrote his first book, *Il mito asburgico nella letteratura austriaca moderna* (1963). He turned to more creative forms of writing after publishing further critical studies, and the collections of newspaper articles in *Dietro le parole* (1978) and *Itaca e oltre* (1982). His best-known book, *Danubio* (1986), is an account of a journey to the sources of the river, which blends history, anecdote, memoir, and scenic evocation, focusing on fusions and overlaps between different nationalities and cultures. The interest in borders is even more prominent in the novel *Un altro mare* (1991) and the memories of people and places in and near Trieste in *Microcosmi* (1997). He is also the author of the short novel *Illazioni su una sciabola* (1984) and the play *Stadelmann* (1988), which recount episodes of collective and individual defeat at the margins of greater historical events.   [KP]

MAI, ANGELO (1782–1854). Scholar and cleric, born near Bergamo, who became *librarian at the Biblioteca Ambrosiana in *Milan and then at the *Vatican Library in *Rome. He was made Cardinal in 1838. He discovered important texts by Fronto, Eusebius, and others. His discovery of *Cicero's *De re publica* inspired *Leopardi's *canzone* 'Ad Angelo Mai'.   [FD'I]

Maia, see D'ANNUNZIO, GABRIELE.

MAIA MATERDONA, GIAN FRANCESCO (1590–c.1650). Poet born near Brindisi and a priest, he proved the most notable, and occasionally the most original, of the first wave of Southern imitators of *Marino. He skilfully appropriated Marino's language, though he tended towards small-scale descriptive cameos and lacked the underlying corrosive *irony of his model. His *Rime* (1629) went through several reprints, and he also published a devotional treatise, *L'utile spavento del peccatore* (1649).   [MPS]

MALABAILA, DAMIANO, see LEVI, PRIMO.

MALAPARTE, CURZIO (1898–1957) (pseud. of Kurt Eric Suckert). Controversial writer and *journalist. Born in Prato, and already politically active before *World War I, he was a volunteer who saw service on various fronts. He first became widely known for his highly polemical defence of the common Italian soldiers at Caporetto in *La rivolta dei santi maledetti* (1921). He was an early and highly active convert to *Fascism and prominent as a journalist throughout the Fascist period, working for *La Stampa* and *Il *Corriere della sera* and founding and editing the reviews *900* (*Novecento*) (1926), *La Conquista dello stato* (1924), and *Prospettive* (1937). In his essay *Italia barbara* (1925) he presented a vision of Italy as an essentially rural country whose inhabitants were distrustful of innovation, with Fascism defending it against foreign corruption much as the *Counter-Reformation had done four centuries earlier.

He became a leading figure in the *strapaese* movement, producing a collection of chauvinistic popularizing verse in *L'Arcitaliano* (1928). But his outspokenness got him into trouble. His book (in French) on the strategies used by Fascism to achieve power, *Technique du coup d'état* (1931), earned him arrest and a brief spell of confinement on Lipari. But he continued to publish, including the *autobiographical *Fughe in prigione* (1936). His experiences during *World War II, particularly as a correspondent in Russia, gave him the substance for his two most widely read works, *Kaputt* (1944) and *La pelle* (1949). He continued to write after the war, as well as working in the *theatre and *cinema, publishing a vigorous characterization of his fellow *Tuscans in *Maledetti Toscani* (1956) and the *travel writing of *Io in Russia e Cina* (published posthumously in 1958). Postwar criticism of both Left and Right has tended look on him with suspicion.   [CFB]

See G. B. Guerri, *L'Arcitaliano* (1980); G. Pardini, *Curzio Malaparte: biografia politica* (1998).

MALATESTA. The Malatesta were a family of landlords and soldiers from the Romagna. They established a lordship (*signoria*) in Rimini in 1296, and extended their rule in the Romagna. Although temporal subjects of the Pope, the family were de facto rulers of Rimini until 1500, when Cesare *Borgia's defeat of Pandolfo effectively ended their rule. Carlo I Malatesta (1368–1429), military commander of *papal forces and married to Elisabetta *Gonzaga, was instrumental in ending the Great Schism in 1415. Their greatest political and military influence came with Sigismondo (1417–68), a poet and an innovative *patron of letters, architecture, and the arts, who built the Malatesta Temple in Rimini replete with classical iconographic decorations. Exaggerated charges of paganism, immorality, and political duplicity led to his excommunication (1463) by Enea Silvio *Piccolomini, Pope Pius II, an action which helped ensure his notoriety as a '*Renaissance despot'.   [JEL & SJM]

MALATESTA, BATTISTA, DA MONTE-FELTRO (*c.*1384–1447) was daughter of the Count of *Urbino and grandmother of Costanza *Varano, whom she helped educate. Leonardo *Bruni addressed to her his treatise on women's *education, *De studiis et litteris* (1424). Her marriage to Galeazzo *Malatesta, lord of Pesaro, ended on his assassination (1431); she returned to Urbino and her literary interests.   [AR]

MALATESTI, ANTONIO (1610–72). *Florentine comic poet. He studied *astrology and painting but worked in commerce until Ferdinando III de' *Medici's *patronage allowed him to dedicate himself to writing. He composed a collection of riddles, *Enigmi* (1640) and another of rustic *sonnets, *La Tina*, which he dedicated to Milton and presented to him in manuscript. Many of the toasts and riddles in his often original *Brindisi dei Ciclopi* (1673) reflect contemporary Florentine life. He also wrote traditional sonnets, *ottave*, and quatrains, which he collected in *La sfinge* (1673). [FC]

Malavoglia, I (1881). *Verga's greatest novel and the first novel of *verismo* was planned as the first in the cycle of 'I Vinti'. It is the story of a family of *Sicilian fishermen, shortly after *Unification. After the father's death, five young people and their grandfather, Padron 'Ntoni, have to struggle against natural disasters and against usury which progressively impoverishes them. The honest, hardworking grandfather is contrasted with one of the grandsons, 'Ntoni, who dreams of wealth, gets drunk in the tavern, and is involved in smuggling. At the end Padron 'Ntoni dies alone in hospital whilst the grandson, having completed five years in gaol, leaves the country for good. [RL]

Malebolge. Ten subdivisions of the circle of the fraudulent in *Dante's *Inferno*.

Male oscuro, Il, see BERTO, GIUSEPPE.

MALERBA, LUIGI (pseud. of Luigi Bonardi) (1927–). Best known as a *novelist but also a dramatist and *children's writer of note. He was a member of the *Gruppo 63 and already displays an imaginative interest in *modernist ideas on literary self-reflexiveness in his first novel, *La scoperta dell'alfabeto* (1963). But social critique is at least as important a strand in his work. Already in *Il serpente* (1966) the play of wit and sarcasm is couched in deliberately unsophisticated language in a attempt to represent the disappearing *peasant society of his native Emilia. His work remained intellectually demanding, however. In *Il pianeta azzurro* (1986) the targets have become the corruption and malaise of the political system of the First Republic. *Il fuoco greco* (1990) is a *historical novel set in 10th-c. Byzantium, while *Le pietre volanti* (1992), is cast as a diary in which a painter reflects on his life against the background of an intriguingly futuristic world. [PBart]

MALISPINI, RICORDANO. According to the text, the author, with his nephew Giacotto, of a *Storia fiorentina*. It was formerly thought that this *chronicle, which appears to stop at 1286 (though in one truncated manuscript it continues until at least 1317), was written in the late 13th c. It is now known, however, to be a late 14th-c. forgery copied from the *Libro fiesolano* and from an abridgement of Giovanni *Villani's *Nuova cronica*, with insertions designed to glorify certain *Florentine families, especially the obscure but newly rich Bonaguisi. If Ricordano and Giacotto ever existed, it does not appear that they were writers. [JCB]

Malombra (1881). *Fogazzaro's first and most dramatic novel. It follows the emotional and spiritual progress of the weak-willed aesthete, Corrado Silla, torn between the unexciting but self-sacrificing Edith and the beautiful, deranged Marina di Malombra, convinced that she reincarnates one of her ancestors who was driven by passion to commit murder. [AM]

MALPAGHINI, GIOVANNI (1346–1417). Rhetorician and grammarian, originally from Ravenna. He began his career very young as copyist for *Petrarch, helping him to transcribe and order his letters and the *Canzoniere*. He left Petrarch in 1368 and went on to teach in the *Florentine *studio*, where he had important *humanists amongst his pupils. [MP]

MALPICA, CESARE (1800–48). Versatile writer, who was born in Capua, and spent his career in *Naples. He wrote poetry, short stories, and *novels, but was better known for books about his *travels in *Tuscany, *Umbria, and *Sicily. His journalistic activities included founding the *Giornale dei giovanetti* (1844) and then editing the *Giornale delle madri e dei fanciulli*. [FD'I]

MALPIGHI, NICOLÒ (14th c.–15th c.). Notary from *Bologna, who moved to *Rome in 1409, and became secretary to Pope John XXIII and then a *papal secretary (*abbreviator*) under Martin V. The author of amorous, encomiastic, and political verse in the *Petrarchan style, he retained close links with *Bolognese intellectuals, notably *Panormita. [ELM]

Malta and its diminutive archipelago underwent similar racial and political changes to those experienced by *Sicily; influences came from

Malvezzi, Virgilio

Phoenicians, Greeks (in two stages), Carthaginians, Romans, Arabs, Normans, and the Houses of *Anjou and *Aragon. Malta's most important event was the shipwreck there of the Apostle Paul in AD 60; his conversion of the islanders bequeathed an unswerving adherence to Christianity, now exclusively of the Roman variety. In 1530 the Knights of St John assumed government, and for over 250 years, until France invaded in 1798, imposed a militantly religious oligarchy, creating a university (1769), and Europe's then most impressive fortifications. In 1800 Britain was welcomed in after French anti-religious outrages, and following 1813 Malta became a British protectorate until 1964, when it voted for independent status within the Commonwealth.

Malta produced a considerable body of literature in Italian under the Knights of St John, but is of greater interest to Romance philologists than to critics of Italian literature. Maltese morphology and vocabulary is akin to North African Arabic (their word for God is *Allah*), with heavy lexical admixtures, mainly Italian, but also taken from other European languages. Until 1934 Maltese remained in most respects a spoken language, English and Italian having joint official status under the British after 1850; in 1934 Italian's status was abolished. Malta's heroic anti-*Fascist stance in *World War II was recognized by accolades from the Allies, including Britain's George Cross. Subsequently the use of Italian declined, but since 1960, Italian *television beamed from Sicily (61 miles away) has increased Italy's cultural influence. [JRW]

MALVEZZI, VIRGILIO (1595–1654). A *Bolognese aristocrat whose family traditionally supported the *papacy and the Spanish monarchy, Malvezzi was a prolific political writer and moralist. He spent most of his life in *Spain, from 1639 as royal *historiographer to Philip IV. His vast œuvre was praised by Quevedo and Gracián among others. It includes a treatise on Tacitus, monographs on figures from ancient and Spanish history and *Ritratto del privato politico cristiano* on Spanish royal absolutism (1635). [PBert]

Mambriano, Il, see FRANCESCO CIECO DA FERRARA.

MAMELI, GOFFREDO (1827–49). *Genoese poet, most famous for 'Fratelli d'Italia', which since 1949 has been the Italian national anthem, though it became widely known soon after its composition in

Genoa during the revolution of *1848. Mameli went on to fight in *Milan and then with *Garibaldi in *Rome. He died as result of a wound received there. [FD'I]

MAMIANI DELLA ROVERE, TERENZIO (1799–1885). Aristocratic politician and writer from Pesaro, who took part in the 1831 insurrection in *Bologna and was subsequently *exiled in France. After *Unification he was minister of *education and a member of the senate. He first wrote poetry, and then dedicated himself to philosophy, becoming professor in *Turin and *Rome. [FD'I]

MANARA, MILO, see COMICS.

MANCINI, POLIZIANO (16th c.–17th c.). *Tuscan writer of whom little is known. He published a trilogy of *novels—*Il principe Altomiro di Lusitania fortunato, Il principe Altomiro travagliato,* and *Il principe Altomiro regnante*—between 1641 and 1650. They follow the fortunes of a Catholic prince who succeeds in converting the Far East to Christianity. [MC]

Mandragola, La (1518). *Machiavelli's best-known *comedy centres on the attempt of an amorous *young *Florentine, Callimaco, to seduce Lucrezia, the *young wife of an elderly and apparently sexually impotent lawyer, Messer Nicia. Callimaco disguises himself as a doctor and plays on Messer Nicia's desire for offspring by offering the lawyer a magic potion derived from the mandrake root from which the play takes its title. In order to gain access to Lucrezia, Callimaco convinces Nicia that a sacrificial victim is required, as the potion has the unfortunate side-effect of killing the first male to sleep with the recipient. In another disguise he assumes this role and, after achieving his desired objective, reveals the deception to Lucrezia. Despite initial protests she agrees to accept what fortune and the Gods have brought upon her and takes Callimaco as her lover. The play has been interpreted as a commentary on the corruption of contemporary Florence. It is certainly one of the most lively of Italian *Renaissance comedies, largely thanks to Machiavelli's exploitation of contemporary Florentine idiom. [SJM]

MANESCALCO, MARIANO, see CONGREGA DEI ROZZI.

MANETTI, ANTONIO (1423–97). *Florentine politician, scientist, and man of letters, who belonged to the circle of *Ficino. Best known for his studies of *Dante's works, which were used by *Landino and *Benivieni, he was also the author of a *Vita di Filippo *Brunelleschi*, which accompanied a version of the *Novella del grasso legnaiuolo*, and of a collection of *biographies of eminent Florentine personalities, *Uomini singulari in Firenze dal MCCCC innanzi*. He combined a philological approach to the Florentine poetical tradition of the 14th c. with a *Neoplatonic reading of the texts.
[LB]

MANETTI, GIANNOZZO (1396–1459), from a leading *Florentine patrician family, came to *humanist studies only as an adult, his father, Bernardo, a rich merchant and banker, having opposed his Latin *education. Nevertheless, Giannozzo not only learned Latin and Greek, but also became one of the first humanists to learn Hebrew. He is most famous for his eclectic treatise *De dignitate et excellentia hominis*, a humanist response to the widely known *De miseria humanae conditionis* by the 13th-c. Pope *Innocent III. Manetti also enjoyed an active political and diplomatic career in Florence, cut short by his estrangement from the leaders of the *Medici regime in 1453; thereafter he retired to *Rome and *Naples.
[RDB]

MANFREDI (1232–66). Illegitimate son of the Emperor *Frederick II, he was King of *Sicily from 1258 until his death at the battle of Benevento (1266). He continued *patronage of the *Sicilian School of poets. Though a Ghibelline [see GUELFS AND GHIBELLINES] and twice excommunicated, he is presented by *Dante as an example of a man who is saved by repentance at the point of death (*Purg.* 3.103–45).
[PA]

MANFREDI, EUSTACHIO (1674–1739). Astronomer and poet, who was a founder member of *Arcadia in *Bologna and became the city's intellectual leader. His own Accademia degli Inquieti (founded in 1690) eventually merged with *Marsigli's Instituto delle Scienze. A mathematics professor from 1699 and from 1711 head of the university observatory, in 1715 and 1725 he published important ephemerides and in 1728 was elected to the Royal Society. His poetry is marked by its strict *Petrarchism, which in 1706 earnt him membership of the *Crusca Academy.
[JMAL]

MANFREDI, MUZIO (1535–c.1607). Poet and *courtier of Ferrante II *Gonzaga. He was particularly known for his violent *tragedy *Semiramide* (1593), which is indebted to Sperone *Speroni and Seneca. He also wrote numerous *madrigals, a *pastoral play, and letters on literary topics, *Lettere brevissime* (1605).
[FC]

MANGANELLI, GIORGIO (1922–90), *novelist, essayist, *journalist, and teacher of English literature, began his literary career as one of the most admired and respected members of the *Gruppo 63 and of the *Neoavanguardia*; in a famous essay, *Letteratura come menzogna* (1967), he characterized literature as a negation of bourgeois reality, a rhetorical, ceremonial ritual of the unconscious celebrated by the artist as priest of the underworld, who through language liberates life's inexorable leaning towards death. This is an accurate description of *Hilarotragoedia* (1964), an essay-novel that is a disquisition on man's 'Hades-bound' state of being. In the tradition of Carlo Emilio *Gadda, he deployed an extraordinary linguistic and rhetorical inventiveness to create erudite *satires of contemporary society's 'mythological bad faith'. His creative writings in this vein include *Agli dèi ulteriori* (1972), *Lunario dell'orfano sannita* (1973), *A e B* (1975), *Discorso dell'ombra e dello stemma* (1982), and *Encomio del tiranno* (1990). Critical and theoretical writings include *Angosce di stile* (1981), *Laboriose inezie* (1986), and the intriguing *Pinocchio: un libro parallelo* (1977). His travels produced *Cina e altri Orienti* (1974), and a selection, *Improvvisi* (1989), of his newspaper articles. *Antologia privata* (1989) is his personal selection from among all his writings.
[CGW]

Manganello, see MISOGYNY.

MANGIABOTTI, ANDREA DE', see ANDREA DA BARBERINO.

Manifesti romantici, see ROMANTICISM.

Manifesto degli intellettuali fascisti, see GENTILE, GIOVANNI.

Mannerism was until recently a term of disparagement. It is probably best defined as the style that prevailed in art and architecture in Central Italy, including *Rome and *Florence, from about 1520 to about 1590. This is characterized by elegant, elongated, unnatural figural forms, and often irrational approaches to space. It is closely associated with *Castiglione's concept of *sprezzatura* as an ideal of courtly behaviour: so too a primary aim of the Mannerist artist was to convey highly complex forms in an apparently effortless way. But it also has artificial qualities comparable to those evident in developed *pastoral writing, notably Battista *Guarini's *Pastor fido* (1586, published in 1590). Shearman (1967) summed it up as the 'stylish style'.

Its origins lie partly in Rome, especially in the late work of *Raphael (for example, his *Transfiguration* of 1520), and *Michelangelo's nude figures on the Sistine Chapel ceiling (1508–12). Another, often bizarre, though always graceful strand of Mannerism originated in Florence, notably in the work of Iacopo da Pontormo (1494–1556) and Rosso Fiorentino (1494–1540). A second generation of Mannerists, including *Vasari and Francesco Salviati (1510–63), succeeded in fusing these strands into a highly complex illusionistic style. Through the travels of Mannerist artists, as well as the dissemination of engravings, Mannerism spread rapidly to the *courts of Europe. In the 1580s the style came increasingly to seem at odds with *Counter-Reformation ideas on art, and the new naturalism of the Carracci and Caravaggio became increasingly fashionable as the foundation of the *Baroque style. The term is often used of literature, particularly poetry, of the later 16th c. that shows similar characteristics, notably in the lyrics of Torquato *Tasso and the younger Giovan Battista *Strozzi. [CR]

See J. Shearman, *Mannerism* (1967).

MANNI, DOMENICO MARIA (1690–1788). Director of the Biblioteca Strozzi in *Florence, who edited early texts and published works of *antiquarian and literary scholarship, including a useful *Istoria del *Decamerone* (1742). But his *Veglie piacevoli, ovvero notizie de' più bizzarri e giocondi uomini toscani*, in the style of *Boccaccio, was dismissed by *Baretti. [JMAL]

MANNONI, REMO, see ALTOMARE, LIBERO.

MANOELLO GIUDEO (or EBREO), see IMMANUEL ROMANO.

MANSO, GIAMBATTISTA (1569–1645) was for many years the leading figure in *Neapolitan poetic and intellectual circles, and the first biographer of Torquato *Tasso. Of noble origin, in 1611 he founded the Accademia degli *Oziosi, to which he introduced John Milton in 1638. But it was as protector of Italian poets that he played crucial roles. He helped *Marino out of many scrapes, and in return made free with Marino's poetry, plagiarizing it in his *Poesie nomiche* (1635). He helped Tasso personally on several occasions, and Tasso repaid the debt with his *dialogue *Il Manso overo de l'amicitia*. In his wanderings round Italy after his imprisonment, Tasso stayed with Manso in 1592, and the relationship remained firm until Tasso's death in 1595. Like most *biography of the time, Manso's *Vita di Tasso* (begun in 1604 and finished by 1619) is not reliable: it romanticizes and dramatizes Tasso's life, broadcasting the myth that he was imprisoned for his love of Leonora d'*Este, making of Tasso a knight whose verbal and military dexterity, heroism, and honour all now seem sadly at odds with the Tasso we know, and playing down the poet's degradation and difficulties. In line with classical practice, Manso quotes in the final chapter a series of Tasso's famous sayings, but even to contemporaries these appeared to owe more to Erasmus. [PBD]

MANTEGAZZA, PAOLO (1831–1910). *Darwinian *positivist thinker, originally from Monza. He occupied from 1870 the first chair of anthropology in Italy (at *Turin) and is best known for his numerous works in social anthropology. His publications include a novel of eugenics, *Un giorno a Madera* (1874), and, in collaboration with *Neera, an influential *Dizionario di igiene per le famiglie* (1895). [AHC]

MANTOVANO, IL, see SPAGNOLI, BATTISTA.

Mantua (Mantova). Surrounded by the lakes of the river Mincio and set in the plains of *Lombardy, the city was the dynastic centre of the *Gonzaga family, who ruled uninterrupted between 1328 and the invasion of imperial forces in 1629. Boasting a population of some 25,000 in 1500, Mantua had a largely agrarian economy, although much work was provided by the Gonzaga building projects. Despite not having a *university or any indigenous artistic culture, the city benefited from the proximity of *humanists and artists in other centres, especially *Venice, *Florence, *Ferrara, and *Padua, as well as from the enlightened reputation of the ruling family as *patrons. Ludovico Gonzaga (1412–78) was educated by the humanist pedagogue *Vittorino da Feltre, and Leon Battista *Alberti was employed in the construction of S. Sebastiano and S. Andrea, as well as overseeing the replanning of the city. Pisanello and Mantegna both executed commissions there, the latter remaining from 1460 to the end of his life and completing the famous *Camera degli sposi* fresco cycle. For twenty years Giulio Romano supervised the construction and decoration of the sumptuous Palazzo del Tè on the western side of the city.   [SJM]

Manuscripts and Manuscript Production. The Latin scripts in which Italian literature was copied were the descendants of the hierarchical system of scripts which the Romans bequeathed to the peoples of the early *Middle Ages in the West. These ranged from book or 'rustic' capitals to late Roman cursive, a documentary hand full of complicated ligatures (strokes linking letters). Between these extremes came the bookhands now known as uncial (another upper-case script) and half uncial (the first lower-case or minuscule book script), as well as a scholarly hand incorporating elements of the cursive, but used in books. By the 7th–8th c. numerous pre-Caroline hands, basically cursive and using many ligatures, had emerged from the cursive styles of the earlier hierarchy. The distinctive form developed in South Italy is now known as Beneventan. It had a long life, and survived in the South long after the pre-Caroline styles had been superseded elsewhere in Italy. Some of the earliest examples of written Italian, datable to the 12th c., are in this script. The pre-Caroline scripts of Northern and Central Italy yielded to the *Carolingian script (a combination of elements from the late Roman half uncial and cursive hands), which emerged in Northern France in the late 8th c. This well-spaced minuscule script was much more legible than the old cursive hands, and spread rapidly throughout the Carolingian empire. In Central Italy a distinctive version of it known as *romanesca* retained more cursive features.

Over time the original small-module Carolingian script grew larger in proportion and more compressed, especially in Northern Europe. Changes in the cut of the pen led to a more angular script, often heavily abbreviated. This new type of script, called *littera moderna* in the late Middle Ages, as opposed to the *littera antiqua* (Carolingian script), and especially associated with the new *universities, became known as Gothic in the 16th c. This script took many forms. The rotunda form prevalent in Italy was less angular and compressed than the North European types. Alongside the book scripts a

'chancery' script (*cancellaresca*) was developed in the 13th c., to cope with ever increasing documentation. This cursive hand soon became the common script of educated people. Scribes, who were often also notaries, started using it to copy texts, and during the 14th c. the *cancellaresca* became the usual script for texts in the vernacular, including notably *Dante's *Divine Comedy*. Mercantesca, another version of Gothic cursive developed in the 13th c. by *merchants for accounts and correspondence, was being used by the end of the 14th c. for vernacular texts of all kinds that the merchant class copied for themselves, and continued to be widely used during the succeeding century.

Already in the late 13th c. some scholars were seeking out copies of classical authors to study. The manuscripts they found were usually copied in Carolingian script, which influenced their own hands. In the mid-14th c. *Petrarch explicitly criticized even the finest Gothic hands as being handsome but trying to read, and developed his simplified semi-Gothic script—small, clear, and well spaced. This reformed Gothic was very influential, especially in North Italy, and continued to be used well into the 15th c. Meanwhile in *Florence, the Chancellor, Coluccio *Salutati, who also found Gothic hands tiresome to read, encouraged Niccolò *Niccoli and his protégé Poggio *Bracciolini to experiment further. Modelling their hands on late Carolingian 11th- and 12th-c. hands, of which there were many examples in the library of Salutati, they 'invented' the so-called *humanistic script at the turn of the 14th c. (a copy of Valerius Maximus in the *Vatican Library, still experimental and perhaps copied by Poggio, is dated 1397).

At first the use of the new script (called *littera antiqua* by contemporaries, the same term as had been used for Carolingian script) was restricted to a small circle, but it soon spread outside Florence, to scholars in *Rome (Poggio went to the *papal curia in 1402/3), *Venice and the North-East (through *Guarino da Verona), *Milan, and elsewhere. By the 1440s it was being used generally to copy literary texts in Latin, and its success was assured in the late 1460s, when the earliest printers used it as the model for their 'Roman' type. However, although the *Divine Comedy* was among the earliest texts transcribed in the new script, for most of the 15th c. vernacular texts, apart from the *Canzoniere* and *Trionfi* of Petrarch, were normally copied either in some version of Gothic or in semi-humanistic hands. In the 1420s Niccoli had developed a humanistic cursive which was soon adopted by other scholars for their drafts and correspondence, and later also as a bookhand. In the second half of the century the italic style of cursive, the model for the italic fount of Aldo *Manuzio, emerged in the Veneto as a rival bookhand. The documentary version used in the early 16th-c. papal chancery by calligraphers such as Ludovico Arrighi provided the model (partly through printed writing books) for another bookhand, the new *cancellaresca*, which prevailed in the 16th c.

It is rarely possible to date and localize a written text from the evidence of script alone. Few manuscripts are securely dated, and a palaeographer's judgement, based on personal experience and visual memory, may be mistaken. The complementary discipline of *codicology* calls on the physical aspects of a piece of writing and its context to provide further evidence. In a codex, or manuscript in book form, the constituents to be considered by a diligent researcher are mostly physical: the material used—generally parchment or paper—and the way in which it has been manufactured, the folding and arrangement of quires, the method of ruling used to guide the scribe's writing, notes by the original scribe, decoration, binding, later annotation, and other signs of ownership, but should also include the text itself or the exemplar on which it is based (which from the 1460s onwards might be a printed text). Just as script evolved, so did methods of manuscript production. For example, until the 14th c. the material used for manuscripts in Western Europe was normally parchment, in Italy generally produced from young goatskins (*capretti*), which had to undergo a long preparation of soaking, shaving, and stretching. Parchment is durable, and provides a good writing surface when well prepared, but it was expensive. Paper, made from rags and cheaper to produce, was introduced to Western Europe by the Arabs, but was not manufactured there until the 13th c., when the first papermill opened at Fabriano. It was rarely used for text manuscripts before the later 14th c., by which time its manufacture was widespread and its quality had greatly improved. From then on its use increased rapidly, especially for cheaper books in the vernacular. [See also PRINTING.] [ACdelaM]

See B. Bischoff, *Latin Palaeography: Antiquity and the Middle Ages* (1990); L. E. Boyle, *Medieval Latin Palaeography: A Bibliographical Introduction* (1984); A. Petrucci, *Breve storia della scrittura latina* (1989); id., *Writers and Readers in Medieval Italy: Studies in the History of Written Culture*, ed. C. M. Rading (1995).

MANUZIO, ALDO (*c.*1452–1515) was one of the most influential figures in the early history of *printing, and his creative innovations have left a permanent mark on printing and *publishing. Born in Bassiano, near *Rome, he received a *humanist training, and first earned his living as a teacher; in the 1480s he tutored the young aristocrat Alberto Pio of Carpi. In 1490 he moved to *Venice, and in 1495, in partnership with the printer Andrea Torresani, who later became his father-in-law, began an ambitious programme of publishing Greek texts in the original. In 1496 Francesco Griffo cut for him a roman type (the so-called Bembo), whose influence has lasted to this day. Griffo also cut the first italic type, one of the several innovative features of the series of octavo editions of the Greek and Roman classics (together with *Petrarch's *lyric poetry and *Dante's *Divine Comedy*), which Aldo began to publish in 1501. These, the world's first pocket classics, though not cheap, provided scholars and persons of culture with texts to be read outside the study or library. Their success can be seen in the many imitations they provoked, inside and outside Italy. Aldo published a total of 126 editions. [CF]

MANZINI, GIAMBATTISTA (1599–1664). A *Bolognese who displayed his literary talents in a variety of works. He came to prominence in a polemic against Matteo *Peregrini over the role of the intellectual at *court (*Il servire negato al savio*, published in 1626). His dramatic works, a *tragedy (1631) and a *comedy (1633), reflect the moral aims of the *Counter-Reformation; his one *novel, *Il Cretideo* (1637), shows a passion for the new genre. He also published two rhetorical manuals. [PBD]

MANZINI, GIANNA (1896–1974). *Novelist. Born in Pistoia, she studied literature in *Florence and spent some years there. She became one of the group of innovative, experimental writers and intellectuals associated with *Solaria*, and after its closure contributed to *Letteratura* and *Campo di Marte*. She made *Tuscany the setting for her first novel, *Tempo innamorato* (1928). The collections of stories that followed show her absorbing the influence of modern European fiction, Virginia Woolf in particular. After her marriage failed, she moved permanently to *Rome in 1933, where she embarked on a lifelong relationship with the critic Enrico *Falqui. Her second novel, the highly innovative work-in-progress *Lettera all'editore*, caused a critical stir on publication in 1945. From then until her death she published a steady stream of novels and stories, including the autobiographical *Sulla soglia* (1971) and *Ritratto in piedi* (1971), a powerful account of her relationship with her anarchist father who died in 1925 after being stalked and stoned by *Fascist thugs. Her work as a whole crosses the boundaries between fiction, history, and *autobiography, while drawing stylistically on stream-of-consciousness techniques, cinematic devices to break up narrative time, and other means of problematizing the relationship between author, reader, and text. [AHC]

MANZONI, ALESSANDRO (1785–1873) is by general consent Italy's greatest *novelist. He was born in *Milan, and spent most of his life there, alternating between his house in Via Morone (now the Centro Studi Manzoniani), and his villa in Brusuglio, on the outskirts of the city. He lived in Paris between 1805 and 1810 in the freethinking household of his mother, Giulia Beccaria (the daughter of Cesare *Beccaria), and was there again sporadically until 1820. This enabled him to acquire a first-hand knowledge of the French *encyclopédistes* and of European *Romantic culture. He also became thoroughly familiar with 17th-c. French Catholic moralists. His personal life was scarred by the deaths of his first wife, Enrichetta Blondel, his second wife, Teresa Stampa, and four of his daughters. He appears to have suffered from chronic anxiety, which sometimes prevented him from writing for long periods. He was, however, little inclined to discuss his personal problems, and was outwardly given to *humour and understatement. The large number of letters he left are a precious source of information regarding his views and his work, but not as regards his private afflictions.

In Paris, around 1810, he experienced the religious crisis which led him from agnosticism to an austere form of *Catholicism, and from then on all his writings bore the mark of his religious beliefs. His Catholicism, however, never implied automatic acceptance of the dictates of the Church establishment. Politically, he was a progressive *liberal, who opposed the continuing temporal power of the *papacy and supported the annexation of *Rome to the Italian state. Theologically, he inclined to a form of *Jansenism. He was a severe judge of the shortcomings of the Catholic Church and consistently distanced himself from the *Jesuit tradition. His Catholicism was founded on an uncompromising ethical concern, and alien to the more blatant trappings and paraphernalia of mass religiosity. His *Osservazioni sulla morale cattolica* (1819), intended to respond to the critique of Catholicism put forward by the Swiss Protestant historian Sismondi in his *Histoire des républiques italiennes du Moyen-Âge*, argued that true Catholic ethics were based exclusively on the Christian gospels.

He shared the cultural and political aims of the Milanese Romantics, but was always cautious in his overt pronouncements. He declined an invitation to contribute to their weekly journal *Il *Conciliatore*. In his only public utterance on the subject, *Lettera sul Romanticismo*, which appeared in 1823 when the movement had already disbanded, he expressed agreement with the Romantics' condemnation of the incessant use of classical mythology, unconditional imitation of classical writers, and normative rules such as the dramatic unities, but he judged their constructive suggestions to be far too vague and ill-defined [see also CLASSICISM; NEOCLASSICISM]. He also was scathing towards the Gothic aspects of Romantic writings. On the other hand, the very fact of writing a novel, arguably the first modern Italian novel, implied at least a willingness to engage with Romantic ideas—as did indeed the whole drift of Manzoni's literary career, with its concern to uncover the hidden parts of history and to communicate with a wide readership rather than with a narrow circle of fellow writers.

His first writings after returning to Milan were the *Inni sacri* (1815, but then supplemented by 'Pentecoste' of 1822). These were followed by the historical *tragedies, *Il *conte di Carmagnola* (1820) and *Adelchi* (1822). In 1821 he wrote 'Marzo 1821', which became one of the most famous patriotic poems of the *Risorgimento, and 'Il cinque maggio', in which he reflected on the vicissitudes of the life of *Napoleon, who had just died. *Adelchi* was a direct result of the new perspectives on medieval history, and on literature as an exploration of historical reality, acquired during his renewed contacts with French cultural circles in 1819–20. His stated aim in the play was to cast light on the lives of the native Italians subjected to the Longobards, and to shift the focus from illustrious to ordinary people. But the protagonists turned out to be famous Longobards and Franks, while the indigenous masses only appeared as the object of comment in one of the choruses.

The aim of highlighting the lives of ordinary people, frustrated by the medium of drama, found fulfilment in *I *promessi sposi*, which he began writing in 1821. His decision to attempt a *historical novel was influenced by the enthusiastic belief of Parisian friends, such as Augustin Thierry and Claude Fauriel, in the epistemological potential of the genre. He was convinced that the function of literature was that of enhancing truth. All his statements concerning the portrayal of history in fiction point to a single-minded preoccupation with truth. Historical characters, events, and situations must be presented just as they were in reality, and fictional elements must comply with the criterion of verisimilitude. But literature was also to focus on moral truth, on the ideal behind the real, and for him moral truth defined itself in terms of his own special brand of Catholicism.

This uncompromising attitude towards the duties of the writer soon led him to abandon creative writing altogether. In spite of composing the greatest of Italian historical novels, he came to reject the genre in *Del romanzo storico, e in genere de' componimenti misti di storia e d'invenzione* (1850, but developing from ideas first formulated two decades earlier), claiming that in future only *historiography, correctly undertaken, could fulfil the aim of providing a true interpretation of reality. After 1827 his writings consisted mainly of essays on philosophy, history, politics and economics, literature, and above all language—most notably *Sentir messa* (1836), *Storia della colonna infame* (1842), the unfinished *Saggio comparativo sulla rivoluzione francese del 1789 e la rivoluzione italiana del 1859*, begun in 1862, in which he condemns violent political upheavals, and *Della lingua italiana*, which he began in the 1840s and also left unfinished.

Manzoni argued that language was a fundamental aspect of Italian *Unification, in various studies and articles of the period 1845–68, as well as in numerous unpublished earlier writings. He considered the normative criterion for languages to be living usage; a language could only be considered such if it could be used for communication at all levels, from the domestic to the scholarly and scientific. He considered that spoken *Florentine was the only Italian idiom to fulfil these criteria. This belief was the main driving force behind his rewritings of his novel. The first draft, entitled *Fermo e Lucia*, was written in 1821–3 and never published. About a year after its completion he began a drastic process of revision, which was to lead to the first publication of *I promessi sposi* in 1825–7 (the so-called *ventisettana*), and then to the definitive edition of 1840 (the so-called *quarantana*). The transition from *Fermo e Lucia* to *I promessi sposi* involved an attempt to move to a supraregional language based on Tuscan, as well as extensive recasting and restructuring, while the differences between the *ventisettana* and the *quarantana* consist almost entirely of linguistic changes, often involving no more than single words, and dictated by Manzoni's wish to move closer to spoken Florentine.

In 1868, seven years after Unification, he chaired a parliamentary committee with the remit of suggesting ways of spreading a common language among Italians of all regions and social classes. The resulting recommendations, embodied in *Dell'unità della lingua italiana e dei mezzi di diffonderla* (1868), included the drafting of a dictionary of contemporary spoken Florentine, the maximum use of Tuscan teachers in all schools, and the rewriting of textbooks and catechisms by Tuscans. The new dictionary, *Novo vocabolario della lingua italiana secondo l'uso di Firenze*, was completed in 1897, and the suggested educational policy was partly implemented for a while, but the continuing deficiencies and uneven development of the school system prevented any real achievement. Such applications of Manzoni's linguistic theories as there were produced only new forms of *purism and pedantry, which were to last well into the 20th c. [See also QUESTIONE DELLA LINGUA.]

Manzoni has cast a long shadow over Italian culture at all levels. *I promessi sposi* is still required reading in secondary schools. It has shaped Italians' ways of thinking, often in unconscious ways, more than any other novel. It is responsible for the received view of 17th-c. politics and culture, and verbal borrowings from it have become embedded in everyday language, as well as constantly resurfacing in films, books, and *journalism.   [VRJ]

Tutte le opere, eds. A. Chiari and F. Ghisalberti, 7 vols. (1957–90). See E. Sala di Felice, *Il punto su Manzoni* (1989); S. S. Nigro, *Manzoni* (1989); B. Reynolds, *The Linguistic Writings of Alessandro Manzoni* (1950).

MARAINI, DACIA (1936–) is one of Italy's best-known contemporary *women writers. Born in *Florence, she spent her childhood in Japan, including a period of internment (1943–5), before the family returned to her mother's native *Sicily. She has lived in *Rome since leaving home at 18, and was for a long time the partner of Alberto *Moravia.

Her immensely productive career has involved creative writing, film work, *journalism, and feminist

activism; indeed since the 1970s her *feminism forms the matrix of the majority of her fictional and other writings, and she has addressed virtually all of the major feminist issues such as abortion, sexual violence, female sexuality, and father–daughter and mother–daughter relations. Her prose works, many of them prize-winning, include fiction, non-fiction and *autobiography, for example: *L'età del malessere* (1963), *Memorie di una ladra* (1972), *Donna in guerra* (1975), *Lettere a Marina* (1981), *Il treno per Helsinki* (1984), and *Isolina* (1985). Of her more recent work, *La lunga vita di Marianna Ucrìa* (1990) and *Bagheria* (1993) arise out of her *Sicilian connections, *Voci* (1994) is a feminist *detective story, and *Un clandestino a bordo* (1996) addresses abortion and maternity. Maraini has collaborated with several *theatre groups, founding the women's experimental Teatro Maddalena in Rome in the 1970s, and writing more than thirty plays. She has also produced several volumes of poetry from *Crudeltà all'aria aperta* (1966) to *Viaggiando con passo di volpe* (1991). [JHB]
    See C. Lazzaro-Weis, 'Dacia Maraini', in R. Russell (ed.), *Italian Women Writers* (1994); P. Gaglianone, *Conversazione con Dacia Maraini* (1995).

MARAMAURO, GUGLIELMO (c.1317–c.1380). *Neapolitan noble with strong literary interests. He was a friend of *Petrarch, and the addressee of two of the poet's *Seniles*. He wrote a history of *Naples, now lost, and a *commentary on *Dante's *Inferno*, which he began in 1369 [see also DANTE COMMENTARIES]. A small number of *lyric poems also survive. [PH]

MARANA, GIOVANNI PAOLO (1642–93), a poor noble from *Genoa, was imprisoned for taking part in the Della Torre conspiracy. By 1683 he was in France, where he worked as a *journalist and was probably pensioned by Louis XIV. His principal claim to fame is *L'esploratore turco* or *L'espion du Grand Seigneur*, published in both Italian and French versions in Paris in 1684. This is a collection of thirty letters, claiming to be secret reports on France sent to the Sultan and 'translated from the Arabic'. The reports continued, whether or not written by the same author, reaching eight volumes in the English translation (1687–94). The presentation of a *satire on contemporary manners in the guise of an account by an outsider appealed to readers, and inspired Montesquieu's more famous *Lettres persanes*. [UPB]

MARATTI ZAPPI, FAUSTINA (1679/80–1745) was celebrated as the most accomplished woman poet of her age. The illegitimate daughter of the Roman painter Carlo Maratta, she received an exceptional *education in the *liberal arts, and entered the *Arcadia Academy as Aglauro Cidonia. Her poems, published with those of her husband Giovan Battista *Zappi in 1723, display a predilection for domestic intimacy in their choice of subjects. [CCa]

MARCELLO PAGNINI, see SEMIOTICS; STRUCTURALISM AND POST-STRUCTURALISM.

MARCHESA COLOMBI (pseud. of Maria Antonietta Torriani) (1846–1920). *Novelist and *journalist who married and later separated from Eugenio Torrelli Viollier, the founder and editor of the *Corriere della sera*. Though best known for her novels, she was also an active campaigner for women's *education. Her social concerns are reflected in novels such as *In risaia* (1878), an early example of *verismo, which details the conditions of women workers in the rice fields. Her best-known novel, *Un matrimonio in provincia* (1885), is an ironic anatomization of bourgeois marriage. She also published poems and *children's stories. [See also FEMINISM.] [UJF]

Marchese di Roccaverdina, Il (1901). Luigi *Capuana's best *novel, considered to be a masterpiece of Italy's naturalist tradition. It focuses on the violence and irrationality of a *Sicilian marquis, who, having killed his mistress's husband out of jealousy, is gradually driven to insanity by the guilt he suffers. [RSD]

MARCHETTI, ALESSANDRO (1633–1714). *Tuscan scientist and man of letters. Being a lifelong anti-*Aristotelian did not prevent his holding chairs of philosophy and mathematics at *Pisa (1660–1714), where he continued *Galileo's investigations into elasticity. The verse translation of Lucretius' *De rerum natura*, which he completed in 1669, circulated only in manuscript until it was published in 1717 in London by *Rolli, but it was an important stimulus to intellectual heterodoxy in Italy. He also translated from Anacreon (1707). He published his own collected *Rime* in 1704. [JMAL]

MARCHETTI, GIOVANNI (1790–1852). Politician who became Pope Pius IX's foreign minister in *1848, and also a poet, *translator, and critic. His co-edition of the *Divine Comedy* (1819) includes an important essay on the poem's *allegory, which he regards as primarily political.

[MPC]

Marciana, Biblioteca Nazionale, see LIBRARIES.

Marco Lombardo. One of the wrathful in *Dante's *Purgatorio*, and the bearer of a central political message about *papacy and empire.

MARCONI, GUGLIELMO, see ACCADEMIA D'ITALIA, REALE.

MARDERSTEIG, GIOVANNI, see PRINTING.

Mare amoroso, Il. A loosely structured love poem of 334 lines, composed in Western *Tuscany in the late 13th c., and the earliest known example of unrhymed *hendecasyllables. In addition to a conventional detailing of the physical features of the beloved, it contains *bestiary material, astronomical lore, and allusions to heroes and heroines from the *romance tradition. It has been variously interpreted as a *parody of *courtly themes, a rhetorical handbook for novice love poets, an attempt to bring together all possible ways of celebrating the beloved's beauty and virtues, and an *encyclopedia of amorous themes and images. It has been proposed that the author is Brunetto *Latini. [CK]

Marfisa bizarra, see DRAGONCINO, GIOVAN BATTISTA.

Margutte, see MORGANTE, IL.

Marianna Sirca, see DELEDDA, GRAZIA.

MARIN, BIAGIO (1891–1985). *Dialect poet, born between *Venice and *Trieste in the coastal village of Grado, which was under *Austrian rule at the time. After studying philosophy in Vienna, he moved to *Florence, where he got to know various Triestine writers and contributed to *La *Voce*, though he eventually took his degree with *Gentile in *Rome. He fought as a volunteer in *World War I, and was subsequently a teacher and then a librarian in Trieste before retiring to Grado.

His first collection, *Fiuri de tapo* ('Cork-Tree Blossoms', 1912), like the many which followed, is in the dialect of Grado. Overall his poems, which he

collected in *I canti dell'isola* (1981), are centred on a small number of thematic nuclei—personal happiness and tragedy, a deeply religious sense of the fragility of the individual's existence, the events of daily life, love for Grado and the archaic culture of its sea-going families. Nor does his style change significantly. He remains true to simple, melodic metres and to a purified form of his dialect which seems to acquire a virginal freshness and authenticity. In going against the *hermetic tendency of much 20th-c. Italian poetry, he is similar to some other poets from the North-East, notably *Saba and the early *Pasolini. [RD]

MARINELLA, LUCREZIA (1571–1653). Prolific *Venetian poet and polemicist, and probably the most learned woman of letters of her day. Her father, Giovanni Marinelli, a noted physician who wrote on women's health and beauty, amassed a large library that benefited his daughter's *education. As a poet she attempts to put high artistic quality at the service of morality and religion in accordance with *Counter-Reformation thinking. She wrote lives of the saints in *ottava rima*, allegorizing *commentaries on sacred verse, including her own, and a *pastoral drama, *Felice Arcadia* (1605), mixing prose and poetry. Her greatest poetic achievement was an *epic in the manner of Torquato *Tasso, *L'Enrico, overo Bisantio acquistato* (1635), celebrating the capture of *Byzantium during the 12th-c. *Crusades by the Venetian Enrico Dandolo.

Marinella stepped out of the above genres in the most powerful and learned defence of women yet penned by a woman, *La nobiltà et l'eccellenza delle donne, co' difetti e mancamenti de gli huomini* (1600). It was a response to Giuseppe Passi's deeply *misogynistic *I donneschi difetti* (1599). Marinella shows by examples, quotations from authorities, and argument that women are more virtuous than men and that men are far more culpable of the vices of which Passi accuses women. In the 1601 and 1620 editions she extends her refutation of Passi, and an entire *Aristotelian tradition behind him, to embrace misogynist writings from *Boccaccio to Sperone *Speroni, Ercole Tasso, and Torquato Tasso. No woman before had dared to attack the reasoning of named illustrious and learned men, and find it wanting, if not ludicrous. [See also FEMINISM; WOMEN WRITERS, 1.] [LAP]

The Nobility and Excellence of Women and the Defects and Vices of Men, ed. and trans. A. Dunhill (1999).

MARINETTI, FILIPPO TOMMASO (1876–1944). Poet, *novelist, dramatist, and, above all, founder and prime mover of *Futurism.

Born in Alexandria in Egypt, Marinetti attended a French *Jesuit college there, and then studied for his *baccalauréat* in Paris, later graduating in law at the University of *Genoa. He composed his earliest works in the *symbolist manner in French, which at the time he considered the only means of expressing complex late 19th-c. sensibility. The French connection lasted, although his views changed considerably. *Poesia* (1905–9), the magazine which he founded in *Milan with Sem *Benelli, published new foreign and Italian writing. His founding Futurist Manifesto appeared in *Le Figaro* (20 February 1909), as well as in *Poesia,* and his famous Futurist novel first appeared in French as *Mafarka le futuriste* (1909). The manifesto reflected both French post-symbolist literary developments and growing Italian *nationalist opposition to *Giolitti's political system: it proclaimed that poetry should espouse the values of the new century—action, violence, and industrial change—and boasted that Futurism marked the much-longed-for resurgence of Italian culture.

As his ideas spread to other branches of the arts, Marinetti helped shape the relative manifestos in the movement's challenging, iconoclastic style and masterminded their distribution, subsequently publishing works of members of the movement in his *Edizioni futuriste.* He organized boisterous Futurist *serate* (which grew out of his own earlier recitations of French poetry) throughout Italy, and from 1912 onwards arranged art exhibitions and other Futurist performances in many European cities. His own most significant literary contribution was his 1912 invention of *parole in libertà,* which 'freed' words not only from verse forms but also from conventional syntax. An early demonstration of the possibilities, and the limitations, of the technique is his long, 'Zang Tumb Tumb' (1914) on the recent siege of Adrianopolis. He also composed various innovative 'sintesi teatrali'.

Marinetti campaigned vigorously for Italian intervention in *World War I. He himself fought in Northern Italy and was wounded. In 1919 he played a prominent part in early *Fascist subversion, but temporarily broke with *Mussolini in 1920 as the latter became less revolutionary. He restored his support after Fascism gained power, becoming a member of the *Accademia d'Italia in 1929 whilst continuing to defend modern art. Contradictory to the end, he attacked the regime's anti-Semitic legislation in the later 1930s but then (after following the Italian army to Russia) he gave his support to the Salò republic. [SV]

See L. De Maria (ed.), *F. T. Marinetti. Teoria e invenzione futurista* (1983); G. Baldissone, *Filippo Tommaso Marinetti* (1986).

MARINI, GIOVANNI AMBROSIO (before 1600–after 1667). *Genoese priest and author of edifying writings and three *novels—*Le gare de' disperati* (1644), *Gli scherzi di fortuna a pro dell'innocenza* (1662), and, most importantly, *Il Calloandro fedele* (first part 1640, final edition 1653, then frequently reprinted up until 1887). This tells the story of two star-crossed lovers, Calloandro and Leonilda, who are heirs to the empires of Constantinople and Trebizond, and ends with their wedding and the union of the two empires. The intricate, constantly surprising plot includes voyages, duels, mysteries, disguises, and recognition scenes. The ambiguous and outlandish situations, all expertly managed, include Calloandro being believed dead four times and at one point expected to fight against himself as the champion of two opposing armies. In clear, vigorous prose, without laboured conceits, Marini offers his readers a mixture of aristocratic and *chivalric heroism and tear-jerking emotion. [MC]

Marinismo refers to the poetic manner of *Marino and his followers, a heterogeneous group who aimed to be innovators, although in fact they were still dependent in fundamental ways on the poetic tradition from Torquato *Tasso to *Petrarch. Marino himself, as he declared in the Preface to *La lira,* wished to be a new leader and model for other poets. Second, he wished to surprise and shock the reader through the marvellous (*meraviglioso*) and the unusual (*peregrino*). The qualities he and his followers most valued were *ingegno* and *acutezza,* as demonstrated through far-fetched metaphors and conceits, often ones that would assault the reader's senses [see BAROQUE; CONCETTISMO]. This meant being ready, in fact eager, to break literary rules and precepts. It also meant a rapacious and indiscriminate attitude towards literary imitation, ranging, as Marino expounded in a letter to Claudio *Achillini, between translation, imitation, and bare-faced theft.

In practice Marino and his followers mixed tradition and innovation. They worked with existing poetic forms, notably the *sonnet, the *sestina,* the *canzone,* the *madrigal, and less frequently the

Marino, Giovanbattista

ottava rima, but developed new, more fluid structures and line lengths. They also treated hallowed themes (love, woman, nature), but they made the senses and sensuality the dominant element. The passions, which had attracted the attention of *Paduan writers and theorists in the mid-16th c. as well as of Tasso, take centre stage, and are depicted in extreme forms in representations of subjects such as martyrdom, sacrifice, heroic grandeur, and abysmal existential fear. The Marinists also take up new themes—notably the visual and musical arts and indoor scenes—with a new repertoire of references embracing modern scientific advances, other specialized branches of knowledge, and exotic locations and animals.

There are similarities with Tasso, but the balance between form and content in Tasso is deliberately unbalanced by Marino and his followers, who very often forget all concerns about unity in their poems (witness the *Adone*). The most striking difference, however, is the intensified role of metaphor. Marino and his followers looked for metaphors that would arrest the reader by suggesting a likeness between two apparently disparate things, thus producing startling metamorphoses, conceits (*concetti*), and far-fetched images that send sparks flying as they create a friction between two apparently diverse objects [see TESAURO, EMANUELE; PEREGRINI, MATTEO].

The extent to which this new metaphorical freedom reveals a new world is still open to critical debate. In some ways it seems to make poetry a form of intellectual game or puzzle; in others it suggests new ways of perceiving and describing reality, parallel to the mathematical measures emloyed by *Galileo and his followers in the experimental sciences. [See CIMENTO, ACCADEMIA DEL; LINCEI, ACCADEMIA DEI; QUERELLE DES ANCIENS ET DES MODERNES.] Apart from Marino himself, Marinists of note include Claudio Achillini, Giuseppe *Artale, *Ciro di Pers, Vincenzo da *Filicaia, Girolamo *Fontanella, Giacomo *Lubrano, Marcello *Macedonio, Gian Francesco *Maia Materdona, Bernardo Mornado, Girolamo *Preti, and Giovan Leone *Sempronio.   [PBD]

See G. G. Ferrero (ed.), *Marino e i marinisti* (1956); G. Getto, 'Lirici marinisti', in *Barocco in prosa e in poesia* (1969) ; A. Asor Rosa, *La lirica del Seicento* (1975).

MARINO, GIOVANBATTISTA (1569–1625) was the outstanding poet of his day. He showed in his life and in his works a thrust towards novelty and unconventionality, and is commonly seen as the major voice in the overlapping and intertwined developments variously termed *marinismo, *concettismo, *secentismo, and the *Baroque. Born in *Naples, he interrupted his studies in *law, like many Italian poets, in order to cultivate poetry. From 1592 he was Secretary in the Neapolitan *court of Conca Matteo di Capua, having already in 1588 been elected a member of the Accademia degli Svegliati, where he met Giambattista *Manso, Torquato *Tasso, and Camillo *Pellegrino. His early *epic *Anversa liberata* (1595–1600), in the style of Tasso's *Gerusalemme liberata,* was never finished. After a two-year prison sentence (1598–1600) he fled to *Rome, where he was welcomed into literary and religious circles. His *Rime* were published in two volumes in *Venice in 1602, and reissued in 1608 in a single volume as *La lira.*

He travelled widely in Italy in the service of Pietro Aldobrandini, the Pope's nephew, accompanying him on a visit to the court of *Turin in 1608, where he found favour with Carlo Emanuele I and disfavour with the resident poet Gaspare *Murtola, whose *Creazione del mondo* he fiercely attacked. An exchange of *satirical *sonnets between the two poets ensued, and the animosity grew to such a pitch that Murtola made an attempt on Marino's life. After a further one-year stretch in prison, Marino settled down in the court of the Duke of *Savoy to a period of intense creative work, drafting his most famous work, *Adone,* an epic without war, and publishing a further collection of lyrics, the *Dicerie sacre* (1614), divided into three books, 'Pittura', 'Musica', and 'Cielo'. In 1615 he moved to the French court of Louis XIII, where he completed his other major works: *La Galeria* (1619 and 1620), a wide-ranging survey in poetry of contemporary artists; and the important collections of idylls and *pastoral poetry, *La sampogna* (1620) and the *Egloghe boscherecce. Adone,* begun before 1600, was published by Marino in 1623 in a magnificent edition at Louis XIII's expense. Soon afterwards he returned to Italy to great acclaim, and was elected head of the Accademia degli *Umoristi in Rome in May 1623, and, in early 1624, head of the Accademia degli *Oziosi in Naples. Like Tasso, he spent his final years working on a religious poem, *La strage degli innocenti,* published posthumously in 1632.   [PBD]

See J. Mirollo, *The Poet of the Marvelous* (1963); M. Guglielminetti, *Tecnica e invenzione nell'opera di Giambattista Marino* (1964); P. Cherchi, *La metamorfosi dell'Adone* (1996).

Marito di Elena, Il, see VERGA, GIOVANNI.

MARLIANI, BARTOLOMMEO, see ANTI-QUARIANISM.

MARMORI, GIANCARLO (1926–82). Born in La Spezia, but resident in Paris after 1951, he wrote in both French and Italian. His interest in *psychoanalysis and *fin-de-siècle *eroticism is evident in his poetry and in critical works such as *Le vergini funeste* (1966). [JJ]

MAROTTA, GIUSEPPE (1902–64). *Neapolitan writer who went to *Milan in 1925 to work in *journalism. He contributed humorous articles and stories to the *Corriere della sera* and *L'Europeo*, as well as writing film scripts and *cinema criticism. He published various collections of stories in the 1930s but achieved most success with *L'oro di Napoli* (1947). His work centres on everyday life in Naples and Milan. Though broadly *Neorealist, it has strong veins of melancholy and caricature. [GP]

MARRADI, GIOVANNI (1852–1922). *Lyric poet whose early collections of verse, including *Canzoni moderne* (1879) and *Ricordi lirici* (1884), offered idyllic evocations of country life and of his home town of Livorno. Later in his career he wrote the grandiose and patriotic *Rapsodie garibaldine* (1899), which enjoyed considerable success. [CFB]

MARRASIO, GIOVANNI (1400/4–52). *Latin poet from Noto in *Sicily, who studied at *Siena, where he became friendly with *Panormita and Enea Silvio *Piccolomini. His most important work is the *Angelinetum*, a series of seven elegies dedicated to Leonardo *Bruni, and treating the author's love for Angelina Piccolomini. [ELM]

MARSIGLI, LUIGI FERDINANDO, COUNT (1658–1730). *Bolognese scientific writer. He based his work (epoch-making in the field of oceanography) on observations made during his extensive travels. In 1692 he was elected to the Royal Society. His scientific collections became the nucleus of the Bologna Instituto delle Scienze. [JMAL]

MARSILI, LUIGI (1342–94). Augustinian friar and man of letters, who travelled extensively between *Florence and France, particularly to *Avignon. A close friend of *Petrarch, he followed his mentor's scholarly interests, establishing the monastery of Santo Spirito in Florence as a centre of *humanistic studies. [LB]

MARSILIO DA PADOVA (1275/80–1342/3). Author of the *Defensor pacis* (1324), which defined peace as the aim of the state, and the *papal claim to plenitude of power as the cause of civil strife. In his vision of the state, based on the popular will under an elected prince, priests would be subject to the secular power, and the Pope would likewise be subject to General Councils of the Church. Marsilio accompanied the Emperor Louis of Bavaria to *Rome in 1327–8 and later wrote further works concerning the empire. Controversial and suspected of *heresy, he influenced reformers from Wyclif to Luther. [PA]

MARSUPPINI, CARLO (1398–1453). *Humanist from a leading Arezzo family, and an intimate friend of Cosimo de' *Medici. He was appointed to teach rhetoric, poetry, philosophy, and Greek at the Florentine *studio in 1431. Succeeding Leonardo *Bruni as *Florence's Chancellor in 1444, he had a high reputation as a classical stylist, although his literary production was slight, his projected Latin *translation of the *Iliad* being left unfinished. [RDB]

Martelliano, Verso, see MARTELLO, PIER IACOPO.

MARTELLO, PIER IACOPO (1665–1725). Eclectic man of letters from *Bologna. A *lyric poet and playwright of average quality, Martello was above all a singularly sharp drama critic and theoretician. Following the tastes of the Accademia dell'*Arcadia, he distanced himself from the sensual *Baroque poetry and rich imagery of *Marino. At the same time he dissented from the more radical expressions of French aesthetic rationalism, and defended *epic and *pastoral poetry in the Italian tradition. He composed several plays of various kinds (*comedies, *satirical and historical dramas) and on various subjects, emulating Corneille and Racine. His aim was to create a theatre tailored to Italian culture and taste. He also devised, on the analogy of the French alexandrine, the fourteen-syllable *verso martelliano* named after him. Martello's criticism is worthy of attention mainly in the works *Del volo* (1710) and *Della tragedia antica e moderna* (1715), both in the form of the *Galilean dialogue. A close friend of Bolognese scientists, Martello found support for his Baroque

369

empiricist aesthetics in the thought of Francis Bacon, with its interest in images, fantasy, and invention. He was also an advocate of the dissemination of science through the *Jesuits' techniques of rhetorical communication. [See also ROCOCO; THEATRE, 2; VERSIFICATION.] [IMC]

MARTINELLI, TRISTANO (1557–1630), the first actor known to have played *Arlecchino in the *commedia dell'arte, was famous and sought after in both Italy and France. His career with various companies reflects tensions between the independent ambitions of the solo comedian and new demands for a more corporate approach to the *theatre profession. [RAA]

MARTINI, FAUSTO MARIA (1886–1931). Poet and dramatist. A friend of *Corazzini in *Rome, he published verse characteristic of the *Crepuscolari in Le piccole morte (1906) and Poesie provinciali (1910). The plays which he wrote in the 1920s also show an interest in the humble details of provincial life. [CFB]

MARTINI, FERDINANDO (1841–1928). Dramatist, *journalist and politician. He was minister for *education (1892–3) and minister for the colonies (1915–19). His theatrical writings, mainly collected in Al teatro (1895), criticized the cultural divisions persisting after *Unification, called for state support for the Italian *theatre and exhorted dramatists to return to imitating life. [DF]

MARTINO DA CANALE, see CHRONICLES.

MARTOGLIO, NINO (1870–1921). *Sicilian playwright, poet, and *theatre director, who put Sicilian theatre on the Italian map, encouraging both *Pirandello and *Rosso di San Secondo to stage their plays. He turned to film direction from 1913, and is known particularly for his direction of *Bracco's Sperduti nel buio. [JAL]

MARULLO, MICHELE (Michele Marullo Tarcaniota) (c.1453–1550). Outstanding *Latin poet, who was born in Constantinople but moved to Italy after the fall of the city. He lived in Ancona and above all in *Naples, where he knew prominent *humanists such as Giovanni *Pontano and Iacopo *Sannazaro. He combined work as a literary scholar and humanist with that of mercenary, taking part in various military operations. He went to *Rome in

1488, where he associated with Paolo *Cortesi, and to *Florence in 1489, where he was involved in a literary polemic with Angelo *Poliziano and forged a deep friendship with *Pico della Mirandola. Apart from one poem in Italian of uncertain attribution, all his work was in Latin, consisting of four books of epigrams dedicated to Giovanni di Pierfrancesco de' *Medici, a book of laments (Neniae), the treatise De principum eruditione, and the four books of Hymni naturales, which are considered his most important work. The refined poetry of the Hymni, modelled on the ancient philosophical hymns by poets such as Cleanthes, combines themes from the philosophy of Plotinus and the *Neoplatonism of Pico and *Ficino, with reminiscences of contemporary works (such as Pontano's Urania) and other ancient texts, above all the De rerum natura of Lucretius, of whom Marullo was an assiduous and acute student. [LChi]

Marxism. As elsewhere in Europe, Marxism in Italy first became influential in intellectual circles rather than in the labour movement. But the Italian reception of Marx was unusual in being shaped by *idealist theories of the state.

The first Italian Marxist of stature, Antonio *Labriola, like many of his successors, combined Marxist political economy and sociology with the ideas of the *Neapolitan Hegelians (such as Silvio and Bertrando Spaventa). He attempted to transform Hegel's idealist dialectic into a material force and at the same time to rescue Marx from *positivist interpretations of his thought. Drawing also on *Vico's ideas of 'corsi' and 'ricorsi' in history, he developed a version of historicism which saw history as both being creatively made by human beings and having knowable law-like tendencies, if not positive laws.

This non-positivist version of historical materialism had a major impact on Italy's best-known Marxist, Antonio *Gramsci, and, through him, on the workers' movement. With Palmiro *Togliatti and Amadeo Bordiga, Gramsci was one of those who broke with *Socialism at Livorno in 1921 and founded the Italian *Communist Party (PCI), which, like other political parties, was forced underground throughout the *Fascist period. After *World War II Togliatti's popularization of Gramsci's Quaderni del carcere and the mass electoral support for the Communist Party made Marxism a major political and cultural force. Many intellectuals left the party in the 1950s in the wake of Khrushchev's denunciation of Stalin and Soviet

repression in Eastern Europe, but they continued to be drawn to Marxist terminology and concepts. Within the party Galvano *Della Volpe elaborated a Marxist aesthetics, whilst figures outside the party such as *Pasolini and *Fortini gave Marxist thinking more unorthodox twists. Extraparliamentary revolutionaries of the 1960s and 1970s did their best to ground their utopian visions in Marx, but the terrorism to which some of them resorted only contributed to the steep decline in Marxism's status during the 1980s. All the same some of the most important *literary criticism (such as that of Alberto *Asor Rosa) of the late 20th c. evidenced the continuing vitality of Marx's influence. [See also POLITICAL THOUGHT.] [DS]
See P. Spriano, *Storia del Partito Comunista Italiano* (1967–75).

Marzocco, Il (1896–1932). *Florentine literary review founded by Angiolo *Orvieto. The title—the lion emblem of Florence—was suggested by *D'Annunzio. It was associated from early on with *nationalism and published, among other well-known names, *Corradini, *Pascoli, and *Ojetti.
[DF]

MASCARDI, AGOSTINO (1590–1640). From Sarzana in Liguria, Mascardi studied in *Rome and joined the *Jesuits for a time. A client of *Urban VIII, a member of the Accademia degli *Umoristi, a professor of rhetoric at the University of Rome, a *Latin poet, and a writer on ethics and the passions, Mascardi was and remains best known as a *historian. His *Arte istorica* (1636) expounded the theory of a rhetorical history, while his *Congiura del conte Fieschi* (1629) provided an example of the practice, which was translated into French and English.
[UPB]

Maschera e il volto, La, see CHIARELLI, LUIGI; GROTTESCHI.

MASCHERONI, LORENZO (1750–1800). Illustrious mathematics professor at Pavia, who is also remembered for his *Invito a Lesbia Cidonia* (1793), an elegantly enthusiastic verse description of Pavia's scientific collections, cast as an epistle to Countess Paolina *Grismondi (in the *Arcadia *academy named Lesbia Cidonia). He was active in public life during the Revolution (1797–1800), and celebrated by Vincenzo *Monti in his *Mascheroniana* [see NAPOLEON AND THE FRENCH REVOLUTION].
[JMAL]

MASCIONI, GRYTZKO, see ITALIAN WRITERS IN SWITZERLAND.

MASETTI, PIRRO, see MASTRI, PIETRO.

MASINO, PAOLA, see 900 (*Novecento*).

MASSINI, FILIPPO (1559–1617/18). Successful academic lawyer from *Perugia who also taught at *Pisa, *Bologna, and Pavia. His collected *lyrics (1609) reflect the conservative *Petrarchist inclinations of 16th-c. Perugia, but also experiment with a mild form of *concettismo. He was a friend of Torquato *Tasso and *Marino, and also composed a *Lezione del madrigale* (1588). [MPS]

MASTRI, PIETRO (pseud. of Pirro Masetti) (1868–1932). *Florentine poet. He was associated as young man with Angiolo *Orvieto's literary journal, *Il *Marzocco. His early rustic poetry was influenced heavily by *Pascoli, while the later verse of *La meridiana* (1920) and *La via delle stelle* (1927) was largely religious in character. [CFB]

MASTRIANI, FRANCESCO (1819–91). Underrated Neapolitan novelist who now seems an important figure in 19th-c. Italian fiction. He undertook medical studies in *Naples but turned to literature, and initially earned his living working for the Customs Office and as a tourist guide. He wrote more than 100 *novels, beginning with *Sotto altro cielo* (1847) and publishing them from 1875 onwards in serial form in the Naples paper *Roma*. Some he subsequently adapted as highly successful plays. He owed his appeal as a novelist partly to his skill with melodrama, the nature of which can be gauged from some of his best-known titles—*La cieca di Sorrento* (1852), *Il mio cadavere* (1853), *I misteri di Napoli* (1875) (which was indebted to Eugène Sue), and *La sepolta viva* (1889). But his work also documents Neapolitan customs and attitudes, and gives a remarkable picture of social structures and conflicts in the city. In these respects he is close to *Verga, but he is also far more openly on the side of the oppressed, denouncing the abuse and injustice to which they are subject. In the ten volumes of *I Vermi* (1862–4), with its subtitle, *Studi storici sulle classi pericolose in Napoli*, both his scope and his social commitment are particularly apparent. [DO'G]

Mastro-don Gesualdo. The second in *Verga's *novel-cycle 'I Vinti' appeared in magazine-form in

1888 and as a book in 1889. Set in *Sicily, the story tells of a bricklayer (*mastro*) who through sheer ruthlessness and hard-work makes himself a rich landowner and entrepreneur, earning the honorific title 'don'. However with every economic success comes an inner defeat. Having married into the nobility for material reasons, he dies alone and in despair in the house of his daughter Isabella, Duchess of Leyra. It is the most bitter and harshly pessimistic of Verga's novels. [RL]

MASTRONARDI, LUCIO (1930–79). *Novelist, who wrote about his home town of Vigevano in *Lombardy, where he was a primary schoolteacher, exploiting the comic and expressive potential of contemporary Northern Italian speech in ways that sometimes bring him close to *Gadda. His first novel, *Il calzolaio di Vigevano* (1959), is set in the 1940s, and treats its chorus of *dialect voices with affectionate sarcasm. *Il maestro di Vigevano* (1962) gives a more problematic and angry account of the family life and neurotic tensions of an individual divided between a formalistic *educational system and the new consumerist values of a thrusting provincial town. *Il meridionale di Vigevano* followed in 1964. [DieZ]

MASUCCIO SALERNITANO (Tommaso Guardati) (1410–75), a member of a noble Salerno family employed at the *court of *Naples, was the first storyteller from outside *Tuscany to imitate *Boccaccio. His *Novellino* has a great deal in common with the *Decameron*: fifty stories marshalled in tens, misdeeds of the clergy, practical jokes on jealous husbands, satire on women, tragic and funny stories alternating, and stories with happy endings; but there is no frame, and the author is the sole narrator. Each story is prefaced by a rubric and a dedication to a figure known to the Neapolitan court. At the end the author comments on the tale, often axe-grinding rather than moralizing. He includes two 'Romeo and Juliet' stories: in 31, set in Nancy, the eloping lovers are gruesomely murdered by lepers, whose colony is burnt down in revenge; 33 is closer to Shakespeare's plot, and in the tradition of the courts of love that Boccaccio had known in Naples, Masuccio requires his readers or listeners to decide which of the two lovers loved best. Masuccio's tone is sensational and spine-chilling. His language is recognizably *dialectal, belonging to the age before attempts at standardization. [See also NOVELLA AND RACCONTO.] [JR]

MATAZONE DA CALIGANO. The apparent author of a late 14th- or early 15th-c. poem of 284 *settenari* [see VERSIFICATION] in an eastern *Lombard vernacular, mocking the character and behaviour of rustics (*villani*). It is the earliest known example in an Italian vernacular of this type of verse *satire. Matazone (from *matto*, 'mad') claims to hail from Caligano, which may be Calignano near Pavia. [PH]

Matelda, the guardian of the Earthly Paradise in *Dante's *Purgatorio*.

MATRAINI CONTARINI, CHIARA (1514–1604). *Lyric poet from Lucca who wrote love poems (first published as *Rime* in 1555) for a young lover who was apparently murdered. She also composed *religious verse, short meditational works, and a body of *letters. Long thought simply a well-educated *Petrarchist, she is now seen as possessing greater stylistic and thematic individuality. [ABu]

MAURO, GIOVANNI (1490–1536), was a vernacular poet of Friulian origin who favoured *terza rima*. He worked for various cardinals in *Rome, where he became an enemy of Pietro *Aretino by writing ironically at his expense in *Della bugia*. A member of the Accademia dei Vignaiuoli, he died in a hunting accident. [GPTW]

MAZZA, ANGELO (1741–1817). Poet, who became Professor of Greek at the *university of his native Parma. His verse tends towards lofty and sonorous abstraction, and poems such as 'L'aura armonica' of 1772 led to his being dubbed 'il poeta dell'armonia'. He derived themes such as the power of music from *English literature, to which he was introduced by his teacher and friend *Cesarotti. He subsequently *translated and imitated English poets, notably Akenside, Dryden, Mason, and Pope. His example left its mark on *Foscolo and other poets of the next generation. [JMAL]

MAZZANTINI, CARLO, see RESISTANCE.

MAZZEO DI RICCO (b.?1235). Poet from Messina in *Sicily, and chronologically one of the last of the *Sicilian School. Six of his *canzoni* survive, demonstrating a good knowledge of *troubadour poets such as *Folchetto di Marsiglia. *Guittone addressed his *canzone* 'Amor, tant'altamente' to him. [JU]

MAZZINI, GIUSEPPE (1805–72). Revolutionary, social and *political thinker. His appearance with the significant name of Fantasio as a character in his friend Giovanni *Ruffini's novel, *Lorenzo Benoni* (1853), is evidence both of the strong impact his message, personality, and staunch moral principles had on his contemporaries, and of the recognized impracticality of his ideals—even if some of them, such as a democratic republican government in Italy and a European union, have come to fruition in markedly different historical circumstances.

Born of a middle-class family in *Genoa, already a refugee at 26 because of his political activism, he founded his revolutionary organization, *Giovine Italia*, in Marseilles in 1831. But he lacked the firsthand experience of Italian society at all levels, and never translated his principles into effective political action. His involvement in the *1848 *Milan uprising, the *Tuscan and *Roman Republics of 1849, and various earlier and subsequent revolutionary attempts, all ended in failure. Nevertheless he exerted enormous influence on the *Risorgimento, perhaps because he stopped short of proposing radical social change. His best-known work, *Dei doveri dell'uomo* (1860), the first four chapters of which were written in 1841–2 just a few years before the Communist Manifesto, emphasizes not human rights in the context of class struggle but human duties in a religious perspective. He wrote copiously and continuously mostly on political subjects, but also on history, music, Italian and European literature. Variously persecuted, imprisoned, sentenced to death, banned, and exiled by governments throughout his life, after some years in England he returned to Italy as Joseph Brown shortly before his death in *Pisa. [GC]

See D. Mack Smith, *Mazzini* (1994).

MAZZOLÀ, CATERINO (d.1806). *Librettist, originally from Longarone near Belluno. He was an acquaintance of *Da Ponte, and, from 1781 to 1796, court poet at Dresden, where he published some half-dozen libretti that were *Metastasian in moral earnestness, if not mellifluousness. In 1791 he adapted Metastasio's *Clemenza di Tito* for Mozart. [JMAL]

MAZZUCHELLI, GIOVANNI MARIA (1707–65). Scholarly *biographer. He was a pupil of Domenico *Lazzarini and Francesco Saverio *Quadrio, and ran an *academy at his aristocratic home in Brescia. His incomplete dictionary of Italian writers, *Gli scrittori d'Italia* (1753–63), though confined to letters A and B, is a landmark in the history of Italian *literary historiography. [JMAL]

MEDICI. The Medici were a *Florentine *banking family who first came to prominence at the end of the 13th c., but after Salvestro de' Medici's leading role in the Ciompi revolt of 1378, the family lost political credibility until his cousin, Giovanni di Bicci (1360–1429), was made *papal banker in the early 15th c. Giovanni now became the focus of a political alliance, which was given even more direction by his son Cosimo (1389–1464), and by the mid-1420s began to attract the animosity of the oligarchic leadership. In 1433 the factional conflict came to a head, when Cosimo was sentenced to thirty years' exile. With the removal of the Medici and their partisans, the oligarchic leadership believed they had restored the status quo, but they complacently failed to purge the electoral lists of Medici partisans, a majority of whom were selected by lot for the city's chief magistracy in 1434. The new government promptly recalled Cosimo from exile, banishing the oligarchic leaders. In order to secure its position the Medici regime embarked on a series of ad hoc constitutional innovations, which provoked underlying opposition. After 1454, anti-Mediceans secured the gradual abandonment of Medicean constitutional controls, Cosimo's position becoming perilously weak, and it was only in 1458 that the Medici regime retook power.

On his death Cosimo's position as head of the regime was assumed by his son Piero (1416–69), whose leadership, however, was challenged by a conspiracy in 1465–6. Again, superior political organization and decisive action secured another Medici triumph, ensuring the smooth succession of Piero's son, Lorenzo de' *Medici (1449–92). In the early years of his predominance, Lorenzo had to share power with other leading oligarchs, but this made him even more determined to enhance his control. The *Pazzi conspiracy of 1478, when Lorenzo was wounded and his brother Giuliano was killed, led at first to a dangerous war, but Lorenzo's diplomatic triumph in securing a separate peace treaty with *Naples ended the challenge to his leadership. On his return to Florence, the city's constitution was once again overhauled, resulting in a further concentration of power at the centre of the regime. When Lorenzo died in 1492, power passed smoothly to his son Piero (1472–1503), who, however, unable to cope with

Medici, Lorenzo De'

the diplomatic and military confusion caused by the invasions of Italy in 1494, was driven from the city that November, so ending sixty years of Medici dominance.

When Piero was drowned in 1503, leadership of the Medici family in exile passed to his brother, Cardinal Giovanni (1475–1521), who, aided by Pope Julius II and a Spanish army, was allowed to return to Florence in 1512; shortly afterwards, a *coup d'état* abolished the popular government which had ruled Florence after 1494, restoring a strengthened version of the old Medici regime. Early in 1513 Cardinal Giovanni was elected Pope Leo X, and the Medici reached the height of their prominence; Florence now became largely a satellite of the *Roman papacy, a situation which hardly changed after Leo's death, when his cousin Cardinal Giulio de' Medici (1478–1534) became Pope Clement VII. The continued dominance of Florence by Rome made the Medici regime highly unpopular; when Rome was *sacked by imperial troops in 1527, the Medici were once again expelled, and the popular republic was restored. Besieged by the imperial army, the Florentines were forced to restore the Medici in 1530, and Alessandro de' Medici became Duke of Florence, only to be assassinated in 1537; his successor was Cosimo I (1519–74), one of the ablest Italian rulers of the 16th c., who founded a dynasty which lasted until 1737, when, on the death of the seventh Medici ruler, the state passed to the house of Lorraine.   [RDB]

See D. Kent, *The Rise of the Medici* (1976); N. Rubinstein, *The Government of Florence under the Medici (1434 to 1494)* (1997).

MEDICI, LORENZO DE' (1449–92). Leader of the oligarchic regime founded by his grandfather, Cosimo de' *Medici, which, in the later 15th c., controlled *Florence by subtle manipulation of the city's republican constitution and by the cultivation of networks of loyal friends and clients. Despite the widespread impression that the young Lorenzo was something of a playboy prince— which is not to deny his accomplished delight in pastimes such as music, dancing, and hunting—he was in fact thoroughly trained as a domestic politician and budding Italian diplomatist by his ambitious family during his teens. This arduous and even dangerous apprenticeship, which he sometimes resented, nevertheless suited a young man determined to excel and fully conscious of the dynastic burden he might soon inherit.

On assuming leadership of the Medici 'party' in December 1469 upon the death of his father Piero, Lorenzo managed to repulse internal and external challenges to his precarious position, not least from members of his own family and from ambitious Medicean oligarchs. Early reported by the *Milanese ambassador as wanting to govern as much as possible by constitutional methods, in July 1471 Lorenzo and his friends had passed legislation to set up a *balìa*, or council with extraordinary powers, which consolidated his control. Further significant constitutional change—the creation of a powerful Council of Seventy—came in 1480, in the bellicose aftermath of the *Pazzi conspiracy, during which Lorenzo was wounded and his younger brother, Giuliano, murdered. Even so, the early 1480s were a difficult time for Lorenzo and his city. Only in the years preceding his death, and despite frequent illnesses and a reiterated longing to wash his hands of public affairs, did he truly become the more or less undisputed leader of the regime and party boss of Florence—the 'maestro della bottega', as admiring contemporaries said—and a statesman much esteemed throughout Italy for his skill at representing the interests of his rich but militarily vulnerable city.

Lorenzo's largely diplomatic correspondence, written in a masterful style which became increasingly direct as he gained maturity, is also distinguished by an intelligence at once sharp and subtle, and won the approval of Francesco *Guicciardini, whose critical style of political analysis Lorenzo himself in some respects anticipated. For Lorenzo was an intellectual politician who took literature and his own writing seriously indeed. Despite frequent claims to the contrary, he was neither a poet who dabbled in politics nor a politician dabbling in poetry. Well, if conventionally, educated in the Latin classics by his tutor, Gentile *Becchi, Lorenzo began to write poetry at the age of 14 or so, no doubt with the encouragement of his mother, Lucrezia *Tornabuoni, herself the author of religious stories and poems, and of her protégé, Luigi *Pulci. Steeped as he was in the *Tuscan poetic tradition, Lorenzo's early verses were in a sense exercises which, inevitably, adopted the amorous themes and reworked the poetic techniques of *Dante and *Petrarch. Lorenzo's experimentation with other literary genres reveals a serious intellectual commitment touched by a desire to demonstrate a precocious virtuosity. His juvenile *Simposio*, or *I beoni* ('The Boozers'), is a burlesque poem, describing a journey through a Florentine suburban landscape peopled by drunkards, which *parodies late medieval *epic poems of spiritual quest, while the more or less contemporaneous *novella, *La Ginevra*, springs from the tradition of *Boccaccio, and his *Uccellagione di Starne* is a *hunting poem indebted to Pulci. If he is indeed the author (as is now commonly agreed), it is also during this period that he composed the mock-idyll *Nencia da Barberino*.

If during the early 1470s, the period of his first political battles, his muse lay dormant, from about 1472/3 Lorenzo began to write again, turning to more philosophical and *religious poetic themes. Throughout the rest of his short life, and despite his numerous other preoccupations, he continued to write poetry in a number of different genres, and with increasing power and virtuosity. Moreover, he tinkered with his creations almost obsessively, reworking them to their advantage but to the dismay of his later editors. Even now, after the recent labours of a brilliant generation of editors, the chronology of Lorenzo's works remains a subject of debate. His self-conscious reflection upon his own literary output is also revealed in his *Comento*, of uncertain date, an academic *commentary on a collection of his own poetry which also yields precious autobiographical data. This major poet's later works include bawdy *carnival songs (*canti carnascialeschi*) which, it has been speculated, may have served the political purpose of helping Lorenzo endear himself to the popular classes. Also late is a work in yet another genre, *La rappresentazione di San Giovanni e Paolo*, a mystery play which has also been read as a political *allegory [see also SACRA RAPPRESENTAZIONE]. More personal among his later works was the long poem known variously as the *Descriptio hiemis* or *Ambra*, a dramatic narrative which reveals both Lorenzo's own sensual nature and his skill at describing wintry, uncontrollable nature. It is probably contemporary with the *Selve*, which are influenced by *Poliziano's expositions of *Statius' *Silvae*, and also with Lorenzo's forays into popular carnivalesque poetry and the rather more refined *canzoni a ballo*. In the months preceding his death (of uricaemia) in April 1492, Lorenzo also wrote several stark devotional poems (*laudi*), reminding us that he was, among other things, an important religious poet.

Lorenzo's contemporary and enduring reputation as a *patron of the arts is on the whole justified. His relationship with the *Neoplatonic philosopher *Ficino was more troubled than traditional scholarship would allow, as is perhaps reflected in the *Altercazione*, a debate in *terza rima* between himself and Ficino on the highest good. But the close personal and intellectual alliance Lorenzo shared with Poliziano offered this major philologist and poet much-appreciated security and leisure. Lorenzo himself found in Poliziano a vernacular poetic example to be emulated and a learned adviser without peer. He was as much a patron of scholarship as of literature, supervising with an awesome eye for detail the re-establishment of the University of *Pisa from 1472 onwards. From a similarly young age, Lorenzo continued to build up the already excellent Medici private *library, especially by acquiring Greek *manuscripts. To his passion for artistic patronage he devoted more time, money, and intelligence than some recent scholarship has given him credit for. The contemporary praise of Lorenzo's architectural taste and expertise was not mere flattery. As a youthful member of works committees and commissioning bodies, he mixed with artisans and learned about building. As early as 1474, he acquired the spectacular site on which, towards the end of his life, he began to build his villa of Poggio a Caiano, a truly innovative classicizing structure. In such novel projects, his own and those of others, Lorenzo, possessed of a creative temperament and long experience, was as much the learned collaborator of the architects Giuliano da Maiano, Luca Fancelli, and Giuliano da San Gallo as he was their patron.   [FWK]

Tutte le opere, ed. P. Orvieto (2 vols., 1992); *Lettere*, ed. N. Rubinstein (1977–). See B. Toscani (ed.), *Lorenzo de' Medici: New Perspectives* (1992); M. Mallett and N. Mann (eds.), *Lorenzo the Magnificent: Culture and Politics* (1996).

Medicine. Italy played a prominent role in medical studies from the early *Middle Ages until the end of the 16th c. The school of Salerno, whose Rule for health was still being used in the 17th c., is credited with having introduced Arabic medicine into Western Europe in the 11th c., and the early 13th c. saw a great flourishing of medicine as a *university discipline. In about 1315, *Pietro d'Abano of *Padua harmonized *Aristotelianism and Galenic medicine in his *Conciliator*, which set the agenda of medical enquiry for several centuries [see also SCHOLASTICISM]. 15th-c. doctors were among the first to use the techniques of *humanist scholarship; Marsilio *Ficino was a medical author as well as a *Neoplatonist, but his contribution to the revival of medical studies was surpassed by Niccolò

Medusa

Leoniceno (1428–1524) of the University of *Ferrara, who collected *manuscripts of Greek medicine, and *translated much of Galen's voluminous output into Latin. Giambattista da Monte (1498–1551), Leoniceno's pupil, took with him his humanist learning to Padua, and combined it there with solid methodological teaching and clinical instruction at the bedside; his tenure as professor of medical theory coincided with the founding of a botanical garden at the University, and the flourishing of anatomical studies under Andreas Vesalius (1514–64), among whose successors were Realdo Colombo (d.1559), Gabriele Falloppia (1523–63), and Girolamo Fabrizi di Acquapendente (1533–1619), the teacher of William Harvey. Through these developments, Padua became the foremost centre of medical studies in Europe, and attracted many foreign students, especially from Germany.

What distinguished Paduan professors of medicine was their logical and linguistic sophistication, their adherence to Aristotelian natural philosophy, and their sturdy independence from theology. They strongly resisted the controls which the *papacy attempted to place on them by bulls in 1513 and 1564, and subscribed to the heterodox doctrine associated with Pietro *Pomponazzi that different truths apply to theology and philosophy. Elsewhere in Italy other innovative doctors were at work. Girolamo *Fracastoro produced a novel theory of contagious diseases, a long poem in Latin on syphilis, and *dialogues on the operation of the mind; Giovanni Argenterio (1512–72), a sceptical Galenist, produced a new medical methodology; and Gerolamo *Cardano enjoyed an international reputation as a clinician, an *astrologer, and a popularizer of new scientific discoveries. All of these writers, and many others, could justify the claim that, as a profession, doctors were humanists with an unusually thorough command of Greek. Together with their colleagues in natural philosophy such as Pomponazzi and Iacopo Zabarella (1533–89), they constitute one of the most notable intellectual strengths of Italian culture before the modern period.   [IWFM]
See N. G. Siraisi, *Medieval and Early Renaissance Medicine* (1990); L. I. Conrad, M. Neve, V. Nutton, R. Porter, and A. Wear, *The Western Medical Tradition, 800 BC to AD 1800* (1995).

Medusa, see GRAF, ARTURO.

MEGLIO, ANTONIO DI (1384–1448), herald of the *Florentine government (1417–46) and minor vernacular poet, wrote amorous *sonnets, religious *frottole*, and political poems, many to commission. His *Rappresentazione del dì del giudizio* (on the Last Judgement) was expanded by Feo *Belcari [see also SACRA RAPPRESENTAZIONE]. Antonio's verse is noteworthy for its formal elegance and for some pleasing descriptions of landscapes.
                                                                        [GPTW]

MELANDRI, LEA (1941–). *Feminist thinker, who gives particular emphasis to *psychoanalysis. With *L'infamia originaria* (1977) she developed the idea of the 'pratica dell'inconscio' amongst women, exploring the erasure of women's sexuality as the basis of their socio-economic marginalization. Subsequent studies include significant rereadings of Sibilla *Aleramo.   [SW]

MELI, GIOVANNI (1740–1815). *Sicilian *dialect poet, who was born and spent his life in Palermo, where he was a doctor and later a professor of chemistry. He devoted himself to dialect poetry from an early age. Though his work includes shorter lyrics, his narrative and discursive poems in *ottava rima* are of much greater interest. These generally blend irony and philanthropic reasonableness. In *La fata galanti* (1759) a wide-ranging flight on a winged horse becomes the means for ironic reflections on *Arcadia. *L'origini di li munnu* (1770) argues against the setting-up of pointless metaphysical systems. *Don Chisciotti e Sanciu Panza* (1787) contrasts an abstract model of enlightened reason with popular, instinctive wisdom.

Meli published a first five-volume edition of his *Poesie siciliane* in 1787–9, which he later expanded (1814), adding in particular the fables of *Favuli murali*. After 1765 his real interests lay in authors such as Bacon, Locke, Hobbes, Voltaire, Condillac, and above all Rousseau, whose works were more freely available in *Enlightenment circles in mainland Italy. One result was his *Riflessioni sul meccanismo della natura in rapporto alla conservazione e riparazione dell'individui* (1777), an essay on man's position in the world which combines medical and philosophical ideas, and was quickly accused of atheism. [See also DIALECT WRITING.]   [SC]

Melinconici, Accademia dei, see UMORISTI, ACCADEMIA DEGLI.

MELLITI, MOHSEN, see IMMIGRANT LITERATURE.

Melodramma. In Italian the equivalent of '*opera' in English. It can refer particularly to the written text or *libretto that is set to music, for which the expression *dramma per musica* was also traditionally used.

MELOSIO, FRANCESCO (1609–70). Poet who turned the wordplay of *concettismo* to politely humorous *parody. He also published academic discourses and opera *libretti. A lawyer by training, he served Cardinal Spada in *Rome, then moved to the *court of *Turin, where he became administrator of the ducal army. Late in life he took holy orders and retired to his native Città della Pieve in Umbria.
[MPS]

Memoriale, see VOLPONI, PAOLO.

Memoriali bolognesi (*Libri Memorialium*). Official registers of legal transactions in *Bologna, of which the volumes from 1265 to 1436 survive. The scribes were bound to fill any blank spaces to preempt illicit codicils, and included poetry from the *Sicilian School, contemporary Bolognese poets, and the *dolce stil novo, as well as early examples of passages from the *Divine Comedy. More popular, often ribald material is also present. The texts are frequently different from those transmitted by other sources and often obviously imperfect. It is not clear whether they were transcribed from memory, perhaps with *dialect interference, or copied carelessly from other written sources. [JU]

Menabò di letteratura, Il (1959–67). Literary review edited by Elio *Vittorini and, after his death, by Italo *Calvino. It was receptive to avant-garde ideas, and published numerous texts of contemporary poetry and narrative. Amongst its chief contributors were Franco *Fortini, Paolo *Volponi, and Francesco *Leonetti, as well as Vittorini and Calvino. It promoted a socially and morally committed literature and attempted to redefine the role of the intellectual in the context of modern science and industrial capitalism. The solutions it offered, however, did little more than propose new literary treatments of alienation in the workplace. The title is a typesetters' term for the mock-up of a newspaper page or similar and was intended as an allusion to the modern workplace. [See also IMPEGNO.]
[RSD]

MENEGHELLO, LUIGI (1922–). Writer who was also the founder of the Department of Italian Studies in the University of Reading (UK), where he taught from 1947 to 1980. Born at Malo, near Vicenza, his voluntary '*exile' in England has shaped both his style as writer and his ambiguous relationship with the history and culture of 20th-c. Italy. His books are a unique blend of *novel, *autobiography, and social and literary essay which escape categorization. They also combine Italian, Veneto *dialect, and English in an expressive pastiche in which each separate language, and its culture, is both valorized and relativized. Language is the protagonist of his numerous books, whether it be employed to dissect Italian history through the portrait of his native village, most famously in *Libera nos a Malo* (1963), or to subvert national myth and rhetoric, as in *I piccoli maestri* (1964), a witty and irreverent account of his experiences as a partisan during the *Resistance. His later writing focuses on the history of the formation (and deformation) of the Italian intellectuals of his generation, with *Pomo pero* (1974), *Fiori italiani* (1976), *Jura* (1987), *Bau-sète!* (1988), *Maredè, maredè . . .* (1990), *Il dispatrio* (1993), and *La materia di Reading* (1997). [LPer]

Meneghino, see MAGGI, CARLO MARIA; PORTA, CARLO.

MENGHINI, LUIGI, see SCIENCE FICTION.

MENINNI, FEDERICO (1636–1712). A native of Gravina di Puglia, he studied and practised *medicine in *Naples. He was one of the last exponents of *concettismo in his unexceptional *Poesie* (1669). He is remembered more for the *Ritratto del sonetto e della canzone* (1677), a survey of the Italian *lyric important as one of the earliest historical accounts of the genre, as well as for its claims that it had attained the peak of its 'perfection' with the 'moderns' *Marino and *Chiabrera. [See also QUERELLE DES ANCIENS ET DES MODERNES.] [MPS]

MENOCHIO, IACOPO, see LAW.

MENZINI, BENEDETTO (1646–1704). *Satirical and *lyric poet. In his *Arte poetica* in *terza rima* (1688), he attacks the *Baroque poetic in the name of an archaic style based on the cult of *Dante and 14th-c. Italian. This return to traditional forms foreshadows the aesthetics of the Accademia dell'*Arcadia, which Menzini joined in 1691, before joining the Accademia Fiorentina in 1699 and the Accademia della *Crusca in 1702 as well.

He taught rhetoric at *Florence, Prato, and *Rome, and served *Christina of Sweden from 1685 until her death.

Menzini never forgot his humble origins, and a certain down-to-earth quality survives in his best work, the *Satire*, completed before 1685 and published posthumously. Though he relied on classical satire for his subject matter, he also used the form to launch scathing attacks on poets, the clergy, women, philosophers, hypocrisy, vices, and even personal enemies. Of all the 17th-c. satirists he is the most bitter, with a no-nonsense directness aided by his sober style. His lyric poetry (1674 and 1680) earned him the sobriquet 'saviour of Tuscan poetry' for its linguistic *purism; and his other poetic works look back consciously to earlier models: *Del paradiso terrestre*, written in *ottava rima* (1691) to Torquato *Tasso's creation poetry; and *Accademia tusculana* (published posthumously), a mixture of archaicizing prose and poetry, to *Sannazaro. [PBD]

Menzogna e sortilegio, see MORANTE, ELSA.

MEO ABBRACCIAVACCA (13th c.). *Pisan Ghibelline [see GUELFS AND GHIBELLINES] and author of three *canzoni* and a small number of *sonnets, some included in vernacular prose letters addressed to *Guittone. He deploys Guittonian rhetoric and a certain lexical dexterity, but his imitations are basically pedestrian. [JU]

MEO DE' TOLOMEI (*c.*1260–after 1310). *Sienese poet who wrote *poesia giocosa* in the manner of his contemporary, Cecco *Angiolieri. A member of a leading family, he was apparently overshadowed in public life by his brother. His seventeen surviving *sonnets contain bizarre accounts of family conflicts, especially with his brother and mother. [JP & JMS]

MERCANTINI, LUIGI (1821–72). Patriotic poet. Born near Ascoli Piceno, he trained as a priest but taught literature in various cities, except when exiled in Greece for taking part in the revolution of *1848. His poetry is facilely traditional and was remarkably successful. 'La spigolatrice di Sapri' (1857), long inflicted on Italian schoolchildren, is a poetic manifesto of the *Risorgimento. [FD'I]

Merchants. Trade was the motor behind the prosperity of medieval Italian cities, beginning with the

rise of *Venice in the 10th c. *Genoa, *Pisa, and Amalfi (until captured by the Normans in 1073) quickly competed with Venice for trade in the Mediterranean and beyond, though inland cities developed more slowly. By 1300 *Milan, Venice, Genoa, and *Florence (which boomed in the 13th c.) were the major trading cities in Europe. In most cities the nobility and the merchant class were not clearly distinguishable, even if many successful merchants were self-made adventurers. There was less social mobility from the mid-14th c. onwards, though new families (such as the *Medici) did sometimes emerge.

Trade requirements contributed to the spread of *literacy and to the foundation of lay schools. Some merchants wrote practical guides to trading abroad, with enlivening notes on the customs of places visited, a notable example being Francesco di Balduccio *Pegolotti's *La pratica della mercatura*. Romanticized accounts of merchant adventures are frequent in literature, though the *Decameron* also offers a complex representation of the merchant-aristocratic ethos. [See also BANKERS; POLO, MARCO; TRAVEL WRITING.] [CEH]

MERICI, ANGELA, see WOMEN WRITERS, I.

Meridiano di Roma, see FIERA LETTERARIA, LA.

MERINI, ALDA (1931–). Poet born in *Milan, who published her first collection, *La presenza di Orfeo*, in 1953, but who has achieved most acclaim since *Vuoto d'amore* (1991). Her poetry is highly charged and much of it concerned with the mental instability for which she was hospitalized in the 1960s and 1970s. [See also LYRIC POETRY.] [PH]

Merope, see ALFIERI, VITTORIO; MAFFEI, SCIPIONE.

MESSINA, MARIA (1887–1944). Author of somewhat Dickensian *novelle* about the petite bourgeoisie of her native *Sicily, collected principally in *Pettini fini* (1909), *Piccoli gorghi* (1911), and *Le briciole del destino* (1918). Her work was well thought of by *Verga and Ada *Negri. [PBarn]

Mestiere di vivere, Il, see PAVESE, CESARE.

METASTASIO, PIETRO (Pietro Trapassi) (1698–1782). A dramatist of enormous talent, he was born in *Rome and, as an adolescent, taken under the protection of *Gravina, who became a second father to him, bringing him up along strictly rationalistic lines, hellenizing his surname, sending him to study classical literature with the Calabrian scholar Caloprese, and leaving him a substantial inheritance on his death.

Metastasio's talent soon showed itself in a collection of *Poesie* (1717) and the *tragedy *Giustino* (1718), and gained him a precocious notoriety with the performance in *Naples of the *dramma per musica Didone abbandonata* (1724) [see also LIBRETTO; OPERA]. From this moment onwards his name and literary activity are tied to the production of *drammi per musica* that served as models of the genre up to the middle of the 18th c. In 1729 he was appointed imperial poet in Vienna, and in the following ten years not only organized court entertainments but also published *lyric poetry in the *Arcadian style as well as his most famous dramas, including *Demetrio* (1731), *Demofoonte* (1733), *Olimpiade* (1733), *La clemenza di Tito* (1734), *Achille in Sciro* (1736), *Ciro riconosciuto* (1736), and *Attilio Regolo* (1740). With the accession to the *Austrian throne of Maria Theresa in 1740, and then of Joseph II in 1765, the cultural climate of Vienna became more concerned with civic matters and at the same time more interested in formal experimentation. The effect of this was to make the dramas of Metastasio's second period (1745–73) considerably less interesting, as can be seen from the orientalizing *L'eroe cinese* (1752), and from *Il trionfo di Clelia* (1762) and *Ruggiero* (1771). Much more important in this period are his critical reflections on literature in general, on the theatre of the ancient world, and on techniques for the staging of opera: for instance in his *Estratto dell''Arte poetica' di Aristotile e considerazioni su la medesima*, the *Osservazioni sul teatro greco*, and the *Note alla traduzione dell''Epistola ai Pisoni' di Orazio*, in which he abandons classical prejudices on the subject of literary genre in favour of a much more empirical spirit.

In Metastasio's *drammi per musica* the language, with its extreme simplicity and frequent repetition of particularly melodious words, is by far the most important element. But his libretti—which were published as such for the first performance of each work, then modified in various ways according to the demands of producers—also have strong theatrical and musical elements, though he was not involved in the composition of the music itself. His plots are generally taken from existing but not well known mythological or historical narratives. They are divided into three acts, and involve six main characters: two pairs of lovers, a wise man as helper and adviser, and a wicked opponent. The lovers are acted by tenors and sopranos, the two other male characters by baritone or base voices. Love is a constant element in the plots, and frequently takes precedence over everything else, determining the dramatic development through the clash of opposing passions, and sometimes in conflict with virtue, social position, or political necessity: for instance in *Olimpiade*, performed in Vienna in August 1733, the young Megacle has to intercede with the beautiful Aristea in order for her to accept the love of Licida, Prince of Crete, who has saved Megacle's life in the past; the drama turns on the frustrated passion of Megacle, who is also in love with Aristea, but is obliged by gratitude to put duty before desire. Obstructed in the fulfilment of their love, the figures in these dramas appear unsatisfied, restless, and changeable, and the happy ending in the third act is only brought about by an act of virtuous renunciation on the part of one of the characters, or by the classical device of recognition, the final revelation of the true identity of one or more of the participants.

The literary form of Metastasio's dramas is based on general human situations and simple parallels, and is characterized by a rigid division between *aria*, with short, rhythmical, melodious lines, easy to sing, and involving the expression of passions, and *recitativo*, the part of the text concerned with the development of the plot. It is in the *arie* that the Arcadian poetry of the period attains a clarity and simplicity of language that will be imitated for decades to come in Europe, even though Metastasio's taste was for more markedly expressive poets such as Torquato *Tasso or even *Marino. The language of Metastasio's dramas was to revolutionize the expression of feelings by a process of simplification, and using a symmetrical system of oppositions between pleasure and pain, reality and illusion, sincerity and mendacity, rationality and irrationality. This is his main contribution to the lyric and drama of the first half of the 18th c. [See also AUSTRIA; THEATRE, 2.] [SC]

See G. Nicastro, *Metastasio e il teatro del Settecento* (1973); A. Beniscelli, *Felicità sognate: il teatro di Metastasio* (2000).

Metello, see PRATOLINI, VASCO.

METHNANI, SALAH, see IMMIGRANT LITERATURE.

Metre, see VERSIFICATION.

MEZZANI, MENGHINO (*c.*1295–1375/6). A notary who held various public offices in his native Ravenna. He was a friend and admirer of *Dante, writing summaries in *terza rima* of *Inferno* and *Purgatorio*, and a friend also of *Petrarch, with whom he exchanged *sonnets. His main poetic correspondent, however, and closest literary friend was *Antonio da Ferrara. [PH]

Mezzogiorno. The term is used most often to refer to the southern mainland within the boundaries of the pre-*Unification Kingdom of the Two Sicilies. However, the 'Questione meridionale', which is the optic through which the *Mezzogiorno* has tended to be viewed, is often taken to embrace the problems of *Sicily and *Sardinia as well. In reality the *Mezzogiorno*, like the 'North' with which it is often contrasted, is internally quite heterogeneous.

In one form or another the Southern question has been a constant of Italian political life since the 1870s and has occupied the attentions of many of Italy's greatest political and cultural figures, including Pasquale Villari, *Sonnino, Francesco Saverio *Nitti, Gaetano *Salvemini, Antonio *Gramsci, Luigi Sturzo, Carlo *Levi, and Manlio *Rossi-Doria. Only under *Fascism was the existence of the question denied. Yet the issues involved are as diverse and changing as they are important. In the *Liberal period of the later 19th and early 20th c. they included brigandage, malaria, illiteracy, *peasant poverty, and *emigration. Today they have become de-industrialization, organized crime, drug-trafficking, and the weakness of 'civic sense' (*senso civico*). In the postwar period, the growth rate of the South's gross domestic product has matched that of the North and Centre, and yet there is a persistent gap between the 'two halves' of the peninsula in terms of standard of living, unemployment, and efficiency of services.

Despite the diversity of the South and the profound transformations that have occurred, there has been a very strong tendency to portray the *Mezzogiorno* as a homogeneous, static, and backward social world. Still today, there is disagreement about the extent to which the very term *Mezzogiorno* refers to any distinctive social reality. Moreover, stereotypical images of the *Mezzogiorno* as a theatre for the exotic, tragic, comic, dangerous, or primitive have been part of Italian culture at all levels at least since Unification. [JD]

See P. Bevilacqua, *Breve storia dell'Italia*

meridionale (1993); R. Lumley and J. Morris (eds.), *The New History of the Italian South* (1997).

MICANZIO, FULGENZIO (1570–1654) was trained as a theologian and summoned to *Venice in 1606 by Paolo *Sarpi, to whom he remained loyal for the rest of the latter's life. During the famous Interdict, when Sarpi fought against the excommunication of Venice by the Pope, he lent support to Sarpi's case, and later wrote a life of Sarpi in which he displays naïve admiration, even worship, for his master. [PBD]

MICHELANGELO BUONARROTI (THE ELDER) (1475–1564). Sculptor, painter, architect, and poet. While in the service of Lorenzo de' *Medici, he became acquainted with the doctrines of *Neoplatonism and the poetry of *Dante and *Petrarch; he was strongly influenced also by *Savonarola. His major works of art include the *Pietà* (*Rome, 1498), *David* (*Florence, 1504), the Sistine Chapel ceiling (Rome, 1508–12), sculptures for the tomb of Pope Julius II (Rome and Florence, 1513–45), the *Medici tombs and Laurentian Library (Florence, 1519–34), the *Last Judgement* (Rome, 1536–41), and architectural designs for the Capitoline Hill and St Peter's (Rome, 1549–64).

Michelangelo's poems belong mostly to the later part of his life. They remained unpublished until 1623, when Michelangelo *Buonarroti the Younger issued a selection, revising them according to 17th-c. taste and substituting female subjects in those addressed to men. Full editions were published by Guasti (1863), Carl Frey (1897), and Enzo Noè Girardi (1960), who includes 302 poems, mostly *sonnets and *madrigals (many unfinished), and forty-one fragments and quotations. The collection includes a satirical description of Michelangelo's discomforts when painting the Sistine ceiling (5), an attack on the venality of *papal Rome (10), two sonnets on Dante (248, 250), and fifty poems, mostly epitaphs in quatrains, written on the death of Cecchino Bracci (179–228). There are also *allegories in *ottava rima* (67–8), and *capitoli* [see CANTO] in *terza rima* (85–6). Several poems from the 1530s and 1540s express Michelangelo's suffering in love for an unknown 'donna bella e crudele', but the most celebrated are those addressed to Tommaso Cavalieri and Vittoria *Colonna, in which Michelangelo adopts the Neoplatonic concept of earthly beauty as an image of heavenly beauty and conveys his desire to transcend the sinful mortal body and attain to the divine (e.g. 83,

106), a process of extracting the ideal from the material which he compares to the work of the sculptor (151). The later poems reveal Michelangelo's sense of sin and his desire for God's grace in the face of his approaching death (285, 293).

The most important influence on Michelangelo's poetry was Petrarch. However, its introspective directness and intensity of personal feeling, together with its Neoplatonic and religious themes and syntactic complexity (even at times obscurity), set it apart from contemporary *Petrarchism. As *Berni wrote, addressing the Petrarchists: 'e' dice cose, e voi dite parole'. Michelangelo was the subject of *biographies by *Vasari (1550 and 1568) and Ascanio *Condivi (1553), and is an interlocutor on the subject of painting in Francisco de Hollanda's *Dialogues* (set in Rome in 1538), and on the subject of Dante in Donato *Giannotti's *Dialogi* (set in 1546). In 1547, *Varchi lectured to the Florentine Academy on his sonnet, 'Non ha l'ottimo artista alcun concetto'. His statue of Moses inspired poems by *Marino and *Alfieri.   [PA]

Rime, ed. E. N. Girardi (1960). See R. J. Clements, *The Poetry of Michelangelo* (1965); C. Ryan, *The Poetry of Michelangelo* (1998).

MICHELSTAEDTER, CARLO (1887–1910). Thinker and writer who lived through the transition from the 19th to the 20th c. with dramatic intensity, and whose philosophizing is in the pessimistic tradition of Schopenhauer, Nietzsche, Weininger, and *Leopardi. Born in Gorizia into a *Jewish family, he registered at Vienna University in 1905 to read mathematics, but moved after a year to *Florence to read literature and philosophy. He completed his degree, but shot himself in Gorizia after an argument with his mother. His friends Vladimiro Arangio Ruiz and Gaetano Chiavacci, who had brought him into contact with some of, the *La *Voce* group, edited *Il dialogo della salute* (1912) and his dissertation, *La persuasione e la rettorica* (1913). The second in particular provoked intense critical debate. Living, in Michelstaedter's vision, is an empty, inauthentic experience, generated by 'rhetoric' or 'inadequate persuasion'. A genuinely 'persuaded' individual accepts the pessimism inherent in the human condition, remaining untouched by social rituals and conventions, and striving to live in the dimension of the present.
                [KP]

MICHIEL, PIETRO (17th c.). *Venetian patrician and a founding member of the Accademia degli *Incogniti, who composed numerous works in prose and verse, including *novelle*, *pastoral eclogues, and verse epistles. *Licida* (1644) is a *dialogue treatise imitating Pietro *Bembo's *Asolani*, whilst his lyrics try out variations on all the stock topics of *Baroque love poetry.   [MPS]

MICO DA SIENA is said by *Boccaccio in the *Decameron* (10.7) to be the poet who wrote the *ballata*, 'Muoviti, Amore', at the request of a Minuccio d'Arezzo who set it to music [see MINO D'AREZZO]. His existence has been doubted and the poem may well be by Boccaccio himself.   [PH]

Middle Ages. Italian literature and, more broadly, Italian culture are indelibly marked by the literary heritage left by the so-called *Tre Corone*, *Dante, *Petrarch, and *Boccaccio, who were all active during the 14th c. With the *Divine Comedy*, Dante had made the long poetic narrative his own and apparently left little room for others, while Petrarch's *Canzoniere* ensured his dominion over the *lyric. The *Decameron*, too, quickly became canonical, demonstrating that the vernacular could be the language not only of great verse but also of great prose. Given their exemplary status, which time has consolidated, ever since the 14th c. the *Tre Corone* have also fundamentally affected the ways in which key cultural questions have been addressed and resolved: from the *questione della lingua* to the duties of writers and intellectuals, and from *educational curricula to ideas relating to notions of *italianità*. Yet their most fundamental and lasting contribution to the shaping of Italian culture and history is linguistic. Thanks largely to the excellence of their writing, the essentially *Tuscan vernacular which they all employed has been widely considered from the 14th c. until the present as the basis of a national literary language, thereby countering the problems caused by the proliferation of different *dialects in the peninsula. As a result, there is much greater and more obvious continuity between medieval Tuscan and present-day Italian than exists, for instance, between Chaucer's language and the forms of English current in Britain today.

In literary histories the rest of medieval Italian literature is normally treated as subservient and separate. However the 13th c. in particular stands as one of the great centuries of Italian literature. It saw major writers—Brunetto *Latini, *Iacopone da Todi, *Guittone d'Arezzo, Guido *Cavalcanti, Cecco *Angiolieri. It is difficult, in fact, to imagine the *Tre Corone* as somehow disconnected from this vital and complex literary ferment, of which they themselves were well aware.

Dante, Petrarch, and Boccaccio have also had the distorting effect of appearing both to bring the Middle Ages in Italy to a close and to prepare for the *Renaissance. But the thousand years of the Middle Ages were complex and varied, marked by sharp changes in intellectual, political, and social life. The rapid urbanization that took place in the Italian peninsula from the 11th c. onwards contributed to the development of new types of government, which, by involving significant sections of the citizenry, supplanted *feudal structures, and led to the emergence of a new bourgeois class, with its great wealth based on trade and a sophisticated *banking system. It also led to the creation of new types of schooling whose highest expression was found in the *universities. [See also COMMUNES; MERCHANTS; SIGNORIA.]

In Italy, it is generally accepted that the Middle Ages stretches approximately from the collapse of Roman authority between the 4th and 5th c. to the birth of *humanism in the latter part of the 14th, though different academic disciplines have different perceptions of what constitute the limits of the Middle Ages, just as the epoch is seen as coming to an end at different times in different countries. Petrarch, Boccaccio, and most of the humanists were convinced that they were heralding a new era of 'light'; and there is no doubt that a major intellectual change did occur in Italy during the latter part of the 14th c. and during the course of the 15th. A seismic shift occurred from a theologically determined view of knowledge, based on a detailed hermeneutics of the *Bible and on a providential sense of history, to a non-theological, historicist, and philologically centred epistemology. Yet, despite this shift, the process did not entail a precise cleavage, as the humanists claimed, but is marked by continuities between the classical world and the medieval period, as well as between the latter and the Renaissance. Equally, notions of 'rebirth' and 'renewal' are not features unique to humanist ideology. Similar ideas proliferated throughout the Middle Ages, not least with St *Francis of Assisi and *Gioachino da Fiore. In any case, it is at the very least open to question whether, for instance, the humanists' *antiquarian and thus conservative cult of classical culture is more original, effective, and intellectually challenging than medieval attempts creatively to assimilate, imitate, and emulate the works of the great pagan *auctores* [see

LITERARY THEORY, 1]. Medieval literature, both in Latin and in vernacular, is much more formally inventive than that produced during the Renaissance, precisely because the Middle Ages had a much more elastic notion of poetics than that fostered by humanist culture. Ironically, Dante, rather than Petrarch or Boccaccio, introduces the real 'renaissance' of Western literature.

Throughout the Middle Ages the culture of Italy—as in the rest of Europe—predominantly found expression through Latin, which enjoyed the unique role of serving as the 'universal' language binding Christendom together. Latin's hegemony ensured that the concept of (competing) 'national cultures' was alien to medieval thought. Thus, it did not matter where a text was produced; what mattered was the degree of its 'usefulness' (*utilitas*) in ethical terms, a notion which is at the core of all medieval thinking about writing. This Latin writing (and the same is, of course, true of medieval Latin culture in general) is important not only because of the impact it had on vernacular culture, but also in itself, as the product of some of the finest minds of the West from *Boethius to *Pier Damiani, from Gregory the Great to *Marsilio da Padova, and from Cassiodorus to the doctors of Salerno [see MEDICINE]. Two 13th-c. theologians born and active in Italy, *Bonaventure of Bagnoregio and Thomas *Aquinas, emblematically represent two very different expressions of *scholasticism and of Christian reactions to the recovery of Aristotle, an event which had a determining effect on the progress of European culture, not least because it challenged both Roman and Christian systems of thought. Bonaventure championed a scripturally based, divinely inspired hermeneutics, while Aquinas supported rationalist ways of thinking.

Probably more than to the lasting power of Rome's patrimony, Latin owed its position of predominance to its intimate association with the Church, which remained the main centre of intellectual life, and hence the principal custodian of the classical Latin heritage. In Italy the monastery of Montecassino, founded by St *Benedict around 530, was for centuries a major hub of cultural activity. Some of the earliest documents containing attestations of the Italian vernacular are linked to the monastery, most notably the famous *Placito capuano* of 960, the oldest of the four *Placiti campani*; and one of the very few Italian literary texts of the (late) 12th c., the so-called *Ritmo cassinese*, was discovered in Montecassino, where it was possibly composed. Indeed, Italy's oldest surviving literary vernacular compositions are primarily religious in character, for instance the *Ritmo su sant'Alessio* (end of 12th c.) [see HAGIOGRAPHY; PAPACY AND THE CATHOLIC CHURCH; RELIGIOUS LITERATURE]; and St Francis' *Cantico di Frate Sole* (1224), which anticipates the subsequent flowering of sacred *laudi*. The mass of ordinary people, being illiterate, were excluded from Latin culture. Modern scholarship tends to associate popular oral composition with the professional entertainers known as *giullari* in Italian. The *Ritmo laurenziano*, which until recently was considered the oldest extant text with literary ambitions written in an Italian vernacular, comes from this milieu.

The problem of establishing when the different Italian vernaculars emerged from spoken Latin remains unsolved. All that can safely be said, on the basis of the surviving documentation, is that evidence of an awareness of Latin and vernacular as distinct languages emerges at the Council of Tours of 813, when priests were encouraged to translate their sermons into the 'rustic Roman language' in order to make them accessible to the faithful. [See also HISTORY OF THE ITALIAN LANGUAGE.]

The appearance in the Romance area generally, towards the middle of the 9th c., of texts containing sections or expressions in the vernacular formally codified the opposition between Latin on the one hand and vernacular on the other—an event which can be said to herald the beginnings of 'modern' culture. The opposition between Latin and vernacular became ever more pronounced during the subsequent centuries, though it was only by drawing on Latin literature that vernacular writing could develop and achieve its own legitimacy. In any case, even in the 13th and 14th c., most texts continued to be written in Latin. Nevertheless the impact of vernacular literature was dramatic. Most significantly, it destroyed for ever the idea of cultural unity fostered by Latin's 'universalism', and highlighted instead its fragmentation and mobile specificities. Thus, a tradition of plurilingual writing developed in which different languages, including Latin, were dialectically brought together [see PLURILINGUISMO]. *Raimbaut de Vaqueiras, for instance, combined Italian with other Romance languages in two of his poems. In Italy many of the different regionally based vernaculars produced literary texts during the 13th and 14th c., mirroring the peninsula's geopolitical fracturing into a variety of *communes and *signorie.

Although a minority, some natives of Italy chose to write in either French or Provençal. Brunetto

*Latini used French for his *Tresor*, as did Rustichello da Pisa when he recorded Marco *Polo's *Milione*; while, in North-East Italy, a hybrid mix of French and Veneto dialect was created for the *chivalric epic [see FRANCO-VENETO LITERATURE; FRENCH INFLUENCES, 1]. *Sordello and other poets and the grammarian *Terramagnino da Pisa had recourse to Provençal. In the same way, non-Italians used their own vernacular while resident in Italy. The reasons for this linguistic eclecticism are complex and varied, but plainly both French and Provençal literature had acquired much prestige and influence in Italy. In addition, beginning in the 12th c., France exerted considerable sway over all aspects of cultural activity in Italy, including the dissemination of Latin texts. It was also the case that the linguistic option confronting a writer was primarily that of choosing between Latin and vernacular, rather than between Latin and his own vernacular. Although it became widely accepted that an individual vernacular could achieve special success in a certain area, such as Provençal in the field of poetry, it was only with Dante's *De vulgari eloquentia* that the idea of seeing and evaluating vernacular literature in geographical terms was actively propounded, and a hierarchy of vernaculars, based on their artistic efficacy, was established. Italian literary historiography, as well as the notion of an 'Italian literature' and that of an Italian literary language, find their first serious articulation in Dante. [See also HISTORIES OF ITALIAN LITERATURE; TROUBADOURS.]

It is not immediately obvious why Italian literature should have lagged behind those in French and Provençal, which developed impressively during the 12th c. The contributions, naturally in Latin, that Italy made at this time in the areas of *law, rhetoric, *education, *medicine, philosophy, and theology are of the highest order. The main reason for the delay is probably the lack of a strong and intellectually enlightened centre which was not institutionally closely involved with Latin culture. It was—as Dante noted in the *De vulgari eloquentia*—with the establishment of such a centre, the *Magna curia* in *Sicily of the Emperor *Frederick II, that an explicitly Italian literary consciousness and a sophisticated literary tradition emerged. Before the appearance, some time during the early 1230s, of the *Sicilian School of poets, vernacular writing, as evidenced by its paucity, was essentially occasional in character, though two recently published texts indicate that secular love poetry was already being written in the North of Italy in the years before

Migliorini, Bruno

1190. These poems, a *canzone ('Quand eu stava in le tu' cathene') and a text of five verses ('Fra tuti quî ke fece lu Creature'), could thus represent the oldest surviving literary compositions in Italian.

The poetic lessons of the Sicilian School spread rapidly northwards and were reworked in an original manner across Central Italy. The so-called *Siculo-Tuscan poets, with leading figures in Guittone d'Arezzo and *Bonagiunta da Lucca, tended to privilege experimentation. Then, by the 1280s, in *Florence the poets of the *dolce stil novo, especially Guido *Cavalcanti and Dante, championed a philosophically and psychologically sophisticated view of love which they presented in a refined and elegant language that is largely devoid of regionalisms, and that marks the beginnings of Tuscan, and specifically Florentine, dominance over Italian literature and its literary language. Regardless of the success of love poetry, a vast panoply of literature was composed from about the middle of the 13th c. onwards in a wealth of regionally based Italian vernaculars—didactic poetry, vernacular *translations of Latin and Romance works (volgarizzamenti), sacred verse, *allegorical prose, political poetry, *chronicles, the 'comic' *sonnets of *poesia giocosa, and narratives in both prose and verse. Didactic poetry was particularly associated with the North and the laudi with *Umbria and the Marche.

By the end of the 13th c., Italian literature can be said to have superseded its Romance rivals, even before the arrival of Dante, Petrarch, and Boccaccio. After the Tre Corone most 14th-c. vernacular writing was the work of epigones rather than of original literary imaginations. The Middle Ages, and not the Renaissance—as too often has been asserted—is the key defining moment for Italian culture; and it is important to remember that the merit for this should not be restricted to Italy's three greatest writers.   [ZB]

Le origini, ed. A. Viscardi et al. (1956); La prosa del Duecento, ed. M. Marti and C. Segre (1959); Poeti del Duecento, ed. G. Contini (1960); Letteratura italiana delle origini, ed. G. Contini (1970). See E. R. Curtius, European Literature and the Latin Middle Ages (1953); J. Larner, Italy in the Age of Dante and Petrarch, 1216–1380 (1980).

MIGLIORINI, BRUNO (1896–1975). Major figure in Italian linguistics (particularly etymology and lexicology) and a highly successful and influential popularizer of his subject. He was the first professor of the *history of the Italian language (at *Florence University), co-founder of the journal Lingua nostra, and president of the Accademia della *Crusca (1949–63). His Storia della lingua italiana (1960) remains the most authoritative single-volume history of the language.   [MM]

Milan

1. Before 1700

Milan is strategically situated, close to Alpine passes and the rivers and lakes of Northern Italy. Celtic in origin, it was of importance before it was acquired by Rome in 197 BC. Within the later Empire it became an imperial capital. It was here that Constantine declared toleration for Christianity in 313 and, later in the century, Ambrose, the city's Bishop and eventual patron saint (339–97), confronted the Arian heresy. On the Empire's decline, Milan suffered repeatedly in the barbarian invasions. However, its position and the wealth of its hinterland in foodstuffs and raw materials aided its recovery. This can be measured in population growth: around 1300 Milan reached its medieval peak of some 100,000 inhabitants, making it one of the largest cities of Western Europe. In 1288, the Milanese *Bonvesin de la Riva celebrated its size, wealth, resources, and activity. In the *Renaissance, Milan was famed for its textile and metal industries as well as for its trade.

Economic growth had religious and political consequences. In the 11th c. Milan was central in the struggle between Pope and Emperor over the reform of the Church. It was also central to the struggle for greater autonomy. *Communal rule emerged in the 11th c., and saw its triumph when Milan led the Lombard League that defeated the Emperor Frederick I (Barbarossa) at Legnano (1176), securing virtual independence in the Peace of Constance (1183). However the commune was undermined by social unrest and faction. In the 13th c. two families, the Della Torre and the *Visconti, struggled to impose their lordship or *signoria, a contest which was won in 1311 by the latter. On the death of Filippo Maria Visconti (1402–47), Milan reverted to communal rule—the Ambrosian Republic—until forced to surrender in 1450 to the *condottiere Francesco *Sforza. Sforza rule lasted until Milan was captured for Louis XII of France in 1498. Thereafter Milan became largely a prize in the struggle between the French and the Habsburgs. The city finally passed to the *Spanish *Habsburgs in 1535, and was held by them until the 18th c.

The Visconti and the Sforza *courts had helped make Milan a leading cultural centre. The absence of a court, foreign governors, the restricted influence of the Milanese elite, and severe outbreaks of *plague (1566, 1629–33) have cast Spanish rule in a negative light. However Milan's economic importance remained. Its archbishopric continued to be influential: Carlo *Borromeo (1538–84) was a key figure in the *Counter-Reformation. Though Milan had no *university until the modern period, the *printing press flourished and cultural institutions were founded, like the Biblioteca Ambrosiana (1609) [see also LIBRARIES]. [JEL]

2. 1700 onwards

In 1707 Milan passed from *Spanish to *Austrian rule. Both *Habsburg emperors, Maria Theresa and her son Joseph II, were influenced by *Enlightenment ideas, and made important economic and legal reforms, curbing ecclesiastical privileges and strengthening agriculture and the manufacturing industries. During the 18th c. Milan became a cosmopolitan city. Alongside *Naples, it was the most influential centre of the Italian Enlightenment, with *Muratori, *Parini, *Beccaria, the *Verri brothers, and the Accademia dei Pugni, and the journal *Il* *Caffè*. Milanese culture also looked upon its own *dialect tradition with confidence and pride, an outlook which was to last into the 19th c., with Carlo *Porta, and later with playwrights like *Bertolazzi.

Milanese intellectuals were well placed to form the ruling group of the *Napoleonic regimes (1796–1814)—the *Jacobin Repubblica Cisalpina, followed by the Repubblica Italiana and the Regno Italico. After the Napoleonic period, which encouraged the formation of an embryonic entrepreneurial middle class, the Habsburg restoration in 1814 was not welcome, especially as it became increasingly oppressive in response to successive waves of patriotic conspiracies. Linked to the newborn patriotic movement were the first Italian *Romantics, with their journal *Il* *Conciliatore* (1818–19). In *1848 the people of Milan rose against the Habsburg regime, but were eventually defeated. Milan and the surrounding region of *Lombardy were annexed to *Piedmont-Sardinia in 1859 at the end of the Second War of Independence, thereby automatically becoming part of the Kingdom of Italy when this was established in 1861 [see UNIFICATION].

In the new Italy, Milan's commerce, banking, and industry made it economically the most advanced city in the country. It has also become a major centre for fashion and design and for the *publishing industry, with *Bompiani, *Feltrinelli, *Garzanti, *Mondadori, and *Rizzoli all having their main offices there. Milan has been a pivotal city for all modern cultural movements, including the *Scapigliatura*, *verismo*, *Futurism, and the *Neoavanguardia*. [VRJ]

See G. Treccani degli Alfieri, *Storia di Milano* (1953–62).

MILANI, LORENZO (1923–67). Campaigning priest and teacher. Born of a *Tuscan landowner and a *Jewish mother, he entered the priesthood in 1947 and dedicated his ministry to combating social injustice, largely through his own teaching of working people in San Donato di Calenzano, near Prato. Transferred to Sant'Andrea di Barbiana in the Apennine foothills, he established his own free school, which attracted visitors from all over Italy. Under his guidance his pupils published the collective *Lettera ad una professoressa* (1967), which is a clear critique of the Italian school system [see EDUCATION]. He became equally famous for championing conscientious objection to military service and proclaiming that the notion of a just war was now defunct. [JG-R]

MILELLI, DOMENICO (1841–1905). Poet from Catanzaro. As a young man he fought with *Garibaldi's troops. In both his life and his poetry he displayed a polemical temperament and an impatience with convention. His collections include *In giovinezza* (1873), *Poemi della notte* (1899), and, arguably his best work, *Fior d'infanzia* (1904). [CFB]

Milione, Il, see POLO, MARCO.

MILIZIA, FRANCESCO (1725–98). Originally from Otranto, he established himself in *Rome as a leading authority on the fine arts, especially architecture. His writings combine *neoclassical admiration for Greek art with *Enlightenment rationalism and utilitarianism, showing also a taste for the expressive and the dramatic, and appreciation of Roman and Gothic art. [JMAL]

MINO D'AREZZO (13th c.). A musician who apparently composed settings for various contemporary *lyric poems, though none of his work survives. He has been identified with the Mino Mocato of *Siena mentioned by *Dante (*DVE* 1.13), and with the Minuccio d'Arezzo of *Decameron* 10.7 [see MICO DA SIENA]. [PH]

MINTURNO, ANTONIO (Antonio Sebastiani) (1500–74), named after his birthplace North of *Naples, was a bishop in Calabria, a poet in the *Petrarchist mode, and a literary theorist and critic. Two treatises, *De Poeta* (1559) and *L'arte poetica* (1564), present his views on literary matters. The latter is shorter but includes valuable discussion on aspects of vernacular poetry. His position is strongly *Aristotelian, and critical of the vernacular *romance. [See also LITERARY THEORY, 2.]

[DG]

MINZONI, ONOFRIO (1734–1817). *Ferrarese priest and poet once admired for descriptive *sonnets on the model set by Carlo Innocenzo *Frugoni and Giuliano *Cassiani. His grandiose manner is inflated and Frugonian, rather than *Dantesque as claimed by Vincenzo *Monti, who imitated his best-known sonnet, 'Sulla morte di Cristo'. [JMAL]

Mio Carso, Il, see SLATAPER, SCIPIO.

Mirabilia urbis Romae. A Christianized topographical description of the 'marvels' of the city of *Rome compiled c.1140. It also gives its name to a genre which flourished in both Latin and vernacular versions down to the late 17th c. [SD]

Miracoli della Vergine Maria, I. *Hagiographic text which appears in different versions throughout Europe from the 12th c. onwards. Notable 14th-c. Italian versions are the anonymous *Libro dei cinquanta miracoli* from the Veneto and the *Miracoli della Vergine* of Duccio di Gano of *Pisa. [JT]

Mirra, see ALFIERI, VITTORIO.

MISASI, NICOLA (1850–1923). Calabrian writer. He was a persuasive advocate of *verismo. Many of his own *novels and short stories, notably *Racconti calabresi* (1883) and *La badia di Montenero* (1902), depend upon the realistic description of rural life in Calabria. [See also NOVELLA AND RACCONTO.] [CFB]

Misogallo, see ALFIERI, VITTORIO.

Misogyny in the *Middle Ages and *Renaissance was founded in deeply entrenched cultural attitudes, codified in civil and canon *law, intellectually supported by *Aristotelianism and scholasticism, and reinforced by the structures of political and ecclesiastical institutions. Prejudices which had long been nourished by the authority of St Jerome and which chimed with medieval ascetic practices and preferences were largely exacerbated by recovery of ancient and early Christian texts in the Renaissance. The *Counter-Reformation encouraged giving greater dignity to marriage for lay people, but never backed down on the subjection of women to their husbands as the law of God. Only in the 19th c. would serious changes of attitude begin to emerge.

The most important of earlier Italian misogynist invectives is *Boccaccio's *Corbaccio* of about 1355, which draws on *Ovid's *Remedia amoris*, Juvenal, and the *Roman de la rose* for its antidotes to poisonous sexual infatuation as concocted by women (in this case a scheming widow) to debilitate men's rationality. It also draws on some well-known Latin fragments originally from a treatise by Theophrastus denouncing marriage, and utilized by St Jerome, which were later *translated into Italian by Leon Battista *Alberti. In the 16th c. treatises such as Giovanni *Della Casa's *Dialogus de uxore non ducenda* (1537) and Ercole Tasso's *Dello ammogliarsi* (1594) continue to make the same points, a new crescendo being reached in Giuseppe Passi's *I donneschi difetti* (1599). They could also be used to advance homosexual practices, as in the anonymous *Manganello*, though it was regularly printed together with Antonio *Cornazzano's refutation.

Ostensibly less polemical writing drew on Aristotle and Xenophon. Sperone *Speroni's misleadingly titled *dialogue, *Della dignità delle donne* (1542), has a woman argue that a woman's dignity is found in her natural condition of servitude. Torquato *Tasso's *Della virtù donnesca* (1582) sees speculative and public virtues as appropriate for men, and chastity for women, though women rulers who must practise manly virtues are allowed a virile soul.

All these arguments were vigorously opposed by some Renaissance writers, both male (*Castiglione, *Ariosto, Lodovico *Domenichi), and female (Veronica *Franco, Moderata *Fonte, Lucrezia *Marinella, Arcangela *Tarabotti). But misogyny was ever resurgent. Later appeals were to spurious biological evidence about women's natural weakness of the kind voiced in Ferdinando *Galiani's *Dialogo sulle donne* of 1772. [See also FEMINISM; WOMEN WRITERS.] [LAP]

See I. Maclean, *The Renaissance Notion of Woman* (1980).

Mock-Heroic Poetry. The genre which parodies the elevated style and conventions of *epic by applying them incongruously to trivial subject matter. The *chivalric poems of the *Renaissance, especially Luigi *Pulci's *Morgante*, have mock-heroic elements, with high-flown sentiments in love and war offset by an undercurrent of earthy humour; but Pulci's attitude, and even more that of *Ariosto in the *Orlando furioso*, is one of amused detachment rather than direct parody. A more openly subversive effect is apparent in *Folengo's *Baldus* (1521), written in a *macaronic (half-Latin, half-vernacular) language which reflects the pervasive uncertainty of an age where established norms were everywhere under attack.

The work which initiated the mock-epic as a distinct genre was *Tassoni's *La secchia rapita*, substantially written in 1614–15, published in 1622 and in a final revised edition in 1630. The poem, in the traditional epic twelve books, recounts a war between Modena and *Bologna over a wooden bucket which Modenese soldiers had stolen as a trophy; the narrative uses incidents from the medieval history of the two cities to satirize the events and personalities of Tassoni's own day. The poem set a fashion which produced many more or less pedestrian imitations in Italy; in France it inspired Boileau's *Le Lutrin* (1674–83), and in England Pope's *Rape of the Lock* (1712–14). Contemporary with Tassoni's poem, but rather different in intention, was Francesco *Bracciolini's *Lo scherno degli dei* (1618), a parody deflating classical mythology as unworthy of the attention of Christian poets. Giovan Battista *Lalli's *Franceide* (1629) parodies the famous contest between French and Spanish knights at Barletta in 1503, with a Franco-Italian contest to decide whether the disease which first spread among the French army in *Naples in 1495 should be called *mal francese* or *mal napoletano* (the French lost, so *mal francese* was the name which stuck). The same author's *Moscheide* recounts the Emperor Domitian's war against the assembled armies of flies. Different again was Lorenzo *Lippi's *Malmantile racquistato* (published posthumously in 1676), a poem whose inconsequential story provides a showcase for the richness of popular *Florentine language, and which was the subject of several linguistic *commentaries. Diverse as they are, these poems reflect a common impatience with literary and social conventions which were felt to be stifling and inflexible. [See also PARODY AND PASTICHE; SATIRE.]
[RMD]

See C. Previtera, *La poesia giocosa e l'umorismo* (1942); *Studi tassoniani* (1966).

MODENA, LEONE, see JEWS AND JUDAISM.

Modernism. As a term used to encompass a set of international cultural movements or tendencies in the first thirty or so years of the 20th c., *modernismo* is rarely employed in Italy. Italian critics prefer categories such as *avanguardia* and *Neoavanguardia* to refer to those art forms or artistic figures whose formally innovative work expresses or reflects the crisis in modernity experienced through the phenomena of urbanization, industrialization, and the growth of a common mass culture. The term also suffered through association with *decadentismo* and certain aspects of *Fascist thought and aesthetics.

Nevertheless, Italy did produce a number of key figures in what is internationally known as modernism. The theatre of Luigi *Pirandello, with its dual emphasis on the crisis in traditional artistic form and on fractured notions of selfhood, typifies its concerns. Similarly, the fiction of Italo *Svevo, set in the plurilingual city of *Trieste, challenges *realist conventions of plot and characterization. Both authors express the confusion felt in the face of rapid social change. *Futurism, often seen as the first modernist movement, represented the opposite response, embracing the modern world and applauding the aesthetic innovations which developing technology allowed. [See also GRUPPO 63.]

The term *modernismo* is also used of the Catholic reform movement of the early 20th c., condemned by Pius X.
[DD]

MOGGI, MOGGIO DE' (*c*.1325–after 1388). Early *humanist, grammar teacher, and notary from Parma. His patrons included Benintendi de' *Ravagnani and the *Visconti. Some of his Latin verse and prose, mostly letters, have survived, but he is best known as a friend and correspondent of *Petrarch. He was the latter's son Giovanni's teacher in Parma from 1343 to 1345.
[PH]

MOLZA, FRANCESCO MARIA (1489–1544) is best known for his classicizing vernacular verse. Born in Modena, he studied in *Rome and *Bologna, where he learnt Latin, Greek, and Hebrew. His *humanist training and literary activities brought him into contact with Pietro *Bembo, and after 1529 he entered the *court of Cardinal Ippolito de' *Medici. Despite a turbulent private life he produced a considerable body of writing, which includes *Boccaccesque *novelle, an oration against Lorenzino de' Medici, and Latin lyrics and letters. In Italian he experimented with the burlesque style and the *Petrarchan lyric, but achieved his most impressive results in *La ninfa tiberina* of c.1537, a *pastoralizing celebration in *ottava rima of the beauties of Faustina Mancini. [PLR]

MOLZA, TARQUINIA (1542–1617). The granddaughter of Francesco Maria *Molza, she wrote poems in Latin and Italian and *translated some Platonic *dialogues. She served as a gentlewoman at the *court of *Ferrara (1583 to 1595) and knew Torquato *Tasso, who addressed various *sonnets to her, and wrote a dialogue, *La Molza overo de l'amore.* [ABu]

MOMIGLIANO, ATTILIO (1883–1952), professor of Italian at Catania, *Pisa, and *Florence, studied at *Turin under Arturo *Graf, whose historical and aesthetic principles he used in prolific and influential critical work, notably *Alessandro *Manzoni: la vita e le opere* (1919), *Saggio su l'*Orlando furioso* (1928), and *Storia della letteratura italiana* (1934–5). [See also HISTORIES OF ITALIAN LITERATURE; LITERARY CRITICISM.]
[JRW]

Monaca di Monza. Gertrude, the female antiheroine in *Manzoni's *I *promessi sposi,* who has been forced to become a nun by her aristocratic family and is blackmailed by her lover into betraying the heroine, Lucia. Based on a historical figure, she played a more prominent part in the first version of the novel. [VRJ]

MONACHI, VENTURA (d.1348) *Florentine notary and Chancellor of the Republic in 1340. He is also the author of nineteen *lyric poems heavily dependent on the modes and techniques of the *dolce stil novo,* which by his time were becoming old-fashioned. [SNB]

MONACI, ERNESTO, see POSITIVISM.

Monarchia. *Dante's Latin prose treatise on political philosophy addresses the central issue of medieval political debate: the relationship between secular and spiritual power as embodied in Emperor and Pope, their supreme earthly representatives. The 'monarchy' Dante advocates signifies government of the whole human race by a single secular ruler to whom all lesser rulers (kings,

princes) are answerable, and whose authority comes to him directly from God: such a figure alone can guarantee peace and justice, and thus allow humanity to flourish. Dante's argument is firmly anchored in medieval and classical thinking, especially the authoritative texts of Aristotle (notably in book 1, which establishes the need for a universal world-ruler) [see also SCHOLASTICISM], *Virgil (in book 2, which demonstrates not just the legitimacy but the providential role of the Roman Empire), and the *Bible (in book 3, which proves the emperor's independence of *papal overlordship, dismissing the arguments from biblical exegesis and from history—notably the so-called '*donation of Constantine'—on which papal apologists traditionally based their claims).

The treatise's originality lies both in the attempt to argue the case from first principles and in the way the argument is structured: the three books with their separate yet linked theses function as a quasi-syllogism; if we accept the conclusions of books 1 and 2 as premises, only then can we truly understand the force of the argument in book 3. At first glance *Monarchia* may strike modern readers as remote from the practical realities of politics and arid in its remorseless syllogistic reasoning; yet closer acquaintance reveals both the passionate engagement and the powerful shaping intelligence which are the hallmarks of the poet of the *Divine Comedy.* It is now thought that the treatise was written during the period of composition of the *Paradiso,* probably around 1318. [PS]

Monarchy. Until 1860 monarchs in Italy were essentially foreign implantations, and rarely loved by their subjects. The *Risorgimento saw all Italy's other absolute rulers supplanted by the House of *Savoy. Required to symbolize Italy's nationhood, the monarch was enabled by the constitution to interfere in almost all the major policy decisions taken by government. But none of Italy's four kings—*Vittorio Emanuele II (1861–78), Umberto I (1878–1900), Vittorio Emanuele III (1900–46) and Umberto II (1946)—were politically able or clearsighted. Vittorio Emanuele III was instrumental in Italy's intervention in *World War I, and then in both the rise and fall of *Mussolini. By a narrow majority the monarchy was abolished in the referendum of 1946. [RAbs]

Monasticism, see BENEDICTINES; DOMINICANS; FRANCISCANS; PAPACY AND THE CATHOLIC CHURCH; RELIGIOUS LITERATURE.

Mondadori. *Milanese *publishing firm since 1911, founded in 1907 by Arnoldo Mondadori as a printing firm. He and his rival *Rizzoli were the first modern industrial publishers in Italy but, unlike Rizzoli, Mondadori always made books the centre of his operations. He acquired rights to leading writers, including *D'Annunzio, *Verga, and *Pirandello. He simultaneously developed his magazine sector, from literary reviews to Disney *comics, and built an integrated company which owned and controlled all stages of production—paper-making and printing in Verona, distribution and retail through the Mondadori 'per voi' bookstores. In 1965 Mondadori started a revolution in book distribution by selling its Oscar paperbacks through newsstands (*edicole*). After Arnoldo's death (1971) the firm was controlled by his heirs until taken over by Silvio Berlusconi's Fininvest group in 1994. [See also LITERARY PRIZES.]

[DF]

Mondo, Il (1949–66). Literary and political weekly founded and edited in *Rome by Mario Pannunzio, who had previously written for the clandestine *Resistance press. It attracted contributions from most of Italy's liberal intellectual elite—articles from the likes of *Praz and *Moravia, fiction from *Calvino, *Cassola, and others—and tried to create an independent position that was neither *Communist nor *Christian Democrat. It ceased publication partly for financial reasons, but also because state monopolies made its autonomy untenable. It was revived in 1969 by *Rizzoli under the editorship of Arrigo *Benedetti, and then again in 1975, as a weekly supplement of the *Corriere della sera.*

[DCH]

Mondo nuovo, see STIGLIANI, TOMMASO.

MONELLI, PAOLO (1891–1984). *Journalist who worked for the *Corriere della sera* and other papers. He wrote valuable reportage in *Roma 1943* (1945) and *Mussolini: piccolo borghese* (1952). He also published fiction and a neo-*purist defence of the Italian language, *Barbaro dominio* (1921).

[DF]

Monolinguism, see DIALECT; PLURILINGUISMO.

MONTALE, EUGENIO (1896–1981). By common consent the most important Italian poet of the 20th c. Born into a middle-class *Genoese family, he abandoned the business career for which he was

destined and dedicated himself to independent literary studies. He served in *World War I as an infantry officer and then returned to Genoa.

His first collection of poems, *Ossi di seppia*, was published by *Gobetti in 1924 and reissued with some additional poems in 1928. In 1927 he moved to *Florence, where he worked for the *publishing house *Bemporad until he was appointed director of the Gabinetto *Vieusseux in 1928, a post he held until he was dismissed in 1938 on the grounds that he was not a member of the *Fascist party. His second book of poems, *Le occasioni*, appeared in 1939. He spent the war mostly in Florence, but afterwards moved to *Milan to write for the *Corriere della sera.* Milan was his home for the rest of his life. In 1956 he published his third book, *La bufera e altro*, containing poems written between 1939 and 1954, some of which had been published as *Finistère* in Lugano in 1943. He now entered a phase of poetic silence which was to last, barring a few isolated poems, for over a decade. But the importance of his work was also being recognized inside and outside Italy. In 1967 he was made a Senator for life and in 1975 he was awarded the Nobel Prize for literature. By this stage he was publishing poetry again, but in a new much more prosaic style which he first demonstrated in *Satura* (1971), containing poems going back to the earlier 1960s. Two other collections followed in this new manner, *Diario del '71 e del '72* (1973) and *Quaderno di quattro anni* (1977), as well as *Altri versi*, which was included in his collected *Opera in versi* (1980). This late productivity had a surprising epilogue with a *Diario postumo*, part of which was first published in 1991. The authenticity of this collection of unpublished poems, apparently left by Montale to a friend, Annalisa Cima, has been much debated. In any event they are insignificant texts which add little or nothing to Montale's œuvre.

Ossi di seppia is a composite work in which various influences are visible—*symbolism, the group around La *Voce, *D'Annunzio, and *Gozzano being the most obvious. Yet the fundamental features of Montale's subsequent poetry are also evident—the ability to handle the modern 'male di vivere' (as he called it one poem) in poetic forms that retain a classical decorum in their choice of words, metres, and syntax, and also the ability to catch a sense of the universal implications in particular experiences, bringing together the physical and the metaphysical, the poverty of individual lives and grand symbolic values. The language is already precise, concrete, technically exact, naming the ordinary things that the symbolists and D'Annunzio had excluded from poetry, but simultaneously overdetermining them and endowing them with a deeply tragic significance.

For all the importance of *Ossi di seppia*, Montale's central position in 20th-c. Italian poetry is due above all to *Le occasioni* and *La bufera e altro*. In these two collections his modern *classicism achieves its definitive form, his lexicon is more controlled and more unitary, and the modernity of certain themes and techniques has its fullest realization. In the *Ossi* Montale concentrated on the intermittent and discontinuous nature of authentic awareness and self-knowledge; now poetic epiphanies become the principle underlying a new order and a new style. At the same time, Montale's classicizing idea of form involves explicit recourse to Browning, Valéry, and Eliot, whilst his implicit poetics comes close to Eliot's notion of the objective correlative. A further innovation is the constant presence (or absence) of a female figure who is addressed by the 'I' speaking in the poems. In the *Occasioni* and for the first five sections of the *Bufera* the *tu*-figure is almost always Clizia, the name which Montale adopted for Irma Brandeis, an American scholar studying in Florence with whom he had a relationship between 1933 and 1938, when she was forced by the race laws to return to the USA. Clizia personifies humanist values of decency, self-control, and formal elegance, which are set against the the absurdity of existence and the violence of Fascism.

*Allegorical references or allusions to the regime are few in the *Occasioni*. Only in the *Bufera* does Montale speak directly of public history. But the latter collection is his most complex and the most ambiguous in its implications, as he opens his classically contained idiom to the tragic reality of war and then to the drabness of the years that followed. In the last part of the collection Clizia is replaced by another figure, Volpe, Montale's name for Maria Luisa *Spaziani, whom he met in 1949 and who, as Volpe, represents earthly vitality and sensual passion in contrast to the spiritual and humanist values represented by Clizia.

During the years after 1954 when Montale was not writing poetry, his contributions to the *Corriere della sera* greatly increased in frequency. He used them to develop a critique of the modern world, displaying an outlook that was conservative and ultimately nihilistic in its implications. He saw postwar mass culture as having very quickly destroyed the old high culture and true writers as having no salvation left to them. His own poetic silence was consistent with such an attitude. When he did begin to write poetry again in the mid-1960s, he seemed largely to have abandoned classical poetic values. The *Xenia* of *Satura* were unpretentious elegies for his dead wife, Drusilla Tanzi, using her nickname, Mosca. Items from the news or day-to-day happenings, *satire and neo-*crepuscolare* gloom now ousted the grand style and with it much of what was so splendidly poetic in Montale's work. Critics are agreed about the value of his first three books, but judgements on his later production are divided; some hold that he remained a great poet, whilst others see clear decline.

Montale's extensive and influential literary *journalism has been collected as *Il secondo mestiere* (1996). He wrote much less imaginative prose, but came close to prose poetry in the deliberately slender anecdotes of *Farfalla di Dinard* (1956).

[GM]

See G. Contini, *Una lunga fedeltà* (1974); R. Luperini, *Storia di Montale* (1986); M. A. Grignani and R. Luperini (eds.), *Montale e il canone poetico del Novecento* (1998).

MONTANARU (Antioco Casula), see SARDINIA.

MONTANELLI, INDRO (1909–2001). Right-wing *journalist who joined *Il *Corriere della sera* in 1938, leaving it only in 1973 in protest at the paper's leftward shift. He championed an explicitly right-wing politics as a founder (with Leo *Longanesi) of *Il Borghese* in 1950, and again in *Il Giornale nuovo*, which he founded in 1974. As a correspondent, his reports were a model of clear, pungent prose; as an editor he created a fiercely loyal readership, as is demonstrated by the replies to readers' letters assembled in *Caro direttore* (1991). Disgusted by Silvio Berlusconi, he showed unsuspected sympathy for his old enemies on the Left in the early 1990s. Montanelli has also written extensively as a popular historian, novelist, and playwright. [RE]

MONTANI, GIUSEPPE (1789–1833). *Literary critic and poet. Originally from Cremona, he became a Barnabite, until the order was suppressed under *Napoleon. A sympathizer with the *Milanese *Romantics and *liberals, he moved in 1824 to *Florence, where he became one of the principal contributors to *Antologia*, with responsibility for the literary pages. He was a sensitive and unpedantic critic, at his most expressive when he could feel himself at one with his author. This was the case, for example, with *Leopardi, whose poetry and *Operette morali he was one of the first to appreciate. [MPC]

MONTE ANDREA (13th c.). An important and undervalued *Florentine poet of the generation before *Dante, who decisively ignored him, probably because his poetic and philosophical outlook was so different. He was a moneylender and at some stage went bankrupt. He exchanged poems with *Guittone d'Arezzo, Chiaro *Davanzati, and many other lesser figures.

His surviving poems—eleven *canzoni and more than 100 *sonnets, almost all of sixteen lines—are remarkably varied. Some are love poems celebrating the angelic qualities of the lady in a way that seems to anticipate the *dolce stil novo; others are quasi-comic representations of violent desire and frustration. There are also fictitious sonnet exchanges between the lover and his lady. He is at his fiercest in political *tenzoni, voicing partisan support for the *Guelf cause, and making the political contest a contest of poetic form with invincible accumulations of equivocal and internal rhymes. His most powerful poems are five weighty and metrically complex canzoni, which create a dramatic image of his despair at his own financial collapse, and proclaim the penalties of penury and the omnipotence of money in the world at large. [PH]

Montecassino, see MIDDLE AGES.

MONTECUCCOLI, RAIMONDO (1609–80). Military writer. Born into a noble family near Modena, he became a general in the imperial army, fighting in the Thirty Years War and then against Sweden and Turkey. His Trattato della guerra, written during captivity in Sweden in 1639–42, like the Della guerra col Turco in Ungheria of 1670, considers both the political and military dimensions of war. He also took account of new technical developments. His works began to be published after his death and influenced 18th-c. military thought. [FC]

MONTEFELTRO. *Feudal family from the Romagna who established control of *Urbino in the 13th c. but had to continue to earn money elsewhere as *condottieri. Though Guidantonio promoted civic and economic reform in the earlier 15th c., it was his illegitimate son, *Federigo, who brought stable government, proving an enlightened ruler

and one of the most munificent *patrons of his time. His physically feeble son Guidobaldo succeeded in 1482, but died childless in 1508. Rule then passed to Francesco Maria della Rovere. [LChe]

MONTEVERDI, CLAUDIO (1567–1643) was the most significant Italian composer of his time. His music moves away from the a cappella vocal polyphony of the *Renaissance towards more emotional styles for solo voice(s) and accompaniment typical of the *Baroque. His nine books of *madrigals, three of church music, and three surviving *operas both summarized and revolutionized their fields.

Born and trained in Cremona, he moved to *Mantua in 1590–1 as *court musician of Duke Vincenzo *Gonzaga. His fourth (1603) and fifth (1605) books of madrigals reflect new developments influenced by the poetry of Torquato *Tasso and Battista *Guarini. Monteverdi justified their contrapuntal licence by the notion of a seconda pratica (with music subservient to word). His two Mantuan operas, Orfeo (1607) and Arianna (1608; now mostly lost), established the genre newly invented by the *Florentines, while the mammoth Sanctissimae Virgini Missa ac vespere (the so-called 1610 Vespers) is a masterpiece of the modern church style. Monteverdi was dismissed by the Gonzagas in 1612 and moved to *Venice in 1613 as director of music at St Mark's. Late in life, he returned to the stage, exploiting the development of public opera in Venice to produce Il ritorno d'Ulisse in patria (1640) and the remarkable L'incoronazione di Poppea (1642–3). [TC]
See P. Fabbri, Monteverdi (1994).

MONTI, AUGUSTO (1881–1966). Writer and schoolteacher. In the 1920s he joined the anti-*Fascist movement *Giustizia e libertà, and exerted a powerful influence on his pupils at the Liceo Massimo d'Azeglio in *Turin, including Leone *Ginzburg and Cesare *Pavese. In 1935 he was sentenced to five years' confino [see EXILE]; he fought in the *Resistance and later wrote for *Belfagor and Il *Ponte. [DF]

MONTI, VINCENZO (1754–1828). Versatile *neoclassical poet, part of whose versatility was the ability to adapt rapidly to changing political circumstances in a way that was already criticized by his contemporaries.

Born into a landowning family near Ravenna, he studied at *Ferrara but won the favours of Cardinal

Scipione Borghese with *La visione di Ezechiello* (1779). He went to *Rome in 1778, becoming a member of the *Arcadia academy as Antonide Saturniano. He estabished a reputation in *papal circles with poems such as those included in *Saggio di poesie* (1779), and won a degree of favour with a wider public with *tragedies such as *Aristodemo* (1787). The repercussions of the French Revolution in Italy drove him to *Milan, where he supported the idea of a *Napoleonic Empire. When the Cisalpine Republic fell in 1799, he moved to Paris, where he stayed until 1801. Famous by the time he returned to Italy, he obtained the chair of eloquence at Pavia University (1802–4) and composed various works celebrating Napoleon, such as *Il bardo della selva nera* (1806). When the Restoration arrived, he endeavoured to show his loyalty with *theatre pieces such as *Mistico omaggio* (1815) and *Il ritorno di Astrea* (1816).

The impulse to please whoever was in power dominates Monti's work, and he could produce mythological or *religious poems as required. But his imagination was easily fired. He wrote an ode *Al Signore di Montgolfier* (1784) on the occasion of the famous balloon flight, in which he shows sympathy for progressive ideas. In the *Sciolti a Sigismondo Chigi* (1782) he creates melodious pathos in tune with contemporary *pre-Romantic feeling. *In morte di Ugo di Bassville*, or the *Bassvilliana* (1793), is an anti-revolutionary poem, in which an angel displays to the shade of Hugo de Bassville the horrors of the Revolution. Conversely, *La Musogonia* (1797) is a celebration of myths and the Muses which anticipates *Foscolo's *Le grazie*, whilst *In morte di Lorenzo *Mascheroni*, or *La Mascheroniana* (1801), shows a surprisingly appealing sentimentality.

Monti *translated parts of the *Aeneid*, Perseus' *Satires* (1804), and Voltaire's *Pucelle d'Orléans*, but is more famous for his *Iliad* (1811), though, as Foscolo remarked, he was not so much original as a translator of translators of Homer. He was also interested in linguistic questions, holding that the national language should be a written language somewhere between the modern and the classical, rather than a contemporary spoken language. [See also QUESTIONE DELLA LINGUA.]   [GDP]

See F. Allievi, *Vincenzo Monti* (1954); W. Binni, *Monti, poeta del consenso* (1981).

MORANDINI, GIULIANA (1938–). *Novelist, critic, and essayist, originally from Udine. Her interest in points of interaction between Austro-German, Slav, and Italian cultures, especially as experienced by women, is evident in her first three novels, *I cristalli di Vienna* (1978), *Caffè specchi* (1983), and *Angelo a Berlino* (1987). Later novels have extended her historical range. . . . *E allora mi hanno rinchiusa* (1977) is an investigation into women in mental hospitals and prisons. Much of her critical work is in German, or on German literature.   [SW]

MORANDO, BERNARDO (1589–1656), born into a rich *Genoese family, worked in commerce in Piacenza, where he also enjoyed the *patronage of the Dukes of Parma. He later took holy orders. His poems include many texts for music. His major success, the *novel *La Rosalinda* (1650), tells of a young Catholic girl living in London, who is forced by religious persecution to flee England with the man she loves and other Catholics. Subsequent Mediterranean adventures include shipwrecks, pirate attacks, slavery, separations, and reunions, with theatrical, poetic and musical interludes. But fundamentally the novel is strongly religious. When the two protagonists are reunited for the last time, they draw a spiritual lesson from their vicissitudes, and he enters a monastery, she a nunnery.   [MC]

MORANTE, ELSA (1912–85). One of the most interesting of postwar Italian *novelists, who established her reputation with *Menzogna e sortilegio* (1948), which won the Viareggio prize [see LITERARY PRIZES] and attracted the attention of the leading *Marxist theorist Georg Lukács. It tells the story of a young woman who is obsessed in equal measure by her personal and family past and by the need to reorder and embellish it in writing. In part it reflected the early career of a writer who was always to regard her writing as a high calling, and publicized it as such. She had previously published a serialized novel, *Qualcuno bussa alla porta* (1935–6), a collection of short stories showing traces of the *realismo magico* of the 1930s, *Il gioco segreto* (1941), and a children's story, *Le bellissime avventure di Caterì dalla trecciolina* (1941, revised and expanded 1959). She had also published a *translation of Katherine Mansfield's notebooks, *Il libro degli appunti* (1941).

Her next novel, *L'isola di Arturo* (1957), is an extraordinary study of the evolving relationship between a young boy approaching adolescence and the lordly yet absent father whom he hero-worships. The theme of unsatisfactory, ultimately compromised relationships between single parents and difficult children is then continued in the title story of *Lo scialle andaluso* (1963). Morante also published a volume of short lyric verse, *Alibi* (1958), before trying her hand at an experimental kind of extended narrative poetry with *Il mondo salvato dai ragazzini* (1968). During the 1950s and 1960s she travelled extensively and wrote newspaper and magazine articles, many of which were collected posthumously in *Pro e contro la bomba atomica* (1987), as well as a brief but illuminating essay on Fra Angelico, *Il beato propagandista del Paradiso* (1970). She returned to the full-blown novel form with *La *Storia* (1974) and *Aracoeli* (1982), her last and most despairing novel, which focuses (not for the first time) on the figure of a failing and defeated mother. Her style is one of the most wrought, some would say overwrought, in 20th-c. Italian fiction; at her best (and there is some of her best in all of her novels) she came as close as any of her contemporaries to capturing in prose the rhythms of the torment of mutual dependence.

Morante lived most of her life in *Rome, where she was born. In 1941 she married Alberto *Moravia, from whom she eventually separated.

[MPC]

See G. Rosa, *Cattedrali di carta: Elsa Morante romanziere* (1995).

MORASSO, MARIO (1871–1938). *Journalist and essayist. His writings for the periodical *Il *Marzocco*, and essays like 'La nuova arma: la macchina' (1905) and 'Il nuovo aspetto meccanico del mondo' (1907), are considered part of the *nationalist, right-wing criticism of bourgeois democracy, which is associated with *Futurism in the arts and, later, with *Fascism in politics. [CGW]

MORAVIA, ALBERTO (1907–90) (pseud. of Alberto Pincherle). One of Italy's most famous and prolific 20th-c. *novelists. Born in Rome, he suffered from a form of tuberculosis during his childhood and adolescence, and was therefore often confined to home and hospitals. His early literary debut in 1929, with the novel *Gli *indifferenti*, marked him as one of the most promising narrators of his generation. The novel showed the extent to which Moravia had successfully assimilated various foreign influences, that of Dostoevsky being the most central. It also distinguished itself for its dry, analytical style which contrasted sharply with the *prosa d'arte* in vogue at the time; but its depiction of the moral apathy of an Italian middle-class family was unfavourably received in *Fascist

circles. Moravia's following novels—*Le ambizioni sbagliate* (1935), *L'imbroglio* (1937), *I sogni del pigro* (1940), *La mascherata* (1941), and three collections of short stories—confirmed his talent, although none them equalled the intensity and structural cohesion of *Gli indifferenti*. More successful is the short novel *Agostino* (1943), centred on the sensual anxieties of an adolescent. The friction with the Fascist authorities also continued, to the point that the publication in 1941 of the second edition of *La mascherata* (which is an *allegory of the Fascist establishment) was halted by the *censors.

In the years before *World War II Moravia was also active as a reviewer and, more importantly, as a *travel writer following a series of trips abroad, to Britain, Greece, China, and the USA. After the promulgation of the anti-Semitic laws in 1938, since his father was *Jewish, he was prevented from signing his articles and reviews with his own name. After the war, he became an influential figure as a militant intellectual. His essay *La speranza, ossia cristianesimo e comunismo* (1945) was a first sign of his interest in *Marxism as a utopian ideology, although he produced a more influential essay in 'L'uomo come fine' (1946), which developed a poetics based on individual *stoicism in the face of social and political uncertainty. Critics often point to parallels between Moravia's ideas, particularly at this period, and French *existentialism. His *Neorealist novel about the life of a Roman prostitute, *La *romana* (1947), marked the beginning of his exploration of working-class life, which continued in the 1950s with the highly praised *Racconti romani* (1954) and the novel *La ciociara* (1957), the story of a shopkeeper and her daughter who take to the countryside on the collapse of the *Fascist government in Rome in 1943. During these years Moravia was also drawing a critical portrait of the moral apathy and progressive alienation of the middle classes in novels such as *L'amore coniugale* (1949), *Il conformista* (1951), and *Il disprezzo* (1954).

As a militant intellectual, Moravia publicly positioned himself on the left, although he never joined the Italian *Communist Party. In 1953 he and Alberto *Carocci founded the literary monthly *Nuovi argomenti*, which attempted to create a bridge between Communist and *liberal culture. In 1955 he started to write a weekly film review for the magazine *L'Espresso*, which he continued almost without interruption until his death. In the mid-1950s he also wrote his first two plays, a *theatre adaptation of *La mascherata* (1954) and *Beatrice Cenci* (1958). He later wrote four more plays, including *Il dio Kurt* (1968), set in a German concentration camp. The novel *La *noia* (1960) was welcomed by critics as one of Moravia's most accomplished postwar works. Once more centred on the alienation and moral apathy of a middle-class protagonist, it remained faithful to his Marxist and Freudian perspective, while at the same time absorbing the lessons of the French *nouveau roman*.

In 1963, after his separation from his first wife, Elsa *Morante, Moravia went to live with the younger author Dacia *Maraini. He continued to write popular travel books, among them *Un'idea dell'India* (1962) and *A quale tribù appartieni?* (1972). As for his fiction, if sexuality is an explicit theme in all his novels (the Catholic Church put his work on the *Index in 1952), it is particularly explicit in *Io e lui* (1971), in which the protagonist's penis is endowed with a personality and voice of its own. In the 1970s and 1980s, Moravia continued with the formal and thematic patterns of his earlier work, but also addressed contemporary issues such as the student movement, anti-nuclear protest, *feminist theories, and post-Freudian *psychoanalysis. The constant flow of novels and stories includes *La vita interiore* (1978), *1934* (1983), and *L'uomo che guarda* (1985), though collections of short stories such as *Il paradiso* (1970), *Boh!* (1973), and *La villa del venerdì* (1990) were generally given a more favourable reception. In 1984 he became a European Member of Parliament as an independent candidate for the Communist Party, and in 1986 he married a young Spanish woman, Carmen Llera.

Critical response to Moravia's fiction has varied. Although novels such as *Gli indifferenti*, *La romana*, and *La noia* are considered masterpieces, many critics have dwelt on his unsophisticated prose style, the repetitiveness of his characterization and plots, and the constant recourse to sexual themes. Moravia's intellectual stature, however, is undisputed, as is his influence on public opinion during the postwar years. [GUB]

See C. Benussi (ed.), *Il punto su Moravia* (1987); S. Wood, *Woman as Object: Language and Gender in the Work of Alberto Moravia* (1990); T. E. Peterson, *Alberto Moravia* (1996). .

MORELLI, GIOVANNI (1371–1444), a wool *merchant from a middle-ranking *Florentine family, was the author of a series of family memoirs (*ricordi*), covering the years 1393 to 1421. Intend-

ed to provide moral instruction as well as to preserve his family's memory, they also offer invaluable insights into Florentine social customs and attitudes. [RDB]

MORELLI FERNANDEZ, MARIA MADDALENA (1727–1800). Official poetess to the grand ducal *court in *Florence (1765–75) and better known by the *Arcadian pseudonym Corilla Olimpica, she achieved celebrity as Italy's foremost female *improviser. Her controversial coronation on the Capitol (1776) was later idealized by Mme de Staël in *Corinne*. [JMAL]

MORETTI, MARINO (1885–1979). Poet and *novelist. Born in Romagna, he moved to *Florence in 1902, where he became a friend of *Palazzeschi, *Papini, and *Prezzolini. Much influenced as a poet by *Pascoli, his *Poesie scritte col lapis* (1910) led *Borgese to coin the term *crepuscolare*. By then he was already turning more to prose. His novels frequently portray the struggles against adversity of women rather like his mother, who was responsible for his literary *education, and who directly inspired *Mia madre* (1923). Later novels, such as *La vedova Fioravanti* (1941), in keeping with his declared anti-*Fascist opinions, show a greater and more pessimistic social conscience. He withdrew to his native Cesenatico after the war and continued to write fiction until the end of his life.

[JJ]

MORETTI, NANNI, see CINEMA.

Morgante, Il. A long narrative poem by Luigi *Pulci, begun in the early 1460s and printed, in twenty-three cantos, probably in 1478; the definitive version, in twenty-eight cantos, was printed in 1483. The poem begins with a promise to honour the life of Charlemagne in a manner worthy of *Florence, which according to tradition he had refounded after its destruction by the Goths. It quickly becomes apparent, however, that the Emperor is a largely ineffective figure in the story, which follows the adventures of *Orlando and *Rinaldo in the Orient, including Orlando's adoption of the giant Morgante as his companion after defeating him and converting him to Christianity. Usually as a result of the treachery of Gano (the Ganelon of the *Chanson de Roland*), the heroes meet a series of Saracen adversaries, in encounters which are regularly complicated by the amorous attraction between one of the paladins and a Saracen princess. In a

self-contained episode which was reprinted independently of the rest of the poem, Morgante meets a half-giant, Margutte, who in a mock-confession boasts of his rejection of all moral and religious codes. The five cantos added in 1483 return to the theme promised at the outset with an account of the death of Orlando at Roncesvalle (Roncevaux) and a tribute to the career of Charlemagne.
[RMD]

MORNADO, BERNARDO, see MARINISMO.

MORONI, GIOVANNI BATTISTA (d.1645). Lawyer from *Ferrara who undertook political missions to *Rome and *Venice. He was a member of the Accademia degli *Incogniti, and published two *novels, *I lussi del genio esecrabile di Clearco* (1640) and *Il principe santo* (1641). The unctuously religious tone of both masks a turbid eroticism. The second deals with the theme of incest and owes much to Torquato *Tasso's *Torrismondo*.
[MC]

MOROVELLI, PIETRO, see SICULO-TUSCAN POETS.

MORPURGO, FORTUNA, see DIAS, WILLY.

MORRA, ISABELLA DI (1520–46). Poet whose life was almost unremittingly tragic. Born into an aristocratic Southern family, she was held against her will in their isolated castle after her father joined with the French. She found an admirer in Diego Sandoval De Castro, a Spanish noble who was himself a poet. When the relationship was discovered, she was murdered by her brothers, as later was De Castro. Her sensitive *Rime*, first published in 1552, seek to render the frustration and melancholy of her extreme circumstances. Though she remains within the limits of the *Petrarchist canon, her more reflective poems anticipate later *Mannerism.
[ABu]

MORSELLI, GUIDO (1912–73). Outstanding *novelist, whose reputation is entirely posthumous. Born in *Bologna, apart from war service he lived a relatively secluded life in Varese, where the family fortune (his father was a leading *Milan industrialist) gave him the freedom to devote his time to writing. A monograph on Proust (1943) and a speculative duologue, *Realismo e fantasia* (1947), made no impact, and not one of his novels had found a publisher before his suicide at the age of 60.

Speculations surrounding his death combined with revelations of editorial blindness or bias stoked a literary furore.

His versatility is remarkable. He wrote two substantial novels in *realist mode which are set at opposite ends of the social spectrum, *Un dramma borghese* of 1961–2 and *Il comunista* of 1964–5. Then followed *Roma senza papa*, a timely *satire of trendiness in the Catholic Church, *Contropassato prossimo*, an ingeniously plausible version of European history as it might have been if *World War I had had a different outcome, and the joyous *Divertimento 1889*, about an entirely fictitious escapade in the life of Umberto I. The final unnerving *Dissipatio HG*, written in 1972–3, is a cry for both solitude and companionship, and also a denunciation of humankind as an alien species blighting the planet Earth.
[HS]

Morte accidentale di un anarchico (1970), a farce by Dario *Fo, was inspired by the death in police custody in December 1969 of Giuseppe Pinelli, after his arrest in connection with the bomb incident in Milan's Piazza Fontana. A self-confessed madman impersonates figures of authority to expose a corrupt judicial and political system.
[JAL]

MOSCA, GAETANO (1854–1941). Political theorist from Palermo, who taught at various *universities and became a parliamentary deputy, and then senator. From his early *Elementi di scienza politica* (1884) onwards, he saw political science as an outgrowth of historical knowledge [see also POLITICAL THOUGHT]. He thought society should be run by small intellectual elites, but maintained a belief in law, which led him to oppose *Fascism and to withdraw from politics in 1926.
[DCH]

MOSCA, GASPARE, see MAFIA.

MOSCA, GIOVANNI, see BERTOLDO, 2; GUARESCHI, GIOVANNI.

MOSCONI CONTARINI, ELISABETTA, see WOMEN WRITERS, 2.

Motti, see FACEZIE.

Motti e facezie del piovano Arlotto (1460s–1470s). Vernacular collection of droll and ribald stories concerning the rustic wit and homespun morality of Arlotto de' Mainardi (1396–1484), a

395

priest in the Mugello region whose unconventional reputation is well attested in the historical record, which confirms with surprising precision the accuracy of many of the facetious tales circulating about him in this (and other) collections. The *Motti*'s anonymous author should probably be sought in the rather old-fashioned *Florentine circles in which the historical Arlotto moved, among countrified gentlemen possessed of broad social sympathies and a certain scepticism about the benefits of *Medici rule. [See also FACEZIE.]   [FWK]

MOZZONI, ANNA MARIA, see FEMINISM.

Mulino, Il. Political and social science *periodical founded in *Bologna in 1952. It was instrumental in introducing Anglo-American social science into Italy in a period dominated by *Marxism and the anti-scientism of *Croce. Since 1954 il Mulino (written with the 'il' in lower-case) has also been a publishing firm covering various academic disciplines.   [DF]

MURATORI, LUDOVICO ANTONIO (1672–1750). Historian, librarian, and man of letters. Born and educated in Modena, he was ordained priest in 1695, the year he went to *Milan to take charge of the Biblioteca Ambrosiana. He returned to Modena in 1700 as court librarian for the *Este family, a post he retained until his death. [See LIBRARIES.]

His writings are vast in quantity and range from *literary theory to history and social reform. His initial plan, outlined in *Primi disegni di una repubblica letteraria d'Italia* (1703), was to marshal and mobilize Italy's most creative intellects in a project of cultural and historical renewal of the peninsula, which he thought could not be met by *Arcadia, of which he was a member. It remains a key to his work as a whole. His numerous writings on literature, from his most important work, *Della perfetta poesia* (1706), to the *Riflessioni sopra il buon gusto nelle scienze e nelle arti* (1708) and *Osservazioni alle 'Rime' di Petrarca* (1712), were a comprehensive response to aesthetic problems raised by Arcadian rationalism. Muratori championed the reality of human feelings as intrinsic to poetry, and defended both the rhetorical and living elements of language against the excessive abstractions of Cartesian derivation.

The clash between the Este and the Holy See over the possession of Comacchio (1708–9) marked a change in Muratori's political outlook. He

had previously espoused neo-*Guelf ideas [see also GIOBERTI, VINCENZO]. He now undertook the historical research which became a landmark in *historiographical methodology. Developing the empiricism already evident in his literary writings, he set out to construct a 'civic' history based on the careful accumulation and sifting of evidence in opposition to rationalist and theologically impregnated schemes of development. His monumental historical labours in Latin consisted of the twenty-five-volume *Rerum italicarum scriptores* (1723–51) and the six-volume *Antiquitates italicae medii aevi* (1738–42). His twelve-volume *Annali d'Italia* (1745–9) made available to a wider reading public a less erudite and scholarly account of Italian history from the 5th c. to his own day, whereas the Latin histories finished at 1500. The treatment of the *Middle Ages, to Muratori the key to understanding modern developments in Italy, was the most systematic and critical in 18th-c. Italy. In his *Della pubblica felicità* (1749) he brought together the themes of his lifelong political, civil, and religious reflections into an advice manual for moderate reform which was to find fame at home and abroad.   [GLCB]

Opere, ed. G. Falco and F. Forti (1964). See F. Forti, *Ludovico Antonio Muratori* (1953); S. Bertelli, *Erudizione e storia in L. A. Muratori* (1960).

MURTOLA, GASPARE (mid-16th c.–1624). *Genoese writer who owes his fame to Giovan Battista *Marino. When Marino displaced him as secretary and court poet to Carlo Emanuele I of *Savoy, the two engaged in an exchange of vituperative *sonnets, which degenerated into a failed attempt on Marino's life. Murtola was forced to flee *Turin, but found favour and modest employment in *Rome under Paul V. His poetry is more conservative than that of his rival, and heavily influenced by Torquato *Tasso, but it remains within the parameters of early *concettismo. His most important work, *La creazione del mondo* (1608), follows Tasso and Du Bartas in retelling the seven days of Creation. It has long been mocked on the basis of Marino's rather selective criticism. Despite occasional lapses into bathos (such as some oft-quoted verses in praise of cabbages), it constitutes a dignified attempt to combine orthodox religious views with the new proto-scientific interest in the taxonomy of nature which had been sparked off by New World discoveries.   [MPS]

MUSA, GILDA, see SCIENCE FICTION.

MUSCETTA, CARLO, see LITERARY CRITICISM.

MUSCETTOLA, ANTONIO (1628–79). *Neapolitan nobleman and copious writer of *lyrics, *tragedies, prose discourses, and didactic verse letters. He managed to imitate both *Marino and *Chiabrera, favouring a mild sententiousness founded on antithesis rather than extended metaphor. [MPS]

Music. The long and fruitful collaboration between literature and music in Italy is closely related to the fact that phonetically Italian has changed only slowly since the later *Middle Ages and that the rules of Italian *versification have remained correspondingly stable.

In the *De vulgari eloquentia* (2.10), writing under *troubadour influence, *Dante commented on the close connection between the accentual and metrical properties of verse and the properties of the melody to be attached to it. In the 14th c. many poets wrote verse specifically designed to be set to music, giving rise to the genre of 'poesia per musica', which enjoyed a long popularity in Italian literature. Since the early *humanists believed that serious poetry should be written in Latin, much 15th-c. popular vernacular poetry was disseminated through musical renditions using standard formulae which only seldom required musical notation. Notable musician-poets included Leonardo *Giustinian, *Serafino Aquilano, Angelo *Poliziano, and Antonio *Tebaldeo.

Around 1500, under Isabella d'*Este's *patronage at *Mantua and *Ferrara, a written tradition of *strambotti* and *frottole* emerged, receiving a significant boost in popularity through the invention of music *printing. Under the influence of Pietro *Bembo a number of 16th-c. composers made *Petrarch their preferred poet for sophisticated musical settings and created the musical genre of the *madrigal, which dominated Italian secular music for over eighty years and had a strong impact outside Italy, particularly in Elizabethan England. *Ariosto, Torquato *Tasso, Battista *Guarini, *Chiabrera, and *Marino were also favoured by madrigal composers, who included Adrian Willaert, Cipriano de Rore, Jacques de Wert, Luca Marenzio, and *Monteverdi. Poliziano's *Orfeo* had combined recited poetry with music. In the course of the 16th c. it became increasingly popular to fashion musical settings of dramatic episodes, known as *intermedi*, which were inserted between acts of plays. These grew more and more lavish and, especially in *Medicean *Florence, became associated with important state occasions. *Pastoral plays such as Tasso's *Aminta* and Guarini's *Il *pastor fido*, also relied on musical numbers. These strands meshed with the theories of Florentine humanists interested in reviving the supposed Greek unity of drama and music. The result was the 'dramma per musica', as early *opera was called, whilst in the early 17th c. the opera *libretto emerged as a new literary genre.

*Arcadia responded enthusiastically to the development of the new genre, and Apostolo *Zeno and Pietro *Metastasio ensured the dominance of the Italian operatic libretto throughout Europe for the best part of the 18th c. With the rise of *Romanticism Italian opera lost its international monopoly but became a national literary and dramatic institution. Although relying on libretti written or adapted for him by Italian poets, *Verdi always chose themes from French, German, and English literature. A reaction against this was operatic *verismo*, a short-lived attempt at *realism, featuring the harsh and tragic life of Italian *peasants or else bohemian artists. *Puccini, though fond of non-Italian models, turned to Carlo *Gozzi for his last opera, *Turandot*. Gozzi's fantastic subjects appealed to 19th- and 20th-c. composers more than they did to his 18th-c. contemporaries.

Interaction between literature and music has been less striking since the later 19th c., though *D'Annunzio exerted an influence on contemporary composers and was influenced in his turn by Wagner. His enthusiasm for national traditions also contributed to the rediscovery of Monteverdi. In the second half of the 20th c. Luciano Berio created an original style of composition based on phonetic components of language and the expressive features of the human voice. [BB]

See J. Haar, *Essays on Italian Poetry and Music in the Renaissance* (1986); L. Bianconi, *Music in the Seventeenth Century* (1987); D. Kimbell, *Italian Opera* (1994).

MUSSATO, ALBERTINO (1261–1329). The best known of the *Paduan circle of pre-*humanist scholars and a friend and pupil of Lovato *Lovati. He was a notary, and played an active role in the government of his city. In 1302 he was sent as an ambassador to Pope *Boniface VIII, and in 1311 he was present in *Milan at the coronation of the Emperor *Henry VII. He played an active role, both as a diplomat and as a soldier, during the wars between Padua and Verona (1312–28). He was captured by the Veronese in 1314 and finally exiled from Padua in 1325.

Mussato's literary production is extremely varied, ranging from *historiography to *tragedy, and comprising also religious poetry, moral and philological treatises, *letters in both prose and verse (all in Latin), and at least one *sonnet in the vernacular. The *Historia Augusta de gestis Henrici VII* deals with the events of 1313–15, while his (possibly unfinished) *De gestis italicorum post Henricum VII Caesarem* continues the account up to 1321. Although Padua provides his principal focus, Mussato succeeds in presenting a broader view of recent history and, modelling his work on *Livy, aims at accuracy and impartiality. His tragedy *Ecerinis* celebrates the Paduan struggle against the earlier Veronese tyrant, Ezzelino da Romano, and takes Seneca as its literary model. Here impartiality is abandoned, for the figure of Ezzelino is a thinly disguised portrayal of the contemporary Veronese leader, Cangrande *della Scala. In 1315 Mussato was crowned as the historian and poet of Padua in a mock-classical ceremony.   [CEH]
   See G. Ronconi, *Le origini delle dispute umanistiche sulla poesia* (1976).

MUSSOLINI, BENITO (1883–1945). Founder and leader of *Fascism and head of Italy's government from 1922 to 1943. Born in Predappio (Romagna), he was a left-winger in the *Socialist Party until his expulsion in 1914 for his support for intervention in *World War I. He had been editor of the party newspaper *Avanti!* from 1912 until 1914; he then set up the pro-war *Il Popolo d'Italia*. He founded the Fascist movement in 1919 and seized power in October 1922, subsequently dismantling parliamentary democracy and assuming special powers as *Duce* (leader). A charismatic demagogue, he retained his personal popularity until the alliance with Germany and the disastrous conduct of *World War II brought about his downfall. The King had him arrested in July 1943 after a revolt of his ministers. Rescued by German paratroops on Hitler's orders, he became head of the Repubblica Sociale Italiana with its seat in Salò. In April 1945 he was executed by partisans. His body was brought to *Milan, and publicly desecrated, together with that of his lover, Claretta Petacci.

Mussolini's personal impact on literary culture is difficult to disentangle from that of Fascism. His own writings include an early bodice-ripper, *Claudia Particelli o l'amante del cardinale* (1910), and three historical plays co-written (or at least co-signed) with Giovacchino *Forzano—*Campo di maggio* (1930), *Villafranca* (1931) and *Cesare* (1939). More significant are the *autobiographical *Il mio diario di guerra, 1915–1917* (1931) and *La mia vita* (1947), and the rich rhetorical quarry of his *journalism, speeches, and political writings, collected in *Opera omnia* (54 volumes, 1951–63). The vast quantity of contemporary writing about him, from the early *biographies by *Beltramelli and *Sarfatti to Franco Ciarlantini's *Mussolini immaginario* (1933), testifies to the extraordinary cult of his personality.   [DF]
   See R. De Felice, *Mussolini* (1965–92);
   L. Passerini, *Mussolini immaginario* (1991).

MUZIO, GIROLAMO (1496–1576), born in *Padua, served as a courtier and wrote on *courtly topics (e.g. *Il duello*, *Il gentilhuomo*), as well as composing verse and an art of poetry (1551). Works on the language from the 1530s onwards, published as the *Battaglie per diffesa dell'italica lingua* (1582), include a defence of the vernacular against claims for the superiority of Latin, and the *Varchina*, in which Muzio attacks *Varchi's pro-*Florentine *Ercolano* while upholding his own ideal of an Italian learned from books. [See also QUESTIONE DELLA LINGUA.]   [BR]

Myricae, see PASCOLI, GIOVANNI.

Mysticism. The term commonly relates to a sense of the soul's transcending the material circumstances of historical selfhood and emerging into a world of pure consciousness, into the presence of an Absolute unqualified by time and space. The experience may encourage a more or less severe asceticism, but often presupposes a lively sense of the variety and dignity of the world as points of departure for the mystical ascent.

Few of the major works of Italian literature are specifically mystical in character, though a certain mystical urgency, strengthened by his reading of the Cistercians and Victorines, is discernible in *Dante. The *Neoplatonism of *Ficino, *Pico della Mirandola, Lorenzo de' *Medici, and other 15th-c. writers is fundamentally a matter of idealism rather than of mysticism proper, that is, of knowing rather than of unknowing as the object of spiritual endeavour. The powerful and widespread attraction of the mystical way, however, continues to be felt in more popular forms of literature, such as the lives of saints, *laudi*, *sacre rappresentazioni*, and *sermons. In such contexts it frequently offered a challenge to the institutional authority of the Church, which took measures to control and limit mysticism during the *Counter-Reformation. Species of mystical sensibility are discernible in modern poets from *Leopardi to *Ungaretti, Clemente *Rebora and Margherita *Guidacci. [See also HAGIOGRAPHY; PAPACY AND THE CATHOLIC CHURCH; RELIGIOUS LITERATURE.]

[JT]

N

NADAL, GIOVANNI GIROLAMO (also Natali) (d.1383). *Venetian *merchant and politician, and presumed author of the *Leandreide*, a retelling in *terza rima*, heavily influenced by *Dante, of the story of Hero and Leander. It includes a famous catalogue of poets ancient and modern, partly delivered by a character representing Dante himself. [SNB]

NADI, GASPARE (1418–1504). Master mason, whose *diary, written in idiomatic *Bolognese, records not only details of the architectural projects he oversaw for the city's pre-eminent family, the Bentivoglio, but also personal and political comments. In this, as in other respects, his *Diario bolognese* resembles the family diaries which survive more abundantly in *Tuscany. [CJ]

NALATO, G. UGO, see GIAN DAULI.

NALDI, NALDO (*c*.1436–1513). *Florentine poet of considerable refinement and a scholar of Greek and Latin culture. Received at the *court of the *Medici, and mentioned in Angelo *Poliziano's poetry, he was a friend of Pietro *Bembo and mixed with the scholars of the *Platonic Academy. In 1476 he entered the service of Pino Ordelaffi in Forlì. After a period in *Venice, he was appointed professor of humanities at the University of Florence, and then at *Pisa. He wrote various Latin poems, including *Bucolica* modelled on *Virgil, an *epic poem on the capture of Volterra by *Federigo da Montefeltro (*Volaterrais*), and a poem on a the Medici tournament of 1475 (*Hastiludium*). [LChi]

NANI, GIAMBATTISTA (1616–78). *Venetian patrician and historian. Nani combined intellectual activities with a distinguished public career, notably as member of the Venetian senate, where his speeches were heard with great attention, and as

ambassador to France between 1643 and 1648. Appointed historian to the Republic in 1652, he wrote about the period 1613–71. His *Istoria della Repubblica Veneziana*, composed in a deliberately plain style, was published between 1662 and 1679, and translated into French and English. [See also HISTORIOGRAPHY.] [UPB]

NANNINI, REMIGIO (*c*.1521–81). *Dominican friar, author of secular and religious works, including *Poesie in lode della Madonna*, editor, and translator. His *translations include the biblical *Epistole e Evangeli con annotazioni morali* (1570), *Ovid's *Heroides* (which he afterwards disowned), Aemilius Probus, and *Petrarch. He edited works by *Guicciardini, *Pontano, and St Thomas *Aquinas. [CG]

Naples

1. Before 1600

Consisting roughly of the southern half of the Italian peninsula, the Kingdom of Naples, during the *Renaissance, was the largest state in Italy and its key political player. Founded in 1130 as a single entity with *Sicily by Norman invaders, who had united the various Greek and *Lombard principalities of the area, it was subsequently ruled by the *Hohenstaufen (1189–1266), the House of *Anjou (1266–1435), and the House of *Aragon (1435–1501), before falling to the kings of *Spain, who ruled it as a colony, under a viceroy, from 1504 until 1713. When the Anjou kings were expelled from Sicily and their capital Palermo in 1282, Naples became a separate and independent kingdom, and remained so until the advent of the Spanish, except for a brief period of reunion (1442–58) under Alfonso I 'the Magnanimous', who took the title of 'King of the Two Sicilies' in 1403. The city of Naples became the capital, and other cities, some of which had once flourished as independent states, gradually succumbed to the centralizing policies of the monarchy and the relentless exactions of the powerful *feudal lords who held sway in most areas of the kingdom. A cosmopolitan and multilingual country, it was the scene of much violence and warfare, suffering repeated invasions and internecine feuding. Consequently there was little solidarity between or within classes, and only minimal loyalty to the state.

The cultural life of the kingdom was largely dependent on royal patronage, and thus centred on the capital and *court, though some feudal lords did promote cultural activity in the provinces (the *Acquaviva at Atri and Nardo for instance, or the Sanseverino at Salerno—which also boasted one of the oldest *universities in Europe, famous for its *medical school). Under the Hohenstaufen the court, in Sicily, was at the avant-garde of what was to become Italian literature [see FREDERICK II; SICILIAN SCHOOL]. Under the Anjous, in Naples, it mainly functioned as a vehicle for the transmission of French culture [see FRENCH INFLUENCES, I], but it continued to enjoy great renown (*Petrarch elected King Robert to be his examiner for the laureateship), and reached its apogee under the Aragonese, who, to boost their legitimacy and enhance their prestige, promoted *humanism (*Panormita, *Valla, *Pontano), though the Kingdom always remained a lively centre of *Aristotelian and *scholastic studies, based on the universities of Salerno and Naples [see NIFO, AGOSTINO]. Throughout the centuries it also kept alive its Greek heritage [see GREEK INFLUENCES; GREEK WRITING IN ITALY], especially in Terra d'Otranto (Il *Galateo), and it witnessed the production of a wealth of literature in Latin, especially at the time of humanists such as Pontano and *Sannazaro.

Much was also written in the local vernaculars, right up to the Renaissance and beyond (*Masuccio Salernitano, Diomede *Carafa, *Passero), but from the mid-14th c., when the *Florentines acquired a monopoly in economic and political affairs, Naples gradually succumbed to the linguistic hegemony of Tuscan, whose victory is normally dated to the publication of Sannazaro's *Arcadia [see also QUESTIONE DELLA LINGUA]. Under the Spanish, who sought to impose cultural and religious conformity, the court lost its cultural prominence, but by then, and despite its political separateness, Naples had come to participate fully in the cultural trends of the rest of Italy. *Petrarchism enjoyed a great vogue in the 16th c., with Vittoria *Colonna, *Tansillo, *Terracina; there was

hot debate, here as elsewhere, between the supporters of *Ariosto and Torquato *Tasso (Tasso, of course, lived in the South for many years); and in the second half of the century Naples produced some of the more original Italian writers of the day (*Della Porta, *Bruno, *Campanella, *Marino).

[EGH]

See *Storia di Napoli* (1967–78); J. H. Bentley, *Politics and Culture in Renaissance Naples* (1987); F. Tateo, *L'umanesimo meridionale* (1976).

2. 1600 onwards

In the early 17th c. *marinismo and *dialect literature (*Cortese and *Basile) both flourished in Naples. In the 18th c. a thriving civic, political, and philosophical culture of European importance (the elder *Giannone, *Vico, *Genovesi) developed alongside a literature which operated as a closed circuit of communication between political elites and intellectuals in the Court (from 1734 the *Bourbon dynasty ruled the Kingdom of Naples, embracing all the mainland South and *Sicily), as well as in theatres, salons, and *academies. This was characterized by displays of technical dexterity in various registers of Italian, Neapolitan, and Latin.

The triumph of the reactionary movement *sanfedismo* (led by Cardinal Ruffo) after the revolution of 1799, and the subsequent restoration of the Bourbons (1815–60) after the *Napoleonic regime (1805–15), deepened the rift between *liberal intellectuals and the political system. *Publishers and *journalists geared literary production increasingly to the market and an enlarged reading public. Intellectuals emphasized the social uses of literature (Genovesi), the need to go beyond *purism (*Puoti), and the close link between content and form (*De Sanctis), and drew attention to the inadequacies of literary Italian and its remoteness from everyday language, which was still, for all classes and all purposes, dialect. Various forms of hybridism emerged, particularly after *Unification (1860). *Theatre, poetry, and song (*Di Giacomo) used an Italianized form of Neapolitan comprehensible in the rest of the peninsula, whereas prose fiction and journalism used Italian with dialect interferences (*Mastriani, *Serao). The best results of the interweaving of dialect and literary Italian are in Di Giacomo's prose fiction. There was also a new tendency for Neapolitan culture (evident in *Croce's historical work) to present itself as at once detached from and bound to the rest of the nation. The literary tradition was imbued with a sense of

Napoleon and the French Revolution

daily life in Naples as a form of spectacle or theatre in itself (as Goethe was one of the first to note). The feeling that Naples was 'outside history' was related to the sense of provincial isolation produced by the Bourbon restoration and confirmed by the Unification, after which the city and its intellectuals became ever more marginalized with respect to wider Italian economic and political realities.

From the late 19th c. the cultural industry in the city favoured the development of close relations (and conflicts) between Neapolitan writers, which led to striking family resemblances in their work, whatever genre they practised. Figures such as Mastriani, Di Giacomo, Serao, *Bracco, Ferdinando *Russo, Raffaele *Viviani, and the *Futurist *Cangiullo were often at the same time journalists, novelists, *diarists, and dramatists. Nearly all of them also wrote songs, as if the Neapolitan literary language demanded to be recited or sung. The song-publishing business in the city distributed its products internationally in this pre-mass media period, and perfected a form of self-presentation in which otherness and marginality were translated into the eternal typology of 'art'.

After *World War II Neapolitan culture was subjected to the industrialization and modernization that occurred in the country as a whole. Its fiction, song, and *cinema became 'genres' produced in *Rome or *Milan. Local cultural production collapsed, and many intellectuals left the city, including *De Filippo, *La Capria, *Marotta. Those who remained (such as *Pomilio, and *Prisco) tended to find themselves alienated from the nation and from the city itself. By the 1990s, however, there were some welcome signs of local cultural regeneration. [See also POPULAR SONG.]

[MLS]

Napoleon and the French Revolution. Although the *Enlightenment ideas which fostered the French Revolution were widespread among Italian intellectuals, many were horrified by the course it took, though some tried vainly to promote middle-of-the-road reformist projects. A few welcomed the Revolution—for instance Filippo Buonarroti, an Italian *Jacobin émigré who agitated for the invasion of Italy. The Directory, however, was more concerned with French security than with exporting revolution, and launched Napoleon's Italian campaign of 1796–7 as a way to acquire both military bases and counters to be used in truce or peace negotiations. One of Napoleon's first acts was to hand *Venice over to *Austria with the

Treaty of Campoformio, arousing the odium of *Foscolo and other Italian patriots. The first and most important of the Italian republics, the Repubblica Cisalpina, was founded in 1797. By 1805 it had become the Kingdom of Italy, with Napoleon himself crowned in *Milan. Similarly the Parthenopean Republic, founded in *Naples in 1799, became the Kingdom of Naples under the rule first of Joseph Bonaparte and then of Joachim Murat.

French government, particularly in Naples, was not always unpopular, but in general it subordinated the interests of the Italian people to those of France. French laws and regulations were often introduced, high taxes were imposed in the occupied regions, and large numbers of art works were expropriated to the Louvre. Nevertheless, between 1799 and 1814 most of the Italian peninsula had its first taste, if not of freedom and autonomy, at least of political unity. Many *Risorgimento fighters trained in Napoleon's army, and many protagonists of *Romanticism were, at some time or other, officials in his bureaucracy. Many influential Italian writers, including Vincenzo *Monti, *Giordani, *Gioia, and the young Foscolo, praised him publicly at some stage in their career, whatever their reservations and later criticisms; the most balanced assessment of his impact was offered by *Manzoni in 'Il cinque maggio', the poem he wrote on Napoleon's death in 1821. Napoleon used modern forms of patronage, such as state bureaucracy, incentives to publishers and printers, better educational provisions to gain the consensus of the intellectuals, with the result that more writers than ever could derive an income, or even make a living, from their work. The benefits of Napoleonic rule for Italy's cultural life, social and political cohesion, and economic advancement can be measured by the failure of *Restoration governments to set the clock back. [GC]

See S. Woolf, *A History of Italy 1790–1870* (1979); J. A. Davis, 'War and Society in Napoleonic Italy', in J. A. Davis and P. Ginsborg (eds.), *Society and Politics in the Age of the Risorgimento* (1991).

NAPOLI-SIGNORELLI, PIETRO (1731–1815). *Neapolitan polygraph [see POLIGRAFI] who was long resident abroad, notably in Madrid (1765–88). His *Storia critica dei teatri antichi e moderni* (ten volumes in its definitive 1813 edition) was the first and for a long time the only work of its kind in Italian. A rich but uneven compilation, it asserts Italian *theatrical supremacy but is stronger in other areas such as Spanish drama.   [JMAL]

NAPPI, CESARE (*c.*1440–1518). *Bolognese notary who collected in his vast *Palladium eruditum* both his own literary works, the best known of which is the facetious tale *I negromanti*, and the correspondence and poetry of his friends and fellow members of the Bolognese literary circle around Battista *Spagnoli. His *Memoriale* is among the few family *diaries surviving from Bologna.   [CJ]

NARDI, BRUNO (1884–1968) was the first modern scholar to insist, against *Croce, on a knowledge of medieval science and philosophy for a correct understanding of *Dante's texts. His principal collections of writings are *Saggi di filosofia dantesca* (1930), *Dante e la cultura medievale* (1942), and *Dal 'Convivio' alla 'Commedia'* (1960).   [DF]

NARDI, IACOPO (1476–1563) was an influential Florentine politician and patriot, eventually exiled for his anti-*Medici views. He wrote a history of *Florence, and two occasional *theatre compositions based on stories from the *Decameron; like those of *Galeotto del Carretto, they represent a transition between medieval and *humanist conceptions of dramaturgy. [See also COMEDY.]   [RAA]

NATALI, GIOVANNI GIROLAMO, see NADAL, GIOVANNI GIROLAMO.

Nationalism. Italian often restricts the term 'nazionalismo' to the ideology of the *Associazione nazionalista italiana* (see below), but the term may also refer to all kinds of thought about the Italian nation. The history of the terms 'nazione' and 'nazionalismo' is closely linked with further terms such as 'italianità', 'Italia', 'patria', 'popolo', and, from *Unification to the *Fascist period, 'razza' or 'stirpe italica'. This loose and protean vocabulary has been used to talk about a whole range of personal and collective problems.

It is *Dante's writings which effectively mark the beginnings of national or (on some readings) nationalistic discourse in Italy. Over the five centuries between Dante and the French Revolution the question of Italy keeps recurring, sometimes being given famous literary expression, as in *Petrarch's 'Italia mia' (*Canz.* 128), or the last chapter of *Machiavelli's *Principe*. There are in this period three dimensions to the issue. The first is

linguistic and concerns the choice of a form of Italian as an intellectual and literary medium in preference to Latin or other European vernaculars (notably French). By the 16th c. that meant choosing the literary language of Dante, Petrarch, and *Boccaccio over other regional vernaculars. [See HISTORY OF THE ITALIAN LANGUAGE; QUESTIONE DELLA LINGUA]. The second dimension was a pride in Italians' cultural achievements and their privileged relationship to classical antiquity. The third was political: whilst it was only in rare cases (*Cola di Rienzo, for example) that any form of unified Italian polity was projected, the name of Italy did come to encode a concern to maintain local peace and freedom within the North and Centre of the peninsula in the face of external influences and intercommunal strife. But throughout this period the words 'nazione' and 'patria' were at least as likely to refer to a municipal community or place of origin—*Florence or *Siena, for example—as to Italy.

It is only with the *Enlightenment, and more dramatically with the French Revolution and the *Napoleonic era, that the language of nationalism is used to think about social issues and to express aspirations for an Italian state. French domination of most of the peninsula after 1796 introduced notions of national sovereignty and the popular will into government, and gave Italy's elites glimpses of the benefits (and dangers) of administrative and economic modernization. But those very developments were often frustrated by the arbitrary, expansionist nature of the regimes installed by Napoleon. Ugo *Foscolo is perhaps the emblematic literary figure to emerge from this contradiction. A soldier, *journalist, academic, and *exile, he attempts in *De' sepolcri* (1807) to found a patriotic myth, at once elegiac and defiant, around the tombs of the nation's great men.

During the *Risorgimento, different groups used the language of nationhood to project often diametrically opposed visions of a future Italy. For *Mazzini, for example, the Italian people had a divine mission to shake off the rule of monarchs and priests and become a unitary republic based on individual liberty. For Vincenzo *Gioberti, a socially conservative confederation of states under *papal leadership could re-establish the peninsula's cultural and religious primacy. After *1848, moderate opinion in Northern and Central Italy increasingly associated nationhood with law and order, monarchy, and a paternalistic vision of progress.

After Unification, the language of nationalism becomes implicated in a whole variety of ways with the problems of the new state. Even if many intellectuals and leaders could now wield that language with confidence, the same could not be said of the majority of the population. Some *peasants encountered during *Garibaldi's invasion of *Sicily in 1860 apparently thought that when the General invoked 'la Talia' he was referring to his wife. Nevertheless, the language of nationalism came to be used by the elites in describing, and disagreeing about, a wide variety of problems associated with cultural modernity, state formation, and the state's legitimacy in the eyes of the population. Following a famous dictum of Massimo *D'Azeglio that, with Italy made, there remained the need to 'make the Italians', many saw their task as precisely that. Nationalism also became both the sign of loyalty to the state and a means of identifying threats and outsiders.

On the other hand, many individuals and groups dissatisfied with the Italian state voiced their opposition in national terms. For the followers of Garibaldi and Mazzini before 1870, the new '*Piedmontized' Italy, lacking Rome, was a betrayal of the nation. Enrico *Corradini's Associazione nazionalista italiana (1910–23) based its anti-democratic, imperialist ideology on an idea of the nation conceived in racial and spiritual terms. The state also made many efforts to Italianize its citizens. The nation-building drive is exemplified by Edmondo *De Amicis' school-reader *Cuore (1886). Violent, sentimental, and hugely popular for decades after its publication, this fictional diary of a school year reflects contemporary efforts to make patriotism into a civic religion. The social regimentation and leadership cult of the Fascist regime, which made a militaristic nationalism its official credo, have also been seen as an attempt to 'make Italians'.

Italy is unusual in the degree to which jingoistic nationalism has been politically and culturally marginalized since *World War II. Furthermore, the ideas associated with nationhood were in some respects marginal to the great Catholic and *Communist sub-cultures, which were both international in their outlook, and had sub-national roots in particular regions. Nevertheless, it is in the postwar era that mass *education, industrialization, migration, the spread of spectator sport, and the introduction of *television have helped transform collective identities in a way that the deliberate efforts of the state could not achieve alone. The language of nationhood has been used in many different and conflicting ways to describe these changes and make sense of them as collective experiences.

Today almost all Italians, even secessionists, or intellectuals who lament that Italy is not a 'normal' nation, or politicians who wholly disagree with each other, use the vocabulary of nationalism. [See also PAPACY AND THE CATHOLIC CHURCH.]   [JD]

See G. Bollati, 'L'italiano', in R. Romano and C. Vivanti (eds.), Storia d'Italia, vol. i: I caratteri originali (1972); M. Serena Sapegno, '"Italia" "Italiani"', in A. Asor Rosa (ed.), Letteratura italiana, vol. v: Le questioni (1986).

NATOLI, LUIGI (1857–1941). *Novelist and *journalist, who wrote scrupulously researched *historical novels set in his native *Sicily, under the name William Galt. The most successful, I Beati Paoli (1909–10), relates the adventures of an early 18th-c. secret society. Praise from Umberto *Eco has led to the recent republication of several of his novels.   [PBarn]

NATTA, ALESSANDRO, see WORLD WAR II.

Naturalism, see FRENCH INFLUENCES; REALISM; VERISMO.

NAVAGERO, ANDREA (1483–1529) was a *Venetian *humanist, poet, *historian, and diplomat. He succeeded Marcantonio *Sabellico as historian of the Venetian Republic and was involved in important diplomatic missions. His classical learning led him to editorial collaboration with Aldo *Manuzio. He wrote *Latin poetry in the style of Catullus, official orations for the Venetian senate, and vernacular poems in the *Petrarchist mode.   [PLR]

Neapolitan, see NAPLES.

'Nedda', see VERGA, GIOVANNI.

NEERA (pseud. of Anna Zuccari) (1846–1918). *Novelist and poet. Her *autobiographical writings tell of a poor, isolated childhood near *Milan. She married in 1871 and entered Milanese literary circles. Her fiction, beginning with Un romanzo (1876), extols maternity as the only proper vocation for women as well as a source of surprising passion. She summarized her conservative views in Idee di una donna (1903), having given them more practical form in the Dizionario d'igiene per le famiglie (1881), written jointly with Paolo *Mantegazza. She was a friend of *Capuana and her work was admired by *Croce. Recent criticism focuses on the ambivalence of her anti-*feminist defence of women. [UJF]

NEGRI, ADA (1870–1945). Poet, *novelist, and one of the first significant working-class voices in Italian literature. Brought up in poverty in *Milan by a widowed mother, as she describes in her *autobiographical novel, *Stella mattutina* (1912), she became a teacher through her own and her mother's determination. She married in 1896, though the marriage did not last. The birth of a daughter occasioned *Maternità* (1904), a collection of poetry in the late *Romantic manner which both celebrates her motherhood and expresses pain at her own mother's death. Other poetry, beginning with *Fatalità* (1892), voiced social and political protest, though her later work was blander. Like many other *women writers of her time, she bemoaned women's lot, yet criticized all but the poorest working women and *feminists. She won the *Mussolini prize for artistic achievement in 1931 and was made a member of the Reale *Accademia d'Italia in 1940. Her enthusiasm for *Fascism has damaged her subsequent reputation. [UJF]

NEGRO, MARIN (16th c.). Nothing is known of this author of the *Venetian *comedy *La pace*, performed in 1561. In terms of contemporary *theatre polemic, this play takes an anti-academic line, making use of *dialects, like the *commedia dell'arte*, and rejecting formal theory in favour of proven audience appeal. [RAA]

NELLI, FRANCESCO (d.1363). *Florentine notary close to both *Petrarch and *Boccaccio. Petrarch wrote many letters to him, addressing him as 'Simonides' and dedicating his *Seniles* to him. He died of the *plague in *Naples, where he was part of the entourage of the seneschal Niccolò *Acciaiuoli. [MP]

NELLI, IACOPO ANGELO (1673–1767). *Sienese writer, and a priest and tutor in *Rome. He is best known as a precursor of *Goldoni, and is somewhat closer to him than his fellow *Tuscans Girolamo *Gigli and Giovanni Battista *Fagiuoli. Between 1731 and 1758 he published sixteen *comedies, though some, such as *La serva padrona* (1709), had been written much earlier. They combine Molièresque treatment of character with *commedia dell'arte* intrigue and racy colloquial dialogue. The liveliest, *Serve al forno*, anticipates Goldoni's *Le massere*, with its brawling housemaids.

He also wrote humorous verse, a *tragedy, *Il Pompeiano*, and an Italian grammar. [JMAL]

Nencia da Barberino (c.1470). Poem in *ottava rima* attributed to Lorenzo de' *Medici, or sometimes to Bernardo *Giambullari, and certainly a product of Lorenzo's circle in the early years of his rule. In its absorption and transformation of popular rustic themes, it is close to *lyric poetry of this period by Lorenzo and his associates. Surviving in four manuscripts, each with a version of differing length, the poem is cast as a monologue by the *peasant lover Vallera to his beloved shepherdess Nencia, in a light-hearted *parody aimed at a sophisticated audience. Its language, the aspirations attributed to Vallera, and the description of Nencia and her interests satirize the artificial tradition of the classical *pastoral as much as the humble rustic and his clumsy passion. [JEE]

NENCIONI, ENRICO, see AMERICAN INFLUENCES.

Neoavanguardia. Avant-garde movement, dated approximately 1956–68, in Italian literature, but not covering all avant-garde art of this period, and termed 'neo' to distinguish it from the 'historic' avant-gardes (as they were called) of *Futurism, Dada, and *Surrealism of the 1910s. The founding of Luciano *Anceschi's *il *verri* in 1956 brought together a group of writers who took up a challenge posed by Elio *Vittorini in *Il *Menabò* in 1961. Vittorini had argued that the French *nouveau roman* was much closer to the reality of the industrial world, through its new use of language, than literature which explicitly took the industrial world for its subject matter. The group around *il verri* held that form, as opposed to content, offered the only possibility of bringing about ideological change. A writer who attempts to criticize or delve behind the images promoted by and for a given social and economic system, and who uses, to do so, the language of that system, merely reproduces that system and perpetuates a mystification. Therefore the avant-garde artist innovates at the level of form, by destroying the ordered system of conventional language. The disorder that he creates is an open expression of conflicts in reality which the system wishes to homogenize into a spurious harmony.

The *Neoavanguardia* aimed to 'de-provincialize' Italian culture by disseminating the most innovative ideas current in the Western world (in economics, sociology, ethnology, linguistics, and aesthetics),

Neoclassicism

while at the same time using their own literary works to subvert the comfortable place literature (and particularly poetry) had in Italian culture and ideology. The 1961 anthology *I novissimi* programmatically collected poems by Alfredo *Giuliani, Antonio *Porta, Edoardo *Sanguineti, Nanni *Balestrini, and Elio *Pagliarani, which subverted conventional linguistic, stylistic, and imaginative norms. The five very different poets had in common a desire to open up *lyric poetry to the meanings carried by the objects and institutions of the modern world, rather than impose a subjective sensibility on reality. Meanwhile Umberto *Eco and Sanguineti wrote essays explicitly expounding the theories behind the artistic practice. A meeting of these and other writers in October 1963 led to their adopting the name *Gruppo 63, and from June 1967 to July 1969 the periodical *Quindici* was the movement's mouthpiece.

The theoretical polemics of the *Neoavanguardia* targeted *Neorealism for its attempt to bring about change in the real world without first challenging the rationality and homogeneity of the language and thought which buttressed the status quo. Where the culture of the anti-*Fascist *Resistance had abhorred irrationality and formalism, the *Neoavanguardia* explored precisely these elements in pre-Fascist Italian culture, nurturing a deep suspicion of coherence in literature. One of the characteristic ways in which the poets of the movement brought the real world into lyric poetry was by either including in their poems, or building their poems out of, 'found' material—texts or fragments of texts having a totally non-literary provenance. In the *novel, the movement's major contribution was to introduce the aesthetics and techniques of the French *nouveau roman* into Italian narrative. As is often the case with avant-gardes, the writers were regarded as a spectacle for amusement and bewilderment, while their works of art were rarely, if ever, subjected to serious analysis or appreciation. Exactly the same fate befell the Italian historical avant-garde of *Futurism.

[CGW]

See C. Wagstaff, 'The Neo-Avantgarde', in M. Caesar and P. Hainsworth (eds.), *Writers and Society in Contemporary Italy* (1984).

Neoclassicism. The term points to a revival of interest in Graeco-Roman authors and a fresh wave of *imitation of their work, but it has such a wide reference and interpretation that its usefulness in literary history (as distinct from art history) is limited.

In established English and French usage it refers to writers operating as early as the 1660s, but it has been applied in Italy to authors flourishing a good century later, on the strength of some analogies between the contents of their work and what was being produced by visual artists at the time. The best-known connection is between *Foscolo's unfinished poem *Le grazie* and *Canova's group in the Woburn marbles, but one might also mention the increasingly available folios of line-drawings reproducing ancient masterpieces, which had a strong impact on *Leopardi's imagination, and *Giordani's descriptions of sculptures by Canova and Tenerani.

The prefix 'neo-' suggests that the principles of order, decorum, propriety, and balance prevailing during the *Renaissance needed to be affirmed anew when the *Enlightenment had curbed much of the flamboyance of the *Baroque age. It alludes also to the new finds from the excavations of Herculaneum and Pompeii, which had begun in the late 1730s and which inspired theorists like Winckelmann and Francesco *Milizia and artists like Canova, Mengs, David, and Piranesi, not to mention countless craftsmen and engravers who supplied an extensive international market and fostered a new taste for artefacts and decorations based on ancient works of art. It is further applied to the idealizing celebration of a fictitious *pastoral society in an equally fictitious *Arcadia. Some forms of neoclassicism were generally conservative, insisting on the imitation of ancient art as an immutable criterion of excellence. But there is too a revolutionary neoclassicism which affirms a moralizing conception of political renewal derived from the writings of Plutarch. Initially it takes its models from republican Rome, but, in its orientation towards a new aristocracy, it turns more to the imperial age and creates the *style Empire*.

Overall the concept of neoclassicism seems to imply a set of attitudes that are not only aesthetic but social—elitism, a reliance on well-tested tradition, a sense of balance and propriety usually associated with good breeding and education. Nevertheless, Italian literary neoclassicism is hardly distinguishable from *classicism, most of whose adherents and advocates during *pre-Romanticism and early *Romanticism saw themselves as part of a tradition going back at least to the Renaissance. The very term was unknown to them, and is not even recorded in the *Tommaseo–Bellini dictionary of 1865.

[GC]

See A. Frattini, *Il neoclassicismo e Ugo Foscolo*

(1965); M. Praz, *On Neoclassicism* (1972); H. Honour, *Neoclassicism* (1973).

Neo-Guelfism, see GIOBERTI, VINCENZO; GUELFS AND GHIBELLINES; POLITICAL THOUGHT.

Neoplatonism. A number of *Renaissance Italian thinkers, artists, and poets, among them *Pico della Mirandola, *Benivieni, *Michelangelo, Francesco *Patrizi the Younger, and *Bruno, were much influenced, if often only indirectly, by the thought of Plotinus (AD 205–70) and by the ancient Platonists who followed his interpretation of Plato. But Marsilio *Ficino was pre-eminent, given the depth of his understanding and the ardour of his enthusiasm, and given his unequalled mastery of the ancient texts, many of which, including Plato's collected *dialogues and Plotinus' *Enneads*, he rendered into Latin for the first time, supplying them with *commentary. He thus initiated in 15th-c. *Florence a Neoplatonic revival which subsequently influenced European *court culture, literary, artistic, and social, from Portugal to England and Hungary.

The Italian Neoplatonists came to Plato and Plotinus by way of *Augustine in the twin beliefs that Plotinus was the arch-interpreter of Plato—at times even more profound—and that Plato himself was the culminating 'theologian' of a line that stretched back, by way of Philolaus, Pythagoras, and Orpheus, to Hermes Trismegistus [see HERMETICISM] and Zoroaster. This gentile succession was parallel to, and consonant with, the succession of Hebrew prophets beginning with Moses. Both prophetic traditions were preparatory for Christianity and for the Platonic philosophy adumbrated in the opening of St John's Gospel, in St Paul's Epistles, and in the writings then attributed to St Paul's disciple, Dionysius the Areopagite (but now assigned to a late 5th-c. follower of Proclus). For the Italian Neoplatonists read back into both traditions the unitary metaphysics which Plotinus had extracted from Plato's diverse works, and which elevates the One beyond all being as the supreme principle, ineffable, unknowable, the goal of mystical union, of the flight of the alone to the alone, in the famous closing phrase of the *Enneads*.

Hence they were drawn to the *via negativa*, central to the thought of the Areopagite, but which they supposed Plato had set out earlier in the negative propositions in the second half of the *Parmenides*, long revered in the Plotinian tradition as the 'inmost sanctuary' of his philosophy-theology. Hence too

their fascination with theologizing ancient mythology and poetry in order to discover the metaphysics of the One (identified with Uranus) and, subsequent to the One, of pure Mind (identified with Cronos or Saturn, and the principle of being and intelligibility and the first existent), and then of Soul (identified with Zeus or Jupiter, and the source of all motion as the self-moved). Their Neoplatonic psychology is similarly triadic: the soul's crown or flower is its unity; its highest faculty is intuitive understanding (as with the angels); and in itself it is life and motion. We therefore exercise a providential, Jovian care over those below us, a Saturnian meditation on the intelligible realm within us, and a Uranian yearning—defined in terms both of eros and of the will—for the One which is our first and final cause. Indeed, this triadic structure is found at every level of reality, and the Italian Neoplatonists were able to think of it, following *Augustine, as 'the footsteps of the Trinity'. The system suggested, however, a unique role for Soul as All Soul or as the World Soul, and thus (depending on its various identifications) for the Holy Ghost (or Sophia or the Son or Nature), both as the animating principle and as the whole of which all creatures, including the star spirits and demons, are parts. Moreover, following various striking axioms in Plato, Plotinus, and Proclus, each animate part can be thought of as the whole, though each according to its capacity: thus each of us, in a way, is the cosmos, is Soul, with all the various Christological and pantheistic implications.

Given Porphyry's captivating portrait of Plotinus as a sage attended by a guardian deity, Ficino in particular was also moved to set out a refined Platonic demonology and to revive the ancient hermetic and gnostic notion that each soul is a fallen star demon yearning to fly back to its celestial home, to escape its slavery in matter. Arguably indeed, Renaissance Neoplatonism resurrected several ancient heretical ideas, those we associate with Gnosticism, Origenism, Arianism, and Pelagianism. Certainly, by emphasizing the occult, *magical, *astrological, *numerological, and demonological elements in Plato, especially as highlighted by such post-Plotinian Neoplatonists as Iamblichus, Synesius, Hermias, and Proclus, Ficino and his followers produced an Orphic-Pythagorean-Platonic-Proclan-Christian vision of the world, its beings, and its animation that many at the time considered unorthodox (though Ficino was able to fend off any official condemnation of his views).

Neorealism

The revival of Neoplatonism's light metaphysics and its deployment of solarian imagery and motifs may have prepared the way for Sun-centred thinking even if did not cause the Copernican revolution, but a more obvious and lasting impact resulted from its other emphases: on the disciplinary and ascetic role of eros as love and desire; on the primacy of Beauty as the splendour of the Ideas in their collectivity as Truth; on the notion of divine madness or rapture (*mania* or *furor*); on the need to bring the intellectual person to visionary faith by way of Platonic dialectic using Plato's works both as a propaedeutic (as in Augustine) and as a theological curriculum in their own right. In such a visionary scheme Plotinus thus becomes a Church Father, an evangelist, even a beloved son—Ficino transposes God's words in the Gospel accounts of Christ's baptism and transfiguration—in whom Plato is well pleased. This bold trope is indicative of the daring claims attending the Italian Neoplatonists' revival of Plato and of the Christian Neoplatonism which they believed he and his predecessors had anticipated, and to which Dionysius, Plotinus, and Augustine especially had borne subsequent witness.

[MA]

See P. O. Kristeller, *Studies in Renaissance Thought and Letters* (1956–93); J. Hankins, *Plato in the Italian Renaissance* (1990); M. Allen, *Synoptic Art: Marsilio Ficino on the History of Platonic Interpretation* (1998).

Neorealism. The struggle against *Fascism was widely felt to involve a renewal of Italian culture— hence 'neo'—and the search for a specifically Italian discourse with which to represent social reality, the source being identified in the *verismo* of Giovanni *Verga's *Sicilian narratives—hence 'realism'. In the desire to de-provincialize Italian narrative, models were also sought in North American writers from Herman Melville to John Steinbeck [see AMERICAN INFLUENCES]. As a rule, Neorealism's literary and cinematic narratives dealt with contemporary subject matter, anchored their stories in well-defined geographical and cultural locations, and concentrated on those sections of society which felt the effects of political and economic power rather than on individuals who wielded it. Neorealists belonged to a deep and widespread tendency in Italian culture which held literary formalism in deep suspicion for its elitism, its political irresponsibility, and its associations with what *Marxists called 'bourgeois decadence'— bourgeois culture's obsession with the ideal and the

irrational, and its privileging of form over content. Nevertheless it is probably more useful to see Neorealism in terms of a historical moment, from the start of the anti-*Fascist struggle in the 1930s to the 1960s, than in terms of specific characteristics.

The cultural tide of which Neorealism is a component embraced not only literary narrative but also poetry, fictional and documentary *cinema, painting (notably the work of Renato Guttuso, 1912–87), *photography, and non-fiction *publishing. In literary narrative memoirs, *autobiography and the essay-novel featured every bit as prominently as conventional fiction. Poets whose defence against Fascist conformity had been a *hermetic style, owing much to French *symbolism, evolved a more demotic manner, most noticeably Salvatore *Quasimodo. Cinema established Italy as a force to be contended with even in Hollywood, the very citadel of the victors and occupiers of a defeated Italy. In publishing, *Einaudi brought out a series of Italian *translations of books on anthropology and primitive myths and religions. Where the state held sway, Neorealism did not penetrate, and instead the exploitation of the media for propaganda purposes continued as though the lesson of Fascism had not been learnt—in *radio and *television broadcasting, and in cinema newsreels. Indeed, the conservative, Catholic state, which was deeply implicated in the Cold War against *Communism, was hostile to Neorealism; a powerful and influential junior minister of the time, Giulio Andreotti, publicly upbraided Vittorio *De Sica for depicting, in his film, *Umberto D.* (1952), a shameful picture, devoid of optimism and hope, of Italy's social provision for the vulnerable [see also CHRISTIAN DEMOCRATS]. For the state, culture's role was to guide the public with both political and ecclesiastical propaganda, and to provide consolation, entertainment, and escape from the hardships of daily life and work. For the Neorealists, culture's role was to provide knowledge and understanding of the realities of political, economic, and social life. In the cinema the state played a not inconsiderable role in killing off Neorealism by starving it of funds.

Even though many of its artists were *Communists, and the Italian Communist Party doggedly attacked anything it saw as non-realist art (for example, *Fellini's *La strada* of 1954), Neorealists were not doctrinaire *Marxists. With the exception of Luchino *Visconti, they were not Marxist historicists, nor did they espouse Soviet socialist realism. In the cinema, their politics were often *populist, the belief in the political force of the spontaneous goodness of the common people being classically demonstrated in *Rossellini's *Roma città aperta* (1945), although De Sica's films provided biting critiques of capitalism in the margins of his images, and De Santis and Visconti carried on open polemics over the class struggle. However, Marxist intellectuals used Neorealist works as weapons in political debate: Visconti's *Senso* (1954) was hailed as historical realism (in the Lukácsian sense), while De Sica was dismissed as a naturalist, and Fellini and Rossellini as bourgeois spiritualists.

Neorealism was never reportage, though Cesare *Zavattini aspired to it in the film he sponsored, *Amore in città* (1953). As is made plain by Italo *Calvino in his preface to the second edition (1964) of *Il *sentiero dei nidi di ragno* (1947), Neorealists aspired to a poetical expression of a personal vision and experience, albeit one shared by many who had experienced anti-Fascism and the war. In this perspective the range of Neorealist narrative can be seen to embrace narratives as diverse as *Silone's *Fontamara* (1930), *Pavese's *Paesi tuoi* (1941, but written in 1939), *Vittorini's *Conversazione in Sicilia* (1938–41), *Pratolini's *Il quartiere* (1944), Carlo *Levi's *Cristo si è fermato a Eboli* (1945), Primo *Levi's *Se questo è un uomo* (1947), Carlo *Cassola's *La ragazza di Bube* (1960), and *Fenoglio's *Il partigiano Johnny* (published in 1968). Rossellini's *Paisà* (1946), De Sica's *Ladri di biciclette* (1948), Visconti's *La terra trema* (1948), and De Santis' *Riso amaro* (1949) are all examples of Neorealist cinema at its best.

Only a small percentage of Italian films produced in the postwar decade were Neorealist, and yet that small body of work has probably had as much influence on the art of cinema as any body of work has ever had in any art form. Literary Neorealism, on the other hand, exerted its influence primarily in Italy. In the 1960s a new generation of writers and film makers had to make a brutal break with the Neorealist past in order to have any hope of acquiring an individual cultural identity [see NEO-AVANGUARDIA.]   [CGW]

See D. Heiney, *Three Italian Novelists: Moravia, Pavese, Vittorini* (1968); G. Tinazzi and M. Zancan (eds.), *Cinema e letteratura del neorealismo* (1983).

NERI, BONACCORSO, see HOUSEHOLD TREATISES.

NERI, IPPOLITO (1652–1708). Poet who studied *medicine at *Pisa and then was a pupil of Francesco *Redi, before becoming court doctor to the *Medici. He published a collection of *Rime* (1700) on various subjects and a *mock-heroic poem, *La presa di San Miniato* (1760), which draws on both Torquato *Tasso and *Tassoni. Some *libretti and *comedies have also been attributed to him.   [FC]

NERI, POMPEO, see ENLIGHTENMENT.

NERI MOSCOLI, see POESIA GIOCOSA.

NERLI, FILIPPO DE' (1485–1556). *Florentine patrician who wrote a chronicle of events in the city from 1215 to 1537. He was a member of the Orti Oricellari literary group, whose discussions provided the catalyst for *Machiavelli's writing of the *Discorsi*, and which furnished the conspirators of the 1522 anti-*Medicean plot. [See also RUCELLAI, BERNARDO.]   [SJM]

NERUCCI, GHERARDO (1828–1907). Pistoian teacher who collected traditional *Tuscan tales in *Sessanta novelle popolari montalesi* and songs, lullabies, and riddles in *Cincelle dei bambini* (both 1880). He related his experiences of the *1848 revolutions in *Ricordi storici del battaglione universitario toscano* (1891).   [PBarn]

NESI, GIOVANNI (1456–1506). *Florentine *Neoplatonist and disciple of *Ficino, active in civic affairs in the later 15th c. His *dialogue *De moribus* of 1484 treats *Aristotelian ethics as a prelude to Ficinian theology. His *Oraculum de novo saeculo* (1497) and his vernacular religious poetry press Neoplatonic elements into the service of *Savonarola's spiritual reforms. He also wrote *Petrarchist love lyrics in a Neoplatonic vein and, some time before 1499, a philosophical poem in imitation of *Dante.   [DK]

Newspapers, see JOURNALISM.

NIBBI, GINO, see ITALIAN WRITERS IN AUSTRALIA.

NICCODEMI, DARIO (1874–1934). Playwright, theatre director, and novelist, who staged the first production of *Pirandello's *Sei personaggi in cerca d'autore* in 1921. He wrote two novels and several plays in the manner of the 19th-c. French *pièce bien faite* [see THEATRE, 2], the best known being *Scampolo* (1916), and also left a volume of

Niccolai, Giulia

illuminating theatrical memories, *Tempo passato* (1929). [JAL]

NICCOLAI, GIULIA (1934–). *Milanese poet, who played a prominent part in avant-garde developments in the 1960s and 1970s [see NEO-AVANGUARDIA]. In 1972 she founded the review *Tam Tam* with Adriano *Spatola. Her particular interests were sound-poetry, visual, and nonsense poetry. *Harry's Bar e altre poesie (1969–80)* (1981) includes work in English, French, German, and Latin as well as Italian, all with a playfully absurd intent. [CO'B]

NICCOLI, NICCOLÒ (*c.*1365–1437) belonged to the generation of *Florentine *humanists gathered around *Salutati. An extraordinary collector of antiquities and classical books, he was considered an intransigent *classicist, and in this guise appears as a character in Leonardo *Bruni's *Dialogi ad Petrum Histrum*. Although involved in numerous disputes with fellow humanists, he was one of the great promoters of classical studies. No writings by him survive. [LB]

NICCOLINI, GIOVAN BATTISTA (1782–1861). Dramatist. Born near *Pisa into an aristocratic *Florentine family, he was an ardent republican as a young man. After a degree in law at Pisa, he lived and worked in Florence, partly for the Accademia della *Crusca. He was a friend of *Manzoni and defended the use of Florentine as a literary language. His earlier, more *neo-classical tragedies, beginning with a Euripidean *Polissena* (1810), already displayed patriotic, anti-absolutist ideas. His major successes, *Antonio Foscari* (1827), *Giovanni da Procida* (1830), and the anti-clerical *Arnaldo da Brescia* (1843), were historical *tragedies and even more forceful. He took little part in actual politics from *1848 onwards and eventually accepted the idea of an Italian *monarchy. [DO'G]

NICCOLINI, LAPO, see HOUSEHOLD TREATISES.

NICCOLÒ CIECO D'AREZZO (15th c.). *Improviser and writer of panegyric verse in a variety of metres, that reveals influences from both *Dante and *Petrarch. His presence is attested in *Venice, *Rome, *Florence, *Siena, and *Perugia, where he composed an encomiastic poem dedicated to the Emperor Sigismund (1433). His other panegyrics include praise of several of the states in which he was resident, of Popes Martin V and Eugenius IV, and of Francesco *Sforza (1435). His poetry was much admired in his day. [JEE]

NICCOLÒ DA CASOLA (d.*c.*1380). *Bolognese notary who wrote *Franco-Veneto poetry at the *Este *court in *Ferrara in the 1350s. *La guerra d'Attila*, of more than 37,000 lines, celebrates his patrons' ancestors as defenders of Italy against the Hun, and looks forwards to *Boiardo and *Ariosto in its mixture of battles, magic, and love adventures. [JP & JMS]

NICCOLÒ DA CORREGGIO (1450–1508). *Court poet. From the provincial nobility of *Ferrara, he became a courtier at a young age, serving first Borso and then Ercole d'*Este. He served as *condottiere* for the *Sforza of *Milan, and married the daughter of the famous soldier Bartolommeo Colleoni. An associate at Ferrara of *Boiardo and Il *Pistoia, he was court poet to Beatrice d'Este while at Milan, a friend and correspondent of Isabella d'Este, and later master of revels and theatrical producer for Lucrezia *Borgia in Ferrara. His main literary accomplishment is the play *Favola di Cefalo* (1487), in five acts in *ottava rima*, interspersed with choral interludes in other metres; though of less merit than *Poliziano's *Orfeo*, which it seeks to imitate, it played a part in the development of theatrical spectacles in Ferrara, introducing modern vernacular drama alongside *translations from the classics. Subsequently Correggio composed a poem in *ottava rima* dedicated to Isabella d'Este, the *Fabula Psiches et Cupidinis*. He also wrote a *canzoniere* in a variety of metres. Correggio's verse lacks stylistic merit, but is inventive and fluent. [JEE]

NICCOLÒ DA VERONA (mid-13th c.). Author of two large narrative poems in a relatively refined form of *Franco-Veneto. The *Prise de Pampelune* deals with Carolingian material, whilst the *Pharsale* presents a *romance version of material from Lucan. Both were written for the *Este *court in *Ferrara. [See also EPIC.] [PH]

NICCOLÒ LEONICENO, see MEDICINE.

NICHOLAS V, see LIBRARIES; PAPACY AND THE CATHOLIC CHURCH; RENAISSANCE; VATICAN LIBRARY.

NICHOLAS OF CUSA (1401–64) was a German philosopher, church reformer, and cardinal. Born at Kues on the Moselle, he attended the University of *Padua from 1417 to 1423, receiving a doctorate in canon *law. His exposure to *humanism in Italy made him an enthusiastic *manuscript hunter—he later discovered twelve lost plays by Plautus—and book collector, though he never mastered classical Latin or acquired knowledge of Greek. Returning to Germany, he studied briefly at Cologne before becoming secretary to the Archbishop of Trier in 1427. At the Council of Basel he began as a leading spokesman of conciliarism, but by 1436 had shifted his allegiance to the *papal party. He was elevated to the cardinalate in 1449 and the following year was appointed papal legate to Germany and Bishop of Bressanone (Brixen), where he attempted, unsuccessfully, to reform the clergy and monasteries. Influenced by the *Neoplatonism of Proclus and Pseudo-Dionysius the Areopagite, he wrote several treatises developing the theme of learned ignorance: the paradoxical notion that the highest form of human knowledge is the recognition that our finite minds can never know the infinite God, in whom there is a coincidence of opposites, or meeting of all contradictions. [JK]

NICOLETTI, PAOLO, see PAOLO VENETO.

NICOLINI, GIUSEPPE (1788–1855). A youthful follower of *neoclassicism, who embraced *Romanticism while criticising its excesses in *Del fanatismo e della tolleranza* (1820). He contributed to *Il *Conciliatore*, but lost his teaching post after the 1821 insurrection. He translated from Byron and published a biographical essay on him (1834). [MPC]

NICOLÒ DA CASOLA, see NICCOLÒ DA CASOLA.

NICOLÒ DA VERONA, see NICCOLÒ DA VERONA.

NICOLUCCI, GIOVAN BATTISTA, see PIGNA, IL.

NIEVO, IPPOLITO (1831–61). The most important Italian *novelist of the mid-19th c., and a man of action whose dynamic personality sets him apart from the conservative majority of Italian writers. He was born in *Padua, but spent his childhood between *Mantua and the Friuli, where his family owned the castle of Colloredo di Montalbano, his life there later providing the material for the earlier chapters of the *Confessioni di un italiano*. As a teenager he took an active part in the *1848 revolution in Mantua, and then continued with anti-*Austrian subversion as a law student at Pavia. In 1857 he was forced to flee to *Milan, where he wrote for various reviews and fell in love with his cousin. Having played a leading role in *Garibaldi's expedition to *Sicily in 1860, he was drowned when the ship on which he was returning to *Naples was wrecked.

His short literary career, prosecuted in tandem with his political career, was remarkably prolific and diverse, whilst at the same time underscored by consistent moral and political principles. He began as a poet with two collections of lyrics, *Versi* (1854 and 1855), modelled on *Parini and *Giusti, both of whom had emphasised the educative force of poetry. He published further collections of verse, *Le lucciole* (1858) and *Gli amori garibaldini* (1860), and two verse *tragedies, *I Capuani* (1857) and *Spartaco* (1857). He was nevertheless mainly a prose writer, producing many *novelle* (collected as *Novelliere campagnolo* (1956)) and three *historical novels—*Angelo di bontà* (1856), set against the background of the decline and fall of the Venetian republic, *Il conte pecoraio* (1857), set in contemporary Friuli after 1855, and *Le confessioni di un ottuagenario* (published posthumously in 1867 and later retitled *Confessioni di un italiano*) which returns to the setting of *Angelo di bontà*. His political writings include *Venezia e la libertà d'Italia*, published anonymously after the disappointing armistice of Villafranca in 1859, an important *Frammento sulla rivoluzione nazionale*, and two accounts of the Garibaldi expedition. All this is in addition to *journalism, an extensive correspondence, a *comedy (*Le invasioni moderne*, written in 1857), and *translations from Heine, Hugo, Lermontov, and Greek popular poetry.

In *Studii sulla poesia popolare e civile massimamente in Italia* (1854) Nievo lays down the distinctively post-*Romantic premises of his subsequent fiction, demanding that the writer should be socially and politically engaged, and alert to developments in other European literatures and cultures. At the same time he asserts the decisive role of the lower classes in the construction of a new national identity, and recognizes the importance of *dialects and dialect culture. His *novelle* are based partly on his personal experiences and emphasize the harshness of *peasant life, contrasting it with bourgeois ease and problematizing the issue of the contribution of the peasantry to the formation of the new Italian state. His clear-eyed *realism qualifies the religious element in his writing and distinguishes his work from that of *Manzoni, to whom he is in other ways much indebted. Though he is by no means a *positivist, in some ways he strongly anticipates the *verismo of *Verga, particularly in his use of dialect and often irregular Italian.   [FD'I]

See P. De Tommaso, *Nievo e altri studi sul romanzo storico* (1976); M. Gorra, *Manzoni e Nievo* (1976).

NIFO, AGOSTINO (*c*.1470–1538). Natural philosopher who was also known as Eutichio, taught at the University of *Padua from 1492 to 1499, then held teaching posts at *Naples, Salerno, *Rome, and *Pisa. He is particularly important for commentaries on *Aristotle and for his work, which he dedicated to Pope Leo X, attacking the writings of Pietro *Pomponazzi (1518). He also wrote treatises on the duties and attributes of a prince and on the role of the courtier.   [PLR]

1968 was the year of protest par excellence. As in *1848, social revolt spread through the peninsula while also taking place in other countries, as movements from below challenged centres of political and economic power. The leading role was played by students, who in January occupied thirty-six *universities in protest at government *education policies. Their actions led to changes in educational practice, though not to further funding. But their support for industrial workers, especially in *Turin and *Milan, helped create the Hot Autumn of strikes in 1969 (which provided the scenario for Nanni *Balestrini's *Vogliamo tutto*, 1971). For some, 1968 marked the beginning of a period of democratization and modernization of Italian society, represented by the new rights acquired by workers and women. Others saw the events as the cradle of the left-wing terrorism that besmirched public life in the following decade. Culturally the immediate effect of 1968 was to politicize almost all forms of cultural activity from the *Venice Biennale to the school history lesson. The *Neoavanguardia too was thrown into crisis, with its members finding themselves having to choose between political revolution and acceptance of academic and other institutions. [See also EDUCATION, 2; FEMINISM.]   [REL]

Ninfale fiesolano, Il (1344–?46). Poem in *ottava rima* by *Boccaccio, telling of the love of the shep-

herd Africo for the nymph Mensola. When Mensola half-willingly succumbs, and then gives birth to baby Pruneo, she is destroyed by her mistress, the goddess Diana, at which Africo kills himself. Their names become the names of the two streams of Fiesole. Their son, taken in by Africo's parents, goes on to perform epic deeds connected with the founding of Fiesole and *Florence. The poem draws heavily on *Ovid's *Metamorphoses* and on *Statius' *Achilleid*, but the nymphs and goddesses are portrayed in human terms and in a simple country setting, with the two main characters showing an appealing freshness and innocence.   [VB]

NITTI, FRANCESCO SAVERIO (1868–1953). Economist at *Naples University, who advocated a high-wage economy and government intervention, particularly to encourage the industrialization of the South [see MEZZOGIORNO]. Elected as a radical to parliament, he held various ministerial posts and was Prime Minister for a troubled year in 1919–20. He was forced into *exile during the *Fascist period, which he spent mostly in Paris.
          [JD]

NIZOLIO, MARIO (1498–1576). Philosopher and man of letters, who was an outstanding expert on *Cicero. His *Observationes in M. T. Ciceronem* were reprinted several times, also with the title *Thesaurus ciceronianus*. Though defending a rigid *classicism of form, he refused to regard classical antiquity as the only source of authority and truth. His most important work, *De veris principiis et de vera ratione philosophandi contra Pseudophilosophos libri IV* (1553), criticizes *Aristotelian philosophy in the interests of freedom of thought.   [CG]

Nobile vigonze opus, see MACARONIC LITERATURE.

NOBILI, GUIDO (1850–1916). *Florentine lawyer, devoted to writing and *hunting. He published *De profundis clamavi ad te, Domine* (1891), a pamphlet fiercely criticizing imperialist expansionism, and the *novel *Senza bussola* (1906). Some regional sketches and the ironic but lyrical *Memorie lontane* of 1914 were published posthumously.
          [PBarn]

NOGAROLA, ISOTTA (1418–66). Religious writer who lived her entire life in Verona. Martino Rizzoni, pupil of *Guarino da Verona, taught her Latin and some Greek, and introduced her to the *studia humanitatis*. From 1434 she wrote letters to various *humanists, of which the most famous was to Guarino, who did not respond until she complained. Slandered with the accusation of incest in 1438, she made her home a religious retreat, for which she was praised especially by Ludovico Foscarini, humanist and *Venetian governor of Verona. Her most famous composition was a *dialogue with him on the relative guilt of Adam and Eve for the Fall (1451). She defended Eve on the ground of her weakness (imperfection), while Foscarini argued for her guilt because of her pride. Her subsequent works include a *biography of St Jerome, a letter urging a *Crusade (1459), and a consolatory letter to a father on the death of his child. She was honoured posthumously by two *sonnets praising her chastity, but not her learning. [AR]

Noia, La (1960). Novel by *Moravia, on the theme of alienation. Dino, a young middle-class man, strives to become an artist only to realize the extent of his isolation from reality. The novel is strongly influenced by the French *nouveau roman*. [GUB]

NOLFI, VINCENZO (early 17th c.). *Librettist and a member of the Accademia degli *Incogniti in *Venice. He accepted the sung drama then current, but recognized the libretto as a new genre, denying classical authority and giving precedence to the scenographer. Though based on Homer, his *Bellerofonte* (1642) was the first *opera set in Venice. [FC]

Nome della rosa, Il (1980). Umberto *Eco's first novel and his most successful commercially and aesthetically. Its plot centres on a murder investigation carried out in 1327 by an English *Franciscan with Sherlock Holmes characteristics and his young *Benedictine novice assistant in a remote Italian abbey, which is also the scene of violent theological disputes with more than a hint of *heresy. The combination of *detective novel, *historical novel, literary teaser, and vehicle for the philosophical probing of some of the cognitive issues raised by *semiotics, proved unexpectedly appealing to a worldwide audience. [MPC]

NOMI, FEDERICO (1633–1705). Poet born in Anghiari in *Tuscany who lived most of his life in or near Arezzo, eventually becoming a parish priest in the small town of Monterchi. He was a friend of Francesco *Redi and a member of the Accademia

degli Insensati. His major works were *Buda liberata* (1703), modelled on Torquato *Tasso's *epic, and the *mock-heroic *Il catorcio d'Anghiari*, written about 1684 in imitation of *Tassoni. Other works include strictly non-*Marinist lyrics, religious poetry, translations of Horace's *Odes* and *Epodes*, and Latin imitations of Juvenal. [FC]

NONO, LUIGI (1924–90). Composer, teacher and writer on *music. His works are explicitly political; among the most successful is *Il canto sospeso* (1956), a setting of letters from imprisoned anti-*Fascists. He wrote music to a variety of texts, including his own for *Liebeslied* (1954) and *Al gran sole carico d'amore* (1975). [RS]

Nostri antenati, I, see BARONE RAMPANTE, IL; CALVINO, ITALO; CAVALIERE INESISTENTE, IL; VISCONTE DIMEZZATO, IL.

NOTA, ALBERTO (1775–1847). *Turinese playwright, who had a successful career in the *Piedmontese magistracy and civil administration, eventually being made a baron by Carlo Felice. His forty or so *comedies, much performed at the time, now seem lifeless imitations of *Goldoni. [DO'G]

NOTAIO, IL, see GIACOMO DA LENTINI.

NOTARI, UMBERTO (1878–1950). *Journalist and *novelist, originally from *Bologna, who founded various *periodicals and newspapers in *Milan, among them *L'Ambrosiano*. He also founded the publishers Istituto Editoriale Italiano. He was charged with obscenity for his novel *Quelle signore* (1906), but acquitted. [AHC]

Note azzurre, see DOSSI, CARLO.

Notturno, Il, see D'ANNUNZIO, GABRIELE.

NOVARO, ANGIOLO SILVIO (1866–1938). A Ligurian Catholic writer from Diano Marina who enjoyed a considerable reputation in his own time. His works include the *novel *L'angelo risvegliato* (1901) and the poetry for children collected in *Il cestello* (1910). [See also CHILDREN'S LITERATURE.] [PH]

NOVE, ALDO, see CANNIBALI.

900 (*Novecento*) (1926–9). Literary journal founded in *Rome by Curzio *Malaparte and

Novel

Massimo *Bontempelli, though Malaparte quickly lost interest. It initially appeared as a quarterly in French (it had an editorial office in Paris), but it became a monthly, published in Italian, in the period leading up to its demise. It was avowedly anti-provincial and published work by modern European writers, including James Joyce, D. H. Lawrence, and Virginia Woolf. As such it proclaimed itself 'stracittà' in opposition to the *strapaese tendency of much *Fascist culture. Bontempelli defended the journal's Europeanism, claiming that the aim was to break with 19th-c. literary tradition, and drawing an analogy with Fascism's break with 19th-c. concepts of democracy. 900 had affinities with earlier Milanese *Futurism, and was also at odds with the notion of literary culture which La *Ronda had defended. But its most interesting aspect was the way in which Bontempelli used it as a vehicle for his own views of literature, emphasizing the role of the imagination, the importance of realistic detail, and, above all, the cultivation of a magical atmosphere [see REALISMO MAGICO]. These ideas influenced a number of writers who began as contributors to 900, including Antonio Aniante, Paola Masino, and Corrado *Alvaro. [CFB]

Novel. In modern usage the term romanzo usually refers to a literary narrative in prose, which is distinguished from the novella or racconto by its length and complexity [see NOVELLA AND RACCONTO]. But the word derives from the French adjective meaning 'Neo-Latin' and in a medieval context is used (like English 'romance') to designate works of narrative, sometimes didactic narrative, which were written in the vernacular and intended to be read for pleasure, notable 14th-c. examples being *Boccaccio's *Filocolo and his Elegia di madonna *Fiammetta [see also ROMANCE]. Cesare *Segre has argued that all the structural ingredients of the modern novel are already present in the medieval romance, whereas others situate the rise of the modern Italian novel in the 17th c. or even later. What is certain is that the novel has always been protean in nature, having emerged in a postclassical age and never having been subject to the strict rules of codification that were applied to genres with precedents in classical Greek literature, such as the *epic and *tragedy.

The modern novel as such does indeed develop in 17th-c. Europe. A long history of *chivalric narrative reaching back to the *Middle Ages had been brought to a close by Rabelais and Cervantes.

In France the roman précieux now offered an aristocratic society a way of seeing itself in idealized form, whilst in Spain the picaresque novel drew on traditional representations of a society in crisis. Italy witnessed the development of the *Baroque novel, which *Asor Rosa has suggested came about through the secularization of chivalric poetry and the increasingly literary character of the novella. There were a few developments in other directions. *Marini presented an idealization of aristocratic life in his highly successful Calloandro fedele (1640–1), and, in a radical move, *Brusoni's Trilogia di Glisomiro (1657–62) replaced the lives and loves of the aristocracy with those of the contemporary bourgeoisie [see also BIONDI, GIAN FRANCESCO].

The Italian 18th c. was marked by an astonishing number of *translations of novels, thus introducing a practice which has continued unabated to this day. Voltaire and Rousseau were particularly popular, but the market was dominated by the English—Defoe and Swift, Sterne and Richardson. Although their success testifies to the presence of a reading public with catholic tastes, the indigenous novel continued to have difficulty in getting established. It appears to have drawn heavily on the *theatre, with melodramatic exploitation of coincidence and arbitrary turns of plot. Both the prolific abbot Pietro *Chiari and Antonio *Piazza regularly had recourse to protagonists who were themselves readers of novels. They thus anticipated the early 19th-c. debate over *reading and the novel which saw the *Romantics cautiously in favour of the new genre and the *classicists adamant in their hostility. The beginnings of a new subjectivity are evident in Alessandro *Verri's *neoclassical novels and in the *autobiographical narratives of *Casanova, *Goldoni, and Carlo *Gozzi. But the Italian novel emerged from the shadows only with *Foscolo's *Ultime lettere di Jacopo Ortis (1802), which combines in the figure of its hero the Romantic lover and the Romantic patriot.

The works of Sir Walter Scott, which were quickly read and translated in Italy, led to the introduction of the *historical novel and at last the establishment of a strong native novel tradition. Little more than a decade saw *Grossi's Marco Visconti (1834), Massimo *D'Azeglio's Ettore Fieramosca (1833), Cesare *Cantù's Margherita Pusterla (1838), *Guerrazzi's La battaglia di Benevento (1827), and *Manzoni's I *promessi sposi (1827), this last constituting a narratological and intellectual tour de force that has become identified with both the birth of the modern Italian novel and the birth of a national written language. The heyday of the historical novel lasted from the mid-1820s to about 1840, though it has remained one of the most popular and prolific narrative genres in Italy. Novels of contemporary life began to emerge around the mid-century. *Rovani's *Cento anni* (1856–63) offers a fresco of the preceding hundred years, *Nievo's *Le *confessioni d'un italiano* creates a first-person protagonist who is emblematic of his age, *Tommaseo's *Fede e bellezza* (1840) explores the inner world of its characters, while *Ranieri and *Tarchetti developed the social humanitarian novel.

The professional novelist-journalist comes into being in Italy largely after *Unification in 1860, thanks to a combination of social and economic factors—rapid urbanization, the rise of a bourgeoisie, the spread of *literacy (albeit very uneven in terms of geography, class, and gender), and the expansion of a regionalized but active periodical press [see JOURNALISM; PERIODICALS; PUBLISHING]. The novel for children was introduced with *Collodi's *Le avventure di *Pinocchio* (1883) and *De Amicis' *Cuore* (1886) [see also CHILDREN'S LITERATURE]. *Verismo* presented the realities of the new Italy to its largely Northern readership: *Verga in I *Malavoglia* (1881) and I *Mastro-don Gesualdo* (1889), *De Roberto in I *viceré* (1894) and *Capuana, all wrote of *Sicily, whilst *Serao depicted life in *Naples, *De Marchi *Milan, and *Neera and the *Marchesa Colombi the Northern provinces. At the same time *D'Annunzio and *Fogazzaro were having greater commercial success with novels based on the more sensational aesthetics of decadence [see DECADENTISMO].

The *modernist novel quickly achieved outstanding results in Italy with *Pirandello's *Il *fu Mattia Pascal* (1904) and his subsequent fiction, and *Svevo's *La *coscienza di Zeno* (1923), but was slow to receive the attention it deserved, although between the 1930s and 1950s European modernism was to have a profound influence on writers such as *Borgese, *Tozzi, *Manzini, and *Banti. But the dominant current came to be *Neorealism, which was already cultivated in the *Fascist years by younger writers as a particular form of modernism, and which addressed the more immediate issues raised by *World War II and the *Resistance in novels by *Pavese, *Fenoglio, *Vittorini, and *Calvino. In the 1950s a more self-doubting, intimate vein becomes dominant, especially in Natalia *Ginzburg and *Bassani. But a violently assertive modernism, though with roots in *Dossi and the

*Lombard tradition, had long been cultivated by *Gadda. *Quer pasticciaccio di via Merulana* (1957) and *La *cognizione del dolore* (1963), in particular, provided the starting point for writers of the 1960s such as *Manganelli and the experimentalists of the *Neoavanguardia, who were determined to resist the general tendency to reduce the language and techniques of fiction to a common norm.

Since the early 1970s the Italian novel has maintained its protean fluidity, showing, as it did throughout the 20th c., an openness to literatures from elsewhere, but generally proving difficult to categorize in terms of overall tendencies. Major figures such as *Morante, *Sciascia, and Calvino followed their distinctive individual paths during the 1970s, though the later Calvino and *Eco's *Il *nome della rosa* (1980) ushered in a phase of knowing *post-modernism. At one extreme has been the magic realism of Latin American writing in *Ortese and *D'Arrigo [see REALISMO MAGICO], at the other American minimalism in *Celati and *Del Giudice. Between them are figures as varied as *Sanvitale, *Tabucchi, *Vassalli, and *Maraini. A currently emerging tendency is represented by the so-called *cannibali, who incorporate pulp culture and visual media into their writing.   [AHC]

See A. Asor Rosa (ed.), *Letteratura italiana*, vol. iii: *Le forme del testo*, 2: *La prosa* (1984); G. Tellini, *Il romanzo italiano dell'Ottocento e Novecento* (1998).

Novella and *Racconto*

1. To 1700

The *novella* is a specifically Italian form of the tale, and overlaps with the fable and parable, with the anecdote and joke [see FACEZIE], and with myth. It was the predominant form of prose fiction in the Italian vernacular during the *Middle Ages and *Renaissance. The name, related to *nuova* (plural *nuove*, 'news'), ties it to narratives on the borders of information and fiction, the area of verisimilitude, of what has the appearance of truth. The traditional *novella* is usually about known historical people of a particular locality and time. It deals with human events both comic or tragic, and operates according to rational causality. In this it is distinct from narratives of the fantastic, where magic and extra-human forces hold sway. Most characteristically, *novelle* boast affinity with oral culture. They are mediated by storytellers, presented as the faithful reporters of events and dialogue, and therefore of the rich variety of linguistic registers and codes of their protagonists, from *dialect to jargon, from sublime rhetorical declamations to lowly and scurrilous quips. The author's role is thus often seemingly reduced to that of a mere scribe. The fact that the. *novella* creates an illusion of reality should not, however, blind the reader to its long literary tradition, going back to Latin, Greek, and Oriental models.

Even before *Boccaccio's masterpiece, the *Decameron* (set in 1348, during the *plague), the homeland of the Italian *novella* was *Florence and *Tuscany, where there also flourished manuals of *exempla* in the vernacular, with short anecdotes illustrating moral and religious points, as exemplified in writings by Domenico *Cavalca and Iacopo *Passavanti. The anonymous *Novellino*, the first secular collection, had already appeared in the 13th c. None of these pre-Boccaccio types displayed a frame-story, and even in the half-century after the *Decameron*, Franco *Sacchetti's varied *Trecentonovelle* still has no frame, though making abundant use of a moral point attached to each story. From this time on, however, the frame becomes the most permanent legacy of the *Decameron*. Giovanni *Sercambi's *Novelle* keep close to the *Decameron* with a group of storytellers who flee plague-stricken Lucca in Tuscany; and the Florentine Ser Giovanni's *Pecorone* sets his story-telling in a convent with only two narrators recounting fifty *novelle* over twenty-five days. Florentine quick-wittedness is celebrated in the anonymous collection of anecdotes and practical jokes, *Motti e facezie del piovano Arlotto*.

In the 15th c. two non-Tuscan collections appear: *Il novellino* of *Masuccio Salernitano, and *Le porretane* by Giovanni Sabbadino degli *Arienti, which was completed in 1468. Both authors were courtiers, writing for the entertainment and instruction of aristocratic *patrons at *Naples and *Bologna respectively; but while the former is heavily didactic, and replaces the frame with a dedicatory letter for each tale as well as a moral commentary following, the latter celebrates local traditions and dialect in the 'low' setting of the nearby spa of Porretta.

The 16th c. was typified by substantial collections that were translated and disseminated all over Europe. They show a debt to the *Decameron*, but with diverse emphases, and especially with respect to the frame story. *Grazzini bends Boccaccio's love of the *beffa* or practical joke—another Florentine specialty—to cruel and macabre extremes, recounted by a group of storytellers calmly awaiting

their supper. In the same vein are *Giraldi Cinzio's *Hecatommithi*, gloomy, if not savage tales of revenge published after Grazzini's in 1565, though set earlier in the cataclysmic 1527 *Sack of Rome. Undoubtedly the most famous collection was by Matteo *Bandello, a courtier at various Northern *courts as well as in France. Called simply *Novelle*, it was published in sections beginning in 1554. By prefacing each tale by a long dedicatory letter explaining how he came to know of the events recounted, he strives more than any other writer of the genre to give an air of historical veracity to his tales.

Further innovations in the frame can be found in Agnolo *Firenzuola's use of embedding *novelle*; that is, inserting tales within larger narratives, all within the main 'frame' narrative—a technique used in antiquity by *Ovid and Apuleius, but also by Oriental collections of animal fables such as the *Panchatantra*. Renaissance authors also place *novelle* within other genres: *Castiglione within the *dialogue in his *Cortegiano*, and *Ariosto within his narrative poem, *Orlando furioso*. The same century and the next bring in reactions to the historical *novella*. *Le piacevoli notti* of Giovan Francesco *Straparola introduce magical, folk elements, as well as some stories in dialect, into thirteen nights of story-telling at *carnival time. Some well-known fairytales first find their formulation here: Puss-in-Boots (11.1), a magic doll excreting money (5.2), and a pig turning into a prince (2.1). A carnival setting, this time in *Siena, also proves suitable for Scipione *Bargagli's light-hearted *Trattenimenti* of 1587.

Tuscan cultural dominance and the Tuscan literary language suffer further setbacks in the 17th c. The *Venetian Accademia degli *Incogniti produced *Cento novelle amorose* (1651), perhaps the first example of collective authorship in that a frameless collection is made up of *novelle* by individual members. Unity is provided by a new *erotic naturalism, inspired to some degree by Boccaccio, and a corresponding lack of moralistic lessons. But the other two major collections reject the Tuscan language itself. The Bolognese Giulio Cesare *Croce, a blacksmith by trade and oral storyteller, appears to write as he speaks in the *Sottilissime astuzie di Bertoldo* (1606); the foolish adventures of the *peasant *Bertoldo and his idiot son Bertoldino, while bringing us close to popular oral culture and its crude humour, are decidedly anti-literary. Rebellious features characterize Giambattista *Basile's *Cunto de li cunti*, published in 1636 after his death. The largest collection of *fiabe* ever written in the Italian peninsula, it was composed entirely in a highly crafted Neapolitan dialect. Here the illusion of tales told by ignorant old women hides a wealth of cultural and literary traditions to counter Tuscan hegemony.

Some individual *novelle* have achieved a life of their own. For example the **Novella del grasso legnaiuolo*, an anonymous Florentine narrative dated around 1409, describes an elaborately contrived *beffa* played on a fat cabinet-maker by the architect of Florence's dome, Filippo *Brunelleschi, and his set. Luigi *Da Porto wrote the most famous single *novella* of all, the story of Romeo and Juliet. Analogues of young thwarted lovers, who die by a tragic mistake, go back to Ovid's Pyramus and Thisbe. Masuccio Salernitano (*novella* 33) tells a recognizable form of the story about rival Italian families, with an obliging friar who delivers a sleep-inducing drug. Matteo Bandello (2.9), who adapted Da Porto, was translated into English in William Painter's collection *The Palace of Pleasure* (1566–7), a reservoir of plots and motifs for English literature, including *Shakespeare.
[LAP]

2. 1700 onwards

By the mid-18th c. the *novella* was associated mostly with *dialect or *folk and popular literature, and a writer of literary *novelle* such as Gasparo *Gozzi was very much the exception. Though novels continued to be written and published, major writers (*Goldoni, *Parini, *Alfieri) focused more on poetry and the *theatre, reserving prose for the essay or the memoir. When the status and character of narrative was revised with the advent of *Romanticism, it was the prose novel that first took pride of place; the *novella* appeared principally as the *novella in versi*. However, the mid-19th c. saw short prose narratives in abundance. While the term itself continued to be used, the *novelle* that were written increasingly resembled the short stories produced in other European countries, and were similarly encouraged and conditioned by the demands of the *periodicals in which they usually first appeared.

Yet the tradition of the concise, forceful *novella* proved surprisingly hardy, partly because its closeness to folk literature made it seem the appropriate vehicle for the aspirations of both Romantic *realism and *verismo*. The drive to represent rural life shows itself already in the mid-1830s and even more in *Nievo's stories. In the second half of the

century it often turns into *bozzettismo*—the creation of 'sketches' that hover between the poetic, the moral, and the photographic. But it achieves much fuller and more complex expression in *Verga's **Vita dei campi* (1880), a collection that moves between techniques of folk narrative and sophisticated social and psychological analysis partly inspired by Zola, and which proved a test-bed for much that Verga would develop in his later novels and stories. Other *veristi*, from *Capuana to *Deledda, followed in his footsteps in their *novelle*, as they did in their novels.

The realist *novella* was seriously challenged by *Pirandello from the mid-1890s onwards. Taken together, his **Novelle per un anno* present a startling wealth of new ideas and techniques without parallel in subsequent *novella* writing. That does not mean that Pirandello had anything like the last word. The realist *novella* was itself poetically renewed in the 1930s by *Pavese and *Vittorini and then continued in starker form in *Moravia's **Racconti romani* (1954), whilst the *surreal *novella*, of which there are examples in Pirandello, was particularly cultivated by *Bontempelli and then by *Buzzati. With the collapse of *Neorealist programmes in the 1950s, *fantasy fiction emerged as one of the acknowledged alternatives to realism. Both modes are particularly exploited by *Calvino, though from *Le *città invisibili* (1972) onwards he returns to older practices of framing, linking, and patterning collections of stories.

Modern writers tend to prefer the term *racconto*, which can also embrace short novels. At the same time the term *novella* has come to be used increasingly loosely. Since at least *Gadda's (exceptionally long) *Novella seconda* (1971), it may be nothing more than a gesture towards an almost vanished tradition.
[PH]

See *La novella italiana: atti del convegno di Caprarola, 19–24 settembre 1988* (1989).

Novella del grasso legnaiuolo, La (early 15th c.), by an unknown author, is one of the most famous *novelle* of the *Renaissance. It concerns a practical joke, like many of *Boccaccio's stories in the **Decameron*. The protagonists are the famous artists *Brunelleschi and Donatello. The joke, which was purportedly carried out in 1409, consisted of making a fat wood-inlayer, Manetto Ammannatini, known as Grasso, believe that he had become someone else. The whole of *Florence was enlisted, Grasso's workshop was literally turned upside down, and he was so shamed that he disappeared to Hungary. [See also BEFFA; MANETTI, ANTONIO; NOVELLA AND RACCONTO.]   [JR]

Novella in versi. The term is a 19th-c. invention, but the phenomenon of the verse story existed from at least the 14th c., although largely as a marginal and popular sub-genre. It was dependent on *fabliaux*, *exempla*, and prose *novelle*, particularly *Boccaccio's *Decameron*, as is evident in *Brusantino's *Cento novelle*. Generally it perpetuated a provincial oral tradition of moralizing narrative and remained unpublished in book form, as was the case with Antonio *Pucci's *cantari*, and the *Liber solactii* of Simone Prodenzani (first half of the 15th c.), though episodes in *Boiardo and *Ariosto are also effectively verse stories.

In the 19th c. the *novella in versi* became an established *Romantic genre, in which writers struggled to reconcile narrative structure and *lyric tonality, frequently using *ottava rima* and writing in *dialect. Subjects were commonly historical and influenced by Byron rather more than *Manzoni. Tommaso *Grossi's *Ildegonda* (1820) is typical in combining a medieval setting and traditional poetic language in a way that made the genre acceptable to both Romantics and *classicists. Other practitioners were Ignazio *Cantù, Silvio *Pellico, Bartolomeo *Sestini, Luigi *Carrer, Giovanni *Torti, and Vincenzo *Padula. Giovanni *Prati took a firm step towards bourgeois *realism in his blank verse *Edmenegarda* (1841), and Niccolò *Tommaseo introduced a degree of psychological analysis in *Una serva* (1837). The genre subsequently waned, but continued in poems such as *Pascoli's 'Italy', *Gozzano's 'La signorina Felicita', and, more recently, *Pagliarani's 'La ragazza Carla'.   [FD'I]

Novelle della Pescara, see D'ANNUNZIO, GABRIELE.

Novelle morali, see ALBERGATI CAPACELLI, FRANCESCO; SOAVE, FRANCESCO.

Novelle per un anno (1922–37). The title *Pirandello chose for his collected short stories, suggesting a year's reading of a story a day. They encompass a vast array of characters and human experiences, and range from early *veristic tales to the *modernist prose of his later years.   [JAL]

Novelle rusticane, see VERGA, GIOVANNI.

NOVELLI, ENRICO, see YAMBO.

Novellino, see MASUCCIO SALERNITANO.

Novellino, Il. The modern name for a collection of *novelle, put together in *Florence around the end of the 13th c., probably by a single author. Entitled (in the oldest manuscript) the *Libro di novelle e di bel parlare gientile*, the work is addressed to the 'minori', that is, people of limited culture but ready to improve themselves. The first printed edition, published in 1525 by Carlo *Gualteruzzi in *Bologna, under the title *Le ciento novelle antike*, became the basis for subsequent editions. The *Novellino* presents 100 tales, deriving from many sources—some classical and medieval, but mainly French and to a lesser extent Provençal and Italian. Their distinctive rhetorical and stylistic ideal is the brief, effective, and elegant turn of phrase (*motto*), which is made to dominate a series of traditional narrative genres—*exemplum, fabliau, vida* (*biography), courtly *romance, and city *chronicle.   [MP]

NOVENTA, GIACOMO (pseud. of Giacomo Ca' Zorzi) (1899–1960). Poet and critic. Born into a noble *Venetian family in Noventa di Piave in the Veneto, he fought as a volunteer in *World War I, and then studied law in *Turin, where he frequented the circle around *Gobetti and made lasting friendships with *Soldati and *Debenedetti. After travelling widely in Europe between 1926 and 1934, he became a contributor to *Solaria. When it was suppressed by the *Fascist authorities, he founded *La riforma letteraria* (1936–8) with Alberto *Carocci. Before it too was suppressed, and Noventa banished from all university cities, he published in it various essays vehemently criticizing all aspects of 'official' Italian culture, in particular proclaiming the fundamental identity of Fascism and anti-Fascism.

After *World War II, he founded *La Gazzetta del Nord* (1946–7) and *Il Socialista moderno* (1945–50), and argued the case for Catholic social democracy until withdrawing from the political arena in 1956. That year he published *Versi e poesie*, containing poems going back to the 1930s but hitherto known only through letters or magazines (until 1933 published under the name of Emilio Sarpi). They are written in a form of Veneto *dialect which Noventa created from diverse sources, and totally reject *hermetic poetry, expressing instead a *Romantic sensibility, influenced particularly by Goethe, Heine, and Novalis. As a poet Noventa can be as political, polemical, and sarcastic as he is in prose, but at his most lyrical he achieves a clarity and forcefulness of expression without parallel in modern Italian poetry. [JJ]

Numerology. For the Christian West, the *Bible is the primary source of the notion that God created all things 'in number, weight and measure', and both Testaments attribute significance to such numbers as 3, 4, 7, 10, 12, 40, 70, and 144. The other major source is the Platonic tradition, itself the bearer of various Pythagorean ideas and of number symbolism from classical mythology and poetry. In the *Timaeus* (39C ff.) Plato presents the structure of the world-soul as two connected quaternaries, 1-2-4-8 and 1-3-9-27 (the so-called *lambda*), with their intervening geometric means, 6, 12, and 18, and thus as containing the musical harmonies of the octave (2:1), the perfect fifth (3:2), and the perfect fourth (4:3). *Augustine and the *encyclopedists of late antiquity—Macrobius, Martianus Capella, Boethius, Cassiodorus, and Isidore of Seville—eventually wove the two traditions together and established numerology as one of the keys to interpreting the Bible, the natural world, and man, and thus as a principle for organizing all human artefacts. Augustine's *City of God*, for example, has 22 books, the number of the letters in the Hebrew alphabet.

The pre-eminent numerological poet is *Dante. In *Vita nova* 29 he links Beatrice with the number 9, because she was 'uno nove, cioè uno miracolo' rooted in the Trinity itself; and his *Divine Comedy* has a complex numerical structure based on the number 3: witness its *terza rima* and its 3 books consisting of 33 cantos each (the years of Christ's life). Along with an introductory canto (Christ died in his 34th year), this sums to 100 or 10 squared cantos, 10 being the number of the law and its commandments and the sum of the first 4 numbers (the Pythagoreans' *tetractys*), and 100 being the ideal length of earthly life. Similarly *Petrarch may be drawing on numerology as an organizing principle for his *Rime* and *Trionfi* (as well as on related calendrical schemata—natural and astrological, ecclesiastical and secular), and *Boccaccio may be toying with the symbolism of 10 and 100 in his *Decameron*.

In the 15th and 16th c. the numerological tradition was enriched by the introduction of additional Orphic, *hermetic, Pythagorean, *Neoplatonic, and cabalistic elements; by the rediscovery of Vitruvius' work *De architectura* (which argued that the human body's proportions consists of ratios that

should be imitated in the design of buildings); and by a renewed interest on the part of theorists such as *Minturno and Iacopo Pontano both in classical prosody and in *Virgil's numerology. Witness such important synthesizing works as *Ficino's commentaries on the *Timaeus* and on the nuptial or fatal number in Plato's *Republic* 8 (1496), *Pico della Mirandola's *Conclusiones* and his *Heptaplus* (an intricate sevenfold interpretation of the 7 days of Creation), Francesco Giorgio's *De harmonia mundi* (1525), Francesco Barozzi's *Commentarius in locum Platonis obscurissimum* (1566), and Pietro Bongo's *Mysticae numerorum significationis liber* (1583).

Italian *Renaissance poets, followed by their French and English emulators, refer to the 'mysteries'—mythological, *allegorical, and typological—of particular numbers: Giangiorgio *Trissino, for example, in the descriptions of the palaces of Acratia and Areta in his *Italia liberata da' Goti* (1547), and Torquato *Tasso, predictably, in his *Le sette giornate del mondo creato* (1592). But the extent to which they and others intended to organize their works on numerological and/or musical principles as a way of imposing form and therefore beauty (*grazia*) remains an open and contentious question. Did *Marino, for instance, intend the 648 lines of his epithalamium *Venere pronuba* (1616) to signify 3 times 6 cubed, with 6 being the marriage number (as 2 times 3) and the first perfect number (as the sum of its aliquot parts of 1, 2, and 3), and 6 squared being the interval between rebirths? In the 20th c. *Pirandello (*Il *fu Mattia Pascal*), *Calvino (*Palomar* and *Le città invisibili*), and others have occasionally revived the tradition. [MA]

See V. F. Hopper, *Medieval Number Symbolism* (1938); M. Allen, *Nuptial Arithmetic: Marsilio Ficino's Commentary on the Fatal Number in Book VIII of Plato's Republic* (1994).

Nuns are relevant to the history of Italian culture for two major reasons: for the crucial role they played in the *education of women, and for their contribution to literature and the arts. In the *Middle Ages and the early modern period nunneries were the most important places for female education outside the family. As well as being an honourable place for mainly upper-class women to live, convents provided religious and domestic training, and sometimes taught reading and writing (above all the Poor Clare and Ursuline convents). The most prestigious institutions could offer access to small collections of books. The large number of nuns amongst *women writers, particularly in the *Renaissance, is evidence of the convents' role as intellectual centres. The educational and cultural significance of convents began to decline in the 18th c., a decline which culminated in the abolition of monastic communities by the French authorities at the end of that century. Nuns turned to active roles in society, such as charity, assistance, and missionary work.

Nuns widely contributed to spiritual and mystical writing. St Clare (Chiara) of Assisi (1193–1253) was the author of a Rule for female monastic life. The learned S. Caterina da Bologna [see VIGRI, CATERINA] wrote a devotional work which was printed several times; the ecstatic visions of Maria Maddalena de' *Pazzi were carefully transcribed by her companions; and Veronica Giuliani (1660–1727) kept a long spiritual diary. Nuns devoted themselves to the writing of the Lives of their fellow nuns, and the history of their communities. Illuminata Bembo (d.1496) recorded the life and miracles of S. Caterina da Bologna. Angelica Baitelli (1588–1650) wrote two historical works both focused on her convent and based on Latin medieval documents, and some chronicles were collectively and continuously written by nuns (the *Memoriale di Monteluce*, published in 1983, covered nearly four centuries).

Nuns also contributed to literature. Beatrice del Sera (1515–85) and Maria Clemente Ruoti (c.1609–90) both wrote plays to be performed within the cloister. Others contributed to different genres: Arcangela *Tarabotti authored polemical works, and Camilla Faà *Gonzaga (1599–1662) wrote her memoirs. Nuns' creativity went beyond writing, to include painting (Plautilla Nelli), engravings (Isabella Piccini), and musical composition (Lucrezia Orsina Vizzana). [See also FEMINISM; RELIGIOUS LITERATURE.] [SE]

See C. A. Monson (ed.), *The Crannied Wall: Women, Religion and the Arts in Early Modern Europe* (1992); E. A. Matter and J. Coakley (eds.), *Creative Women in Medieval and Early Modern Italy* (1996).

Nuova antologia (1866–). Literary periodical, published in *Florence until 1878, then in *Rome. Its founding editors sought to continue in newly united Italy the work of *Vieusseux' *Antologia*. Early contributors included *Carducci, *D'Annunzio, and *De Sanctis. Among the novelists it serialized were *Verga (*Mastro-don Gesualdo*) and *Deledda. During the *Fascist period it was given a pro-regime orientation under the editorship of Luigi *Federzoni. [DF]

Nuova Italia, La, see PUBLISHING.

Nuovi argomenti (1953–). Review founded in *Rome by *Carocci and *Moravia. Other members of the editorial board have included *Pasolini, *Sciascia, and *Siciliano. In its early years it published various important literary inquiries, including a series of questionnaires on *Neorealism. Stimulated in part by the emergence in the 1980s of popular literary magazines such as *Leggere* and *Wimbledon*, it modernized its graphic design, moved over to a larger format, and devoted an increasing amount of space to the work of new writers. [MPC]

O

Occasioni, Le, see MONTALE, EUGENIO.

Occhiali d'oro, Gli, see BASSANI, GIORGIO.

OCHINO, BERNARDINO (1487–1564). *Sienese religious reformer, popular preacher, and Vicar-General of the *Cappuccini* [see FRANCISCANS], who fled to Protestant Geneva in 1542. In England he wrote the ingenious *dialogues he entitled *Tragoedie* (1549), which influenced Milton. But his speculative anti-Trinitarianism made him unwelcome among confessional Protestants, and he died an outcast from orthodox sects in Moravia. [PMcN]

ODASI, TIFI, CORRADO, AND LUDOVICO. Three brothers, of whom the first two were part of a late 15th-c. literary *humanist circle at *Padua that cultivated linguistically hybrid poetry. Tifi— Michele di Bartolomeo (d. after 1492), who took the name of the helmsman of the Argonauts, Typhis—composed the incomplete *Macaronea*, the first example of a *macaronic poem and the source of the term. It was printed in *Milan in about 1490 and emulated by Teofilo *Folengo. The third brother, Ludovico (1455–1509), was a *courtier of Guidubaldo da *Montefeltro at *Urbino. [LAP]

ODDI, SFORZA (1540–1611) was a *law teacher and dramatist from *Perugia. His *Erofilomachia* ('Battle of Love and Friendship') (1572) and *I morti vivi* (1576) set a pattern for *comedies with a serious moralistic central plot—a format which he then defended in the Prologue to *La prigione d'amore* (1589). [RAA]

Odi barbare, see CARDUCCI, GIOSUE.

Officina (1955–8). Review edited in *Bologna by Francesco *Leonetti, Pier Paolo *Pasolini and Roberto *Roversi, with the subsequent involve-ment of Angelo Romanò, Gianni Scalia, and Franco *Fortini. *Marxist in orientation and indebted to the experience of *Vittorini's *Politecnico*, the review mounted an important challenge to the literary canon, declaring itself equally hostile to *hermetic ideas of the autonomy of art and to *Neorealist *impegno*. Whilst the polemics staged by the review were politically charged, the emphases and concerns remained essentially literary and individualistic, ultimately divisively so. A short-lived new series was published by *Bompiani in 1959. [See also PERIODICALS, 1.] [MPC]

OGNIBENE DA LONIGO (1412–c.1500). *Humanist, who was a pupil of *Vittorino da Feltre and, in *Venice, of *Chrysoloras. He taught eloquence in Treviso and Vicenza, at the *court of *Mantua and, perhaps, in Venice. He commented on *Cicero, Lucan, Lucretius, Quintilian, and *Ovid, and translated many works of grammar, rhetoric, and prosody from the Greek. [CG]

OJETTI, UGO (1871–1946). Literary *journalist, *novelist, and art critic. His early work for *La Tribuna* included important interviews with well-known Italian writers, such as *Verga and *D'Annunzio, which he then collected as *Alla scoperta dei letterati* (1895). From 1898 until the end of his life he wrote articles on culture and art criticism for the *Corriere della sera*, which were collected in the seven volumes of *Cose viste* (1924–39). He also wrote articles for the *Illustrazione* (1904–9), which he republished as *I capricci del conte Ottavio* (1909), incorporating the pseudonym under which they originally appeared in the title.

Though occasional in nature, all of Ojetti's journalistic writing is couched in elegant prose, comparable, at least in the 1920s and 1930s, to *prosa d'arte*. His novels, starting with *Senza Dio* (1894) are mostly early, and bear the stamp of late 19th-c. conventions. One stands out, *Mio figlio ferroviere*

Olimpica, Corilla

(1922), which is set in post-*World War I Italy. Ojetti's art criticism is concerned mostly with Italian *Renaissance painters, and includes separate volumes on *Raphael (1921) and Mantegna (1931). Ojetti founded the art journal *Dedalo* (1920–33) and the literary journals *Pegaso* (1929–31) and *Pan* (1933–5), which display both his refined cultural conservatism and his *Fascist sympathies.   [AC]

OLIMPICA, CORILLA, see MORELLI FERNAN-
DEZ, MARIA MADDALENA.

OLIVETTI, ADRIANO (1901–60) brought to his position as president of one of the great Italian industries (Olivetti, founded by his father Camillo) a visionary commitment to the renewal of society. He founded the movement of *Comunità* (and the *periodical of the same name), and offered employment or *patronage to many urbanists, architects, designers, and writers, among them Libero *Bigiaretti, Ottiero *Ottieri, Geno *Pampaloni, and Paolo *Volponi.   [LL]

Olschki. Florentine *publishers, founded in 1886 as an antiquarian booksellers by Leo Samuel Olschki, whose family were printers in Prussia. The bookshop functioned initially as a sort of literary salon. The publishing business specialized in *Dante and other early literature. The two arms were divided after *World War II.   [DF]

Ombra d'Argo, L', see PERIODICALS, I.

Omnibus (1937–9). Current affairs weekly, founded by Leo *Longanesi, which numbered among its contributors established figures such as *Malaparte and *Alvaro, as well as younger writers such as Vitaliano *Brancati and Arrigo *Benedetti. The printing techniques, format, photographs, and political cartoons looked forward to the illustrated magazines of the postwar period. It was suppressed by the *Fascist regime for its nonconformism, following an inquiry carried out by former contributor Alberto *Savinio.   [DCH]

ONESTO DA BOLOGNA (*c.*1240–*c.*1303) is cited by *Dante (*DVE* 1.15) for the excellence of his now lost *canzone*, 'Più non attendo il tuo soccorso, amore'. His surviving poems (three *canzoni*, one *ballata*, and twenty or more *sonnets, fifteen of them in *tenzoni*) are influenced by both *Guittone d'Arezzo and Guido *Guinizzelli, whilst his poetic

correspondents include *Cino da Pistoia. Probably a money-changer, Onesto is mentioned several times in *Bolognese legal records.   [CK]

ONGARO, ANTONIO (*c.*1560–1600) was born in *Padua, and spent most of his life in *Rome in the service of the *Farnese family. His *Alceo* (performed in Nettuno in 1581) was dubbed 'l' *Aminta* bagnato', thanks to its close imitation of Torquato *Tasso's *Aminta* and its seaside setting, which is also used in his *piscatorial eclogue *Filide*.
[CPB]

ONOFRI, ARTURO (1885–1928) wrote poetry and literary *journalism whilst working for the Red Cross in his native *Rome. *Liriche* (1907), *Poemi tragici* (1908), and *Canti delle oasi* (1909) draw on Bergson and William James and reveal an affinity with the *symbolists and *Crepuscolari*. Between 1910 and 1912 he was an important presence in *Nuova antologia*, and founded his own journal, *Liriche* (1912–13). His critical essays included articles on contemporary French culture for *Il Popolo romano* and studies of *Pascoli, which were collected by Emilio *Cecchi (1953). After the poetic fragments of *Orchestrine* (1917) and *Arioso* (1921), he was led, via the work of Rudolf Steiner, to theosophy and the theosophical poetry of *Terrestrità del sole*, a cycle of five volumes mostly published posthumously.   [AHC]

ONOFRI, FABRIZIO (1917–). Fiction writer and essayist from *Rome. He fought in the *Resistance in *World War II, and was a leading member of the *Communist party until he quarrelled with *Togliatti in 1956. His fiction reflects his political *impegno*. He is better known for socio-political studies such as *Classe operaia e partito* (1957).
[VS-H]

Opera is the generic term for dramas set wholly or in large part to *music. It embraces a multitude of sub-types—*intermezzo, opera seria, opera buffa*, etc.—and a multitude of distinctive national forms—*tragédie lyrique, Singspiel*, etc. The Italian mainstream form comprises a fusion of poetry, music, and spectacle in which music commonly has the upper hand. Lyrical and virtuoso singing (arias, ensembles), the musically heightened declamation of poetry (recitative), and music incidental to spectacle and stage action (dances, marches, etc.) all play their part.

Opera emerged in Italy at the close of the 16th c.

from a synthesis of various *theatrical forms in which music played an important role: the *interme-dio*, the *pastoral drama, the revived classical *tragedy; crucial musical ingredients were the monodies cultivated by the *Camerata de' Bardi in *Florence and the *madrigal. At first a rarified entertainment for great occasions at *court (the *Medici in *Florence) and in private palaces (the Barberini in *Rome), opera established itself as a public art form through touring companies, mod-elled on the *commedia dell'arte* troupes; during the 1630s a number of theatres opened in *Venice to provide them with permanent, commercially organ-ized homes. In this environment opera underwent rapid change: mythological subjects lost their popularity in favour of historical ones, the cult of beautiful singing (*bel canto*) shifted the emphasis from recitative to aria and downgraded the status of the poet; the spectacle was enlivened with stage machines and episodes of broad *comedy.

During the 17th c. opera became the most popu-lar and prestigious of art forms: in Venice alone close on 400 operas were produced in some dozen different theatres. In emulation of Italian practice, distinct national genres of opera were established in Paris, London, and Hamburg; elsewhere Italian opera was imported wholesale, notably at the *Habs-burg court in Vienna. During the 18th c. opera underwent a series of 'reforms'. Apostolo *Zeno and his *Arcadian contemporaries devised a new style of *libretto—literary and high-minded, and with the roles of music and poetry strictly rational-ized. This type—the *dramma per musica*—was transformed into great art by *Metastasio. In *opera buffa* (the comic genre which emerged as a distinct type as a result of this reform), *Goldoni's libretti enjoyed comparable esteem. In the third quarter of the century a number of operatic reformers, notably Gluck and *Calzabigi in Vienna, achieved a rapprochement of the song-dominated Italian tradition with the French tradition, in which ballet and chorus had continued to play a conspicuous part. Throughout the 18th c. Italian opera was an international art form, and much of the finest Italian opera was composed oustide Italy by non-Italian composers, notably Handel, Gluck, and Mozart.

After the upheavals of the Revolutionary period, *Rossini opened up Italian opera to new *Romantic subject matter, and fused elements from *opera buffa* and *opera seria* in a structural synthesis handled with such flair and authority that it came to be known (by analogy with the Code Napoléon) as the

Code Rossini. The 'code' provided a framework for the full-blooded Romantic work of *Bellini and *Donizetti, and for *Verdi down to the 1850s. Opera remained a broadly popular art; it was one of Verdi's most remarkable achievements that, during a productive career of more than fifty years, in the course of which he transformed Italian opera, upholding the supremacy of the composer over the singers, creating a continuously enthralling musico-dramatic continuity in place of number-opera, and absorbing elements from French and German traditions, he should have carried popular audi-ences with him almost to the end. But, by the third quarter of the 19th c. new operas appeared more rarely and fewer composers made their mark. *Puc-cini was the last whose career consisted almost entirely of the composition and successful staging of opera. The national fascination with opera con-tinued in the 20th c., and for some composers, such as Malipiero and *Dallapiccola, it remained a cen-tral concern. But there was much more experimen-tal self-consciousness, as composers sought new syntheses of music, poetry, and theatrical spectacle. Commonly they have collaborated with poets and writers of distinction; for the librettist's *métier* died with Puccini's collaborators.   [DRBK]

See L. Bianconi and G. Pestelli (eds.), *Storia dell' opera italiana* (1987–); D. Kimbell, *Italian opera* (1991); R. Parker (ed.), *The Oxford Illustrated History of Opera* (1994).

Operette morali (1827). *Leopardi's major cre-ative work in prose. The final (posthumous) edition of 1845 comprises twenty-four *operette*—fables, *dialogues, essays, and collections of aphorisms. The great majority were written in 1824, though the idea of writing dialogues in the manner of Lucian goes back to 1819 or 1820. The whole book, which was Leopardi's own favourite amongst his works, expresses a deeply pessimistic perspective on the world but one that is expressed with much humour, and also with total confidence.   [MPC]

Orality, see DIALECT; DIALECT WRITING; LITER-ACY; SPOKEN LANGUAGE IN LITERATURE.

Oraziana, Scuola, see HORACE; SCUOLA ORAZIANA.

Orbecche, see GIRALDI CINZIO, GIAMBATTISTA.

ORBICCIANI, BONAGIUNTA, see BONA-GIUNTA DA LUCCA.

Orcagna, Andrea

ORCAGNA, ANDREA, see BURCHIELLO, IL.

ORCHI, EMANUELE (*c.*1600–49) was a theologian and philosopher. He is most famous for his *sermons, in which he employed a style characterized by *concettismo*. His *Prediche quaresimali* were published posthumously in 1650. [PBD]

Ordinati, Accademia degli, see UMORISTI, ACCADEMIA DEGLI.

Ordine nuovo, L'. Famous left-wing *periodical with three successive incarnations: a weekly (May 1919–December 1920), a daily (January 1921–December 1922), and a fortnightly (March 1924–April 1925). The weekly, founded and edited in *Turin by *Gramsci, *Togliatti, and others, supported the movement of factory councils as organs of workers' self-government and nuclei of a *Communist 'new order'. It published writings of the international Left, from Lenin to Max Eastman, Karl Liebknecht, and Sylvia Pankhurst, and the *theatre criticism of *Gobetti. The daily was from 22 January 1921 the organ of the newly founded Communist Party of Italy. The fortnightly, also edited by Gramsci, was forced to cease publication after repeated harassment by the *Fascists. [DF]

ORELLI, GIORGIO, see ITALIAN WRITERS IN SWITZERLAND.

ORENGO, NICO (1944–). *Novelist and short-story writer who was born and works in *Turin. His work often evokes the landscape of Liguria as the setting for both personal and historical memory. He has edited *Tuttolibri*, the literary supplement of *La Stampa*. [MPC]

Orfeo, Fabula di (1480). Early vernacular *pastoral play written in the *sacra rappresentazione* form by *Poliziano for *court entertainments at *Mantua during *carnival. Based on a fusion of *Virgilian and *Ovidian sources, it tells the story of Orpheus's loss of Eurydice. [JAL]

ORIANI, AFREDO (1852–1909). *Novelist and essayist. Born in Faenza, he was educated in *Bologna, where after further studies in *Rome and *Naples he worked briefly in the legal profession before withdrawing to the family villa and rarely interrupted rural isolation. His early fiction, which he published as Ottone di Banzole, begins with *Memorie inutili* (1876), a collection of auto-

biographical *novelle* in a violently anarchic mode indebted to the *Scapigliati*. But his negative anarchism, which is at its strongest in the novel *No* (1881), took a sharply authoritarian turn. He polemicized against the idea of divorce in *Matrimonio* (1886), whilst *La lotta politica in Italia* (1892) expressed a strongly *nationalist vision of the newly unified Italy's historic role. Novels of the 1890s, such as *Gelosia* (1895), were influenced by Dostoevsky and Zola, and dwelt on obsessive psychological states and the clash between the real and the ideal. In the last decade of his life he turned to the *theatre, enjoying a certain success with *L'invincibile* (1902). He also gave fullest expression to a Nietzschean vision of a society ruled by a new aristocracy in *La rivolta ideale* (1908). Largely ignored during his lifetime, he was celebrated by the *Fascists as an important precursor. The 30-volume edition of his works (1923–33) was ostensibly edited by *Mussolini himself. [PH]

ORLANDI, LEMMO, see SICULO-TUSCAN POETS.

Orlando is the Italian name of the obscure figure in the massacre of Charlemagne's rearguard at Roncevaux (Roncesvalle) (15 August 778), who became the martyr-hero of the *Chanson de Roland* (*c.*1098). He is celebrated by *Dante in *Inferno* 31 and *Paradiso* 18. In the 15th c. the *epic figure of the French poem underwent a transformation, as the Carolingian material was increasingly contaminated with Arthurian *romance, notably in *Andrea da Barberino's *Reali di Francia* and Luigi *Pulci's *Morgante* (1478). The culmination of this process was reached when *Boiardo portrayed the paladin as in love with the pagan princess *Angelica in his *Orlando innamorato* (1483). Unrequited, this love led to madness in *Ariosto's *Orlando furioso* (1516), where it is eventually cured, and Orlando is returned to his former role. His defeat in love rather than in battle is a distinctive feature of the reception of the Roland legend in Italy, and has caught the imagination of various modern writers. Italo *Calvino revisited the Orlando theme particularly in *Il *cavaliere inesistente* (1959). [MGD]

ORLANDO, FRANCESCO, see LITERARY CRITICISM.

Orlando furioso (1532). *Chivalrous *epic in forty-six *cantos of *ottava rima* by Ludovico *Ariosto, taking its point of departure from

*Boiardo's *Orlando innamorato*. *Orlando, who had fallen in love with the enemy princess *Angelica in Boiardo's poem, goes mad (*furioso*) when he discovers that his beloved has gone off with a Moorish soldier, Medoro. He is only restored to sanity when the English knight Astolfo flies up to the moon on a winged horse (the hippogriff) and recovers his senses for him. Orlando's return to the Christian ranks allows Charlemagne's army to raise the pagan siege of Paris and the long war against the combined African forces to end. A further strand in Ariosto's poem concerns the love of the Christian warrior-maiden Bradamante and the pagan prince Ruggiero: with the defeat of the pagan army Ruggiero is converted to the Christian faith and marries Bradamante, thus initiating the long line of the *Este family, Ariosto's patrons. Interwoven among these three main strands (the war, Orlando and Angelica, and Bradamante and Ruggiero) are a host of secondary tales of an amorous nature involving both Christian and pagan characters.
[CPB]
Ed. L.Caretti (1954).

Orlando innamorato (1483 and 1495). Unfinished *chivalric *romance in *ottava rima* by Matteo Maria *Boiardo. The work is built on a multiplicity of interlacing stories, dominated by that of *Orlando and his love for *Angelica in book 1 (29 cantos), and that of Rugiero in books and 2 and 3 (31 and 9 cantos respectively). In book 1 the Emperor Charlemagne invites all knights to Paris for the Pentecost festivities. These are disrupted by the sudden appearance of *Angelica, a virgin pagan princess who, in order to lure the paladins away from the Christian cause, announces that she will give herself to whoever can defeat her brother Argalia. One by one all the principal knights, Christian and pagan, fall in love with her, especially Orlando and his cousin Ranaldo [see also RINALDO]. But when Feraguto kills Argalia, Angelica flees, and the ensuing quest will take the male pursuers through a multitude of diverse adventures.

Book 2 introduces Rugiero, a new protagonist, progenitor of the House of *Este. Without his prowess Agramante's expedition to invade France cannot succeed. Atalante, who has raised Rugiero knowing he is destined to die by betrayal, frustrates the search until Brunello, a master thief, seeks him out. In book 3, as Paris is besieged, Rugiero meets the Christian Bradamante; a romance flourishes, but the two are soon separated. Later, in a wood, Fiordespina comes upon Bradamante and, thinking her a knight, falls in love with her. The poem ends with the poet blaming the present (1494) French invasion of Italy for the suspension of his tale. The story is taken up by *Ariosto in the *Orlando furioso*.
[MGD]

Orlando laurenziano, see PULCI, LUIGI; RINALDO.

Orphism. Esoteric current in European *Romanticism, which views poetry as an act of pure creativity that exploits the analogies that bind the material and spiritual universes. In discussions of modern Italian poetry, particularly *hermetic poetry, the term is often used to indicate language treated as an absolute value, that is, purely lyrical language, without documentary residue.
[SPC]

ORSINI. A leading *Roman baronial family. They came to prominence in the 12th c. as *Guelf opponents of the *Colonna, towards whom their animosity prevailed through to the 16th c. Major landowners north of Rome, the family was heavily involved in *papal politics, providing three popes: Celestine III (1191–8), Nicholas III (1277–80), and Benedict XIII (1724–30), as well as the 15th-c. papal *condottieri* Paolo and Niccolò Orsini. Clarice Orsini was married to Lorenzo de' *Medici in 1469. The family's power was forcefully challenged by the *Borgia Pope Alexander VI (1492–1503) through the agency of Cesare *Borgia, as mentioned in *Machiavelli's *Principe* (chapter 7).
[SJM]

ORSINI, FULVIO, see ANTIQUARIANISM.

ORSINI, GIULIO, see GNOLI, DOMENICO.

ORSINI, PAOLO GIORDANO (1591–1656). Duke of Bracciano, and grandson of the homonymous wife-murderer in Webster's *White Devil*. He published at his own expense a slight collection of verse (1648), usually assigned to the ranks of *concettismo*. But he really practises a moralizing and sententious late *Petrarchism, with only occasional hints of *Baroque wit.
[MPS]

ORTESE, ANNA MARIA (1914–98). *Novelist. Born in *Rome, she spent much of her life in *Naples, where she played an active part in literary culture, particularly in the years immediately following *World War II. Her most famous collection of stories, *Il mare non bagna Napoli* (1953), is a

Orti Oricellari

passionate denunciation of continuing poverty and corruption there. In other *Neorealist works Ortese deplores the postwar rush to modernity, with its destruction of traditional communities and alienation from the land, whilst at the same time remaining untouched by the temptation to nostalgic idealization. But she went beyond *realism in much of her subsequent writing. *L'iguana* (1965) is one of the most original modern Italian novels. Hovering between fairy story, romance, and *allegory, it presents a dystopian version of *Treasure Island* and *The Tempest*, in which innocence and hope are corrupted by treachery and greed, and destroyed. *Il cardillo addolorato* (1993) is a dazzlingly beautiful historical fantasy of mysterious, metamorphosing identity, with the linnet itself a symbol of innocent love lost and abandoned. As in *L'iguana*, Ortese reveals herself hostile to a rationalism which would destroy nature in the name of progress. Outside all schools and movements and making few concessions to contemporary taste, Ortese's fables have an extraordinary seriousness of purpose and depth of vision. [SW]

Orti Oricellari, see ACADEMIES; MACHIAVELLI, NICCOLÒ; RUCELLAI, BERNARDO.

ORVIETO, ANGIOLO (1869–1968). *Florentine poet who wrote on biblical and exotic themes, but is more important for having founded the reviews *Vita Nuova* (1889) and *Marzocco* (1896), as well as the British Institute in Florence (1917). He also wrote *libretti and literary essays and translated English Romantic poets. [FD'I]

Osservazioni letterarie, see PERIODICALS, 1.

Osservazioni sulla morale cattolica, see MANZONI, ALESSANDRO.

Ossian. Legendary Gaelic bard, reputedly living in the 3rd c. AD, whose work was reinvented by James Macpherson on the basis of a mixture of Scottish folk poetry and his own imagination. *Cesarotti published a *translation of *Poesie di Ossian* (1762), which was itself notable for its stylistic and formal novelty. In its 1801 edition it was accompanied by historical essays arguing for the authenticity of the original. It launched a vogue for Ossianism, that is, for poetry built on *lyric and *epic imagery, alternating exuberance and melancholy and freely mixing different metric forms. Its influence is visible in *Foscolo and beyond. [SC]

Ossi di seppia, see MONTALE, EUGENIO.

Ottava rima. A form of narrative poetry, consisting of strophes or *stanze* of eight *hendecasyllables with the rhyme scheme ABABABCC. The oldest examples are *Boccaccio's *Filostrato* and the *cantare Fiorio e Biancifiore*. It is not clear whether the form was 'invented' by Boccaccio (who could have adapted the stanza of the *canzone as a narrative metre) or if the *cantari* existed earlier (they could have drawn on forms of the *lauda-*ballata). The *ottava rima* is frequently used for narrative verse in all centuries, reaching its zenith in the poems of *Ariosto, Torquato *Tasso, and *Marino. [See also VERSIFICATION.] [PGB]

OTTIERI, OTTIERO (1924–). *Novelist. After a degree in literature in *Rome, he worked in *publishing in *Milan and then for *Olivetti in Ivrea. A contributor to the discussion of 'Letteratura e industria' in *Il *Menabò* (1961), he was one of the leading exponents, with Nanni *Balestrini, of 'industrial literature' in the late 1950s and early 1960s. His novels of the period, the most successful being *Donnarumma all'assalto* (1959), are closer to politically committed sociological analysis than to fiction. From *L'irrealtà quotidiana* (1966) onwards, his novels explore the neurotic behaviour of individuals oppressed by industrial society. The effort to express this leads him in his recent work to poetry, or to combinations of prose and verse, such as *Diario del seduttore passivo* (1995). [JEB]

Ottimo commento, see DANTE COMMENTARIES; LANCIA, ANDREA.

OVID (43 BC–AD 17) (Publius Ovidius Naso). Arguably the most widely influential of Roman poets during the *Middle Ages and *Renaissance. Love poetry was indebted to his love lyrics proper (*Amores*), to his poetry on the art of seduction (*Ars amatoria*), and to his palinodes (*Remedia amoris*). The *Metamorphoses*, with their immense web of stories of transformation, including Apollo and Daphne, Pyramus and Thisbe, Orpheus and Eurydice, Andromeda and Perseus, and Diana and Actaeon, were commonly interpreted as moral and even theological *allegories during the Middle Ages, and were exploited, not always with allegorical intent, by all major poets (and artists) from *Dante to at least *Ariosto. Only with *Counter-Reformation condemnations of ancient mythology did Ovid's direct influence seriously wane. [LAP]

OXILIA, NINO (1888–1917). *Turinese poet and playwright, killed fighting in *World War I. As a poet he moved from the *crepuscolarismo* of *Canti brevi* (1909) to the *Futurism of *Gli orti* (1918). He wrote various plays, mostly with his friend, Sandro Camasio (1886–1913), the best-known being *Addio! Giovinezza* (1911). The two of them also directed a number of films. [PBarn]

Oziosi, Accademia degli. The most famous of the *Neapolitan literary *academies, founded in 1611 by Giambattista *Manso. It played a key role in reintroducing *concettismo* to Naples, where orthodox *Petrarchism had displaced the richly experimental poetry produced there in the previous decades. When *Marino returned to his native city in 1624, he was elected the academy's *principe*. After this it became the launching platform for the literary careers of a long series of poets who moved *concettismo* towards ever more elaborate, ornately erudite extremes, a direction possibly taken as a result of the strongly aristocratic outlook of its members. [MPS]

P

PACI, ENZO, see AUT-AUT; PHENOMENOLOGY.

PACIAUDI, PAOLO MARIA (1710–85). *Turinese antiquary and reformer. A *Theatine, he served the dukes of Parma as librarian during the Duchy's golden age as the 'Athens of Italy', and collaborated with Du Tillot in the reform of *education, drawing up the new *Costituzione per i regi studii* (1768). The printer *Bodoni was his protégé.   [JMAL]

PACIOLI, LUCA (*c*.1445–1517). Mathematician, and author of a treatise on proportion, *De divina proportione* (1509), inspired by *Neoplatonic thought and illustrated by his friend *Leonardo Da Vinci. His scholarly writings on mathematics also included a *Summa de arithmetica* and an edition of Euclid's works (1509).   [LB]

Padrone sono me!, Il, see PANZINI, ALFREDO.

Padua. Though according to legend Padua (Italian Padova, Latin Patavium) was founded by Trojan refugees led by Antenor, a palaeo-*Venetian provincial town had developed on an ox-bow of the Brenta by 500 BC. The settlement came under Roman rule in 49 BC and soon became a major commercial and cultural centre of Northern Italy. Padua was largely destroyed by the barbarian invasions of the early 7th c., eclipsed by *Lombard centres at Verona and Pavia. Lay political leaders wrested power from Padua's bishops in the 12th c., with the vast town hall, the Palazzo della Ragione, constructed in 1218 as a symbol of the *commune's growing authority. Soon after, dissident students and professors from *Bologna established a *university in the city, and the thaumaturgic friar, Anthony of Lisbon, introduced the teachings of St *Francis; hence, from early in the 13th c., Padua flourished both as a centre of learning in *law and *medicine and as a focus of mendicant spirituality.

The harsh rule of the Ghibelline tyrant Ezzelino da Romano in the second quarter of the century destroyed many of the leading *feudal families [see GUELFS AND GHIBELLINES]. Following his fall in 1259, the Paduan commune enjoyed its heyday for the next half-century, with the construction of public buildings at the civic centre and large preaching churches on the periphery, and the extension of the city's authority over the surrounding countryside (*contado*) and neighbouring Vicenza. To meet the strife caused by the the descent of Emperor *Henry VII in 1310 and the expansionist policies of his vicar, Cangrande *della Scala, lord of Verona, Padua's commune elected Giacomo da Carrara as its lord and protector in 1318. Though the city fell under the rule of German or Scaliger vicars for the next two decades, the Carrara lords used their alliances with *Florence and *Venice to recapture it in 1337.

These momentous events in Padua's expansion and defence were recorded by major local historians, Rolandino [see CHRONICLES] and Albertino *Mussato, who were also leaders of a circle of early *humanists dedicated to the study of Latin literature and Roman history. The Carrara dynasty's rule was marked by notable *patronage of learning and art, with *Petrarch, Pier Paolo *Vergerio the Elder, and Giovanni *Conversino fixtures at the *court, and Guariento, Altichiero, and Giusto de' Menabuoi the main painters of the Carrara circle. In addition, *Franco-Veneto *epics, popular in 14th-c. Padua, betokened the Carrara family's devotion to *chivalric ideals. The expansionist designs of the last Carrara lords, Francesco il Vecchio and his son, Francesco Novello, led to a series of wars with Venice and the eventual conquest of the city in 1405.

For the next four centuries, Padua settled into the role of Venice's 'left bank'. Its university was renowned throughout Europe for the study of science, medicine, and philosophy, including

428

among its members *Nicholas of Cusa, *Pompon-azzi, Harvey, and *Galileo. Alongside this learned culture, popular literature flourished in Padua, where *Ruzante developed as its principal *dialect writer in the early 16th c. Padua's elite continued its tradition of artistic patronage with the Mantegna frescos in the Church of the Eremitani and Donatello's sculptures both outside and on the altar of S. Antonio. Padua's growth and prosperity in the early modern era were witnessed by the founding of a number of *academies and literary societies and a vital musical life, which produced, along with *madrigals and *opera, a dance known as the *padovana*. In recent centuries, Padua's past has been studied and documented, both within and outside the university, by one of the most vital school of local historians in all of Italy, from F. S. Dondi dall'Orologio and Andrea Gloria in the 19th c. down to Paolo Sambin, Sante Bortolami, and Silvana Collodo in our own time.   [BK]
See J. K. Hyde, *Padua in the Age of Dante* (1966); A. Simioni, *Storia di Padova* (1968); B. G. Kohl, *Padua under the Carrara* (1998).

PADULA, VINCENZO (1819–93). Calabrian poet, priest, and teacher, active on behalf of the Southern *peasantry as a young man and then a member of anti-*Bourbon intellectual circles in *Naples. He offers a realistic depiction of social inequalities in the South in his drama *Antonello capobrigante calabrese* (1864), first published in *Il Bruzio*, a *periodical focused on Southern issues and culture which he founded and edited (1864–5). He also wrote *dialect poetry, *novelle in versi*, such as *Il monastero di Sambucina* (1842), and verse fables drawing on *folk traditions, such as *La castagna, la noce e l'acciarino* and *L'Orco*.
[DO'G]

PAGANI CESA, GIUSEPPE URBANO, COUNT (1757–1835). Poet and *tragedian from Belluno. He sought to outdo Vincenzo *Monti with his tragedy *Gracco tribuno* (1808), and in 1816 he anticipated Giovan Battista *Niccolini's patriotic *Nabucco* (1819) with a homonymous tragedy dedicated to Italy but praising the *Austrian Emperor. His essay *Sovra il teatro tragico italiano* (1826) championed classical tragedy as written by *Alfieri against Schlegel and the *Romantics.
[JMAL]

PAGANO, FRANCESCO MARIO (1748–99). Southern intellectual, whose most important

work, *Saggi politici* (1783–5), combined a philosophy of history with hopes of reform for the South. He also wrote *tragedies. His *Jacobin-inspired draft of a constitution for the Parthenopean Republic [see NAPLES, 2; NAPOLEON AND THE FRENCH REVOLUTION] led to his execution in 1799. [See also MEZZOGIORNO; POLITICAL THOUGHT.]
[GLCB]

PAGLIARANI, ELIO (1927–). Poet born in Forlì who has been a teacher in *Milan schools, magazine editor, reviewer, and critic. He has published some dozen collections of poems showing his commitment to experimentalism and self-renewal. Lengthy extracts from his 1960 poem *La ragazza Carla* were included in Alfredo *Giuliani's *anthology *I novissimi*, where their documentary representation of a Milan office worker's perceptions might have seemed out of place, but in fact exemplified the *Neoavanguardia*'s critique of contemporary society through the demystification of its languages and their ideological function. Subsequent collections include *Lezione di fisica* (1964), in which Pagliarani played with the very long didactic line in the manner of Mayakovsky, *Lezione di fisica e Fecaloro* (1968), *Rosso Corpo Lingua* (1977), which introduced strong percussive repetitions into his poetry, the more restrained *Esercizi platonici* (1985), and *Epigrammi* (1988).   [MPC]

PAGLIARESI, NERI (*c.*1350–1406). *Sienese nobleman and poet. He became St *Caterina's secretary and *translated *Raimondo da Capua's biography of her. He wrote *hagiographical *cantari*, including a *Leggenda di Santo Giosafà*, and other *religious verse.   [SNB]

Painting, see VISUAL ARTS AND LITERATURE.

PALANDRI, ENRICO (1956–). *Novelist, originally from *Venice. His earlier novels focused directly on the post-*1968 generation of Italians. The first, *Boccalone* (1977), centred on the student movement in *Bologna in 1977. More complex and disquieting is the retrospective *La via del ritorno* (1990). *Le colpevoli ambiguità di Herbert Markus* (1997) and *Angela prende il volo* (2000) give his concerns with contemporary political and moral unease a more philosophical dimension.   [PH]

PALAZZESCHI, ALDO (pseud. of Aldo Giurlani) (1885–1974). *Florentine poet and *novelist who made distinctively whimsical and ironic contributions to *crepuscolarismo* and *Futurism. His privately published early poetry reworks *symbolist and Crepuscular motifs, often in apparently childlike tones, but with a growing sense of absurdity and the grotesque. In *Poemi* (1909) he went against both *symbolism and traditional views of the poet's public or moral role, by presenting himself as a circus performer and making personal suffering a matter of *humour.

When *Marinetti was sent this volume, he warmly welcomed Palazzeschi into Futurism. For a few years Palazzeschi found Futurism's iconoclasm and solidarity congenial, although he never adopted its political ideology, machine aesthetics, or most radical literary techniques. Futurism stimulated the lively and subversive poems of *L'incendiario* (1910; enlarged 1913). They included *parodies of the *Romantic treatment of nature ('I fiori') and death ('La fiera dei morti'), and a *modernistic treatment of the convention of the lovers' walk beloved by *D'Annunzio ('La passeggiata'). His aesthetics of humour are expressed in his manifesto 'Il controdolore' and the poem 'E lasciatemi divertire', which, beneath apparent meaninglessness, poses fundamental questions about the nature of poetry in the modern world. His *fantastic Futurist novel *Il codice di Perelà* (1911) has a quasi-Messianic protagonist, a man made of smoke and the epitome of 'leggerezza', who is in fact an *allegory of the poet.

Palazzeschi helped establish the fruitful alliance between Futurism and the *Lacerba* group in 1913, which in turn brought him into closer contact with the Parisian avant-garde. However, he broke with Marinetti in April 1914 and associated himself with *Papini and *Soffici, the editors of *Lacerba*, when they ended the alliance in 1915, claiming polemically that, with their ironic approach to literature, they were the true Futurists. His experience of military life during *World War I brought a new humanity to his writing, as is evident in his attacks on war in *Due imperi . . . mancati* (1920). He subsequently enjoyed a successful career as a novelist and short-story writer, especially with *Le sorelle Materassi* (1934), which is typical in using more traditional forms but maintaining a comic tone in its presentation of unexceptional characters. He moved to *Rome in 1941. Towards the end of his life, amused by the new scholarly interest in such an anti-academic movement as Futurism, he returned briefly to poetry and the free-floating fantasy writing of his youth.   [SV]

See L. De Maria, *Palazzeschi e l'avanguardia*

(1976); F. Livi, *Tra crepuscolarismo e futurismo: Govoni e Palazzeschi* (1980).

PALEARIO, AONIO, see EPICUREANISM.

PALLADIO, ANDREA (1508–80). One of the major architects and writers on architecture of the *Renaissance. His real name was Andrea di Pietro della Gondola. Born in *Padua, he worked as a stonemason in Vicenza until he met Giangiorgio *Trissino, who educated him and gave him his classical name. He studied contemporary architecture as well as the ruins of antiquity, making sketches which were intended as practical tools for his own work. He is most famous for his *Venetian churches (in particular S. Giorgio and the Redentore) and his rural villas for the Venetian aristocracy. He produced a description of ancient Roman remains, *Le antichità di Roma* (1554), contributed drawings to Daniele Barbaro's edition of Vitruvius (1556), and etched the illustrations for an edition of Caesar's *Commentaries* (1575). His most famous publication is the *Quattro libri dell'architettura* (1570), a landmark in the evolution of the architectural treatise, which sets out the principles of classical architecture and also surveys his own practice.
                    [PLR]

PALLAMIDESSE DI BELLINDOTE (mid 13th c.). *Florentine author of a *canzone* and two *sonnets, one in *tenzone* with *Monte Andrea. His style is involved and eccentric, and looks back to the *Sicilian School. He was a friend of Brunetto *Latini and *Rustico Filippi, and fought at the battle of Montaperti in 1260.   [JU]

PALLAVICINO, FERRANTE (1615–44). Prolific *satirist and *novelist. He was protected in *Venice by the founder of the Accademia degli *Incogniti, Gian Francesco *Loredan, after he abandoned religious orders. But he was eventually beheaded by *papal henchmen for his attacks on the nepotism, venality, and licentiousness of the Barberini Pope *Urban VIII.

His early novels mix romantic adventure and political messages. In *Il principe hermafrodito* (1640) a Spanish royal couple hide the sex of their only daughter to preserve their dynasty, but the daughter at the end reveals her true nature and changes the law so that women can succeed to the throne. The satire of sexual and political depravity in the Church and in the *Spanish court becomes more intense in *Il corriero svaligiato* (1641), in which four

*Milanese nobleman read and comment on letters taken from a mailbag en route from Milan (then under Spanish rule) to *Rome and *Naples. It reaches its extreme point in *Il divortio celeste* (published anonymously in 1643), in which Christ is so appalled by the depravities of his bride, the Church, as detailed by St Paul after a fact-finding mission, that he decides not only to divorce the Catholic Church but never to marry another. The work is indebted to *Aretino's *pasquinate*, *Boccalini's *Ragguagli di Parnaso*, Erasmus' *Colloquies*, and Protestant satires, but has its own vitality and originality. Though Pallavicino's friends denied that he was the author, he became a legend within Italy and all over Protestant Europe as a martyr to freedom of expression. But he was also violently *misogynistic, as in his *parody of a whore's instruction manual, *La retorica delle puttane* (1642), and was one of the figures criticized by Arcangela *Tarabotti. [See also LIBERTINES AND LIBERTINISM.]   [LAP]

See G. Spini, *Ricerca dei libertini* (1983).

PALLAVICINO, PIETRO SFORZA (1607–67). Born and educated in *Rome, Pallavicino entered the Church and governed Iesi, Orvieto, and Camerino before joining the *Jesuits. A professor of philosophy and theology at the Collegio Romano, he wrote poems, a *tragedy, and a work of *literary criticism, *Considerazioni sopra l'arte dello stile* (1646) [see LITERARY THEORY, 3]. He also published a vindication of the Jesuits and, best-known of all his works, the *Istoria del Concilio di Trento* (1656–7), defending the Council from the criticisms of Paolo *Sarpi [see also COUNTER-REFORMATION].   [UPB]

PALMIERI, GIUSEPPE, see ENLIGHTENMENT.

PALMIERI, MATTEO (1406–75) was a *Florentine apothecary of modest family who became a significant political and diplomatic figure in the *Medici regime. He received a *humanist *education, although his acquaintance with Greek authors seems to derive mainly from *translations. His most widely diffused work was the *Liber de temporibus*, a tabular universal chronology based on historical works by Sozomeno and Leonardo *Bruni. His mystical poem, *Città di vita*, written in *terza rima*, was found to be heretical. He is now most famous for his political treatise, *Della vita civile*, a work mainly concerned with the life of a citizen active

in public affairs and inspired by classical ideals of learning and virtue; it is primarily based on Quintilian's *Institutio oratoria*, *Cicero's *De officiis*, and *Aristotle's *Nicomachaean Ethics* (in Bruni's translation).   [RDB]

Palomar (1983). *Post-modern work by *Calvino, composed of twenty-seven short prose pieces, hovering between the short story and the essay, whose arrangement in groups of three owes something to the *Divine Comedy*. The eponymous protagonist, named after the Californian telescope, tries to observe and describe the world he inhabits, but never manages to penetrate beneath the surface of things.   [MMcL]

PALUMBO, NINO (1921–83). *Novelist, who turned to writing after an economics degree at *Milan's Bocconi University and a brief commercial career. Beginning with *Impiegato d'imposte* (1957) his predominantly *realist fiction centres on craftsmen and clerical workers struggling to maintain moral values against economic constraints. He later moved towards psychological drama, in, for example, *Il serpente malioso* (1977).   [JEB]

PAMPALONI, GENO (1918–2001). *Literary critic, who wrote extensively on 20th-c. Italian authors and for a time ran the publishing house *Vallecchi. Writers he helped to promote include *Vittorini, *Pavese, *Fenoglio, *Moravia, and *Calvino.   [SVM]

Pan, see OJETTI, UGO; PERIODICALS, 1.

PANANTI, FILIPPO (1766–1837). *Tuscan poet. Exiled for his *liberal republicanism in 1799, he settled in London, where he published burlesque poetry and prose, including his masterpiece, the mordant verse novel *Il poeta di teatro* (1808). Returning to Italy in 1814, he was captured by pirates, as he describes in *Avventure e osservazioni sopra le coste di Barberia* (1817).   [EAM]

PANCRAZI, PIETRO (1893–1952). *Literary critic, originally from Cortona, who worked principally in *Florence. He contributed regularly to *Il Corriere della sera* and other papers, as well as to literary *journals, most notably *De Robertis' *La *Voce* and *Ojetti's *Pegaso*, of which he was co-editor. He co-edited with *Papini the polemical anthology *Poeti d'oggi* (1920), and wrote extensively and subtly about modern Italian literature, particularly in the articles gathered in the six volumes of *Scrittori d'oggi* (1942–53). He was among the first serious critics to discuss *Montale and *Moravia. He also edited older Italian authors and published some fiction and *travel writing of his own. [DCH]

PANDOLFINI, AGNOLO (1360–1446), from a *Florentine family first prominent in the 14th c., was a leading *Medici partisan. An amateur Latinist whose learning was praised by Leon Battista *Alberti and *Vespasiano da Bisticci, he encouraged Leonardo *Bruni and appears as principal interlocutor in Matteo *Palmieri's *Della vita civile* and Alberti's *Della tranquillità dell'animo*. [RDB]

PANDONI, GIOVANNI ANTONIO DEI, see PORCELIO, IL.

Pane e vino, see VINO E PANE.

PANIGAROLA, FRANCESCO, see SERMONS.

PANIZZI, ANTONIO (1797–1879). The most influential *library administrator in Britain of the 19th c. Born near Modena, he became a *carbonaro* after graduating in law at Parma. He was arrested but escaped to London in 1823, to be welcomed by *Foscolo. He became professor of Italian at University College London, but joined the British Museum Library in 1831, becoming Principal Librarian in 1856. He was knighted in 1869. He published an important combined edition of *Boiardo and *Ariosto (1830–4). [See also ITALIAN BOOK AND MANUSCRIPT COLLECTIONS OUTSIDE ITALY.] [DER]

PANNARTZ, ARNOLD, see PRINTING.

PANNUNZIO, MARIO, see MONDO, IL.

PANORMITA, IL (Antonio Beccadelli) (1394–1471). *Latin poet and *humanist, who was born in Palermo and studied *law at *Bologna. While practising law in *Florence he began to write poetry, and dedicated to Cosimo de' *Medici a collection of obscene epigrams (*Hermaphroditus*), which was universally condemned as pornographic [see also EROTICISM AND PORNOGRAPHY]. He served as court poet and diplomat to Filippo Maria *Visconti at Pavia, before returning to *Sicily in 1434, where he was employed by King Alfonso V of *Aragon. He

was named Panormita (man from Palermo) after he moved to *Naples, where he expanded the royal *library and planted the seed that eventually developed into the Accademia *Pontaniana, attracting intellectuals and writers to the city. [PLR]

PANSA, GIAMPAOLO, see RESISTANCE.

Pantalone. A mask of the *commedia dell'arte*, and a type of the old man or *vecchio*, who is also known as 'Il Magnifico', and is a figure of *Venetian provenance. Performers wore a leather half-mask together with a long, hooked nose and pointed beard; characteristic costume was a black cape over a scarlet doublet and hose, black slippers and skullcap, with a short dagger and leather purse. Initially a vigorous and amorous bourgeois *merchant, the type was increasingly domesticated, and in the 18th c. was translated into the conservative *paterfamilias* of *Goldonian *comedy. [KR]

PANUCCIO DAL BAGNO (13th c.). *Pisan poet, directly influenced by *Guittone d'Arezzo, whose twenty-two poems make up in terms of technical complexity and bravura for what they lack in poetic inspiration. Panuccio's precise use of philosophical terminology makes him a forerunner of the *dolce stil novo*, but his excessive concern with reasoning makes his work cleverly versified rhetoric. Within these limitations, however, he was a major innovative force in both the formal and the syntactic language of *Tuscan poetry. [JU]

PANVINIO, ONOFRIO, see ANTIQUARIANISM.

PANZACCHI, ENRICO (1840–1904). Poet, critic, and essayist. He taught art history at *Bologna University, and for a time was also a member of parliament. He wrote extensively on literature, art, and music. His most important volume of poetry, *Poesie* (1894), is in the manner of *Carducci. [CFB]

PANZINI, ALFREDO (1863–1939). Best known as a novelist, he published some forty-six volumes of narrative, *belles-lettres*, and literary, historical, and linguistic studies. He was born in the Romagna, studied literature at *Bologna under *Carducci, and then worked as a schoolteacher in *Milan and *Rome. In 1929 he was made a member of the *Fascist Reale *Accademia d'Italia.

*Croce and *Gramsci dismissed him as a historian, linguists deny him any standing, and his

admirers made no intellectual claims on his behalf and deplored his attempts to engage with contemporary issues, such as *World War I in *Il romanzo della guerra nell'anno 1914* (1915) and agrarian conflict in the entertaining novel *Il padrone sono me!* (1922), which is recounted in the voice of a *peasant boy and was published as Fascism rose to power. A petit bourgeois humanist rooted in Graeco-Roman and *Renaissance *classicism, Panzini is representative of a generation of teachers and writers. He achieved his reputation by bringing classical lightness and grace to contemporary or trans-historical phenomena. Thus *La lanterna di Diogene* (1907) is the account of a bicycle tour from Milan to the Adriatic, and *Santippe* (1914) is about Socrates' much-maligned wife. The latter also exemplifies Panzini's fascination with women as men's downfall, which is pursued with even greater intertextual vaudeville (as Giacomo *Debenedetti was to call it) in *Il bacio di Lesbia* (1937), and had already figured in *Io cerco moglie!* (1920), Panzini's first popular success. His limitations are least evident in essayistic or diaristic works, such as *Il diavolo nella mia libreria* (1920), fairy-tale creations, such as *I tre re con Gelsomino buffone del re* (1927), and literary studies, such as *Matteo Maria Boiardo* (1918) and his *translation of Hesiod (1928). His *Dizionario moderno* (1905) of neologisms was reprinted up to 1942, the *purist sarcasm being progressively edited out. His *Guida alla grammatica italiana* (1932) is a poetically couched guide to Italian usage and style. [JG-R]
See E. Grassi (ed.), *Alfredo Panzini nella cultura letteraria fra '800 e '900* (1985).

PAOLAZZI, LEO, see PORTA, ANTONIO.

PAOLETTI, FERDINANDO, see ENLIGHTENMENT.

PAOLI, GINO, see CANTAUTORI.

PAOLI, PIER FRANCESCO (*c.*1585–1637/42). Poet who espoused a moderate *concettismo* and is best known for prefatory verses attached to works by *Marino, though he published several copious collections in his own name. Born in Pesaro, he spent most of his literary career in *Rome, where he was a member of the Accademia degli *Umoristi, and served the Savelli family. [MPS]

PAOLIERI, FERDINANDO (1878–1928). *Florentine writer, principally of *novelle*. In 1913–14 he also contributed to the *Sienese Catholic journal, *La Torre*. His first work of note was a series of lively sketches, *Scopino e le sue bestie* (1914). The later *Novelle incredibili* (1920) and *Novelle agrodolci* (1925) have mostly rustic *Tuscan settings and a somewhat *strapaese* character.
[CFB]

PAOLINI MASSIMI, PETRONILLA (1663–1726). *Arcadian poet. Born in Tagliacozzo near L'Aquila, she was known in the Arcadia as Fidalma Partenide, and was a member of the Accademia degli *Intronati in *Siena and the Infecondi in *Rome. A pupil of Alessandro *Guidi, she favoured the metre and the tragic style of the *canzone*. Her poems were published in various anthologies and are characterized by moving autobiographical themes, including the murder of her father, the death of her son, and her own entry into a convent.
[CCa]

PAOLINO VENETO, see BOCCACCIO, GIOVANNI.

PAOLO DA PERUGIA, see BOCCACCIO, GIOVANNI.

PAOLO DELL'ABACO (*c.*1300–1372). The leading *Florentine abacus teacher of his time and author of works on arithmetic, *astrology, and astronomy. His early vernacular *Regoluzzi* was composed probably in 1329 for practical use by *merchants, and is of mathematical interest since it proposes a ternary grouping of arithmetical numbers. [JP & JMS]

PAOLO LANFRANCHI (late 13th c.). Author of seven Italian *sonnets, which are jocular, uncomplicated reworkings of traditional motifs. A Ghibelline from Pistoia [see GUELFS AND GHIBELLINES], banished from the city for affray in 1291, he spent some time at the court of Pedro III of *Aragon, to whom he dedicated a sonnet in Provençal. [JU]

PAOLO VENETO (1369–1429), or Paolo Nicoletti, was a *scholastic philosopher and logician. An Augustinian friar, he studied in *Padua and Oxford. In addition to teaching philosophy and theology at Padua, *Siena, and *Perugia, he went on diplomatic missions for the *Venetian Republic. He wrote numerous *Aristotelian commentaries and the influential *Logica parva*. [JK]

Papacy and the Catholic Church

Papacy and the Catholic Church

1. Before 1870

The papacy and the Catholic Church have traditionally been the target of invective in much of the historiography of Italian literature. Influenced, above all, by the polemics of *Dante (notably in his *Monarchia*) and *Machiavelli (e.g. *Discorsi* 1.12), the papacy has been seen as the obstacle *par excellence* in the way of Italy's self-realization as a united political nation. The grounds for linking this with a perception of the resulting cultural and literary decadence experienced by the peninsula since the *Renaissance were set out fully by Simonde de Sismondi in his influential *Histoire des républiques italiennes* (1807–18). The literary criticism of both *De Sanctis and *Croce was heavily indebted to Sismondi's Hegelian view of history as pre-eminently the history of freedom of the human spirit, to which the papacy and Catholic Church were regarded as necessarily opposed. *Manzoni replied to Sismondi's critique in his *Osservazioni sulla morale cattolica* as early as 1819 (revised in 1855), and recent historical and critical studies have undermined entrenched negative views of Italian *Baroque literature and learning. But the broad lines of what is essentially an anachronistic (Whig) narrative still obstruct understanding of the relationship between the papacy, the Catholic Church and the literary history of the Italian peninsula.

The prominence of *religious literature from the very beginnings of Italian vernacular writing (e.g the *Ritmo su Sant'Alessio* [see HAGIOGRAPHY; MIDDLE AGES] and St *Francis' *Cantico di frate sole*) on the one hand, combined with the subsequent protean character it took on the other (faithfully anatomized by the indefatigable *Tiraboschi in his *Storia della letteratura italiana* of 1772–82), eloquently testify to the breadth, vitality, and variety of ecclesiastical *patronage. Moreover, aside from the distinctive literary interests of individual popes, such as the *humanist Nicholas V (1447–55), the poet and author of religious dramas *Clement IX (1667–9), or the cosmopolitan scholar Benedict XIV (1740–58), the opportunities for advancement offered by the papal bureaucracy and cardinals' households were numerically unrivalled within Italy from at least the 14th to the late-18th c., and provided financial support for generations of writers from *Petrarch to Vincenzo *Monti.

Recent research has confounded established prejudices regarding the *Counter-Reformation. It has been now firmly established that Paul IV's 1559 *Index was unworkably severe. And the subsequent Tridentine Indexes of 1564 and 1596, which reflected a pragmatic awareness of the limitations of blanket prohibition and were the product of tensions between rival interest groups, were of limited effectiveness. It has also been shown that the Roman *Inquisition (refounded 1542), unlike its Spanish cousin, was directly dependent on the cooperation of the local, secular authorities for its operation, and that its procedures were in important respects fairer and more rigorous than those found in secular jurisdictions. Overall, tribunals were scrupulous and sceptical as regards witchcraft, and the low number of prosecutions is in stark contrast with northern Europe. Of perhaps even greater significance, the refurbishment of local religion that ensued from the Council of Trent (1545–63) led to a renaissance in ecclesiastical erudition (c.1550–c.1750) that gave a strong impetus to vernacular writing. The Oratorian historian Cesare Baronio (1538–1607) and his local counterparts sought to (re)discover and justify their devotional traditions in the eyes of the papacy. A potent symbol of their collective achievement, to which many of them contributed advice and information, was Ferdinando Ughelli's *Italia sacra* (1644–62)— the first comprehensive framework of history which is truly Italian in geographical scope to be compiled since classical times. [See also CONCORDAT; RELIGIOUS LITERATURE; RISORGIMENTO; ROME; UNIFICATION; VATICAN LIBRARY.] [SD]

See M. Fumaroli, *L'Âge de l'éloquence* (1980); E. Duffy, *Saints and Sinners: A History of the Popes* (1987); P. Levillain (ed.), *Dictionnaire historique de la papauté* (1994).

2. From 1870

The occupation of *Rome by Italian troops in September 1870 ended the temporal power of the popes, that is, their territorial sovereignty over Central Italy. It also created the 'Roman Question', a dispute between the papacy and the Italian state which was not resolved until 1929. Until then, the popes would be the self-declared 'prisoners of the Vatican'. Italy tried to reach an agreement by means of the Law of Papal Guarantees of 1871, which gave legal immunity to the Vatican and other papal palaces, sovereign honours to the Pope, and an annual income. But Pius IX rejected it: in protest, he forbade Italian Catholics to vote or stand in national elections. The ensuing social, political, and cultural struggle between Catholicism and the new *liberal Italy was sometimes very bitter: writers as diverse as *Carducci, *D'Annunzio, and the youthful *Mussolini all dipped their pens in anticlerical venom.

The pre-*World War I *nationalists were the first movement to break with the traditional anticlericalism of Italian political culture and hail the potential contribution of Catholicism to Italian unity. The war itself also helped integrate Catholics into national life. But though the Partito Popolare Italiano sought to place Italian Catholics in the mainstream of democratic development, it was defeated by *Fascism. It was thus Mussolini who signed the Lateran Pacts [see CONCORDAT] with Pius XI in 1929, ending the 'Roman Question'. This helped consolidate the Fascist regime, but also made concessions to the Church in the areas of *education and marriage.

After the fall of Fascism, the Church managed to keep its gains, in part because of Catholic participation in the *Resistance. The confirmation of the 1929 pacts in the Republican Constitution (1948) inaugurated a period of Catholic 'triumphalism' under Pope Pius XII. Postwar Italy became a kind of Papal State of the 20th c., governed by the secular arm of the Church, the *Christian Democrat Party. Its rule, in diluted form, lasted almost exactly fifty years.

Italy's economic 'miracle' in the 1950s and 1960s set in motion processes of change—industrialization, urbanization, and migration—which, aided by the contemporaneous invasion of American culture, led to the secularization of Italian society. This was confirmed by the results of the divorce referendum (1974), the abortion referendum (1981), and the new Concordat (1983) which abolished the role of Catholicism as the 'sole religion of the State'. But Catholicism remains an important social and cultural force, and, though to a lesser extent since the collapse of the Christian Democrats in 1994, a political force too. Nevertheless, Italy has growing Protestant and Islamic minorities, and is rapidly becoming a multi-religious society.
[JP]

See A. C. Jemolo, *Church and State in Italy, 1850–1950* (1960); M. Clark, *Modern Italy 1871–1995* (1996).

PAPANDREA, VINCENZO, see ITALIAN WRITERS IN AUSTRALIA.

PAPINI, GIOVANNI (1881–1956), writer and *journalist, was one of the principal figures in the radical *Florentine culture of the early 20th. He co-founded and edited with *Prezzolini the periodical *Leonardo*, collaborated on the *nationalist *Il Regno* (1903–6) and on *La *Voce*, and founded and edited *Lacerba*. Despite his lack of formal training in philosophy he was alert to new developments and was largely responsible for introducing into Italy the work of Henri Bergson and the American philosophers John Dewey and William James. He was an unremitting polemicist who took strong positions for and (more frequently) against contemporary literary and intellectual figures, including *Croce and *Gentile, notably in the articles collected in *24 cervelli* (1912) and *Stroncature* (1916). A blasphemy suit was threatened against him in 1913 for an article in *Lacerba*, 'Gesù peccatore', suggesting that Christ was homosexual.

He wrote, aged 30, an autobiographical stock-taking, *Un uomo finito* (1912), before starting a new phase of activity which included a brief alliance with *Futurism (1913–14), documented in *L'esperienza futurista* (1919), and sabre-rattling for intervention in *World War I. The war shocked him into a sense of guilt which contributed to his conversion to Catholicism, announced in 1919. His *Storia di Cristo* (1921) was an international bestseller. He became a supporter of *Fascism, which honoured him in 1937 by appointing him to the *Accademia d'Italia and which he eulogized in *Italia mia* (1939). He was one of the main voices of the Fascist-Catholic periodical *Il *Frontespizio*. From 1935 he was professor of Italian literature at the University of *Bologna.
[DF]

See M. Isenghi, *Papini* (1972).

PARABOSCO, GIROLAMO (1524–57). *Madrigal composer, musician, and poet. Born in Piacenza, he worked in *Venice and various Northern *courts, becoming first organist at St Mark's in 1551. He was a friend of *Doni, *Aretino, and Titian, and published poems, *comedies [see THEATRE, I], and *novelle.
[FC]

PARADISI, AGOSTINO (1736–83). *Enlightenment intellectual and poet. He became professor of political economy at Modena University (1772–80) and influenced the reforms of Duke Ercole III (1780–96). As a poet he coupled imitation of *Horace with philosophical aspirations in the blank-verse epistles of *Versi sciolti* (1762) and in his odes, and set the example for the Emilian *Scuola oraziana.
[JMAL]

Paradisi, Giovanni

PARADISI, GIOVANNI (1760–1826). Poet. The son of Agostino *Paradisi, he rose to prominence in the *Milanese cultural establishment under *Napoleon. He was heir to the Emilian *Scuola Oraziana, but anticipated *Manzoni's *Inni sacri* in 'Ode sulla Passione' and 'Inno a San Pietro'.

[JMAL]

Paradiso. The third of the three *cantiche* of *Dante's *Divine Comedy*. Dante, guided by *Beatrice, ascends through the various heavens until he reaches the Empyrean, the real seat of God beyond time and space. The blessed souls whom he meets all have their being in the Empyrean, but they appear to Dante in the nine lower heavens, according to their particular spiritual qualities. The lower heavens are still touched by the shadow of the earth. The virtuous souls in the Heaven of the Moon were forced to break religious vows, those in the Heaven of Mercury were over-given to fame and glory, and those in the Heaven of Venus surrendered too much to love. Subsequent heavens have no similar limitations. The Heaven of the Sun presents lovers of wisdom (principally Christian philosophers and saints), the Heaven of Mars *crusaders (including Dante's ancestor Cacciaguida), the Heaven of Jupiter lovers of justice, and the Heaven of Saturn contemplatives. In the Heaven of the Fixed Stars Dante sees the Triumph of Christ and is examined on the virtues of Faith, Hope, and Charity by St James, St John, and St Peter respectively. In the Crystalline Heaven he sees the various Angelic Orders, before the blessed reveal themselves arrayed in the Celestial Rose in the Empyrean. Beatrice now resumes her place amongst them and Dante is guided on the last stage of his journey to the Godhead by St Bernard.

If Dante is concerned in the *Paradiso* to articulate as far as possible ineffable beatitude and produces his most amazing poetry in the process, he also never loses sight of this world and its iniquities. Throughout the *cantica* invective, lyricism, and doctrinal disquisition merge and alternate in a startlingly powerful and original way. The final vision is couched in terms of an expressive failure, but it achieves perfect circularity. After it Dante, having understood the *forma universal* of creation and the mystery of the Trinity, returns to this earth, to tell the story of his journey through the afterlife and all that it entailed, including the vision of which he cannot speak.

[PH]

Paradiso degli Alberti, Il, see GIOVANNI DA PRATO.

Paragone, see BANTI, ANNA; BASSANI, GIORGIO; LONGHI, ROBERTO.

Paralipomeni della Batracomiomachia, see LEOPARDI, GIACOMO.

PARETO, VILFREDO (1848–1923). Economist and sociologist. He trained as an engineer and transferred principles from mechanics (such as equilibrium and system) to societies. In 1897 he became professor of political economy at Lausanne and wrote *Cours d'économie politique* (1896), *Les Systèmes socialistes* (1901–2), and *Manuale d'economia politica* (1906). He retired early in 1907. Initially a fervent democrat, he became increasingly anti-democratic and cynical about historical change. In his major work, *Trattato di sociologia generale* (1916), he conceived of society as a system moving between states of equilibrium, where people often acted irrationally but masked this with pseudo-logical justifications (which he called 'residui') and where one elite displaced another over time ('circulazione delle elites'). He applauded the *Fascist seizure of power in 1922. [DF]

PAREYSON, LUIGI (1918–). Author of a large range of philosophical works, mainly on aesthetics, interpretation, *existentialism, and German *idealism. Appointed professor of aesthetics and philosophy in *Turin from 1952, he published his influential *Estetica: teoria della formatività* in 1954. This argued that the essence of the work of art lay in its 'mode of forming' or style, a process understood as incorporating the full range of the artist's individuality. While Pareyson opposed many tenets of the then-dominant aesthetics of Benedetto *Croce, he also shared many of Croce's fundamental assumptions. He was an important influence on his pupil Umberto *Eco. [DR]

PARIATI, PIETRO (1695–1733) was brought up in Reggio Emilia and Modena; then, exiled from his home state, he moved to *Venice in 1699, and finally to Vienna, where he was appointed imperial poet. The author of prose *tragedies, comic *intermezzi*, verses of various kinds, and *pastoral fables, he is mainly known for his *libretti, of which he composed at least ten as sole author, and many more in collaboration with the more famous Apostolo *Zeno; the most successful of these, performed in theatres up to the end of the century, were *Sesostri re d'Egitto* (1709) and *Arianna e Teseo* (1726). [See also AUSTRIA; OPERA.]   [SC]

PARINI, GIUSEPPE (1729–99). Italy's foremost *Enlightenment poet. He was born in Bosisio near Como, the tenth son of a *peasant family, and was brought to *Milan by his great-aunt, who guaranteed his *education (with the Barnabites) on condition that he become a priest. Tutored also by Cesare *Beccaria and Pietro *Verri, two of the most enlightened members of Milan's Accademia dei Trasformati [see ACADEMIES], Parini was constrained at the same time to give lessons in order to support his parents. In 1752 he wrote *Alcune poesie di Ripano Eupilio*, a miscellany of his own *pastoral poems along with *translations from classical authors (Catullus, Anacreon, Moschus, *Horace), a typically *Arcadian *anthology which was immediately welcomed by the Trasformati, who accepted him as a member.

Ordained priest in 1754, he at once became a tutor in the rich ducal household of the Serbelloni, where he remained until 1762, when he resigned in protest after the Duchess Vittoria petulantly slapped her choirmaster's daughter. His ironic reflections on the fatuities of the nobility began with the *Dialogo della nobiltà* (1757), a *dialogue between the corpses of a poverty-stricken poet and a nobleman, now equal in death. Painfully and obviously the poet succeeds in convincing his former adversary that nobility in itself is worthless without virtue. At the same time his *Lettere del conte N.N. ad una falsa divota* attacked fashionable but insincere religiosity. Parini's contributions to the Milanese Enlightenment continued with odes in *neoclassical style underlining the importance of civic and moral values and celebrating social and scientific innovations, notably 'La vita rustica', 'La salubrità dell'aria', 'L'innesto del vaiuolo', 'L'educazione', 'L'impostura', and 'La musica', a polemic against the castration of boy sopranos. The odes show his Rousseauistic view linking the beneficial laws of nature with higher human values, visible particularly in wholesome family ties. Parini's sense of the essential equality of man challenged his experience of the corrupt aberrations of the parasitic class he had to serve.

In 1763 he became tutor to the young Carlo Imbonati and published *Il mattino*, the first part of his great *satire, *Il *giorno*, a poem in unrhymed *hendecasyllables about a day in the life of a young nobleman, who is taught the arts of fatuous behav-

iour by his tutor, the narrator Parini. The narrative deals with such behaviour in pedantically minute detail (how, for instance, to form one's lips into a Cupid's bow in order to give an elegant yawn), treating every moment of the young gentleman's day with advice on the countless activities dictated by social fashion, from powdering a wig to conversing on such subjects as commerce, fashion, food, and philosophy. The style of the poem is elevated, containing many references to classical and contemporary culture. The irony works through the hyperbolic neoclassical similes, manipulated much as in Alexander Pope's *Rape of the Lock* to create disproportionate contrasts between content and style. It is at its most felt when it operates on the continual disparity between, on the one hand, the wholesome if poverty-stricken peasant life and the wretched state of the urban poor, and, on the other, the debauchery and lavish extravagance of the irresponsible nobility, eager to conform to current French ideas of conspicuous consumption, and followers of the inept social mode of *cicisbeismo*—the 'gallantry' of the courtier in fashionable service to another man's wife, and a social evil which preoccupied other enlightened writers, including Carlo *Goldoni and Vittorio *Alfieri. The poem thus presents an interesting sociological view of the period, as well as of Parini's wholesome prejudices, those of an enlightened if powerless and frustrated intellectual. Thus the exploited if developing peasant class is seen to have potential for improvement, thanks to technical advances in agriculture, while the urban poor live in more squalid conditions, dependent inevitably in a parasitic way upon the extravagances of Parini's main target in that society, the nobles, whose existence is viewed in a wholly negative light.

Only the first two parts of *Il giorno* (*Mattino* and *Mezzogiorno*) were published during Parini's lifetime; the two later parts, *Vespro* and *Notte*, were left in a disorganized state at his death, and have been the subject of much editorial dispute since their publication in the first complete edition of his works (1801–4). These sections continue describing the day of the 'Giovin Signore', though much of the earlier élan is lost as the portrait of the protagonist becomes more and more one-sided, and his vices and fatuities become a list of hobbies and diversions of the noble class. After the publication of the earlier parts Parini needed no more from his satire, and was moreover becoming an establishment figure himself. Indeed, it was an indication of the liberality of the *Austrian administration of Milan, and of the tolerance of the nobility, that publication of the *Giorno* brought some prosperity to Parini, as his targets bought it and laughed at themselves. In 1768 he was appointed editor of the Austrian-backed *Gazzetta di Milano*, though he soon left that post to take up the chair of belles-lettres at Milan's Scuole Palatine, transferred in 1774 to Brera, where in 1787 Parini was nominated superintendent of state schools. In 1771 he had composed the *libretto of Mozart's *Ascanio in Alba*, written to celebrate the wedding of the Austrian Archduke Ferdinand, and in 1777 he had been elected a fellow of *Rome's Accademia dell'*Arcadia. In 1791 he published the first edition of the *Odi*, which in addition to the earlier poems also contained occasional compositions, such as 'In morte del Maestro A. Sacchini'; others reflected his more comfortable lifestyle, and his frank appreciation of female beauty.

Following the French invasion of May 1796, Parini participated in the *Municipalité* set up by the revolutionary forces, but by July withdrew, condemning the *Directoire* for indifference to the wellbeing of *Lombardy, and for predatory attitudes to what had become a French colony. A year later the Austrians re-entered the city, just before Parini's death on 15 August. [See also NAPOLEON AND THE FRENCH REVOLUTION.]   [JRW]

Poesie e prose, ed. L. Caretti (1951). See G. Petronio, *Parini e l'illuminismo lombardo* (1972); E. Bonora, *Parini e altro Settecento* (1982).

PARISE, GOFFREDO (1929–86). *Novelist who had a varied career in *journalism and literature, mostly in the Veneto and *Milan. He also travelled widely as a foreign correspondent in the 1960s, the fruits of which were *Cara Cina* (1966), *Due, tre cose sul Vietnam* (1967), *Biafra* (1968), and *New York* (1977). Much of his fiction is located around his native Vicenza, but is not narrowly regionalistic. For many readers his best work is to be found in the early novels, *Il ragazzo morto e le comete* (1951) and *Il prete bello* (1954), and the later *Sillabario n. 1* (1972) and *Sillabario n. 2* (1982), these last being collections of short, distilled exempla of moral or psychological behaviour, which seem merely to suggest the outlines of a story and yet require no further elaboration. He published other novels and stories, as well as a play, *L'assoluto naturale* (1967), and won most recognition for the uncharacteristic *Il padrone* (1964), a savagely grotesque *satire of the economic jungle of contemporary Milan and its inhabitants.   [MPC]

PARODI, ERNESTO GIACOMO (1862–1923), a pupil of the literary historian Pio *Rajna, taught at *Florence University and was editor of the *Bullettino della Società Dantesca*. His principal scholarly interests included *Dante, the influence of classical culture, *dialect, and problems of literary style. Together with Michele *Barbi, he developed new techniques in *textual criticism which helped to establish the impressive Italian 'nuova *filologia', of which his edition of Dante's *Convivio* is a notable example.   [ZB]

Parodia sacra, see PARODY AND PASTICHE.

Parody and Pastiche. The distinction between parody and pastiche (and other notions such as *humour and irony, and *satire), although fairly clear in principle, is difficult to make in individual cases. Both parody and pastiche involve a connection between texts. According to Genette (1982) the manner in which a text ('hypotext') is treated by another ('hypertext') has two aspects or dimensions: the relation between the two texts, and the function of the hypertext. The relation can be of transformation (the hypertext modifies the hypotext) or of imitation (the hypertext is written 'in the manner of' the hypotext). The function of the hypertext, the attitude that it reveals towards the hypotext, can be ludic, satirical, or serious. We accordingly obtain a grid with six categories, designated by Genette with terms for which he adopts a specific meaning: (1) parody (ludic transformation); (2) disguise or travesty (satirical transformation); (3) transposition (serious transformation); (4) pastiche (ludic imitation); (5) caricature (satirical imitation); (6) forgery (serious imitation). If we need a more delicate classification of the functions, we may consider intermediate categories such as ironic (between the ludic and the satirical), polemical (between the satirical and the serious), and humorous (between the serious and the ludic).

In Italian literature we find examples of parody from the very beginning, encouraged by Italy's multilingual tradition, in which the coexistence of Latin, literary Italian, and a multitude of different vernaculars has privileged the use of linguistic effects, for instance in polyglot texts [see HISTORY OF THE ITALIAN LANGUAGE; POLYGLOT THEATRE]. The bilingual exchange (*contrasto*) of the 12th-c. *troubadour *Raimbaut de Vaqueiras offers one of the earliest examples of a parodic use of an Italian vernacular, in a *Genoese woman's rejection of a jongleur's advances [see GIULLARI]. In *Cielo d'Alcamo's 'Contrasto' we find the juxtaposition of high and low registers within the *Sicilian School. In *Renaissance plays and in the *commedia dell'arte different *dialects are used, not only to identify individual characters, but also to 'place' them, exploiting their dialects' comic connotations. The linguistic contrast between the rustic and the urban fits into the tradition of the satire against *peasants, and is also relevant in many poems making use of *Paduan and Bergamo dialects in Northern Italy, and in the *Tuscan poems in the tradition of the *Nencia da Barberino ascribed to Lorenzo de' *Medici.

In the *Middle Ages we find examples of 'Parodia sacra', on which there is an important study by Novati (1889) concentrating on the *Cena Cypriani*. Very well known are parodies of *Folgore da San Gimignano's by *Cenne dalla Chitarra. In the *Renaissance *Boiardo's and *Ariosto's poems offer a parody of the *Arthurian and *Carolingian traditions, not to speak of Luigi *Pulci, in whose *Morgante the comic element is particularly visible. *Tassoni's Secchia rapita is openly satirical. Explicitly parodistic are the *macaronic texts by *Folengo, mocking not so much *Virgil as his Renaissance imitators. Other famous parodies are the *Petrarchan travesties in the tradition of *Berni and *Burchiello. [See EPIC; MOCK-HEROIC POETRY; ROMANCE.]

On the other hand the *translation of famous texts, such as those of *Dante and Ariosto, into dialects has often been executed not so much with the ludic or satirical purpose of lowering the hypotext, as to raise the level of the hypertext and of the dialect it uses. In cases such as Carlo *Porta's translations from Dante's *Inferno, we recognize a ludic and humorous transformation of the original, and also a committed homage to the power and versatility of Porta's own Milanese. For the modern period, obvious targets of parody are influential poets such as *Carducci, *Pascoli, *Gozzano, and especially *D'Annunzio. See some felicitous transformations and imitations in L. Folgore, Libro delle parodie (1965); P. Vita-Finzi, Antologia apocrifa (1961); G. Almansi, G. Fink, Quasi come (1976). [GCL]

See G. Genette, Palimpsestes (1982); G. Gorni and S. Longhi, 'La parodia', in A. Asor Rosa (ed.), Letteratura italiana, vol. v (1986); G. Barberi Squarotti (ed.), Lo specchio che deforma: le immagini della parodia (1988).

Parole in libertà, see FREE VERSE; FUTURISM.

PARRONCHI, ALESSANDRO (1914–). *Florentine art critic and poet. One of the younger Florentine *hermetic poets, he published his first collection, I giorni visibili, in 1941. His poetry as a whole, anthologized in L'incertezza amorosa (1992), retains hermetic features in its *Petrarchism, literary artifice, and themes, with religious questioning becoming more insistent with the onset of old age. His criticism includes studies of *Rosai and other 20th-c. *Tuscan artists, and essays uniting his literary and artistic interests. [SPC]

PARTENIO, BERNARDINO (d.1589), contributed to one of the most important literary debates of the 16th c. with his Della imitazione poetica (1560). It deals exclusively with *imitation in the older, *Ciceronian sense of imitating the style of other authors, and discusses the problem of avoiding plagiarism when imitating. [See also LITERARY THEORY, 2.] [DG]

Parthenopean Republic, see NAPLES, 2; NAPOLEON AND THE FRENCH REVOLUTION.

Partigiano Johnny, Il, see FENOGLIO, BEPPE.

Partisans, see RESISTANCE.

Partito d'Azione. Anti-*Fascist party, founded in 1942, which grew out of the *Giustizia e libertà movement. It played a major role in the *Resistance, particularly in *Piedmont, and provided Italy with its first postwar prime minister, Ferruccio Parri. Internal wrangling, and a disastrous electoral result in 1946, led to its collapse. [PC]

PARUTA, FILIPPO (d.1629). A lawyer from Palermo, and secretary to the senate, Paruta was best known as a scholar, a member of several *academies, and the author of a numismatic study, La Sicilia descritta con medaglie (1612). He was also the author of the *pastoral Tirsi et Fillide (1614), and of posthumously published poems in *Sicilian *dialect. [UPB]

PARUTA, PAOLO (1540–98), *Venetian patrician and historian. Following the publication of his Perfezione della vita politica (1579), a discussion of civic life, Paruta was appointed historian to the Republic. Following the political changes of c.1580, he turned towards the active life, becoming ambassador to *Rome from 1592 to 1595 and procuratore di San Marco. His later works appeared

Parzanese, Pietro Paolo

posthumously: the *Discorsi politici* (1599), the history of the Cyprus war, and the *Istoria veneziana* (1605). These texts, translated into English in the 1650s, reveal the author's admiration for the Venetian system of government and his suspicion of generalizations about politics.   [UPB]

PARZANESE, PIETRO PAOLO (1809–52). Poet who was a priest in his home town, Ariano, but also had *liberal connections in *Naples. He composed lyrics, longer poems, and *tragedies in the *Romantic popular manner, including some patriotic odes. He also *translated English and French Romantic writers.   [FD'I]

PASCARELLA, CESARE (1858–1940). Important *Roman *dialect poet, but one who took his cue from *Carducci rather than from *Belli. He began his career as a *journalist and illustrator for the Rome-based *Capitan Fracassa* and *Fanfulla della domenica*. His first works of note, *Er morto de campagna* (1881) and *La serenata* (1882), were short narrative *sonnet cycles, both in dialect, and with a darkly realistic colouring. The twenty-five sonnets of *Villa Gloria* (1886) retell a celebrated episode of the *Risorgimento, the defeat of the Cairoli brothers just outside Rome, from the point of view of a plebeian Roman. Carducci thought the result raised dialect to an epic level. But Pascarella's best-known work is *La scoperta dell'America* (1894), an account of Columbus' voyage, which is both shrewdly humorous and deeply *nationalistic. Pascarella spent the later part of his life working on *Storia nostra*, a sonnet sequence with *epic pretensions, which aimed to narrate, through the language of a simple inhabitant of Rome, the history of the city from its origins to the present. The 267 sonnets which he completed were published posthumously in 1941. Pascarella was an impressive reciter of his verse and highly rated as a poet in his lifetime. He was elected to *Mussolini's Reale *Accademia d'Italia in 1930.   [CFB]

PASCOLI, GIOVANNI (1855–1912) was one of the most important and original, if controversial, poets of his time. He was born at San Mauro, near Rimini, into a family afflicted and impoverished by misfortune: by the murder of his father in 1867 and the premature deaths of his mother and five brothers and sisters. In the poet's youth his native Romagna was one of the regions most troubled by political agitation after the *Unification of Italy. His own active work on behalf of the Italian *Socialist Party was terminated by a brief period of imprisonment in 1879, though he never abandoned his humanitarian ideals.

In 1891, as a mature poet of 35, Pascoli published his first collection of *lyric poetry, *Myricae*. At this time he was teaching classics at a secondary school in Livorno. Promotion to a university post came in 1895, when he acquired a permanent home for himself and his sister Maria at Castelvecchio in the foothills of the Apuan Alps. After holding posts at *Bologna, Messina, and *Pisa, he succeeded *Carducci in the chair of Italian at Bologna in 1905.

His reputation as an innovator rests on four collections, all permeated by sad memories and dominated by images of the landscapes and country life of Romagna and *Tuscany. The title *Myricae* alludes to Virgil's 'humble tamarisks' (*Eclogues* 4.2), and indicates both his subject-matter and his treatment of it. The definitive edition, augmented from twenty-two to 150 poems, appeared in 1903. The other collections are *Poemetti* (1897), later renamed *Primi poemetti*, *Canti di Castelvecchio* (1903), and *Nuovi poemetti* (1909). The title *Poemetti*, or 'miniature epics', was suggested by the narrative-descriptive structure of the poems, all written in *terza rima. By contrast, the stanzaic structure of the poems in *Canti di Castelvecchio* links them with *Myricae*, though individual poems are ampler in scope and more complex metrically.

These early collections broke with traditional poetic language, discarding lofty diction in favour of a more conversational idiom and exploiting, for the first time in the history of Italian poetry, words for commonplace objects, from agricultural machinery and domestic utensils to flower-names and bird-names, as well as onomatopoeic representations of bird-calls and other sounds. His technical precision may be a source of incomprehension even for an Italian reader. He even borrowed non-Italian words (for instance, 'chicken-house', 'pie', 'flavour' in his poem 'Italy', about Italian emigrants returning from America) and local *dialect words (which forced him to supply glossaries). Pascoli did not always avoid banality. At his best, however, the relatively prosaic nature of his diction is offset by the use of symbols, the power of suggestion, and the emotional charge that even his simplest lyrics may hold. The other distinguishing feature of his manner is the attention paid to musical effects, achieved partly through assonance, partly through refrains, partly through the use of shorter metres (especially the *novenario* of the folk tradition) neglected by earlier poets.

Pascoli aimed to capture the essence of things in all their particularity, and produced a theory of poetry as a purely intuitive act. His essay *Il fanciullino* (the first chapters of which were published in 1897, the definitive version in 1903) sees the poet as having a childlike vision, but is now linked by most critics with the poetics of *symbolism and *decadentismo*, though Pascoli effected his quiet revolution independently of developments in France. He admired Wordsworth and Tennyson, and recent research has established his indebtedness to other English sources: Herbert Spencer's *Philosophy of Style* (1852), Max Müller's 1861 *Lectures on the Science of Language*, published in Italian in 1864, and James Sully's *Studies of Childhood* (1895).

The remaining five collections of Pascoli's Italian verse explore a variety of metres ranging from blank verse (*endecasillabi sciolti* [see HENDECA-SYLLABLE; VERSIFICATION]) to imitations of classical lyric stanzas and the *laisses* of old French *epic poetry. The evocations of classical antiquity comprising *Poemi conviviali* (1904) have been likened to the *Poèmes antiques* of the French Parnassian poet Leconte de Lisle. The earliest poems in the collection first appeared in Adolfo *De Bosis's *Il Convito*, and Pascoli's volume evinces the literary aestheticism which the anthology helped to make fashionable. The *Poemi conviviali* also anticipated the high literary style of Pascoli's late poetry. During these last years of his life he vigorously supported Italy's *colonial ventures in North Africa, and some of the poems echo the *nationalist spirit of the time. The *Odi e inni* (1906) are mostly commemorative poetry, and though many of the *odi* are personal and reflective, the *inni* deal with heroic figures and momentous happenings. The other collections are all inspired by people and events of the Italian past. The unfinished *Canzoni del re Enzio* reconstruct the events that led to the defeat and death of *Manfredi, son of *Frederick II, at the battle of Benevento in 1266, celebrating Bologna and the virtues of the Italian people as demonstrated by the men from the democratic *communes who defeated the imperial army. Of the three compositions constituting *Poemi italici* (1911) the most striking is 'Paulo Ucello', a philological tour de force that uses archaic Italian to give an aura of *Franciscan simplicity to the 15th-c. Florentine painter. The uncompleted *Poemi del *Risorgimento*, celebrating people, places, and events associated with the movement towards a united Italy, was published posthumously. Pascoli

also wrote some significant poetry in Latin (*Carmina*).

During his lifetime Pascoli's poetry was adversely criticized by Benedetto *Croce, and he was overshadowed by his younger contemporary Gabriele *D'Annunzio. Nevertheless his innovations influenced *Futurists, *Crepuscolari*, and later poets from *Saba to Attilio *Bertolucci.

[PRH]

Tutte le opere (1944–52). See M. Biagini, *Il poeta solitario* (1963); W. Binni, 'La poetica di G. Pascoli', in *La poetica del decadentismo* (1969); P. R. Horne, Introduction to *Pascoli. Selected Poems* (1983).

PASINETTI, PIER MARIA (1913–). Novelist, who has divided his life between his native *Venice and California, where he taught Italian literature. Publishing fiction since 1942, he found critical success with *Rosso veneziano* (1959), an intricate saga of two Venetian families, one artistic and libertarian, the other practical and politically engaged, at odds with each other during *Fascism. Later works, such as *Il ponte dell'Accademia* (1968), and the articles collected in *Dall'estrema America* (1974), exploit the author's dual identity, and contrast the ancient (Italy) and modern (USA). Plots straddle the Atlantic and combine 19th-c. breadth with the structural originality of contemporary narrative.

[JEB]

PASINI, PACE (1583–1644). Author of an interesting prose *romance, *L'historia del cavalier perduto* (1644), which may have been a source for *Manzoni's *Promessi sposi*, and combines *chivalric, picaresque, and political themes. His *Rime* (1642) are characterized by a conventional *concettismo*, but have appended to them the *Trattato de' passaggi dall'una metafora all'altra e degli innesti dell'istesse*, which is one of the earliest theoretical discussions of the style. A *Padua-trained lawyer, he lived mostly in his native Vicenza, but was also a frequent visitor to *Venice, where he was associated with the Accademia degli *Incogniti. [MPS]

PASOLINI, PIER PAOLO (1922–75). A figure of major significance in Italian literary and cinematographic culture between the 1940s and the 1970s. He worked in a large number of forms and media—*dialect poetry, poetry in Italian, the *novel and short story, *cinema, *theatre, *journalism, *literary criticism, *semiotics, even drawing—and explored in interesting ways hybrid genres such as

Pasolini, Pier Paolo

the written screenplay or the 'notebook' film, as, for instance, in *Appunti per un'Orestiade africana* (1968). His work combines an obsessive scrutiny of the self with a heterodox *Marxist vision of the world and of history, as epitomized in his most famous poem, 'Le ceneri di *Gramsci' (1954). Uniquely for a literary intellectual of his formation, Pasolini was lionized by and mythologized for a mass public, both through media scandal, implicitly or explicitly driven by hostility to his homosexuality, and through his own exploitation of the media in the 1960s and 1970s. His violent death served only to enhance the process of mythologization.

He was born in *Bologna in 1922, and had a peripatetic childhood. He grew particularly attached to his mother's home region, Friuli. He attended Bologna University, taking courses in art history with Roberto *Longhi, contributing to *Fascist student reviews, and writing a thesis on *Pascoli. In 1942, he published a first volume of poetry, *Poesie a Casarsa*, in Friulan dialect. The poems are lyrical and bucolic, charged with the sublimated *eroticism of the landscape and its youthful inhabitants. Much to Pasolini's delight, Gianfranco *Contini praised the book fulsomely. Living in Friuli between 1943 and 1950, Pasolini worked as a teacher, setting up a Friulan cultural association, l'Academiuta Furlana, and subsequently becoming involved with the politics of local autonomy and then the *Communist Party. He continued to write dialect poetry in *La meglio gioventù* (1954), as well as the poems in Italian of *L'usignolo della chiesa cattolica* (1958), *diaries, and the stories of *Il sogno di una cosa* (1962), *Amado mio* and *Atti impuri* (1982). In general, his Friulan work has grown in reputation in the years following his death.

In 1949 he was accused of propositioning minors, sacked from his teaching job, and expelled from the Communist Party. He moved to *Rome in 1950, where for several years he lived in poverty, teaching and cultivating contacts in Rome's literary and film worlds, notably with Giorgio *Bassani and Attilio *Bertolucci. The experience of living in Rome's poorest areas provided him with the material for his most characteristic work of the 1950s and 60s. The period 1955–9 saw Pasolini's literary career at its peak: his first two novels, *Ragazzi di vita* and *Una vita violenta*, were controversial but successful; his collection of poems, *Le ceneri di Gramsci* (1958) set out a new course for poetry, and for the long poem in particular, in its integration of traditional forms and committed ideological con-

tent; his journal, *Officina* (1955–9), co-founded with his old Bologna friends, Roberto *Roversi and Francesco *Leonetti, used a combination of Gramscian and Continian influences to open up interesting new paths for literary debate after the stale postwar polemics over *Neorealism and *hermetic poetry.

Officina collapsed in 1959, his planned third Roman novel had stalled, and the poetry of *Religione del mio tempo* (1961), although full of lively narrative pieces and showing a new satirical edge, was poorly received. At this point his career moved in two striking new directions. First, between 1960 and 1965, he wrote a column in a mass-circulation, Communist Party magazine, *Vie nuove*, in which he answered readers' letters. Secondly, he moved into film-making. His first film, *Accattone* (1961), offered a poetic glimpse of the world of his novels, populated by pimps, prostitutes, and thieves but given a sublime purity by the setting, static camerawork, and sacred music. The same world was portrayed in *Mamma Roma* (1962), with Anna Magnani, and *La ricotta* (1963), a sparkling short about a film version of the Gospel story. *La ricotta* was prosecuted in a famous trial for blasphemy, but Pasolini went on to make his *Vangelo secondo Matteo* (1964), filmed in Southern Italy with the same direct and sublime intensity as the previous films, but using the Gospel text as film-script. Far from being seen as blasphemous, it was hailed by the Church, and is commonly seen as the most spiritual of all Bible adaptations on screen.

In the same year he published a large poetry collection, *Poesia in forma di rosa*, heralding the disintegration of the controlled poetic forms of earlier work, in favour of hybrid, provisional, diaristic forms. In the mid-1960s he made one full-length film, *Uccellacci e uccellini* (1966), and two shorts with the comic actor *Totò, which showed a new brio, and also a new manner of integrating ideology into cinema through *allegory and fantasy. He became an editor of the influential journal, *Nuovi argomenti*, alongside *Moravia and Alberto *Carocci, and he wrote a number of much-discussed essays in film *semiotics, later collected as *Empirismo eretico* (1972). In 1966 he also began his six verse *tragedies, all meditations on subjectivity, sexuality, and mythical-cum-psychoanalytical archetypes, such as the father and the son. In parallel to his theatre, after 1967 his cinema was initially dominated by ancient and modern myths, for instance in *Edipo re* (1967) and *Teorema* (1968). His final collection of poems in Italian, *Trasumanar* *e organizzar* (1971), took the process of disintegration evident in *Poesia in forma di rosa* still further, with its sprawling forms and grating, caustic style. Its principal subject was a love–hate dance with the *1968 student movements, by turns acclaiming them as revolutionary and despising their bourgeois hypocrisy.

In the early 1970s his search for a pre-bourgeois authenticity led him to make a trilogy of films of early narrative texts centred on the body and the open expression of its sexuality—*Decameron* (1971), *I racconti di Canterbury* (1972), and *Il fiore delle Mille e una notte* (1974). In the final three years of his life, his work seemed to take on a sort of visionary fervour, as his polemics against consumerist modernity, gathered in *Lettere luterane* (1975) and *Scritti corsari* (1976), reached a mass audience, and irritated intellectuals on both left and right. He made his final film, *Salò o le centoventi giornate di Sodoma*, in 1976; it is an awful, degrading allegory of Fascism and consumerism as sadomasochistic torture, displayed in horrific and schematic detail. At the same time he was working these themes into a massive allegorical and visionary novel, a large fragment of which was published in 1992 as *Petrolio*. Alongside his nihilistic rewriting of his Friulan poetry in *La nuova gioventù* (1975), these works indicate an extraordinary, dark crescendo of creativity in his last years.

He was murdered, by one or more young men, at Ostia in November 1975. [RSCG]
See R. Rinaldi, *Pier Paolo Pasolini* (1982); N. Greene, *Pier Paolo Pasolini: Cinema as Heresy* (1990); B. D. Schwartz, *Pasolini Requiem* (1992).

PASQUALI, GIORGIO (1885–1952) was the main Italian classical philologist of the 20th c. He absorbed the finest German tradition, and made of *textual criticism a contribution to cultural history. Among his best-known works, influential also on Italian philology, are *Storia della tradizione e critica del testo* (1934) and the four collections of *Stravaganze* (1933–51). [See also FILOLOGIA.] [GCL]

Pasquinate is the name given to anonymous verse and prose compositions which, during the first half of the 16th c., were attached to a Hellenistic statue called Pasquino in *Rome on the feast of St Mark (25 April), or during a *papal enclave. They regularly contained biting political and social *satire, were aimed at both secular and religious personalities and institutions, and were often of a very high literary standard, with contributions from writers of

the calibre of Pietro *Aretino. They were extremely popular, and circulated widely in manuscript form. From 1509 to 1544 they were often collected and published. [PLR]

PASSAVANTI, IACOPO (*c.*1302–57). *Florentine preacher and *religious writer. He entered the *Dominican convent of S. Maria Novella at 14 and held important positions in the order in the course of his life, becoming, for instance, prior in Pistoia and Florence. He studied in Florence and later in Paris (1330–3) before teaching philosophy and theology in *Pisa, *Siena, and *Rome. He returned to Florence in 1340, and during the Black Death (1348) was in charge of the rapidly growing convent library. He supervised the completion of S. Maria Novella and was partly responsible for the founding of the Florentine Certosa.

Some of his *sermons survive but he is best known for the *Specchio di vera penitenza*, an elaborate reworking of homilies he delivered in Lent 1354. Through its vivid treatment of the nature of sin and its consequences, it aimed to provide a lay audience with a practical guide to repentance. Passavanti shows impressive doctrinal expertise. He also develops the forty-eight examples with which he illustrates his message into what are in effect *novelle*, his artistry bearing comparison with that of *Boccaccio in the *Decameron. [CK]

PASSERINI, LUISA, see AUTOBIOGRAPHY; PSYCHOANALYSIS.

PASSERO, FELICE (16th–17th c.). *Benedictine monk and poet, born in *Naples, who became prior and then abbot of Montecassino. He wrote religious poems in *ottava rima, including a *Vita di S. Placido* (1589), *L'Essamerone overo l'opra de' sei giorni* (1608), and *L'Urania ovvero la costante donna* (1616). [FC]

PASSERONI, GIANCARLO (1713–1803). Poet. Born near Nice, he lived most of his life in *Milan as a poor priest. In *Il Cicerone* (1755–74), in 101 cantos of *ottava rima, he *satirizes manners via a humorous tissue of digressions which recalls and may have influenced *Tristram Shandy* (1759–63). In his targets and values he has much in common with his lifelong friend *Parini, but his verse lacks the latter's vigour and refinement. [JMAL]

PASSI, GIUSEPPE, see MARINELLA, LUCREZIA; MISOGYNY.

Passione. Vernacular versions of the ancient liturgical passion survive in a few Provençal fragments and, in Italian, in the *Laudario di Cortona* [see LAUDI]. They encourage participation in the agony of the Gospel narrative, and draw on patterns and techniques of secular poetry. From the mid-13th c. the vernacular *passione* is absorbed into the **sacra rappresentazione*.   [JT]

Passione di Cristo, La, see CANTARI.

Passion Plays, see SACRA RAPPRESENTAZIONE.

Pastiche, see PARODY AND PASTICHE.

PASTONCHI, FRANCESCO (1877–1953). Born near Imperia, he published a first volume of verse, *Saffiche*, in 1892. Like much of his subsequent work it was heavily influenced by **D'Annunzio. The *decadent mood persists in *Il violinista* (1908). He also published plays and short stories. He was professor of Italian literature at *Turin University from 1935.   [DCH]

Pastoral. From classical Latin literature to the end of the 18th c., pastoral occupied a significant position on the Italian literary scene, though its forms—eclogue, narrative poem, *novel, *favola pastorale*, and drama—altered from century to century. Italian pastoral has bequeathed at least three masterpieces of European dimensions: *Sannazaro's **Arcadia*, Torquato *Tasso's **Aminta*, and Battista *Guarini's *Il *pastor fido*. It was also a genre where, late in the *Renaissance, *women writers made their mark.

Two classical Latin poems laid the foundations for the pastoral, and provided enduring features: *Virgil's *Eclogues*, and the frame story from *Ovid's *Metamorphoses*. The former gave pastoral the timeless landscape of woodlands, meadows, and streams; names of poet-shepherds such as Mopsus, Tityrus, and Meliboeus, and their beloveds such as Galatea and Amaryllis; the recurring themes of vehement passion, unrequited love, loss and melancholy; covert political references; and the self-conscious celebration of *lyric poetry as the means to alleviate personal sorrow. Ovid gave Italian pastoral the four ages of mankind in their moralized form: the Golden Age of bliss, justice, and communal living in harmony with nature without the need for law, followed by the Silver, Bronze, and finally Iron Ages. Most pastoral is set in or yearns nostalgically for the lost Golden Age. In the Iron Age there is greed, conflict, violence, and private property. The law of cyclical transformation holds out the hope, however, that disintegration and decay will lead on to harmonious renewal. Christians soon equated the Golden Age with the Garden of Eden before the Fall, and read a prophecy about the Saviour into the lines of Virgil's fourth Eclogue about justice returning to earth and a New Age, thus adding to pastoral a theological dimension. Virgil had located his shepherds in *Sicily; when the Greek pastoral poet Theocritus was read and *translated in the 15th c., the more distant Arcadia in Greece became the ideal *locus amoenus*.

*Dante, *Petrarch, and *Boccaccio all wrote Latin eclogues so densely *allegorical that commentaries were needed to unravel them. But the vernacular poetry of Petrarch and Boccaccio also spread pastoral along different paths, especially in the later 15th c. Petrarch's brooding over past memories, his sense of death and of ephemeral beauty, and his love of wild natural settings far away from city life were all seen as typically pastoral. Boccaccio, on the other hand, heightened the erotic element of pastoral, especially in stories recounted by the nymphs in the **Ameto*, and introduced a new element of coarseness and violence in the rape scene in the **Ninfale fiesolano*. Many *Florentines in Lorenzo de' *Medici's circle wrote pastoral poetry, both serious and *satirical; *Poliziano created the first pastoral drama, **Orfeo*, which he called a *favola*, with choruses and mixed poetic forms. Like the shepherds, his Orpheus sang lyrics of lost love, pointing to the power of poetry to hold death itself in abeyance, at least temporarily.

The *Neapolitan Iacopo Sannazaro weaves together classical and vernacular motifs and genres in the first pastoral novel of international renown, *Arcadia*, a mixture of traditional lyric verse forms and prose narrative. When Sannazaro claimed that he was reviving pastoral after a thousand years, he set himself apart from and above all earlier vernacular pastoral, abandoning religious and moral allegory as well as chases of nymphs by satyrs, and satirical parody. Sannazaro's tone is melancholic; one finds solace for unrequited love, painful separation, and death through poetry performed out loud with friends. In *Arcadia*, furthermore, rank, money, and political power have no place. His refined laments found favour in Italy, where sixty editions were printed from 1504, as well as with imitators and translators in other major European countries, such as Sir Philip Sidney, whose *Arcadia* appeared late in the century.

In the second half of the 16th c., the *court at *Ferrara became the focus of new developments in pastoral. Short, loose episodic performances of pastoral myths gave way to dramas conforming to *Aristotelian unities. It is in this century that pastoral and musical drama also combine, leading to *opera. *Niccolò da Correggio's long narrative poem, *Fabula Psiches et Cupidinis*, continues the fondness for mythological subject matter in pastoral. Far more distinguished were the two most celebrated pastorals of the century, both written by courtiers at Ferrara and performed there: Tasso's *Aminta* (first performed in 1573) and Guarini's *Pastor fido* (first published in 1589). The novelty in both these pastoral dramas was in the *intermezzi* or choruses, borrowed from classical drama and woven into plots following Aristotelian unities. The result was a new hybrid genre, *tragicomedy.

Guarini deliberately rivalled and strove with reforming zeal to surpass Tasso's *Aminta*, with the result that although few years separate the dramas chronologically, an abyss separates them ideologically. In *Aminta* the law of nature, operating according to pleasure and instinct, is exalted over laws designed to control fallen humankind. The 'golden law' is 'S'ei piace ei lice' ('Whatever brings pleasure is right'). Guarini denies his Golden Age the supremacy of pleasure: souls of the Golden Age were accustomed to doing good; the law of honour, not Nature, was a happy one, and its rule was 'Piaccia, se lice' ('Let it give pleasure, if it is right'). Significantly, the shepherds and nymphs are strictly monogamous, both in love and in marriage. The Golden Age and the ideals of *Counter-Reformation Italy coincide. Guarini's interpretation of Arcadia and the Golden Age is heavily coloured by religious overtones and metaphors of blindness applied to the human condition. Only after suffering does the heaven-ordained wedding at the end bring joy, and even then the joy is born of virtue. For the entire 17th c. and beyond, *Il pastor fido* was a *theatrical reference point. Both plays, however, focus on the moral aspects of shepherds' lives and loves, marginalizing Sannazaro's sense of pastoral as the lyric poet's special province, expressing mood.

Although the pastoral drama involved women playing equal roles in the unfolding and resolution of erotic conflicts, the first dramas written by women were late in the 16th c. Isabella *Andreini Canali, a poet and leading actress, composed and performed in *Mirtilla* (1588); and in the same year, Maddalena *Campiglia composed her *Flori*. In

their plots' complexity, unreciprocated loves, misunderstandings, and final resolutions, the two dramas are related to Tasso and especially Guarini; Mirtilla, the leading nymph, is the literary sister of Mirtillo, Guarini's 'faithful shepherd' and male lead. Like Guarini, Andreini Canali announces her intention to celebrate 'true' love which leads to marriage, and condemns sensual passion as a blind mistake killing reason. But comic elements abound, with nymphs playing games with satyrs, and Andreini gives herself plenty of set soliloquies. The female character, Flori, explores a range of dramatic emotions, from extremes of grief to erotic yearning to madness—the latter quality frequently found in female pastoral drama.

The third main woman writer of the period, Lucrezia *Marinella, seems to have drawn inspiration not just from Sannazaro, but from Virgil's *Eclogues* and *Georgics*, and a long tradition of poets celebrating nature and natural philosophy, including Tasso and his *Mondo creato*. In her pastoral novel, *L'Arcadia felice* (1605), composed in a mixture of prose and verse, her shepherds and nymphs are enlightened agriculturalists bent on understanding nature's secrets. The central character, Erato (named after the Muse of scientific poetry), tends a magic garden and enjoys prophetic powers—the most remarkable role of any woman in pastoral. No erotic complications trouble her or the band of nymphs she supervises. [LAP]

See E. Carrara, *La poesia pastorale* (1905); P. V. Marinelli, *Pastoral* (1971); L. G. Clubb, *Italian Drama in Shakespeare's Time* (1989).

Pastor fido, Il (1593). Battista *Guarini's immensely influential *pastoral drama interweaves three love stories of *Arcadian nymphs and shepherds. The play mixes comic, pastoral, and tragic motifs, as well as sensuality and moralism. It has often been judged cumbersome in comparison with Torquato *Tasso's *Aminta*, which it is plainly attempting to supersede. [CEJG]

PATERNÒ, LODOVICO (b.1533). Poet who was born into the provincial nobility near Caserta and studied *law at *Naples. His varied output includes eclogues and *satires, often in unusual metrical forms. He is particularly noted for his attempts to outdo *Petrarch as a love poet, at least in scale, in the first instance with his *Nuovo Petrarca* (1561) which contains more than a thousand poems. His particular *Petrarchism displays interesting *Mannerist features. He was in frequent contact with writers such as Berardino *Rota and Bernardo *Tasso. [ABu]

Patriotism, see NATIONALISM; RISORGIMENTO.

PATRIZI, FRANCESCO (THE ELDER) (Francesco Patrizi da Siena) (1413–94). Major Sienese *humanist, who held high offices in *Siena before being exiled for political conspiracy in 1457. He was made Governor of Foligno and then Bishop of Gaeta in 1461 by his friend Enea Silvio *Piccolomini. He is principally known for his influential political tracts, De institutione reipublicae (1518) and De regno et regis institutione (1519). His other humanist works, largely unpublished, include epitomes, treatises on philosophy, *letter-writing, and metrics, collections of Latin poems and epigrams, diplomatic orations, and a history of Siena. He also wrote important early vernacular *commentaries on *Petrarch's *Canzoniere and *Trionfi. [PBert]

PATRIZI, FRANCESCO (THE YOUNGER) (Francesco Patrizi da Cherso) (1529–97) was one of the most important *Neoplatonic philosophers of the 16th c. After travelling widely, he taught Platonic philosophy at *Ferrara University between 1578 and 1592, and at *Rome from 1592. His first work, La città felice (1553), was followed by many treatises, on military history, poetics [see RENAISSANCE], rhetoric, history, and mathematics. He *translated Greek texts of Philoponus and Proclus, and treatises attributed to Hermes Trismegistus [see HERMETICISM] and to Zoroaster, and edited in Latin the pseudo-*Aristotelian Theologia. His chief work, influenced by *Ficino and *Pico della Mirandola, was the Nova de universis philosophia (1591), which was condemned by the *Inquisition. Patrizi spent his final years revising it. [PBert]

Patronage. The word generally used by historians to describe the financial and moral support premodern elites in Italy and elsewhere gave to writers, scholars, and artists. Whereas the commissioning of paintings and sculpture was almost invariably subject to legal contracts, which protected the interests of both artist and patron, the support offered to literary figures and scholars was, more often than not, casual and intermittent, despite the enduring reputation for munificence enjoyed by celebrated *Renaissance patrons. To be sure, some (usually very distinguished) literary figures received handsome remuneration for works dedicated to, or laudatory of, patrons, while a few became their long-time associates and even familiars. The historian Giovanni Simonetta was not only a trusted chancellor to the *Sforza of Milan but the author of De rebus gestis Francisci Sfortiae commentarii (1473–6). The *Aragonese *court at *Naples employed a series of notable *humanist scholars, including Lorenzo *Valla, Giannozzo *Manetti, and Giovanni *Pontano, as both bureaucrats and eulogists. The brilliant poet and philologist Angelo *Poliziano was from 1471 onwards the intellectual companion of his protector, Lorenzo de' *Medici, whose political cause he also championed after the *Pazzi conspiracy in the Coniurationis commentarium (1478).

It is telling that such examples as much demonstrate the workings of social and political patronage as of literary patronage. For the majority of writers and scholars, indeed, the quest for a patron was as grinding and never-ending as it was often fruitless. The minor *Latin poet Naldo *Naldi showered prospective patrons, including *Federigo da Montefeltro, with praises they largely ignored; he, and many other more distinguished literary figures, perforce became itinerants who hawked their intellectual wares around the Grub Streets of Italy. The adaptability required is well illustrated by the career of the *Bolognese secretary, Giovanni Sabadino degli *Arienti, who managed to live precariously under the protection of many patrons and wrote (with very uneven results) in almost every known prose genre. Like some other of his late 15th-c. contemporaries, Arienti discovered that aristocratic women such as Isabella of Spain and Ginevra Sforza Bentivoglio, to the latter of whom he dedicated his book praising women, the Gynevera de le clare donne, were more likely to offer him encouragement and reward than were their kinsmen. Nevertheless, it was proverbial to say that 'chi vive a corte more al spedale' ('live at court, die in the poorhouse'). [FWK]

See G. F. Lytle and S. Orgel (eds.), Patronage in the Renaissance (1981); G. Ianziti, Humanistic Historiography under the Sforzas (1988); C. James, Giovanni Sabadino degli Arienti (1996).

PATTI, ERCOLE (1905–76). *Rome-based writer who published several collections of *journalistic writing between the wars, and also nostalgically *satirical sketches of high society under *Fascism in Quartieri alti (1940). He turned to fiction after the war, with popular comic novels that were readily adapted for the *cinema. [JEB]

PAVESE, CESARE (1908–50) was a poet, reviewer, *translator, *journalist, and *diarist, though it is probably as a *novelist that he will be remembered by public and critics alike, with *La *luna e i falò* (1950) generally felt to be his finest work. There is a strong autobiographical and confessional vein in his writing, with many of his major characters being based on himself. This does not always make for comfortable or appealing reading, but allows an authentic, self-critical voice to emerge, speaking honestly of a complex individual's response to the turbulent times in which he lived.

The contrast between town and country that is characteristic of most of his work has an obvious autobiographical origin. He grew up in *Turin, but with often lengthy visits to the village of S. Stefano Belbo, in the Langhe region of *Piedmont, where he was born. After his father's death in 1914 he was brought up by his mother and sister, an experience of female influence that may not have been entirely positive, judging by his difficulties with women as an adult and the *misogynistic strand in his work. Reclusive and incommunicative in his personal life, he found refuge and an outlet in writing from an early age. He made a first attempt at suicide in 1927 after a friend killed himself.

At *university in Turin, he became interested in American and English literature. He wrote a thesis on Walt Whitman and began what would become a series of *translations, principally of contemporary American fiction, including Sinclair Lewis, John Dos Passos, Sherwood Anderson, and William Faulkner. He also wrote essays on these and other authors, published principally in *La Cultura*, which both presented them to an Italian public and became a a way of developing a poetics of his own. At this stage he thought of himself principally as a poet. In 1930, he wrote 'I mari del sud', a poem which contains the stylistic and thematic nucleus of *La luna e i falò* and which led to his first and most important collection of poems, *Lavorare stanca* (1936). [See also AMERICAN INFLUENCES.]

After his degree Pavese taught as a private tutor, since he had not joined the *Fascist party and was ineligible for employment as a teacher in state schools. His friends Leone *Ginzburg (whom he replaced as editor of *La Cultura* for a year when the latter was arrested in 1934) and Augusto *Monti, his former teacher, were active in the *Giustizia e libertà* movement. Largely thanks to a relationship with a woman in the movement, Pavese found himself arrested and then sent as an internal *exile

to an isolated Calabrian village. In Calabria he started the *diary which became at least as much a commentary on the creative process as a means to self-examination and which he eventually prepared for posthumous publication as *Il mestiere di vivere* (1952). On returning to Turin in 1936 he discovered that the woman effectively responsible for his exile had decided to marry someone else. The broken love affair confirmed the pattern of self-pity, alienation, and a sense of his own destiny which is amply documented in his diaries, letters, and creative work. He now moved towards prose, writing short stories and, in 1938–9, a first novel, *Il carcere*, which is a poetic account of his imprisonment and exile. In 1939 he also wrote *Paesi tuoi*, published in 1941, a novel of the encounter between a Turinese worker and the asocial violence of *peasant life in the Langhe.

Quite what Pavese's political stance was during *World War II is still unclear, though there is some evidence of more sympathy with Fascism and even Nazism than was long suspected. He was declared medically unfit for the army and in 1942 joined the editorial staff of *Einaudi in Turin, working alongside Leone and Natalia *Ginzburg, Italo *Calvino, Giaime *Pintor, Elio *Vittorini, and other semi-dissidents. After the fall of the Fascist government in 1943 and the setting up of the Republic of Salò in the North, he withdrew to the *Piedmontese countryside, eventually working as a tutor in an isolated convent school but never participating in the *Resistance. The retreat into the hills, with its accompanying guilt and uncertainty, forms the basis of *La *casa in collina*, written in 1947 and eventually included with *Il carcere* in *Prima che il gallo canti* (1949). But, as is also reflected in the novel, his painful awareness of the savagery of the war around him led to a new interest in myth as a way of articulating the relationship between literature and the darker sides of human nature and experience. After the war he developed a complex theory of myth to which he gave imaginative realization in *Dialoghi con Leucò* (1947). With typical contradictoriness he was also a member of the *Communist party for a while, writing for *L'Unità* and stressing the importance of *impegno*. But though he forced himself to produce an orthodox committed novel, *Il compagno* (1947), these last highly creative years focused more on his own dilemmas and those of a society caught between traditional rurality and the changes wrought by modern urban culture and thought patterns, most evidently in the three short novels published as

Pavolini, Corrado

La bella estate (1949). *La luna e i falò* brings together the themes of his work as a whole, including his American phase, which is represented by vivid, troubled evocations of a landscape he only knew through literature.

After the failure of his relationship with the American actress Constance Dowling, for whom he wrote the poems of *Verrà la morte e avrà i tuoi occhi* (1951), he plotted his own death meticulously and took an overdose of barbiturates in a Turin hotel on the night of 25–6 August 1950.

[NMS]

See D. Thompson, *Cesare Pavese* (1982); T. Wlassics, *Pavese falso e vero* (1985); A. O'Healy, *Cesare Pavese* (1988).

PAVOLINI, CORRADO (1898–1980). *Florentine dramatist, poet, and critic. Though he published several volumes of verse, he was a director and drama teacher in *Rome with avant-garde interests and wrote more for and about the *theatre. In the 1920s he published studies of *Marinetti, as well as *Cubismo futurismo espressionismo* (1927).

[PC]

PAZIENZA, ANDREA, see COMICS.

PAZZI. The Pazzi, a noble *Florentine family, became *papal *bankers in the mid-15th c., but this led to rivalry with the *Medici and to the famous Pazzi conspiracy of 1478, when Lorenzo de' *Medici was wounded and his brother Giuliano killed. The Pazzi returned to some prominence in Florence after the exile of the Medici in 1494. Piero de' Pazzi (1416–64) was an amateur *humanist and one of *Ficino's early *patrons. [See also PAZZI, MARIA MADDALENA DE'.]

[RDB]

PAZZI, MARIA MADDALENA DE' (1566–1607), originally Caterina de' Pazzi, pursued an early vocation, becoming a Carmelite *nun in *Florence in 1583. A serious illness was followed by ecstatic experiences, subsequently dictated to colleagues in a series of five books, which have been claimed to be one of the major monuments of Catholic *mystical literature. She was canonized in 1669. [See also PAZZI.]

[JHB]

PAZZI, ROBERTO (1946–). Poet and *novelist working in *Ferrara. His four volumes of poetry show the influence of *Saba. He is better known for his narrative works, notably *Cercando l'imperatore* (1985), *Vangelo di Giuda* (1989), and *Domani sarò

Re (1997), which create a stimulating blend of history and *fantasy.

[PC]

PEA, ENRICO (1881–1958). *Novelist. Born in Serravezza near Lucca and brought up by his grandfather (a figure who recurs in his fiction), he worked as a blacksmith, farm labourer, and deckhand before emigrating to Alexandria in 1896. There he met Giuseppe *Ungaretti, who helped him get the early stories of *Fole* published in Pescara in 1910. He returned to Italy in 1914 and became an active organizer of *Tuscan folk musicals, or *maggi*, in Viareggio. After publishing two collections of verse, he turned to autobiographical fiction, much of which he first published in serial form in reviews such as *Pegaso* and *Nuova antologia*. Writing in a lexically rich Italian, which mixes a measure of highly literary items with *dialect words from the Tuscan Apennines, he tends to undermine normal chronology, and to introduce elements of magic or legend which blur the boundaries between reality and fable. His most important novels, *Moscardino* (1922), *Il volto santo* (1924), and *Il servitore del diavolo* (1929), seem to oscillate between *expressionism, *realismo magico*, and *verismo*. [DieZ]

Peasants (*contadini*) formed the overwhelming majority of the Italian population from the earliest times until the late 19th c. and were reduced to a tiny minority only in the second half of the 20th c. They are already dismissed as bestial, sullen, and devious *villani* in medieval literature, and would generally have been perceived by the literate classes as at odds with urban civility and intelligence. Only with *Romanticism and more particularly with *verismo* did the peasantry come to represent simple, fundamental values which more sophisticated society had lost or corrupted.

In reality the Italian peasantry was never a homogeneous body, either legally or socially, beyond being those who worked the *contado* (the land of a count and then the land around a town) and the countryside generally. Already by the end of the 13th c. most peasants in Italy were no longer serfs bound to work their lord's land, although until at least the 14th c. many remained legally bound to a lord or even a *commune. All over Italy there were some peasants who owned and worked their own land or who held land on hereditary lease from the Church. In the South, however, there tended to be more landless labourers, working for lords owning large estates (*latifondi*). And from the 13th c. onwards there were various systems of short-term leasing. *Mezzadria* (share-cropping), a contractual arrangement by which half the produce of the land was paid to the landowner, became particularly widespread, usually proving crippling to the peasant and simultaneously useful as a method of social control. Though of course many peasants lived in the countryside, in hamlets, farms, or villages, many agricultural workers in fact lived in towns, and went out to work the land as required. Overall, whilst there was always a minority of well-off independent farmers, the great majority of peasants throughout the country were already in the 14th c. living in poverty, often at a subsistence level. Though there were fairly frequent uprisings against individual lords, there was never a major peasant revolt, such as that of 1381 in England.

Social and intellectual developments in town and *court brought little change. Only under *Enlightenment influence did landowners in states under *Habsburg rule begin to take a serious interest in more rational forms of cultivation and husbandry. But in 1860 agriculture still occupied some 90 per cent of the population. For *liberal Italy the peasants seemed open both to clerical reaction and anarchistic revolution, and represented the main impediment to a strong national identity. *Fascist rural policy sought to 'nationalize' them through propaganda, while keeping them on the land or settling them in the colonies. In the 1943–5 *Resistance most peasants in the centre and north of Italy concentrated on survival, their participation limited to withholding food from enforced collections and supplying black-market produce to the towns.

At the end of *World War II peasants still accounted for almost half the working population of the country. During the 'economic miracle' of the early 1960s a significant proportion of the sharecroppers and small peasant proprietors of the Central and Northern regions left the land and became workers or independent producers in small and medium industry. In the South, agricultural production in 1945 was still dominated by *latifondi*, unemployment often approached 40 per cent, and the only exit was *emigration. In spite of piecemeal agrarian reforms, and the creation of the Cassa per il *Mezzogiorno in 1950, the mass exodus of adults of working age to industry in Northern Italy and Europe proved unstoppable.

The ex-peasant family firm could set wages and conditions without reference to national norms laid down by authority or in collective bargaining, and invest in new technology from high rates of saving through sacrifices of living standards. Real prosperity was attained by millions of Italian ex-peasants of the North and Centre who had emerged from a poverty-stricken agriculture only a few years earlier. The peasant migrants from the South had a less happy transition to industrialization, and their total uprooting drained the South of enterprise, leaving it open to corruption and organized crime.
[RAbs]

See R. M. Bell, *Fate and Honor, Family and Village: Demographic and Cultural Change in Rural Italy since 1800* (1979); D. L. Kertzer, *Family Life in Central Italy, 1880–1910* (1984).

Pecorone, Il. *Florentine collection of fifty *novelle*. According to the proem and a self-deprecatory concluding *sonnet, which reveals the title ('Big Sheep', but its significance is disputed), the work was begun in 1378 at Dovàdola, near Forlì, by a certain Ser Giovanni, evidently in *exile. Eight plausible identifications of Giovanni have been proposed, but none is decisive. Two-thirds of the stories are taken—in places verbatim—from Giovanni *Villani's *Nuova cronica*, while other sources for single stories include *Boccaccio. The *Decameron's* influence is also seen in the establishment of a framing situation and in the conclusion of each session with a *ballata*. The stories are told by two narrators, a nun named Saturnina and her Florentine lover Auretto (an anagram of 'auttore', 'author'), who has become a friar and the chaplain of Saturnina's convent in Forlì in order to be able to meet her with the desired frequency in the convent's parlour. There are twenty-five of these meetings, during which the narrators each tell the other a story. The *novelle* have well-controlled plots, but characterization, descriptions and style are banal. The most famous is the story of Giannetto or the pound of flesh (4.1), which is imitated by Shakespeare in *The Merchant of Venice*. [JCB]

Pegaso, see OJETTI, UGO; PERIODICALS, I.

PEGOLOTTI, FRANCESCO DI BALDUCCIO (14th c.). *Florentine *merchant in the service of the *Bardi company until their bankruptcy in 1345. He wrote a handbook for merchants, later given the title *Pratica della mercatura*, which is an important source of information about Florentine mercantile life. [JP & JMS]

PEIRE DE LA CAVARANA, see TROUBADOURS.

Pellegrino, Camillo

PELLEGRINO, CAMILLO (*c.*1527–1603), stirred up a furious literary debate with his *Il Carrafa o vero della epica poesia* (1584), in which he praised Torquato *Tasso's *Gerusalemme liberata* at the expense of *Ariosto's *Orlando furioso*. He was immediately opposed by Lionardo *Salviati and other members of the newly formed Accademia della *Crusca. [CPB]

PELLICO, SILVIO (1789–1854). Dramatist most famous for his prison memoirs. *Piedmontese by origin, he settled in *Milan in 1809 and was part of the circle that gravitated towards *Foscolo and *Monti and included such contemporaries as Ludovico *Di Breme, Giovanni *Berchet, and Pietro *Borsieri. His *tragedy *Francesca da Rimini*, staged in Milan in 1815, and published three years later, is one of the first and one of the most successful to be inspired by the famous episode in the fifth canto of *Dante's *Inferno*. Pellico did not take a direct part in the polemics around *Romanticism which erupted in 1816, but he was to the fore in the promotion and editing of *Il *Conciliatore* to which he also contributed. His review articles included essays on Chénier (February–April 1819) and Schiller's *Maria Stuart* (July 1819), in which he elaborated his theory of the importance of historical themes in drama.

Though another tragedy, *Eufemio di Messina*, was published in 1820, in the meantime Pellico had become involved with the *carbonari. He was arrested in October 1821 and sentenced to death the following February, the sentence then being commuted to fifteen years' labour, to be served in the notorious Moravian fortress of Spielberg. The story of his arrest, sentence, and imprisonment and the rediscovery of his religious faith is told in *Le mie *prigioni* (1832), the book he wrote after his release in 1830, which was a best-seller of its day inside Italy and also abroad. He continued subsequently to write for the *theatre, as well as undertaking editorial and secretarial work, becoming librarian to the Marchioness of Barolo in his later years. Though his piety was evident in everything that he published, he was never able to recapture the élan which had marked his earlier plays and critical essays. [MPC]

See E. Bellorini, *Silvio Pellico* (1916); M. Stival, *Un lettore del Risorgimento: Silvio Pellico* (1996).

PENNA, SANDRO (1906–77). Poet. Born in *Perugia, he trained as an accountant, but then lived mostly in *Rome, taking various temporary jobs, including bookshop assistant, proof reader, and art dealer. His first collection of poems, *Poesie* (1939), was successful, and he began to contribute to literary *periodicals such as *Letteratura*, *La Rassegna d'Italia*, and *Paragone*. He went on to produce nine poetry collections, three of which appeared posthumously. His main theme is his undisguised homosexuality. While his love for young men is for the most part a subject for celebration, some poems also lament the marginalization and solitude he suffers as a result of his sexual preferences. Conversely, his solitude is often felt to be a source of freedom and joy, and his shunning of contemporary Italian society is largely voluntary. Although Penna probably owes something to *Pascoli and *Saba (who helped him as a young man), his poetry, much of it in ostensibly simple quatrains, has a lucidity and spontaneity which much modern Italian poetry does not have. [VS-H]

Pensiero debole, Il. The title of an influential collection of philosophical essays edited by Gianni *Vattimo and Pier Aldo Rovatti in 1983. The term has become the label for a current of *post-modern Italian thought, associated especially with Vattimo, which draws particularly on Heidegger, Gadamer, and Derrida. Broadly speaking it rejects demands for certainties in the fields of knowledge and ethics, and privileges the individual's awareness of, and interaction with, a constantly changing, collective horizon of messages, memories, and projects. Where 20th-c. ideological systems had grand projects, it envisages only a modest degree of personal intervention as either possible or desirable. [GS]

Pentamerone, see BASILE, GIAMBATTISTA.

PEPOLI, ALESSANDRO, COUNT (1752–96). *Venetian dramatist. A self-styled champion of liberty, he systematically sought to outdo *Alfieri in his numerous *tragedies—often on subjects Alfieri had already treated—and in his extravagant lifestyle. He also imitated Voltaire and *Shakespeare, and drew on English subjects in *Eduigi* and *Anna Bolena*. [JMAL]

PEPOLI, CARLO (1796–1881). *Bolognese aristocrat who was also a scholar and writer. After being active in the 1831 Bologna uprising, he left for France, where he wrote for *Mazzini's *Giovine Italia* and composed the *libretto of Vincenzo *Bellini's *I puritani* (1835). Though he returned to

Italy to fight in the revolution of *1848, he spent many of the years up to 1859 as a teacher of Italian literature in London. *Leopardi addressed one of his *Canti* to him. [FD'I]

PERCOTO, CATERINA (1812–87). Short-story writer. She was born into a cultured but financially imperilled noble family in San Lorenzo, a village near Udine, and lived there most of her life, very much in the manner of the *peasants she wrote about. All the same she published stories in *Milanese reviews and was in touch with important literary figures, largely thanks to Francesco *Dall'Ongaro, who became her literary mentor after receiving an essay she had written on Andrea *Maffei's *translation of Klopstock's *Messiade*. *Tommaseo, for instance, wrote a preface to her first collection of *Racconti* (1858). Some of her stories are in Friulan, particularly the very short ones. In these, and in her stories in Italian, she offers a humane and sensitive picture of peasant life. Like other writers associated with contemporary *letteratura rusticale* [see also CARCANO, GIULIO; CORRENTI, CESARE], she emphasizes the natural virtues of the peasants in contrast with the vices and artificiality of the urban upper classes. Though her *realism is exact, its moralizing aspects link her more firmly to *Manzoni than to *Verga, for whom she wrote a preface to his *Storia di una capinera* (1871). Those stories in which she represents *Austrian repression in the Friuli are amongst her most uncompromisingly realistic and most heartfelt in their patriotism. [DO'G]

PEREGRINI, MATTEO (sometimes Pellegrini) (1595–1652) was the first Italian theorist of *concettismo*. Educated at the University of *Bologna, where he later taught logic and natural philosophy, he was a leading light of the city's cultural life, a member of the Accademia dei *Gelati and the Accademia della Notte, under whose auspices he published his first Latin and Italian poetry (1621 and 1627). He stirred up a polemic over the role of the intellectual at *court: *Che al savio è convenevole il corteggiare* (1624) provoked a reply from his fellow-citizen Giambattista *Manzini. He also entered the debate (current since the time of *Castiglione) over how the courtier should solve the delicate problem of telling his master the truth (*Della pratica comune a prencipi e servidori loro* of 1634).

In 1637 he left Bologna for *Genoa, where, until 1649, he served the Republic. There he completed his most important work, *Delle acutezze*, published in 1639, on the subject of poetic conceits. Paradoxically for such a 'modern' work, Peregrini extrapolates from premises given or hinted at by the ancients, from whom all its many examples and illustrations are taken. Such is the nature of modernism in the 17th c.: the ancients are not so much rejected as reappraised and supplemented. Conceptually, the work is muddled, but the core of Peregrini's theory is that unadorned truth appeals to the Intellect, while rare and beautiful artifice (not necessarily linked to truth) appeals to Wit (*Ingegno*). In its search for the artificial and the marvellous *Ingegno* must concentrate on making connection between disparate objects; the resulting conceits will be the more effective the more they are removed from everyday reality, and are most effective when founded not on truth but on appearances. Peregrini has often been described as a 'moderate' *Baroque figure. His work clearly influenced *Tesauro's more focused theory, but both have been more often mentioned than read. [See also QUERELLE DES ANCIENS ET DES MODERNES.] [PBD]

PERFETTI, BERNARDINO (1681–1747). Poetic *improviser and a professor of *law in his native *Siena, he was crowned poet laureate on the *Roman Capitol in 1725. His poems, partly transcribed during his performances, were published in 1748 in *Florence as *Saggi di poesie, parte dette all'improvviso e parte scritte*. [CCa]

PERI, GIAN DOMENICO (1564–1639) was famous for an *epic poem *Fiesole distrutta*, published in 1619, which tells of the foundation of *Florence upon the ruins of Fiesole. He was born of *peasant stock and only once moved out of his home town of Grosseto. This, together with his lack of learning, made it possible for him to preserve here and there in his epic a popular authenticity, which rubs shoulders, however, with less convincing erudite features. He wrote another epic, *La rotta navale* (1642), *pastoral dramas, a Creation poem, and prose pieces on mythological and pastoral subjects. [PBD]

PERI, IACOPO, see CAMERATA DE' BARDI.

Periodicals

1. Literary Periodicals

Influenced by English and French models, periodicals concerned with literary matters and written for

Periodicals

a specialized public of literati began appearing throughout Italy in the second half of the 17th c. The *Giornale de' letterati* was published in *Rome from 1668 to 1683, the *Giornale veneto de' letterati* in *Venice during the years 1671–80 and 1687–90, and the *Giornale de' letterati* in Parma from 1686 to 1690 and in Modena from 1692 to 1697.

In the 18th c., the *Enlightenment culture of the North produced a significant number of journals edited by such well-known writers as Scipione *Maffei (*Osservazioni letterarie*, Verona, 1737–40), Giuseppe *Baretti (*La *Frusta letteraria*, Venice and Ancona, 1763–5) and Girolamo *Tiraboschi (*Nuovo giornale de' letterati d'Italia*, Modena, 1773–90). The more important reviews of the period, Gasparo *Gozzi's *Gazzetta veneta* (1760–2) and Pietro and Alessandro *Verri's *Il *Caffè* (1764–6), were less literary and more sociopolitical in outlook.

In the early 19th c., three journals played a prominent role in the literary and cultural debates of the time. *Biblioteca italiana* (Milan, 1816–25), supported by the *Austrian government which ruled *Lombardy, was essentially conservative and *classicist in orientation. *Il *Conciliatore* (*Milan, 1818–19), a politically moderate biweekly, was the principal medium for Italy's *Romantic school. It discussed openly the state of literature and saw in Romanticism a means of cultural and social progress. The *Antologia* (Florence, 1821–33), founded by Giovan Pietro *Vieusseux, while continuing the *liberal legacy of *Il Conciliatore*, maintained a more European perspective and fostered a progressive and socially oriented culture. From 1860 to the end of the century, the literary reviews with the greatest circulation were *Nuova antologia* (1866–), the *Scapigliatura* magazines *Cronaca grigia* (1862–82) and *Figaro* (1864), *Rivista minima di scienze, lettere ed arti* (1865–6), *La Farfalla* (1876–83), *Fanfulla della domenica* (1879–1919), *La Cultura* (1881–1912), *La Domenica letteraria* (1882–5), and three journals associated with aestheticism: *Cronaca bizantina* (1881–5), *Il Convito* (1895–6), and *Il *Marzocco* (1896–1932).

At the turn of the century, reviews promoting social activism began to appear, especially in *Florence, which had been Italy's capital from 1865 to 1871 and had become the country's prime centre of literary culture. *Leonardo* (1903–7) represented the aspirations of a group of young intellectuals led by Giovanni *Papini and Giuseppe *Prezzolini; *Il Regno* (1903–6), under the direction of Enrico

*Corradini, spread the ideology of *nationalism; *Hermes* (1904–6) was *D'Annunzian in orientation and edited by the novelist and critic Giuseppe Antonio *Borgese. These years also saw the appearance of Benedetto *Croce's *La *Critica* (1903–44), which promoted the *idealism of its founder and chief contributor, as well as that of Croce's early philosophical ally Giovanni *Gentile. *La Critica* was to become the single most influential Italian periodical of the first half of the 20th c. But the journal that had the greatest immediate effect on the literary intellectuals of the time was the *La *Voce* (1908–16), edited by Giuseppe Prezzolini until 1914 and thereafter by Giuseppe *De Robertis. *La Voce* advanced a conception of literature based on the 'fragment', which it considered the most immediate, spontaneous, and concentrated form of literary and poetic expression.

Numerous reviews were founded in the wake of *La Voce*. From a literary standpoint, the prime centre was Florence and the most significant were *Lacerba* (1913–15), *La *Ronda* (1919–23), *Primo tempo* (1922–3), *Il *Selvaggio* (1924–43), *Solaria* (1926–34), *900* (*Novecento*) (1926–9), *La *fiera* (later *L'Italia*) *letteraria* (1925–36), *Pegaso* (1929–32), *Il *Frontespizio* (1929–40), *Il *Bargello* (1929–43), *Pan* (1931–5), *Letteratura* (1937–68), *Campo di Marte* (1938–9), and *Primato* (1940–3). Of these, *Solaria* played an important role in the Europeanization of Italian culture during *Fascism, and was a forum and outlet for *Gadda, *Vittorini, *Montale, and others, its legacy being continued into the 1960s by *Letteratura*. Other periodicals too showed a surprising degree of independence, even if (as was the case with *Primato* and *Il Bargello*) they were closely connected with the Fascist regime.

All the same, the fall of Fascism marks a watershed. From 1945 onwards numerous reviews were created to debate the relation of literature to society, the commitment of culture to social causes, and the role of the avant-garde in furthering progressive social ideals [see also NEOAVANGUARDIA; NEOREALISM]. The greater number of them were conceived on the political Left and animated by the conviction that the social function of literature was to promote a more informed, free, and humane society. How such a goal was to be achieved became the thematic matter of such periodicals as *Il *Ponte* (1945–), *Società* (1945–61), *Il *Politecnico* (1945–7), *Il *Contemporaneo* (1954–65), *Officina* (1955–9), and *Ragionamenti* (1955–7). In the 1970s and 1980s, essentially the same questions were approached in the context of neo-capitalism on the pages of *Problemi* (1967–), *Lavoro critico* (1975–), *L'Ombra d'Argo* (1983–7), and *Allegoria* (1989–). Reviews in which political issues were couched in terms of experimentalism versus tradition, such as *Il* *Menabò (1959–67) and *Quindici (1967–9) had a strong impact on the culture of the 1960s, while journals devoted more specifically to poetry and questions of criticism and literary form, such as *il* *verri (1956–) and **Strumenti critici* (1966–), still enjoy wide circulation. [RSD]

See G. Luti, *Cronache letterarie tra le due guerre 1920–1940* (1966); V. Castronovo and N. Tranfaglia (eds.), *Storia della stampa italiana* (1976).

2. Learned Periodicals on Italian Studies

Usually when one refers to learned periodicals one means those journals used by scholars to publish their findings and to keep abreast of current research and new publications in general. For this purpose normally journals also include book reviews, and sometimes bibliographical sections. Among the best-known journals in the field of Italian literature the following should be mentioned: **Giornale storico della letteratura italiana* (1883–); *Rassegna bibliografica della letteratura italiana* (1893–), later *Rassegna della letteratura italiana* (1953–); *Lettere italiane* (1949–); *Italia medioevale e umanistica* (1958–); *Studi e problemi di critica testuale* (1970–); *Italianistica* (1972–); *Filologia e critica* (1976–); *Rivista di letteratura italiana* (1983–). Among those published outside Italy: *Italica* (1924–); *Revue des études italiennes* (1936–); *Italian Studies* (1937–); *Italian Quarterly* (1957–); *Forum Italicum* (1967–); *Quaderni d'italianistica* (1980–); *The Italianist* (1981–); *Annali d'italianistica* (1983–); *Spunti e ricerche* (1985–).

It is useful for students of Italian literature also to consult journals devoted to philological and linguistic studies, such as *Romania* (1872–); *Zeitschrift für romanische Philologie* (1877–); *Studi di filologia italiana* (1927–); *Lingua nostra* (1939–); *Romance Philology* (1947–); *Studi linguistici italiani* (1960–); *Studi di grammatica italiana* (1971–); *Studi di lessicografia italiana* (1979–). Some of the major figures of Italian literature have periodicals devoted to their work, such as *Giornale dantesco* (1893–1943); *Bullettino della Società Dantesca Italiana* (1889–1921); *Studi danteschi* (1920–); *L'Alighieri* (1960–); the *Deutsches Dante-Jahrbuch* (1916–); the American *Dante Studies* (1966–), formerly *Annual Report of the Dante Society*

(1882–1965); *Annali manzoniani* (1939–); *Studi petrarcheschi* (1948–); *Studi tassiani* (1951–); *Studi sul Boccaccio* (1963–); *Studi goldoniani* (1968–). [LL & GCL]

See G. Ricuperati, *Periodici eruditi, riviste e giornali di varia umanità dalle origini a metà Ottocento*; and L. Mangoni, *Le riviste del Novecento*, in A. Asor Rosa (ed.), *Letteratura italiana*, vol. i (1982); A. Martinoli (ed.), *Periodici dei secoli XVIII e XIX* (1990).

PERLEONI, GIULIANO (15th c.) (Rustico Romano) fled from *Rome after the closure of Pomponio *Leto's *Academy, and entered the service of Ferrante of *Aragon. In *Naples he was an active member of a group of *lyric poets including *De Jennaro. His own collection of poetry, the *Compendio di sonecti* (1492), shares with them the striving for a language transcending regional usage. [ELM]

PERODI, EMMA (1850–1918). Children's author. She embraced *realism in novels emulating *De Amicis, such as *Cuore del popolo* (1892) and *fantasy in fairy tales, such as *Le novelle della nonna* (1892), which derived from contemporary folklore research. She became editor of *Il giornale per i bambini* in Rome in 1883. [ALL]

PEROTTI, ARMANDO (1865–1924). A poet whose two most successful collections of verse were *Dal Trasimeno* (1887) and *Il libro dei canti* (1890). He spent much of his life in his native Bari, of which he wrote a history, *Bari ignota* (1908). [CFB]

PEROTTI, NICCOLÒ, see CALDERINI, DOMIZIO.

Perpetua. Don *Abbondio's housekeeper in *Manzoni's *Promessi sposi, now the common term in Italian for the housekeeper of a priest.

PERRI, FRANCESCO (1885–1974). Calabrian *novelist, who wrote two books suppressed by *Fascism: *I conquistatori* (1925) and *Emigranti* (1928). The latter is the story of a fictitious Calabrian village, Pandore; an attempt by *peasants to occupy the land is suppressed by the *carabinieri*, and many of the younger generation emigrate to the USA. [DF]

PERTICARI, GIULIO, COUNT (1790–1822). Poet and scholar from Savignano near Forlì

Perucci, Andrea

and son-in-law to Vincenzo *Monti. In debates on the *questione della lingua*, he became Monti's chief supporter against *purism with *Degli scrittori del Trecento e de' loro imitatori* (1818) and *Dell'amor patrio di *Dante e del suo libro intorno il Volgare Eloquio* (1820).   [JMAL]

PERUCCI, ANDREA (1651–1704), from Palermo, wrote a wide range of poetry and theatrical material, in a variety of languages and *dialects. His treatise on performing art, *Dell'arte rappresentativa* (1699), is an important document: it deals with both scripted and improvised *theatre, and accords higher status to the latter because of the creative responsibility which it gives to actors. His 'revised' version of *Il convitato di pietra* (1678) is an item in the stage history of the Don Juan story. [See also BERTATI, GIOVANNI; CICOGNINI, GIACINTO ANDREA.]   [RAA]

Perugia. An Etruscan and then Roman city, which was an independent *commune from the 11th c. and came to dominate much of *Umbria. It was strongly *Guelf, and with *papal help became a major *university and cultural centre which, in the 14th c., developed its own strand of *poesia giocosa. In the 15th and 16th c. painting of the Umbrian School flourished more strongly, largely thanks to the dominant Baglioni family. Internal struggles resulted in conquest by Paul III in 1540. Papal rule was maintained, sometimes bloodily, until 1860. Modern Perugia has the important Università per Stranieri, founded in 1926 by *Mussolini.   [SCS]

PES, GAVINO (1725–96). *Sardinian poet from Tempio in the centre-north of the island. He made his mark in youth with Anacreontic poems. These later gave way to religious verse, such as the ode 'Lu pentimentu'.   [JMAL]

PETER MARTYR, see VERMIGLI, PIETRO MARTIRE.

PETITO, ANTONIO (1822–76). *Neapolitan actor who, like his father, became famous as *Pulcinella. In spite of being almost illiterate, he wrote several *comedies, of which the best known was *Palummella, zompa e vola* (1873) and an *autobiography, *Io Pulcinella*, published by Salvatore *Di Giacomo in 1905.   [DO'G]

PETRACCO, see PETRARCH, FRANCESCO.

PETRARCH, FRANCESCO (Petrarca) (1304–74). Latin *humanist and arguably the greatest Italian *lyric poet. He was born in Arezzo of a family of *Florentine exiles, and spent his first years in *Tuscany, before moving in 1312 to *Avignon where his father, a notary called Ser Petracco, had realized there were openings at the *papal *court. After basic grammar studies, he was sent with his younger brother Gherardo to study *law first at Montpellier and then at *Bologna. He returned to Avignon in 1326, after the death of his father, and decided to abandon legal studies in order to concentrate on literature and scholarship. To this end he embarked on a church career (limiting himself to minor orders), as the only way to guarantee economic independence and the possibility of cultivating his humanist interests. In 1330 he entered the service of the powerful Cardinal Giovanni *Colonna, making on his behalf frequent European journeys, which led to some important scholarly discoveries.

About this time he bought a house in Vaucluse on the left bank of the Sorgue, as a haven of tranquillity and solitude. He had already started to make a collection of his Italian lyrics. But there in 1338 he embarked on the major Latin works—his *epic, the *Africa*, and the historical *biographies of *De viris illustribus*, which he hoped would make him the new *Virgil and new *Livy. It was about this time that he began to use the classical-sounding and euphonious name Francesco Petrarca, rather than Francisco Petrachi, which is found in some early documents. His reputation soon crossed the Alps, and in 1341 he fulfilled his ambition of being crowned poet laureate on the Campidoglio in *Rome.

The next few years were divided between Italy and Provence, and saw some decisive events in his life. He was caught up in the failed attempt by *Cola di Rienzo to install an anti-noble government in Rome; his brother Gherardo entered a monastery; he fathered an illegitimate daughter (an illegitimate son having already been born to him in 1337); and there was the existential crisis of his 40th birthday. Above all the *plague of 1348 brought about a succession of deaths of friends, including his protector, Giovanni Colonna, and his beloved *Laura. In 1350 he made his one visit to Florence and met his great admirer Giovanni *Boccaccio, thus setting in train a friendship with extraordinary cultural implications.

In 1353, weary of the corruption and polemic of the papal court, he decided to leave Avignon for good and settle in Italy. His first home was *Milan, where he was welcomed and honoured by the *Visconti family, who allowed him to carry on his literary work whilst employing him on diplomatic missions. In 1362, he moved briefly to *Padua, and then to *Venice, where he was a guest of Benintendi de' *Ravagnani, who obtained from the Republic a palazzo for him on the Riva degli Schiavoni. In 1367, after some local philosophers had challenged his competence, he decided to go back to Padua and accept the *patronage of the Carrara family. He had a house built on some land in Arquà in the Colli Euganei which he had been given by Francesco da Carrara. He spent his last years there, absorbed in the task of completing his various unfinished works. It is there that he died and is buried.

Petrarch is a completely new type of writer and literary figure, particularly with respect to *Dante, who was from the same city as his father and was similarly exiled as a White *Guelf [see BLACKS AND WHITES]. Petrarch lives out his *exile not as a punishment but as a normal condition, eventually calling himself 'a stranger everywhere' ('peregrinus ubique'), and constantly striving to extend his cultural horizons and make himself a citizen of the world. He succeeds in distancing himself from his immediate historical environment, looking for the support of the powerful only in order to safeguard his intellectual freedom; service given to various different lords does not imply restriction for his literary work, but its liberation. He addresses a public that is not of one country but universal, using Latin to express philosophical and moral ideas of a general nature and reserving Italian for the representation in verse of his personal meditations on love and religion. This radical division in his work accounts for his refusal to recognize Dante as a model to be imitated, as he makes plain in a letter to Boccaccio (*Familiares* 21.15), and also explains how in Italian he reacts against the *Vita nova* and the *Divine Comedy* in both the lyric poetry of the *Canzoniere* and the *allegorical *Trionfi*.

Most of Petrarch's works are in Latin, the language of his much-loved classical authors and the fathers of the Church, St *Augustine first and foremost, whom he revered, and also a language in which to communicate with the learned of every place and time. He was above all a letter-writer and cultivated all forms of epistolography [see also LETTER-WRITING AND EPISTOLARI]. He began as early as 1349 to collect and arrange the letters sent by him to friends and well-known personalities, following the example of *Cicero and Seneca. The

first collection, comprising 350 letters written before 1361, becomes the twenty-four books of the *Rerum familiarum libri* (commonly referred to as the *Familiares*), dedicated to Ludwig van Kempen, the friend to whom he gave the name Socrates. He withheld the nineteen letters of violent polemic against the papal court at Avignon, which were prudently released separately as the *Sine nomine*. He then gathered 120 letters composed after 1361 in the seventeen books of *Rerum senilium libri* (or *Seniles*), which he intended to round off with an autobiographical letter to posterity, though this last never progressed beyond the draft stage. Many other letters which he excluded from his formal collections, presumably as uninteresting or irrelevant, were preserved by their recipients, and have long been known as the *Epistole varie*. Petrarch also composed verse-letters; sixty-six of these, all in hexameters and thematically related to the *Familiares*, form the three books of the *Epistole metrice*. These have features in common with the twelve eclogues of the *Bucolicum carmen*, which also deal with personal and contemporary issues, though under a veil of dense allegory. Petrarch's polemical bent shows itself at its most violent in the four prose *Invective*, in which he defends his new idea of culture and poetry against the attacks of his rivals. The most interesting of these is undoubtedly the *De sui ipsius et multorum ignorantia*, in which he denounces the false culture of *Aristotelian philosophers, and upholds the fundamental human values of literature which is inspired by Christian truth.

The other important genre which Petrarch cultivated in Latin is *historiography, which allowed him to revive the culture and life of ancient Rome. The *De viris illustribus* initially comprised twenty-three biographies of significant Romans ranging from Romulus to Cato the censor. Another twelve figures from the *Bible and mythology (Adam, Jason, Hercules, etc.) were added later. The work was revised many times and extended, in part because it was to provide the ideological basis for the decoration of the Sala dei Giganti in Padua; it was completed after Petrarch's death by Lombardo *della Seta. Petrarch also failed to complete his other major historical work, the *Rerum memorandarum libri*, a collection of *exempla after the model of Valerius Maximus. The original project was to construct a series of ancient and modern tales which would illustrate the four cardinal virtues and the relative vices, but Petrarch never progressed past the first virtue, Prudence. The *Africa* is also

Petrarch Commentaries

inseparable from his historical writings, *De viris illustribus* having probably begun as notes made during its composition. Whilst the model is Virgil's *Aeneid*, the poem retells the history of the Second Punic War, praising the figure of Scipio Africanus to the skies. Only nine of the projected twelve books were written, two of them still having notable gaps.

As a moralist and philosopher, Petrarch is more concerned with problems of his own time than with ancient Rome. His most serious work in this field is undoubtedly *De remediis utriusque fortune*, a vast prose treatise in *dialogue form, divided into two parts, which aims to help human beings deal with the problems of both good and bad fortune. The *De vita solitaria* and *De otio religioso* both celebrate the secluded life, lived in contact with nature, in the company of a few friends and many books. But the really decisive work in this part of Petrarch's production is the *Secretum*, which is both his spiritual testament as a writer and the key to understanding all his work. In particular it rehearses the main themes of the *Canzoniere* and the *Trionfi*—the passage of time, the transience of human passions, especially love and glory, the need to meditate on death, and hence to undertake confession and repentance.

Although Petrarch expected renown for his Latin works, he devoted as much care to the composition of his Italian poetry as he did to his collections of letters. In fact, the Italian poems which he called trifles (*nugae*), not his weighty Latin tracts and histories, were to be imitated in succeeding centuries, as having created a new model for poetic language and modern artistic sensibility. He worked on the *Canzoniere* or *Rerum vulgarium fragmenta*, as he called it, over a period of forty years. Some nine forms of the collection succeeded each other. The final one, which he may not have intended to be definitive, contains 366 poems, divided into two parts, though their traditional titles, 'in vita di Laura', and 'in morte di Laura', are not Petrarch's. There are significant precedents for collections of this sort in the Romance lyric, the most important being the *Libre* of Guiraut Riquier, the two-part *canzoniere* of *Guittone d'Arezzo, and Dante's *Vita nova*. But Petrarch's *Canzoniere* is unique. It brings together a variety of metrical forms, not only *sonnets and *canzoni but also *sestine, * ballate, and *madrigals; it has a highly complex architecture as a collection; and thematically it explores in depth the contradictions and convergences between classical myth and Christian conversion, creating always

unresolved tensions between love as desire and love as charity.

His other work in Italian, the *Trionfi*, which remained not quite finished, even though Petrarch worked on it from 1340 until his death, is more ambitious but also less successful in artistic terms. It is an allegorical poem in *terza rima, clearly imitating Dante's *Divine Comedy*. It takes elements of Petrarch's individual biography, notably his love for Laura and his cult of poetry, and by relating them to experiences of exemplary figures of the past gives his life a general allegorical significance. Six triumphal processions are depicted in sequence—Love, Chastity, Death, Fame, Time, and Eternity—each yielding to the one that follows until Eternity triumphs over all. But here, in contrast with the poem to the Virgin at the end of the *Canzoniere*, the ideal journey from earth to heaven ends with the vision of Laura in glory and the hope of joining her there. [MP]

Canzoniere and Trionfi, rime estravaganti, codice degli abbozzi, ed. M. Santagata (1996). See also E. H. Wilkins, *The Making of the Canzoniere* (1951); K. Foster, *Petrarch, Poet and Humanist* (1984); U. Dotti, *Vita di Petrarca* (1987).

Petrarch Commentaries. *Petrarch's two collections of poems in Italian, the *Canzoniere* [see CANZONIERE; CANZONIERE, IL] and the *Trionfi*, did not have *commentaries written for them until almost seventy years after Petrarch's death, no doubt mainly because it was as a Latin writer that Petrarch was initially most valued by *humanist culture. Reservations about his writing love poems, and in Italian, are evident in early commentaries, which also are neither as thorough nor as knowledgeable as later ones; but the issues which are investigated, and often discussed in general terms, remain fundamentally the same until the end of the 16th c.—the literal meaning of the poems, the sense of Petrarch's love for *Laura, parallels in earlier poetry, and the order or lack of order of the poems.

The first complete commentary to the *Canzoniere* is now lost. It was compiled in 1443 by Pietro Lapini da Montalcino for Francesco Maria *Visconti, and apparently argued for an *allegorical interpretation of Laura. The most important 15th-c. commentary followed in 1444–7, again compiled for the same Visconti; it is by Francesco *Filelfo, who has doubts about the acceptability of love as the major theme, and covers only poems 1–135, discussing linguistic difficulties, classical sources, and poetic technique, though he recognizes only *sonnets and *canzoni*, and treats the overall structure of the collection as arbitrary. First published in 1476 in *Bologna, Filelfo's commentary was completed by G. Squarciafico in 1484. By 1500 the full commentary had been reprinted another eight times. Editions from 1503 onwards also include another much shorter commentary, attributed to *Antonio da Tempo, which had first been published separately in 1477 in Bologna by Domenico Siliprandi, who may have been its author. This commentary (which is the first to use the term *canzoniere* of Petrarch's lyrics) deals principally with the themes of the poems and their classical sources, and again shows a limited understanding of Italian metre (on which Antonio da Tempo had written an exhaustive treatise). The 1477 edition also included a *biography, attributed to Pier Candido *Decembrio, which was then reprinted in most 16th-c. editions. Other complete commentaries on the *Canzoniere* were produced in the later 15th c. at the *Aragonese *court in *Naples by Acciapaccia and Francesco *Patrizi the Elder, who, though a former pupil of Filelfo, treated the order of the poems as significant.

The most popular and most reprinted commentary of the 16th c. was that by Alessandro *Vellutello, first published in *Venice in 1525. Having failed to recognize Petrarch's original manuscript, he rearranged the whole collection, dividing it into love poems written during Laura's lifetime, those written after her death, and poems on other subjects. Vellutello's edition also included the *Trionfi*, on which previously there had been only the commentary of Lapini's son, the doctor Bernardo Ilicino, written soon after 1463, and first published in Bologna in 1473. Cavalier though he may have been, Vellutello is more approachable than his more learned and cautious contemporaries. Sebastiano Fausto da Longiano (1532) brings in parallels with Petrarch's Latin works, as does Gesualdo (1533). Bernardino *Daniello (1541) examines in detail Petrarch's sources and precedents, both in Latin and Greek literature and in earlier Italian poetry. The list of variants given in his 1549 edition shows a new interest in the processes of composition and in the application of *textual criticism to Petrarch's poetry. But the best and most original examination of Petrarch's language, style, thought, and sources is provided by *Castelvetro (1582), although his subsequent influence was limited. No other full commentaries were published in the middle and second half of the 16th c., but many editions—notably *Sansovino (1546), *Brucioli

(1548), *Dolce (1553), and *Ruscelli (1554)—included biographies, rhyming dictionaries, glossaries, etc., both to make Petrarch more understandable and to facilitate imitation.

A major work of summary and integration of the commentary tradition was carried out by *Carducci and Severino *Ferrari in their edition of 1899. Previously in the 19th c. the most interesting (though, as Carducci pointed out, unscholarly) commentary on Petrarch is that by *Leopardi, who tries to read the text much as the ancients might have read their classics, and also to make the work accessible to a wide public, including women, children, and foreigners. [NC]

See F. Petrarca, *Le Rime*, ed. G. Carducci and S. Ferrari (1899); C. Dionisotti, 'La fortuna del Petrarca nel Quattrocento', *Italia medievale e umanistica*, 17 (1974); B. Richardson, *Print Culture in Renaissance Italy* (1994).

Petrarchism. During the 15th and 16th c. *Petrarch's vernacular *lyric poetry—the *Canzoniere* rather than the *Trionfi*—was widely imitated both inside and outside Italy. The theory and practice of *imitation varied greatly until the early 16th c. *Aragonese Petrarchism in *Naples is quite different from Petrarchism in Northern *courts, for instance. After 1530, however, practice became much more uniform as the rules proposed by Pietro *Bembo in the *Prose della volgar lingua* (1525) became widely accepted.

Petrarch was already famous as a vernacular poet in the 14th c., but there was no suggestion that he was to be the sole or main model. Other poets drew on his vocabulary and imagery as they drew on those of *Dante. During the 15th c., however, his metrical forms began also to be imitated, as did the narrative structure of his *Canzoniere*. The 150 poems of Giusto de' *Conti's *La bella mano* (1440) and the 180 poems in *Boiardo's *Amorum libri* (1499) both include imitations of the metrical patterns of Petrarch's *canzoni*, and both assume the form of narrative collections telling the story of the author's love for a woman, though Boiardo draws also on *Ovid's *Amores*. But these are in many ways exceptions. In the courts of Northern Italy during the second half of the 15th c. a form of poetic *improvisation flourished which was characterized by the almost mechanical recycling of images and rhetorical devices from Petrarch, principally for social entertainment. The most striking practitioner is *Serafino Aquilano, but the main distinguishing feature of the poems of Antonio

Petro De Barsegapè

*Tebaldeo, Panfilo *Sasso, *Niccolò da Correggio, and Gasparo *Visconti is the use of Petrarch's *Canzoniere* as a lexicon of imagery and rhetoric from which to select at will, with attempts to produce unitary collections on the Petrarchan model being few and far between. In *Florence, during the same period, the poetry of Lorenzo de' *Medici, *Poliziano and others does not show Petrarch occupying a comparably dominant position. Although his greatness was widely acknowledged—for example, in the preface written to the *Raccolta aragonese* of 1476 by Poliziano in Lorenzo's name— the Florentine tradition identified its models more in Dante and the *dolce stil novo* than Petrarch. The Aragonese court in Naples, with its scholarly interest in *Spanish and Provençal poetry as well as poetry in the Italian vernacular, was perhaps the place where the imitation of Petrarch came closest to the actual model, in the *canzonieri* of Giuliano *Perleoni, *Cariteo, Iacopo *Sannazaro, and others.

With the introduction of *printing, geographical divisions become less significant. Most poetry produced came also to be published in book form, hence assuming some of the features of Petrarch's unitary collection. But the resemblances were often purely formal. Petrarch's ordering of his poems was often very imperfectly understood [see PETRARCH COMMENTARIES], but there was no other obvious model for a book of vernacular lyric verse.

The progress of 16th-c. Petrarchism was helped by the emergence of a new vernacular *humanism, which identified classics in the vernacular in the same way as it did in Latin and Greek. A milestone in this process is represented by the 1501 edition of Petrarch's poems and the 1502 edition of Dante's *Divine Comedy*, published in *Venice by Aldo *Manuzio, devoid of commentary and printed in the same small format as he was using for his editions of *Virgil, Catullus, and other ancient classics.

The editor of these ground-breaking editions of Petrarch and Dante was Pietro Bembo, who is responsible for the codification of Petrarchism in the 16th-c. In his *Prose della volgar lingua* he theorized the need to apply the humanist theory of imitation in Latin to the vernacular. Just as Virgil and *Cicero were the models for writing poetry and prose in Latin, the models for vernacular poetry and prose were to be Petrarch and *Boccaccio, if Italian vernacular literature was to achieve the same degree of excellence as Latin. Eclectic imitation, as theorized by Poliziano, was ruled out. Instead,

Bembo offered a kind of grammar for poetic writing, though one which actually allowed considerable flexibility and individuality within a set of rhetorical, linguistic, and stylistic restraints. It was subsequently exploited by poets from the most diverse backgrounds, including Trifon *Gabriele, Giovanni *Guidiccioni, *Michelangelo, Torquato *Tasso, and *Della Casa. Women poets, such as Veronica *Franco, Veronica *Gambara, and Vittoria *Colonna, also conformed to the norm, even if in other ways their poetry changes the poetic scenario of Italian *Renaissance literature.

Petrarchism as such ends with the 16th c., but Petrarch remains an ineliminable presence in Italian poetry. With some justification, critics single out in particular *Leopardi for having returned to Petrarch for inspiration in his *idilli*, though not at all in the Renaissance manner. The same is true of the Petrarchism of *Ungaretti and other 20th-c. poets, though Andrea *Zanzotto and Patrizia *Valduga take up 16th-c. Petrarchism in startlingly modern ways.   [NC]

See L. Baldacci, *Il Petrarchismo nel Cinquecento* (1956); N. Cannata, *Il canzoniere a stampa 1470–1530* (1998).

PETRO DE BARSEGAPÈ (13th c.). *Milanese soldier who composed a verse *Sermon*, as he calls it, dated 1274. It paraphrases parts of the *Bible in three sections (Creation, Incarnation and Passion, Last Judgement). It is written in pedestrian but linguistically interesting Milanese.   [JU]

PETROLINI, ETTORE (1886–1936). *Roman variety actor who became also a playwright and film-maker. He created a new kind of comic *theatre that drew on *Futurism and avant-garde culture in general, and combined modern variety techniques with elements of *commedia dell'arte*.
[SVM]

PETRONIO, GIUSEPPE, see LITERARY CRITICISM.

PETROSELLINI, DOMENICO OTTAVIO (1683–1747). Priest and poet from Corneto Tarquinia, who founded the Accademia dei Quirini (1717–64), which gathered the disaffected followers of *Gravina after they left *Arcadia. His *satire *Il Giammaria, ovvero l'Arcadia liberata* (1892) recounts the schism, said to have been provoked by the tyranny of *Crescimbeni.
[JMAL]

PETRUCCELLI DELLA GATTINA, FERDINANDO (1815–90). Lucanian writer and politician. Active in the *1848 uprising in *Naples, he subsequently fled to London, where he met *Mazzini. He was elected a deputy on his return in 1860. He wrote *novels based on his experiences as well as works of contemporary political history.
[EAM]

PETRUCCI, GIOVANNI ANTONIO (1456–86). *Neapolitan *humanist and secretary to Ferrante of *Aragon, who was a member of the *Accademia Pontaniana, and friend of *Pontano and *Cariteo. Arrested (and subsequently decapitated) for his part in a baronial conspiracy against the Aragonese monarchy, he composed a collection of eighty-three *sonnets in prison, inspired by his experiences.
[ELM]

PETRUCCI, OTTAVIANO, see PRINTING.

PEZZANA, ANGELO, see AFFÒ, IRENEO.

Phenomenology. Philosophical movement originating in the work of Edmund Husserl in the first decade of the 20th c., according to which the phenomenon is conceived not as the sign of some hidden essence but rather as the emergence of reality to consciousness. In a phenomenological approach to literature, reading is seen as beginning in the familiar context of the reader's experience, but then as gradually discovering the otherness, or alternative consciousness, of the text. Thus an inseparable bond is created between the text and its reception, which reflects the general phenomenological tenet that the relationship between the subject and the objects of consciousness constitutes the focus of philosophical investigation.

Antonio *Banfi (1886–1957) played an important part in introducing phenomenology into Italian philosophy. Its presence is evident then in the work of Enzo Paci (1911–76), who approached the crisis of the subject in modernity within an eclectic perspective that brought together phenomenology, science, and *Marxism—most importantly in *Funzione delle scienze e significato dell'uomo* (1963) and *Idee per una enciclopedia fenomenologica* (1973). He also applied phenomenology to the study of literature (especially Mann, Proust, and Rilke), and to architecture and music. An interest in phenomenology is evident in *literary criticism of the 1970s and in the poetry of Andrea *Zanzotto.
[RSD]

Philology, see FILOLOGIA.

Photography. Although Italy was not involved in its invention, Italian photography flourished in the later 19th c. with commercial studios specializing in the reproduction of topographical and architectural views, and of works of art for the rapidly growing tourist market. *Florence became one of the main centres, following the establishment in the 1850s of the studios of Giacomo Brogi and the Fratelli Alinari, who aimed at systematic photographic documentation of the whole of Italy. Among the portrait photographers was Mario Nunes Vais, who photographed the most important personalities of his time.

The *positivists held that photography was the most accurate and faithful means of capturing reality, but most Italian artists responded by moving away from surface *realism. *Futurism was one of the few movements which made any attempt to exploit the new medium. Most writers of note (from *Verga onwards) were similarly mistrustful of 'photographic' realism in literature, though by the 1930s a reconciliation of writers and photographic images was occurring through the *cinema, which had its fruits particularly in *Neorealism. Photographs were only widely used in popular *journalism in the 1930s—notably in *Longanesi's *Omnibus*—but were wildly exploited in the postwar years, Italian *paparazzi* leading the world with their invasive pictures of the famous in *Rome in the 1950s. [See also FOTOROMANZO.]
[GP]

Piacere, Il (1889), Gabriele *D'Annunzio's semi-autobiographical first novel, narrates the amours and society adventures of the aesthete Andrea Sperelli, set against the *decadent backdrop of contemporary *Rome. The book breaks spectacularly with the *realism of his earlier *novelle*, creating new aesthetic fashions in language, style, and content.
[JRW]

PIAVE, FRANCESCO MARIA (1810–76). *Librettist. Born on Murano, he studied in *Rome and then returned to *Venice. He worked for the Fenice theatre, and later for La Scala. He wrote the libretti for some of *Verdi's most famous operas, starting with *Ernani* (1844) and including *Rigoletto* (1851), *La traviata* (1853), and *La forza del destino* (1862).
[DO'G]

PIAZZA, ANTONIO (1742–1825). *Venetian writer who, following on from the wave of success

Picciola, Giuseppe

enjoyed by Pietro *Chiari, wrote his first *novel in the 1760s, a genre which he approached in sentimental and picaresque vein. Travelling with companies of actors, from 1773 to 1778 he moved from *Genoa to *Milan, and *Florence to Brescia, writing plays and accumulating a rich store of *theatrical experience, and involving himself in the polemics of the day. From 1787 to 1798 he was the sole author of the *Gazzetta urbana veneta*, a biweekly newsletter in support of the democratic municipality of Venice.   [IC]

PICCIOLA, GIUSEPPE (1859–1912). Exiled from his native Istria, he wrote patriotic poetry in *Versi* (1884), strongly influenced by *Carducci, for whom he worked as secretary for a while. He was well known also for his *irredentist oratory, and also published studies of contemporary Italian literature.   [PBarn]

PICCOLO, LUCIO (1901–69). Poet and cousin of *Tomasi di Lampedusa who lived a secluded life in his native *Sicily. His first collection, *Canti barocchi*, appeared in 1956, after he had sent some poems to *Montale, who appreciated their intensity and verbal music. His complex natural symbolism displays a profound assimilation of 20th-c. European poetry.   [CO'B]

PICCOLOMINI, ALESSANDRO (1508–79). *Humanist who wrote on astronomy and the natural sciences as well as on literature and philosophical matters. He studied in his native *Siena, moving to *Padua in 1538 and then to *Rome in 1546. A member of the Accademia degli *Intronati in Siena, he is thought to be one of the authors of *Gli *ingannati* (1532). He went on to write other *comedies, *L'amor costante* (1540) and *Alessandro* (1545). He also composed treatises on women and love, and a *canzoniere* following the rules of 16th-c. *Petrarchism, and *translated from *Virgil, *Ovid, Xenophon, and *Aristotle. In later life he published commentaries on Aristotle's *Rhetoric* (1571) and *Poetics* (1575).   [NC]

PICCOLOMINI, ENEA SILVIO (Pius II) (1405–64). Renowned *humanist and poet, who was elected Pope in 1458. He studied humanities in *Siena, where he wrote a collection of lascivious epigrams, *Chinti*, in the manner of *Marrasio and *Panormita. He attended Francesco *Filelfo's Greek lectures in *Florence in 1429, and was secretary to several prominent churchmen. He travelled

extensively, attending and writing accounts of the Council of Basel (1432). In 1442 he was crowned poet laureate by the Emperor Frederick III, but in 1446 he took holy orders. During these years he produced a collection of *dialogues on politics (*Pentalogus*), a *novella* in Latin (the *Historia de duobus amantibus*), a Latin *comedy (*Chrysis*), and the short treatise *De curialium miseriis*.

His devotion to humanism was continued in a large number of works of *biography, *educational theory, topography, and historical geography as he climbed the ecclesiastical ladder, becoming Bishop of *Trieste (1447), of Siena (1450), *papal ambassador and Cardinal (1456). In 1462–4, as Pope, he composed his masterpiece, the *Commentarii rerum memorabilium*, twelve lively books of *autobiography and a *chronicle of his papacy. He died in Ancona waiting to embark on a *Crusade against the Turks.   [PBert]

Piccolo mondo antico (1895). Novel by *Fogazzaro, which lovingly evokes the Valsolda of the 1850s. Its protagonists, Luisa and Franco Maironi, are educated through the suffering caused by the drowning of their daughter. Franco becomes a true Christian and patriot who goes off to fight for Italian *Unification, whilst Luisa learns to accept the prospect of new motherhood.   [AM]

Piccolo mondo moderno, see FOGAZZARO, ANTONIO.

Piccolo Teatro, see STREHLER, GIORGIO.

PICO, GIOVANFRANCESCO (1469–1533), the nephew of Giovanni *Pico della Mirandola, edited his uncle's works (1496) after his death, with a *biography, although he did not share his ideas. He himself rejected *Aristotle's natural philosophy, wrote treatises against *astrology and *witchcraft, and proposed that salvation depended on the divine wisdom of scripture rather than on human reason. He was a follower of *Savonarola, writing his biography and various works in his defence in the 1490s. In 1511 in *Rome he took part in a famous debate with Pietro *Bembo on the *imitation of the classics. [See also SCEPTICISM.]   [PLR]

PICO DELLA MIRANDOLA, GIOVANNI (1463–94), uncle of Giovanfrancesco *Pico, was born the younger son of the Count of La Mirandola and Concordia and became the *Wunderkind* of his time. A dazzling aristocrat, precocious scholar, and budding poet, he attended the *universities of *Bologna, *Ferrara, and *Padua, where he studied *Aristotle and his commentators and a number of medieval texts. In 1482 he began to study Greek, and in 1484 made important contacts in *Florence before spending nine months at the University of Paris. In 1486 he took up Hebrew, and conceived the *scholastic enterprise of defending various philosophical and theological propositions in a public disputation. But he came up with an unprecedented and inordinate 900 such *conclusiones* culled from a rich variety of ancient and medieval texts, including the Orphic Hymns, the Chaldean Oracles, and the cabbala (selectively *translated for him by a converted Jew, Flavius Mithridates). He then declared he would defend them, not at a university where the enterprise might have been less remarkable, but in *Rome and against all comers, whose expenses he offered, as a munificent prince, to pay. For this intended disputation, he composed an introductory oration (only later subtitled *De hominis dignitate*), which is now famous because of its opening pages on the making of Adam as a being free to ascend or descend the ladder of creation. In March 1486, on his way to Rome, he eloped in Arezzo with the willing wife of a minor Medici *signore*, and was forced to surrender her after a pursuit and a fight in which several retainers were killed. He retired to *Pisa and then Fratta, and wrote his *Commento* on a love poem by his close friend Girolamo *Benivieni, in the process taking issue at times with his quasi-mentor and friend *Ficino.

On 7 December the *Conclusiones* were published as *Conclusiones sive theses DCCCC*, and controversy erupted. On 20 February 1487 a review commission was set up by Pope Innocent VIII, which proceeded in early March to condemn just seven and to question just six of the 900 theses (all thirteen treating of ticklish theological matters such as the real presence). Uncompromisingly, Pico rushed to defend these in an *Apologia* which he dedicated to Lorenzo de' *Medici, and the Pope then condemned the whole enterprise in a bull whose publication he delayed until 15 December. Pico made for Paris but was arrested and briefly imprisoned in *Savoy. A few weeks later he was invited back to Florence, at the intercession of Ficino among others, and Lorenzo gave him asylum at the villa of Querceto near Fiesole.

Pico's mood now darkened and he devoted the remaining years of his tragically brief life to the study of the *liberal arts and theology, in the mean-

while becoming drawn to, if not spellbound by, *Savonarola. In 1489 he finished a *commentary on the opening of Genesis, the *Heptaplus*, important for its Christological ideas and a cabbalistic appendix. Subsequently he wrote various commentaries on the psalms, a brief but important philosophical paper in 1491 propounding an *Aristotelian position on the identity of the One and being, and finally a huge sophisticated work attacking *astrology, *Disputationes adversus astrologiam divinatricem* (published posthumously in 1496). In June 1493 he requested and received from the new *Borgia Pope, Alexander VI, a full pardon on the matter of the disputation. On 17 November 1494, he died at the age of 31 (poisoned by a disappointed retainer?) and was buried in Savonarola's church, S. Marco, universally mourned as the phoenix of learning. Apart from his dramatic life, his phenomenal memory (still a byword in Italy), and his much cited oration, he is famous, not for being a *Platonist, an Aristotelian, or a *Scholastic, though all three allegiances have been ascribed to him, but for his brilliant attempt to synthesize a vast amount of eclectic material, and for his pioneer work on incorporating cabbalistic learning into Western philosophy. [See also NEOPLATONISM.]   [MA]

Opera Omnia (1572–3 and 1971). See E. Garin, *Giovanni Pico della Mirandola: vita e dottrina* (1937); G. Di Napoli, *Giovanni Pico della Mirandola e la problematica dottrinale del suo tempo* (1965).

Piedmont. Until the early 19th c. Piedmont was a relatively backward, largely agricultural region, whose inhabitants spoke *dialects with marked Gallo-Romance features, or else French if they were educated. Politically, too, as part of the Dukedom of *Savoy, it looked more to France than to the rest of the peninsula. But Savoyard expansion in Northern Italy in the 18th c. and the acquisition of *Sardinia led to *Turin being developed as the capital of what was now a kingdom. This was quickly restored in 1815 after the *Napoleonic period and strengthened by being given *Genoa. Despite bigotry, repression, and the militarism of its aristocracy and monarchy, by the 1840s Piedmont had a forward-looking political class and a leader, in *Cavour, who was able to steer Italy to *Unification. Piedmont furnished most of the troops who fought the campaigns of 1859–60, a king for the new Italy, *Vittorio Emanuele II [see also MONARCHY], and, in its 1848 *Statuto*, a constitution that would last a century. The region has since been at the forefront of Italian industrial development, particularly with FIAT in Turin and *Olivetti in Ivrea. But rural poverty and *peasant culture persisted at least until the 1950s, as is witnessed in the fiction of *Pavese and *Fenoglio, who also write powerfully about the ferocious partisan struggles that took place in the region during *World War II [see RESISTANCE].

[RAbs]

PIER DAMIANI (1007–72). Camaldolese monk from Ravenna, and later a cardinal (1057). His writings deal with the perfection of the monastic life, attacking sexual practices in monasteries (*Liber Gomorrhianus*) and advocating asceticism and reform. *Dante meets him among the contemplatives in Paradise (*Para.* 21.43–135). [PA]

PIER DELLA VIGNA (1190–1249) rose from humble beginnings to become, from 1230 onwards, a senior minister and confidant of the Emperor *Frederick II. In 1249 he was arrested on a charge of treason and blinded; his subsequent death in prison near *Pisa was widely believed to be suicide. *Dante puts him in hell for killing himself, but has him eloquently protest his innocence of treason (*Inf.* 13.55–78). Pier was also one of the *Sicilian school of poets, though only three elegant *canzoni* are attributable to him with any certainty. His Latin correspondence is interesting historically and shows great rhetorical expertise.

[JP & JMS]

PIERI, MARIO (1776–1852). Born in Corfu, he became a pupil of *Cesarotti, and a fanatical opponent of *Romanticism. His writings include original verse, *translations from Latin (notably Propertius), a *Storia del risorgimento della Grecia*, and an *autobiography. He courted celebrity by association, cultivating the famous, whose letters to him were published in 1863. [JMAL]

PIERRO, ALBINO (1916–95). Lucanian poet, from the village of Tursi near Matera, who studied in *Rome and became a teacher. After various volumes of verse in Italian, he turned to his native *dialect in *'A terra d'u ricorde* ('The Land of Memory', 1960) and subsequent volumes. He had no predecessors, and used the dialect in a creative and sometimes experimental fashion. He expresses the responses of an 'exile' to the destruction of traditional communities and moral values by industrialization, finding in recollection an ambiguous emotional refuge. [JJ]

PIETRO D'ABANO (1257–?1315). Writer on *medicine, natural philosophy, and *astrology, who learnt Greek and studied Greek and Arab philosophy. Born in Abano near *Padua, he travelled widely, including visits to Constantinople and Paris, before obtaining a teaching post in Padua. He held rationalist and determinist views, derived principally from Averroes, which led to his being accused of *heresy. [JP & JMS]

PIETRO DA EBOLI (late 12th c.). Cleric who wrote a Latin poem in elegiac couplets, the *Liber ad honorem Augusti* or *De rebus siculis* (1195). It supports the conquest of *Sicily by the *Hohenstaufen Emperor Henry VI and expresses the ideal of the Empire as a unifying institution. [JP & JMS]

PIETRO DA FOSSOMBRONE, see ANGELO CLARENO.

PIETRO DA MOGLIO (d.1383). *Humanist teacher. Possibly a pupil of *Giovanni del Virgilio, he opened a private school of grammar and rhetoric in *Bologna which was attended by figures such as Coluccio *Salutati and *Giovanni Conversino. In 1362 he obtained the chair of rhetoric at *Padua, where he came into contact with *Petrarch and *Boccaccio. In 1368 he transferred to Bologna. His teaching of classical and modern authors, in particular the *pastoral poems of *Dante and Petrarch, included history as well as grammar and rhetoric. His pupils' notes (*recollectae*) have preserved some of his comments on *Cicero, Seneca, Terence, and *Boethius. He wrote a Latin poem, *De Anna sorore Didonis*, inspired by *Virgil. [MP]

PIETRO DA MORRONE, see CELESTINE V.

PIETRO LOMBARDO (Petrus Lombardus) (1090/5–1160). From near Novara, he became professor of theology in Paris, where he was later bishop. His four books of *Sententiae*, compiled from the opinions of the *Church Fathers, systematized the whole of Christian theology, and were an authoritative source for St Thomas *Aquinas. *Dante puts him among the theologians in Paradise (*Para.* 10.106–8). [PA]

PIETRO OLIVI (*c.*1248–98). Provençal philosopher and theologian belonging to the Spiritual *Franciscans. His writings press for rigorous commitment to poverty, and include a *commentary on the *Apocalypse* drawing on *Gioachino da Fiore,

Pinocchio

parts of which were condemned as *heretical after his death. He taught in *Florence in 1288 and probably influenced *Dante. [JP & JMS]

PIGNA, IL (Giovan Battista Nicolucci) (1530–75), *Ferrarese *court poet and ducal secretary, author of *I romanzi* (1524), a treatise defending *Ariosto against *Aristotelian critics, and asserting the independence of the *romance from the rules of *epic. He quarrelled with his fellow Ferrarese *Giraldi Cinzio, driving him from the court. Torquato *Tasso was wary of him, calling him 'il saggio Elpino' in the *Aminta*, and complimenting him in his *Considerazioni intorno a tre canzoni di G. B. Pigna*. [CPB]

PIGNATELLI, ASCANIO (1533–1601). *Petrarchist poet in the tradition of Pietro *Bembo. He was of a noble family, and studied *law at *Padua, where he attended the Accademia degli Eterei. In recognition of his exploits during the Turkish campaign of 1566, he was given the title of Duke of Bisaccia by King Philip II of Spain. A friend of both Celio *Magno and Torquato *Tasso, he joined the *Naples-based literary circle of Camillo *Pellegrino, Giambattista *Manso, and the young Giovanbattista *Marino. [PLR]

PIGNOTTI, LAMBERTO (1926–). Poet and critic who was born and grew up in *Florence and has taught at *Bologna and Florence universities. He was active in the *Gruppo 63 and helped to found the Gruppo 70. He has written extensively on visual and film poetry. His own practice is highly experimental, aiming to expand the spatial and sensory dimensions of poetry in collections such as *Nozione di uomo* (1964), *Una forma di lotta* (1967), and *Parola per parola, diversamente* (1976). [GM]

PIGNOTTI, LORENZO (1739–1812). Born in Figline, he taught physics at *Pisa University, where from 1809 he was also Rector. He achieved a literary success with the verse fables of *Favole e novelle* (1782), inspired by those of La Fontaine. English influence is reflected in his *pre-Romantic poem, *La tomba di Shakespeare* (1779), and in *L'ombra di Pope* (1781) and *La treccia rubata* (1808), which is an imitation of *The Rape of the Lock*. In his later years he wrote an official *Storia della Toscana sino al principato*, which was published posthumously. [JMAL]

Pilgrims, see ROME; TRAVELLERS IN ITALY.

PINCHERLE, ALBERTO, see MORAVIA, ALBERTO.

PINCHETTI, GIULIO (1845–70) abandoned a career in law to become a *journalist in *Milan. He joined the *Scapigliatura*, publishing a collection of poems, *Versi* (1868), which show the influence of Byron and *Leopardi. Two years later he committed suicide. [AHC]

PINDEMONTE, GIOVANNI (1751–1812). Veronese playwright. Unlike his younger brother Ippolito *Pindemonte, he played an eventful part in revolutionary politics and turned his pen to patriotic verse. His varied *tragedies enjoyed a considerable stage success. Typically they exploited spectacle, as in *I Baccanali*, his first great stage success in 1782, or pathos, as in *Adelina e Roberto* (1805). They display *Shakespearian influence in *Ginevra di Scozia, Elena e Gerardo*, and *Cincinnato*. [JMAL]

PINDEMONTE, IPPOLITO (1743–1828). *Pre-Romantic poet. Born into a noble Veronese family, he studied in Modena and Verona, travelling to *Rome in 1780 where he entered the *Arcadia as Polidete Melpomenio. He wrote a first *tragedy, *Ulisse*, in 1777, which was followed by others, and by various poems and *translations. In 1788–90 he visited Switzerland, France, England, and Germany, drawing on his experiences for a novel, *Abaritte* (1790). A brief flirtation with revolutionary ideas led to *La Francia* (1790), but he quickly withdrew from politics and spent much of the rest of his life in his villa near Verona. During his career he tried various styles of poetry in his efforts to achieve formal perfection, from the narrative of *Gibilterra salvata* (1782) to the discursive *Epistole in versi* (1804) and *Sermoni* (1819). He finds his own pre-Romantic voice best in rustic poetry, publishing a first *Saggio di poesie campestri* in 1788. Though he abandoned his *Cimiteri* when he learnt of the imminent publication of *Dei sepolcri* (which *Foscolo dedicated to him), the unfinished poem was published with Foscolo's in a single volume in 1807. From 1805 to 1819 he worked on his remarkable *translation of the *Odyssey* (1822), which, rather than *epic verve, displays the combination of melancholy and classical grace characteristic of pre-Romantic poetry. [GDP]

Pinocchio (1883). Classic *children's story by Carlo *Collodi. This highly literary, funny,

463

compassionate work takes up the *commedia dell'arte* tradition and presents a wooden puppet who rebels against conventional morality and tutelage. He goes through a series of picaresque adventures, turning into a donkey before his final metamorphosis into a real, good boy.   [ALL]

PINTOR, GIAIME (1919–43). Writer and intellectual who was killed soon after joining the *Resistance. As a *literary critic and militant anti-*Fascist, he forged an important link between prewar *hermetic writers and the Resistance generation with its *Marxist ideals and insistence on the need for political action. He began publishing essays on Italian and German literature at a very young age; these were collected posthumously in *Il sangue d'Europa (1939–1943)* (1950). The letter written to his brother shortly before his death is often cited as an eloquent expression of the ideals of the Resistance.   [SVM]

PIO, GIOVAN BATTISTA, see BEROALDO, FILIPPO (THE ELDER); LATIN PROSE IN ITALY.

PIOVANO ARLOTTO, see MOTTI E FACEZIE DEL PIOVANO ARLOTTO.

PIOVENE, GUIDO (1907–74). *Novelist. An aristocrat from Vicenza, he studied literature in *Milan under G. A. *Borgese. From 1927 he published reviews and short stories in *Il Convegno*, and from 1930 in *Solaria*, his first book of fiction being the short stories of *La vedova allegra* (1931). During the 1930s he lived in various parts of Italy, particularly *Florence and *Rome, where he was editor of *Ojetti's *Pan*, but travelled widely in Europe as a newspaper correspondent, covering the Spanish Civil War from the Franco side.

His fiction surveys depths of guilt with aristocratic aloofness. The *epistolary novel *Lettera di una novizia* (1941) and the interlocking stories of *La gazzetta nera* (1943) include confessions of murder by individuals in holy orders. The novels *Pietà contro pietà* (1946), about the cataclysm of 1943, when Piovene himself took part in the liberation struggle, and *I falsi redentori* (serialized in 1946–7), are obsessively guilt-ridden and pessimistic about human redeemability. During the Cold War, though nicknamed 'il conte rosso', Piovene took the Western side, returning to *journalism for *Epoca* and *La Stampa*. He travelled round Italy for Italian *radio, which led to *Viaggio in Italia* (1957), while a long trip round Europe led to

Europa semilibera (1973). His 1962 essay, *La coda di paglia*, an unremitting confession of his collusion with *Fascism, caused a furore that cost him the 1963 Viareggio prize for the novel *Le Furie*, but the quasi-narrative meditation on death, *Le stelle fredde*, won the Strega prize in 1971 [see LITERARY PRIZES]. He left unfinished the novel *Verità e menzogna* and the essays *Idoli e ragione*.   [JG-R]

See G. Catalano (ed.), *Guido Piovene* (1980).

PIRA, MICHELANGELO, see SARDINIA.

Piramo e Tisbe, see CANTARI.

PIRANDELLO, LUIGI (1867–1936) is best known as a playwright. But as well as forty-four plays, his vast production includes eight volumes of poetry, seven *novels, over 200 short stories (most of which were collected as *Novelle per un anno*) [see NOVELLA AND RACCONTO], a philological thesis, essays, reviews, and film scripts.

The second child (but first son) of six children, he was born in a house called Caos on the southern coast of *Sicily near Agrigento. His father Stefano was the owner of a sulphur mine, one of the few thriving industries in a declining island economy; his mother Caterina came from a Sicilian anti-*Bourbon family, providing her son with some of the material for his long *historical novel, *I vecchi e i giovani* (1913). Although he spent his working life outside Sicily, Pirandello never forgot his origins nor the symbolism inherent in the name of his birthplace. After secondary education in Palermo, he enrolled in the city's university, then transferred to the University of *Rome in 1887, and moved again in 1889 to the University of Bonn, where he graduated with a thesis on the *dialect of Agrigento in 1891. In Palermo there had been an erotic attachment to a cousin, Lina Pirandello; in Bonn he had fallen in love with a young German woman, Jenny Schulz-Lander; but in 1894, three years after his return to Italy, his family arranged his marriage to Antonietta Portulano, daughter of a business associate of his father's. Three children were born: Stefano in 1895, Lietta in 1897, and Fausto in 1899.

After his marriage Pirandello settled with his family in Rome, and in 1897 took the post of professor at the Istituto Superiore di Magistero (a teacher-training institute) to supplement his father's allowance. Six years later, disaster struck the family. Flooding in the sulphur mine led to the loss of Pirandello's father's capital and his wife's dowry, both of which had been invested in the mine. This disaster was a major turning point in Pirandello's life: his wife became unstable, developing a persecution mania fed by obsessive jealousy, and financial concerns became acute. He had made his literary debut as a poet in 1889 with *Mal giocondo*, and by the time of the mine disaster was already a respected member of the Rome literary intelligentsia with several publications to his name, concentrating his ambitions on prose writing after advice from Luigi *Capuana. With a sick wife and three children to support, he now turned to writing with a frenzied earnestness. The first fruits of these labours were the novel *Il *fu Mattia Pascal* (1904), considered a major example of European *modernism. Nine volumes of short stories appeared between 1903 and 1915, and three further novels: *Suo marito* in 1911, *I vecchi e i giovani* in 1913, and *Si gira* in 1915, revised as *Quaderni di Serafino Gubbio* (1925). In 1908, with a collection of critical essays that included the important *L'*umorismo*, Pirandello won the competition for a permanent post at the Magistero.

Until 1917 it thus seemed that Pirandello's name would be associated with fiction. Interest in *theatre was not entirely absent from his life, however. The year 1910 witnessed the first performances of his plays *La morsa* and *Lumie di Sicilia*, both drawn from short stories. *Se non così* was presented in *Milan in 1915, *Pensaci, Giacomino!* and *Liolà* in 1916 in Rome by Angelo Musco's company. His first major play, *Così è (se vi pare)* was performed in 1917, and from then until his last years theatre was the dominant activity in his life. Pirandello himself explained his turning to theatre in relation to *World War I. Narrative was too passive a mode of expression for the intense emotions he was experiencing: a family in turmoil with his wife mentally sick, accusing him of liaisons with his students and incest with his daughter, and two sons at the front. His theatre, always polemical, deliberately disturbing his audience, was, he felt, better able to utter the restless dissatisfaction he experienced.

Once started, he engaged wholeheartedly in theatrical life. In 1924 he set up his own company, the Teatro d'Arte, partly funded by a grant from the *Fascist state. Pirandello had strategically joined the Fascist Party at its moment of crisis after the Matteotti affair (June 1924) and reaped his rewards in government support for his theatrical venture. The Teatro d'Arte opened in April 1925 but succumbed to some of the very characteristics of Italian theatre that Pirandello had hoped to correct: the star system, the use of a prompter, and touring.

When the company disbanded in the summer of 1928, however, Pirandello could count a number of achievements: fifteen world premières and nine Italian premières of foreign plays, the raising to star status of the company's leading actress, Marta Abba, with whom he had developed an intense relationship, innovatory lighting and stage design from his two designers, Virgilio Marchi and Guido Salvini, and numerous tours in Italy, Europe, and South America.

Sei personaggi in cerca d'autore (1921) made Pirandello an international dramatist, and during the years 1918–28 he was at the peak of his dramatic and theatrical powers. He wrote twenty-two plays in this period, including *Il *giuoco delle parti* (1918), *Enrico IV* (1922) with Ruggero Ruggeri in the main role, *Vestire gli ignudi* (1922), *La vita che ti diedi* (1923), and the second play (after *Sei personaggi*) in what became a theatre trilogy, *Ciascuno a suo modo* (1924). The summer of 1928 marked a major break in Pirandello's career. At the age of 60 and with no long-term commitments, he went to Germany for two years, and then settled in Paris, but always in hotels or rented accommodation. In Berlin he wrote the third play of the theatre trilogy, *Questa sera si recita a soggetto* (1930), and saw it performed in Königsberg and Berlin. Before his death he completed and had performed seven others; *I giganti della montagna* remained unfinished. During this long period of playmaking, however, fiction was not entirely neglected. *Uno, nessuno e centomila* (1926) was written alongside the dramas, and Pirandello continued to write, revise, and edit short stories, creating in his last years a different kind of symbolic fiction in, for instance, 'La tartaruga' (1936) and 'Una giornata' (1936).

Pirandello's difficult life exacerbated a personal pessimism. Beneath the articulate ratiocination of many of his characters, whether in fiction or drama, lies a cry of anguish concerning the purpose of human suffering and indeed, the purpose of life. At the heart of Pirandello's thought lies a tragic paradoxical tension between life and form (*vita* and *forma*). Form gives a lasting quality to aspects of life but in so doing arrests its essential movement and spontaneity; thus art, which is pure form, and life are fundamentally opposed. Pirandello's ideas concerning identity and knowledge are closely related to this opposition, and are central to his writing. For him identity is a collection of masks, forms imposed on the life within us by ourselves and by others. Behind the masks, however, there is no face; Pirandello entitled his collection of plays with the sinister phrase *Maschere nude*. The title of his last novel, *Uno, nessuno e centomila*, states this theme succinctly: we are one body (*uno*), we have no self (*nessuno*), and we comprise a multiplicity of personae (*centomila*), depending on the situations in which we find ourselves. Like identity, all knowledge is relative. The raisonneur character Laudisi in *Così è (se vi pare)* (Right You Are (If You Think So): another emblematic title) can recognize himself as brother to his sister but cannot say who he is. It is the pain deriving from these two areas of identity and knowledge that distinguishes Pirandello's thought—the 'pena di vivere così' (the 'pain of living like this'), according to the title of another of his stories.

Pirandello considered this revolution in the view of identity and knowledge as devastating as the Copernican revelation of the place of the earth in the cosmos. One of his major achievements, however, is to make comic creations from such a profoundly pessimistic vision. Humour comes from situations. The short story 'Il capretto nero' (1913) is typical: the English lady who visits Sicily discovers that the little goat with which she has fallen in love is a hairy monster by the time it reaches her in London. Humour also comes from characters: Pirandello is master of the grotesque caricature, for instance the two inquisitive ladies of the town in *Così è (se vi pare)*, or Dr Genoni, the psychiatrist in *Enrico IV*; and he has a fine line in grumbling landladies. But his humour is blended with compassion, as the poetics of *L'umorismo*, elaborated in polemic with Benedetto *Croce, maintains it must be. To be aware of discrepancy and incongruity provides material for the comic; to think about them and feel them leads to the humorist's vision. The example given in the essay is of an elderly lady (one of his many caricatures), overdressed and heavily made-up. The effect is incongruous and therefore laughable; but think of her possible situation—trying to please a younger man friend, to deceive herself in the face of encroaching death—and the laughter becomes suffused with compassion.

Pirandello's drama writing and playmaking engaged with the theatrical movements of his time, naturalism and the avant-garde. His major iconoclastic piece, *Sei personaggi in cerca d'autore*, is a critique of naturalism, masquerading as a denial of the possibility of theatre. The play dramatized ideas expressed in the essay 'Illustratori, attori e traduttori' (1908) and repeated often during his life, concerning the actor's inability to present an author's text on stage, thus focusing on issues at the centre of the theatrical debate in Europe. However, after the 1925 revisions to *Sei personaggi*, which show a link with symbolist theatrical techniques, and particularly after the invention of the talking *cinema (1927), Pirandello saw the dangers posed by the avant-garde for the very survival of theatre, a concern evident in his essay 'Se il film parlante abolirà il teatro' (1929). In his later years, he sought the meaning of theatre rather than questioning its viability, and championed its actors, as is clear in *Questa sera si recita a soggetto* (1930), the last play in his theatre trilogy.

As a promoter of self-conscious theatre, particularly through *Sei personaggi in cerca d'autore*, Pirandello was a major influence on theatrical developments of the 20th c. Leading theatre directors have presented his plays in the capitals of Europe, including Max Reinhardt, Georges Pitoëff, Giorgio *Strehler, and Franco Zeffirelli. His theatrical debates on reality and illusion, identity, the relativity of knowledge, and his dramatization of time make of him a forerunner of the 'theatre of the absurd' and have found echoes in many dramatists, including Anouilh, Beckett, Pinter, Albee, and Boal. He was awarded the Nobel Prize in 1934. [JAL]

Maschere nude, ed. A. D'Amico (1986–93); *Novelle per un anno* (1956–7); *Saggi, Poesie, Scritti varii*, ed. M. Lo Vecchio-Musti (1960). See G. Giudice, *Pirandello: A Biography* (1975); C. Vicentini, *Pirandello: il disagio del teatro* (1993); A. H. Caesar, *Characters and Authors in Luigi Pirandello* (1998).

Pisa. Already a military port in Roman times, Pisa enjoyed a period of commercial and military power in the 12th and 13th c., when it competed with Amalfi, *Genoa, and *Venice. It was in this period that its major monuments were constructed and that it was a centre of the sculptural activity of Niccolò Pisano and his circle. Its decline began with defeat by Genoa at Meloria (1284). The Gherardesca family, who ruled from 1316 to 1341, founded a *university, which, when the city passed under the control of the Florentines in 1405, became effectively the university of *Florence. From then on Pisa was otherwise something of a backwater, famous for its tower and for being *Galileo's city of birth. In 1810 a *Napoleonic decree established a branch of the Paris École Normale in the city. The Scuola Normale Superiore di Pisa was initially a teacher-training institution. By the later 19th c. its focus had become advanced scholarly research. Its activities and reputation were consolidated, rather than undermined, during the *Fascist period under the direction of Giovanni *Gentile. It is now considered the foremost scholarly and scientific institution in Italy. [PH]

PISACANE, CARLO (1818–57) originally trained as an engineer in the *Bourbon army but became a leader and analyst of the *socialist Left in the *Risorgimento. More radical than *Mazzini, he analysed the failure of the *1848 revolutions in *La guerra combattuta in Italia negli anni 1848–9*. He was killed at Sapri leading an ill-fated attempt to provoke *peasant insurrection in the Kingdom of the Two *Sicilies. [LR]

PISANI, BALDASSARRE (b.1650). A lawyer and a late *Neapolitan practitioner of *concettismo*, who was included by Federico *Meninni in his anthology of lyrics. He published *Poesie liriche*, in their first form in 1669, some Latin verse and several *sacre rappresentazioni*. [MPS]

PISANI, UGOLINO (mid-15th c.). Courtier and poet laureate. He studied *law at Pavia, where he knew *Panormita and wrote his *Confabulatio coquinaria* (1435), a *parody of doctoral degree ceremonies. His comic vein is to be seen in *Philogenia*, which imitates classical *comedies of intrigue, and has some well-realized characters. [SR]

PISANÒ, GIORGIO, see RESISTANCE.

Piscatorial Eclogue. Marine sub-genre of *pastoral poetry which flourished in the 16th c., particularly in *Naples and the South. It originates in the late 1490s with *Sannazaro's *Eclogae piscatoriae*, which substitute sometimes dramatic sea scenes and fishermen for woods and shepherds. [PH]

PISTOIA, IL (Antonio Cammelli) (1436–1502) gravitated unhappily among the *courts of Northern Italy, losing posts as quickly as he got them. He is best known for his lively occasional *sonnets, which follow in the tradition of popular *satirical poetry established by Il *Burchiello, and later associated with Francesco *Berni. His political poems target the corruption of the Church, the immorality prevalent in public life and, in his later years, the shame of foreign invasion. Other sonnets, of a personal nature, are based on incidents and characters of everyday life, often sharply and wittily observed. The style is popular, slangy, frequently slanderous,

but invariably amusing or engaging, and makes particularly effective use of witty dialogue. He also wrote a clumsy verse *Tragedia nominata Pamphila*, an early dramatization of *Boccaccio's story of Ghismonda and Guiscardo (*Decameron 4.1). [CPB]

PITIGRILLI (pseud. of Dino Segre) (1893–1975). Writer of slick collections of short stories and *novels, superficially libertine but substantially conformist. His production has been divided into three periods: erotic (1920–3), lay-sceptical (1929–36), sceptical-religious (1948–71). The first includes some of his most successsful works, later repudiated (such as *La cintura di castità* and *Cocaina*, both 1921); the second includes *L'esperimento di Pott* and *Dolicocefala bionda*; the third is marked by his conversion to Catholicism (he came from a *Jewish family). He was publicly denounced as a spy of the *Fascist secret political police, OVRA. [LL]

PITRÈ, GIUSEPPE (1841–1916) a founding figure in the study of folk culture in Italy, especially of his native *Sicily, though he graduated and worked as a medical doctor. He published collections of Sicilian folk poems and stories and wrote on popular traditions and customs. He founded, with Salamone Morpurgo, the *Archivio per lo studio delle tradizioni popolari* (1882–1909). [See also FOLK AND POPULAR LITERATURE.] [AWM]

PITTI. Old *Florentine *merchant family who rose to prominence in the later 13th c., achieving political pre-eminence with the triumph of the *Medici in 1434. Luca Pitti assumed a role in the ruling group second only to Cosimo himself, presiding when the Medici regime retook power in 1458 after several years' severe decline. After Cosimo's death in 1464, Luca's relations with his son and successor Piero became strained, and he led the conspiracy which attempted to oust the Medici in 1465–6. When Piero prevailed in September 1466, Luca was allowed to remain in Florence but without political power; thereafter, the family's position declined rapidly. Buonaccorso *Pitti wrote a famous vernacular *Cronaca*, while Iacopo (1519–89) was the author of the important *Istorie fiorentine* [see CHRONICLES; HISTORIOGRAPHY]. [RDB]

PITTI, BONACCORSO (1354–c.1430) led a turbulent life, travelling extensively and holding

Piumini, Roberto

numerous public posts, particularly in *Florence. He left a record of his experiences in his *Cronaca* (1412–30), one of the finest examples of the Florentine tradition that combined private memoirs with an account of public events [see also AUTOBIOGRAPHY; CHRONICLES; PITTI]. [LB]

PIUMINI, ROBERTO, see CHILDREN'S LITERATURE.

PIUS II, see PICCOLOMINI, ENEA SILVIO.

PIVATI, GIANFRANCO, see ENCYCLOPEDIAS.

PIZZICOLLI, CIRIACO DE', see CIRIACO D'ANCONA.

PIZZUTO, ANTONIO (1893–1976). *Novelist. Originally from Palermo, he took degrees in law and philosophy and followed a successful career in police administration before starting to write seriously in the 1950s, well after the early *Sul ponte di Avignone* (1938). The formal experimentation of his first mature novel *Signorina Rosina* (1956) anticipates the 1960s *Neoavanguardia*. Subsequent works, such as *Paginette* (1964) and *Sinfonia* (1966), take the dismantling of traditional narrative even further through neologisms and syntactic disruptions. The aim is partly to express the absurdity of modern bourgeois existence, but Pizzuto now appears abstract and rarefied, in contrast with *Gadda, with whom he was once frequently compared. [JEB]

PLACCI, CARLO (1859–1941). *Florentine noble, born in London, who travelled Europe as a foreign correspondent and as an enthusiastic participant in literary salons. He was a successful popular *novelist in his day, with works such as *Un furto* (1892), but is now most remembered for his correspondence with *D'Annunzio, *Salvemini, and other writers and critics. [PBarn]

Placiti campani (960 and 963). Four Latin legal texts from Campania, which employ a distinctively Southern Italian vernacular to cite witnesses' acknowledgements of land-titles, each citation being a single, formulaic sentence, of virtually identical content. These are the earliest uncontroversial attestations of written use of the vernacular, but the reasons for this short-lived experiment in its use remain obscure. The oldest of the four is known as the *Placito capuano* [see also MIDDLE AGES]. [MM]

Placito capuano, see MIDDLE AGES; PLACITI CAMPANI.

Plague. The Black Death, unknown in Italy since the 8th c., was reintroduced by trading ships returning from *Byzantium. The bubonic form (causing excruciating swellings) was accompanied by septicaemic and pneumonic forms. None could be analysed or treated by medieval medicine. Plague struck Messina in 1347 and by 1348 had spread to Northern and Central Italy, where some cities lost up to half their population. Giovanni *Villani and *Petrarch's *Laura were amongst the victims. But civil society held up well and *Boccaccio's famous description of *Florence in chaos in the Introduction to the *Decameron* is not to be taken literally. Further sporadic outbreaks followed and plague was not finally eliminated until the 18th c. [CEH]

PLATINA, IL (Bartolomeo Sacchi) (1421–81). *Humanist and *historian. After lengthy stays in *Mantua and *Florence, he moved in 1462 to *Rome, joining the College of Abbreviators; his protests against its abolition by Pope Paul II led to his imprisonment. He was jailed again when Paul suppressed the *Accademia Romana, whose members he suspected of conspiring against him. The new Pope, Sixtus IV, reinstated him in the curia and in 1475 appointed him prefect of the *Vatican Library. His writings, all in Latin, include a history of the popes and of *Mantua, political and ethical treatises, and a cookbook [see COOKERY BOOKS]. [JK]

PLATO, see NEOPLATONISM; PLATONIC ACADEMY.

Platonic Academy. The Platonic Academy, also known as the Florentine or, more rarely, the Careggian Academy, has always been linked to the figure of Marsilio *Ficino. Indeed, it has become an attractive historiographical commonplace that Cosimo de' *Medici, having been inspired by the *Byzantine intellectual *Pletho in 1439 during the Council of *Florence, then founded a Platonic Academy in 1462 at Careggi and gave Ficino a villa there and appointed him its head, and that over 100 statesmen, diplomats, lawyers, ecclesiastics, patricians, and poets, including *Landino, *Pico della Mirandola, *Poliziano, Chalcondylas, Alessandro *Braccesi, Sebastiano Salvini, and Lorenzo de' *Medici himself, belonged to it as to a quasi-religious confraternity. It is, however, somewhat of a myth invented, not by Ficino or his contemporaries, but by later pro-Medici propagandists, after the flowering in the 16th c. of a number of learned societies. It received its definitive articulation in a 1902 study by Arnaldo Della Torre, though he was challenged at the time.

The Latin word *academia* (*accademia* in Italian) had a number of meanings in the *Renaissance, and could refer to the newly refounded *university (*studio*) of Florence, and most appositely to a gathering of *litterati* around figures such as *Bessarion, *Salutati, or *Pontano. Ficino's own usage varied but in the main he seems to have used it to refer either to his school for patrician pupils (his *academici*), or to the spirit, or to the actual works, or to manuscripts, of Plato and the Platonists or *Neoplatonists. True, Cosimo gave him in April 1463 a farm property at Montevecchio near Careggi, to which over the years he retreated in the summer heat to study and write; and unquestionably, though a client priest, he became famous as a scholar and a luminary in the Medici and other signorial circles, and must have played a leading part at times in celebrations, debates, discussions, and musical recitals (though whether the 1468 Plato birthday banquet actually occurred is debatable). Witness the magisterial roles assigned him in Lorenzo's *Altercazione* and in book 2 of Landino's *Disputationes camaldulenses*, and various contemporary testimonies to his singing to an Orphic lyre. Moreover, he cultivated and advised a huge and influential circle of friends and correspondents, pupils, and admirers, even though few if any adopted his radical Platonism. Nevertheless it is misleading to refer to this informal eclectic group as the Platonic or the Florentine Academy, though we might think of it as the Accademia Ficiniana, on the model, say, of the *Accademia Pontaniana. Even so, Ficino and his Neoplatonism had a wide-ranging if diffused impact on his contemporaries, including artists such as *Botticelli, and on three generations of the Medici, who were among his *patrons; and he was singularly successful in a variety of ways in evoking the ethos and even something of the setting and practice of the ancient Athenian Academy. [See also ACADEMIES.]   [MA]

See A. Della Torre, *Storia dell'Accademia Platonica di Firenze* (1902); A. Field, *The Origins of the Platonic Academy of Florence* (1988).

PLETHO, GEORGE GEMISTOS (1355/60–1452/4) was a *Byzantine philosopher who taught in Mistra, in the Peloponnese, including among his students the future Cardinal *Bessarion. Accompanying the Greek delegation to the Council of *Ferrara-*Florence from 1438 to 1439, he lectured to Italian *humanists, arguing that Plato was superior to *Aristotle, in an effort to renew interest in Platonism among Western scholars. His major work, *The Laws*, was a Greek treatise modelled on Plato's dialogue of the same name, in which he promoted *Neoplatonic paganism as the philosophical basis for a revived Byzantine empire; it was burned by the Patriarch of Constantinople as heretical and survives only in fragments.   [JK]

Plurilinguismo was first used as a critical and historiographical designation in 1951 by Gianfranco *Contini in an essay on *Petrarch's language, 'Preliminari sulla lingua di Petrarca'. The term has since become widely established in Italian *literary criticism. It refers both to a particular manner of writing (experimental, theoretically self-reflective, and stylistically, structurally, and linguistically eclectic) and to the literary tradition embodying these characteristics. In Italy, this tradition finds its origins and supreme articulation in *Dante's œuvre. However, it constitutes a minority tradition, since the predominant voice of Italian literature is characterized by *monolinguismo* (or *unilinguismo*), whose greatest exponent was Petrarch. The division of Italian literature into a Dantean and a Petrarchan line goes back at least to the 15th c. *Plurilinguismo* is closely associated with the notion of *Expressionism (*espressionismo* or *espressivismo*). [See also LITERARY THEORY, I; POLYGLOT THEATRE.]   [ZB]

***Podere, Il*,** see TOZZI, FEDERIGO.

Podestà. Originally indicating an imperial agent appointed by the Emperor Frederick I, the term (from the Latin *potestas*, 'power') came to designate the formal head of government in the medieval Italian *commune from the early 13th to the early 15th c. He was normally an outsider and appointed for a fixed period. The term was revived under *Fascism for the centrally appointed heads of local administration.   [PH]

Poema. In Italian used of narrative poetry; *poesia* is used of lyrics, and of poetry in general [see also EPIC; ROMANCE].

***Poemetti*,** see PASCOLI, GIOVANNI.

***Poemi conviviali*,** see PASCOLI, GIOVANNI.

Poerio, Alessandro

POERIO, ALESSANDRO (1802–48). *Neapolitan poet and patriot, who spent much of his life in *exile (partly in *Florence) and died of wounds during the revolution of *1848 in *Venice. He *translated works by Goethe (whom he met in Germany). Some of his poems were published anonymously by Parisian friends in 1843, but much of his work was not edited until long after his death.   [FD'I]

Poesia (1). Forms of the learned Latin term *poesis* (from Greek *poiésis*, the noun from *poiéin*, 'to make') enter the vernacular in the 13th c., referring, like *poeta*, to higher forms of verse-writing, that is, frequently verse in Latin. In modern usage 'poesia' can mean either literary creativity in a general sense, whether in prose or verse, or composition in verse as opposed to prose. In this latter sense it often indicates a single poetic composition, usually brief, and hence normally distinguished from the long 'poema'.

In its broader sense 'poesia' suggests aesthetic emotion, artistic creation, and a particular attentiveness to the signifier and to polysemic expression. There is still a tendency to see poetry as the result of codified strategies for composition, but there is also an opposite tendency to privilege spontaneous inspiration, or a state of grace, which is possible even in the absence of *education or technical and rhetorical ability. In the first half of the 20th c. particular weight was given to *Croce's view that 'poesia' is 'intuizione lirica' distinct from '*letteratura' (or 'non poesia'), that is, from all those aspects of a text which have a structural, historical, cultural, or philosophical, but not aesthetic, value. Current academic interest is centred on the issue of the specificity of poetic language.   [NG]

Poesia (2), see MARINETTI, FILIPPO TOMMASO.

Poesia giocosa, or *poesia comico-realistica* (both designations are modern), emerges in Italy in the later 13th c. as a consciously *parodic response to the linguistic and thematic conventions of serious love poetry (*poesia aulica*), inherited from the *troubadour poetry of Provence and established in Italy by the *Sicilian School and their successors. The *poeti giocosi* cheerfully throw overboard refinement of language, elevation of tone, and lofty abstraction of subject matter. Instead they use a broader range of language, embracing a certain amount of obscenity and abuse, and frequently incorporating colloquialisms and direct speech. They take as their themes the most ordinary and physically concrete aspects of everyday life in tavern, marketplace, and bedroom, treating the body and its functions with often scatological gusto. Among the most interesting consequences of this reversal of stylistic norms is the space it opens up for women—not yet as authors, but at least as speaking subjects and agents in the poetic narrative. The distinction between the two genres is encapsulated in the contrast between *Dante's *Beatrice (as she appears in the *Vita nova*) and *Petrarch's *Laura, both of whom are idealized, ethereal, spiritually charged, and almost always silent at least in life, and on the other hand Cecco *Angiolieri's Becchina—realistically portrayed, earthy, carnal, and highly (often hilariously) loquacious.

Angiolieri is among the best known of the *poeti giocosi*, but the earliest recorded poems in the genre are the *sonnets (always the preferred form for *poesia giocosa*) of *Rustico Filippi. Both were *Tuscans (Angiolieri from *Siena, Filippi from *Florence), and the genre was most extensively practised in that region. A significant exception is constituted by the circle of mid-14th-c. *Perugian poets centred on *Cecco Nuccoli, Neri Moscoli, and Marino Ceccoli. Other figures commonly associated with *poesia giocosa* include *Meo de' Tolomei, *Immanuel Romano, *Cenne dalla Chitarra, and Pietro de' *Faitinelli. *Folgore da Sangimignano is also commonly classed as a *poeta giocoso*, though his sonnet sequences present a degree of idealization which is unusual for the genre. But more famous names, including Guido *Guinizzelli, Guido *Cavalcanti, and Dante, all wrote occasional comic poems, just as vice versa some *poeti giocosi* (notably Rustico Filippi) also wrote a certain amount of *poesia aulica*.

Scholarly discussion of *poesia giocosa* was hampered for many years by the assumption that the poets who practised it were essentially naïve autobiographers, transcribing their own experience of wine, women (or men), and song straightforwardly into poetry. In fact, the reverse seems more likely to be true. Such biographical data as has come to light in recent decades shows that many of the most colourful and apparently realistic details that occur in *poesia giocosa* are fictitious. Though there may be some kind of autobiographical connection between the poet and his work, it seems clear that both *poesia giocosa* and *poesia aulica* were the work of intelligent, well-read, and highly sophisticated artists, skilled in manipulating a set of conventions and their audience's generic expectations in order to produce literary artefacts. The genre itself has a long pedigree, though as far as we are concerned a discontinuous one, with isolated examples appearing amongst the *Sicilians, notably *Cielo d'Alcamo, and Provençal poets, and more frequently in medieval Latin verse. The tradition of *poesia giocosa* survived in Florence at least as far as the mid 15th-c. in the work of *Burchiello and others.

[SNB]

Poeti giocosi del tempo di Dante, ed. M. Marti (1956). See M. Marti, *Cultura e stile nei poeti giocosi del tempo di Dante* (1953).

Poetica. The poetic or literary intentions, or theory, that underlie a work, typically distinguished in 20th-c. Italian criticism from the *poesia* that may or may not be the outcome [see also LITERARY CRITICISM; LITERARY THEORY].

Poetics, see IMITATION; LITERARY THEORY.

Poeti giocosi, see POESIA GIOCOSA.

Poetry, see EPIC; LITERARY THEORY; LYRIC POETRY; POEMA; POESIA; ROMANCE.

POLENTON, SICCO (1375/6–1447) wrote a bulky history of Latin literature, *Scriptorum illustrium latinae linguae libri XVIII*, around 1437. It is mostly an uncritical compendium of *biographies of ancient authors, but there are some interesting asides on modern writers: Polenton's *Paduan connections make him single out Lovato *Lovati and Albertino *Mussato as *Dante's predecessors in the revival of letters, while after *Petrarch the most important figures are Giovanni *Conversino and the *Venetian Francesco *Barbaro. It also provides evidence for the low ebb of Petrarch's fortune in the early 15th c., but Polenton lacks the acumen and terminology to provide a genuinely critical account of Latin literature. [See also CLASSICAL SCHOLARSHIP; HISTORIES OF ITALIAN LITERATURE; HUMANISM.] [MMcL]

POLI, UMBERTO, see SABA, UMBERTO.

Police, see ARMED FORCES AND POLICE.

Poligrafi. This term traditionally designates a few versatile and unscrupulous 16th-c. intellectuals who were willing and able to write on any subject (hence their name) and for (or against) anyone, so long as they were paid for their work. To attract *patronage the *poligrafi* employed with equal flair courtly flattery and criminal threats; they indulged in obscenity, the bizarre, and the outrageously slanderous. The existence of the *printing press was essential for the development of this phenomenon—not by chance particularly rife in *Venice—for it needed an ever growing body of readers in order to achieve the public exposure on which it thrived. Best known are Pietro *Aretino, indisputably the most brilliant and successful among the *poligrafi*, Nicolò *Franco, and Anton Francesco *Doni. [LPer]

Politecnico, Il (1), see CATTANEO, CARLO; LITERARY THEORY, 5; PERIODICALS, 2.

Politecnico, Il (2) (1945–7). Important literary and cultural *periodical, first a weekly and then from May 1946 a monthly. It was founded and directed by Elio *Vittorini and a team of editors that included Franco *Fortini, Franco *Calamandrei, Vito Pandolfi, Albe Steiner, and Stefano Terra. It hosted the writings of many intellectuals active in the *Resistance, and its overriding theme was that of cultural renewal, which it believed could be achieved by bringing Italy up to date on the development of European and American culture. This policy sparked an intense debate between Vittorini, then a member of the *Communist Party, and the Party's general secretary, Palmiro *Togliatti, as well as other Communist intellectuals, who did not agree with the journal's openness to experimental and avant-garde work. In its second phase as a monthly, the review became somewhat less committed to transmitting world culture and more militant in pursuing its stated objectives of cultural independence. [RSD]

POLITI, ADRIANO (1542–1625). *Sienese nobleman known for his *Dittionario toscano*, published in 1613–14, and for his place in the *questione della lingua*. Like *Beni and *Tassoni, he was inspired to contribute to the debate about the Italian language by the publication of the *Vocabolario della Crusca* in 1612. He resented the *Florentine bias of the dictionary, and brought out his own version, which gives the Sienese equivalent for each Florentine word. He also *translated the *Annals* of Tacitus, whose popularity increased greatly in 17th-c. Italy. [PBD]

Political Thought. A self-consciously Italian political tradition only developed in the 19th c., when the *Risorgimento inspired a number of

Political Thought

contrasting visions of a united Italy. Prior to that, political theorists tended to identify with the regimes and traditions of their region and were often in the service of local rulers. Nonetheless, one can detect three general themes which recur from the post-Roman period up to the present. The first concerns the competing attractions of the two Romes (Emperor versus Pope, active versus contemplative life, social emancipation versus heavenly contemplation). The second relates to the respective strengths and weaknesses of *signorie and *communes, monarchies and republics, authoritarian and democratic rule. The first theme reflects the fact, peculiar to the Italian situation, that the *papacy operated as a territorial as well as a spiritual power. The second is equally specific to Italy in that it is a classical theme which acquired new life with the rise of the city-states and principalities in the later *Middle Ages. The third theme arises from the struggles in which these polarized conceptions of politics partook and which they partly generated: namely a recurrent linking of the idea of Italian unity with order and an end both to sectarian and inter-state strife and to the foreign domination that often accompanied them.

These themes are intertwined, mixing in all available combinations as circumstances change, and can be found in all significant thinkers of a broadly empiricist or rationalist persuasion. Thus the autocratic ambitions of the *papacy between the 13th and 15th c. engendered an intermittent conciliarist reaction within the Church that urged the need for consultation with the Council of Bishops, an argument that drew on and fed into debates about the benefits of oligarchical and republican governance in the *communes. Likewise, the theocratic aspirations of Popes to establish a right to the temporal power of the Roman Empire, and to assert their spiritual ascendancy over all civil rulers, came to be matched by similar claims to a universal secular authority on the part of Emperors. From the beginning, communes and principalities aligned themselves with both camps—most notably in the clash between *Guelfs and Ghibellines. These ideological battles continued in new configurations up until the Risorgimento, when the neo-Guelfism of *Rosmini Serbati, and most particularly of *Gioberti, who advocated that the papacy should take the lead in Italian *Unification, was counterposed by the largely anti-clerical views of *liberal *monarchists and radical democrats, and then endured as the postwar rivalry between *Communists and *Christian Democrats.

The clash between Church and Empire, commune and principality, informs the writings of the three major political thinkers of the Middle Ages and *Renaissance: *Dante, *Marsilio da Padova, and *Machiavelli. All worked within the largely secular and neo-*Aristotelian paradigm of politics that had been established by *Aquinas. Writing in the wake of *Henry VII's abortive Italian expedition, Dante envisaged him taking on the mantle of the Roman Empire and establishing the universal peace and political unity between the different peoples of the world necessary for the collective enterprise of human knowledge and culture to achieve its full potential [see MONARCHIA]. Marsilio, by contrast, framed his case in the *Defensor pacis* against the disruptiveness of clerical pretensions to rule in the context of communal assertions that popular government was the bastion of freedom against tyranny. Yet the 'Defender of the Peace' proved to be his work's dedicatee, Ludwig of Bavaria, in his successful Italian invasion of 1327–30. However, the full separation of Church from state in the form of a neat distinction between politics and morals, Christian or otherwise, only came with Machiavelli a century afterwards. For him politics was essentially instrumental to the establishment of order and civic liberty, depending on qualities that were specific to the political arts. Although an advocate of the commune in his *Discorsi*, the conclusion of the *Principe* repeats the call for a princely figure capable of liberating Italy from the flood of foreign invasions.

The elaboration of Machiavellian '*ragioni di stato' by thinkers such as Gaspare Scioppio (1576–1649), Giovanni *Botero and Ludovico *Zuccolo continued into the 17th c. It was counterposed by the religious, if heretical, *Platonic utopianism of *Bruno and *Campanella. The *Counter-Reformation gave new impetus to the battle between Church and state, culminating in the defences of toleration and civil authority by *Sarpi and *Giannone. The development of a secular science of politics during the 18th c. continued to oscillate between the radical, republican utopianism of figures such as Francesco Mario *Pagano (1748–99) and the drive of reformists like *Genovesi and *Beccaria to enlighten despotic rulers. Both identified the Church as the chief barrier to social and political change.

The French Revolution [see NAPOLEON AND THE FRENCH REVOLUTION] reopened the question of Italian Unification. Whilst radical democrats such as *Cattaneo, Giuseppe *Ferrari, and *Pisacane adopted a *positivist position and looked to the empiricist and realist tradition of Machiavelli and the *Enlightenment reformers, *liberal supporters of Pius IX (such as Gioberti) or of *Cavour (such as Bertrando Spaventa, 1817–83, and his brother Silvio, 1822–93) tended to be philosophical *idealists, who constructed an Italian heritage going back to *Ficino and *Vico. Not surprisingly, the most important figure of the period, *Mazzini, straddled the various traditions, identifying God with the people and supporting both republicanism and *monarchy. With Italy finally united, the aim became to 'make Italians', with *liberalism, *Fascism, and *Communism drawing prominent support from both idealists (such as *Croce, *Gentile, and *Gramsci respectively) and positivists (such as Gaetano *Mosca, Alfredo Rocco, and Achille Loria). The defenders of democracy were relatively thin on the ground, though Carlo Rosselli [see ROSSELLI, AMELIA] and *Gobetti, both killed by Fascists, are honourable exceptions. Postwar Italian politics was dominated by the two Romes represented by Communism and *Christian Democracy. Their decline since 1990 has yet to inaugurate a new paradigm of Italian political thought. [RPB]

See E. A. Albertoni, *Storia delle dottrine politiche in Italia* (1985); R. Bellamy, *Modern Italian Social Theory* (1987); N. Bobbio, *Ideological Profile of Twentieth-Century Italy* (1995).

POLIZIANO, ANGELO (1454–94), Florentine scholar, *humanist, and poet, took his name from the Latinization (Mons Politianus) of his birthplace, Montepulciano in *Tuscany. The first of five children born to Benedetto Ambrogini, a *Medici man, and Antonia Salimbene, Poliziano went to *Florence after his father's violent death in 1464. Though unmentioned in his writings, his father's death shaped Poliziano's future life, which was linked to the fortunes of the Medici.

By 1473 he was a member of the Medici household, by 1475 Lorenzo de' *Medici's secretary and tutor to his son Piero; later he tutored another son, Giovanni, the future Pope Leo X. His economic position was further consolidated by a number of ecclesiastical benefices. Poliziano's identity as a Medici man was confirmed after the plot (1478) by a rival Florentine family, the *Pazzi, to murder both Lorenzo and his brother Giuliano. Giuliano was killed but Lorenzo escaped with an injury, and Poliziano composed in Latin his first published (and printed) work, the *Pactianae coniurationis commentarium* (1478). The following year, hurt by difficulties in the relationship with Lorenzo's wife, Clarice *Orsini, and with Lorenzo himself, Poliziano left Florence and sought the *patronage of Cardinal Francesco *Gonzaga of *Mantua, for whose his *court he wrote the play *Fabula di *Orfeo*. Back in Florence in 1480 as professor of oratory and poetry at the *university or *studio*, he remained there, apart from visits to *Rome and *Venice, until his death in 1494, two years after that of his patron. He was taken back into the Medici household as librarian some time after the death of Clarice Orsini in 1488.

Poliziano's death, with those of Giovanni *Pico della Mirandola and Matteo *Franco, signalled the end of an era. Charles VIII of France entered Florence the same year and the Medici were forced to leave. The era, characterized by faith in human abilities, a sense of purpose, and burgeoning wealth, had flourished in the peace made possible by Lorenzo's diplomacy and was shattered by the presence of the French in Italy. A typical sense of optimism and faith in the future is evident in the letter Poliziano composed in Lorenzo's name as a preface to the *Raccolta aragonese*, a collection of Tuscan poetry sent to Frederick of *Aragon: his argument is that the Tuscan language, already graced with a distinguished and abundant literature, will take its place alongside Greek and Latin as it develops further its capacities for expression. Poliziano's own vernacular writing consists of short poems (the *Rime*), the *Orfeo*, and the *Stanze per la giostra*. Some of the *Rime* slip easily into the genre of light verse and are indistinguishable from those of his contemporaries; others are recognizable for the easy grace with which classical allusion combines with literary and popular language. For instance, in 'Io mi trovai, fanciulle, un bel mattino' the poet speaks in the person of a young woman collecting flowers in a garden on a fine May morning, integrating both the rose motif from the poem 'On roses' attributed to Ausonius and a Greek poem which describes Venus preferring roses to all other flowers. The fable of Orpheus, hastily composed for the Mantuan court, stands poised between the *sacra rappresentazione* and the later *pastoral play: Poliziano uses the form of the Tuscan religious didactic drama to provide a classical court entertainment, signalling his intention from the beginning by the ironic substitution of Mercury for the Christian angel. His poetic dexterity is shown here in the variety of his metre, and his control of

473

classical allusion in the integration of different versions of the Orpheus myth.

The *Stanze*, written to celebrate the joust in honour of Simonetta Cattaneo won by Giuliano de' Medici on 29 January 1475, also combined the popular and the classical. Written in *ottava rima*, which hitherto had been used exclusively for popularizing narrative verse, it combines philosophical thought and classical erudition with a grace that belies its depth. The work, thought to have been begun soon after the joust, was left unfinished probably due to the deaths of the protagonists (Simonetta's in 1476 is alluded to in book 2). Rather than a description of the joust, it is a celebration of love and a tribute to the Medici. The poem, like the designs for the joust created by Botticelli, owes much to discussions among members of the *Neoplatonic circle to which Poliziano and Botticelli belonged, and its fascination lies largely in its apparently effortless syncretism of classical and vernacular allusion with *Neoplatonic ideas.

Poliziano was one of the greatest *classical scholars of the *Renaissance and one of its most accomplished *Latin poets, as he demonstrated particularly in his *Miscellanea* (1489) and in the verse prolusions (*Silvae*) to his lecture-courses for the Florentine *studio*. He practised in verse and prose the stylistic eclecticism which he argued for in a famous exchange of letters on *imitation with Paolo *Cortesi, though he tended generally to cultivate Silver Latin usage rather than that of Golden Age poets such as *Virgil. He was also one of the first humanists to compose verse in convincing classical Greek. [See also GREEK INFLUENCES.]   [JAL]

   Stanze, Orfeo, Rime, ed. D. Puccini (1992). See G. Ghinassi, *Il volgare letterario del Quattrocento e le 'Stanze' del Poliziano* (1957); I. Maïer, *Ange Politien: la formation d'un poète humaniste* (1966).

POLLASTRA, GIOVANNI (1465–1540), also known as Pollastrino and Pollio Lappoli, an ardent *Medicean partisan and bitter enemy of the *Borgias, was the leading literary figure in Arezzo in his day. A prolific Latin and vernacular writer, his *comedy *Partenio* (1516) was the first vernacular play to be performed at the University of *Siena.   [RDB]

POLO, MARCO (1254–1324). *Venetian *merchant whose *Divisament dou Monde* ('Description of the World') recounts his journey to China and back, and his sojourn (1271–95), along with his father and uncle, at the court of Kublai Khan. The alternative title, *Il Milione*, may conceal Polo's nickname (perhaps Emilione) given to distinguish him from other Venetian homonyms. Polo dictated the work to Rustichello da Pisa, who copied it in Franco-Italian, during their imprisonment together in *Genoa in 1298 [see also FRENCH INFLUENCES, 1]. The Prologue boasts that no man since Creation had travelled so extensively: from Zanzibar to Japan and from the Arctic to Java. Christopher Columbus was aware of the book in an annotated Latin edition of 1506.   [JRW]

Polyglot Theatre. Performance-oriented genre, characterized by verbal virtuosity, which flourished in *Venice in the mid-16th c. and prefigured the *commedia dell'arte*. Its outstanding exponents were the actor-playwrights Andrea *Calmo and Gigio Artemio *Giancarli (d. before 1561). Formative influences were the cosmopolitan character of Venice, the routines of popular Venetian performers (*buffoni*), and the experiments of *Ruzante. In polyglot theatre the conventional love intrigue and characters of literary *comedy became the pretext for farcical action and the pell-mell juxtaposition of languages, *dialects, and accents (including Venetian, Paduan, Bergamask, pidgin Greek, and Spanish) for expressionistic or comic effect. [See also THEATRE, 1; PLURILINGUISMO.]   [RGF]

POMBA, GIUSEPPE (1795–1876). *Turinese *publisher and bookseller. With new techniques of production and new promotional initiatives, he attracted a growing middle-class readership. He launched several successful series of ancient and modern classics, and widely read reference works such as the thirty-five-volume *Enciclopedia storica*, edited by Cesare *Cantù (1838–46). Pomba retired in 1849. His firm eventually became the Unione Tipografico-Editrice Torinese (UTET) in 1854.   [MPC]

POMILIO, MARIO (1921–90). Christian *novelist, closely connected with *Naples for much of his life. He already focuses on religious themes in *L'uccello nella cupola* (1954), but extends his ethical and political scope in novels such as *La compromissione* (1965) and *Il quinto evangelio* (1974), which has huge historical and moral scope. Though he had been a member of the *Partito d'Azione and then a *socialist, his conservative style and his *Manzonian concern with issues of faith and doubt were firmly opposed to the ideology of 1960s experimentalism.   [JEB]

POMPEI, GEROLAMO (1731–88). A prominent figure in Veronese literary circles of his time, he published elegant *pastorals in *canzone form as *Canzoni pastorali* (1764). He also published *tragedies on the Greek model and *translations from the classics, notably *Le vite di Plutarco volgarizzate* (1772–3). Ippolito *Pindemonte was his pupil and friend. [JMAL]

POMPONAZZI, PIETRO (1462–1525) was born into a noble family and studied at *Padua, where he graduated in *medicine in 1487, and where he taught natural philosophy from 1488 to 1499, before moving to *Ferrara, and finally to *Bologna in 1512. He is best known for his defence of *Aristotelianism and for his recourse to natural causes for the explanation of supernatural effects. This stance led to a heated controversy after the publication of his *De immortalitate animae* in 1516. In this work he maintained that it was impossible to demonstrate the immortality of the soul by reason, and that it had to be taken as a matter of faith. [PLR]

POMPONIO GAURICO (1481/2–1530) taught Greek and Latin at the University of *Naples betweem 1512 and 1519, where he was a friend of Iacopo *Sannazaro and Giovanni *Pontano. He wrote a collection of *Latin poetry (elegies, eclogues, epigrams), and treatises on poetry and sculpture. He disappeared, and is presumed to have died, while on a journey between Salerno and Castellammare. [PLR]

PONA, FRANCESCO (1595–1655). Veronese doctor closely linked with the Accademia degli *Incogniti and a prolific writer. He produced scientific works, including *Il gran contagio di Verona nel 1630* (1631) and *Trattato de' veleni* (1643), some scholarly historical studies, such as *XII Caesares* (1641) and *Galeria delle donne celebri* (1641), and drama, oratory, and fiction. His best-known work is *La lucerna di Eureta Misoscolo* (1665, subsequently enlarged and reprinted several times). This is a lively *dialogue, full of outspoken *libertine ideas, between a schoolboy, Eureta, and his oil-lamp. Over four evenings a soul imprisoned in the lamp tells of its many reincarnations (famous historical figures, ordinary people, animals, and objects), often emphasizing the pathological and cruel aspects of its experiences. Pona also translated *Ovid's *Metamorphoses* and John Barclay's *Argenis* (1629). The latter had a significant influence on the Italian *novel. [MC]

PONTANO, GIOVANNI (1429–1503) was the most renowned *humanist at the *Aragonese *court in *Naples. Born in Umbria, he studied first at *Perugia, entering the service of the Aragonese royal family in 1447, and moving to Naples in 1448, where he became engaged in diplomatic, administrative, and political activities. In Naples he studied poetry and science under Lorenzo Buonincontri, and literature and Greek with Gregory of Tifernus and *Trapezuntius. He also came under the influence of Antonio Beccadelli (Il *Panormita). In 1458, after the death of Alfonso of Aragon, he became counsellor to King Ferdinand I; he was appointed his secretary in 1466, and undertook a number of important diplomatic missions. He was made President of the Camera della Sommaria in 1474 and secretary to Ippolita *Sforza, Duchess of Calabria. The period of the French invasion and the occupation of Naples saw the end of his active participation in public life. After this he devoted himself to study and writing, though he maintained his position at the centre of Neapolitan intellectual life.

He wrote almost exclusively in Latin, in a style that was widely praised during his lifetime, and in almost all contemporary humanist genres. His poetry embraced elegies, *pastoral eclogues, idylls, and epigrams, erotic themes coming to the fore in the *Amorum libri* (later entitled *Parthenopei*) and in the Catullan *Hendecasyllabi seu Baiae*. His most engaging poetry is his most personal; he wrote poems for his wife in *De amore coniugali*, incorporating *naeniae*, or cradle-songs, for his son, and later laments for both, as well as for many other friends, in his *Tumuli*. The breadth of his interests is remarkable. He wrote on philology and orthography in the *De aspiratione*, scientific topics in *De hortis Hesperidum*, and *Meteororum liber*, *astrology in various works, including *Urania*, a poem imitating the recently discovered Manilius, and *De fortuna*, which only just manages to reconcile astrological determinism with the idea of divine Providence. As well as histories, such as the *De bello neapolitano*, he composed *De principe*, an advice book for rulers based on Xenophon's *Cyropaedia*, which he dedicated in 1468 to Duke Alfonso of Calabria. He also wrote ethical and moral treatises, centred on ideas of equanimity and the golden mean, and various short treatises on the best uses of wealth, such as *De liberalitate* and *De beneficentia*. He is at his liveliest and most down-to-earth in his satirical prose *dialogues, notably the *Asinus*, in which he berates himself for loving an ass (who may

just represent Ferdinand II). Under his leadership the *Accademia Pontaniana (originally founded by Antonio Beccadelli and called the Accademia Porticus Antoniana) became the focal point of Neapolitan intellectual life.   [PLR]
See C. Kidwell, *Pontano* (1991).

Ponte, Il. Monthly magazine published in *Florence, founded in April 1945 by Piero *Calamandrei, who edited it until his death in 1956. In this period it was closely identified with the former *Partito d'Azione and with Calamandrei's personal aims of economic and social reform and integral application of the 1948 Constitution. Among its principal early political contributors were Ferruccio Parri and *Salvemini; its literary contributors included *Dessì, *Montale, *Saba, *Scotellaro, and Carlo *Levi. It has since retained its character as an independent voice of liberal *socialist traditions.
[DF]

PONTI, CARLO, see CINEMA.

PONTIGGIA, GIUSEPPE (1934–). *Novelist and essayist based in *Milan. Initially aligned with the *Neoavanguardia, he respects conventional novel structures, but experiments with language and syntax to render an alienated, disturbed vision of a superficially stable society, for instance in *Il giocatore invisibile* (1978).   [JEB]

PONTORMO, IACOPO DA, see DIARIES; MANNERISM.

Ponzela Gaia, La, see CANTARI.

Popes, see PAPACY AND THE CATHOLIC CHURCH.

Popular Literature, see FOLK AND POPULAR LITERATURE.

Popular Song in Italy has been mainly identified with the melodic tradition even in the postwar period. Both at home and abroad, melody is seen as an authentic and typical product, the particular physiognomy of which is quite distinct from the more rhythmic feel of international pop music. Born towards the end of the 19th c. from two robust sources, the *bel canto* tradition and *Neapolitan popular song, it frequently lent itself to rhetorical celebrations of established values and institutions. However, this did not prevent melody from winning popularity among the population at large. In

the 1930s it was artificially promoted, with French and American influences being combated or censored. After the fall of *Fascism and the spread of jazz and swing during the Allied occupation, it was widely felt that efforts to reinforce national musical traditions would come to nothing. Instead, melody returned and encountered great success in the 1950s, favoured by the climate of restoration which followed the victory of the *Christian Democrats in the 1948 election.

New singers, such as Luciano Tajoli, Nilla Pizzi, and Claudio Villa, became enormously popular, thanks to the growth of *radio and *television, an expanding record market, and the San Remo festival of Italian song, which became a yearly event from 1951. Even today their voices have an extraordinary quality and expressiveness, a remarkable fact considering that not one of them had had a formal training. Their actual songs were less attractive. In keeping with the desire to forget tragedies and political conflicts of the war years, they were mainly nostalgic and escapist in tone; there were innumerable references to flowers, mammas, the bell towers of small villages and the carefree happiness of timeless youth. Anyone keen to sample novelty or more challenging fare was obliged to look to French popular song or to the Latin American rhythms which became popular due to *cinema and the Xavier Cugat orchestra, which toured the country and appeared on television. It was in the nightclubs that the Americanisms, irony, and humour of singers like Renato Carosone and Fred Buscaglione found an outlet.

From the late 1950s, rock and roll and pop music presented a major challenge to the music industry, but rather less to such institutions as the Church, the family, and schools [see EDUCATION], despite some signs of a moral panic. The advent of youth music did not signal a break with preceding styles and tastes. 'Beat' remained fundamentally 'light music', and was relatively easily absorbed by the San Remo Festival, which underwent a slow process of renewal after Domenico Modugno's surreal 1958 hit 'Nel blu dipinto di blu' ('Volare'). Subsequent innovations, including the *cantautori*, rock music, and, more recently, rap, could not be contained within either the melodic tradition or San Remo; indeed, they explicitly stood in opposition to both. By the 1970s the melodic tradition had run out of steam and with it San Remo. Although state television and the record companies relaunched the festival in the 1980s, they could not force a diet of sugary themes and kitsch on the public and the music became more internationalist, though the performers remained mostly Italian. However, Italian melody lived on among artists who took up the creativity of Modugno and the moderate rhythms of international pop—in the 'soft rock' of Lucio Dalla and I Pooh, in the equally 'soft' singer-songwriters Riccardo Cocciante, Claudio Baglioni, and Renato Zero, and in younger voices like Eros Ramazzotti and Laura Pausini. [SG]

See G. Baldazzi, *La canzone italiana del Novecento* (1989); G. Borgna, *Storia della canzone italiana* (1992).

Populism, as a literary movement, originated in Russian literature of the late 19th c., notably with Herzen and Tolstoy. It generally suggests the representation of the *peasantry or the poor as a positive ideal. In Italy, the influence of *Manzoni has meant that the 'umili' have figured prominently in literature. But the term 'populismo' has most often been used pejoratively by *Marxist writers and critics to describe paternalistic bourgeois representations of the poor as vessels of the authentic, universal values of the earth and of the nation, destined never to change. Franco *Fortini, for example, writing in 1953, dismissed *Neorealism as lacking all revolutionary grit for this reason, and relabelled the movement 'neo-populismo'. The most sustained polemical attack on Italian literature from this perspective is Alberto *Asor Rosa's *Scrittori e popolo* (1965), which takes on the entire sweep of modern Italian literature, from Manzoni to *Cassola and *Pasolini, by way of *nationalists, Neorealists, and others, accusing all of them of being guilty in varying degrees of the sin of populism. He makes the same claim regarding political thinkers such as *Mazzini, *Gioberti, and *Gramsci. [RSCG]

PORCELIO, IL (Giovanni Antonio dei Pandoni) (*c*.1405–after 1485). *Humanist who travelled from *court to court, earning his living by writing *Latin poetry in honour of the resident ruler. A copious, though at times clumsy, versifier, he was crowned poet laureate by the Emperor Frederick III in 1452. [JK]

Pornography, see EROTICISM AND PORNOGRAPHY.

Porretane, Le, see ARIENTI, GIOVANNI SABADINO DEGLI.

PORTA, ANTONIO (1935–89) (pseud. of Leo Paolazzi). Poet and critic. Born and educated in *Milan, he became part of the circle around *il *verri* and then of the *Gruppo 63. He and *Balestrini were the youngest of the poets anthologized in *I novissimi* (1961). The title of his first collection, *La palpebra rovesciata* (1960), reflects the anti-ironic openness which attracted him to the *Neoavanguardia and which drew him to confront flesh-and-blood issues in a poetic language underscored by percussive rhythms. Though he was programmatically opposed to any cult of the poetic self, at the core of much of his poetry lies an obscurely tragic existential trauma. *I rapporti* (1966), which brings together his earlier collections, tackles difficult subjects—sadism, violence against women, and the ambiguities of his own sexual identity. Subsequent collections, notably *Passi passaggi* (1980) and *Invasioni* (1984), maintain a high level of poetic energy whilst allowing the changing patterns of life to 'invade' the verse and create diary-like structures.

Porta was a skilled anthologist, both of others' work in *Poesia italiana degli anni Settanta* (1979) and of his own in *Nel fare poesia* (1985), which with its self-commentary becomes almost an *autobiography. He also published two *novels, *Partita* (1967) and *Il re del magazzino* (1978), and a collection of short stories, *Se fosse un tradimento* (1981). [MPC]

PORTA, CARLO (1775–1821). One of the greatest Italian *dialect poets. Born in *Milan, he worked as a civil servant most of his adult life, except for a brief interlude (1800–4) when he was a comic actor at the Teatro Patriottico. He was a leading member of Milanese intellectual circles. In 1816 he opened his own *cameretta*, a gathering of friends, including *Berchet and other *Romantics, who met once a week to discuss political and literary matters. His first composition, *El lavapiatt del Meneghin ch'è mort* ('The Dead Meneghino's Dishwasher') (1792), pays homage to the Milanese mask Meneghino and to Carlo Maria *Maggi, who had invented him. Veneration for Maggi as the forefather of the *Lombard tradition and reworkings of the Meneghino character as the embodiment of the Milanese man of the people run throughout his poetry. The next landmark in his poetic production was a partial *translation into Milanese of *Dante's *Inferno* (1802–5), the first ever known dialect translation of Dante.

His most famous poems were written from 1812. These include *Desgrazzi de Giovannin Bongee* ('The Misfortunes of Giovannino Bongeri') (1812), with its follow-up, *Olter desgrazzi de Giovannin Bongee*

Positivism

('More Misfortunes of Giovannino Bongeri') (1814), *Lament del Marchionn di gamb avert* ('The Lament of Bandy-Legged Melchior') (1816). All three are narrative poems about poor, ill-treated, unassuming, Milanese lower-class men, such as long-suffering Marchionn, who tells of the misdeeds of his gorgeous and vivacious wife, 'la Tetton' ('Big Tits'). But the most famous of a series of low-life female characters is Ninetta, the prostitute who is the protagonist of *La Ninetta del verzee* (1814).

The *verzee*, the main vegetable market in Milan, already immortalized by Maggi as the locus of Milanese popular culture, looms large throughout Porta's poetry. In *On funeral* ('A Funeral') (1816) he celebrates the 'scoeura de lengua del Verzee' ('language school of the vegetable market'), from which he returns with a shopping basket laden with popular erudition freely given by maidservants and barrow-boys. Porta also overtly affirms the superiority of his dialect over the national language in 'Calca l'aratro è ver, fatica e suda', which alternates lines of Italian and Milanese, and contrasts the flimsy sentiment that fizzles out in teasing games, as expressed in the codified, rarefied *Tuscan of the lyrical tradition, with the sincere and straightforward love which the rural proletarian voices in Milanese dialect.

Anti-clerical satire is the focus of *Ona vision* ('A Vision'), *Fraa Zenever* ('Friar Juniper'), *Fraa Diodatt* ('Friar Godgiven') (1813–14), and *El viacc de fraa Condutt* ('Friar Condutt's Trip') (1816). Porta's last poems, *La nomina del cappellan* ('The Appointment of the Chaplain') (1819), *Meneghin biroeu di ex monegh* ('Meneghino Servant of the Former Nuns') (1820), and *La guerra di prett* ('The Priests' War') (1821), portray a bitterly sarcastic picture of the effects of the *Austrian *Restoration on Milanese life.

Porta's favourite metre is *ottava rima*, especially in the narrative poems, which follow oral modes of verse narrative in other ways too, employing formulas which suggest gestures to listening spectators or at times developing direct addresses to them. The result is a striking air of immediacy and humour. [VRJ]

Poesie, ed. D. Isella (1975). See *La poesia di C. Porta e la tradizione milanese* (1976); G. Bezzola, *Vita di Carlo Porta nella Milano del suo tempo* (1980).

Positivism was a philosophical system developed in France in the first half of the 19th c. by Auguste Comte (1798–1857), which then spread throughout Europe, mainly in the work of the English philosopher Herbert Spencer (1820–1903). In contrast to traditional philosophies concerned with the study of essences and first principles, positivism held that the only valid objects of knowledge were empirically testable facts and their interrelations. It extended its model of scientific inquiry to different fields and promoted the empirical study of social phenomena to which Comte gave the name 'sociology'.

In Italy, positivism exerted its greatest influence in the area of historical and literary scholarship. Appealing as it did to the secular mentality of the *Risorgimento, it laid the basis for the reconstruction of Italian history by means of detailed archival research. In literary studies, the emphasis was placed on erudition and philological accuracy. Inspired by the positivist belief in factual evidence, the Scuola Storica, as it was called, explored the literary past often with the purpose of tracing the evolution of poetic forms, at times tending toward rigid social determinism. Following on the work of such prominent *literary critics and philologists as Domenico Comparetti (1835–1927), author of the renowned *Virgilio nel medio evo* (1882), Alessandro D'Ancona (1835–1914), Ernesto Monaci (1844–1918), and Pio *Rajna (1847–1930), the research methods of the Scuola Storica have been widely deployed in Italian academic criticism throughout the 20th c. The *Giornale storico della letteratura italiana*, founded in 1883, attests today to the lasting vitality of the kind of historical criticism inspired by positive science. [See also FILOLOGIA.]

In prose fiction, positivism played a significant role in the formation and practice of the poetics of *verismo. Luigi *Capuana, Giovanni *Verga, and Federico *De Roberto all at some point in their careers, if with different emphases, conceived of literature as representative of a documentable reality and of the literary text as a medium for conveying the inner truths of humanity's struggle for survival.

The impact of positivism on the social sciences in Italy can be seen in the work of at least three internationally known thinkers: Cesare *Lombroso, Vilfredo *Pareto, and Gaetano *Mosca. Lombroso, a psychiatrist who taught at the University of *Turin, advanced the theory that traits of criminal personalities are determined by particular somatic features. Although this theory is no longer accepted, the emphasis Lombroso placed on the criminal, rather than on the crime committed, paved the way for the modern science of criminology. Pareto's debt to positivism consists in his rigorous study of social phenomena, based on the notion of elites, according to which the balanced operation of social systems is ensured by the constant control exerted by the governing elite groups over the governed. For Pareto, the ideal society is one in which the continuity of elites is guaranteed. Mosca applied a similar orientation to the field of politics, advancing the theory that in all forms of government there exists a minority political class which holds power over the majority of citizens, who have no real presence in the workings of government. In the field of philosophy, Roberto *Ardigò introduced the fundamental themes of European positivism into Italian culture. Influenced to a large extent by Spencer, he maintained that concrete, scientifically verifiable experiences constituted the outer limit of any philosophical theory of reality.

In many respects, positivism continues the great heritage of *Enlightenment thought, as it too was based on the hope that science could provide new methods for increasing knowledge which would enhance social life and further the quest for a universal brotherhood of free and equal human beings.
[RSD]

See T. Iermano (ed.), *Positivismo, naturalismo, verismo: questioni teoriche e analisi critiche* (1996).

POSSEVINO, ANTONIO (1534–1611). *Jesuit missionary and *papal legate from *Mantua, who opposed the Protestant *Reformation and conducted unsuccessful missions of reconciliation to Sweden, Russia, and Poland. His *Moscovia* (1586) is a pioneering account of Russian history. He later lectured in *Padua, where Francis de Sales was his pupil. [PMcN]

Post-modernism is a broad and highly contested term that had particular currency in the 1980s. It is used to designate both changes in the social and economic structures of contemporary society, particularly in the light of globalization, and forms of contemporary artistic practice that appear to respond to, or take part in, such changes. Post-modernist works express on a formal and thematic level the diversity and uncertainty of contemporary life. Tradition is not rejected and experimentalism for its own sake is regarded with suspicion. No one set of aesthetic or moral standards has general validity, and the search for valid forms, if undertaken, is more important than their outright proclamation. In Italy this condition has been theorized by

the philosopher Gianni *Vattimo, using his concept of '*pensiero debole'.

In literature, the *detective fiction of Leonardo *Sciascia is a relatively early dramatization of postmodern anxiety. Reason and justice are no longer adequate tools for apprehending reality, and his detectives find no solutions. Umberto *Eco, regarded by many as Italy's major post-modern writer, also uses the detective genre in *Il *nome della rosa* (1980). He is less concerned than Sciascia with his detective's failure; what he admires is the pursuit of possibilities rather than assertions of monolithic truth. *Il nome della rosa* is also a *historical novel, reflecting the critical, ironic revisiting of history characteristic of an important strand of postmodern fiction. Writers such as Sebastiano *Vassalli and Dacia *Maraini have attempted reconstructions of Italy's forgotten past, aware that their versions, however plausible or moving, are only provisional and partial accounts.

Post-modern works exhibit a renewed interest in narration. Writers such as Gianni *Celati, Andrea *De Carlo, and Roberto *Pazzi propose storytelling as a valid means of understanding the world. There is a new awareness also of the ways language shapes the world we inhabit; this awareness links the semantic richness of Aldo *Busi with the spare, precise prose of Antonio *Tabucchi. Some critics view the very accessibility of much post-modernist fiction as proof that it is complicit with the market interests of capitalism, a complicity satirized by Italo *Calvino in *Se una notte d'inverno un viaggiatore* (1979). Yet this openness has altered the face of Italian literature as more women and younger writers have achieved recognition. The hybrid voice of Eritrean-born Erminia Dell'Oro can be seen as symptomatic of the post-modern democratization of culture. [See also STRUCTURALISM AND POST-STRUCTURALISM.] [DD]

See G. Mari (ed.), *Moderno postmoderno* (1987); J. Cannon, *Postmodern Italian Fiction* (1989).

Post-structuralism, see STRUCTURALISM AND POST-STRUCTURALISM.

POZZA, NERI (1912–88) founded the publishing house in Vicenza for which he is best known in 1945. As well as memoirs, he wrote poetry dominated by his experiences as a *Fascist prisoner, and a *novel, *Processo per eresia* (1970), which combines passion for *Venetian art with profound knowledge of his native province. [JJ]

Pozzi, Antonia

POZZI, ANTONIA (1912–38). *Milanese poet, who committed suicide soon after completing her thesis (on Flaubert) at Milan University. Her poems, which she had been writing since the age of 17, were published posthumously, as *Parole* (1939), to some critical acclaim. In them she concentrates on her emotional states, but her attention to style and form leads to the creation of a quite definite and recognizable poetic voice. Her points of reference are not just the standard *D'Annunzio and *Pascoli but the *Crepuscolari*, *Ungaretti, Rilke, and other modern French and German poets. The result in her best work is an individual form of *symbolism. [RD]

POZZO DE' ZORZI, MODESTA, see FONTE, MODERATA.

PRAGA, EMILIO (1839–75). The archetype of the Italian version of the *poète maudit*. The son of a wealthy *Milanese industrialist, and an enthusiast of Baudelaire and Heine, he destroyed himself largely through alcohol and drugs after his father's death plunged the family into poverty. He had been a painter before turning to poetry with *Tavolozza* (1862). He became a leading presence in the Milanese *Scapigliatura*, writing its artistic manifesto with *Boito in 1864. He published stories and *libretti, as well as the poems of *Penombre* (1864) and *Fiabe e leggende* (1867). A *novel, *Memorie di un presbiterio*, was completed after his death by Roberto *Sacchetti. [AHC]

PRAGA, MARCO (1862–1929). Playwright son of the poet Emilio *Praga. Scarred by his father's self-destruction, he trained as an accountant in *Milan. His first play, *Le due case*, written with Virgilio Colombo in 1885, was followed over the next thirty years by a further eighteen plays. In 1889 came public success with *Le vergini*, followed a year later by his most famous play, *La moglie ideale*, premièred with Eleonora Duse in the lead role.

The most talented of the practitioners of *teatro borghese*, who included *Giacosa, *Rovetta, *Antona-Traversi and *Bracco, Praga depicted the everyday life of the bourgeoisie, showing how morality often descends into social posturing, and with a strong emphasis on psychological analysis, though he was unimpressed by *positivist theories. He was president of the Società degli Autori ed Editori and won royalties for playwrights upon performance of their work. In 1912 he became director of the *Manzoni theatre in Milan, staging various new plays, including *Pirandello's *È stato così*; he was also, briefly, director of the Silentium Film company founded in Milan in 1916. He was theatre critic for the *Corriere della sera* and *Lettura*, and contributed to *L'Illustrazione italiana* under the pseudonym Emmepì. He committed suicide in hospital in Varese. [See also THEATRE, 2.] [AHC]

PRAMPOLINI, ENRICO (1894–1956). Experimental *theatre designer and painter from *Futurism's second generation. Already in 1915 he proposed replacing realistic backcloths with an interplay of evocative coloured light. He later developed Futurist Pantomime, blending lighting, music, painting, mime, and mechanical models. [SV]

PRATELLA, FRANCESCO BALILLA (1880–1955). Composer, *literary critic, and musicologist. He published several *Futurist essays, notably the *Manifesto dei musicisti futuristi* (1910), but withdrew from the movement after *World War I. A choral piece, *La chiesa di Polenta*, is a setting of a poem by *Carducci, but his *operas use texts he himself composed. [RS]

PRATESI, MARIO (1842–1921). *Tuscan *novelist, who worked as a schoolteacher until 1906. His portrait of a venal society in *L'eredità* (1883) and *Il mondo di Dolcetta* (1895) combines the scientific rigour of *verismo with a *Scapigliato denunciation of the betrayal of *Risorgimento hopes, whilst his sketches of Tuscan life in *In provincia* (1883) display a moral and political commitment lacking in *Fucini, to whom he is often compared. His disillusionment gradually led him away from socio-political commitment to existential pessimism. Some critics have detected a new religious idealism in his later novels. [PBarn]

PRATI, GIOVANNI (1814–84). Poet who attempted to recapture the ardour of *Romanticism at a time when it was already in crisis. He was born in Campomaggiore near Trento and studied at *Padua, where he became a friend of Aleardo *Aleardi, with whom his name is commonly linked. He established his reputation when he moved to *Milan in 1840 and wrote *Edmenegarda* (1841). This *novella in versi* about bourgeois passion and hypocrisy, had great success with the public, though critics were less convinced. Subsequent narrative and philosophical poems such as *Satana e le Grazie* (1855) and *Armando* (1864) also had a mixed reception on account of the schematic treatment of their characters' psychology. His various collections of *lyric poetry derived their appeal mainly from their sentimental qualities, although the charm and grace of some poems looks forwards to *Pascoli, and the late *Psiche* (1876) and *Iside* (1878) show a new realism of approach. Prati was a convinced monarchist—leading to embittered relations with republicans like Daniele Manin in *Venice—and wrote various celebratory poems for the House of *Savoy. He became official royal historian in *Turin in the early 1860s and later a parliamentary deputy and senator. [DO'G]

PRATOLINI, VASCO (1913–91). One of the most important *novelists of the immediate postwar years, whose reputation has suffered, however, since the decline of *Neorealism. Of working-class *Florentine origin, he took various jobs as a young man. In the early 1930s he became a sub-editor for *Il *Bargello*, to which he contributed articles emphasizing the revolutionary aspects of *Fascism. He also wrote more literary articles for *Il Bargello* and other reviews. Disquiet at the direction Fascism was taking led to *Campo di Marte* (1938–9), the dissenting and largely *hermetic periodical which he founded and edited with Alfonso *Gatto. In 1940 he moved to *Rome, initially to work for the the ministry of education. He took part in the Roman *Resistance, and after the war lived largely in Rome and *Naples.

His early stories, collected in *Il tappeto verde* (1941) and *Le amiche* (1943), are more lyrical than narrative. But during the war years, whilst never abandoning lyricism completely, he developed a more urgent voice which found its material in the Florence of his youth. *Il quartiere* (1944) is a first attempt to articulate the coming to political consciousness of his generation, and their recognition of the need to take up arms against Fascism. *Cronache di poveri amanti* (1947), his most successful novel and a canonical text of Neorealism, recounts the not quite total triumph of Fascism over the Florentine working class in the 1920s. In *Metello* (1955), which provoked an intensely politicized debate about Neorealism and *impegno*, he went a little further back to present a romanticized account of the struggle between Florentine workers and their bosses in the years before *World War I. *Metello* became the first volume of a trilogy entitled *Una storia italiana*: the others are *Lo scialo* (1960), another portrayal of 1920s Florence, but on a vast scale, and arguably the one Italian novel which

attempts in any depth to analyse Fascism in practice; and the *autobiographical *Allegoria e derisione* (1966), which attempts to understand the emotional and political evolution of a Florentine intellectual from boyhood to the present. A profound concern with the irrational shows itself in these works, and in the earlier exploration of personal family trauma in *Cronaca familiare* (1947). It is also a major element in Pratolini's novels about the young of postwar Florence, caught between the need for *impegno*, resurgent Fascism, and new cultural pressures: *Un eroe del nostro tempo* (1949), the semi-comic *Le ragazze di Sanfrediano* (1952), and *La costanza della ragione* (1963). As well as novels Pratolini wrote plays, film scripts (for *Visconti and *Rossellini amongst others), and the poems collected in *Il mannello di Natascia* (1985). [PH]

See G. Bertoncini, *Vasco Pratolini* (1987).

PRATT, HUGO (1927–95). Popular *comic-book artist. In the postwar years he developed (partly in Argentina) a new satirical and witty style, with highbrow references to *cinema and literature. His best-known creation, the lone adventurer Corto Maltese, made him famous internationally. [SVM]

PRAZ, MARIO (1896–1982) was professor of Italian at Liverpool (1924–32), Manchester (1932–4), and *Rome (1934–66), the influential editor of *English Miscellany*, and joint editor of *Cultura, London Mercury, Criterion*, and *English Studies*. An internationally known prize-winning *literary critic, he wrote many brilliant essays on Italian, English, and comparative literary problems, of particular importance being *La carne la morte e il diavolo nella letteratura romantica* (1930) (better known as *The Romantic Agony*, 1933), *Studi sul concettismo* (1934) (*Studies in Seventeenth-Century Imagery*, 1938), *Gusto neoclassico* (1940), and *Mnemosine: parallelo tra la letteratura e le arti visive* (1971). [JRW]

PRENDILACQUA, FRANCESCO, see VITTORINO DA FELTRE.

Pre-Romanticism. The second half of the 18th c. sees various developments occurring in European literature which are commonly regarded as anticipating *Romanticism. In the Italian context pre-Romanticism chiefly refers to the reception of foreign models, mainly English and German, which were perceived as exotic at the time. The new vogue reached the peninsula via France, usually through French *translations, and was fostered by the unprecedented openness of *Enlightenment cosmopolitanism to foreign influences.

The sentimental moralism of Richardson's *Pamela* makes an early appearance in *Goldoni's *Pamela nubile* and *Pamela maritata* (1750), based on the Abbé Prévost's translation of the novel. A new response to nature, expressed in unfamiliar descriptive guises, comes to be known through French translations of Thomson's *The Seasons* and Gessner's *Idylls*, as well as through the writings of Rousseau, which also promote the cult of sensibility. Goethe's despairing *Sorrows of Young Werther* circulate first in French translation, then in an inaccurate Italian version (1781) of the inaccurate French. Exceptionally, *Cesarotti, with English assistance, translates directly from the original in his remarkable and uniquely influential Italian versions (1763–72) of *Fingal* and the other prose poems attributed by James Macpherson to the Celtic bard *Ossian.

The typical products of Italian pre-Romanticism are mainly poetry. They naturalize either the soulfully magniloquent manner of Ossian/Macpherson and Gray in *The Bard* or the more meditative melancholy vein of the English 'graveyard poets'— Young, Hervey, the Gray of the *Elegy*—as in *Bertola de' Giorgi's *Notti clementine* (1771), *Fantoni's *Notti* (1785–92) and Alessandro *Verri's novel *Notti romane* (1792–1804). A parallel rediscovery and reappraisal of *Dante is reflected in *Varano's imitative *Visioni* (1749–66) and later in the poetry of Vincenzo *Monti.

Much in Italian pre-Romanticism remains at the superficial level of a fashionable pursuit of novelty. It was attacked as such by *Parini, and also as a threat to the purity of the classical tradition. Yet it represents an essential transition in taste from *Arcadia and *classicism to Romanticism. In reflecting their aspiration to the sublime, it made an undeniably formative contribution to the work of the major writers active in the decades preceding the birth of doctrinal Romanticism (1816). *Alfieri modelled his tragic verse on the *hendecasyllables of Cesarotti's Ossian; Monti adapted part of *Werther* in his *Sciolti a Sigismondo Chigi* (1783) and drew on Gray for his celebration of *Napoleon in *Il bardo della selva nera* (1806); *Foscolo's *Ultime lettere di Jacopo Ortis* (1802) were a politicized *Werther*, the antidote to which he found in Sternian irony and in his splendid translation of Sterne's *Sentimental Journey* (1813). In Alfieri and

Foscolo pre-Romanticism is radicalized into post-Enlightenment pessimism and revolt, going far beyond mere fashion to become a Romanticism *ante litteram*.   [JMAL]

See W. Binni, *Preromanticismo italiano*, 2nd edn. (1959).

Press, see JOURNALISM; PERIODICALS; PUBLISHING.

PRESSBURGER, GIORGIO (1937–). *Novelist. Born in Budapest, he left Hungary after the Russian invasion of 1956 and studied biology in *Rome. He was initially more concerned with the *theatre. His first notable fiction, co-written with his brother Nicola (who died in 1985), appears in *Storie dell' ottavo distretto* (1986) and *L'elefante verde* (1988), both concerned with the *Jewish experience in Hungary. Subsequent novels, such as *La coscienza sensibile* (1992), have drawn more evidently on his scientific training.   [PH]

PRETI, GIROLAMO (*c*.1582–1626). Born probably in *Bologna, he was destined for a legal career, but broke off his studies to become one of the most accomplished of early 17th-c. poets. He is best known for his idylls, a genre which he established with the mythological *Salmace* of 1609, and then extended to more straightforwardly amorous subjects. His *lyric *Poesie* (1614) are characterized by a cautious yet original adaptation of the models offered by *Marino, whom he knew from the early 1600s, when Marino was a frequent visitor to Bologna. He makes moderate use of complex metaphors and *acutezze* [see CONCETTISMO], inclining to a gently sensuous style, which captures physical detail (his description of the nymph Salmace bathing is exemplary), while avoiding the more intense and disturbing erotic charge to be found in Marino. His ideas were similarly conservative: in his brief treatise *Intorno all'onestà della poesia* (1618) he reasserts the *Renaissance *Neoplatonist view of the moral functions of love poetry. More than any other of Marino's friends, he was perplexed by *L'*Adone*. He was one of the few *concettisti* to find favour in the *Rome of *Urban VIII; he served as secretary to Cardinal Francesco Barberini, and was accompanying him on a Spanish embassy when he died suddenly.   [MPS]

PREZZOLINI, GIUSEPPE (1882–1982). Prolific cultural commentator, best known for founding the highly influential *Florentine *periodical *La *Voce* in 1908, and editing it for most of its first six years of existence. Together with his close friend Giovanni *Papini, he had already edited *Leonardo* (1903–7), a journal exploring various international anti-*positivist philosophical currents which was inspired by the desire for Italian cultural resurgence. This desire found less inward-looking and more practical expression in *La Voce* and its associated *publishing house. Influenced by *Croce, Prezzolini led a diverse group of intellectuals in an attempt to address Italy's moral and political problems in rational terms and to improve its cultural and civic life. The group dissolved in 1913–14, and Prezzolini lost faith in his intellectual mission. During *World War I he came close to *Mussolini, but subsequently left Italy.

He was professor of Italian literature at Columbia University (1930–50), and took American citizenship in 1940. From 1968 he lived in Lugano. His publications include the important *Repertorio bibliografico della storia e della letteratura italiana (1937–42)*, several studies of *Machiavelli, and many *autobiographical works, *diaries, collections of letters, and other studies documenting the experience of *La Voce*, especially the monumental *La Voce 1908–1913* (1974). [SV]

Prigioni, Le mie (1832). The memoirs of Silvio *Pellico, documenting his arrest after the troubles of 1821 and his incarceration in *Venice and the Spielberg fortress. The book proved a rallying cry for the *Risorgimento; it survives because of its warm depiction of Pellico's own spiritual quest and the accuracy of some of his pen-sketches. [MPC]

Primato (1940–3). Fortnightly *periodical, based in *Rome, founded by Giuseppe *Bottai and edited by Bottai and Giorgio Vecchietti. Its aim was to draw the best writers and critics of the time, whatever their political outlook, into making a serious contribution to the war on which *Fascist Italy was embarking, without constraining them simply to produce propaganda. In the event political and general issues were examined with considerable detachment, whilst the *literary criticism published was often more stringent than in many prewar journals. Early issues, for example, included an important debate on *hermetic poetry to which *Montale, *Contini, Corrado *Pavolini, Francesco *Flora, Giuseppe *De Robertis, and other names of note contributed. Later issues published various poems that Montale would include in *La bufera e altro*. [PH]

Primavera di bellezza, see FENOGLIO, BEPPE.

Primo tempo, see PERIODICALS, I; SOLMI, SERGIO.

Principe, Il, see MACHIAVELLI, NICCOLÒ.

Principe hermafrodito, Il, see PALLAVICINO, FERRANTE.

Printing was brought to Italy by two German clerics, Conrad Schweynheym and Arnold Pannartz, who set up a press in 1465 in the Benedictine monastery of Subiaco and printed four books, before moving to *Rome in 1467. Their Subiaco production—a Donatus (the Latin schoolbook), of which no copies survive, the works of the early Christian writer Lactantius, *Cicero's *De oratore*, and St *Augustine's *De civitate Dei*—sums up the direction of the earliest printing in Italy and the reasons for its success. Italy was the centre of Christendom and the home of the new *humanist learning, and printing put down roots and flourished on Italian soil by serving these pre-existing markets. About 30 per cent of books printed in Italy in the 15th c. were religious in character; something like 80 per cent were in Latin or in another learned language.

As well as instruments of culture, books are also merchandise, and successful printing and publishing entreprises must also meet commercial imperatives. From the outset, the production of printed books in Italy was centred, not in the great *university towns of *Padua, *Bologna, and Pavia, but in the major commercial centres of Rome, *Venice, *Milan, *Florence, and *Naples. Of these, Venice, with its international trade routes and *merchant community and its proximity to central Europe, quickly became the most important; indeed, for about fifty years from 1470, it was the centre of European printing, and it retained its leading place in the Italian peninsula until the Republic fell in 1797. It was from here that the first highly organized international publishing and bookselling concern, the Compagnia di Venezia, was run; here also that the two founts, roman and italic, which have dominated Western European printing down to the present, were brought to perfection, and, in the case of italic, invented. It was in Venice, too, that the printed book first achieved emancipation from the *manuscript model, which had conditioned its early years, and began to develop its own rationale.

Meanwhile, the percentage of works published

in the vernacular steadily increased. Many of these were slim, popular works of piety, information, or entertainment, liable, like schoolbooks, to be used to destruction: without doubt many early editions in these categories have disappeared without trace. But great works of literature also began to appear in print. The first editions of *Petrarch's *Canzoniere* and of the *Decameron* were published in 1470; the *Divine Comedy* followed two years later. *Poliziano's *Stanze per la giostra* and *Orfeo* were printed only a few years after composition, though their first dissemination was through manuscript. Many editions of contemporary poetry and prose followed in the last two decades of the 15th c. By the middle of the 16th c. the balance of printed production had shifted from Latin to the vernacular. Even at the beginning of the century, vernacular writers wrote their works in the expectation of their being printed: Pietro *Bembo, *Castiglione, *Ariosto, all financed the first editions of their works and, when circumstances permitted, closely followed their progress through the press. By the middle of the century vernacular editions were the mainstay of the leading publishing houses, particularly in Venice, and many men of letters made their living out of the printing industry, as authors, editors, translators, and correctors. However, even during this flourishing period, leadership in quality book production and type design had already passed from Italy to Switzerland and France.

The *Counter-Reformation put a brake on the variety and vigour of the publishing market, and Italian printing went into a slow, centuries-long decline, from which it was only briefly rescued at the end of the 18th c. by the genius of Giambattista *Bodoni. Because of the pre-industrial nature of the Italian economy, modern printing methods were slow to reach Italy; only in the second half of the 19th c. did the major publishing houses begin to use machines and stereotype for the production of books. The contemporary Italian printing industry has remained distinctively small-scale, though often of high quality; the influence of outstanding modern hand-press printers and type designers such as Giovanni Mardersteig of Verona has been formative.

Until the advent of *photography, printed books were illustrated by woodcuts or metal engravings. Woodcuts, being relief carvings, can be printed together with the text they illustrate, and are thus cheaper and easier to produce than metal engravings (usually copper), which require a different sort of press. In the first 100 years of printing, woodcut illustrations predominated, and they continued to be used after 1550 for works requiring large numbers of illustrations. But *Mannerist and then *Baroque taste preferred the greater delicacy and contrast of engraving, and various forms of engraving dominated the illustration of printed books from the middle of the 16th c. until the revival of woodcuts at the end of the 18th.

*Music printing presents special problems, because the representation of music requires two elements, staves and notation, with the latter superimposed on the former. Some early music printers printed each page from woodcuts. Others sought a typographical solution. At first, each sheet was printed twice, or sometimes three times, once for the staves, a second time for the notes and once again for any text. The first Italian printer to specialize in music printing, Ottaviano Petrucci (Venice, b.1501), quickly realized he could dispense with the third round of printing by printing text with the staves. The final solution was to cast sections of the stave with each note, thus enabling stave, notes, and text to be printed together. Introduced to Italian printing by the Frenchman Antoine Gardane (Antonio Gardano) in the early 1540s, this allowed the printing of polyphonic and instrumental music to flourish as never before, and thus probably played a significant part in the development of Baroque music. From the 17th c. typographical music printing was largely superseded by the use of engraving. [See also GIUNTI; MANUZIO, ALDO; PUBLISHING.]   [CF]

See L. Febvre and H. J. Martin, *The Coming of the Book: The Impact of Printing (1450–1800)* (1976); B. Richardson, *Print Culture in Renaissance Italy* (1994); M. Santoro, *Storia del libro italiano* (1994); S. H. Steinberg, *Five Hundred Years of Printing* (1996).

PRISCO, MICHELE (1920–). *Novelist. Born near *Naples, he graduated in law there and went on to contribute to *Alvaro's *Risorgimento* and *Bilenchi's *Il nuovo corriere*. His abundant fiction is largely set in Naples, much of it going against Neapolitan stereotypes. The stories of *La provincia addormentata* (1949), for example, give a slow-motion close-up of the inertly respectable middle class of the area. The novel *La dama di piazza* (1961) views the history of Naples from the end of *World War I to the end of *World War II through the experiences of one family. *Una spirale di nebbia* (1966) is a form of psychological detective story.
                                                          [JG-R]

Problemi, see PERIODICALS, I.

PRODENZANI, SIMONE, see NOVELLA IN VERSI.

Progresso, Il (1832–46). *Neapolitan journal, founded by Giuseppe *Ricciardi after the closure of *Antologia*. Its full title was *Il Progresso delle scienze delle lettere e delle arti*. Ricciardi, who put his faith for progress above all in the sciences, maintained contact with *Vieusseux, and attracted writers from all over Italy. He was succeeded as editor by R. Liberatore. [MPC]

Promessi sposi, I. *Manzoni's masterpiece and his only novel. First drafted as *Fermo e Lucia* in 1821–3, it was recast as *I promessi sposi* in 1825–7 and first published in 1827 (the 'ventisettana'). After detailed linguistic revision, the definitive edition was published in 1840 (the 'quarantana').

The novel is set in Spanish-dominated *Lombardy in the 1620s, against the background of the *Counter-Reformation and the Thirty Years War. The betrothed couple, Lucia Mondella and Renzo Tramaglino, are prevented from marrying because Don Rodrigo, the local *feudal lord, wants Lucia for himself. All initial efforts to solve the problem fail. Lucia and Renzo are forced to flee and become separated. Their eventual reunion is delayed by a series of vicissitudes triggered by the initial act of oppression. In the course of these they are aided or impeded by a variety of characters. Don Rodrigo's initial aim of preventing the wedding succeeds because the cowardly Don Abbondio, the parish priest, bows to his intimidations. After the separation Lucia shelters in a convent under the protection of the nun Gertrude, the *Monaca di Monza, but Gertrude betrays her, and Lucia is abducted and carried off to the castle of a powerful lord known only as the Innominato, who has organized the kidnapping on behalf of Don Rodrigo, But the Innominato undergoes a conversion, partly through meeting Cardinal Federico *Borromeo, and frees Lucia, who goes to live in *Milan in the house of a well-to-do couple. There she is struck down by the *plague, but recovers, and is found by Renzo in the plague hospital. The last obstacle is the vow of perpetual virginity that she made to the Virgin Mary during her imprisonment in the castle of the Innominato. This is rescinded by the timely intervention of the Capuchin Fra Cristoforo, and the way is open for the wedding and a future life of prosperity and serenity.

The ultimate archetype of the story is the quest of the fairy tale, but most of the characters correspond to types found in the 18th-c. European *novel, with subtle modifications stemming from Manzoni's committed Catholicism and his decision to take his protagonists from the lower classes— Lucia and Renzo are *peasants-cum-silk workers. The figure of the *libertine is split between Don Rodrigo and the Innominato, with only the latter, who repents, being portrayed in a glamorous light. Renzo is the questing hero of the fairy tale and also the character who undertakes the 'epic of the road' typical of many male protagonists of 18th-c. European novels. Gertrude reproduces the 'corrupt nun' of Gothic novels; a detailed sub-narrative explains the family pressures which led to her entering the convent and charts her subsequent misdemeanours. Lucia herself, the personification of female virtue and intuitive trust in God, is the Redeeming Virgin (as in Richardson's *Clarissa*), and the Persecuted Maiden (as in Richardson, De Sade, and the Gothic novel). Together the two characters can be seen as reproducing the Mary/Eve dichotomy which runs throughout Western culture.

Making lower-class characters the protagonists is original to Manzoni. Aside from the cultural innovativeness of the gesture, it also supports his documentary concerns. Renzo is used as the vehicle for the portrayal of social reality and its impact on the lower strata of society. Lucia is held more aloof and encounters the great and powerful. Together they enable Manzoni to explore history from above and history from below and to present a picture of 17th-c. Lombard society, which is then supplemented and developed in explicitly historical accounts of the *bravi*, the invasions of German troops and ultimately the *plague.

The story is narrated mainly through the voice and from the perspective of an external, (almost) omniscient narrator, with occasional shifts to one or other of the characters. The omniscience of the narrator is diminished by the pretence that the fictional story was found in an anonymous 17th-c. manuscript (the 'Anonimo'), references to which are woven into the narration. They have the function of limiting the inventing capacity of the narrator, and enhancing the illusion of reality: not only is the story supposed to have been written soon after the events, but it is also presented as a transcript of Renzo's own oral narration to the anonymous author.

The text of the novel makes frequent references

to historical sources in order to underline the authenticity of the portrayal of historical characters, events and situations. Manzoni did consult a vast amount of material, both published works and archival documents, which is however inevitably manipulated and transformed in the process of transition to the literary text. Choosing to set a fictional story involving a peasant couple within the period of the *Counter-Reformation meant taking on board the whole question of the validity and effectiveness of this new beginning for the Church of Rome. The resulting picture is interestingly ambivalent. Manzoni produced a severe critique of both political and ecclesiastical authorities in 17th-c. society, while at the same time enhancing the positive nature of Cardinal Borromeo, and censoring those aspects of the historical material which suggested a basic failure of the Church's bid for the hearts and minds of the rural masses. His peasantry are what the Counter-Reformation would see as good Catholics, led by competent (if not heroic) pastors at parish level, such as Don Abbondio, and (almost) cleansed of superstition and magic; they live in a society without spectacular liturgy, without *Jesuits, without religious repression and fundamentalism, aided by heroic Capuchins, and led by a virtually faultless Cardinal Archbishop. In this respect *I promessi sposi* can be read as a project for a future society, freed of the worst features of the *ancien régime* through the action of enlightened leaders, and imbued with a Catholicism which has learned the lesson of the *Enlightenment, and whose leaders demand not temporal power but the moral authority which stems from heroic virtue.

[VRJ]

I promessi sposi nelle due edizioni del 1840 e del 1825–7 raffrontate tra loro, ed. L. Caretti (1971). See G. Baldi, *I promessi sposi* (1985); E. N. Girardi, *Strutture e personaggi dei 'Promessi sposi'* (1994); V. R. Jones, *Le dark ladies manzoniane* (1998).

Propugnatore, Il (1868–93) was published in *Bologna and edited first by Francesco Zambrini and from 1888 by *Carducci. It was an erudite journal of *medieval and *Renaissance literature. It featured historical essays, editions of unpublished or unknown texts (in strict accordance with the principles of modern *positivist philology), and other archival material. One of its main enterprises was a catalogue of early Italian printed books. Contributors included the major scholars of the time, such as Francesco D'Ovidio, Ernesto Monaci, Pio *Rajna,

and Alessandro D'Ancona [see LITERARY CRITICISM; LITERARY THEORY, 5; PERIODICALS, 2; POSITIVISM]. [GP]

Prosa d'arte was one of the most distinctive literary phenomena of the 1920s and 1930s. It derived from the poetics of the *prose poem and verse fragment, as developed in *La *Voce* under the editorship of Giuseppe *De Robertis in 1915–16. Eschewing any form of narrative, *prosa d'arte* cultivated a precious, polished style, with a rarefied, poetic aura. It aimed more to evoke an aesthetic than an emotional response, often hiding lines of verse in the prose texture as part of its efforts to heighten effects of beauty and harmony. Its major exponent, Vincenzo *Cardarelli, who was the motive force behind *La *Ronda* (1919–22), wanted *prosa d'arte* to reinvent the movement of classical prose, and to rise to a kind of abstract absolute of fine style. Each 'chapter' or 'capitolo' (*Capitoli* was the title of an anthology published by Enrico Falqui in 1938) was to be a miniature masterpiece in its own right, devoid of reference to contemporary— that is, *Fascist—reality and the seeds of conflict inherent in it.

Prosa d'arte was soon widely cultivated and gained wide currency through *elzeviri,* the articles on art and literature published on the cultural page (*la terza pagina*) of many daily newspapers. Apart from Cardarelli, masters of the form included Antonio Baldini and Emilio *Cecchi, who both wrote regularly for the *Corriere della sera.* [AC]

Prose della volgar lingua, Le, by Pietro *Bembo (1525), established the basis for the subsequent development of literary Italian. The *dialogue, set in 1502, justifies in books 1 and 2 the principle of imitating the usage of the greatest authors (the *Florentine of *Petrarch rather than *Dante in verse, *Boccaccio in prose). Bembo considered this the only enduring model for vernacular writers, rejecting a language based on the unstable Italian *courts or one open to popular influences, as was contemporary literary Tuscan. Book 3 describes this usage in detail. The work demonstrates an exceptional knowledge of Italian literary history. [See also GRAMMARS; IMITATION; LINGUA CORTIGIANA; PURISM; QUESTIONE DELLA LINGUA.] [BR]

Prose Poem (*poesia in prosa*). Italian practitioners have been strongly influenced by the archetypal example of Baudelaire, who showed a way of bringing to what was formally prose the qualities of a poem. In Italy the prose poem was not clearly separated from *prosa d'arte*; it flourished first in the ambit of *La* *Voce* of Giuseppe *De Robertis; hence, for example, Carlo *Linati's *Doni della terra* (1915) and Arturo *Onofri's *Trombe d'argento* (1924). It was taken up by the writers of *La* *Ronda*, with collections being published subsequently by *Cardarelli, *Malaparte, *Soffici, and others. The highly literary prose poem's success under *Fascism has worked against it in the postwar period.   [CFB]

Prostitutes, see COURTESANS.

Provence, see FRENCH INFLUENCES, 1; TROUBADOURS.

Proverbs, that is, short maxims or sententious sayings, usually kept alive through oral transmission. In Italy vernacular collections were made as early as the 13th c. They were widely used, especially in *novelle* and *comedies. In the 15th c. facetious or lubricious explanations of proverbs compiled in *novella* form, for example, by Ludovico *Carbone and Antonio *Cornazzano.   [DieZ]

Psychoanalysis. The theories of Sigmund Freud, often elaborated through reference to literary texts and artistic figures, initially received a cool reception in Italy or were simply not studied. A figure like *Pirandello, who was concerned with divisions and delusions in the individual personality, drew his ideas principally from late 19th-c. French psychological thought rather than from Freud. Benedetto *Croce did express an interest, though he was critical of the way psychoanalysis appeared to encroach on the concerns of philosophy. Giovanni *Gentile was less sympathetic: his *educational reforms of 1924 ensured that psychoanalysis, and psychology in general, were kept well out of schools. Left-wing figures were scarcely more encouraging; *Togliatti, the long-time leader of the *Communist Party, deplored what he saw as the excessive importance Freud gave to sex.

A more encouraging response came from *Trieste, which, as part of the Austro-Hungarian Empire until 1919, was strongly affected by *Austrian culture. Italo *Svevo probably read Freud as early as 1908 and went on to write *La* *coscienza di Zeno* (1923), Italy's first, and certainly best known, psychoanalytic *novel. The novel was criticized by Edoardo *Weiss, a student of Freud's and Italy's first psychoanalyst, who perhaps saw himself in the novel's Dr S. Weiss, however, was an

influential figure in spreading Freud's ideas. His patients included Sandro *Penna and also Umberto *Saba, whose poetry bears a strong Freudian imprint.

Despite official disapproval Freud's influence did spread. In 1946 *La* *Fiera letteraria* dedicated an entire issue to psychoanalysis. Alberto *Moravia argued that in the 20th c. it is impossible not to be influenced in some sense by Freud's theories, and proved the point thematically, if not in other ways, in his own work. His short novel *Agostino* (1943) deals with the oedipal crisis of an adolescent boy who is initiated simultaneously into the realities of sex and class politics. In *Il conformista* (1951) the political choices of the protagonist are worked out implicitly in terms of Freud's theory of repression. However, the language and narrative structure of Moravia's work remains untouched by Freudianism.

Moravia was typical of writers of his generation in looking to psychoanalysis for a means of deepening pre-existing concerns rather than as a way of opening up new dimensions of experience. *Pavese was particularly interested in Freud's theories of collective myth-making, while *Vittorini saw in psychoanalysis a means of deciphering the hidden messages of the body. The somewhat younger *Pasolini enthused about the ways in which psychoanalysis brought together politics and sexuality, again providing a framework for the articulation of views already held.

Jacques Lacan's rereading of Freud had some impact in the 1960s and 1970s, being drawn on by Umberto *Eco in *La struttura assente* and in some avant-garde creative writing by figures as different as Andrea *Zanzotto and Edoardo *Sanguineti. But since the late 1960s, it is the *feminist movement which has made a particularly significant contribution to psychoanalysis. Although contesting the masculine bias of many of Freud's premises, a number of women, notably Lea *Melandri in her 'pratica dell'inconscio', were able to adapt his theories as a means of thinking through questions of sexual difference. Elena Giannini Belotti's *Il fiore dell'ibisco* (1985) and Luisa Passerini's *Autoritratto di gruppo* (1988) bear witness to the role of psychoanalysis in feminist practice. Of great significance to this contestation and reappropriation of Freud has been the influence in Italy of the French feminist writer Luce Irigaray. In the USA, the Italian-born theorist Teresa De Lauretis has made a major contribution to the feminist reappraisal of Freud's work.   [DD]

Publishing

See M. David, *Letteratura e psicanalisi* (1967);
T. De Lauretis, *The Practice of Love* (1994).

Publishing. In the modern sense of the activity of issuing works for sale to the public after acquiring the legal title to their reproduction, publishing did not emerge in Italy as a business activity separate from typesetting and *printing until the 19th c., though it had started to become divided from book-selling already during the 16th c. As late as 1920 there were still many firms which combined printing and publishing on the same site, and several of the most prominent 20th-c. publishers (*Laterza, *Mondadori, *Rizzoli, *Vallecchi) started as printers. Some modern publishing firms have subsequently integrated printing, as well as bookselling and other media, like film and newspapers, into their overall activities, but they have done so as large-scale industrial enterprises, with a physical division between the different branches.

The history of publishing in Italy begins with the first printed books in the 1460s. The principal centres from the late 15th to the 18th c. were *Florence, *Naples, *Rome, *Milan, and, most important of all, *Venice. It was here that Aldo *Manuzio began printing and publishing his octavo editions of classical texts in 1501 and that the international publishing and bookselling firm Compagnia di Venezia was founded. Throughout the 16th c. there was effectively a single European market for printed books. This began to break up in the 17th c. with the declining importance of Latin and the growth of vernacular publishing. A division emerged between the Catholic south of Europe, including Italy, and the Protestant north. Venice, together with the Iberian peninsula, dominated the southern area and also distributed in the markets of the eastern Mediterranean: Turkey, the Levant, Greece and the Balkans, the Ukraine.

The situation changed again in the second half of the 18th c. with the growing importance of French and German publishing, the commercial and cultural rise of Britain, the contraction of the market for religious books (the religious orders were in decline; the *Jesuits were expelled from Portugal and Spain), and increased competition from other Italian centres of book production, including *Bologna, Parma, Lucca, and Livorno. The declining sales of religious texts were not offset in Italy, as they were in northern Europe, by sufficient increased sales of secular texts to keep the trade buoyant, and Italy thus began to lose its European role. Despite this, the dominance of Venice within

Italy was maintained until the fall of the Venetian Republic in 1797, thanks in large part to the Remondini firm, based in Bassano but with its publishing offices on the lagoon, which expanded in 1760–80 to become the largest firm of its kind in Europe. Remondini used hand presses but had a proto-industrial organization, employing over 1,000 people, supervising their work with strict timekeeping, and integrating the whole production cycle in one business, from paper-making to printing, engraving, and binding.

After the end of the *Napoleonic occupation (1814) Milan and, in second place, *Turin emerged as the new principal centres of Italian publishing. It was in Turin in 1830 that Giuseppe *Pomba (whose firm eventually became the Unione Tipografico-Editrice Torinese or UTET) pioneered the mechanization of printing in Italy when he bought a Cowper's Patent Machine capable of printing ten sheets (320 octavo pages) a minute. In Milan Sonzogno (founded 1818) and Fratelli Treves (1861) came to dominate, respectively, the popular and quality literature markets; Hoepli (1870) became a leading publisher of science, manuals, and encyclopedias. In the course of the century important firms were founded in other cities, including *Le Monnier (1836) and Sansoni (1873) in Florence and Zanichelli (1859) in Bologna. Rome, on the other hand, became marginal to the publishing world in this period, despite its elevation to capital city in 1870 and notwithstanding the brief success of Angelo *Sommaruga as publisher of periodicals and books there in the early 1880s.

In the 20th c. the dominant position of Milan was consolidated as new, more powerful firms emerged there, beginning with *Mondadori (a publisher from 1911), which, in the decade after *World War I, overtook Treves as market leader and bought the rights to several of Treves's most successful authors, including *D'Annunzio and *Verga. *Rizzoli (1909) at first concentrated on *periodicals, but later diversified into books (as well as newspapers) and built a strong list after *World War II. Smaller but prestigious firms developed elsewhere, notably *Laterza (1901) in Bari, *Bemporad (1906), *Vallecchi (1913) and La Nuova Italia (1926) in Florence, and *Einaudi (1933) in Turin. *Fascism exerted a number of controls on publishing: it curbed the activities of the firms linked to the *Socialist Party that had emerged between the 1890s and the 1920s, increased *censorship, and from 1938 imposed changes of management and name on firms owned by *Jewish families, including Treves (which became *Garzanti) and Bemporad (which was merged with Barbera to become *Marzocco). At the same time, a non-Jewish publisher like Mondadori managed to negotiate quite successfully with the Fascist state, publishing some of the regime's favoured authors while pursuing its own commercial goals. A national publishers' federation was set up in the 1920s to further the collective interests of the industry, for instance by control of paper prices and reduction of export tariffs; it later became, particularly under the presidency (1940–3) of Attilio Vallecchi, an instrument to bring publishers into line with the autarkic policy of promoting Italian authors and reducing *translations.

The period after 1945 saw increased expansion of the existing larger firms, the emergence of a major new player, *Feltrinelli (1955), and a proliferation of small firms, some linked to the parties of the left, like Editori Riuniti, publisher of the *Communist Party from 1953 to 1991 (after which it became autonomous), or (in the 1960s and 1970s) to the far Left. By the 1980s the market had become highly dualistic, with around 3,700 registered publishing firms but just five of them (Mondadori, Rizzoli, Einaudi, Garzanti, Feltrinelli) accounting for 30 per cent of total turnover. The 1990s were marked by a series of takeovers (Mondadori by Berlusconi), mergers (Rizzoli absorbed Sansoni; Garzanti annexed UTET), and diversification into publishing on CD-ROM. By the second half of the 1990s almost all the larger publishers and several of the smaller ones had developed an electronic publishing division.   [DF]

See M. Berengo, *Intellettuali e librai nella Milano della Restaurazione* (1980); A. Postigliola (ed.), *Libri editoria cultura nel Settecento italiano* (1988); G. Ferretti, *Il mercato delle lettere* (1994).

PUCCI, ANTONIO (*c.*1310–88). *Florentine public servant (he was the city's town crier) and prolific poet. He wrote many *sonnets, including some on moral themes, but he is best known for his narrative poems. These are swift-moving and linguistically vivacious, especially his *cantari on legendary subjects, such as *Brito di Bretagna* and *Gismirante*. He also produced shorter and metrically varied *sirventesi on contemporary themes.
[SNB]

PUCCI, FRANCESCO (1543–97) was an advocate of religious tolerance and political reform who took a degree at Oxford, and for a brief period converted to Protestantism. The Catholic Church

deplored his treatises opposing excessive dogma and asserting that, free from laws, mankind was naturally immortal, good, and innocent. Calvinists despised his views on predestination. Pucci was executed by the Roman *Inquisition for *heresy. [See COUNTER-REFORMATION; REFORMATION.]
[GPTW]

PUCCIANDONE MARTELLI, see SICULO-TUSCAN POETS.

PUCCINI, GIACOMO (1858–1924). The most distinguished and popular composer of Italian *opera after *Verdi. His first mature work, *Manon Lescaut* (1893), achieved a remarkable blend of Italian, Wagnerian, and French elements. Later operas reflect the innovations of Debussy and Stravinsky. His greatest triumphs were collaborations with the *librettists *Giacosa and Illica—*La Bohème* (1896), *Tosca* (1900), *Madama Butterfly* (1904)—in which elements of *verismo are less important than his genius for creating for each a distinctive sound world. Later operas enjoyed less success, though the musico-dramatic range in *Il trittico* (1918) marks one of his finest achievements. The unfinished *Turandot* was prepared for performance by Franco Alfano.   [DRBK]

PULCI, ANTONIA (1452–1501) was the wife of Bernardo *Pulci and sister-in-law of *Luigi Pulci and *Luca Pulci. The first woman author of *sacre rappresentazioni, with three plays securely attributed to her, in 1488 she became an Augustinian tertiary, founding a lay order of *nuns, the sisters of Santa Maria della Misericordia, in *Florence in 1500.   [JHB]

PULCI, BERNARDO (1438–88). Born in *Florence, the younger brother of Luca *Pulci and Luigi *Pulci and husband of Antonia *Pulci, Bernardo took over the business affairs of the family when Luca was imprisoned for debt. He is best known for his *sacra rappresentazione Barlaam e Josafat*. His other works include a *Petrarchan *canzoniere, a poem, *La passione di Cristo*, in *ottava rima*, and a *Vita della Gloriosa Vergine Maria* in *terza rima*. His *translations of *Virgil's *Eclogues* into *terza rima*, dedicated to Lorenzo de' *Medici, influenced the development of the vernacular *pastoral, in spite of their poor quality.   [JEE]

PULCI, LUCA (1431–70). Brother of Luigi *Pulci, and like him a contributor to the revival of

Pulci, Luigi

vernacular poetry in *Florence in the 1460s. His *Driadeo d'amore* is a mythological poem in a *Tuscan setting in *ottava rima*, a genre subsequently developed in Lorenzo de' *Medici's *Ambra*. His *Pistole* are a series of letters from classical and contemporary heroines modelled on *Ovid's *Heroides*, in *terza rima*. He probably also began the *Ciriffo Calvaneo*, a chivalric poem continued (but not completed) by Luigi after his death. [RMD]

PULCI, LUIGI (1432–84). Author of the *Morgante*, a long narrative poem ostensibly on *Carolingian themes but with numerous digressions, including many comic episodes involving the giant Morgante. Born into a noble but impoverished *Florentine family, Pulci's career was closely linked with the *patronage of the *Medici. Lucrezia *Tornabuoni, mother of Lorenzo de' *Medici, commissioned the *Morgante* as a tribute to Charlemagne in the context of the Florentine rapprochement with the French crown in 1461. But Lorenzo increasingly took her place; forty-seven of Pulci's letters to him survive, ranging in date from 1465 (when Lorenzo was just 16) to 1484, shortly before Pulci's death. Passages of the *Morgante* were known among Lorenzo's friends by the late 1460s, although there is no contemporary evidence for the tradition that Pulci read the poem aloud for their entertainment. Pulci's other contributions to the poetry of Lorenzo's circle up to the early 1470s included *La Beca*, a variation on the style of rustic poetry exemplified by Lorenzo (or one of his associates) in the *Nencia da Barberino*, but with a more pronounced *dialectal character; and *La giostra di Lorenzo de' Medici*, a description in *ottava rima* of the joust which had launched Lorenzo's public career in 1469, though the poem was still unfinished in 1474.

Lorenzo's relationship with Pulci changed after his accession to power on his father's death in 1469. In the early 1470s he sent Pulci on diplomatic errands to *Naples, *Rome and *Milan, but in the growing competition for the young ruler's attention Pulci was outshone by more sophisticated figures like *Ficino and *Poliziano (although he remained on friendly terms with the latter). The quarrels in which he was embroiled from the mid-1470s are recorded in his vituperative *sonnets against Ficino, whose abstruse speculations were an easy target for Pulci's robust humour, and in his protracted *tenzone* with Matteo *Franco, chaplain to Lorenzo's wife, Clarice. These sonnets, together with others mocking conventional religion, gave

Pulci a reputation for impiety which he never lost, despite later attempts to establish his orthodoxy. From 1473 onwards he was intermittently employed by the *condottiere* Roberto Sanseverino, with whom he travelled extensively in Northern Italy, often also acting as an intermediary between Sanseverino and Lorenzo. In 1481 a proposal for him to be made Captain of Val di Lugana under Sanseverino's patronage came to nothing, and he apparently remained in Florence until his last journey with Sanseverino, in late summer 1484. He died suddenly in *Padua, where according to local tradition he was buried in unconsecrated ground.

The *Morgante* was probably first printed, in twenty-three cantos, in 1478, although the earliest surviving edition dates from 1481. It is apparent from the first canto that the poem is not the celebration of Charlemagne which is promised in its opening lines, but a series of disconnected adventures involving *Orlando, *Rinaldo, and their companions in the Orient, in which energetic battles alternate with Gargantuan meals and love affairs with Saracen princesses. This can be partly explained by Pulci's use of an anonymous poem in sixty *cantari*, the *Orlando laurenziano*, which appears to be the source for much of his narrative (although the exact relationship between the two texts is debated). Pulci's gift is less for coherent narrative than for verbal embellishment prompted either by his source text or by a stock situation. It is a gift shown to most dazzling effect in the mock creed and confession of Margutte, a half-human, half-giant figure who is Morgante's companion in a succession of anarchic exploits until he dies from an uncontrollable fit of laughter.

From this point onwards Pulci's anxiety to return to his supposed theme is apparent, and in canto 23 he abruptly interrupts his narrative to announce the imminence of the fateful battle of Roncesvalle. The definitive version of the poem, printed in 1483, has five extra cantos in which Pulci finally fulfils his commission to retell the Roncesvalle story and, in the last canto, to pay tribute to the life of Charlemagne. But the new cantos also reflect Pulci's changed relationship with the mainstream of Florentine culture after 1478, with passages defending himself against hostile critics and demonstrating both his awareness of current theological debates and his embracing of orthodoxy. These include a riposte to an unnamed preacher who had attacked his irreligious writings, probably *Savonarola on his first visit to Florence in 1482; this episode is also reflected in Pulci's *Confessione*, an unexceptionable declaration of religious belief written in *terza rima* in 1483–4. In the last years of his life Pulci probably also worked inconclusively on the *Ciriffo Calvaneo*, a *chivalric poem left unfinished by his brother Luca *Pulci at his death in 1470.

The 1483 additions to the *Morgante* reflect Pulci's unresolved ambivalence about the status and nature of his poetry: was it to be confined to the comic style, or could it be a vehicle for more weighty historical and religious themes? It was this very ambivalence which was the most distinctive quality of the new genre of chivalric poetry which Pulci effectively created, and which was to have such a huge success in the poems of *Boiardo and *Ariosto, in which Pulci's influence is clearly visible. His acceptance into the *Tuscan literary canon is confirmed by his citation in the 1611 dictionary of the Accademia della *Crusca. His most influential admirer outside Italy was Byron, who called him 'sire of the half-serious rhyme', *translating the first canto of the *Morgante* and adopting it as the model for his own style in *Don Juan*. [RMD]

Morgante e Opere minori, ed. A. Greco (1997). See P. Orvieto, *Pulci medievale* (1978); M. Davie, *Half-serious Rhymes: The Narrative Poetry of Luigi Pulci* (1998).

Pulcinella. This Southern Italian variant of the *zanni* mask of the *commedia dell'arte* probably emerged at the end of the 16th c. in *Naples, but may have taken on distinctive stage form only early in the 17th c. in the performances of Silvio Fiorillo, who transferred to it from the *Capitano role. It remained characteristic of performance in the Naples region and, clad in distinctive dress of white, loose-fitting tunic and black mask with a beak-shaped nose, it has come to be seen as an icon of the Neapolitan stage. In the 18th c. it was translated, if at some remove, to the Punch of the English popular booth theatre. [KR]

PUOTI, BASILIO (1782–1847). *Neapolitan *educator. In 1825 he established a school of Italian which was inspired by *neoclassical ideals of linguistic *purism. He published numerous works in favour of this approach. *De Sanctis, in his account of the school, includes a memorable description of a visit by *Leopardi. [See also GRAMMARS.] [MPC]

Purgatorio. The second of the three *cantiche* of *Dante's *Divine Comedy. Dante and his guide,

*Virgil, have emerged from the darkness of Hell at the foot of Mount Purgatory, the mountain on which the souls of those who have repented before death purge themselves of the stains of sin. Dante envisages the mountain as having been created at the fall of Lucifer and now reaching up into the Southern sky directly opposite Jerusalem. Dante and Virgil encounter its guardian, Cato, and some new arrivals, and then begin an ascent during which they meet a succession of penitent souls much as they had met sinful souls in *Inferno. Only here the atmosphere is quite different: the souls are submitting willingly to the torments of purgation, since sooner or later they will become free to ascend to *Paradise.

On the lower slopes (commonly called *Antepurgatorio*) there are souls of excommunicates and those who delayed repentance until the last moment, now waiting until the time comes for them to begin their purgation proper. The main part is divided into seven terraces (*cornici*), corresponding to the seven deadly sins—Pride, Envy, Anger, Accidy (spiritual weakness or sloth), Miserliness (coupled with Prodigality), Greed, and Lust. The higher the terrace, the less onerous the sin and the less difficult Dante finds the climb. For the later part of the climb he and Virgil are accompanied by the Roman poet *Statius, whose release from purgation they witness. At the top they enter the Earthly Paradise. Here they see a remarkable symbolic pageant, representing the whole of biblical and Christian history, with, at its centre, the figure of *Beatrice, who now replaces Virgil as Dante's guide. She subjects Dante to a sharp examination and ritual purification before completing the action of the pageant. Dante is now ready to ascend to Paradise. [PH]

Purism aims to exclude undesirable elements (especially lexical ones) from a language in order to maintain a purity which may be identified with a past golden age, and it generally arises in response to change within a language and/or language contact. Purism in Italy until the 19th c. stemmed from the doctrine, developed in the 16th c. mainly by Pietro *Bembo and *Salviati and supported by *dictionaries and *grammars, that literary usage should *imitate 14th-c. *Florentine. This view was contested by the *Enlightenment, and the terms *purismo* and *purista* (first recorded 1758–9 but not used in print until 1838) were introduced to denote linguistic affectation or archaism. The 19th-c. purism of Antonio *Cesari and others was based both on veneration for the 14th c. and on distaste for neologisms and foreign borrowings, especially from French. Purism in the 20th c. resisted unassimilated borrowings from French and later from English and was at its height during the second half of the *Fascist period. The *neopurismo* promoted by Bruno *Migliorini from the late 1930s sought a compromise between the needs of Italian to evolve and to maintain its structures. [See also QUESTIONE DELLA LINGUA.] [BR]

PUSEK, DUBRAVKO, see ITALIAN WRITERS IN SWITZERLAND.

PUSTERLA, FABIO, see ITALIAN WRITERS IN SWITZERLAND.

Q

Quaderni del carcere, see GRAMSCI, ANTONIO.

Quaderni piacentini (1961–84). *Periodical founded by Piergiorgio Bellocchio with an extra-parliamentary Left agenda. It not only carried articles devoted to political and union matters, but also took a leading role in stimulating new thinking in the 1960s and 1970s on issues such as immigration, the family, and the treatment of psychiatric patients. [MPC]

QUADRIO, FRANCESCO SAVERIO (1695–1756). Literary scholar born in the Valtellina, who eventually settled in *Milan. His *Della poesia italiana* (1734), expanded into *Della storia e della ragione d'ogni poesia* (1739–52), is considered the earliest attempt to produce a universal literary *encyclopedia. In 1733 he published and attributed to *Dante the apocryphal *Rime spirituali.*
[JMAL]

Quadrivio (1933–43). Roman literary weekly founded and edited by Telesio *Interlandi. Its aim was to promote and celebrate *Fascist literature and culture, with an emphasis on what it saw as the 'healthy' aspects of the modern. It published articles and poems at one time or another by a vast range of contributors, including *Cardarelli, *Comisso, *Falqui, *Govoni, *Montale, and *Ungaretti; but it narrowed its appeal to both contributors and readers as Interlandi encouraged more and more articles favouring Hitler and the anti-*Jewish policies of the Fascist regime. In 1938 Interlandi founded the explicitly racist *La difesa della razza* as a sister paper. [PH]

Quadrivium, see LIBERAL ARTS.

Quaestio de aqua et terra (1320) presents *Dante's discussion of an important problem in medieval cosmology, namely the physical causes which, seemingly against the laws of nature, allow the earth, as the heavier element, to rise above water. The Latin treatise reveals an excellent understanding of *Aristotelian science and is a model of contemporary syllogistic analysis. It examines and rejects the relative merits of different possible solutions to the problem, before demonstrating that the earth is pulled upwards by the influence of the Heaven of the Fixed Stars. Dante's proposal and arguments are not original, and most scholars agree that the work was written not so much as a dispassionate contribution to a scientific debate, but as a way of dealing with criticisms voiced by philosophers regarding the *Divine Comedy*'s poetic treatment of doctrinal matters. Nevertheless, Dantists are divided as to whether the poet, in the treatise, was establishing his poem's empathy with Aristotelianism or repudiating this as a system of thought inimical to his visionary poetry. [See also SCHOLASTICISM.] [ZB]
Ed. F. Mazzoni (1979).

QUARANTOTTI GAMBINI, PIER ANTO-NIO (1910–65). *Novelist and *journalist born in Pisino d'Istria (now Pazin, Croatia) and an advocate of the Italian identity of his homeland, which was assigned to Yugoslavia after *World War II. Closely associated with *Trieste (though he took a law degree in *Turin), he became a friend of Umberto *Saba in 1929, and partly as a result published his first significant stories in *Solaria. These were later collected in *I nostri simili* (1939).
The favourite themes of his quite large body of work are nostalgic contemplation of the Istrian landscape and rites of passage from childhood to adulthood against the backdrop of the war. Some of his best writing is to be found in the autobiographical novels *Le trincee* (1939), *Il cavallo Tripoli* (1956), and *Amor militare* (1955), posthumously published together (with some changes of title) as *Gli anni ciechi* (1971). His *Primavera a Trieste*

Quasimodo, Salvatore

(1955) is an impressive account of the four-week Yugoslav occupation of the city in 1945. Quarantotti Gambini had directed the city library during the war and taken part in the *Resistance. In the face of accusations of compromising himself with the *Fascist regime, he left Trieste in 1945 and spent the rest of his life in *Venice. [KP]

QUASIMODO, SALVATORE (1901–68). With *Montale, one of the most important of the second generation of 20th-c. poets. Born in Modica near Ragusa in *Sicily, the son of a Sicilian station-master, he went to school in Palermo and Messina, and studied engineering in *Rome without taking his degree. From 1926 to 1938 he held posts with the ministry of public works in a variety of cities. He entered literary circles in *Florence in 1929, initially through *Vittorini, who married his sister; here he came into contact with Montale and the early *hermetic poets. He also had contacts in *Genoa from 1931 with Adriano *Grande and other Ligurian writers connected with the review `Circoli`. From 1938 onwards he lived in *Milan, closely linked to a group of painters and musicians distinguished by their involvement in civic affairs. On the strength of his literary reputation he was appointed professor of Italian literature at the Conservatorio Verdi in 1941, a post he held until his retirement in 1968.

From the beginning his poetry was strongly tied to his native island, a lost, 'incomparable' land, evoking distant myths of classical Greece. His first collections, *Acque e terre* (1930), *Òboe sommerso* (edited by Montale in 1932), *Erato e Apòllion* (edited by Sergio *Solmi in 1936), and *Poesie* (1938), which were all collected and in part re-written in *Ed è subito sera* (1942), enthused hermetic critics such as Macrì, who found in it the 'poetica della parola', and the absoluteness and purity that they were looking for in poetry. It has a refined and rarefied classical style, indebted to French *symbolism, the best of *D'Annunzio, and *Ungaretti; it is populated by angelic female figures reminiscent of the *dolce stil novo*; its recurrent images of water, air, and wind evoke an enchanted, innocent, lost landscape, in which the Narcissus figure of the poet loses himself in uncontaminated Nature. All this did not prevent a wider public—and Quasimodo became a suprisingly popular poet—from appreciating the melancholy underlying this dream of purity and perfection, the sense of religion and existential abandonment encapsulated in the famous three-line poem: 'Ognuno sta solo sul

cuor della terra / trafitto da un raggio di sole: / ed è subito sera'.

*World War II and its immediate aftermath seemed to inject a new concern with contemporary reality into a poetry that hitherto had been preoccupied with formal issues. Milan becomes an emblem of the *Resistance, and, with the example particularly of Lorca and other major modern European poets in view, intellectual and civic *impegno* become paramount themes. *Con il piede straniero sopra il cuore* (1946), *Giorno dopo giorno* (1947), *La vita non è sogno* (1949), *Il falso e vero verde* (1956), *La terra impareggiabile* (1958), and *Dare e avere* (1966) win public approval and recognition, culminating in the Nobel prize in 1959, but are given a mixed reception by *literary critics, themselves currently at odds with each other over the value and significance of the hermetic movement. These either privileged the elegiac and idyllic mode of the earlier poetry against what they dismissed as the naïve or partisan rhetoric of the later, or contrasted the force of *Neorealist commitment with the mournful chants of the seeker for mythic rebirth. Recent assessments have been more balanced, and stressed the significant elements of continuity, seeing a resistance to the negative aspects of modern experience in the verbal texture of the earlier work, and in the later poetry a tenacious concern with the Italian poetic tradition as exemplified by *Foscolo and *Leopardi, and a continued interest in inward, lyrical writing. The fact remains, however, that in spite of his undoubted influence on younger poets such as *Luzi and *Gatto, Quasimodo is perhaps even today more quoted than read.

In the postwar years Quasimodo's important essays and discourses on poetry, gathered principally in *Il poeta e il politico e altri saggi* (1960), develop alongside his actual poetic work as its necessary complement. As well as recognizing the dramatic impact of the catastrophic historical events of the first half of the century, and the emergence of an increasingly technological society, he articulates the need to renew the ethical impulse that seemed to have faded from Italian poetry after Leopardi, reconnecting literature and life through a return to the epic forms of Homer and ancient Greece. There is a similar civic or political motivation underlying his activities as a literary translator, which he had first embarked on as a young man. Apart from his important *translations of *Shakespeare, Ruskin, Greek tragedy, and Homer, his *Lirici greci* (1940), *Fiore delle Georgiche* (1942), and *Canti di Catullo* (1955) have the qualities and status

of original poetic works—no doubt in part because Quasimodo's own style, with its prevalence of substantival forms, subject–verb inversions, and absolute constructions, displays formal features directly indebted to Homer and *Virgil.   [AD]
Poesie e discorsi sulla poesia, ed. G. Finzi (1983). See G. Zagarrio, *Quasimodo* (1969); O. Macrì, *La poesia di Quasimodo* (1986).

QUATRARIO, GIOVANNI (1336–1402). *Humanist and friend of *Salutati. Born in Sulmona, he lived in *Rome from 1368, where he served as a secretary at the *papal curia. He wrote Latin eclogues, verse letters, and elegies, including one on the death of *Petrarch.   [PH]

Querelle des anciens et des modernes. The name for the debate that took place in France from the mid-17th c. onwards is a convenient designation for similar, earlier developments in Italy, beginning in the first decades of the 17th c., but traceable back to *Renaissance writers such as *Castiglione and *Aretino. Paolo *Beni in his linguistic writings and his work on Torquato *Tasso (1612–16), Alessandro *Tassoni in book 10 of his *Pensieri* (1620), and Secondo *Lancellotti (1623 and 1636), all share a belief that late 16th- and early 17th-c. culture, including poetry, art, science, and history, had by their day reached greater perfection than that of classical times. It is in the works of these authors that the idea of progress is born, the notion that all human institutions and creative activities improve with time.

Such a view replaces the quasi-pagan idea of *fortuna*, that of cyclic historical patterns (as in *Machiavelli, for instance), and the belief in a prelapsarian Golden Age. The modernism of Beni, Tassoni, Lancellotti, and many others is the result of considerable knowledge of the ancient world, and is proposed, despite the often jocular titles of their works, in all seriousness. One has only to think of *Galileo's case, or *Di Capua's, to see that the problems of reconciling ancient authority with modern experience could be a matter of life and death. What all these writers had in common was that they believed they had reached the dead end of the *humanist discovery and imitation of the ancients that had satisfied the 15th and most of the 16th c. By the early 17th c. the authority of ancient examples seemed irrelevant and unreasonable. The modern world had literally outgrown the ancient models: space, new continents, new poetic and linguistic possibilities had finally forced at least some

thinkers to begin to revise their views on the usefulness of learning. In this way, paradoxically, humanism burned itself out, and from the ashes the modern world, with all its uncertainties and relativities, was born.   [PBD]
See G. Margiotta, *Le origini italiane de 'La Querelle des anciens et des modernes'* (1953).

Quer pasticciaccio brutto de via Merulana. Novel by Carlo Emilio *Gadda, first published in *Letteratura* in 1946, and reissued in book form, with important changes and additions, in 1957. It is ostensibly a *detective story, though the investigation by Francesco Ingravallo, a police inspector in *Fascist *Rome, into the murder of a wealthy married woman reaches no satisfactory solution. The novel is also a philosophical meditation on the causes of evil, a gallery of masterly characters, a portrayal of a society, and a linguistic and stylistic tour de force. It brought Gadda to the attention of the general public as a novelist.   [GS]

Questione della lingua. The name given to the centuries-long debate about the nature of the linguistic practice to be adopted in the written language. Literary Italian developed in various forms in the 13th and 14th c. Unlike English and French, its development did not follow that of a national spoken language, since this emerged only after the *Unification of Italy in 1860. Thus writers mostly had to acquire a knowledge of the written language by literary *imitation, instead of drawing on their native speech. It was the lack of a national spoken language on which to base the language of literature that gave rise to the protracted and controversial debate about what the standard literary language should be.

The first person to turn his attention to the matter was *Dante, who in his *De vulgari eloquentia* (*c.*1303–*c.*1305) put forward the view that language of literature should be based on no single *dialect, but should draw on the best elements of all, in order to achieve the universal quality to which he aspired as a stylistic ideal (though in practice he himself wrote in an enriched form of his own *Florentine variety of Tuscan). The critical period of the debate came in the 16th c., when writers' minds were focused on the urgent need to agree on a standard by the impact of *printing. We can distinguish four main positions in the debate, though the various participants cannot always be fitted neatly into one or other of them: (1) favouring archaic Tuscan, to be learnt by literary imitation (e.g. Pietro

Quietism

*Bembo); (2) writing in a language drawn from contemporary Tuscan (e.g. Claudio *Tolomei); (3) employing an archaic common language, based on literary imitation, but not solely of Tuscan (e.g. Girolamo *Muzio); (4) adopting a contemporary common language (the *lingua cortigiana), based on the usage of the main *courts of Italy (e.g. *Trissino). The decisive influence was that of Bembo, who argued in his *Prose della volgar lingua (1525) that writers of Italian should model themselves on *Petrarch in verse and *Boccaccio in prose, just as the *humanists wrote their Latin by imitating *Virgil and *Cicero. Florentine Tuscan, learnt by imitation of the great writers of the past, was almost universally adhered to thereafter as the basis of literary Italian. Bembo's ideas were of crucial importance, because they provided Italians with a practical means of acquiring a common literary language in a divided nation with no national spoken tongue to draw on. [See also DICTIONARIES; GRAMMARS; PURISM; VOLGARE AND VOLGARE ILLUSTRE.]

Subsequently the debate ceased to be concerned with the problem of which dialect to choose as the basis of the written language, but concentrated instead on what kind of Florentine should be used and how far it should be allowed to develop from its base: whether it should remain an archaic language with a narrow literary vocabulary, learnt by imitation; or display a less rigid adherence to its base, as *Cesarotti urged in the 18th c., and enrich the traditional vocabulary by borrowing from other European languages such as French, as argued by Pietro *Verri and other contributors to the *Enlightenment journal *Il Caffè; or whether one should adopt a more modern standard based on the contemporary speech of educated Florentines, as *Manzoni believed. Those who proposed such alternatives to Bembo's solution were in the minority, however; the majority continued to learn their Italian by imitating the great writers of the past, and from 1612 the Florentine model was also supported by the authority of the purist *Vocabolario della Crusca. As a consequence, written Italian remained a very bookish language, far removed from the realities of speech. Manzoni reacted against its archaic, artificial nature, and sought to rejuvenate it by making the language of his novel I *promessi sposi conform in its second edition, as far as he was able (for he was *Milanese), to the educated Florentine spoken in his day. But while this solution was more satisfactory to him personally as a writer, there is no doubt that Bembo's was more practical, since all

those who had access to *education could learn Italian from books, while not everyone had the opportunity or the inclination to go to *Florence for long periods to learn from the speech of its inhabitants.

There is another and more important reason why Manzoni's solution was not acceptable on a national basis. Italian has always been more than a written form of Florentine dialect. Though national languages generally originate in the speech of a particular area, they are also the product of education and culture, and outgrow their local origins, absorbing features from elsewhere, to become the property of the whole nation. When, in the years immediately following Unification, Manzoni and his followers tried to make Italian conform to certain local peculiarities of contemporary Florentine usage not found in the literary language, their efforts were unsuccessful, and the futility of the exercise was exposed by the great 19th-c. linguist *Ascoli in his preface to the first volume of the Archivio glottologico italiano (1873). Ascoli understood that the problem could no longer be solved artificially by imposing a model, if Italian was to become the spoken and written possession of the whole nation, instead of the preserve of an educated elite. He knew that it was not possible to get ordinary people to adopt an educated standard, Florentine or otherwise, unless the level of their culture was raised so that they could absorb it. The solution lay therefore not in trying to persuade people to accept Florentine or any other model, but in raising the nation's general level of education and allowing the process of natural selection to take its course. This is substantially what has happened, and as a result the language has actually become less rather than more Florentine since Unification, because of the influence of *Rome in government administration and the media, and of Northern Italy in the economic life of the nation. [RABGH]

See R. A. Hall, The Italian 'Questione della lingua' (1942); M. Vitale, La questione della lingua (1960); B. Migliorini and T. G. Griffith, The Italian Language (1984).

Quietism refers to a 17th-c. religious trend towards inner contemplation and mysticism. Instead of searching for God through prayer, it emphasizes the passive and complete surrender of the self in the act of quiet inner contemplation. This doctrine comes close to denying the value of the sacraments and of good works, and seems to allow the soul spiritual self-sufficiency. The Catholic

Church condemned it in 1687, maintaining the value of active prayer and petition to God. [PBD]

QUILICHINO DA SPOLETO, see ALEXAN-DER ROMANCES.

Quindici (1967–9). Review published in *Rome, initially monthly, and edited first by Alfredo *Giuliani and then from 1968 by Nanni *Balestrini. It developed from the *Gruppo 63, from whom it drew both its editors and contributors such as Umberto *Eco and Edoardo *Sanguineti. It foundered on the challenge of whether to align itself as an organ of avant-garde culture with the student and factory movements of 1968–9, or to stay with a more narrowly cultural mission. In the event it opened its pages to the protesters, but was overtaken by the speed with which events unfolded on the streets. [MPC]

QUIRINI, GIOVANNI (early 14th c.). Member of a powerful *Venetian dynasty, who is among the earliest recorded *lyric poets to have written vernacular love poetry in Venice. More than 120 lyric poems survive. They are strongly influenced by the styles and techniques of *Dante, whom he may have known personally. He is cited respectfully in Giovanni Girolamo *Nadal's *Leandreide*. [SNB]

QUIRINI, LEONARDO (17th c.). *Venetian nobleman and amateur poet. He wrote *madrigals on amorous themes, which tread a cautious path between Torquato *Tasso and *Marino. He was also a friend of Gian Francesco *Loredan and a member of the Accademia degli *Incogniti.
[MPS]

QUIRINI, PIERO (1479–1514), from the noble *Venetian family, studied philosophy and theology in *Padua and held high offices in the Venetian Republic, which sent him as ambassador to France (1504) and Castile (1506). In 1512 he entered the order of the Camaldulenses and became an ardent supporter of reform and innovation within the Church, proposing the use of Italian vernacular for Scripture and liturgy. He died in *Rome. [LPer]

R

RABONI, GIOVANNI (1932–). *Milanese poet and critic, who once practised as a lawyer. Particularly influenced by *Parini and Baudelaire, Raboni's introspective urban poetry, with its regrets for lost Milanese traditions and culture, is also a commentary on general social and political disorientation in the second half of the 20th c. His earlier poems had an epigrammatic incisiveness. Much of his work from *Versi guerrieri e amorosi* (1990) onwards is more personal but in strict *sonnet form. He has been theatre and *literary critic for the *Corriere della sera* and has *translated Proust and other modern French authors. [CO'B]

Raccolta aragonese is the name of a collection of early and contemporary Tuscan poems, assembled by Lorenzo de' *Medici in 1476–7 to send to Federico of *Aragon, the younger son of the King of *Naples. The first Italian *anthology of its kind, the collection was accompanied by a letter now generally agreed to have been written by *Poliziano, which constitutes, after *Dante's *De vulgari eloquentia*, the first critical reflection on Italian poetry. The project was part of Lorenzo's cultural diplomacy, which sought to gain prestige for *Tuscany through the promotion of its language and literature. [JAL]

Racconti romani (1954) is a collection of short stories by *Moravia, previously published in the newspaper *Il *Corriere della sera*, depicting working-class and lower middle-class life in *Rome. *Nuovi racconti romani* (1957) brought the entire collection to a total of about 150 stories. Each story recounts an anecdotal event exposing the protagonist's daily struggles with questions of money or love. [See also NOVELLA AND RACCONTO.] [GUB]

Racconto, see NOVELLA AND RACCONTO.

Radio. The viability of radio as a technology for the long-distance communication of sounds was first demonstrated in 1901 by Guglielmo Marconi's experimental 'wireless telegraph' transmission of Morse Code across the Atlantic. It became a medium for broadcasting in many countries after *World War I. A regular service began in Italy in 1924; the early schedules consisted mainly of music, with a small proportion of spoken programmes. Given the high cost of the receivers and the licence fee, the initial family audience was mainly middle-class, though amateurs could build crystal receivers cheaply, and some cafés and restaurants with a working-class clientele installed sets, which became particularly popular for sports broadcasts.

*Marinetti was probably the first Italian writer to seize on radio as a revolutionary medium for literature, first as a metaphor (in 1912 he coined the phrase 'immaginazione senza fili' ('wireless imagination') to designate a new kind of rapid poetic communication freed from syntax and literary convention), then with his experimental radio broadcasts from the late 1920s. In 1933 he co-authored a manifesto of radio. Not all writers shared his *Futurist vision of the creative and literary possibilities offered by radio (and film), and many dramatists and actors initially snubbed the new medium on the grounds of its acoustic inadequacies and the audience's allegedly fluctuating attention. Nevertheless, schedules began to include literary works either adapted or specially written for radio: the first purpose-written Italian radio play was Luigi *Chiarelli's *L'anello di Teodosio*, broadcast in 1929. *Pirandello's *Il piacere dell'onestà* was broadcast in 1934, despite his reservations about plays on radio.

By the early 1930s the *Fascist regime had come to recognize the potential of radio as a means of mass communication, and consequently exerted more direct control over schedules and programme content, subsidized sets for use in schools and other public places, and attempted to increase the penetration of radio in rural areas. This policy partly backfired during *World War II, when the cheaper sets were bought and used to listen clandestinely to the anti-*Fascist broadcasts of the BBC and The Voice of America, as documented in the work of *Fenoglio and others. In 1944 the former EIAR (Ente Italiano Audizioni Radiofoniche) was renamed RAI (Radio Audizioni Italia), and in 1951 the network was divided into three separate services or 'programmes'. Literary broadcasts, including discussions by critics, were devolved to the cultural Terzo Programma, which at first had a limited geographical coverage. Despite this, radio audiences grew to an all-time peak in the decade 1945–55 and brought drama, poetry, and discussions of literature to an unprecedently large number of people. Among the writers involved in arts programmes was *Gadda, who joined the RAI in 1950 and commissioned and wrote many talks and interviews. Some postwar radio plays used the medium innovatively to comment on itself: an example was *La domenica della buona gente*, *Pratolini's play about football pool mania, broadcast on the Terzo Programma on 12 March 1952, in which characters listen obsessively to sports programmes and results. When *television began a regular service in 1954, it gradually depleted the audience for radio and took over or competed with some of its genres, including drama. Television, however, was always pitched at a mass audience, and even after the introduction of a second, more cultural television channel in 1961, radio remained the more important medium for literary broadcasting.   [DF]

See G. Isola, *L'ha scritto la radio: storia e testi della radio durante il fascismo (1922–1944)* (1998); F. Malatini, *Cinquant'anni di teatro radiofonico in Italia, 1929–1979* (1981).

Ragazzi di vita (1955). *Pasolini's first published novel is a series of gritty stories set amongst the underclasses of *Rome's 'borgate' (or shanty towns) after *World War II. The main character, 'er Riccetto, and his companions steal, gamble, fight, pay and get paid for sex. Large parts of the book's dialogue are in Roman *dialect.
[RSCG]

Ragguagli di Parnaso, see BOCCALINI, TRAIANO.

Ragionamenti, see PERIODICALS, I.

Ragionamento, see ARETINO, PIETRO; SEI GIORNATE.

Ragion di stato refers to the debate between the rival claims of politics and Christian morality in the *political theory of the late 16th and 17th c. While, in the *Principe*, *Machiavelli had decided the question by placing political considerations above and beyond moral ones, political writers after the Council of Trent and the *Counter-Reformation felt constrained to observe the laws of morality in their published work; during this period, in fact, Machiavelli's works were prohibited. The work of a writer like Paolo *Paruta (1579) shows to what extent the debate between Christian morality and political necessity depended upon a judicious and complex weighing of both elements, often in what appears to be impractical compromise, as is most clearly exemplified in 1589 in the work of Giovanni *Botero. The works of *Boccalini in the early years of the 17th c. unmask the hypocrisy and deceit which underlay Botero's concept of *ragion di stato*: against the expedient immorality of monarchical *ragion di stato*, Boccalini places the ideal of a free and tolerant republic intent on the pursuit of moral virtue, knowledge, and wisdom. A clever and influential solution came from Ludovico *Zuccolo, who argued in 1621 that, if the political solution is morally good one, whether the outcome be monarchy or republic, oligarchy, or tyranny, it is necessarily sanctioned by Christian morality. In this way, Zuccolo achieves Machiavelli's solution of having the end justify the means, but with the crucial difference that the end must be a morally acceptable one. Lodovico *Settala (1627) depended heavily on Zuccolo, as did later writers on the subject.   [PBD]

RAIMBAUT DE VAQUEIRAS (1155/60–c.1205). *Troubadour born in Vaqueiras in the Rhone valley, who spent much of his career in the service of Italian rulers. Though briefly in *Genoa with Obizzino Malaspina, he served principally with Bonifacio I of Monferrato, whom he followed to *Sicily (1194) and on the fourth *Crusade (1201). His poems (twenty-seven are certain) include love songs, *satirical and *allegorical poems, an epic verse letter in three parts addressed to Bonifacio on their various exploits together, and a remarkable dancesong, 'Kalenda maia'. A taste for linguistic experiment is shown particularly in a humorous dialogue poem (*contrasto*) from about 1190, in which a woman speaking Genoese resists the blandishments of a *giullare* speaking Provençal, and in a multilingual *discordo*, which deploys Provençal, Genoese, French, Gascon, and Portuguese in successive stanzas.   [LM]

Raimondo Da Capua

RAIMONDO DA CAPUA (*c.*1330–99). *Dominican friar, who was confessor to St *Caterina of Siena from 1374 to 1378 and accompanied her to *Avignon in 1376. He wrote an account of her life, the *Legenda maior*, between 1374 and 1378. He became head of the order in 1380, and was beatified in 1899. [JP & JMS]

RAJBERTI, GIOVANNI (1805–61). *Milanese poet and doctor of liberal political views, who worked in Milan, Monza, and Como. He published gently ironic poems in *dialect, and comic prose in Italian, such as *Cenni fisologici-morali* (1845) and *Sul gatto* (1846). He translated some of *Horace's satires into Milanese, as well as producing a version of the *Arte poetica* (1836). [EAM]

RAJNA, PIO (1847–1930). *Positivist literary critic, who produced important editions and studies of *medieval and *Renaissance texts, most famously studies of the sources of *Pulci's *Morgante* and *Ariosto's *Orlando furioso*. [See LITERARY CRITICISM; LITERARY THEORY, 5; TEXTUAL CRITICISM.]

RAMBERTINO BUVALELLI (d.1221). *Bolognese who was *podestà* in various Northern Italian cities, and the first known Italian *troubadour in Provençal. He was an exponent of the more accessible *trobar leu*, apparently learnt from reading rather than direct contact with Provence. He influenced Lanfranco *Cigala and Percivalle *Doria. [JU]

RAME, FRANCA (1929–). Actress raised in a family of travelling players where she learnt the actor's craft, and who married Dario *Fo in 1954. She has since been a partner in his *theatrical and political enterprises, and from the mid-1970s has developed her own monologues based on *feminist issues. [JAL]

RAMONDINO, FABRIZIA (1936–). *Neapolitan novelist, who lived in Spain, France, and Germany before returning to Naples in 1960. Her first book, *Napoli: i disoccupati organizzati* (1977), developed out of her work as a political activist committed to social issues. Her first and best-known novel, *Althénopis* (1981), takes its title comes from the name (meaning 'old woman's eye') that the German occupiers gave to war-torn Naples. The novel centres on the relationship between a mother and her daughter, to which Ramondino gives an intense, bitter-sweet texture through incorporating memories of the people, food, smells, and other personal experiences of those years. She published a collection of stories, *Storie di patio* (1983), which addresses themes of *exile, marginalization, and childhood, and a second novel, *Un giorno e mezzo*, in 1988. Her interest in *travel led to *Taccuino tedesco* (1987), the diary of a journey through Germany, and *In viaggio* (1995), a collection of thirteen tales positing travel or the journey as a necessary condition of human existence. [AHC]

RAMUSIO, GIOVANNI BATTISTA (1485–1557). Geographer, *historian, and man of letters. Taught by *Pomponazzi in *Padua, he had a deep knowledge of classical and oriental languages, carried out many delicate political missions, and became a secretary of the *Venetian senate in 1515. He is known mainly for his three-volume *Le navigationi et viaggi* (1550, 1556, 1559), which collects the most famous accounts of *travels from antiquity to his own time. [CG]

RANDAZZO, NINO, see ITALIAN WRITERS IN AUSTRALIA.

RANIERI, ANTONIO (1806–88). Neapolitan writer best known for his friendship with *Leopardi, whom he met in *Pisa whilst exiled from *Naples for his *liberal ideas. He was Leopardi's host in Naples and cared for him from 1833 until his death in 1837. He wrote an acount of their friendship in *Sette anni di sodalizio con Giacomo Leopardi* (1880). His other work includes the novel, *Nunziata* (1839), *Frate Rocco* (1842: a collection of stories denouncing conditions in the foundlings' hospital in Naples which earnt him a short spell in prison), an edition of Leopardi (1843–5), and writings on history and the Southern question [see MEZZOGIORNO]. He became a parliamentary deputy in 1860 and a senator in 1882. [DO'G]

RANIERI DA PERUGIA (early 13th c.). Notary teaching at *Bologna between 1219 and 1245, who wrote an influential *Ars notaria*, as well as works on contract *law. [JP & JMS]

RAPHAEL (Raffaello Sanzio) (1483–1520), from *Urbino, became one of the most influential and celebrated painters of his time (and of the whole *Renaissance), working principally in *Rome for Popes Julius II (1503–13) and Leo X (1513–21). His literary friends, many of whose portraits he painted, included Baldassarre *Castiglione, Pietro *Bembo, Andrea *Navagero, and Agostino Beazzano. [CR]

RAPISARDI, MARIO (1844–1912). Poet and critic, famous for his anticlerical and anti-*monarchist writing. His poem *Lucifero* (1877), significant as an expression of *positivist thought in Italian poetry, led to a public disagreement with *Carducci and earned him the chair of Italian at Catania University. *Giustizia* (1883), banned under *Fascism, was highly polemical in its irreverent secularism and republicanism. Its themes were developed in his most important work, *Giobbe* (1884), and in *Poesie religiose* (1887), *Poemetti* (1892), and *Epigrammi* (1897). *L'Atlantide* (1894), inspired by *Leopardi's *Paralipomeni*, is an attack on corruption in contemporary Italian society. Rejected during Fascism, his work has been revived by scholars such as Concetto Marchesi and Alberto *Asor Rosa. [RS]

RASY, ELISABETTA (1947–). Novelist, critic and *journalist. Her earlier *feminist writings include the important *La lingua della nutrice* (1978). Her novels, the first of which was *La prima estasi* (1985), range from the apparently autobiographical *Posillipo* (1995) to *L'ombra della luna* (1999), which re-creates the experiences of Mary Wollstonecraft in revolutionary France. [PH]

Rationes dictandi, see ARS DICTAMINIS.

RAUDENSE, ANTONIO, see ANTONIO DA RHO.

RAVAGNANI, BENINTENDI DE' (c.1318–60). Notary and Chancellor of the *Venetian Republic and a personal friend of *Petrarch. In 1362 he endeavoured to obtain a residence in Venice for him in return for the bequest of his *library. He also helped Andrea *Dandolo to draft his two *chronicles of the city. [MP]

RAVERA, LIDIA (1951–). *Turinese novelist. She and Marco Lombardo Radice created a sensation with *Porci con le ali* (1976), a *satire of youthful sexual fantasies set against student protest [see 1968] and terrorism, which they published in the guise of two 15-year-olds, Rocco and Antonia. Subsequent fiction explores the myths and legacy of the 1960s generation. [SW]

REA, DOMENICO (1921–94). Neapolitan novelist, whose typical subjects are the poor of *Naples and the South [see MEZZOGIORNO]. The seven short stories of *Spaccanapoli* (1947), with their mixing of *dialect and Italian, established him as a *Neorealist. Then came tales such as those collected in *Ritratto di maggio* (1953)—which deals with the social destinies of the subjects of a 1929 junior school photo—and in *Quel che vide Cummeo* (1955). He underwent a creative crisis after the publication of the novel *Una vampata di rossore* (1959), about a family facing the wife and mother's terminal cancer. But he eventually wrote more short stories, collected in *Fondaco nudo* (1985). A last novel, *Ninfa plebea* (1992), has sensual themes absent from his previous work. His one play, the early *Le formicole rosse* (1948), is an experimental, densely symbolic family drama. [JD]

Reading, as distinct from *literacy, designates a variety of practices of scanning and comprehending written, engraved, or embossed symbols. In Italy, from late antiquity to the advent of printing, it consisted of the reading of handwritten texts or inscriptions, either silently, murmured, or aloud, according to the reader's purpose and situation. Latin texts predominated throughout the *Middle Ages, with a much smaller number of texts in Greek, Hebrew, Arabic, and, from the 13th c., vernacular. Book reading was often slow by modern standards because most *manuscripts were produced in continuous writing, without spaces between words and with arbitrary punctuation, and were frequently interpreted and annotated in detail. In the 12th and 13th c. manuscript production was revolutionized by the separation of words, division into paragraphs, and extensive use of abbreviations, coloured initials, and headings, all of which aided visual recognition and memorization of passages and enabled faster reading. The main habitual readers belonged to the scholarly, religious, and monastic communities, *courts, and the legal and *medical professions. *Merchants, shopkeepers, and artisans also had to deal with written words and numbers, though generally they understood the vernacular only. The majority of the population read nothing.

From the late 15th c. printing not only vastly increased the numbers of copies of books in circulation and diversified their size and format; it also introduced new kinds of vernacular reading, from pamphlets and placards (16th c.) to gazettes, newspapers, and magazines (18th c.). The distribution

Reading

of printed materials was extended by itinerant vendors, the reading public was enlarged in the towns, and to a much smaller extent in villages, and its social composition began to change, as did the 'practices of reading', to use historian Roger Chartier's expression. When vernacular texts were read by semi-educated readers they did not necessarily read them in the same way as learned readers. In his reconstruction of the readings of religious texts by the Friulian miller Domenico (Menocchio) Scandella, burnt for *heresy in 1600, Carlo Ginzburg (*Il formaggio e i vermi*, 1976) suggested that Menocchio's unorthodox interpretations were partly the effect of his assimilating print culture into a pre-existing popular culture with its own beliefs and oral traditions.

In towns, the street, the *café, and the bookseller's reading room (*gabinetto di lettura*) all became sites for the distribution and consumption of print, and the new popular reading public was served by cheap devotional texts and almanacs. In *Milan by the 1840s almanacs were being printed in editions of 20,000–40,000 copies, up to twenty times more than the average novel. Women also started to be recognized as a distinct market: Silvio *Pellico in 1819 noted that a public of female readers had emerged who required (so he claimed) books targeted specifically at them. These came to include romantic *novels and guides to good conduct. Unmarried women's reading in aristocratic and bourgeois families was generally kept under surveillance because of prevailing anxieties about corrupting effects of unsuitable novels. By the end of the 19th c. there was an identifiable lower middle-class reading public in the towns, particularly for the *romanzo d'appendice* and new genres like the *romanzo rosa* (popular romantic fiction), as well as a working-class public. The latter was served additionally by the publications circulated by the Catholic Church, and by the labour movement through its *biblioteche popolari* (set up in the 1890s).

Over a long period one can trace two major shifts in practices of reading in the print era. The first was from intensive to extensive reading, by which frequent readers, such as writers and scholars who read for professional reasons, dealt with more texts faster. The practice of writing detailed glosses and commentaries declined and was replaced by more rapid annotation. This may be attributed not just to an increase in the number of publications but also to a changing attitude to the written word: as *journalism and *publishing grew and as the scientific revolution spread, so did a characteristically modern sense of print as transient rather than permanent. The trend was deplored by defenders of intensive reading: *Leopardi wrote in the fifth chapter of 'Il Parini, ovvero della gloria' (in *Operette morali*, 1827) that so many books were now being produced that the scholar had no time to read them all once, let alone reread them.

The second shift was the decline in reading aloud and the spread of silent reading. Individual silent reading appears to have been characteristic of educated readers since antiquity (though in certain situations they also read aloud), but among the lower social classes reading aloud remained the norm, not only for announcements, newspapers, and placards but also for religious texts, verse, and popular fiction. In communities with high levels of illiteracy those individuals who could read and write tended to be called upon to read aloud or compose letters. In rural areas readers aloud included not only priests and labour movement orators but also *poeti a braccio* and *cantastorie*, who recited poetic texts and songs, of both popular and erudite origin, to a non-literate public. These itinerant figures were to survive until the demise of *peasant culture in the 1960s and 1970s. With their disappearance and with the general rise in literacy and school attendance, a whole world of reading aloud was largely eclipsed by silent reading. The most important exception has been the development since the 1950s of the talking book (*libro parlato*) and audio editions of magazines for the blind and partially sighted.

Despite the enlargement of the reading public it was repeatedly remarked, from the late 18th c. until recently, that Italy remained a country of few readers, particularly of books and newspapers, in comparison with countries like Britain or Germany. Five main reasons were given: Italy's comparatively high levels of illiteracy and semi-literacy until the late 1950s; low rates and short duration of school attendance by the lower classes, the peasantry in particular, until the raising of the minimum school-leaving age to 14 in 1962; limited distribution of printed paper outside towns; the relatively high cost of books (still cited as a barrier to mass book reading in the 1930s); the insufficient number of local lending libraries. In 1927 out of 9,148 *comuni* only 1,200 (13 per cent) had a public library. Another long-standing complaint, supported from 1906 by survey evidence, was that novels in *translation were often read in preference to those by Italian authors. This led to calls for protectionism in the *Fascist period, but such measures as were taken

502

had no lasting effect. A survey of 1949 found that thirteen out of the twenty novels read most recently were translations; the most cited author was A. J. Cronin.

Insofar as a mass reading public did exist it was for illustrated magazines, which emerged in the late 19th c. and took on their modern appearance in the 1930s with rotogravure printing. Weekly magazines consolidated and enlarged particular communities of readers, for instance young women and children, and then defined more specialized constituencies such as sports and science enthusiasts. Overall, weekly magazines had sales far larger than those of newspapers or books. Nevertheless, book reading also increased steeply after the 1960s: the number of people who declared they read books doubled from 12 to 24 million between 1973 and 1983. The main reasons were probably that more people stayed on at school and went to *university, incomes rose, and books were better distributed.

Some media analysts claim that electronic publishing and the Internet have started to bring about, particularly for the generation growing up with these technologies, another major shift in reading practices: from traditional linear reading, with its direction of movement from start to finish through a text, to reading without a pre-given direction, whereby the user explores an interactive hypertext or surfs a network. This practice may increasingly supplement linear reading but is unlikely to replace it. At the same time computer technology has significantly increased blind people's access to printed texts through scanners, character recognition, and Braille translation software and voice synthesizers. [See also EDUCATION; JOURNALISM; LIBRARIES; PRINTING.] [DF]

See A. Petrucci, *Writers and Readers in Medieval Italy* (1995); R. Chartier (ed.), *Pratiques de la lecture* (1985); S. Piccone Stella and A. Rossi, *La fatica di leggere* (1964).

Reali di Francia, I, see ANDREA DA BARBERINO.

Realism. Though one can speak in general terms of realism in *Dante, *Boccaccio or *Machiavelli, as an identifiable literary tendency realism comes into being in the early 19th c. as part of *Romanticism. It first emerges in the *Milanese *dialect poetry of Carlo *Porta and in *Manzoni's *historical novel *I *promessi sposi*. Aiming at a new readership amongst the ordinary people of Italy, both writers felt they had to invent a popular literary language and take up themes of general interest, derived

from historical fact and plainly recounted in a way that could be felt to correspond with reality. As Manzoni writes in a letter to Cesare *D'Azeglio in 1823, the subject of Romantic art is the 'truth'. *I promessi sposi* is very much a realist novel: the two protagonists are ordinary people, the style and the language are prosaic and everyday, and the narrative situations are drawn from everyday life. But the strength of the drive towards realism is shown by the fact that even Giacomo *Leopardi, whose poetry is written primarily according to classical criteria, includes some realistic elements in his depiction of ordinary people's lives. A much stronger realism is evident in *Belli's *sonnets in *Roman dialect, which represent the way of life and speech of the Roman populace.

In the 1840s and 1850s there was a tendency to prefer the everyday to the larger historical perspective, which shows itself particularly in tales and novels of the countryside with a *populist, philanthropic air, as typified by the work of Giulio *Carcano and Caterina *Percoto, and the *Novelliere campagnolo* of Ippolito *Nievo. During these same years Giuseppe *Rovani, in *Cento anni*, and Nievo, in *Le *confessioni di un italiano*, attempt large historical novels with contemporary settings, that are rich in realistic depictions of Italian life since the later 18th c.

A more decisive shift towards realism occurs with the *Scapigliatura* (1860–75), whose Lombard members called themselves the 'soldati del Realismo'. In practice however they often tend to prefer out-of-the-ordinary themes and formal experimentation. The only one who approaches a kind of realism is the *Piedmontese Giovanni *Faldella, whose *Figurine* consists of twelve short sketches of rural life. All the same the *Scapigliati* opened Italian literature to contemporary foreign influences, and broke with the reassuringly safe forms of Manzonian narrative. It is not surprising that *verismo* began in Milan, or that its originators, Giovanni *Verga and Luigi *Capuana, though *Sicilians, were close to the *Scapigliati*.

Verismo as they created it depicts the world of *peasants, shepherds, and fishermen and the realities of provincial life, and aims at the impersonality of presentation laid down as desirable by Flaubert, Zola, and other French Naturalists. Its language draws on the vocabulary, idioms, and syntactic structures of popular speech, without, however, having recourse to dialect. Philosophically *verismo* looks to the determinist and scientific principles of *positivism, which at this period drew the major

Realismo magico

Romantic critic of the time, Francesco *De Sanctis, to look kindly on Zola and '*Darwinism in art', even though he was still drawn more to a Romantic version of realism than to a Naturalist one.

The outstanding *veristi* are Sicilians—Verga, Capuana, and also Federico *De Roberto, the author of *I Vicerè* (1894). In Campania, Matilde *Serao and Salvatore *Di Giacomo describe working-class life in *Naples. In *Tuscany there are Renato *Fucini and Mario *Pratesi, though both are more peripheral with respect to *verismo* proper. In *Lombardy the main realist writer is Emilio *De Marchi, who reconciles a Manzonian approach with the realist emphasis on the social and economic environment.

Verismo proper lasts little more than a decade, from 1878 to around 1890. This is the period of Verga's masterpieces, *I *Malavoglia* and *Mastro-don Gesualdo*, a period when the young Gabriele *D'Annunzio also writes under the influence of Verga and Maupassant in the stories of *Terra vergine*, and *Le novelle della Pescara*. But it was also D'Annunzio who, with *Il *piacere* (1889), set in motion the *decadentist reaction against *verismo*.

Decadentism is closer to *symbolism than to realism, and the early 20th-c. avant-garde developments such as *Futurism and *expressionism also took off in quite different directions. One author who does continue from *verismo* is Federigo *Tozzi in his depiction of rural scenes and in his provincial settings, especially in *Il podere* and *Tre croci* (both written in the years 1915–20), though in general Tozzi is an expressionist who is more interested in the psychology of his characters than in their social environment.

A revival of realist themes occurs in various forms in the 1930s. *Vittorini and *Pavese fuse realism, myth, and symbolism; *Moravia's more analytical realism, which he first explores in *Gli *indifferenti* (1929), aims at creating an Italian form of the bourgeois novel; whilst realism in Southern fiction finds a social orientation in *Silone's *Fontamara* (1933) and Carlo *Bernari's *Tre operai* (1934). These forms of realism lead into the *Neorealism of the fiction written, broadly speaking, between the fall of *Fascism in 1943 and 1948, though the development is largely spontaneous and has no overarching theory or programme in these years. Characteristic forms are the memoir and the testimony, exemplified above all by Carlo *Levi's *Cristo si è fermato a Eboli* and Primo *Levi's *Se questo è un uomo*, though a more open and experimental writing appears in *Calvino's *Il *sentiero dei nidi di ragno*. From 1948 to 1955 Neorealism is officially promoted by parties of the Left and tends to become 'Socialist Realism', with a return to the traditional model of the novel and overt ideological *impegno*, as is typified by Francesco *Jovine's *Le terre del Sacramento* (1952) and Vasco *Pratolini's *Metello* (1955). However distinctive they are, Beppe *Fenoglio's novels and stories of partisans, beginning with *I ventitré giorni della città di Alba* (1952), are also conditioned by this Neorealist climate.

Experimentalism combines with Neorealism in *Ragazzi di vita* and *Una vita violenta* of Pier Paolo *Pasolini and in some other 1950s fiction. But the *Neoavanguardia* comes into being as a polemical rejection of Neorealism and *verismo* and in its actual literary practice favours abstract narrative forms over realistic representation.   [RL]

See N. Sapegno, *Ritratto di Manzoni e altri saggi* (1960); M. Corti, *Il viaggio testuale* (1978).

Realismo magico. The term designates the aesthetic theory and practice of a group of young writers, in particular Massimo *Bontempelli, associated with the avant-garde journal *900* (*Novecento*), founded in 1926 by Bontempelli and Curzio *Malaparte. Bontempelli was drawn to French *surrealism and the avant-garde theories of Giorgio *De Chirico and the Metaphysical painters. Unlike André Breton, he believed that the individual should learn to control the irrational rather than be drawn into it. 'Realismo magico' argues for the construction of a new reality based on the apprehension of of the 'surreal within the real', the magic that is concealed from us by the mundane and quotidian. Bontempelli cited 15th-c. artists such as Mantegna, Masaccio, and Piero della Francesca as having created a visual *realism that has a precision and a solidity of its own, while retaining an aura of mystery and magic. He saw the writer as having a similar task, the ideal result (as with *Pirandello) being literary works quite independent both of their author and of normal versions of real life. He puts the theory into practice in works such as *Il figlio di due madri* (1929) and *Gente nel tempo* (1937).   [AHC]

REBORA, CLEMENTE (1885–1957). *Milanese poet, whose earlier work is particularly associated with the ethical and artistic renewal promoted by *La *Voce*. His *Frammenti lirici* (1913) and *Canti anonimi* (1922) use highly *expressionistic language, setting against the chaos and banality of urban existence the authentic and sometimes overwhelming life of nature, with intimations of the divine, and a belief in human goodness and the value of human effort.

Conversion to Catholicism in 1929 led Rebora to destroy many of his papers, including the poems he had written since 1922. In 1930 he entered the *Rosminian order and in 1936 was ordained priest. Thereafter he produced poems of purely religious inspiration. The most striking, for imagery and expressive power, are to be found among the *Canti dell'infermità* (1957), which he composed during his protracted final illness. Critics have often regarded his conversion as the end of his career as a poet, but recent assessments, following the publication of his voluminous correspondence in 1982, have evaluated the later work more sympathetically, seeing it as expressing the moral commitment to human improvement which characterizes his life as a whole. [SPC]

Reception of Italian Literature in Britain.
Before the arrival of the printed book, in the second half of the 15th c., access to Italian writers was difficult for English readers, and interest in Italian literature slight. The important exception was Chaucer, whose works reveal his knowledge and admiration of *Dante's *Divine Comedy*, of *Petrarch's lyric poetry, and of *Boccaccio's *Filostrato*, *Filocolo*, and *Teseida* (but not of the *Decameron*, as far as we know, at least in its entirety), thus initiating the English interest in the Italian masters.

It was not until the 15th c., however, with the new wave of *humanist scholarship in Italy, that Englishmen in considerable numbers began to attend Italian *universities in search of the new learning, and to bring back with them a taste for modern vernacular authors which soon spread to a wider audience. Petrarch's lyric poetry in particular came to enjoy a huge vogue in 16th-c. England, following the imitations and translations of Wyatt and Surrey; but many of the minor Italian lyricists were also admired, and contributed to developments in English *Petrarchism similar to those on the Continent—developments that later drew *Shakespeare's protest 'My lady's eyes are nothing like the sun'. The *epic poets too were widely known and appreciated, thanks to the much-admired translations of *Ariosto's *Orlando furioso* by John Harington (1591) and of Torquato *Tasso's *Gerusalemme liberata* by Edward Fairfax (1600), and to Spenser's imaginative adaptations in *The Faerie Queene*;

Tasso's 'grand' style would significantly influence *Paradise Lost*. *Pastoral also played a part, with *Sannazaro's *Arcadia* inspiring Sidney, and the plays of Tasso and Battista *Guarini leading the way for Marston and Fletcher. The Elizabethan and Jacobean playwrights drew heavily for plots on the Italian *novella* tradition from Boccaccio to *Giraldi Cinzio and *Bandello, often via French intermediaries, the latter remaining for generations to come the gateway to Italian literature for many English readers. And the outpouring of *literary theory in Italy in the latter half of the 16th c. made a significant impact on the English theorists of epic and *tragedy.

By the 17th c. the tide was turning against the Italians, however, as religious differences and national pride asserted themselves. In addition to the distaste for the excesses of Petrarchism there was suspicion of Italian deviousness, seen in *Castiglione's *Cortegiano*, widely known thanks to a successful version by Sir Thomas Hoby (1561). And 'the murd'rous Machiavel' (*Henry VI* III.iii.3) was demonized on the English stage and has never recovered. Roger Ascham, who quoted in his *Scholemaster* (1570) the famous 'Inglese italianato è un diavolo incarnato' ('The Italianate Englishman is a devil incarnate'), counselled against any familiarity with Italian books. It was the fashionability of the Grand Tour and the changes in taste that came with the *Romantics that revived Italian fortunes in the mid-18th c. The *travellers' growing fascination with Italian art and music spilled over into literature: *Metastasio, for example, was very popular with young ladies learning to sing in Italian. The Romantic taste for horror brought the *Inferno* into prominence, and *Ugolino and *Francesca da Rimini became household names. But a more serious understanding of Dante and of other Italian authors was diffused by a group of Italian *exiles in England, *Foscolo and *Mazzini among them, and Antonio *Panizzi published in England the first edition of *Boiardo's *Orlando innamorato* unencumbered by *Berni's revision. The leading English Romantic poets were all familiar with the major Italian writers, as were most of the educated public. That interest, however, centred almost entirely on medieval and *Renaissance authors, and contemporary Italian writers were largely ignored.

The fashionable interest in Italian language and literature declined after the mid-19th c., but if the general public deserted the Italians, the foundations of a new and more serious understanding had been established, and a more or less continuous line of scholarly study and appreciation has led to the present day, when Italian literature is taught in most British universities and a pool of skilled *translators in Britain and America has made Italian writers more accessible to English readers than ever before. [CPB]

See R. Marshall, *Italy in English Literature 1755–1815* (1934); C. P. Brand, *Italy and the English Romantics* (1957); R. Kirkpatrick, *English and Italian Literature from Dante to Shakespeare* (1995).

REDI, FRANCESCO (1626–98). All-rounder who excelled in both letters and science. His early *education was with the *Jesuits in *Florence; he studied *medicine and philosophy at *Pisa from 1643 to 1647. After travelling throughout Italy he was appointed to the post (previously held by his father) of court doctor to the Grand Duke of *Tuscany, a position he held until his death. In 1655 he was elected to the Accademia della *Crusca in Florence, and began work in 1658 as one of the revisers for the third edition (1691) of the *Vocabolario della Crusca*. In 1657 he was a founder member of the Accademia del *Cimento. In 1666 he was appointed to a lectureship at the University of Florence in the Tuscan language, and much later, in 1685, he entered the Academy of *Christina of Sweden and the Accademia dell'*Arcadia.

The versatility of his appointments is reflected in his work. His *Poesie toscane* show him as a competent but unoriginal *purist. His most famous poetry is the dithyramb, *Bacco in Toscana*, which began as a toast for an academic gaudy in 1666 and was progressively enlarged and published in 1685. The work sings the praises of wine, displaying an intoxicating verve in its witty play on words and its experimental metrical structure. Redi's linguistic talent is apparent too in his work on the *Vocabolario della Crusca* and in his *dictionary of words and phrases of his native Arezzo. He knew Hebrew, Greek, Latin, Arabic, French, and German. He discredited once and for all the doctrine of spontaneous generation in *Esperienze intorno alla generazione degl'insetti* (1668); he laid the foundation for the modern study of parasites in *Osservazioni intorno agli animali viventi che si trovano negli animali viventi* (1684); he identified the nature of viper poison in *Osservazioni intorno alle vipere* (1664). With such works, and his *Consulti medici*, he laid the ground for the modern study of biology. His method owes much to *Galileo's, but focuses on smaller-scale questions. His Italian prose, like

Galileo's, is vivid and clear, unlike much of the writing of the later 17th and the 18th c. [PBD]

RE ENZO (*c.*1220–72). Italian name for King Heinrich, illegitimate son of the Emperor *Frederick II, who was captured by the *Bolognese in 1249, and remained their prisoner until his death. His few surviving poems treat of unhappy love and prudent resignation. He was probably an important intermediary between the *Sicilian School and early Bolognese poets. [PH]

Reformation. Between Luther's protest of 1517 and the Roman *Inquisition's reconstitution in 1542, Italians were free to accept or reject the crucial doctrine of justification by faith. By 1519 Lutheran literature was already circulating in Italy, and innumerable highly placed Catholics (including bishops and cardinals) became crypto-Lutherans. *Ochino's evangelism and the anonymous tract *Beneficio di Cristo* proved very persuasive. But the Protestant Reformation took shallow root in Italy, and never enjoyed popularity except in certain well-defined centres such as Lucca, Modena, *Naples, and *Venice, where it flourished briefly in the mid-16th c. Crisis of conscience caused many converts to flee abroad; many more remained as 'Nicodemites' (Calvin's contemptuous term for believers in Reformation doctrine who were outwardly still Catholic), and untold numbers were liquidated; for after 1542 the Inquisition and the *Index effectively eradicated Protestantism from Italy, which was even more *papal in 1600 than in 1500. [See also COUNTER-REFORMATION.] [PMcN]

REFRIGERIO, GIOVAN BATTISTA (*c.*1447–*c.*1491). *Bolognese notary and secretary, who wrote poems in Italian and Latin in the style of Antonio *Tebaldeo and Serafino *Aquilano. Most of his surviving verse was preserved by his friend and fellow notary, Cesare *Nappi. Refrigerio was forced to flee Bologna in 1488, after being implicated in a plot against the Bentivoglio. [CJ]

REGINA DI LUANTO (pseud. of Guendalina Lipperini) (1862–1914). Once married to her noble *Florentine husband, Alberto Roti, she soon left him for a more unconventional existence. Her *novels, beginning with *Salamandra* (1892), are centred on female protagonists and depict aristocratic society from the point of view of a critical outsider. [UJF]

REGIO, PAOLO (1541–1607) was a *Neapolitan lawyer and cleric, becoming Bishop of Vico Equense in 1583. Author of a *piscatorial prose work, the *Siracusa* (1569), inspired by *Sannazaro's *Arcadia*, his later works are mainly spiritual and theological, including lives of saints and the eschatological poem *La Sirenide*. [ELM]

Regno, Il, see PERIODICALS, 1.

Reina di Scotia, La, see DELLA VALLE, FEDERICO.

Religion, see BIBLE; CLERGY; COUNTER-REFORMATION; HAGIOGRAPHY; INQUISITION; PAPACY AND THE CATHOLIC CHURCH; REFORMATION; RELIGIOUS LITERATURE.

Religious Literature occupied a pre-eminent place in vernacular writings from the very beginning (notably the *Ritmo su Sant'Alessio* and the *Cantico di frate sole* of St *Francis) and continued to be an important point of reference right through to the 19th c. in such widely read writers as Alessandro *Manzoni and Antonio *Fogazzaro. This was achieved despite the fact that the strong legacy of classical civic culture in Italy ensured that the Church never possessed the near-monopoly of *literacy and learning it enjoyed north of the Alps. Such a long-lasting and pervasive influence on the forms and content of vernacular literature cannot just be explained by the evangelistic, missionary ideology of the Roman Catholic Church combined with its prominent public role and extensive *patronage network. One needs to consider the full range of genres encompassed by religious literature (and chronicled by Girolamo *Tiraboschi with a coverage never subsequently matched for acuity and range). They included not only *hagiography, *sermons, *sacre rappresentazioni, and *translations of the *Bible (in particular the Psalms), but also catechisms, *romances, and sacred history (of towns, churches, and religious orders). In all but the last of these genres, oral delivery rather than the written form was the more usual means of dissemination. Significantly, the models for these writings were invariably Latin (ultimately scriptural and patristic) and their authors, not infrequently, non-Italian members of international religious orders. Thus religious literature functioned as an important vector for foreign literary influences, from the early 14th-c. translation of the 6th-c. *Vite dei Santi Padri* overseen by the *Dominican Domenico *Cavalca, to the works of Ignatius of Loyola and Luis de Granada in the 16th c. and Francis De Sales and Jacques Bossuet in the 17th c.

Recent scholarship has altered our understanding of Italian religious literature in two important respects. First, it has demolished the myth that *printing was exploited by Protestants more than by Catholics. Although the Italian biblical translations by the crypto-Protestant Antonio *Brucioli (?1498–1566) and the Calvinist Carlo Diodati (1541–1625) enjoyed numerous contemporary editions, no fewer than sixty confession manuals in 185 editions were published between 1465 and 1550, and 208 editions of Italian catechisms appeared between 1547 and 1599. Moreover, several significant printing presses were founded by leading Catholic institutions in response to the Protestant *Reformation (for example, at the *Jesuit Collegio Romano in 1556 and the Vatican in 1587), which printed numerous apologetical works in Italian and other languages. Secondly, recent and current trends in *literary criticism have led to fresh assessments of forms of writing which have collective or anonymous authorship, which recycle literary topoi, and whose combinations of oral, written and often visual modes of composition reveal a highly developed interest in the processes of audience reception. Literary models long considered essentially 'medieval' in nature are in fact relevant to Italian literature in general and demonstrated their vitality through the 17th and 18th c., as is testified by the sermons of Paolo *Segneri the Elder and Alfonso de' Liguori. [See also COUNTER-REFORMATION; PAPACY AND THE CATHOLIC CHURCH.] [SD]

See G. Tiraboschi, *Storia della letteratura italiana* (1787–94); C. Dionisotti, *Geografia e storia della letteratura italiana* (1967); S. Ditchfield, *Liturgy, Sanctity and History in Tridentine Italy* (1995).

REMIGIO DE' GIROLAMI (d.1319) was *Dominican *lector* at S. Maria Novella in *Florence. His writings on civic matters include *De bono communi,* on the public good as preferable to the private good, and *De bono pacis,* on the need to achieve peace even at the expense of refusing to apply just punishments. [PA]

Remondini, see PUBLISHING.

Renaissance. Volume 7, *La Renaissance* (1855), of Jules Michelet's *Histoire de France* was the decisive step towards the modern concept of the Renaissance. Michelet's view of the Renaissance as

Renaissance

the 'discovery of the world and the discovery of man' was soon confirmed by Jakob *Burckhardt's landmark book, *The Civilization of the Renaissance in Italy* (1860), but with a shift of emphasis from the emergence of national consciousness (especially in France) to the concept of 'unbridled individualism' and the resulting 'state as a work of art'. For Burckhardt it was not the revival of antiquity alone (masterfully emphasized just a year earlier, in 1859, by Georg Voigt in *The Revival of Classical Antiquity*), but 'its union with the genius of the Italian people which achieved the conquest of the Western world'. Thus Burckhardt presented a Renaissance that was essentially Italian and which other countries, starting with France, simply imported from Italy more than a century later, around 1500. In this view, the second and definitive edition of *Vasari's *Vite* (1568) sanctioned the self-consciousness of the Renaissance in polemical opposition to the preceding *Middle or Dark Ages.

These paradigms are more useful to emphasize and explain the cultural hegemony of Italy until 1650 than for our historical judgement. For we know that capitalism and urban societies (the largely 'democratic' *communes) were born in the Middle Ages rather than in the Renaissance, so that 'modern man' owes his birth to both epochs. Nevertheless, although we no longer argue much about periodization, the Renaissance remains a most fertile ground for such theorizing because of its relationship with the Middle Ages, *Mannerism, the *Baroque, *modernism and *post-modernism (if we accept Toulmin's authoritative definition of post-modernism as the anti-Cartesian current to be traced at least as far back as Montaigne, and which includes at least Giordano *Bruno and Giambattista *Vico).

Contemporaries rightly saw the series of military events that afflicted the peninsula between 1494 and 1559 as the political end of Italy, *finis Italiae*, and it was a glaring paradox that the Italian states' independence came to an end at the very moment of their highest cultural productivity. The events that brought about their demise were indeed the occasion for the establishment of Italian cultural hegemony in the Western world, since the spread of the Italian Renaissance was triggered by the movements of armies and diplomats that brought thousands of leading Europeans within close reach of Italy's wonders. The 1492 discovery of America also contributed to displacing the centre of commerce away from the Mediterranean.

Inseparable from the Renaissance is the move-

ment we know as *humanism, which, on the philosophical plane, consisted of the revival of a Socratic stand in favour of focusing on moral behaviour, against the naturalistic (physical) and theological concerns that characterized previous schools of thought. Humanism had a technical side, philology. As applied to the newly found ancient *manuscripts (often simply 9th- and 10th-c. Carolingian products), a philologist's work entailed the successive stages of discovery, collation, edition, exegesis, and hermeneutics. The most impressive documents of humanist philology were undoubtedly Lorenzo *Valla's (1407–57) *Elegantiae* of the Latin language and his debunking of the *Donation of Constantine as a medieval forgery, and Angelo *Poliziano's *Miscellanea* (1454–94) [see CLASSICAL SCHOLARSHIP]. Poliziano was also the best poet of his century both in the vernacular and in Latin—and Greek.

The humanities or *studia humanitatis*—more specifically what we call literature, then known as poetry, eloquence, and history—loomed largest, but the most conspicuous asset of the Renaissance was its art, including the exhilarating sight of the new cities, with their splendid architecture and their urban planning, the most systematic example of which was Biagio Rossetti's (d.1516) 'new' *Ferrara, the *addizione erculea* ordered by the *Este Duke Ercole I and started around 1492. If *Giotto had marked a new beginning around 1300, it was another Florentine, Masaccio (1401–28), who awoke the attention of all Europe. This new art went together with decisive technical developments. Renaissance painting and sculpture, especially in the bas-relief (Ghiberti, Donatello, Iacopo della Quercia, Desiderio da Settignano, the Della Robbias, Mino da Fiesole, the Rossellinos, Verrocchio), received strong impulse from the development of perspective, first geometric (Piero della Francesca, Leon Battista *Alberti, Paolo Uccello, Andrea Mantegna) and then 'aerial' (*Leonardo da Vinci). An application of optics, perspective was achieved not by pure scientists but by the artists themselves, thus witnessing their inventiveness and intellectual breadth. Brunelleschi's miraculous *cupolone* for the Florentine cathedral resulted from the advanced state of Italian and especially Tuscan engineering, duly inherited by Leonardo, who was soon flanked by the other two masters of the High Renaissance, *Raphael and *Michelangelo. As for other technological developments, even though *printing first took root in Germany (Mainz, with Gutenberg, c.1450), the early German printers found it natural to move to Italy (first to Subiaco, south of Rome, where Sweinheim and Pannartz arrived in 1464), as the country that offered the best environment for technological innovation and the best markets. *Venice and *Florence soon became the most active centres of printed books.

Philosophy boasted such bold experimenters as *Pico della Mirandola, as well as the stunning achievement of the total recovery and Latin *translation of Plato's and the *Neoplatonists' works by the Florentine Marsilio *Ficino, but the *universities remained tied to the *Aristotelianism and Averroism the humanists so loudly despised. Both Pico and Ficino valiantly worked at the harmonization of ancient pagan thought with Christianity. The recovery of Greek culture received powerful aid from the arrival of Eastern scholars escaping from the Turkish occupation of the *Byzantine Empire (Constantinople fell in 1453). Cardinal *Bessarion brought to Venice his invaluable library of Greek manuscripts [see LIBRARIES]. But other scholars had arrived earlier, including the leading Platonist George Gemistos *Pletho, whose manifesto was issued in Florence in 1439. The new science found imaginative witnesses of note, Giordano Bruno being especially memorable among them, with his bold vision of endless universes in the wake of Copernicus.

To imitate the ancients or to be oneself, that was the question. Poliziano insisted that he expressed himself—'me ipsum exprimo'—not *Cicero. Valla as well as Erasmus proposed an eclectic programme of *imitation of the best masters, citing the way in which bees can turn into honey any kind of pollen they find. Imitation was a form of rivalry, more emulation than reproduction or approximation. And eclecticism was a form of tolerance, which, in the midst of the theological polemics that would lead to civil wars in other countries, was the greatest wish of the most open Italian minds (exemplified by Bernardino *Ochino, and Fausto Socini, principal founder of Unitarianism, starting in the 1560s). The humanists were aware that they were creatively different from the ancients, and rather than considering the ancient masters holders of a permanent truth, as the medieval use of authorities clearly implied, they did not hesitate to question them, starting with Aristotle himself, as *Petrarch had so forcefully begun to do. This was the work of humanist philology, and its focus was more on the discovery of the relative values of history than on the 'discovery' of merely 'literary' texts.

Pico della Mirandola's oration 'De hominis dignitate' (1486) is the most admired document in a typical humanist genre: the hymn to the dignity or nobility of the human condition. *Castiglione's *Cortegiano* (1528) is the most influential treatise on the merits, functions, and aptitudes of the new courtier, the 'modern' social role model for the monarchic societies that sprang out of the medieval communes and *signorie*. This model produced the French *gentilhomme* or *honnête homme* and the English 'gentleman'.

Florence, *Rome, Venice, Ferrara, *Mantua, *Milan, *Urbino, and a host of other Central and Northern cities were the focal points of Renaissance culture in Italy, but the South was also rich in resources, especially the large centres of Palermo [see SICILY] and *Naples. In Naples the *Aragonese dynasty after Robert of Anjou saw the likes of *Pontano, statesman and prolific humanist, and Iacopo *Sannazaro, begetter of the European *pastoral, which was thoroughly dominated by the example of his *Arcadia* (1504). At Rome the Tuscan Poggio *Bracciolini left his imprint on the Chancery under Nicholas V (1447–55) and Pius II (1458–64) [see PICCOLOMINI, ENEA SILVIO]. Leonello d'Este had been a pupil of *Guarino da Verona at the Ferrarese *court school started in 1429, and as Duke proceeded to reform the local university according to Guarino's humanist teachings. This was an exceptional event in the light of the general conservatism of universities which, as elsewhere in Europe, remained a stronghold of medieval interests. So too Francis I was prompted by the humanists to found a *Collège des lecteurs royaux*, later *Collège de France*, as a counterpart to the University of Paris.

The *educational field witnessed the appearance of a movement of great consequence worldwide, the foundation of the *Jesuit Order (1540), dedicated primarily to education through the establishment of colleges and universities. The first successful Jesuit undertakings were the public University of Messina (1548) and the Collegio Romano (1551), followed by the takeover of so many educational institutions throughout the world that it sometimes appeared as though the Jesuits had the monopoly in the field. They contributed to the spread and preservation of the humanist heritage, since they insisted on teaching exclusively in the Latin of Cicero and mostly in the humanities [see LATIN POETRY IN ITALY; LATIN PROSE IN ITALY].

*Ariosto embarked on the manneristic adventure of an 'open work', expressing the vision of a

Renaissance

world of multiplicity, relativity, and pluralism. It paralleled the decentred, centrifugal composition that in painting and sculpture replaced the vanishing point of 'classical' composition. The four corners, traditionally empty, become full. This was analogous to Michelangelo's design of an inner hall (the vestibule to the Library in S. Lorenzo in Florence) where, against the classical Vitruvian rules of 'rational' architecture, the hanging piers cannot support the ceiling because they do not touch the ground, the windows are not openings on nature because they are blind, and the massive staircase is out of proportion with the mere need to reach a second storey.

The *lyric was a prolific genre in the 16th c., and was signally patterned after Petrarch's *Canzoniere, following the doctrine successfully propounded by Pietro *Bembo in De imitatione (1513) and *Prose della volgar lingua (1525), setting up *Virgil and Cicero as absolute models for, respectively, Latin verse and prose, and Petrarch and *Boccaccio respectively for vernacular verse and prose. Bembo, *Della Casa, *Tansillo, *Galeazzo di Tarsia, Michelangelo, and Torquato *Tasso are the foremost lyrical poets of the century, but the *Manneristic or counter-Renaissance current is well represented by Francesco *Berni and Pietro *Aretino. The same century also saw a remarkable flowering of women poets, among whom one must mention the noble ladies Vittoria *Colonna and Veronica *Gambara, alongside the 'honest' *courtesans Gaspara *Stampa, *Tullia d'Aragona, and the Venetian Veronica *Franco [see also WOMEN WRITERS, 1].

*Theatrical genres have not been strong in Italy, but the lively interest in the revival of ancient forms that characterized the Renaissance led to many works that, even though of limited aesthetic merit, influenced later theatre, even in England and France, because of their exemplary embodiment of what came to be regarded as the rules of 'regular' theatre. Giangiorgio *Trissino's *tragedy Sofonisba (1515) took its place in this classicistic modelling process alongside his *epic poem Italia liberata dai Goti (1547). Giambattista *Giraldi Cinzio's Senecan tragedy Orbecche (1541) was especially influential in England. Other influential works are of considerable artistic merit, such as *Sannazaro's *Arcadia (1504) and Battista *Guarini's Il *Pastor fido (1590). Tasso produced a gem of a *pastoral play in his *Aminta (1573). The *comedy had a more complex history, and *Machiavelli and Ariosto were the more talented authors in this genre.

During the Renaissance *literary criticism came to the fore as an autonomous and committed discipline, and Italy's role in this vast corpus was central and decisive. The crucial event was the (re)discovery of Aristotle's Poetics, which had been practically ignored in antiquity and distorted through Averroes's Arabic interpretation in the medieval period. Critical developments were triggered by both Alessandro de' *Pazzi's Greek and Latin edition in 1536 and Francesco *Robortello's commentary of 1548, followed by a host of others, the most important of these being perhaps Giulio Cesare *Scaligero's Poetices libri septem (published posthumously in 1561) and Ludovico *Castelvetro's Poetica (1570). It was Scaligero who enunciated and fixed the un-Aristotelian principle of imitation or mimesis of (ancient) ideal literary models (especially Virgil) rather than directly of nature. Castelvetro, in turn, canonized the three 'unities' of plot, time, and place, equally un-Aristotelian yet equally decisive for the '*classicism' to come, especially in France. Somewhat by himself yet powerfully original was Francesco *Patrizi the Younger, who in his seven books Della Poetica (the last five discovered only in 1949) canonized the Neoplatonic verbum he derived from Ficino and, together with Castelvetro, erected the marvellous to the level of a major poetic task, thus foreshadowing Giambattista *Marino and the poetics of the Baroque. [See also LITERARY THEORY, 2.]

All in all, 'Aristotelian' literary criticism was the creation of Italian 16th-c. philologists. But the consciousness of an original 'modernity' forced some alert critics, first and foremost Giraldi Cinzio, to proclaim the canonicity of new forms and irregular authors, such as, especially, Ariosto and the *Orlando furioso. If the *chivalric poem did not conform with the 'Aristotelian' idea of an *epic, there must be room for such 'modern' new forms in the new Parnassus. In his turn, Tasso would try to produce a 'regular' national Italian epic that combined the classical prerequisites and themes with modern needs, by choosing a Christian subject matter (the *Crusades) and a multiplicity of central characters, even involved in distracting love affairs. His *Gerusalemme liberata (1582), because of its profoundly contradictory inspiration and form, turned out to be a Mannerist rather than a 'classical' masterpiece. His heroes and heroines are torn between their sense of duty to sublime collective missions and their need to satisfy their private passions. In such ways an age that once appeared as a dream of self-satisfied, serene perfection turns out to be an

Resistance

opening into varied and even contradictory later developments. [See also ACADEMIES; QUERELLE DES ANCIENS ET DES MODERNES.]   [AS]
See H. C. Haydn, *The Counter-Renaissance* (1950); E. R. Curtius, *European Literature and the Latin Middle Ages* (1953); E. Garin, *Italian Humanism* (1965); P. O. Kristeller, *Renaissance Thought*, vol. ii (1965); A. Scaglione, *The Liberal Arts and the Jesuit College System* (1986); C. Schmitt and Q. Skinner (eds.), *The Cambridge History of Renaissance Philosophy* (1988).

RENIER MICHIEL, GIUSTINA (1755–1832). *Venetian noblewoman, who held one of the most vigorous literary salons in Venice. Her interests included literature, science, and local history and culture, to which she devoted her major work, *Origine delle feste veneziane* (1817–27).
[CCa]

Renzo. Artisan protagonist of *Manzoni's *Promessi sposi.*

Re Orso, see BOITO, ARRIGO.

REPACI, LEONIDA (1898–1985). Writer known for his semi-autobiographical novel cycle, *Fratelli Rupe*. He trained in *Turin as a lawyer, joined the *Socialist Party and later the *Communist Party. In 1926, he was accused of murdering a local *Fascist in his native Calabria; on release he withdrew from political life until after *World War II.   [DF]

Repubblica Cisalpina, see NAPOLEON AND THE FRENCH REVOLUTION.

Repubblica Sociale Italiana, see FASCISM; MUSSOLINI, BENITO; RESISTANCE.

Rerum memorandarum libri, see PETRARCH, FRANCESCO.

Rerum vulgarium fragmenta, see CANZONIERE, IL.

Resistance. There were Italians who resisted *Fascism in the course of the twenty years of *Mussolini's regime, but the term is normally used of the armed resistance to Nazi and Fascist forces in the last twenty months of *World War II.
After the occupation of most of Central and Northern Italy by German troops in September

1943, many young men took to the hills often in order to avoid conscription, deportation, forced labour, or death, creating almost by default the first partisan bands. In the initial stages such bands were disorganized and naïve, but the organizational capabilities of, above all, the *Communist Party and the *Partito d'Azione helped shape them into more effective forces. In late 1943 Mussolini re-established a Fascist state as the Repubblica Sociale Italiana (RSI), with its headquarters in Salò on Lake Garda, which attracted a large number of adherents. The Resistance movement received a certain amount of material help from the Allies, who were pushing up the peninsula after the invasion of *Sicily in the summer of 1943, but was largely independent under the direction of Comitati di Liberazione Nazionali (CLN).

The Resistance has been officially celebrated since the war for its part in the defeat of Nazism–Fascism, but there has been constant debate about its nature, worth, and effectiveness. The historian Claudio Pavone's thesis, which has now been generally accepted, is that the movement was fighting three wars at the same time—a war of liberation against the Germans, a civil war against the Fascists, and a class war. Many have questioned partisan activities which led to reprisals against civilians, such as that at the Fosse Ardeatine in Rome in March 1944, which is described in detail in Robert Katz's *Death in Rome* (1967). Equally contentious have been the cases of post-Liberation executions of Fascists by partisans, who retained their organization and weapons for some time after the end of hostilities.

Though there were clandestine papers, little fiction and poetry was printed during the Resistance itself. There is no Italian equivalent of Vercors's *Le Silence de la mer* (1942). Although a few poems such as Alfonso *Gatto's 'Per i morti di piazzale Loreto' circulated clandestinely, the number of Resistance poems written in Italy was far smaller than in France. A large number of songs were, however, composed and the most famous of these ('Bella ciao' and 'Fischia il vento') have become part of national culture. But there was a flood of memoirs, novels, and short stories from 1945 to the mid-1950s, although it is films such as *Rossellini's *Paisà* (1946) and *Roma città aperta* (1945) which are better known.

Memoirs, by far the most published genre at the time, have proved to be the least enduring. Many were written in the heat of the moment, and were so vitiated by personal obsessions as to have become quickly unreadable. The resurgence of interest created by the fiftieth anniversary celebrations led to republication of some of the more successful examples: Pietro Chiodi, *Banditi* (1946); Leo Valiani, *Tutte le strade conducono a Roma* (1947); Dante Livio Bianco, *Guerra partigiana* (1954); Ada Gobetti, *Diario partigiano* (1952). Memoirs of RSI Fascists have also been recently published for the first time, such as Carlo Mazzantini's *A cercar la bella morte* (1992) and Giorgio Pisanò's *Io, fascista* (1997).

Most Resistance fiction from this period has also dated, though there are exceptions. The first Resistance novel proper was *Vittorini's *Uomini e no* (1945), which mixes the activities of the GAP (Gruppi di Azione Patriottica) and the existential crises of its otherwise nameless protagonist, Enne 2, with interestingly problematic juxtapositions of Hemingwayesque narration and passages of lyrical introspection. Italo *Calvino's first novel, *Il *sentiero dei nidi di ragno* (1947), tries for another fresh slant by depicting the Resistance through the eyes of its child protagonist, Pin. Of more obviously *Neorealist works, one which still enjoys critical approval is Renata *Viganò's *L'Agnese va a morire* (1948). It has often been felt, however, that the Resistance is best written about in short stories, which were regularly published by newspapers and encouraged through competitions run by partisan organizations. Calvino, whose stories written at this time are far better than his novel, and Marcello Venturi, whose collection *Gli anni e gli inganni* appeared in 1965, both contributed regularly to *L'Unità*, whilst Beppe *Fenoglio began his career with the stories of *I ventitré giorni della città di Alba* (1952).

Interest in the Resistance waned (or according to some was suppressed) in the mid-1950s, but returned in the 1960s. In literature notable high points were Luigi *Meneghello's *I piccoli maestri* (1963) and Fenoglio's posthumously published *Il partigiano Johnny* (1968). There was also room for more distanced reflection on the phenomenon of Resistance and neorealist writing, most interestingly carried through by Calvino in a 1964 preface to *Il sentiero dei nidi di ragno*. Increasing recognition of the part played by women in the Resistance led to the publication of works such as Giovanna *Zangrandi's *I giorni veri* (1963). In the 1980s the Resistance seemed increasingly remote. However, the 1990s saw a certain resurgence of literary interest, with novels such as Giampaolo Pansa, *Ma l'amore no* (1994), Ferdinando *Camon, *Mai visti sole e luna* (1994), Alessandro Gennari, *Le ragioni del sangue*

(1995), and Giancarlo Governi, *Hai visto passare un gatto nero* (1998). [PC]

See G. Falaschi, *La resistenza armata nella narrativa italiana* (1976); C. Pavone, *Una guerra civile* (1993); P. Cooke (ed.), *The Italian Resistance: An Anthology* (1997).

Restoration. The term refers both to the territorial and political settlement of 1814–15 ending *Napoleonic government in Italy, and to the period before the *1848 revolution. Most of the old dynasties were restored, as were many of the pre-1792 boundaries. Hence the Restoration period is usually associated with ill-considered attempts to return to the *ancien régime* and with a short-sighted intolerance of political and religious freedoms. In reality, however, reaction was short-lived and confined to *Piedmont, Modena, and a few other states. Elsewhere, interesting, if ultimately failed, attempts were made to create modernized forms of absolutism by integrating Napoleonic legislation with old regime conservatism. [LR]

RESTORO D'AREZZO (13th c.). Aretine author of an important prose treatise in the vernacular, *La composizione del mondo colle sue cascioni*, dated 1282, divided into two books, the first and shorter one describing the world and the second discussing the causes (*cascioni*) of phenomena. The work covers astronomy, geography, and natural sciences, making use of Arabic sources in Latin translation, and is unusual and original in the importance it attaches to observation, and to the description of curiosities such as fossils and ancient remains. The treatise marks an important advance in the use of the vernacular for scientific purposes. Autobiographical hints suggest that Restoro was a friar, goldsmith, and painter. [JU]

REVELLI, NUTO (1919–). Memorialist and social historian. His earlier books recount his experiences during *World War II—the retreat from Russia, the development of his political ideals, and his leadership of a partisan band in his native *Piedmont. Subsequent work, such as *Il mondo dei viventi* (1977), includes oral history projects that document the lives and politics of the Piedmontese *peasants. [SVM]

Revolution, see 1848; 1968; NAPOLEON AND THE FRENCH REVOLUTION; RISORGIMENTO.

Revolverate, see LUCINI, GIAN PIETRO.

REZZONICO, CARLO CASTONE DELLA TORRE DI (1742–96). Born in Como and a cousin to Pope Clement XIII, he combined literary pursuits with army and *court service, chiefly at Parma. There he inherited the mantle of Carlo Innocenzo *Frugoni, whose works he edited, adding a *Ragionamento* (1779) expounding the 'scientific' poetic underlying his own poems on Newtonian gravitation and sensationalist epistemology, *Il sistema dei cieli* (1775), and the unfinished *L'origine delle idee* (1778). He also wrote *lyric poetry, a *libretto, essays, and *travel accounts, including the *Giornale del viaggio d'Inghilterra* (1787–8), describing a fashionable tour of the English provinces with their country estates, private art collections, picturesque scenery, and industrial wonders. [JMAL]

Rhetoric, see ARS DICTAMINIS; LITERARY THEORY.

Rhyme, see VERSIFICATION.

RICCARDO DI SAN GERMANO (early 13th c.). Imperial notary during the reign of the Emperor *Frederick II. His Latin *Chronica*, influenced by the historiographical tradition of Montecassino, is a major source for the history of Southern Italy under the *Hohenstaufen dynasty. [JP & JMS]

RICCHI, AGOSTINO (1512–64) made a career in *medicine; but as a student in *Bologna he produced the stage *comedy *I tre tiranni*, which was performed before both Pope and Emperor in 1530. The 'tyrants' are the allegorical ones of Love, Fortune, and Money; and the play shows a rather awkward intrusion of these symbolic concepts into the normally mimetic *humanist drama. [RAA]

RICCI, BERTO (1905–41). *Florentine poet and writer, and a *Fascist who struggled against the reactionary tendencies of official Fascism. He founded the polemical review *L'Universale* (1931–5), which aimed to break free from narrow versions of cultural *nationalism, but also to shape and define a 'Fascist' literature. He was killed in North Africa. [SVM]

RICCI, SCIPIONE DE' (1741–1809). Bishop of Pistoia and Prato (1780–91), who introduced, with the support of Grand-Duke Peter Leopold of *Tuscany, a series of ecclesiastical reforms inspired by a combination of *Jansenism and the enlight-

ened Catholicism of *Muratori. Local and *Roman opposition prevailed and Ricci was forced to retract. His *Memorie* (not published until 1865) are an important source for an understanding of Jansenism in Italy. [GLCB]

RICCIARDI, GIUSEPPE (1808–82) was born into a *liberal family in *Naples, and founded *Il *Progresso* in 1832. *Exiled in France in 1834–48 and 1849–59, he was close to *Garibaldi and was elected to the chamber of deputies after *Unification. He published historical works and memoirs dealing with the *Risorgimento campaigns. [MPC]

RICCIARDO DA BATTIFOLLE (d.1374). Tuscan *lyric poet. He took *Cino da Pistoia and *Petrarch as models for his own love poetry, which also acts as a vehicle for the display of his classical erudition. [SNB]

RICCIO, PIETRO, see CRINITO, PIETRO.

RICCOBONI, LUIGI ANDREA (1676–1753). Modenese actor and dramatist. After the failure of his own company in Italy, from 1716 to 1729 he directed in Paris the *comédiens italiens*, collecting the scenarios written for them in *Nouveau théâtre italien* (1733). His Parisian publications include a remarkable *Histoire du théâtre italien*, with a treatise *Dell'arte rappresentativa* (1728–31), and *Réflexions historiques et critiques sur les différents théâtres de l'Europe* (1738). [FF]

Ricordi. Based on the *Florentine tradition of family *ricordanze* and of shrewd political advice recorded by diplomats and secretaries, *Guicciardini's collection of maxims or rules represent a new genre of writing, later developed by Tommaso *Campanella, as well as more famously by French writers like Montaigne, Pascal, and La Rochefoucauld. Written at different periods of his life, between 1512 and 1530, and constantly reworked, they demonstrate the reflective process by which Guicciardini articulated a novel, unprescriptive view of life and politics. [See also HOUSEHOLD TREATISES.] [ABr]

Ridicolosa, Commedia, see COMMEDIA RIDICOLOSA.

Riforma letteraria, La, see NOVENTA, GIACOMO.

RIGHETTI, CARLO, see ARRIGHI, CLETTO.

Rigoni Stern, Mario

RIGONI STERN, MARIO (1921–). Veneto novelist and writer. As a sergeant in an Alpine regiment, he took part in the Russian campaign during *World War II, and survived the terrible retreat from the Don in which thousands of Italian soldiers lost their lives. His account of his experiences, *Il sergente nella neve* (1953), was immediately acclaimed on publication, and remains his most famous work. This moving testimony of the horrors of the retreat is written in a pared-down style that focuses, not on anger, blame, and the bitter collapse of national pride, but on the courage and humanity of many he encountered. Rigoni Stern did not publish another book for nearly a decade, and the theme of war and the tragedy of war continues to dominate his later work. Many of his short stories, such as those collected in *Il bosco degli urogalli* (1962), are centred on the experiences of the Alpine troops. *Ritorno sul Don* (1971) recounts his return to the site of the now unrecognizable Russian camps of World War II. *Storia di Tönle* (1978) looks back instead to *World War I.

[SVM]

Rime nuove, see CARDUCCI, GIOSUE.

Rime of Dante. Even if *Dante had written nothing else, his lyrics—almost ninety in number—would have assured him an outstanding place in European literature. His most productive period in this field was from 1283 to 1293, when he changed the course of Italian love poetry. Influenced by *Guinizzelli and Guido *Cavalcanti, the young poet praised the beauty of *Beatrice but lamented the sufferings he incurred. Then he directed his love exclusively to praise, and revolutionized his art with the *canzone* 'Donne ch'avete intelletto d'amore' (cited as the beginning of Dante's *dolce stil novo* in *Purgatorio* 24.51), soon followed by the *sonnet 'Tanto gentile e tanto onesta pare': both masterpieces of their genre, selected in 1293/4 for his *Vita nova*.

The study of philosophy and Dante's entry into politics (1295) led to a broadening of his poetic horizon. After the restricted vocabulary of the early love poems, the poet began a complex process of experimentation. 'Le dolci rime d'amor' (*Conv.* 4) claims that he will abandon *allegory to treat of the controversial topic of true nobility (in a city that had deprived aristocrats of their political rights). The *tenzone* with Forese *Donati gives us the thrust and parry of vulgar insults. 'Amor che ne la mente mi ragiona' is later (*Conv.* 3) described

as a love poem in praise of Lady Philosophy. Technical innovations include the harsh poetry of the *rime petrose,* which include the *sestina 'Al poco giorno' and the double *sestina* 'Amor, tu vedi ben'.

Whereas the young poet had claimed that vernacular poetry should deal only with love (*VN* 25), after his exile Dante extended its sphere to include Arms, Love, and Rectitude (*De vulgari eloquentia* 2.2)—with the latter as the inspiration behind the great *canzone* 'Tre donne intorno al cor mi son venute'. The last lyrics known to us are a sonnet (*c.*1305), addressed to *Cino da Pistoia and proclaiming that love destroys free will; and a *canzone* (*c.*1307), 'Amor, da che convien', in which the 40-year-old poet complains of the tyranny of his new love for an unknown woman.

[JAS]

Dante's Lyric Poetry, ed. K. Foster and P. Boyde (1967). See P. Boyde, *Dante's Style in his Lyric Poetry* (1971).

Rime petrose. A group of four lyric poems by *Dante, written probably in *Florence before his exile in 1302. They focus on unyielding desire for a resistant 'donna di pietra' ('woman of stone'), and experiment with stylistic harshness and metrical difficulty after the model of the *troubadour *Arnaut Daniel. They include the first known *sestina* in Italian, as well as a unique double *sestina*.

[PH]

RINALDI, CESARE (1559–1636). *Bolognese writer whose elaborate love poetry anticipated that of Giambattista *Marino (whom he knew) and went through a number of editions. He also wrote moral treatises. His house in Bologna became a meeting point for writers and artists.

[ABu]

Rinaldo, son of Amone, brother of Ricciardetto, Alardo, and Guicciardo, and a leading figure in *chivalric narratives, first appeared in the French *Renaus.* Favoured by *Florentine authors, he is routinely banished by Charlemagne at the traitor Gano's instigation, and becomes a highwayman or enjoys adventures with *Orlando in the Orient, before returning to save France from Saracen attack. Rinaldo is protagonist of the *cantari *Rinaldo di Montalbano* and the *Orlando laurenziano,* as well as of Luigi *Pulci's *Morgante,* all 15th-c. poems. He also appears in *Boiardo's *Orlando innamorato* (as Ranaldo) and *Ariosto's *Orlando furioso,* and in Torquato *Tasso's

Gerusalemme liberata, where he is an ancestor of the *Este family. [GPTW]

RINALDO D'AQUINO (early 13th c.). Poet of the *Sicilian School. He was perhaps the brother of St Thomas *Aquinas and falconer at the *court of *Frederick II. His surviving poems (ten *canzoni* and two *sonnets) reflect the conventional themes of *troubadour love poetry, though *Dante twice praises the *canzone* 'Per fino amore vo sì letamente' (*DVE* 1.12 and 2.5). There is a more popular air to his best-known *canzone*, 'Già mai non mi conforto', in which a woman plaintively voices her despair over her lover's departure for the Holy Land and blames her anguish on Christ and the Cross. [CK]

Rinaldo di Montalbano. *Tuscan text in fifty-one *cantari*, preserved in a 15th-c. *Florentine *manuscript, narrating the military and amorous adventures of *Rinaldo in the Orient after his rebellion against Charlemagne. Variant versions of the text, some as long as seventy-three *cantari*, were frequently printed in the 16th c., with the title *Inamoramento de Rinaldo*. [RMD]

Rinascita (1944–91) was founded by Palmiro *Togliatti as the cultural monthly of the *Communist Party (PCI). Highbrow in content, it was the organ through which the PCI established its intellectual credentials and sought to implement its project of integrating *Marxism into the national culture. Although it was relatively open in the views it hosted, it nonetheless reflected the party's subservience to Soviet positions. Togliatti himself wrote short articles, signed Roderigo di Castiglia, reproving those who stepped out of line. In the 1960s, *Rinascita* became a weekly dedicating more space to social and political issues. Alberto *Asor Rosa was its last editor. [SG]

RINUCCINI, ALAMANNO ZANOBI (1426–99). *Humanist and member of a *Florentine family first prominent in the 14th c. He himself gained a second-rank political position under Cosimo de' *Medici. Siding with the anti-Mediceans in the revolution of 1466, he was subsequently marginalized politically. Embittered, he denounced Lorenzo de' *Medici as a tyrant in his *De libertate* (1479). He studied Greek and philosophy under *Argyropoulos, composing Latin works and translating Greek texts into Latin. Together with Donato *Acciaiuoli, he disseminated Argyropoulos' *Byzan-tine view of a broad philosophical culture, preparing the way for the revival of speculative philosophy in Florence under *Ficino and *Pico. [RDB]

RINUCCINI, CINO (1350–1417). *Florentine poet. Little is known of his life other than that he was a member of a wealthy noble family. He was a fervent admirer of the Florentine literary tradition represented by *Dante, *Petrarch, *Boccaccio, and the *dolce stil novo*, which he defended in a Latin *Invectiva* against certain *humanist detractors. His own poems correspondingly take his Tuscan predecessors as models. They are technically skilled and often delicately graceful, though tending to impose a certain static quality on *dolce stil novo* and Petrarchan topics. A *sestina* ('Quando nel primo grado il chiaro sole'), which develops the image of a beautiful woman in an exquisite rural setting, becomes a lament for the fragility of earthly beauty. In one of his best-known poems, the *madrigal* 'Un falcon peregrin dal ciel discese', the peregrine falcon represents unending desire.

Rinuccini's poetry is often neglected, but he played an important part in the formation of a vernacular literary canon and anticipated 16th-c. *Renaissance attitudes to literature in Italian. He also acted as a link between the early Florentines and 15th-c. poets such as Lorenzo de' *Medici and *Poliziano: it is from Lorenzo's collection that early manuscripts of Rinuccini's poems are derived. [JP & JMS]

RINUCCINI, OTTAVIO (1562–1621). The leading poet of his time in *Florence, closely associated with the rise of *opera. Encouraged by the patron Iacopo Corsi, he produced two *libretti set to music by Iacopo Peri, *Dafne* (1598) and *Euridice* (1600), the latter performed during the festivities celebrating the wedding of Henri IV of France and Maria de' *Medici (whom Rinuccini later served in Paris). He also wrote libretti for Claudio *Monteverdi, including *Arianna* and the *Ballo delle ingrate* (1608).

Although he claimed to be reviving ancient dramatic practices, he was more influenced by contemporary *pastorals. His flexible mixing of unrhyming *versi sciolti* and more structured, strophic verse to distinguish musical recitative and *aria* established important principles for later libretti. His posthumously published *Poesie* (1622) also contains *lyric poetry which had been set by contemporary musicians. [See also CAMERATA DE' BARDI; VERSIFICATION.] [TC]

RIPA, CESARE, see ICONOGRAPHY.

RIPAMONTI, GIUSEPPE (1574–1643). A priest and a professor of rhetoric at the seminary of *Milan, and a client of Federico *Borromeo, Ripamonti was appointed chronicler to the city in 1609. He published three major *historical works, on the church of Milan (1617–28), on the *plague of 1630 (1640), and on the city itself (1641–3), works which were utilized by *Manzoni.   [UPB]

RIPELLINO, ANGELO MARIA (1923–78) taught Russian language and literature at the University of *Rome. An energetic and innovative critic, who at times blurred the boundaries between critical and creative writing, he *translated several major Russian authors, including Chekhov and Pasternak. He also wrote *lyric poetry and collaborated with the *Gruppo 63.   [ZB]

RISI, NELO (1920–). *Milanese poet. After serving on the Russian front during *World War II, he has worked as a *journalist, *translator, and (like his brother Dino) film director. From his first volume, *Polso teso* (1956), which was quickly associated with the so-called *linea lombarda* [see also ERBA, LUCIANO] in modern poetry, his verse has been deliberately anti-lyrical, with marked epigrammatic and ironic tendencies. Later discursive poetry treats issues such as consumerism and the Cold War, but there are also evident debts to *Montale and French *surrealism, whilst collections such as *Dentro la sostanza* (1965) can embrace contemporary experimentation with language and form.   [JJ]

Risorgimento. The complex process leading to the *Unification of Italy, much mythicized inside and outside Italy, both at the time and later. In reality it enabled the Kingdom of *Piedmont-Sardinia, which was one of the Italian states in the new European order dictated in 1815 by the Congress of Vienna after the fall of *Napoleon, to annex the other six—*Lombardy-Venetia which had been under direct *Austrian rule, the Duchies of Parma and Modena and the Grand Duchy of *Tuscany indirectly ruled by Austria, the *Papal States, and the quaintly named Kingdom of the Two Sicilies which included most of Southern Italy and *Sicily. The process was formally completed in 1860 (1866 for Venetia), when transitional governments in the six states sanctioned their union to Piedmont-Sardinia through a round of plebiscites. These reflected a widespread desire for *national unity while effectively endorsing the Piedmontese takeover. The Act establishing on 17 March 1861 the Kingdom of Italy was passed by Parliament on behalf, not of the Italian people, but of the King's government. The first King of Italy continued to be known as *Vittorio Emanuele II.

According to the Austrian Foreign Minister, von Metternich, Italy was in 1815 a 'geographical expression'. The reverse would have been truer: for centuries this geographical expression, whatever the regional allegiances and often ferocious rivalries of its inhabitants, had somehow been aware of being Italy. It had a literary language which, though used mostly in writing by a tiny minority of educated people, was recognized even by illiterates as the vehicle of a common culture, much as Latin was accepted by Catholic churchgoers everywhere as the hallowed language of their religion, even if they could not use or understand it. The exciting though brief experience of having large areas of Italy unified under Napoleon had left a mark even among ordinary people. Hence the ideal of national unity not only inspired the thought and guided the actions of a small number of politicians, ideologues, and men of action (such as *Cavour, *Mazzini, and *Garibaldi), promoting contrasting and often incompatible views and aims, but also surfaced here and there among otherwise uncomprehending masses not particularly interested in the political aspirations of their betters.

It would be wrong, nevertheless, to view the Risorgimento as a mass movement, or as a coherent movement at all. Nearly all its protagonists belonged to the educated upper and middle classes. Most of their failures, such as the various ill-prepared Mazzinian uprisings and the disastrous expeditions by the Bandiera brothers (1844) and Carlo *Pisacane (1857), derived from the lack of inter-class solidarity and of a common ideological basis between the leaders and the would-be led. Vittorio Emanuele II and Cavour paid lip service to the noble ideal of Italian unity because it was compatible with their aims of dynastic consolidation and territorial expansion. A number of wealthy landowners favoured Piedmont-Sardinia because they knew it to be an even more conservative monarchy than Austria, and hoped they could best safeguard their interests by shifting their allegiance from a distant sovereign, known to have problems in Central Europe, to one nearby. The budding Northern industrialists and traders were more interested in freeing their commercial operations from Austrian control than in having them regulated and taxed by a new united kingdom. Those who believed that their own political purposes, whatever they might be, would best be served by unification did not necessarily agree on whether the new state should be a monarchy or a republic, or whether it should have a centralized or federal structure. The bourgeoisie wanted constitutional government merely to limit the powers of absolute rulers, certainly not to upset the old social order.

Many enthusiastically embraced the principle, later codified in *Tomasi di Lampedusa's *Il *gattopardo* by Tancredi Falconeri, that everything should change so that everything should stay the same. Some of those who wanted reforms clearly saw that the unification of the country would not in itself bring them about. A few democrats, like Mazzini, Garibaldi, Pisacane, and *Nievo, knew that no real progress could be made unless the millions of exploited and disenfranchised *peasants were granted some political rights and better living conditions. The peasants, on the other hand, tended to resist change like a very sick person who finds any movement atrociously painful. Hence they handed the Bandiera brothers over to the police, slaughtered Pisacane's expedition, and waged a bloody guerrilla warfare against the Piedmontese army (1861–5) that claimed more victims than the three wars of independence (*1848, 1859, 1866) put together.

The best-known Italian *novel of the age, *Manzoni's *I *promessi sposi*, projected burning issues of social injustice and political corruption onto a much earlier and less controversial historical period, and skilfully balanced its strictures against the sins of the powerful with preaching the Christian virtues needed to bear their misrule, a message which some of Manzoni's contemporaries, let alone later readers, found unpalatable. This message, repeated and simplified in various forms of 'popular' literature after 1861, was timely, since the new government was no better than those it replaced and markedly worse than some. The least underdeveloped regions of the new Italy were those formerly under Austrian rule, which had at least been paternalistic, tolerably honest, and efficient, as well as blinkered and bureaucratic. The general disillusionment with the new regime (known to Italian historians as 'la delusione risorgimentale') is clearly mirrored in *Carducci's poetry. For a striking fictional panorama of Risorgimento history one must look to Nievo's *Confessioni di un italiano* (1867), though, in the aftermath of the defeats by the Aus-

trians at Lissa and Custoza in 1866, it failed to appeal to readers needing a less radical and realistic picture of events. Three decades later, at a time of great stress for the new nation torn between banking scandals, social unrest, and disastrous colonial adventures, they favoured *Fogazzaro's cosy description of Northern provincial life in the decade before unification in *Piccolo mondo antico* (1896).

The Risorgimento inspired a number of interesting even if not entirely reliable *autobiographical memoirs by *Abba, Masssimo *D'Azeglio, Garibaldi, *Pellico, and *Settembrini. [See also MONARCHY.]   [GC]

See D. Beales, *The Risorgimento and the Unification of Italy* (1981); S. Woolf, *A History of Italy 1790–1870* (1979); Lucy Riall, *The Italian Risorgimento* (1994).

Rispetto, see STRAMBOTTO.

Ritmo cassinese (late 12th c.). Metrical text, of *Benedictine production, intended for public recitation as moral instruction. Although sometimes obscure, the text is substantially in a central Italian *dialect. However it is probably based on a Latin original, and is interspersed with Latin phrases, which suggests that the intended audience had some acquaintance with Latin.   [MM]

Ritmo laurenziano (1188–1207), a poem composed of three stanzas, each made up of monorhymed eight-syllable lines, and originating probably from Volterra, was long considered to be the oldest extant text with clear literary aims written in an Italian vernacular. Recent research, however, has moved its date of composition from the middle of the 12th c. to the period 1188–1207, thus making it the contemporary of the other two surviving *ritmi*: the *Ritmo cassinese* and *Ritmo su Sant'Alessio*. Its author, an anonymous *giullare*, praises the generosity of Bishop Grimaldesco di Iesi and that of a bishop of Volterra. The poem survives in a single manuscript in the Biblioteca Laurenziana in *Florence (hence the designation), and, according to some scholars, it was transcribed by its author. If this is the case, the manuscript would constitute the oldest Italian poetic autograph.   [ZB]

Ritmo su Sant'Alessio (early 13th c.). Incomplete narrative poem recounting the life of St Alexis in irregular strophes, similar to those of the *Ritmo cassinese*. It is preserved in a manuscript in

Ascoli Piceno and was probably composed in central Italy. Its language shows features of *Umbria and the Marche, but also Latin elements. It probably derives from a lost Latin source.   [PH]

Riviera ligure (1895–1919). Established originally as a publicity magazine of the Sasso oil company at Oneglia in Liguria, it became a literary quarterly under the editorship of Angiolo Silvio *Novaro, who was succeeded in 1899 by his brother Mario. Its approach was eclectic, but it published poems and writings by all the important writers of the period (except the *Futurists), including *Bontempelli, *Cecchi, *Govoni, *Sbarbaro, *Soffici, and *Ungaretti, though a certain predilection for Ligurians remained to the end. It became particularly well known with the caustically perceptive reviewing of Giovanni *Boine from 1912 to 1917.   [GP]

Rivista minima di scienze, lettere ed arti, see PERIODICALS, 1.

Rivoluzione liberale, La (1922–5). *Turinese weekly journal. Its founder and editor, Piero *Gobetti, wanted it to articulate a non-reactionary, *liberal-*socialist theory of elites. Going against the theories of Vilfredo *Pareto and Gaetano *Mosca, he aimed to combine the critique of the Italian state found in *Salvemini's *L'Unità* and the council-*communism which *Gramsci was proposing in *L'*Ordine nuovo*. But Gobetti published a wide variety of political and cultural articles, in particular bringing contemporary Russian writers to the attention of Italian readers, though in 1924 he founded another journal, *Il *Baretti*, with a specifically cultural orientation. *La Rivoluzione liberale* was closed in November 1925 by the Prefect of Turin on the direct orders of *Mussolini.   [DS]

Rizzoli. *Publishing firm founded (as a printing firm) by Angelo Rizzoli in *Milan in 1909. From 1927 it published magazines, diversified in 1934 into film production and distribution, and after 1945 developed its book publishing and bookselling divisions. The Biblioteca Universale Rizzoli, started in 1949, was Italy's first series of cut-price paperback classics. The firm recovered from financial collapse and scandal in the 1980s to become the leading media conglomerate RCS (Rizzoli Corriere della Sera). In the 1990s it acquired the *Florentine publisher Sansoni (founded 1873).   [DF]

RIZZOTTO, GIUSEPPE, see MAFIA.

ROBERT, ENIF, see WOMEN WRITERS, 3.

ROBERTI, GIOVANNI BATTISTA (1719–86). *Jesuit and writer. Born in Bassano, he taught in the Society's academies in Parma and *Bologna. He displays a moderately enlightened outlook in didactic poems, such as *Le fragole* (1752) and *La commedia* (1756), which praises *Goldoni, the *Favole esopiane* (1782), and pamphlets denouncing the slave trade, swaddling bands, and other contemporary evils.   [FF]

ROBORTELLO, FRANCESCO (1516–67). *Humanist literary theorist and commentator. Born in Udine, he studied at *Bologna and subsequently taught eloquence at *Pisa and other Northern *universities. His historical and philological writings include a discussion of the principles of *textual criticism, *De arte sive ratione corrigendi veteres authores.* His *In librum Aristotelis De arte poetica explicationes* (1548) is the first full *commentary on *Aristotle's *Poetics*, albeit in the Latin translation of Alessandro *Pazzi, as emended by Robortello himself. An appendix contained discussions of genres not considered in the surviving text of the *Poetics*, including *satire, the epigram, *comedy, and elegy. [See also LITERARY THEORY, 2.]   [DK]

ROCCA, GINO, see SCIENCE FICTION.

ROCCATAGLIATA CECCARDI, CECCARDO (1871–1919). Poet and anarchist, who abandoned law studies in *Genoa for *journalism and wrote for various Ligurian *periodicals and newspapers. His poetry is indebted to *Carducci and *D'Annunzio, but lacks their formal discipline. He was charged with incitement to violence for the pamphlet *Dai paesi dell'anarchia* (1894).   [AHC]

ROCCO, ANTONIO, see LOREDAN, GIAN FRANCESCO.

ROCCO E ANTONIA, see RAVERA, LIDIA.

Rococo. The Italian *Rococò* derives from the French, itself a distortion of *rocaille*, that is, the use of stones to ornament artificial grottoes. The term spread from visual arts to indicate an aesthetic tendency common to 18th-c. literature in several European countries, although with local differences in both extent and chronology. Its hallmarks are a light-hearted hedonism, irony, and escapism. It is characterized by the use of mythological and love themes and the treatment of social rituals and manners, such as taking coffee or chocolate and wine-tasting, brilliant conversation, clever jokes. Other recurrent motifs are the *carpe diem* call to enjoy the present, the fear of ageing and of oblivion, and an infatuation with precious art objects.

The style of Rococo is often colloquial, with a common tendency to ironize social conventions. Typical literary forms are the Anacreontic verse, the idyll, and the *mock-heroic poem. While Italian poets combined these features of European Rococo with classical tendencies, a more international Rococo style is in the *Feste* and dramas written by *Metastasio in Vienna (particularly those of 1732–40). Rococo elements of language can be traced in P. I. *Martello's prose works, and typical Rococo themes and stylistic traits in his dramas such as *Il Davide in corte* or *Lo starnuto d'Ercole*. There are also Rococo tastes in Paolo *Rolli's *Endecasillabi* (1717), and in Ludovico *Savioli Fontana's *Amori* (1758 and 1765), as well as in *Parini's *Il *giorno*, with its satirical representation of contemporary society.   [IMC]

RODARI, GIANNI (1920–80). Italy's pre-eminent children's writer of the 20th c. After a brief career in teaching, he devoted himself to *journalism and writing. From *Il libro delle filastrocche* (1950) onwards he combines utopian *Marxism and *fantasy, which he saw as a key to reality, not an escape from it. Earlier condemned by the Church, he worked with teachers and schoolchildren in the 1960s through the Movimento di Cooperazione Educativa. His most innovative works are collections of (sometimes very short) stories and fables, such as *Favole al telefono* (1962), *Il libro degli errori* (1964), and *Novelle fatte a macchina* (1973). His *Grammatica della fantasia* (1973) explains his educational and literary thinking and proposes techniques for fostering creativity. [See also CHILDREN'S LITERATURE.]   [ALL]

Rodomonte. Pagan champion in *Ariosto's *Orlando furioso*.

Rodrigo, Don. Local lord and villain in *Manzoni's *Promessi sposi*.

ROLANDINO DA PADOVA, see CHRONICLES; PADUA.

ROLLI, PAOLO (1687–1765). *Arcadian poet and *translator. Born in *Rome and a pupil of Gian Vincenzo *Gravina, he entered the Arcadia academy as Eulibio Brentiatico, quickly gaining a reputation as an *improviser. In 1716 he moved to London, where he became a private tutor to children of the nobility and the royal family, and stayed until 1744. He wrote *libretti for Handel, Giovanni Bononcini, Nicola Antonio Porpora, and others, and published various collections of shorter poems, becoming the most famous author of lyrics for music of the century apart from *Metastasio. He translated Milton's *Paradise Lost* (1733), and edited Italian classics that were under ecclesiastical *censorship in Italy itself, including Alessandro *Marchetti's translation of Lucretius (1717) and the *Decameron* (1725). [See also ROCOCO.]   [CCa]

ROMAGNOSI, GIAN DOMENICO (1761–1835). Lawyer and philosopher who held chairs at Parma and Pavia universities during the *Napoleonic period. His political ideas (and his *freemasonry) led to his resignation from teaching after the *Restoration. He contributed to *Il *Conciliatore*, *Antologia*, and *Biblioteca italiana*, and exerted an immense influence on younger patriots.   [EAM]

Romana, La (1947) is *Moravia's first *novel with a first-person female narrator. Adriana, a lower-class girl from *Rome, comes into contact with the world of the urban middle classes, through her occupation first as an artist's model and later as a prostitute. The positive qualities of this working-class heroine contrasted with the mediocrity of the bourgeoisie, together with the plain naturalistic narrative technique, marked *La romana* as a striking example of *Neorealist attitudes.   [GUB]

Romance. A French term originally used to refer to compositions in the vernacular as opposed to Latin, *roman* came to be applied in the 12th c. specifically to works of narrative fiction. The romance is distinguished from *epic by its prevailing ethos, which focuses on the individual hero rather than on the common cause of a nation or society; the motivation for the action is internal and emotional rather than national or religious, and indeed the tension between public and private loyalties is often a central theme. In the course of the 13th c. the narrative structure of the French romance became increasingly complex, and the fictitious world which it created correspondingly self-contained. The romance is thus an exceptionally fluid genre, both in form (a variety of verse forms, or prose) and content; and there is a recognizable continuity between the medieval romance and its modern descendant, the *novel, still called *roman* in French and *romanzo* in Italian.

The first extended narrative fiction in Italian, in the first half of the 14th c., draws on all the main bodies of French material as well as on classical and medieval Latin texts. In verse, the mostly anonymous *cantari* narrate incidents drawn from or modelled on *Arthurian and classical myths. The Carolingian stories are developed first in *Franco-Veneto verse texts and later in the prose compilations of *Andrea da Barberino. Also in prose are two compilations of Arthurian stories, the *Tristano riccardiano* and the *Tavola ritonda*, and a version of the *Alexander romance, *Li nobili fatti di Alessandro*. A key figure in the development of both verse and prose narrative is *Boccaccio, who spent a formative decade at the *Anjou court in *Naples in the 1330s. In verse, his *Filostrato*, an influential version of the Troilus and Cressida story, draws on the French *Roman de Troie* and *Guido delle Colonne's *Historia troiana*; the *Teseida*, which makes use of *Statius' *Thebaid* and probably also the *Roman de Thèbes*, tells the story of Emilia, Arcita, and Palemone which is reproduced in Chaucer's *Knight's Tale*. In prose, the tale of Floire and Blanchefleur provides the core narrative of the *Filocolo*, but the work also includes numerous other stories illustrating the nature and dilemmas of love. This anticipates Boccaccio's most original work before the *Decameron, the *Elegia di Madonna Fiammetta*, which explores the emotional turmoil of a woman deceived in love, in a work which has been called the first modern psychological novel.

Boccaccio's psychological *realism was combined with the traditional elements of love, magic, and the exotic, together with a touch of humorous irony, in the *chivalric poems of the *Renaissance. The great popularity of these poems, especially *Ariosto's *Orlando furioso*, established the romance as a genre, albeit one unknown to the ancients, as was clear with the renewed currency of Aristotle's *Poetics* in the 1540s. The perceived need for a theoretical justification of the genre was met by G. B. *Giraldi Cinzio's *Discorso intorno al comporre dei romanzi* and *Pigna's *I romanzi*, both published in 1554. Encouraged by this new legitimacy, Bernardo *Tasso gave free rein to the taste for complex interwoven plots in his *Amadigi* (1560), an adaptation of the Spanish

Amadis de Gaula, the romance which had pride of place in Don Quixote's library. Bernardo's son Torquato *Tasso was less fortunate, struggling in his *Gerusalemme liberata* to find a compromise between the luxuriance of the romance and epic solemnity. But the romance was to have an enduring influence on fiction down to modern times. [See also LITERARY THEORY, 2; NOVEL.] [RMD]

See D. Delcorno Branca, *Il romanzo cavalleresco medievale* (1974).

ROMANCE EPIC. Term commonly used for the *chivalric poems of the *Renaissance, which combine the martial and religious material of the *epic with elements of *romance, notably love.

Roman de la rose, see ALLEGORY; FIORE, IL; FRENCH INFLUENCES, I.

ROMANI, FELICE (1788–1865). *Librettist and writer. Born in *Genoa, he took a degree in law at *Pisa and another in literature at Genoa. After a period of teaching and travelling, he moved to *Milan, where he became a friend of Vincenzo *Monti, though his work shows more the influence of *Foscolo and *Leopardi. From 1814 to 1834 he was under contract to write libretti for La Scala. He produced more than 100, including those for Vincenzo *Bellini's *Norma* and *La sonnambula*, and *Donizetti's *Anna Bolena*, *L'elisir d'amore*, and *Lucrezia Borgia*. He later worked in *journalism, mostly as a *literary critic. He also published stories and lyric poems. [DO'G]

ROMANÒ, ANGELO, see OFFICINA.

ROMANO, LALLA (1906–2001). Novelist from *Piedmont. After studying literature at *Turin University, she taught in secondary schools in Turin and *Milan before concentrating on writing. Her initial interest in poetry, as shown by *Fiore* (1941), led to more potent results in the *prose poems of *Le metamorfosi* (1951). But the experience of *translating Flaubert's *Trois contes* drew her to fiction. Her first novel, *Maria* (1953), is influenced by Flaubert's *Un cœur simple*, and studies the relationship between a servant and his mistress. Generally in the 1950s she resisted *Neorealist orthodoxies. Partly in consequence there was a mixed critical reception to novels such as *Tetto murato* (1957), which is set during *World War II but depicts the experiences of two couples magically cut off from the violence around them. However, she won the

Strega prize [see LITERARY PRIZES] with *Le parole tra noi leggère* (1969). This novel is unusual in Italian literature in exploring the complexities and ambiguities of a mother–son relationship, showing the power struggle between them and their mutual hostility and attraction. Humorous and tragic by turns, it includes letters, school compositions, and fragments of dialogue. *Una giovinezza inventata* (1979) evokes her youth, *Inseparabile* (1981) her marriage. She also wrote *travel memoirs in later life. [SW]

Romanticism. The terms 'Romanticism' and 'Romantic' may be drawn on in a generic sense to refer to much Italian writing of the 19th c., and even the late 18th c., but they are specifically linked in Italy (in a way not replicated in other European countries) to a period of literary debate and experimentation which broadly corresponds to the first dozen years or so of the post-*Napoleonic *Restoration (roughly 1815–27). In this perspective Romanticism acts as a focus, and in some cases a rallying cry, for a confrontation over the modernization of Italian literature.

The immediate trigger for the debate came from an article by Mme de Staël published in *Biblioteca italiana* in 1816, in which she called for a renewal of Italian letters and enjoined her readers to use *translation, not least of modern *English and *German poetry, as a way of broadening their literary horizons. The article provoked *nationalistic attacks on Staël and passionate interventions in her defence, notably *Di Breme's *Intorno all'ingiustizia di alcuni giudizi letterari italiani*, *Borsieri's *Avventure letterarie di un giorno*, and *Berchet's *Lettera semiseria di Grisostomo al suo figlio*, all of them published within a few months of each other in 1816. Although the word 'Romanticism' was not mentioned in de Staël's article, the notion of the *romantique* popularized by her in *De l'Allemagne*, and by her circle in such works as A.W. Schlegel's *Course of Dramatic Literature* and Sismondi's *Sulla letteratura del mezzogiorno d'Europa*, is implicit in her remarks. The recodification whereby the far more nuanced German 'romantisch' or English 'romantic' become simplified into an identification between Romanticism and the modern, and the modern placed in dialectical opposition to the ancient (or antique), the Romantic to the classical, the historical to the mythological, proved eminently exportable to Italy. Romanticism is adopted in 1816 as the banner of a literary modernization which is seen first and foremost in socio-political terms— modern literature must be popular—and, following

Schlegel and Sismondi, is given a particularly 'Southern' colouring: Italian Romanticism will find its roots in the 'romance' traditions of the *communal *Middle Ages, rather than emerging from 'Northern' mists.

Along this path, to whose mapping an influential cohort of moderate *classicists such as *Giordani and *Londonio also contributes, Italian Romanticism will quite quickly reach a broadly consensual, or 'conciliatory', position which will be reflected in the programme at least, if not in every detailed argument, of *Il *Conciliatore*. On this centre ground, Romanticism comes to represent a degree of openness to the demands of the present and a certain progressivism which in many respects corresponds, at least in Northern Italy, to a reiteration and continuation of the *Enlightenment values of *Il *Caffè* and the *Verri brothers. This does not mean that the term is emptied of intellectual and artistic force. As in France, Romanticism in Italy is particularly engaged in challenging the canon and the rules of literary composition which had been largely inherited from the late 16th c. Italian Romanticism, furthermore, develops original and productive reflections on the relation between literature and history, initially with the interventions of *Pellico and others on historical drama in the late 1810s, and then with the continuing debate in the following decade over the *historical novel. The key figure at all stages of this discussion is *Manzoni, who brings to it not only unusual intellectual rigour, but also the ability to turn theory into practice. Paradoxically, it is also Manzoni who most quickly proclaims the limitations of Italian Romanticism, assessing it as more 'negative' than 'positive' in his *Lettera sul romanticismo* (1823), and who negates his own practice of the historical novel in *Del romanzo storico* (first drafted in 1830).

The consensual nature of Italian Romanticism excluded the extremes of classicist xenophobia and Romantic fashionableness. But it also marginalized important European debates on the nature of modernity and its impact on reason and sensibility, and hence on the role and nature of literature, which Di Breme in particular sought to introduce with his reflections on the sentimental and the 'pathetic' in poetry. *Leopardi strenuously opposed his arguments in the *Discorso di un italiano intorno alla poesia romantica* (written in 1818 but left unpublished), but he was more attuned than any of his contemporaries to the vast territory opened up by the new sensibility, a territory which he explored in the *Zibaldone*—perhaps the most representative

Romanzo d'appendice

document of the age of Romanticism in Italy, if not of Italian Romanticism as a movement.   [MPC] See E. Bellorini (ed.), *Discussioni e polemiche sul romanticismo* (1943); C. Springer, *The Marble Wilderness: Ruins and Representation in Italian Romanticism, 1775–1850* (1987); E. Raimondi, *Romanticismo italiano e romanticismo europeo* (1997).

Romanzo d'appendice. The term is used, like the French *feuilleton*, of *novels published in instalments in newspapers (usually on the lower half of a page or in a separate section) or in magazines, and written to suit the demands both of the format and of a readership wanting heightened emotion and excitement. Its literary origins lie in 18th-c. English Gothic tales, but it was the simultaneous publication in *Milan and *Naples in 1845 of Eugène Sue's *Les Mystères de Paris* that launched the genre in Italy. The Milanese *Corriere della sera* came to dominate the field with the *translations from French that it began to publish in 1876. *Gramsci saw the *romanzo d'appendice* as a medium of education appealing to the popular imagination. More recently Umberto *Eco has emphasized its escapist functions.   [AHC]

Romanzo giallo, see DETECTIVE FICTION.

Romanzo rosa. Common term for popular romantic fiction [see DANDOLO, MILLY; LIALA; READING].

Rome has been capital of Italy only since 1871, a decade after *Unification [see also RISORGIMENTO]. Before that it was a provincial town that was also the seat of a universalizing religious institution, the Catholic *papacy, which was also its temporal ruler, and simultaneously the seat, notionally at least, also of the other universalizing institution of Western Europe, the Holy Roman Empire. This unique history has not only always made Rome a powerful multivalent symbol; it has also shaped both the physical configuration of the city and the role it has played in Italian culture.

As capital of the Roman Empire, and then for two centuries the hub of a new Christian empire, the city became a unique palimpsest of classical ruins and Christian (re)building, which regularly cannibalized existing structures. The juxtaposition and superimposition of the pagan with the Christian deeply affected subsequent perceptions of the historical and mythical past, inspiring writers to

reflect simultaneously on its meanings and their own cultural identity. The earliest instance in the vernacular that we know is a mid-13th-c. translation into Roman *dialect of the *Liber ystoriarum Romanorum* (itself is a compilation of the *Storie de Troia e de Roma*). From the same anonymous source came a Roman dialect version of the *Mirabilia urbis Romae*, a Christianized topographical description, which was to influence pilgrim guidebooks down to the 17th c. Imaginative interest in Rome's classical heritage took on an explicitly political significance in the *Cronica di anonimo romano* (written 1357–60 and now attributed to Bartolomeo di Iacovo di Valmontone), which centres on an eyewitness account of *Cola di Rienzo's attempt in 1347 to free Rome from papal control and refound the Roman republic.

Six years earlier *Petrarch had been crowned poet laureate on the Capitoline Hill and declared a citizen of Rome. The event symbolizes the city's central place in the Western literary imagination. But it also drew those who wished to recover and understand the material (as well as literary) monuments of antiquity. Once the papal *court finally returned in 1420 from *Avignon where it had been 'exiled' since 1305, there was a constant stream of immigrant scholars and artists which lasted well beyond Italian Unification. The most influential verbal and visual representations of the city are, for the most part, by non-Romans, from Leon Battista *Alberti and Flavio *Biondo to Carlo Emilio *Gadda and Pier Paolo *Pasolini.

The *humanists' belief that ancient Rome's greatness rested as much on her art and letters as on her military power lay behind the papacy's deployment of their eloquence to enhance its own image and thereby its authority. A linguistic counterpart to its claim to be the supreme judge of religious orthodoxy might be found in curial writers such as Pietro *Bembo and *Sadoleto, who declared *Cicero the sole model for *imitation by the writer aspiring to excellence in his prose. However, the humanist insistence on treating texts (including the *Bible) as sources to be philologically scrutinized rather than as authorities to be uncritically accepted, ensured the demise of papal humanism even before the devastating sack of the city in 1527 by unpaid soldiers from the army of Emperor Charles V. [See also ANTIQUARIANISM; SACK OF ROME.]

Vernacular literary production in the city during and after the *Counter-Reformation was more vigorous and varied than has traditionally been allowed, even if Rome was the artistic, not the literary, capital of Europe from about 1550 to 1650. The important precondition was the presence of numerous cardinals' courts vying with each other for prestige and overseen by what was effectively an elective monarchy, whose sovereign was invariably an old man in a hurry to consolidate his family's fortunes. Such a polycentred *patronage network was further enhanced by the fact that numerous religious orders had their headquarters in the city, several of which supported significant cultural institutions of international standing, such as the *Jesuit Collegio Romano and the Oratorian Vallicelliana library. By the close of the 17th c. Rome boasted over fifty *libraries, and 132 *academies had been founded there since 1600 (out of a total 870 for the peninsula as a whole). The Accademia dei *Lincei (1603) reflected the city's importance as a pre-eminent European centre for the collection and study of the natural (as well as the ancient) world, while the *Arcadian academy (1690) testified to the enduring power of *classical influences on Italian vernacular literature. The flourishing state of Rome's cultural life at this time was reflected in the publication of the first Italian learned *periodical, the *Giornale de' letterati* (1668–83).

During the following century, the papacy's diminishing political prestige, combined with the city's increasing popularity as classical playground for Northern European gentlemen on the Grand Tour [see TRAVELLERS IN ITALY], was reflected in the progressively more provincial and drily antiquarian nature of much Roman literary production. All the same, the quality of writings by the critic and art theorist Francesco *Milizia and the archaeologist Ennio Quirino Visconti (1751–1818), as well as those of Alessandro *Verri and Vincenzo *Monti, all active at the century's end, warns us against constructing any simplistic decline-and-fall narrative. That said, the restoration of the Papal States in 1815 (which had been occupied, on and off, by French troops since 1798) did not see a corresponding revival in Roman literary life. As a temporal ruler the Pope was dependent on French support down to 1870, and his weakness was reflected in a policy of vigorous *censorship which was only lifted briefly just before the Roman Republic of *1848–9. Significantly, the most impressive literary achievement of this period is to be found in G. G. *Belli's sardonic dialect *sonnets.

As capital of Italy since 1871, the city has undergone a physical, social, and cultural transformation unprecedented since the time of Augustus, the pace only beginning to slow down in the 1970s. *Mussolini made particularly drastic interventions in the centre, and founded a modern administrative and residential zone for the *Fascist Esposizione Universale Romana (EUR). Numerous attempts to make the city Italy's literary capital—*Sommaruga's journal *Cronaca bizantina* (1881–5) is an early example—have had limited success. If Rome has assumed a central place in national cultural production and representation, it has been as undisputed capital of the Italian *cinema industry and as subject of several cinematic masterpieces. Otherwise the city has continued to be significant either at a universal level or at a local one. With the possible exceptions of *D'Annunzio's *Il *piacere* (1889) and *Ungaretti's poetry of the 1920s and 1930s, the most effective and successful literature to come out of the city since Unification concerns itself very much with the specific city and in many cases with its language, as is instanced by the fiction of Gadda, Pasolini, and *Moravia. Certainly for much of the 20th c. *Florence and *Milan were at least as important as centres of literary culture.　　[SD]

See N. Purcell, 'The City of Rome', in R. Jenkyns (ed.), *The Legacy of Rome: A New Appraisal* (1992); C. Edwards, *Writing Rome: Textual Approaches to the City* (1996); C. Edwards (ed.), *Roman Presences* (1999).

RONCONI, LUCA, see THEATRE, 2.

Ronda, La (1919–23). *Roman literary monthly. Regular contributors included Vincenzo *Cardarelli, Emilio *Cecchi, Riccardo *Bacchelli, and Alberto *Savinio. The journal was founded as a consciously reactionary response to the avant-garde culture of *Futurism and La *Voce which had flourished immediately before *World War I. Though its programme was never fully carried through, it proposed classical perfection in place of experimentation, pointing to *Leopardi and *Manzoni as stylistic models and advocating detachment from political realities. Many of the writers who wrote for La *Ronda* later published collections of their elegant short prose-pieces. [See also PROSA D'ARTE; PROSE POEM.]　　[CFB]

ROSA, GIOVANNI BATTISTA, see TITTA ROSA, GIOVANNI.

ROSÀ, ROSA, see FUTURISM; WOMEN WRITERS, 2.

Rosa, Salvator

ROSA, SALVATOR (1615–73) was the foremost *satirical poet of his age, as well as a famous painter and an actor. His early years up to 1635 were spent in *Naples, where, like other members of his family, he devoted himself to painting. From 1635 to 1640 he showed his talents as a comic actor and as a satirical painter. On moving in 1640 to *Florence as court painter to Gian Carlo de' *Medici, he came face to face with the literary world of the Accademia della *Crusca, and began work on his seven *Satire* in *terza rima, after *Ariosto's example. *La musica* criticizes the pompous display of the music in *Urban VIII's *Rome, and condemns the mixture of sacred and profane elements in contemporary music. *La poesia* criticizes the roles of literary *academies and condemns the excesses of *Baroque style. *La pittura* argues the superiority of historical and religious paintings over paintings representing everyday life, at that time increasingly a speciality of the Flemish painters. *La guerra* rails against the submission of Italy's leaders to foreign invaders. *L'invidia* hits back at those who had dared to accuse Rosa of plagiarism. *La Babilonia* condemns *papal corruption. *Tirreno*, the last and seventh satire, composed in 1657–8 and redrafted in Rosa's final years, shows the author bitterly reviewing his failure as a poet and vowing to give up writing as a dangerous waste of time.

Though critical of contemporary art and poetry, Rosa is part of his age in his frequent weighty classical allusions, his lexical freedom, and his liking for ornate rhetorical structures. His poetry also shows here and there a directness and accuracy of expression that drives home the satiric point, often laconically. [PBD]

Satire, ed. Danilo Romei (1995). See U. Limentani, *La satira nel Seicento* (1961); J. Scott, *Salvator Rosa: His Life and Times* (1995).

ROSAI, OTTONE (1895–1957). *Florentine painter. After a *Futurist (1914–17) phase, he went on to still lifes, landscapes, and figures. A member of the *Selvaggio* group in 1926–9, he painted a memorable series of players of street and café games. In the 1950s he provided a series of haunting self-portraits. [DF]

ROSELLI, ROSELLO (1399–1451). Lawyer, priest, friend of the *Medici, and servant of Popes Martin V and Eugenius IV. He was an imitator of *Petrarch, whose *Canzoniere* he transcribed, adding fifty-seven *sonnets, twelve *ballate, and

four *canzoni of his own. He exchanged *tenzoni and other compositions with *Burchiello and wrote *Petrarchist love poems to commission. [GPTW]

ROSELLINI FANTASTICI, MASSIMINA (1789–1859) was born in *Florence, the daughter of the poetic *improviser Fortunata Fantastici Sulgher, and was herself encouraged by *Foscolo to write poetry. She eventually completed a substantial narrative poem, *Amerigo* (1843), but is remembered more for her collection of *Dialoghi e racconti pei fanciulli* (1851). [FD'I]

ROSEO, MAMBRINO (da Fabriano) (16th c.). Soldier, author of a narrative poem on the siege of *Florence (1530), and a prolific adapter and *translator of *romances, many from *Spanish originals belonging to the cycle of *Amadís de Gaula*, popular in the later 16th c. His translations also include serious works, in particular the *Institutione del prencipe cristiano* of A. Guevara. He is the author of a continuation of Suetonius' *Vitae*, and of Tarcagnota's history of the world. [JEE]

ROSI, FRANCESCO (1922–) began his film career as assistant to Luchino *Visconti on *La terra trema* in 1948, making the step to direction with *La sfida* ten years later. Although he has experimented with various genres, the heart of Rosi's work has always been the investigation film or political thriller. Beginning with *Salvatore Giuliano* (1962) and *Mani sulla città* (1963), he has shown a particular interest in the South of Italy and the Southern Question [see MEZZOGIORNO], as, for instance, in his 1979 *television adaptation of Carlo *Levi's *Cristo si è fermato a Eboli*. His lasting reputation, however, will remain based on films such as *Il caso Mattei* (1972), about the mysterious death of an oil millionaire, and *Cadaveri eccellenti* (1976), a story of corruption in the judicial system taken from Leonardo *Sciascia's novel *Il contesto*. [See also CINEMA.] [GN-S]

ROSINI, GIOVANNI (1776–1855). *Historical novelist, poet, dramatist, and art historian, who was professor of rhetoric at *Pisa for most of his career. His novels comprise *La monaca di Monza* (1829), *Luisa Strozzi* (1832–3), and *Il Conte Ugolino della Gherardesca e i Ghibellini di Pisa* (1843). [DO'G]

ROSMINI SERBATI, ANTONIO (1797–1855). Influential philosopher who made a major contribution to the diffusion and assimilation of

*German *idealism in Italy, and worked tirelessly to reconcile contemporary Catholicism and *liberalism. Born into an aristocratic family in Rovereto, he studied theology at *Padua. He then entered the Church, and quickly founded more than one reforming lay order. His subsequent relations with the Church authorities were troubled by his association with *Cavour and *Balbo, though he also went on to argue strongly against the secularism of the Italian state. His prolific writings range from philosophy, theology, and jurisprudence to pedagogy, anthropology, literature, and politics, and influenced all other moderate Catholic intellectuals, including *Manzoni, *Fogazzaro, and *Gioberti.   [FD'I]

ROSPIGLIOSI, GIULIO, see CLEMENT IX.

ROSSANDA, ROSSANA (1924–). Prominent *Communist intellectual, who was one of the founders of the newspaper *Il Manifesto* following her expulsion from the party in 1969. Her books on contemporary politics and society include *L'anno degli studenti* (1968), *Le altre* (1979), and *Un viaggio inutile o della politica come educazione sentimentale* (1981).   [REL]

ROSSELLI, AMELIA (1930–96). Perhaps the most important Italian woman poet of the 20th c. She was the daughter of an English mother and Carlo Rosselli, the prominent anti-*Fascist assassinated near Paris on *Mussolini's orders in 1937 [see also GIUSTIZIA E LIBERTÀ]. She was born in Paris and grew up in France, England, and the USA, studying literature, philosophy and, above all, music. She moved to Italy only after *World War II. Long a prey to various forms of depression, she eventually took her own life in her flat in *Rome.

Her first poems were in French and English, the English being published much later as *Sleep* (1992). Her poetry in Italian was written mostly in the 1960s and 1970s, beginning with *Variazioni belliche* (1964). Her work is thoroughly aware of the Italian tradition, but owes more to European *symbolism and *surrealism. The page becomes the place for lacerating self-confession, in an idiom which runs counter to normal word usage and syntax, and which, through stripping away all protective conventions, aims to voice primary drives and emotions, in particular, erotic desire and the fear of illness and death. But the spontaneous disorder that ensues is counterbalanced by rigid formal control, above all through metrical patterns modelled on those of modern music. The overall effect is of a densely *expressionistic poetry for which it is hard to find parallels in 20th-c. Italy.   [GM]

ROSSELLI, CARLO, see GIUSTIZIA E LIBERTÀ; ROSSELLI, AMELIA.

ROSSELLINI, ROBERTO (1906–77) was precipitated to worldwide fame by the unexpected success of his film *Roma città aperta* in 1945/6. Two more films about the *Resistance and the aftermath of war followed, *Paisà* (1946) and *Germania anno zero* (1947), firmly establishing him at the forefront of the *Neorealist movement. But a group of films with Ingrid Bergman (who became his wife) alienated public opinion in Italy—though *Viaggio in Italia* (1954) in particular was greatly admired in France, especially by the forerunners of the *nouvelle vague*. Rossellini reinvented himself in the late 1960s with a series of didactic films about history made for television, including *La prise de pouvoir par Louis XIV* (1966) and *L'età di Cosimo de' Medici* (1972). He returned to the large screen with a biography of the *Christian Democrat leader Alcide *De Gasperi, *Anno uno* (1974). [See also CINEMA.]   [GN-S]

ROSSETTI, DANTE GABRIEL (1828–82). Son of the exiled *carbonaro* and Dantist Gabriele *Rossetti (1783–1854), he published the first English translation of *Dante's *Vita nova* (with *Early Italian Poets*, 1861), and used the text as inspiration for paintings, which then enjoyed a vogue in Italy. He was the major pre-Raphaelite influence on the culture of Rome in the 1880s, for example on the artistic movement *In arte libertas* (1887), and on *D'Annunzio, who spread his influence by recreating Rossetti's heroines verbally, especially in *Il *piacere* and in his *Tribuna* articles.   [JRW]

ROSSETTI, GABRIELE (1783–1854). Born in Vasto but educated in *Naples, he became a *carbonaro* and was forced into *exile in 1821. He settled in London, where he taught Italian literature at King's College. The father of Dante Gabriel *Rossetti and his sister Christina, he was a poet in his own right, as well as a critic who interpreted the *Divine Comedy* as a secret sectarian *allegory.   [MPC]

ROSSI, ADRIANO DE' (mid-14th c.). *Florentine friend and colleague of Antonio *Pucci. He wrote a set of glosses on *Boccaccio's *Teseida*.   [SNB]

Rossi, Gian Vittorio

ROSSI, GIAN VITTORIO (pseud. Janus Nicius Erythraeus) (1577–1647). *Jesuit-educated Latinist and poet, member of the Accademia degli *Umoristi in the Barberini circle of *Roman *litterati*, and author of various works of biblical scholarship (*dialogues, *homiliae, exempla virtutum et vitiorum*). He also wrote portraits of contemporaries in the *Pinacotheca imaginum illustrium doctrinae vel ingenii virorum* (1643), and a long *satire on Roman society in the 1630s and 1640s, *Eudemia*, influenced by Barclay's *Argenis*. [PBert]

ROSSI, NICOLÒ (second half of 16th c.) lived in Vicenza and was a member of the Accademia Olimpica. He studied classical and Italian literature and showed an interest in poetics. His most important works are the *Discorsi intorno alla tragedia* (1590), in which he discusses Giangiorgio *Trissino's *tragedy *Sofonisba*, and the two treatises *Discorsi intorno alla comedia* (1589), centred on Giovan Battista Calderari's *Armida*. In both cases he reviews the standard *Aristotelian positions in the light of his own interpretations. [See also LITERARY THEORY, 2.] [PLR]

ROSSI, NICOLÒ DE' (1290–c.1350). Poet, originally from Treviso, who became professor of jurisprudence in *Bologna. He composed a *canzoniere* for a certain Floruça, which is preserved in two partially autograph manuscripts and contains some 400 *sonnets and a few *canzoni*, arranged in roughly chronological order. Though the narrative element is much less prominent and the variety of metrical forms much more limited, the collection clearly anticipates that of *Petrarch, and may have been one of its models. [NC]

ROSSI, ROBERTO (c.1355–1417). Born into an ancient *Florentine magnate family, he eschewed political involvement in favour of *humanist studies, learning Greek from *Chrysoloras and himself teaching members of the Florentine elite, including Cosimo de' *Medici and the *chronicler Domenico Buoninsegni. He is chiefly noted as a *translator of Greek authors into Latin. [RDB]

ROSSI, VITTORIO, see HISTORIES OF ITALIAN LITERATURE.

ROSSI-DORIA, MANLIO (1905–88). Leading authority on agrarian problems of the *Mezzogiorno*. Imprisoned under *Fascism, he fought in

the *Resistance after 1943. From 1948 he taught agrarian policy and economics at the University of *Naples (Portici). Particularly important are his *Riforma agraria e politica meridionalista* (1948) and *Scritti sul Mezzogiorno* (1982). [JD]

ROSSINI, GIOACCHINO (1792–1868). The most internationally successful and influential composer of *opera in the earlier 19th c. By the time he was 21 he was already famous for five one-act farces and the full-length *Tancredi* and *L'italiana in Algeri*, all composed for *Venice. His mature comedies, *Il barbiere di Siviglia* (1816) and *La Cenerentola* (1817), are the most perfect specimens of purely Italian *opera buffa*, while the heroic operas of 1815–23, composed mostly for *Naples, introduced new *Romantic themes (*Otello* after *Shakespeare, *La donna del lago* after Scott) and established a format for Italian opera that was exemplary until the 1850s. His last operas were written for Paris, where *Guillaume Tell* (1829) powerfully influenced grand opera. [DRBK]

ROSSO DI SAN SECONDO, PIER MARIA (1887–1956), from Caltanissetta in *Sicily, wrote over thirty plays in addition to short stories and one novel, *La fuga*. His works explore contrasts—between passion and reason, the overpowering heat of the south and the cool lucidity of the north, personal freedom and social convention. His *theatrical form is based as much on the sensuous expression of atmospheric detail as on the communicative quality of words. A younger contemporary of *Pirandello, by whom he was both supported and overshadowed, and influenced by Ibsen, Maeterlinck, and Wedekind, he is now recognized as an Italian *expressionist. An early play, *Marionette che passione!* ... (1918), dramatized the different stages of passion through three characters, the 'puppets' of the title, and was an important contribution to the *teatro *grottesco*. Some of his later plays, often set in Sicily, including the impressive *La bella addormentata* (1919), have the quality of fable in their colourful presentation, but are also fierce indictments of a grasping, materialistic society. [JAL]

'Rosso Malpelo', see VERGA, GIOVANNI.

ROTA, BERARDINO (1508–75). *Humanist and poet, born into a privileged *Neapolitan family, who made an important contribution to *Petrarchism in Naples. His poems include *piscatorial eclogues (1560), which are much indebted to *Sannazaro, and a collection of *sonnets—celebrated at the time—written on the death of his wife in 1559. He also wrote Latin elegies and epigrams.   [ABu]

ROVANI, GIUSEPPE (1818–74). *Milanese novelist and *journalist. He was an active republican, exiled in Switzerland with *Mazzini and *Cattaneo after the revolution of *1848, but was eventually driven by debts to agree to write the official account of the visit of the Emperor Franz Joseph in 1857. By that stage he was closely associated with the *Scapigliati, Carlo *Dossi in particular, and a prey to the alcoholism that would eventually kill him.

His *historical novels, which begin with Lamberto Malatesta (1843), replace *Romantic idealism with scepticism, and focus on the glamour and squalor of bohemian existence rather in the manner of *operatic *realism. His major work, Cento anni, which appeared first in serial form in 1857–8, attempts to reproduce the successes of Balzac and Dumas. Basically the memoirs of a thief turned banker, it tells in a somewhat episodic manner the history of a family over five generations. Rovani had always been interested in the relations between the arts, and in the essays gathered in Le tre arti (1874) he theorized his ideas on synaesthesia. These are already discernible in Cento anni and become more evident in his late novels, from La Libia d'oro (1868) onwards.   [DO'G]

ROVATTI, PIER ALDO, see AUT-AUT; PENSIERO DEBOLE, IL.

ROVERSI, ROBERTO (1923–). Poet and owner of the Palmaverde antiquarian bookshop in *Bologna. He was one of the founders of *Officina, and then of Rendiconti (1961), and has generally refused to allow his work to be appropriated by the *publishing and cultural industries. His poetry is best represented by Dopo Campoformio (1962), the title of which refers to the treaty abolishing *Venetian independence in 1793. A sense of a historic political defeat pervades all his mature writing, in which anger, despair, bitterness, and sheer bloody-mindedness all play a part. He has also written novels, short stories, and plays.   [MPC]

ROVETTA, GEROLAMO (1851–1910). Novelist and playwright. Born in Brescia, he lived and worked principally in *Milan. His early commercially successful novels, Mater Dolorosa (1882),

Le lacrime del prossimo (1888), and La baraonda (1894), portray a world of unfettered capitalism and corrupt speculation in which a decadent aristocracy has given way to a class of parvenus. Regarded by contemporaries as amoral and pessimistic, Rovetta's fiction is also a denunciation of the betrayal of *Risorgimento ideals. It is true, however, that he perceives no possibility of redemption, and denies the proletariat any power of resistance.

Although unarguably powerful, his novels are psychologically weak and stylistically careless. He is best remembered for his *verista *theatre. After some sparkling *comedies and traditional melodramas, he came to maturity with the Trilogia di Dorina (1891), in which a victimized woman defeats society with its own venal weapons. Subsequently, Marco Spada (1892), La realtà (1893), I disonesti (1894), and Papà Eccellenza (1903) depict a society in which compromise always wins out over duty. He also wrote historical dramas; his most successful play, Romanticismo (1901), portrays Italian resistance to *Austrian rule and contains some celebrated, if grandiloquent, patriotic speeches.   [PBarn]

Rozzi, Congrega dei, see CONGREGA DEI ROZZI.

RUBBI, ANDREA (1738–1807). *Venetian literary *journalist. A former *Jesuit, in reaction to the prevailing gallomania he systematically championed Italian literature by editing twelve volumes of Elogi italiani, a vast poetic compendium, Il Parnasso italiano (46 vols., 1784–91), and an anthology of work by 160 living poets, Il giornale poetico (1789–92).   [JMAL]

Rubé, see BORGESE, GIUSEPPE ANTONIO.

RUCELLAI, BERNARDO (1448–1514). Public servant and *humanist, prominent in *Florentine life before and after the death of Lorenzo de' *Medici, whose sister he married. He wrote erudite works in Latin, including the first *history of Italy, De bello italico, to cover the years 1494–9. In 1502–5 his gardens (the Orti Oricellari) became a meeting place for writers and thinkers. [See also ACADEMIES.]   [JCB]

RUCELLAI, GIOVANNI (1403–81). *Florentine *merchant and *banker, related by marriage to the *Strozzi family and to Cosimo and Lorenzo de' *Medici, and a *patron of artists and architects. He wrote a Zibaldone quaresimale, a commonplace book of family history, moral reflection, and

Rudesindo Salvado

excerpts from *chroniclers, which is a valuable source of information about contemporary Florence. [FWK]

RUDESINDO SALVADO, see ITALIAN WRITERS IN AUSTRALIA.

RUFFINI, GIOVANNI (1807–81). *Genoese republican, who was condemned as a *carbonaro and *Mazzinian in 1833, and lived most of the rest of his life in London and Paris. He wrote the *libretti for *Donizetti's *Don Sebastiano* (1842) and *Don Pasquale* (1847) and novels and stories in English about *Risorgimento Italy, enjoying success with both the autobiographical *Lorenzo Benoni* (1853) and the historically informative *Don Antonio* (1855). [DO'G]

RUGGIA, GIROLAMO, see ITALIAN WRITERS IN SWITZERLAND.

RUGGIERI APUGLIESE (mid-13th c.). Professional *giullare, probably a *Sienese, whose five surviving poems may well preserve features of oral performance. His joking *sirventese 'Tant'aggio ardire e canoscenza' parades all the trades he knows (carpentry, brothel-keeping, law, astrology, etc.), and the vast range of topics he can write poems about. [JU]

Ruggiero. Protagonist, along with *Orlando, of *Ariosto's *Orlando furioso, and supposed progenitor of the House of *Este.

RUOTI, MARIA CLEMENTE, see NUNS.

RUSCELLI, GIROLAMO (*c*.1504–66), of Viterbo, first sought a career in *Rome, *Naples, and elsewhere, but in 1549 moved permanently to *Venice, where he became one of the leading editors and writers for the *printing industry. The Italian works he edited include *Boccaccio's *Decameron* (1552), *Petrarch's verse (1554), *Ariosto's *Orlando furioso* (1556), and *anthologies of verse, letters, and *comedies. Professional rivalry provoked a polemic with Ludovico *Dolce. Ruscelli's interests in correct writing are seen in his *Del modo di comporre in versi* (1559) and his *Commentarii della lingua italiana* (1581). Other original works include a treatise on the *emblem, *Le imprese illustri* (1566). [BR]

RUSCONI, CARLO, see SHAKESPEARE.

RUSSO, FERDINANDO (1868–1927). *Neapolitan *dialect poet. Unlike his contemporary Salvatore *Di Giacomo, in collections such as *Sunettiate* (1887), *Gente 'e malavita* (1897), and the narrative poem *O cantastorie* (1895), he voices popular discontent with Italy after *Unification, as well as denouncing conditions in his native city. He also wrote novels and plays. [PBarn]

RUSSO, LUIGI, see BELFAGOR; LITERARY CRITICISM.

RUSSOLO, LUIGI (1885–1947). One of the first painters to join *Futurism. While some of his works evoke moods and memories, his modern urban works suggest speed or the energy of crowds through thrusting abstract shapes. He was also a theorist of Futurist music. His manifesto *L'arte dei rumori* (1913) and the performances of his 'intonarumori' anticipated *musique concrète*. [SV]

Rusticale, Letteratura or Poesia, see CARCANO, GIULIO; CORRENTI, CESARE; PERCOTO, CATERINA.

RUSTICHELLO DA PISA, see ARTHURIAN LITERATURE; MIDDLE AGES; POLO, MARCO.

RUSTICI, CENCIO DE' (1380/90–1445). *Roman *humanist, whose literary activities primarily involved *translations from the Greek. He was with Poggio *Bracciolini in the monastery of San Gallo when the latter made his discoveries of ancient texts. He participated in the debate on the language spoken in ancient Rome, defending Leonardo *Bruni's thesis, that the vernacular had always existed alongside Latin, against Flavio *Biondo's view that it had developed from it. [LB]

RUSTICO FILIPPI (or Rustico di Filippo) (*c*.1235–before 1300). Little is known about his life, except that he was a *Florentine and a Ghibelline [see GUELFS AND GHIBELLINES]. He is mentioned in *Francesco da Barberino's *Documenti d'amore* and by Brunetto *Latini, though never by his contemporary *Dante. His fifty-eight surviving *sonnets fall into two roughly equal groups: one consists of conventional love poetry in serious vein, the other of the earliest recorded examples of *poesia giocosa. Rustico specializes in grotesquely comic portraits of individuals, whom he derides with often astonishing linguistic virtuosity. [SNB]

RUZANTE (Angelo Beolco) (c.1496–1542), a *Paduan actor-director-playwright, was one of the most vigorous *theatrical talents of the Italian *Renaissance. The illegitimate son of a wealthy mercantile family, he rose to prominence in the 1520s, supported by the polymath Alvise *Corner. He entertained Corner's circle, projecting his *patron's image as enlightened Maecenas. Between 1520 and 1526 he played at venues in *Venice, during *Carnival, accompanied by one of the first troupes of semi-professional actors. He enjoyed the patronage of the *Este court in *Ferrara (c.1528–32), where he collaborated with *Ariosto.

Beolco's fourteen surviving plays reveal a practitioner's feel for staging, timing, and character, exemplified in the evolving figure of the *peasant-clown 'Ruzante', with whom he became synonymous in the public mind. He was consistently controversial, treading a fine line between enter-tainment and provocation, which appealed to his patrician audiences. Challenging the linguistic hegemony of Tuscan, he championed the rustic *dialect of Padua, employed expressionistically or realistically alongside Tuscan, Venetian, and the dialect of Bergamo in early examples of *polyglot theatre. He polemicized against high culture, sometimes obscenely, in favour of peasant naturalness. Experimenting insistently, he spanned elite and popular genres, from patter monologues to five-act adaptations of Roman *comedy, and prefigured the *commedia dell'arte, particularly in L'Anconitana (c.1534–5). His stagecraft and socio-psychological exploration are most telling in La Moscheta (c.1528–32), a black comedy of sexual manipulation, in Bilora (c.1530), a sombre drama of peasant/city conflict, and in the anti-war one-act play Parlamento de Ruzante (c.1530). [RGF]

See L. Zorzi, Ruzante: Teatro (1967).

S

SABA, UMBERTO (pseud. of Umberto Poli) (1883–1957). One of the most important 20th-c. Italian poets, distinguished from contemporaries such as *Montale and *Ungaretti by his anti-*hermetic and overtly *autobiographical stance. He was born in *Trieste, then under *Austro-Hungarian rule, to an Italian father and a *Jewish mother abandoned by her husband before he was born, and in infancy felt closest to his Slovene Catholic nurse, separation from whom proved immensely painful. His relationships with his parents and nurse, his love for his wife Lina and daughter Linuccia, and his affection for Trieste, with its mixture of Italian and German cultures, are recurrent themes in his work.

He spent much of his life in Trieste, returning frequently even when he lived in other cities. Before *World War I he did military service in Southern Italy, and spent periods in *Florence, *Bologna, and *Milan. In Florence he published his first collection, *Poesie*, in 1910, using his pseudonym for the first time, and got to know some of the contributors to La *Voce. From 1917 he ran an antiquarian bookshop in Trieste, becoming a major presence in Triestine culture and a friend in particular of Virgilio *Giotti and Giacomo *Debenedetti, though he maintained contacts with Florence, especially with the writers of the *Solaria group, an issue of the review being dedicated to his work in 1928. On the fall of *Mussolini in 1943, he fled Nazi persecution, first to Florence and then to Lugano. For the ten years following *World War II his base was Milan.

He first collected his poems together as *Il canzoniere* in 1919. Though he continued to publish separate collections, he gradually built it up until, in its definitive 1961 edition, the *Canzoniere* represents over fifty years of literary activity. From the 1947 version onwards he included a third-person self-commentary, *Storia e cronistoria del Canzoniere*, intended to remedy what he perceived

as critical neglect of his work. In many ways the project is primarily *autobiographical, an attempt to exorcize neuroses engendered by his childhood experiences, which assumes an unmistakably Freudian character after *psychoanalysis in 1929–30, the clearest demonstration of this being *Il piccolo Berto* of 1929–31. But Saba is unusual amongst modern authors in finding partial resolution for inner conflicts in immersion in the organic unity of life and in erotic delight in its beauties.

Part of the pleasure and the resolution is contemplation of the everyday existence of ordinary men and women. Saba addresses general human sympathies with both intimacy and reserve. Instrumental in this respect is his markedly traditional poetic language and the formality of his metres, rhymes, and his preference for strict forms such as the *sonnet. Poetically his roots are in the tradition of *Parini, *Foscolo, *Leopardi (and Heine), the *libretto and the poetry of *verismo, rather than in *symbolism. He dismissed hermetic poems as crossword puzzles, though he was influenced by Montale and 'pure' lyricism in *Parole* of 1933–4 and *Ultime cose* of 1935–43.

His prose works complement his poetry. *Scorciatoie e raccontini* (1946) consists mostly of penetrating Nietzschean aphorisms (the 'short cuts' of the title) about life. *Ernesto*, left unfinished in 1953 and published posthumously, is an autobiographical memoir in the form of a story about a boy's first experiences of sexual love. The protagonist is endowed with the innocent sensuality and love of life which, despite the evident hurt, contribute greatly to the strength and appeal of Saba's poetry.

[SPC]

Tutte le poesie, ed. A. Stara (1988). See J. Cary, *Three Modern Italian Poets: Saba, Ungaretti, Montale* (1969); L. Polato, *L'aureo anello* (1994).

SABELLICO, MARCANTONIO COCCI (c.1436–1506). *Historian and *humanist, who lived in *Rome where he was a pupil of Pomponio *Leto and Domizio *Calderini. Later he moved to Udine as a teacher of rhetoric and settled at last in *Venice. The works that won him fame are the *Rerum venetarum ab urbe condita libri XXXIII*, a history of Venice, and the *Enneades sive Rapsodiae historiarum*, a world history which starts from the most remote times and ends in 1504. Sabellico's history is humanistic, modelled on Livy and following Flavio *Biondo, by whom he was deeply influenced. But his selection and use of sources lacked critical rigour. [CG]

SACCHETTI, FRANCO (?1330–1400). Writer of *novelle* and poet. He was born into an old *Florentine *Guelf family, possibly in Ragusa (Dalmatia). He became a *merchant, and then after 1363 turned to politics, undertaking numerous diplomatic missions on behalf of the Florentine state. He was also *podestà and *papal representative in various cities in *Tuscany and Romagna. He died at San Miniato, probably of the *plague.

His literary career proceeds in tandem with his busy public life and is partly a commentary on it. His first work is an encomiastic poem in *ottava rima, La battaglia delle belle donne di Firenze con le vecchie* (1354). This mixes popular and literary features; its metre is that of the marketplace improvisers, but the models are *Boccaccio's early *Caccia di Diana*, which paid homage to the belles of the *Neapolitan *court, and *Dante's (lost) *sirventese on the sixty most beautiful ladies in Florence mentioned in the *Vita nova* (6). Sacchetti began collecting his *lyric poems around the same time, eventually producing a *Libro delle rime*, which contains more than 300 poems covering a variety of topics and written in a variety of metres. It is a kind of poetic diary, in which Sacchetti notes, usually in chronological order, reflections and musings linked to his daily life. The earlier poems are on love or political themes or are comic in character, whilst those of his mature years are more moralistic and religious. [See also ARS NOVA.]

Sacchetti is best known as a writer of *novelle*. His narrative abilities are already evident in the *Sposizioni di vangeli* (c.1381), a lay equivalent of the kind of *sermon-writing practised by contemporary preachers. It is modelled on sermons for Lent. Its forty-nine chapters are each divided into three parts: the *quaestio*, proposing the theme to be treated, the *exemplum* developing the narrative proper, and the *absolutio* which states the moral to be drawn. The *Trecentonovelle*, Sacchetti's master-

piece of *novella* writing, has something of the same stamp. It was planned as early as 1385, but the stories were written and gathered together between 1392 and 1397. The title presupposes the inevitable comparison with the 100 stories of the *Decameron*, with which it does not aim to compete stylistically, but which it assumes can be supplemented and updated in terms of narrative material. The *Proemio* announces that the collection includes not just traditional *novelle*, but accounts of events which the author witnessed or which happened to him personally. Although there is no frame, the presence of the author as narrator, or on occasion as a character, gives the work its narrative unity. The action of memory links the stories together and a sturdy moral approach extracts practical lessons from them. The result is a full, lively depiction of Florence as it was at the end of the 14th c. The *Trecentonovelle* has survived only in a 16th-c. transcription, containing 222 out of the original 300 *novelle*. [MP]

Il Trecentonovelle, ed. E. Faccioli (1970); *Il libro delle rime*, ed. F. Brambilla Ageno (1990).

SACCHETTI, ROBERTO (1847–81). *Piedmontese *journalist, lawyer, and novelist, who wrote for *Rivista minima*, *Il Pungolo*, and the *Gazzetta piemontese*. He published two novels, the autobiographical *Cesare Mariani* (1876) and *Entusiasmi* (1881) set in *1848 *Milan. He became close to the Milanese *Scapigliatura and completed Emilio *Praga's *Le memorie del presbiterio* after Praga's death. [AHC]

SACCHI, ANTONIO, see COMMEDIA DELL'ARTE; GOZZI, CARLO.

SACCHI, BARTOLOMEO, see PLATINA, IL.

Sack of Rome. The events leading up to the Sack of *Rome in 1527 are complex. Contributing factors were the antagonism in the city towards Pope Clement VII, the activities of the *Colonna faction, the contest between the Emperor and the *papacy, and the breakdown of the League of Cognac of 1526. The result was that the Constable of Bourbon led an imperial army to Rome with the intention of ransoming the city. He was, however, unable to control his German and Spanish troops, who engaged in a savage sack. The Pope saved himself by taking refuge in Castel Sant'Angelo, though his eventual ransom brought him to the point of bankruptcy.

Sacra rappresentazione

The Sack had a devastating effect on the business, social, and cultural life of Rome. It led to disease and famine, the despoiling of palaces and of the cultural patrimony of the city, and to the loss of many of its artists and intellectuals, who fled to safer havens. Contemporary accounts are furnished by *Castiglione, *Guicciardini, Marin *Sanudo the Younger, Benvenuto *Cellini, Pietro Corsi, Iacopo *Sadoleto, Pierio *Valeriano, Pietro Alcionio, and Pietro *Aretino in *Sei giornate. [PLR]

Sacra rappresentazione. *Theatre form popular in 15th-c. *Tuscany and central Italy, based on biblical stories and Christian legends. A development of the dramatized *laudi, the plays were staged by confraternities and were intended to educate participants, often children, and audience alike. The *sacra rappresentazione* follows a pattern: an angel announces the play, addressing the public directly; the story is then acted out, and the moral drawn at the end by the angel or another character. The self-consciousness evident in the frame is sometimes emphasized by audience participation: at the end of the *Rappresentazione di *Santa Uliva,* stage directions indicate that the banquet can include the audience; while the opening to the *Rappresentazione di Abramo e Agar* includes a hunchback master of ceremonies who guides two boys to their seats, who in turn will see their stories acted out in the biblical tale of Isaac and Ishmael. The plays are in verse, both spoken and sung, mostly in *ottava rima* but sometimes employing other forms, in particular that of the *laudi,* at a celebratory point towards the end. The scenery is symbolic and the representation of time linear but not naturalistic, while the characters are often given recognizable contemporary characteristics. The texts can be presented with the minimum of scenery; however, it is known that a number included the elaborate stage machinery that was developed during the 15th c.

Though mainly anonymous, a number of the *sacre rappresentazioni* can be attributed to specific writers, predominantly in Tuscany. Feo *Belcari's *Abraam* is an early example and the best known of his eight texts; Castellano *Castellani's *Figliuol prodigo,* one of seven by the author, shows sophistication both in its adaptation of the parable and in its use of the octave. Two of the Pulci family contributed to the genre, Antonia *Pulci with five and Bernardo *Pulci with one, while the most famous example of the genre is Lorenzo de' *Medici's *Rappresentazione di San Giovanni e Paolo.* A form of popular theatre, the *sacra rappresentazione* did not

disappear with the coming of the *commedia erudita* [see COMEDY], largely because the latter, presented in *courts and patrician houses, served a different audience. Continuous reprinting testifies to its popularity, mainly in *Florence but as far afield as Palermo and *Venice. [JAL]
Sacre rappresentazioni del Quattrocento, ed. L. Banfi (1968); *Nuovo corpus di sacre rappresentazioni fiorentine del Quattrocento,* ed. N. Newbigin (1983). See A. D'Ancona, *Origini del teatro italiano* (1891).

SADOLETO, IACOPO (1477–1547). Ecclesiastic and *humanist. He studied in *Ferrara, then moved to *Rome to develop his knowledge of Greek, also applying himself to the study of ethics and theology. He made a rapid and successful career in the Church; a papal secretary, he was appointed Bishop of Carpentras and later cardinal. He wrote poems and short works in elegant Ciceronian prose (notably the *De Laocoontis statua*), which made him, along with his friend Pietro *Bembo, the leading exponent of *Ciceronianism in his time. He also composed treatises on theological, philosophical, and *educational topics, the most notable of which are the *Phaedrus de liberis recte instituendis* and the *De laudibus philosophiae.* A deeply religious man, he was a prominent figure in the *Counter-Reformation and a proponent of reform in the Church. [CG]

SAGREDO, GIOVANNI (1617–82). *Venetian writer and politician who served as ambassador in Paris, London, and Vienna, from each of which he sent perceptive reports. He published only the first volume of his *history, *Memorie istoriche de' monarchi ottomani* (1673), but completed *L'Arcadia in Brenta* (1667). This recounts the journey down the river Brenta of a group of ladies and gentlemen, who spend their time playing games and indulging in pleasant conversation. About forty short *novelle* are recounted in the course of the journey, deriving from literary and popular precedents, *biographies of artists, and *humanist collections of *facezie and witticisms. [MC]

SAIBANTE, BIANCA LAURA (1723–97) founded the Accademia degli Agiati, with her husband Giuseppe Valeriano *Vannetti, in her native Rovereto. She made her house an important meeting-point of Italian and *German cultures. She herself wrote verse and studied the sciences and philosophy. [CCa]

SAINT-PONT, VALENTINE DE, see
WOMEN WRITERS, 3.

Saints, see HAGIOGRAPHY.

SALFI, FRANCESCO SAVERIO (1759–
1832). Born in Cosenza, he became a priest,
freemason, teacher, and *Jacobin in *Naples.
Exiled after 1794, he lived mostly in *Milan where
he composed *Alfierian *tragedies, and a pantomime satirizing the Church, *Il general Colli in Roma*
(1797). He subsequently moved to Paris, and
published studies (in French) on Italian literary
history.   [DO'G]

SALGARI, EMILIO (1862–1911). Leading
Italian travel and adventure novelist for the young.
Born in Verona, he was briefly a merchant navy
cadet before turning to writing while living mainly
in Verona and *Turin. His early serialized novels of
1883–4, including a version of *Le tigri di Mom-
pracem* (published in book form only in 1900),
already went against the current of European *colonialist literature, with black heroes, strong women,
and a sympathy for all underdogs.

These early novels were intended for adults, but
from 1891 Salgari conscientiously attuned his writing to young readers, embracing all the adventurous archetypes and inventing splendid pirate
heroes in the figures of Sandokan, a dispossesed
sultan in 19th-c. Borneo, and the Corsaro Nero,
who sails the 17th-c. Caribbean. He also created
exuberant descriptions of every topography from
the tropics to the polar regions. Italian children's
literature had previously been constrained by the
national focus of the *Risorgimento, and Salgari
had quite exceptional sales for the time. He edited a
children's newspaper, wrote hundreds of stories
and articles and nearly eighty novels, and was
widely imitated. His reputation has suffered from
his being taken up by *Fascist propaganda and he
still awaits due critical recognition. [See also CHIL-
DREN'S LITERATURE.]   [ALL]

SALIMBENE DA PARMA (Salimbene de
Adam) (1221–*c.*1288). *Chronicler. He was a
member of the Order of the Friars Minor who
travelled widely in Italy and France. His *Chronicon
Parmense*, covering the years 1167–1287 in Parma,
takes into account the Italian and European contexts. It is a lively and anecdotal work, written in a
Latin strongly influenced by vernacular usage.
                                                        [CEH]

SALIMBENI, ANGELO MICHELE (d.1517)
was a notary from *Bologna, and an active member
of the city's literary circles. Some poems, mainly
*sonnets and eclogues [see PASTORAL], have sur-
vived, alongside a quantity of letters; but he is best
known for his epithalamium on the marriage of
Annibale II Bentivoglio.   [ELM]

SALINARI, CARLO, see CONTEMPORANEO, IL;
DECADENTISMO; LITERARY CRITICISM.

SALTARELLI, LAPO (late 13th–early 14th c.).
*Florentine lawyer who as White *Guelf *priore*
opposed *Boniface VIII, but then joined the Blacks
[see BLACKS AND WHITES]. *Dante cites him as an
example of contemporary corruption (*Para.*
15.128). Four *sonnets by him survive.   [JU]

SALUSTRI, CARLO ALBERTO, see
TRILUSSA.

SALUTATI, COLUCCIO (1331–1406) was
the key figure in the transition from *Petrarchan to
15th-c. *humanism. Like *Petrarch, he was a major
exponent of Latin *letter writing, particularly after
his discovery of *Cicero's *Epistulae ad familiares*
(1392); but unlike his mentor, he embraced public
office, ending up as Chancellor of *Florence
(1375–1406), and championing the republican
ideology and the mixture of scholarship with the
active life that became the basis of so-called 'civic'
humanism.

His *De laboribus Herculis* (*c.*1390) continued the
humanist tradition of defences of poetry inaugurated
by Petrarch and *Boccaccio, drawing heavily on a
long-standing practice of *allegorical interpretation; but it was in his public and private Latin letters
that Salutati emerged as a stylist of some note in the
late 14th c.: it was famously said that in the war
against *Milan his eloquence was more powerful
than Giangaleazzo *Visconti's army. However, by
the mid-15th c. his Latin, according to Flavio
*Biondo, already seemed too harsh. His other
major achievement was his invitation (1397) to
Manuel *Chrysoloras to give lessons in ancient
*Greek in Florence, a formative experience for
younger humanists such as Leonardo *Bruni. Very
much an intermediary figure, Salutati wrote nothing in the vernacular, but he did defend *Dante,
Petrarch, and Boccaccio against the attacks of
the humanist avant-garde of Bruni and Poggio
*Bracciolini. [See also LATIN PROSE IN ITALY;
LITERARY THEORY, 2.]   [MMcL]

SALUZZO ROERO, DIODATA (1775–1840). A *Piedmontese noblewoman brought up on *Dante and Torquato *Tasso, she won unanimous admiration among her male contemporaries for her varied but distinctive *Poesie* (1796), which often anticipate *Romanticism in their heartfelt personal quality. The ode 'Le rovine' was held up by *Di Breme (1816) as a model of *lyric poetry. She also wrote *tragedies (*Erminia, Tullia*), *comedies, and *novelle*. Her would-be *magnum opus*, however, was a novel in *terza rima*, *Ippazia, ovvero delle filosofie* (1827), set in 5th-c. Egypt and interspersed with lyrical and doctrinal passages.   [JMAL]

SALVADORI, GIULIO (1862–1928). Poet and literary academic, originally from Arezzo, though he taught in *Rome and *Milan. After publishing a first collection of verse, *Minime* (1882), he became an enthusiastic convert to Catholicism in his mid-20s. The subsequent *Canzoniere civile* (1889) and *Ricordi dell'umile Italia* (1918) are strongly religious in theme and inspiration.   [CFB]

SALVATORELLI, LUIGI (1886–1974). Anti-*Fascist historian and journalist. In 1921 he left his his post at *Naples University to become editor of *La Stampa*, returning to academic work in 1925 but coming back to *journalism after *World War II. His *Nazionalfascismo* (1923) interpreted Fascism as a reactionary phenomenon that reflected the confused hopes of petty bourgeois social groups.   [RAbs]

SALVEMINI, GAETANO (1873–1957). *Historian and one of the most authoritative, upright, and independent of Italy's political writers. As a *Socialist in the late 1890s, he was as much influenced by Carlo *Cattaneo as by Karl *Marx. He was himself from Molfetta near Bari, and saw the vital importance of the *Mezzogiorno*, denouncing violence and malpractice by *Giolitti's candidates in the South. Leaving the Socialist Party in 1911, he worked briefly for *La *Voce*, and founded the weekly *L'Unità* (1911–20), in which he argued against the invasion of Libya and for intervention in *World War I. He was elected to parliament in 1919. He was a leading anti-*Fascist, and went into *exile in 1925. From London, Paris, and Harvard he campaigned ceaselessly against *Mussolini's regime and wrote influential analyses of it. He returned to Italy in 1947 as professor of modern history at *Florence University.   [JD]

SALVI, ANTONIO (1664–1724). *Medici *court physician-cum-*librettist until 1715, and thereafter active in the *Venetian *theatre. Some of his twenty-five works, such as *Arminio, Il Gran Tamerlano*, and *Scanderberg* (1703–18) are on 'exotic' subjects. Others derive from Corneille and Racine, such as *Amore e maestà* (1715) and *Astianatte* (1718), which were two of six adapted for staging in London (in 1721 and 1727 respectively) in settings by Handel. In Italy his works were set by leading composers such as Alessandro Scarlatti, Vivaldi, and Galuppi.   [JMAL]

SALVIATI, LIONARDO (1539–89), through his scholarship and his role in establishing the Accademia della *Crusca, helped to reassert the influence of *Florence over the development of Italian. He claimed as early as 1564 in his *Orazione in lode della fiorentina favella* that Florentine was superior to the classical languages in 'sweetness' and achievement. His linguistic ideas are most fully expressed in *Degli avvertimenti della lingua sopra 'l Decamerone* (1584–6), which arose from his 1582 expurgated edition of Boccaccio's *Decameron*.

Salviati, like Pietro *Bembo, favoured imitation of 14th-c. authors, blaming the 15th-c. decline of the language on excessive Latin influence [see QUESTIONE DELLA LINGUA; PURISM]. Unlike Bembo, he included non-literary works in his canon and, influenced by *Varchi, he stressed the underlying identity of 14th-c. and contemporary spoken Florentine. As an editor, Salviati used his outstanding knowledge of Florentine texts to preserve genuine readings, but did not hesitate to modernize spelling, unlike his lifelong enemy *Corbinelli. Salviati wrote two *comedies on classical Roman models, *Il granchio* in verse (1566) and *La spina* in prose (published in 1592). He moved to a university post in *Ferrara in 1587, but in 1588 illness forced him to return to Florence.   [BR]

SALVINI, ANTON MARIA (1653–1729). As professor of Greek in *Florence, he was a prolific but inaccurate translator from ancient Greek, but also turned his hand to French (Boileau) and English (Addison). He became a leading authority on the Italian language, and was wedded to 14th-c. literary usage [see HISTORY OF THE ITALIAN LANGUAGE; QUESTIONE DELLA LINGUA].   [JMAL]

SAMIGLI, E., see SVEVO, ITALO.

SANESI, ROBERTO (1930–2001), poet, translator and critic, with a special interest in British and American poetry, particularly that of T. S. Eliot, all of whose works he translated into Italian. [DR]

Sanfedismo, see NAPLES, 2.

SANGUINACCI, IACOPO (mid-15th c.). *Paduan poet and *improviser of verses who lived in *Ferrara at the court of Lionello d'*Este, where he was known and esteemed by *Guarino da Verona. Poems by him are to be found in several codices; of note is a *canzone* on the joys and pains of love, dedicated to Lionello d'Este. [CG]

SANGUINETI, EDOARDO (1930–). Known principally as the foremost theorist and creative artist of the *Neoavanguardia*, Sanguineti was born in *Genoa, and is professor of Italian literature at the *university there. He is a poet, novelist, and *journalist, but also a dramatist (with Stefano Roncoroni), *librettist (for Luciano Berio), and parliamentarian (1979–83).

Already in his early work he constructed a counter-ideology to that of neo-capitalism on the basis of Jung's notion of the collective unconscious, proposing that myths and dreams form a language in which the mind can forge order and identity out of disorder and madness. *Laborintus* (1956) recounts a *Dantesque descent through a chaotic unconscious in search of integration and wholeness, in rich, hypermetrical verses and in a dense, dream-like mixture of languages from which threads and themes spiral out. The procedure continued in *Erotopaegnia* (1961) and *Purgatorio de l'Inferno* (1964), as well as in his first novel, *Capriccio italiano* (1961), which uses a deliberately impoverished diction with the aim of allowing the dream images to take on the status of an expressive language. The title of his 1965 collection of essays, *Ideologia e linguaggio*, identifies the two interlocked concerns which have characterized his approach up to the present day both as artist and as critic, whether the subject is Dante or the *Crepuscolari*, whose lyricizing of daily life has affinities with his own. His 1970 anthology of 20th-c. Italian poetry, *Poesia italiana del Novecento*, has been influential in provoking a reassessment of the modern tradition. His earlier poetry is collected in *Segnalibro* (1982). [CGW]

SANI, GINO MITRANO, see COLONIAL LITERATURE.

SANMINIATELLI, BINO (1896–1984). *Florentine novelist. In spite of an enthusiasm for *Futurism, his first short fiction was in the tradition of *Tuscan *verismo*. Perhaps his best work is the novel *Fiamma a Monteluce* (1938), which centres on his favoured theme of the generational struggle within the family. Sanminiatelli was also a painter and art critic. [SVM]

SANNAZARO, IACOPO (1458–1530). Outstanding *Renaissance poet and *humanist. He spent most of his life in *Naples, as part of the circle of humanists, writers, and artists first brought together by Alfonso of *Aragon. He joined the household of his successor, Ferdinand, in 1481, and served him and subsequently his son, Federigo, whom he accompanied into exile in 1501.

His intellectual mentor was *Pontano, whose *academy he joined in 1478. He followed him in cultivating the Latin eclogue, but transformed it in his *Eclogae *piscatoriae* (composed before 1500) by replacing the usual figures and settings with fishermen and dramatic marine events, such as seastorms and shipwrecks in the bay of Naples. His Latin love poetry, *Elegiae*, also differs from Pontano's often joyous verse in its suffused melancholy.

He spent more than twenty years on his last major humanist work, *De partu virginis*, published in 1526 in *Rome and Naples and dedicated to Pope Clement VII, who made him a defender of the faith for his efforts. It is a Latin *epic in hexameters, intended as a Christian rival to *Virgil's *Aeneid* and classicizing the Gospel accounts almost out of recognition. Not even the proper names survive; Mary, for instance, is indicated as a virgin, maid, queen, and goddess. At the Annunciation she is depicted as a maid on the sea-shore of a Greek island gathering shells, terrified at the arrival of a sailor in a boat bringing her news. The poem's literary qualities and its celebration of the triumphant arrival of the world's saviour, rather than the suffering Christ, made Pope Leo X and humanist ecclesiastics deem it the answer to Protestant *heresy and the reaffirmation of *papal magnificence and authority.

Unlike Pontano, Sannazaro also wrote extensively in the vernacular. His most famous work, *Arcadia*, with its mixture of prose and lyric poems, launched a new kind of *pastoral that was imitated all over Europe. He composed a *canzoniere* of *Petrarchist lyrics (not published as a collection until just after his death), which is largely dedicated to Cassandra Marchese, a noble Neapolitan lady with whom he maintained a close friendship over many years. Benedetto *Varchi thought that the poems carried out much of Pietro *Bembo's programme for the *lyric before it had actually been drawn up. Sannazaro also left texts for theatrical spectacles at court, and a vernacular correspondence. [LAP]

See C. Kidwell, *Sannazaro and Arcadia* (1993).

SANSEVERINO, AURORA (1669–1730). *Sicilian noblewoman, who entered the *Arcadia Academy as Lucinda Coritesia, and wrote *Petrarchan *sonnets which were included in the *Rime degli Arcadi* (1716). [CCa]

Sansoni, see PUBLISHING; RIZZOLI.

SANSOVINO, FRANCESCO (1521–83), son of the sculptor Iacopo, was a scholar *printer in *Venice, who published *translations of the classics and *anthologies of Italian literature and history. His most original works are his Venetian guide books and a collection of letters to his contemporaries loosely linked to the *Decameron* (1542). [ECMR]

SANTAROSA, SANTORRE DI (1783–1825). *Piedmontese patriot. He expressed his hopes for a new Italy in *Delle speranze degli italiani* (1820) and was a leader of the 1821 rising in Piedmont. He then lived in *exile in London, but died in Greece fighting against the Turks. [EAM]

Santa Uliva, Rappresentazione di. 16th-c. *sacra rappresentazione*, first printed in 1568, which presents the adventures of the daughter of the Emperor Julian. Having rejected the marriage proposed by her father, she survives extraordinary dangers before marrying the King of Castile. It is distinguished for its length, explicit stage directions, and elaborate *intermezzi* including audience participation in a banquet. It received a memorable production by Jacques Copeau (1933) in the cloisters of Santa Croce, Florence. [JAL]

SANT'ELIA, ANTONIO (1888–1916). Architect who joined *Futurism in 1914 and wrote the manifesto *L'architettura futurista*. He was killed in action soon afterwards, but his designs for an integrated Futurist city of steel and concrete skyscrapers, linked by rapid escalators to power stations and airports, reveal his prescience. [SV]

Santo, Il (1905). Novel by *Fogazzaro. It follows the painful spiritual progress of Benedetto, formally Piero Maironi, as he renounces the world and the temptations of love and learns to live a modern form of saintliness. The novel's progressive attitudes towards science, church organization, and Church–state relations led to its being placed on the *Index in 1907. [AM]

SANTUCCI, LUIGI (1918–99). *Milanese novelist. Having begun as an academic *literary critic, he published his first story, *In Australia con mio nonno*, in 1947. His fiction is strongly religious, but with a vein of irony and humour. His most popular novel, *Il velocifero* (1965), depicts Milanese life around the end of the 19th c. [PBart]

SANUDO, MARIN (THE ELDER) (c.1270–c.1343). *Venetian aristocrat, who undertook five expeditions to the Middle East, studying economic and political conditions and military preparedness. He made a map of the Mediterranean and wrote three versions of his *Conditiones Terrae Sanctae*, presenting one to Clement V in 1309 and another to John XXII in 1321, in the hope that they would be used on *Crusades. [JCB]

SANUDO, MARIN (THE YOUNGER) (1466–1536) was born into a *Venetian patrician family and in a long political career held a number of government posts, though he never attained high office. He moved in *humanist circles and collected manuscripts, books, and paintings. He wrote a number of historical works in Latin and Italian on Venice and its subject territories, including the *Vite dei Dogi* and the *Diarii*, the work for which he is best known. The *Diarii* incorporate letters and contain a wealth of historical and documentary information covering the period from 1496 to 1533; however, their length, unstructured nature, and indiscretions helped ensure that Sanudo never became the official *historian of Venice. [JEL]

SANVITALE, FRANCESCA (1933–). Novelist. Born in *Milan, she studied literature at *Florence University, and then moved to *Rome, where for many years she worked on cultural programmes for Italian *television and wrote for *Il Messaggero* and *Nuovi argomenti*.

The first of her novels and collections of stories, *Il cuore borghese* (1972), is an unsparing analysis of the bourgeoisie of the 1950s. Her next, justly acclaimed novel, *Madre e figlia* (1980), is autobiographical; it traces the evolution over three decades of an all-enveloping love–hate relationship between mother and daughter in a poetic prose which combines emotional intensity with intellectual acuity. Similarly intense, *L'uomo del parco* (1984) represents the phantasmagoric world of a woman fighting to stave off psychological disintegration against the social and political realities of Rome during the kidnapping and murder of the *Christian Democrat politician Aldo Moro. It was followed in 1991 by *Verso Paola*, a short novel recounting a rail journey south from Bolzano by a former 1960s activist. Sanvitale's first *historical novel, *Il figlio dell'Impero* (1994), draws extensively on archives and contemporary documents to evoke early 19th-c. Europe, especially Vienna and Paris, through the rootless existence of Napoleon's son. In 1995 she published an anthology of 19th-c. women's writing from *Fonseca Pimentel to Matilde *Serao.   [AHC]

SANZIO, RAFFAELLO, see RAPHAEL.

SAPEGNO, NATALINO (1901–90), one of the major *historians of Italian literature and a specialist in the 14th c. He studied in *Turin and from 1937 taught in *Rome. He belonged to Piero *Gobetti's *Rivoluzione liberale* group, and was influenced by Benedetto *Croce and later Antonio *Gramsci. Among his works is the influential three-volume manual *Compendio di storia della letteratura italiana* (1936–47), with its one-volume version *Disegno storico* (1949). He produced important editions of *Petrarch (1951), *Boccaccio (1952), *Poeti minori del Trecento* (1952), and *Dante's *Divine Comedy* (1955–7), considered by many to contain the best *Dante commentary available.   [LL & GCL]

Sardinia. The island's formal connection with Italy dates from 1720, when the Treaty of London assigned it to the Duchy of *Savoy. For the three preceding centuries it had been dominated by *Aragon and *Spain, and earlier by *Genoa and *Pisa. Thus it has a long tradition of linguistic heterogeneity, with *Dante considering Sardinian an uncouth aping of Latin (*DVE* 1.11). Writing of any significance in Italian or Sardinian only began to appear after 1720; poetry in Sardinian then became a continuous stream, while Italian was the medium for historical and didactic writing, often with the express aim of contributing to Sardinia's socio-economic development.

Since 1861 the island has been increasingly drawn into the Italian literary sphere, but has also shown a growing concern with its own cultural identity. The conflicting tendencies are evident in the work of the 19th-c. poet Sebastiano *Satta, and continue in authors such as Grazia *Deledda and Giuseppe *Dessì. Other notable modern writers include Montanaru (Antioco Casula, 1878–1957), whose poetry in Sardinian was fully in touch with developments in modern poetry elsewhere, and Salvatore Cambosu (1895–1962) and Maria Giacobbe (1928–), both of whom lucidly explore their island's culture in Italian. In the 1970s fresh energy invigorated writing in Sardinian, which now came to be used for novels by, for example, Michelangelo Pira (1928–80). [See also GRAMSCI, ANTONIO; LEDDA, GAVINO; LUSSU, EMILIO.]   [JCB]

SARFATTI, MARGHERITA (1880–1961). Famous as *Mussolini's mistress and *biographer, Sarfatti was from a wealthy Northern Italian *Jewish family, and a *feminist and *Socialist in pre-*Fascist days, who became art critic for *Avanti!*, and a supporter of the *900 (*Novecento*) group. She edited Mussolini's magazine *Gerarchia* (1924–34), and helped write articles for American journals published under Mussolini's name. Her *biography of him—the first 'official' one—appeared in English in 1925 and then was widely read in the modified Italian version, *Dux*, of 1926. Their affair lasted into the 1930s. She later fled to Argentina in the wake of the race laws. She published her memoirs as *Acqua passata* (1955).   [RSD]

SARPI, EMILIO, see NOVENTA, GIACOMO.

SARPI, PAOLO (1552–1623). *Historian. Born in *Venice, Sarpi spent most of his life in the monastery of the Servite friars there, though he gained experience of affairs as Vicar-General of the order from 1599 to 1604. He became famous when he was appointed theological adviser to the Republic (1606) after it had been placed under interdict by Pope Paul V.

As a historian, Sarpi is remembered for three works. The strongly anti-papal *Istoria del Concilio di Trento* was published in London, in Italian, in 1619, after the manuscript had been smuggled out with the help of the British embassy. Translated into Latin, English, and French, the history, built around the contrast between appearance and reality in human affairs, became a classic which survived the attempt to refute it by Pietro Sforza *Pallavicino. The *Istoria dell'Interdetto* (produced

Sarrocchi, Margherita

to aid Sarpi's friend Jacques-Auguste de Thou in writing his history of his own time) and the *Trattato delle materie beneficiarie*, an account of the gradual enrichment and corruption of the Church and the rise of *papal power, were published posthumously in Geneva. Sarpi was a man of wide interests, including philosophy, theology, *law, mathematics, and *medicine. His cell was the centre of a network of international correspondents, many of them Protestants, who shared his fear and hatred of Rome, *Spain, and the *Jesuits. His religious opinions are more elusive; he has been variously viewed as a crypto-Protestant, a secret atheist, or more simply as a pre-Tridentine Catholic in a post-Tridentine world [see also COUNTER-REFORMATION].

[UPB]

SARROCCHI, MARGHERITA, see WOMEN WRITERS, I.

SASSETTI, FILIPPO (1540–88) studied philosophy at the University of *Pisa from 1568 to 1573, and was a member of the Accademia Fiorentina and the Accademia degli Alterati [see ACADEMIES]. After 1578 his trade as a *merchant took him on journeys to Spain and Portugal, and eventually to the East. He wrote on *Dante, *Aristotle's poetics, and *imprese. His letters, which show his *humanist background, are of particular interest with their detailed historical and anthropological descriptions. One is famous as a very early statement of the thesis that what will become known as the Indo-European languages share a common origin. [See also TRAVEL WRITING.]

[PLR]

SASSO, PANFILO (1455–1527). *Humanist and poet, originally from Modena, who composed several collections of vernacular poetry and a book of Latin epigrams. His poetry, like that of *Serafino Aquilano and *Tebaldeo, is typical of 15th-c. *Petrarchism as practised in North Italian *courts. He was tried for *heresy in 1523 but acquitted.

[NC]

SASSOLO DA PRATO, see VITTORINO DA FELTRE.

Satire (1)

1. Before 1700

Satire in Italy is indebted throughout its history to *Horace, and Juvenal, though the former's tem-

pering of moral indignation with humour is more influential than the vitriol of the latter.

The *Divine Comedy* determines the political and anticlerical emphases that will dominate Italian satire. *Dante purports to deliver a message from God about last-minute reform of a wayward, perverted state and Church, with *Florence the city of Lucifer and Simoniac Popes putting earthly riches before Christ. *Petrarch's letters *Sine nomine* (1343–59) are close to Dante in their relentless exposure of worldliness and hypocrisy at the *papal *court in *Avignon, though they follow classical models in adopting a human moral perspective rather than a divine one. In his *Decameron* *Boccaccio similarly homes in on clerical hypocrisy. Though usually humorous—the story of Fra Cipolla (6.10) is exemplary—he can be more trenchant, as in the long invective against mendicant friars introducing the story of the unscrupulous Frate Alberto (4.2).

A new brand of ironic, learned, and yet light satire emerged in the *Renaissance with the translations of Lucian, first into Latin in the 15th c. and then into the vernacular in the 16th. Leon Battista *Alberti's *Intercenales* are masterpieces of this new style, targeting not only social vices and hypocrisy, but also religion itself. His *dialogue *Momus*, named after the god of satire, similarly treats the vanity and folly of the human race.

The Lucianic mode continues in the 16th c., now mediated through Erasmus's *Colloquies* and Thomas More's *Utopia*. Niccolò *Franco, Anton Francesco *Doni, and Giovan Battista *Gelli write satirical dialogues about moral, political, and religious reform during the *Reformation and *Counter-Reformation. But satire was also entering dangerous waters by mentioning specific events and people. *Aretino's savage and mostly obscene *pasquinate* (first series 1521), which ridiculed the Pope and curia, were put on the *Index. Later scurrilous attacks earned the death penalty for Franco and, in the 17th c., for Ferrante *Pallavicino. From now on criticism of secular and sacred authority had to be clandestine.

[LAP]

2. From 1600

If satire is the weapon of the disenfranchised, then *Spanish and *Austrian dominance made Italy its natural home in the 17th and 18th c. Anti-Spanish satire begins with *Boccalini's *Ragguagli di Parnaso*, and continues with Fulvio *Testi, who also satirizes *Jesuits and corrupt clergy. The *Renaissance *epic becomes satire in *Tassoni's *La secchia rapita*, which reduces a real dispute of 1393 between *Guelfs and Ghibellines to farce. More wide-ranging was the *Neapolitan Salvator *Rosa, whose seven long satires follow in the footsteps of *Ariosto. *Arcadians such as *Gravina and *Rolli used satire to attack the excesses of *Marino's followers; Rolli also edited an anthology of Italian satire in London. On stage, *Maggi's *Milanese *dialect satires ushered in a genre continued by the *Sienese Girolamo *Gigli, whilst *Goldoni's plays emphasize the moral superiority of the merchant class through satirizing the idle, arrogant nobles in Venetian society.

Satire of the nobility continues in the elaborate blank verse of *Parini's Il *giorno. But satire as a weapon against rivals and contemporary pretensions is used far more vigorously in prose by *Baretti in La Frusta letteraria. A characteristically bleak philosophical twist is given to satirical writing by *Leopardi in his Paralipomeni and *Operette morali. Though the *Risorgimento preferred the heroic mode, satire of the Church, foreign fashions, and social pretensions flourished in the 19th c. in dialect poetry, most notably in Carlo *Porta and *Belli, but it was also cultivated successfully in Italian by *Giusti and *Carducci. The *Scapigliatura largely initiated in Italy the satire of bourgeois behaviour and attitudes that would reach a high point in the 20th c. in *Gadda's novels.

Political and social satire, which flourished in late 19th and 20th c. reviews and journals, survived surreptitiously under *Fascism in fiction by *Moravia and *Brancati, though it could only be used openly by writers in *exile such as *Silone. Satirical accounts did appear after the event, most notably Gadda's Eros e priapo, but it has mostly been modern postwar Italian society that has been most fiercely satirized, for instance by *Mastronardi and *Volponi, though lighter and, for many readers, more appealing notes were struck in the 1950s by *Guareschi and *Flaiano. Whilst Dario *Fo's highly successful *comedies laid into state institutions and modern capitalism in the 1960s, one of the few examples of satire in Italy having real political repercussions was a 1973 article mocking Colonel Qaddafi by *Fruttero and Lucentini, who then gave their version of the subsequent upset in Italo-Libyan relations in L'Italia sotto il tallone di Fruttero e Lucentini (1974). [See also MOCK-HEROIC POETRY; PARODY AND PASTICHE.] [GT]

See U. Limentani, La satira nel Seicento (1961); F. Ratano, La satira italiana nel dopoguerra (1976).

Satire (2), see ARIOSTO, LUDOVICO.

SATTA, SALVATORE (1902–75). *Sardinian writer, known in his lifetime as a prominent jurist and professor of civil law at the University of *Rome. He became famous as a novelist after his death with the publication of Il giorno del giudizio (1977), which he had written towards the end of his life. The story of the aristocratic Sanna Carboni family, it provides a complex and multi-faceted portrait of the inhabitants of Nuoro in Sardinia in the early 20th c. Also published posthumously was La veranda (1981), a dark and intense love story set in a tuberculosis sanatorium, which was composed in the 1920s and found by chance among Satta's papers. Less well known is De profundis, published in 1948 but written on the eve of the liberation of Italy, which presents an unusual and penetrating analysis of the social origins of *Fascism. [SVM]

SATTA, SEBASTIANO (1867–1914). *Sardinia's most celebrated poet. He was principally influenced by *Carducci, and, writing in Italian, considered himself the 'poeta-vate' of his island. His Canti barbaricini (1910) and posthumous Canti del salto e della tanca (1924) embody traditional Sardinian values, but are tinged with deep anxiety about their future. [JCB]

Saul (1782), a *tragedy in five acts by Vittorio *Alfieri, is recognized as his masterpiece. The King of Israel is depicted at the point of his decline from power. Abandoned by God, he is oppressed by the prospect of encroaching old age. Paradoxically he both loves and persecutes David, in whom he sees his own youthful self, and who he knows is destined to succeed him. [ADiB]

SAVARESE, NINO (1882–1945). *Sicilian novelist. Though he associated with writers of La *Voce and La *Ronda in the first three decades of the 20th c., he subsequently lived mostly in his native Enna. His lyrically melancholic work treats his provincial Sicilian world as a paradigm of human solitude. He is best known for I fatti di Petra (1937) and Cronachetta siciliana dell'estate del 1943 (1945). [AWM]

SAVINI DE' ROSSI, ARETAFILA, see WOMEN WRITERS, 2.

SAVINIO, ALBERTO (pseud. of Andrea De Chirico) (1892–1952). Writer, composer, and

Savioli Fontana, Ludovico Vittorio

painter. Born in Greece, he lived in Munich (1906–10) and, with his brother, Giorgio *De Chirico, in Paris (1910–15), where he met Apollinaire and Picasso. In 1914 he published *Les Chants de la mi-mort*, launched the musical movement *sincérisme*, then concentrated on writing and art criticism.

In 1918 he moved to *Rome, where he published *Hermaphrodito* (1918) and wrote for *Valori plastici* and *La *Ronda*. In 1926 he married, returned to Paris, and devoted himself to painting, with his first one-man show in 1927. In the same year he published the novel *Angelica o la notte di maggio* and became close to Cocteau and the *surrealists; his dream-like pictures, influenced by Otto Weininger's analogies between human and animal psychology, merged human forms with those of animals or birds. In 1933 he returned definitively to Italy, where he painted mythological murals in the Istituto Nazionale delle Assicurazioni in *Turin and wrote the fictions *Gradus ad Parnassum* (1938), *Dico a te, Clio* (1940), and *L'infanzia di Nivasio Dolcemare* (1941). After the war he resumed musical composition with a ballet and *opera, and produced radical set and costume designs for productions of Stravinsky and Offenbach at La Scala.   [DF]

SAVIOLI FONTANA, LUDOVICO VITTORIO
(1729–1804). Bolognese aristocrat and member of the *Bologna Academy of Sciences, who is the best-known and most original *erotic poet of the period. His interests spread also to history and the visual arts. In his youth he composed *Gli amori* (1758 and 1765), a collection of twenty-four *canzonette* [see VERSIFICATION] inspired by the Latin elegiac poets (*Ovid, Catullus, Propertius), reinterpreted in a *classicistic-*Rococo vein that effectively combines the classical with a modern style and sensibility. Savioli was also influenced by the love poems of Pope (*The Rape of the Lock* and *Eloisa to Abelard*) and by French poetry (*Le temple de Gnide* by Montesquieu), as well as by French Rococo painting. In his maturity Savioli focused exclusively on *historical studies. His *Annali bolognesi* (1784–95), in six volumes, imitate the style of *Livy and Tacitus.   [IMC]

SAVIOTTI, GINO (1891–1980). Born in
Arpino, he edited *Pagine critiche* in Parma (1923–5) and *L'Indice* in *Genoa (1930–1). In 1939 he became director of the Italian Cultural Institute in Lisbon and spent the rest of his life there. He published various *novels in the 1930s; the two

most successful were *Mezzo matto* (1934) and *Il fratello* (1936).   [DCH]

SAVIOZZO, IL, see SERDINI, SIMONE.

SAVONAROLA, GIROLAMO (1452–98) was a *Ferrarese *Dominican who preached ardently for moral reform and came to prominence during his second stay (1490–8) in *Florence, his adoptive city, where he was prior of the monastery of San Marco. He foretold the coming in 1494 of the new Cyrus, the French King Charles VIII. Having criticized Medicean rule, he set about reforming the constitution after Piero de' *Medici's expulsion in November 1494, and his supporters publicly destroyed exterior signs of profanity. His invectives against Pope Alexander VI resulted in excommunication in 1497. When an interdict was threatened, public opinion turned, San Marco was stormed, and Savonarola burnt at the stake on 23 May 1498.

His devotees included many intellectuals (Giovanni *Nesi, Giovanfrancesco *Pico, the *Benivieni brothers) and he influenced both Giovanni *Pico della Mirandola and Marsilio *Ficino, although the latter, whose *Neoplatonism he disapproved of, turned against him. Savonarola is important not so much for his Latin and Italian tracts as for the power of his *sermons and his belief in Christian government. His movement helped to shape Florentine political history in the early decades of the 16th c., and his continuing influence is attested by numerous editions of his life and sermons. He was seen by many as a precursor of Martin Luther. [See also REFORMATION.]   [RDC]

Savoy. The Savoy dynasty first emerged in the 11th c., when Umberto Biancamano established control over the passes of the Mont Cenis and the Little and Great St Bernards. These passes would remain at the core of what became a duchy and eventually a kingdom, embracing much of modern French Savoy and Italian Piedmont, and at various times reaching out into Burgundy, Switzerland, Liguria, and *Lombardy. It was a precarious buffer-state, whose name, status and borders kept changing, preserved more by great-power rivalry than by its mountainous remoteness. But from 1559, when the treaty of Cateau-Cambrésis brought the Franco-Spanish war in Italy to a conclusion and restored to Duke Emanuele Filiberto the control of his territory, there began a process of slow accretion.

With the treaty of Aix-la-Chapelle (1720)

Savoy-Piedmont was formally assigned *Sardinia and became the Kingdom of Sardinia, whose orientation was now firmly towards Italy. After the *Napoleonic conquest of 1796–8 and the *Restoration of 1815 (which brought control of *Genoa), the kingdom (now commonly referred to as Piedmont) developed into the dominant military power in the peninsula, whilst remaining a bastion of religious and political intolerance. At *Unification the region of Savoy, including Nice, was ceded to France, but the Savoy kings now became the (unfortunately inadequate) kings of Italy. [See also CAVOUR; MONARCHY; PIEDMONT; TURIN.] [RAbs]

SBARBARO, CAMILLO (1888–1967). Poet. Born in Santa Margherita near *Genoa, he worked in industry before serving as a soldier in *World War I. Afterwards he taught classics at a school in Genoa, but was eventually forced to resign when he refused to join the *Fascist party. He spent much of the rest of his life living with his sister on the Ligurian coast.

His first major collection, *Pianissimo* (1914), was published by the *Florentine journal *La *Voce*. Written, as its title suggests, in the low-key, anti-rhetoric of *Crepuscolare poetry, it was an early example of poetry on the theme of the 'waste land', emphasizing somnambulism, alienation, the objectivization of the self in things, but suggesting that poetry might be a way to salvation. Much of the repertoire of later modern poets was here; notably enough, his friend *Montale dedicated two poems in *Ossi di seppia* to him. Sbarbaro's subsequent poetry of note is found mostly in *Trucioli* (1920)— brief *prose poems in the Vocian manner whose privileging of slight details of natural phenomena seems to reflect his study of lichens, on which he was an authority. Sbarbaro also *translated Greek classics (Sophocles, Aeschylus, and Euripides) and French literature (Balzac, Stendhal, Flaubert, and Zola). [VS-H]

SCALA, ALESSANDRA (1475–1506), daughter of Bartolomeo *Scala, had access to the literary circle around Lorenzo de' *Medici. We have from her hand a Greek epigram written to *Poliziano in response to one he had written to her, and a letter to Cassandra *Fedele. She married the poet Michele *Marullo in 1494, and after his death in 1526 retired to a convent. [AR]

SCALA, BARTOLOMEO (1430–97). First Chancellor of *Florence from 1465 until his death

and a person of considerable power and prestige both under the *Medici and under the Florentine republic. Despite his humble origins (for which he was famously criticized by Francesco *Guicciardini and also by *Poliziano), he enjoyed the friendship and respect of a wide circle of public men and *humanists including Francesco *Filelfo, *Platina, *Ficino, and *Marullo. In addition to his letters and orations, his writings include two *histories, one an incomplete *Historia florentinorum* (printed in 1677), humanist treatises on philosophical sects, marriage, etc. (1458–c.1465), two important collections of 100 fables (1481, ?1488–92), a *dialogue on the nature of *law (1483), a defence of *Savonarola (1496), and various poems, including an unfinished one on trees (1496–7), interesting for its Lucretian account of civilization. [ABr]

SCALA, FLAMINIO (1552–1624) was a *commedia dell'arte actor, manager, and dramatist. He published a unique collection of scenarios, *Il teatro delle favole rappresentative*, in 1611. The Prologue to *Il finto marito* (1618) assesses the relative importance of dramatist and actor in theatrical creation. [See also THEATRE, 1.] [RAA]

SCALFARI, EUGENIO (1924–). Politically radical *journalist, who has also served as a *Socialist deputy. After writing regularly for *La Stampa*, *L'Europeo*, and *Il Mondo*, he founded *L'Espresso* with Arrigo *Benedetti in 1963 and edited it until 1968. He founded *La Repubblica* in 1976 and became its editor. He has written several books of political commentary. [REL]

SCALIA, GIANNI, see OFFICINA.

SCALIGER, JOSEPH (in Italian Scaligero) (1540–1609). Son of Giulio Cesare *Scaligero and a more important figure in European terms. Forced repeatedly to move from one country to another on account of his Calvinism [see REFORMATION], he made a major contribution to *humanist studies in Paris, Geneva, and Leiden. His works include *commentaries on classical writers and chronological studies in which he seeks to reconcile ancient and Copernican thinking. [FC]

SCALIGERI, see DELLA SCALA.

SCALIGERO, GIULIO CESARE (1484–1558). *Humanist critic of Erasmus, literary theorist, and writer of *commentaries. He studied

Scaligero Della Fratta, Camillo

philosophy at *Padua (1515–19), then settled at Agen in France as physician to the Bishop Angelo Della Rovere.

He began his career with two polemicals against Erasmus' *Ciceronianus*, the *Pro M. T. Cicerone contra Desiderium Erasmum orationes duo* (1621). He wrote several commentaries on works of *Aristotle, including the *Historia animalium* and the *De plantis*, as well as a polemic against *Cardano (1557). He also left a collection of poems in Latin, some epistles, and an important tract on language, *De causis linguae latinae* (1540), in which he attempted a scientific exposition of the rules of Latin grammar. His chief work was *Poetices libri septem* (1561), a posthumously published treatise on Aristotelian principles, in which he surveys and analyses, often with a polemic intent, writers and works, genres, verse forms, and styles, giving precise rules for composition [see also LITERARY THEORY, 2]. The work exercised an immense influence on French *classicism.   [PBert]

SCALIGERO DELLA FRATTA, CAMIL-LO, see BANCHIERI, ADRIANO.

SCALVINI, GIOVITA (1791–1843). Patriot and man of letters, who spent much of his adult life in *exile. Born near Brescia, he studied at *Bologna and Pavia before moving to *Milan. He was influenced by *Foscolo, and had peripheral connections with *Biblioteca italiana, Il *Conciliatore, and the beginnings of *Antologia. In 1822 he fled Italy as a suspect *liberal, ending up in England, where he remained until 1827. He was then in Paris until 1833, and finally became a tutor with the Arconati family in Gaesbeek in Belgium, until he was amnestied in 1838.

His experiences as a political exile play a large part in his liberal-patriotic poetry, notably in *Il fuoruscito* (begun in 1824) and *Ultimo carme*. Although many of his papers were destroyed at his express wish after his death by his literary executor, Niccolò *Tommaseo, he has come increasingly to be appreciated as a critic and a *translator. His 1829 essay on *Manzoni, comparing him to Scott, is one of the most perceptive of the period on the then modish topic of the *historical novel. His translation of *Faust*, part 1 (1835) has been admired even by so exacting a modern translator of Goethe as Franco *Fortini.   [MPC]

SCANDELLA, DOMENICO, see COSMOLOGY.

Scapigliatura. Collective name given to a loose-knit, numerically fluctuating group of writers, *journalists, and artists who lived and worked in *Milan in the years immediately following the *Unification of Italy in 1860, with an offshoot developing a little later in *Turin. They were the first Italian avant-garde movement, and a product of the ideological disquiet that came in the wake of Unification and was felt particularly acutely in now rapidly expanding entrepreneurial Milan.

The term, deriving from *scapigliato* meaning 'dishevelled' or 'unkempt', first appeared in Cletto *Arrighi's heavily censored novel *Gli ultimi coriandoli* (1857). It is in the introduction to his next novel, *La scapigliatura e il sei febbraio* (1862), that there is a first delineation of the group—young patriots between 20 and 35 years old, independent in thought and lifestyle, restless, living in a city from which they feel excluded but of which they form the avant-garde. In this novel they participate in the unsuccessful *Mazzinian insurrection against the *Austrians that took place in Milan on 6 February 1853. Historically the *Scapigliatura* was the Italian counterpart to the French *bohème*, and similarly combined patriotism with hostility towards the bourgeoisie and the status quo, making a cult of disorder, improvidence, flamboyance, and dandyism which at least some of them were willing to live out to the extreme. The short-lived journal *Lo Scapigliato*, founded by Cesare *Tronconi under the pseudonym Dottor Etico on 17 December 1866, emphasized the group's anti-conformism and intellectual independence, but it was only in 1865 in the journal *Cronaca grigia* that Arrighi, in a letter accompanying Arrigo *Boito's poem *Ballatella*, referred for the first time to the *Scapigliatura* as an artistic movement.

Members included the writers Iginio Ugo *Tarchetti, Antonio *Ghislanzoni, and Carlo *Dossi, the painter Tranquillo Cremona, the composer Giuseppe Grandi, and the composer and conductor Franco Faccio, as well as others active in more than one artistic field, such as Emilio *Praga and Giovanni Camerata, who were poets and painters, Arrigo Boito, who was a poet, composer, and *librettist for *Verdi, and his older brother, Camillo Boito, who was an architect, art historian, and writer. When the movement established itself in *Piedmont, it attracted the writers Roberto *Sacchetti, Giovanni *Faldella, and Achille Giovanni Cagna, all of whom shared the literary and ideological aspirations of the Milanese *Scapigliati*. The mentor of the whole movement was felt to be the author of the five-volume *historical novel *Cento anni*, Giuseppe *Rovani, whose open-air 'lessons' in aesthetics held at an inn in Milan entered into the mythology of the group.

What united them aesthetically were aspirations rather than artistic practices, but they shared a common desire to de-provincialize Italian culture, which was furthered by their creative receptivity to literatures from abroad. Tarchetti and Camillo Boito, influenced by Mary Shelley, Radcliffe, Hoffmann, and Poe, were the first Italian writers to publish tales of the *fantastic, while in poetry Arrigo Boito and Emilio Praga turned to Heine and Baudelaire to forge a new poetics mixing *realism and the macabre. Influenced by Sue and Dickens among others, the social novel, often published in instalments and marked by a strong humanitarianism, evolved through Tarchetti into *Valera's works of social investigation. A separate line of linguistic experimentalism is also visible in the Lombard Dossi and the Piedmontese Faldella and Cagna. [AHC]
See G. Mariani, *Storia della Scapigliatura* (1967); G. Rosa, *La narrativa degli Scapigliati* (1997).

SCAPPI, BARTOLOMEO, see COOKERY BOOKS.

SCARFOGLIO, EDOARDO (1860–1917). Writer and newspaper editor. In *Rome he wrote for *Cronaca bizantina* (1881–4) and edited *Il Corriere di Roma* (1885–7). In 1887 he moved to *Naples and in 1892 founded and edited *Il Mattino*, to which his wife, Matilde *Serao, contributed until their separation in 1902. He at first backed *Giolitti but then embraced the *nationalist Right and put *Il Mattino*'s weight behind Italy's *colonialist war in Libya (1911–12). In *World War I he urged support for Germany and Austria (which gave him financial backing) to counter British maritime supremacy and further Italy's Balkan and Mediterranean influence. [DF]

SCARPETTA, EDUARDO (1853–1925). Highly successful *Neapolitan actor-dramatist, who departed from traditional Neapolitan *theatre by using scripts and by portraying the petite bourgeoisie rather than the contrast between rich and poor and between city and country. Though criticized by Salvatore *Di Giacomo, his reforms led directly to the work of Eduardo *De Filippo.
[PBarn]

SCATAGLINI, FRANCO (1930–94). *Dialect poet from Ancona, though his first book, *Echi* (1950), was a *hermetic collection. His poetry treats events from his own life sometimes in an interestingly *psychoanalytic manner, most notably in the autobiographical *El sol* ('The Sun') (1995). But the poems collected in *Rimario agontano* ('Anconan Rhymes') (1987) and the reworking of the *Roman de la rose* in *La rosa* (1992) are most striking for distancing their language from normal spoken dialect, as if Scataglini were recreating or inventing the archaic language of Ancona. His work has links with other anti-*modernist poets, such as *Saba, *Penna, *Noventa, and *Pasolini, and also with the prose experiments of *Gadda. [RD]

Scepticism is the philosophical tradition which questions our ability to obtain knowledge. By claiming that the content of human certitude bears no necessary relationship to any truth, scepticism is the direct antithesis of realism, which postulates that correctly acquired subjective certitude apprehends objective truth. The history of scepticism is normally divided into two broad periods, ancient and modern. Sources for our knowledge of ancient scepticism, which lasted from the 4th c. BC to the 2nd c. AD, are the writings of Sextus Empiricus, particularly his *Outlines of Pyrrhonism* (1st c. AD), Diogenes Laertius' *Lives and Opinions of Eminent Philosophers* (3rd c. AD), and *Cicero's *De natura deorum* (1st c. BC).

Although not unfamiliar to medieval thought, scepticism was not a major philosophical issue. Modern scepticism first appeared during the *Renaissance in connection with moral, religious, and scientific themes. In Italy, Giovanfrancesco *Pico was the first to make liberal use of the arguments of Sextus Empiricus, in his *Paragone fra la vanità della scienza pagana e la verità dell'istruzione cristiana* (1520), in order to highlight the contradictions into which reason is constantly led, and defend the appeal to faith as the basis of Christian belief. Generally, however, scepticism has been hostile to Catholicism. In the Italy of the *Enlightenment, sceptics were lumped together with atheists, *libertines, and deists as enemies of the Church, even by enlightened religious figures such as *Muratori. During the period which spanned the writings of Descartes, Locke, Hume, and Kant, when the major philosophical issues concerned the foundations of knowledge itself, scepticism became the epistemological malaise to conquer. In 19th- and 20th-c. philosophy the sceptical argument,

presented as the 'philosophical doubt' that we 'know' little or nothing but can continue to act on the basis of 'belief', has become redundant, given the common currency of relativist and *post-modern perspectives.   [GLCB]
See M. Burnyeat (ed.), *The Skeptical Tradition* (1983).

SCERBANENCO, GIORGIO (1911–69). Born in Kiev to a Russian father and Italian mother, he lived in Italy from childhood. He edited women's magazines and wrote more than sixty novels and countless short stories. He was acclaimed as Italy's leading writer of classic *detective fiction for a series (1966 onwards), featuring Duca Lamberti, an ex-doctor disqualified for practising euthanasia.   [JEB]

SCHEIWILLER, VANNI (1889–1965). *Milanese *publisher specializing in contemporary art and poetry. His later publications carried the words 'All'Insegna del Pesce d'Oro', from a *trattoria* in Milan favoured by poets such as *Quasimodo, *Gatto, and *Sereni, all of whom he published.
[DF]

SCHETTINI, PIRRO (1630–78). Italian and Latin poet from Cosenza whose early lyrics were written in a moderately sensual *Baroque style akin to that of Girolamo *Preti. Subsequently he reverted to a moralizing *Petrarchism. To promote his conservative views, he established in Cosenza an Accademia Parrasiana (1668), which was much lauded for rejecting 'corrupt' Baroque taste, though it also concerned itself with philosophical and scientific investigations. But his influence was small and his poetry merely accomplished. In his last years he completed his recantation by taking holy orders and burning many of his works.   [MPS]

SCHIFF, PAOLINA (19th c.). *Feminist writer. She wrote the novel *Il profugo* (1880) and a history of German literature. Her essays include one on 'La donna e la legge civile'.   [AHC]

SCHMITZ, ETTORE ARON, see SVEVO, ITALO.

Scholarship, see CLASSICAL SCHOLARSHIP; FILOLOGIA; TEXTUAL CRITICISM.

Scholasticism. The theological and philosophical teachings of the university 'Schoolmen' in late medieval Europe. It achieved its fullest systematization in the works of Albertus Magnus (1193–1280) and *Aquinas. Other important proponents included the Scottish *Franciscan John Duns Scotus (c.1264–1308).

While maintaining the supremacy of the truths of the Christian faith, as revealed in the *Bible and interpreted by the Church Fathers, Scholasticism sought to confirm the role of reason in investigating and explaining all fields of human knowledge—metaphysics, physics and the natural world, epistemology, ethics, law, and government—and to consider philosophy as the handmaiden of the queen of the sciences, theology. In its methods of argumentation through syllogisms and distinctions and in its philosophical foundations, it developed the rationalizing doctrines of Aristotle (known through Latin translations), applying such concepts as person and nature, substance and accident, form and matter to explain, in however limited a way, the theology of the Trinity, the Incarnation, Transubstantiation, and the human soul. Inevitably, its rationalism came into conflict at times with *Augustinian Platonism and the tradition that privileged God's transcendence and the primacy of the will and love over the intellect and reason.

Though it aimed at a comprehensive synthesis, Scholasticism was by no means monolithic, but proceeded by constant debate and employed public disputations as an educational tool. The principal controversy in the 13th c. concerned Islamic interpretations of Aristotle, particularly those of ibn Rushd (Averroes) (1126–98), who separated the truths of faith and reason, and proposed that all humans share in a collective intellect. Such propositions were condemned by the Bishop of Paris in 1277. In the 14th c., the doctrine of the Pope's supremacy in the sphere of temporal jurisdiction, advanced most notably by Egidio Romano (Giles of Rome) (1247–1316), was opposed by William of Ockham (c.1285–1349) and *Marsilio da Padova. The dispute on Nominalism, which relegated universal concepts and words to the realm of logic rather than the science of things, may have contributed to Scholasticism's subsequent reputation for hair-splitting and sophistry, but it continued to form the basis of orthodox Catholic thought and education throughout the *Renaissance [see ARISTOTELIANISM] and into the 20th c. Its methods of argument, philosophy, and theology strongly influenced *Dante, especially the *Convivio*, the *Monarchia*, and many passages in the *Divine Comedy*.   [PA]

See N. Kretzmann, A. Kenny, and J. Pinborg (eds.), *The Cambridge History of Later Medieval Philosophy* (1982).

SCHÖNBECK, VIRGILIO, see GIOTTI, VIRGILIO.

SCHWEYNHEYM, CONRAD, see PRINTING.

SCIASCIA, LEONARDO (1921–89). *Novelist. He lived all his life in the village of Racalmuto in western *Sicily, where he was born. From 1975 to 1977 he was a city councillor in Palermo as an independent linked with the *Communist Party. In 1979 he was elected to parliament with the Radical Party. Otherwise his life was outwardly uneventful, yet through his literary writing and his *journalism he participated in the great political and literary *causes célèbres* of the Sicily and Italy of his time.

Though his first work, *Le favole della dittatura* (1950), drew the praise of *Pasolini, it was with *Le parrocchie di Regalpetra* (1956) and *Gli zii di Sicilia* (1958) that he found his own voice. The first was based on his experiences as a teacher, and is an investigation into the way of life in a Sicilian town, while the second is a collection of four stories, each probing aspects of 19th- and 20th-c. Sicilian experience. From these early works onwards Sciascia evinces a deeply rooted and profoundly knowledgeable pessimism about Sicilian history and the ability of human beings in general to implement improvements in society. The Sicily he describes is prey to many of the most oppressive forces in history, with the *Inquisition, the *Mafia, and *Fascism present literally or metaphorically in all his works. The title of a book-length interview, *La Sicilia come metafora* (1979), is significant in a writer who came to view Sicily as a universal metaphor for human life.

The complexity of his shifting viewpoints on Sicily is evident in the succession of books and articles he dedicated to Luigi *Pirandello, though, where Pirandello was an irrationalist, Sciascia aimed at rationalism. From what he saw as the social and ontological disorder of Sicily, he sought refuge in a myth of reason and a dedication to Voltaire and 18th-c. France. Voltaire and Pirandello are frequent, countervailing presences in his work. *Candido* (1977) is an act of homage to both, and is also the most subtly autobiographical of his works. With gentle but pungent irony, the story depicts a young boy, born in Sicily at the Liberation, struggling with the two great institutionalized

systems of belief, Christian and *Marxist, which contended for supremacy in Italy, and eventually coming to be dissatisfied with both.

Sciascia became best known for his idiosyncratic *detective stories. The earliest, *Il *giorno della civetta* (1961) and *A ciascuno il suo* (1966), begin as investigations into Mafia crimes but widen out to expose corruption in the society which tolerates or instigates crime. In *Il contesto* (1971) and *Todo modo* (1974), the criminality affects high levels of society, with politicians, judges, and industrialists operating in a Mafia manner. The criminal is never brought to justice inside the fiction, but the reader is made detective and uncovers the network of corruption. After a considerable gap Sciascia returned to detective fiction with *Il cavaliere e la morte* (1988) and *Una storia semplice* (1989), both of which unite transcendental quest with criminal investigation.

Many of his other works are cast in a style of the essay-enquiry inspired by *Manzoni's *Storia della colonna infame*. *Morte dell'inquisitore* (1964), his own favourite book, tells of the killing of a 17th-c. inquisitor by a native of Racalmuto, Fra Diego La Matina. Sciascia is no objective historian, and presents Fra Diego as a fighter for liberation against a force which could be Fascism as much as the historical Inquisition. *L'affaire Moro* (1978) examines the kidnapping and murder of the *Christian Democrat statesman Aldo Moro, criticizing the Red Brigades as successors of the Inquisition, but casting doubt also on the uprightness of Moro's political colleagues. All Sciascia's work is a cry of protest against such anti-life forces.   [JF]

See M. Onofri, *Storia di Sciascia* (1994); J. Farrell, *Leonardo Sciascia* (1995).

Science Fiction. At the beginning of the 20th c. there were hints of science fiction in Italian authors such as *Salgari and Gino Rocca (1891–1941), but in Italy science fiction was long considered a typically Anglo-Saxon genre. Most texts were *translated from English for what was considered a popular readership and the few Italian science fiction authors used English pseudonyms.

Though interest increased through the 1930s, the boom came with *Mondadori's *Urania* series, launched in 1952 on the pattern of their *gialli* [see DETECTIVE FICTION] as *periodicals on sale in newsstands (*edicole*). Towards the end of the 1950s educated Italians also began to pay attention to science fiction. *Calvino accepted for *Einaudi *Le meraviglie del possibile* (1959), an anthology of Italian science fiction writing edited by *Fruttero e Lucentini, with an introduction by Sergio *Solmi. In 1960 *Buzzati published *Il grande ritratto*, the first science fiction novel by an established Italian author. Around the same period other authors, such as *Landolfi, *Berto, *Soldati, *Flaiano, and Calvino, began to include science fiction themes in their work. From the 1960s onwards Italian science fiction has been strengthened by figures such as Vittorio Catani, Luigi Menghini, Gilda Musa, and Valerio Evangelisti. Evangelisti created a cult protagonist in *Nicholas Eymerich, inquisitore* (1994), who appears in a number of his subsequent novels. [NG]

Scienza nova, La, see VICO, GIAMBATTISTA.

SCIOPPIO, GASPARE, see POLITICAL THOUGHT.

SCIPIONE (pseud. of Gino Bonichi) (1904–33). Painter with surreal, grotesque tendencies who was one of the founders of the so-called Scuola Romana. He was a friend of *Ungaretti (whose portrait he painted), *Sinisgalli, and other writers. He died from tuberculosis. His writings—poems, notes, diary entries, and visionary prose pieces— were published as *Le civette gridano* (1938) and *Carte segrete* (1943). [RD]

SCOLARI, DOMENICO, see ALEXANDER ROMANCES.

Scoperta dell'America, La, see PASCARELLA, CESARE.

SCOTELLARO, ROCCO (1923–53). Poet and writer who was committed to the cause of the Southern poor, and elected *Socialist mayor of his home town, Tricarico near Matera, in 1946. Almost all his poems were published posthumously. *È fatto giorno* (1954) and *Margherite e rosolacci* (1978) use a popular register to deal with private suffering and social injustice, though they also echo sophisticated modern poetry. Poor labourers of the southern countryside are given a voice in his sociological inquiry *Contadini del Sud* (1954). The unfinished autobiographical novel *L'uva puttanella* (1956) is an elegiac treatment of his characteristic themes of personal and social transformation and struggle. [See also MEZZOGIORNO.] [JD]

Scripta. Philological and palaeographic term indicating purely written varieties of Italian vernacu-

lars, occurring especially before 1500. These are much more localized and idiosyncratic than the equivalents emerging from Latin *scriptoria* (writing workshops) in view of the instability of the usage which scribes were attempting to represent. [DieZ]

SCROFFA, CAMILLO (*c.*1526–65). A poet from Vicenza who, under the pseudonym Glottocrisio Ludimagistro Fidenzio, published the *Amorosa elegia di un appassionato pedante al suo amatissimo Camillo* (1562), which started the genre of burlesque poetry known as *fidenziana*. The poetry parodies *classicism, and the pedant of the title is ridiculed in a language full of hyperbole and incongruous Latinisms. In its lively portrayal of the pedant and its witty language, however, Scroffa's *satire shows an attachment to the world of studies that it satirizes. Between 1540 and 1545 he also published, in the same vein, the *Cantici di Fidenzio*. *Fidenziana* verse, whose antecedents are Francesco *Belo's *Il pedante* and *comedies such as *Aretino's *Il marescalco*, lasted through the 17th and the 18th c., turning into a more broadly burlesque mode as the polemical motives behind it died away. [CG]

Sculpture, see VISUAL ARTS AND LITERATURE.

Scuola Normale Superiore, see PISA.

Scuola oraziana. Group of late 18th-c. minor poets from the *Este Duchy of Modena and Reggio Emilia (hence also the label 'Scuola Classica Estense') first identified by *Carducci as a 'school' linked by common values—*classicism, with *Horace as chief model, yet modernity, concreteness and utility in contrast to *Metastasian vacuity. They looked to *Milan and were influenced by *Parini and *Beccaria. The lead was given by Agostino *Paradisi and Luigi *Cerretti, who were followed by a second generation that included Francesco *Cassoli, Luigi Lamberti, and Giovanni *Paradisi. [JMAL]

Scuola storica, see LITERARY CRITICISM; POSITIVISM.

SEBASTIANO FAUSTO DA LONGIANO, see PETRARCH COMMENTARIES.

SECCHI, ANGELO, see DARWINISM.

Secchia rapita, La, see TASSONI, ALESSANDRO.

Secentismo. Term usually applied in a derogatory sense to the far-fetched metaphorical nature of much literary style in the prose and poetry of the 17th c., or 'Seicento'. Since such a style was thought, from the late 17th c., to mask a lack of any serious content or moral intention, the word soon came to indicate moral decline, decadence, and triviality in literature on the one hand, and stylistic fireworks and artifice on the other, as occurred also with the related terms *Marinismo*, *concettismo*, and the *Baroque.

Secentismo came to be applied to the whole of Italian literature of the time, with the invariable exception of the works of *Galileo, *Sarpi, and *Campanella. This negative view tended to stereotype the period and to prevent in some cases a clear-eyed understanding of its individual writers. It must be said that such writers themselves did much to foster the view that they wished, in comparison with the *Renaissance writers and authorities they often mocked, to be outrageous, modern, even shocking. Literary historians and critics are now beginning to take a more positive view of the phenomenon, as the stylistic reflection of many of the uncertainties and intellectual discomforts of the age. [See also QUERELLE DES ANCIENS ET DES MODERNES.] [PBD]

Secretum. Latin *dialogue by *Petrarch, set in 1342 but probably composed between 1347 and 1353. The dialogue lasts three days and is conducted in the presence of a female figure representing Truth. The speakers are the author, designated Franciscus, and his alter ego represented by St *Augustine. Together they examine Petrarch's moral and spiritual failings, identifying the most dangerous as weakness of will and perennial indecision (*acedia*) and arguing over how far love for *Laura and the desire for glory are distractions from a truly religious life and from God. But the unresolved conclusion is a typically Petrarchan assertion of his inability to change and to follow Augustine's example. [MP]

SEGNERI, PAOLO (1624–94). Leading *Jesuit preacher and theologian. He entered the order in 1637, moving after a two-year novitiate to the Collegio Romano to study philosophy and rhetoric, and then, from 1642 to 1645, to teach humanities. Ordained priest in 1653, he moved to Pistoia to teach grammar, and undertook, from 1665 to 1692, a gruelling annual eight-month preaching tour of Italy. Fruit of this is his most famous work, the *Quaresimale*, published in 1679 but written from

1655 to 1665, a collection of *sermons addressed to a public blinded, in Segneri's view, by prejudice and depravity. He adopts a strongly exhortatory but rational tone on both theological and topical questions, and brutally exposes many of the hypocrisies, sophistries, and injustices of his age. The style is modelled on *Cicero, but shows a Jesuit-inspired directness.

Segneri's later, now underestimated, moral treatises have a concise and lively appeal: *Il parroco istruito* (1642), *Il penitente istruito* (1669), *Il confessore istruito* (1672), *Manna dell'anima, per tutti i giorni dell'anno* (1673–80), *Il cristiano istruito nella sua legge* (1685), and *L'incredulo senza scuse* (1690), were all printed many times in the 17th c., and some were translated into English and French as well as Arabic and Chinese. Segneri also contributed to the theological polemics over *quietism and probabilism, in both cases emphasizing that man has to take responsibility for his own thought, actions, and will. [PBD]

SEGNI, BERNARDO (1504–58). *Florentine *humanist, who translated Aristotle's *Nicomachean Ethics, Politics, De Anima, Rhetoric,* and *Poetics* into Italian from the Greek with commentaries. He also composed a Florentine *history from 1527 to 1555 with a life of the prominent politician Niccolò Capponi attached, and a verse *translation of Sophocles' *Oedipus Rex*. [SJM]

SEGRE, CESARE (1928–). Scholar and semiotician, who studied in *Turin and has taught romance philology in *Pavia. He produced a memorable critical edition of the *Chanson de Roland* (1971), and editions of *Ariosto (1960) and *Bono Giamboni (1968). He has also published important studies of the *history of the Italian language, most famously *Lingua, stile e società* (1963). He played a fundamental role in the development of *semiotics in Italy, with a series of volumes beginning with *I segni e la critica* (1969) and *Le strutture e il tempo* (1974), and has remained a valuable commentator on recent developments in literary studies, as in *Notizie dalla crisi* (1993). [See also FILOLOGIA.] [LL & GCL]

SEGRE, DINO, see PITIGRILLI.

Sei giornate is the collective title of Pietro *Aretino's *Ragionamento* (1534) and *Dialogo* (1536), and the archetypal erotic work from which virtually all subsequent European *erotic (and pornographic) production derives. It was inspired by heterodox *classical models (notably Lucian's *Dialogues of the Courtesans*), as well as by vernacular narrative, including *Boccaccio's. *Ragionamento* deals with the three main conditions of women, that of the nun, the wife, and the prostitute. In the *Dialogo* Nanna teaches her still-virgin daughter how to become a prostitute, then gives her examples of men abusing women, and finally talks with a procuress about the latter's job. The work portrays a cynical society, and can be read as a *parody of *Neoplatonic treatises on love. [GAq]

Sei personaggi in cerca d'autore (1921), *Pirandello's most innovatory and best-known play, explores a number of his key themes: the failure of language to effect true communication, the multiple nature of personality, and the tragic conflict between form and the flux of life.

The play, initially conceived as a novel, opens on a rehearsal of Pirandello's *Il *giuoco delle parti*, which is interrupted by the arrival of the Six Characters: the Father, who states that they are characters looking for an author, the Mother, Son, Stepdaughter, Boy, and Little Girl. The director of the company is persuaded to stage their tragic story of poverty, family strife, and death, but this proves impossible. The play, carefully constructed to appear spontaneous, is a critique of the tradition of the 'well-made play' and a deconstruction of naturalism [see FRENCH INFLUENCES; REALISM; VERISMO], showing *theatre to be an impossible art: the Characters, unique creations of the artist's imagination, cannot live within the theatre's material restrictions. Pirandello revised the play in 1925, suggesting masks for the Characters, and adding alterations to the third part. Pitoëff's production of 1923 brought Pirandello European recognition. [JAL]

SELLA, QUINTINO (1827–84). Geologist and politician of the right, who was three times minister of finance after *Unification. He was a strong proponent of *Rome as national capital. His plans for city institutions included a national *library and a prominent role for the *university, both intended to give Rome a strong lay identity. [JD]

Sellerio. *Publishing firm founded in Palermo in 1969 by Enzo and Elvira Sellerio. It specializes in books on Sicilian culture and history. *Sicily is its principal market but it distributes its essay and literature titles nationwide. It has been closely identified with new Sicilian writing, and its authors include *Consolo, *Bufalino and *Sciascia. [DF]

Selvaggio, Il (1924–43) was founded in Colle di Val d'Elsa by the vintner Angiolo Bencini and Mino *Maccari as a fortnightly paper for the local *Fascist militia. Maccari took sole control in 1926 and made *Il Selvaggio* the voice of the *strapaese* movement within Fascism. With its vigorous cartoons and etchings, popularizing poems and humorous articles, it voiced in a way acceptable to the regime the grievances of rebellious *squadristi* who wanted *Mussolini to carry through the promised revolution. It advocated regionalism and ruralism as the ways to protect the true character of Italy against the corruption of modern life and culture which it saw embodied in *Bontempelli's *900 (*Novecento*) movement, or *stracittà*. Its criticisms of institutionalized Fascism led to its increasing isolation, especially after it spoke out against anti-Semitism in the later 1930s. Contributors included *Malaparte, *Soffici, and *Bilenchi, but the main presence was always Maccari, who took the paper with him to *Siena, to *Turin, and finally, in 1932, to *Rome. [DCH]

SELVAGGIO PORPORA, see BENTIVOGLIO, CORNELIO.

Semiotics or semiology, the general theory of signs, is important for the study of literature in two major ways: because it views the literary text as an act of communication, and because it places the text within a theory embracing all aspects of cultural life. It has a special importance for Italian literature because of its impact on the practice of *literary criticism in Italy from the late 1960s onwards; in the 1970s and 1980s semiotics was generally recognized in the Italian academic world as one of the leading approaches, if not the leading approach, to literature, and has continued to be a major influence since.

As the theory of signs, semiotics grows out of *structuralism and the work of Ferdinand de Saussure. Its Italian versions also draw heavily on the Americans C. S. Peirce and Charles Morris, as well as reflecting the strong influence of *Marxism on Italian academic culture. Its most influential theorist, in Italy and possibly worldwide, is the philosopher Umberto *Eco, whose seminal introduction, *La struttura assente*, was published in 1968, and who in 1974 was appointed by the University of *Bologna to the first chair in the subject in any country. But its impact on literary criticism resulted directly from its adoption by a number of more traditional academics, particularly in the field of Romance philology [see FILOLOGIA], the most prominent of whom were Cesare *Segre, Maria *Corti, D'Arco Silvio *Avalle, Marcello Pagnini, and Stefano Agosti. Thanks to the prestige of this group, and more generally to the high status traditionally assigned to theory by Italian critics, semiotic criticism acquired an importance in Italy unparalleled in any other country.

Italian semiotics takes over from structuralism a focus on the specific properties of the verbal medium of literature, which it integrates into a framework embracing all the factors in the process of literary communication. The concern with sign theory produces a special interest in codes, particularly literary codes such as genre conventions and the rules governing plot structures. At the same time due attention is given to author and reader, and above all to the text's relation to the ideological and material context in which it is produced. The result is a complex, multi-layered model of literary communication, dominated by the notion of a series of 'mediations' (author, reader, codes, ideology) between text and context, each layer being closely connected to the others, but also possessing its specific characteristics and functions.

While open to, and inspired by, the most advanced developments in modern literary and cultural theory, Italian semiotics has a strikingly consensual, even establishment character. It was deeply opposed to many aspects of the *critica estetica*, emanating from the philosophy of Benedetto *Croce, which dominated Italian criticism from the *Fascist period up to the late 1950s, and whose neglect of both the verbal medium and the social context of literature the semioticians aimed to correct. At the same time it maintained a traditional respect for philological precision, history, and the established literary canon, that contrasts with the radicalism of much of the work on which it drew, particularly French structuralist theory, and also helps to explain its academic impact. Italian semiotics has produced few novel revelations about literature; it offers a 'prudent and realistic' (Segre) set of guidelines for the practice of literary history and criticism, characterized by comprehensiveness, balance, flexibility and a high degree of practical common sense. [See also LITERARY THEORY, 6.] [DR]

See C. Segre, *Semiotics and Literary Criticism* (1973); M. Corti, *An Introduction to Literary Semiotics* (1978).

Sempione strizza l'occhio al Fréjus, Il, see VITTORINI, ELIO.

SEMPRONIO, GIOVAN LEONE (1603–c.1646). Poet whose *concettismo* is perhaps the closest in spirit to that of *Marino. He ironically celebrates aberrant loves, such as fair dwarves, giantesses, dark ladies, and servant girls, and systematically extrapolates from established conceits—as when he compares a lady with her hair in a towel to an Ottoman warrior; her face is crowned by the stars of her eyes, whilst the warrior has only the crescent moon on his turban. In addition to the lyrics of *La selva poetica* (1633–48), he wrote an *epic, *Il Boemondo* (1651), imitating Torquato *Tasso, but also echoing Marino's *Adone*, and a *tragedy drawn from *Dante, *Il conte Ugolino*. Little is known of his life except that he was born in *Urbino. [MPS]

Seniles, see PETRARCH, FRANCESCO.

Senilità (1898). Italo *Svevo's deflationary version of the novel of destructive passion. It tells the story of the over-literary insurance clerk Emilio Brentani's fanciful love affair with the working-class girl Angiolina Zarri, which turns obsessive and costs him the friendship of the sculptor Stefano Balli and the life of his sister Amalia. [JG-R]

Sensismo (French *sensisme*) is the doctrine which reduces all the contents of knowledge and consciousness to sense impressions. Its major exponent was Condillac (1715–80), who spent the years 1758–67 in Parma. From the late 1750s du Tillot, the most powerful minister at the court, used the presence of Condillac to secure a constant flow of French visitors to the city. Thus, for a short while, Parma became an important centre of *Enlightenment thought in Italy.

In his *Traité des sensations* (1754) Condillac, in opposition to the Cartesian theory of innate ideas, developed John Locke's conception of their empirical origin. Rejecting Locke's distinction between sensation and reflection, he went on to reduce the whole of psychic experience to combinations of sense impressions. An important corollary of these ideas was the notion that since all sensations are either pleasurable or unpleasing, we inevitably seek the former and avoid the latter.

The *sensismo* of Condillac influenced the juridical and ethical thinking of such figures as *Genovesi, *Romagnosi, *Gioia, *Beccaria, and

Sentiero dei nidi di ragno, Il

Pietro *Verri. It also influenced the development of Beccaria and Verri's aesthetic and literary theories, as well as those of *Algarotti and *Bettinelli. In the case of Verri, moreover, *sensismo* was fundamental to his thinking on pain and pleasure and to his theory of progress. In general, aided by the popularizing manuals of Francesco *Soave, it played an important part in replacing Cartesian rationalism as the dominant perspective informing reflections on the nature of language.

In Beccaria's *Dei delitti e delle pene, sensismo* informs his discussions of the nature of punishment for crimes. In his linguistic writings in *Il *Caffè*, he goes beyond the theory of words as simple signs for thoughts, which are the same for everybody, and stresses their nature as representing amalgams of sense impressions which are individually determined. This theme is developed by *Cesarotti, who argues, in his *Sopra i progressi dell'arte poetica* (1762), for a new art of poetry and criticism. He accepts the principle that poetry imitates nature, but observes that given the inexhaustible and varied impressions nature makes on the human mind, poetic imitation cannot be restricted within predetermined limits.   [GLCB]

See D. W. Hamlyn, *Sensation and Perception* (1961); D. Carpanetto and G. Ricuperati, *Italy in the Age of Reason 1685–1789* (1987).

Sentiero dei nidi di ragno, Il (1947), *Calvino's first novel, became the canonical *Neorealist fiction about the *Resistance. The urchin Pin's involvement with unheroic partisans is narrated from his viewpoint: the novel's success is mostly due to Calvino's creative blend of a *realist *Bildungsroman* with Stevensonian and fairy-tale motifs. [MMcL]

Sentimento del tempo, see UNGARETTI, GIUSEPPE.

Se questo è un uomo (1947, revised 1958). Primo *Levi's first and most important work. It is a powerful *autobiographical account of his deportation to the Nazi concentration camp at Auschwitz-Monowitz. Episodic and meditative in form, the book examines the qualities of life and human character revealed by the hideous cruelty of the camp system.   [RSCG]

SERAFINO AQUILANO (Serafino Ciminelli) (1466–1500). Poet who was highly successful in his own time and is now considered one of the more extreme representatives of 15th-c. *Petrarchism. Born into a noble family in L'Aquila, he moved in 1478 to *Naples, where he studied music and poetry. He moved to *Rome in the service of Cardinal Ascanio *Sforza, and there made his name as a poet and singer. He was subsequently invited to the courts of Naples, *Milan, *Mantua, and *Urbino, and performed in front of Charles VIII. His facile and fluid verse found its best expression in *strambotti*. He also wrote comic poems in the manner of *Burchiello, as well as imitations of *Sannazaro's eclogues.   [DieZ]

SERAO, MATILDE (1856–1927). One of the major literary figures of her time. Born in Greece, with a Greek mother, she grew up in *Naples, qualifying as a schoolteacher. She was introduced to *journalism by her father and was soon publishing reviews and short stories in various papers. She moved to *Rome in 1882, became a friend of *D'Annunzio, *Boito, and other literary figures, and wrote—amongst much else—an often provocative society column for *Cronaca bizantina*. She married Edoardo *Scarfoglio in 1885. The two of them returned to Naples, where they founded and ran *Il Corriere di Napoli* and *Il Mattino*. She separated from Scarfoglio in 1904, subsequently founding the weekly *La Settimana*, and the daily *Il Giorno*.

In some ways her more serious journalism seems simply to support the status quo. She kept her distance from the *feminist movement and ridiculed the notion of extending suffrage to women in articles such as 'Votazione femminile' (1883), though since a mere 6 per cent of Neapolitans had the vote anyway, any extension of suffrage would only have been to a privileged minority. However the articles collected in *Il ventre di Napoli* (1884) show a campaigning journalist, taking the government to task for its handling of the cholera epidemic in Naples and bearing witness to the appalling living conditions of the proletariat and the sub-proletariat at that time.

Much of Serao's creative work concentrates on the subjectivity of women. She gives sentimental fiction a twist in earlier novels such as *Cuore infermo* (1881) and *Fantasia* (1883), which explore dissatisfactions with heterosexual relationships and juxtapose them with possibly more fulfilling relationships between women. She saw herself as a *verista* writing alongside *Verga, *Capuana, and *De Roberto, and her best work has often been considered the *realist novels of her middle years, notably *Il paese di cuccagna* (1891), which depicts popular Neapolitan society fantasizing and scheming around the lottery. In later Gothic novels such as *La mano tagliata* (1912) she unexpectedly shifts the focus from the heterosexual couple to the complexities of mother–daughter relations. Though she was well thought of by Henry James amongst others, her reputation declined after her death. There has been a justified revival of interest in her in recent years.   [UJF]

See A. Banti, *Matilde Serao* (1965); W. de Nunzio Schilardi, *Matilde Serao giornalista* (1986).

SERCAMBI, GIOVANNI (1348–1424) is best known for his **novelle*, though he also wrote an important *chronicle of his native Lucca. Of modest origins, he rose to become *gonfaloniere*. After playing a key role in the ascent to power of the Guinigi family in 1400, he found himself excluded by the new **signori*, and henceforth devoted himself to writing. Following the **Decameron*, he represents the 155 stories in his *Novelliere* as being told to a group of people fleeing Lucca during the *plague of 1374, with himself as sole narrator. The stories are remarkably varied in their sources, but written in a perhaps deliberately unelaborate fashion, with morals appended that can seem at odds with their sometimes scabrous contents. They were first published in their entirety in the 20th c.   [PH]

SERDINI, SIMONE (Il Saviozzo) (*c.*1360–1419/20). *Lyric poet. He was exiled from his native *Siena in 1389 for involvement in a quarrel, and led a wandering life in the service of various *Tuscan warlords for the next three decades, including a brief return to Siena in 1400. He committed suicide in prison near Viterbo. He is an accomplished and erudite lyric poet in several genres, including the amorous, the political, and the burlesque. His most original works, such as the *canzone 'Le 'nfastidite labbia' ('The nauseated lips'), are laments in a rhetorically heightened style, or *disperate.   [SNB]

SERENI, VITTORIO (1913–83). Poet of considerable importance in his own right who also played a significant role in redirecting Italian poetry away from the *hermetic movement to more concrete engagement with contemporary realities. Born in Luino on the Lago Maggiore, he spent his childhood there and in Brescia, moving with his family to *Milan in 1932. He studied literature at Milan University and became part of the group associated with the review *Corrente*, which was responsible for publishing his first collection, *Frontiera* (1941), in which hermetic self-absorption

already shows signs of turning outwards. He was called up in 1941 and captured by the Allies in *Sicily in 1943, spending the rest of the war in a prison camp in North Africa. *Diario d'Algeria* (1947) was born of this experience, and is marked by the sense of enforced separation from the world and from the possibility of moral rebirth that the *Resistance offered his contemporaries in Italy. He returned to Milan in 1945 initially as a schoolteacher, moving to public relations at Pirelli in 1952 and to *Mondadori in 1958.

His postwar poetry as a whole attempts to take hold of day-to-day realities and issues in modern life without totally abandoning recognizably poetic features of the traditional Italian *lyric. *Gli strumenti umani* (1965) is impressive for its depth of feeling as much as for the steadiness and warmth of the writing, which marked out a new path without calling attention to itself. His last collection, *Stella variabile* (1982), is similar, though more openly prosaic in manner; the disillusionments of age do nothing to cloud Sereni's firm sense of moral responsibility or undermine the fineness of his style. As well as essays on poetry and some stories, he published important *translations of René Char and William Carlos Williams.   [EE]

Poesie, ed. D. Isella (1995). See A. Luzi, *Introduzione a Sereni* (1990).

SERGARDI, LUDOVICO (1660–1726) is best known as a *satirist. Born in *Siena, he moved to *Rome and embarked on a successful career in the *papal bureaucracy. He published his satires of Roman society under the name of Quinto Settano. They first appeared in Latin in 1694 and were subsequently translated by Sergardi into **terza rima*. A further satire on the hypocrisy of the clergy, *Conversazione delle dame di Roma*, seems to anticipate *Parini's *Il *giorno*. He is more openly vitriolic in his *letters and *sermons, denouncing not only the clergy but the linguistic doctrines of the Accademia della *Crusca and the theories of *Gravina. He also had artistic and medical interests; he designed the pavement for Piazza S. Pietro and the position of the obelisk, and sketched the kidney-stones found in Innocent XI's body after his death.   [FC]

SERIMAN, ZACCARIA (1708–84). *Novelist, *journalist, and *publisher. A Venetian from a noble family of Armenian extraction, he was educated in *Bologna in a *Jesuit college. In *Venice he was a member of the group of *Enlightenment thinkers headed by Marco Foscarini, Andrea Memmo, and

Sermini, Gentile

Angelo Querini, all of whom were influenced by the encyclopedic interests of the *Franciscan Carlo Lodoli in their project for cultural renewal. His novel *Viaggi di Enrico Wanton* appeared anonymously in 1749; modelled on the work of Swift as mediated by the French writer Desfontaines, it uses the novel form to express philosophical and pedagogical ideas. [IC]

SERMINI, GENTILE (early 15th c.). Little is known of his life except for his association with *Siena. Around 1424 he composed a collection of forty *Novelle*, largely risqué and scandalous tales with no unifying cornice, and interspersed with other types of writing in both prose and poetry. The collection is dedicated to his brother and is obstensibly intended to provide entertainment for him during a stay near Siena. [JEE]

Sermons have been written in the vernacular since at least the 13th c. In the *Middle Ages and *Renaissance, however, their authors were predominantly members of international religious orders who drew extensively on non-vernacular sources, and sometimes (*Savonarola is one instance) made prelimary sketches in Latin. Many vernacular sermons survive only in Latin summaries, such as St Antonio of Padua's *Sermones dominicales et festivi* (1221–31), or else in vernacular reports, such as the *Quaresimale fiorentino* of *Giordano da Pisa. These examples reflect the two principal audiences for sermons throughout their history: respectively, the preacher's fellow clergy and the laity. Many of the vernacular sermons of the *Franciscan St *Bernardino of Siena were known only in Latin printed versions until the 19th c. By contrast, Savonarola was unusual for his time in overseeing the publication of his sermons.

Such mendicant preachers changed the sermon from a monastic, Scripture-focused homily into a broader thematic discourse, which made extensive use of *exempla* to persuade lay and urban audiences. After a *humanist-inspired flirtation with neo-*Ciceronian Latin in the late 15th c., an evangelical revival led to a return to Scriptural roots. The Roman *Inquisition (refounded 1542) saw the dangers of doctrinal controversy in this, and redirected the sermon to the affirmation of orthodoxy. A key figure here was St Carlo *Borromeo. His brand of sacred oratory, in the hands of preachers such as Francesco Panigarola (1548–94), brought sermons into the domain of literature, and led to works such as *Marino's *Dicerie sacre* (1614).

The 17th and 18th c. was the golden age of penitential sermons, which formed the centrepiece of rural missions throughout Italy. Collections by the *Jesuit Paolo *Segneri and Alfonso de' *Liguori became best-sellers, and during the following century were cited as examples in standard manuals for parish priests. The latter began to play a significant role as preachers with the temporary abolition of the religious orders in 1810. The trend was reinforced when Leo XIII (1878–1903) and Pius X (1903–14) took measures to ensure their adequate training and to emphasize the catechistical role of the sermon. Such a role remains fundamental today, although sermons given by laypeople are increasingly common. [SD]

See R. Rusconi, 'Predicatori e predicazione (secoli IX–XVIII)', *Storia d'Italia*, *Annali* vol. iv (1981); G. Martina and U. Dovere (eds.), *La predicazione in Italia dopo il Concilio di Trento* (1996); M. Sodi (ed.), *Dizionario di omiletica* (1998).

SERRA, MICHELE, see TRAVEL WRITING.

SERRA, RENATO (1884–1915). One of the most important Italian *literary critics of the early 20th c. After a degree in literature at *Bologna University, he worked for a while in *publishing. But he was already active as a critic when he became head of the important Biblioteca Malatestiana in his home town of Cesena in 1909.

After contributing to provincial reviews, he wrote articles for *Prezzolini's *La *Voce*, collecting those on Giovanni *Pascoli and Antonio *Beltramelli and a discussion of *Carducci and *Croce as *Scritti critici* (1910). His extensive writings on contemporary literature, many not published until after his death, include a long essay on Kipling. In *Le lettere* (1914) he gives an overview of early 20th-c. literature, divided into older masters and new writers. He was called up in April 1915 and wounded fatally a few months later. *La Voce* had just published his long 'Esame di coscienza di un letterato', which discusses the contradictions faced by the Italian writer, torn between love of literature and the tragedy of war. Many young post-*World War I writers saw Serra as their mentor, admiring his elegance of style and the fineness of his critical insights. [AC]

Sestina. A form of *canzone made up entirely of *hendecasyllables, in six stanzas each of six lines and with a final verse or *congedo* of three lines, introduced into Italy by *Dante (who adapted a *canso* by the *troubadour Arnaut Daniel) and codified by *Petrarch. The lines do not rhyme with each other within the stanza, but each stanza has the same rhyme words, which rotate in the following sequence in relation to the stanza before: last, first, second from last, second, third from last, third, giving the pattern ABCDEF, FAEBDC, etc. In the *congedo* three of the same words are in rhyme position and three within the lines, according to varying schemes. [See also VERSIFICATION.]

[PGB]

SESTINI, BARTOLOMEO (1792–1822). Poetic *improviser. Born in *Florence, where he studied fine art, he had immense success throughout Italy. He was also a *carbonaro* and was arrested in 1819, after which he fled to France where he died. He also composed plays and a *novella in versi*, *La Pia* (1822), derived from *Purgatorio* 5.

[FD'I]

SETTALA, LODOVICO (1552–1633). Doctor who specialized in problems of public hygiene. He studied with the *Jesuits in *Milan and graduated in *medicine at Pavia. As a young doctor he treated the sick during the *plague that swept Milan in 1576, and did much in the region to prevent contagion and heal the sick during the outbreak of 1630, though he himself succumbed and remained handicapped.

He published his *De peste et pestiferis affectibus libri quinque* in 1622, and followed that in 1630 with his *Della preservazione della peste*. He appears in *Manzoni's *Promessi sposi* as an exemplary physician who, because of his foresight and rare knowledge of hygiene, was actually accused of creating and spreading the plague. Settala published Latin commentaries on Hippocrates, and his interest in social issues led to the publication of a Latin work on the management of the family (1626), and a seven-book treatment in Italian of the contemporary political debate on *ragion di stato*. [PBD]

SETTANO, QUINTO, see SERGARDI, LUDOVICO.

SETTE, GUIDO (d.1367). Long-standing friend of *Petrarch, and eventually Archbishop of *Genoa. Petrarch addressed numerous important letters to him, such as *Familiares* 19.9, on the warfare endemic in contemporary Italy, and *Seniles* 10.2, in which he gives an appraisal of his own life.

[MP]

SETTEMBRINI, LUIGI (1813–76). A major figure of the *Risorgimento, who spent his life fighting for his *liberal ideals, and was repeatedly arrested in his native *Naples or forced into *exile. In prison after the revolution of *1848, he spent five years translating Lucian's works. Dispatched in 1859 with other prisoners to America, he ended up teaching Italian in London for two years. From 1861 he was professor of Italian literature at the University of Naples, composing *Lezioni di letteratura italiana* (1866–72) for the young of the new Italy. His still enjoyable memoirs, *Ricordanze della mia vita*, were published by his friend Francesco *De Sanctis in 1879. [FD'I]

Settenari, see VERSIFICATION.

SETTIMELLI, EMILIO, see FUTURISM.

Se una notte d'inverno un viaggiatore (1979). Novel by *Calvino indebted to *semiotic and reader response theory, and centred on a male and female reader who read ten novel fragments. The frame-tale deals self-reflexively with the production and consumption of literature, while the novel fragments, in typical totalizing fashion, encapsulate contemporary narrative styles. [MMcL]

Sexuality, see EROTICISM AND PORNOGRAPHY; HOMOSEXUALITY.

SFORZA. The family name (denoting strength) derived from the nickname of Muzio Attendolo (1369–1424), a *condottiere* from the Romagna. An illegitimate son, Francesco (1401–66), served as *condottiere* under Filippo Maria *Visconti (1401–66), and acquired the Duchy of *Milan after the Ambrosian republic of 1447–50; his brother, Alessandro (1409–73), became lord of Pesaro in 1445. Francesco was succeeded by his sons Galeazzo Maria (1444–76) and Lodovico 'il Moro' (1451–1508). Galeazzo Maria's illegitimate daughter Caterina Sforza (c.1462–1509) achieved fame as ruler of Imola and Forlì, after the murder of her husband (1488), and offered a heroic, though doomed, resistance to Cesare *Borgia in 1499.

The Sforza dukes were among the most powerful rulers of Italy, but they failed to survive the Italian Wars of 1494–1559, Milan falling to the Habsburgs in 1535; the Pesaro branch ended in 1519. Both *courts were centres of *patronage for architecture, letters, and the arts; *Filarete, Francesco *Filelfo, Pier Candido *Decembrio,

Sforza Bentivoglio, Ginevra

*Leonardo da Vinci, and Bramante all frequented that of Milan, whilst the University of Pavia thrived, particularly under the guidance of Lodovico.
[JEL & SJM]

SFORZA BENTIVOGLIO, GINEVRA, see ARIENTI, GIOVANNI SABADINO DEGLI; PATRONAGE.

SGORLON, CARLO (1930–). Novelist who has enjoyed considerable popular success. His fiction centres on his native Friuli. In some novels, such as *Il trono di legno* (1973), he gives to the ostensibly *realistic representation of archaic *peasant culture a mythic and magical aura. In others he achieves an accessible and engaging combination of real facts and fantasy, old legends and modern tragedy. One of his most impressive books, *L'armata dei fiumi perduti* (1985), mediates an account of *Jewish persecution during *World War II and the displacement of the Cossack people through the customs and myths of a remote Italian village and its visionary female protagonist, Marta. Sgorlon has a degree in German literature from the Scuola Normale in *Pisa, and has published studies of Kafka and Elsa *Morante. The influence of both is evident in his work. [PBart]

SGRICCI, TOMMASO, see IMPROVISED POETRY.

SGRUTTENDIO DE SCAFATO, FILIPPO. The author—otherwise unidentified but sometimes thought to be Giulio Cesare *Cortese—of *De la tiorba a taccone* (1646), a vigorous *parody of *Marino's poetry in *Neapolitan *dialect. Its ten sections are termed *corde*, that is, the strings of the guitar-like *tiorba* (which is played with a *taccone* or plectrum). [DO'G]

SHAKESPEARE often uses Italian settings and characters in his plays. Eight have major Italian sources (*Ariosto, *Bandello, and *Giraldi Cinzio among them), all available to him in English or French translations. It is unlikely that he visited Romeo's Verona and Shylock's *Venice, or that he knew more than a few words of Italian. Local details in the plays were probably supplied by Italian acquaintances and by John *Florio, who is the source of phrases in *The Taming of the Shrew*. Yet Shakespeare's Italy is notably less conventional and *Machiavellian than Marlowe's or Webster's. *Castiglione's *Cortegiano* provided him with an image of accomplished courtly life and even instructions on the kinds of puns appropriate for a courtier, though Shakespeare disregarded Castiglione's prohibition of obscene quibbles. The *Sonnets* show him well versed in 'the numbers that *Petrarch flowed in' (*Romeo and Juliet* II. iv) and in the conceits of *Petrarchists like *Serafino Aquilano.

The first Italian to mention 'Shakespier' was *Magalotti (1667), but it was only as a consequence of Voltaire's appraisal and aspersions that Shakespeare became familiar to Italian writers. Paolo *Rolli compares him to *Dante in his *Osservazioni in risposta al Saggio del Voltaire sulla poesia epica* (1728); *Baretti repeated Johnson's and Addison's anti-*classicist arguments in *Discours sur Shakespeare et sur Monsieur de Voltaire* (1778). *Goldoni had satirized a foolish imitator of 'Sachespir' in *I malcontenti* (1754). *Alfieri, Vincenzo *Monti, and *Foscolo all admired and imitated Shakespeare, whom they read in P. F. Letourneur's French, as did *Manzoni, the most authoritative of the bard's Italian champions. There are Shakespearean scenes in *Adelchi*, and a famous ironic allusion in *I *promessi sposi* (ch. 7) to Voltaire's 'barbaro non privo di ingegno'. *Mazzini in 1830 and *De Sanctis (in twelve lectures of 1846–7) celebrated Shakespeare's presentation of personalities and harmonious vision of life's contradictions. This reading was developed by *Croce in a lucid and influential philosophical study (1919). Meanwhile, *Verdi's *operas *Macbeth*, *Otello*, and *Falstaff* (based on *The Merry Wives of Windsor*) showed a profound poetic and theatrical understanding of Shakespeare, and made the three plays, often produced on the Italian stage, more familiar to popular audiences.

The earliest partial prose *translation, by Giustina *Renier Michiel, appeared in 1798 in *Venice. Michele *Leoni then published fourteen volumes of *Tragedie* (1819–22). Carlo Rusconi's complete but faulty prose version (1839) was widely read until Mario *Praz produced a modern edition of the plays (1943–7). *Pasolini brilliantly adapted *Othello* as a puppet play with the comedian Totò as Iago in his short film *Che cosa sono le nuvole?* (1968).
[MB]

See B. Croce, *Ariosto, Shakespeare e Corneille* (1920); M. Praz, *Caleidoscopio shakespeariano* (1969).

Short story, see NOVELLA AND RACCONTO.

SICILIANI, PIETRO, see DARWINISM.

SICILIANO, ENZO (1934–). *Literary critic, *novelist, and a notable figure in the intellectual and cultural life of *Rome since the mid-1960s. His first work was *Racconti ambigui* (1963). He is one of the editors of *Nuovi argomenti*, and director of the Gabinetto *Vieusseux in *Florence. He was a controversial president of Italian state *television and *radio (RAI) in the late 1990s.   [RSCG]

Sicilian School. A loosely organized group of some twenty poets, who were active at the *court of *Frederick II in *Sicily and Southern Italy in the first half of the 13th c. They have been seen since *Dante as the originators of the Italian tradition of *lyric poetry.

The majority were Sicilians, though a few came from as far north as *Tuscany. Writing in an elevated form of the Sicilian *dialect, they imitated Provençal *troubadours, with some debts also to French *trouvères* and German *Minnesinger*. The subject of their poetry was refined love (*fino amore*) and they generally treat the beloved lady, the role of the lover, and the effects of passion according to established patterns. Most of them were in effect imperial civil servants, including *Giacomo da Lentini (who is generally considered the leader of the school), *Guido delle Colonne, *Iacopo Mostacci, and *Pier della Vigna, but their poetry recreated the *feudal trappings of their predecessors: the lady was a lord and the poet-lover played the faithful vassal who served in order to gain her affection or a token of it ('guiderdone'). Departures from this refined and noble courtly manner are to be found in certain poems by *Giacomino Pugliese and *Compagnetto da Prato, which have a more popular, realistic air. *Cielo d'Alcamo's 'Rosa fresca aulentissima' is a uniquely comic dialogue poem which stands apart from the other poems we have.

The more elevated poems are permeated with Provençal features. As well as rarer items, there are repeated word-forms such as 'intendanza' ('love', Prov. 'intendansa'), 'sollazzo' ('pleasure', Prov. 'solatz'), 'coraggio' ('heart', 'courage', Prov. 'coratge'), etc.; metrical techniques, such as 'coblas capfinidas' (beginning a stanza with the last word of the stanza preceding) and 'coblas unissonans' (using the same rhyme-sounds throughout a *canzone*); and devices such as the use of a secret name (*senhal*) to hide the lady's identity. The *canzone* and *discordo* are both adaptations of Provençal metrical forms, though the *sonnet is an invention of the Sicilians, probably of Giacomo da Lentini.

The *canzone* by *Stefano Protonotaro, 'Pir meu

cori alligrari' ('To gladden my heart'), is the only complete poem to have survived in its original linguistic dress. Virtually all the rest survive in manuscripts compiled and written by Tuscan scribes who adapted the texts to Tuscan usage.

Dante speaks highly of Guido delle Colonne, Giacomo da Lentini, and *Rinaldo d'Aquino in the *De vulgari eloquentia*. *Petrarch suggests that the pre-eminence of the Sicilian poets is now merely chronological priority (*Trionfo d'amore* 4.35–6). Most subsequent assessments also tended to emphasize historical importance over aesthetic excellence, though in recent years the aesthetic qualities of their work have been increasingly acknowledged.   [CK]

Le rime della scuola siciliana, ed. B. Panvini (1962). See E. Pasquini and A. E. Quaglio, *Le origini e la scuola siciliana* (1971); C. Kleinhenz, *The Early Italian Sonnet* (1986).

Sicily. The fact of being a large island at the centre of the Mediterranean has meant that since antiquity Sicily has had a history and culture distinct from those of mainland Italy. All the same, the bonds between the two have always been stronger than those between Sicily and other countries to which it has been often forcibly linked. Sicilian is an Italic *dialect, and since medieval times most Sicilian writers have written in Italian, Sicilian dialect, or Latin, rather than in the language of one or other of their invaders.

Ancient Sicily remained strongly Greek under the Romans and was part of the *Byzantine empire from the 6th to the 9th c. But in 827 it was invaded by the Arabs, who ruled the whole island from 902 until being driven out by the Normans in the later 11th c. During the Arab occupation Sicily was an important centre of Arab science and thought. The poet Ibn Hamdìs, who was born in Syracuse in 1055 but who died in Majorca in 1133, has often been treated as an emblematic figure of *exile by later Sicilian writers.

Thanks to dynastic marriages, Sicily passed under German control at the start of the 13th c. and entered on arguably the most splendid period of its post-classical history. *Frederick II founded *universities, built castles and cities, and established an intellectually and culturally sophisticated cosmopolitan *court, one feature of which was the *Sicilian School of poets, the founders of the Italian tradition of *lyric poetry. But the defeat of German power by Charles of *Anjou in the 1260s brought cultural disarray and political turmoil. The revolt of the

Siculo-Tuscan Poets

Sicilian Vespers (1289) led to the island passing to the *Aragonese, though conflicts with the *Naples house of Anjou and their supporters continued until the Aragonese also became rulers of Naples in 1442. They in turn were succeeded by the Spanish in 1504, who ruled, sometimes with *Baroque splendour, for the next two centuries. Some cultural activity continued throughout this period. *Humanism showed itself in the work of figures such as Antonio Cassarino (1379–1447) of Noto, who translated Plutarch and Plato's *Republic*. And there were *Petrarchists such as Argisto Giufreddi (1535–93) and Antonio *Veneziano, who also wrote verse in Sicilian dialect.

With the emergence of French *Bourbons as rulers of Naples and Sicily in the 18th c., *Enlightenment ideas began to take hold through figures such as Francesco Paolo Di Blasi (1753–95) and the viceroy Domenico Caracciolo, who at last abolished the *Inquisition in 1792, whilst in literature Giovanni *Meli was an *Arcadian of advanced ideas and another notable dialect poet. Ferdinand of Naples managed to maintain a relatively liberal government in Sicily when the rest of Italy was under *Napoleonic control, becoming somewhat more authoritarian on his return to Naples to rule over what was generally known as the Kingdom of the Two Sicilies. Sicilian *liberals rebelling against the Bourbons led to the *1848 revolutions in Italy, but it was *Garibaldi's expedition of 1860 which brought about their fall and the integration of the island in the kingdom of Italy. But the *Risorgimento and *Unification, however enthusiastically embraced by the minuscule middle class, were for most Sicilians a failed revolution, leading to *Piedmontese taxation and exploitation and the *emigration of a large proportion of the population to the USA and South America.

All the same, the later 19th c. saw a cultural resurgence. New historians emerged, such as Isidoro La Lumia (1823–79) and the historian of Arab Sicily, Michele Amari (1806–89). *Verismo was the creation (outside Sicily) of the Sicilians Giovanni *Verga and Luigi *Capuana, with Federico *De Roberto as its third principal exponent. In the early 20th c. *modernism had one of its major figures in Luigi *Pirandello, whilst Italian *idealism had its major philosopher after *Croce in Giovanni *Gentile. At the other extreme Alessio Di Giovanni (1872–1946) reaffirmed the strength of dialect poetry.

*Fascism, which boasted that its Prefetto Mori had done away with the *Mafia, was embraced by writers such as *Vittorini and *Brancati as young men, though both then turned fiercely against it. But to many it seemed that Sicily had been caught in an unchangeable torpor since at least 1860, a view best captured in *Tomasi di Lampedusa's *Il *gattopardo* (1958). Leonardo *Sciascia tried to present a counter-case and to work actively for real change on the island, though a tragic view of Sicilian history remains in his work and in that of his younger successor, Vincenzo *Consolo. A less politicized, though equally intellectual, form of writing is evident in the fiction and essays of Gesualdo *Bufalino. Perhaps one of the major signs of real cultural change in recent decades is that, unlike almost all their predecessors, significant writers like Sciascia and Bufalino lived and worked in Sicily itself, and had the support of a Palermo publisher, *Sellerio, with a national distribution network.

[AWM]

See D. Mack Smith, *A History of Sicily* (1968).

Siculo-Tuscan Poets. Fairly loose modern term designating those poets who lived in the prosperous mercantile city-states of central Italy—*Tuscany in particular—and who, despite their very different cultural milieu, imitated the poetry of the *Sicilian School, as well as that of the Provençal *troubadours. They are usually (but not always) distinguished from *Guittone d'Arezzo and his many followers. Some figures (*Bonagiunta da Lucca, in particular) demonstrate a certain freshness of sentiment and expression, but on the whole the Siculo-Tuscans limit themselves to conventional imagery and a generally less complicated style than that of Guittone.

Bonagiunta is probably the earliest member of this non-existent 'school' and may well have played a pivotal role as an intermediary between the Sicilian School and Tuscany, both for other Siculo-Tuscans and for Guittone and the Guittonians. *Florence, however, quickly becomes one major centre for Siculo-Tuscan poetry with figures such as Chiaro *Davanzati, La *Compiuta Donzella, Carnino Ghiberti, Neri de' Visdomini, Pietro Morovelli, Megliore degli Abati, and Mastro Francesco. The other major centre is *Pisa, with *Galletto, Tiberto Galiziani, Pucciandone Martelli, and Lunardo del Guallacca. But the fashion was widespread to the west of Florence. In *Siena there were Folcacchiero dei Folcacchieri and Caccia; in Pistoia, Lemmo Orlandi; and in Lucca, *Inghilfredi, as well as Bonagiunta.

The Siculo-Tuscan manner gave way to the

dolce stil novo in Florence in the later 13th c. A late practitioner was *Dante da Maiano, who exchanged poems with *Dante Alighieri, himself writing in the old style at the very start of his poetic career. [CK] *Poeti del Duecento*, ed. G. Contini, vol. i (1960). See E. Pasquini and A. E. Quaglio, *Le origini e la scuola siciliana* (1971); C. Kleinhenz, *The Early Italian Sonnet* (1986).

Siena became a great medieval commercial and *banking centre, as well as the hub of the Ghibelline alliance, particularly rivalling *Guelf *Florence; but after the Ghibelline victory at Montaperti in 1260, Siena's history was a tale of decline in favour of Florence. Sienese politics in the 14th and 15th c. were dominated by the *monti*, a type of class into which the citizenry were divided. Although the city came under the one-man rule of Pandolfo Petrucci at the turn of the 16th c., republican government was restored until it became subject to the Florentine Duke Cosimo de' *Medici in 1559. [RDB]

Signora di Challant, La, see GIACOSA, GIUSEPPE.

Signoria. Term used to describe the lordship of a single family or individual over a specific territory. The political landscape of medieval and *Renaissance Italy was characterized by the struggle between the rival forms of republic or *commune and principality or *signoria*. During the course of the 13th c., the liberty of the city-states was increasingly eroded by older *feudal families re-establishing hegemony over the previously self-governing popular communes that had sought to dominate them. Beginning with the *Montefeltro in *Urbino (1234), and continuing to the Carrara in *Padua (1318), these dynastic families led the so-called refeudalization of much of the Italian peninsula. [SJM]

SIGONIO, CARLO (also Sigone) (1523/4–84). Erudite philologist and *historian, whose works include a twenty-volume history of early medieval Italy (1574 and 1591). He was born in Modena and studied with Francesco Porto and Ludovico *Castelvetro. At the *University of *Padua he was involved in an acrimonious dispute with Francesco *Robortello. In 1562 he published his *De dialogo* on poetics, a work which had an influence on the young Torquato *Tasso, who had followed his lectures in 1560–2. A man of independent thought, he

had close links with the Catholic reform movement [see COUNTER-REFORMATION]. [PLR]

SILONE, IGNAZIO (Secondino Tranquilli) (1900–78) was born in Pescina de' Marsi in Abruzzo. His father was a republican, his mother a weaver. Educated as a 'candidate for the clergy', as he said, he became politically active in the aftermath of the 1915 earthquake, in which he and his younger brother Romolo were orphaned. Via the *Peasant Leagues he went to *Rome, discovered *Marxism, and joined the *Socialist Youth, then the *Communist Party at its foundation in 1921. He helped to run the clandestine press. In Spain he was imprisoned several times and took his pseudonym. In Russia he met Lenin, Trotsky, and Stalin. He writes in *Uscita di sicurezza* (1965) of his final disillusionment with Stalinism when in 1927 *Togliatti and he were expected to sign a document condemning Trotsky. Equally he disliked the treatment of the Moscow poor. New but currently (2001) contested evidence has been produced that he acted as a *Fascist double agent in the later 1920s. He was expelled from the Party in 1931. In 1929, when he had taken refuge in Switzerland with suspected tuberculosis, Romolo was captured trying to join him and died in Procida; there have been suggestions that Silone may have offered to spy for the Fascist police in order to save him. The circumstances of Romolo's death are reminiscent of that of Berardo in *Fontamara* (1933), Silone's best-known work, written at a clinic in Davos, and a powerful fictional indictment of Fascism as seen through the eyes of the *cafoni*, the peasant inhabitants of an Abruzzi village.

Fontamara was followed by five short stories, published in Zurich as *Die Reise nach Paris* (1934), and by *Der Fascismus* (1934), a history of Fascism; Silone allowed neither to appear in Italian. *Pane e vino* (1936) and its sequel, *Il seme sotto la neve* (1942), follow the life of a left-wing agitator living incognito in Abruzzo and finally sacrificing himself; the mixture of political and religious values are typical of Silone's idealism. *Ed egli si nascose* (1944) is the dramatic version of *Pane e vino. La scuola dei dittatori* (1938), a skit on dictatorship, came out in Italy in 1962. Because of *censorship, during the Fascist period these works were only known abroad, in translation, where they were very popular. Silone also ran the Socialist Foreign Centre in Zurich until 1940, and was imprisoned briefly in 1942 for contravening Swiss neutrality by smuggling an anti-Fascist newspaper into Italy. In

Silvia

October 1944 he returned to Rome and worked in the Socialist Party with his friend Saragat, later President of Italy. He became editor of the Socialist paper *Avanti!*, and was elected as an Abruzzi member of the constituent assemby. He left active politics in 1949.

From 1945 onwards he rewrote his early works: *Fontamara* (1949), *Vino e pane* (1955, the revised version of *Pane e vino*), *Il seme sotto la neve* (1961), *Ed egli si nascose* (1965). The result is a more universal view and an acknowledgement of the failure of the looked-for revolutionary action against Fascism in the South. The first version of the *autobiographical *Uscita di sicurezza* appeared in 1949 in *Umanità*, and in translation in Richard Crossman's *The God that Failed* (1950). *Una manciata di more* (1952) further reflects Silone's disillusionment with Communism; *Il segreto di Luca* (1956) considers personal honour in the figure of a peasant ex-convict; *La volpe e le camelie* (1960), his only novel set outside Abruzzo, explores the conscience of a Fascist spy in Switzerland. *L'avventura di un povero cristiano* (1968) is a play about the Abruzzi Pope *Celestine V who abdicated, sacrificing political power for private ideals. *La speranza di suor Severina* (1981, unfinished, edited by Darina Silone) is about a nun who leaves her convent having acted as a witness against police brutality, losing her faith but keeping her hope alive. Silone also edited *Tempo presente* from 1956 to 1968 with Nicola Chiaromonte. They both resigned when they discovered it was CIA-funded.   [JR]

See L. d'Eramo, *L'opera di Ignazio Silone, saggio critico e guida bibliografica* (1971); I. Origo, *A Need to Testify* (1984); M. N. Paynter, *Ignazio Silone: Beyond the Tragic Vision* (2000).

Silvia. Heroine of Torquato *Tasso's *Aminta*; also the name of the subject of a famous poem by *Leopardi, 'A Silvia'.

SIMONE DA CASCIA (c. 1295–1348). *Augustinian friar and religious writer. From 1317 onwards he was particularly active as a preacher in *Tuscany. In 1333, on a preaching visit to *Florence, he composed an *Ordine della vita cristiana*. His Latin works include letters and a life of Christ, *De gestis Domini Salvatoris*.   [JP & JMS]

SIMONETTA, GIOVANNI, see PATRONAGE.

SIMONI, RENATO (1875–1952), playwright and man of the *theatre, was well respected for his

plays and as a theatre director, particularly for his productions of *Goldoni's *comedies. He is now best remembered for his theatre criticism, five volumes of masterly reviews providing a useful resource for historians of the Italian theatre.
                                                            [JAL]

Sine nomine, see PETRARCH, FRANCESCO.

SINISGALLI, LEONARDO (1908–81). Poet, best known for his *hermetic work. Born near Potenza, he graduated as an engineer in *Rome and worked in industrial design for Pirelli, Alitalia, and other firms in the North and Centre. He published his first collection, *Quaderno di geometria*, in 1936. His poetry as a whole is elegant and epigrammatic, recalling in sharply etched images the mythic immobility of his native Lucania, and contrasting with it his later nomadic working life. He also published *autobiographical stories on similar themes and essays on mathematics, science, and the figurative arts.   [SPC]

Sirventese (or *serventese*). A form of poetic composition which originated among the *troubadours in the 'service' of their lord. In 13th- and 14th-c. Italy, *sirventesi* covered a wide variety of subjects—historical, political, civic, and didactic—often taking the form of a diatribe or invective. Early examples include the historical *sirventesi* describing the strife between *Guelfs and Ghibellines in *Bologna and Romagna in the 1270s.   [PA]

Sistema periodico, Il, see LEVI, PRIMO.

Slang (*gergo*). As a conventional, often deliberately cryptic idiom or vocabulary, used within a restricted social group, slang usually originates as a parasitic formation within a given language or *dialect. In the 15th c. thieves and other groups on the fringes of society used a *lingua zerga*, or *lingua furbesca* or *furbesco*, which served as a vocabulary resource for comic writing. Luigi *Pulci, by whom we have a slang letter to Lorenzo de' *Medici, also compiled a short list of words and phrases in *furbesco*. In the 16th c. the *Nuovo modo de intendere la lingua zerga*, a dictionary of slang probably by Antonio Brocardo, became many writers' vade mecum. Because of its expressive force, slang was also used sporadically in the *theatre and in poetry. The *Milanese Carl'Antonio *Tanzi wrote a *Dialegh in lengua furbesca e milanesa tra Sganaffa e Gaböt* (1766). Though Carlo *Dossi was in favour

558

of using *gerghi*, modern urban slang is extensively exploited for the first time in Italian fiction by *Gadda and *Pasolini. In the 1980s the language of young city people—slang in a loose sense—was cultivated by writers such as *Tondelli and the *cannibali who followed. [See also DIALECT WRITING; SPOKEN LANGUAGE IN LITERATURE.]   [DieZ]

SLATAPER, SCIPIO (1888–1915). *Triestine writer. Like others of his generation from Trieste, he found his point of cultural reference in *Florence, where he studied at the university (1908–12) and came into direct contact with *La * Voce*, eventually becoming its editor (1909–10). His extensive *journalism enthusiastically supported *irredentism and Italian intervention in *World War I. He is best known for *Il mio Carso* (1912), a lyrical *autobiography with a diary-like air, written in brief, fragmentary chapters in a variety of literary and linguistic registers. It is both a romantic and an experimentally modern work, which explores a complex dialectic between nature and culture; nature in the form of the Carso offers an ideal mirror in which the writer-protagonist can see himself, but there is also a conflicting pull of the city of Trieste, representing culture, and a consequent fragmentation of the wholeness which seemed to be promised. Slataper returned from a period in Hamburg as Italian lector in 1913 more *nationalist than ever. He enlisted in the Italian army in May 1915 and was killed on the Austrian front a few months later. His writings were published posthumously by his friend Giani *Stuparich.   [KP]

SOAVE, FRANCESCO (1743–1806). *Educationalist. Born in Lugano, he entered the Order of the Somaschi and became a teacher. His pupils included (briefly) *Manzoni. He organized the first state elementary schools in *Lombardy (1786–89), pioneered the school textbook, and published humanitarian *novelle morali* that were a landmark in Italian *children's literature and went through over 100 editions between 1782 and 1909. In philosophy he influentially promoted an eclectic empiricism (derived from Locke, Condillac, and Bonnet) through *translations and his popular *Istituzioni di logica, metafisica ed etica* (1791). [See also GRAMMARS.]   [JMAL]

SOCCI, ETTORE (1846–1905). *Pisan republican who wrote an account of his part in *Garibaldi's 1870 campaign in France in *Da Firenze a Digione: impressioni di un reduce*

garibaldino (1871). A *journalist and novelist, he was elected to parliament in 1892 and campaigned to extend the suffrage, especially for women.   [JD]

Socialism in Italy is inseparable from the Italian Socialist Party (PSI), which was founded in 1892 in *Genoa. It was led for many years by its reformist, leader Filippo Turati, though it was divided into maximalist (revolutionary), reformist, and syndicalist wings. *Mussolini was a maximalist leader until he was expelled for supporting Italy's entry into *World War I at a time when the party was alone amongst European socialist parties in being opposed to the war. Divisions came to a head at the 1921 Congress at Livorno, when the maximalists left to form the Italian *Communist Party (PCI). Left disunity was a major contribution to *Fascist success after the March on Rome in October 1922 and continued unresolved from then onwards. After the war *Christian Democrat (DC) and Socialist alliances kept the Communists out of power between the 1960s and the redrawing of the Italian political map in the early 1990s. But the Socialist Party never developed a convincing political culture of its own, though its share of the votes rose to about 15 per cent. Like the DC, it was destroyed by corruption scandals. Its leader and former Prime Minister, Bettino Craxi, fled to Tunisia, and its supporters moved to the new parties that emerged from the collapse of the First Republic.   [DS]

Società (1945–61) had a complex history. It was founded in *Florence as the independent equivalent of *Rinascita*. Edited by the archeologist Ranuccio Bianchi Bandinelli (with Romano *Bilenchi and Cesare Luporini as deputies), it drew in idealist intellectuals who joined or allied themselves with the *Communist Party (PCI). Internationalist in outlook and eager to tackle general political themes, it came under pressure from *Togliatti to treat Italian issues of a purely cultural nature and contribute more actively to the study of *Marxism. From 1946 to 1953 the PCI played a strong supervisory role. After that date the journal was much more independent.   [SG]

SOCINI, FAUSTO, see RENAISSANCE.

SOFFICI, ARDENGO (1879–1964). Poet, painter, and critic, once influential and admired. Born into a farming family near *Florence, he

559

began to study fine art there but moved to Paris in 1900. He became part of its avant-garde culture, which he then did much to popularize in Italy. Back in Florence in 1907, he was one of the founders of *La *Voce* (1908), together with *Prezzolini and *Papini. His first autobiographical novel, *Lemmonio Boreo* (1911), traces the exploits of Lemmonio as he goes through his native region setting perceived wrongs violently to rights in a way that seems to look forwards to *Fascist *squadrismo*. Soffici again joined with Papini to found the more *Futurist *Lacerba* (1913) and began to experiment with Futurist ideas and techniques in his paintings and writings, notably *BIF$ZF+18*. *Simultaneità*. *Chimismi lirici* (1915).

After fighting in *World War I, he wrote a fictionalized version of his experiences in *Kobilek* (1918) and published a journal, *Rete mediterranea*, which he single-handedly wrote and edited. But his thinking and creative work now took a narrowly traditionalist turn. He became a convinced supporter of *Fascism and attempted to elaborate the principles of a distinctively Fascist art. He was a leading figure in the *strapaese* movement, but writings such as *Taccuino d'Arno Borghi* (1933) display clear anti-Semitism as well as regional chauvinism.

[CFB]

See L. Corsetti, *Nuovi contributi critici su Ardengo Soffici* (1994).

Sofonisba, see TRISSINO, GIANGIORGIO.

SOGRAFI, SIMEONE ANTONIO (1759–1818). Dramatist. Born in *Padua, where he took a degree in law, he moved to *Venice and became a successful *librettist and writer of *comedies. He is best known for the one-act comedies *Le convenienze teatrali* (1794) and *Le inconvenienze teatrali* (1800).

[DO'G]

Solaria (1926–34, though the last issue only appeared in 1936). Important literary journal, founded in *Florence by Alberto *Carocci, with the help of Raffaello Franchi, Bonaventura *Tecchi, and Eugenio *Montale at a time when the *Fascist regime was clamping down on press freedom. The title, taken from *Campanella's utopian *Città del sole*, was indicative of the group's aspiration to construct an autonomous republic of literature. The opening number disclaimed a literary programme, but indicated continuity with *La *Ronda* and *Il *Baretti*, for both of which some early contributors had written. The review also opened itself up to

other more innovative figures, most notably *Gadda.

Though eclectic, *Solaria* was decidedly antiprovincial. It introduced to Italy writers such as Joyce, Proust, and Kafka, and it recognized the importance of the *novel (as opposed to *prosa d'arte*), especially the work of *Svevo and *Tozzi. Though there were internal differences between Carocci and the assistant editor, Alessandro *Bonsanti, the end came when the Fascist authorities censored publication of *Vittorini's *Il garofano rosso* and Enrico Terracini's *Le figlie del generale*, ostensibly on moral grounds.

[DCH]

SOLDANI, IACOPO (1579–1641) is known for his eight *Satire* (published posthumously). His targets included the *court, hypocrisy, inconstancy, luxury, and avarice. The fourth *satire, composed in 1623, is particularly important for its anti-*Aristotelian, pro-*Galilean views; and the sixth is interesting for its *Stoic outlook on life. A *Florentine through and through, he was a member of the Accademia della *Crusca (and its head for some time), and, like other *Tuscan satirists, avoided the style associated with *Secentismo* and *concettismo*. The balance and purity of his Tuscan language caused his work to be used as source material for the third edition (1691) of the *Vocabolario della Crusca*. He was a friend of the younger *Buonarroti, with whom he shared a romantic feeling for nature.

[PBD]

SOLDANIERI, NICCOLÒ DI NERI (d.1385). *Florentine poet and supporter of the Ghibellines [see GUELFS AND GHIBELLINES]. He ranged widely across genres, owing much in his moralizing *canzoni* to *Petrarch, but he is best known for his *cacce, *ballate*, and *madrigali*, short poems intended for performance with musical accompaniment and dancing.

[SNB]

SOLDATI, MARIO (1906–99) was prolific and highly successful both as a writer and as a film director. A period studying in America indelibly marked him, giving rise to *America, primo amore* (1935), while one of his characteristic veins was memorialistic. From 1940 onwards he published a book every two or three years. His first novel, *Salmace* (1929), was followed by novels and short stories strong on complex and skilful plots, and vividly evoked settings, including *Smeraldo* (1974, a darkly apocalyptic novel of fantasy politics), *Lo scopone* (1982, with M. Corgnati, almost a manual on the card game of that name), and *Nuovi racconti del maresciallo* (1984, which was turned into a highly successful popular *television series). He was best known as a film director for his literary adaptations, particularly of *Fogazzaro: *Piccolo mondo antico* (1940) and *Malombra* (1942), are both examples of the style dubbed *calligrafismo*. *Fuga in Francia* (1948) was his contribution to *Neorealism. He worked as second unit director on King Vidor's *War and Peace* (1955) and William Wyler's *Ben Hur* (1959). [See also CINEMA.] [CGW]

SOLMI, SERGIO (1899–1981). Poet and critic. After a degree in law from *Turin, he fought in *World War I and then went on to a career in banking in *Milan. He was a founder of *Primo tempo* in 1922, in which his friend Eugenio *Montale published his first poems. His own first collection, *Fine di stagione* (1932), was in the classicizing manner of *La *Ronda*, though his later verse became stylistically more relaxed and more deeply meditative. He fought in the *Resistance in *World War II and was twice imprisoned. His criticism focused on modern French literature and on *Leopardi, but he also wrote on art and *science fiction. [CO'B]

SOMMARIVA, GIORGIO (second half of the 15th c.). Poet. From an old Veronese family, he practised *law, held civic office, and in 1488 was sent by the *Venetian Republic to Gradisca as governor. As well as love verses imitating *Petrarch, he composed poetical works in the *dialects of Verona, Venice, Bergamo, *Padua, and Friuli as well as in Tuscan, using a simple and lively language which reflects the vivacity of the spoken idiom. [CG]

SOMMARUGA, ANGELO (1857–1941). Publisher. He founded the *Roman literary magazine *Cronaca bizantina* (1881), then branched into book *publishing and increased his periodical holdings. In 1885 the Depretis government, attacked in one of his magazines, suspended his activities and brought him to trial. He spent most of the rest of his life in self-imposed *exile. [DF]

SOMMI, LEONE DE' (1525–92) was a *Mantuan *Jew and a semi-professional practitioner of *theatre, who wrote in both Italian and Hebrew. His *Wedding Comedy* in the latter language is an interesting sign of the spread of *humanist culture. In his *Dialoghi in materia di rappresentazioni sceniche* he gives a thorough treatment of dramaturgy, acting, and staging, making equal use of scholarship, the-

ory and practical experience to demand the highest possible standards. [RAA]

Sonnet (*sonetto*). The normal form, from its beginnings to the present day, is of fourteen *hendecasyllables, divided into two parts of eight and six lines (in the earliest examples usually linked by the repetition in line 9 of a word or concept taken from the first part). The first part (called the *fronte, ottava, ottetto,* or *quartine*) originally had the rhyme scheme ABABABAB, but from the *dolce stil novo* onwards the scheme ABBAABBA is more common, emphasizing the division of the *fronte* into two quatrains that remains dominant in the work of Petrarch and his followers. Other rhyme schemes for the *fronte* are very rare. The second part (called *sirma, sestina, sestetto, terzine,* and in the past also *mute*) initially had the rhyme scheme CDCDCD or CDECDE; CDEEDC, CDEDCE or even CDCCDC are also quite common; the scheme for the *sirma* is allowed to vary considerably, much more than that of the *fronte,* provided that no line remains unrhymed.

The sonnet form originates in the *Sicilian School, most probably in the work of *Giacomo da Lentini. The name means 'little melody' or 'little song' (from the Provençal *sonet,* diminutive of *so* meaning 'melody'); the original general meaning is replaced by the modern sense in the course of the 13th c. However it was not a form specifically intended for setting to music, though sonnets were often set to music subsequently, like *madrigals. The form does not correspond exactly in its structure to stanzas of known *canzoni,* but it is the equivalent of the stanza in terms of poetic genre, corresponding to the Provençal *cobla esparsa*; there is no basis at all, for chronological reasons, for the hypothesis that the sonnet derives from the fusion of two *strambotti.* Like the *cobla,* the sonnet in the early period is used particularly for poetic correspondence (*tenzoni*); it can also be used as an element, virtually a strophe, of more extended texts, either a collection of sonnets (already in *Guittone d'Arezzo) or a proper narrative poem (the *Fiore*). In its normal form, it is widely used in Italian poetry in all centuries in all literary genres, and still survives today, sometimes treated quite freely (*Caproni, *Zanzotto, *Raboni), despite the decline of traditional versification. The success of the original form or its modifications in all the main European literatures is well known.

Of the variants of the sonnet, the only one to have any importance beyond the 14th c. is the *sonetto caudato* or sonnet 'with a tail', the tail being the addition of a *settenario* that rhymes with the four-teenth line followed by a rhyming couplet; the *sirma* normally follows the scheme CDCDCD dEE (where the lower-case letter marks the *settenario*). The first examples occur at the beginning of the 14th c.; it is common in the 'comic' poetry of the 16th c. (*Berni) and still in use in the 19th c., also with the addition of further 'tails' (a sonnet with several 'tails' is also called a *sonettessa*). An older but less common variant is the *sonetto ritornellato*, or sonnet with a refrain, which has the addition of a rhyming couplet (Guido *Cavalcanti). In the 13th and 14th c. there was a great deal more experimen-tation with variants; a detailed description of the numerous possible forms can be found in the treatise of *Antonio da Tempo. Examples are the sonnet with an ABABABAB *fronte* extended by one or more AB couplets, and/or with a CDCDCD *sirma* extended by one or more CD couplets, or with a *sirma* of three tercets (Guittone and *Monte Andrea); also the 'double' sonnet (*doppio* or *rinter-zato*), with a *settenario* rhyming with the preceding line inserted after the odd lines of the *fronte* and after the first and second lines of each tercet, or, in the tercets, only after the second line (Guittone and also *Dante). Occasionally the sonnet can have lines shorter than the hendecasyllable: in such cases it is called a *sonetto minore* (versions of these 'dis-guised' by the page layout can be found in *Pas-coli's *Myricae*). [See also VERSIFICATION.] [PGB]

See L. Biadene, *Morfologia del sonetto nei secoli XIII–XIV* (1888 and 1977); R. Antonelli, 'L'invenzione del sonetto', in *Miscellanea di studi in onore di Aurelio Roncaglia* (1989); N. Tonelli, *Aspetti del sonetto contemporaneo* (2000).

SONNINO, GIORGIÓ SIDNEY (1847–1922). *Tuscan politician of the *liberal Right. He founded and edited the *Rassegna settimanale* (1878–82). His *Torniamo allo Statuto* (1897) called for a restoration of the monarchy's powers in order to end parliamentary corruption. He had two spells as Prime Minister during the *Giolittian era. As Foreign Minister he negotiated Italy's entry into *World War I. [See also MAFIA.] [JD]

Sonzogno, see PUBLISHING.

SORDELLO (*c.*1200–?1269). The most cele-brated and perhaps the best Italian *troubadour. Born into the lesser nobility in Goito, near *Man-tua, he served the *Este family in *Ferrara and was later at Verona. His notorious amorous adventures

included running off with Cunizza, wife of Rizzar-do di San Bonifacio. In 1229 he left for the courts of Spain and Provence, only returning in 1265, as a now prestigious follower of Charles of *Anjou. His forty-two surviving poems, which include satirical, moral, and didactic poetry as well as love poems, show a predilection for often violently polemical debates. These, and his celebrated lament for Blacatz d'Aulps (1236/7), are his best poems, and may well have motivated the esteem for his proud nobility of character which *Dante shows in *Purgatorio 6. [LM]

SOUTH, see MEZZOGIORNO.

Spaccio de la bestia trionfante, see BRUNO, GIORDANO.

Spagna, La. The most comprehensive Italian verse narrative of Charlemagne's legendary cam-paigns in Spain, culminating in the treachery of Gano and the tragic battle of Roncesvalle (Ronce-vaux). The poem, in *ottava rima*, exists in two ver-sions, of thirty-four and forty cantos, which probably reflect the work of two anonymous mid-15th c. poets. *Manuscript evidence shows that the *Spagna* circulated in both Northern Italy and *Tus-cany; Luigi *Pulci drew on it in the second part of the *Morgante*, and episodes such as Orlando's combat with the giant Ferraù form part of the narrative background to the poems of *Boiardo and *Ariosto. [RMD]

SPAGNOLI, BATTISTA (1447–1516). Latin poet, known as Il Mantovano after his native city, *Mantua, where he completed his literary studies. In 1464 he entered the Carmelite Order, in which he rose to high office. His enormous literary output includes eclogues, *religious verse, and narrative poems whose balance between classical and Chris-tian elements justifies the name of 'Christian *Virgil' given to him by Erasmus. [SR]

Spain and Spanish Influences. The literary influence of Italy on Spain has been far stronger than Spain's on Italy, particularly in certain periods. In the *Middle Ages Italians knew little of Spain. Even *Dante was unable to say what lan-guage was spoken in the Iberian peninsula. But Spain acted as a mediator between Arab culture (flourishing especially around Cordoba) and Italian culture. It may be possible in this way to account for the presence of Arab thought in the

Divine Comedy, as well as for some otherwise puzzling aspects of medieval Italian metrics.

In 1442 Alfonso V of *Aragon established his brilliant and cultured *court in *Naples, which opened the way for Spanish writers (Castilian and Catalan) and Italian writers to come into contact with each other. Similar opportunities emerged in *Rome and *Florence. But only a few Spanish authors, such as Enrique de Villena and Juan de Mena, were known in the 15th c. However, in the next century Spain became the dominant power in Italy, ousting the French after a long and complex period of conflict and sealing its supremacy with the Treaty of Cateau-Cambrésis in 1559. An ever-growing stream of Spanish writers now visited Italy, including Juan del Encina, Torres Naharro, Garcilaso de la Vega, Antonio de Guevara, and Juan de Valdés. Their work was occasionally read in Italy, though more often it was they who assimilated Italian literary fashions. In 1506 the first *translation of *Celestina* was published in Rome, and in a few highly cultured courts such as *Ferrara and *Urbino some *cancioneros* and Spanish *chivalric *romances were known and read. *Amadís* and *Palmerín* had considerable success; so too did the work of Antonio de Guevara, some sentimental romances (such as the *Carcél de Amor*), religious writers (such as Luis de Granada), and chroniclers of the Indies (such as Fernandez de Oviedo and López de Gómara). In the 17th c. Spanish influence strengthened. Italian dramatists learnt from Lope de Vega, Calderón, and Tirso de Molina, and novel writers, from the picaresque novel and even more from Cervantes.

The Spanish language was widely known in Italy in the 16th and 17th c. and a large number of Hispanisms—many ephemeral—infiltrated Italian. *Castiglione advised his courtier to study Spanish, and the first Spanish grammars for Italians were published. Writers often put Spanish in the mouths of characters in plays, or in some cases adopted the language as their literary medium.

Spanish influence continued into the 18th c. Major dramatists such as *Metastasio, *Goldoni, and Carlo *Gozzi clearly knew Spanish *theatre well. In 1767 the *Jesuits were expelled from Spain and took refuge in Italy, where figures such as Hervás y Panduro continued their important scientific studies.

Spain fascinated the *Romantics. In Italy Giovanni *Berchet was drawn to its poetry and romances. These, together with the dramatists (particularly Calderón) and *Don Quixote* formed

the basis for the Italians' renewed interest, whilst the best-known of contemporary Spanish authors was perhaps Angel de Rivas. Edmondo *De Amicis' *Spagna* (1873) is a mine of information regarding Spanish literature and culture, and shows a limited acquaintance with authors such as Pérez Galdós, Palacio Valdés, and Bécquer.

In the 20th c. authors as different as Giovanni *Papini and Benedetto *Croce have been great cognoscenti of Spanish literature. And there has been widespread interest in modern philosophers and poets, especially Unamuno, Machado, Valle Inclán, J. R. Jiménez, García Lorca, and Alberti. Echoes of these are to be found scattered through much modern poetry.   [MCD]

See F. Meregalli, *Presenza della letteratura spagnola in Italia* (1974); G. L. Beccaria, *Spagnolo e spagnoli in Italia: riflessi ispanici sulla lingua italiana del Cinque e del Seicento* (1985).

SPALLANZANI, LAZZARO (1729–99). One of the founders of modern experimental biology. Born at Scandiano near Reggio Emilia, he taught in Reggio Emilia and Modena before becoming professor in Pavia (1769). His writings are remarkable for their lucidity and literary refinement, the most important on a non-scientific subject being his *Viaggi alle Due Sicilie* (1796).   [JMAL]

Spanish Influences, see SPAIN AND SPANISH INFLUENCES.

SPATOLA, ADRIANO (1941–88). Born in Croatia, he became a member of the *Gruppo 63 and founded the review *Tam Tam* with Giulia *Niccolai in 1972. He was a leading exponent of avant-gardism and aimed at a total poetry with visual, gestural, and phonic dimensions, in which normal meanings of words were secondary.

[CO'B]

SPAVENTA, BERTRANDO, see POLITICAL THOUGHT.

SPAVENTA, SILVIO, see CROCE, BENEDETTO; IDEALISM; MARXISM; POLITICAL THOUGHT.

SPAZIANI, MARIA LUISA (1924–). Poet born in *Turin, who taught French literature at Messina University before moving to *Rome. Her first collection, *Le acque del sabato* (1954), was *hermetic and *Montalian in manner, but the poems of collections such as *Luna lombarda* (1959) and

Specchio di vera penitenza

Utilità della memoria (1966) have dreamlike textures that recall Dylan Thomas. Her later work, for instance *Giovanna d'Arco* (1990), prefers longer forms and tends to verse narrative.   [GM]

Specchio di vera penitenza, see PASSAVANTI, IACOPO.

SPEDALIERI, NICOLA (1740–95). *Sicilian priest and polemicist, who settled in *Rome under Pius VI. He distinguished himself by his refutations of 'Fréret' (really D'Holbach and Naigeon, 1778) and Gibbon (1784) on Christianity. His controversial *Dei diritti dell'uomo* (1791) grounded the rights of man and popular sovereignty in religion.
                                                              [JMAL]

Spelling. The modern Italian system is phonetic rather than etymological, i.e. it does not generally preserve spellings which represent either a pronunciation no longer used or the root forms of classical borrowings. But there is no perfect correspondence between letters and sounds: twenty letters of the Latin alphabet, singly or in combination (*j, k, w, x, y* are not normally used, and *h* has no independent phonetic function), represent a much higher number of phonemes (thirty in the Florentine system: twenty-one consonants, two semiconsonants, and seven vowels). Problems for learners include the lack of a stress accent in polysyllabic words except on the final vowel (e.g. *città*). This system was established chiefly in the 16th c. Previously, spelling had become increasingly etymological under the influence of *humanism, but, with new-found confidence in the autonomy of the vernacular, phonetic spelling was adopted, e.g. *dissi, oscuro* instead of *dixi, obscuro*. Reading was made easier with enhanced punctuation and some limited accentuation. *Printing helped to standardize these practices, through *dictionaries, *grammars, and the collaboration of editors with printers. Particularly influential were Pietro *Bembo's editions of *Petrarch and *Dante (1501–2), which introduced the distinction between *è* ('is') and *e* ('and'), and the apostrophe to indicate elision and aphaeresis; and the usage adopted by *Salviati and the *Vocabolario della Crusca*, the third edition of which (1691) helped to spread the modern distinction between *u* and *v*.

With these exceptions, the numerous attempts to improve the system have failed, partly through the difficulty of changing ingrained habits which have strong cultural associations, partly because many proposals were linked with specific pronunciations; the imperfections of Italian spelling do have the virtue of allowing some regional variation. The reforms proposed have involved additional letters (variant forms of existing letters, some of which might be based on handwriting, or more rarely new letters) and/or diacritic signs. An isolated early attempt at reform was made in Leon Battista *Alberti's grammar, but experimentation was encouraged above all by print. Would-be 16th-c. reformers included *Trissino, Claudio *Tolomei, and Pier Francesco *Giambullari. Giovanni *Gherardini (1778–1861) suggested a spelling closer to Latin (e.g. *academia, commodo*) and hence more 'European'. The spread of Italian as a national language after *Unification encouraged further proposals, for example those of Policarpo Petrocchi, Pietro Gabriele Goidànich, and Arrigo Castellani, all based, however, on Florentine pronunciation. [See also QUESTIONE DELLA LINGUA.]   [BR]

See N. Maraschio, 'Grafia e ortografia: evoluzione e codificazione', in L. Serianni and P. Trifone (eds.), *Storia della lingua italiana*, vol. i (1993).

SPERANI, BRUNO. Pseudonym under which the Dalmatian Beatrice Speratz (1839–1923) published both immensely popular pedagogical tales for girls and novels of working-class life, such as *La fabbrica* (1894), which combined Christian *Socialism and the naturalism of Zola (whom she translated). She was *Milanese correspondent for *La Nazione*, and a prolific *journalist.   [PBarn]

SPERATZ, BEATRICE, see SPERANI, BRUNO.

SPERONI, SPERONE (1500–88). *Paduan philosopher and scholar, who was a prolific writer but such a perfectionist that only two works, *Dialoghi* (1542) and his *tragedy *Canace* (1546), were published during his lifetime, both without his permission. Many of his works were only published by Forcellini in 1740.

Although a good classical scholar (he studied *Aristotle with *Pomponazzi) he always wrote in Italian and, while Principe of the Accademia degli Infiammati (1541/2), he decreed that all proceedings should be conducted in the vernacular. He developed his views on language and style in two *dialogues, *Delle lingue* and *Della retorica*, the former being extensively used by Du Bellay in his defence of the French language (1549). *Canace* (written in 1542) exemplifies his linguistic theories and his

emotional interpretation of Aristotle's catharsis. It was criticized for its immorality and artifical verse forms by *Giraldi Cinzio, writing anonymously in *Giudizio sopra una tragedia* (1550). Speroni's replies produced a major polemic on tragic theory. Later works include studies on *Dante and *Virgil and an unfinished *Dialogo dell'istoria*, while his letters give a fascinating insight into his family life. His epitaph, composed by himself, emphasizes his devotion to scholarship and to the Italian language.
[ECMR]

SPIRITO, LORENZO GUALTIERI (c.1426–96) from *Perugia was a mercenary soldier in the service of the *condottiere* Piccinino, whom he celebrated in his poem *Altro Marte* (1489). His prolific writings include a *canzoniere* for a certain Fenice, whose name also provides the title and theme for an allegorized poem imitating *Petrarch's *Trionfi*. He also wrote a longer poem on his native city.
[ELM]

Spoken Language in Literature. Traditionally, literature in Italian maintained a notable distance from colloquial language, in prose as well as verse, even before the literary language was codified in the 16th c. *Dialect writing, on the other hand, tended to be closer to popular speech, though in many cases—for instance in the Veneto—a regional literary language became well established. But at least some *Renaissance *letters (for instance those of *Machiavelli) seem to reflect spoken usage, whilst a *dialogue such as *Castiglione's *Cortegiano* offers an image of ideal but not necessarily totally unreal conversational practice. However, it is hard to be sure how far educated speech is echoed or reproduced in Italian writing, in part because it no doubt varied according to social contexts and purposes, as well as according to region and class usage.

Obvious imitation of popular speech occurs most in the *novella* and *comedy to indicate spontaneity and liveliness, though there are numerous conscious examples elsewhere—even in a 13th-c. Latin *chronicle like that of *Salimbene da Parma. From the early 19th c. one of the major problems for *realist novelists, from *Manzoni through *Verga to *Vittorini and *Pavese, was the convincing representation in Italian of *peasant speech, when in reality all peasants spoke dialect. *Gadda was one of the first novelists to exploit the riches offered by Italy's linguistic multiplicity. With the spread of Italian as the spoken language of the country in the last thirty years, it has become possible for novelists to base their writing on spoken practice, though much fiction preserves the traditional distance, as does academic and critical writing. Dialects, on the other hand, which are now in steep decline throughout the country, have been shaped into highly literary forms by poets from *Noventa to Franca *Grisoni. [See also DIALECT WRITING; FOLK AND POPULAR LITERATURE; QUESTIONE DELLA LINGUA; SLANG.] [DieZ]

SPOLVERINI, GIAMBATTISTA (1695–1762). Man of letters and enlightened administrator of his family estates near Verona. He shows agricultural as well as literary expertise in *La coltivazione del riso* (composed 1744–6). It is generally regarded as the finest Georgic poem in Italian after *La coltivazione* of *Alamanni, on which it is modelled. [JMAL]

Stabat Mater. Latin hymn which evokes Mary's grief as a mother at the foot of Christ's cross. Usually attributed to *Iacopone da Todi, it has been set to music by many composers, including Palestrina, Vivaldi, Pergolesi, Haydn, *Rossini, Schubert, *Verdi, Poulenc, and Penderecki. [PA]

STAËL, MADAME DE, see FRENCH INFLUENCES, 2; PRE-ROMANTICISM; ROMANTICISM.

STAMPA, GASPARA (1523–54). Poet whose character and importance has been much debated, though it is now generally recognized that her work gives *Petrarchist conventions a new twist whilst remaining very much within them. Born in *Padua, she lived most of her life in *Venice. She was in close contact with musicians and writers, but was probably not the *courtesan she was said to be even in her own lifetime. In 1548 she entered into a relationship with Count Collaltino di Collalto, who became her lover but broke with her three years later, after which she briefly contemplated the religious life before forming a new, short-lived attachment with one Bartolomeo Zen, an old family friend.

Her *Rime*, published in 1554 soon after her death by her sister Cassandra and dedicated to Giovanni *Della Casa, are mostly concerned with her love for Collaltino, a high 'colle' with whom she repeatedly contrasts her own 'bassezza', not least as a poet. This emphasis on inferiority, reflecting her ambiguous position as a woman and poet, leads to impressions of spontaneity and new depths of feeling that particularly affected *Romantic readers,

but also to a certain repetitiveness, even within individual poems. Her self-awareness and cultural aspirations are apparent in poems addressed to other poets, in which she praises their education and wisdom and makes learning an essential basis for worthwhile artistic expression. [See also WOMEN WRITERS, 1.] [ABu]
Rime, ed. R. Ceriello (1994).

Stampa, La, see JOURNALISM.

Stanze per la giostra (1494). *Poliziano's unfinished narrative poem in *ottava rima*, written in 1475–8 to record the victory of Giuliano de' *Medici in the *Florentine joust (1475) in honour of Simonetta Cattaneo. Iulio, an over-confident adolescent admirable for his physical prowess and cultural inclinations, arrogantly rejects love. Cupid plots his conversion. While out hunting, the young man follows a white doe, which disappears and is replaced by a beautiful woman (Simonetta) by whom Iulio is captivated. The reader is then transported to the kingdom of Venus as Cupid travels back to report to his mother the success of his plot. In the second book a change of tone suggests that chaste sublimation is the prevailing theme: Iulio is prepared by a symbolic dream to fight in the joust in which he will gain honour and glory for himself and his loved one. At this point the poem breaks off. [JAL]

STATIUS (Publius Papinius Statius) (*c*.45–?96). Latin poet, author of two *epics, the *Thebaid* (on the war of the seven kings against Thebes) and the unfinished *Achilleid*. *Dante alludes to numerous events and characters, especially from the *Thebaid*, and presents Statius as having been a secret convert to Christianity (*Purg.* 21–2). The *Thebaid* also influenced *Boccaccio's *Teseida* and hence Chaucer. Statius' shorter poems, the *Silvae*, inspired *Poliziano's Latin poems with the same title. [PA]

STECCHETTI, LORENZO, see GUERRINI, OLINDO.

STEFANESCHI, IACOPO GAETANO (*c*.1270–1343). A cardinal who wrote two works in Latin—*Opus metricum*, a poem on *Celestine V, and *De centesimo seu jubileo anno liber*, a prose account of the Jubilee of 1300. He commissioned *Giotto's *Navicella* for St Peter's in *Rome and later served in the curia in *Avignon. [PA]

STEFANI, BARTOLOMEO, see COOKERY BOOKS.

STEFANO PROTONOTARO (da Messina) (13th c.). Poet of the *Sicilian School. 'Protonotaro' ('First Notary') suggests that he was a legal official of some importance. His three surviving *canzoni* are love poems, celebrating the superior quality of his passion and showing a correspondingly refined compositional expertise. The most important, 'Pir meu cori alligrari' ('To rejoice my heart'), is the only complete Sicilian poem to have survived in its original linguistic form, and has a stylistic complexity and formal unity rare in Sicilian School poetry as it has survived today. [PH]

STELLA, ANTON FORTUNATO (1757–1833). *Printer and bookseller who worked initially in his native *Venice but transferred to *Milan in 1810. He was a friend of various writers, including *Giordani, Vincenzo *Monti, and most notably *Leopardi, who undertook various editorial tasks for him, and whose *Operette morali* he published in 1827. The firm continued until 1850. [MPC]

STELLUTI, FRANCESCO (1577–1652) was, with Federico *Cesi, one of the founder members of the Accademia dei *Lincei. After the death of Cesi in 1630 he tried unsuccessfully to continue the activities of the academy, but managed to get its *Tesoro messicano* published in 1651. He published scientific treatises (on fossilized wood, for example), *lyric poetry, and a blank-verse *translation of the *satires of Persius (1630). [PBD]

STERBINI, CESARE (1784–1831). *Roman *librettist, best known for collaborating with *Rossini on *Il barbiere di Siviglia* (1816). He also wrote the libretti for *Paolo e Virginia* (1812) and *Torvaldo e Dorliska* (1815). He worked in the *papal administration and was a friend of G. G. *Belli. [DO'G]

STIGLIANI, TOMMASO (1573–1651). Poet and *literary critic, best known for his enmity with *Marino. Born in Matera and educated in *Naples (where they first met), he antagonized literary circles there and moved to *Venice, publishing a brief collection of *Rime* (1601) which is arguably the earliest printed example of full-blown *concettismo.

After unsuccessfully seeking *patronage in *Milan and *Turin, he became secretary to the Duke of Parma, publishing an expanded version of

the *Rime* in Parma in 1605, which alternates the serious practice of *concettismo* with parodies of its excesses. This ambivalence characterized all his works, including the *Mondo nuovo* (1617), a highly fictionalized account of the discovery and Christianization of the Americas, whose epic and encyclopedic aspirations flounder in the conflict between heavy-handed moralism and titillating sensationalism. Tensions with Marino erupted in a public falling-out in 1617, as did those with the historian Enrico Caterino *Davila, which ended dramatically in a duel and Stigliani's expulsion from Parma (1621). Moving to *Rome, he recast himself as a Roman classicist, with definitive editions of his lyrics (1623), the revised and completed *Mondo nuovo* (1628), and various literary-theoretical works. But he continued his feud in the *Occhiale* (1627), which is a virulent critique of Marino's *Adone*. Even his collected letters (1664) include forgeries to present his quarrels with the long-dead Marino in a better light. But his verse never really broke free of the conventions and mannerisms of the early 17th c., and he himself never overcame his resentment at his rival's (to him) inexplicable success. [MPS]
See M. Pieri, '*Contre* Stigliani', in *Per Marino* (1976).

Stilus gregorianus, see CURSUS.

Stoicism, as filtered through *Cicero and Seneca, exercised a formative role on early Christian writers, who saw similarities between Stoic and Christian asceticism, and then on *Renaissance *humanists, especially from 1350 to 1450. A key text was *Petrarch's *De remediis, which pitted reason against the emotions of joy, hope, dread, and melancholia in the struggle to rise above both adverse and prosperous fortune. Self-sufficiency and aloofness went on to become the model for an educated elite with figures like *Salutati and Leon Battista *Alberti stressing the importance of duty, or of performing virtue for its own sake. But an *Epicurean like Lorenzo *Valla opposed Stoic pessimism, and disputed the spurious connection between Seneca and St Paul which had been accepted earlier. In the 16th c. the Greek writings of Epictetus gained favour, though towards the end of the century there was renewed interest in Seneca, for preserving moral integrity in times of tyranny and persecution. Cicero's *De natura deorum* also contributed to discussions of a divine Providence ordering and guiding the cosmos, as did Seneca's

De providentia, which goes through various arguments justifying why the good suffer in life.
[LAP]

STOPPANI, ANTONIO (1824–91). Priest, geologist, museum curator, and veteran of the conflicts of the *Risorgimento, who is best known for his illustrated guide *Il bel paese* (1873). His other writings include essays on nature in the *Divine Comedy* and on *Manzoni's youth, as well as poetry and short stories. [JD]

Storia, La (1974). Elsa *Morante's third novel, and one of Italy's first industrially programmed best-sellers. Set principally in *Rome in 1943, it has a slow-witted young woman, her child, and a dog as its main protagonists. It depicts the violence of history and (more convincingly) the alternative, more authentic worlds which ordinary people create to overcome their victimhood. [MPC]

Storia della colonna infame (1842). Historical essay by *Manzoni. The title refers to the pillar erected in *Milan to shame two men executed on the charge of spreading the *plague epidemic in 1628. Manzoni denounces the judges and examines in detail the documents of the trial, which is mentioned briefly in *I *promessi sposi*. [VRJ]

Storia della letteratura italiana, see DE SANCTIS, FRANCESCO; HISTORIES OF ITALIAN LITERATURE; TIRABOSCHI, GIROLAMO.

Storia di una capinera, see VERGA, GIOVANNI.

Stornello, see FOLK AND POPULAR LITERATURE.

Stracittà, see 900 (NOVECENTO); STRAPAESE.

STRADA, FAMIANO (1572–1649). *Jesuit writer. Born in *Rome, Strada taught rhetoric at the Collegio Romano. He is best known for his *history of the revolt of the Netherlands, *De bello belgico decades duae,* written at the request of the Duke of Parma, published in 1632–47, and translated into Dutch, French, Italian, English, and Spanish before the end of the century. [UPB]

Strambotto. A short poem set to music, also called a *rispetto* (mainly in *Tuscany), normally made up of eight rhyming *hendecasyllables according to the scheme ABABABAB (the *ottava siciliana,* or in *Sicily *canzuna*: the first example is

Strano, Luigi

by *Boccaccio in the *Filocolo), or ABABABCC (ottava toscana), or ABABCCDD, or with rarer rhyme schemes. It is most common in the 15th and 16th c. In 'popular' poetry it is regularly divided into two parallel parts, as also in *Pascoli's rispetti (in Myricae). The musical form of the strambotto can be used for other metres, for example *sonnets. [See also VERSIFICATION.]   [PGB]

STRANO, LUIGI, see ITALIAN WRITERS IN AUSTRALIA.

Strapaese. The vision of *peasant wholesomeness and a corresponding earthy pithiness of style which was promoted particularly by Mino *Maccari apropos of *Tuscany and Tuscan in Il *Selvaggio in the interwar years. It was polemically opposed to the internationalism of stracittà associated with *Bontempelli and the *900 (Novecento) group. Both tendencies claimed to be in tune with the true spirit of *Fascism, but strapaese gained the ascendency in the 1930s.   [PH]

STRAPAROLA, GIOVAN FRANCESCO (c.1480–before 1557). *Novelliere from near Bergamo, of whose life very little is known. His first publication was a *Petrarchist *canzoniere (1508), but his reputation rests on Le piacevoli notti, the first part of which came out in 1550, followed by a second part in 1553, and a complete edition in 1556.

The work was an immediate success and saw numerous editions and translations. It comprises seventy-five fables told by ten ladies and various men on the thirteen nights of *carnival, while guests of the Bishop of Lodi on the island of Murano near *Venice. Each fable ends with a verse riddle, 73 of them in *ottava rima. There are debts to *Boccaccio, *Andrea da Barberino's Reali di Francia, the Latin novelle of Giovanni Morlini, and the writings of Jacopo da Varazze. The fables are most interesting and important, however, for their retellings of magical and fantastic folk stories, including some of the most famous in European literature. Though the Piacevoli notti was a best-seller, the obscene nature of parts of the text and inclusion of clerical protagonists resulted in its being placed on the *Index of prohibited books in 1624. [See also FOLK LITERATURE.]   [PLR]

Strega, see LITERARY PRIZES.

STREHLER, GIORGIO (1921–97). *Theatre director, who founded with Paolo Grassi the

Piccolo Teatro of *Milan, Italy's longest-lasting repertory theatre, opening in 1947 with Gorky's Lower Depths. Strehler's productions are legendary; in particular, *Goldoni's Il servitore di due padroni, *Pirandello's I giganti della montagna, and *Shakespeare's Tempest. Strehler was responsible for introducing Brecht to Italian audiences. His style, described as lyrical realism, impressed for its combination of social detail and aesthetic beauty. He directed *opera at La Scala in Milan and in the 1980s plays at the Paris Odéon.   [JAL]

STRIGGIO, ALESSANDRO. Father and son of the same name. The elder Alessandro (c.1537–92) was a *Mantuan musician who spent much of his career in *Florence. He wrote music for *court entertainments (including the intermedi for the wedding of Grand Duke Francesco I de' *Medici and Johanna of Austria in 1565), directed the court singers, and was renowned for his viol playing. He published some eight books of *madrigals including the comic Cicalamento delle donne al bucato, and a remarkable forty-part motet. His son Alessandro (?1573–1630) was also an instrumentalist, but preferred the career of court secretary in Mantua. He was the *librettist of Claudio *Monteverdi's first *opera, Orfeo, and wrote other entertainment texts for the *Gonzaga. His diplomatic mission to *Venice seeking support against the imperial invasion of Mantua unwittingly brought the *plague to the city.   [TC]

STROCCHI, DIONIGI (1762–1850). Poet born in Faenza, who studied in *Rome, and then, like his friend Vincenzo *Monti, pursued a teaching and political career in the North. Under *Napoleon he celebrated public events in verse. He translated Callimachus (1805) and Virgil's Eclogues (1831) and Georgics (1834). He was an opponent of *Romanticism.   [JMAL]

STROZZI. One of the largest and most important *Florentine families, coming to prominence in the later 13th c. *Bankers, international *merchants, and great landowners, they assumed a pre-eminent position in the city's political life until 1434, when, because of their leading role in the preceding oligarchic regime, several leading family members were exiled; under the 15th-c. *Medici, the Strozzi never resumed a significant place in the regime, although financially and commercially the family prospered in the later part of the century. The Strozzi had a rapprochement with the Medici in the early 16th c., but eventually prominent family members fell out with them and were conspicuous among the opposition to the establishment of the Medici duchy in the 1530s. The family spread to other Italian cities, most notably *Ferrara, in the 15th c. Although never resuming their former political prominence, the Strozzi numbered several important soldiers, musicians, painters, and writers in ducal Florence.

Particularly noteworthy family members include Palla (1372–1462), the richest man in the city in the 1420s; he was largely responsible for the appointment of *Chrysoloras in 1397, becoming one of his first Greek pupils and one of the most important bibliophiles of the early Florentine *Renaissance. After he was banished to *Padua by the Medici regime in 1434, he devoted himself to the study of Greek, employing Andronicus Callistus and Johannes *Argyropoulos as his tutors and amassing a major private *library; his return to Florence was always blocked by the Mediceans. Filippo Strozzi the Elder (1428–91), son of the famous letter-writer Alessandra Macinghi *Strozzi, returned from *exile to become one of the richest men in Laurentian Florence, building the huge Palazzo Strozzi. His son, Filippo the Younger (1489–1538), married into the Medici family and became one of the most prominent financiers of Medicean Florence and *Rome, but after Clement VII's death he lost his influential position; he became an opponent of Cosimo I at the battle of Montemurlo in 1537, when he was captured, later committing suicide in prison. [RDB]

See M. Bullard, *Filippo Strozzi and the Medici* (1980).

STROZZI, ALESSANDRA MACINGHI (1408–71). Wife of Matteo Strozzi, a member of the patrician *Florentine family. Her extensive correspondence with her exiled sons, written in fresh and vivid Tuscan, is one of the earliest surviving Italian private *letter collections. Comparable in scope and human interest to the contemporary English letters of the Paston family, Alessandra's correspondence, which reveals her to have been as shrewd a judge of public as of family affairs, constitutes a capital source for students of *Renaissance Florence and of women's history. [See also STROZZI.] [FWK]

STROZZI, ERCOLE (1470/5–1508). Latin poet from the branch of the *Florentine *Strozzi family which had established itself in *Ferrara. He

was a friend of the young *Ariosto and Pietro *Bembo. As well as Latin elegies, a few vernacular *sonnets have survived. He died a violent death, perhaps murdered on the orders of the *Este family. [PH]

STROZZI, GIOVAN BATTISTA. The name of two important writers of *madrigals from the famous *Florentine family of the *Strozzi, 'il vecchio' (1505–71) and his son, 'il giovane' (1551–1634). In many cases it is uncertain which of the two is the author. But the younger Strozzi was particularly prolific, with more than 1,000 madrigals to his name. He further developed the skill shown by his father in investing *Petrarchan motifs with a new *Mannerist grace and inventiveness. His prose writings include a treatise on madrigal composition. Many of the poems of both Strozzi are still unpublished. [See also GAREGGIAMENTO POETICO, IL.] [PH]

STROZZI, GIULIO (1583–1652). *Librettist and poet. He hailed from a branch of the *Florentine *Strozzi family which had settled in *Venice. He spent most of his life there and played an important part in the development of Venetian *opera. He is best known for the libretti for *Monteverdi's *Proserpina rapita* (1630) and Francesco Sacrati's *La finta pazza* (1641). Other texts include *madrigali* set to music by his adopted daughter, the composer and singer Barbara Strozzi. [FC]

STROZZI, TITO VESPASIANO (1424–1505) of *Ferrara, descendant of the *Florentine *Strozzi and educated by *Guarino da Verona, is known as a scholar, poet, and financial administrator. In this capacity he served under three *Este generations, and held the highest administrative office in Ferrara from 1497 to 1505. Strozzi's surviving Latin poetry consists of three eclogues (1513), fragments of his *Borsias* (c.1460), on Borso d'Este, and his *Erotica* (1443). The latter have been admired for their elegant fusion of classical elegy (especially Tibullus) and *Petrarchan elements. [JAL]

Structuralism and Post-structuralism. Structuralism in France was developed in the 1960s by figures working in various disciplines—linguisticians (Benveniste), psychoanalysts (Lacan), psychologists (Piaget), philosophers (Althusser, Foucault), and anthropologists (Lévi-Strauss). Modern structuralists took their basic assumptions

Strumenti critici

from the linguistician Ferdinand de Saussure (whose *Cours de linguistique générale* was published by his pupils in 1916) and to a lesser extent from Russian formalism and the Linguistic Circle of Prague. The basic structuralist conviction is that any meaningful object (languages and literary texts are two examples) is a system or an organism, and either has a deep structure that must be discovered or can be given one by the scientist. In either case, only by means of structures can the world be rationally understood. In the case of literary products, structuralism invites the reader to look at each text as a complete and autonomous system of stylistic, syntactic, and conceptual relationships, and tends to neglect the wider historical and cultural context, as well as the biographical substratum. On the other hand, it encourages a theoretical (that is, rational, abstractive, and exhaustive) approach.

The structuralist revolution was welcomed by some of Italy's foremost critics. At the same time, those who most drew on structuralist ideas were practising philologists, concerned with linguistic and literary history and the editing of texts, often from the medieval period. Notable instances are *Contini, *Varianti e altra linguistica* (1970), *Segre, *Le strutture e il tempo* (1974), *Avalle, *Modelli semiologici nella Commedia di Dante* (1975), and *Corti, *Metodi e fantasmi* (1969). Italian structuralist criticism has therefore generally managed to avoid the pitfalls of extreme abstraction or empty formalism, while introducing more modern and efficient methods of textual analysis. It also developed a theoretically well-grounded alternative to *De Sanctis' romantic historicism, *Croce's *idealism, and *Marxist ideology which still dominated *literary criticism and *literary theory in Italy in the 1950s.

Post-structuralism is not a philosophical school or homogeneous critical methodology, but a term indicating a loosely related array of theoretical positions that take structuralism's attention to language, textuality, and the process of signification as their point of departure, but reject its systematic core and generally denounce its ultimately idealist allegiance. Again, it was in Paris in the 1970s and 1980s that the most significant developments occurred, with the work of Derrida, Deleuze, Barthes, Kristeva, and Lyotard. In literary studies, Derrida's deconstruction has become the dominant note within post-structuralism, particularly in the United States. Stefano Agosti (*Les styles de Nietzsche*, 1976), Maurizio Ferraris (*Differenze*, 1981), and Gianni *Vattimo (*Le avventure della differenza*, 1988) have done most to introduce post-structuralism, especially Derridean deconstruction, to Italy. But interest has been more limited than elsewhere, at least as regards literary studies. The simultaneous development in Italy of *semiotics, in particular the work of Umberto *Eco, provided an alternative answer to structuralist abstraction and elitism and one which paid greater attention to wider cultural contexts and specific forms of communication, such as the mass media, without falling back into idealist traps. [GS]

See M. Corti and C. Segre, *I metodi attuali della critica in Italia* (1970); C. Segre, *Avviamento all'analisi del testo letterario* (1985); R. Capozzi and M. Ciavolella (eds.), *Scrittori, tendenze letterarie e conflitto delle poetiche in Italia (1960–1990)* (1993).

Strumenti critici was launched in 1966 as a four-monthly journal 'of culture and literary criticism' by four scholars, D'Arco Silvio *Avalle, Maria *Corti, Dante Isella, and Cesare *Segre, who, as well as having collaborated with Gianfranco *Contini, shared an interest both in traditional philology [see FILOLOGIA] and in recent developments in *literary theory, such as *structuralism and *semiotics. Their aim was to demonstrate, against the abstract and ahistorical developments of French and North American structuralism and semiotics, that such new methods could successfully be merged with historically and linguistically sensitive approaches to literature. The editors and their collaborators found particular support and inspiration for their positions in the writings of the Russian Formalists, Bakhtin, and the Moscow-Tartu School. A new series of the journal, which is less critically committed and is still running, was launched in 1986. [ZB]

Studia humanitatis. The *Renaissance term, derived from the work of *Cicero, for the study of grammar, poetry, history, rhetoric, and moral philosophy, so called in the belief that these subjects made men more human. The term was often interchangeable with that of 'liberal' studies, and was understood to refer only to Greek and Latin, not vernacular, learning. It was the root of the contemporary Latin word *humanista*, meaning one who studied or taught these disciplines, and thence also of the modern term *humanism as applied to the Renaissance. [DR]

Studio, see UNIVERSITIES.

STUPARICH, CARLO (1894–1916). *Triestine writer who enlisted in the Italian army in *World War I and killed himself rather than be captured by the *Austrians. He had been a member of the group round *La *Voce* in Florence. His verse, prose, and *letters, all vibrantly patriotic, were collected by his brother Giani *Stuparich as *Cose e ombre di uno* (1919). [KP]

STUPARICH, GIANI (1891–1961). *Triestine writer. After studying briefly at Prague University (1913), he took a degree in literature at *Florence (1915), where he was a friend of *Slataper and wrote for *La *Voce*. He and his brother Carlo *Stuparich were volunteers in *World War I. He later published a terse war diary, *Guerra del '15* (1931), and a choral novel, *Ritorneranno* (1941), based on his experiences. A schoolteacher for many years, he was opposed to *Fascism and during *World War II was arrested and deported for his presumed Judaism [see JEWS AND JUDAISM]. As well as *autobiographical memoirs, notably *Trieste nei miei ricordi* (1948) [see DIARIES], Stuparich wrote stories and short novels, one of the most successful being *L'isola* (1942), which focuses on a tragic father–son relationship. *Simone* (1953), his last novel, is a highly literary foray into *fantasy. [KP]

SUCKERT, KURT ERIC, see MALAPARTE, CURZIO.

Summa artis rithimici vulgaris dictaminis, see ANTONIO DA TEMPO.

Suppositi, I (1509). Five-act *comedy by Ludovico *Ariosto. Erostrato changes places with his servant Dulippo so as to be near his beloved Polinesta, who is also courted by the more eligible elderly Cleandro. When the latter discovers that Dulippo is his long-lost son, he withdraws his claim on Polinesta, allowing the young couple to marry. An English version by George Gascoigne (1566), said to be the first prose comedy in English literature, provided the subplot for *Shakespeare's *Taming of the Shrew*. [See also RECEPTION OF ITALIAN LITERATURE IN BRITAIN.] [CPB]

Surrealism. The literary and artistic movement founded in Paris in the early 1920s, and given theoretical definition principally by André Breton (1896–1966), never enjoyed widespread success amongst Italian writers and intellectuals. All the same, the Italian artist and writer most closely associated with the movement, Alberto *Savinio, said that in 1937 Breton had attributed the origins of surrealism to him and his brother, Giorgio *De Chirico. Also influenced by surrealism were Antonio Delfini, who claimed that his *Fanalino della Battimonda* (1933) was produced by automatic writing, and Tommaso *Landolfi in his short-story collections *Dialogo dei massimi sistemi* (1937) and *Il mar delle blatte e altre storie* (1939). The Italian critics most receptive to surrealism between the wars were Giacomo *Debenedetti and Carlo *Bo, who in 1944 published a critical study and anthology of surrealist texts in translation, while the art and literature journal *Prospettive* devoted a special issue to surrealism on 15 January 1940. Postwar Italian writers influenced by surrealism included *Fortini, for whom the Left surrealists provided a model of a poetry that could be political without being falsely lucid (his translation of Éluard's *Poésie ininterrompue* appeared in 1948 and a critical study in 1959), and the poets of the *Neoavanguardia. Other poets, especially Alfonso *Gatto and Vittorio *Bodini, absorbed surrealist practices into their particular forms of Italian *hermetic poetry. [DF]
See C. Bo, *Bilancio del surrealismo* (1944); F. Fortini, *Il movimento surrealista* (1959).

SVEVO, ITALO, meaning 'Italian Swabian (or German)', was the defiant pseudonym adopted by Ettore Aron Schmitz (1861–1928) on the cover of his novel *Una vita* (1892), when his native *Trieste, then in *Austria-Hungary, was riven by national rivalry between Italians, Slavs, and Germans. The suggestions of *Socialism and cross-national bonds in the pseudonym largely explain the writer's neglect in his native city, in whose literary life he long remained a fish out of water. Though Schmitz was an *irredentist, Svevo's writings eschew *nationalist rhetoric and subvert the competitive values of mercantile Trieste. The pseudonym also recognizes Schmitz's mixed parentage; his parents were both *Jewish, but his father was of German origin and his mother, Allegra Moravia, Italian. It also signals his education from 1874 to 1878 at a freethinking Jewish school at Segnitz-am-Main, near Würzburg, in Germany. His headmaster was Samuel Spier, a founder of the German Social Democratic Workers' Party, who had been imprisoned for his opposition to Bismarck's prosecution of the war against France. Ettore's Socialist-leaning universalism leads him also to ignore Jewishness in his writings and is already apparent in an 1880 fragment of a play in *Martellian verse, *Ariosto governatore*, hingeing on the *Ariosto's social and political conscience.

At Segnitz, Ettore conceived his passion for literature—above all, *Shakespeare and the great German writers. On his return to Trieste, at the behest of his father, a self-made businessman, he studied business and in 1880 took up a position in a bank, where he remained until 1899, dealing with French and German correspondence. Svevo's 'Profilo autobiografico' proclaims that he sacrificed his literary vocation to save the family from ruin after the collapse of his father's business, but this is not borne out by the evidence. He simply fell in with his father's wishes, while throwing himself into the study of the Italian classics. He tried to prove himself as a verse playwright, but consigned all his dramatic efforts to the flames until he found his way after reading Zola's *Le Naturalisme au théâtre* in 1881. Svevo kept returning to writing plays, though by 1887 he had despaired of the Italian *theatre and the theatre-going public. The only one of his plays to be performed during his lifetime (in 1927) was *Terzetto spezzato*, written around 1901, a sardonic triangular *comedy in which a deceased wife is summoned up in a spiritualist séance by her bickering widower and former lover. Of the other plays, *Un marito*, from the period of Svevo's wedding, is a psychologically pitched critique of the notion of the crime of honour; *L'avventura di Maria* is a prewar work on a middle-class husband's ignominious failure to escape from comfort and conformity to live with the actress he loves.

Up to the mid-1880s Svevo wrote occasional literary articles, signed 'E.S.', for the outspokenly nationalist Triestine daily, *L'Indipendente*. They centre on the pursuit of truth in a *positivist spirit but grow increasingly paradoxical, culminating in an acceptance of Schopenhauer's theory of irrational will or self-interest. Gradually his literary interests shifted to the Russians and Scandinavians, and his writing to the narratives of self-exploration. Using the pseudonym E. Samigli, Ettore Schmitz published the story 'Una lotta', in *L'Indipendente*, in 1888, and the more substantial, somewhat Dostoievskian, tale of crime and punishment, 'L'assassinio di Via Belpoggio', in 1890. The notion of strife in a *Darwinian and Schopenhauerian (and later in a Freudian) sense runs through all his fiction. In fact he was then also writing *Un inetto*, which became *Una vita* (1892). This combines a solidly *realist study of the non-survival of the unfit, represented in the over-literary bank clerk, Alfonso

Nitti, in mercenary Trieste, with a Schopenhauerian exploration of the protagonist's self-delusions and compulsions. The plot centres on Alfonso's complexly motivated seduction and then abandonment of the banker's daughter, Annetta Maller, leading to the would-be noble gesture of his suicide. But the publication of *Una vita* passed virtually unnoticed. Svevo's stylistic polar opposite, *D'Annunzio, was by then the rising star of the Italian *novel.

A diary note of 1889 expresses Ettore Schmitz's sense of total isolation and failure. But he soon found a brother-in-art in the young, irreverent, swashbuckling post-Impressionist painter, Umberto Veruda, who probably encouraged Svevo to publish *Una vita* at his own expense (as he was also to do with his other novels). The two men shared socialist sympathies and the pleasure of *épater les bourgeois*. This was when Ettore lost his head over a circus girl, an episode which he then caustically dissected in *Senilità* (serialized in *L'Indipendente* prior to volume publication in 1898, and revised in 1927). The novel presents an ironical psychological close-up of the protagonist, Emilio Brentani, a failed novelist and insurance clerk in his 30s, and systematically explores human interaction as a process of deception of oneself and of others. The circus girl Giuseppina Zergol appears as Angiolina Zarri, and the sculptor in the novel, Stefano Balli, presents some characteristics of Veruda. Emilio's unmarried sister Amalia is the casualty of her brother's 'senile' passion for Angiolina. The few critics who reviewed the novel were almost all offended by its apparent moral negativity.

In 1896 the financially struggling Ettore Schmitz married his wealthy first cousin's daughter, the uncomplicated Livia Veneziani, who was thirteen years his junior and did not share his intellectual outlook. However, they always remained passionately attached, and Livia soon gave Ettore a daughter, though numerous miscarriages then followed. The *diary which he kept during his betrothal and the many hundreds of *letters he wrote his wife give tantalizing insights into his personality. In 1899 Ettore entered employment with the Veneziani firm, which manufactured ships' paint, and stayed with them for the rest of his life. He eventually became a prosperous partner, but, until *World War I, family finances remained fairly tight. The 'Profilo autobiografico' again suggests that Svevo sacrificed writing to the necessity of supporting his family, and speaks of his twenty-five years' silence until the publication of his third and most daring novel, *La *coscienza di Zeno,* in 1923. In fact, he opted for security and comfort, but never gave up writing plays, stories, and essays, even when busily engaged at the firm's paint factories in Trieste, *Venice, and London.

In 1907 Svevo engaged James Joyce, over twenty years his junior, as his English-language tutor. He thus became midwife to *Dubliners* and *Portrait of the Artist as a Young Man,* and also the model for Leopold Bloom in *Ulysses.* In return he derived enormous encouragement from Joyce's admiration for *Senilità,* as well as a privileged entry into literature in English. Svevo, the wandering free-thinking Jew who always came back home to Trieste, was apparently quite unlike Joyce, the voluntary exile from Dublin: yet both were obsessed with probing themselves, the life of their home town, and the suppressed drama of the everyday. Between 1907 and 1915 each was the other's only serious literary interlocutor. Svevo's literary sophistication gained further from his study of Freud's writings and his contacts with the *psychoanalytical movement, beginning in 1908 and culminating in his third novel, with its explicitly psychoanalytical title.

The writing of *La coscienza di Zeno*—Svevo's intensely funny and profoundly serious masterpiece—was triggered by the end of World War I, which had seen a distressed Schmitz both profit financially from business deals with both sides and attempt to outline a pacifist programme in a more than ever nationalistic Trieste, which after the war finally became part of Italy. The novel hilariously describes the attempt by the shifty Zeno Cosini, a wealthy but ineffectual Triestine, to cure his complexes (and his smoking) through psychoanalysis. In writing down his key recollections, Zeno is unable to suppress his sense of guilt over having wished for the death of his father and his father-in-law, as well as that of his rival in love. His guilt feelings appear not quite unfounded. Svevo's use of Freudian and psychoanalytical motifs, his counterpoint between Zeno's consciousness and his unconscious, between startling candour and consummate lies, is turned to account as a source of narrative and epistemological irony in this study of modern man. Values disintegrate as the words that designate them are turned inside out. Narrative time, as Joyce was quick to observe, is skewed and spliced by the narrating Zeno's shifting perspectives and motives. In the diaristic finale, Svevo's anti-hero proclaims himself cured by his success as a profiteer in wartime Trieste and prophesies the self-destruction of diseased humanity by an ultimate weapon. Zeno's antics beguile the reader into complicity with the character, and his biography parallels Svevo's in his compulsive smoking of last cigarettes and in the conformist character of his wife, Augusta. But, as Svevo was to point out, the novel is Zeno's autobiography, not the author's.

Svevo's ostracism from the Italian literary world continued with the silence which greeted his third novel. Where criticism was voiced at all, it centred on his supposed inability to write good Italian. The silence was broken by Joyce, now in Paris, who brought Svevo's works to the attention of French literary circles. Reports of the impending revelation percolated back to Italy, where Eugenio *Montale presented the writer to the world in an essay in *L'Esame* late in 1925, just ahead of the French launch by Benjamin Crémieux in *Le Navire d'argent* early in 1926. Svevo thus for the last two and a half years of his life enjoyed celebrity among the international and Italian literary avant-garde, and in his native Trieste attracted a literary circle that included *Saba, Virgilio *Giotti, and Giani *Stuparich. *Senilità* and *La coscienza di Zeno* soon came out in French translation, and, after Svevo's death, in other languages, and a revised edition of *Senilità* was brought out in Italian, with some linguistic and other amendments.

Other writings were now published in journals—the brief fable 'La madre', about an incubator chick, Curra, who is driven off by the free-range hen he takes for his mother; 'Vino generoso', a story close to the world of Zeno Cosini; 'Una burla riuscita', a long tale studded with minuscule bird fables about the neglected writer duped into thinking he has become a best-seller, who nevertheless makes a killing in the volatile currency markets. Svevo also worked on new stories and plays. The unfinished long tales 'La novella del buon vecchio e della bella fanciulla' and 'Corto viaggio sentimentale' each show a wealthy, ageing protagonist trying to imagine himself a philanthropist while seducing a working-class girl or bestowing cheap sympathy upon a tragic youth. *Con la penna d'oro* and *La rigenerazione* are late plays thematically close to the sequel to *La coscienza di Zeno* that Svevo was working on when he died: the former explores the power exercised by a benefactress on her family circle through her wealth; the latter, about the ageing protagonist's rejuvenation operation, has a dream sequence that goes beyond the usual limits of Svevo's drawing-room drama.

Despite Svevo's fascination with the impersonality of drama, he achieves greater penetration

Switzerland

via intimate first-person, or quasi first-person, narrative. In the splendid slabs of his unfinished fourth novel, published posthumously with two different openings as *Il vecchione* and *Le confessioni del vegliardo*, we read an ageing Zeno using diaristic writing as a tonic to compensate for the frustrations of his losing battles with his business manager, his wife and son, his mistress, smoking, and old age. It is Zeno's subtle but futile revenge against a world whose critique and satire ultimately rebound against him. The real author, Svevo, as ever, remains aloof, elusive, maintaining an ultimate layer of quizzical but ethically challenging irony.

In a disapproving *Fascist Italy, the more or less dissident writers grouped around the journals *Solaria* and *Il Convegno* acclaimed Svevo for his astringent, deflationary style and stance, his unnerving irony and existential seriousness, even seeing him as a moral master. Svevo's works thus helped redirect the mainstream of Italian literature and have now entered the canon of literary *modernism. [JG-R]

See B. Moloney, *Italo Svevo: a Critical Introduction* (1974); J. Gatt-Rutter, *Italo Svevo. A Double Life* (1988); N. Cacciaglia and L. Fava Guzzetta (eds.), *Italo Svevo scrittore europeo* (1994).

Switzerland, see ITALIAN WRITERS IN SWITZERLAND.

Symbolism. Having begun in France in the early 1880s with the poetry of Mallarmé and Verlaine, symbolism became a European literary and artistic movement in the 1890s. In Italian *literary criticism the term is generally restricted to poetry. Though English poets, such as Swinburne, and theorists, such as Pater, were as influential as the French, it is particularly French symbolist attitudes and concerns—the stress on the power of music, the preference for evocation over description, with the consequent privileging of impressions, intuitions, and sensations—which are evident in *Pascoli, *D'Annunzio, and other poets publishing in the *Cronaca bizantina* and *Convito*. [See also DECADENTISMO; PERIODICALS, I.] [GP]

TABUCCHI, ANTONIO (1943–). *Novelist who studied in *Pisa and teaches Portuguese literature at the University of *Siena. He translated and introduced into Italian culture the work of Fernando Pessoa.

In his own fiction Tabucchi was influenced by the tradition of *realismo magico* of *Pea and *Bontempelli, as well as by authors such as Conrad, Henry James, Borges, Márquez, *Pirandello, and also Pessoa. His characters, like Pirandello's and Pessoa's, are endowed with a multitude of personalities, and his plots are full of reversals. He is particularly effective both in suggesting a dreamlike atmosphere of mystery and ambiguity and in conveying a message of libertarian commitment. He often presents an intellectual quest, which may take the form of travel to exotic places or purely of a journey in the mind, which allows him to create enigmatic and ephemeral realities. After the oblique complexities of books such as *Il gioco del rovescio* (1981), *Notturno indiano* (1984), *Il filo dell'orizzonte* (1986), and *L'angelo nero* (1991), he achieved popular success with the ostensibly simpler *Sostiene Pereira* (1994), the story of an ageing journalist finding himself having to make fundamental choices in the totalitarian world of late 1930s Lisbon.
[LL]

TADDEO ALDEROTTI (1223–95). *Florentine doctor and medical writer, who helped to revitalize the study of ancient *medicine. He made a Latin *translation of Aristotle's *Ethics* (judged ugly by *Dante in *Convivio* 1.10), and wrote one of the earliest vernacular medical texts, *Sulla conservazione della salute*. Other writings include *comment-aries and *Consilia* (case studies). [JP & JMS]

TAGLIAZUCCHI, GIROLAMO (1674–1751). Born in Modena, he became professor of Italian at *Turin University. He nurtured the cult of *Petrarch, and by precept and example—notably *Prose e poesie* (1735)—worked to instil good taste in the young. *Baretti was his pupil. [JMAL]

TAMARO, SUSANNA (1957–). *Triestine *novelist. After a relatively experimental debut in *La testa tra le nuvole* (1989), she became famous worldwide with the much more straightforward and emotionally appealing *Va' dove ti porta il cuore* (1994). Her next novel, *Anima mundi* (1997), heightened the religious dimension in her writing, which is even more explicit in *Non vedo l'ora che l'uomo cammini* (1997), a collection of articles originally published in *Famiglia cristiana*. [AC]

Tam Tam, see NICCOLAI, GIULIA; SPATOLA, ADRIANO.

TANA, CARLO GIAMBATTISTA (1649–1713). *Turinese nobleman who became a prominent general and administrator for the House of *Savoy. He wrote one of the first *comedies in *Piedmontese *dialect, *'L cont Piolet*, which was originally performed by aristocrats, and only published in 1784. [DO'G]

Tancredi. Christian champion in Torquato *Tasso's *Gerusalemme liberata*.

TANFUCIO, NERI, see FUCINI, RENATO.

TANSILLO, LUIGI (1510–68). *Petrarchist poet. Born into the *Neapolitan aristocracy, he held various posts at the court of Naples, some in the service of the Spanish viceroy. He was in contact with Annibale *Caro and Benedetto *Varchi, and became a member of the *Florentine Accademia degli Umidi in 1540 [see ACADEMIES]. He is considered the most important Southern Italian Petrarchist, and was admired by Torquato *Tasso and *Marino, no doubt for his anticipations of the *Baroque manner. His *canzoniere* was the result of a lifetime's work and only published in 1711. His published work included an eclogue, *I due pellegrini* (1530), an erotic poem in *ottava rima* entitled *Il vendemmiatore* (1532), laudatory poems addressed to various high-ranking figures, and *Le lagrime di San Pietro* (1580), a poem in fifteen cantos of *ottava rima* imbued with *Counter-Reformation moral and religious fervour. [NC]

TANUCCI, BERNARDO (1698–1783). *Tuscan lawyer, who followed Charles of *Bourbon to *Naples, becoming a minister (1739–77) and an important cultural figure under Charles and Ferdinand IV. He promoted socio-economic reforms, with greatest success in the sphere of Church–state relations. He left an extremely valuable correspondence with Charles. [GLCB]

TANZI, CARL'ANTONIO (1710–62). *Milanese poet. He was secretary of the Accademia dei Trasformati in Milan [see ACADEMIES]. His poems, in Italian and in *dialect, were edited in the year of his death by Giuseppe *Parini. [CCa]

TARABOTTI, ARCANGELA (1604–52) (pseud. Galerana Baratotti or Barcitotti). *Venetian prose writer, advocate of women's liberty and equality, critic of contemporary patriarchy within the family, state, and Church, social satirist, and polemicist. Tarabotti's protests sprang from bitter experience. As a young girl she was sent to the *Benedictine convent of S. Anna, and pressured into taking vows at 16 that bound her for life. She died in S. Anna, probably of tuberculosis. Some of her works, such as *L' Inferno monacale*, were only published in the 20th c.

Tarabotti had no formal *education, and repeatedly blames lack of schooling, brought about by men, as the greatest single reason for women's subjection. She was nevertheless befriended by members of the Accademia degli *Incogniti, who were known for their *libertine tendencies, and the founder, Gian Francesco *Loredan, assisted her with the publication of her correspondence (1650). Her first work, *La tirannia paterna* (published posthumously in 1654 as *La semplicità ingannata*, and quickly placed on the *Index) is the most radical indictment of patriarchy before modern times. It argues a philosophy and theology of women's intellectual and moral equality and liberty. Tarabotti draws on the *Bible, and in equal measure on *Dante, to exalt free will as God's greatest gift to men and women alike. It is therefore criminal

for fathers, the state, or the Church to force women into convents. In marriage it is likewise criminal for a husband to treat his wife as if she were by nature a servant or slave. When Francesco Buoninsegni published a *Satira contro il lusso donnesco* (1638), Tarabotti answered with an *Antisatira* (1644), exposing men's even greater extravagance. In her final most philosophical polemic, *Che le donne siano della spezie degli uomini* (1651), she rebutted long-standing arguments that women do not have a rational soul and are incapable of moral choice or of being saved. [See also FEMINISM; MISOGYNY; WOMEN WRITERS, 1.] [LAP]
Che le donne siano della spezie degli uomini, ed. L. Panizza (1994).

TARCANIOTA, MICHELE MARULLO, see MARULLO, MICHELE.

TARCHETTI, IGINIO UGO (1839–69). *Novelist. Born into an impoverished *Piedmontese family, thoughout his life he was dogged by financial difficulties which contributed to his early death from typhus and consumption. His experiences as a volunteer officer in the army between 1859 and 1865 led to the novel *Una nobile follia* (1867), which provides a courageous denunciation of the conscript army at a time when the armed forces were a potent, if fragile, symbol of Italy's *Unification. In his last few years Tarchetti lived a peripatetic existence between *Turin and *Milan, eventually settling in the latter and working frenetically to earn enough to be a full-time writer. He set up two short-lived journals, the *Piccolo giornale* and *Palestra musicale*, and contributed to many others. He was a member of the *Scapigliatura, producing serialized novels and stories which reveal a restless, eclectic personality and aspire, like other works of the group, to deprovincialize Italian literature by turning to foreign literary models. After the social humanitarianism of *Paolina: mistero del coperto Figini* (1865), he introduced the *fantastic to the Italian reading public, five of his stories being posthumously collected as *Racconti fantastici* (1869). His last novel, *Fosca*, written when he was dying, is a study of its eponymous heroine's sexuality and sickness and the morbid attraction–repulsion she holds for the narrator. His close friend Salvatore *Farina completed the crucial missing chapter so that Tarchetti could be paid on its serialization. [AHC]

TARCHIANI, ALBERTO, see CORAZZINI, SERGIO.

TARTUFARI, CLARICE (1868–1933). *Roman *novelist who began as a poet with *Versi nuovi* (1894) and then wrote extensively for the *theatre. Her novels, such as *Roveto ardente* (1905) and *Il miracolo* (1909), are set amongst the petite bourgeoisie of Rome, and debate moral and religious issues in the manner of *Fogazzaro. [UJF]

TASSO, BERNARDO (1493–1569), father of Torquato *Tasso, led a chequered career as courtier, soldier, and man of letters in the service of Ferrante Sanseverino, the exiled Prince of Salerno. Bernardo published *Horatian odes, a collection of *letters, and works of *literary theory, but is best known for his narrative poem *Amadigi* (1560), loosely based on the successful Spanish romance *Amadís de Gaula* by Garcia Ordóñez de Montalvo. The Italian poet aimed to combine the unity, seriousness, and moral tone of the classical *epics with the amorous and fantastic material of the *Ariostesque *romance, but most readers have found his poem laboured and tedious. [CPB]

TASSO, ERCOLE, see MISOGYNY.

TASSO, TORQUATO (1544–95), son of Bernardo *Tasso, is almost as famous for the circumstances of his unhappy life as for the international acclaim he won for his two masterpieces, the *pastoral play *Aminta* (1573) and the *epic poem *Gerusalemme liberata* (1581). After a disturbed childhood he found a home for some twenty years at the *Este *court in *Ferrara, the last seven of which were spent in confinement for apparent insanity, which manifested itself principally in an acute sensitivity to slights, resulting in outbursts of abuse against the Duke and his fellow courtiers. His condition was exacerbated by concerns about the reception of his poem and the fate of his manuscripts, over which he lost control while confined, and also by fears of being charged with *heresy by the *Inquisition. The various legends that arose, especially in the age of *Romanticism (see Goethe's *Torquato Tasso*), that the 'imprisonment' was a punishment meted out by the Duke because of the poet's passion for the Princess Leonora, are now discredited. Tasso regained some measure of composure in his later years, but wandered restlessly between various protectors in *Mantua, *Naples, *Florence, and *Rome, where he died in 1595.

Despite these difficult circumstances he wrote throughout his life, composing a large body of prose and verse, much of it of the highest quality. He was given to frequent revision of his drafts and was slow to release them for publication, so that a good deal of his work either was published without his consent or remained in *manuscript, posing enormous problems for editors, who are still struggling to resolve textual problems and produce satisfactory editions. In addition to the masterpieces mentioned above he composed a youthful *romance, *Rinaldo* (1562); a late revision of his epic under the new title of *Gerusalemme conquistata* (1593); a long poem on the Creation, *Le sette giornate del mondo creato* (published in 1607); a *tragedy, *Il re Torrismondo* (1587); a much admired series of prose *dialogues; and several influential treatises on poetics [see LITERARY THEORY, 2], as well as a large number of *letters. He also wrote more than 1,700 short poems, and is considered today as one of the best *lyric poets of the 16th c. Tasso attached great importance to these compositions, which he planned to publish in three collections of amorous, encomiastic, and sacred verse, a plan only partially realized in his lifetime. His facility in and mastery of lyric forms, particularly the *sonnet and *madrigal, is remarkable—the latter, a free combination of long and short, rhymed and unrhymed lines, seems best to have reflected his belief that music was the soul of poetry, and his verse has been the source of innumerable musical settings. The amorous poems, while *Petrarchan in inspiration, extend the Petrarchan lexicon and themes; the lyrics in praise of *patrons and others adapt the grand style of his epic to occasional subjects; the religious poems reflect *Counter-Reformation tastes, but are also at times personal and moving.

The *Aminta*, Tasso's pastoral play, was written for the Ferrarese court, and performed in the court retreat on the island of Belvedere del Po in July 1573. It was an immediate success, although no printed edition appeared until 1582. The *Aminta* crowned a series of recent pastoral plays produced at the Ferrarese court, and stimulated the other acknowledged masterpiece of the genre, Battista *Guarini's *Pastor fido* (1590). A French translation appeared in 1584, an English version, by Abraham Fraunce, in 1591 and it was soon translated and imitated all over Europe. The beauty of Tasso's delicately modulated verse with its patterns of seven- and eleven-syllable lines, rhymed and unrhymed, and particularly of a series of lyric interludes sung between the acts, is reported to have delighted the court audience. They were further entertained by scattered allusions to the Duke and

Tasso, Torquato

his circle, and by discovering some of themselves thinly disguised among the shepherds. So the court is transported to the woods, where the myth of a Golden Age is celebrated with a hedonistic dream of freedom: 'S'ei piace ei lice' ('You can do what you like'), especially in love. The dream, however, is soon seen to clash with reality: the Golden Age is not one the shepherds currently enjoy, and they look back nostalgically to the simple innocent pleasures of the past, before the intrusion of the court and its values corrupted the countryside. The pastoral setting becomes a landscape of the mind, where courtiers and shepherds alike recreate the fantasies of the poet and his audience.

It has been the formal, lyric beauties of the *Aminta* which have mostly captivated readers down the ages: the 'musicality' of Tasso's verse has always been admired. But modern critics have also stressed the play's considerable dramatic qualities, perhaps inspired by contemporary *tragicomic theory. Tragic passion and violence dominate the stage until the happy ending, and the structural balance is finely tuned as the protagonists are shuttled between love and death. Aminta's adolescent sensuality gives way to modesty and reverence when he saves Silvia from the Satyr's attempted rape, and this softens the aloof maiden, while the Satyr's initial respect (he brings flowers) turns fatally to violence—processes to which the experiences of the worldly Dafne and Tirsi supply a counterpoint. Tasso also holds his audience by the engaging appeals of the Chorus, the clarity and simplicity of the plot, and an unusual blend of the popular and the literary in a style sensitively adjusted to the *theatre.

The *Aminta* was written and staged within a few months, and without any of the theoretical controversy which accompanied the long gestation of the *Gerusalemme liberata*, the prime motivation for which was the creation of an epic poem that would rival, possibly even excel, the *Iliad* and the *Aeneid*. The problem facing Tasso was to repeat the popular success of *Ariosto's *Orlando furioso* while also meeting the *Aristotelian criteria for the epic, of which Ariosto was considered to have fallen short, and at the same time not falling foul of the Inquisition. Tasso wrestled almost all of his adult life with this challenge, from his early apprenticeship with his experimental romance, *Rinaldo*, the *Discorsi dell'arte poetica* (1570) on epic theory, and his composition of the *Liberata* (1560–81), which involved him in a lengthy correspondence with a team of 'revisers', to his rewriting of his epic as the

Gerusalemme conquistata, the reformulation of his epic theory as the *Discorsi del poema eroico* (1594), and his defence of the revised epic, published posthumously as the *Giudizio sovra la Gerusalemme conquistata*.

In accordance with his published theories Tasso chooses a historical subject of epic proportions, the capture of Jerusalem by the *Crusaders in 1099, broadly following classical precedent, but replacing a pagan with a Christian subject as the current Counter-Reformation ethos required. The period of time, he believed, should be one near enough to the time of writing for the characters and customs to be recognizable, but sufficiently remote to allow the poet scope for invention. Thus while many of the details of the action derive from *chronicles, others come from literary sources or from the poet's own imagination, and he manipulates his historical sources to meet the traditional epic criteria, in particular to ennoble the Christians and enhance their stature; he omits, for example, their subsequent failure to hold the city. The military action is the prime focus of the poem: the title highlights the 'liberation' of Jerusalem (in contrast with Ariosto's amorous Orlando). War is of course the traditional subject matter of the epic, and Tasso gives great prominence both to the large-scale clash of Christian and pagan forces, and to the encounters of individual men of arms. The thrill of the Christians' first glimpse of Jerusalem (canto 3), the excitement of the pagan sortie to fire the huge siege-tower threatening the city (12), the tension of the final assault (19–20)—all are vividly conveyed, as is the heroism of the knights, and especially of the pagan leaders Argante (19) and Solimano (20) as they face their end. Indeed, the pathos of defeat and the horror of death on the battlefield, so blithely ignored in the popular romances, seem to inspire the poet as much as the glory of victory in arms.

At the same time Tasso was resolved to follow Ariosto's successful precedent in combining the theme of arms with that of love, and his opening stanzas proclaim his intention of softening the 'bitter truth' of history with the 'sweet drafts' of his own invention. So the Christian knight Rinaldo falls victim to the charms of the pagan Armida in her enchanted garden, while the pagan warrior Clorinda inspires a fatal passion in the Christian Tancredi. Classical and Italian sources are prominent here, but Tasso's treatment is largely original: a moralizing urge has the poet reconcile Rinaldo with Armida at the end, thus showing his superiority to Aeneas, who deserted Dido; while a morbid,

*Baroque sensibility pervades other scenes, as when Tancredi unwittingly pierces Clorinda's breast (20.64), and Sofronia and Olindo are bound together at the stake (2.32). Tasso also interprets in his own way the epic theorists' insistence on 'meraviglie' or incidents arousing wonder in the reader, such as magic and the supernatural. These, in accordance with Counter-Reformation taste, are to be brought under the authority of the Christian religion—so while individual episodes such as Armida's garden (canto 16) and the enchanted wood (13) repeat the magic devices of the romances, the whole action is shown as controlled by God and the angels, opposed by Beelzebub and his devils (compare Homer's council of deities). The depth and sincerity of the poet's faith inspires some fine passages, both those depicting the splendour of church ceremonial and liturgy and others expressing the lonely sinner's sense of mystery and awe before God's handiwork.

Lengthy discussions about style occur in Tasso's theoretical writings, mostly inspired by the poet's reading of Aristotle and Demetrius. The 'grand style' he judges appropriate for the epic and employs in the *Liberata* is characterized by an elevated lexicon and a density of rhetorical devices such as periphrasis, hyperbole, antithesis, displaced word order, and occasional conceits such as would become normal in later Baroque poetry. Tasso's is a highly expressive style in which the psychological effect is stressed and the poet's own emotional reaction to his narrative is declared. Tasso excludes Ariosto's lowly, sometimes down-to-earth style as well as his predecessor's ironic commentary on his own process of composition, which lowers the emotional charge that Tasso by contrast seeks constantly to raise. The Accademia della *Crusca attacked his language as not adequately conforming to Pietro *Bembo's principles, but posterity has largely vindicated Tasso's lexicon, and his 'grand style' was enormously influential.

Indeed, despite the carping of admirers of Ariosto who conducted a furious campaign against it, Tasso's poem was quickly recognized as the epic masterpiece for which Europe had been waiting, and which could challenge the great classical epics. Tasso himself, however, was not convinced. It was not only the criticism of Ariosto's supporters which worried him but his own sense that the version he had been forced to publish in 1581, following an earlier illicit edition, had not received his final revision; and in his later years he set about the substantial rewriting of his poem, which he published

in 1593 as *Gerusalemme conquistata*. This was the only version of the work which he explicitly approved, but it was a sad disappointment to his admirers, and has been discarded by later generations in favour of the poem we read as the *Liberata*. The revised version in fact implements many of the stylistic changes he was contemplating in the 1570s, but it is too heavily constrained by moral considerations and poor aesthetic judgement. The poem he rejected was widely applauded, however, and a succession of highly successful translations (into Spanish in 1587, French in 1595, English (Fairfax) in 1600) brought it into the mainstream of European literature. A profusion of Christian epics followed in Tasso's wake: Ronsard's *Franciade*, Lope de Vega's *Jerusalén conquistada*, and Milton's *Paradise Lost* among them. Indeed, Tasso's reputation has withstood the vagaries of critical fortune better than Ariosto's *Furioso*, appealing to *classicists and Romantics alike, and stands as high today as ever. [CPB]

Poesie, ed. F. Flora (1952); *Prose*, ed. E. Mazzali (1959). See C. P. Brand, *Torquato Tasso* (1965); L. Caretti, *Ariosto e Tasso* (1967); A. Fichter, *Poets Historical: Dynastic Epic in the Renaissance* (1982).

TASSONI, ALESSANDRO (1565–1635). A multifaceted and complex writer, he was born into a noble family in Modena, studied in *Bologna, *Pisa, and *Ferrara, and moved to *Rome in 1597, where he entered the service of Cardinal Ascanio *Colonna, and took an active part in the cultural life of the city. From 1620 he was employed at *court in *Turin, subsequently returning to Modena, where he was also employed at the court and where he died.

Nowadays valued much more for his 'light' side, as a poet, than as the 'serious' philosopher which he laid claim to be, he is known mainly as the inventor of the *mock-heroic genre with his poem *La secchia rapita*, which he began in 1614/15, and which deals in burlesque mode with the events of the Modena-Bologna war of 1325. Though superficially structured along classical lines, the work is permeated throughout by a *Baroque poetic. Its author characterized it as a 'mixture of the serious and the humorous, the solemn and the burlesque, the heroic and the comic'. But 'serious' figures such as the tragic Enrico and the epic Oceano show it to be a degraded form of the *epic genre, which ceases here to act as a positive reflection of social and ethical values, and serves instead as a negative measure of the extent to which these values have been lost. At the same time *La secchia rapita* presents an anti-ideal, anti-heroic world with its own picturesque and provincial geography, where the everyday is projected into the exaggerated proportions of the sublime. [See also UMORISTI, ACCADEMIA DEGLI.]

The complex and substantial nature of Tassoni's literary interests is reflected in the range of forms which he attempted, writing in a variety of modes, by his own account as a legal scholar, secretary, philosopher, historian, politician, and poet, and varying, expanding and adapting the intellectual resources he possessed. As a thinker (*Pensieri e pre-redazioni*), he is notable not so much for the content of his work as for the playful approach with which he makes knowledge into a kind of reckless intellectual gymnastics, a boundless field for the exercise of his sharp intelligence. As a historian (*Difesa di Alessandro Macedone, Guerra della Valtellina, Annali*), he demonstrates a fundamentally ethical vision, inspired by Tacitus, which in its positive aspect interprets history in heroic terms as the product of exceptional personalities, but in its negative moments offers a pessimistic picture of events as the dark fruit of human passions, of men's vices rather than their virtues. As a political commentator (*Filippiche, Risposta al Soccino*), he sides with *Piedmont against *Spain and expresses his hostility to foreign rule with inspired eloquence. As a linguist (*Postille al *Vocabolario della Crusca*), he takes a stand against the 14th-c. models of Pietro *Bembo and the Accademia della *Crusca, finding the basis of good expression in common usage, drawing on a variety and range of sources, and on the spontaneity of spoken language. [See QUESTIONE DELLA LINGUA.] As a critic and polemicist (*Considerazioni sopra le Rime di Petrarca*), he constantly takes issue with contemporary orthodoxies, whether derived from *Aristotle, *Petrarch, Bembo, or anyone else, rejecting appeals to authority and *Renaissance rules regarding literary models, and advocating a poetics of freedom. [PP]

Opere, ed. P. Puliatti (1986–93). See P. Puliatti, *Bibliografia di A. Tassoni* (1969–70).

Tavola ritonda, see ARTHURIAN LITERATURE.

Teatro comico, Il. *Comedy in three acts by *Goldoni, performed in *Venice as the prologue to the sixteen plays produced in 1750–1. Following French examples of meta-theatre, the actors of Orazio's company rehearse on stage, discussing the author's—that is, Goldoni's—ideas on reform of

the *theatre, and condemning *Baroque affectations. [FF]

TEBALDEO, ANTONIO (1462–1537). *Petrarchist poet and a central figure in Italian literary culture of the 16th c. Born in *Ferrara, he joined the *Este *court and in 1490 followed Isabella d'Este to *Mantua after her marriage, as her preceptor. He presided over her network of literary relationships and became the leading name in contemporary vernacular poetry.

His own work does little more than plunder *Petrarch's abstract metaphorical language and recycle it in what now seems an extremely laboured fashion, but it was immensely popular—he published at least twenty-seven editions of his *canzoniere between 1498 and 1510—and came to be seen as a paradigm of courtly literature. In 1513 he was forced to move from Mantua and settled in *Rome. He now had the esteem of *Ariosto (who cited him among the greatest living poets in *Orlando furioso 42), Pietro *Bembo, *Colocci, *Castiglione, and *Raphael, who put him among the greatest poets in his painting of Parnassus in the Stanza della Segnatura. Whilst in Rome, he abandoned his increasingly dated poetic style of vernacular poetry and acquired a well-deserved reputation as a neo-Latin poet. Bembo and Colocci edited his *Latin poems after his death, though their edition, published probably in 1546, is now lost. They also projected a revised edition of his vernacular poetry which may never have been printed. [NC]

TECCHI, BONAVENTURA (1896–1968). Critic, Germanist, and novelist. During *World War I he was captured and imprisoned in Germany with Ugo *Betti and Carlo Emilio *Gadda, who became lasting friends. Gadda later encouraged his collaboration with *Solaria. He was director of the *Vieusseux library in *Florence (1925–31), and later taught German literature in Italy and abroad. Apart from studies of German and contemporary Italian literature, he wrote *novels and short stories. He is best known for *Gli egoisti* (1959). [SVM]

TEDALDI FORES, CARLO (1793–1829). Poet and dramatist. From a modest Cremona family, he was able to study law at *Bologna thanks to a generous *Jesuit, Padre Fores (whose name he took), and subsequently moved to *Milan. A *Romantic from 1816, he composed the Byronic *Romanzi poetici* (1820) and argued against Vincenzo

*Monti's defence of mythology in *Meditazioni poetiche* (1825). Of his historical *tragedies, *Beatrice da Tenda* (1825) is the most notable. [MPC]

TELESIO, ANTONIO (1482–1534) from Cosenza was a *humanist and author of a variety of Latin works. Celebrated by *Giovio, he is best known for a collection of elegies, *Poemata*, a *tragedy on the myth of Danae, the *Imber aureus*, and a *commentary on the works of *Horace. [ELM]

TELESIO, BERNARDINO (1509–88). Natural philosopher. Born in Cosenza, he studied in *Milan and *Rome with his uncle, Antonio *Telesio. He then moved to *Venice and supposedly to *Padua, before returning south. He established in Cosenza an Accademia Cosentina, which was then renamed the Accademia Telesiana. In 1564 Pope Pius IV offered him the Bishopric of Cosenza, which he refused.

His most famous work is a treatise on natural science, with the Lucretian title *De rerum natura iuxta propria principia* in the final 1586 version, though earlier versions with slightly different titles had appeared in 1565 and 1570. Telesio is important for his anticipation of later scientific thinking, rejecting traditional *Aristotelian categories and methods of argument, and proposing the thoroughly materialistic theory that all knowledge is sensation and that the soul itself is matter rather than spirit. The book was placed on the *Index in 1596. [PLR]

Television officially began broadcasting in Italy in 1954. Modelled on the BBC, state television (RAI-TV) aspired to inform, educate, and entertain. Politics was granted no place outside news programmes before 1963, in keeping with the *Christian Democrats' desire to avoid making any concessions to the Left. The main output consisted of solid middlebrow fare including plays and adaptations of literary classics. Religious broadcasts and some adult education programmes added an uplifting tone. Entertainment consisted of variety shows and quizzes, the most memorable of which were *Lascia o raddoppia?*, a local version of *The 64,000 Dollar Question*, and the musical game show *Il Musichiere*. Some changes occurred in the 1960s when the *Socialists joined the government and a second RAI channel was created. At this time, news became less overtly biased, there was acknowledgement of the *Resistance, and some *Neorealist films were broadcast. Broadly speak-

ing, however, little changed until the mid-1970s, when the Constitutional Court opened the way to the liberalization of the air waves. Despite a reform of RAI passed in 1975, which transferred control from the government to parliament in an attempt to legitimize the state monopoly, private and commercial broadcasting at local level was permitted.

In the space of just a few years the old paternalistic pattern of broadcasting broke down and a new, commercial ethos won out. In the private sector, a process of concentration led to Silvio Berlusconi winning control by 1983 of the three leading networks, Canale 5 (his flagship), Rete 4, and Italia 1. In order to compete, RAI was compelled to cast aside its old values and adopt a commercial approach which saw an increase in broadcasting hours, daily rather than weekly scheduling, the domination of entertainment, in-programme sponsorship, an emphasis on star presenters, and the use of imported films and soap operas. At the same time RAI was weakened by the influence of the Italian parties' system for sharing out the spoils of government (*lottizzazione*), into which even the Communists were integrated with the creation of a third RAI channel. Following repeated pressure from the Constitutional Court and the European Commission to regulate the broadcasting sector, the Mammì law of 1990 was introduced, which in substance confirmed the status quo. Although Italian television in the 1990s conserved something of its origins (notably a taste for variety-style shows and a certain provincial atmosphere), it evolved into a powerful medium through which much of the political, cultural, and family life of the country passed. [See also CINEMA; RADIO.] [SG]

See R. Monteleone, *Storia della radio e della televisione in Italia* (1992); S. Gundle, 'Television in Italy', in J. Coleman and B. Rollet (eds.), *Television in Europe* (1997).

TENCA, CARLO (1816–83). Committed *Risorgimento *journalist and *literary critic, active in his native *Milan and elsewhere. Initially a *Mazzinian, during the 1850s he became increasingly close to *Cavour, though he was also strongly influenced by Carlo *Cattaneo. His main concern was the popularization and modernization of Italian literature. He wrote for many *periodicals during his long career, and edited *Il 22 marzo*, the official organ of the provisional revolutionary government in Milan in *1848 (after which he went into *exile in Lugano). Most famously and successfully, he was editor from 1850 to 1859 of *Il *Crepuscolo*, in

Tenco, Luigi

which he published his own most important essays. He was in charge of *education in Milan from 1860 to 1867 and a served also as a parliamentary deputy. His *historical novel, *La Ca' dei cani* (1840), poked gentle fun at the genre. [MPC]

TENCO, LUIGI, see CANTAUTORI.

Tenzone. Poetic exchange, usually in *sonnet form, in which the respondent(s) repeat the rhymes of the first poem, usually in their entirety. Most 13th- and 14th-c. poets took part in *tenzoni.* Many reformulate commonplaces about love; others are more personal, with sometimes polemical statements of poetics. Political *tenzoni* can be virulently partisan and (in the case of *Monte Andrea's circle) extended contests in formal virtuosity. [PH]

TEOTOCHI ALBRIZZI, ISABELLA (1760–1836). Born in Corfu, she became the most admired hostess in *Venice. Her salon was frequented by such figures as *Cesarotti, *Foscolo, *Bertola de' Giorgi, Byron, and Ippolito *Pindemonte, who became her companion. She portrayed her guests in *Ritratti* (1807). She also left a voluminous correspondence. [JMAL]

TÉRÉSAH (1877–1964) (pseud. of Corinna Teresa Ubertis Gray). Prolific *novelist and poet and a popular speaker. *Sergina o la virtù* is still striking as an analysis of social conditions during *World War I. The stories of *La casa al sole* (1917), which has often been thought her best book, evoke the complex emotions hidden beneath the surface of everyday life. [UJF]

TERRACINA, LAURA (1519–?1577). *Neapolitan poet. Of noble birth, she entered the Accademia degli *Incogniti as Febea. Her nine volumes of poetry, written in Tuscan with traces of Neapolitan and inspired by *Petrarch and *Ariosto, enjoyed enormous popularity at the time, running to some thirty editions, but have found little favour with modern critics. [EGH]

TERRACINI, BENVENUTO, see LITERARY CRITICISM.

TERRAMAGNINO DA PISA (13th c.). Author of a versified Provençal *grammar, *Doctrina de Cort,* of about 1280. His surviving Italian writing is confined to a *sonetto doppio* [see SONNET] in a *tenzone* (perhaps with *Meo Abbracciavacca)

arguing about which of them best follows *Guittone d'Arezzo. [JU]

Terra vergine, see D'ANNUNZIO, GABRIELE.

Terre del sacramento, Le, see JOVINE, FRANCESCO.

Terza pagina ('third page'), the cultural page of newspapers [see JOURNALISM; LITERARY CRITICISM; PROSA D'ARTE; TRAVEL WRITING].

Terza rima. Considered an invention of *Dante's, it was the metre of the *Divine Comedy,* afterwards much used in didactic and narrative poetry in competition with the *ottava rima.* The first line of every tercet or *terzina* rhymes with the third of the same tercet, and the second line rhymes with the first and third lines of the next tercet, producing the scheme ABA BCB CDC, etc. With rare exceptions, each unit of text concludes, as in every *canto of the *Comedy,* with a single line rhyming with the second line of the last tercet. In *pastoral poetry from the 15th c. onwards there is frequent use of *terza rima* with *sdrucciolo* lines. [See also VERSIFICATION.] [PGB]

TESAURO, EMANUELE (1592–1675) was the most important *Baroque literary theorist in Italy. Born in *Turin and educated by the *Jesuits, whose order he entered in 1611, he studied theology at *Naples and *Milan and began preaching. In 1634 he left the Jesuit Order and in 1635 entered the service of the *court of *Savoy. There he composed histories of *Piedmont, Flanders, Turin, and Italy under barbarian rule, two *tragedies, panegyrics, and works of moral philosophy. His main work was *Il cannocchiale aristotelico,* first published in 1654 and reprinted at least ten times in the 17th c. Developing ideas adumbrated in *Renaissance poetics, and using the Aristotle of the *Rhetoric* rather than of the *Poetics,* Tesauro builds up a vast theory of metaphor and *concettismo.* His theory depends on a distinction between *intelletto* and *ingegno*: *intelletto* apprehends facts and communicates them via literal signs directly and unadorned to the mind; *ingegno* apprehends facts and transforms them, through processes of analogy and lateral thinking, into pleasing, witty rhetorical conceits.

Tesauro is conscious of the dangers of slippage between truth and language, but he appreciates the sensuous and intellectual pleasure and wonder that non-literal, non-transparent words and signs can create. For him, all language is inherently metaphorical in that it involves transference from thought to the senses. The role of *ingegno* is to investigate the hidden connection between all things, treating the world as a storehouse of potentially marvellous analogies. Metaphor is central to this metamorphosing process; and Tesauro shows how in kaleidoscopic fashion one metaphor can generate an infinite number of others in such a way that the scope of poetic and rhetorical analogy is extended, in theory, as never before. In this way he subverts Aristotle while paying lip-service to him, and opens up a new literary world which is akin to the new scientific and geographical worlds of the early 17th c. [See also ARISTOTELIANISM; LITERARY THEORY, 3; MARINISMO.] [PBD]

See M. Zanardi, *Contributi per una biografia di Emanuele Tesauro* (1979); D. Aricò, *Il Tesauro in Europa* (1987).

Teseida (1339–41). Narrative poem by *Boccaccio with *epic aspirations. It consists of twelve canti in *ottava rima*, with a similar number of lines to *Virgil's *Aeneid*. The plot centres on two faithful friends, Arcita and Palemone, competing for the love of Emilia, the younger sister of Ippolita, Queen of the Amazons, who is married to Theseus, the ruler of Athens. Theseus arranges a grand tournament to decide between them. Though Arcita emerges victorious, he is fatally wounded and Emilia is married to Palemone. Boccaccio's literary ambitions are shown by the erudite glosses which he himself added. His principal sources were probably *Statius, the *Roman de Thèbes*, and an unnamed *Byzantine work, perhaps the *Digenes Akritas*. The Greek aura may have led to the poem's success in 15th-c. Greece. It was also taken up by Chaucer in the *Knight's Tale*. In Italy it established *ottava rima* as the canonical form for epic verse and the thematic union of arms and love in *chivalric poetry which would continue up to *Ariosto and Torquato *Tasso. [VB]

TESSA, DELIO (1886–1939). *Milanese *dialect poet, who practised law in Milan and reviewed for Milanese and Swiss papers. Anti-*Fascist and anti-social, he published only one collection of his poetry, *L'è el dì di mort, alegher!* ('It's the day of the dead, cheer up!', 1932), during his lifetime. His verse looks back explicitly to Carlo *Porta, but is violently *expressionistic in its language and representations of contemporary society. [JJ]

TESTI, FULVIO (1593–1646). Poet and diplomat. Born in *Ferrara and educated by the *Jesuits, he served the *Este family, the Pope, and, above all, the dukes of Modena. In his youth he courted polemic, and the displeasure of his master, the Duke of Modena, by writing an anti-Spanish poem, the *Pianto d'Italia* (1617), which was mistakenly hailed in the *Risorgimento as an early expression of *nationalist aspirations, and by launching thinly veiled accusations of plagiarism at his poetic elders and betters. But he was essentially an establishment figure. Poetically, alongside Gabriello *Chiabrera, he was the major exponent of the Hellenizing strand of *Baroque *classicism, combining *Horatianism with the imitation of Anacreon and Pindar. But his harmonious yet ultimately platitudinous moral verses betray little originality of feeling or expression. His dignified, undemanding odes may have helped his rise to high office at the *court of Modena, though ultimately he fell out of favour, dying in prison in equivocal circumstances. His most important and interesting writings are not, however, his lyrics (only collected in 1653), but his extensive correspondence, which is a major document of Baroque politics and letters. [MPS]

Testimonianza di Travale (1158). A report of some legal depositions offering the earliest surviving example of a non-formulaic utterance in an Italo-Romance vernacular. In mid-text it abruptly and unaccountably abandons Latin to quote some of the witnesses' own (Tuscan) words. Of particular linguistic interest are the partitive pronoun *de* (Latin *inde*) and *ma'* (Latin *magis*), apparently meaning 'only'. [See also HISTORY OF THE ITALIAN LANGUAGE.] [MM]

TESTONI, ALFREDO (1856–1931). *Bolognese playwright who almost single-handedly revived Bolognese drama, enjoying a great commercial success with the historical *comedy *Il Cardinale Lambertini* (1906). He also wrote humorous *dialect verse in the persona of 'Sgnera Cattareina'. In 1880 he co-founded with Antonio *Fiacchi the humorous weekly *Ehi ch'al scusa*. [PBarn]

TESTORI, GIOVANNI (1923–93). *Milanese *novelist, poet, and dramatist. His earlier fiction, for instance, *Il fabbricone* (1961), centres on dramatic, violent representations of the lives and minds of the sub-proletariat of industrial Milan, and makes expressive use of a mixture of Italian and *dialect. His dramas of the same period are similar.

Textual Criticism

L'Arialda (1961), as directed by Luchino *Visconti, was censored and provoked a national debate on freedom of expression. Linguistic violence and artifice—it has been called *mannerism—continues in his subsequent work. In diverse ways he attempts to express the atrocious, often self-mutilating condition of humanity bereft of God, and at the same time he aims to find temporary redemption and solace in art, notably in poetry, as shown especially in *Diademata* (1986). Some striking plays, for instance *L'Ambleto* (1972) and *Macbetto* (1974), are deliberately distorted rewritings of *Shakespeare. He later wrote religious verse dramas, such as *Confiteor* (1985). Testori was also a painter of some note. [PBart]

Textual Criticism. The purpose of textual criticism is to reconstruct texts as nearly as possible in their original form. The first stage, recension, sets out to reconstruct the text which lies behind surviving witnesses by deducing their genealogical interrelationship and reconstituting the common ancestor or 'archetype'. This genealogy is established through the identification of significant errors, and it may be expressed as a *stemma codicum*, or family tree. The stemma may be complicated by changes introduced by the author or by contamination, the process of copying from more than one source. A choice between variants may be resolved through study of the author's language and style or by adopting the more difficult reading, less likely to have been altered. The second stage is the examination of the archetype, the identification of any errors, and, where possible, their emendation. The editor must also decide how far spelling and punctuation are to be standardized or modernized. [See also FILOLOGIA.]

This method was developed in the 19th c. by the German scholar Karl Lachmann (1793–1851) and others in biblical and *classical scholarship, though the genealogical principle was anticipated by *humanists such as *Poliziano. Before the 1890s, editors of Italian literature depended largely on emendation by contamination and conjecture, and tended to make the language of texts conform with their own criteria, although in the *Renaissance, emulating classical scholarship and spurred on by the advent of *printing, editors such as Pietro *Bembo, *Borghini, *Salviati, and *Corbinelli began to seek out the best available witnesses and to use conjecture sparingly. The application of the 'Lachmannian' method to Italian authors was established in particular by the pioneering edition of *Dante's *De vulgari eloquentia

(1896) carried out by Pio *Rajna, also author of the first Italian synthesis of the method (1906), and by Michele *Barbi's edition of Dante's *Vita nova (1907). Barbi's approach to the problem of spelling was to eliminate forms not corresponding with contemporary pronunciation; subsequently, more conservative criteria were introduced, since spelling can have cultural and stylistic significance. Because Italian textual criticism developed its techniques primarily in the context of the medieval canon, it was slow to incorporate the techniques of textual bibliography as developed in Anglo-American scholarship, i.e. textual criticism as applied to texts diffused in print. [BR]

See G. Pasquali, *Storia della tradizione e critica del testo* (1952); F. Brambilla Ageno, *L'edizione critica dei testi volgari* (1975); C. Fahy, *Saggi di bibliografia testuale* (1988).

Theatines. The first of the post-*Reformation orders, they derive their name from the city of Chieti (Latin *Theate*) where their first community was established in 1517 by St Gaetano Thiene and Giampietro Carafa to improve clerical behaviour and promote evangelism. The new order was formally constituted in 1524 and immediately attracted many like-minded secular priests. It then was further boosted by Carafa's election to the *papacy as Paul IV (1555). He gave them permanent use of what became their mother-church, S. Andrea della Valle in Rome.

But the Theatines were prevented by statute from holding property, or even begging for alms, trusting rather in God's providence. They also refused to establish schools of their own, devoting themselves instead to charitable and missionary activity within and beyond Christendom—they inspired the founding of the College of Propaganda Fide, supplying its first early rectors and masters. Their emphasis on poverty, piety, and good works, ministering to the poor and sick, was seen by many as the antithesis to the *Jesuits' close links with the upper classes and perceived intellectual arrogance. Writers were lavish in their praises of Theatine preachers, but, given the nature of the order, their influence on literary culture was largely indirect, and is still to be explored. [MPS]

Theatre

1. Before 1600

After thundering denunciations from the early Christian Fathers, performed art in the medieval period was culturally and morally devalued unless it could be adapted to a liturgical function. Theatre activity thus became linked to a precise celebratory context, either devotional and localized or (if secular) very ephemeral; and the texts performed were not seen as having a broader transferable cultural validity. Commercial street theatre probably continued to exist, but in most cases it belonged to an oral tradition performed by illiterates, and so its material is not now directly accessible. In Italy, after very few surviving strictly medieval playscripts, religious drama began to be more textually focused in 15th-c. *sacre rappresentazioni*; there is a considerable body of these from *Florence in particular, many attributed to named single authors rather than being collective compositions. Their development seems to coincide with the increasing attention also paid to production values, in terms of elaborate staging (in churches or other venues) with ingeniously engineered mechanical and visual effects. On the secular side, from the first decades of the 16th c., a number of plays have come down to us, especially from the so-called 'Pre-Rozzi' dramatists of Siena [see CONGREGA DEI ROZZI], which mingle popular, religious, *epic, and romantic themes in a loose structure like that of early Tudor theatre in England.

*Humanist *educators, with their classical models, were determined to revive a notion of a play script as a culturally respectable form of literature, with the same prestige as was possessed by Greek and Roman drama [see GREEK INFLUENCES; LATIN INFLUENCES]. This ultimately meant detaching such texts from a particular occasion of performance, and offering them for general perusal in the new medium of *print. It also, in their eyes, meant re-establishing the strictly separate genres of *comedy and *tragedy; giving the content of a play some universal (but secular) interest and significance; and adhering closely to the structural formulae found in the ancient models. For some it also meant the reconstruction of the dedicated classical theatre building; but resources did not permit experiments of this sort until the 1580s, and by that time the spatial layout, and especially the scenography, of the new drama had acquired an independent character and momentum which was entirely of its own time.

To begin with, the new drama was a province of the aristocracy, who mounted amateur performances to invited audiences in princely *courts, private houses, and *academies or clubs. *Comedy was favoured initially, starting with *translations of

Plautus and Terence from the 1480s on, and then blossoming into original classical-style compositions with *Ariosto's *Cassaria* in *Ferrara in 1508. It was also in Ferrara that the ground was laid for the new scenography; the fixed setting of classical comedy was represented as a careful perspective view of a townscape, which lent a rational, self-contained air to the world enacted in the drama. This innovation, already half-way to 'picture-frame' or 'fourth wall' staging, was highly appreciated, and it undermined later attempts to reconstruct a theatre building on ancient models. Nevertheless, courtiers in particular still demanded an element of pure spectacle with less of a narrative element, and in many courts the five acts of a classical comedy were separated by *intermezzi*, lavish song-and-dance performances with mythological content and sometimes symbolic political messages. This produced a revived demand for engineering skills: movable scenery, special effects, and changes of scene were common in *intermezzi* (and later in *opera), while still regarded as banned in ordinary drama by the classical 'unities'.

The first classical *tragedy, *Giraldi Cinzio's *Orbecche*, was performed in Ferrara in 1541; and Ferrara also saw the beginnings of *pastoral drama with a classical five-act structure, in Giraldi's *Egle* (1545) and Agostino de' *Beccari's *Sacrificio* (1554). It was in *Venice, which had a different performing tradition, that professional, popular, and commercial theatre practices intervened on, and to some extent took over, the classical plots and material which the courtly amateurs had created. Figures such as *Ruzante, Andrea *Calmo, Gigio Artemio *Giancarli, and Girolamo *Parabosco wrote and performed for wider publics and sometimes on a commercial basis. By 1550, fully professional companies had been formed, and were touring both public and private venues, not only pioneering the new improvised *commedia dell'arte* but also willing to perform written texts in all theatrical genres. Apart from their improvisation from scenarios, their second major innovation, still often undervalued by historians, was their admission of women on the stage in the roles of comic lovers and tragic or pastoral heroines: the existence of star actresses would eventually transform and characterize European theatre.

By 1600 there was tension, but also regular interchange, between the academic upper-class vision of theatre and of dramaturgy and the livelier but less respectable practices and insights of the professionals. In Venice, some full-time commercial theatre

Theatre

buildings had been opened by aristocratic impresarios. The situation was complicated by the increasing tendency of the *Counter-Reformation Church to disapprove of theatre altogether, as the Christian Fathers had done. But performance arts were by now an entrenched part of the ruling classes' self-image, and the Church had to accept the fact. In addition, the new century was going to bring an exciting fusion between music, acting, and spectacle in the irresistible new genre of opera.

[RAA]

See N. Pirrotta, *Music and Theatre from Poliziano to Monteverdi* (1982); M. Pieri, *La nascita del teatro moderno in Italia tra XV e XVI secolo* (1989).

2. 1600 onwards

From the late 16th c. the masked, improvised, and dialect speaking *commedia dell'arte* was the dominant Italian theatrical form, sustained both by the popular travelling players and by a new class of actor that included men and women of culture. Flaminio *Scala's collection of scenarios (1611) is indicative of this new class's interest in written culture as well as improvised theatre. The *commedia dell'arte* remained popular entertainment until the mid-18th c., when Carlo *Goldoni began his gradual reform, making of elaborate and sometimes obscene farce a family entertainment through elimination of the mask, improvisation, and vulgar language. His *Venetian rival, Carlo *Gozzi, tried to preserve the spirit of the *commedia dell'arte* in written plays. *Pastoral and *tragedy also developed during this period. Early tragedies had been imitations of Greek and Roman models, e.g. *Trissino's *Sofonisba* (1515) and *Giraldi Cinzio's *Orbecche* (1541). It was Federico *Della Valle who accommodated tragic feeling to the *Counter-Reformation mood in verse tragedies based on biblical as well as classical themes, the most dramatic of which is *Iudit* (1627); but it was not until the early 18th c. that an Italian tragedy, Scipione *Maffei's *Merope* (1713), attracted European attention, with its combination of classical and *French influence and the quality of its poetry. The best of the nineteen tragedies of Vittorio *Alfieri, *Saul* (1784) and *Mirra* (1786), project Alfieri's theme of the struggle between tyranny and freedom through subjects taken from the ancient world, but reflect the organization of French tragic drama rather than heralding a new Italian tragic form.

In the 19th c. Italian *comedy and drama was also influenced by French dramatic practice. The *pièce bien faite*, known in English as the 'well-made play', was first developed by Auguste Eugène Scribe (1791–1861) and became a dominant form in France by the mid-19th c. Beginning with a simple exposition, the 'well-made play' is skilfully crafted to build and maintain suspense, its tension dependent on a secret that is revealed in an obligatory scene (*scène à faire*) towards the end of the play. The formula was well suited to dramas about the family, and often focused on adultery. Achille *Torelli, Paolo *Ferrari, Giuseppe *Giacosa, and Marco *Praga all wrote plays within this genre, some of which have been revived after their time. Torelli, a *Neapolitan, provided a stringent analysis of the decadent Neapolitan aristocracy in his best play, *I mariti* (1867), while Giacosa and Praga reflected the concerns of the Northern Italian middle classes with plays that deal with marriage, adultery, and money. Ferrari's later plays, such as *Il duello*, *Il ridicolo*, and *Il suicidio*, develop the 'well-made play' into the thesis or problem play, highlighting issues of concern for his times.

*Risorgimento themes lie behind the tragedies of the period, e.g. Silvio *Pellico's *Francesca da Rimini* (1815), Alessandro *Manzoni's *Il *conte di Carmagnola* (1819) and *Adelchi* (1892); while Pietro *Cossa's plays later in the century fuse tragic themes with the tenets of *verismo. The 20th c. brought changes. Ideas explored in *Futurist theatre and by the *grotteschi have lasted better when reworked by *Pirandello, whose *Sei personaggi in cerca d'autore* was the most challenging and seminal play of the period. It was also Pirandello who wrote a tragedy of European status, *Enrico IV* (1922), which has lasted better than Gabriele *D'Annunzio's attempts to revive tragedy in a form acceptable to the 20th c. American avant-garde theatre in the 1960s inspired further theatrical developments in Italy, and much imaginative work appeared in the 1970s and 1980s, with, for instance, reworkings of the classics by Carmelo *Bene (1937–2002), and explorations of performance space by Luca Ronconi (1933–). The 1960s also saw the development of a different kind of audience, in the form of politicized students and workers who saw in theatre a place for counter-culture, and flocked to Dario *Fo's performances.

3. Organization and Management

There were no permanent theatres in Italy before the Teatro Olimpico of Vicenza (1585), soon followed by theatres in Sabbioneta (1588) and Parma (1618). In the 17th c. Giovanbattista Aleotti

(1546–1636) and Giacomo Torelli (1608–78) were European leaders in theatre and stage design. During this period the organization of theatre in Italy remained largely as it had been in the 16th c., with *court performers and itinerant players. Political *Unification in 1860 brought changes. The *court theatre companies disappeared with the royal houses, a host of new companies came into being, and many a city council thought fit to commemorate Unification with the building of a theatre. By 1873 there were said to be 940 theatres in Italy. The new government decided that theatre was not one of the nation's essentials, and therefore not to be funded from the national purse. The result of this decision led to an increase in competition; the rise of the star actor, the *mattatore*, is probably due to the resulting economic situation. Italy is at least as well known for its performers as for its writers; Eleonora Duse, Ernesto Rossi, and Tommaso Salvini became household names in the 19th c., as Dario *Fo has become for his performances in the 20th.

Until the end of *World War II, the internal organization of theatrical companies also remained similar to that of the *commedia dell'arte* troupes of the 16th c. Actors were employed by annual contract as 'roles' (e.g. leading actor or actress, comic actor) with the constricting result that plays were written with these roles in mind. The opening of the Piccolo Teatro in Milan (1947) by Paolo Grassi and Giorgio *Strehler began the institution of the municipal repertory theatre, the *teatro stabile*. Concentration in one place allowed for the development of stage design and scenery, repertoires broadened, and as in other European countries Italian directors (e.g. Orazio Costa, Luchino *Visconti, Giorgio Strehler), rather than actors, became the dominant theatrical figures. [JAL]
See J. S. Kennard, *The Italian Theatre* (1932); M. Carlson, *The Italian Stage from Goldoni to D'Annunzio* (1981).

Theologia platonica, see FICINO, MARSILIO.

Theology, see AQUINAS, ST THOMAS; BIBLE; COMMENTARIES; HERESIES; LITERARY THEORY, 1; MIDDLE AGES; RELIGIOUS LITERATURE; SCHOLASTICISM.

THOVEZ, ENRICO (1869–1925). *Turinese *literary critic and poet. Whilst his first collection of poems, *Il poema dell'adolescenza* (1901), is notable for its rigidly classicizing metre, it was his polemical crit-ical writing which made his name. Early articles

accused *D'Annunzio of plagiarism, for instance, and his fierce judgements and direct, forceful style won the approval of the writers around *La *Voce* group in *Florence. His most successful critical work was *Il pastore, il gregge e la zampogna* (1910), which attacked *Carducci's view of the civic role of the poet and proposed an ideal of pure lyricism, though one infused still with lofty moral ideals.
[CFB]

Tigre reale, see VERGA, GIOVANNI.

TILGHER, ADRIANO (1887–1941). Philosopher, moralist, and *literary critic, originally from *Naples. Influenced by contemporary vitalism and relativism, he proposed an influential aesthetics at odds with both *Croce and *positivism, seeing a work of literature as a synthesis of the tensions of its day. He was particularly drawn to *Pirandello, and, in *Studi sul teatro contemporaneo* (1922), was the first critic to stress the opposition between 'vita' and 'forma' in his drama. Tilgher's vision of life as a perennial flux influenced the writings of Salvatore *Gotta and Fausto Maria *Martini. He was persecuted during the *Fascist period for his opposition to the regime. [PBarn]

TIMPANARO, SEBASTIANO (1923–2000). Scholar and *literary critic. Born in Parma, he studied classical philology in *Florence under Giorgio *Pasquali, but rapidly extended his intellectual range. Much of his major work was on 19th-c. culture and scholarship, including *La filologia di Giacomo Leopardi* (1955), *La genesi del metodo di Lachmann* (1963), and his fundamental *Classicismo e illuminismo nell'Ottocento italiano* (1965). He articulates an intellectually complex *Marxism in *Sul materialismo* (1970), and in *Il lapsus freudiano* (1974) he uses the theory of textual scholarship to criticize the idea of the Freudian slip. He remained outside the university world, working first as a schoolteacher and then for the *publishers La Nuova Italia in Florence. [See also TEXTUAL CRITICISM.] [DieZ]

TIRABOSCHI, GIROLAMO (1731–94). Literary historian and scholar. He was born in Bergamo, and became a *Jesuit at an early age. In 1755 he was appointed to the chair of rhetoric at the Brera in *Milan, publishing his inaugural lecture, *De patriae historia* (1760), and the *Vetera humiliatorum monumenta* (1766–8). In 1770 he became director of the *Estense *library in Modena. He then published various scholarly and historical works on Modena, such as *Notizie de' pittori, scultori, incisori, architetti natii degli stati del duca di Modena* (1786), and between 1773 and 1790 wrote for the *Nuovo giornale dei letterati d'Italia*, a literary bulletin published in Modena, of which he became the editor.

He began his *Storia della letteratura italiana* in 1772, completing it in 1782 and publishing a corrected and enlarged ten-volume edition in 1787–94. It marks the transition from the compilations characteristic of the 18th c. to a broader vision based on factual research, though it still relies on the accumulation of material, embracing all fields of learning and high culture, and the Italy which it presupposes is ill-defined as a political entity. The book's vastness of purpose and the writer's interest in language (in vol. iii) make it one of the most important documents of late 18th-c. Italian culture. [See also HISTORIES OF ITALIAN LITERATURE.]

[GDP]

TIRRENO, see LUSSU, EMILIO.

TITTA ROSA, GIOVANNI (pseud. of Giovanni Battista Rosa) (1891–1972). Poet, *literary critic, and fiction writer. He was from near L'Aquila, but studied in *Florence and went on to a career in *journalism. He wrote landscape poetry, notably in *Le feste delle stagioni* (1928) and *Alta luna* (1935), with a sense of *Leopardian solitude and melancholy. The short stories of *I giorni del mio paese* (1941) and *Paese con figure* (1942) are similarly descriptive. He contributed to debates on modern literature with *Narratori contemporanei* (1921) and *Invito al romanzo* (1930). [RSD]

TITTONI, TOMMASO, see ACCADEMIA D'ITALIA, REALE.

TOBINO, MARIO (1910–91). *Tuscan writer who was also head of a psychiatric hospital near Lucca until he retired in 1980. Though he published *Poesie* (1934) and another volume of poems, *Asso di picche* (1955), he first attracted attention with *Il figlio del farmacista* (1947). Then came *Il deserto della Libia* (1952), an account of his experiences as a soldier in *World War II, and *Le libere donne di Magliano* (1953), based on his asylum experiences, as is the later *Gli ultimi giorni di Magliano* (1987). The *autobiographical focus is characteristic, but Tobino is capable both of poetic intensity and of forceful *parody. The measured *Il clandestino* (1962) is one of the most complete

presentations of the early phase of the *Resistance. The versatility of his abundant production ranges from the overt political *satire of *Fascism in *Bandiera nera* (1950, reprinted in *L'angelo del Liponard* in 1951) to the lively travelogue *Due italiani a Parigi* (1954) and a late play, *La verità viene a galla* (1987). [JG-R]

TOFANO, SERGIO, see CHILDREN'S LITERATURE.

TOGLIATTI, PALMIRO (1893–1964). Italian *Communist Party (PCI) leader from 1926 to his death. Born in *Genoa, he worked closely with *Gramsci in *Turin after *World War I. He spent most of the *Fascist years in Russia (1926–44), becoming a leading figure in the Communist International. He is credited with having turned the PCI into a mass party and a constitutional force after 1945. [SG]

TOLOMEI, CLAUDIO (1492–1556). *Humanist, linguistic scholar, and poet. Banished from his native *Siena for supporting the *Medici, he travelled extensively, mostly in the service of Ippolito de' Medici, and had a successful ecclesiastical career. As a linguist, he shows a modern, empirical approach to language, which he views as a complex, living system. His *dialogues, *Polito* (1525) and *Cesano* (1555), discuss the origins of language, the relation between oral and written speech, and the phonology of Tuscan. He also applied classical metrics to Italian poetry in *Versi et regole de la nuova poesia toscana* (1539). [BG]

TOMASI, TOMMASO (1608–58). Author of political tracts and *comedies. Born in Pesaro, he trained as a cleric in *Rome. He lived in *Florence under *Medici *patronage, and *Venice, where he was a member of the Accademia degli *Incogniti, before returning to Rome. He was best known for a clandestine *Vita del Duca Valentino* (1655), which, though put on the *Index, was repeatedly reprinted. [FC]

TOMASI DI LAMPEDUSA, GIUSEPPE (1896–1957). The author of *Il *gattopardo* (1958) was from an old *Sicilian aristocratic family. He served with the artillery during *World War I. Captured and imprisoned in Austria, he escaped and returned to Italy on foot. He spent much of the *Fascist period travelling, publishing a small number of reviews in the early 1920s in Northern Italy.

He met his wife, Alessandra Wolff Stomersee, an Italo-Latvian *psychoanalyst, in London and they married in Riga in 1932. After *World War II he lived quietly in Palermo, and gave classes on European literature to a dedicated group of young friends. Some of his notes were published after his death, including *Lezioni su Stendhal* (1977), *Invito alle lettere francesi del Cinquecento* (1979), and *Letteratura inglese: dalle origini al Settecento* (1989).

A brief meeting with Eugenio *Montale and Emilio *Cecchi at a conference in *Lombardy in 1954 was the catalyst for the intense creativity of the last two and a half years of his life, though he had had a long-standing desire to write a *novel set in Sicily at the time of *Garibaldi's expedition. Incomplete versions of *Il gattopardo* were rejected for publication by *Mondadori and *Einaudi (the reader in the latter case being *Vittorini). Giorgio *Bassani then accepted the full text for *Feltrinelli, integrating two further chapters which Lampedusa had completed not long before his death from lung cancer.

Three stories, also written in 1956–7, were published after Lampedusa's death as *I racconti* (1961). 'La gioia e la legge' deals with questions of patronage and social status through the person of a Palermo clerk. In 'Lighea' an elderly classicist tells the story of his youthful relationship with a mermaid. 'Il mattino di un mezzadro' was to have been the first chapter of a novel, *I gattini ciechi*, tracing the rise and fall of the Ibba family. [JD]

See D. Gilmour, *The Last Leopard* (1988).

TOMASO DA FAENZA (later 13th c.). Judge from the Romagna by whom we have nine poems in the *Guittonian manner. One *canzone is a reply (using the same rhymes) to *Monte Andrea, whilst one *sonnet is addressed to *Cino da Pistoia. *Dante cites him as a poet moving away from local usage in his language (*DVE* 1.14). [JU]

TOMITANO, BERNARDINO (1517–76) taught logic in the *university of his native *Padua, and belonged to the Accademia degli Infiammati [see ACADEMIES]. He was strongly influenced by Sperone *Speroni. His *Ragionamenti della lingua toscana* (1545, republished with a supplement in 1546) were expanded into the *Quattro libri della lingua toscana* (1570). Books 1 and 2 argue that philosophy is necessary to the orator and the poet. Books 3 and 4 discuss eloquence in writing and speech. Speroni is a speaker in the *dialogues, and argues for moderation in the vernacular: one should avoid both excessive imitation of 14th-c. Tuscan and the language of the common people. [See also QUESTIONE DELLA LINGUA.] [BR]

TOMIZZA, FULVIO (1935–99). *Novelist whose life and work are closely bound up with the North-East border region of Italy. He was born in Materada d'Umago in Istria (now Umag, Croatia). In 1955, one year after the area became part of Yugoslavia, he moved to *Trieste and worked for Italian state broadcasting (RAI). His novels, from *Materada* (1960) to *La miglior vita* (1977), are mainly autobiographical and set in Istria during *World War II and its aftermath, when much of the local population was forced to emigrate, mainly to Italy. They evoke a lost Istrian rural society, with protagonists who are torn between Italian and Slav identities. His more recent writing has a historical colouring. *Franziska* (1998), for instance, reconstructs the story of a Slovene girl born in Trieste in 1900, whose love for an Italian officer comes tragically to nothing, reflecting the history of Italy's relationship with its North East in the 20th c. [KP]

TOMMASEO, NICCOLÒ (1802–74). Complex and versatile writer, whose life and work display a mixture of *Romantic creativity and exact scholarship, strong religious belief, and patriotic commitment, all of which he struggled repeatedly to bring into harmony with each other. Born and brought up in Dalmatia, he studied first in Split and then in *Padua, where he graduated in law in 1822. He also developed his knowledge of both Italian and Latin literature, whilst the Catholicism of his upbringing was reinforced by reading *Rosmini Serbati.

In 1824 he settled in *Milan, where he worked for the *publisher A. F. *Stella and contributed to major *periodicals including *Antologia. He met *Manzoni (his *Colloqui col Manzoni* were finally published in 1929), and declared for Romanticism in literature with *Il Perticari confutato da Dante* (1825) and essays on the *historical novel. In 1827 he moved to *Florence at the invitation of *Vieusseux, and developed his already existing interests in lexicography in the *Nuovo dizionario de' sinonimi della lingua italiana* (1830). He also compiled an *anthology of popular poetry, *Canti popolari toscani, corsi, illirici e greci* (1841–2) [see FOLK AND POPULAR LITERATURE]. When *Antologia* was closed down in 1833, he moved to France for a period of voluntary *exile (1834–9), which was also one of intense social life and political involvement. Out of this period come a retrospective collection of verse, *Memorie poetiche e poesie* (1838), two historical novels, *Il sacco di Lucca* and *Il Duca d'Atene* (1837), his *commentary on the *Divine Comedy* (1837), and his best-known work of fiction, the largely *autobiographical *Fede e bellezza* (1840).

Back in Italy, he settled in *Venice in 1839. He now published collections of philosophical and critical essays, a *Dizionario estetico* (1840), and *Iskrice* (1844), a collection of prose pieces in Serbo-Croat, of which Italian versions had already appeared in *Scintille* (1841). He was arrested along with Daniele Manin in *1848, freed, and installed as minister of public *education in the provisional government. When the latter fell in 1849 he went into exile on Corfu, where he wrote about the events he had just experienced in *Venezia negli anni 1848 e 1849* (first published in 1931), and argued for the ending of the temporal power of the *papacy in *Rome et le monde* (1851). After a stay in *Turin, he settled definitively in Florence in 1859. His sight was progressively deteriorating; almost blind, he nevertheless persevered in the compilation of his major dictionary, which, with the collaboration of Bernardo *Bellini, was published as the *Dizionario della lingua italiana* between 1858 and 1879. [See also DICTIONARIES.] [MPC]

See G. Debenedetti, *Niccolò Tommaseo* (1973).

TOMMASO DA CELANO (13th c.). *Franciscan friar, appointed official *biographer of St *Francis by Pope Gregory IX in 1228. His *Vita prima* (1229) was supplemented in 1246–7 by a *Vita secunda*, based on reminiscences of Francis's close companions; in 1253 he added an account of the saint's miracles. [See also HAGIOGRAPHY.] [JP & JMS]

TONDELLI, PIER VITTORIO (1955–91). Gay novelist interested in kitsch and youth art and culture. Born in Correggio, he graduated at *Bologna University, and lived in *Milan.

His first book, *Altri libertini* (1980), comprises six stories about members of the lost student generation of the 1970s, with drugs, sex, and travel as their main interests. It successfully mimics their particular idiom and is one of the first Italian examples of physical, emotional writing which implicitly denies ideological involvement. It was followed by *Pao Pao* (1982), a moderately entertaining *autobiographical account of national service, interwoven with stories of gay love. His contrived

beach novel, *Rimini* (1985), which is partly a parody of soap operas, was a commercial success, although the attempt to touch on the theme of political intrigue seemed to misfire. He returned to the solitude of the artist, and the theme of death, in his sombre *Camere separate* (1989). His collection of essays, *Un week-end postmoderno* (1990), contains numerous lively and incisive *journalistic pieces. [See also HOMOSEXUALITY.] [DieZ]

TORCIGLIANI, MICHELANGELO (1618–79). Poet from Lucca who studied in *Rome, where he enjoyed considerable literary *patronage, even though his tastes were not fully consonant with the dominant *classicism. When conflicts developed between Lucca and the *papacy he moved to *Venice, which was altogether more receptive to *concettismo. There he championed *Marino, befriending his Venetian followers *Loredan and *Busenello, and particularly imitating his idylls and epithalamia. But paradoxically he is better appreciated for the idiosyncratic classicism he developed in Venice in his Italian paraphrases of Anacreon, and two verse *dialogues on natural science, *L'astronomia* and *La chimica*. [MPS]

TORELLI, ACHILLE (1844–1922), *Neapolitan author of numerous plays, including a popular masterpiece, *I mariti* (1867), which conveyed a critique of the old decadent order and an endorsement of the new Italy with impressive lightness of touch. His *Scrollina* was revived by *Pirandello in 1928 with Marta Abba in the title role. [See also THEATRE, 2.] [JAL]

TORELLI, GIACOMO, see THEATRE, 3.

TORELLI, GIUSEPPE (1816–66). Writer and politician from Novara. He was secretary to Massimo *D'Azeglio, whose *autobiography he completed. He wrote for various papers as Ciro D'Arco, becoming editor of *Il Risorgimento* and the *Gazzetta ufficiale*, and was elected to the *Turin Parliament. He also wrote *novels and his memoirs. [EAM]

TORELLI, POMPONIO (1539–1608) was a nobleman from Parma, an occasional diplomat, but mainly a man of letters. His principal legacy is five stage *tragedies published between 1597 and 1605, which are now seen as showing a certain penetration in handling political themes. In his dramaturgy, as well as following *Aristotle's *Poetics* he showed an uncommon preference for Greek (rather than Roman) structural and compositional features, with no scene divisions and a strong role given to the chorus. [See also LITERARY THEORY, 2; THEATRE, 1.] [RAA]

TORINI, AGNOLO (c.1315–98). *Florentine layman and clothworker, who was also a poet and the author of two *religious prose treatises: *Brieve collezione della miseria della umana condizione* (based on *Innocent III's *De contemptu mundi*) and *Brieve meditazione de' beneficii di Dio.* [SNB]

TORNABUONI, LUCREZIA (1427–82), born into a noble *Florentine *banking family, was the wife of Piero di Cosimo de' *Medici, mother of Lorenzo de' *Medici, and grandmother of Popes Leo X and Clement VII. She was a literary *patron, notably of Luigi *Pulci, and author of religious poetry, including *laudi* and five long narrative poems on biblical subjects: St John the Baptist, Judith, Susanna, Esther, and Tobias. She was actively involved in advancing the Medici client network, as her letters demonstrate, and was also the manager or promoter of a number of business enterprises, notably the redevelopment of the Baths at Morba. [JHB]

TORNIMPARTE, ALESSANDRA, see GINZBURG, NATALIA.

TORRACA, FRANCESCO, see LITERARY CRITICISM.

Torre, La, see TOZZI, FEDERIGO.

TORRESANI, ANDREA, see MANUZIO, ALDO.

TORRIANI, GIOVANNI, see ITALIAN WRITERS IN SWITZERLAND.

TORRIANI, MARIA ANTONIETTA, see MARCHESA COLOMBI.

TORRICELLI, EVANGELISTA (1608–47). Mathematician and physicist. Born in Faenza, he became a student of *Galileo's pupil Castelli, and briefly secretary to Galileo himself. He then entered the service of the *Medici Grand Duke and lectured at the *Florentine *studio*. Only part of his *Opera geometrica* was published during his lifetime. He contributed to the development of infinitesimal calculus, and researched on optics, ballistics,

hydrodynamics, and atmospheric pressure, his experiments with mercury leading to the invention of the barometer. After his death, France rather than Italy became the centre of advanced mathematical research. [FC]

TORTELLI, GIOVANNI (c.1400–66). *Humanist who spent two years in Constantinople (1435–7) and made one of the first attempts to *translate Greek drama (c.1439). He became the first prefect of the *Vatican Library under Nicholas V. His important lexicon, *De orthographia* (1449), on the spelling of Greek words in Latin, also supplied a history of Greek philosophy and contributed to the formation and more precise use of Latin philosophical terminology. He was indebted to Lorenzo *Valla, who in turn dedicated his *Elegantiae* to him. [See also CLASSICAL SCHOLARSHIP.] [LAP]

TORTI, FRANCESCO (1763–1842). *Umbrian author of an interesting *history of Italian literature, *Prospetto del Parnaso italiano* (3 vols., 1806–12). He was a friend of Vincenzo *Monti, but gradually distanced himself from his linguistic *purism. He gathered together his polemical essays on the subject in *Antipurismo* (1829). [MPC]

TORTI, GIOVANNI (1774–1852). *Milanese poet. As a young man he celebrated the Revolution and *Napoleon. *La visione di Parini* (1806) is a tribute to his deceased mentor *Parini, whilst his *Sepolcri* is an appendix to the poems of *Foscolo and Ippolito *Pindemonte of the same title and was published with them in 1808. Highly esteemed by *Manzoni and *Grossi, he shows more moral character than talent in mature works such as *La torre di Capua* (1829), a romantic verse narrative reminiscent of the *Promessi sposi*. [JMAL]

TOSCANELLA, ORAZIO (d.?1579) taught near Rovigo before moving to *Venice by the mid-1560s. From 1558 onwards he wrote over fifty works for the press but earned little from them. He specialized in introducing readers to the elements of rhetoric and poetry, sometimes making ideas more easily memorable through diagrammatic summaries. [BR]

TOTÒ (pseud. of Antonio De Curtis) (1898–1967) was born in poverty, but of noble antecedents, in *Naples. Primarily a star of the revues, he became Italy's best-loved comic actor due to the many films he made between 1948 and

Tozzi, Federigo

the early 1960s. One of his last performances was in *Pasolini's *Uccellacci e uccellini* (1966). [SG]

TOZZI, FEDERIGO (1883–1920). *Sienese novelist. He has been highly rated by various critics, especially by the *Solaria* group, for whom he was to be ranked alongside *Pirandello and *Svevo. But his work has never excited the same interest, largely because of the austerity of his subjects and approach.

Tozzi failed to complete his secondary *education, and read his way into Italian literature in Siena public library. In 1900 he founded the literary journal *La Torre* with his friend and long-time collaborator Domenico *Giuliotti. His first published works were the undistinguished poems of *La zampogna verde* (1911) and *La città della vergine* (1913). In 1914 he took up a precarious existence as a literary *journalist in *Rome, where he knew Pirandello. His literary acquaintances expanded to include Grazia *Deledda, Goffredo *Bellonci, and Sibilla *Aleramo. He now completed his most important works, *Con gli occhi chiusi* (1919), *Tre croci* (1920), and *Il podere* (1921). All three are deeply rooted in the countryside around Siena, which provides the setting and basic constraints for the characters, though there is also a strong autobiographical element deriving from Tozzi's conflicts with his *peasant father. The narrative minutely investigates the passions and dysfunctions of individuals torn between greed and disabling psychological weaknesses as they struggle vainly to gain and hold onto property and to realize dreams that ultimately can only destroy them.

In literary terms Tozzi is indebted to the provincial *Tuscan narrative tradition represented by *Paolieri and *Fucini, but he also learnt from *Verga and Dostoevsky, from the new psychology of William James, and from the neurological research of Paul Janet. His original blend of naturalism, psychologism, and autobiography had a strong influence on later Tuscan writers such as *Benedetti, *Bilenchi, *Cassola, and *Pratolini.

[PBart]

See G. Debenedetti, *Il romanzo del Novecento* (1971); G. Luti, Introduction to F. Tozzi, *Opere*, ed. M. Marchi (1987).

Tragedy. The restoration of *comedy and tragedy as theatrical genres based on *classical models was the result of *humanist scholarship in the 15th and 16th c. However, tragedy took longer than comedy to find a place in the new *Renaissance classicizing

*theatre. It is arguable that classical tragedy was a much harder model to decipher, and to adapt to contemporary circumstances, than any form of comedy: its original roots in ancient Greek religion and social ritual were far removed from anything which the humanists, for all their scholarship, could readily conceive. Even the Roman tragedies of Seneca, written for a society more similar to that of Renaissance Italy, needed some heavy modification to harmonize them with current taste and religious views. The insistence that tragedy was an upper-class genre depicting princely characters was acceptable to a courtly audience, but pagan concepts of destiny and of punishment needed to be assimilated to Christian notions of Providence and divine retribution.

The earliest original Italian tragedy, *Sofonisba* by Giangiorgio *Trissino, was composed in 1515 but not performed until 1556. It established the unrhymed *hendecasyllable [see also VERSIFICATION] as the normal metre for dialogues and soliloquies, with more varied lyrical metres for the choruses—whose inclusion was regarded as imposed by classical precedent, even though their function must have been hard to envisage at first. Later writers rejected other aspects of the work, such as the continuous open-ended structure regarded as 'Greek' in origin: there was soon a general preference for a five-act structure with an external Prologue, which was seen as 'Roman'. The story of *Sofonisba* is a simple one of noble resistance, whereby the heroine prefers death to humiliation. This inaugurated an unbroken tendency for Italian tragedy to present models of the most high-flown aristocratic values and sensibilities.

The production of *Giraldi Cinzio's *Orbecche*, in *Ferrara in 1541, was the inauguration of performed tragedy for Italian *court audiences. It was a significant success; but Giraldi himself immediately reviewed his practice by the introduction of tragedies with a happy ending (*tragedie a lieto fine*), which he saw as more readily adaptable both to audience taste and to contemporary moral and religious demands. Poetic justice, in his view, demanded that grisly Senecan deaths should be reserved for the evil characters, while the more virtuous ones should find a last-minute reprieve or fortunate reversal of fortune. His published views were opposed by the theory and practice of Sperone *Speroni, whose unfinished *Canace* was also then influential—except perhaps in its choice of superhuman classical deities, rather than noble or legendary humans, as its protagonists.

The second half of the 16th c. saw a considerable amount of theoretical precept about tragedy, based mainly on *Aristotle and *Horace, as well as a substantial number of tragic plays—over seventy between 1540 and 1600 [see also LITERARY THEORY, 2]. Leading authors were Giraldi himself, Pietro *Aretino, Ludovico *Dolce, Torquato *Tasso, and Luigi *Groto. Stories were taken, as recommended, from history or legend; great emphasis was placed on the long, rhetorically composed speech (with messenger roles often being given to the best actors); and from the start there was a tendency to explore the conflict between love and duty in a principal character. However, one significant exception to this last point would be Dolce's *Marianna* of 1565, which deals with the unmerited victimization of a virtuous queen at the hands of her tyrannical husband, Herod. In fact female roles were given more focus in tragedy than in comedy: many plays have eponymous heroines, and it is clear that the earliest actresses made their reputation in this genre as well as in *pastoral and *commedia dell'arte*. The resolute or pathetic heroine was then transferred to become an essential feature of the new genre of *opera—which also found a more comfortable place for the chorus.

Sixteenth-century tragedy never managed to break free from close detailed *imitation and borrowing from classical sources. In 1585 Sophocles' *Oedipus Rex* in *translation, rather than an original composition, was chosen as the opening production for the new, purpose-built Teatro Olimpico in Vicenza, which in its own eccentric way aimed to reproduce theatre designs of antiquity. Although tragedies continued to be written throughout the 17th and 18th c. (with authors such as Prospero *Bonarelli, Giacinto Andrea *Cicognini, Federico *Della Valle, Andrea *Perucci, and Pomponio *Torelli), they were constantly contending as 'serious' theatre with the prestige of French dramatists, such as Corneille and Racine; and, at home, with more mixed genres such as *tragicomedy, plays modelled on more flexible Spanish models, and opera seria, which became the aristocratic choice for culture and entertainment throughout Europe. Italy's only tragic dramatist of lasting repute, Vittorio *Alfieri, contributed the swan-song of the classical genre in the late 18th c. Composed with immense labour, in many stages, his tragedies present, with sometimes remarkable intensity, the tensions between a determinedly aristocratic sense of individual moral pride—which can inspire an enlightened ruler but also, paradoxically, an un-

enlightened tyrant—and a recognition of new tendencies towards collective rights, democracy, and nationalism. Or, when they are not so clearly political in content, they explore a psychological struggle within a single protagonist, caused by an appalled recognition of his or her own immoral desires (*Mirra, Saul*).

Alfieri's fierce concentration on individual dilemmas eliminated the chorus altogether from tragedy. It was brought back, in a dying gasp, by Alessandro *Manzoni, whose *Risorgimento tragedies attempt among other things to bring onto a theatre stage the collective presence of a whole people. But this effect could ultimately be better achieved in patriotic operas, such as the *libretti of Solera set to music by *Verdi. In effect, in the 19th c. opera provided the serious drama, including the tragic drama, which captured the imaginations of a vast majority of Italian theatregoers. By the time that real creative attention was being given once more to *teatro di prosa* (non-musical theatre), in the last decades of the century, the classical distinctions of genre had become permanently superseded.

[RAA]

La tragedia del Cinquecento, ed. M. Ariani (1977); *Teatro del Cinquecento*, ed. R. Cremante, vol. i (1988). See S. Carandini, *Teatro e spettacolo nel Seicento* (1990); F. Angelini, *Il teatro barocco* (1975).

Tragicomedy. After the *humanist resurrection of the strictly differentiated genres of *comedy and *tragedy, their limitations quickly came to be felt, and practitioners tried to loosen the straitjackets they imposed. *Giraldi Cinzio insisted in his *Discorsi* (1554) that tragedies could have happy endings; Sforza *Oddi explicitly pioneered a form of comedy in which more noble and sentimental themes were mixed with scurrility. The moulds were broken even more by the popular but uncanonical genre of *pastoral drama; and it was on the strength of his play *Il pastor fido* that Battista *Guarini finally theorized a new genre called *tragicommedia* (the word itself being taken from the Prologue of Plautus' *Amphitryo*). Guarini's views were summarized in his *Compendio della poesia tragicomica* (1601), in which the strongest motivation was perhaps that of harmonizing *Aristotelian notions of catharsis with moral lessons more suitable to a Christian society. The subsequent history of European *theatre was increasingly to favour the mingling of genres, until the genres themselves disappeared and the word 'tragicomedy' became redundant. In Italy in particular, 17th-c. 'serious' drama was progressively influenced not only by pastoral but by *opera, and by the less rigid forms of *Spanish *comedia*, thus often becoming tragicomic in fact if not always in name. [See also LITERARY THEORY, 2; THEATRE, 1.]   [RAA]

See M. T. Herrick, *Tragicomedy: Its Origin and Development in Italy, France and England* (1955).

TRANQUILLI, SECONDINO, see SILONE, IGNAZIO.

Translations. For a multilingual tradition such as the Italian one, the issue of translation has always been central. Thus, in the polyglot environment of *Frederick II's enlightened and itinerant *court, translating between different languages (Latin, Greek, Arabic, Hebrew, German, French, and Provençal, not to mention Sicilian and other Italian idioms) must have been a common experience. Indeed, there is a growing body of evidence to suggest that the refined language used by the poets of the *Sicilian School constitutes an attempt, in advance of *Dante's *volgare illustre*, to create a supraregional form of Italian which, in imitation of Latin, could overcome the peninsula's linguistic fragmentation. However, long before the emergence of texts written in the vernacular, throughout Europe the problem must have existed for educated people of the relationship between their native spoken language and Latin. The latter, as the principal medium of cultural expression, was exclusively a written language and, as such, was not anyone's mother tongue. In 1931, discussing the relationship between German and Roman law, the German scholar Heck went as far as to suggest that any text written in medieval Latin ought to be deemed a 'translation'. Interestingly, the same notion can be said, in general, to hold good for texts written in Italian. Until the 20th c., the *dialects were Italy's mother tongues, and Italian was learnt as a written, literary language. It has been suggested that, in order fully to understand *Manzoni's *Promessi sposi*, one needs to know the author's native *Milanese expressions which underlie his Italian phraseology.

Italian vernacular literature owes one of its primary originating stimuli to translation. Surrounded both by a long-established Latin culture and a fast-growing French one, 13th-c. Italian intellectuals reacted by adapting and translating into Italian Latin texts of every kind, including the works of poets, philosophers, *hagiographers, historians,

and rhetoricians. An equally fruitful relationship linked Italian translators to Old French texts. Though many of the translations were certainly written with practical and educational ends in mind, it is also the case that such texts not only enriched the possibilities of the nascent literary language but also encouraged literary experimentation and self-confidence. In terms of medieval reflection on literature, one way of establishing authority was by becoming closely associated with a confirmed authoritative text or author. Translations were an ideal way of achieving this goal, as is evident from the important role which translation plays in the 13th-c. Italian *lyric tradition, best evidenced by the *Fiore's* reworking of the *Roman de la rose*. [See FRENCH INFLUENCES, 1.]

Translating has been so vital in Italian cultural life that Gianfranco *Folena stressed the need to distinguish between *volgarizzare*, which concerns the rendering of a Latin text into the vernacular, and *tradurre*, which involves the version from one vernacular into another. The term *tradurre* comes from the Latin *traducere*, which seems to have been introduced in a letter of 1400 by Leonardo *Bruni (prior to this, the verbs *convertire, explicare, exprimere, mutare, transmutare, transferre, translatare* had been commonly used). Just as translation had a determining effect upon medieval literature, so too *humanist and *Renaissance culture is largely defined by its translating practices. The sophistication and ambition of these far outstrip the activities of the medieval *interpretes*. The translations of Greek texts into Latin and Italian, and of Latin works into Italian are noteworthy for their philological rigour and for the theoretical thinking—such as that found in Leonardo *Bruni's *De interpretatione recta*—which underpins them.

Translation theory also fundamentally affected 19th-c. Italian attitudes to literature. Mme de Staël's article 'Sulla maniera e l'utilità delle traduzioni', which, not inappropriately, became known in Italy thanks to Pietro *Giordani's translation in the first volume of the *Biblioteca italiana* (1816), marks the 'official' start of the Italian *Romantic movement. In her article, de Staël took a line very close to the views which Goethe and Humboldt were propagating during the same years, regarding the important function which translators could exercise in widening and enriching the expressive potential of the language. All three were in favour of an 'estranging' rather than a 'naturalizing' kind of translation, namely one that brought the reader towards the original (the option favoured by German Romanticism), rather than the original towards the reader (the solution supported by French *classicism). *Leopardi made important observations on this question in his *Zibaldone; however, the real impact of such ideas is to be sought in the rich development of Italian literary language during the 19th c. [See also GERMAN INFLUENCES.]

The idea that translation should encourage creativity finds notable fulfilment in Ippolito *Pindemonte's 1822 version of the *Iliad*, which introduces a contemporary melancholic and effusive dimension lacking in the original. Other, earlier translations had already made significant contributions to the poetic language and art of their day: especially important were the translations into Italian of the *Aeneid* by Annibale *Caro (published posthumously in 1581) and of the *Iliad* by Vincenzo *Monti (1810). During the 20th c., too, this tradition continued to flourish, as in the cases of *Quasimodo's renderings of classical Greek lyric poets and of *Pasolini's translation of Plautus' *Miles gloriosus* into Roman *dialect. Pasolini's work belongs to an interesting genre. Given the age-long division in Italy between literature in Italian and in dialect, a tradition has long existed of dialect versions of classic texts, normally Italian ones. These dialect adaptations have often been composed with *parodic and realistic intent, as occurs in Carlo *Porta's brilliant Milanese versions of several of the opening *canti* of Dante's *Inferno*. A very different response to the Italian classics is constituted by attempts to render their antiquated language in a modern idiom. These versions, instances of intralingual translation whose aim is not just to make the classics accessible but also to provide a *commentary on them, have recently caused considerable dispute between traditionalists and modernizers. Given present-day trends in literary scholarship, it is hard to imagine that the number of such paraphrases will not continue to grow or that they will not increasingly be read.

Translations affect every area of modern Italian intellectual and cultural life. Their quantitative importance can be gathered from the following data relating to 1971, which are quite typical of recent decades. Of the 11,095 books published, over one fifth (2,282) were translations—a figure which placed Italy in sixth place internationally as regards the number of translations in that year. The proportional weight of translations becomes even heavier if one considers specific disciplines. In the 1969 Einaudi *Guida alla formazione di una biblioteca*

pubblica e privata, among the titles proposed there is a clear majority of translations as regards disciplines such as economics (70 out of 119), chemistry (23 out of 33), and psychology (67 out of 71). [GCL & ZB]

See G. Folena, *Volgarizzare e tradurre* (1991); G. Lepschy, 'Traduzione', in *Enciclopedia Einaudi*, vol. xiv (1981).

TRAPASSI, PIETRO, see METASTASIO, PIETRO.

TRAPEZUNTIOS, GEORGE (1395–c.1472), or George of Trebizond. Leaving his native Crete for Italy in 1416, he taught Greek in Vicenza, *Venice, and *Rome. He became a Roman Catholic and was employed at the *papal curia, producing Latin *translations of *Aristotle, Plato, Ptolemy, and the Cappadocian Fathers. His influential rhetoric textbook (*Rhetoricorum libri V*) drew on classical Greek authors unknown to Western scholars. A fanatical Aristotelian, he published an attack on Plato which provoked Cardinal *Bessarion to defend the philosopher against his 'slanderer'. George's attempt to convert Sultan Mehmed II to Christianity in 1465 led to imprisonment in Rome on suspicion of apostasy. [See also GREEK INFLUENCES.] [JK]

Trasformati, Accademia dei, see ACADEMIES.

Trattatello in laude di Dante (*De origine vita studiis et moribus viri clarissimi Danti Aligerii florentini poete illustris et de operibus compositis ab eodem*). Celebratory *biography of *Dante by *Boccaccio, which marks the emergence (in modern times) of great artists as worthy subjects for life-stories, alongside kings and heroes. A first version was drafted some time after 1351, and a second around 1360, the latter being again slightly revised some time before 1372. [VB]

Trattato del Beneficio di Cristo, see BENEFICIO DI CRISTO, TRATTATO DEL.

Travale, Testimonianza di, see TESTIMONIANZA DI TRAVALE.

Travellers in Italy have produced a formidable body of writings, the majority of which preceded the formation of an Italian national identity, and contributed to the creation and persistence of stereotypes concerning the national character and cultural heritage. Documentation about journeys to

595

Travel Writing

Italy includes travelogues, guides, treatises of advice, *diaries, and *letters, but also sketches, drawings, and paintings, whether produced by the travellers themselves or collected.

Travel to Italy was at its most prestigious during the 18th c., the age of the Grand Tour, but important precursors are to be found among the pilgrims, scholars, diplomats, *merchants, and adventurers of the *Middle Ages and the *Renaissance. Poets such as Chaucer, Milton, and Sidney visited Italy and contributed to the spread of Italian *humanism in Britain, while travellers such as Thomas Coryate (*Coryat's Crudities*, 1611) and Fynes Moryson (*An Itinerary Written by Fynes Moryson*, 1617) were among the creators of visions of Italy which, combined with historical and religious events, soon produced the myth of the *Machiavellian Italian, and the mirroring stereotype according to which 'an Englishman Italianate is a devil incarnate'. Since then, the contrast between a glorious past and a decadent present has characterized most images of Italy produced by foreign travellers.

The increased popularity of travel to Italy affected not just Britain but also other European cultures, as testified by the travels of Montaigne, De Brosses, Goethe, and Stendhal; and the first guides to the Grand Tour, such as Lassels' *Voyage of Italy* (1670) and Misson's *Nouveau voyage d'Italie* (1691), were translated into various languages. Yet the Grand Tour was predominantly a British phenomenon, and grew to involve a large sector of the aristocracy first, and of the upper and middle classes later. Books on the tour were popular, and by the end of the 18th c., after the publication of Addison's *Remarks on Several Parts of Italy* (1705), Samuel Sharp's *Letters from Italy* (1766), Smollett's *Travels through France and Italy* (1766), and numerous other volumes, the tradition was so established that Sterne could write both a masterpiece of *travel writing and its most successful parody ever: *A Sentimental Journey through France and Italy* (1768). In the 19th c. Italy was also 'the paradise of exiles', and poets such as Byron, Shelley, and Browning spent large parts of their lives in the peninsula. Before them Gray, Wordsworth, and Coleridge had all made their own tours, while later on the flow of scholars, artists, art lovers, and eccentrics continued with John Ruskin, Norman Douglas, Aldous Huxley, D. H. Lawrence, and Hilaire Belloc, as well as Americans such as Mark Twain, Henry James, and Edith Wharton. Many women also travelled to Italy, and some of their accounts, such as those left by Lady Mary Wortley Montagu (1689–1762),

Esther Lynch Piozzi (1741–1821), Frances Trollope (1780–1863), or Vernon Lee (1856–1935), are among the most perceptive, while Mariana Starke's *Letters from Italy* (1800) was one of the most popular guides of its century and underwent continuous rewritings and editions.

In recent years a number of British authors have published travel books on Italy (among them Jan Morris, Eric Newby, and Duncan Fallowell), and in each case it is possible to trace links with established traditions. Italians, on the other hand, have traditionally produced few travel accounts of Italy. The trend is now being reversed, however [see also TRAVEL WRITING].   [LPol]

See C. De Seta (ed.), *Storia d'Italia: Annali*, vol. v: *Il paesaggio* (1982); A. Brilli, *Quando viaggiare era un'arte* (1995); M. Pfister (ed.), *The Fatal Gift of Beauty* (1996).

Travel Writing is not traditionally included in the canon of Italian literature, yet numerous examples of the genre can be found from the *Middle Ages to the present. Marco *Polo's *Il milione* (1298) and Christopher Columbus's *Diary* (1492–3) constitute two unconventional yet significant archetypes: neither was written in Italian, both belong to a Western rather than strictly national tradition, and they remain on the margins of literary conventions and canons; both also highlight fundamental characteristics of travel writing, such as its links with *autobiography and the issue of its factual or fictional nature.

Among early Italian works are G. B. *Ramusio's collection *Le navigationi et viaggi* (1550–9), and accounts written by explorers, *merchants, diplomats, and clergy, such as Filippo *Sassetti's *Lettere da vari paesi* (1570–88), Francesco *Carletti's *Ragionamenti sopra le cose da lui vedute* (1606), and Pietro *Della Valle's *Viaggi* (1650–63). The 18th c. marked an increase in the number of Italians who travelled in Europe and in the popularity of travel literature, often written in the form of *letters, as in the case of *Baretti's *Lettere familiari* (1762–3), *Algarotti's *Viaggi di Russia* (1764), or Pietro and Alessandro *Verri's *Viaggio a Parigi e Londra* (1766–7). Scientists like Alessandro *Volta also wrote accounts of their travels, while autobiographies such as *Alfieri's *Vita* (1806) share many features with travelogues.

The *Restoration brought along restrictions on travel, but the 19th c. eventually became a new age of explorations, and Italian travel writing acquired a stronger taste for the adventurous and the exotic as well as the descriptive and learned. At the end of the century Edmondo *De Amicis and Emilio *Salgari marked the two opposite directions in which the genre would move: Salgari's exotic adventures transported the Italian public into a fantastic and entirely fictional dimension, while De Amicis's reportages announced the close links between 20th-c. Italian travel writing and the development of the national press. Most prominent contemporary writers have written for the *terza pagina* or cultural page of newspapers, and travel articles have been among the most common contributions. *Cecchi, *Malaparte, *Comisso, *Piovene, *Pasolini, *Moravia, and *Parise all wrote travel reportages, and their travel books, even when they do not directly derive from articles, bear the traces of *journalistic experience.

Travel writing also documents the attraction exercised by particular places at specific moments in time, as in *Gozzano's *Verso la cuna del mondo* (1917), a picture of India, or Parise's *Odore d'America* (1990), a portrait of the USA in the 1960s and 1970s. On the other hand, Italian travel writing about Italy is a recent development. Early exceptions are Giuseppe Baretti's *An Account of the Manners and Customs of Italy* (1768), written in response to British criticisms, Lazzaro *Spallanzani's *Viaggi alle Due Sicilie e in alcune parti dell'Appennino* (1792–7), and Carlo *Collodi's *Un romanzo in vapore da Firenze a Livorno* (1856). Contemporary works, from *Pancrazi's *Donne e buoi dei paesi tuoi* (1934) to *Gadda's *Meraviglie d'Italia* (1939) and Piovene's *Viaggio in Italia* (1957), include socio-historical observation as well as heritage celebration, and are closely linked to the construction of models of national and regional identity.

In recent years the amount of travel writing published in Italy has increased in direct proportion to the growth of the tourist industry and of critical interest in the genre. Recent works range from Michele Serra's satirical tour of Italian seaside resorts, *Tutti al mare* (1986), to Fabrizia *Ramondino's episodic *diary, *In viaggio* (1995), and Claudio *Magris's large- and small-scale geographical epics, *Danubio* (1986) and *Microcosmi* (1997). [See also TRAVELLERS IN ITALY.] [LPol]

See M. Farnetti, *Reportages* (1994); L. Monga (ed.), *L'odeporica / Hodoeporics: On Travel Literature*, *Annali d'italianistica*, vol. xiv (1996).

TRAVERSARI, AMBROGIO (1386–1439). *Humanist and monk, who translated many Greek *Church Fathers into Latin. He lived in the monastery of S. Maria degli Angeli in *Florence and participated in the cultural life of the city, dedicating his Latin version of Diogenes Laertius' compendium on the lives of the philosophers to Cosimo de' *Medici. In 1431 he became General of the Camaldulensian order and worked assiduously for Church reform. [JK]

TREBIZOND, GEORGE OF, see TRAPEZUNTIOS, GEORGE.

TRECCANI DEGLI ALFIERI, GIUSEPPE, see ENCICLOPEDIA ITALIANA.

TRECCANI, ERNESTO (1920–). *Milanese painter and writer, who founded *Corrente* in Milan in 1938. It was a cultural and political weekly which adopted an independent *liberal stance though it also saw *Fascism as a bulwark against *Communism. The paper was banned in 1940, when Treccani's editorials became too critical. Treccani became well known as a painter. He also published poetry. [DCH]

Trecentonovelle, Il, see SACCHETTI, FRANCO.

Tre corone, Le, phrase designating *Dante, *Petrarch, and *Boccaccio as the three 'crowns' of Italian literature; see MIDDLE AGES.

Trent, Council of, see COUNTER-REFORMATION; PAPACY AND THE CATHOLIC CHURCH; REFORMATION.

Tre operai, see BERNARI, CARLO.

Treves, see GARZANTI; PUBLISHING.

Trieste. From 1382 to 1918 Trieste was part of *Austria and came to flourish as an international port, and as an industrial and financial centre. As a result of Italian *irredentism and the Treaty of Versailles, it became Italian in 1918 and has steadily declined economically since then. Being at the crossroads of three languages and cultures (Italian, Germanic, and Slav), the city has a distinctive cultural identity and vitality, evident especially in the earlier part of the 20th c. Triestine writers include *Svevo, *Saba, *Slataper, Carlo and Giani *Stuparich, Virgilio *Giotti, Giorgio and Guido *Voghera, Fulvio *Tomizza, and Claudio *Magris. [ES]

Trilussa

TRILUSSA (pseud. of Carlo Alberto Salustri) (1871–1950). *Roman poet who spent most of his life in the capital. His voice was already apparent in his first collection, *Stelle di Roma* (1889), which consisted of *madrigals in Roman *dialect offering good-humoured *satirical vignettes of life in the city. In the wake of its success he became a columnist for various Roman newspapers and developed into a keen observer of the foibles of different individuals and different classes.

Although he also wrote lyrical and idyllic poetry, his satirical verse, mostly dialect *sonnets, won most success with the public. He published four collections in quick succession, including *Caffè concerto* (1901) and *Er serrajo* (1903), which have often been compared with the work of *Belli and Carlo *Porta, though Trilussa is by no means as cutting. He also developed an interest in fable, and achieved a new popularity for his poems comparing human society and the world of animals, in collections such as *Ommini e bestie* (1908), *Lupi e agnelli* (1919), and *Giove e le bestie* (1932).   [CFB]

Trionfi (*Triumphi*). A sequence of six allegorical poems in *terza rima* by *Petrarch, and his only substantial work in Italian apart from the *Canzoniere*. Taking his cue ultimately from the *Divine Comedy*, Petrarch worked on the *Trionfi* at intervals from 1340 until his death, but never quite finished them. He describes, one after the other, dream visions of 'triumphs' of Love, Chastity, Death, Fame, Time, and Eternity. Each in turn yields to the following as its superior in the ultimate order of things. Petrarch's central themes of poetry and high culture are first celebrated and then gradually left behind. An exemplary itinerary is delineated from profane to divine love and from earthly to eternal glory. In the last poem, in contrast to the *canzone* to the Virgin in the *Canzoniere*, Petrarch imagines *Laura in heaven, and expresses the hope of joining her there.   [MP]

Trionfo della morte, see D'ANNUNZIO, GABRIELE.

TRISSINO, GIANGIORGIO (1478–1550). Patrician *humanist from Vicenza, determined to follow *Greek as well as Latin models in his attempts to give Italian literature examples of genres which had flourished in the ancient world. His *Sofonisba* (composed 1513–14, published 1524) is usually considered the first modern European *tragedy to follow classical practice. In it Trissino observed the unities of time and action, and established the use of

blank verse in Italian tragedy [see VERSIFICATION]. Translated into French by Mellin de Saint-Gelais (c.1559), the play was influential outside Italy as well as within.

In his likewise influential *Poetica*, Trissino advocated the use of blank verse for both tragedy and *epic, and contributed to the diffusion of largely *Aristotelian poetic theory [see LITERARY THEORY, 2]. Trissino also made proposals for *spelling reforms, and was a major participant in the *Questione della lingua* as a proponent of an Italian rather than Tuscan solution to the issue. In spite of the promise of the early verse included in his *Rime*, Trissino's most ambitious poetic venture was to prove a vast disappointment: his *Italia liberata da' Goti* (1547–8), in which he hoped to give Italy an epic of Homeric character, is more notable for its learning than for its poetic qualities.   [TGG]

Tristan, see ARTHURIAN LITERATURE; TRISTANO RICCARDIANO.

Tristano riccardiano. Late 13th-c. Tuscan version of the prose *Roman de Tristan*, contained in a manuscript in the Biblioteca Riccardiana in *Florence. It is a free retelling in semi-oral vein of the tragic love story of Tristano and Isotta la bella. [See also FRENCH INFLUENCES, I.]   [PH]

Tristi amori, see GIACOSA, GIUSEPPE.

Triumphs, see FESTIVALS; TRIONFI.

Trivium, see LIBERAL ARTS.

TROMBA, FRANCESCO (b. late 15th c.) was in the service first of Gentile Baglioni and then of his rival Giovanni at the *court of *Perugia. His poem (1525) on the siege of Marseilles celebrates the exploits of Renzo di Ceri, the Perugia *condottiere*. A *cantastorie* and professional *improviser and entertainer, Tromba also had links with the *printing industry in Perugia. His narrative poem *La dragha di Orlando* (1525/7), a standard story of the *Rinaldo cycle, is unfinished; book I is virtually identical with the *Rinaldo furioso* (1526) attributed to Marco Cavallo in its first edition, but subsequently to Tromba. Tromba is also the author of versions of the *Trabisonda* and the *Altobello* stories, both popular subjects for *romance *epics. [JEE]

TROMBONCINO, BARTOLOMEO (1470–1535). Composer mainly of *frottole*, but also of

sacred and theatrical music. His settings of poems range from *Petrarch to his contemporaries. Born in Verona, he worked principally in *Mantua.
[FC]

TRONCONI, CESARE (1836–94). *Milanese *novelist, *journalist, and polemicist. In 1866 he founded the *Gazzettino* (later the *Gazzettino rosa*) and *Lo *Scapigliato*, for which he wrote as Dottor Etico. Influenced by Zola, his novels address social issues, but the morbid details earned him a reputation for obscenity.
[AHC]

Troubadours. The term, from *trobar*, 'to compose' or 'to versify', designates composers of verse and music in Provençal. These were usually educated professional poets, dependent on the generosity of noble patrons, though in some cases themselves feudal lords. They were quite distinct from the *joglares* (*giullari*) whose role was limited to performing the troubadours' compositions. Troubadour poetry was known and often composed in Italy from at least the 12th c., and exerted an enormous influence on early Italian *lyric poetry.
    The main centres of troubadour activity were the feudal courts of Occitan- (i.e. Provençal-) speaking France, an area much larger than modern Provence. The central theme of the poetry, *fin'amors*, transposes into the field of eros the pact between lord and vassal and its accompanying rituals, the lady being cast as the lord, the poet as the vassal. The audience too is (initially at least) the restricted and culturally homogeneous one of the courts. The lyrics, though composed on the page, are intended to be sung. They are written in a literary, supra-regional form of Provençal, and display refined and rigorously strict metrical and musical techniques, ultimately linked with Latin liturgical practice, but having from the beginning their own autonomy. The principal types of poem are *canso* (reserved for love poetry), *sirventes* (moral or political verse), *tenso* and *partimen* (poetic debates), *pastorela* (addresses to shepherdesses), *alba* (dawn-poems), *balada* (dance-songs), and *descort* (songs with irregular structures). All of these are drawn upon in Italian poetry, though not all are codified as poetic forms. [See BALLATA; CANZONE; DISCORDO; SIRVENTESE; TENZONE; VERSIFICATION.]
    The first recognized troubadour is Guillem IX of Aquitaine (1071–1126), who is followed by Jaufre Rudel and Marcabru. The golden age, from 1140 to 1250, includes the names of most importance for Italian poetry—Peire d'Alvernhe, Bernart de Ventadorn, Raimbaut d'Aurenga, Guiraut de Bornelh, *Arnaut Daniel, *Folchetto di Marsiglia (Folquet de Marselha), Bertran de Born, *Raimbaut de Vaqueiras, and Peire Vidal. But the Albigensian Crusades of the early 13th c. fatally undermined the Occitan courts and their culture. The last recorded Provençal troubadour is Guiraut Riquier (c.1230–c.1295). Due to the itinerant lives lived by many troubadours and the dense network of relationships between the geographically scattered courts, the troubadour lyric was easily taken up and imitated in the whole of Western Europe.
    Troubadours were active in Italy, particularly in the Northern courts of the Malaspina, the *Este, the da Romano, and others, from the end of the 12th c. Troubadour poetry provided the formal, linguistic, stylistic, and thematic models and resources for the *Sicilian School and then was drawn on afresh by poets from *Guittone d'Arezzo to *Dante and *Petrarch. In the North there were a number of 'Italian troubadours', of whom about thirty are known—mostly judges, notaries, and civil servants, who composed Provençal poems in the Provençal manner and in some cases won fame and prestige outside Italy. The first was probably Peire de la Cavarana (middle or late 12th c.), followed by the *Bolognese Rambertino Buvalelli and the *Genoese poets Percivalle *Doria, *Bonifacio Calvo, and Lanfranco *Cigala. Cigala and the *Mantuan *Sordello are probably the most important of the Italian troubadours. Perhaps the last is the early 14th-c. Ferrarino da Ferrara.
    The eastern Po valley became a centre for the transcription and compilation of anthologies of Provençal poems, producing from the 13th c. onwards most of the oldest and richest *canzonieri* which have survived. Because the audience was now also more heterogeneous, a new body of *vidas* (*biographies) and *razos* (explanatory *commentaries) also came into being in this area, largely thanks to Uc de Saint Circ, who was active at the da Romano court in Treviso between 1220 and 1257.
[LM]

R. T. Hill and T. G. Bergin, *Anthology of the Provençal Troubadours* (1973). See M. L. Meneghetti, *Il pubblico dei trovatori* (1992); F. R. P. Akenurst and J. M. Davis (eds.), *A Handbook of the Troubadours* (1995).

Trovatori, see TROUBADOURS.

Truffaldino, see COMMEDIA DELL'ARTE.

Tullia D'Aragona

TULLIA D'ARAGONA (1510–56). Well-educated poet and *courtesan, who was born in *Rome but lived in *Florence, *Ferrara, *Venice, and *Siena before returning to Rome in her later years. She had relationships with Girolamo *Muzio and Bernardo *Tasso, and a wide circle of poets dedicated poems to her. In some cases they also helped her with her own poems, which are more given over to praise of her patrons than to love, and display a desire to impress with their cultural sophistication. She may also have written a *dialogue, *Della infinità di amore*, published in Venice in 1547. [ABu]

TURAMINI, ALESSANDRO, see LAW.

TURATI, FILIPPO, see DARWINISM; SOCIALISM.

TURCI, PAOLA, see CANTAUTORI.

Turin (Torino) began to gain importance in 1563 when the Dukes of *Savoy made it the capital of their state. They developed it architecturally mostly in the 18th c., when the city became one of the major centres of the *Baroque through the work of Guarino Guarini and Filippo Juvarra. Their rigid cautious rule gave way to four years of relative freedom from 1798, with a French-backed regime inspired by *Jacobin ideals. But in 1802 Turin was annexed to France, an event which caused disillusionment among many Turinese Jacobins. In 1814, the restored Savoy dukes introduced a harsh reactionary regime.

Paradoxically for a city which was on the frontier of Italy and the capital of a transnational state, Turin became the epicentre of the successful strand of the patriotic movement, largely thanks to the leadership of *Cavour. After *Unification it was the first national capital (1861–4). The loss of this status encouraged a mood of resentment and retrenchment, which remains to this day a feature of some sections of Turinese society. Notable among the founding elements of Turinese identity in the second half of the 19th c. were *Bersezio's *dialect play *Le miserie d'Monsu Travet*, which celebrates the humdrum life of a humble clerk, and *De Amicis' *Cuore*.

The rise of FIAT changed the character of the city, which became the centre of the Italian car industry, and experienced considerable demographic growth through immigration, at first from the surrounding countryside. The result was a new working-class culture. In the aftermath of *World War I Turin was the centre of the factory councils movement led by *Gramsci. In the 1950s and 1960s there were new waves of immigrants from Southern Italy, and more recently from Africa and Eastern Europe. Contemporary Turin is ethnically and linguistically mixed, but still largely dependent on FIAT.

The *Fascist period witnessed the rise of the (anti-Fascist) *publishers *Einaudi, who eventually became a crucial opinion-maker on the Left, and of the *Giustizia e libertà* movement. The Liceo Massimo D'Azeglio counted Augusto *Monti among its teachers, and *Pavese and *Primo Levi among its students. [See also PIEDMONT; MONARCHY.] [VRJ]

See L. Firpo, *Storia di Torino* (1971).

TUROLDO, DAVID MARIA (1916–92). Christian poet and dramatist from Friuli. Ordained a priest in 1940, he took part in the *Resistance in *Milan, where he founded a clandestine paper, *L'Uomo*, in 1941. From his first collection onwards (*Io non ho mani*, 1948), his distinctly personal poetry explores the relationship between the divine word and concrete human reality. [CO'B]

Tuscany. The region of Tuscany (Toscana) includes the cities of *Florence, Lucca, *Pisa, Arezzo, and *Siena. Understandably, it has often been connected in the historical imagination of Tuscans with the ancient Etruria, the area inhabited by the Etruscans, which did include modern Tuscany but also extended further to the south into modern Lazio. Etruscan remains are abundant at Volterra, Populonia, and elsewhere, and the connection with ancient Etruria was emphasized in the *Renaissance period by Annio da Viterbo and others. The modern conception of Tuscany derives, however, from the pretensions of the Dukes of Tuscany, who ruled approximately this area in the 9th c. AD, in the period of the break-up of the Carolingian empire, which had earlier maintained a more centralized control over Northern Italy. It was not yet, of course, a region of great cities.

The 11th and 12th c. saw the emergence of the *communes which were to become important as economic centres. This process was under way in the lifetime of the 'Great Countess' Matilda of Tuscany, who controlled much of Northern Italy before her death in 1115. Thereafter centralization was not an important factor. The separate communes, frequently at war with each other, were much involved in the conflicts of empire and *papacy in the 12th and 13th c., Pisa generally taking the Ghibelline (imperial) and Florence the *Guelf (papal) side. Pisa was at this period the most wealthy and powerful city. Its position on the coast enabled it to vie with *Genoa and *Venice in the imperialist expansion of Italy, and to acquire some landed possessions in the Eastern Mediterranean. But Pisa's early rise to prominence was to lead to an equally early decline. The naval defeat by Genoa at Meloria in 1284 has usually been seen as the turning point. The cities now to take the lead in industrial and commercial wealth were Florence, Siena, and Lucca. Florence and Siena depended on a similar expertise in woollen cloth manufacture and international finance, though Florence was by this time much larger. Lucca was also a city of international merchants, its wealth depending on the early development of the silk industry, which remained its staple throughout the *Renaissance period.

Florence was already growing to predominance with the defeat of Arezzo at Campaldino in 1289, to be followed a century later by Arezzo becoming a possession. Siena suffered perhaps more than any other Italian city from the Black Death of 1348 [see PLAGUE] and entered serious decline. Pisa was added to the Florentine dominion in 1406. In the 15th c., therefore, Tuscany was effectively the area dominated by Florence, with the exception of Siena and Lucca, which retained independence. Volterra was ruthlessly suppressed by Lorenzo de' *Medici in 1472, and the recently analysed Florentine *catasto* (tax return) of 1427 has shown how completely Florentines dominated Tuscan wealth, by owning property outside Florence itself and by taxing the subject towns more heavily than the capital. Siena was finally conquered by Cosimo I of Florence in 1555. Tuscany became for practical purposes equivalent to the *Medici grand duchy. Only Lucca remained independent into modern times.

Tuscany remained under the control of the Medici Grand Dukes until 1735. They were succeeded by the *Habsburg–Lorraine family, including the enlightened despot Leopold, Grand Duke from 1765 to 1790, when he became Holy Roman Emperor. During the *Napoleonic period Tuscany became briefly a kingdom of Etruria and then a French department. Renewed Habsburg–Lorraine rule after 1815 ended finally in 1859, when Tuscany became part of the new Italy.   [GH]
See Touring Club Italiano, *Guida d'Italia: Toscana, non compresa Firenze* (1948); A. von Reumont, *Geschichte Toscanas* (1976–7).

TUSIANI, JOSEPH, see ITALIAN WRITERS IN THE UNITED STATES.

Twelfth-Century Renaissance. The intellectual and spiritual revival which took place in various centres in Europe in the 12th c. had an important influence on subsequent Italian literature, particularly *Dante. Like all renaissances, it is difficult to define with any chronological or geographical precision. All the same certain facets are clearly identifiable.

The revival and study of the Latin classics already under way in the Carolingian age was now consolidated and brought to new heights under the supervision of Bernard Silvester and John of Salisbury in the great centres of Chartres and Orléans. Latin grammar and rhetoric were cultivated afresh on the basis of *Cicero and Quintilian. Knowledge of ancient science (Euclid, Ptolemy, Galen, and Hippocrates) was boosted through an assiduous labour of *translation from both Greek and Arabic. The study of ancient philosophy was revived, with an emphasis both on Platonic idealism and on *Aristotelian dialectics (by the end of the century the West was in possession of the entire *Organon* and much of Aristotle's natural science). There was a renewed interest in sacred and secular historiography, shown in the work of Robert of Torigni, Odericus Vitalis, and Otto of Freising. Roman *law was given a new prominence under the auspices of Irnerius at *Bologna but also at *Rome, Pavia, and Ravenna.

In none of these respects does the 12th c. exhaust its own possibilities. Both ideologically and methodologically, as well as in its characteristic institutions, it anticipates 13th-c. *scholasticism, which achieved a more elaborate and more searching resolution of the problems implicit in Christian *humanism. All the same, its thinkers were outstanding by any standards. They include Anselm (d.1109), with his desire to give rational form, as far as possible, to the substance of faith; Roscelin (d.1125), among the earliest representatives of medieval nominalism; Abelard (d.1142), with his decisive intervention in the question of universals; and, among the representatives of Chartrian humanism, William of Conches (d.1145), Gilbert de la Porrée (d.1154), and John of Salisbury (d.1180). In the area of dogmatics and theological method there are the important figures of *Pietro Lombardo (d.1160), Ivo of Chartres (d.1117), and Gratian (whose *Decretum* belongs to the middle part of the century), while prominent in the area of

Two Sicilies, Kingdom of the

mystical theology are Bernard of Clairvaux (d.1153) and the various representatives of the Abbey of St Victor in Paris, especially Hugh of St Victor (d.1141) and Richard of St Victor (d.1173). [See also MIDDLE AGES; RENAISSANCE.]

[JT]

See C. H. Haskins, *The Renaissance of the Twelfth Century* (1927); P. Dronke, *A History of Twelfth-Century Western Philosophy* (1988).

Two Sicilies, Kingdom of the, name of the realm of the King of *Naples, including both *Sicily and Southern Italy [see also ARAGON; MEZZO-GIORNO].

U

UBALDI, SERGIO, see ITALIAN WRITERS IN AUSTRALIA.

UBERTI, FAZIO DEGLI (?1302–?1367). *Lyric and didactic poet. The Uberti had been a famous and powerful *Florentine family in the 13th c. [see FARINATA], but Fazio was born in *exile (probably in *Pisa) and spent his life in the *courts of Northern Italy—Verona, *Milan, *Bologna, and *Mantua.

His allegorical-didactic poem, the *Dittamondo* (the title is adapted from the Latin *Dicta mundi*) turns *Dantesque ideas and techniques to different ends. It recounts, in *terza rima, a journey of the protagonist-poet through the continents of Europe, Asia, and Africa that made up the known world, guided not by *Virgil but by the ancient geographer Solinus, and with the aim of discovering not divine truth but geographical, historical, and environmental facts about the places visited. Fazio's lyric poems (fourteen *canzoni, twelve *sonnets, two *laudi, and a *frottola) are mostly on love or political themes. The love poetry echoes both the *dolce stil novo and *popular song. It is centred on a certain Ghidola, whom he calls Spina, an allusion to her family, the Malaspina, who were lords over the Lunigiana. His political poetry is strongly Ghibelline, willing Italy to become subject once again to imperial authority [see GUELFS AND GHIBELLINES]. [MP]

UBERTINO DA CASALE (*c.*1259–after 1325). A leader of the Spiritual *Franciscans. In book 5 of his *Arbor vitae crucifixae Jesu* (1305) he uses imagery from Revelation and *Gioachino da Fiore to present St *Francis as a new Christ, who has been sent in the last age before the end of the world to reform the corrupt 'carnal' Church ruled by the 'Antichrists' *Boniface VIII and Benedict XI. He is a character in *Eco's *Il *nome della rosa* (1980). [PA]

UBERTIS GRAY, CORINNA TERESA, see TÉRÉSAH.

UC DE SAINT-CIRC, see TROUBADOURS.

UDA, MICHELE (1830–98). *Sardinian dramatist who joined with the *Scapigliati in *Milan. He enjoyed a popular triumph with his historical drama *Gli spostati* (1859). Its success was never repeated, and Uda turned to stories and *romanzi d'appendice, which portrayed the urban reality of Milan in garish colours. [PBarn]

UDENO NISIELY, see FIORETTI, BENEDETTO.

UGHELLI, FERDINANDO, see PAPACY AND THE CATHOLIC CHURCH, I.

Ugolino. Sinner in the circle of the Traitors in *Dante's *Inferno 33, who recounts his death by starvation with his children.

UGOLINO DA MONTEREGIO, FRA, see FIORETTI DI SAN FRANCESCO.

UGOLINO DA SORMANO, FRA, see FIORETTI DI SAN FRANCESCO.

UGUCCIONE DA LODI (13th c.). Author of one definite surviving work, the so-called *Libro*, a poem of 702 verses written in a form of Veneto-Lombard, though more *Venetian than *Lombard. It is a meditation on the creation of the world, the pains of hell, and a range of moral issues. Uguccione passes virulent comments on the contemporary Church, and may have had links with the Paterines or *Waldensians. A *Florentine version of his poem was made in 1265. [JT]

UGUCCIONE DA PISA (d.1210). Canon lawyer, later Bishop of *Ferrara, who compiled the

Ultime lettere di Jacopo Ortis

Derivationes, an alphabetical lexicon in Latin, giving the etymology and meanings of words and proper nouns (including those from Greek) which are used in the *Bible, the classics, and the *Church Fathers. The work was known to *Dante and *Boccaccio. [PA]

Ultime lettere di Jacopo Ortis. Influential *epistolary novel by *Foscolo. Begun in 1796 after the model of Goethe's *Werther*, it was recast and completed in 1802 as an anti-*Napoleonic protest, with a libertarian drama (derived from *Alfierian *tragedy) superimposed upon the original love plot. The *autobiographical hero commits suicide because of Bonaparte's 'betrayal' of *Venice to *Austria with the Treaty of Campoformio (1797) [see NAPOLEON AND THE FRENCH REVOLUTION], as well as out of love for the unhappily betrothed Teresa. Intended as Foscolo's 'book of the heart', it displays an effusiveness and sentimental hyperbole, which signal a new era in Italian literature. [JMAL]

Ulysses. The protagonist of Homer's Odyssey is also the only legendary hero to whom *Dante devotes a major episode of his *Divine Comedy (*Inf.* 26.85–142). Instead of returning home to Ithaca, Dante's Ulysses sails into the unknown, beyond Gibraltar, until he is shipwrecked in sight of a solitary mountain rising high above the sea (the mountain of Purgatory and Earthly Paradise). Critical interpretation is traditionally divided between those who view Ulysses' voyage as a symbol of a heroic quest for knowledge, though destined to fail for lack of grace, and those who view it as Dante's indictment of vain curiosity, a deceitful thirst for self-fulfilment at the expense of all civic, social, and moral duties. Dante's rewriting left an indelible mark on the figure of the Homeric hero, as can be seen in some of its 20th-c. revisitations by *Pascoli, *D'Annunzio, *Gozzano, *Savinio, and Primo *Levi. [LPer]

Umbria was the Roman name for the region, but fell out of general use until it was reinstated after *Unification in 1861. Early medieval Umbria was *Byzantine in the west, but otherwise closely linked with the dukedom of Spoleto. From 756 it was absorbed into the *Papal States, where (apart from the *Napoleonic period) it remained until Unification. St *Benedict founded the Benedictine order there in 529, St *Francis the Franciscans in 1209. The strong Franciscan tradition found expression in the *laude—most notably in those of *Iacopone da Todi—and the spirituality of Umbrian art remains striking well into the *Renaissance. [SCS]

Umidi, Accademia degli, see ACADEMIES; GRAZZINI, ANTON FRANCESCO.

Umorismo, L' (1908, revised in 1920) contains *Pirandello's major theoretical statement on the kind of writing that he himself practised. *Umorismo* (*humour) is differentiated not only from more serious kinds of writing but also from *comedy, irony, and *satire; it is distinguished by involving the writer's sympathetic participation and reflection, enabling the comic to be visible within the tragic and the tragic within the comic. [JAL]

Umoristi, Accademia degli enlivened literary circles in *Rome after its foundation in 1603 by Paolo Mancini on the advice of Gasparo Salviani. As its name implies, the academy was dedicated to the celebration of the burlesque and *mock-heroic poetry. Members included Francesco *Bracciolini, *Chiabrera, Anton Francesco *Doni, Secondo *Lancellotti, *Magalotti, *Marino, and *Tassoni. The activity of the academy included the composition and recitation of poetry that mocks established poetic traditions and particularly the serious use of mythology and pagan deities in Italian verse. It played an important role in focusing the 17th-c. development of the style of *Berni, particularly through the invention of the mock-heroic *epic poem, written in *ottava rima. Tassoni was the first to use the new manner, in his *Secchia rapita*, though Bracciolini's *Lo scorno degli dei* (1618) was published first.

The academy did not remain unified for long: in 1608 a dissenting faction founded the Accademia degli Ordinati, and in 1614 another faction founded the Accademia dei Melinconici. The anti-authoritarian and modern ethos of the Umoristi may be seen as part of the growth of modernism in the first two decades of the 17th c. in Italy. [See also ACADEMIES; QUERELLE DES ANCIENS ET DES MODERNES.] [PBD]

Una donna (1906). Novel by Sibilla *Aleramo, and the first unequivocally *feminist novel to be published in Italy. An *autobiographical first-person narrative of a passage through childhood, marriage, and motherhood to a painful affirmation of independence, the book is a compelling denunciation of women's legal and social subordination. [AHC]

Una partita a scacchi, see GIACOSA, GIUSEPPE.

Una peccatrice, see VERGA, GIOVANNI.

Una vita (1892). Italo *Svevo's first novel, largely ignored on publication. Its anti-hero, Alfonso Nitti, a bank clerk, enters the rat-race, seduces his employer's daughter, then withdraws and chooses suicide. Upper and lower middle-class *Triestine milieux and Alfonso's home village are shown to be equally governed by mercenary motives. [JG-R]

Una vita violenta (1959). *Pasolini's second published novel. Like *Ragazzi di vita,* it is set in the Roman 'borgate' (or shanty towns). It is the *Bildungsroman* of a single, weak-willed 'ragazzo di vita', Tommaso Puzzilli, who moves from neo-*Fascism to *Communism and martyrdom, but also from sub-proletarian vitality to bourgeois conformism. [RSCG]

UNGARETTI, GIUSEPPE (1888–1970). One of the most innovative and influential Italian poets of the first half of the 20th c. He was born in Egypt in Alexandria, into a modest family from Lucca. He grew up there with his mother after his father had died in an accident working on the Suez canal. He was educated in French at a Swiss-run school, but also read his way rapidly into Italian literature and corresponded as a very young man with eminent figures such as *Prezzolini. He also mixed with expatriate Italian anarchists and intellectuals, such as Enrico *Pea, and wrote his first poems (now lost without trace). Another good friend was Mohammed Sceab, whose suicide in Paris some years later occasioned the poem 'In memoriam' in *L'allegria.*

In the wake of financial problems, Ungaretti left Egypt for Europe in 1912, visiting Italy but moving quickly to Paris, where he attended philosophy lectures at the Sorbonne and got to know Apollinaire, Picasso, De Chirico, Modigliani, Léger, and other artists and writers. Amongst these were Italian *Futurists, and, on the invitation of *Papini, *Soffici, and *Palazzeschi, he published some poems with Futurist colourings in *Lacerba,* though he would soon rewrite or reject them and move away from Futurism. The outbreak of *World War I brought him from Paris to fight against the *Austrians as a private in the Italian army. He served on the Northern Italian and later the French fronts. Thanks to the financial help of a fellow soldier, Ettore Serra, he published his first collection of poems, *Il porto*

sepolto, in 1916. In retrospect it was a remarkable event: the poems had a powerful simplicity and concentration of language, owing more to Rimbaud, Mallarmé, and Apollinaire than to Italian poets, and were on powerful, moving subjects (mostly *exile and the experience of war), and yet voiced a profound faith in the value of poetry and in human solidarity. All in all, they did not correspond to either traditional or avant-garde assumptions in Italy at the time. Ungaretti would continue to revise and expand on them. A second edition was published in 1923, with a short preface by *Mussolini (subsequently removed). Eventually they were integrated into *L'allegria* (1931, but published in its final form only in 1942), which also absorbed *Allegria di naufragi,* another collection mainly of war poems published in Paris in 1919 at the same time as an overlapping collection of poems in French (*La guerre*).

After the war Ungaretti married and worked in Paris, first as a correspondent for *Il Popolo d'Italia* and later in the press office of the Italian embassy. In 1921 he moved to *Rome, and made a living working for the foreign affairs ministry and various newspapers. He also travelled extensively, producing *travel *journalism and lecturing on poetry. In 1933 he published his second major collection, *Sentimento del tempo,* consisting of poems written since the end of the war, many of which underwent several detailed rewritings. It is an impressive and demanding work: Ungaretti deliberately widens his linguistic, metrical, and thematic range, introducing expressions of intense religious anguish, and drawing more explicitly on the Italian poetic tradition, especially *Petrarch and *Leopardi. His analogies became more daring and hard to follow; in some poems he pursued an ideal of literary purity that brought him to the more obscure reaches of the *hermetic movement.

From 1936 to 1942 he lived in Brazil, where he taught Italian literature at the University of São Paulo. After his return to Italy he taught at Rome University, and became a member of the *Accademia d'Italia. In 1942 he started republishing his works under the general title *Vita d'un uomo,* which remained unchanged from that moment on and was to be applied to his entire œuvre. This was also a period of activity as a *translator—particularly from *Shakespeare, Mallarmé, Paulhan, Góngora, and Racine. In 1947 he published *Il dolore,* the poems of which are quite different from his previous work, being an emotionally direct representation of the harrowing experience of the illness and

Unico Aretino

death of his 9-year-old son in Brazil. In the 1950s he became more widely recognized as a major poet both in Italy and abroad. Later collections—*La terra promessa* (1950), *Un grido e paesaggi* (1952), *Il taccuino del vecchio* (1960), and *Il deserto e dopo* (1961)—offer progressively more general meditations on the human condition, particularly on the idea of man as a traveller in search of an Ithaca or a promised land. The themes are familiar from his previous work but are now more composed. In most cases the search for formal perfection led to revised second editions, though there are sequences in the last collections which demonstrate a new diaristic, ironic vein.

As well as including expositions of his own poetics, Ungaretti's many essays, articles, and lectures cover a wide range of Italian and European literature. They are characteristically vigorous and at times eccentric. Ungaretti always played an active part in cultural debates and controversies, particularly in his prewar newspaper journalism and his contributions to *periodicals ranging from *Solaria and *Primato to the *Nouvelle revue française*, *Commerce*, and *Mesures*, which, though French, had an international orientation and readership. He was, however, a man and a writer of many contrasts—uprooted emigrant, curious vagabond, cosmopolitan intellectual on the one hand and, on the other, *Fascist academician and standard-bearer of his nation's cultural identity, veering between sincerity and ostentation, simplicity and artfulness, clumsiness and perfection. Such contradictions, nevertheless, do not lead to an ideological or artistic impasse, but to a tension which is fruitful because it is permanently unresolved. They signal a rare contact between poetry and life and give rise to a constantly evolving œuvre, which is at the same time the story of an individual and an exploration and re-creation of the essential forms of poetry.   [GS]

Vita d'un uomo: tutte le poesie, ed. L. Piccioni (1969); *Saggi e interventi*, ed. M Diacono e L. Rebay (1974). See F. J. Jones, *Giuseppe Ungaretti: Poet and Critic* (1977); G. Guglielmi, *Interpretazione di Ungaretti* (1989).

UNICO ARETINO (Bernardo Accolti), see IMPROVISED POETRY.

Unification of Italy was formally completed in 1860 (1866 for the Veneto). The nation's first King was *Vittorio Emanuele II of *Piedmont. *Turin was the first national capital, then *Florence from 1864 to 1870, then *Rome, with the occupation of the city by Italian troops in September 1870. [See also LIBERALISM; MONARCHY; NATIONALISM; PAPACY AND THE CATHOLIC CHURCH, 2; RISORGIMENTO.]

Unità, L'. Daily newspaper of the *Communist Party, published in *Rome; also a weekly *periodical founded by Gaetano *Salvemini.

United States, see AMERICAN INFLUENCES; ITALIAN WRITERS IN THE UNITED STATES.

Universale, L', see RICCI, BERTO.

Universities

1. Before 1600

Universities were a medieval creation, in which Italy—especially *Bologna—played a key role. The consolidation of demand for expertise in *law crystallized into institutional form during the 12th and early 13th c. In Bologna, with an international community of students taught by a body of entirely 'citizen' professors, collective bargaining by students for protection, rights, and privileges led to the formation of the celebrated 'student-universities', in which student paymasters allegedly exercised considerable control over their teachers. The true extent of student power is debatable, and in any case the phenomenon was short-lived. A more significant factor was determined competition from other towns and rulers, which led to the proliferation of attempts at university foundation during the 13th and 14th c. in particular. By 1500 a dozen universities were functioning, under the increasingly tight control of their sponsors, towns, and princes. The competitiveness of the system meant increased choice for students, who were not restricted to studying at a single university. Late medieval Italy thus saw the influx of large numbers of foreigners coming to study (especially at Bologna, *Padua, Pavia, *Siena, and *Perugia); from Germany and Iberia above all, but also from France, England, and not infrequently Scandinavia and Eastern Europe.

More controversial is the universities' cultural role. *Humanists' attacks on *scholastic culture as conservative and restrictive were part of their attempt to make a break with medieval culture; yet these attacks have all too readily been taken at face value by modern historians who have seen the universities as the traditional enemies of humanism. The explanation is more sociological. The Italian

universities were traditionally vocational training grounds, for law, *medicine, and, later, on the Parisian model, theology. Such teaching of the *liberal arts as existed—primarily philosophy and logic—was as preparation for medicine, and was less regulated than the 'higher' subjects. Humanists—the vast majority of whom, incidentally, had university training—thus had to be content with a relatively humble place in the academic hierarchy. Much of their stridency, particularly in the early 15th c., can be ascribed to professional insecurity and rivalry. In fact many humanist centres benefited greatly from salaried university posts, particularly in *Florence, *Ferrara, and *Rome. In due course, too, the ideas and methods of the humanists, particularly their philological approach, also permeated the system, gaining ground in the law faculties of France and the theological and arts faculties of Germany from the end of the 15th c. and eventually finding their way back home. Italian universities may have had a tendency to be a force for conservatism, but perhaps this is also a measure of the importance they had as educators of the elite and of professionals. [See also ACADEMIES; EDUCATION, I; MIDDLE AGES; RENAISSANCE.]
[PRD]

See J. Davies, *Florence and its University during the Early Renaissance* (1998).

2. From 1600

The modern history of universities in Italy has been essentially one of gradual secularization and modernisation against the resistance of Church, state, and vested academic interests. The language of teaching remained Latin until the late 18th c., and student enrolment was centred on *law and *medicine until the early 20th c. The study of fundamental sciences was strongly inhibited by both Church and state: the Casati Law of 1859 laid down that university teachers could be dismissed if 'in their teaching they impugned the truths upon which religious and moral order rests'. In 1923 the *Gentile reform consolidated academic elitism in ways which continue to impede democratization of university education.

The student movements of the 1960s and early 1970s [see 1968] failed to alter the fundamental character of the system and its values. The forty-seven Italian universities have a student population of well over a million; anyone with the *maturità* can enrol for a course. With no systematic check on attendance, wastage rates are high. Faculties, headed by an elected *preside*, are divided into

departments responsible for the different subjects in a degree. Degrees may consist of as many as twenty subjects, five being done per year over four years.

Apart from full professors, who have great prestige and influence, posts are divided between researchers and associate professors, appointed by examination as well as assessment of publications. Recent years have seen the establishment of research doctorates, as distinct from the all-purpose undergraduate *tesi di laurea*. Reforms put before parliament in 1999 envisage greater autonomy for individual universities, shorter degrees, and some element of modularization. [See also EDUCATION, 2–3.]
[RAbs]

See G.-P. Brizzi (ed.), *L'università in Italia fra età moderna e contemporanea* (1991).

Uomini e no (1945). Novel by *Vittorini about the partisan *Resistance in *Milan. In its ambitious exploration of the struggle between humanity and inhumanity, the novel focuses partly on *Communist group actions and partly on the existential crisis of one of their leaders, known as Enne 2 (N2), deploying experimental techniques that recall *Conversazione in Sicilia*.
[JU]

Urania, see FRUTTERO E LUCENTINI; SCIENCE FICTION.

URBAN VIII (Maffeo Barberini) (1568–1644). A *Florentine patrician and *lawyer, active as a diplomat, Barberini became Pope in 1623 at the age of 55. He is most famous as an intellectual and a friend of *Galileo, before he turned against him. He published poems in Latin (1620) and Italian (1635), and was a leading *patron of literature (of Agostino *Mascardi, for example) and of art. Caravaggio painted his portrait, while Bernini, a personal friend, designed the Palazzo Barberini for him and also the *baldacchino* in St Peter's.
[UPB]

Urbino is a hilltop city in the Marche, the birthplace of *Raphael and the setting for *Castiglione's *Cortegiano*. Without noticeable economic or political resources, the city flourished artistically and culturally in the second half of the 15th c. under *Federigo da *Montefeltro, who constructed his famous palace there, employing Piero della Francesca and other outstanding artists. *Patronage continued under Federigo's son Guidobaldo and his della Rovere successors, though Urbino became a secondary centre again by the mid-16th c. Guidobaldo founded a Collegio dei Dottori in 1502, which was given *university status in 1671 by Clement X. The university has remained private; it was expanded in the 1960s and 1970s by the leading architect Giancarlo De Carlo.

[LChe]

UTET, see POMBA, GIUSEPPE; PUBLISHING.

UZZANO, NICCOLÒ DA (1359–1431), from a prominent *Florentine *banking family, became leader of the oligarchic regime after the death of Maso degli Albizzi (1417). He was the reputed author of a vernacular poem anonymously attached to the Palazzo Vecchio in 1426, denouncing the *gente nuova*, the 'new' Florentine families, and calling for the reassertion of oligarchic dominance.

[RDB]

V

VALCIECO, RAFFAELE, see BOIARDO, MATTEO MARIA.

VALDÉS, JUAN DE, see COUNTER-REFORMATION.

VALDUGA, PATRIZIA (1952–). Poet from the Veneto currently living in *Milan. From her first collection, *Medicamenta* (1982), her work has obsessively blended themes of death, suffering, and passionate sexuality. The anger and provocativeness of her verse is both controlled and flaunted by her use of the metre and language of the classic *Petrarchan tradition. [CO'B]

VALERA, PAOLO (1850–1926). *Journalist and anarchist. He founded the *Milan *periodicals *La Plebe* and *La Folla* (two series: 1901–4 and 1913–15). His *Milano sconosciuta* (1879) belongs to the genre of prurient 'investigations' of low life. He spent ten years *exiled in London following a libel conviction. His last book, *Mussolini* (1924), was immediately impounded. [DF]

VALERI, DIEGO (1887–1976). Poet who was at least as well known as a *literary critic and scholar of French and Italian literature. Born in *Padua, he taught at the *university there, and later became director of the Accademia delle Belle Arti in *Venice. In poetry he continued from *Pascoli, *D'Annunzio, and the French *symbolists, and remained apart from the main literary trends of his time, preferring a simple, pure style and taking for his subjects reflections on everyday life and common human problems. [RD]

VALERI, NINO (1897–1978). *Historian who was professor in various *universities. He is best known for his work on the princely states of the *Renaissance [see also SIGNORIA]. After *World War II he concentrated on post-*Unification history, especially the policies of *Giolitti, whose correspondence he edited. His work stresses links between socio-economic, political, and cultural history. [RAbs]

VALERIA, IRMA, see FUTURISM.

VALERIANO, PIERIO (1477–1558) was the *humanist name of Giovanni Pietro Bolzani of Belluno. He studied in *Venice before moving to *Rome. In Latin he wrote a study of the text of *Virgil (1521), a *dialogue, *De litteratorum infelicitate* (1620), and the *Hieroglyphica* (1556), a study of animal and other symbols. Valeriano's *Dialogo della volgar lingua* (written probably in the 1520s, first printed 1620) leans towards *Trissino's views on the Italian, rather than strictly Tuscan, nature of the literary language. [See also QUESTIONE DELLA LINGUA.] [BR]

VALERINI, ADRIANO (16th c.) was one of the earliest known professional actors, taking the mask of the lover, Aurelio: he formed his own company, the Uniti, but retired from the stage in 1584. He wrote one *tragedy, *Afrodite* (1578), and some *madrigals. He is also known for his association with the actress Vincenza *Armani, for whom he composed a celebratory *Orazione* (1570) after her death. [See also THEATRE, 1.] [RAA]

VALGIMIGLI, MANARA (1876–1965). *Positivist-oriented scholar and *literary critic, professor of Greek literature in Messina, *Pisa, and *Padua, and then director of the Biblioteca Classense in Ravenna. He is known for the *translations of *Poeti e filosofi di Grecia* (1964). His editions include *Pascoli's Latin poems (1951). [AHC]

VALIANI, LEO, see RESISTANCE.

VALLA, LORENZO (1407–57). The outstanding *humanist of the first half of the 15th c. Born in

Vallecchi

*Rome, he was mainly self-taught, although he received some tutoring from Leonardo *Bruni. He formed friendships with northern Italian humanists while at the University of Pavia (1431–33), and spent a long period as secretary to Alfonso of *Aragon in *Naples before returning to Rome in 1448.

He chose the *dialogue as the vehicle for arguing for and against all views in order to arrive at the closest approximation to the truth. His first dialogue, clearly intended as a model, was *De vero falsoque bono*, originally called *De voluptate* and produced in three versions (1431, 1433, 1444–9). It aimed at restoring pleasure or happiness as the motivation for Christian behaviour, in opposition to *Stoic emphasis on duty and renunciation, and paints a vivid picture of even the heavenly community enjoying charity as the ultimate moral good. [See also EPICUREANISM.]

Valla believed that the reformation of Latin would herald a renewal of intellectual life. The *Elegantiae linguae latinae* (first version completed in 1440) is the first *Renaissance reference work of correct Latin usage. Inspired by *Cicero and Quintilian and based on a staggering range of classical sources, it enjoyed wide diffusion for three centuries. Similarly, the *Dialecticae disputationes*, which aims to reform medieval syllogistic reasoning based on *Aristotle's *Organon*, emphasizes how slovenly usage had led even the greatest *scholastic thinkers astray and crowns rhetoric, not dialectic, as the queen of the liberal arts.

Valla likewise undermined scholastic theology and canon *law. *De libero arbitrio* of 1439–40 dismisses medieval theologians who try to find rational solutions to the issue of the compatibility of free will with divine predestination as futile attempts to use language to enter into God's mind. In *De professione religiosorum*, written at the same period (but only published in 1869), he deplores the claims of the religious orders to spiritual superiority on the basis of their vows of poverty, chastity, and obedience; instead, anticipating much Protestant thinking, he praises the active life of service to the community. More publicly, he demonstrated on historical and linguistic grounds that the *Donation of Constantine (the document purporting to be from the Emperor Constantine to Pope Sylvester which was used to validate claims by the Church to secular authority) was in fact a forgery [see also MONARCHIA].

Valla pioneered the application of textual analysis to the *Bible, subjecting it to the same methods humanists were applying to all ancient texts. He compared the Latin *Vulgate* to the Greek original, and dared to note ambiguities in the translation. Erasmus would embrace Valla's method, printing the latter's notes on the New Testament for the first time (1505). Valla also translated Thucydides from the Greek, proposing him as a model historian, and himself wrote the history of the Aragonese dynasty in Naples. He was relentless in composing invectives against those who attacked him, especially on philological issues—notably *Panormita, Poggio *Bracciolini, Bartolomeo *Facio, and *Antonio da Rho. [See also CLASSICAL SCHOLARSHIP.]   [LAP]

See S. Camporeale, *Lorenzo Valla, Umanesimo e teologia* (1972); M. Lorch, *A Defense of Life: Valla's Theory of Pleasure* (1985).

Vallecchi. *Printing and later *publishing firm founded by Attilio Vallecchi. From 1913 to the 1940s it was the publisher of the *Florentine avant-garde, including the magazine *Lacerba* and the books of *Papini, *Prezzolini, *Soffici, and *Malaparte. After the war it nearly collapsed, but was revived in the 1960s by an injection of capital from the Montecatini chemical company.   [DF]

VALLINI, CARLO, see CREPUSCOLARI.

VALORI, NICCOLÒ (1464–1526/30) was a *Florentine patrician and politician. His teacher Marsilio *Ficino dedicated his *commentaries on Plato to him. His friendship with Niccolò *Machiavelli is attested by their important correspondence. In 1512 he was involved in an anti-*Medici conspiracy and was imprisoned, though later freed, by Pope Leo X. His *biography of Lorenzo de' *Medici, *Laurentii Medici vita*, is evidence of his attempts to win back Medici favour.   [PLR]

Valori plastici (1918–20). Artistic *periodical founded in *Rome by Mario Broglio, which articulated the theory of 'metaphysical' painting through articles by *De Chirico and *Savinio, but was more concerned to resist modern movements such as *Futurism, Cubism, and Impressionism. It advocated instead a return to the formal, technical, and spiritual values of the *Renaissance tradition. The title quickly became a label for the new *classicism of artists such as Morandi and *Carrà (who were also associated with the periodical) as well as De Chirico. As such it was not clearly differentiated from artistic versions of *realismo magico*.   [GP]

VALPERGA DI CALUSO, TOMMASO (1737–1815). Polymath. An Oratorian, he became professor of Oriental languages and Greek in *Turin. He also published as a mathematician and poet, and was instrumental in the creation of Turin's Royal Academy of Sciences. From 1772 he was a friend of *Alfieri, who dedicated *Saul to him. [JMAL]

VAMBA (pseud. of Luigi Bertelli) (1858–1920). *Florentine *journalist, illustrator, and *children's author. In 1906 he founded *Il Giornalino della domenica*, a children's magazine combining texts by famous writers with avant-garde illustrations. It originally published the pieces that became his best-known book, *Il giornalino di Gian Burrasca* (1912). [KP]

VANI, BERTO, see VIGEVANI, ALBERTO.

VANINI, GIULIO CESARE LUCILIO (1585–1619) is considered to be Italy's first out-and-out *libertine, He studied philosophy, theology, and *medicine in *Naples, *Rome, and *Padua. He read *Pomponazzi, *Cardano, and the pantheistic and Averroist tradition, then became a Carmelite, and travelled to Paris and London, where he converted to Anglicanism in 1612, before being imprisoned in the Tower of London and reconverting a year later. In 1615 he published his *Amphiteatrum aeternae Providentiae* against the Greek philosophers, and in 1616 the unorthodox treatise *De admirandis naturae reginae deaeque mortalium arcanis*. He was forced to flee to Prague and then to Toulouse, where he was accused of atheism and died at the stake. [PBert]

VANNETTI, CLEMENTINO (1754–95). Man of letters, active principally in his native Rovereto, but influential through his wide range of correspondence as secretary to the Accademia degli Agiati, whose members included Carlo *Gozzi and *Goldoni. He was a precursor of *purism, and a defender of classical orthodoxy against foreign *pre-Romantic influences. His major work was *Osservazioni intorno ad Orazio* (1792). [JMAL]

VANNICOLA, GIUSEPPE (1877–1915). Writer, who in his youth was a concert musician and then a novice monk. He frequented *symbolist and *Futurist circles in *Florence, and wrote for and edited avant-garde journals. His own mystical vision of poetry is best expressed in the prose poems of *Corde della grande lira* (1906). [PBarn]

Vanni Fucci. Sinner in the *bolgia* of the Thieves in *Dante's *Inferno 24.

VARALDO, ALESSANDRO (1876–1953). Author of plays, *theatre criticism, and novels of love and adventure. Two of these, *La grande passione* (1920) and *Mio zio il diavolo* (1923), were adapted for the screen. He was also president of the Società Italiana degli Autori (1920–8). [DF]

VARANO, ALFONSO (1705–88). *Ferrarese man of letters. He wrote four *tragedies, including a noteworthy *Giovanni di Giscala* (1754), but was more admired for his *Visioni sacre e morali*, written in 1749–66. These are *terza rima* poems, drawing on *Dante and the *Bible, of a kind popularized by Vincenzo *Monti. [JMAL]

VARANO, COSTANZA (1426–47) grew up in Pesaro, where she was partly educated by her grandmother, Battista *Malatesta da Montefeltro, and became an accomplished Latinist; several *letters, orations, and poems are preserved. In 1444 she married Alessandro *Sforza, lord of Pesaro, which ended her studies. Her daughter Battista later married Federico da *Montefeltro. [AR]

VARCHI, BENEDETTO (1503–65). *Humanist man of letters. The son of a wealthy Florentine notary, he studied at *Florence and *Pisa, and joined the anti-Medicean republicans after the *Sack of Rome (1527), but left Florence during the siege of 1529–32. Returning in 1532, he rejoined the republicans, and wrote a series of *sonnets in 1537 to celebrate the (presumed) tyrannicide, Lorenzino de' *Medici. Cosimo de' Medici's seizure of power that year forced him into *exile in *Bologna, *Venice, and *Padua, where he studied *Aristotelian philosophy and gave public lectures, including an academically *Petrarchist exposition of a sonnet of Pietro *Bembo. In 1543, his patrimony exhausted, he accepted Duke Cosimo's invitation to return to Florence. Elected to the conservative Accademia Fiorentina in 1543, he subsequently delivered and published papers on contemporary cultural issues: on the relative pre-eminence of sculpture or painting, on *Petrarch's *Rime* and *Dante's *Purgatorio and *Paradiso, and in particular on Platonic love. His published papers on this last subject, *Sopra alcune quistioni* *d'amore, Dei sensi, Della pittura d'amore,* and his *Sopra i setti dubbi d'amore* (1554), helped to keep 15th-c. *Neoplatonic themes alive, fashionably if pedantically, until the final quarter of the century.

Regarded by now as a safe conservative, in 1546 Varchi was commissioned by Cosimo to compile a *history of contemporary Florence, the *Storia fiorentina* which, despite its flattery of the Medici, is written in a lively style and contains original historical research, if largely based on documents provided by Duke Cosimo; finished by 1565, it was not published until 1761. Encouraged by fellow academicians such as Giovan Battista *Gelli and Pier Francesco *Giambullari, and advised by Vincenzio *Borghini (who urged him to counter the non-Tuscans' usurpation of Florence's classical language), he wrote the *dialogue *L'Ercolano* (written in 1564 and published in 1570), making Borghini one of his interlocutors in defence of a literary language which combined Florentine spoken usage with linguistic criteria derived from the Tuscan classics; at the same time Varchi paid tribute to Bembo for his attempts to achieve the same result (Varchi was instrumental in publishing the second edition of Bembo's *Prose della volgar lingua*). Borghini tried in vain for years to get the printer *Giunti to remove from the text an opinion foisted on him by Varchi: that Dante was superior to Homer. [See also QUESTIONE DELLA LINGUA.]

[JRW]

See U. Pirotti, *B. Varchi e la cultura del suo tempo* (1971).

VARESE, CARLO (1792–1866). *Novelist. Born in Tortona, he qualified as a doctor at Pavia and practised in Voghera and *Genoa, becoming eventually a parliamentary deputy. He wrote several *historical novels influenced by Walter Scott, beginning with *Sibilla Odaleta* (1827). He also wrote novels with a contemporary setting, such as *Il proscritto* (1830), and an eight-volume history of Genoa (1835–8). [DO'G]

VASARI, GIORGIO (1511–74). Painter, architect, and writer. He is best known for *Le vite de' più eccellenti architetti, pittori, e scultori italiani da Cimabue insino a' tempi nostri,* first published in *Florence in 1550, and reissued in revised and expanded form in 1568. This was the first attempt to write a systematic history of art and architecture in Italy in the *Renaissance from its beginnings.

Born in Arezzo, Vasari received a good classical *education, which led to his being invited in 1524 to

study alongside the young *Medici, Alessandro (1511–37) and Ippolito (1511–35). This early connection with the Medici was to prove vital to the success of his career. At the same time he began to study art with the painter Andrea del Sarto (1486–1530) and the sculptor Baccio *Bandinelli (1493–1560). His fame as a writer has often obscured his talents and his achievement as *Mannerist painter and architect. Travelling extensively in Italy, he worked for Popes Paul III (1534–49) and Julius III (1550–5), and for *patrons in *Venice, *Bologna, *Naples, and *Tuscany. His career culminated in his appointment as *court painter to Duke Cosimo de' Medici, for whom he painted extensive fresco cycles in the Palazzo Vecchio in Florence. His buildings include the Villa Giulia in Rome (with *Ammannati and Vignola) and the Uffizi in Florence.

The *Vite* are much influenced by his artistic practice. A preface sets out his theoretical views on art, together with a history of classical art and a long account of artistic techniques. The *biographies themselves are arranged roughly chronologically and gather together an astonishing amount of information. They are divided into three periods, according to Vasari's view of the achievements of each: the first, from the late 13th c. to about 1400, marks a new beginning in art; the second, from about 1400 to about 1480, sees the great advances in naturalistic representation, proportion, and perspective; in the third period, running up to Vasari's own day, artistic achievement has been perfected, above all in the work of his hero, *Michelangelo. The 1568 edition included biographies of many of Vasari's contemporaries.

Vasari's views on history are remarkably sophisticated, and owe much to the ideas and advice of friends such as Paolo *Giovio and Annibale *Caro. His account of Italian art shaped subsequent perceptions of the Renaissance, and remains highly influential today. [CR]

See L. Corti, *Vasari: catalogo completo* (1989); P. L. Rubin, *Giorgio Vasari: Art and History* (1995).

VASSALLI, SEBASTIANO (1941–) is among the most interesting, prolific, and innovative Italian *novelists to have emerged since the beginning of the 1980s. Although his earliest works, a mix of verse and prose, were inspired by the experimentalism of the *Neoavanguardia, in the mid-1970s he turned to the more traditional form of the novel in order to reach a wider audience. All his books, which have drawn on a wide range of novel genres from the *historical novel (*La chimera*, 1990) to *science fantasy (*3012*, 1995) and the comic novel (*Mareblu*, 1982), have dealt critically with the history, culture, and ideology of Italy since *Unification—topics which Vassalli has also explored in a series of polemical yet carefully researched non-fiction works, most notably *Il neoitaliano: le parole degli anni ottanta* (1989).

[ZB]

VASSALLO, LUIGI ARNALDO (1852–1906). Satirical *journalist from Liguria. Self-taught, he worked in *Genoa and *Rome, where he was one of the founders of magazines such as *Capitan Fracassa* and *Don Chisciotte*, often signing himself Gandolin. He became editor of *Il secolo XIX* in Genoa, and published six novels between 1882 and 1903. [AHC]

Vatican Library. One of the most important research libraries of modern Italy, the Vatican Library began life as the private collection of the Popes. As we know it, the library dates from the 15th c., previous papal collections having fallen victim to the vicissitudes of history. Its founding father is Nicholas V, and the conventional founding date 1450. At his death in 1455 it already comprised more than 800 Latin and about 400 Greek *manuscripts, making it the biggest library in the Western world at the time. The bull *Ad decus militantis Ecclesiae* (1475) of Sixtus IV set out the library's constitution. It was to have premises, funds, and staff, and to be open to scholars for the furtherance of the faith and the advancement of knowledge—conditions and aims which it still fulfils today. By 1481 the collection had grown to 3,500 items, had a full-time librarian in the *humanist *Platina (Bartolomeo Sacchi), and was used by churchmen and scholars. The library continued to grow by purchase and acquisition throughout the *Renaissance, until Sixtus V (1585–90) was obliged to commission a new building, which the library still occupies, in the complex of the Vatican palace.

For Italianists one of the most important acquisitions of its first century and a half of life was the library of Fulvio Orsini. This contained a wealth of literary material, including the library of Pietro *Bembo, and its greatest treasure, the autograph manuscripts of *Petrarch's *Canzoniere*. But the library's largest and most prestigious acquisitions were still to come. In 1623 it acquired as spoils of war the Palatinate Library from Heidelberg, rich in

ancient manuscripts from disbanded monasteries in Protestant Germany. In 1658, with the extinction of the dukedom of *Urbino, the Vatican acquired the ducal library, including the marvellous series of illuminated manuscripts commissioned in the 15th c. by the library's founder, *Federigo da Montefeltro. Another notable collection acquired at this time was the library of Queen *Christina of Sweden. Many other collections followed in the succeeding centuries, much increasing (among other things) the library's holdings of Near Eastern and Oriental material. Among modern acquisitions the most important has been the Barberini library (1902), with its many manuscripts and early printed books. The Vatican library today contains about 75,000 manuscripts and 2,000,000 printed books. [See also LIBRARIES; MAI, ANGELO; PAPACY AND THE CATHOLIC CHURCH.] [CF]

See J. Bignami Odier and J. Ruysschaert, *La Bibliothèque vaticane de Sixte IV à Pie XI* (1973); A. M. Stickler and L. E. Boyle (eds.), *The Vatican Library, its History and Treasures* (1989).

VATTIMO, GIANNI (1936–) is the best-known contemporary Italian philosopher, and teaches at *Turin University. He studied with Luigi *Pareyson and then Gadamer (publishing an Italian translation of his *Truth and Method* in 1972), and has worked in particular on *existentialism, hermeneutics, and aesthetics. In the 1970s he reinterpreted Nietzsche in a perspective which united *Marxist revolution and sexual liberation. Then, in the light especially of his readings of Heidegger and Derrida, he attempted to formulate a non-dogmatic, anti-systematic approach to knowledge and action. More recently, in *Credere di credere* (1996), he has written also on religious belief. [See also PENSIERO DEBOLE, IL.] [GS]

VECCHI, OMERO, see FOLGORE, LUCIANO.

VECCHI, ORAZIO (*c*.1550–1605). Composer, best known for his numerous *canzonette* [see VERSIFICATION]. He grew up and worked in Modena, though he published most of his work in *Venice. His major *madrigal *comedy, *L'amfiparnaso* (1597), has a text written jointly with Giulio Cesare *Croce. He also wrote *lyric poems and plays.

[FC]

Vecchi e i giovani, I (1913). Pessimistic *historical novel by *Pirandello, depicting individual and collective failures in both the older and younger generations, while charting the history of *Sicily in the 1890s. It challenges late 19th-c. values, and conventional interpretations of post-*Unification history. [JAL]

VEGIO, MAFFEO (1407–58). Lombard *humanist and priest, active at Pavia and later *Bologna, who became *papal secretary in *Rome. He is remembered mainly for adding a thirteenth book with a happy, moral ending to *Virgil's *Aeneid* (1428). He also wrote three *satirical Latin *dialogues in the manner of Lucian (and Leon Battista *Alberti) and a treatise on *education. Perhaps because he combined moral rectitude and a fondness for learned jokes, Lorenzo *Valla made him the *Epicurean spokesman in his *De vero falsoque bono*. [LAP]

VELLUTELLO, ALESSANDRO (15th–16th c.) published a *commentary on *Petrarch in 1525, and one on *Dante in 1544. The Dante commentary demonstrates a willingness to resist the prevailing views of Pietro *Bembo; it was intended to supersede *Landino's commentary, but its success was limited. His Petrarch commentary, with its inventive reordering of the *Canzoniere and romanticized biographical reading of the poems, was one of the most popular of the century. [See also DANTE COMMENTARIES; PETRARCH COMMENTARIES.] [DG]

VELLUTI, DONATO, see AUTOBIOGRAPHY; HOUSEHOLD TREATISES.

VENEZIANO, ANTONIO (1543–93). *Sicilian poet and adventurer who trained as a *Jesuit in Palermo and *Rome but took up a life of fraud and rape, with frequent spells in prison. In 1578 he was captured by pirates and got to know Cervantes in Algiers. He later held civic office in his native Monreale, but died in a fire in a Palermo prison. He wrote Latin epigrams, love poetry, and *sacre rappresentazioni, but was famous for his Sicilian *dialect lyrics. Collected principally in *La Celia* (1638), these are in a form of *ottava rima* and combine freshness and *humanist refinement. [ABu]

Venice. Unusually for Italy, Venice had not been a Roman city. It was named after the Roman province of Venetia, whose inhabitants fled from the *Lombards to the shores and islands of the lagoons in the 6th c.; the name Venice came to be associated with the most secure of these refugee communities, founded in the centre of the lagoons on the 'high bank', the *rivus altus* or Rialto. Security was a principal reason for the growth and survival of the city; other reasons lay in the nature and location of its site. The Venetians were forced to trade in necessities: building materials, foodstuffs, and even water. However, the lagoons produced game, fish, and salt. They also afforded a relatively safe anchorage and, at the head of the Adriatic and near such navigable rivers as the Po, Venice was well placed to be an entrepôt port between the Mediterranean and Europe.

Venice's emergence as a commercial power was gradual, but by the 9th c. its *merchants traded in the intercontinental market at Alexandria. Political and naval links with *Byzantium brought other commercial opportunities, extended by Venetian participation in the Fourth *Crusade which captured Constantinople in 1204, laying the foundations of a Venetian empire in the east, the *stato di mar*. In the 13th and 14th c. these developments led to rivalry with *Genoa, which Venice survived. At its height in the late *Middle Ages, Venetian trade reached from the English Channel to the Black Sea—though individual merchants like the *Polo family could travel even further—and the Rialto became a centre for international finance and commerce. The city was also one of the largest in Western Europe, with a population reaching some 120,000 in 1300, and recovering from outbreaks of bubonic *plague to reach that figure again in 1500. However, from the 15th c. Venice faced a formidable adversary in the Ottoman Turks, and from the 16th c. the Spanish, Portuguese, English, and Dutch increasingly altered the pattern of world trade. But the city's economic decline was gradual, and partly offset by the development of new industries (textiles, printing) and survival as a regional market.

Supporting that market was the mainland empire acquired in the 15th c., the *stato di terra*, a gain which persuaded Venice to style itself as a lordship or *dominium* rather than a *commune. Early in its history the tribunes and then the duke or *doge* who ruled Venice had acknowledged the authority of Byzantium, but with the decline of the Byzantine empire, Venice emerged in the 9th c. as a self-governing city with sovereignty resting—de facto—with the community itself. In practice, authority was exercised by a narrow oligarchy of long-established merchant families, but c.1300, in a period of commercial instability and naval threats from

Genoa, its ranks were greatly increased and given the hereditary right to sit in the commune's Greater Council, the *Maggior Consiglio*. That a self-created nobility ruled the Republic until 1797 was due to a range of factors. Some were negative: the pursuit of internal and external enemies by a police magistracy, the Council of Ten. Some were positive: the maintenance of affordable food supplies; the creation of a citizen class with privileged access to secretarial positions in the government and encouragement of the city's influential confraternities, the *scuole*. Some were unintended: strict control of admission to the *Maggior Consiglio* was put in place only in the 16th c. The city's unusual situation possibly fostered social cohesion, while the security it afforded prevented external enemies from fomenting faction or social unrest.

Venice fell in 1797, intimidated by *Napoleon's revolutionary armies. Consigned to *Habsburg rule, the city rose in rebellion against the Austro-Hungarian empire and in sympathy with the *Risorgimento in *1848, but joined a united Italy only in 1866.

The presence of a *university at *Padua— acquired by the Republic in 1405—helped prevent Venice from becoming a centre of learning, in a formal sense, until comparatively recently. Moreover for some contemporaries and later historians the nobility's mercantile and political preoccupations made it slow to respond to *Renaissance *humanism: *Petrarch's gift of his library (1362) was neglected. More generally, however, the city's wealth, security, empires in the east and Italy, and wider international connections attracted talent, creating a cosmopolitan society and a rich cultural history. For example, the early importance of Venice for the *printing and distribution of books drew the Roman Aldo *Manuzio to the city in 1490. His editorial assistants included Greeks and Cretans, and the Aldine Press contributed greatly to the diffusion of Greek, Latin, and Italian literature.

The cosmopolitan character of the city was an aspect of the 'myth of Venice'. This dates from the Middle Ages and was the creation of foreigners and Venetians seeking to celebrate the city's site, wealth, independence, stability, and good government. The myth also stressed Venetian piety, though for Protestants the city could be praised for its tolerance and readiness to resist the secular authority of the Church. It is hardly surprising, therefore, that an anti-myth developed criticizing the Venetians as morally lax and more eager to

expand their own frontiers than to defend Christendom. Attacks on the city's government as a decadent, corrupt, but ruthless oligarchy increased, especially in the 18th c. The decline of Venice as an economic and imperial power, its fall in 1797, and growing environmental threats to its existence, have made decay and nostalgia common themes in 19th- and 20th-c. accounts.   [JEL]

See D. S. Chambers, *The Imperial Age of Venice* (1970); F. C. Lane, *Venice: A Maritime Republic* (1973).

VENIER, DOMENICO (1517–82). *Venetian poet and politician, who dedicated himself to *patronage and cultural activity following his withdrawal from public life through illness in 1546. His own verse is conventionally *Petrarchist for the most part, but his house became a meeting point for other writers and poets.   [ABu]

VENIER, LORENZO, see EROTICISM AND PORNOGRAPHY.

VENIER, MAFFIO (1550–86) was one of the most original *Venetian poets of the 16th c. His love lyrics are, in turn, restless, passionate, humorous, and disenchanted. Written in Venetian *dialect, often in an anti-*Petrarchist spirit, they are earthy and, notably in his verse dispute with the poet-courtesan Veronica *Franco, sometimes obscene.   [RGF]

Venexiana, La (*c*.1535–7). Anonymous, powerfully erotic *Venetian drama, and one of the most original plays of the *Renaissance. The plot concerns Giulio, a *Lombard passing through Venice, who woos Valiera, a young married noblewoman. She consents, and arranges a rendezvous. A widow, Anzola, also attracted by Giulio, tricks him into going to her palace for a night of love. Furious, Valiera none the less gives herself to Giulio. Highly unusual in its employment of Tuscan, Venetian, and the Bergamo *dialect, as well as in its mainly indoor action, the play is remarkable for its psychological exploration of the power of love over its female protagonists. [See also THEATRE, I; COMEDY, I.]   [RGF]

VENTURI, LIONELLO (1885–1961). Art critic and historian. Though he had written on Giorgione and the Italian primitives, he was committed to modern internationalism as professor in *Turin (1915–31), and associated with Carlo *Levi and others in his group. He was one of the very few academics to refuse to take the oath of obedience to the *Fascist regime, and left for France in 1932. He spent the war years in the USA, returning to become professor of art history in Rome in 1945.

[GP]

VENTURI, MARCELLO, see RESISTANCE.

VENTURI, POMPEO, see DANTE COMMENTARIES.

VERDI, GIUSEPPE (1813–1901). One of the supreme figures in the history of *opera. Having established his reputation with *Nabucco* (1842), in which themes of nationhood and faith resonated irresistibly with the mood of the *Risorgimento, he towered over his Italian contemporaries for half a century. By artistic temperament at once conservative, radical, and idealistic, Verdi found inspirational models in the plays of Hugo, Schiller, and *Shakespeare, and brought the operatic tradition which he had inherited to a glorious culmination in *Rigoletto* (1851), *Il trovatore* (1853), and *La traviata* (1853). By the 1860s his operas had become grander in form and more cosmopolitan in musical language; each of them—*La forza del destino* (1862), *Don Carlos* (1867), *Aida* (1871)—was a cultural event of international importance. After a period of disillusioned silence in the 1870s, he was coaxed out of retirement to compose two Shakespearean operas with Arrigo *Boito as *librettist, *Otello* (1887) and *Falstaff* (1893).

[DRBK]

VERDINOIS, FEDERICO (1844–1927) specialized in impressionistic sketches of *Neapolitan popular life, but also wrote *fantastic tales inspired by spiritualism which have awakened recent critical interest. He taught English and Russian in Naples, and published some of the first Italian *translations of Turgenev, Dostoyevsky, Tolstoy, and Gorky.

[PBarn]

VERDIZZOTTI, GIOVAN MARIO (1537/40–1604/07). *Venetian painter and poet, friend of Torquato *Tasso, and author of *Cento favole morali* (1570). An admirer of *Ariosto, he discussed narrative poetry in correspondence with Orazio Ariosti, the poet's great-nephew, and in a treatise, *Della narrazione poetica* (1588). His poems *Aspramonte* (1591) and *Boemondo* (1607) are both fragmentary.

[RMD]

VERGA, GIOVANNI (1840–1922). Founder of *verismo and the most important Italian writer of the second half of the 19th c. Born in Catania into a *Sicilian family of noble extraction, he had the patriotic ideals of the *Risorgimento instilled into him from an early age. These are plainly displayed in his first youthful *novels, *Amore e patria, I carbonari della montagna,* and *Sulle lagune,* all written between 1857 and 1863.

A first turning point comes with a visit to *Florence in 1865, during which he writes *Una peccatrice.* This is not a patriotic, *historical novel, but a novel about romantic love. The hero, an artist, falls in love with a *femme fatale*; he becomes a success and wins her, but once the woman is his, he tires of her and eventually she kills herself. Plainly Verga's attention has shifted from society and political passions to the passions of the individual.

In 1869 Verga settled in Florence, which was then the capital of Italy. Francesco *Dall'Ongaro, who belonged to the older *Romantic generation, took him under his wing, and suggested he write about the plight of a girl obliged to become a nun. The result was the highly successful *epistolary novel *Storia di una capinera* (1871). Verga moves away from schoolbook rhetoric and assumes the ingenuous tone of a young girl, Maria, writing to a friend. Furthermore, as later with *verismo*, the determining motivations are economic. Maria's father, a widower, marries again and leaves his daughter without a dowry or inheritance, both being set aside for the new stepsister, whilst the only option for Maria is to become a nun. Maria falls in love with a young man, but he pursues his own financial interests and abandons her for the stepsister. Maria has now no escape from the nunnery; she goes mad and dies.

Whilst still in Florence, Verga began to be influenced by the *Scapigliatura, as is evident from *Eva* (1873). The theme of this novel, which played a vital role in his development as an author, is the fate of art in modern society, particularly in relation to economic factors. Eva is a dancer who sells her art to the public. The painter Enrico Lanti, in order to succeed financially, must also abandon his romantic ideals and learn to produce a vulgar form of art, which is the only sort that the public likes. When Enrico convinces Eva to live with him in poverty in a garret, she loses the appeal given her by the stage and wealth. After their separation, Enrico tries to get her back and is wounded in a duel with her new lover. Totally defeated, he returns to Sicily to await death.

In 1872 Verga settled in *Milan and had direct contact with *Scapigliatura* writers. His next novels, *Tigre reale* (1874) and *Eros* (1875), are typical *Scapigliato* products. In both, a contrast is drawn between the false, cynical life of the urban upper classes and family virtues embodied in a female character. However, also in 1874, he wrote 'Nedda', a *novella* with a Sicilian setting, which is in a much more *realist vein than anything else he had so far written, though the narrative impersonality which will distinguish his *verismo* is still absent. It tells the story of a poor olive-gatherer and her love for a young peasant, Janu, who dies when she is pregnant with his child. Abandoned by everyone, Nedda has to watch her baby daughter die in dire poverty.

In 1877 Verga published a collection of his stories—all either late Romantic or *scapigliato* in manner—as *Primavera e altri racconti*. At the end of the same year, his most important friend, the Sicilian writer and critic Luigi *Capuana, also settled in Milan. The two were deeply impressed by Zola's *L'Assommoir*, also published that year, and decided to take it as a literary model. Thus, in late 1877 and early 1878, as a result of the encounter with French Naturalism, *verismo* came into being as an avant-garde movement aiming to create the modern novel which Verga and Capuana felt Italy lacked. They made it a prerequisite that the writer should assume a scientific stance, as proposed by contemporary *positivism; reality should furnish inspiration and the work of literature should be a document created with the impersonality that had already been theorized in France by Flaubert and Zola.

The first example of the new manner was 'Rosso Malpelo', a story written between spring and summer 1878 about an orphan boy who works as a miner and is tormented by everyone else (including, it seems, the narrative voice) on the grounds that his red hair signals an evil character. It was included in *Vita dei campi* (1880), a collection of *novelle* with Sicilian *peasant settings. This is Verga's first work of *verismo* and includes other famous stories such as 'Jeli il pastore', 'Cavalleria rusticana', and 'La lupa'. Another *novella*, 'L'amante di Gramigna', opens with a brief exposition of the theory of *verismo*.

Verga had already been working on a 'bozzetto marinaresco', or seafaring sketch, called provisionally 'Padron 'Ntoni'. After the decision to espouse *verismo*, he destroyed the manuscript and rewrote the work from scratch. The rewriting grew into *I *Malavoglia* (1881), which is one of the great works of Italian fiction after *Unification. It is the story of the gradual decline of the Malavoglia family, brought about by a mixture of factors—natural disasters, usury, of which the head of the family, Padron 'Ntoni, is the victim, and the corruption of the grandson, the young 'Ntoni. As in *Vita dei campi*, impersonality means adopting the point of view of the community of fishermen and peasants. This view from below is maintained rigorously throughout the novel, and constitutes its fundamental stylistic innovation. But the novel blends naturalism, symbolism, a realism which is accurate in every detail, and a narrative movement with both epic and lyric qualities. In focusing on the plight of small-scale property owners in thrall to usury and laws regarding military service (which removed sons of working age from the land), it also articulates one of the most explosive issues regarding the Italian South at the time [see also MEZZOGIORNO].

I Malavoglia was to be the first of 'I vinti', a cycle of five novels about modern Italian life, from the lowest to the highest social classes. After the fishermen and peasants of *I Malavoglia*, *Mastro-don Gesualdo* would depict the provincial bourgeoisie of Sicily, *La duchessa di Leyra*, the Palermo nobility, *L'onorevole Scipioni*, the world of parliamentary government in Rome, and *L'uomo di lusso*, the vain luxury of contemporary art. Only the first two were completed. Though Verga made a start on the third, he did not even sketch out the last two. Other considerations aside, he would always have difficulty using *verismo* to depict the upper classes.

Whilst in *I Malavoglia* the values of the family, honesty, and hard work, as practised by old Padron 'Ntoni, prevail, ideal values fade from the picture of society presented in subsequent works. The dominant motif is 'la roba', the accumulation without moral scruples of goods, land, and money. The pessimism evident in all Verga's fiction now becomes radical. Economic considerations are paramount in the two collections of *novelle* published in 1883—*Novelle rusticane*, again set amongst the poor of Sicily, and *Per le vie*, about the urban proletariat of Milan. Some of the *Novelle rusticane* are intensely powerful: 'Libertà', for instance, is the story of a bloody peasant revolt during *Garibaldi's expedition of 1860, whilst 'La roba' anticipates *Mastro-don Gesualdo* in portraying a peasant who grows rich enough to supplant a noble feudal owner and take over his land.

This was a highly productive phase. Verga was now also writing fiction probing the urban bourgeoisie and the nobility. *Il marito di Elena* (1882) has a distinctly Flaubertian orientation, with its condemnation of the vain romantic whims of a bourgeois wife who betrays her husband and is finally killed by him. The stories of *Drammi intimi* (1884) return to the romantic passions of earlier novels but now with sceptical and ironic detachment. He also gave birth to veristic drama with a stage version of *Cavalleria rusticana*, which, with Eleonora Duse in the main role, enjoyed great success in 1884.

He was now at work on **Mastro-don Gesualdo* and published a series of preparatory *novelle* in 1887 as *Vagabondaggio*. The novel itself, first serialized in **Nuova antologia* in 1888, was extended and revised for publication in book form in Milan the following year. It is the story of a jobbing builder who makes money, becomes middle-class and, in order to climb further socially, marries a woman from the nobility, Bianca Trao. However he only becomes a hybrid of builder (*mastro*) and noble (*don*), and every outward success leads to an inner failure. The tyranny of economic logic forces Gesualdo to abandon the people closest to him and condemns him to inner isolation. In the end he dies alone and in despair in the house of his daughter Isabella, Duchess of Leyra (who was to have been the protagonist of the third novel of the 'Vinti' cycle). There is a notable narrative shift as well as a shift of class. Whilst remaining faithful to the principle of impersonality, Verga abandons the choral perspective and the epic and lyric movement of *I Malavoglia*. Events are recounted in a bare but actively disapproving fashion by a narrative voice from the provincial bourgeoisie, and the ultimately circular structure of the earlier novel is broken up into a series of disconnected episodes.

Times were changing. At the end of the 1870s Verga was in the intellectual and cultural forefront. He knew right-wing intellectuals, such as Leopoldo Franchetti and Sidney *Sonnino, who were working on the Southern question, and wrote for their *Rassegna settimanale*. He was also in touch with *Scapigliati*, such as Luigi *Gualdo and Arrigo and Camillo *Boito, whilst he and Luigi Capuana were the motive forces behind an advanced literary movement whose importance was quickly fully acknowledged. By the mid-1880s he was already becoming more isolated. Now *Decadentismo arrived, signalled by the publication in 1889 of *D'Annunzio's *Il *piacere*. Verga, however, remained faithful to *verismo*. At the same time, he was even more inclined to assume the reactionary political attitudes characteristic of a landowner belonging to the middle class of the rural South.

In 1891 he published the stories of *I ricordi del capitano d'Arce*, which are set amongst the nobility and urban upper classes. In 1893 he returned to Catania, and largely isolated himself from literary society. He worked on the third novel in the 'Vinti' cycle, but, despite the documentary material which his notes show he collected during the 1890s, he completed just one chapter of *La duchessa di Leyra*. The silence of his last years was rarely broken. He wrote some isolated stories, the most noteworthy being *La caccia al lupo*, which he also made into a play. There was also a collection of *novelle*, *Don Candeloro e C.i* (1894), the themes and techniques of which seem to look forwards to *Pirandello, and an anti-*socialist drama, *Dal tuo al mio* (1903), which he then turned into a novel. He was made a senator for life in 1920. To celebrate his 80th birthday, Pirandello gave a lecture in Catania in which he praised his work—and *I Malavoglia* in particular—over that of D'Annunzio.

For a long time Verga was best known to the general public for the *Storia di una capinera* rather than for the great works of *verismo*. Only after *World War I, when Pirandello and *Tozzi hailed him as their master, did he enter into the literary canon. Luigi Russo's monograph of 1934 also contributed to his elevation to classic status. His influence was strongest during the years of *Neorealism, particularly on *Pavese, *Fenoglio, the early *Calvino, and Luchino *Visconti, who filmed *I Malavoglia* as *La terra trema*. But it is evident in more recent years in Sicilian writers such as *Sciascia and *Consolo.

[RL]

See L. Russo, *Giovanni Verga* (1934); G. Debenedetti, *Verga e il naturalismo* (1976); N. Borsellino, *Storia di Verga* (1982); R. Luperini, *Simbolo e costruzione allegorica in Verga* (1989).

VERGANI, ORIO (1899–1960). *Milanese *journalist and novelist who worked on *Roman newspapers and then (from 1926) for the *Corriere della sera*. He published various collections of his articles. The rapid pace of his journalism contrasts with the *crepuscular mood of his novels, of which the first was *Soste del capogiro* (1927). [DCH]

VERGERIO, PIER PAOLO (THE ELDER) (1370–1444). *Humanist and author of one of the most widely circulated treatises on *education in the *Renaissance, the *De ingenuis moribus* *et liberalibus studiis adulescentiae*. Born in Istria, he spent his most productive years in *Padua (1390–1405), where he attended the *university and possibly taught. During this period he also visited *Florence, coming into contact with younger humanists such as Leonardo *Bruni, with whom he attended the Greek classes of *Chrysoloras, and who dedicated to him his *Dialogi ad Petrum Histrum*. From 1405 he was employed at the *papal Curia, then after a period of wandering left Italy in 1417 in the service of the Emperor Sigismund of Hungary, where he ended his days.

His educational treatise was composed in Padua in 1402 or 1403, and dedicated to the son of the ruling lord. It has much in common with the practice of the famous humanist teacher *Vittorino da Feltre, and was lectured on by the other great humanist educator, *Guarino da Verona. As its title indicates, it deals with both moral and intellectual education, to which it adds a section on physical education. In this and in the range of subjects it covers it reflects contemporary practice. Its novelty lies in its strongly classical and secular morality, which assigns a very restricted role to religion, and in its clear preference for the humanist disciplines of history, rhetoric, moral philosophy, and poetry. As well as fragmentary works of a more medieval character, Vergerio composed a series of characteristically humanist *letters, including a defence of *Cicero against the accusation of excessive involvement in civic affairs levelled against him by *Petrarch. [DR]

VERGERIO, PIER PAOLO (THE YOUNGER) (1498–1565) was nephew of the Elder Pier Paolo *Vergerio. A reformist, he was made *papal nuncio to Germany in 1533 and Bishop of Capodistria in 1536. Following his conversion to Lutheranism, he faced a trial for *heresy conducted by Giovanni *Della Casa. He defended himself with a memorable written attack on the licentious writings of his prosecutor's youth. Della Casa replied with a defence of his own work and a denigration of Vergerio, who took refuge first as a pastor in the Grisons in Switzerland and then in Tübingen. There, from 1553, he wrote *Bible *commentaries and anti-Catholic invective.

[GPTW]

Vergini delle rocce, Le, see D'ANNUNZIO, GABRIELE.

VERINO, UGOLINO (1438–1516). Latin poet and notary of noble birth, who held important public positions in Medicean *Florence, particularly after 1464. He was a pupil of *Landino, and dedicated his main poetical work, the *Flametta*, first to Cosimo de' *Medici (1463) and then to Lorenzo de' *Medici (1464). He also wrote a poem in memory of Cosimo, *Paradisus* (1468–9), and the *Carlias (De gestis Magni Caroli)*, an *epic composed between 1469 and 1480. After 1487, along with many learned members of Lorenzo's circle, he became a follower of *Savonarola, to whom he dedicated his *Carmen de christiana religione ac vitae monasticae felicitate* (1491), in which he affirms the utility of poetry, but only when it is used to celebrate religion. [LB]

Verismo. The Italian literary movement corresponding to French Naturalism. It started in *Milan between late 1877 and early 1878 with the encounter of former *Scapigliati, such as Felice Cameroni and Roberto *Sacchetti, and the *Sicilians Giovanni *Verga and Luigi *Capuana, who had settled in the city. The aim was to create a modern *novel in Italy, on the model of the work of Émile Zola.

The principles of canonical *verismo* are as follows: (1) the form must be impersonal; (2) the language and style must accord with the subject matter (if the setting is working-class, so too must be the lexis and the syntax); (3) the aim is to study modern Italy from the lowest classes to the highest; (4) the method must be scientific, based on a study of the environment (social, economic, geographical, etc.) and in accordance with the determinist criteria theorized by *positivism and Naturalism. Although the dependence on French Naturalism is plain, there are important differences: (1) the stylistic aspects of the literary work are emphasized more than scientific ones; (2) it is less manual workers and the city environment which are represented than the *peasantry and provincial life; (3) the political ideology of the *veristi* is not democratic but conservative, even reactionary.

Verismo flourished in Italy between 1878 and 1890, though one of its major works, *I Viceré* by Federico *De Roberto, appeared in 1894, when the *decadentist psychological novel was already dominant. The first novel of *verismo* was Capuana's *Giacinta* (1879), followed in 1880 by Verga's collection of *novelle, *Vita dei campi*, which were actually written between 1878 and 1880. In early 1881 Verga published his masterpiece, *I *Malavoglia*. His second great novel, *Mastro-don Gesualdo*, appeared as a book in 1889 when *verismo* was

Vermigli, Pietro Martire

already beginning to be superseded as an avant-garde movement.

The main exponents of *verismo* were Sicilian— Giovanni Verga, its founder, Luigi Capuana, its most cultured and impassioned theorist, and their pupil, Federico De Roberto. But the movement had successful followers throughout Italy. Matilde *Serao and Salvatore *Di Giacomo wrote about the working class of *Naples. In the Abruzzi the young Gabriele *D'Annunzio followed *verismo* in *Terra vergine* and *Novelle della Pescara*. The *Tuscan peasantry was the main inspiration for Renato *Fucini and Mario *Pratesi, most importantly in the latter's novel *L'eredità* (1889). In *Lombardy Emilio *De Marchi attempted to reconcile the *Manzonian tradition with *verismo* by describing the lives of the lower middle class, most notably in *Demetrio Pianelli* (1888). In the North there was also some cross-fertilization between *verismo* and the *Scapigliatura* in, for instance, Remigio *Zena's *La bocca del lupo* (1892), Gian Pietro *Lucini's *Gian Pietro da core* (1885), and Paolo *Valera's *La folla* (1901). A certain form of *verismo* is also visible in verse: Lorenzo Stecchetti (Olindo *Guerrini) makes deliberate attempts to shock in his treatment of erotic and social themes, and Vittorio *Betteloni writes about the bourgeoisie in a deliberately prosaic manner. In the *theatre it was again Verga who established veristic drama, with the 1884 stage version of *Cavalleria rusticana*, which was a personal triumph for the actress Eleonora Duse.

Traces of the poetics of *verismo* persist in the early *Pirandello, in *Il turno*, *L'esclusa*, and his first *novelle*, in the *Sardinian Grazia *Deledda and, a little later, in the Tuscan Federigo *Tozzi. But the major subsequent influence was on *Neorealism (1943–55). [RL]

See M. Musitelli Paladini, *Nascita di una poetica: Il verismo* (1974); P. Pellini, *Naturalismo e verismo* (1998).

VERMIGLI, PIETRO MARTIRE (Peter Martyr) (1499–1562). Religious reformer. Born in *Florence and educated in *Padua, he became an *Augustinian prior in Lucca, but renounced Rome and fled to Protestant Zurich in 1542. As Regius Professor of Divinity at Oxford, he helped shape the English *Reformation under Cranmer. His voluminous exegetical writings influenced the Puritans. [PMcN]

VERNANI, GUIDO (d. after 1344). *Dominican theologian, who wrote a commentary on *Boniface VIII's Bull *Unam sanctam*, a treatise on *papal power, and a polemical refutation of *Dante's *Monarchia*. In this last he argued that Christ alone is the true Monarch and his supreme vicar on earth is the Pope. [PA]

VERONA, GUIDO, see DA VERONA, GUIDO.

VERRI, ALESSANDRO (1741–1816). One of the editors of the journal *Il *Caffè* founded by his younger brother, Pietro *Verri, and an active figure in the *Lombard *Enlightenment. From a noble *Milanese family, he was distinguished by a refined aesthetic and philosophical sensibility far removed from the optimistic and progressive beliefs of the age, and by an innovative approach to linguistic matters (see the *Rinunzia avanti notaio . . . al *Vocabolario della Crusca*).

In his youth he shared the historical, legislative, and juridical interests of the circle of Cesare *Beccaria, with whom he travelled in 1766–7 to Paris and London. Here he came into contact with the most lively and cosmopolitan society that Europe could offer: his correspondence with his brother Pietro is an invaluable document of this journey and the social and cultural openings it offered. After his return, with the decline of the Lombard Enlightenment, he chose not to return to his family and settled instead in *Rome, where he adopted a conservative and pro-*papal stance. Following the literary fashions and debates of the later part of the century, which tended towards a darker kind of *neoclassical sensibility, he turned to writing *novels. *Le avventure di Saffo poetessa di Mitilene* (1781), *Le notti romane* (1792–1804), and *La vita di Erostrato* (1815) show a refined sense of formal and stylistic decorum, and a Winckelmannian perspective, in which architectural ruins and chiaroscuro have a symbolic function, and an aesthetics of the sublime reinterprets the modern world in the light of that of antiquity. [IC]

verri, il. Literary *periodical (always written in lower-case), with a strong philosophical component, founded as a quarterly in *Milan in 1956 by Luciano Anceschi. It attracted many of the writers and intellectuals who would be associated with the *Neoavanguardia in the 1960s, such as Edoardo *Sanguineti, Umberto *Eco, and Alfredo *Giuliani. Created in the spirit of *phenomenology, it was highly intellectual, but also anti-dogmatic and pluralist from the start, questioning the certainties of contemporary *idealism, the ideological fetters of *Neorealism, and the obscurities of the *hermetic movement, and exploring the possibilities of more experimental writing and *psychoanalytic criticism. It has remained a forum for discussing innovatory tendencies in literature and *literary criticism. [GS]

VERRI, PIETRO (1728–97). *Milanese philosopher and economist. With his brother Alessandro *Verri, he founded the discussion group known as the Accademia dei Pugni and the *periodical *Il*Caffè*, which attacked the conservative and aristocratic attitudes of the times. He was one of the main exponents of the *Lombard *Enlightenment, and helped to promote reforms both through his philosophical and economic writings and as an official in the local *Austrian-controlled public administration, in which he was employed from 1764. He was an economist of some originality, and moved from an early mercantilist protectionism towards a free-market philosophy, anticipating some of the ideas of Adam Smith in his *Meditazioni sull'economia politica* (1771).

His economic theory was grounded in typical cultural themes of the Enlightenment. In his *Meditazioni sulla felicità* (1763) he developed a theory of cultural and social progress based on the concept of an inborn human dissatisfaction with existing conditions. This early expression of the concept of relative unhappiness, fed by a desire for continual improvement, meant that progress was written into the fabric of historical development, and led Verri to reject the possibility of any Rousseauesque return to happier, more natural times. In his *Discorso sull'indole del piacere e del dolore* (1773), a work admired by Kant, he explored in detail the nature of happiness. Pleasure, he maintained, is always the result of the sudden release from *dolore*—the semantic breadth of which ranges from physical pain to psychological dissatisfaction. In this work, profoundly influenced by the *sensismo* of the period, he also developed an aesthetic theory which purported both to explain appreciation of the arts and to suggest artistic techniques for inducing desired effects. In both works he expressed the idea that happiness can only be achieved by adapting our expectations, anxieties, and disappointments to the balancing perspectives of rational reflection.

Verri's other works include numerous minor economic writings, a discussion of the French Revolution, a correspondence with his brother, and a *Storia di Milano*, which had only reached 1559 when he died and remained unpublished until

1851. Equally notable are his *Osservazioni sulla tortura* (1777), which constitutes a moral indictment of the judicial sytem and its use of torture, and his *Ricordi a mia figlia* (1777), an advice manual for his daughter, which is also a reflective, moving, and finely written account of how his theories of happiness could be applied within the society of his time. [GLCB]

Del piacere e del dolore ed altri scritti di filosofia e di economia, ed. R. De Felice (1964). See N. Valeri, *Pietro Verri* (1969).

Versification. One can broadly distinguish between two main periods of versification: that of regular versification and that of *free verse. In the latter (20th c., with some early examples in the 19th c.), regular versification still exists, but is integrated with free forms: for example the *hendecasyllable is still important and there are many examples of *sonnets, but the regular forms are 'marked', there being no obligation at all to use them, and they are subject to all sorts of irregularity. As for regular versification, this can in turn be divided into two periods, up to the 16th c. and from the 16th c. onwards: in the first, rhyme is compulsory, with rare exceptions; in the second, unrhymed verse is allowed, gradually assuming greater importance, and Italian versification is profoundly influenced by the *humanists' rethinking of it according to classical categories. A further division occurs with the establishment in the 16th and 17th c. of oxytonic rhymes (*rime tronche*, with the accent on the final syllable) and proparoxytonic rhymes (*rime sdrucciole*, with the accent on the antepenultimate), as well as a greater variety of verse in the elevated style. The basic rules, already laid down in practice in *Dante's time, are an Italian development of the principles of 12th- and 13th-c. Provençal and French versification, which served as a powerful model for early Italian poetry in terms both of literary content and of form. Certain forms, such as the *ottonario* (eight-syllable line) of the *laudi*, are probably derived directly from medieval Latin versification, from which Provençal and French verse are also derived [see TROUBADOURS.]

The structure of the Italian verse line is based on the number of syllables, in its turn defined by the final accent of the sequence. Lines count as having the same number of syllables if the final accent is in the same position; it does not matter if that is the last syllable in the line (*verso tronco*) or if it is followed by one unaccented syllable (*verso piano*) or by two (*verso sdrucciolo*). The names of the lines refer to the

Versification

numbers of syllables in the *verso piano*: for example a *settenario* is a line of seven syllables if it is *piano* (*Petrarch's 'Chiare, fresche e dolci acque', *Canz.* 126.1), six if it is *tronco* and eight if *sdrucciolo*, but the sixth syllable will always carry the final stress. Lines longer than the *settenario* require, to be recognizable, one or two additional accents in fixed positions. This is particularly true of the *hendeca-syllable (*Dante's 'Nel mezzo del cammin di nostra vita'); in the *ottonario* the third syllable is usually accented as well as the seventh, from the earliest times onwards. In the 19th c. other kinds of verse line established themeselves: the decasyllable (accented on the third and sixth syllables as well as the ninth), the *novenario* (on the second, fifth, and eighth syllables), and the *senario* (on the second and fifth). Lines longer than the hendecasyllable are made up of two smaller lines (hemistichs); the most important is the alexandrine, made up of two *settenari*.

There are also instances of 'anisosyllabic' versification, in which lines are considered equivalent even with a difference of one syllable (or sometimes two) between them: this occurs in the work of the *giullari* and the didactic poetry of the 13th c., the *laudi* of the 13th c. and later, and perhaps also in the 14th-c. *cantari*. Characteristic examples are the *ottonario-novenario* (based on the *ottonario*) of the *laudi*, and the *novenario-ottonario* and the alexandrine with hemistichs of both seven and six syllables used by the *giullari* and in didactic poetry.

In the syllable count, the treatment of adjacent vowels is critical. The combination of accented plus unaccented vowel (*mia, mai, andai*, etc.) is always treated as two syllables at the end of a line, but within the line as one syllable and only exceptionally as two, depending on the period and the style. Otherwise, as a general rule, two adjacent vowels that constitute a single syllable in Italian can count as two syllables (diaeresis) if they were two syllables in the Latin word from which they derive (e.g. *celestïale*); though in the 18th and 19th c. greater licence (censured by the theoreticians) develops in this respect, a licence whose remote origins lie in the freer treatment of the endings of *versi sdruccioli*. On the other hand it is rare for a normally bisyllabic combination (e.g. in *paura*) to be counted as monosyllabic (synaeresis); but *-aio* (*migliaio*), *-oia* (*gioia, noia, Pistoia*), and similar combinations can count as one syllable in the 13th c. and sporadically in later centuries as well. A final vowel in one word followed by an initial vowel in the next usually counts as a single syllable (*sinalefe*, for example, in

'dolci acque' cited above); counting them as two (*dialefe*) is relatively common in the 13th c., particularly when the first is accented, but from Petrarch onwards this is avoided in the elevated style, and even 18th- and 19th-c. poetry is quite inflexible on this score.

There is no rule that the end of a line should coincide with the end of a syntactic unit, but this is the case more normally than not. Interrupting a syntactic unit at the end of a line is termed *enjambement*, as in French, but though the frequency of this varies according to the style, it is never considered an infraction of the rules, in contrast to 'classical' French versification.

Rhyme consists in the last part of two words or of two lines having the same sound from the accented vowel onwards, as in *cuore* and *amore*. Throughout the poetic tradition a rhyme of closed *é* with open *è* or of closed *ó* with open *ò* is judged 'perfect', despite the phonological opposition (*légge* 'law' vs *lègge* 'he reads', *vólto* 'face' vs *vòlto* 'turned'). In the 13th c. it was permitted, though infrequent, to rhyme *i* with closed *é* and *u* with closed *ó* (*rima siciliana*), and sometimes with open *è* and open *ò* respectively (*rima guittoniana*). This second usage becomes negligible from the 14th c. on, and both are related to linguistic peculiarities of the early tradition, mainly to the generally agreed fact that while the texts of the *Sicilian School were written in Sicilian, they were known and imitated in Tuscanized versions. Stylistic value is attached to the distinction between 'easy' and 'difficult' rhymes (respectively, those involving very common endings, e.g. inflexions or suffixes, and those involving rare endings). 'Identical' rhymes, where a word rhymes with itself, are always avoided, except in the *sestina* and in forms with a refrain. On the other hand the *rima equivoca*, involving different words with the same form, is a stylistic feature, for example *parte* ('part') rhyming with *parte* ('he/she leaves'). A characteristic of earlier poetry (up to the 14th c.) is the search for special, so-called 'technical' rhymes; for example the *rima composta* (with displacement of the accent: *nón ci ha* and *oncia* in Dante), the 'false' *rima equivoca* (*l'aura* and *Laura* in Petrarch), 'tmesis' (*tmesi*), where the rhyme word is split (*appo- / rta* ('he brings') rhymes with *accappo* ('I grasp') in *Monte Andrea). 'Rich' rhymes, in which one or more sounds before the accented vowel are also identical (*secondo* and *giocondo* in Petrarch), have never been used systematically (with a few rare exceptions) in Italian, in contrast to French.

Like the verse line, rhyme can be *piana* (*andare*,

cuore, etc.), *tronca* (ending in a vowel: -*à*; in a consonant: -*ar*) or *sdrucciola* (-*àbile*). In early poetry line and rhyme are usually *piani*, and *tronche* or *sdrucciole* rhymes are mainly an indication of minor-genre status (or of a particular genre, such as the *pastoral eclogue written in *sdruccioli* in the 15th and 16th c.). The same is true, from Dante and Petrarch to the 16th c., of the use of verse lines other than the hendecasyllable and the *settenario*; in this respect Italian poetry marks, from as early as the 13th c., a reduction in the range of verse lines available to the Provençal poets and the Sicilian School. The use in the elevated style of all kinds of lines and rhymes, especially of short lines and *rime tronche* and *sdrucciole*, is an innovation spearheaded above all by *Chiabrera, and which enjoyed considerable success right up to the 19th c.; a parallel development was the use of the *rima tronca* ending in a consonant with words that would normally have a *piano* ending (*andar* and *parlar* instead of *andare* and *parlare*): *Pascoli was the first to reject this decisively .

On the subject of the origins of Italian *lyric poetry, importance is normally given to the fact that, unlike Provençal poetry, it was not written to music. This is true, in the sense that the link between poetry and music was no longer indissoluble at the moment of composition, though texts could be and often were set to music at a later stage. Certain forms retain the link with music, such as, from the 13th c., the *ballata* (more so than the *canzone*), the *laudi*, from the 14th c. the *madrigal and the *strambotto*.

In the 13th c. the most significant lyric forms were the *canzone*, the sonnet, and the *ballata*. The latter, very common in the musical poetry of the 14th c., tends to move towards a more popular style, along with the *laudi*, becoming a minor genre in the secular poetry (the *canzonetta*) of the 15th c.; it falls out of use in the 16th c. The *canzone* is the most prestigious metrical genre, the basis for all strophic lyric forms, that is, those divided into strophes or *stanze* with an identical scheme. In its early guise it remains a living form, with occasional variants, up to the work of Torquato *Tasso. In the 16th and 17th c. new forms are derived from it, inspired by the imitation of Latin poetry, by new demands on the poetic medium, and, in the case of the *ode-canzonetta*, by an interest in French poetry on the one hand and popular sung poetry on the other. One such innovation is the 'pindaric ode', in triple stanzas made up of two metrically identical parts, strophe and antistrophe, followed by a third, the *epodo* or epode; introduced by *Trissino,

*Alamanni, and *Minturno (with units that are *canzone* stanzas), used by Chiabrera (with an *ode-canzonetta* strophe), it remains in use up until Pascoli (where it is closer to the classical model). Another more important form is the *canzone-ode*, established by Pietro *Bembo and above all by Bernardo *Tasso, in simplified stanzas without any internal divisions; from this there derive all the types of strophic lyric poetry in hendecasyllables or hendecasyllables and *settenari* in use up until the 19th c. (one outcome that enjoyed great success was the quatrain of hendecasyllables in the rhyme-scheme ABBA, or ABAB). A third, even more important development, is the *ode-canzonetta* introduced by Chiabrera, a strophic form that allowed the use of all kinds of verse line, with a preference for the shorter kind, and with frequent use of *rime tronche* and *sdrucciole*: this was very successful from the 17th to the 19th c., for example in *Metastasio, in the odes of *Parini and *Foscolo, and the lyric poetry of *Manzoni and the *Romantic poets.

Of the early non-lyric forms, the most important are the *quartina monorima* in alexandrines (AAAA, in imitation of the French) and the *sirventese caudato* (AAAb BBBc . . ., with long lines of between 9 and 14 syllables and short lines with from 4 or 5 up to 7—the latter indicated by the lower-case letters in the normal schematic notation). From this there probably derived the *capitolo quadernario* of the 14th c. (ABbC CDdE . . .). From the 14th c. onwards narrative or discursive poetry can be in *terza rima* or *ottava rima*; these same forms are also used, together with lyric forms, in sacred and profane verse drama. At the beginning of the 16th c., these genres also produce the first examples of unrhymed verse, the *endecasillabo sciolto*, or 'free' hendecasyllable, which Trissino proposes as the medium for *epic poetry, but which is initially most successful in didactic texts and translations, and gradually gains ground over the other two forms. The 16th c. also sees the emergence of poetry in which freely ordered rhymes are mixed freely with unrhyming lines in varying combinations of hendecasyllables and *settenari*, a form which becomes fundamental to verse drama (up to and including the recitative of the *melodramma and *cantata), and is adopted into the lyric in the 16th-c. madrigal. On the other hand the *endecasillabo sciolto* does not pass into lyric poetry until Carlo Innocenzo *Frugoni and, most important of all, *Leopardi. The latter draws on 17th- and 18th-c. experiments with modifications of the early *canzone* as well as on the 16th c. madrigal, to create his 'free' *canzone*

623

(or *canzone leopardiana*), comprising strophes with free combinations of hendecasyllables and *settenari*, a form which still influences modern poetry.

19th-c. poetry makes wide use of the metrical schemes, inherited from the 18th c., of the *canzone-ode* and *ode-canzonetta*, along with the sonnet, still a vigorous element of the whole tradition; but it also displays an almost archaeological interest in the reclamation of old forms that had fallen into disuse, such as the *ballata, canzone*, and *sestina*. In the work of *Carducci, Pascoli, and the young *D'Annunzio, there is an important attempt to construct an Italian verse that corresponds to Latin quantitative metres; after Carducci's *Odi barbare*, this is known as *metrica barbara*. There is a long tradition in this respect, dating back to Leon Battista *Alberti (the *Certame coronario* of 1441) and above all Claudio *Tolomei (*Versi et regole de la Nuova Poesia Toscana* of 1529) and other 16th-c. poets, continuing through Chiabrera and, in the 18th and 19th c., *Fantoni; the last two served as Carducci's models. After the idea of assigning quantitative value to Italian syllables is abandoned, Carducci uses combinations of Italian lines to reproduce on the one hand the schemes of *Horace's odes and on the other the classical hexameter and pentameter. In the latter case the introduction of lines of variable length is significant, since it is thought to have influenced the beginnings of free verse. Even if this is only partially true, the *metrica barbara* reflects the calls for metrical innovation which lead, mainly via foreign influences, to the poetic revolution of the 20th c. [PGB]

See P. G. Beltrami, *La metrica italiana* (1991 and 1994); A. Menichetti, *Metrica italiana: fondamenti metrici, prosodia, rima* (1993); G. Gorni, *Metrica e analisi letteraria* (1993).

Verso la cuna del mondo, see GOZZANO, GUIDO.

Verso libero, see FREE VERSE.

VERUCCI, VIRGILIO, see COMMEDIA RIDICOLOSA.

VESALIO, ANDREA (Andreas Vesalius) (1514–64). Medical writer, born into a family of doctors in Brussels, where his father was an imperial apothecary. After studying at Louvain and Paris he took his medical degree in *Padua in 1537, and was made professor of surgery, which included the teaching of anatomy. The success of his use of woodcut illustrations to explain the text in his *Tabulae anatomicae* (1538) encouraged him to produce the seven books of the *De humani corporis fabrica* (1543). The clarity resulting from the combination of text and illustration has made this a landmark in the medical sciences. [See also MEDICINE.] [PLR]

VESPASIANO DA BISTICCI (1421–98) was the leading bookseller of *Renaissance *Florence, and his bookshop, behind the Badia Fiorentina, became the hub of the Florentine literary world. Attached to an older generation of *humanists and adjusting neither to the avant-garde tastes of Lorenzo de' *Medici's city nor to the *printing press, he retired to his farm in the early 1480s, and began to compose his renowned vernacular *biographies of the great men (and a few women) he had known.

Vespasiano's *Vite d'uomini illustri* consist often of disjointed anecdotes, but sometimes (as in the case of the life of Giannozzo *Manetti) they were conceived as extended *commentaries, providing the raw material for later literary biographers. Vespasiano was gifted with a remarkable memory: although he frequently errs in simple chronology or names, his detailed information, recalled sometimes after half a century, can often be confirmed by documentary sources. His political observations, moreover, are often more accurate than the reports of foreign ambassadors living in Florence. Vespasiano's lives are one of the most precious historical sources of the 15th c. and despite, or perhaps because of, their lack of literary finish, they are one of the great monuments of Renaissance biographical literature. [RDB]

VETTORI, FRANCESCO (1474–1539) came from a noble *Florentine family and made a career as a politician, diplomat, and *historian. He received a solid education in the humanities, and was well versed in classical history and literature and in the vernacular literary traditions. He wrote a *dialogue on the *Sack of Rome, and a history of Italy for the period 1511–27, which contains portraits of Popes Leo X and Clement VII. His correspondence with Niccolò *Machiavelli (whose superior he was in 1508–9) is important for the light it sheds on the development of Machiavelli's *political ideas and on the nature of his literary experimentation. [PLR]

Via del rifugio, La, see GOZZANO, GUIDO.

VIALARDI, GIOVANNI, see COOKERY BOOKS.

VIANI, LORENZO (1882–1936). Painter and writer from Viareggio. Poor and ill-educated, he trained in *Florence with the help of local artists and became successful as a painter in the 1920s, when he also began to write stories, *novels, and autobiographical pieces. His collections of short stories, of which *Gli ubriachi* (1923) and *I Vàgeri* (1926) are the best, portray popular types. Like his paintings, they have a vigorous, *expressionistic style, which he enriches with Versilian *dialect.
[SVM]

Viareggio, see LITERARY PRIZES.

VIASSOLO, GIAMBATTISTA, see FEDERICI, CAMILLO.

Viceré, I (1894). Federico *De Roberto's masterpiece is a *historical novel which tells the story of the Uzeda family against the background of the *Risorgimento and the *Unification in *Sicily. Its themes are the violence, greed, and will to power of the landed classes, and the general servility of the popular masses. Its main thrust is that the Risorgimento did not change the socio-economic structures of Sicily in the least; the Uzedas, descendants of the Spanish viceroys, retain their power and privileges within the democratic state, and the novel ends with the election to parliament of the reactionary Prince Consalvo.
[RSD]

VICO, GIAMBATTISTA (1668–1744). Philosopher and *historian, who held the chair of rhetoric at the University of *Naples from 1699 until 1741. After failing several times to obtain a more prestigious academic position, in 1735 he was appointed royal historiographer by the new king, Charles of *Bourbon.

Vico's uneventful life was in sharp contrast with the extraordinary power and fertility of his theoretical labours. His intellectual boldness was not understood by his contemporaries. His major work, *La scienza nuova* (1744), only received European recognition after Michelet's abridged translation of 1824. Despite the enormous attention given to his work this century, especially after *Croce launched him onto the wider intellectual scene with *La filosofia di Giambattista Vico* (1911), many aspects of *La scienza nuova* are still open to contrasting interpretations. Given the religious climate of Vico's Naples, his *Autobiografia* (1725), which describes his intellectual itinerary, is not entirely reliable for our understanding of influences which he could not openly declare. Explicit allusions in his writings to Polybius, Lucretius, Spinoza, and others consist of anodyne references and ritual condemnations, masking a more profound reflection on their ideas and serious indebtedness to them. Many commentators, however, prefer to take Vico's protestations of orthodoxy at face value, and discount the religious pressures on him and on Neapolitan contemporaries such as the elder Pietro *Giannone and Grimaldi.

The last of Vico's seven Latin *Orazioni inaugurali*, which he revised for publication as *De nostri temporis studiorum ratione* (1708), together with the slightly later *De antiquissima italorum sapientia* (1710), mark the authentic beginning of his interest in epistemological questions, and his critique of Cartesian rationalism. The first of these raises the question which was to be at the centre of his subsequent intellectual labours: does the unpredictable nature of human behaviour mean that human history cannot be studied with anything approaching the rigour with which we are able to investigate physical phenomena?

His major achievement lay in demonstrating that all aspects of the human condition are subject to connected patterns of historical development. It was in the discovery of these patterns that he laid claim to a new science of history. In his first important theoretical work, the *Diritto universale* (1720–2), he questions the traditional conception of 'natural law' as the moral foundation of social existence. Since the study of 'real' legal systems, from primitive times, demonstrated that moral legitimacy was not based on a set of universally accepted eternal principles, there had to be an alternative source of authority. In *La scienza nuova*, developed through three editions between 1725 and 1744, the last not appearing until a few months after his death, Vico argues that the authority bestowing legitimacy on society's codes is to be found in the 'senso comune', that is, the structures of thought, feeling, and values common to a whole nation or people. He also sets about demonstrating that all aspects of human existence (language, laws, customs, thought) are interconnected according to a tripartite scheme of development which characterizes the 'senso comune' of successive historical epochs, from a primitive age of sense, through an era of imagination, to one of reason. This pattern of development, determined by Vico's still disputed notion of 'providence', is not linear but cyclical,

Vida, Marco Girolamo

incorporating a theory of decline and return to origins after the third period.

Given his excursions into a wide variety of disciplines, Vico's thought was studied in the 20th c. by specialists in aesthetics, linguistics, mythology, historiography, sociology, and anthropology.

[GLCB]

Opere filosofiche, ed. P. Cristofolini (1971). See G. Tagliacozzo, M. Mooney, and D. P. Verene (eds.), *Vico and Contemporary Thought* (1979); G. Bedani, *Vico Revisited: Orthodoxy, Naturalism and Science in the Scienza Nuova* (1989).

VIDA, MARCO GIROLAMO (d.1566). Neo-*Latin poet and theorist. Two early poems earned him the favour of Pope Leo X, who encouraged him to write a Latin *epic on the life of Christ. The *Christias* (1535) earned its author a place on *Ariosto's poetical ship (*OF* 46.13), and influenced Torquato *Tasso. Vida dedicated the work to Leo's cousin Clement VII, who in return granted him the bishopric of Alba, after which Vida dedicated himself primarily to pastoral duties until his death. He was also author of an influential *De arte poetica* (1527). [See also LITERARY THEORY, 2.]   [DG]

VIERI, FRANCESCO DE', see COMMENTARIES.

VIEUSSEUX, GIOVAN PIETRO (1779–1863). An inventive and energetic cultural organizer, born in Liguria of a Swiss banking and business family. He travelled extensively before settling in *Tuscany and establishing in *Florence (1819) a reading room ('gabinetto di lettura') which was to become a meeting place for artists and intellectuals from all over Italy and Europe. He was at the heart of the creation of *Antologia* and of other *periodicals such as *Il Giornale agrario* and the *Archivio storico italiano*. He left a huge correspondence which is still in the process of being edited. The Gabinetto Vieusseux continues as a *library in Florence. Directors have included Bonaventura *Tecchi, Eugenio *Montale, and Alessandro *Bonsanti.   [MPC]

VIGANÒ, RENATA (1900–76). *Bolognese *novelist. She published two books of poems in her teens, but was then forced for economic reasons to work as a hospital nurse. She turned her training to good account as an active member of the *Resistance. Her 1949 novel, *L'Agnese va a morire*, describes the vicissitudes of a *peasant woman who joins a partisan brigade. Its success, and that of the subsequent film, has tended to overshadow her other novels and stories, which also focus on women and the war. She was a member of the *Communist Party and wrote extensively for *L'Unità* and left-wing *periodicals.   [PC]

VIGEVANI, ALBERTO (1918–). *Milanese *novelist, who contributed (as Berto Vani, to conceal his *Jewishness) to *Prospettive* and *Letteratura* before *World War II. Much of his prolific production is autobiographical recollection, looking both to Proust and to an established *Lombard tradition, most successfully in *Estate al lago* (1957).   [JEB]

VIGNALI, ANTONIO (1501–59). Born in *Siena, he was one of the founders of the Accademia degli *Intronati. His *dialogue, *La cazzaria* (1530/40), both discusses in philosophical detail the prerogatives of different sexual organs and satirizes the Sienese political factions of the 1530s. After a brief period in *Spain, he spent his last years in *Milan.   [DieZ]

VIGOLO, GIORGIO (1894–1983) *Roman poet and composer of lyrical prose, who was openly hostile to the *hermetic movement. His poetry centres on the architecture and people of Rome, and seeks for classical form and clarity. He completed the first critical edition of *Belli and translated Hölderlin. Both poets strongly influenced his own work.   [JJ]

VIGRI, CATERINA (St Caterina of Bologna) (1413–63) of noble Ferrarese origin, left the *Este court for a female lay religious community in 1426. She founded nunneries in *Ferrara (1431) and *Bologna (1455–6), becoming abbess of the latter. She wrote the semi-autobiographical mystical treatise, *Le sette armi spirituali*, destined to be an example to her sisterhood. [See also NUNS.]

[GPTW]

VILLA, CARLO (1931–). *Roman poet and *novelist. His first collection, *Il privilegio di essere vivi* (1962), is in an aggressively experimental vein, whilst his earlier novels, beginning with *La nausea media* (1964), attack social and literary conformism. His vigorous and sometimes sensual pessimism continues in his extensive subsequent production.   [JJ]

VILLANI. *Florentine mercantile family which produced three writers in two generations.

Giovanni (c.1276–1348), the author of the important *Nuova cronica*, initially worked in the Peruzzi trading company, first as an employee and then as a partner. He was in the company's Bruges branch for much of 1302–7 but based in Florence from 1308 onwards, eventually dying in the *plague of 1348. He had long left the Peruzzi when in 1322 he became a partner in the Buonaccorsi company, which went bankrupt two decades later. He represented it in subsequent negotiations with creditors, and in 1346 spent a period in the debtors' prison. A moderate *Black *Guelf, he was three times prior between 1316 and 1328 and (especially between 1322 and 1331) held numerous administrative positions. At one time or another, for instance, he managed the mint, the city walls, and taxation. His public service gave him access to statistical information and official documents which provided valuable material for his *chronicle.

The *Nuova cronica* has many other sources, including earlier chronicles of Florence and elsewhere, as well as Giovanni's own wide experience. Although the spotlight falls primarily on Florence, it is a history of the known world from the Tower of Babel onwards (1280 is not reached until book 8, ch. 56), in thirteen books of increasing length. Giovanni displays a respectable classical *education and a considerable knowledge of the *Bible. Though archaic as a historian in his superstition and his providential view of history, he is forward-looking in his concern with causes and effects and in his attention to practical detail, not least as regards finances, while book 8, ch. 94 contains a famous statistical account of Florentine society in 1339. Despite the major disasters he recounts, his is an optimistic story of Florentine prosperity and greatness.

After his death his chronicle was continued, in eleven additional books, by his younger brother Matteo, who extended the record to 1363, the year of his own death. He is inferior as a writer to Giovanni, and far more pessimistic, seeing Florentine history after the plague of 1348 as reflecting a crisis of moral values. The chronicle was extended again to cover one further year by Matteo's son Filippo (1325–1407/9), who also wrote, in Latin, a *Liber de origine civitatis Florentiae et eiusdem famosis civibus* (among whom he includes *Dante) and a *commentary on the opening canto of the *Inferno*. [See also DANTE COMMENTARIES.]

[JCB]

G. Villani, *Nuova cronica*, ed. G. Porta (1990–1).
See L. Green, *Chronicle into History: An Essay on the Interpretation of History in Florentine Fourteenth-Century Chronicles* (1972).

VILLANI, NICCOLA (or Niccolò) (1590–1636). *Literary critic and poet. He is best known for his part in the polemics over *Marino's *Adone*; his contributions (1630 and 1631) were published under the pseudonyms of Vincenzo Foresi and Messer Fagiano, and argued against *Stigliani in favour of Marino. As a critic he sets Homer and *Virgil above all the moderns, though he ranks Marino above *Dante and *Petrarch [see also QUERELLE DES ANCIENS ET DES MODERNES]. He began an *epic poem, *Fiorenza difesa*, left incomplete at his death and published in 1641; and he composed *satirical poems in Latin and Italian against poets and customs of his age. [PBD]

VILLARI, PASQUALE, see GIORNALE STORICO DELLA LETTERATURA ITALIANA; HISTORIES OF ITALIAN LITERATURE; MEZZOGIORNO.

VINCIGUERRA, ANTONIO (also known as Cronico) (c.1440–1502). *Venetian man of letters known for his *Satire* in *terza rima*, characterized by linguistic experimentation and a rigid religious morality. He is also author of a (lost) *Libellus de Principe* (1501) and of political *sonnets, of which only two have survived. [LB]

Vino e pane (1955, originally published as *Pane e vino*, 1937), *Silone's second novel, concerns a *socialist exile, Pietro Spina, who returns to Abruzzo disguised as a priest to escape the *Fascists. Some of his followers become martyrs. He vanishes, to return in the sequel, *Il seme sotto la neve*. [JR]

Vinti, I, see VERGA, GIOVANNI.

VIRGIL (Publius Vergilius Maro) (70–19 BC). The greatest poet of ancient Rome, author of the *Aeneid*, the *Eclogues*, and the *Georgics*. The *Aeneid* an epic in twelve books, recounts Aeneas' journey from Troy, his love for Queen Dido of Carthage (4), his descent to the Underworld to meet the spirit of his father (6), and his establishment of a kingdom in Latium whose descendants founded *Rome. In the *Middle Ages, it inspired *romances on Troy, Aeneas, and Dido; *Dante used it as evidence of the divine and providential destiny of the Roman Empire, and recreated his own version of Virgil as his guide through the *Inferno and up to the summit of *Purgatory. It profoundly influenced the *Renaissance *epic from *Petrarch's *Africa* to *Ariosto and Torquato *Tasso, was studied by *humanists such as *Salutati and *Landino, and was *translated into Italian *hendecasyllables by *Caro.

Of the ten *Eclogues*, the fourth, celebrating the Golden Age in Augustan Rome, with the return of the Virgin (Astraea, Justice) and the birth of a heavenly child, appeared to some Christian writers to have been an unconscious prophecy of the birth of Christ. More generally, Virgil's *allegorical setting of his subject matter among shepherds in the countryside was taken up in the exchange of Latin poems between Dante and *Giovanni del Virgilio, in *Eclogues* by Petrarch and *Boccaccio, and in *pastoral poetry up to the 18th c.

The *Georgics* influenced later rustic poetry, particularly in the 16th c., with Giovanni *Rucellai's *Le api* and *Alamanni's *La coltivazione*.   [PA]

See D. Comparetti, *Virgilio nel medio evo* (1896); C. Kallendorf, *In Praise of Aeneas: Virgil and Epideictic Poetry in the Early Italian Renaissance* (1989).

VIRGILIO, POLIDORO (*c.*1470–1555). Cleric, diplomat, and historian. He taught humanities at *Bologna before entering the service of Pope Alexander VI, who sent him to England in 1502 to collect taxes. His most popular work was a history of inventions since classical times, the *De inventoribus libri tres* (1499), which was widely translated and saw over 100 editions. He spent much of his life in England at the court of King Henry VII, and displayed his knowledge of *humanist *historiographical methodology in his *Historiae anglicae*, which covers the period from the origins to 1538.   [PLR]

Visconte dimezzato, Il (1952), *Calvino's *allegorical tale about the bad and good halves of a viscount cloven in two by a cannonball, is indebted to Stevenson's *Dr Jekyll and Mr Hyde*. This first part of Calvino's *fantasy trilogy, *I nostri antenati*, uses fairy-tale motifs in exploring Cold War thematics and the question of maturity.   [MMcL]

VISCONTI. Ruling dynasty in *Milan between 1349 and 1447. The family's pre-eminence within *Lombardy was confirmed by continual territorial expansion which saw *Genoa, Bergamo, Brescia, Como, Cremona, and Pavia all subject to their authority. Under Giangaleazzo 'il Conte di Virtù'

(1351–1402)—Duke of Milan (1395) and Lombardy (1397)—their dominions covered most of Northern Italy. They engaged in three wars against *Florence between 1390 and 1402, attempting to establish hegemony over the peninsula. But their state was threatened by dynastic rivalries, ambitious *condottieri, external enemies, and subjects jealous of their autonomy; on the death without male heirs of Filippo Maria (1392–1447), it virtually collapsed. The Visconti were *patrons of the arts and letters, and their *court was home to *Petrarch from 1353. They founded the *University of Pavia (1361) and created a *library. However, their expansionist policies and sometimes eccentric personal-ities attracted criticism, especially from writers sympathetic to republicanism such as the Florentine *humanist *Salutati. Some later historians saw them as precursors of Italian *Unification.   [JEL & SJM]

VISCONTI, BRIZIO (d.1357). Illegitimate son of the *Milanese warlord Luchino, *podestà of Lodi, and *Crusader, who died an impoverished exile in the Veneto. Seven *lyric poems of his survive. They are notable for their linguistic vigour and their classical culture. Some reflect their author's turbulent political experiences.   [SNB]

VISCONTI, ERMES (1784–1841). One of the subtlest thinkers among the *Milanese *Romantics. He was an intimate of *Manzoni, and a frequent contributor to *Il *Conciliatore*, notably with *Idee elementari sulla poesia romantica* (1818) and a *Dialogo sulle unità di luogo e di tempo* (1819), which had considerable resonance.   [MPC]

VISCONTI, GASPARO (1461–99). One of the leading poets at the *Sforza *court at *Milan, he was a friend and associate of *Niccolò da Correggio and enjoyed the *patronage of Beatrice d'*Este. He composed three *canzonieri and a narrative poem, *Paulo e Daria amanti*, but is nowadays best known for his *pastoral play *Pasitea* in *ottava rima. One of the most important products of the early *Renaissance *theatre in Milan, the play is clearly set out in acts and scenes, and infuses contemporary elements into the classical plot.   [JEE]

VISCONTI, LUCHINO (1906–76) was born into a rich aristocratic family but was radicalized by the experience of working with Jean Renoir in Popular Front France in the 1930s. Returning to

Italy, he directed a remarkable first film, *Ossessione* (1943), widely regarded as a precursor of *Neorealism. Except in *La terra trema* (1948, based on *Verga's I *Malavoglia*) and perhaps *Bellissima* (1951), however, he was not a realist by inclination. From *Senso* (1954) his preferred style combined a broadly *Marxist approach to history with melodramatic form. Beginning with *Il *gattopardo* (1962, from *Tomasi di Lampedusa), an elegiac note enters his work, as his belief in the need for change comes into conflict with his emotional attachment to the old order. As time went on he also found it easier to combine this with a recognition of his *homosexuality and his sense of being the last of a line, which found its richest expression in *Ludwig* (1972). Throughout the 1950s and 1960s he alternated film-making with *opera and *theatre production, but during the making of *Ludwig* he suffered a severe stroke which curtailed his activity. [See also CINEMA.] [GN-S]

VISCONTI VENOSTA, GIOVANNI (Gino) (1831–1906). *Milanese writer. His *Ricordi di gioventù* (1904) are an account of his experiences during the *Risorgimento in Milan, with the inclusion also of his burlesque narrative poem *La partenza del crociato* (1856). He published his short stories as *Novelle* (1884) and *Nuovi racconti* (1897). [JD]

VISDOMINI, NERI DE', see SICULO-TUSCAN POETS.

Visual Arts and Literature. Major writers show an interest in art from the 14th c. onwards. *Dante, discussing fame, cites *Giotto as having ousted Cimabue, and goes on to compare human and divine pictorial art in *Purgatorio* 12; Giotto appears again in a story of the *Decameron; *Petrarch becomes a friend in *Avignon of Simone Martini, and writes two *sonnets on the portrait of *Laura which the artist apparently painted for him.

Petrarch may have fantasized the portrait in his desire to be like the ancients. Aspirations to recreate classical art become a major motive force in the 15th c.; the *humanist recovery and interpretation of classical texts inevitably conditioned artistic practice, given the absence of ancient painting except as images on coins or pottery. Though surviving buildings and monuments in *Rome and the discovery of sculptures (such as the Laocoön) provided practical examples for sculptors and architects, these too were inevitably read in human-

ist terms. The interplay between humanist scholarship, literary ability, creative thinking, and practical expertise had its most striking and far-reaching results in the work of Leon Battista *Alberti, who, in addition to his specifically literary work and his architectural projects, effectively established the science of perspective that determined the evolution of subsequent *Renaissance art.

An iconography emerged that was substantially indebted to humanist readings of classical texts for its representations of mythological scenes, its allegorical subtexts, and its ideals of Roman *virtus*. In *Medicean *Florence art and literature were particularly close, with *Botticelli and *Poliziano reflecting *Neoplatonist sensibility (and perhaps ideas) in certain works, most famously Botticelli's *Primavera* and Poliziano's *Stanze per la giostra*, either of which might hold the key to the other. Botticelli was also the first major artist to produce a set of illustrations to the *Divine Comedy*. [See also DIVINE COMEDY: ILLUSTRATIONS.]

The status of artists increased enormously in the 16th c., not least through the figure of *Michelangelo, whose poetry was esteemed, at least by some, as highly as his architecture, painting, and sculpture. A major step in this respect is taken with the *Vite* of *Vasari, which establishes the idea that great creative artists are as fully worthy of *biographies as great men of antiquity, modern rulers, and learned writers such as Dante and Petrarch. In the case of Michelangelo a second biography was written by *Condivi, confirming the stature he already had in Vasari. But throughout the century literature and art are complementary, a tendency supported by *Horace's parallel of poetry and painting in the *Ars poetica*. *Ariosto celebrates great artists in the *Orlando furioso*: Titian paints scenes from Ariosto and Torquato *Tasso. More than that, in much of the art and literature of the time there seems to be a shared set of aesthetic assumptions about order, ease, naturalness, richness, and diversity, as well as a common iconographic and moral vocabulary. [See also EMBLEMS.]

It is generally agreed that by the end of the century, taken as a whole, painting and sculpture are showing a greater inventiveness and complexity than literary production in Italian. But the *Counter-Reformation, combined with the development of *Baroque ideas and sensibility, affects all the arts. *Marino, whose commitment to an art which outdoes nature is evident in all he writes and especially in the *Adone*, introduces a new type of poetry collection with *La galleria*; at the same time,

Vita

through the adoption of the pictorial metaphor of a gallery of portraits, he implicitly acknowledges poetry's inferiority to painting. The classical reaction, which in painting leads to Guercino and artists of similar stature, in literature leads to the rather less interesting decorum of *Arcadia, and to the establishment, in sharp contrast with the Renaissance, of clear boundaries between the arts that will last until the end of the 19th c.

The meeting of *neoclassical sensibilities in the work of *Foscolo and *Canova in the first years of the 19th c. was unusual. The major writers of the *Romantic period, and *Leopardi and *Manzoni in particular, were oriented almost exclusively towards the written word and literary culture, and wrote only generically about other media. From the mid-19th c. there is more of a convergence, partly under the influence of the shared ideology of the *Risorgimento, which promoted verbal, sculptural, and painterly representations of heroic action. But the widespread drive to *realism, which in literature leads to *verismo, is visible in painters such as Filippo Palizzi, and in a more technical way in painters not primarily concerned with social or heroic subjects such as Giovanni Fattori and other *Macchiaioli. A move towards psychological and technical *modernism is visible in both the painters and the writers of the *Scapigliatura movement, whilst late in the century *D'Annunzian *decadentismo is paralleled in the work of Divisionist painters such Giuseppe Pellizza and Gaetano Previati.

The *Futurists break down the barriers between painting and literature at the most fundamental level in their *parole in libertà* (in effect concrete poems), just as they attempt to break down and revolutionize relationships between all the arts and between the arts and society. One of the few members of the group who is convincing both as a poet and as a painter is Ardengo *Soffici, at least in his earlier work. But an interplay between painting and literature continues well after the decline of the movement and amongst figures not closely associated with it, such as *Scipione and Alberto *Savinio (the brother of *De Chirico). Others, such as Mino *Maccari or Luigi *Bartolini, make themselves felt as graphic artists and poets in literary *periodicals of the *Fascist period, whilst the artist Ottone *Rosai was a pivotal figure for a group of energetic Fascist-oriented writers in Florence in the 1920s and 1930s. More generally the *richiamo all'ordine* of the years immediately after *World War I, proposing *modernist forms of *classicism as appropriate to the new Italy of *Mussolini, finds closely related

expressions in the poetry of *Ungaretti and *Cardarelli and in the paintings of *Carrà and Sironi. Indeed, the revolutionary impulse in Fascism is supported and articulated in all the arts until the late 1930s, a particular victory over reaction, celebrated by all modernist writers and artists, being Michelucci's railway station in Florence.

The years since *World War II have seen many artists and writers continue to work together, but in a less programmatic way than in the preceding half-century, in part with the rise of *cinema and *television. Renato Guttuso was in a sense the artist of *Neo-realism, but many writers who emerged during the neo-realist years (such as *Pratolini, *Pasolini, and even the poet Attilio *Bertolucci) turned to film. Late painter-writers were Carlo *Levi and Toti Scialoja. While the *Neoavanguardia, unlike Futurism, did not include notable artists or have strong artistic concerns, it actually chimed with some of the provocative work produced in the 1960s by Lucio Fontana, Piero Manzoni, and others. Since then self-denying *Arte povera* of the late 1960s anticipated the deliberate tentativeness of *il *pensiero debole*, though the new *expressionism of artists such as Francesco Clemente and Enzo Cucchi finds little resonance in literature.   [PH]

See A. Franceschetti (ed.), *Letteratura e arti figurative* (3 vols., 1988).

Vita, see ALFIERI, VITTORIO.

Vita dei campi (1880). Collection of eight *novelle* by *Verga and his first work of *verismo. The stories adopt simple, popular language to represent the life, loves, and customs of *Sicilian *peasants and shepherds, but achieve great depth as well as forcefulness, especially in 'Rosso Malpelo', 'Jeli il pastore', 'Cavalleria rusticana', and 'La lupa'.
      [RL]

Vita di Alberto Pisani scritta da Alberto Pisani, see DOSSI, CARLO.

Vita di un uomo, see UNGARETTI, GIUSEPPE.

Vita nova (the Latin title preferred by modern scholars to the Italian *Vita nuova*). In 1293/4, *Dante selected thirty-one of his *lyric poems and explained their circumstances, meaning, and purpose through a prose *commentary intended to exalt the 'new life' inspired by his love for *Beatrice, whom he had first met in his ninth year and who had died in June 1290. The work was written at the instigation of Guido *Cavalcanti, yet from the very beginning its author emphasizes the gulf separating his experience of love—governed by 'reason's faithful counsel' (2.9)—from Cavalcanti's tragic vision. An ideal chart is offered whereby the lover progresses from a traditional, courtly attitude and Cavalcantian suffering to the experience of disinterested love. This essential discovery leads him to change the subject matter of his poetry: with no hope of external reward, the latter will now consist solely 'in quelle parole che lodano la donna mia' (18.8–9). The immediate result is 'Donne ch'avete intelletto d'amore' (19), Dante's first great *canzone, singled out in *Purgatorio 24.49–57 as the beginning of the *dolce stil novo. The lover-poet's resolve is further tested by Beatrice's death (28) and the sight of a compassionate 'donna gentile' (35–9), but the work ends with his wholehearted return to his early love. Her life had been highlighted by the number 9 to show that she was a miracle rooted in the Trinity. Her appearance to her lover, preceded by Giovanna, the *donna* of Cavalcanti, indicated that her role in Dante's life was somehow analogous to that of Christ (preceded by the Baptist) on a universal plane. The final chapter speaks of a 'mirabile visione' that makes Beatrice's lover resolve to write about her 'what has never been written of any other woman'.   [JAS]

VITTORELLI, IACOPO ANDREA (1749–1835). Poet known as 'l'ultimo degli Arcadi' [see ARCADIA (2)]. Born in Bassano del Grappa, he wrote occasional, burlesque, and satirical verse. But the love lyrics of the *Anacreontiche ad Irene* (1784) are remarkable for their refined simplicity and musicality, and were in fact often set to music. Byron appreciated his work and translated one of his *sonnets.   [JMAL]

VITTORINI, ELIO (1908–66). *Novelist, critic, *translator, and literary editor, and one of the most influential figures in postwar Italian culture. Born into a *Sicilian railway worker's family, he was originally destined for a career as an accountant, but fled to the North and clerical jobs in various cities. He married the sister of *Quasimodo in 1927 and settled in *Florence a year or two later, working as a typesetter for *La Nazione* and as a sub-editor for *Solaria* and *Il *Bargello. His first article had appeared in *Malaparte's *La Conquista dello stato* in 1926.

With his restless intelligence, untrammelled by conventional education, he was intrigued by the

possibilities of moral and social renewal promised by *Fascism, and now wrote extensively (as Abulfeda) for *Il Bargello* on the social and political role of literature and on Fascist policies in general, whilst fully supporting *Solaria*'s efforts to give a modern European direction to Italian literature. He published, in *Solaria*'s editions, a collection of short stories, *Piccola borghesia* (1931), which adopt non-realist techniques in their evocations of contemporary urban life. In *Viaggio in Sardegna* (published with the story *Nei Morlacchi* in 1935) he presents an account of a visit to *Sardinia which already shows poetic and cultural values in conflict with those favoured by the regime.

Though Vittorini actively supported Italian invasion of Ethiopia, he demonstrated his unorthodoxy with *Il garofano rosso*, a poetic but aggressively populist novel of the Fascist revolution, whose publication in *Solaria* in 1933–4 was a major contributing factor to the review's being closed down. His sympathies for the Republicans in the Spanish Civil War led to his effective detachment from Fascism in the later 1930s. By this stage he was living in *Milan and existing largely through his work as a translator from English, mostly of American novelists such as Poe, Caldwell, Faulkner, Saroyan, and Steinbeck, but also Defoe and, adventurously, D. H. Lawrence. His first major novel, *Conversazione in Sicilia (published as *Nome e lagrime* in 1941), demonstrates this outward-looking tendency, with a substantial homage to American fiction, romantically seen as a source of mythic simplicity, within which the need for a new morality can be allusively articulated. His anthology of contemporary American writing, *Americana* (1942), encountered hostility from the Fascist authorities after printing was completed, but enjoyed clandestine distribution [see AMERICAN INFLUENCES]. After being briefly imprisoned in 1943, he joined the *Resistance, working principally for the underground press and writing in 1944 a *modernist Resistance novel, *Uomini e no (1945).

Now a *Communist, Vittorini was briefly editor of the Milan edition of *L'Unità* in 1945. His militant but individualistic approach to culture led him to found *Il *Politecnico* (1945–7), whose debates on culture, economics, politics, and society set much of the Left's cultural agenda, but were as out of line with Communist Party thinking as his prewar writing had been with respect to orthodox Fascism. He caused a stir with the republication of *Il garofano rosso* (1948), accompanied by an important confessional introduction. He also published or

Vittorino Da Feltre

republished various other works from the Fascist years, notably *Erica e i suoi fratelli* (1954) and *La Garibaldina* (1956). But his two completed postwar novels have generally been judged disappointing; *Il Sempione strizza l'occhio al Fréjus* (1947) is a highly allusive *allegory of the role of culture; *Le donne di Messina* (1949) offers a choral portrayal of a town traumatized by the recent hostilities and trying to find a social and economic path forwards. However, the unfinished *Le città del mondo* (1969) has been cited by *Calvino as one of the primary influences on his *Le *città invisibili*.

Vittorini played a vital role as commissioning editor for *Einaudi's *Gettoni* series of new novels and as joint editor (with Calvino, who was one of his protégés) of *Il *Menabò di letteratura*. In 1957 he published *Diario in pubblico*, an anthology of his *literary criticism and essays tailored to present his version of his ideological and cultural progress. In the posthumously published sociological essay *Le due tensioni* (1967) he tries to set a rational, intellectualizing agenda for literature, in contrast to what he saw as a contemporary tendency to gratuitous expressionism. Despite the changed political and moral climate, it represents a return to the polemical stance he had adopted in his articles for the Florentine reviews of the 1930s.

In spite of his public role Vittorini is often judged solely by *Conversazione in Sicilia*, as he himself ruefully acknowledged. But his importance as a creative writer is considerable: he introduced Italian fiction to American techniques of dialogue and narration that exploited short, powerfully suggestive sentences, and to experimental forms of narrative organization, alternating passages of unvarnished, externalized *realism and wishful, internalized magic, in which conventional distinctions of time and place are dissolved to reveal an elemental world of primary relations and primal values. Following in the direction indicated by *realismo magico*, his work uses myth and symbol to transmute ordinary events into essential experiences. However, though well-intentioned and important in themselves, the moral issues are treated somewhat ingenuously and presented with rather too much insistence.   [JU]

Le opere narrative, ed. M. Corti (1982). See S. Briosi, *Vittorini* (1970); S. Pautasso, *Guida a Vittorini* (1977); F. De Nicola, *Introduzione a Vittorini* (1993).

VITTORINO DA FELTRE (1373/9–1446). The most famous of the *humanist *educators.

From the 1390s he studied grammar, then dialectic, mathematics, and natural philosophy at *Padua, where he was a pupil of *Giovanni Conversino and probably knew the elder *Vergerio. He studied Greek in *Venice with *Guarino da Verona. He also taught, and in 1422 succeeded to Gasparino *Barzizza's chair at Padua *University. In 1423 he was summoned to *Mantua to act as tutor to the *Gonzaga children, and remained there for the rest of his life.

Apart from a few letters and a treatise on spelling, no writing of his survives; his fame is due almost wholly to his work as a teacher, celebrated in four humanist *biographies by Francesco Prendilacqua, Francesco da Castiglione, Sassolo da Prato, and *Platina, the first two of whom had been his pupils. At the Ca' Giocosa, as Vittorino named his school, the curriculum centred on the humanistic disciplines, the *studia humanitatis*, but encouraged children also to study mathematics or the natural sciences if they were inclined to these by nature. Training in the disciplines was also combined with physical and moral education, the latter resting on an austere but humane *Stoic ethics. Despite Vittorino's renowned piety, the curriculum is striking for its substantially secular nature; in this and most other respects Vittorino's practice had much in common with the educational treatise of Vergerio. His former pupils included aristocrats, notably *Federigo da Montefeltro, as well as prominent churchmen and humanists.   [DR]

VITTORIO EMANUELE II (1820–78). The first King of Italy on *Unification. His reign over *Piedmont (from 1849) saw a gradual increase in ministers' independence from the crown. But he demonstrated his dynastic view of his role by keeping the same title when he became King of Italy in 1861. He was the beneficiary of a lavish civil list, and used his extensive powers under the constitution, particularly in foreign and military affairs, to engage in independent, unrealistic, and bellicose policy initiatives which threatened to discredit both state and monarchy. Known as the 're galantuomo', after his death he became the 'padre della patria' in mythical reworkings of the *Risorgimento.   [JD]

VIVALDI, CESARE (1925–99). Poet. Born in Imperia but resident in *Rome, Vivaldi was associated with a number of different movements during his career. He employed both traditional and experimental forms, was close to both *Neorealism and the *Neoavanguardia, and wrote in both Italian and Ligurian *dialect. [JJ]

VIVANTI, ANNIE (1868–1942). *Novelist and poet. Born in London to an Italian father and German mother, Anna Lindau (who was also a writer), she travelled extensively before going to Italy to study. There she entered into a close friendship with *Carducci, who wrote the introduction to her first collection of poetry, *Lyrica* (1890). She subsequently married an Irish journalist and spent some years in America before making her home near *Turin in 1918. Her first novel, *Marion, artista di caffè concerto*, had appeared in 1891. Subsequent fiction was dramatically adventurous and erotically charged, though it also concerns itself with the dilemmas of the woman artist. *The Devourers* (1910), written and first published in English, is a story of children as devourers of their mothers. Vivanti was a *Jew and an English citizen, and suffered a period of *confino* (internal *exile) in Arezzo near the end of her life. [UJF]

VIVIANI, CESARE (1947–). Poet born in *Siena but resident in *Milan, where he practises and writes on *psychoanalysis. His first collection, *L'ostrabismo cara* (1973), makes linguistic and psychological abnormality the material for poetry, though with a much more positive approach than the 1960s *Neoavanguardia. Later verse, especially *L'opera lasciata* (1993), looks to more obviously spiritual values. [JJ]

VIVIANI, RAFFAELE (1888–1950). *Neapolitan actor who became a playwright and poet. He was best known for *dialect representations of Neapolitan types. These led to *'O Vico* ('The Alleyway') (1917) and other short plays. He went on to write *tragedies and dramas still centred on Neapolitan popular life. The poems of *Tavolozza* (1931) and ... *E c'è la vita* (1940) are also in dialect. [AC]

VIVIANI, VINCENZO (1622–1703). *Florentine mathematician, and a pupil of *Galileo and *Torricelli. He remained in Florence, though his contacts with advanced research in Paris, London, and elsewhere led to invitations to work abroad. His own geometric studies, in Latin and Italian, rely on classical principles of geometry. He also wrote on physics and mechanics. [FC]

Vocabolario della Crusca (full title *Vocabolario degli accademici della Crusca*). The first dictionary of the *Florentine Accademia della *Crusca, begun in 1591 and printed in *Venice in 1612, was based on *Salviati's canon of 14th-c. Florentine texts, quoting other authors only if they used good Florentine. Fuller and better organized than earlier *dictionaries, the *Vocabolario* provided a model for the Académie Française and for projects in Germany and Spain; but it excluded many technical terms, and its archaizing *purism aroused hostility in Paolo *Beni and others. After a largely unchanged second edition (Venice, 1623), the third (Florence, 1691) drew on more modern authors, listed more scientific and everyday terms, and marked some words as archaic. The fourth edition (Florence, 1729–38) was somewhat more hostile to scientific terms but added some authors and improved some definitions. *Cesari brought out an unofficial expanded edition (Verona, 1806–11), attacked in *Monti's proposal for additions and corrections (1817–24). The fifth edition was never completed: a series of fascicles (1843–52) was abandoned and work on a second series of volumes (1863–1923) was terminated by the state. In 1955 the Accademia announced plans for a new, broadly based *Vocabolario storico della lingua italiana*, on which work began in 1964. [See also ACADEMIES; QUESTIONE DELLA LINGUA.] [BR]

Voce, La (1908–16). *Florentine *periodical founded by Giovanni *Prezzolini with the aim of modernizing Italian culture. While not advocating specific ideas, it tried to promote informed, unrhetorical debate on issues such as *educational reform, the *Mezzogiorno, sexual morality, and Catholic modernism. It approached the burning questions of *nationalism and *irredentism pragmatically and published discussions of foreign innovations, such as *Soffici's articles on Impressionism. Following Charles Péguy's *Cahiers de la quinzaine*, it published a series of *Quaderni*, including *translations of foreign literature. However, the journal's formula was unstable; the concerns of some contributors, like *Salvemini, were predominantly political, while those of others were moral, religious or artistic. From 1914, under the editorship of Giuseppe *De Robertis, the Florentine periodical focused solely on literature, while in 1915 Prezzolini ran the interventionist *Voce politica* in *Rome. [SV]

VOGHERA, GUIDO (1884–1959). The probable author of *Il segreto*, published under the pseudonym Anonimo Triestino in 1961. Apparently inspired by the life of his son, this remarkable introspective novel is set in *Trieste, as *Austrian rule gives way to Italian rule and *Fascism. Voghera was a *Jewish mathematician and physicist who spent the years 1939–53 in Palestine. [KP]

Vogliamo tutto, see BALESTRINI, NANNI.

VOLATERRANO, RAFFAELE MAFFEI, see ANTIQUARIANISM.

Volgare and ***volgare illustre.*** The noun and adjective *volgare* (vernacular) is used, especially from *Dante onwards, to denote, without pejorative overtones, the mother tongue of Italians, as opposed to Latin. *Volgare illustre* (illustrious vernacular) translates 'vulgare illustre', the Latin phrase with which Dante describes in *De vulgari eloquentia* (1.17) the most exalted and exalting form of the vernacular, above regional *dialects and belonging to all of Italy. [See also QUESTIONE DELLA LINGUA.] [BR]

Volgarizzamenti. Term used primarily of 13th- and 14th-c. vernacular versions of Latin, French, and Provençal texts. [See TRANSLATIONS.]

VOLLO, GIUSEPPE (1820–1905). *Venetian writer and dramatist who moved to *Genoa after the revolutions of *1848. After some historical dramas, he enjoyed immense success with scandalous contemporary *comedies such as *La birraia* (1853) and *I giornali* (1855). His most significant works are *Gli ospiti* (1865), a novel based on his experience of *exile, and a monograph on Daniele Manin (1860). [PBarn]

VOLPE, GIOACCHINO (1876–1971) was professor of history at the universities of *Rome and *Milan. His *Il medioevo* (1927) focused on economics as the driving force of social change in the *Middle Ages and was extremely influential. He advocated Italian intervention in *World War I and went on to support *Fascism, becoming a member of parliament (1924–9) and a member of the *Accademia d'Italia. His *Storia del movimento fascista* (1939), along with Giovanni *Gentile's philosophical publications, gave academic credibility to the movement. Unlike Gentile, Volpe

survived the war, completing his most ambitious historical project, *L'Italia moderna,* in 1953. [PC]

VOLPONI, PAOLO (1924–94). Left-wing *novelist and poet. Born in *Urbino, he took a law degree there in 1947, and subsequently worked for *Olivetti in Ivrea and for the Fondazione Agnelli in Milan. In 1975 he gave himself over to a mixture of writing and politics. He was one of the founders of *Alfabeta*, and was elected to the senate as an independent within the *Communist Party in 1983, joining the hard-line Rifondazione Comunista when the party split in 1991. He thought of himself primarily as a poet, though his four main collections were too discursive to win much critical acclaim.

His name was made with his first novel, *Memoriale* (1962), the story of a young worker finding an absurd sublimation of his deepest desires in the very factory conditions which alienate him from himself and others. The mixture of pathos, realism, lyricism, caricature, and anger made the novel one of the test cases in debates about literature and society in the early 1960s [see MENABÒ, IL]. *La macchina mondiale* (1965) treats the same themes, though with more peasant pith. In the more *modernist *Corporale* (1974), an intellectual tries to square the contradictions between his mind and the everpresent body to which the title alludes. The autobiographical element here is plain, and becomes more pronounced in the generally traditional novels that followed, which include a fictionalized portrayal of his old employer Adriano Olivetti in *Le mosche del capitale* (1989). His last book, *Il leone e la volpe* (1995), consists of conversations between himself and Francesco *Leonetti, about the changes they have seen in Italy and its culture during their lives.

[PH]

VOLTA, ALESSANDRO (1745–1827). Scientist born in Como, who held the chair of physics at Pavia from 1778 to 1819 and achieved major advances in the study of electricity. His considerable poetic talent is displayed in his 1787 poem on de Saussure's ascent of Mont Blanc, *Omaggio al Sig. di Sossure.* [JMAL]

Vulgate, see BIBLE.

W

Waldensians. Followers of a 12th-c. evangelical movement founded by Peter Waldo, a merchant of Lyons who, in 1173, obeyed Christ's command to the rich young man to sell all his possessions and give to the poor. He attracted disciples dedicated to obey and proclaim the gospel. These 'Poor Men of Lyons' began in the context of Catholicism, but, coming under *papal condemnation, turned schismatic, and were persecuted by both church and state before and after the *Reformation. In 1532 they made common cause with the Reformers, and survive to this day as 'la Chiesa Evangelica Valdese', mainly in the Cottian Alps. [PMcN]

WEISS, EDOARDO (1889–1970). *Triestine *psychoanalyst who treated *Saba and was a friend of *Svevo. He studied in Vienna with Freud and was the first practising psychoanalyst in Italy, founding the Associazione Psicanalitica Italiana. His books include *Elementi di psicoanalisi* (1931). He emigrated to the United States after the racial legislation of 1938. [ES]

WERTMUELLER, LINA, see CINEMA.

Whites, see BLACKS AND WHITES.

Witchcraft, see MAGIC; PAPACY AND THE CATHOLIC CHURCH, I.

Women Writers

1. Before 1700

Writing by women in Italy before the 15th c. is sparse. There is a small amount of love poetry, beginning with the *Compiuta Donzella in the 13th c., and some *religious and moral texts. It is indicative that St *Caterina of Siena dictated (rather than wrote) the *letters attributed to her. In the *Renaissance, however, there was a flourishing of women writers, fostered by two cultural developments.

The invention of *printing brought a widening of the reading public and a popularization of the kind of literature made available; and secondly, the approval eventually given to writing in the vernacular meant that women did not have to acquire classical learning in order to gain status as writers. They were, nevertheless, slow to enter the literary arena, not just because of the brute facts of early marriage, frequent childbirth, and no effective means of contraception, but also because of their lack of education, and their exclusion from all forms of literary or learned associations. Some gifted women had their genuine writings denied by unbelieving male critics, whilst others had their writings appropriated by men.

In the 15th c. women's writing is conditioned by contemporary *humanism, and almost all is in the form of Latin letters, some amounting to long essays. Isotta *Nogarola argued that men unfairly condemned Eve for the fall of the human race. Laura *Cereta praised marriage as ideally a state of friendship, not subjection, and also yearned for 'respublica mulierum', a literary community of women in which all would be equal; in more intimate vein there are the letters of Alessandra Macinghi *Strozzi to her sons in *exile. Letters continued to be a public as well as a private genre for women in the following century. Vittoria *Colonna used the letter for conveying an intense spiritual life, whilst the *courtesan Veronica *Franco, taking her title from *Cicero, composed a collection of fifty moral and didactic *Lettere familiari* (1580) Isabella *Andreini Canali, the first woman 'star' of the stage, wrote poems and letters with the explicit aim of gaining lasting fame.

*Petrarchism was also appropriated. In her poetry Vittoria Colonna channelled the conventional adulterous desire of male poets into a sublimated love for her dead husband and, later, for Christ. Chiara *Matraini Contarini consciously 'invented' herself after her example, whilst to others who did not share her austere spirituality Colonna bequeathed a language of the emotions. The unmarried Gaspara *Stampa wrote of unrequited passion for a count; Veronica Franco, who preferred *terza rima capitoli*—usually reserved for satire—to the *sonnet [see CANTO], expressed the pleasures of sexual passion more explicitly than any other woman in Italy. At the end of the 16th c. and well into the 17th, women were also writing various kinds of narrative poetry, such as Moderata Fonte's *chivalric Floridoro (1581) and Margherita Sarrocchi's historical *epic Scanderbeide (1623). They also composed *pastoral dramas and *novels.

The vast range of women's devotional and religious writing is only now coming to light. St Caterina *Vigri of Bologna brought 15th-c. Flemish and German mystical writings into Italy, and her Le sette armi spirituali became one of the best known spiritual treatises written by a woman. St Caterina Fieschi Adorno's treatises, published posthumously in 1551, established a whole religious movement devoted to charitable works. Angela Merici's treatises argued for women to remain in communities without taking vows. Only in the 17th c. did writings by women given to mystical and ecstatic experiences become suspect.

Women writers were often what we would call feminists. Laura Cereta wrote a Latin genealogy of women writers from earliest antiquity to her day. Others focused on overthrowing the subjection to men laid down in Genesis, in civil and canon *law, and in moral and political philosophy of an Aristotelian cast. For the courtesan *Tullia d'Aragona, friendship between men and women, based on sexual equality, was possible only outside marriage. Her Dialoghi d'amore (1547) proposed that the professional courtesan alone could be a truly independent woman. Moderata Fonte's all-woman *dialogue, Il merito delle donne (1600), argued that freedom for women to study and write was possible only if they remained single, and that they would be self-sufficient only by teaching themselves the arts and sciences such as *medicine. The versatile and prolific Lucrezia *Marinella provided a thorough rebuttal of women's 'natural' subjection in all moral and intellectual spheres in the Della nobiltà et eccellenza delle donne (1600). And Arcangela *Tarabotti spent her entire life protesting against women's lack of freedom to choose marriage, the convent, or the single state, and developing theories of women's rights, above all the right to *education. In theory these women had rebutted all the objections to their subordination; in practice nothing would change until the institution of marriage did. [LAP]

See L. Panizza (ed.), Women in Italian Renaissance culture and society (2000); L. Panizza and S. Wood (eds.), The Cambridge History of Women's Writing in Italy (2000).

2. The 18th c.

Though much remained unpublished, more women wrote in the 18th c. than ever before, venturing into areas hitherto considered male preserves as educational opportunities increased, and as class structures and prevailing attitudes became less rigid.

Aretafila Savini de' Rossi took part in a debate on women's *education in the Accademia de' Recovrati in Padua in 1729, defending the idea of education for all, irrespective of sex and social class, in an Apologia in favore degli studj delle Donne and Annotazioni al discorso accademico del Signor P. Giovanni Antonio Volpi. In the *Jacobin period more women proclaimed in writing the rights of women, including Rosa Califronia in Breve difesa dei diritti delle donne (1794), Carolina *Lattanzi in Schiavitù delle donne (1797), and many others who remained anonymous. For the first time women wrote on philosophical and scientific matters, among them the *Milanese mathematician Maria Gaetana Agnesi and the *Bolognese physicist Laura *Bassi. Agnesi also wrote on the more traditional subject of religion, as did others such as Veronica Giuliani.

Most women who wrote belonged to the upper classes and did not treat writing as a source of income. For a small minority it offered a career. Elisabetta *Caminer Turra, the first Italian woman *journalist, became editor of literary *periodicals which played a crucial role in the transmission of *Enlightenment culture. Gioseffa Cornoldi Caminer was the first woman editor of an Italian women's magazine, La Donna galante ed erudita (1786–8). Eleonora *Fonseca Pimentel was the editor and sole writer of Il Monitore napoletano, the chief political journal of the *Neapolitan Jacobin republic of 1799. Women gained full membership of *Arcadia in 1708. Women poets admired in their time include Faustina *Maratti Zappi, Petronilla *Paolini Massimi, and Paolina *Grismondi. But women also produced literary portraits (Isabella *Teotochi Albrizzi), drama (Luisa *Bergalli, who also published an *anthology of women poets, Componimenti delle più illustri rimatrici d'ogni secolo, 1726), *letters (Elisabetta Mosconi Contarini), and philosophical and utopian *novels (Giuseppina di Lorena Carignano). [VRJ]

See L. Ricaldone, *La scrittura nascosta: donne di lettere e loro immagini tra Arcadia e Restaurazione* (1996).

3. 1800 onwards

Women's writing in Italy in the first half of the 19th c. is notable neither for quality nor for quantity. But with the social and political changes following on *Unification, a much stronger tradition began to develop. Writers such as *Neera and Carolina *Invernizio emerged as popular *novelists of romantic love, conventional moralism, and patriotic fervour. Others began to take more serious looks at economic and social issues. Matilde *Serao, though an anti-*feminist, wrote tellingly of the expectations and experience of a newly literate generation of young girls in *Naples. Grazia *Deledda, who was even less of a feminist, created unprecedented *realist portrayals of rural *Sardinia which earned her the Nobel prize for literature in 1926. Other women novelists, including *Marchesa Colombi and Sibilla *Aleramo, explored the importance of *education for women, using fiction to deplore the rhetoric of marriage, maternity, and romantic love.

Under *Fascism the possibilities of exposing the real conditions of women's lives receded, though popular romantic fiction enjoyed increasing success. Some notable women writers, such as Sibilla Aleramo and Ada *Negri (who became a member of the *Accademia d'Italia), were enthusiastic about the regime. In spite of its rhetoric, Fascism did allow room for literary *journalism by women—Margherita *Sarfatti, *Mussolini's mistress, being a noteworthy example. Some *Futurist women (such as Enif Robert, Rosa Rosà, Maria Ginanni, and Valentine de Saint-Pont) also produced interesting if minor work, but poetry by women, with rare limited exceptions (such as Antonia *Pozzi), was generally unexciting in every way in the 1920s and 1930s.

After *World War II, a new wave of women writers of real weight and merit emerged. Women from a variety of classes wrote about the *Resistance, in which women had played a significant part, remarkable results being achieved in the work of Renata *Viganò and Giovanna *Zangrandi. Fausta *Cialente and Alba *De Cespedes wrote about women with a new incisive realism; Anna *Banti, Anna Maria *Ortese, and Elsa *Morante brought a new intellectual depth and control; Natalia *Ginzburg proved one of the most penetrating

analysts in Italy of the changing relations between individuals in modern society. The tension, evident particularly in Morante and Ortese, between women's concerns and orthodox politics exploded with the emergence of modern feminism in the 1960s. New forms of poetry, *theatre, and prose came into being and new feminist presses to promote them, though the most successful feminist writer in Italy, Dacia *Maraini, has worked consistently within mainstream media organizations. Over the past few decades women writers, many not expressly feminist, have achieved both popular and critical success and become powerful figures in the media and academia. Contemporary Italy's outstanding novelists include Dacia Maraini, Gina *Lagorio, Fabrizia *Ramondino, Francesca *Sanvitale, and Rosetta *Loy. But it is indicative that the best-selling Italian author in the mid-1990s was Susanna *Tamaro, with her blend of easy *modernism and religious moralizing. Poetry by women has, however, acquired a new rigour and daring, whether in the *dialect of Franca *Grisoni, the experimentalism of Amelia *Rosselli, or the self-destructiveness of Alda *Merini. [SW]

See C. Lazzaro-Weiss, *From Margins to Mainstream* (1993); S. Wood, *Italian Women's Writing, 1860–1994* (1995).

World War I. Italy entered the war on the Franco-British side in May 1915. Behind the intervention were diplomatic manœuvrings aiming to secure Trent and *Trieste for Italy, and motivated by the fears for political stability if a peace were made which did not include Italian gains. Most people, including most politicians, were against intervening, but a bellicose climate had been created by a vocal minority to which all but a few of the country's major writers belonged. Although some, like Gaetano *Salvemini, supported intervention for democratic reasons, the predominant desire, which had grown through the *Giolittian era, was for social, political, and psychological renewal through conflict. Conspicuous interventionists included Enrico *Corradini, the *Futurists, and Giuseppe *Prezzolini. Giovanni *Papini invoked the country's need for a 'caldo bagno di sangue nero', and Gabriele *D'Annunzio made a series of grandiloquent, inflammatory speeches in the weeks before intervention actually occurred.

The war itself rapidly settled into trench warfare between *Austrian and Italian forces. They were deployed on two fronts, facing each other north to south in the mountains of Trentino and Cadore and east to west along the Isonzo River, where the desolate rocky plateau of the Carso was the scene of continuous fighting and became the privileged landscape of Italian war literature. Italian offensives led to high casualties in return for little territorial gain. Over half of the conscripts were *peasants, many from the South. Rations were poor, leave was rare, and morale-raising efforts wholly inadequate. On occasion the harsh disciplinary regime prescribed decimation. In October 1917 the Austrians, supported by German units, broke through the Italian lines at Caporetto. Defeat became a rout as thousands of troops downed arms and headed for home. A new front was established on the River Piave, but large areas of the Veneto had been overrun. In the predominantly defensive campaign which followed, more attention was paid to morale, with many interventionist intellectuals being employed in the trench newspapers and propaganda agencies (Uffici P.). Italian recovery culminated in the victory at Vittorio Veneto in the last days of the war.

Some 680,000 Italian soldiers died in the war. The economy was transformed by the immense effort of war production, which led to an increased concentration of industry and investment in conglomerates based in the North-West. The state also contracted huge debts and inflation set in. Though there had been widespread hopes for social transformation, the prewar divisions in Italian society were in fact exacerbated, and its military and political leadership discredited. Undoubtedly the travails caused by the war played a major part in the rise of *Fascism.

Many books of war memoirs were published. Two of the best known are Piero *Jahier's lyrical Con me e con gli alpini (1920) and Emilio *Lussu's Un anno sull'altipiano (1938). No Italian poet is identified with the war in the manner of a Wilfred Owen or a Siegfried Sassoon. The most famous collection of Italian poetry with a basis in war experience, *Ungaretti's L'allegria, based around his Porto sepolto of 1916, is not obviously opposed to war and is at least as concerned with existential and poetic themes. D'Annunzio had the highest profile of any literary combatant; Notturno (1921), which he wrote after almost being blinded in a flying accident, is his most remarkable war work. The irrationalist vein of war writing is given Futurist realization in such works as *Marinetti's technophilic celebration, Alcova d'acciaio (1921).

[JD]

See G. Candeloro, Storia dell'Italia moderna,

vol. viii (1978); M. Isnenghi, Il mito della Grande Guerra (1989).

World War II. *Fascist Italy was bound to Nazi Germany by the Pact of Steel of 1939, and *Mussolini entered the war in June 1940, when it seemed that Hitler's invasion of France would rapidly lead to total victory. Mussolini was confident that he had the support of the majority of Italians, including many writers, artists, and intellectuals. But the *armed forces were under-equipped, badly led, and rapidly demoralized. After disastrous and costly campaigns in Greece, North Africa, and Russia, *Sicily was invaded by the Allies in mid-1943, Mussolini was deposed by the Fascist Grand Council in July, and an armistice declared by the Allies on 8 September. At this point German troops invaded to stop the Allied advance, which did not reach the far North of the country until the end of the war. Mussolini, who had been rescued by German paratroops, was established as head of an unofficial Fascist government, the Repubblica Sociale Italiana (RSI), with its headquarters at Salò on Lake Garda. From late 1943 the South was under Allied control, whilst an increasingly strong *Resistance movement fought against Fascist and German troops in the Centre and North. By the time the war was declared over in Italy (25 April 1945), the country was in economic and material chaos and politically divided. Many people were unable to make sense of the rapid changes in political alliances which now took place, beyond recognizing the fact that Fascism had lost (the party was outlawed) and that the country was no longer a *monarchy. One strong spectre was of open civil war between Left and Right, which did not recede until the elections of 1948.

The fragmented nature of the war is clearly reflected in its cultural legacy. Those who had fought against the Fascists and the Nazis had access to cultural spaces and produced a large number of films, *novels, short stories, memoirs, and *history books. Those who had fought for Fascist Italy in the early stages of the war, often finishing in forced labour camps in Germany, were largely constrained to remain silent. Oreste *Del Buono's Racconto d'inverno (1945) is an exception in being an account of labour camp experiences, whilst his La parte difficile (1947) deals with the problems faced by soldiers returning home—a subject treated also in Eduardo *De Filippo's Napoli milionaria! (1945) and, more recently, in Sebastiano *Vassalli's L'oro del mondo (1987). Mario *Rigoni Stern and Mario

*Tobino are among the few who have written on their experiences as soldiers in Mussolini's army abroad, whilst Nuto *Revelli has published collections of oral testimonies of the Russian campaign in *La strada del davai* (1966) and *La guerra dei poveri* (1962). In recent years some prisoner-of-war memoirs have been published, such as Alessandro Natta's *L'altra Resistenza* (1997). Even ex-Fascists have preferred to concentrate on the Salò period rather than the earlier war years. [PC]

See F. W. Deakin, *The Brutal Friendship. Mussolini, Hitler and the Fall of Italian Fascism* (1962); G. Bocca, *Storia dell'Italia nella guerra fascista* (1969).

Y

YAMBO (pseud. of Enrico Novelli) (1876–1943). Prolific and best-selling writer and illustrator of adventure stories for *children, beginning with *Dalla terra alle stelle* (1890). *Le avventure di Ciuffettino* (1902) was popular until the 1970s. He was also a *journalist and playwright, and had his own film company, Novelli Film. [KP]

YORICK (pseud. of Pietro Francesco Leopoldo Coccoluto Ferrigni) (1836–95). Lured away from a legal career into *journalism, he became the *theatre critic of *La Nazione* in *Florence, but also wrote for *Fanfulla* and *Nuova antologia*. His criticism is collected in *La morte di una musa: vent'anni di teatro* (1884–5). [JD]

Z

ZA, IL, see DANTE, 2.

ZABARELLA, IACOPO, see ARISTOTELIANISM; MEDICINE.

ZAMMARANO, VITTORIO TEDESCO, see COLONIAL LITERATURE.

ZAJOTTI, PARIDE (1793–1843). Born in Trento and a law graduate of *Bologna and Pavia, he occupied important posts in the *Austrian administration of Lombardy-Venetia, and led the prosecution against the patriots of *Mazzini's *Giovine Italia* in *Lombardy in 1831. His articles on *Manzoni and the *historical novel, published in book form in 1828, nevertheless received Mazzini's praise. [MPC]

ZAMBECCARI, PELLEGRINO (1350–c.1400). Chancellor of *Bologna from 1389 to 1399, he was a friend of *Petrarch and studied in *Florence with *Salutati. Combining his administrative duties with literary interests, he is best known for his vernacular poems (of which only a few have survived) and his extended correspondence in Latin. [LB]

ZANAZZO, LUIGI (1860–1911). *Roman *dialect poet and dramatist, who learnt much from *Belli and, in turn, influenced *Pascarella. A librarian by profession, he also published a collection of *Novelle, favole e leggende romanesche* (1907) and compiled *Usi, costumi e pregiudizi del popolo di Roma* (1908). [PBarn]

ZANELLA, GIACOMO (1820–88). Poet and *literary critic. He was born near Vicenza and spent most of his rather uneventful life as a priest and school and *university teacher in the Veneto, becoming eventually rector of the university of *Padua in 1871. He first became known as a poet for *Versi* (1868). His mild *Romanticism avoids formal experiment even of a modest kind and puts a premium on content. Many poems focus on working-class life, which he depicts with Christian piety; others display his interest in science, although he had trouble reconciling scientific fact and religious faith. In his last years, after a nervous breakdown, he retired to the country, and abandoned social and scientific themes for a more detached poetry of nature.

Zanella *translated classical and modern *English poetry, including Theocritus, Anacreon, *Ovid, Gray, Shelley, and Longfellow, and wrote extensively on art and on literary history. His *Paralleli letterari* (1885) develop interesting comparisons between Italian and English writers. [FD'I]

ZANGRANDI, GIOVANNA (1910–88). *Novelist and *journalist, best known for the account of her *Resistance experiences in the Belluno region in *I giorni veri* (1963). Her other major work is *I Brusaz* (1954), a formidable *Neorealist novel about *peasant hardship in the Alpine valleys. [PH]

Zanichelli, see PUBLISHING.

Zanni. This mask of the *commedia dell'arte*, the name possibly deriving from the *dialect of Bergamo, was the male servant, often conspiring with adventurous youth against cautious middle age, serving but also deceiving master or mistress, generating imbroglios, and generally complicating the stage action. One of the earliest of the masks, its origins may lie in the trestle stage comic antics of a master and a servant. Practitioners were often adept at singing, dancing, acrobatics, and playing musical instruments. Garb varied according to the kind of servant played, and many scenarios call for at least two *zanni*—one quick, astute, and with an eye to the main chance, the other naïve and easily led [see also ARLECCHINO; BRIGHELLA]. The female equivalent was the *servetta*, often named Franceschina. [KR]

ZANOBI DA STRADA (d.1361). Early *Florentine *humanist, who became secretary to Niccolò *Acciaiuoli in *Naples and was a friend and correspondent of *Petrarch and *Boccaccio. He was crowned poet laureate for his Latin verse in *Pisa in 1355. He also discovered the texts of various ancient authors (notably Tacitus and Apuleius). [MP]

ZANOTTI, FRANCESCO MARIA (1692–1777). A pupil of Eustachio *Manfredi, he became professor of philosophy at *Bologna and was secretary to Luigi Ferdinando *Marsigli's Instituto delle Scienze. He was a modern in physics and attempted to apply the theory of universal gravitation to epistemology in *Della forza attrattiva delle idee* (1747), though he remained an *Aristotelian in his long-popular *Filosofia morale* (1754) and *Arte poetica* (1768). [JMAL]

ZANOTTI, GIAMPIETRO (1674–1765) Painter and man of letters, and elder brother of Francesco Maria *Zanotti. He wrote a history of *Bologna's Academy of Fine Art (1739), which Luigi Antonio *Lanzi leaned heavily on for his account of the Bolognese School. The best of his mostly *Petrarchist *Poesie* (1741–5) is to be found in the humorous *capitoli* [see CANTI]. [JMAL]

ZANZOTTO, ANDREA (1921–) is widely recognized as Italy's greatest living poet. He was born near Treviso in the village of Pieve di Soligo where he still lives and where he worked for over forty years as a secondary-school teacher. His work ranges from simple poems in *dialect to experimental compositions informed by difficult philosophical and *psychoanalytical thinking. Almost every volume of poems is of equal importance.

His earliest collections, *Dietro il paesaggio* (1951) and *Elegia e altri versi* (1954), ran counter to contemporary *Neorealism and, in their idyllic but highly literary depiction of Zanzotto's local landscape, looked back both to Italian *hermetic poetry and to the French *symbolist and *surrealist traditions. *Vocativo* (1957) and *IX Egloghe* (1962) keep much of the same imagery, but contain more questioning of the act of writing poetry and of presenting the self in language. At the same time the poems acknowledge that the landscape and the idyllic vision are under threat, taking cognizance of the fact that both *World Wars saw fighting in the region, and that technology and the economic miracle were changing the lives of the *peasant community. The tensions explode in *La beltà* (1968) This is one of the most original works of poetry of

Zappi, Giovan Battista Felice

the postwar era. Zanzotto's linguistic experimentations now mean facing up to the Saussurean thesis that there is no necessary relationship between signifiers and signifieds [see STRUCTURALISM AND POST-STRUCTURALISM]. Poetically the result is a systematic attempt to thwart meaning; the pleasure of sound is allowed to run riot over sense, sometimes in lines of baby-language ('petèl' as Zanzotto calls it in the local dialect), more often in disturbing linguistic juxtapositions and distortions, of high and low literature, for example, or of Lacanian psychoanalytical citations and advertisement jingles. The linguistic confusion is also a representation of social, political, and personal crises which the poems are not at all sure that they can resolve or escape. *Pasque* (1973) takes the crisis a stage further. Its first, more discursive part reflects ruefully on the frustration, perhaps impossibility, of communication, especially in *education. The second part focuses with a mixture of horror and pleasure on notions of birth and rebirth which Zanzotto finds hidden in the word for Easter.

After *Pasque* Zanzotto's interest in dialect came to the fore and was a vital stimulus in the general rebirth of modern Italian dialect poetry. *Filò* (1976) contains two short poems in a pseudo-archaic *Venetian dialect, written originally for *Fellini's 1976 film *Casanova*, and a long poem in the dialect of the Soligo valley, reflecting on the nature and function of dialect itself. Dialect returns in *Idioma* (1986), the third volume of a 'pseudo-trilogy', whose other volumes are *Il Galateo in bosco* (1978), and *Fosfeni* (1983). In *Idioma* dialect is put on a par with the 'official' language (Italian), and used as the idiom' in which to celebrate both local inhabitants and celebrities such as *Montale and *Pasolini. *Il Galateo in bosco* centres on the search for the rules of both natural and civilized behaviour, achieving its most striking results in the sixteen *sonnets of 'Iperonetto', a kind of parodic homage to 16th-c. Petrarchists who retreated to the countryside (the woods) to write their poems. *Fosfeni*, on the other hand, focuses on scientific language, interspersed with logarithms and other symbols, and searches for clear-sighted vision through a largely metaphorical contemplation of the icy Dolomites. A subsequent collection, *Meteo* (1996), is lighter, and follows, according to Zanzotto himself, the rhythms of the weather rather than those of clock-time; as always, the poems are grounded in the local landscape.

Zanzotto has also published some short stories, and brought together many of his numerous critical writings in *Fantasie di avvicinamento* (1991) and *Aure e disincanti* (1994). [VS-H]

See V. Hand, *Zanzotto* (1994).

ZAPPI, GIOVAN BATTISTA FELICE (1667–1719). Poet from Imola, and a successful lawyer in *Bologna and *Rome. He was one of the founders of the *Arcadia Academy, under the name Tirsi Leucasio. He was an excellent *sonneteer, and embodied the Academy's lighter vein. In 1705 he married Faustina *Maratti. Their poems were published together in *Venice in 1723. [CCa]

ZARLINO, GIOSEFFO (1517–90). Composer and important music theorist. He worked first in his native Chioggia and from 1541 in *Venice. His major treatise, *Le istituzioni armoniche* (1558), re-examines the traditional philosophical bases of music, and proposes a more modern system to replace the Greek tones. Vincenzo *Galilei, however, pointed out numerous misunderstandings of ancient sources. [FC]

ZAVATTINI, CESARE (1902–89). Author of film scripts, *novels, short stories, newspaper articles, essays on film theory, volumes of *dialect poetry, and a monumental collection of letters, as well as film director. He worked on scripts for almost every kind of film, but especially comedy. *Darò un milione* (Mario *Camerini, 1935) showed him wringing out of the conventions of comedy an incisive critique of social injustice. His work on *De Sica's *Sciuscià* (1946), *Ladri di biciclette* (1948), *Miracolo a Milano* (1950), *Umberto D.* (1952), make him one of the most influential figures in world *cinema, theorizing and embodying a realist aesthetic [see NEOREALISM] that would inspire filmmakers everywhere to draw poetry from the unspectacular reality before the camera. [CGW]

ZAZZARONI, PAOLO (17th c.). A lawyer and town clerk in his native Verona, who was typical of the provincial rank and file of the third, mid-17th-c. generation of *concettisti. He collected his unremarkable *lyrics in a *Giardino di poesie* (1641), divided into six sections, each with a plant or flower name ('Mirtilli', 'Violette', 'Rose', etc.). [MPS]

ZEICHEN, VALENTINO (1938–). Poet born in Fiume (now Rijeka in Croatia) who has lived most of his life in *Rome. His various collections, from *Area di rigore* (1974) to *Gibilterra* (1991), return to key obsessions—war, love, and a sense of the fundamental solitude of man—which are always presented in a rational, analytical manner, with moments of frivolity and comedy.   [JJ]

ZENA, REMIGIO (pseud. of Gaspare Invrea) (1850–1917). *Novelist and poet. Born in *Turin into a *Genoese noble family, he left for Paris in 1870 to fight against Prussia, but changed his mind and joined Parnassian and *symbolist literary circles. Returning to Genoa, he published widely on French and Italian literature and wrote poems which were later collected in *Poesie grigie* (1880). He also travelled widely, writing a *travel book, *In yacht da Genova a Costantinopoli* (1887). After contact with the *Scapigliatura*, he published a *realist novel, *La bocca del lupo* (1892), set in Genoa's poverty-stricken back streets, and *L'apostolo* (1901), a psychological novel set partly in the Vatican, as well as some forward-looking poetry.   [AHC]

ZENO, APOSTOLO (1668–1750). *Venetian *librettist but also a critic and scholar of reforming *classicist ideas. He took part in polemical debates on the *Crusca in the 1690s, and was a member of the Accademia dell'*Arcadia. He founded the *Giornale de' letterati d'Italia* in 1710 with his brother Pier Caterino, Antonio Vallisneri, and Scipione *Maffei. His first libretto, *Gli inganni felici* (1696), was followed by the successful *Faramondo* (1699), *Lucio Vero* (1700), and *Atenaide* (1714), which led to his appointment as imperial poet and historian by Charles VI of *Austria. In Vienna from 1718 to 1729, he wrote *Lucio Papirio* (1719), which was set to music by the Venetian Antonio Caldara, and various other successful libretti on classical and historical subjects. On returning to Italy he published the religious *Poesie sacre drammatiche* in 1734. He did not enjoy writing libretti, preferring his work on *classical scholarship, history, and numismatics, which included the *Dissertazioni vossiane* (published in 1752–3) and *Degli istorici delle cose veneziane* (1718). *Crescimbeni credited him with initiating the reform of serious *opera, by excluding the comic characters, such as servants, *peasants, and nurses, who had been introduced in the 17th c.—though in fact he retains them until *Antioco* (1705). His classicism draws him to difficult language full of inversions and enjambements, in contrast to the simplicity of the Arcadians, but he follows Arcadian tastes by reducing the changes of scene and the number of characters in order to restore the *Aristotelian unities of place and action.   [ALB]

ZENONE DA PISTOIA (later 14th c.). *Tuscan who settled as a young man in *Padua, and worked in the ambit of the Carrara court. He composed an *allegorical poem in *terza rima*, *Pietosa fonte*, occasioned by *Petrarch's death in 1374 and dedicated to Francesco da Carrara the Elder.   [MP]

Zibaldone. Miscellany of notes and reflections, often with lengthy quotations. The most famous, and probably the most compendious, is that by *Leopardi, who in the years 1817–32 developed his distinctive *Zibaldone* into an intellectual *diary-cum-*autobiography.   [PH]

ZINANI, GABRIELE (or Zinano) (1564/5– after 1634) studied in *Ferrara with *Cremonini and Francesco *Patrizi the Elder before travelling for long periods. Amongst his friends were Torquato *Tasso, *Marino, and Angelo *Grillo. He was a member of the Accademia degli *Umoristi. His works include much *lyric poetry, in which he experiments with novel metrical structures, such as the four-syllable line, and the use of seven- and eleven-syllable lines in *ottava rima*; a *mock-heroic poem, *La Sassonia domata*, which was intended to combine what he saw as *Ariosto's gravità* and Tasso's *dolcezza*; a number of *pastoral dramas; and the *tragedy *L'Almerigo* (1590). He is best known now as a *literary critic and *literary theorist. His *Discorso della tragedia* (1590) contributed to the debate over whether *tragedy should treat historical or imagined actions; he argues citing Aristotle as authority, that a possible and verisimilar action produces the preferred reaction of pity and fear. He also contributed to the debate over *ragion di stato* with *Della ragion de gli stati* (1626).   [PBD]

ZIPOLI, PERLONE, see LIPPI, LORENZO.

ZOPPI, GIUSEPPE, see ITALIAN WRITERS IN SWITZERLAND.

ZORZI, BARTOLOMEO (mid-13th c.). *Venetian *merchant who was captured by the *Genoese and wrote poems in Provençal during his imprisonment. The majority of his eighteen surviving poems are love *lyrics, but two are devotional, and the three best are political *sirventesi. [See also TROUBADOURS.]   [JU]

ZUCCARI, ANNA, see NEERA.

ZUCCOLI, LUCIANO (pseud. of Luciano von Ingenheim) (1868–1929). Aristocrat of Swiss origin who lived in *Milan and Paris. He wrote numerous highly popular *novels and stories dealing with the emotional and moral torments of the upper bourgeoisie, beginning with *I lussuriosi* (1893). [AHC]

ZUCCOLO, LUDOVICO (1568–1630). A political writer, born into a noble family of Faenza, Zuccolo spent several years at the *Urbino *court of Francesco Maria II della Rovere, adopting the name Il Picentino. In 1621 he returned to Faenza and joined the Accademia dei Filopanti [see ACADEMIES]. He wrote *dialogues, three eclogues, and a treatise on metrics, as well as important works of *political thought: *Considerazioni politiche e morali* (1621) contains the famous short treatise *Della *ragion di stato,* based on Aristotle; his *Dialoghi* (1625) criticize More's utopian model of the ideal state, and praises the moderate republicanism of *Venice and San Marino. In modern times, attention was drawn to Zuccolo's work by Benedetto *Croce. [PBert]